KU-429-548

8

AME

THE AMERICAN READER

THE AMERICAN READER

EDITED BY CLAUDE M. SIMPSON,
Harvard University, AND ALLAN NEVINS,
Columbia University

WITH A FOREWORD AND EDITORIAL ADVICE
BY HENRY SEIDEL CANBY

D. C. HEATH AND COMPANY
Boston

Copyright, 1941, by D. C. Heath and Company. No part of the material covered by this copyright may be reproduced in any form without written permission of the publisher. Printed in the United States of America (4C7).

Offices: Boston,   New York,   Chicago
Atlanta,   San Francisco,   Dallas,   London

FOREWORD

NO reader should read this book without first thinking what *is* America — what makes it a nation; what gives to American writing characteristics of its own; what ideas dependent upon life on this continent belong to the American imagination; what is American style, if, indeed, there is an American style. And no American reader or student will finish this book without knowing better than before the earmarks of the American breed.

The purpose of Mr. Simpson's and Mr. Nevins' work has not been to prepare an outline of American literary history — that has been done before; and it is assumed in the book that the student knows in general, or can readily learn, the broad movements, sometimes slow, sometimes fast, by which American literary expression became, not only literature, but also American. There are th ' nearly two centuries when American writing was strictly and consciously colonial: a poor relation of English literature, and native only, if native at all, in theme, and in an occasional shoot of spirit which betrayed the influence of new ideas in a new life in a new continent. There was, later, the sudden maturity of the Puritan imagination, which Van Wyck Brooks has aptly called the flowering of New England. This local literature of a self-contained region was a true ripening of a civilization, which gave us names still great — Emerson, Thoreau, in one way, Longfellow in another. It had immortal longings in it, and some of it belongs to world literature; but though not colonial it was still not American. It did not make the South or the West or the middle regions articulate. Then came the great demoralization of the Civil War and the equally great demoralization of established societies which accompanied the winning and the exploitation of the West. Mark Twain spoke for the West in its first self-consciousness, Walt Whitman began his epic of the democratic faith, which seemed to him then about to become a democratic reality. But there was still no broadly and inclusively American literature. Our schools, our colleges, our magazines, our publishers still thought of American books as by-products of the great English tradition, not as a part of a new literature, rooted in that tradition but grafted with new thought and new experience. Hence we stayed still semi-colonial, still experimental, still largely local until the first World War brought to a nation, now a conglomerate of races, though still English in tradition and in speech, a consciousness that literature, whatever its traditions, had a job to do in finding voices for a vast country. What had been a new world geographically speaking, was now, for the first time, perhaps, realized as a new world of human experience. From 1920 on the vast majority of the best American books in creative literature could have been written only in America.

The editors of this book have approached the task of selecting from these three centuries of American writing with a purpose which is explanatory and illustrative rather than historical in any chronological sense. They have wished to give, to students in our American colleges, stories, essays, poems, letters, plays, that they can read with pleasure and profit, while at the same time sharpening their sense of what is characteristically American. There is nothing in this book put there just because it contains some American fact or the beginning of some American trend in literary expression. There is nothing here not worth reading for its own sake. Less obvious to the casual reader, but equally important, there is nothing in this book which does not represent a writing man trying to tell the world of the special qualities of his own environment. He may not know that he is doing so; usually he is entirely unaware that he is thinking and imagining under the influence of an environment spiritually, intellectually, and physically different from the old home in Europe. This is as it should be. Yet the reader of this book will not fail to note that there are native traits in all the selections, whether or not they deal with America as a theme. Emerson's " The American Scholar " has rhythms in its prose subtly different from any contemporary English writing. Thoreau's " Where I Lived, and What I Lived For " could never have been written in the same way, I believe, by an Englishman or a Frenchman. When one comes to the colloquialism of Ring Lardner and Sherwood Anderson, it is obvious that the American neither speaks nor writes like an Englishman. But it was really obvious in Mark Twain and Walt Whitman long before. And in every one of the selections in this book there is something that is definitely American.

In order to display American writing for study and pleasure and as samples of the American imagination, the editors of this book have broken down literary history into its elements by kinds and purposes. They have disregarded sequence in time, and given you essays, criticism, stories, and plays, arranged by groups, varied within the groups, and presenting variety in the whole. It is the method of the magazine, which, if not invented here, has been more successfully edited by Americans than by any other nation. The notes and brief biographies (as, again, in a magazine) will keep the reader informed of chronology, if he needs to be kept informed. What he gets is, in each group, the attempts of able and imaginative Americans to handle a literary problem, each one in his own way and for his own time. In the group called *Essays on America* you will find Benjamin Franklin trying to explain how the American workman of the eighteenth century handled himself, Donald Davidson discussing the aftereffects of the Civil War, Louis Adamic stating the problems of the immigrants, and Professor Turner offering one key to the problem of what makes American history so different from the European sequence of events. It is not so important *when* these writers wrote; the importance lies in their common task and their success in doing the job.

The rich group of poetry also is best regarded as poetry first, but as poetry also which is emphatically sparks struck from American experience. The themes are by no means always American; the background of our rich and varied history is the unifying factor. Poe in his way is almost as American as Walt Whitman. Whittier, who borrowed his technique from foreign models, is really as much conditioned by life in New England as Robert Frost. And I do not refer to such passionate nationalism as one finds in Vachel Lindsay but to that deeper experience of a soil, a sky, and a sense of national or racial unity which one finds behind all great literatures.

The reader is advised, therefore, to take up this volume, not as a textbook or a history, nor merely as a set of examples of good English composition, but rather as a storehouse of American writing, in which our most stimulating minds try to tell their story of American experience, or give out the ideas that have come to them while living in the American scene. Such a sympathetic reader will agree that, with only a century and a half of national independence, we can put on a surprisingly good show. He will discover, too, the versatility of his American contemporaries who belong to what is probably the richest, if not the greatest, period of American literary history — that is, our own. And he will get a sense of continuity in American culture, and of the ultimate brotherhood of Henry Adams and H. L. Mencken, of Stephen Vincent Benét and H. W. Longfellow, of Nathaniel Hawthorne and Thornton Wilder, and of Herman Melville, Mark Twain, Ernest Hemingway, and John Steinbeck. Finally, and not least useful, he will meet here many interesting and significant American writers for the first time.

HENRY SEIDEL CANBY

ACKNOWLEDGMENTS

For permission to reprint copyrighted material, acknowledgment is made to the following:

To Carl Becker for "Kansas" from *Essays in American History dedicated to Frederick Jackson Turner,* published by Henry Holt and Company, copyright 1910.

To Stephen Vincent Benét for "The Devil and Daniel Webster" from *Thirteen O'Clock,* published by Farrar and Rinehart, Inc., copyright 1936, 1937 by the author; and for the selections from *John Brown's Body,* published by Farrar and Rinehart, Inc., copyright 1927, 1928 by the author.

To Thomas Hart Benton for a selection from *An Artist in America,* published by Robert M. McBride and Company, copyright 1937 by the author.

To the Bobbs-Merrill Company for "Huckleberry Finn" from *The Delight of Great Books* by John Erskine, copyright 1928, 1935.

To Albert and Charles Boni, Inc., for "One of the Missing" from *In the Midst of Life* by Ambrose Bierce, copyright 1891.

To the estate of Heywood Broun for "Shooting the Young Idea" from *Sitting on the World* by Heywood Broun, published by G. P. Putnam's Sons, copyright 1924 by the author.

To Gerald Bywaters and the Editors of the *Southwest Review* for "Contemporary American Artists" from the issue of April, 1938.

To Coward-McCann, Inc., for *Our Town* by Thornton Wilder, copyright 1938.

To John Dos Passos for a selection from *Nineteen-Nineteen,* published by Harcourt, Brace and Company, copyright 1932.

To Doubleday, Doran and Company for "A Municipal Report" from *Strictly Business* by O. Henry, copyright 1910, 1938.

To Farrar and Rinehart, Inc., for "Fiction Tells All" from *Seven Years' Harvest* by Henry Seidel Canby, copyright 1936 and reprinted by permission of the publishers; for *The Green Pastures* by Marc Connelly, copyright 1930 and reprinted by permission of the publishers; and for "Speech to Those Who Say Comrade" from *Public Speech* by Archibald MacLeish, copyright 1936 and reprinted by permission of the publishers.

To the Editors of *Fortune* for "To Heaven by Subway" from *Fortune,* August, 1938, copyright 1938 by Time, Inc.

To Samuel French for *Green Grow the Lilacs* by Lynn Riggs, copyright 1930, 1931 by the author.

To Harcourt, Brace and Company for a selection from the preface to *The Book of American Negro Poetry,* edited by James Weldon Johnson, copyright 1922; for a selection from *Main Currents in American Thought,* Volume III, by Vernon L. Parrington, copyright 1930; for " He " from *Flowering Judas and Other Stories* by Katherine Anne Porter, copyright 1935 by the author; for "Threes " from *Smoke and Steel* by Carl Sandburg, copyright 1920; for " The Buckskin Harness " from *Paul Bunyan* by Esther Shephard, copyright 1924 by the author; and for a selection from *The Autobiography of Lincoln Steffens,* copyright 1931.

To Harper and Brothers for a selection from *My America* by Louis Adamic, copyright 1938 by the author; for " Crash! " from *Only Yesterday* by Frederick Lewis Allen, copyright 1931 by the author; and for " On the Walpole Road " from *A Humble Romance and Other Stories* by Mary E. Wilkins, copyright 1887.

To Constance Garland Harper and the estate of Hamlin Garland for " The Return of a Private " from *Main-Travelled Roads* by Hamlin Garland, published by Harper and Brothers, copyright 1891.

To the Harvard University Press and to the President and Fellows of Harvard College for " John Henry " from *Folk-Songs of the South* by John H. Cox, copyright 1925; and for " I Got Shoes " from *American Negro Folk-Songs* by Newman I. White, copyright 1928.

To Henry Holt and Company for selections from the *Collected Poems of Robert Frost,* copyright 1939; for the poems of Carl Sandburg from *Chicago Poems,* copyright 1916, and *Cornhuskers,* copyright 1918; and for " The Significance of the Frontier in American History " from *The Frontier in American History* by Frederick Jackson Turner, copyright 1921.

To Houghton Mifflin Company for " The Dinner-Party " from *Men, Women, and Ghosts* by Amy Lowell, copyright 1916.

To Little, Brown and Company for a selection from *The Letters of William James,* edited by Henry James, copyright 1920 by the editor; and for *Remembering Laughter* by Wallace Stegner, copyright 1937.

To John A. Lomax for " The Old Chisholm Trail " from *Cowboy Songs and Other Frontier Ballads,* published by The Macmillan Company, copyright 1910; and to John A. Lomax and Alan Lomax for the texts of five ballads from *American Ballads and Folk Songs,* published by The Macmillan Company, copyright 1934.

To The Macmillan Company for a selection from *The Great Tradition* by Granville Hicks, copyright 1933, 1935; and for the poems of Vachel Lindsay from *Johnny Appleseed and Other Poems,* copyright 1928, and *Collected Poems,* copyright 1923.

To the Editors of the *Nation* for part of a review by Stuart P. Sherman, from the issue of September 11, 1913.

To the University of North Carolina Press for " Still Rebels, Still Yankees " from *The Attack on Leviathan* by Donald Davidson, copyright 1938.

To W. W. Norton and Company for a selection from *Sticks and Stones* by Lewis Mumford, copyright 1924 by Boni and Liveright, Inc.

To the University of Oklahoma Press for " From Longhorn to Combine " from *Deserts on the March* by Paul B. Sears, copyright 1935.

To Louise Pound for the text of " Bury Me Not on the Lone Prairie " from *American Ballads and Songs,* published by Charles Scribner's Sons, copyright 1922.

To Charles Scribner's Sons for a chapter from *Farmington* by Clarence Darrow, copyright 1904; for " The Three-Day Blow " from *In Our Time* by Ernest Hemingway, copyright 1925; for " The Golden Honeymoon " from *How to Write Short Stories* by Ring Lardner, copyright 1924; and for the poems of Edwin Arlington Robinson from *Children of the Night,* copyright 1901, and *Town Down the River,* copyright 1910.

To Simon and Schuster, Inc., for " Humor and America " from *The Enjoyment of Laughter* by Max Eastman, copyright 1936; and for " Music and the Flag " from *Of Men and Music* by Deems Taylor, copyright 1937.

To Wilbur Daniel Steele for " How Beautiful with Shoes," copyright 1932.

To the Viking Press, Inc., for " I'm a Fool " from *Horses and Men* by Sherwood Anderson, copyright 1923 by B. W. Huebsch; and for " The Chrysanthemums " from *The Long Valley* by John Steinbeck, copyright 1938 by the author.

To the Editors of the *Yale Review* and to the Yale University Press for " The American Language " by H. L. Mencken, from the Spring, 1936 issue.

Thanks are due also to Mr. Louis B. Wright and the Huntington Library for permission to reprint the Huntington MS. version of " Annabel Lee."

The editors have incurred many debts of gratitude for advice and assistance, and they wish particularly to thank Mr. Archibald DeWeese of the New York Public Library; Mr. Homer Halvorsen of the Harvard Library; Mr. Henry Seidel Canby and Mr. Courtlandt Canby; Professor James F. Fullington of the Ohio State University; Professor Howard Mumford Jones of Harvard; and Professor Paul V. Kreider of the University of Cincinnati.

CONTENTS

Exposition

Poetry

Carl Sandburg

Archibald MacLeish

Drama

Narration

FOLK TALES   559

SHORT STORIES   593

NOVELETTE

NOTES

EXPOSITION

ᘜᘜᘜᘜᘜᘜᘜᘜᘜᘜᘜᘜᘜᘜᘜᘜᘜᘜ

Lincoln Steffens

I Become a Student

MY father discovered and put me into the best private school in San Francisco as a special student to be crammed for Berkeley — and he retained one of the teachers there, Mr. Evelyn Nixon, to tutor me on the side. Characteristically, too, my father gave me liberty: a room to sleep and work in, with no one to watch over and care for me. I could go and come as I pleased. And I came and went. I went exploring and dreaming alone around that city as I had the country around Sacramento, and the place I liked best was the ocean shore; there I lived over the lives of the Greek heroes and the Roman generals and all the poets of all the ages, sometimes with ecstasy, but never, as in my boyhood, with myself as the hero. A change had come over me.

Evelyn Nixon formed it. He was the first teacher I ever had who interested me in what I had to learn — not in myself, but in the world outside, the world of conscious culture. He was a fanatic of poetry, especially of the classic poets When he read or recited Greek verse, the Greeks came to life; romance and language sang songs to me, and I was inspired to be, like him, not a hero nor even a poet, but a Greek scholar, and thus an instrument on which beautiful words might play. Life filled with meaning, and purpose, and joy. It was too great and too various for me to personify with my boyish imitations and hero-ism. I wrote verses, but only to learn the technique and so feel poetry more perfectly. I wanted to read, not to write; I wanted to know, not to do and be, great things — Mr. Nixon expressed it.

" I'm nobody," he used to say. " I'm nothing but one of the unknown beings Homer and Dante, Shakespeare, Caesar, and the popes and the generals and statesmen have sung and fought and worked for. I'm the appreciator of all good words and deeds."

A new, a noble role, and Evelyn Nixon was a fine example of it: the receiver, not the giver, of beautiful inventions. He was an Englishman; he took a double

From *The Autobiography of Lincoln Steffens,* 1931.

first at Oxford, I heard, and came for his health to San Francisco. There was a group of such men, most of them with one story. There were athletes, as well as scholars, at Oxford and Cambridge; they developed muscles and a lung capacity which they did not need and could not keep up in the sedentary occupations their scholarship put them into. Lung troubles exiled them.

"Keep out of college athletics," they advised. "Don't work up any more brawn there than you can use every day afterward."

Nixon taught me Greek, Latin, and English at school, and at his house he opened up the beauty and the meaning of the other subjects I had to cram up for entrance. I worked for him; I worked more, much more, for myself. He saw this, he saw my craving for the answers to questions, and he laughed.

"I will answer no questions of yours," he shouted. "Men know no answers to the natural questions of a boy, of a child. We can only underline your questions, make you mad yourself to answer them, and add ours to whip, to lash you on to find out for yourself — one or two; and tell us! That is what youth is for: to answer the questions maturity can't answer." And when I looked disappointed and balked, he would roar at me like a demon.

"Go to, boy. The world is yours. Nothing is done, nothing is known. The greatest poem isn't written, the best railroad isn't built yet, the perfect state hasn't been thought of. Everything remains to be done — right, everything."

This said, he said it again and again, and finally, to drive me, he set our private hour from seven until eight o'clock Saturday evenings, so that I could stay on into the night with his group of friends, a maddening lot of cultivated, conflicting minds. There were from four to ten of them, all Englishmen, all Oxford and Cambridge men, all exiles and all interested in any and all subjects, which they discussed with knowledge, with the precise information of scholarship, but with no common opinions on anything apparently. There were Tories among them and liberals and one red: William Owen, a grandson, I think — certainly a descendant — of Robert Owen, the first of the early English socialists. There was at least one Roman Catholic, who showed me so that I never forgot it the Christianity of that church; his favorite thesis was that the Protestant churches were Old Testament, righteous sects and knew nothing really of Christ's teachings of love and forgiveness. And there were Protestants there, all schooled in church history; and when a debate came to a clinch, they could quote their authorities with a sureness which withstood reference to the books. I remember one hot dispute of the Catholic's reference to some certain papal bull. Challenged, he quoted it verbatim in the original Latin. What they knew was amazing to me, and how they knew it; but what they did not know struck me harder still. They could not among them agree on anything but a fact. With all their knowledge they knew no essential truth.

It was conversation I was hearing, the free, passionate, witty exchanges of studied minds as polished as fine tools. They were always courteous; no two ever spoke together; there were no asides; they all talked to the question before the house, and while they were on the job of exposition anyone, regardless of his side, would contribute his quota of facts, or his remembrance of some philosopher's opinion or some poet's perfect phrase for the elucidation or the beautification of the theme. When the differences rose the urbanity persisted. They drank their Californian wine with a relish, they smoked the room thick, and they pressed their views with vigor and sincerity and eloquence; but their good temper never failed them. It was conversation. I had never heard conversation before; I have heard conversation sometimes since, but rarely, and never like my remembrance of those wonderful Saturday nights in San Francisco — which were my preparation for college.

When I went up for my examination this time in Berkeley I passed, not well in all subjects, but I was admitted to the university, and that fall I entered the University of California with a set of examination questions for the faculty, for the professors to answer.

The unknown is the province of the student; it is the field for his life's adventure, and it is a wide field full of beckonings. Curiosity about it would drive a boy as well as a child to work through the known to get at the unknown. But it was not assumed that we had any curiosity or the potential love of skill, scholarship, and achievement or research. And so far as I can remember now, the professors' attitude was right for most of the students, who had no intellectual curiosity. They wanted to be told not only what they had to learn, but what they had to want to learn — for the purpose of passing. That came out in the considerations which decided the choice among optional courses. Students selected subjects or teachers for a balance of easy and hard, to fit into their time and yet " get through." I was the only rebel of my kind, I think. The nearest to me in sympathy were the fellows who knew what they wanted to be: engineers, chemists, professional men, or statesmen. They grunted at some of the work required of them — studies that seemed useless to their future careers. They did not understand me very well, nor I them, because I preferred those very subjects which they called useless, highbrow, cultural. I did not tell them so; I did not realize it myself definitely; but I think now that I had had as a boy an exhausting experience of *being* something great. I did not want now to be but rather to know things.

And what I wanted to know was buried deep under all this " college stuff " which was called " shop." It had nothing to do with what really interested us in common. Having chosen our work and begun to do it as a duty, we turned to the socially important question: which fraternity to join. The upper classmen tried to force our answers. They laid aside their superiority to " rush " those of us whose antecedents were known and creditable. It was all snobbish, secret, and exclusive. I joined a fraternity out of curiosity: What were the secrets and the mystic rites? I went blindfold through the silly initiation to find that there were no secrets and no mysteries — only pretensions and bunk, which so disgusted me that I would not live at the clubhouse, preferring for a year the open doors of a boardinghouse. The next great university question was as to athletics. My ex-athletes from Oxford and Cambridge, with their lung and other troubles, warned me; but it was a mistake that saved me. I went with the other freshmen to the campus to be tried out for football, baseball, running, jumping, etc. Caught by the college and class spirit, I hoped to give promise of some excellence. Baseball was impossible for me; I had been riding horses when the other boys were preparing for college on the diamond. I had learned to run at the military academy and in the first freshman tests I did one hundred yards enough under eleven seconds to be turned over to an athletic upper class-man for instruction. Pointing up to Grizzly Peak, a high hill back of the college, he said: " All you need is wind and muscle. Climb that mountain every day for a year; then come back and we'll see."

I did not climb Grizzly Peak every day, but I went up so often that I was soon able to run up and back without a halt. At the end of the year I ran around the cinder track so long that my student instructor wearied of watching me, but, of course, I could not do a hundred yards much under twelve seconds. Muscle and wind I had, but all my physical reactions were so slow that I was of no real use in college athletics. I was out of the crowd as I had been as a boy.

I shine only in the military department. The commandant, a U. S. Army officer, seeing that I had had previous training, told me off to drill the awkward squad of my class, and when I had made of them the best-drilled company in college, he gave me the next freshman class to drill. In the following years I was always drillmaster of the freshmen and finally commanded the whole cadet corps. Thus I led my class in the most unpopular and meaningless of under-graduate activities. I despised it myself, prizing it only for the chances it gave me to swank and, once a week, to lord it over my fellow students, who named me the " D. S." — damn stinker.

My nickname was won not only as a disciplinarian, however; I rarely pun-ished anyone; I never abused my command. I could persuade the freshmen to drill by arguing that, since it was compulsory, they could have more fun doing it well than badly; and that it was the one exercise in which they could beat and shame the upper classmen whose carelessness was as affected as their su-periority. That is to say, I engaged their enthusiasm. All other student enthu-siasms, athletics, class and college politics, fashions, and traditions I laughed at and damped. I was a spoilsport. I was mean, as a horse is mean, because I was unhappy myself.

It is possible to get an education at a university. It has been done; not often, but the fact that a proportion, however small, of college students do get a start in interested, methodical study proves my thesis, and the two personal experi-ences I have to offer illustrate it and show how to circumvent the faculty, the other students, and the whole college system of mind-fixing. My method might lose a boy his degree, but a degree is not worth so much as the capacity and the drive to learn, and the undergraduate desire for an empty baccalaureate is one of the holds the educational system has on students. Wise students some day will refuse to take degrees, as the best men (in England, for instance) give, but do not themselves accept, titles.

My method was hit on by accident and some instinct. I specialized. With several courses prescribed, I concentrated on the one or two that interested me most; and letting the others go, I worked intensively on my favorites. In my first two years, for example, I worked at English and political economy and read philosophy. At the beginning of my junior year I had several cinches in history. Now I liked history; I had neglected it partly because I rebelled at the way it was taught, as positive knowledge unrelated to politics, art, life, or anything else. The professors gave us chapters out of a few books to read, con, and be quizzed on. Blessed as I was with a " bad memory," I could not commit to it anything that I did not understand and intellectually need. The bare record of the story of man, with names, dates, and irrelative events, bored me. But I had discovered in my readings of literature, philosophy, and political economy that history had light to throw upon unhistorical questions. So I proposed in my junior and senior years to specialize in history, taking all the courses required and those also that I had flunked in. With this in mind I listened attentively to the first introductory talk of Professor William Cary Jones on American constitutional history. He was a dull lecturer, but I noticed that, after telling us what pages of what books we must be prepared in, he mumbled off some other references " for those that may care to dig deeper."

When the rest of the class rushed out into the sunshine, I went up to the professor and, to his surprise, asked for this memorandum. He gave it to me. Up in the library I ran through the required chapters in the two different books, and they differed on several points. Turning to the other authorities, I saw that they disagreed on the same facts and also on others. The librarian, appealed to, helped me search the bookshelves till the library closed, and then I called on Professor Jones for more references. He was astonished, invited me in, and began to approve my industry, which astonished me. I was not trying to be a good boy; I was better than that: I was a curious boy. He lent me a couple of his books, and I went off to my club to read them. They only deepened the mystery, clearing up the historical question but leaving the answer to be dug for and written.

The historians did not know! History was not a science, but a field for research — a field for me, for any young man, to explore, to make discoveries in and write a scientific report about. I was fascinated. As I went on from chapter to chapter, day after day, finding frequently essential differences of opinion and of fact, I saw more and more work to do. In this course, American constitutional history, I hunted far enough to suspect that the Fathers of the Republic who wrote our sacred Constitution of the United States not only did not, but did not want to, establish a democratic government, and I dreamed for a while — as I used as a child to play I was Napoleon or a trapper — I promised myself to write a true history of the making of the American Constitution. I did not do it; that chapter has been done or well begun since by two men: Smith of the University of Washington and Beard (then) of Columbia (afterward forced out, perhaps for this very work). I found other events, men, and epochs waiting for students. In all my other courses — in ancient, in European, and in modern history — the disagreeing authorities carried me back to the need of a fresh search for (or of) the original documents or other clinching testimony. Of course I did well in my classes. The history professors soon knew me as a student and seldom put a question to me except when the class had flunked it. Then Professor Jones would say, " Well, Steffens, tell them about it."

Fine. But vanity wasn't my ruling passion then. What I had was a quickening sense that I was learning a method of studying history and that every chapter of it, from the beginning of the world to the end, is crying out to be rewritten. There was something for Youth to do; these superior old men had not done anything, finally.

Years afterward I came out of the graft prosecution office in San Francisco with Rudolph Spreckels, the banker and backer of the investigation. We were to go somewhere, quick, in his car, and we couldn't. The chauffeur was trying to repair something wrong. Mr. Spreckels smiled; he looked closely at the defective part, and to my silent, wondering inquiry he answered: " Always, when I see something badly done or not done at all, I see an opportunity to make a fortune. I never kick at bad work by my class: there's lots of it and we suffer from it. But our failures and neglects are chances for the young fellows coming along and looking for work."

Nothing is done. Everything in the world remains to be done or done over. " The greatest picture is not yet painted, the greatest play isn't written (not even by Shakespeare), the greatest poem is unsung. There isn't in all the world a perfect railroad, nor a good government, nor a sound law." Physics, mathematics, and especially the most advanced and exact of the sciences are being fundamentally revised. Chemistry is just becoming a science; psychology, economics, and sociology are awaiting a Darwin, whose work in turn is awaiting an Einstein. If the rah-rah boys in our colleges could be told this, they might not all be such specialists in football, petting parties, and unearned degrees.

Clarence Darrow

My Home

MY earliest recollections that I can feel quite sure are real are about my family and home. My father was a miller and had a little gristmill by the side of the creek, just in the shade of some large oak trees. His mill must have been very small, for I always knew that he was poor. Still, it seemed to me that the mill was a wonderful affair, almost as large as the big white church that stood upon the hill. It was run by water and when the creek was not too low, which I am sure was very often, as I think it over now. Above the mill was a great dam, which made an enormous pond, larger than the Atlantic Ocean, and much more dangerous to any of us boys venture-

From *Farmington*, 1904.

some enough to go out upon it in a boat, or even on skates in the wintertime. But the most marvelous part of all was the wonderful water wheel hidden almost underneath the mill. It seemed as if there was a great hollow in the ground, to make room for the wheel; and if I had any opinion on the subject, I must have thought that the wheel grew there, for surely no one could make a monster like that. Often I used to go with my father up to the head of the millrace, when he lifted the big wooden gate and let the waters come down out of the dam through the race and the wooden flume over the groaning wheel. I well remember how I used to stand in awe and wonder while my father opened the gate, and then run down the path ahead of the rushing tide and peep through a hole to see the old wheel start. Then I would scamper over the mill, from the cellar with its cogs and pulleys, up to the garret with its white dusty chutes and its incomprehensible machines. Then I played around the sacks and bins of wheat and corn, and watched the grain as it streamed into the hopper ready to be ground to pieces by the slowly turning stones.

How real, and still how unreal, all this seems today! Is it all a dream? And am I writing a fairy story like " Little Red Riding Hood " or The Three Black Bears "? Surely all these events are as clear and vivid as the theat r party of last week. But while I so plainly see the little, idle, prattling child, looking with wondering eyes at the turning wheel, and asking his simple questions the grave, kind old man in the great white coat, somehow there is no relation between that simple child and the man whom the world has buffeted and tossed for so many years, and with such a rough unfriendly hand, that he cannot help the feeling that this far-off child was really someone else.

My father was a just and upright man — I can see him now dipping his bent wooden measure into the hopper of grain and taking out his toll, never a single kernel more than was his due. No doubt the suspicious farmers who brought their sacks of wheat and corn often thought that he dipped out more grain than he had a right to take; and even many of those who knew that he did not still thought he was a fool because he failed to make the most of the opportunities he had. As I grew up, I learned that there are all sorts of people in the world, and that selfishness and greed and envy are, to say the least, very common in the human heart; but I never could be thankful enough that my father was honest and simple, and that his love of truth and justice had grown into his being as naturally as the oaks were rooted to the earth along the little stream.

The old wheel ceased turning long ago. The last stick of timber in its wondrous mechanism has rotted and decayed; the old mill itself has vanished from the earth. The drying stream and the great mills of the new Northwest long since conspired to destroy my father's simple trade. Even the dam has been washed away, and a tiny thread of water now trickles down over the hill where the rushing flood fell full upon the turning wheel. Last summer I went back to linger, like a ghost, around the old familiar spot; and I found that even the great unexplored pond had dried up, and a field of corn was growing peacefully upon the soil that once upheld this treacherous sea. And the old miller, too, with his kindly, simple, honest face — the old miller with his white coat — he, too, is gone, gone as completely as his father and all the other fathers and grandfathers who have come and gone; the dear, kind old miller who listened to my childish questions and taught me, or rather tried to teach me, what was right and wrong has grown weary and lain down to rest, and will soon be quite forgotten by the world — unless this story shall bring his son so much fame that some of the glory shall be reflected back to him.

Somehow the mill seems to have made a stronger impression than the house on my young mind. Perhaps it was because it was the only mill that I had ever seen or known; perhaps because the memories that clung to the mill and its surroundings were such as appeal most to the mind of a little child. Of course, from the very nature of things the home and family must have been among my earliest recollections; yet I cannot help feeling that much of the literature about childhood's home has been written for effect — or not to describe home as it really is to the child, but from someone's ideal of what home ought to be.

I know that my mother was an energetic, hard-working, and in every way strong woman, although I did not know it or think about it then. I know it now, for as I look back to my childhood and see the large family that she cared for, almost without help, I cannot understand how she did it all, especially as she managed to keep well informed on the topics of the day, and found more time for reading and study than any of her neighbors did.

In the main, I think our family was like the other families of the neighborhood, with about the same dispositions, the same ideas and ideals — if children can be said to have ideals — that other people had.

There were seven of us children, and we must have crowded the little home, to say nothing of the little income with which my father and mother raised us all. Our family life was not the ideal home life of which we read in books; the fact is, I have never seen that sort of life amongst children — or amongst grown people either, for that matter. If we loved each other, we were all too proud and well-trained to say a word about it, or to make any sign to show that it was true. When a number of us children were together playing the familiar games, we generally quarreled and fought much more than was our habit when playing with our neighbors and our friends. In this, too, we were like all the rest of the families that I knew. It seems to me now that a very small matter was always enough to bring on a fight, and that we quarreled simply because we liked to hurt each other; at least I can see no other reason why we did.

We children were supposed to help with the chores around the house; but, as near as I can remember, each one was always afraid that he would do more than his share. I recall a story in one of our school readers, which I read when very young; it was about two brothers, a large one and a small one, and they were carrying a pail on a pole, and the larger brother deliberately shoved the pail nearer to his end, so that the heavier load would fall on him; but I am sure that this incident never happened in our family, or in any other that I ever knew.

Most home life necessarily clusters around the mother; and so, of course, it must have been in our family. But my mother died when I was in my earlier teens, and her figure has not that clearness that I wish it had. She seems now to have been a remarkable combination of energy and industry, of kindness, and still of strong and controlling will; a woman who, under other conditions of life, and unhampered by so many children and such pressing needs, might have left her mark upon the world. But this was not to be; for she could not overlook the duties that lay nearest her for a broader or more ambitious life.

Both my father and mother must have been kind and gentle and tender to the large family that so sorely taxed their time and strength; and yet, as I look back, I do not have the feeling of closeness that should unite the parent and the child. They were New England people, raised in the Puritan school of life, and I fancy that they would have felt that demonstrations of affection were signs of weakness rather than of love. I have no feeling of a time when either my father or my mother took me, or any other member of our family, in their arms; and the control of the household seemed to be such fixed rules as are ordinarily followed in family life, with now and then a resort to rather mild corporal punishment when they thought the occasion grave enough. Both parents were beyond their neighbors in education, intelligence, and strength of character; and with their breadth of view, I cannot understand how they did not see that even the mild force they used tended to cause bitterness and resentment, and thus defeat the object sought. I well remember that we were all glad if our parents, or either of them, were absent for a day; not that they were unkind, but that with them we felt restraint, and never that spirit of love and trust which ought always to be present between the parent and the child.

While I cannot recall that my mother ever gave me a kiss or a caress, and while I am sure that I should have been embarrassed if she had, still I remember that when I had a fever, and lay on my bed for what seemed endless weeks, she let no one else come near me by day or night. And although she must have attended to all her household duties, she seemed ever beside me with the tenderest and gentlest touch. I can still less remember any great affection that I had for her, or any effort on my part to make her life easier than it was; yet I know that I must have loved her, for I can never forget the bitterness of my despair and grief when they told me she must die. And even now, as I look back after all these weary years, when I think of her lying cold and dead in the still front room I feel almost the same shudder and horror that filled my heart as a little child. And with this shudder comes the endless regret that I did not tell her that I loved her, and do more to lighten the burdens of her life.

This family feeling, or lack of it, I think must have come from the Puritanic school in which my father and mother were born and raised. It must be that any intelligent parent who really understands life would be able to make his children feel a companionship greater than any other they could know.

With my brothers and sisters my life was much the same. We never said anything about our love for each other, and our nearness seemed to bring out our antagonism more than our love. Still, I am sure that I really cared for them, for I recall that once when a brother was very ill I was wretched with fear and grief. I remember how I went over every circumstance of our relations with each other, and how I vowed that I would always be kind and loving to him if his life were saved. Fortunately, he got well; but I cannot recall that I treated him any better after his sickness than before.

I remember how happy all of us used to be when cousins or friends came to stay a few days in our house, and how much more we liked to be with them than with our own family. I remember, too, that I had the same feeling when I visited other houses; and I have found it so to this day. True it is, that in great trouble or in a crisis of life we seem to cling to our kindred, and stand by them, and expect them to stand by us; and yet, in the little things, day by day, we look for our comradeship and affection somewhere else.

So I think that in all of this neither I nor the rest of my people were different from the other families about us, and that the stories of the ideal life of brothers and sisters, of parents and children, are largely myths.

Samuel L. Clemens

Learning the River

WHAT with lying on the rocks for days at Louisville, and some other delays, the poor old *Paul Jones* fooled away about two weeks in making the voyage from Cincinnati to New Orleans. This gave me a chance to get acquainted with one of the pilots and he taught me how to steer the boat, and thus made the fascination of river life more potent than ever for me.

It also gave me a chance to get acquainted with a youth who had taken deck passage — more's the pity; for he easily borrowed six dollars of me on a promise to return to the boat and pay it back to me the day after we should arrive. But he probably died or forgot, for he never came. It was doubtless the former, since he had said his parents were wealthy, and he only traveled deck passage because it was cooler.

I soon discovered two things. One was that a vessel would not be likely to sail for the mouth of the Amazon under ten or twelve years; and the other was that the nine or ten dollars still left in my pocket would not suffice for so imposing an exploration as I had planned, even if I could afford to wait for a ship. Therefore it followed that I must contrive a new career. The *Paul Jones* was now bound for St. Louis. I planned a siege against my pilot, and at the end of three hard days he surrendered. He agreed to teach me the Mississippi River from New Orleans to St. Louis for five hundred dollars, payable out of

From *Life on the Mississippi,* 1883.

the first wages I should receive after graduating. I entered upon the small enterprise of "learning" twelve or thirteen hundred miles of the great Mississippi River with the easy confidence of my time of life. If I had really known what I was about to require of my faculties, I should not have had the courage to begin. I supposed that all a pilot had to do was to keep his boat in the river, and I did not consider that that could be much of a trick, since it was so wide.

The boat backed out from New Orleans at four in the afternoon, and it was "our watch" until eight. Mr. Bixby, my chief, "straightened her up," plowed her along past the sterns of the other boats that lay at the levee, and then said, "Here, take her; shave those steamships as close as you'd peel an apple." I took the wheel, and my heart went down into my boots; for it seemed to me that we were about to scrape the side off every ship in the line, we were so close. I held my breath and began to claw the boat away from the danger; and I had my own opinion of the pilot who had known no better than to get us into such peril, but I was too wise to express it. In half a minute I had a wide margin of safety intervening between the *Paul Jones* and the ships; and within ten seconds more I was set aside in disgrace, and Mr. Bixby was going into danger again and flaying me alive with abuse of my cowardice. I was stung, but I was obliged to admire the easy confidence with which my chief loafed from side to side of his wheel, and trimmed the ships so closely that disaster seemed ceaselessly imminent. When he had cooled a little he told me that the easy water was close ashore and the current outside, and therefore we must hug the bank, upstream, to get the benefit of the former, and stay well out, downstream, to take advantage of the latter. In my own mind I resolved to be a downstream pilot and leave the upstreaming to people dead to prudence.

Now and then Mr. Bixby called my attention to certain things. Said he, "This is Six-Mile Point." I assented. It was pleasant enough information, but I could not see the bearing of it. I was not conscious that it was a matter of any interest to me. Another time he said, "This is Nine-Mile Point." Later he said, "This is Twelve-Mile Point." They were all about level with the water's edge; they all looked about alike to me; they were monotonously unpicturesque. I hoped Mr. Bixby would change the subject. But no; he would crowd up around a point, hugging the shore with affection, and then say: "The slack water ends here, abreast this bunch of China trees; now we cross over." So he crossed over. He gave me the wheel once or twice, but I had no luck. I either came near chipping off the edge of a sugar plantation, or else I yawed too far from shore, and so I dropped back into disgrace and got abused again.

The watch was ended at last, and we took supper and went to bed. At midnight the glare of a lantern shone in my eyes, and the night watchman said: "Come! Turn out!"

And then he left. I could not understand this extraordinary procedure; so I presently gave up trying to, and dozed off to sleep. Pretty soon the watchman was back again, and this time he was gruff. I was annoyed. I said: "What do you want to come bothering around here in the middle of the night for? Now as like as not I'll not get to sleep again tonight."

The watchman said: "Well, if this an't good, I'm blest."

The " off watch " was just turning in, and I heard some brutal laughter from them, and such remarks as " Hello, watchman! An't the new cub turned out yet? He's delicate, likely. Give him some sugar in a rag and send for the chambermaid to sing rock-a-by-baby to him."

About this time Mr. Bixby appeared on the scene. Something like a minute later I was climbing the pilothouse steps with some of my clothes on and the rest in my arms. Mr. Bixby was close behind commenting. Here was something fresh — this thing of getting up in the middle of the night to go to work. It was a detail in piloting that had never occurred to me at all. I knew the boats ran all night, but somehow I had never happened to reflect that somebody had to get up out of a warm bed to run them. I began to fear that piloting was not quite so romantic as I had imagined it was; there was something very real and work-like about this new phase of it.

It was a rather dingy night, although a fair number of stars were out. The big mate was at the wheel, and he had the old tub pointed at a star and was holding her straight up the middle of the river. The shores on either hand were not much more than a mile apart, but they seemed wonderfully far away and ever so vague and indistinct. The mate said: " We've got to land at Jones's plantation, sir."

The vengeful spirit in me exulted. I said to myself, I wish you joy of your job, Mr. Bixby; you'll have a good time finding Mr. Jones's plantation such a night as this; and I hope you never *will* find it as long as you live.

Mr. Bixby said to the mate: " Upper end of the plantation, or the lower? "
" Upper."

" I can't do it. The stumps there are out of water at this stage. It's no great distance to the lower, and you'll have to get along with that."

" All right, sir. If Jones don't like it he'll have to lump it, I reckon."

And then the mate left. My exultation began to cool and my wonder to come up. Here was a man who not only proposed to find this plantation on such a night, but to find either end of it you preferred. I dreadfully wanted to ask a question, but I was carrying about as many short answers as my cargo room would admit of, so I held my peace. All I desired to ask Mr. Bixby was the simple question whether he was ass enough to really imagine he was going to find that plantation on a night when all plantations were exactly alike and all the same color. But I held in. I used to have fine inspirations of prudence in those days.

Mr. Bixby made for the shore and soon was scraping it, just the same as if it had been daylight. And not only that, but singing " Father in heaven the day is declining," etc. It seemed to me that I had put my life in the keeping of a peculiarly reckless outcast. Presently he turned on me and said: " What's the name of the first point above New Orleans? "

I was gratified to be able to answer promptly, and I did. I said I didn't know.
" Don't *know*? "

This manner jolted me. I was down at the foot again, in a moment. But I had to say just what I had said before.

"Well, you're a smart one," said Mr. Bixby. "What's the name of the *next* point?"

Once more I didn't know.

"Well, this beats anything. Tell me the name of *any* point or place I told you."

I studied a while and decided that I couldn't.

"Look-a-here! What do you start out from, above Twelve-Mile Point, to cross over?"

"I — I — don't know."

"You — you — don't know?" mimicking my drawling manner of speech. "What *do* you know?"

"I — I — nothing, for certain."

"By the great Caesar's ghost I believe you! You're the stupidest dunderhead I ever saw or ever heard of, so help me Moses! The idea of *you* being a pilot — *you!* Why, you don't know enough to pilot a cow down a lane."

Oh, but his wrath was up! He was a nervous man, and he shuffled from one side of his wheel to the other as if the floor was hot. He would boil a while to himself, and then overflow and scald me again.

"Look-a-here! What do you suppose I told you the names of those points for?"

I tremblingly considered a moment, and then the devil of temptation provoked me to say: "Well — to — to — be entertaining, I thought."

This was a red rag to the bull. He raged and stormed so (he was crossing the river at the time) that I judge it made him blind, because he ran over the steering oar of a trading scow. Of course the traders sent up a volley of red-hot profanity. Never was a man so grateful as Mr. Bixby was: because he was brim full, and here were subjects who would *talk back*. He threw open a window, thrust his head out, and such an eruption followed as I never had heard before. The fainter and farther away the scowmen's curses drifted, the higher Mr. Bixby lifted his voice and the weightier his adjectives grew. When he closed the window he was empty. You could have drawn a seine through his system and not caught curses enough to disturb your mother with.

Presently he said to me in the gentlest way: "My boy, you must get a little memorandum book, and every time I tell you a thing, put it down right away. There's only one way to be a pilot, and that is to get this entire river by heart. You have to know it just like A B C."

That was a dismal revelation to me; for my memory was never loaded with anything but blank cartridges. However, I did not feel discouraged long. I judged that it was best to make some allowances, for doubtless Mr. Bixby was "stretching." Presently he pulled a rope and struck a few strokes on the big bell. The stars were all gone now, and the night was as black as ink. I could hear the wheels churn along the bank, but I was not entirely certain that I could see the shore.

The voice of the invisible watchman called up from the hurricane deck: "What's this, sir?"

"Jones's plantation."

I said to myself, I wish I might venture to offer a small bet that it isn't. But I did not chirp. I only waited to see. Mr. Bixby handled the engine bells, and in due time the boat's nose came to the land, a torch glowed from the forecastle, a man skipped ashore, a darky's voice on the bank said, " Gimme de carpetbag, Mars' Jones," and the next moment we were standing up the river again, all serene. I reflected deeply a while, and then said — but not aloud: " Well, the finding of that plantation was the luckiest accident that ever happened; but it couldn't happen again in a hundred years." And I fully believed it *was* an accident, too.

By the time we had gone seven or eight hundred miles up the river, I had learned to be a tolerably plucky upstream steersman, in daylight; and before we reached St. Louis, I had made a trifle of progress in night work, but only a trifle. I had a notebook that fairly bristled with the names of towns, " points," bars, islands, bends, reaches, etc.; but the information was to be found only in the notebook — none of it was in my head. It made my heart ache to think I had only got half of the river set down; for as our watch was four hours off and four hours on, day and night, there was a long four-hour gap in my book for every time I had slept since the voyage began.

My chief was presently hired to go on a big New Orleans boat, and I packed n. satchel and went with him. She was a grand affair. When I stood in her pilothouse I was so far above the water that I seemed perched on a mountain; and her decks stretched so far away, fore and aft, below me, that I wondered how I could ever have considered the little *Paul Jones* a large craft. There were other differences, too. The *Paul Jones's* pilothouse was a cheap, dingy, battered rattletrap, cramped for room; but here was a sumptuous glass temple; room enough to have a dance in; showy red and gold window curtains; an imposing sofa; leather cushions and a back to the high bench where visiting pilots sit, to spin yarns and " look at the river "; bright, fanciful " cuspadores " instead of a broad wooden box filled with sawdust; nice new oilcloth on the floor; a hospitable big stove for winter; a wheel as high as my head, costly with inlaid work; a wire tiller-rope; bright brass knobs for the bells; and a tidy, white-aproned, black " texas-tender," to bring up tarts and ices and coffee during mid-watch day and night. Now this was " something like "; and so I began to take heart once more to believe that piloting was a romantic sort of occupation after all. The moment we were under way I began to prowl about the great steamer and fill myself with joy. She was as clean and as dainty as a drawing room; when I looked down her long, gilded saloon, it was like gazing through a splendid tunnel; she had an oil picture, by some gifted sign painter, on every stateroom door; she glittered with no end of prism-fringed chandeliers; the clerk's office was elegant, the bar was marvelous, and the barkeeper had been barbered and upholstered at incredible cost. The boiler deck (i.e., the second story of the boat, so to speak) was as spacious as a church, it seemed to me; so with the forecastle; and there was no pitiful handful of deckhands, firemen, and roustabouts down there, but a whole battalion of men. The fires were fiercely glaring from a long row of furnaces, and over them were eight huge boilers! This was unutterable pomp. The mighty engines — but enough of this. I had never felt so fine before. And when I found that the regiment of natty servants respectfully " sirred " me, my satisfaction was complete.

When I returned to the pilothouse St. Louis was gone and I was lost. Here was a piece of river which was all down in my book, but I could make neither head nor tail of it: you understand, it was turned around. I had seen it when coming upstream, but I had never faced about to see how it looked when it was behind me. My heart broke again, for it was plain that I had got to learn this troublesome river *both ways*.

The pilothouse was full of pilots, going down to " look at the river." What is called the " upper river " (the two hundred miles between St. Louis and Cairo, where the Ohio comes in) was low; and the Mississippi changes its channel so constantly that the pilots used to always find it necessary to run down to Cairo to take a fresh look, when their boats were to lie in port a week — that is, when the water was at a low stage. A deal of this " looking at the river " was done by poor fellows who seldom had a berth and whose only hope of getting one lay in their being always freshly posted and therefore ready to drop into the shoes of some reputable pilot, for a single trip, on account of such pilot's sudden illness or some other necessity. And a good many of them constantly ran up and down inspecting the river, not because they ever really hoped to get a berth, but because (they being guests of the boat) it was cheaper to " look at the river " than stay ashore and pay board. In time these fellows grew dainty in their tastes, and only infested boats that had an established reputation for setting good tables. All visiting pilots were useful, for they were always ready and willing, winter or summer, night or day, to go out in the yawl and help buoy the channel or assist the boat's pilots in any way they could. They were likewise welcome because all pilots are tireless talkers, when gathered together; and as they talk only about the river they are always understood and are always interesting. Your true pilot cares nothing about anything on earth but the river, and his pride in his occupation surpasses the pride of kings.

We had a fine company of these river inspectors along, this trip. There were eight or ten; and there was abundance of room for them in our great pilothouse. Two or three of them wore polished silk hats, elaborate shirt-fronts, diamond breastpins, kid gloves, and patent leather boots. They were choice in their English, and bore themselves with a dignity proper to men of solid means and prodigious reputation as pilots. The others were more or less loosely clad, and wore upon their heads tall felt cones that were suggestive of the days of the Commonwealth.

I was a cipher in this august company, and felt subdued, not to say torpid. I was not even of sufficient consequence to assist at the wheel when it was necessary to put the tiller hard down in a hurry; the guest that stood nearest did that when occasion required — and this was pretty much all the time, because of the crookedness of the channel and the scant water. I stood in a corner; and the talk I listened to took the hope all out of me.

One visitor said to another: "Jim, how did you run Plum Point, coming up?"

"It was in the night, there, and I ran it the way one of the boys on the *Diana* told me; started out about fifty yards above the woodpile on the false point, and held on the cabin under Plum Point till I raised the reef — quarter less twain — then straightened up for the middle bar till I got well abreast the old one-limbed cottonwood in the bend, then got my stern on the cottonwood and head on the low place above the point, and came through a-booming — nine and a half."

"Pretty square crossing, an't it?"

"Yes, but the upper bar's working down fast."

Another pilot spoke up and said: "I had better water than that, and ran it lower down; started out from the false point — mark twain — raised the second reef abreast the big snag in the bend, and had quarter less twain."

One of the gorgeous ones remarked: "I don't want to find fault with your leadsmen, but that's a good deal of water for Plum Point, it seems to me."

There was an approving nod all around as this quiet snub dropped on the boaster and "settled" him. And so they went on talk-talk-talking. Meantime the thing that was running in my mind was: "Now if my ears hear aright, I have not only to get the names of all the towns and islands and bends, and so on, by heart, but I must even get up a warm personal acquaintanceship with every old snag and one-limbed cottonwood and obscure woodpile that ornaments the banks of this river for twelve hundred miles; and more than that, I must actually know where these things are in the dark, unless these guests are gifted with eyes that can pierce through two miles of solid blackness; I wish the piloting business was in Jericho and I had never thought of it."

At dusk Mr. Bixby tapped the big bell three times (the signal to land), and the captain emerged from his drawing room in the forward end of the texas, and looked up inquiringly.

Mr. Bixby said: "We will lay up here all night, captain."

"Very well, sir."

That was all. The boat came to shore and was tied up for the night. It seemed to me a fine thing that the pilot could do as he pleased without asking so grand a captain's permission. I took my supper and went immediately to bed, discouraged by my day's observations and experiences. My late voyage's notebooking was but a confusion of meaningless names. It had tangled me all up in a knot every time I had looked at it in the daytime. I now hoped for respite in sleep; but no, it reveled all through my head till sunrise again, a frantic and tireless nightmare.

Next morning I felt pretty rusty and low-spirited. We went booming along, taking a good many chances, for we were anxious to "get out of the river" (as getting out to Cairo was called) before night should overtake us. But Mr. Bixby's partner, the other pilot, presently grounded the boat, and we lost so much time getting her off that it was plain the darkness would overtake us a good long way above the mouth. This was a great misfortune especially to certain of our visiting pilots, whose boats would have to wait for their return, no matter how long that might be. It sobered the pilothouse talk a good deal. Coming upstream, pilots did not mind low water or any kind of darkness; nothing stopped them but fog. But downstream work was different: a boat was too nearly helpless, with a stiff current pushing behind her; so it was not customary to run downstream at night in low water.

There seemed to be one small hope, however: if we could get through the intricate and dangerous Hat Island crossing before night, we could venture the rest, for we would have plainer sailing and better water. But it would be insanity to attempt Hat Island at night. So there was a deal of looking at watches all the rest of the day, and a constant ciphering upon the speed we were making. Hat Island was the eternal subject; sometimes hope was high and sometimes we were delayed in a bad crossing, and down it went again. For hours all hands lay under the burden of this suppressed excitement. It was even communicated to me, and I got to feeling so solicitous about Hat Island, and under such an awful pressure of responsibility, that I wished I might have five minutes on shore to draw a good, full, relieving breath and start over again. We were standing no regular watches. Each of our pilots ran such portions of the river as he had run when coming upstream, because of his greater familiarity with it; but both remained in the pilothouse constantly.

An hour before sunset, Mr. Bixby took the wheel and Mr. W. stepped aside. For the next thirty minutes every man held his watch in his hand and was restless, silent, and uneasy. At last somebody said, with a doomful sigh: "Well, yonder's Hat Island — and we can't make it."

All the watches closed with a snap; everybody sighed and muttered something about its being " too bad, too bad — ah, if we could *only* have got here half an hour sooner! " and the place was thick with the atmosphere of disappointment. Some started to go out, but loitered, hearing no bell-tap to land. The sun dipped behind the horizon, the boat went on. Inquiring looks passed from one guest to another; and one who had his hand on the doorknob, and had turned it, waited, then presently took away his hand and let the knob turn back again. We bore steadily down the bend. More looks were exchanged, and nods of surprised admiration — but no words. Insensibly the men drew together behind Mr. Bixby as the sky darkened and one or two dim stars came out. The dead silence and sense of waiting became oppressive. Mr. Bixby pulled the cord, and two deep, mellow notes from the big bell floated off on the night. Then a pause, and one more note was struck. The watchman's voice followed, from the hurricane deck: " Labboard lead, there! Stabboard lead! "

The cries of the leadsmen began to rise out of the distance, and were gruffly repeated by the word-passers on the hurricane deck.

"M-a-r-k three! M-a-r-k three! Quarter less three! Half twain! Quarter twain! M-a-r-k twain! Quarter less — "

Mr. Bixby pulled two bell-ropes, and was answered by faint jinglings far below in the engine room, and our speed slackened. The steam began to whistle through the gauge cocks. The cries of the leadsmen went on — and it is a weird sound, always, in the night. Every pilot in the lot was watching now, with fixed eyes, and talking under his breath. Nobody was calm and easy but Mr. Bixby.

He would put his wheel down and stand on a spoke, and as the steamer swung into her (to me) utterly invisible marks — for we seemed to be in the midst of a wide and gloomy sea — he would meet and fasten her there.

Talk was going on, now, in low voices: " There; she's over the first reef all right! "

After a pause, another subdued voice: " Her stern's coming down just *exactly* right, by *George!* Now she's in the marks; over she goes! "

Somebody else muttered: " Oh, it was done beautiful — *beautiful!* "

Now the engines were stopped altogether, and we drifted with the current. Not that I could see the boat drift, for I could not, the stars being all gone by this time. This drifting was the dismalest work; it held one's heart still. Presently I discovered a blacker gloom than that which surrounded us. It was the head of the island. We were closing right down upon it. We entered its deeper shadow, and so imminent seemed the peril that I was likely to suffocate; and I had the strongest impulse to do *something,* anything, to save the vessel. But still Mr. Bixby stood by his wheel, silent, intent as a cat, and all the pilots stood shoulder to shoulder at his back.

" She'll not make it! " somebody whispered.

The water grew shoaler and shoaler by the leadsmen's cries, till it was down to " Eight and a half! E-i-g-h-t feet! E-i-g-h-t feet! Seven and — "

Mr. Bixby said warningly through his speaking tube to the engineer: " Stand by, now! "

" Aye, aye, sir. "

" Seven and a half! Seven feet! *Six* and — "

We touched bottom! Instantly Mr. Bixby set a lot of bells ringing, shouted through the tube, " *Now* let her have it — every ounce you've got! " Then to his partner, " Put her hard down! Snatch her! Snatch her! " The boat rasped and ground her way through the sand, hung upon the apex of disaster a single tremendous instant, and then over she went! And such a shout as went up at Mr. Bixby's back never loosened the roof of a pilothouse before!

There was no more trouble after that. Mr. Bixby was a hero that night; and it was some little time, too, before his exploit ceased to be talked about by river men.

Fully to realize the marvelous precision required in laying the great steamer in her marks in that murky waste of water, one should know that not only must she pick her intricate way through snags and blind reefs, and then shave the head of the island so closely as to brush the overhanging foliage with her stern, but at one place she must pass almost within arm's reach of a sunken and invisible wreck that would snatch the hull timbers from under her if she should strike it, and destroy a quarter of a million dollars' worth of steamboat and cargo in five minutes, and maybe a hundred and fifty human lives into the bargain.

The last remark I heard that night was a compliment to Mr. Bixby, uttered in soliloquy and with unction by one of our guests. He said: " By the Shadow of Death, but he's a lightning pilot! "

Henry David Thoreau

Where I Lived, and What I Lived For

I

AT a certain season of our life we are accustomed to consider every spot as the possible site of a house. I have thus surveyed the country on every side within a dozen miles of where I live. In imagination I have bought all the farms in succession, for all were to be bought, and I knew their price. I walked over each farmer's premises, tasted his wild apples, discoursed on husbandry with him, took his farm at his price, at any price, mortgaging it to him in my mind; even put a higher price on it — took everything but a deed of it — took his word for his deed, for I dearly love to talk — cultivated it, and him too to some extent, I trust, and withdrew when I had enjoyed it long enough, leaving him to carry it on. This experience entitled me to be regarded as a sort of real-estate broker by my friends. Wherever I sat, there I might live, and the landscape radiated from me accordingly. What is a house but a *sedes,* a seat? — better if a country seat. I discovered many a site for a house not likely to be soon improved, which some might have thought too far from the village, but to my eyes the village was too far from it. Well, there I might live, I said; and there I did live, for an hour, a summer and a winter life; saw how I could let the years run off, buffet the winter through, and see the spring come in. The future inhabitants of this region, wherever they may place their houses, may be sure that they have been anticipated. An afternoon sufficed to lay out the land into orchard, wood lot, and pasture, and to decide what fine oaks or pines should be left to stand before the door, and whence each blasted tree could be seen to the best advantage; and then I let it lie, fallow perchance, for a man is rich in proportion to the number of things which he can afford to let alone.

My imagination carried me so far that I even had the refusal of several farms — the refusal was all I wanted — but I never got my fingers burned by actual possession. The nearest that I came to actual possession was when I bought the Hollowell place, and had begun to sort my seeds, and collected materials with which to make a wheelbarrow to carry it on or off with; but before the owner gave me a deed of it, his wife — every man has such a wife — changed her mind and wished to keep it, and he offered me ten dollars to release him. Now, to speak the truth, I had but ten cents in the world, and it surpassed my arithmetic to tell if I was that man who had ten cents, or who had a farm, or ten dollars, or all together. However, I let him keep the ten dollars and the farm too, for I had carried it far enough; or rather, to be generous, I sold him the farm for just what I gave for it, and, as he was not a rich man, made him a present of ten dollars, and still had my ten cents, and seeds, and materials

From *Walden,* 1854.

for a wheelbarrow left. I found thus that I had been a rich man without any damage to my poverty. But I retained the landscape, and I have since annually carried off what it yielded without a wheelbarrow. With respect to landscapes —

> I am monarch of all I *survey,*
> My right there is none to dispute.

I have frequently seen a poet withdraw, having enjoyed the most valuable part of a farm, while the crusty farmer supposed that he had got a few wild apples only. Why, the owner does not know it for many years when a poet has put his farm in rhyme, the most admirable kind of invisible fence, has fairly impounded it, milked it, skimmed it, and got all the cream, and left the farmer only the skimmed milk.

The real attractions of the Hollowell farm, to me, were: its complete retirement, being about two miles from the village, half a mile from the nearest neighbor, and separated from the highway by a broad field; its bounding on the river, which the owner said protected it by its fogs from frosts in the spring, though that was nothing to me; the gray color and ruinous state of the house and barn, and the dilapidated fences, which put such an interval between me and the last occupant; the hollow and lichen-covered apple trees, gnawed by rabbits, showing what kind of neighbors I should have; but above all, the recollection I had of it from my earliest voyages up the river, when the house was concealed behind a dense grove of red maples, through which I heard the house dog bark. I was in haste to buy it, before the proprietor finished getting out some rocks, cutting down the hollow apple trees, and grubbing up some young birches which had sprung up in the pasture, or, in short, had made any more of his improvements. To enjoy these advantages I was ready to carry it on; like Atlas, to take the world on my shoulders — I never heard what compensation he received for that — and do all those things which had no other motive or excuse but that I might pay for it and be unmolested in my possession of it; for I knew all the while that it would yield the most abundant crop of the kind I wanted, if I could only afford to let it alone. But it turned out as I have said.

All that I could say, then, with respect to farming on a large scale — I have always cultivated a garden — was that I had had my seeds ready. Many think that seeds improve with age. I have no doubt that time discriminates between the good and the bad; and when at last I shall plant, I shall be less likely to be disappointed. But I would say to my fellows, once for all: As long as possible live free and uncommitted. It makes but little difference whether you are committed to a farm or the county jail.

Old Cato, whose *De Re Rusticâ* is my *Cultivator,* says — and the only translation I have seen makes sheer nonsense of the passage — " When you think of getting a farm turn it thus in your mind, not to buy greedily; nor spare your pains to look at it, and do not think it enough to go round it once. The oftener you go there the more it will please you, if it is good." I think I shall not buy greedily, but go round and round it as long as I live, and be buried in it first, that it may please me the more at last.

The present was my next experiment of this kind, which I purpose to describe more at length, for convenience putting the experience of two years into one. As I have said, I do not propose to write an ode to dejection, but to brag as lustily as chanticleer in the morning, standing on his roost, if only to wake my neighbors up.

When first I took up my abode in the woods — that is, began to spend my nights as well as days there — which, by accident, was on Independence Day, or the Fourth of July, 1845, my house was not finished for winter, but was merely a defense against the rain, without plastering or chimney, the walls being of rough, weather-stained boards, with wide chinks, which made it cool at night. The upright white hewn studs and freshly planed door and window casings gave it a clean and airy look, especially in the morning, when its timbers were saturated with dew, so that I fancied that by noon some sweet gum would exude from them. To my imagination it retained throughout the day more or less of this auroral character, reminding me of a certain house on a mountain which I had visited a year before. This was an airy and unplastered cabin, fit to entertain a traveling god, and where a goddess might trail her garments. The winds which passed over my dwelling were such as sweep over the ridges of mountains, bearing the broken strains, or celestial parts only, of terrestrial music. The morning wind forever blows, the poem of creation is uninterrupted; but few are the ears that hear it. Olympus is but the outside of the earth everywhere.

The only house I had been the owner of before, if I except a boat, was a tent, which I used occasionally when making excursions in the summer, and this is still rolled up in my garret; but the boat, after passing from hand to hand, has gone down the stream of time. With this more substantial shelter about me, I had made some progress toward settling in the world. This frame, so slightly clad, was a sort of crystallization around me, and reacted on the builder. It was suggestive somewhat as a picture in outlines. I did not need to go outdoors to take the air, for the atmosphere within had lost none of its freshness. It was not so much withindoors as behind a door where I sat, even in the rainiest weather. The *Harivansa* says, " An abode without birds is like a meat without seasoning." Such was not my abode, for I found myself suddenly neighbor to the birds; not by having imprisoned one, but having caged myself near them. I was not only nearer to some of those which commonly frequent the garden and the orchard, but to those wilder and more thrilling songsters of the forest which never, or rarely, serenade a villager — the wood thrush, the veery, the scarlet tanager, the field sparrow, the whippoorwill, and many others.

I was seated by the shore of a small pond, about a mile and a half south of the village of Concord and somewhat higher than it, in the midst of an extensive wood between that town and Lincoln, and about two miles south of that our only field known to fame, Concord Battle Ground; but I was so low in the woods that the opposite shore, half a mile off, like the rest, covered with wood, was my most distant horizon. For the first week, whenever I looked out on the pond it impressed me like a tarn high up on the side of a mountain, its bottom far above the surface of other lakes; and as the sun arose, I saw it throwing off its nightly clothing of mist; and here and there, by degrees, its soft ripples or its smooth reflecting surface was revealed, while the mists, like ghosts, were stealthily withdrawing in every direction into the woods, as at the breaking up of some nocturnal conventicle. The very dew seemed to hang upon the trees later into the day than usual, as on the sides of mountains.

This small lake was of most value as a neighbor in the intervals of a gentle rainstorm in August, when, both air and water being perfectly still, but the sky overcast, midafternoon had all the serenity of evening, and the wood thrush sang around, and was heard from shore to shore. A lake like this is never smoother than at such a time; and the clear portion of the air above it being shallow and darkened by clouds, the water, full of light and reflections, becomes a lower heaven itself so much the more important. From a hilltop near by, where the wood had been recently cut off, there was a pleasing vista southward across the pond, through a wide indentation in the hills which form the shore there, where their opposite sides sloping toward each other suggested a stream flowing out in that direction through a wooded valley, but stream there was none. That way I looked between and over the near green hills to some distant and higher ones in the horizon, tinged with blue. Indeed, by standing on tiptoe I could catch a glimpse of some of the peaks of the still bluer and more distant mountain ranges in the northwest, those true-blue coins from heaven's own mint, and also of some portion of the village. But in other directions, even from this point, I could not see over or beyond the woods which surrounded me. It is well to have some water in your neighborhood, to give buoyancy to and float the earth. One value even of the smallest well is that when you look into it you see that earth is not continent but insular. This is as important as that it keeps butter cool. When I looked across the pond from this peak toward the Sudbury meadows, which in time of flood I distinguished elevated perhaps by a mirage in their seething valley, like a coin in a basin, all the earth beyond the pond appeared like a thin crust insulated and floated even by this small sheet of inter-vening water, and I was reminded that this on which I dwelt was but *dry land*.

Though the view from my door was still more contracted, I did not feel crowded or confined in the least. There was pasture enough for my imagination. The low shrub oak plateau to which the opposite shore arose stretched away toward the prairies of the West and the steppes of Tartary, affording ample room for all the roving families of men. "There are none happy in the world but beings who enjoy freely a vast horizon," said Damodara when his herds required new and larger pastures.

Both place and time were changed, and I dwelt nearer to those parts of the universe and to those eras in history which had most attracted me. Where I lived was as far off as many a region viewed nightly by astronomers. We are wont to imagine rare and delectable places in some remote and more celestial corner of the system, behind the constellation of Cassiopeia's Chair, far from noise and disturbance. I discovered that my house actually had its site in such a withdrawn, but forever new and unprofaned, part of the universe. If it were worth the while to settle in those parts near to the Pleiades or the Hyades, to Aldebaran or Altair, then I was really there, or at an equal remoteness from the life which I had left behind, dwindled and twinkling with as fine a ray to my nearest neighbor, and to be seen only in moonless nights by him. Such was that part of creation where I had squatted.

> There was a shepherd that did live,
>   And held his thoughts as high
> As were the mounts whereon his flocks
>   Did hourly feed him by.

What should we think of the shepherd's life if his flocks always wandered to higher pastures than his thoughts?

Every morning was a cheerful invitation to make my life of equal simplicity, and I may say innocence, with Nature herself. I have been as sincere a worshipper of Aurora as the Greeks. I got up early and bathed in the pond; that was a religious exercise, and one of the best things which I did. They say that characters were engraven on the bathing tub of King Tching-thang to this effect: "Renew thyself completely each day; do it again, and again, and forever again." I can understand that. Morning brings back the heroic ages. I was as much affected by the faint hum of a mosquito making its invisible and unimaginable tour through my apartment at earliest dawn, when I was sitting with door and windows open, as I could be by any trumpet that ever sang of fame. It was Homer's requiem; itself an Iliad and Odyssey in the air, singing its own wrath and wanderings. There was something cosmical about it; a standing advertisement, till forbidden, of the everlasting vigor and fertility of the world. The morning, which is the most memorable season of the day, is the awakening hour. Then there is least somnolence in us; and for an hour, at least, some part of us awakes which slumbers all the rest of the day and night. Little is to be expected of that day, if it can be called a day, to which we are not awakened by our Genius, but by the mechanical nudgings of some servitor; are not awakened by our own newly acquired force and aspirations from within, accompanied by the undulations of celestial music, instead of factory bells, and a fragrance filling the air — to a higher life than we fell asleep from; and thus the darkness bear its fruit, and prove itself to be good, no less than the light. That man who does not believe that each day contains an earlier, more sacred, and auroral hour than he has yet profaned, has despaired of life and is pursuing a descending and darkening way. After a partial cessation of his sensuous life, the soul of man, or its organs rather, are reinvigorated each day, and his Genius tries again what noble life it can make. All memorable events, I should say, transpire in morning time and in a morning atmosphere. The Vedas say, "All intelligences awake with the morning." Poetry and art, and the fairest and most memorable of the actions of men, date from such an hour. All poets and heroes, like Memnon, are the children of Aurora and emit their music at sunrise. To him whose elastic and vigorous thought keeps pace with the sun, the day is a perpetual morning. It matters not what the clocks say or the attitudes and labors of men. Morning is when I am awake and there is a dawn in me. Moral reform is the effort to throw off sleep. Why is it that men give so poor an account of their day if they have not been slumbering? They are not such poor calculators. If they had not been overcome with drowsiness, they would have performed something. The millions are awake enough for physical labor; but only one in a million is awake enough for effective intellectual exertion, only one in a hundred millions to a poetic or divine life. To be awake is to be alive. I have never yet met a man who was quite awake. How could I have looked him in the face?

We must learn to reawaken and keep ourselves awake, not by mechanical aids, but by an infinite expectation of the dawn, which does not forsake us in our soundest sleep. I know of no more encouraging fact than the unquestionable ability of man to elevate his life by a conscious endeavor. It is something to be able to paint a particular picture, or to carve a statue, and so to make a few objects beautiful; but it is far more glorious to carve and paint the very atmosphere and medium through which we look, which morally we can do. To affect the quality of the day, that is the highest of arts. Every man is tasked to make his life, even in its details, worthy of the contemplation of his most elevated and critical hour. If we refused, or rather used up, such paltry information as we get, the oracles would distinctly inform us how this might be done.

II

I went to the woods because I wished to live deliberately, to front only the essential facts of life, and see if I could not learn what it had to teach, and not, when I came to die, discover that I had not lived. I did not wish to live what was not life, living is so dear; nor did I wish to practice resignation, unless it was quite necessary. I wanted to live deep and suck out all the marrow of life, to live so sturdily and Spartan-like as to put to rout all that was not life, to cut a broad swath and shave close, to drive life into a corner and reduce it to its lowest terms, and, if it proved to be mean, why then to get the whole and genuine meanness of it, and publish its meanness to the world; or if it were sublime, to know it by experience, and be able to give a true account of it in my next excursion. For most men, it appears to me, are in a strange uncertainty about it, whether it is of the devil or of God, and have *somewhat hastily* concluded that it is the chief end of man here to " glorify God and enjoy him forever."

Still we live meanly, like ants; though the fable tells us that we were long ago changed into men; like pygmies we fight with cranes; it is error upon error, and clout upon clout, and our best virtue has for its occasion a superfluous and evitable wretchedness. Our life is frittered away by detail. An honest man has hardly need to count more than his ten fingers, or in extreme cases he may add his ten toes, and lump the rest. Simplicity, simplicity, simplicity! I say, let your affairs be as two or three, and not a hundred or a thousand; instead of a million count half a dozen, and keep your accounts on your thumbnail. In the midst of this chopping sea of civilized life, such are the clouds and storms and quicksands and thousand-and-one items to be allowed for, that a man has to live, if he would not founder and go to the bottom and not make his port at all, by dead reckoning, and he must be a great calculator indeed who succeeds. Simplify, simplify. Instead of three meals a day, if it be necessary eat but one; instead of a hundred dishes, five; and reduce other things in proportion. Our life is like a German Confederacy, made up of petty states, with its boundary forever fluctuating, so that even a German cannot tell you how it is bounded at any moment. The nation itself, with all its so-called internal improvements, which, by the way, are all external and superficial, is just such an unwieldy and overgrown establishment, cluttered with furniture and tripped up by its own traps, ruined by luxury and heedless expense, by want of calculation and a worthy aim, as the million households in the land; and the only cure for it, as for them, is in a rigid economy, a stern and more than Spartan simplicity of life and elevation of purpose. It lives too fast. Men think that it is essential that the *Nation* have commerce, and export ice, and talk through a telegraph, and ride thirty miles an hour, without a doubt, whether *they* do or not; but whether we should live like baboons or like men is a little uncertain. If we do not get out sleepers, and forge rails, and devote days and nights to the work, but go to tinkering upon our *lives* to improve *them,* who will build railroads? And if railroads are not built, how shall we get to heaven in season? But if we stay at home and mind our business, who will want railroads? We do not ride on the railroad; it rides upon us. Did you ever think what those sleepers are that underlie the railroad? Each one is a man, an Irishman, or a Yankee man. The rails are laid on them, and they are covered with sand, and the cars run smoothly over them. They are sound sleepers, I assure you. And every few years a new lot is laid down and run over; so that, if some have the pleasure of riding on a rail, others have the misfortune to be ridden upon. And when they run over a man that is walking in his sleep, a supernumerary sleeper in the wrong position, and wake him up, they suddenly stop the cars, and make a hue and cry about it, as if this were an exception. I am glad to know that it takes a gang of men for every five miles to keep the sleepers down and level in their beds as it is, for this is a sign that they may sometime get up again.

Why should we live with such hurry and waste of life? We are determined to be starved before we are hungry. Men say that a stitch in time saves nine, and so they take a thousand stitches today to save nine tomorrow. As for *work,* we haven't any of any consequence. We have the Saint Vitus's dance, and cannot possibly keep our heads still. If I should only give a few pulls at the parish bell-rope, as for a fire, that is, without setting the bell, there is hardly a man on his farm in the outskirts of Concord, notwithstanding that press of engagements which was his excuse so many times this morning, nor a boy, nor a woman, I might almost say, but would forsake all and follow that sound, not mainly to save property from the flames, but, if we will confess the truth, much more to see it burn, since burn it must, and we, be it known, did not set it on fire — or to see it put out, and have a hand in it, if that is done as handsomely; yes, even if it were the parish church itself. Hardly a man takes a half hour's nap after dinner, but when he wakes he holds up his head and asks, " What's the news? " as if the rest of mankind had stood his sentinels. Some give directions to be waked every half hour, doubtless for no other purpose; and then, to pay for it, they tell what they have dreamed. After a night's sleep the news is as indispensable as the breakfast. " Pray tell me anything new that has happened to a man anywhere on this globe " — and he reads it over his coffee and rolls, that a man has had his eyes gouged out this morning on the Wachito River; never dreaming the while that he lives in the dark unfathomed mammoth cave of this world, and has but the rudiment of an eye himself.

For my part, I could easily do without the post office. I think that there are very few important communications made through it. To speak critically, I never received more than one or two letters in my life — I wrote this some years ago — that were worth the postage. The penny post is, commonly, an institution through which you seriously offer a man that penny for his thoughts which is so often safely offered in jest. And I am sure that I never read any memorable news in a newspaper. If we read of one man robbed, or murdered, or killed by accident, or one house burned, or one vessel wrecked, or one steamboat blown up, or one cow run over on the Western Railroad, or one mad dog killed, or one lot of grasshoppers in the winter — we never need read of another. One is enough. If you are acquainted with the principle, what do you care for a myriad instances and applications? To a philosopher all *news,* as it is called, is gossip, and they who edit and read it are old women over their tea. Yet not a few are greedy after this gossip. There was such a rush, as I hear, the other day at one of the offices to learn the foreign news by the last arrival, that several large squares of plate glass belonging to the establishment were broken by the pressure — news which I seriously think a ready wit might write a twelvemonth, or twelve years, beforehand with sufficient accuracy. As for Spain, for instance, if you know how to throw in Don Carlos and the Infanta, and Don Pedro and Seville and Granada, from time to time in the right proportions — they may have changed the names a little since I saw the papers — and serve up a bullfight when other entertainments fail, it will be true to the letter and give us as good an idea of the exact state or ruin of things in Spain as the most succinct and lucid reports under this head in the newspapers. And as for England, almost the last significant scrap of news from that quarter was the revolution of 1649; and if you have learned the history of her crops for an average year, you never need attend to that thing again, unless your speculations are of a merely pecuniary character. If one may judge who rarely looks into the newspapers, nothing new does ever happen in foreign parts, a French revolution not excepted.

What news! How much more important to know what that is which was never old! " Kieou-he-yu (great dignitary of the state of Wei) sent a man to Khoung-tseu to know his news. Khoung-tseu caused the messenger to be seated near him, and questioned him in these terms: What is your master doing? The messenger answered with respect: My master desires to diminish the number of his faults, but he cannot come to the end of them. The messenger being gone, the philosopher remarked: What a worthy messenger! What a worthy messenger! " The preacher, instead of vexing the ears of drowsy farmers on their day of rest at the end of the week — for Sunday is the fit conclusion of an ill-spent week, and not the fresh and brave beginning of a new one — with this one other draggletail of a sermon, should shout with thundering voice, " Pause! Avast! Why so seeming fast, but deadly slow? "

Shams and delusions are esteemed for soundest truths, while reality is fabulous. If men would steadily observe realities only, and not allow themselves to be deluded, life, to compare it with such things as we know, would be like a fairy tale and the Arabian Nights' Entertainments. If we respected only what is inevitable and has a right to be, music and poetry would resound along the streets. When we are unhurried and wise, we perceive that only great and worthy things have any permanent and absolute existence, that petty fears and petty pleasures are but the shadow of the reality. This is always exhilarating and sublime. By closing the eyes and slumbering, and consenting to be deceived by shows, men establish and confirm their daily life of routine and habit everywhere, which still is built on purely illusory foundations. Children, who play life, discern its true law and relations more clearly than men, who fail to live it worthily, but who think that they are wiser by experience, that is, by failure. I have read in a Hindoo book, that " there was a king's son, who, being expelled in infancy from his native city, was brought up by a forester, and, growing up to maturity in that state, imagined himself to belong to the barbarous race with which he lived. One of his father's ministers, having discovered him, revealed to him what he was, and the misconception of his character was removed, and he knew himself to be a prince. So soul," continues the Hindoo philosopher, " from the circumstances in which it is placed, mistakes its own character, until the truth is revealed to it by some holy teacher, and then it knows itself to be *Brahme*." I perceive that we inhabitants of New England live this mean life that we do because our vision does not penetrate the surface of things. We think that that *is* which *appears* to be. If a man should walk through this town and see only the reality, where, think you, would the " Milldam " go to? If he should give us an account of the realities he beheld there, we should not recognize the place in his description. Look at a meetinghouse, or a courthouse, or a jail, or a shop, or a dwelling house, and say what that thing really is before a true gaze, and they would all go to pieces in your account of them. Men esteem truth remote, in the outskirts of the system, behind the farthest star, before Adam and after the last man. In eternity there is indeed something true and sublime. But all these times and places and occasions are now and here. God himself culminates in the present moment, and will never be more divine in the lapse of all the ages. And we are enabled to apprehend at all what is sublime and noble only by the perpetual instilling and drenching of the reality that surrounds us. The universe constantly and obediently answers to our conceptions; whether we travel fast or slow, the track is laid for us. Let us spend our lives in conceiving then. The poet or the artist never yet had so fair and noble a design but some of his posterity at least could accomplish it.

Let us spend one day as deliberately as Nature, and not be thrown off the track by every nutshell and mosquito's wing that falls on the rails. Let us rise early and fast, or break fast, gently and without perturbation; let company come and let company go, let the bells ring and the children cry — determined to make a day of it. Why should we knock under and go with the stream? Let us not be upset and overwhelmed in that terrible rapid and whirlpool called a dinner, situated in the meridian shallows. Weather this danger and you are safe, for the rest of the way is downhill. With unrelaxed nerves, with morning vigor, sail by it, looking another way, tied to the mast like Ulysses. If the engine whistles, let it whistle till it is hoarse for its pains. If the bell rings, why should we run? We will consider what kind of music they are like. Let us settle ourselves, and work and wedge our feet downward through the mud and slush of opinion, and prejudice, and tradition, and delusion, and appearance, that alluvion which covers the globe, through Paris and London, through New York and Boston and Concord, through Church and State, through poetry and philosophy and religion, till we come to a hard bottom and rocks in place, which we can call *reality,* and say, This is, and no mistake; and then begin, having a *point d'appui,* below freshet and frost and fire, a place where you might found a wall or a state, or set a lamp-post safely, or perhaps a gauge, not a Nilometer, but a Realometer, that future ages might know how deep a freshet of shams and appearances had gathered from time to time. If you stand right fronting and face to face to a fact, you will see the sun glimmer on both its surfaces, as if it were a scimitar, and feel its sweet edge dividing you through the heart and marrow, and so you will happily conclude your mortal career. Be it life or death, we crave only reality. If we are really dying, let us hear the rattle in our throats and feel cold in the extremities; if we are alive, let us go about our business.

I left the woods for as good a reason as I went there. Perhaps it seemed to me that I had several more lives to live, and could not spare any more time for that one. It is remarkable how easily and insensibly we fall into a particular route, and make a beaten track for ourselves. I had not lived there a week before my feet wore a path from my door to the pond-side; and though it is five or six years since I trod it, it is still quite distinct. It is true, I fear, that others may have fallen into it, and so helped to keep it open. The surface of the earth is soft and impressible by the feet of men; and so with the paths which the mind travels. How worn and dusty, then, must be the highways of the world — how deep the ruts of tradition and conformity! I did not wish to take a cabin passage, but rather to go before the mast and on the deck of the world, for there I could best see the moonlight amid the mountains. I do not wish to go below now.

I learned this, at least, by my experiment: that if one advances confidently in the direction of his dreams, and endeavors to live the life which he has imagined, he will meet with a success unexpected in common hours. He will put some things behind, will pass an invisible boundary; new, universal, and more liberal laws will begin to establish themselves around and within him; or the old laws be expanded, and interpreted in his favor in a more liberal sense, and he will live with the license of a higher order of beings. In proportion as he simplifies his life, the laws of the universe will appear less complex, and solitude will not be solitude, nor poverty poverty, nor weakness weakness. If you have built castles in the air, your work need not be lost; that is where they should be. Now put the foundations under them.

Thomas Hart Benton

Rodeo

THE pioneer West has gone beyond recall. The land is largely fenced. There are no more great cattle treks. Solemn Herefords have taken the place of the wild-eyed longhorns of the old days. There are no more six-shooter belted cowboys. The tough work of the cattle business is done by plain cow hands and fence tenders. On the trails to Wichita and Dodge City, where the hard-riding boys of the old days used to drive their long strings of cattle, the tractors and the combines are chugging.

But the West clings to its past. It does not acquiesce in the official ending of the frontier in 1890. It does not readily let go of the drama of its first wild days. Every dust-blown town that can rake up the money has its yearly rodeo and Wild West party where mighty and brave efforts are made to resuscitate the glamour of yesterday. The big doings of these parties center around the cow business, many of whose common chores have been ritualized and made into well-patterned and exciting competitive games. The Western country supports a large number of men whose main business in life is to perform in these games. They are the cowboys of today as distinguished from ordinary cow hands. They are tough birds. Let no one get the idea that the cowboy of the rodeos is just an actor dressed up and playing a part.

Once during prohibition days I went with a party of Texans over to Juarez, across the river from El Paso. In one of the honky-tonks I met the champion broncobuster of Montana, who had been a goodly prize winner in the El Paso rodeo, just terminated, and who was out celebrating with the proceeds. I made two sketches of him and gave him one. He took a shine to me and insisted on buying me drinks whether I wanted them or not. The Mexican whisky sold over the bars was all dressed up in labeled bottles, but it was the worst sort of tobacco-juice corn and hard stuff to down.

After swilling a couple of Montana's treats, I began shooting the others in

From *An Artist in America*, 1937.

a spittoon on the sly. I didn't want to get drunk on the stuff. But Montana drank his whisky and in about ten minutes got roaring tight. The tighter he got the more love he had for me and I couldn't get away from him. He was a thick fellow, one of the kind that country boys call stout. He didn't look like an athlete but when he put his arm around me in a drunken embrace I felt that I was in a trap. He was as hard as steel all over. Every once in a while when he'd let go of me, I'd make a move to get away. But quick as a flash he'd have one of his arms around me again and insist on another drink. My friends sitting at an adjoining table were having the time of their lives laughing at my predicament but they made no move to help me.

Later in the evening he found me again in another place. He must have been absolutely tireless, for he had ridden wild horses all day and yet was capable of carousing as actively all night as if he had spent the day in bed. He was as tough as they come. The last I saw of him he was in the hands of a couple of pals who were trying to get his lurching body over the Rio Grande bridge before closing time. A few years later I heard he was in some penitentiary in the Northwest for killing a man in a drunken bout.

All of the fellows who do the hard riding and pull off the dangerous stunts of the rodeos are tough — not vicious, but just physically tough. As experts, they are also in a class by themselves. They are artists of a kind, and they have all the vanity of the performing artist. Like boxers, wrestlers, actors, and others whose arts involve personal display, they are highly self-regarding and inclined to give much attention to appearances. The cowboy performer is particular about his shirt, his boots, his spurs, and his saddle. During the rodeo season, he is in the spotlight and must live up to his part. The big shows like the Cheyenne rodeo in Wyoming attract thousands of visitors. They are well-organized affairs and offer big prize money as well as much publicity for the winners of the events. From all over the West, young men come to compete before the crowds that gather. After a while, if they are good, they become thoroughly professional and live for and by their performances — like circus people.

Beside the big nationally advertised rodeos, the small-town ones seem amateurish. But for me they are vastly more entertaining. Most of the performers are local boys who are still actually in the cow business. The competition for prizes, even though the prize money be small, is just as strenuous as in the big highly touted affairs. The riding is just as wild and the enthusiasm of the people in the audience is intensified because they know all the contestants.

In 1930 I went with Glen Rounds to a Fourth of July rodeo in a small town in the middle of Wyoming. Glen and I were riding around the back country making drawings of the West. Glen, like Bill, was an old student of mine. He came from the Dakotas but he knew the ropes in this Wyoming country. He knew where to find a good thing. We got into the rodeo town on the day before the show, on the third of July, and located a cabin which we rented for two bits a night.

There was a cowboy in the cabin next to us, a fellow named Tex something, from Fort Worth, Texas, who was a professional horse-buster and rodeo performer. He and a pal of his from New Mexico were the only professionals in this back-country show. They were limbering up for the Cheyenne games after a winter of loafing down in the Rio Grande country. Tex had a split lip and a wife. (I have a picture of him in the Whitney Museum murals. He's the fellow in the big hat rolling a cigarette.) When we unloaded at our cabin, Tex, his wife, and his pal were playing cards on their doorstep. We made friends with them. I told Tex that we wanted to have the run of the field when the rodeo started so that we could make drawings. He said it would be easy to arrange and directed me to a hotel where he said " the boys " running the show had a room for the registration of contestants. I went to the hotel. It was a regular frame hotel of the Western town, a square box with a porch in front and a lot of old barrels, tin cans, and junk in the back.

I found the boys who were running the rodeo established in a front room overlooking the street, where a traveling carnival was just finishing nailing up its booths. They were all hanging out the windows looking at the activities below. I had to yell to get their attention, for people were beginning to shoot off firecrackers and a brass band near by was making bitter efforts to get tuned up. The directors of the rodeo were young. They had on ten-gallon hats, the first requisite of cowtown officialdom, and gaudy shirts of explosive green and cerise.

" Howdy-do, gentlemen," I said when I got their attention.

" Hello, boy," they replied. " Whatcha want? " They looked me over with broad patronage, trying to size me up.

I explained that I was an artist and that I wanted the run of the rodeo grounds in order to make pictures of the events of the morrow.

" A artist," said one. " Are you a perfessional? "

" Sure," I answered.

" Whut paper you on? "

" I'm from the Denver *Post*," I lied, sensing that they would only recognize professionalism with a publicity value.

" By God — are you, mister? " they chorused. Their patronizing airs evaporated and they turned very suddenly respectful.

" Yes," I said, " I've been sent out to find a good typical Western rodeo. We're going to play it up in a Sunday edition. I heard that you were going to have a good show here."

" By God, mister, you're right. You come to the right place," said another. " Say, Jim, git it out."

Jim went down under the bed and hauled out a gallon jar of bootleg. He filled four dirty glasses on the washstand about to the brim.

" Well, boys," he said, raising his glass, " this here's a break for us." Turning to me, " And it'll be a break fer you, mister, 'cause we shor'll appreciate you. We're havin' a big-time rodeo an' we'll fix it so you can do big-time stuff fer yore paper."

After some wrangling as to the proper procedure, they wrote me out a slip of paper which said, " The bearer of this, Mr. Thomas H. Benton of the Denver *Post,* is the official artist of the day. Every courtesy given to him will be appreciated."

They all signed it.

I said, " Say, I forgot to tell you there's another artist with me. He's working on this job too, and'll have to come with me."

" Oh, that's all right," they replied. " He don't need any paper. We're just givin' this to you to make it official. You and yore pardner just go anywheres you want to. We'll know you."

" Say, boys," said the fellow called Jim, " these boys ain't likely got no horses. Do you need a horse, you think? " He turned to me.

" No, no," I said, " we don't need horses. We couldn't work in the saddle." I was a little uneasy. I knew I couldn't ride the Wyoming cow ponies these fellows were used to, and I knew they would think I was a dude and a sister if I couldn't. " No," I said, " we've tried that — working from the saddle before. It don't go. You've got to have your feet steady on the ground to do our work."

" Yes, guess that's right," they agreed. My mind was eased.

That night there was a big to-do in the town. The band got tuned up and marched around the street playing as loud as it could. There was a crowd. All of the country farmers and ranchmen who could find a place to stay were in with their families. The carnival barkers whooped up their wares and games. Little girls and boys from outlying places looked wide-eyed and scared. The metropolitan din was too much for them and they clung together in little knots for all the world like scared calves. Their folks walked solemnly around the carnival booths. Occasionally someone would take a chance throwing a ring or a ball. They were curious but not very free with their dimes. The carnival made a lot of noise but so far as I could judge very little money. These country Westerners were skeptical and cagey. I heard one fellow say warily, " They ain't no use playin' them bingo games. They's all ribbed up to take you."

Glen and I got up early next day and went out to the fairgrounds where the rodeo was to take place. We followed a string of people who were out to get good places. The fairgrounds were not fenced but there was a little grandstand there. An old-fashioned starting tower faced it across the race track. In the center of the field the corrals were located. The rodeo impresarios in their cerise shirts were already out. So was Tex, our cabin neighbor, and his pardner. They and a crowd of yelling cowboys were busy trying to round up a bunch of wild horses that had broken out of an enclosure in a field adjoining the fairgrounds. It looked for a while as if a good part of the animals were going to get away and make a run for the mountains. There was nothing to stop them if they broke the loose encircling cordon of cowboys. The situation was precarious and our impresarios were obviously uneasy. They didn't dare let the main part of the show get away.

As people began coming into the grounds by horseback and car, they were

ordered to take places in a great half-mile circle around the horses. After a while
it looked safe to start the arrivals toward the fairground corrals. When the boys
got them started I climbed up on a post near one of the corral gates. The cowboy
who opened the gate yelled at me, " Git off, there! " I didn't pay any attention
to him. I was too interested in the oncoming horses. The whole herd in a close,
turbulent knot came pounding toward me raising a cloud of dust. About a hundred feet from me they broke and began turning and milling in all directions. A
voice yelled, " Git that son-of-a-bitch off the fence. Ain't he got no sense! " Realizing suddenly that I was scaring the horses, I climbed down and got out of the
way.

It took three quarters of an hour to get the herd corralled. There was one
handsome black pony that kept breaking away. He'd light out through an opening in the crowd and start for the mountains. My neighbor Tex finally lassoed
him and he was shut up with the others. I climbed back up on the corral gate and
started to draw some of the horses. A truculent cowboy rode up to me. He
shouted, " Git off'n that fence. You done caused us enough trouble already. Who
the hell d'you think you are? "

" I'm the official artist," I shouted back, dragging out the paper confirming it.

" What the hell is that? " he yelled.

" Leave 'im alone, Pat, leave 'im alone." Jim, the impresario, rode up and
saved me. His cerise shirt was streaked with sweat and dust. " That's the artist
from the Denver *Post*. He's a-makin' hand pichures fer the paper."

The crowd on the fairgrounds got thick. Some of them began piling in the
grandstand. Nobody was taking tickets. The rodeo managers got together to
consult on the matter. They hadn't counted on so many people coming out before noon. Spectators were supposed to pay twenty-five cents to come on the fairgrounds and fifty cents to sit in the grandstand. The managers and some extra
helpers who had long yellow ribbons tied to their hats went over to the grandstand.

" You fellows got your tickets? " they yelled. " If you hain't, git out yer
money. We're comin' to collect."

The grandstand sitters rose in a body and fled. They swarmed across the
field and perched on the supporting fences of the corrals, where a big crowd was
already roosting. The managers followed them.

" Say, you fellers can't get away with this," they said. " You got to pay yer
two bits fer this show. This ain't no free show."

" We're paying this afternoon," someone yelled. " This ain't no show this
mornin'. We ain't payin' jist to see you fellers run them ponies in."

Jim, who was apparently the leader among the managers, made a conciliatory
speech.

" Well, that's right, boys," he said. " That's right. But after dinner it's a show
and you fellers must pay yer two bits fer comin' on the grounds. We been at a
lot of expense gittin' up this show an' had plenty trouble gittin' the prize money
donated. You fellers got to help us pay what we owe. Now if you fellers'll go
out of the grounds and come in by the road an' pay yer two bits before the show

begins after dinner, we'll be obliged to you. Now I'm jist a-thankin' you fellers beforehand fer the way you're gonna help us."

Most of the crowd got off the fence and scattered toward the edge of the fairgrounds. Glen and I went to town to get something to eat. Hundreds of people had come in from the country during the morning and the one restaurant of the town was jammed with an impatient army trying to get waited on. The hotel dining room was full also. Ranch people sat on the street curbs and in their cars and ate their lunches out of shoe boxes just as the Missouri farmers used to do in Neosho when I was a kid. Glen and I bought a can of beans at a grocery and some cookies at a lemonade stand and ate our lunch in the middle of the street.

The rodeo was scheduled to begin at two o'clock. By one the road to the fairgrounds was jammed with a string of halting sputtering cars and farm trucks. Five or six hundred people were strung out walking on the side of the road. When we got out to the grounds, we found a line of men on horseback collecting tickets and quarters. A lot of the people on foot would slip past them without paying anything. The collectors would try to catch them.

" Now, boys, you gotta do your part. Come on, pay up yer money." Sometimes they were successful in collecting a quarter or so, but in the confusion of cars, horses, people, and dust, most of the shirkers got by.

Jim, the impresario, in his sweat-streaked cerise shirt was trying to be everything at once. His temper was getting short. A sudden rush of boys and men in overalls down beyond the line of admission collectors raised his ire.

" Head off them damned sheepherders," he yelled. " We ain't gonna let everybody in here fer nothin'." A couple of horsemen tried to head the gate rushers off but they dodged around the crowded cars and trucks and were lost. By two o'clock there must have been between four and five thousand people scattered over the fairgrounds. They perched all over the corrals and all over the race track fence in front of the grandstand. They stood up in trucks. The grandstand with its fifty-cent seats was guarded by a row of ticket collectors. It was about half full. Half a dozen Eastern people from a dude ranch somewhere about were grouped in a knot off on the side of the grandstand. They were about half lit and were in a hilarious mood. They cheered everybody that came in the stand.

About two o'clock a fellow in an A.E.F. suit climbed up in the starting tower and blew on a bugle. Then the three gaudy-shirted impresarios pranced their horses out in the track before the grandstand. The fellow named Jim had a megaphone.

He said, " Ladies and Gentlemen, we're all ready here to start our show. We've got some fine workers here and the boys is rarin' to go. But we ain't gonna make a bit of a start till the corrals is cleared and the track is cleared. Now," and he turned toward the corrals whose fences were lined with grinning men and boys, " if you sheepherders want this show to start you git out of the field on the other side of the track. About half of you sneaked in here anyhow. If you can't pay, at least git out of the way so the people that has paid can see."

A bunch of cowboys began riding around in the crowd urging the sheepherders across the track. Only contestants were allowed to stay about the corrals.

As official artists, Glen and I were permitted to remain on the fence by the main chute through which the bucking horses were to come. When the way was partially cleared, for it was impossible to get all the crowd across the race track, the rodeo started. First a Senator Something-or-other made a Fourth of July speech; then the band marched around the field and filed up on a platform in front of the grandstand. The grandstand itself began to fill up.

Jim got out his megaphone again and addressed the crowd. He thanked the senator for his fine speech and then said he had a special announcement. " Ladies and Gentlemen," he shouted, " after the contests in the field is over, right here in front of this grandstand where the band is, we're going to put on a boxing bout between the Butte Wildcat, that famous Montana boxer, and Wyoming Jack Sullivan. These are famous boys, as you all know, and this here is a grudge fight an' it'll be a good un. All of you that wants to stay can pay a dollar extra for your seat and just stay where you are. Ticket sellers will be around after the field contests."

There was a great cheer. The bugle blew and the rodeo was really on. It was the usual thing — calf-roping, steer-riding, bulldozing, and broncobusting. The contestants wrangled and quarreled, the crowd cheered their favorites and roared at every mishap. A couple of boys got badly thrown in the broncobusting contest, but they came to after a sponge of water was squeezed in their faces by the " official " doctor. They limped off the field under the plaudits of their friends and kinsmen. The crowd of sheepherders had all swarmed back toward the corrals during the progress of the show, and when it was time for the wild horse race, the last event on the program, the business of getting them off the track had to be gone through with all over again. A wild horse race is exciting even in the big standardized rodeos. Here it was an elemental battle. There were ten riders and only one got his horse clear around the track for the prize. The rest were bucked all over the field in and out between scattering sheepherders. It was a good rodeo.

When it came time for the fight only a dozen or more paying spectators remained in the grandstand. The band filed down from the ring, and Jim got up and announced that the boxers " wuzn't gonna fight for two bits and if more folks didn't come through, he didn't think they'd be any fight." He appealed to the sporting instincts of the people, who were hanging around thick as bees, but it didn't do any good.

That Wyoming crowd hung on to its pocketbooks and in the end the fight was called off and everybody went home. I saw the Butte Wildcat that evening in town when they were having the fireworks. He was as fat as a hog; so I judged the crowd knew what it was doing when it refused to disgorge to see him perform.

Glen and I beat it at sunup the next day. We didn't want to answer any questions about when our feature was to appear in the Denver *Post*.

Clarence King

Wayside Pikes

OUR return from Mount Tyndall to such civilization as flourishes around the Kaweah outposts was signalized by us chiefly as to our *cuisine,* which offered now such bounties as the potato, and once a salad, in which some middle-aged lettuce became the vehicle for a hollow mockery of dressing. Two or three days, during which we dined at brief intervals, served completely to rest us, and put in excellent trim for further campaigning all except Professor Brewer, upon whom a constant toothache wore painfully — my bullet mold failing even upon the third trial to extract the unruly member.

It was determined we should ride together to Visalia, seventy miles away, and the more we went the more impatient became my friend, till we agreed to push ahead through day and night, and reached the village at about sunrise in a state of reeling sleepiness quite indescribably funny.

At evening, when it became time to start back for our mountain camp, my friend at last yielded consent to my project of climbing the Kern Sierras to attempt Mount Whitney; so I parted from him, and, remaining at Visalia, outfitted myself with a pack horse, two mounted men, and provisions enough for a two weeks' trip.

I purposely avoid telling by what route I entered the Sierras, because there lingers in my breast a desire to see once more that lovely region; and failing, as I do, to confide in the people, I fear lest, if the camp I am going to describe should be recognized, I might, upon revisiting the scene, suffer harm or even come to an untimely end. I refrain, then, from telling by what road I found myself entering the region of the pines one lovely twilight evening, two days after leaving Visalia. Pines, growing closer and closer, from sentinels gathered to groups, then stately groves, and at last, as the evening wore on, assembled in regular forest, through whose open tops the stars shone cheerfully.

I came upon an open meadow, hearing in front the rush of a large brook, and directly reached two campfires, where were a number of persons. My two hirelings caught and unloaded the pack horse and set about their duties, looking to supper and the animals, while I prospected the two camps. That just below me, on the same side of the brook, I found to be the bivouac of a company of hunters, who, in the ten minutes of my call, made free with me, hospitably offering a jug of whisky, and then went on in their old eternal way of making bear stories out of whole cloth.

I left them with a belief that my protoplasm and theirs must be different, in spite of Mr. Huxley, and passed across the brook to the other camp. Under noble

From *Mountaineering in the Sierra Nevada,* 1871.

groups of pines smouldered a generous heap of coals, the ruins of a mighty log. A little way from this lay a confused pile of bedclothes, partly old and half-bald buffalo robes, but, in the main, thick strata of what is known to irony as comforters, upon which, outstretched in wretched awkwardness of position, was a family, all with their feet to the fire, looking as if they had been blown over in one direction or knocked down by a single bombshell. On the extremities of this common bed, with the air of having got as far from each other as possible, the mother and father of the Pike family reclined; between them were two small children — a girl and boy — and a huge girl, who, next the old man, lay flat upon her back, her mind absorbed in the simple amusement of waving one foot (a cowhide eleven) slowly across the fire, squinting, with half-shut eye, first at the vast shoe and thence at the fire, alternately hiding bright places and darting the foot quickly in the direction of any new display of heightening flame. The mother was a bony sister, in the yellow, shrunken, of sharp visage, in which were prominent two cold eyes and a positively poisonous mouth; her hair, the color of faded hay, was tangled about her head. She rocked jerkily to and fro, removing at intervals a clay pipe from her mouth in order to pucker her thin lips up to one side and spit with precision upon a certain spot in the fire.

I have rarely felt more difficulty in opening a conversation, and was long before venturing to propose, " You seem to have a pleasant camp spot here." The old woman sharply, and in almost a tone of affront, answered, " They's wus, and then again they's better."

" Doos well for our hogs," inserted the old man. " We've a band of pork that make out to find feed."

" Oh! How many have you? " I asked.

" Nigh three thousand."

" Won't you set? " asked madam. Then, turning, " You, Susan, can't you try for to set up, and not spread so? Hain't you no manners, say?"

At this the massive girl got herself somewhat together and made room for me, which I declined, however.

" Prospecting? " inquired madam.

" I say huntin'," suggested the man.

" Maybe he's a cattle feller," interrupted the little girl.

" Goin' somewhere, ain't yer? " was Susan's guess.

I gave brief account of myself, evidently satisfying the social requirements of all but the old woman, who at once classified me as not up to her standard. Susan saw this, so did her father, and it became evident to me in ten minutes' conversation that they two were always at one, and made it their business to be in antagonism to the mother. They were then allies of mine from nature, and I felt at once at home. I saw, too, that Susan, having slid back to her horizontal position when I declined to share her rightful ground, was watching with subtle solicitude that fated spot in the fire, opposing sympathy and squints accurately aligned by her shoe to the dull spot in the embers, which slowly went out into blackness before the well-directed fire of her mother's saliva.

The shouts which I heard proceeding from the direction of my camp were easily translatable into summons for supper. Mr. Newty invited me to return later and be sociable, which I promised to do, and, going to my camp, supped quickly and left the men with orders about picketing the animals for the night, then, strolling slowly down to the camp of my friends, seated myself upon a log by the side of the old gentleman. Feeling that this somewhat formal attitude unfitted me for partaking to the fullest degree the social ease around me, and knowing that my buckskin trousers were impervious to dirt, I slid down in a reclining posture with my feet to the fire, in absolute parallelism with the rest of the family.

The old woman was in the exciting denouement of a coon story, directed to her little boy, who sat clinging to her skirt and looking in her face with absorbed curiosity. " And when Johnnie fired," she said, " the coon fell and busted open." The little boy had misplaced his sympathies with the raccoon, and having inquired plaintively, " Did it hurt him? " was promptly snubbed with the reply, " Of course it hurt him. What do you suppose coons is made for? " Then, turning to me, she put what was plainly enough with her a test question: " I allow you have killed your coon in your day? " I saw at once that I must forever sink beneath her standard, but, failing in real experience or accurate knowledge concerning the coon, I knew no subterfuge would work with her. Instinct had taught her that I had never killed a coon, and she had asked me thus ostentatiously to place me at once and forever before the family in my true light. " No, ma'am," I said; " now you speak of it, I realize that I never have killed a coon." This was something of a staggerer to Susan and her father; yet as the mother's pleasurable dissatisfaction with me displayed itself by more and more accurate salivary shots at the fire, they rose to the occasion and began to palliate my past. " Maybe," ventured Mr. Newty, " that they don't have coon round the city of York "; and I felt that I needed no self-defense when Susan firmly and defiantly suggested to her mother that perhaps I was in better business.

Driven in upon herself for some time, the old woman smoked in silence until Susan, seeing that her mother gradually quenched a larger and larger circle upon the fire, got up and stretched herself, and giving the coals a vigorous poke swept out of sight the quenched spot, thus readily obliterating the result of her mother's precise and prolonged expectoration; then, flinging a few dry boughs upon the fire, illumined the family with a ruddy blaze and sat down again, leaning upon her father's knee with a faint light of triumph in her eye.

I ventured a few platitudes concerning pigs, not penetrating the depths of that branch of rural science enough to betray my ignorance. Such sentiments as " A little piece of bacon well broiled for breakfast is very good," and " Nothing better than cold ham for lunch," were received by Susan and her father in the spirit I meant — of entire good will toward pork generically. I now look back in amusement at having fallen into this weakness, for the Mosaic view of pork has been mine from infancy, and campaigning upon government rations has, in truth, no tendency to dim this ancient faith.

By half past nine the gates of conversation were fairly open, and our part of the circle enjoyed itself socially — taciturnity and clouds of Virginia plug reigning supreme upon the other. The two little children crept under comforters somewhere near the middle of the bed and subsided pleasantly to sleep. The old man at last stretched sleepily, finally yawning out, " Susan, I do believe I am too tired out to go and see if them corral bars are down. I guess you'll have to go. I reckon there ain't no bears round tonight." Susan rose to her feet, stretched herself with her back to the fire, and I realized for the first time her amusing proportions. In the region of six feet, tall, square-shouldered, of firm iron back and heavy mold of limb, she yet possessed that suppleness which enabled her as she rose to throw herself into nearly all the attitudes of the Niobe children. As her yawn deepened, she waved nearly down to the ground, and then, rising upon tiptoe, stretched up her clinched fists to heaven with a groan of pleasure. Turning to me she asked, " How would you like to see the hogs? " The old man added, as an extra encouragement, " Pootiest band of hogs in Tulare County! There's littler of the real sissor-bill nor Mexican racer stock than any band I have ever seen in the state. I driv the original outfit from Pike County to Oregon in '51 and '52." By this time I was actually interested in them, and joining Susan we passed out into the forest.

We walked silently on, four or five minutes, through the woods, coming at last upon a fence which margined a wide circular opening in the wood. The bars, as her father had feared, were down. We stepped over them, quietly entered the enclosure, put them up behind us, and proceeded to the middle, threading our way among sleeping swine to where a lonely tree rose to the height of about two hundred feet. Against this we placed our backs, and Susan waved her hand in pride over the two acres of tranquil pork. The eye, after accustoming itself to the darkness, took cognizance of a certain rigidness of surface which came to be recognized as the objects of Susan's pride.

Quite a pretty effect was caused by the shadow of the forest, which, cast obliquely downward by the moon, divided the corral into halves of light and shade.

The air was filled with heavy breathing, interrupted by here and there a snore, and at times by crescendos of tumult, caused by forty or fifty pigs doing battle for some favorite bed-place.

I was informed that Susan did not wish me to judge of them by dark, but to see them again in full light of day. She knew each individual pig by its physiognomy, having, as she said, " growed with 'em."

As we strolled back toward the bars a dusky form disputed our way — two small, sharp eyes and a wild crest of bristles were visible in the obscure light. " That's Old Arkansas," said Susan; " he's eight year old come June, and I never could get him to like me." I felt for my pistol, but Susan struck a vigorous attitude, ejaculating, " S-S-oway, Arkansas! " She made a dash in his direction; a wild scuffle ensued, in which I heard the dull thud of Susan's shoe, accompanied by, " Take that, doggone you! " a cloud of dust, one shrill squeal, and Arkansas retreated into the darkness at a businesslike trot.

When quite near the bars the mighty girl launched herself in the air, alighting with her stomach across the topmost rail, where she hung a brief moment, made a violent muscular contraction, and alighted upon the ground outside, communicating to it a tremor quite perceptible from where I stood. I climbed over after her, and we sauntered under the trees back to camp.

The family had disappeared; a few dry boughs, however, thrown upon the coals, blazed up, and revealed their forms in the corrugated topography of the bed.

I bade Susan good night, and before I could turn my back she kicked her number eleven shoes into the air and with masterly rapidity turned in, as Minerva is said to have done, in full panoply.

Seated upon my blankets next morning, I beheld Susan's mother drag forth the two children one after another, by the napes of their necks, and, shaking the sleep out of them, propel them spitefully toward the brook; then taking her pipe from her mouth she bent low over the sleeping form of her huge daughter and in a high, shrill, nasal key screeched in her ear, " Yew Suse! Get up and let the *hogs* out! "

The idea thrilled into Susan's brain, and with a violent suddenness she sat bolt upright, brushing her green-colored hair out of her eyes, and rubbing those valuable but bleared organs with the ponderous knuckles of her forefingers.

By this time I started for the brook for my morning toilet, and the girl and I met upon opposite banks, stooping to wash our faces in the same pool. As I opened my dressing case her lower jaw fell, revealing a row of ivory teeth rounded out by two well-developed " wisdoms " which had all that dazzling grin one sees in the show windows of certain dental practitioners. It required but a moment to gather up a quart or so of water in her broad palms and rub it vigorously into a small circle upon the middle of her face, the moisture working outward to a certain high-water mark which, along her chin and cheeks, defined the limits of former ablution; then, baring her large red arms to the elbow, she washed her hands and stood resting them upon her hips, dripping freely, and watching me with intense curiosity.

When I reached the towel process, she herself twisted her body after the manner of the Belvedere torso, bent low her head, gathered up the back breadths of her petticoat, and wiped her face vigorously upon it, which had the effect of tracing concentric streaks irregularly over her countenance.

I parted my hair by the aid of a small dressing glass, which so fired Susan that she crossed the stream with a mighty jump and stood in ecstasy by my side. She borrowed the glass, and then my comb, rewashed her face, and fell to work diligently upon her hair.

All this did not so limit my perception as to prevent my watching the general demeanor of the family. The old man lay back at his ease, puffing a cloud of smoke; his wife, also emitting volumes of the vapor of " navy plug," squatted by the campfire, frying certain lumps of pork and communicating an occasional spiral jerk to the coffee-pot, with the purpose, apparently, of stirring the grounds. The two children had gotten upon the back of a contemplative ass, who stood by the upper side of the bed quietly munching the corner of a comforter.

My friend was in no haste. She squandered much time upon the arrangement of her towy hair, and there was something like a blush of conscious satisfaction when she handed me back my looking glass and remarked ironically, " O no, I guess not — no, sir."

I begged her to accept the comb and glass, which she did with maidenly joy.

This unusual toilet had stimulated with self-respect Susan's every fiber, and as she sprung back across the brook and approached her mother's campfire, I could not fail to admire the magnificent turn of her shoulders and the powerful, queenly poise of her head. Her full, grand form and heavy strength reminded me of the statues of Ceres; yet there was withal a very unpleasant suggestion of fighting trim, a sort of prize-ring manner of swinging the arms and hitching of the shoulders.

It required my Pike County friends but ten minutes to swallow their pork and begin the labors of the day.

Susan, after a second appeal from her mother, ran over to the corral and let out the family capital, who streamed with exultant grunt through the forest, darkening the fair green meadow gardens and happily passing out of sight.

When I had breakfasted I joined Mr. Newty in his trip to the corral, where we stood together for hours, during which I had mastered the story of his years since, in 1850, he left his old home in Pike of Missouri.

It was one of those histories common enough through this wide West, yet never failing to startle me with its horrible lesson of social disintegration, of human retrogression.

That brave spirit of Westward Ho! which has been the pillar of fire and cloud leading on the weary march of progress over stretches of desert, lining the way with graves of strong men; of newborn lives; of sad, patient mothers, whose pathetic longing for the new home died with them; of the thousand old and young whose last agony came to them as they marched with eyes straining after the sunken sun, and whose shallow barrows scarcely lift over the drifting dust of the desert; that restless spirit which has dared to uproot the old and plant the new, kindling the grand energy of California, laying foundations for a state to be, is admirable, is poetic, is to fill an immortal page in the story of America; but when, instead of wresting from new lands something better than the old can give, it degenerates into mere weak-minded restlessness, killing the power of growth, the ideal of home, the faculty of repose, it results in that race of perpetual emigrants who roam as dreary waifs over the West, losing possessions, love of life, love of God, slowly dragging from valley to valley till they fall by the wayside, happy if some chance stranger performs for them the last rites — often less fortunate, as blanched bones and fluttering rags upon too many hillsides plainly tell.

The Newtys were of this dreary brotherhood. In 1850, with a small family of that authentic strain of highbred swine for which Pike County is widely known, as Mr. Newty avers, they bade Missouri and their snug farm good-by, and, having packed their household goods into a wagon drawn by two spotted oxen, set out with the baby Susan for Oregon, where they came after a year's march, tired and cursed with a permanent discontent. There they had taken up a rancho, a quarter section of public domain, which at the end of two years was "improved" to the extent of the "neatest little worm fence this side of Pike," a barn, and a smokehouse. "In another year," said my friend, "I'd have dug for a house, but we tuck ager and the second baby died." One day there came a man who "let on that he knowed" land in California much fairer and more worthy tillage than Oregon's best; so the poor Newtys harnessed up the wagon and turned their backs upon a home nearly ready for comfortable life, and swept south with pigs and plunder. Through all the years this story had repeated itself; new homes got to the verge of completion, more babies born, more graves made, more pigs, which replenished as only the Pike County variety may, till it seemed to me the mere multiplication of them must reach a sufficient dead weight to anchor the family; but this was dispelled when Newty remarked: "These yer hogs is awkward about moving, and I've pretty much made my mind to put 'em all into bacon this fall, and sell out and start for Montana."

Poor fellow! At Montana he will probably find a man from Texas who in half an hour will persuade him that happiness lies there.

As we walked back to their camp, and when Dame Newty hove in sight, my friend ventured to say, "Don't you mind the old woman and her coons. She's from Arkansas. She used to say no man could have Susan who couldn't show coonskins enough of his own killing to make a bedquilt, but she's over that mostly." In spite of this assurance my heart fell a trifle when, the first moment of our return, she turned to her husband and asked, "Do you mind what a dead-open-and-shut on coons our little Johnny was when he was ten years old?" I secretly wondered if the dead-open-and-shut had anything to do with his untimely demise at eleven, but kept silence.

Regarding her as a sad product of the disease of chronic emigration, her hard thin nature, all angles and stings, became to me one of the most depressing and pathetic spectacles, and the more when her fever-and-ague boy, a mass of bilious lymph, came and sat by her, looking up with great haggard eyes as if pleading for something, he knew not what, but which I plainly saw only death could bestow.

Noon brought the hour of my departure. Susan and her father talked apart a moment; then the old man said the two would ride along with me for a few miles, as he had to go in that direction to look for new hog-feed.

I dispatched my two men with the pack horse, directing them to follow the trail, then saddled my Kaweah and waited for the Newtys. The old man saddled a shaggy little mountain pony for himself, and for Susan strapped a sheepskin upon the back of a young and fiery mustang colt.

While they were getting ready, I made my horse fast to a stake and stepped over to bid good-by to Mrs. Newty. I said to her in tones of deference, "I have come to bid you good-by, madam, and when I get back this way I hope you will be kind enough to tell me one or two really first-rate coon stories. I am quite ignorant of that animal, having been raised in countries where they are extremely rare, and I would like to know more of what seems to be to you a creature of such interest." The wet, gray eyes relaxed, as I fancied, a trifle of their asperity; a faint kindle seemed to light them for an instant as she asked, " You never see coons catch frogs in a spring branch? "

" No, madam," I answered.

" Well, I wonder! Well, take care of yourself, and when you come back this way stop along with us, and we'll kill a yearlin', and I'll tell you about a coon that used to live under grandfather's barn." She actually offered me her hand, which I grasped and shook in a friendly manner, chilled to the very bone with its damp coldness.

Mr. Newty mounted, and asked me if I was ready. Susan stood holding her prancing mustang. To put that girl on her horse after the ordinary plan would have required the strength of Samson, or the use of a stepladder, neither of which I possessed; so I waited for events to develop themselves. The girl stepped to the left side of her horse, twisted one hand in the mane, laying the other upon his haunches, and, crouching for a jump, sailed through the air, alighting upon the sheepskin. The horse reared, and Susan, twisting herself around, came right side up with her knee upon the sheepskin, shouting, as she did so, " I guess you don't get me off, sir! " I jumped upon Kaweah, and our two horses sprang forward together, Susan waving her hand to her father and crying, " Come along after, old man! " and to her mother, " Take care of yourself! " which is the Pike County for *Au revoir!* Her mustang tugged at the bit and bounded wildly into the air. We reached a stream bank at full gallop, the horses clearing it at a bound, sweeping on over the green floor and under the magnificent shadow of the forest. Newty, following at a humble trot, slopped through the creek, and when I last looked he had nearly reached the edge of the wood.

I could but admire the unconscious excellence of Susan's riding, her firm, immovable seat, and the perfect coolness with which she held the fiery horse. This quite absorbed me for five minutes, when she at last broke the silence by the laconic inquiry, " Does yourn buck? " To which I added the reply that he had only occasionally been guilty of that indiscretion. She then informed me that the first time she had mounted the colt he had " nearly bucked her to pieces; he had jumped and jounced till she was plum tuckered out " before he had given up. Gradually reining the horses down and inducing them to walk, we rode side by side through the most magnificent forest of the Sierras, and I determined to probe Susan to see whether there were not, even in the most latent condition, some germs of the appreciation of nature. I looked from base to summit of the magnificent shafts, at the green plumes which traced themselves against the sky, the exquisite fall of purple shadows and golden light upon trunks, at the labyrinth of glowing flowers, at the sparkling whiteness of the mountain brook, and up to the clear matchless blue that vaulted over us, then turned to Susan's plain, honest face, and gradually introduced the subject of trees. Ideas of lumber and utilitarian notions of fence rails were uppermost in her mind; but I briefly penetrated what proved to be only a superficial stratum of the materialistic, and asked her point-blank if she did not admire their stately symmetry. A strange, new light gleamed in her eye as I described to her the growth and distribution of forests, and the marvelous change in their character and aspects as they approached the tropics. The palm and the pine, as I worked them up to her, really filled her with delight, and prompted numerous interested and intelligent queries, showing that she thoroughly comprehended my drift.

In the pleasant hour of our chat I learned a new lesson of the presence of undeveloped seed in the human mind.

Mr. Newty at last came alongside and remarked that he must stop about here. " But," he added, " Susan will go on with you about half a mile, and come back and join me here after I have taken a look at the feed." As he rode out into the forest a little way he called me to him, and I was a little puzzled at what seemed to be the first traces of embarrassment I had seen in his manner.

" You'll take care of yourself, now, won't you? " he asked. I tried to convince him that I would.

A slight pause.

" You'll take care of yourself, won't you? "

He might rely on it, I was going to say.

He added, " Thet — thet — thet man what gets Susan *has half the hogs!* "

Then, turning promptly away, he spurred the pony, and his words as he rode into the forest were, " Take good care of yourself! "

Susan and I rode on for half a mile, until we reached the brow of a long descent, which she gave me to understand was her limit.

We shook hands and I bade her good-by, and as I trotted off these words fell sweetly upon my ear, " Say, you'll take good care of yourself, won't you, say? "

I took pains not to overtake my camp men, wishing to be alone; and as I rode for hour after hour the picture of this family stood before me in all its deformity of outline, all its poverty of detail, all its darkness of future, and I believe I thought of it too gravely to enjoy as I might the subtle light of comedy which plays about these hard, repulsive figures.

In conversation I had caught the clew of a better past. Newty's father was a New Englander, and he spoke of him as a man of intelligence and, as I should judge, of some education. Mrs. Newty's father had been an Arkansas judge, not perhaps the most enlightened of men, but still very far in advance of herself. The conspicuous retrogression seemed to me an example of the most hopeless phase of human life. If, as I suppose, we may all sooner or later give in our adhesion to the Darwinian view of development, does not the same law which permits such splendid scope for the better open up to us also possible gulfs of degradation, and are not these chronic emigrants whose broken-down wagons and weary faces greet you along the dusty highways of the far West melancholy examples of beings who have forever lost the conservatism of home and the power of improvement?

Heywood Broun

Shooting the Young Idea

THE very beginnings I have forgotten. I don't know now whether the alphabet was an adventure and counting up to ten a soul-satisfying achievement. My earliest memory is of something unpleasant. The lessons in penmanship were hateful. We worked in copybooks with maxims as models and these may have been sage and helpful. By now they have passed out of my conscious mind, though that does not necessarily mean they may not have shaped my character. Still, as I examine my character impartially, it seems unlikely.

The thing which sticks is the painful recollection of the conflict between my technique and the method of the school. I wanted to crook my forefinger on the penholder and the teacher insisted that I should guide it with the first two fingers. That dispute must have lasted almost a year and, looking back, it is fair to say that here was time wasted, for today at the age of thirty-five when I pick up a pen I still employ the forbidden crook of the forefinger. There might have been some nourishment for self-determination in this, but I had no sense of triumph. I conquered only because it was physically impossible for me to write in any other way. The feeling of shame blotted out any possible thrill of victory. When I passed out of that penmanship class, it was with the definite conviction that I was in some way queer and ignoble. Nobody else in the class crooked his forefinger and so it must be evil.

Not until long afterward did I take pride in the curious mobility of my fingers. I could put my thumb out of joint and also bend it back until it touched my wrist, and there might have been years of elation for me in the possession of these unusual powers. However, I had learned from the writing class that being different only got a person into trouble. By the time I began to admire originality, many years later, approaching age had so stiffened my fingers that I was no longer capable of performing any of the feats.

And there is another respect in which I have been marked by that struggle against the teacher and her orthodoxy. It firmly established in my mind the feeling that the physical business of writing was bitter and unpleasant. Circumstance thrust me into the newspaper business and in fifteen years I have ground out several million words, but all of them have been executed in pain and agony. Of course, I learned to use a typewriter in time, but the symbolic repugnance remains, and I doubt if any other laboring man suffers as I do during those moments in which I try to convince myself that further delay is impossible and that the business of setting words down on paper must begin.

From *Sitting on the World,* 1924.

Naturally, I do not expect the school system to be revolutionized in order to take care of the child who just has to crook his forefinger on the penholder, but a general indictment can be worked up out of this individual idiosyncrasy. In my day, at any rate, all technique and all method was too inflexible. The average child is an almost non-existent myth. To be normal one must be peculiar in some way or other. Post-office clerks and newspapermen who run columns and invite contributions would be much happier if the world wrote legibly. But when I was in school legibility was the least of the demands of the teacher. It was not a resting point. We were driven on from there to master curlicues and rounded graces which cannot possibly have contributed to the spiritual or material welfare of anyone in the class. Indeed, unless my memory is wholly at fault, not a little of that precious impressionistic youth of us all was wasted in the endeavor to make us develop a slanting hand. There were green trees and blue skies and rippling breezes in those days and there we sat in the classroom trying to make our letters lean over like the tower in Pisa.

I am not a handwriting expert, but show me a page of anybody's script in which the characters cringe in this fashion and I will have no hesitation in saying: "Your chief fault is that you are too docile and abject in the face of authority." Most of us in that class emulated the example of the man who bowed down in the house of Rimmon. As long as the gale of authority blew strong our handwriting bent before it, and as soon as admonition died down each *l* and *t* leaped up again.

It may seem captious, but it seems to me that the manner in which grammar was taught to us was almost as ineffective as the system of instilling handwriting, although here the technique was practically reversed. Of course, there were things in between grammar and learning to write, but it is the next subject which I remember vividly. I liked grammar because the teacher made a game of it. From the very beginning we had contests and tournaments in which we stood up and parsed each other down. Perhaps I should not complain because this particular class provided me with one of my most treasured memories. When others talk of tennis trophies they have won and golf cups and broad-jump medals, I need not remain altogether silent, for in the annual spring grammar championship held in our school in the year 1897 I was runner-up. The trouble is that, although I remember these sporting events most vividly and the way the competitors went down one by one, there is something I have forgotten. I am not likely to forget how the last two of us parried back and forth until I tripped over a nominative absolute. The thing that worries me is that, as I set this down, I have not the slightest notion of the nature of a nominative absolute or even whether that is the correct phrase for the particular quirk which threw me on that fateful day.

I would gladly trade off all the time I spent on slanting my letters for a better grounding in "shall" and "will." Rules they gave me, but they must have been lightly applied, for not one remains. For a protracted period during my maturity I lived in a fool's paradise, saying to myself: "I don't make many mistakes even if I have forgotten the rules. My ear and my eye tell me whether I have chosen the right one." And then one day I induced an expert grammarian to look over several pages of casual copy of mine and he reported back that I was right only 53.639 per cent of the time. This was so near an even break that I realized that practically nothing stood between me and error except the law of averages. Or, to be specific, my education had contributed to me an efficiency of 3.639 per cent over illiteracy.

Not until I had been in school seven years did anything of truly epoch-making importance happen to me. That was the year in which I first ran up against the scientific point of view. The teacher had asked us to submit a report the following day on the weather. What else I said I don't know, but I wrote: " The day was warm." For that I was held up to scorn in full view of the class. Precisely what did warm mean, she wanted to know. I was asked to explain how wide a variation of temperature I included under that head, and it finally dawned on me that here was a subject concerning which opinion was a feeble thing in the face of ascertainable fact. I could have consulted a thermometer. This awakening did not rouse me to go into scientific pursuits in later life, but it did leave me not wholly unprepared for that sign which hung on the wall of the city room in later years and which ran: " Accuracy! Accuracy! Accuracy! " To be sure, I found out in time that there were happenings and conditions in life not to be measured by any silver thread, but at least I can remain a little unmoved and impatient at all men who thunder out what they think without peering round corners to look at measuring machines far more credible than any haphazard instinctive feeling.

It was in the same class and from the same teacher that I received the most important single piece of stimulus which came to me out of all school and college. Her name was and is Miss Hotchkiss and she is a Canadian. Probably it went somewhat against the grain for her to teach us American history as it was written in the prescribed textbook. The author I have forgotten, but no patriotic society could possibly have had any objection to the version of events as he set them down. There was nothing done by any Britisher which was not identified as rascality and knavery. All Americans concerned, excepting the Judas, Arnold, behaved in a manner which rather diminished the virtues and glories of the folk of whom I had heard in Sunday school.

I cannot say that this excess of zeal sickened me. On the contrary, it fitted in admirably with the notion which prevailed in my mind that all struggles in the world were fights between villains and heroes, the children of darkness and the children of light. There was no hint of anything else until the end of the last class on the final day of the term. But as I was going out Miss Hotchkiss called me over and handed me a small pamphlet and said: " I want you to read this." She gave it to no one else and I don't know why she picked me, as I was a long way from being the prize pupil of the class. When I got home I read the pamphlet and was shocked to find that, although rather apologetic and timid, it endeavored to say some of the things for the English position, in the matter of our revolution, which the history book had left out. The author granted that the war had been a liberalizing influence in the world, but he speculated as to whether the same forces might not have come into the world just as surely even if there had been no conflict. He wound up by saying that while Washington was a great man who acted from the noblest motives, several of the heroes of whom I had read had become glamorous only through romantic afterglow and were in reality rather small-minded and selfish local politicians.

Now all this would fall under the head of seditious propaganda, according to the most recent textbook investigation in New York City. Nevertheless, after the first shock I realized that something brand-new and enormously valuable had been put into my head. Or, at any rate, I thought it was valuable then and I think that even more strongly today. I am not referring to the fact that here was a new slant on the American Revolution. I mean that for the first time in my life I conceived of any great public question as having two sides. We had the Revolution and the Mexican War and the Civil War in our school, and I can't remember that we ever heard a word of anything except the right side, which was, of course, the American side, or, more specifically, the North American side. What we learned was: " My country always is right." And that, from all I read and hear, is still the slogan of the schools.

It seems to me that the expression of dissent, which our school boards call sedition, ought to be fostered rather than whipped out of textbook and teacher. I don't mean that children should be taught that the Revolution, for instance, was wrong or unfortunate. I don't think it was. But it is important that children learn the two-sidedness of history and from that grow to appreciate the double surface of all controversy. By refusing to present all the available evidence, we turn out into the world men and women who are certainly going to make rotten jurors and not much better voters. I have been told that if the schools let up for an instant on the steady pump, pump of patriotism, Bolshevism and red rebellion will stalk out of the school doors. That I don't believe. Indeed, I hold just the opposite. For it seems to me that if you train a child to think wholly on one side of any problem there's no telling when he may happen to hop off the particular plane on which you have placed him and become just as bigoted in dissent as he has been taught to be in conformity. To my way of thinking, Charles E. Hughes and Leon Trotzky come pretty close to being equally tight-minded. Neither of them seems capable of imagining the existence of any point of view but his own.

Even before we encountered history the teachers had begun to pass out literature to us. All the earliest samples were shed off rather easily, for I remember almost nothing of any prescribed reading before high school. I have, though, a definite memory of what literature seemed to me in the classroom. Literature was prose or verse by somebody who was dead, usually a long time. To the best of my knowledge and belief, no living author was ever mentioned to us. My memory of private and uncompelled reading goes farther back. There were three favorite writers who held my attention at about the same time: G. A. Henty, Horatio Alger, and Walter Scott. I hope that the incidental history which Henty introduced in all his stories is sound, because most of what I think I know about world events came from him. Horatio Alger lasted in my affection for almost three years, and then I discovered that the story which he told of Ragged Dick, the newsboy, was almost precisely the same as his tale of Tony, the bootblack. It had been the same story for a long time, but I was slow in catching on to this. Henty I gave up simply because there wasn't any more, and school put a stop to my interest in Scott. *Ivanhoe* was given to us as something we had to read and then I found that it wasn't fun any more.

Offhand I can name only a few of the school classics. We read *Hamlet* and *Macbeth,* and both were spoiled by the interruption of footnotes and the fact that we had to commit lines to memory and write themes on what we thought of the plays. Naturally, we wrote that these were great and masterly works which we had devoured with rapt eagerness. The teacher had already told us the plays were great and we had caution enough to play safe.

Presently Latin came along and then Greek. The current saying was that if you could learn Latin, any other foreign language would be easy. I am not prepared to testify to the truth of this saying, as I never learned any more Latin than was necessary to skim through a college entrance examination, which is not much. Certainly I learned no other foreign tongue. There were three years of French, and all that abides is the opening sentences of the book: *" Ah! un animal. Cet animal est un cheval. Ce cheval est beau."*

German was a little easier than French, and I absorbed enough to pass it both as an elementary and advanced subject for college entrance, but the best I can do now is to sing the first verse of " The Lorelei." Or, rather, I know the words. I also passed elementary Greek in the Harvard admission examinations, and that is the greatest mystery of all. It was the most fugitive sort of friendship.

Arithmetic I retain pretty well. I can bank a poker game and keep a pretty accurate score for bridge, and in fact do almost anything which does not involve long division, for which I have rather lost the knack. Algebra is gone. Geometrically speaking, I know that a straight line is the shortest distance between two points and that the square of the hypotenuse of a right-angled triangle equals the sum of the squares on the other two sides. But both these facts I now accept by faith alone. I can no longer prove them.

Up till now I have been setting this report down with the thought that it fairly well approximates the experiences of the average American in school. With college I must admit that there comes a turn for the worse. I took a good deal less from Harvard than it gives to most, but even the findings of a lazy and indifferent student represent the experiences of not a few. Harvard said in effect: " Work if you will," and I made another choice.

However, I would have gained my degree if I had passed just one more course, and the marvel to me is that I got through in so many subjects concerning which my present conscious memory is wholly negligible. For instance, I spent a full year under Kittredge, who lectured on three plays of Shakespeare's, and everything is gone except two digressions. I remember that Professor Kittredge said on one occasion that he believed in personal immortality after death and that once he complained about bad ventilation on ocean steamers. Since then, I understand, the latter matter has been attended to.

In economics I learned that a protective tariff is scientifically unsound, but I can't remember why. Professor Carver used to lecture on various theories of social reform, socialism, communism, and the single tax during the first half year. In the second half he explained why the various panaceas could not work. These later lectures I missed, so I went away with nothing but the most friendly thoughts concerning each and every one of the impractical visionary schemes touched upon in the course.

Likewise, in philosophy there was a charge and a counterattack. Professor Palmer was much concerned with the question of whether human conduct was motivated under a dispensation of free will or whether we all operated under determinism. I missed most of the recoil which came in the second half year and showed how wrongheaded were all the determinists, and so I believe implicitly in fate.

American history I had under Hart, and one of his lectures is still vivid because he got excited about it and acted it out. People used to come from all over the yard to hear Hart talk about John Brown. He told of the execution of Brown after the raid on Harpers Ferry and how they tried to break the old man's nerve by making him wait on the scaffold before they sprang the trap. And at that point Hart would pause for a moment and stand with his head thrown back as John Brown might have stood. And he said that they didn't break the old man's nerve.

But there was another man at Harvard in my time, and he's there now and ever will be, I rather imagine, who did most of all to fire the imagination of the youngsters. Hart had just one good performance, but C. T. Copeland played repertoire. He lectured on Dr. Johnson and he taught English composition, and you could go to his room and sit in front of a fire and listen a good deal and talk a little. Copeland has said fifty things that I remember, but, more important than that, I carried away the feel and touch of an enthusiastic personality. He made us know that writing is honorable and alive. Hundreds of men left Copeland and Harvard, eager to sit down and write the great American novel. None of them has done it yet, but some continue to try because they feel, after knowing him, that about the most important thing anybody could do in the world would be to create something fine in words. After fifteen years of newspaper work I still think it would be.

Stuart P. Sherman

George Lyman Kittredge

FIRST of all, let us declare that Professor Kittredge belongs to that generation of great college teachers which well-informed observers tell us is rapidly giving place to a later undergrowth of special investigators. There are, to be sure, a few small colleges left in the land, which, without much regard for "productive scholarship," still bestow their pudding and praise upon the man who can master his classroom, stab the laggards broad awake, and by the venerable inquisitorial methods discover and develop the young men of parts. But generally nowadays the word is passed round among the rising generation of instructors that the way to get on in the academic walk is not to waste time on one's pupils, but to publish — it matters not what. Whatever indirect responsibility Professor Kittredge may share in the propagation of this notion, it is undeniable that his own example has not sanctioned it. When the "efficiency" experts began last spring their abortive inquiries into the time spent by members of the instructional staff in preparation for each lecture, Professor Kittredge said, as it is reported, "I shall refuse to answer; it is my trade secret." A thoroughly characteristic *mot,* and it helped reveal the Philistine futility of the investigation. The special flavor of it lay in one's certainty that the questionnaire would, as a matter of fact, be dropped by him summarily and with perfect impunity into the wastebasket, and in the universal recognition that as a teacher, pure and simple, Professor Kittredge is, as they say in Cambridge, "one of the glories of the University." We are thinking now particularly of that famous course in Shakespeare which for many years has been one of the good reasons for going to Harvard.

There is a persistent tradition that Professor Kittredge formed what we may call his undergraduate manner in his preliminary pedagogic experiments long ago at the Phillips Exeter Academy. It is a manner primarily adapted to young, resistant, "tough-minded" persons, and it is perhaps not unconsciously reminiscent of Dr. Boyer of immortal memory and of that older schoolmaster at whose hands John Dryden received, as he gratefully testified, the only thrashing that he ever deserved. Exponents of the new style of teaching salute their assembled pupils in the French fashion with a courteous "Gentlemen," deliver an essay spiced with epigrams, or twitter extemporaneously through the hour, bow, and disappear. Or — of another type — enter the lecture room weary, dreary, from their private lucubrations, explain that they are but fellow workers with their pupils in the same vineyard, pull out a sheaf of ill-digested notes, and drone away till the welcome bell. The new style is based not merely on the assumption

From the *Nation,* September 11, 1913.

that the student is "interested in his own intellectual welfare," but also on
the far wider assumption that he is interested in his teacher's intricate "special
problem." In dealing with undergraduates, Professor Kittredge is an educational
realist. He assumes nothing but the general ignorance, indolence, and inattentiveness of undisciplined youth. He sees congregated before him, in that curious
mixture fostered by the Harvard system, boys of eighteen and men with hair
as white as his own, hard students and loafers from the "Gold Coast," keen-
eyed freshmen from the Cambridge and Boston Latin Schools and untrained
bachelors from the soft Southern colleges, stiff-necked elderly schoolmasters who
wish to "brush up a bit," and opinionated, unlicked cub professors on leave
from the exuberant West. He does not cast a farewell glance about the room
and dive into a manuscript. He envisages the situation. Before instruction proper
can begin, this unequal conglomeration of alertness and dullness, humility and
conceit, must be subjugated, must be terrorized, must be welded by common
apprehension into one homogeneous whole.

Perhaps the technique of terror is a "trade secret," too, but it is also a rich
legend recited by every group of men that have studied English at Harvard.
After the lapse of a good many years we can call up with perfect distinctness
some of the Black Fridays when there was great slaughter of the Innocents.
A pretty abrupt hush follows his rapid footsteps up the aisle, deepens as he
seats himself sidewise and menaces us thunderously from behind the formidable
blue glasses, becomes painfully intense as he rises to stride to and fro the length
of the platform in a kind of tiger-tread, and the blackboard pointer, overstrained
by his nervous fingers, breaks with an electrifying snap. We are about to
enjoy a bad quarter of an hour. "Mr. A! How does a play begin?" "With
dialogue," hazards Mr. A. "Mr. B! How does a play begin?" "With the introduction of the characters," stammers Mr. B anxiously. "Mr. C! How does a
play begin?" Mr. C, who is from the Gold Coast, quietly mumbles, "I don't
know." The hunt is afoot. The next dozen men go down amid derisive snickers
— no one dares to laugh aloud — like clay pipes before a crack marksman.
Panic spreads. Half of us refuse to answer to our names. The other half, in
desperate agitation between an attempt to conjure up any sort of reply and a
passionate desire to sink through the floor, shudderingly wait for the next
victim, till the pursuer, at last weary of the sport, cries out, "A play begins *in
mediis rebus!*" Then we turn to the text. "'We would not die in that man's
company that fears his fellowship to die with us.' Mr. X! Explain 'that fears
his fellowship to die with us.'" Mr. X proffers something very elaborate and
very confused. "Somebody explain that explanation!" — this with the true
Johnsonian shout. "Mr. Y!" Mr. Y moistens his lips, starts, hems, hesitates,
fumbles for words. "Come! Come! Mr. Y. Time flies! Hell threats! Heaven
invites!" Mr. Y shuns salvation and hangs silent in Limbo. Mr. Z ventures on
a surly pleasantry and is greeted with an invitation to "come over and swap
jests with me at 2:30 this afternoon." We all envy Mr. Z as we should envy a
man invited to take supper in a lion's den. Like many other of the great experiences of life, it was a rigorous ordeal while one was undergoing it, but

it was pleasant to look back upon years afterwards, and, like Purgatory, was very salutary.

The instruction proper had also, as we recall it, a powerful purgatorial quality. What has subsequently seemed to us to be Professor Kittredge's guiding spirit is happily embodied in one of the " golden sayings," to use his own phrase, of Josh Billings: " It ain't the things we don't know that makes such fools of us, but a whole lot of things that we know that ain't *so*." This, despite the vernacular dress, is the spirit of science, and for at least once in a lifetime it was an entirely wholesome spirit to encounter amid the bogs and fens of Shakespearean " interpretation." " War to the death," was the cry in that course, " on gushing Mrs. Jamesons, moralizing clergymen, and fantastic Teutonic metaphysicians." " There are many ways of studying Shakespeare," he told us, " but the object of this course is to ascertain what Shakespeare said and what he meant when he said it." The session ordinarily began with five or ten minutes during which we called out questions on difficult points in the previous day's reading. These he answered instantly, always without consulting the book, and succinctly or copiously as the case required. For the next ten or fifteen minutes he subjected us in our turn to a grilling examination on whatever we had prepared for the day. For the rest of the hour he commented with racy phrase and startling illustration, and left the room at the last minute, talking all the way down the aisle and halfway down the stairs.

For graduate students there was another manner. Jupiter Tonans gave way to benignant Jove, a being of equal or greater fascination, but with his terrors laid by, alert, omniscient as it seemed, a hawk-eyed critic still, but of princely amenity, tireless helpfulness, and the cordialest interest in one's personal destiny. This is the Kittredge of the disciples — the candidates for the doctorate — who hand down his *obiter dicta* from year to year, and speak of his chance commendation of some former pupil or pupil's work as one speaks of the conferring of an Order of Merit.

There was nothing lethargic in the atmosphere of those meetings. When the analysis and destruction of a great piece of German interpretation was completed one felt such a glow of satisfaction as must have thrilled the blood of a red-handed Saxon churl when he had assisted good King Alfred in flaying off a Dane skin and nailing it up on a church door. Nor, under that leadership, did one's interest flag when occasion failed for noble rage and cannibalistic enterprise. Fired by that unrelenting ardor, one fixed one's attention with as intense a concern upon a disputed comma in a Canterbury tale as one could have felt for the most momentous crisis in the affairs of a nation. One could sit for week after week copying down under that dynamic dictation an endless ballad bibliography that one never used, nor ever hoped to use, and yet maintain through it all the spellbound gravity of one hearkening to a seraphic discussion of fate and foreknowledge absolute.

Best of all were the ever memorable individual conferences, when the candidate, now going heavily with his dissertation, visited the arbiter of his fate by special appointment at some hour not far from midnight, and came upon him, in the midst of his study, seated at the center of a great half moon of tomes and treatises, and enveloped and clouded, like a god, in infinite smoke. You began the interview with a half hour of wizardry, during which, while you helped thicken the smoke, he told you of the smoking customs of barbarians or poured out odd stories of witchcraft and alchemy in New England. Then you explained your difficulties and he cleared them up, or you told him what you were hunting for, and he pulled out of some recess or other a box full of references bearing exactly upon the point, and filed away months or years before, when he was working upon the same topic. You returned to your labors with a persuasion that there was no topic which had not, on one occasion or another, engaged his attention. You returned with a feeling, also, that your academic fortune was insured. For it may be said of Professor Kittredge, as it was said of the old Germanic chiefs, who never forgot their friends nor forgave their enemies, he has been a good " Ring-Giver."

James Parton

Charles Goodyear

HE copy before us, of Mr. Goodyear's work upon *Gum Elastic and Its Varieties,* presents at least something unique in the art of bookmaking. It is self-illustrating inasmuch as, treating of India rubber, it is made of India rubber. An unobservant reader, however, would scarcely suspect the fact before reading the Preface, for the India-rubber covers resemble highly polished ebony, and the leaves have the appearance of ancient paper worn soft, thin, and dingy by numberless perusals. The volume contains six hundred and twenty pages; but it is not as thick as copies of the same work printed on paper, though it is a little heavier. It is evident that the substance of which this book is composed cannot be India rubber in its natural state. Those leaves, thinner than paper, can be stretched only by a strong pull, and resume their shape perfectly when they are let go. There is no smell of India rubber about them. We first saw this book in a cold room in January, but the leaves were then as flexible as old paper; and when, since, we have handled it in warm weather, they had grown no softer.

Some of our readers may have heard Daniel Webster relate the story of the India-rubber cloak and hat which one of his New York friends sent him at Marshfield in the infancy of the manufacture. He took the coat to the piazza one cold morning, when it instantly became as rigid as sheet iron. Finding that it stood alone, he placed the hat upon it, and left the articles standing near the front door. Several of his neighbors who passed, seeing a dark and portly figure

From *Famous Americans of Recent Times,* 1867.

there, took it for the lord of the mansion, and gave it respectful salutation. The same articles were liable to an objection still more serious. In the sun, even in cool weather, they became sticky, while on a hot day they would melt entirely away to the consistency of molasses. Everyone remembers the thick and ill-shaped India-rubber shoes of twenty years ago, which had to be thawed out under the stove before they could be put on, and which, if left under the stove too long, would dissolve into gum that no household art could ever harden again. Some decorous gentlemen among us can also remember that, in the nocturnal combats of their college days, a flinty India-rubber shoe, in cold weather, was a missive weapon of a highly effective character.

This curious volume, therefore, cannot be made of the unmanageable stuff which Daniel Webster set up at his front door. So much is evident at a glance. But the book itself tells us that it can be subjected, without injury, to tests more severe than summer's sun and winter's cold. It can be soaked six months in a pail of water, and still be as good a book as ever. It can be boiled; it can be baked in an oven hot enough to cook a turkey; it can be soaked in brine, lye, camphene, turpentine, or oil; it can be dipped into oil of vitriol, and still no harm done. To crown its merits, no rat, mouse, worm, or moth has ever shown the slightest inclination to make acquaintance with it. The office of a Review is not usually provided with the means of subjecting literature to such critical tests as lye, vitriol, boilers, and hot ovens. But we have seen enough elsewhere of the ordeals to which India rubber is now subjected to believe Mr. Goodyear's statements. Remote posterity will enjoy the fruit of his labors, unless someone takes particular pains to destroy this book; for it seems that time itself produces no effect upon the India rubber which bears the familiar stamp, " Goodyear's Patent." In the dampest corner of the dampest cellar, no mold gathers upon it, no decay penetrates it. In the hottest garret, it never warps or cracks.

The principal object of the work is to relate how this remarkable change was effected in the nature of the substance of which it treats. It cost more than two millions of dollars to do it. It cost Charles Goodyear eleven most laborious and painful years. His book is written without art or skill, but also without guile. He was evidently a laborious, conscientious, modest man, neither learned nor highly gifted, but making no pretense to learning or gifts, doing the work which fell to him with all his might, and with a perseverance never surpassed in all the history of invention and discovery. Who would have thought to find a romance in the history of India rubber? We are familiar with the stories of poor and friendless men, possessed with an idea and pursuing their object amid obloquy, neglect, and suffering, to the final triumph; of which final triumph other men reaped the substantial reward, leaving to the discoverer the barren glory of his achievement — and that glory obscured by detraction. Columbus is the representative man of that illustrious order. We trust to be able to show that Charles Goodyear is entitled to a place in it. Whether we consider the prodigious and unforeseen importance of his discovery, or his scarcely paralleled devotion to his object in the face of the most disheartening obstacles, we feel it to be due to his memory, to his descendants, and to the public, that his story should be told. Few persons will ever see his book, of which only a small number of copies were printed for private circulation. Still fewer will be at the pains to pick out the material facts from the confused mass of matter in which they are hidden. Happily for our purpose, no one now has an interest to call his merits in question. He rests from his labors, and the patent, which was the glory and misery of his life, has expired.

Our great-grandfathers knew India rubber only as a curiosity, and our grandfathers only as a means of erasing pencil marks. The first specimens were brought to Europe in 1730; and as late as 1770 it was still so scarce an article that in London it was only to be found in one shop, where a piece containing half a cubic inch was sold for three shillings. Dr. Priestley, in his work on perspective, published in 1770, speaks of it as a new article and recommends its use to draughtsmen. This substance, however, being one of those of which nature has provided an inexhaustible supply, greater quantities found their way into the commerce of the world; until, in 1820, it was a drug in all markets and was frequently brought as ballast merely. About this time it began to be subjected to experiments with a view to rendering it available in the arts. It was found useful as an ingredient of blacking and varnish. Its elasticity was turned to account in France in the manufacture of suspenders and garters — threads of India rubber being inserted in the web. In England, Mackintosh invented his still celebrated waterproof coats, which are made of two thin cloths with a paste of India rubber between them. In chemistry, the substance was used to some extent, and its singular properties were much considered. In England and France, the India-rubber manufacture had attained considerable importance before the material had attracted the attention of American experimenters. The Europeans succeeded in rendering it useful because they did not attempt too much. The French cut the imported sheets of gum into shreds, without ever attempting to produce the sheets themselves. Mackintosh exposed no surface of India rubber to the air, and brought no surfaces of India rubber into contact. No one had discovered any process by which India rubber once dissolved could be restored to its original consistency. Some of our readers may have attempted, twenty years ago, to fill up the holes in the sole of an India-rubber shoe. Nothing was easier than to melt a piece of India rubber for the purpose; but, when applied to the shoe, it would not harden. There was the grand difficulty, the complete removal of which cost so much money and so many years.

The ruinous failure of the first American manufacturers arose from the fact that they began their costly operations in ignorance of the existence of this difficulty. They were too fast. They proceeded in the manner of the inventor of the caloric engine, who began by placing one in a ship of great magnitude, involving an expenditure which ruined the owners.

It was in the year 1820 that a pair of India-rubber shoes was seen for the first time in the United States. They were covered with gilding, and resembled in shape the shoes of a Chinaman. They were handed about in Boston only as a curiosity. Two or three years after, a ship from South America brought to Boston five hundred pairs of shoes, thick, heavy, and ill-shaped, which sold so readily as to invite further importations. The business increased until the annual importation reached half a million pairs and India-rubber shoes had become an article of general use. The manner in which these shoes were made by the natives of South America was frequently described in the newspapers, and seemed to present no difficulty. They were made much as farmers' wives made candles. The sap being collected from the trees, clay lasts were dipped into the liquid twenty or thirty times, each layer being smoked a little. The shoes were then hung up to harden for a few days; after which the clay was removed and the shoes were stored for some months to harden them still more. Nothing was more natural than to suppose that Yankees could do this as well as Indians, if not far better. The raw India rubber could then be bought in Boston for five cents a pound, and a pair of shoes made of it brought from three to five dollars. Surely here was a promising basis for a new branch of manufacture in New England. It happened too, in 1830, that vast quantities of the raw gum reached the United States. It came covered with hides, in masses, of which no use could be made in America; and it remained unsold, or was sent to Europe.

Patent leather suggested the first American attempt to turn India rubber to account. Mr. E. M. Chaffee, foreman of a Boston patent-leather factory, conceived the idea, in 1830, of spreading India rubber upon cloth, hoping to produce an article which should possess the good qualities of patent leather, with the additional one of being waterproof. In the deepest secrecy he experimented for several months. By dissolving a pound of India rubber in three quarts of spirits of turpentine and adding lampblack enough to give it the desired color, he produced a composition which he supposed would perfectly answer the purpose. He invented a machine for spreading it, and made some specimens of cloth which had every appearance of being a very useful article. The surface, after being dried in the sun, was firm and smooth; and Mr. Chaffee supposed, and his friends agreed with him, that he had made an invention of the utmost value. At this point he invited a few of the solid men of Roxbury to look at his specimens and listen to his statements. He convinced them. The result of the conference was the Roxbury India-rubber Company, incorporated in February, 1833, with a capital of thirty thousand dollars.

The progress of this company was amazing. Within a year its capital was increased to two hundred and forty thousand dollars. Before another year had expired, this was increased to three hundred thousand; and in the year following, to four hundred thousand. The company manufactured the cloth invented by Mr. Chaffee, and many articles made of that cloth, such as coats, caps, wagon curtains and coverings. Shoes made without fiber were soon introduced. Nothing could be better than the appearance of these articles when they were new. They were in the highest favor and were sold more rapidly than the company could manufacture them. The astonishing prosperity of the Roxbury Company had its natural effect in calling into existence similar establishments in other towns. Manufactories were started at Boston, Framingham, Salem, Lynn, Chelsea, Troy, and Staten Island, with capitals ranging from one hundred thousand dollars to half a million; and all of them appeared to prosper. There was an India-rubber mania in those years similar to that of petroleum in 1864. Not to invest in India-rubber stock was regarded by some shrewd men as indicative of inferior business talents and general dullness of comprehension. The exterior facts were certainly well calculated to lure even the most wary. Here was a material worth only a few cents a pound, out of which shoes were quickly made, which brought two dollars a pair! It was a plain case. Besides, there were the India-rubber companies, all working to their extreme capacity, and selling all they could make.

It was when the business had reached this flourishing stage that Charles Goodyear, a bankrupt hardware merchant of Philadelphia, first had his attention directed to the material upon which it was founded. In 1834, being in New York on business, he chanced to observe the sign of the Roxbury Company, which then had a depot in that city. He had been reading in the newspapers, not long before, descriptions of the new life preservers made of India rubber, an application of the gum that was much extolled. Curiosity induced him to enter the store to examine the life preservers. He bought one and took it home with him. A native of Connecticut, he possessed in full measure the Yankee propensity to look at a new contrivance, first with a view to understanding its principle, and next to see if it cannot be improved. Already he had had some experience both of the difficulty of introducing an improved implement, and of the profit to be derived from its introduction. His father, the head of the firm of A. Goodyear and Sons, of which he was a member, was the first to manufacture hayforks of spring steel, instead of the heavy, wrought-iron forks made by the village blacksmith; and Charles Goodyear could remember the time when his father reckoned it a happy day on which he had persuaded a farmer to accept a few of the new forks as a gift, on the condition of giving them a trial. But it was also very fresh in his recollection that those same forks had made their way to almost universal use, had yielded large profits to his firm, and were still a leading article of its trade, when, in 1830, the failure of Southern houses had compelled it to suspend. He was aware, too, that, if anything could extricate the house of A. Goodyear and Sons from embarrassment, it was their possession of superior methods of manufacturing and their sale of articles improved by their own ingenuity.

Upon examining his life preserver, an improvement in the inflating apparatus occurred to him. When he was next in New York he explained his improvement to the agent of the Roxbury Company, and offered to sell it. The agent, struck with the ingenuity displayed in the new contrivance, took the inventor into his confidence, partly by way of explaining why the company could not then buy the improved tube, but principally with a view to enlist the aid of an ingenious mind in overcoming a difficulty that threatened the company with ruin. He told him that the prosperity of the India-rubber companies in the United States was wholly fallacious. The Roxbury Company had manufactured vast quantities of shoes and fabrics in the cool months of 1833 and 1834, which had been readily sold at high prices; but during the following summer the greater part of them had melted. Twenty thousand dollars' worth had been returned, reduced to the consistency of common gum and emitting an odor so offensive that they had been obliged to bury it. New ingredients had been employed, new machinery applied, but still the articles would dissolve. In some cases, shoes had borne the heat of one summer and melted the next. The wagon covers became sticky in the sun and rigid in the cold. The directors were at their wits' end since it required two years to test a new process, and meanwhile they knew not whether the articles made by it were valuable or worthless. If they stopped manufacturing, that was certain ruin. If they went on, they might find the product of a whole winter dissolving on their hands. The capital of the company was already so far exhausted that, unless the true method were speedily discovered, it would be compelled to wind up its affairs. The agent urged Mr. Goodyear not to waste time upon minor improvements, but to direct all his efforts to finding out the secret of successfully working the material itself. The company could not buy his improved inflator; but let him learn how to make an India rubber that would stand the summer's heat, and there was scarcely any price which it would not gladly give for the secret.

The worst apprehensions of the directors of this company were realized. The public soon became tired of buying India-rubber shoes that could only be saved during the summer by putting them into a refrigerator. In the third year of the mania, India-rubber stock began to decline, and Roxbury itself finally fell to two dollars and a half. Before the close of 1836, all the companies had ceased to exist, their fall involving many hundreds of families in heavy loss. The clumsy, shapeless shoes from South America were the only ones which the people would buy. It was generally supposed that the secret of their resisting heat was that they were smoked with the leaves of a certain tree peculiar to South America, and that nothing else in nature would answer the purpose.

The two millions of dollars lost by these companies had one result which has proved to be worth many times that sum; it led Charles Goodyear to undertake the investigation of India rubber. That chance conversation with the agent of the Roxbury Company fixed his destiny. If he were alive to read these lines, he would, however, protest against the use of such a word as *chance* in this connection. He really appears to have felt himself "called" to study India rubber. He says himself:

From the time that his attention was first given to the subject, a strong and abiding impression was made upon his mind, that an object so desirable and important, and so necessary to man's comfort, as the making of gum elastic available to his use, was most certainly placed within his reach. Having this presentiment, of which he could not divest himself under the most trying adversity, he was stimulated with the hope of ultimately attaining this object.

Beyond this he would refer the whole to the great Creator, who directs the operations of mind to the development of the properties of matter, in his own way, at the time when they are specially needed, influencing some mind for every work or calling. . . . Were he to refrain from expressing his views thus briefly, he would ever feel that he had done violence to his sentiments.

This is modestly said, but his friends assure us that he felt it earnestly and habitually. It was, indeed, this steadfast conviction of the possibility of attaining his object, and his religious devotion to it, that constituted his capital in his new business. He had little knowledge of chemistry and an aversion to complicated calculations. He was a ruined man; for, after a long struggle with misfortune, the firm of A. Goodyear and Sons had surrendered their all to their creditors, and still owed thirty thousand dollars. He had a family, and his health was not robust. Upon returning home after conversing with the agent of the Roxbury Company, he was arrested for debt and compelled to reside within the prison limits. He melted his first pound of India rubber while he was living within those limits and struggling to keep out of the jail itself. Thus he began his experiments in circumstances as little favorable as can be imagined. There were only two things in his favor. One was his conviction that India rubber *could* be subjugated, and that he was the man destined to subjugate it. The other was that, India rubber having fallen to its old price, he could continue his labors as long as he could raise five cents and procure access to a fire. The very odium in which businessmen held India rubber, though it long retarded his final triumph, placed an abundance of the native gum within the means even of an inmate of the debtor's prison, in which he often was during the whole period of his experimenting. He was seldom out of jail a whole year from 1835 to 1841, and never out of danger of arrest.

In a small house in Philadelphia, in the winter of 1834-1835, he began his investigations. He melted his gum by the domestic fire, kneaded it with his own hands, spread it upon a marble slab, and rolled it with a rolling pin. A prospect of success flattered him from the first and lured him on. He was soon able to produce sheets of India rubber which appeared as firm as those imported, and which tempted a friend to advance him a sum of money sufficient to enable him to manufacture several hundred pairs of shoes. He succeeded in embossing his shoes in various patterns, which gave them a novel and elegant appearance. Mindful, however, of the disasters of the Roxbury Company, he had the prudence to store his shoes until the summer. The hot days of June reduced them all to soft and stinking paste. His friend was discouraged, and refused him further aid. For his own part, such experiences as this, though they dashed his spirits for a while, stimulated him to new efforts.

It now occurred to him that perhaps it was the turpentine used in dissolving the gum, or the lampblack employed to color it, that spoiled his product. He esteemed it a rare piece of luck to produce some barrels of the sap not smoked, and still liquid. On going to the shed where the precious sap was deposited, he was accosted by an Irishman in his employ, who, in high glee, informed him that he had discovered the secret, pointing to his overalls, which he had dipped into the sap, and which were nicely coated with firm India rubber. For a moment he thought that Jerry might have blundered into the secret. The man, however, sat down on a barrel near the fire, and, on attempting to rise, found himself glued to his seat and his legs stuck together. He had to be cut out of his overalls. The master proceeded to experiment with the sap, but soon discovered that the handsome white cloth made of it bore the heat no better than that which was produced in the usual manner.

Satisfied that nothing could be done with India rubber pure and simple, he concluded that a compound of some substance with India rubber could alone render the gum available. He was correct in this conjecture, but it remained to be discovered whether there was such a substance in nature. He tried everything he could think of. For a short time he was elated with the result of his experiments with magnesia, mixing half a pound of magnesia with a pound of gum. This compound had the advantage of being whiter than the pure sap. It was so firm that he used it as leather in the binding of a book. In a few weeks, however, he had the mortification of seeing his elegant white book covers fermenting and softening. Afterwards, they grew as hard and brittle as shell, and so they remain to this day.

By this time, the patience of his friends and his own little fund of money were both exhausted; and one by one the relics of his former prosperity, even to his wife's trinkets, found their way to the pawnbroker. He was a sanguine man, as inventors need to be, always feeling that he was on the point of succeeding. The very confidence with which he announced a new conception served at length to close all ears to his solicitations. In the second year of his investigation he removed his family to the country and went to New York in quest of someone who had still a little faith in India rubber. His credit was then at so low an ebb that he was obliged to deposit with the landlord a quantity of linen spun by his excellent wife. It was never redeemed. It was sold at auction to pay the first quarter's rent; and his furniture also would have been seized, but that he had taken the precaution to sell it himself in Philadelphia, and had placed in his cottage articles of too little value to tempt the hardest creditor.

In New York — the first resort of the enterprising and the last refuge of the unfortunate — he found two old friends, one of whom lent him a room in Gold Street for a laboratory, and the other, a druggist, supplied him with materials on credit. Again his hopes were flattered by an apparent success. By boiling his compound of gum and magnesia in quicklime and water, an article was produced which seemed to be all that he could desire. Some sheets of India rubber made by this process drew a medal at the fair of the American Institute in 1835 and were much commended in the newspapers. Nothing could exceed the smoothness and firmness of the surface of these sheets; nor have they to this day been surpassed in these particulars. He obtained a patent for the process, manufactured a considerable quantity, sold his product readily, and thought his difficulties were at an end. In a few weeks his hopes were dashed to the ground. He found that a drop of weak acid, such as apple juice or vinegar and water, instantly annihilated the effect of the lime and made the beautiful surface of his cloth sticky.

Undaunted, he next tried the experiment of mixing quicklime with pure gum. He tells us that, at this time, he used to prepare a gallon jug of quicklime at his room in Gold Street and carry it on his shoulder to Greenwich Village, distant three miles, where he had access to horse power for working his compound. This experiment, too, was a failure. The lime in a short time appeared to consume the gum with which it was mixed, leaving a substance that crumbled to pieces.

Accident suggested his next process, which, though he knew it not, was a step toward his final success. Except his almost unparalleled perseverance, the most marked trait in the character of this singular man was his love for beautiful forms and colors. An incongruous garment or decoration upon a member of his family, or anything tawdry or ill-arranged in a room, gave him positive distress. Accordingly, we always find him endeavoring to decorate his India-rubber fabrics. It was in bronzing the surface of some India-rubber drapery that the accident happened to which we have referred. Desiring to remove the bronze from a piece of the drapery, he applied aquafortis for the purpose, which did indeed have the effect desired, but it also discolored the fabric and appeared to spoil it. He threw away the piece as useless. Several days after, it occurred to him that he had not sufficiently examined the effect of the aquafortis, and, hurrying to his room, he was fortunate enough to find it again. A remarkable change appeared to have been made in the India rubber. He does not seem to have been aware that aquafortis is two-fifths sulphuric acid. Still less did he ever suspect that the surface of his drapery had really been " vulcanized." All he knew was that India-rubber cloth " cured," as he termed it, by aquafortis was incomparably superior to any previously made, and bore a degree of heat that rendered it available for many valuable purposes.

He was again a happy man. A partner with ample capital joined him. He went to Washington and patented his process. He showed his specimens to President Jackson, who expressed in writing his approval of them. Returning to New York, he prepared to manufacture on a great scale, hired the abandoned India-rubber works on Staten Island, and engaged a store in Broadway for the sale of his fabrics. In the midst of these grand preparations, his zeal in experimenting almost cost him his life. Having generated a large quantity of poisonous gas in his close room, he was so nearly suffocated that it was six weeks before he recovered his health. Before he had begun to produce his fabrics in any considerable quantity, the commercial storm of 1836 swept away the entire property of his partner, which put a complete stop to the operations in India rubber and reduced poor Goodyear to his normal condition of beggary. Beggary it literally was; for he was absolutely dependent upon others for the means of sustaining life. He mentions that, soon after this crushing blow, his family having previously joined him in New York, he awoke one morning to discover that he had neither an atom of food for them, nor a cent to buy it with. Putting in his pocket an article that he supposed a pawnbroker would value, he set out in the hope of procuring enough money to sustain them for one day. Before reaching the sign, so familiar to him, of the three Golden Balls, he met a terrible being to a man in his situation — a creditor! Hungry and dejected, he prepared his mind for a torrent of bitter reproaches; for this gentleman was one whose patience he felt he had abused. What was his relief when his creditor accosted him gaily with, " Well, Mr. Goodyear, what can I do for you today? " His first thought was that an insult was intended, so preposterous did it seem that this man could really desire to aid him further. Satisfied that the offer was well meant, he told his friend that he had come out that morning in search of food for his family, and that a loan of fifteen dollars would greatly oblige him. The money was instantly produced, which enabled him to postpone his visit to the pawnbroker for several days. The pawnbroker was still, however, his frequent resource all that year, until the few remains of his late brief prosperity had all disappeared.

But he never for a moment let go his hold upon India rubber. A timely loan of a hundred dollars from an old friend enabled him to remove his family to Staten Island, near the abandoned India-rubber factory. Having free access to the works, he and his wife contrived to manufacture a few articles of his improved cloth and to sell enough to provide daily bread. His great object there was to induce the directors of the suspended company to recommence operations upon his new process. But so completely sickened were they of the very name of a material which had involved them in so much loss and discredit, that during the six months of his residence on the Island he never succeeded in persuading one man to do so much as come to the factory and look at his specimens. There was thousands of dollars' worth of machinery there, but not a single shareholder cared even to know the condition of the property. This was the more remarkable, since he was unusually endowed by nature with the power to inspire other men with his own confidence. The magnates of Staten Island, however, involved as they were in the general shipwreck of property and credit, were inexorably deaf to his eloquence.

As he had formerly exhausted Philadelphia, so now New York seemed exhausted. He became even an object of ridicule. He was regarded as an India-rubber monomaniac. One of his New York friends, having been asked how Mr. Goodyear could be recognized in the street, replied: " If you see a man with an India-rubber coat on, India-rubber shoes, an India-rubber cap, and in his pocket an India-rubber purse, with not a cent in it, that is he." He was in the habit then of wearing his material in every form, with the twofold view of testing and advertising it.

In September, 1836, aided again by a small loan, he packed a few of his best specimens in his carpetbag and set out alone for the cradle of the India-rubber manufacture — Roxbury. The ruin of the great company there was then complete, and the factory was abandoned. All that part of Massachusetts was suffering from the total depreciation of the India-rubber stocks. There were still, however, two or three persons who could not quite give up India rubber. Mr. Chaffee, the originator of the manufacture in America, welcomed warmly a brother experimenter, admired his specimens, encouraged him to persevere, procured him friends, and, what was more important, gave him the use of the enormous machinery standing idle in the factory. A brief, delusive prosperity again relieved the monotony of misfortune. By his new process he made shoes, piano covers, and carriage cloths, so superior to any previously produced in the United States as to cause a temporary revival of the business, which enabled him to sell rights to manufacture under his patents. His profits in a single year amounted to four or five thousand dollars. Again he had his family around him and felt a boundless confidence in the future.

An event upon which he had depended for the completeness of his triumph plunged him again into ruin. He received an order from the government for a hundred and fifty India-rubber mailbags. Having perfect confidence in his ability to execute this order, he gave the greatest possible publicity to it. All the world should now see that Goodyear's India rubber was all that Goodyear had represented it. The bags were finished; and beautiful bags they were, — smooth, firm, highly polished, well-shaped, and indubitably waterproof. He had them hung up all round the factory, and invited everyone to come and inspect them. They were universally admired, and the maker was congratulated upon his success. It was in the summer that these fatal bags were finished. Having occasion to be absent for a month, he left them hanging in the factory. Judge of his consternation when, on his return, he found them softening, fermenting, and dropping off their handles. The aquafortis did indeed " cure " the surface of his India rubber, but only the surface. Very thin cloth made by this process was a useful and somewhat durable article; but for any other purpose, it was valueless. The public and signal failure of the mailbags, together with the imperfection of all his products except his thinnest cloth, suddenly and totally destroyed his rising business. Everything he possessed that was salable was sold at auction to pay his debts. He was again penniless and destitute, with an increased family and an aged father dependent upon him.

His friends, his brothers, and his wife now joined in dissuading him from further experiments. Were not four years of such vicissitude enough? Who had ever touched India rubber without loss? Could he hope to succeed, when so many able and enterprising men had failed? Had he a right to keep his family in a condition so humiliating and painful? He had succeeded in the hardware business; why not return to it? There were those who would join him in any rational undertaking; but how could he expect that anyone would be willing to throw more money into a bottomless pit that had already engulfed millions without result? These arguments he could not answer, and we cannot; the friends of all the great inventors have had occasion to use the same. It seemed highly absurd to the friends of Fitch, Watt, Fulton, Wedgwood, Whitney, Arkwright, that they should forsake the beaten track of business to pursue a path that led through the wilderness to nothing but wilderness. Not one of these men, perhaps, could have made a reasonable reply to the remonstrances of their friends. They only felt, as poor Goodyear felt, that the steep and thorny path which they were treading was the path they *must* pursue. A power of which they could give no satisfactory account urged them on. And when we look closely into the lives of such men, we observe that, in their dark days, some trifling circumstance was always occurring that set them upon new inquiries and gave them new hopes. It might be an *ignis fatuus* that led them farther astray, or it might be genuine light which brought them into the true path.

Goodyear might have yielded to his friends on this occasion, for he was an affectionate man, devoted to his family, had not one of those trifling events occurred which inflamed his curiosity anew. During his late transient prosperity, he had employed a man, Nathaniel Hayward by name, who had been foreman of one of the extinct India-rubber companies. He found him in charge of the abandoned factory and still making a few articles on his own account by a new process. To harden his India rubber, he put a very small quantity of sulphur into it, or sprinkled sulphur upon the surface and dried it in the sun. Mr. Goodyear was surprised to observe that this process seemed to produce the same effect as the application of aquafortis. It does not appear to have occurred to him that Hayward's process and his own were essentially the same. A chemical dictionary would have informed him that sulphuric acid enters largely into the composition of aquafortis, from which he might have inferred that the only difference between the two methods was that Hayward employed the sun, and Goodyear nitric acid, to give the sulphur effect. Hayward's goods, however, were liable to a serious objection: the smell of the sulphur in warm weather was intolerable. Hayward, it appears, was a very illiterate man; and the only account he could give of his invention was that it was revealed to him in a dream. His process was of so little use to him that Goodyear bought his patent for a small sum and gave him employment at monthly wages until the mailbag disaster deprived him of the means of doing so.

In combining sulphur with India rubber, Goodyear had approached so near his final success that one step more brought him to it. He was certain that he was very close to the secret. He saw that sulphur had a mysterious power over India rubber when a union could be effected between the two substances. True, there was an infinitesimal quantity of sulphur in his mailbags, and they had melted in the shade; but the surface of his cloth, powdered with the sulphur and dried in the sun, bore the sun's heat. Here was a mystery. The problem was how to produce in a *mass* of India rubber the change effected on the surface by sulphur and sun. He made numberless experiments. He mixed with the gum large quantities of sulphur, and small quantities. He exposed his compound to the sun and held it near a fire. He felt that he had the secret in his hands; but for many weary months it eluded him.

And, after all, it was an accident that revealed it; but an accident that no man in the world but Charles Goodyear could have interpreted, nor he, but for his five years' previous investigation. At Woburn one day, in the spring of 1839, he was standing with his brother and several other persons near a very hot stove. He held in his hand a mass of his compound of sulphur and gum, upon which he was expatiating in his usual vehement manner — the company exhibiting the indifference to which he was accustomed. In the crisis of his argument he made a violent gesture which brought the mass in contact with the stove, which was hot enough to melt India rubber instantly; upon looking at it a moment after, he perceived that his compound had not melted in the least degree! It had charred as leather chars, but no part of the surface had dissolved. There was not a sticky place upon it. To say that he was astonished at this would but faintly express his ecstasy of amazement. The result was absolutely new to all experience — India rubber not melting in contact with red-hot iron! A man must have been five years absorbed in the pursuit of an object to comprehend his emotions. He felt as Columbus felt when he saw the land-bird alighting upon his ship, and the driftwood floating by. But, like Columbus, he was surrounded with an unbelieving crew. Eagerly he showed his charred India rubber to his brother and to the other bystanders, and dwelt upon the novelty and marvelousness of his fact. They regarded it with complete indifference. The good man had worn them all out. Fifty times before, he had run to them, exulting in some new discovery, and they supposed, of course, that this was another of his chimeras.

He followed the new clew with an enthusiasm which his friends would have been justified in calling frenzy if success had not finally vindicated him. He soon discovered that his compound would not melt at any degree of heat. It next occurred to him to ascertain at how low a temperature it would char, and whether it was not possible to *arrest* the combustion at a point that would leave the India rubber elastic but deprived of its adhesiveness. A single experiment proved that this was possible. After toasting a piece of his compound before an open fire, he found that, while part of it was charred, a rim of India rubber round the charred portion was elastic still, and even more elastic than pure gum. In a few days he had established three facts: first that this rim of India rubber would bear a temperature of two hundred and seventy-eight degrees without charring; second, that it would not melt or soften at any heat; third, that, placed between blocks of ice and left out of doors all night, it would not stiffen in the least degree. He had triumphed, and he knew it. He tells us that he now " felt himself amply repaid for the past, and quite indifferent as to the trials of the future." It, was well he was so, for his darkest days were before him, and he was still six years from a practicable success. He had, indeed, proved that a compound of sulphur and India rubber, in proper proportions and in certain conditions, being subjected for a certain time to a certain degree of heat, undergoes a change which renders it perfectly available for all the uses to which he had before attempted in vain to apply it. But it remained to be ascertained what were those proper proportions, what were those conditions, what was that degree of heat, what was that certain time, and by what means the heat could be best applied.

The difficulty of all this may be inferred when we state that at the present time it takes an intelligent man a year to learn how to conduct the process with certainty, though he is provided, from the start, with the best implements and appliances which twenty years' experience has suggested. And poor Goodyear had now reduced himself not merely to poverty but to isolation. No friend of his could conceal his impatience when he heard him pronounce the words *India rubber*. Businessmen recoiled from the name of it. He tells us that two entire years passed, after he had made his discovery, before he had convinced one human being of its value. Now, too, his experiments could no longer be carried on with a few pounds of India rubber, a quart of turpentine, a phial of aquafortis, and a little lampblack. He wanted the means of producing a high, uniform, and controllable degree of heat — a matter of much greater difficulty than he anticipated. We catch brief glimpses of him at this time in the volumes of testimony. We see him waiting for his wife to draw the loaves from her oven, that he might put into it a batch of India rubber to bake, and watching it all the evening, far into the night, to see what effect was produced by one hour's, two hours', three hours', six hours' baking. We see him boiling it in his wife's saucepans, suspending it before the nose of her teakettle, and hanging it from the handle of that vessel to within an inch of the boiling water. We see him roasting it in the ashes and in hot sand, toasting it before a slow fire and before a quick fire, cooking it for one hour and for twenty-four hours, changing the proportions of his compound and mixing them in different ways. No success rewarded him while he employed only domestic utensils. Occasionally, it is true, he produced a small piece of perfectly vulcanized India rubber; but upon subjecting other pieces to precisely the same process, they would blister or char.

Then we see him resorting to the shops and factories in the neighborhood of Woburn, asking the privilege of using an oven after working hours, or of hanging a piece of India rubber in the " man-hole " of the boiler. The foremen testify that he was a great plague to them, and smeared their works with his sticky compound; but, though they all regarded him as little better than a troublesome lunatic, they all appear to have helped him very willingly. He frankly confesses that he lived at this time on charity; for, although *he* felt confident of being able to repay the small sums which pity for his family enabled him to borrow, his neighbors who lent him the money were as far as possible from expecting payment. Pretending to lend, they meant to give. One would pay his butcher's bill or his milk bill; another would send in a barrel of flour; another would take in payment some articles of the old stock of India rubber; and some of the farmers allowed his children to gather sticks in their fields to heat his hillocks of sand containing masses of sulphurized India rubber. If the people of New England were not the most " neighborly " people in the world, his family must have starved or he must have given up his experiments. But, with all the generosity of his neighbors, his children were often sick, hungry, and cold, without medicine, food, or fuel. One witness testifies: " I found (in 1839) that they had not fuel to burn nor food to eat, and did not know where to get a morsel of food from one day to another, unless it was sent in to them."

We can neither justify nor condemn their father. Imagine Columbus within sight of the new world, and his obstinate crew declaring it was only a mirage, and refusing to row him ashore! Never was mortal man surer that he had a fortune in his hand than Charles Goodyear was when he would take a piece of scorched and dingy India rubber from his pocket and expound its marvelous properties to a group of incredulous villagers. Sure also was he that he was just upon the point of a practicable success. Give him but an oven, and would he not turn you out fireproof and coldproof India rubber as fast as a baker can produce loaves of bread? Nor was it merely the hope of deliverance from his pecuniary straits that urged him on. In all the records of his career, we perceive traces of something nobler than this. His health being always infirm, he was haunted with the dread of dying before he had reached a point in his discoveries where other men, influenced by ordinary motives, could render them available.

By the time that he had exhausted the patience of the foremen of the works near Woburn, he had come to the conclusion that an oven was the proper means of applying heat to his compound. An oven he forthwith determined to build. Having obtained the use of a corner of a factory yard, his aged father, two of his brothers, his little son, and himself sallied forth, with pickaxe and shovels, to begin the work; and when they had done all that unskilled labor could effect towards it, he induced a mason to complete it, and paid him in bricklayers' aprons made of aquafortized India rubber. This first oven was a tantalizing failure. The heat was neither uniform nor controllable. Some of the pieces of India rubber would come out so perfectly " cured " as to demonstrate the utility of his discovery; but others, prepared in precisely the same manner, as far as he could discern, were spoiled, either by blistering or charring. He was puzzled and distressed beyond description; and no single voice consoled or encouraged him. Out of the first piece of cloth which he succeeded in vulcanizing he had a coat made for himself, which was not an ornamental garment in its best estate; but, to prove to the unbelievers that it would stand fire, he brought it so often in contact with hot stoves that at last it presented an exceedingly dingy appearance. His coat did not impress the public favorably, and it served to confirm the opinion that he was laboring under a mania.

In the midst of his first disheartening experiments with sulphur, he had an opportunity of escaping at once from his troubles. A house in Paris made him an advantageous offer for the use of his aquafortis process. From the abyss of his misery the honest man promptly replied that that process, valuable as it was, was about to be superseded by a new method, which he was then perfecting, and as soon as he had developed it sufficiently he should be glad to close with their offers. Can we wonder that his neighbors thought him mad?

It was just after declining the French proposal that he endured his worst extremity of want and humiliation. It was in the winter of 1839–1840. One of those long and terrible snowstorms for which New England is noted had been raging for many hours, and he awoke one morning to find his little cottage half buried in snow, the storm still continuing, and in his house not an atom of fuel nor a morsel of food. His children were very young, and he was himself sick and feeble. The charity of his neighbors was exhausted, and he had not the courage to face their reproaches. As he looked out of the window upon the dreary and tumultuous scene, " fit emblem of his condition," he remarks, he called to mind that, a few days before, an acquaintance, a mere acquaintance, who lived some miles off, had given him upon the road a more friendly greeting than he was then accustomed to receive. It had cheered his heart as he trudged sadly by, and it now returned vividly to his mind. To this gentleman he determined to apply for relief, if he could reach his house. Terrible was his struggle with the wind and the deep drifts. Often he was ready to faint with fatigue, sickness, and hunger, and he would be obliged to sit down upon a bank of snow to rest. He reached the house and told his story, not omitting the oft-told tale of his new discovery — that mine of wealth, if only he could procure the means of working it! The eager eloquence of the inventor was seconded by the gaunt and yellow face of the man. His generous acquaintance entertained him cordially and lent him a sum of money which not only carried his family through the worst of the winter but enabled him to continue his experiments on a small scale. O. B. Coolidge, of Woburn, was the name of this benefactor.

On another occasion, when he was in the most urgent need of materials, he looked about his house to see if there was left one relic of better days upon which a little money could be borrowed. There was nothing except his children's schoolbooks — the last things from which a New Englander is willing to part. There was no other resource. He gathered them up and sold them for five dollars, with which he laid in a fresh stock of gum and sulphur, and kept on experimenting.

Seeing no prospect of success in Massachusetts, he now resolved to make a desperate effort to get to New York, feeling confident that the specimens he could take with him would convince someone of the superiority of his new method. He was beginning to understand the causes of his many failures, but he saw clearly that his compound could not be worked with certainty without expensive apparatus. It was a very delicate operation, requiring exactness and promptitude. The conditions upon which success depended were numerous, and the failure of one spoiled all. To vulcanize India rubber is about as difficult as to make perfect bread; but the art of bread-making was the growth of ages, and Charles Goodyear was only ten years and a half in perfecting his process. Thousands of ingenious men and women, aided by many happy accidents, must have contributed to the successive invention of bread; but he was only one man, poor and sick. It cost him thousands of failures to learn that a little acid in his sulphur caused the blistering; that his compound must be heated almost immediately after being mixed or it would never vulcanize; that a portion of white lead in the compound greatly facilitated the operation and improved the result; and when he had learned these facts, it still required costly and laborious experiments to devise the best methods of compounding his ingredients, the best proportions, the best mode of heating, the proper duration of the heating, and the various useful effects that could be produced by varying the proportions and the degree of heat. He tells us that many times, when, by exhausting every resource, he had prepared a quantity of his compound for heating, it was spoiled because he could not, with his inadequate apparatus, apply the heat soon enough.

To New York, then, he directed his thoughts. Merely to get there cost him a severer and a longer effort than men in general are capable of making. First he walked to Boston, ten miles distant, where he hoped to be able to borrow from an old acquaintance fifty dollars, with which to provide for his family and pay his fare to New York. He not only failed in this but he was arrested for debt and thrown into prison. Even in prison, while his father was negotiating to secure his release, he labored to interest men of capital in his discovery, and made proposals for founding a factory in Boston. Having obtained his liberty, he went to a hotel and spent a week in vain efforts to effect a small loan. Saturday night came, and with it his hotel bill, which he had no means of discharging. In an agony of shame and anxiety, he went to a friend and entreated the sum of five dollars to enable him to return home. He was met with a point-blank refusal. In the deepest dejection, he walked the streets till late in the night, and strayed at length, almost beside himself, to Cambridge, where he ventured to call upon a friend and ask shelter for the night. He was hospitably entertained, and the next morning walked wearily home, penniless and despairing. At the door of his house a member of his family met him with the news that his youngest child, two years of age, whom he had left in perfect health, was dying. In a few hours he had in his house a dead child, but not the means of burying it, and five living dependents without a morsel of food to give them. A storekeeper near by had promised to supply the family, but, discouraged by the unforeseen length of the father's absence, he had that day refused to trust them further. In these terrible circumstances, he applied to a friend upon whose generosity he knew he could rely, one who had never failed him. He received in reply a letter of severe and cutting reproach, enclosing seven dollars, which his friend explained was given only out of pity for his innocent and suffering family. A stranger, who chanced to be present when this letter arrived, sent them a barrel of flour — a timely and blessed relief. The next day the family followed on foot the remains of the little child to the grave.

A relation in a distant part of the country, to whom Goodyear revealed his condition, sent him fifty dollars, which enabled him to get to New York. He had touched bottom. The worst of his trials were over. In New York he had the good fortune to make the acquaintance of two brothers, William Rider and Emory Rider, men of some property and great intelligence, who examined his specimens, listened to his story, believed in him, and agreed to aid him to continue his experiments, and to supply his family until he had rendered his discovery available. From that time, though he was generally embarrassed in his circumstances, his family never wanted bread, and he was never obliged to suspend his experiments. Aided by the capital, the sympathy, and the ingenuity of the brothers Rider, he spent a year in New York in the most patient endeavors to overcome the difficulties in heating his compound. Before he had succeeded, their resources failed. But he had made such progress in demonstrating the practicability of his process that his brother-in-law, William De Forrest, a noted woolen manufacturer, took hold of the project in earnest and aided him to bring it to perfection. Once more, however, he was imprisoned for debt. This event conquered his scruples against availing himself of the benefit of the bankrupt act, which finally delivered him from the danger of arrest. We should add, however, that as soon as he began to derive income from his invention he reassumed his obligations to his old creditors, and discharged them gradually.

It was not till the year 1844, more than ten years after he began to experiment, and more than five years after discovering the secret of vulcanization, that he was able to conduct his process with absolute certainty, and to produce vulcanized India rubber with the requisite expedition and economy. We can form some conception of the difficulties overcome by the fact that the advances of Mr. De Forrest in aid of the experiment reached the sum of forty-six thousand dollars — an amount the inventor did not live long enough to repay.

His triumph had been long deferred, and we have seen in part how much it had cost him. But his success proved to be richly worth its cost. He had added to the arts not a new material merely, but a new class of materials applicable to a thousand diverse uses. His product had more than the elasticity of India rubber, while it was divested of all those properties which had lessened its utility. It was still India rubber, but its surfaces would not adhere, nor would it harden at any degree of cold, nor soften at any degree of heat. It was a cloth impervious to water. It was paper that would not tear. It was parchment that would not crease. It was leather which neither rain nor sun would injure. It was ebony that could be run into a mold. It was ivory that could be worked like wax. It was wood that never cracked, shrunk, nor decayed. It was metal, "elastic metal," as Daniel Webster termed it, that could be wound round the finger or tied into a knot, and which preserved its elasticity almost like steel. Trifling variations in the ingredients, in the proportions, and in the heating made it either as pliable as kid, tougher than oxhide, as elastic as whalebone, or as rigid as flint.

All this is stated in a moment, but each of these variations in the material, as well as every article made from them, cost this indefatigable man days, weeks, months, or years of experiment. It cost him, for example, several years of most expensive trial to obviate the objection to India-rubber fabrics caused by the liability of the gum to peel from the cloth. He tried every known textile fabric and every conceivable process before arriving at the simple expedient of mixing fiber with the gum, by which, at length, the perfect India-rubber cloth was produced. This invention he considered only second in value to the discovery of vulcanization. The India-rubber shoe, as we now have it, is an admirable article — light, strong, elegant in shape, with a fibrous sole that does not readily wear, cut, or slip. As the shoe is made and joined before vulcanization, a girl can make twenty-five pairs in a day. They are cut from the soft sheets of gum and joined by a slight pressure of the hand. But almost every step of this process, now so simple and easy, was patiently elaborated by Charles Goodyear. A million and a half pairs per annum is now the average number made in the United States by his process, though the business languishes somewhat from the high price of the raw materials. The gum, which when Goodyear began his experiments was a drug at five cents a pound, has recently been sold at one dollar and twenty cents a pound, with all its impurities. Even at this high price the annual import ranges at from four to five million pounds.

Poor Richard informs us that necessity never makes a good bargain. Mr. Goodyear was always a prey to necessity. Nor was he ever a good man of business. He was too entirely an inventor to know how to dispose of his inventions to advantage; and he could never feel that he had accomplished his mission with regard to India rubber. As soon as he had brought his shoemaking process to the point where other men could make it profitable, he withdrew from manufacturing and sold rights to manufacture for the consideration of half a cent per pair. Five cents had been reasonable enough, and would have given him ample means to continue his labors. Half a cent kept him subject to necessity, which seemed to compel him to dispose of other rights at rates equally low. Thus it happened that, when the whole India-rubber business of the country paid him tribute, or ought to have paid it, he remained an embarrassed man. He had, too, the usual fate of inventors, in having to contend with the infringers of his rights — men who owed their all to his ingenuity and perseverance. We may judge, however, of the rapidity with which the business grew, by the fact that, six years after the completion of his vulcanizing process, the holders of rights to manufacture shoes by that process deemed it worth while to employ Daniel Webster to plead their cause, and to stimulate his mind by a fee of twenty-five thousand dollars. It is questionable if Charles Goodyear ever derived that amount from his patents, if we deduct from his receipts the money spent in further developing his discovery. His ill health obliged him to be abstemious, and he had no expensive tastes. It was only in his laboratory that he was lavish, and there he was lavish indeed.

His friends still smiled at his zeal, or reproached him for it. It has been only since the mighty growth of the business in his products that they have acknowledged that he was right and that they were wrong. They remember him, sick, meager, and yellow, now coming to them with a walking stick of India rubber, exulting in the new application of his material, and predicting its general use, while they objected that his stick had cost him fifty dollars; now running about among the comb factories, trying to get reluctant men to try their tools upon hard India rubber, and producing at length a set of combs that cost twenty times the price of ivory ones; now shutting himself up for months, endeavoring to make a sail of India-rubber fabric, impervious to water, that should never freeze, and to which no sleet or ice should ever cling; now exhibiting a set of cutlery with India-rubber handles, or a picture set in an India-rubber frame, or a book with India-rubber covers, or a watch with an India-rubber case; now experimenting with India-rubber tiles for floors, which he hoped to make as brilliant in color as those of mineral, as agreeable to the tread as carpet, and as durable as an ancient floor of oak. There is nothing in the history of invention more remarkable than the devotion of this man to his object. No crusader was ever so devoted to his vow, no lover to his mistress, as he was to his purpose of showing mankind what to do with India rubber. The doorplate of his office was made of it; his portrait was painted upon and framed with it; his book, as we have seen, was wholly composed of it; and his mind, by night and day, was surcharged with it. He never went to sleep without having within reach writing materials and the means of making a light, so that, if he should have an idea in the night, he might be able to secure it. Some of his best ideas, he used to say, were saved to mankind by this precaution.

The catalogue of his successful efforts is long and striking. The second volume of his book is wholly occupied with that catalogue. He lived to see his material applied to nearly five hundred uses, to give employment in England, France, Germany, and the United States to sixty thousand persons, who annually produced merchandise of the value of eight million dollars. A man does much who only founds a new kind of industry; and he does more when that industry gives value to a commodity that before was nearly valueless. But we should greatly undervalue the labors of Charles Goodyear if we regarded them only as opening a new source of wealth; for there have been found many uses of India rubber, as prepared by him, which have an importance far superior to their commercial value. Art, science, and humanity are indebted to him for a material which serves the purposes of them all, and serves them as no other known material could.

Some of our readers have been out on the picket line during the war. They know what it is to stand motionless in a wet and miry rifle pit, in the chilling rain of a Southern winter's night. Protected by India-rubber boots, blanket, and cap, the picket-man performs in comparative comfort a duty which, without that protection, would make him a cowering and shivering wretch, and plant in his bones a latent rheumatism to be the torment of his old age. Goodyear's India rubber enables him to come in from his pit as dry as he was when he went into it, and he comes in to lie down with an India-rubber blanket between him and the damp earth. If he is wounded, it is an India-rubber stretcher, or an ambulance provided with India-rubber springs, that gives him least pain on his way to the hospital, where, if his wound is serious, a water bed of India rubber gives ease to his mangled frame and enables him to endure the wearing tedium of an unchanged posture. Bandages and supporters of India rubber avail him much when first he begins to hobble about his ward. A piece of India rubber at the end of his crutch lessens the jar and the noise of his motions, and a cushion of India rubber is comfortable to his armpit. The springs which close the hospital door, the bands which exclude the drafts from doors and windows, his pocket comb and cup and thimble, are of the same material. From jars hermetically closed with India rubber he receives the fresh fruit that is so exquisitely delicious to a fevered mouth. The instrument case of his surgeon and the storeroom of his matron contain many articles whose utility is increased by the use of it, and some that could be made of nothing else. His shirts and sheets pass through an India-rubber clothes wringer, which saves the strength of the washerwoman and the fiber of the fabric. When the government presents him with an artificial leg, a thick heel and elastic sole of India rubber give him comfort every time he puts it to the ground. An India-rubber pipe with an inserted bowl of clay, a billiard table provided with India-rubber cushions and balls, can solace his long convalescence.

In the field, this material is not less strikingly useful. During this war, armies have marched through ten days of rain, and slept through as many rainy nights, and come out dry into the returning sunshine, with its artillery untarnished and its ammunition uninjured, because men and munitions were all under

India rubber. When Goodyear's ideas are carried out, it will be by pontoons of inflated India rubber that rivers will be crossed. A pontoon train will then consist of one wagon drawn by two mules; and if the march is through a country that furnishes the wooden part of the bridge, a man may carry a pontoon on his back in addition to his knapsack and blanket.

In the naval service we meet this material in a form that attracts little attention, though it serves a purpose of perhaps unequaled utility. Mechanics are aware that, from the time of James Watt to the year 1850, the grand desideratum of the engine-builder was a perfect joint — a joint that would not admit the escape of steam. A steam engine is all over joints and valves, from most of which some steam sooner or later would escape, since an engine in motion produces a continual jar that finally impaired the best joint that art could make. The old joint-making process was exceedingly expensive. The two surfaces of iron had to be most carefully ground and polished, then screwed together, and the edges closed with white lead. By the use of a thin sheet of vulcanized India rubber, placed between the iron surfaces, not only is all this expense saved, but a joint is produced that is absolutely and permanently perfect. It is not even necessary to rub off the roughness of the casting, for the rougher the surface the better the joint. Goodyear's invention supplies an article that Watt and Fulton sought in vain, and which would seem to put the finishing touch to the steam engine — if, in these days of improvement, anything whatever could be considered finished. At present, all engines are provided with these joints and valves, which save steam, diminish jar, and facilitate the separation of the parts. It is difficult to compute the value of this improvement, in money. We are informed, however, by competent authority, that a steamer of two thousand tons saves ten thousand dollars a year by its use. Such is the demand for the engine packing, as it is termed, that the owners of the factory where it is chiefly made, after constructing the largest water wheel in the world, found it insufficient for their growing business and were obliged to add to it a steam engine of two hundred horsepower. The New York agent of this company sells about a million dollars' worth of packing per annum.

Belting for engines is another article for which Goodyear's compound is superior to any other, inasmuch as the surface of the India rubber clings to the iron wheel better than leather or fabric. Leather polishes and slips; India rubber does not polish, and holds to the iron so firmly as to save a large percentage of power. It is no small advantage merely to save leather for other uses, since leather is an article of which the supply is strictly limited. It is not uncommon for India-rubber belts to be furnished, which, if made of leather, would require more than a hundred hides. Emery wheels of this material have been recently introduced. They were formerly made of wood coated with emery, which soon wore off. In the new manufacture, the emery is kneaded into the entire mass of the wheel, which can be worn down till it is all consumed. On the same principle the instruments used to sharpen scythes are also made. Of late we hear excellent accounts of India rubber as a basis for artificial teeth. It is said to be lighter, more agreeable, less expensive, than gold or platina, and not less durable. We have seen also some very pretty watchcases of this material, elegantly inlaid with gold.

It thus appears that the result of Mr. Goodyear's long and painful struggles was the production of a material which now ranks with the leading compounds of commerce and manufacture, such as glass, brass, steel, paper, porcelain, paint. Considering its peculiar and varied utility, it is perhaps inferior in value only to paper, steel, and glass. We see, also, that the use of the new compound lessens the consumption of several commodities, such as ivory, bone, ebony, and leather, which it is desirable to save, because the demand for them tends to increase faster than the supply. When a set of ivory billiard balls costs fifty dollars, and civilization presses upon the domain of the elephant, it is well to make our combs and our paper knives of something else.

That inventions so valuable should be disputed and pirated was something which the history of all the great inventions might have taught Mr. Goodyear to expect. We need not revive those disputes which embittered his life and wasted his substance and his time. The Honorable Joseph Holt, the commissioner who granted an extension to the vulcanizing patent in 1858, has sufficiently characterized them in one of the most eloquent papers ever issued from the Patent Office:

No inventor probably has ever been so harassed, so trampled upon, so plundered by that sordid and licentious class of infringers known in the parlance of the world, with no exaggeration of phrase, as "pirates." The spoliations of their incessant guerilla warfare upon his defenceless rights have unquestionably amounted to millions. In the very front rank of this predatory band stands one who sustains in this case the double and most convenient character of contestant and witness; and it is but a subdued expression of my estimate of the deposition he has lodged, to say that this Parthian shaft — the last that he could hurl at an invention which he has so long and so remorselessly pursued — is a fitting finale to that career which the public justice of the country has so signally rebuked.

When Mr. Goodyear had seen the manufacture of shoes and fabrics well established in the United States, and when his rights appeared to have been placed beyond controversy by the Trenton decision of 1852, being still oppressed with debt, he went to Europe to introduce his material to the notice of capitalists there. The great manufactories of vulcanized India rubber in England, Scotland, France, and Germany are the result of his labors; but the peculiarities of the patent laws of those countries, or else his own want of skill in contending for his rights, prevented him from reaping the reward of his labors. He spent six laborious years abroad. At the Great Exhibitions of London and Paris he made brilliant displays of his wares, which did honor to his country and himself, and gave an impetus to the prosperity of the men who have grown rich upon his discoveries. At the London Exhibition he had a suite of three apartments, carpeted, furnished, and decorated only with India rubber. At Paris he made a lavish display of India-rubber jewelry, dressing cases, workboxes, picture frames, which attracted great attention. His reward was a four days' sojourn in the debtors' prison, and the cross of the Legion of Honor. The delinquency of his American licensees procured him the former, and the favor of the Emperor the latter.

We have seen that his introduction to India rubber was through the medium of a life preserver. His last labors, also, were consecrated to lifesaving apparatus, of which he invented or suggested a great variety. His excellent wife was reading to him one evening, in London, an article from a review, in which it was stated that twenty persons perished by drowning every hour. The company, startled at a statement so unexpected, conversed upon it for some time, while Mr. Goodyear himself remained silent and thoughtful. For several nights he was restless, as was usually the case with him when he was meditating a new application of his material. As these periods of incubation were usually followed by a prostrating sickness, his wife urged him to forbear, and endeavor to compose his mind to sleep. " Sleep! " said he. " How can I sleep while twenty human beings are drowning every hour, and I am the man who can save them? " It was long his endeavor to invent some article which every man, woman, and child would necessarily wear, and which would make it impossible for them to sink. He experimented with hats, cravats, jackets, and petticoats; and, though he left his principal object incomplete, he contrived many of those means of saving life which now puzzle the occupants of staterooms. He had the idea that every article on board a vessel seizable in the moment of danger — every chair, table, sofa, and stool — should be a life preserver.

He returned to his native land a melancholy spectacle to his friends — yellow, emaciated, and feeble — but still devoted to his work. He lingered and labored until July, 1860, when he died in New York, in the sixtieth year of his age. Almost to the last day of his life he was busy with new applications of his discovery. After twenty-seven years of labor and investigation, after having founded a new branch of industry, which gave employment to sixty thousand persons, he died insolvent, leaving to a wife and six children only an inheritance of debt. Those who censure him for this should consider that his discovery was not profitable to himself for more than ten years, that he was deeply in debt when he began his experiments, that his investigations could be carried on only by increasing his indebtedness, that all his bargains were those of a man in need, that the guilelessness of his nature made him the easy prey of greedy, dishonorable men, and that his neglect of his private interests was due, in part, to his zeal for the public good.

An attempt was made last winter to procure an act of Congress extending the vulcanizing patent for a further period of seven years, for the benefit of the creditors and the family of the inventor. The petition seemed reasonable. The very low tariff paid by the manufacturers could have no perceptible effect upon the price of articles, and the extension would provide a competence for a worthy family who had claims upon the gratitude of the nation, if not upon its justice. The manufacturers generally favored the extension, since the patent protected them, in the deranged condition of our currency, from the competition of the foreign manufacturer, who pays low wages and enjoys a sound currency. The extension of the patent would have harmed no one, and would have been an advantage to the general interests of the trade. The son of the inventor, too, in whose name the petition was offered, had spent his whole life in assisting his father, and had a fair claim upon the consideration of Congress. But the same unscrupulous and remorseless men who had plundered poor Goodyear living, hastened to Washington to oppose the petition of his family. A cry of " monopoly " was raised in the newspapers to which they had access. The presence in Washington of Mrs. Goodyear, one of the most retiring of women, and of her son, a singularly modest young man, who were aided by one friend and one professional agent, was denounced as " a powerful lobby, male and female," who, having despoiled the public of " twenty millions," were boring Congress for a grant of twenty millions more — all to be wrung from an India-rubber-consuming public. The short session of Congress is unfavorable to private bills, even when they are unopposed. These arts sufficed to prevent the introduction of the bill desired, and the patent has since expired.

The immense increase in the demand for the gum has frequently suggested the inquiry whether there is any danger of the supply becoming unequal to it. There are now in Europe and America more than a hundred and fifty manu- factories of India-rubber articles, employing from five to five hundred operatives each, and consuming more than ten million pounds of gum per annum. The business, too, is considered to be still in its infancy. Certainly it is increasing. Nevertheless, there is no possibility of the demand exceeding the supply. The belt of land round the globe, five hundred miles north and five hundred miles south of the equator, abounds in the trees producing the gum, and they can be tapped, it is said, for twenty successive seasons. Forty-three thousand of these trees were counted in a tract of country thirty miles long and eight wide. Each tree yields an average of three tablespoonfuls of sap daily, but the trees are so close together that one man can gather the sap of eighty in a day. Starting at daylight, with his tomahawk and a ball of clay, he goes from tree to tree, making five or six incisions in each and placing under each incision a cup made of the clay which he carries. In three or four hours he has completed his circuit and comes home to breakfast. In the afternoon he slings a large gourd upon his shoulder and repeats his round to collect the sap. The cups are cov- ered up at the roots of the tree, to be used again on the following day. In other regions the sap is allowed to exude from the tree and is gathered from about the roots. But, however it is collected, the supply is superabundant; and the countries which produce it are those in which the laborer needs only a little tapioca, a little coffee, a hut, and an apron. In South America, from which our supply chiefly comes, the natives subsist at an expense of three cents a day. The present high price of the gum in the United States is principally due to the fact that greenbacks are not current in the tropics; but in part, to the rapidity with which the demand has increased. Several important applications of the vulcanized gum have been deferred to the time when the raw material shall have fallen to what Adam Smith would style its " natural price."

Charles Goodyear's work, therefore, is a permanent addition to the re- sources of man. The latest posterity will be indebted to him.

John Dos Passos

The Happy Warrior

THE Roosevelts had lived for seven righteous generations on Manhattan Island; they owned a big brick house on 20th Street, an estate up at Dobbs Ferry, lots in the city, a pew in the Dutch Reformed Church, interests, stocks and bonds, they felt Manhattan was theirs, they felt America was theirs. Their son,

Theodore,

was a sickly youngster, suffered from asthma, was very nearsighted; his hands and feet were so small it was hard for him to learn to box; his arms were very short;

his father was something of a humanitarian, gave Christmas dinners to newsboys, deplored conditions, slums, the East Side, Hell's Kitchen.

Young Theodore had ponies, was encouraged to walk in the woods, to go camping, was instructed in boxing and fencing (an American gentleman should know how to defend himself), taught Bible Class, did mission work (an American gentleman should do his best to uplift those not so fortunately situated);

righteousness was his by birth;

he had a passion for nature study, for reading about birds and wild animals, for going hunting; he got to be a good shot in spite of his glasses, a good walker in spite of his tiny feet and short legs, a fair horseman, an aggressive scrapper in spite of his short reach, a crack politician in spite of being the son of one of the owning Dutch families of New York.

In 1876 he went up to Cambridge to study at Harvard, a wealthy talkative erratic young man with sidewhiskers and definite ideas about everything under the sun,

at Harvard he drove around in a dogcart, collected stuffed birds, mounted specimens he'd shot on his trips in the Adirondacks; in spite of not drinking and being somewhat of a christer, having odd ideas about reform and remedying abuses, he made Porcellian and the Dickey and the clubs that were his right as the son of one of the owning Dutch families of New York.

He told his friends he was going to devote his life to social service: *I wish to preach not the doctrine of ignoble ease, but the doctrine of the strenuous life, the life of toil and effort, of labor and strife.*

From the time he was eleven years old he wrote copiously, filled diaries, notebooks, loose leaves with a big impulsive scrawl about everything he did and thought and said;

naturally he studied law.

From *Nineteen-Nineteen,* 1932.

He married young and went to Switzerland to climb the Matterhorn; his first wife's early death broke him all up. He went out to the badlands of western Dakota to become a rancher on the Little Missouri River;

when he came back to Manhattan he was Teddy, the straight shooter from the west, the elkhunter, the man in the Stetson hat, who'd roped steers, fought a grizzly hand to hand, acted as Deputy Sheriff,

(a Roosevelt has a duty to his country; the duty of a Roosevelt is to uplift those not so fortunately situated, those who have come more recently to our shores)

in the west, Deputy Sheriff Roosevelt felt the white man's burden, helped to arrest malefactors, bad men; service was bully.

All this time he'd been writing, filling the magazines with stories of his hunts and adventures, filling political meetings with his opinions, his denunciations, his pat phrases: Strenuous Life, Realizable Ideals, Just Government, *when men fear work or fear righteous war, when women fear motherhood, they tremble on the brink of doom, and well it is that they should vanish from the earth, where they are fit subjects for the scorn of all men and women who are themselves strong and brave and highminded.*

T.R. married a wealthy woman and righteously raised a family at Sagamore Hill.

He served a term in the New York Legislature, was appointed by Grover Cleveland to the unremunerative job of Commissioner for Civil Service Reform,

was Reform Police Commissioner of New York, pursued malefactors, stoutly maintained that white was white and black was black,

wrote the Naval History of the War of 1812,

was appointed Assistant Secretary of the Navy,

and when the *Maine* blew up resigned to lead the Rough Riders,

Lieutenant-Colonel.

This was the Rubicon, the Fight, the Old Glory, the Just Cause. The American public was not kept in ignorance of the Colonel's bravery when the bullets sang, how he charged without his men up San Juan Hill and had to go back to fetch them, how he shot a running Spaniard in the tail.

It was too bad that the regulars had gotten up San Juan Hill first from the other side, that there was no need to get up San Juan Hill at all. Santiago was surrendered. It was a successful campaign. T.R. charged up San Juan Hill into the governorship of the Empire State;

but after the fighting, volunteers warcorrespondents magazinewriters began to want to go home;

it wasn't bully huddling under puptents in the tropical rain or scorching in the morning sun of the sacred Cuban hills with malaria mowing them down and dysentery and always yellowjack to be afraid of.

T.R. got up a round robin to the President and asked for the amateur warriors to be sent home and leave the dirtywork to the regulars

who were digging trenches and shovelling crap and fighting malaria and dysentery and yellowjack

to make Cuba cosy for the Sugar Trust
and the National City Bank.

When he landed at home, one of his first interviews was with Lemuel
Quigg, emissary of Boss Platt who had the votes of upstate New York sewed
into the lining of his vest;
he saw Boss Platt too, but he forgot about that afterwards. Things were
bully. He wrote a life of Oliver Cromwell whom people said he resembled.
As Governor he doublecrossed the Platt machine (a righteous man may have
a short memory); Boss Platt thought he'd shelved him by nominating him
for the Vice-Presidency in 1900;

Czolgocz made him president.

T.R. drove like a fiend in a buckboard over the muddy roads through the
driving rain from Mt. Marcy in the Adirondacks to catch the train to Buffalo
where McKinley was dying.
As President
he moved Sagamore Hill, the healthy happy normal American home, to
the White House, took foreign diplomats and fat armyofficers out walking
in Rock Creek Park where he led them a terrible dance through brambles,
hopping across the creek on steppingstones, wading the fords, scrambling up
the shaly banks,
and shook the Big Stick at malefactors of great wealth.
Things were bully.
He engineered the Panama revolution under the shadow of which took
place the famous hocuspocus of juggling the old and new canal companies by
which forty million dollars vanished into the pockets of the international
bankers,
but Old Glory floated over the Canal Zone
and the canal was cut through.
He busted a few trusts,
had Booker Washington to lunch at the White House,
and urged the conservation of wild life.
He got the Nobel Peace Prize for patching up the Peace of Portsmouth that
ended the Russo-Japanese war,
and sent the Atlantic Fleet around the world for everybody to see that
America was a firstclass power. He left the presidency to Taft after his second
term leaving to that elephantine lawyer the congenial task of pouring judicial
oil on the hurt feelings of the moneymasters
and went to Africa to hunt big game.
Big game hunting was bully.
Every time a lion or an elephant went crashing down into the jungle underbrush, under the impact of a wellplaced mushroom bullet
the papers lit up with headlines;

when he talked with the Kaiser on horseback

the world was not ignorant of what he said, or when he lectured the Nationalists at Cairo telling them that this was a white man's world.

He went to Brazil where he travelled through the Matto Grosso in a dugout over waters infested with the tiny maneating fish, the piranha,

shot tapirs,

jaguars,

specimens of the whitelipped peccary.

He ran the rapids of the River of Doubt

down to the Amazon frontiers where he arrived sick, an infected abscess in his leg, stretched out under an awning in a dugout with a tame trumpeterbird beside him.

Back in the States he fought his last fight when he came out for the republican nomination in 1912 a progressive, champion of the Square Deal, crusader for the Plain People; the Bull Moose bolted out from under the Taft steamroller and formed the Progressive Party for righteousness' sake at the Chicago Colosseum while the delegates who were going to restore democratic government rocked with tears in their eyes as they sang

> *On   ward Christian so old gers*
> *March   ing as to war*

Perhaps the River of Doubt had been too much for a man of his age; perhaps things weren't so bully any more; T.R. lost his voice during the triangular campaign. In Duluth a maniac shot him in the chest, his life was saved only by the thick bundle of manuscript of the speech he was going to deliver. T.R. delivered the speech with the bullet still in him, heard the scared applause, felt the plain people praying for his recovery but the spell was broken somehow.

The Democrats swept in, the world war drowned out the righteous voice of the Happy Warrior in the roar of exploding lyddite.

Wilson wouldn't let T.R. lead a division, this was no amateur's war (perhaps the regulars remembered the round robin at Santiago). All he could do was write magazine articles against the Huns, send his sons; Quentin was killed.

It wasn't the bully amateur's world any more. Nobody knew that on armistice day, Theodore Roosevelt, happy amateur warrior with the grinning teeth, the shaking forefinger, naturalist, explorer, magazinewriter, Sundayschool teacher, cowpuncher, moralist, politician, righteous orator with a short memory, fond of denouncing liars (the Ananias Club) and having pillowfights with his children, was taken to the Roosevelt hospital gravely ill with inflammatory rheumatism.

Things weren't bully any more;

T.R. had grit;

he bore the pain, the obscurity, the sense of being forgotten as he had
borne the grilling portages when he was exploring the River of Doubt, the
heat, the fetid jungle mud, the infected abscess in his leg,

and died quietly in his sleep
at Sagamore Hill
on January 6, 1919
and left on the shoulders of his sons
the white man's burden.

ESSAYS ON AMERICA

Donald Davidson

Still Rebels, Still Yankees

A T a meeting of Southern writers in Charleston some years ago, Laurence Stallings looked belligerently around him and expressed an ardent preference for a " Balkanized America." " What I like about Charleston," he said, " is that it has resisted Abraham Lincoln's attempts to put the country into Arrow Collars. If the South had won the war, the country would have had lots more color."

The rebelliousness of Mr. Stallings need not compel us to suspect him of being an unreconstructed Southerner disguised as a man of letters, who is looking for artistic reasons to justify what arms and politics once failed to secure. Discontent with the uniformity of America is common enough; what is not common is the knowledge that this uniformity, a byword ever since James Bryce looked at the American commonwealth through the spectacles of the Gilded Age, is more a myth than a reality.

As a myth, it probably represents the wishful thinking of those who, for their own designs, want America to become uniform. Actually America is not yet uniform; very likely it is less uniform than it once was, and far more Balkanized than Mr. Stallings dreams. The unreconstructed Southerners have done their part in keeping it Balkan; but there are unreconstructed Yankees, too, and other unreconstructed Americans of all imaginable sorts, everywhere engaged in preserving their local originality and independence.

The only people who do not know this are certain experts who do most of the current talking about American society. They live in a sociological pickle of statistics and progress. They are eternally looking for what they call " social values," but they strangely confine their research to libraries and graduate " projects " at the larger universities. They avoid the places where social values may be encountered in the flesh. If they stumble upon a living social value,

From *The Attack on Leviathan,* 1938.

walking visibly about some spot of earth and drawing its nutriment from a tradition embodied in the houses, speech, crafts, music, folklore, and wisdom of an actual people, their rule is to denounce it as an anachronism and to call for its extermination. For them, nothing must grow according to its nature, but things " develop " by laboratory formulae, which are obtained by inspecting the reactions of the most abnormal and depressed specimens of humankind, too weak to protest against sociological vivisection.

Those of us who still believe in the map of the United States know that it marks the residence of some diverse Americans who had better not go unacknowledged. In Vermont, for instance, are people who are still Yankees; and in Georgia, and elsewhere, there are still Rebels. I remember talking with a certain Virginian who watched a Vermont sunset with me, one summer evening. As the sun passed below the distant Adirondacks, we looked at the Green Mountains around us, and at the trim Vermont fields where all the weeds were flowers and all the grass was hay. In the clear detail of the afterglow we saw the forests of spruce and balsam and maple, and spoke of how the very wilderness, in this New England state, had uprightness and order. The woods were as snug and precise as a Yankee kitchen — no ragged edges, no sprawling, nothing out of place. In the clearings the farmhouses were all painted; and the barns were painted, too. The streams were orthodox streams, almost model streams, with water always translucent and stones rounded and picturesquely placed among moss and ferns. They were often called " brooks " — a word that for Southerners existed only on the printed page.

On this land, the Virginian said, the Yankees had looked so intimately and long that, like the man in Hawthorne's story of the Great Stone Face, they had become the image of what they contemplated. The Yankee genius of Vermont was upright, vertical, and no doubt Puritan. Where the landscape itself enforced consistency and order, how could the people concede much virtue to inconsistency and irregularity? The forebears of the Vermont Yankee had once failed to understand how Southerners could be devoted both to slavery and democracy. That old failure of understanding did not seem queer, or worth more than a passing sigh, to two Southerners who stood looking at sunset upon a land whose gentled wildness suggested the urgent possibility of a well-ordered universe, cut to a discreet Yankee pattern. But the human geography of America had now become a particolored thing, sprawling across the continent in a crazy-quilt of provinces, or sections, each with its private notion of a universe. No longer, as in the sixties, could the Yankee make bold to set up a general pattern for the entire Union. He had enough to do if he would defend and preserve what was peculiarly his own — his very own, surely, in upper New England. In such a purpose of preservation the two Southerners at last could make bold to sympathize, even to help if possible. But preservation could not be achieved without recognizing a principle of diversity in American life. Only by such means could one make any sense out of Lamar's famous epigram in his eulogy on Sumner, " My countrymen, know one another and you will love one another "; it ceased to have meaning if America was to be subjugated to the ideal of uniformity, or to the ideal universe that some one section might generate.

But how could the principle of diversity be inculcated? On the negative side, certain false images, the product of legend or propaganda, must somehow be counterbalanced. Regrettably enough, some of the fairest legends caused the greatest embarrassment. To the Virginian I recalled the horror of a good lady from the Middle West, who was motoring from Washington to Richmond. Mount Vernon was all right, she thought; there the legend was safely frozen. But beyond, on the road to Richmond, what had become of all the great mansions she had read about, the cotton fields with Negroes caroling, the old gentlemen in goatees and white vests, sipping mint juleps in the shade? They were not visible. There were only a few scattered shacks and tumble-down barns in miles of impenetrable wilderness that looked for all the world as it must have looked when John Smith first invaded it. If she could have encountered the legend, the lady would have been content. But not seeing it or knowing how to locate it, she was smitten with a housewifely desire to get at this ragged land with a good broom and whisk it into seemliness.

Other sojourners had been anxious to do a far more drastic tidying-up. The Harlan County visitors, the Scottsboro attorneys, the shock troops of Dayton and Gastonia asked no questions about the genius of place. Wherever they went on their missions of social justice, they carried with them a legend of the future, more dangerously abstract than the legend of the past, and sternly demanded that the local arrangements be made to correspond with it, at whatever cost. The local arrangements, indeed, might well bear some mending. And yet the only America that the visitors offered as a model was an overgrown urban America, forever in process of becoming one laboratory experiment after another.

What could be done about all this? Our answers were shrouded in darkness as we walked back to the log fires and good company of a New England inn. The Virginian, after the fashion of good Southerners who do not want to let anybody know the uncertainty of their minds under modern conditions, did not propose any answer. Instead, he told several good stories. They were his courteous and delightful way of saying that he was being pounded between his own unyielding loyalty and the howling respectability of the great world.

I

If any answer is to be found, if anything positive is to be done, it must surely be through a laborious process of discovering America all over again. When one looks at America, not to see how it does or does not fit the synthetic ideals proposed for its future, but only with the modest purpose of detecting the realities — let us say the social values — that persist in local habitations, he soon realizes that comparisons are more fruitful than condemnations. More specifically, when one has the good fortune to go directly from a summer in Vermont to an autumn and winter in Middle Georgia, he forms a clear picture of sectional differences. This picture is not in the least favorable to the notion that the diverse America of the Rebels and Yankees is in any immediate danger of being submerged.

If on coming to Vermont I had consulted the modern legend of New England that vaguely haunted my mind, I would have received the iconoclastic shock which our advanced thinkers argue is the first step toward salvation. Had not a New England migrant to the South assured me that his ancestral acres were now inhabited by Montenegrins, who had turned them into a goat farm? Had not the sepulchral Eugene O'Neill and others told tales of the poverty and decadence of New England life? The farms were deserted, it was said; the immigrants and mill towns had come; the Yankees had left for parts unknown, or, remaining, had become degenerate. Even the loyalty of Robert Frost gave no comfortable assurance, if one accepted the New York aleck's criticism of *North of Boston;* though there were many wistful asides in which Frost put forth the guarded wisdom of a not yet daunted soul. The New England of Whittier and Webster was supposed to be extinct; it had been replaced by Puritan-baiters and F. Scott Fitzgeraldites who drank cocktails and read Proust when not conducting the insurance business of the United States.

But if the Vermont that I saw was in the least representative of New England, this composite picture was a wild detraction. In Vermont, if nowhere else, a New England like that of Whittier and Webster miraculously persisted, a reality capable of reducing a Southerner almost to despairing envy. I could understand what led Walter Hines Page, a quarter of a century ago, to disparage his native North Carolina and fall in love with New England. But the time was past when one needed to disparage or praise in the interest of the America Page dreamed about, for in the 1930's it seemed impossible of realization, or, where realized, already past saving. To one who did not accept Lincoln's quaint idea that the United States must become "all one thing or all the other," it seemed more than ever true that the unity of America must rest, first of all, on a decent respect for sectional differences.

If Vermont and Georgia could be taken in a broad way to stand for New England and the deep South, one could easily trace out the most general differences. The Vermont towns, like the Vermont landscape, were swept and garnished, as if the Day of Judgment might at any moment summon them into the presence of the celestial inspector. They looked as if Vermonters lived by the adage "Handsome is as handsome does," and one could reflect that this proverb might well have issued from some collaborative effort of Poor Richard and Jonathan Edwards. The most delightful of Southern towns was almost certain to mix a little squalor with its grandeurs. Here, what a Southerner most particularly noticed, was the neatly painted aspect of everything, the absence of ramshackle buildings and litter, the white steeples of churches, the shipshapeness of streets, yards, garages, barber shops, and public buildings. By some special benison of God and the New England conscience, not a billboard had been allowed to sprout between Bennington and the Canadian border. Perhaps by the same double grace, not a weed sprouted, either. All the weeds had turned into ferns and buttercups. Vermont farms were Currier and Ives prints of what good farms ought to look like, with orchards and brooks in exactly the right place and gates that did not need mending. In the background were lakes and mountains where one would put them if he were Aladdin or Wordsworth. It was not surprising to be told that hardly a poison snake, and no poison ivy, existed in the state of Vermont; or to find that there were excellent trails running the whole length of the Green Mountains, with fingerposts at every wilderness crossroads, and tin huts, with beds, firewood, and caretaker, atop of the highest peak. A few nagging irregularities of nature, like blackflies and mosquitoes, seemed really blasphemous in a land to which God had given a monopoly of all things good and precise. No wonder, with all this beneficence around them, that the Yankees remembered the *Mayflower* and forgot John Smith, honored Bunker Hill and neglected King's Mountain. If they could claim such priority in the benevolence of God, their proprietary feeling toward the Revolutionary War and their almost hereditary claim to the direction of the United States government were by comparison insignificant appurtenances, theirs as a matter of course and by general presumption.

Although I did not hold very devotedly to the economic determinism of modern historians, it was a temptation to say that the people were a great deal like the land. There was the climate, which put keenness into a Southerner's veins. Summer was short, and one had to make the most of it; winter was severe, and one had to keep shield and buckler perpetually ready against it — in that matter was God benevolent or ruthless? Short summers and cold winters made the Vermont Yankee frugal and careful. He must watch his corners. If he were caught napping, he would perish. So much and no more was the gift of his seasons; so much and no more was the rule of his nature. And one had to watch over his neighbor as well as work with him if the general security were not to be imperiled by some outrageous letting down of bars. Very likely, the New England civic conscience derived as much from the imperatives of climate as from the Puritan tradition; the one egged on the other.

No great check had ever been put upon the development of qualities that the Southerners recognized as ineradicably Yankee. History had been as kind to the Yankee as God had been kind. Since Revolutionary times no great sudden change had ever swept over these peaceful towns and this quiet landscape. Industrialism had come slowly and somewhat agreeably upon a people who had the ingenuity to use it and the moral force to make it behave. How could they who thought they knew how to tame the monster realize that he might walk unshackled and ravening elsewhere? The Yankees, indeed, had never tasted defeat. Since Burgoyne's expedition no invader had come upon them to ravage and destroy. They had freed the Negroes, replying " I can " to duty's " Thou must "; but they were fortunately exempt from the results of emancipation, for no Negroes lived among them to acquaint them with the disorder of unashamed and happy dirt. One knew that a slum in New England would be a well-managed slum, and that New Englanders would comprehend Secretary Perkins' horror at the lack of plumbing in unreformed America and her notion of saving the barefoot South by building shoe factories. For in New England humanitarianism was the natural flower of good sense. In a land where everything was so right, it was hard to imagine a perverse land where so much could be so wrong without disturbing either a people's composure or their happiness.

But in the plantation country of Middle Georgia the social values required a different yardstick. The genius of Georgia was stretched out, relaxed and easy, in keeping with the landscape, which required a large and horizontal view of mundane affairs. The Georgian assumed that God would have sense and heart enough to take into consideration, when Judgment Day came around, a good deal besides external and man-made appearances. God was a gentleman, indeed, who would certainly know, without being told, that one was a person, a somebody, doing his best among some rather amazing arrangements that had better not be talked about too much. The climate might or might not predispose the Georgia Rebel to laziness; the fact was, he worked and fretted more than the Yankee knew. But the Rebel idea was never to seem to work and fret. You must not let your work ride you, was the saying. In plain truth, you did not need to. The land was bountiful, and the Lord would provide, and in event of the Lord's failure or displeasure you could always fall back on your kinfolks.

Where the seasons were all mixed up, so that autumn merged into spring without any sharp demarcation, and you might have a dubious summer in the middle of winter, it became almost a point of honor not to worry too much about provision. There was no need to watch corners when something was growing all the time. Almost anything would grow in Middle Georgia, and almost everything did grow, including weeds whose invasions could not possibly be repelled from every roadside and ditch if they were to be kept out of cotton and corn.

The Georgia landscape had a serene repose that lulled a man out of all need of conscience. It was anything but swept and garnished. It could be mild or majestic or genial and savage depending on what view you got of pines against red earth, or Negro cabins underneath their chinaberry trees, or sedge grass running into gullies and thence to impenetrable swamps, or deserted mansions lost in oak groves and magnolias. Rivers were muddy and at times unrestrained; they got out of bounds, as all things natural did here. In the pine barrens you might get an impression of desolation and melancholy; but things could grow lushly too, with the overpowering vegetable passion that harrowed the Puritan soul of Amy Lowell when she visited the Magnolia Gardens at Charleston. But finally, it was a well-tilled country, where you were forever seeing the Negro and his mule against the far horizon, or the peach orchards bursting into an intoxicating pink.

The seasons were full of charms and intimidations. Spring, with its dogwood blossoms and soft airs, might deliver a tornado or a flood; summer, full of grown corn and harvest ease, might turn into dusty drouth. The woods that lured you to enter and gave nuts and flowers for the taking were full of hidden terrors. Sit on a mossy bank without precaution, and in a few hours you might be on fire with chigoe bites. Stoop to pick a flower, and you might find a rattlesnake. Indoors the housewife had to fight cockroaches and flies; outdoors were hawks, polecats, weasels, possums, coons, and other varmints to harry the henhouse. Precision, for the Georgian, must rank among the Utopian virtues. If New England encouraged man to believe in an ordered universe, Georgia — and a good deal of the South besides — compelled him to remember that there were snakes in Eden. Nature, so ingratiating and beautiful, which bound the Georgian to his land with a love both possessive and fearful, was a fair but dreadful mistress, unpredictable and uncontrollable as God. The New Englander knew exactly where to find nature yielding, and he could make arrangements accordingly. But the Georgian never knew. His safest policy was to relax, and he readily developed a great degree of tolerance for irregularity in nature and man. At his lowest level, this quality made him lackadaisical and trifling. In this he differed from the New England Yankee, who became a perfectionist, and then at his worst might turn into zealot, strangely intolerant even while, as idealist, he argued for tolerance.

History, like God and nature, had been both generous and unkind to Georgia and the South. The Georgia Rebel must approach his early history through a bloody link of war and reconstruction that was hazy and bygone to the Vermont Yankee. Defeat had possessed him and had rubbed deep into his wounds. Around him were the visible reminders of destruction and humiliation. His land had been ravaged and rebuilt, and he had been told to forget. But he would not and could not forget, and was therefore torn between his loyalty and his awareness that the great world was bored with his not forgetting. He had been rebuked for being inept at administering a newfangled government that he did not understand or like any too well, and in which he had been allowed to participate only by a kind of negligent afterthought. Turning desperately to the industrial civilization against which he had once taken arms, he had played it as a hedge against the problematic future. Though agrarian at heart, he had been forced to wonder whether the ingenious Yankee might not be right after all.

Thus he remembered the faith and hankered after the fleshpots at the same time. But industrialism, declining to be treated as a mere hedge, began Sherman's march to the sea all over again. It piled ugliness upon wreckage and threw the old arrangements out of kilter. The United Daughters of the Confederacy and the Kiwanis Club flourished side by side. Mule wagon and automobile, fundamentalism and liberalism, education and illiteracy, aristocratic pride and backwoods independence disproved the axiom that two bodies cannot occupy the same space. Cities that preserved the finest flavor of the old regime had to be approached over brand-new roads where billboards, tourist camps, filling stations, and factories broke out in a modernistic rash among the water oaks and Spanish moss. And everywhere was the Negro, a cheerful grinning barnacle tucked away in all the tender spots of Southern life, not to be removed without pain, not to be cherished without tragedy. The Georgian, when reproached for his intolerance, told himself that actually nobody outdid him in fond tolerance of the Negro. Lynchings, the work of hotheads and roustabouts, were regrettable; but what did a few lynchings count in the balance against the continual forbearance and solicitude that the Georgian felt he exercised toward these amiable children of cannibals, whose skins by no conceivable act of Congress or educational program could be changed from black to white. The presence of the Negro, which had its advantages in agriculture and domestic service, made the Georgian's life both comfortable and ramshackle; it gave him devoted servants and social problems, cheap labor and hideous slums, an endless flow of folklore and anecdote, and eternal apprehension for the future. But in his own way the Georgian respected the Negro as another irregularity, taking a human and personal form, that had somehow to be lived with. He distrusted all ready-made prescriptions for bringing about regularity. In Georgia, life went along horizontally: you never crossed a bridge until you came to it — and maybe not then.

<h2 style="text-align:center">II</h2>

But sociologists not only cross bridges; they build all imaginable kinds of new ones. The picture of America, as sociologically reformed, does not contemplate any great concessions to Yankee uprightness or Rebel relaxation. Indeed, the sociologist, armed with science, is ready to follow reformation with transformation. In the vast inevitable working of the social forces, sectional differences become irrelevant. With a cold smile the sociologist pronounces a death sentence upon Rebel and Yankee alike. Not that they matter very much — but they will have to yield!

When he talks like this, I am perversely compelled to remember the individuals I have seen, Brother Jonathan of Vermont and Cousin Roderick of Georgia, whom I cannot imagine as yielding to the puny weapons flourished by our social philosophers. They are local incarnations of the Old Adam. They are the immovable bodies that can furnish the irresistible social forces with an incalculable meeting. They are human beings, undebatably alive; and they are different.

Brother Jonathan lives in Yankeetown — for a place name is often a " town " in New England, and less often a " ville " or a " burg " as in the South. He is a wizened little chip of a man, with blue eyes and a bald head, and he looks frail enough for any northwest wind to blow away. But there is not a wind on this planet strong enough to blow Brother Jonathan off his mountain farm. If any wind contrived to do so, he would climb right back again in the matter-of-fact way that Robert Frost describes in *Brown's Descent* — he would " bow with grace to natural law, And then go round it on his feet."

Brother Jonathan is past seventy years, and his wife Priscilla is well over sixty, but between them they still manage to do most of the daily work, in house and field, for a two-hundred-acre farm, most of which is in woodland and meadow. Nathaniel, their adopted son, helps some now and then; but Nathaniel, who is carpenter, mechanic, cabinetmaker, mountain guide, and tax collector combined, is busy putting up the new house into which he and Sophronia, his wife, will soon move — they are building it extra large, to take in summer boarders. Sophronia helps Priscilla as much as she can, but she has her own small children to look after. Later on, Brother Jonathan hopes to get a twelve-year-old boy from the orphanage, who will do the chores for his keep. But now, Brother Jonathan must be up at daylight to start the kitchen fire and milk the cows. If it is haying time, he is out in the meadow early with the mowing machine, which he has sharpened and greased with his own hands or repaired at his own smithy if it needs repairing. The mower bumps and clicks through the rough meadow, tossing the little man to and fro as he warily skirts the outcrops of stone that will have to be circled with a scythe to get the last wisp of hay.

Later, he changes the patient old horses from mower to wagon and starts in with a pitchfork. It is a sight to see him navigating the loaded wagon from the upper field to the barn, past jutting boulders and through deep ruts. But his pace is easy; he keeps it up all day without undue perspiration or agony, and after supper cuts his wood and milks his cows again in unruffled calm. He does not seem tired or bored. As he milks, he philosophizes to the listening stranger. Yes, times are not what they were, but a man can get along if he will be careful and honest. Foolish people, of course, never know how to manage. The harm all comes from people of no character that do things without regard to common decency. The stars are shining when he takes the pails of milk into the kitchen. Under the hanging oil lamp he reads the Burlington *Free Press* or *The Pathfinder* until he begins to nod.

All the arrangements on Brother Jonathan's farm are neat and ingenious — the arrangements of a man who has had to depend largely on his own wits and strength. The barn is cleverly arranged in two stories, with a ramp entering the upper story for the convenience of Brother Jonathan and his hay wagons, and running water on the lower story, for the convenience of the animals. One well, near the barn, is operated by a windmill; it supplies the stock. Another well, higher up, supplies the house, for Brother Jonathan has a bathroom in the upper hall and faucets in the kitchen. He has no telephone or electric lights. A man can dig and pipe his own well, and they are finished; but telephone and electric lights, not being home contrivances, require a never ending tribute to Mammon. He has his own sawmill and his own workshop, where he can mend things without losing time and money on a trip to the village. His garage, occupied at present by Nathaniel's four-year-old car (which is not being used!), contains a carpenter's bench and a small gas engine rigged to do sawing and turning. There are pelts drying on the walls.

The house is built to economize space and retain heat. For all its modest proportions, it is convenient and comfortable. The kitchen is spacious and well equipped. The pantry and cellar are stored with vegetables, fruits, and meats that Priscilla has put up with her own hands. The dining-room, with its long table covered with spotless oilcloth, is eating-room, living-room, and children's playground combined. Here all gather after supper: the women with their tatting and embroidery; the lively dark-eyed boy from the village, with his homemade fiddle; a summer boarder or two, or a visiting relative; and always Brother Jonathan with his newspaper. In one corner is a reed organ, on which Brother Jonathan occasionally plays hymns. In another corner is a desk, filled with miscellaneous papers, books, and old magazines. On the walls hang a glass frame containing butterflies, the gift of a wandering entomologist; an 1876 engraving of General Washington being welcomed at New York, with the pictures of all the Presidents, up to Hayes, around the border; and a faded photograph of a more youthful Brother Jonathan with his fellow baggage-clerks, taken in the days when he went west and got a job in Chicago. Brother Jonathan talks of Chicago sometimes, but he never reveals why he, unlike many other Yankees, came back to Vermont.

The temper of the household is a subdued and even pleasantness which the loud alarms and excursions of the world do not penetrate very far. The progress of Nathaniel's new house; the next morning's arrangements for gathering vegetables and canning; what Brother Jonathan shall say in the speech he is to make at the approaching celebration of the Timothys' golden wedding — such topics take precedence over the epic contentions of Mr. Roosevelt. Priscilla may go so far as to marvel that anybody can doubt the goodness of Mr. Hoover. (She does not add, as she well might, that Mr. Roosevelt, as a " Yorker," inherits the distrust of Vermont.) Or Brother Jonathan may warm up to politics enough to announce his everlasting distrust for liquorish Al Smith and to confess that, out of firm disapproval for vice, he has once or twice bolted the Republican ticket and voted for the Prohibition party's candidate. But in the South, he supposes, he would be as good a Democrat as the next one. They are all curious about the South — about Negroes — and whether the Southern people still have hard feelings against the North (on this point they seem a little anxious and plaintive). But the talk soon shifts to the Green Mountain Boys, from one of whom Brother Jonathan is descended, or to stories of his childhood, when bears were as thick as porcupines are now — he tells of how seven bears were once killed in the same tree. In these stories Brother Jonathan may put in a dry quip or two, by way of garnishment. He has a store of homely jokes and extended metaphors, to which he frequently adds a humorous gloss to be sure the stranger gets the point. Then maybe there is a game of anagrams — or on another evening, a corn roast, with a few cronies and kinfolk from the village, who talk the clipped Yankee-talk that seems, to Southern ears, as pure an English as can be, with only a little of the twang that dialect stories have taught one to expect.

Brother Jonathan is not dogmatic to the point of testiness, but he is firmly rationalistic on many points. He declares it incredible, for instance, that Catholics can believe in transubstantiation — how can bread and wine *actually* turn into the blood and body of Jesus Christ? Yet oddly enough, Brother Jonathan is neither Congregationalist nor Unitarian, but Methodist, and does not mind repeating the Apostles' Creed, with its formidable references to the Trinity and the Resurrection. I am led to suspect that it is not the doctrine but the authority to which Brother Jonathan is temperamentally hostile. He is used to depending on himself; he does not like to be told things. And his independence is of a piece with the whole conduct of his life. Years ago, when a famous local character eccentrically bought up all the surrounding woodland and farm land and turned it into a forest reserve which he bequeathed to a neighboring college, Brother Jonathan did not sell out. He held on then, he holds on now, with a possessiveness that would be the despair of communists. He will continue to hold on, as long as trees yield maple syrup — which he will never, never basely dilute with cane syrup — and boarders return summer after summer.

For Brother Jonathan belongs in spirit to the old republic of independent farmers that Jefferson wanted to see flourish as the foundation of liberty in the United States. To conserve that liberty he has his own Yankee arrangements: the " town," which the Southerner had to learn consisted of a village and a great deal of contiguous territory up to the next " town line "; and the town meeting, at which Brother Jonathan could stand up and tell the government what he thought about it. Of the uses of town meetings Priscilla has something to say, which comes, I reflect, with a little feminine sauciness. A certain individual, she relates, was criticized for not painting the " community house," as he had been employed to do; and when he excused himself on the ground that paint was lacking, his own wife sprang up in the town meeting and cried: " Don't believe a word he says. That paint's setting in the cellar this minute! "

But the Southerner could reflect that such family intimacy might have civic advantages. Brother Jonathan's local government is composed of nobody more Olympic or corrupt than his own neighbors and relations. For him it is not something off yonder, and he visualizes the national government (though a little too innocently) as simply an enlarged town meeting, where good management ought to be a matter of course: it maintains a library, it looks after roads, it sees that taxes are paid and well spent. If the state government does not behave, Nathaniel himself will run for the legislature and see that it does behave.

In all this there was much for a Southerner to savor seriously and learn about — as he savored and learned about the strange food that appeared on Brother Jonathan's table: doughnuts for breakfast, maple syrup on pie and cereal, the New England boiled dinner, the roasting ears that were really roasted in the old Indian fashion. Just as Brother Jonathan's menu suited the soil and the people, so his tidiness and responsibilty suited the unobtrusive integrity of his character. With emphasis, one could say: Vermont is upright, vertical, and, even yet, Puritan — why not?

III

And almost two thousand miles away, with an unconcern about the state of the world that parallels but differs from Brother Jonathan's, Cousin Roderick of Rebelville is achieving another salvation somehow not recorded in the auguries of socialistic planning. Autumn is beginning, the scuppernongs are ripe, and he invites everybody to come over and join him in the scuppernong arbor. In the late afternoon a merry crew gather around the great vine, laughing and bantering as they pick the luscious grapes and crush them against their palates. Sister Caroline is there, with a figure as trim and a wit as lively at eighty as it must have been at twenty. Young Cousin Hector and his wife are there — they are "refugeeing" from the industrial calamity that overtook them in a Northern city. And there are numerous other vague cousins and sisters and children, all munching and passing family gossip back and forth between bites. Cousin Roderick's own Dionysian laughter goes up heartiest of all among the leaves, as he moves to and fro, rapidly gathering grapes and pressing them upon the visitors. "Oh, you are not going to quit on us," he says. "You must eat more than *that*. Scuppernongs never hurt a soul." The scuppernong vine, he declares, is a hundred years old and nearly always fruitful. But not so old, never so fruitful, puts in Sister Caroline, as the scuppernong vine at the old place, that as barefoot children they used to clamber over.

Then the meeting is adjourned to Cousin Roderick's great front porch, where one looks out between white columns at sunset clouds piling up into the deep blues and yellows of a Maxfield Parrish sky. Down the long street of Rebelville, between the mighty water oaks set out by Cousin Roderick's kin after the Confederate War, the cotton wagons are passing, heaped high with the white mass of cotton and a Negro or two atop, and the talk goes on, to the jingle of trace chains and the clop of mule hoofs on the almost brand-new state highway, which is so much better for rubber tires than mule hoofs. Over yonder lives Cousin Roderick's Aunt Cecily, a widow, the single indomitable inhabitant of a stately mansion where economics has not yet prevailed against sentiment. Next door is Uncle Burke Roderick, a Confederate veteran who at ninety still drives his horse and buggy to the plantation each morning; he is the last survivor of three brothers who were named Pitt, Fox, and Burke, after their father's eighteenth century heroes. All around, indeed, are the Roderick kin, for Cousin Roderick, whose mother married a Bertram, bears the family name of his mother's people, a numerous clan who, by dint of sundry alliances and ancient understandings, attend to whatever little matters need attention in the community affairs of Rebelville, where Jefferson's "least government" principle is a matter of course. Before supper, or after, some of the kinfolks may drop in, for there is always a vast deal of coming and going and dropping in at Cousin Roderick's.

As he takes his ease on the porch, Cousin Roderick looks to be neither the elegant dandy nor the out-at-elbows dribbler of tobacco juice that partisans have accredited to the Southern tradition. He is a fairly tall, vigorous man, plainly dressed, with the ruddiness of Georgia sun and good living on his face. His eyes are a-wrinkle at the corners, ready to catch the humor of whatever is abroad. His hand fumbles his pipe as he tells one anecdote after another in the country drawl that has about as much of Mark Twain and Sut Lovingood in it as it has of the elisions and flattenings supposed to belong to Southern patrician speech. In fact, though he is really patrician (as the female members of his family can assure you) he does not look anything like the Old Colonel of legend, and in spirit he, too, belongs to the Jeffersonian constituency. He has some of the bearing of an English squire, and a good deal of the frontier heartiness that Augustus Baldwin Longstreet depicted in *Georgia Scenes*. He assumes that the world is good-humored and friendly until it proves itself otherwise. If it does prove otherwise, there is a glint in his eye that tells you he will fight.

Cousin Roderick is the opposite of Chaucer's Man of Law, who ever seemed busier than he was. Cousin Roderick is busier than he seems. His air of negligence, like his good humor, is a philosophical defense against the dangerous surprises that life may turn up. Really, he is not negligent. He does not work with his own hands, like Brother Jonathan, or his Southern brothers of upcountry and bluegrass; but in the past he has worked aplenty with his hands and knows how it should be done. On his several tracts of land, the gatherings of inheritance and purchase, are some one hundred and fifty Negroes whom he furnishes housing, food, and a little money; they do his labor — men, women, children together — they are his " hands." He is expected to call them by name, to get them out of jail, to doctor them, even sometimes to bury them when " lodge dues " may have lapsed. They are no longer his slaves; but though they do not now utter the word, they do not allow him to forget that he has the obligations of a master.

As Cousin Roderick makes the " rounds " of his fields — no more on horseback, as of old, but in a battered Chevrolet — he sets forth his notions of economy. As for the depression, that is no new thing in Rebelville. People here have got used to ruination. After the Confederate War came Reconstruction, Tom Watson, and the Populist turmoil of the nineties; a while later, the peach boom and its collapse; then the Florida boom with its devastations; and now, this new depression. Like most of his kin, Cousin Roderick has simply retreated into the plantation economy. He tells how, when he was a young fellow just beginning to take charge, his father came out to the plantation one day and asked for a ham. Cousin Roderick explained that hogs were up to a good price; he had sold the entire lot, on the hoof, and had good money in the bank. " Sir," said the old man, " let me never again catch you without hams in your smokehouse and corn in your crib. You've got to make this land take care of itself." " And that," says Cousin Roderick, " is what I aim to do." From the land he feeds his own family, the hundred and fifty Negroes, and the stock. Whatever is left, when taxes and upkeep are deducted, is the profit. Anything that grows, he will plant: asparagus, peaches, pecans, onions, peppers, tomatoes, and of course the great staple crops, grain, hay, and cotton. Especially cotton, for no matter how low the price, cotton is money. It is ridiculous, he thinks, to talk of getting people who are hard-up for money to reduce cotton acreage. For his part, Cousin Roderick intends to make every bale his land will produce. But if cotton fails, he still can sell cattle, or cabbage, or timber from his baronial holdings. Land is the only abiding thing, the only assurance of happiness and comfort. He wants more land, not less.

One suspects that Cousin Roderick, however hard-pressed he may be at the bank, is fundamentally right. If he is not right, how does he manage, in these times, to send a daughter to college, and entertain his friends, and keep a cheerful face before the world? The portraits of his ancestors, looking down from their frames above great-grandfather's sideboard or his wife's new grand piano, eternally assure Cousin Roderick that he is right. They won this Eden of sandy earth and red clay, where all things grow with a vigor that neither winter nor drouth can abate. Not soon, not soon will their son give it up.

To the designs of experts who want to plan people's lives for them, Cousin Roderick gives no more than the indulgent attention of a naturally kindhearted man. He reads the anxious thunderings of the young men who reproduce, in the Macon *Telegraph,* the remote dynamical poppings of the *New Republic,* and is unmoved; the young men are like the mockingbird who sat on the cupola of the courthouse while court was in session and so learned to sing: *Prisoner-look-upon-the-jury! Jury-look-upon-the-prisoner!* GUILTY! GUILTY! GUILTY! It is a little incredible that so much planning should need to be done. Don't people know how they want to live? As for politics, long since it became tawdry and uncertain. Politics is for lawyers. Cousin Roderick would no more think of running for the legislature than he would think of moving to China. In that, perhaps, he lamentably differs from his ancestors. But in Rebelville political action is generally no more than a confirmation of what has been talked around among the clans. If you really want things done, you speak quietly to Cousin So-and-So and others that pass the word to everybody that counts. And then something is done.

In Rebelville the politics and economics of the bustling world become a faint whisper. All that matters is to see one's friends and relatives and pass from house to house, from field to field, under Georgia skies; to gather at a simple family dinner where only three kinds of bread and four kinds of meat are flanked by collards, sweet potatoes, corn, pickles, fruits, salads, jams, and cakes; or at a barbecue for fifty or more, for which whole animals are slaughtered and, it would seem, entire pantries and gardens desolated; or to sit with the wise men in front of the store, swapping jokes and telling tales hour after hour; or to hunt for fox, possum, coon, and quail, in swamp and field; or (for the ladies) to attend meetings of U.D.C.'s, D.A.R.'s, and missionary societies; or church service, or district conference or the tender ceremonies of Confederate Memorial Day, or the high school entertainment; or to hear the voices of Negroes, sifting through the dusk, or the mockingbird in moonlight; or to see the dark pines against sunset, and the old house lifting its columns far away, calling the wanderer home. The scuppernongs are gone, and cotton is picked. But already the pecans are falling. And planting begins again while late roses and chrysanthemums are showing and, even in the first frosts, the camellias are budding, against their December flowering. What though newspapers be loud and wars and rumors threaten — it is only an academic buzzing, that one must yet tolerate for manners' sake. Sowing and harvest go together, and summer runs into winter, and in Georgia one is persuaded to take the horizontal view.

By some it may be said that dark clouds hang over Yankeetown and Rebelville — and clouds of menace, maybe of destruction. I do not deny their presence, but my story is not of such clouds. In this strange modern world it may be observed that men talk continually of the good life without producing a specimen of it, to convince an inquirer. Brother Jonathan and Cousin Roderick do not talk about the good life. They lead it. If government is intended to serve human interests, what does it propose to do about them? I cannot believe that a government or a science which ignores or depreciates them is very trustworthy. I believe that government and science will fail unless they are taken into account. They, and others, are the incarnations of the principle of diversity through which the United States have become something better than Balkan, and without which the phrase " my country " is but a sorry and almost meaningless abstraction.

Frederick Jackson Turner

The Significance of the Frontier in American History

IN a recent bulletin of the Superintendent of the Census for 1890 appear these significant words: "Up to and including 1880 the country had a frontier of settlement, but at present the unsettled area has been so broken into by isolated bodies of settlement that there can hardly be said to be a frontier line. In the discussion of its extent, its westward movement, etc., it cannot, therefore, any longer have a place in the census reports." This brief official statement marks the closing of a great historic movement. Up to our own day American history has been in a large degree the history of the colonization of the Great West. The existence of an area of free land, its continuous recession, and the advance of American settlement westward explain American development.

Behind institutions, behind constitutional forms and modifications, lie the vital forces that call these organs into life and shape them to meet changing conditions. The peculiarity of American institutions is the fact that they have been compelled to adapt themselves to the changes of an expanding people — to the changes involved in crossing a continent, in winning a wilderness, and in developing at each area of this progress out of the primitive economic and political conditions of the frontier into the complexity of city life. Said Calhoun in 1817, " We are great, and rapidly — I was about to say fearfully — growing! " So saying, he touched the distinguishing feature of American life. All peoples show development; the germ theory of politics has been sufficiently emphasized. In the case of most nations, however, the development has occurred in a limited area; and if the nation has expanded, it has met other growing peoples whom it has conquered. But in the case of the United States we have a different phe-

From *The Frontier in American History,* 1921.

nomenon. Limiting our attention to the Atlantic coast, we have the familiar phenomenon of the evolution of institutions in a limited area, such as the rise of representative government; the differentiation of simple colonial governments into complex organs; the progress from primitive industrial society, without division of labor, up to manufacturing civilization. But we have in addition to this a recurrence of the process of evolution in each western area reached in the process of expansion. Thus American development has exhibited not merely advance along a single line, but a return to primitive conditions on a continually advancing frontier line, and a new development for that area. American social development has been continually beginning over again on the frontier. This perennial rebirth, this fluidity of American life, this expansion westward with its new opportunities, its continuous touch with the simplicity of primitive society, furnish the forces dominating American character. The true point of view in the history of this nation is not the Atlantic coast; it is the Great West. Even the slavery struggle, which is made so exclusive an object of attention by writers like Professor von Holst, occupies its important place in American history because of its relation to westward expansion.

In this advance, the frontier is the outer edge of the wave — the meeting point between savagery and civilization. Much has been written about the frontier from the point of view of border warfare and the chase, but as a field for the serious study of the economist and the historian it has been neglected.

The American frontier is sharply distinguished from the European frontier — a fortified boundary line running through dense populations. The most significant thing about the American frontier is that it lies at the hither edge of free land. In the census reports it is treated as the margin of that settlement which has a density of two or more to the square mile. The term is an elastic one, and for our purposes does not need sharp definition. We shall consider the whole frontier belt, including the Indian country and the outer margin of the " settled area " of the census reports. This paper will make no attempt to treat the subject exhaustively; its aim is simply to call attention to the frontier as a fertile field for investigation, and to suggest some of the problems which arise in connection with it.

In the settlement of America we have to observe how European life entered the continent, and how America modified and developed that life and reacted on Europe. Our early history is the study of European germs developing in an American environment. Too exclusive attention has been paid by institutional students to the Germanic origins, too little to the American factors. The frontier is the line of most rapid and effective Americanization. The wilderness masters the colonist. It finds him a European in dress, industries, tools, modes of travel, and thought. It takes him from the railroad car and puts him in the birch canoe. It strips off the garments of civilization and arrays him in the hunting shirt and the moccasin. It puts him in the log cabin of the Cherokee and Iroquois and runs an Indian palisade around him. Before long he has gone to planting Indian corn and plowing with a sharp stick; he shouts the war cry and takes the scalp in orthodox Indian fashion. In short, at the frontier the environment is at first too strong for the man. He must accept the conditions which it furnishes, or perish, and so he fits himself into the Indian clearings and follows the Indian trails. Little by little he transforms the wilderness, but the outcome is not the old Europe, not simply the development of Germanic germs, any more than the first phenomenon was a case of reversion to the German mark. The fact is that here is a new product that is American. At first, the frontier was the Atlantic coast. It was the frontier of Europe in a very real sense. Moving westward, the frontier became more and more American. As successive terminal moraines result from successive glaciations, so each frontier leaves its traces behind it, and when it becomes a settled area the region still partakes of the frontier characteristics. Thus the advance of the frontier has meant steady movement away from the influence of Europe, a steady growth of independence on American lines. And to study this advance, the men who grew up under these conditions, and the political, economic, and social results of it, is to study the really American part of our history.

In the course of the seventeenth century the frontier was advanced up the Atlantic river courses, just beyond the fall line, and the tidewater region became the settled area. In the first half of the eighteenth century another advance occurred. Traders followed the Delaware and Shawnee Indians to the Ohio as early as the end of the first quarter of the century. Governor Spotswood, of Virginia, made an expedition in 1714 across the Blue Ridge. The end of the first quarter of the century saw the advance of the Scotch-Irish and the Palatine Germans up the Shenandoah Valley into the western part of Virginia, and along the piedmont region of the Carolinas. The Germans in New York pushed the frontier of settlement up the Mohawk to German Flats. In Pennsylvania the town of Bedford indicates the line of settlement. Settlements soon began on the New River, or the Great Kanawha, and on the sources of the Yadkin and French Broad. The king attempted to arrest the advance by his proclamation of 1763, forbidding settlements beyond the sources of the rivers flowing into the Atlantic; but in vain. In the period of the Revolution the frontier crossed the Alleghanies into Kentucky and Tennessee, and the upper waters of the Ohio were settled. When the first census was taken in 1790, the continuous settled area was bounded by a line which ran near the coast of Maine, and included New England except a portion of Vermont and New Hampshire, New York along the Hudson and up the Mohawk about Schenectady, eastern and southern Pennsylvania, Virginia well across the Shenandoah Valley, and the Carolinas and eastern Georgia. Beyond this region of continuous settlement were the small settled areas of Kentucky and Tennessee, and the Ohio, with the mountains intervening between them and the Atlantic area, thus giving a new and important character to the frontier. The isolation of the region increased its peculiarly American tendencies, and the need of transportation facilities to connect it with the East called out important schemes of internal improvement, which will be noted farther on. The " West," as a self-conscious section, began to evolve.

From decade to decade distinct advances of the frontier occurred. By the census of 1820 the settled area included Ohio, southern Indiana and Illinois, southeastern Missouri, and about one half of Louisiana. This settled area had surrounded Indian areas, and the management of these tribes became an object of political concern. The frontier region of the time lay along the Great Lakes, where Astor's American Fur Company operated in the Indian trade, and beyond the Mississippi, where Indian traders extended their activity even to the Rocky Mountains; Florida also furnished frontier conditions. The Mississippi River region was the scene of typical frontier settlements.

The rising steam navigation on western waters, the opening of the Erie Canal, and the westward extension of cotton culture added five frontier states to the Union in this period. Grund, writing in 1836, declares: " It appears then that the universal disposition of Americans to emigrate to the western wilderness, in order to enlarge their dominion over inanimate nature, is the actual result of an expansive power which is inherent in them, and which by continually agitating all classes of society is constantly throwing a large portion of the whole population on the extreme confines of the State, in order to gain space for its development. Hardly is a new State or Territory formed before the same principle manifests itself again and gives rise to a further emigration; and so is it destined to go on until a physical barrier must finally obstruct its progress."

In the middle of this century the line indicated by the present eastern boundary of Indian Territory, Nebraska, and Kansas marked the frontier of the Indian country. Minnesota and Wisconsin still exhibited frontier conditions, but the distinctive frontier of the period is found in California, where the gold discoveries had sent a sudden tide of adventurous miners, and in Oregon, and the settlements in Utah. As the frontier had leaped over the Alleghanies, so now it skipped the Great Plains and the Rocky Mountains; and in the same way that the advance of the frontiersmen beyond the Alleghanies had caused the rise of important questions of transportation and internal improvement, so now the settlers beyond the Rocky Mountains needed means of communication with the East, and in the furnishing of these arose the settlement of the Great Plains and the development of still another kind of frontier life. Railroads, fostered by land grants, sent an increasing tide of immigrants into the Far West. The United States army fought a series of Indian wars in Minnesota, Dakota, and the Indian Territory.

By 1880 the settled area had been pushed into northern Michigan, Wisconsin, and Minnesota, along Dakota rivers, and in the Black Hills region, and was ascending the rivers of Kansas and Nebraska. The development of mines in Colorado had drawn isolated frontier settlements into that region, and Montana and Idaho were receiving settlers. The frontier was found in these mining camps and the ranches of the Great Plains. The Superintendent of the Census for 1890 reports, as previously stated, that the settlements of the West lie so scattered over the region that there can no longer be said to be a frontier line.

In these successive frontiers we find natural boundary lines which have served to mark and to affect the characteristics of the frontiers, namely: the fall line; the Alleghany Mountains; the Mississippi; the Missouri where its direction approximates north and south; the line of the arid lands, approximately the ninety-ninth meridian; and the Rocky Mountains. The fall line marked the frontier of the seventeenth century; the Alleghanies that of the eighteenth; the Mississippi that of the first quarter of the nineteenth; the Missouri that of the middle of this century (omitting the California movement); and the belt of the Rocky Mountains and the arid tract the present frontier. Each was won by a series of Indian wars.

At the Atlantic frontier one can study the germs of processes repeated at each successive frontier. We have the complex European life sharply precipitated by the wilderness into the simplicity of primitive conditions. The first frontier had to meet its Indian question, its question of the disposition of the public domain, of the means of intercourse with older settlements, of the extension of political organization, of religious and educational activity. And the settlement of these and similar questions for one frontier served as a guide for the next. The American student needs not to go to the " prim little townships of Sleswick " for illustrations of the law of continuity and development. For example, he may study the origin of our land policies in the colonial land policy; he may see how the system grew by adapting the statutes to the customs of the successive frontiers. He may see how the mining experience in the lead regions of Wisconsin, Illinois, and Iowa was applied to the mining laws of the Sierras, and how our Indian policy has been a series of experimentations on successive frontiers. Each tier of new states has found in the older ones material for its constitutions. Each frontier has made similar contributions to American character, as will be discussed farther on.

Loria, the Italian economist, has urged the study of colonial life as an aid in understanding the stages of European development, affirming that colonial settlement is for economic science what the mountain is for geology, bringing to light primitive stratifications. "America," he says, " has the key to the historical enigma which Europe has sought for centuries in vain, and the land which has no history reveals luminously the course of universal history." There is much truth in this. The United States lies like a huge page in the history of society. Line by line as we read this continental page from West to East we find the record of social evolution. It begins with the Indian and the hunter; it goes on to tell of the disintegration of savagery by the entrance of the trader, the pathfinder of civilization; we read the annals of the pastoral stage in ranch life; the exploitation of the soil by the raising of unrotated crops of corn and wheat in sparsely settled farming communities; the intensive culture of the denser farm settlement; and finally the manufacturing organization with city and factory system. This page is familiar to the student of census statistics, but how little of it has been used by our historians. Particularly in eastern states this page is a palimpsest. What is now a manufacturing state was in an earlier decade an area of intensive farming. Earlier yet it had been a wheat area, and still earlier the " range " had attracted the cattle herder. Thus Wisconsin, now developing manufacture, is a state with varied agricultural interests. But earlier it was given over to almost exclusive grain-raising, like North Dakota at the present time.

The Atlantic frontier was compounded of fisherman, fur trader, miner, cattle raiser, and farmer. Excepting the fisherman, each type of industry was on the march toward the West, impelled by an irresistible attraction. Each passed in successive waves across the continent. Stand at Cumberland Gap and watch the procession of civilization, marching single file — the buffalo following the trail to the salt springs, the Indian, the fur trader and hunter, the cattle raiser, the pioneer farmer — and the frontier has passed by. Stand at South Pass in the Rockies a century later and see the same procession with wider intervals between. The unequal rate of advance compels us to distinguish the frontier into the trader's frontier, the rancher's frontier, or the miner's frontier, and the farmer's frontier. When the mines and the cowpens were still near the fall line the traders' pack trains were tinkling across the Alleghanies, and the French on the Great Lakes were fortifying their posts, alarmed by the British trader's birch canoe. When the trappers scaled the Rockies, the farmer was still near the mouth of the Missouri.

Why was it that the Indian trader passed so rapidly across the continent? What effects followed from the trader's frontier? The trade was coeval with American discovery. The Norsemen, Vespuccius, Verrazani, Hudson, John Smith, all trafficked for furs. The Plymouth pilgrims settled in Indian corn-fields, and their first return cargo was beaver and lumber. The records of the various New England colonies show how steadily exploration was carried into the wilderness by this trade. What is true for New England is, as would be expected, even plainer for the rest of the colonies. All along the coast from Maine to Georgia the Indian trade opened up the river courses. Steadily the trader passed westward, utilizing the older lines of French trade. The Ohio, the Great Lakes, the Mississippi, the Missouri, and the Platte, the lines of western advance, were ascended by traders. They found the passes in the Rocky Mountains and guided Lewis and Clark, Frémont, and Bidwell. The explana-tion of the rapidity of this advance is connected with the effects of the trader on the Indian. The trading post left the unarmed tribes at the mercy of those that had purchased firearms — a truth which the Iroquois Indians wrote in blood, and so the remote and unvisited tribes gave eager welcome to the trader. " The savages," wrote La Salle, " take better care of us French than of their own children; from us only can they get guns and goods." This accounts for the trader's power and the rapidity of his advance. Thus the disintegrating forces of civilization entered the wilderness. Every river valley and Indian trail became a fissure in Indian society, and so that society became honeycombed. Long before the pioneer farmer appeared on the scene, primitive Indian life had passed away. The farmers met Indians armed with guns. The trading frontier, while steadily undermining Indian power by making the tribes ul-timately dependent on the whites, yet, through its sale of guns, gave to the

Indian increased power of resistance to the farming frontier. French colonization was dominated by its trading frontier; English colonization by its farming
frontier. There was an antagonism between the two frontiers as between the
two nations. Said Duquesne to the Iroquois: "Are you ignorant of the difference between the king of England and the king of France? Go see the forts
that our king has established and you will see that you can still hunt under
their very walls. They have been placed for your advantage in places which
you frequent. The English, on the contrary, are no sooner in possession of
a place than the game is driven away. The forest falls before them as they
advance, and the soil is laid bare so that you can scarce find the wherewithal
to erect a shelter for the night."

And yet, in spite of this opposition of the interests of the trader and the
farmer, the Indian trade pioneered the way for civilization. The buffalo trail
became the Indian trail, and this became the trader's " trace "; the trails widened
into roads, and the roads into turnpikes, and these in turn were transformed
into railroads. The same origin can be shown for the railroads of the South,
the Far West, and the Dominion of Canada. The trading posts reached by these
trails were on the sites of Indian villages which had been placed in positions
suggested by nature; and these trading posts, situated so as to command the
water systems of the country, have grown into such cities as Albany, Pittsburgh,
Detroit, Chicago, St. Louis, Council Bluffs, and Kansas City. Thus civilization
in America has followed the arteries made by geology, pouring an ever richer
tide through them, until at last the slender paths of aboriginal intercourse have
been broadened and interwoven into the complex mazes of modern commercial
lines; the wilderness has been interpenetrated by lines of civilization growing
ever more numerous. It is like the steady growth of a complex nervous system
for the originally simple, inert continent. If one would understand why we
are today one nation, rather than a collection of isolated states, he must study
this economic and social consolidation of the country. In this progress from
savage conditions lie topics for the evolutionist.

The effect of the Indian frontier as a consolidating agent in our history is
important. From the close of the seventeenth century various intercolonial
congresses have been called to treat with Indians and establish common measures of defense. Particularism was strongest in colonies with no Indian frontier.
This frontier stretched along the western border like a cord of union. The
Indian was a common danger, demanding united action. Most celebrated of
these conferences was the Albany congress of 1754, called to treat with the
Six Nations, and to consider plans of union. Even a cursory reading of
the plan proposed by the congress reveals the importance of the frontier. The
powers of the general council and the officers were, chiefly, the determination
of peace and war with the Indians, the regulation of Indian trade, the purchase
of Indian lands, and the creation and government of new settlements as a
security against the Indians. It is evident that the unifying tendencies of the
Revolutionary period were facilitated by the previous coöperation in the regulation of the frontier. In this connection may be mentioned the importance of

the frontier, from that day to this, as a military training school, keeping alive the power of resistance to aggression, and developing the stalwart and rugged qualities of the frontiersman.

It would not be possible in the limits of this paper to trace the other frontiers across the continent. Travelers of the eighteenth century found the cowpens among the canebrakes and pea-vine pastures of the South, and the cow drivers took their droves to Charleston, Philadelphia, and New York. Travelers at the close of the War of 1812 met droves of more than a thousand cattle and swine from the interior of Ohio going to Pennsylvania to fatten for the Philadelphia market. The ranges of the Great Plains, with ranch and cowboy and nomadic life, are things of yesterday and of today. The experience of the Carolina cowpens guided the ranchers of Texas. One element favoring the rapid extension of the rancher's frontier is the fact that in a remote country lacking transportation facilities the product must be in small bulk, or must be able to transport itself, and the cattle raiser could easily drive his product to market. The effect of these great ranches on the subsequent agrarian history of the localities in which they existed should be studied.

The maps of the census reports show an uneven advance of the farmer's frontier, with tongues of settlement pushed forward and with indentations of wilderness. In part this is due to Indian resistance, in part to the location of river valleys and passes, in part to the unequal force of the centers of frontier attraction. Among the important centers of attraction may be mentioned the following: fertile and favorably situated soils, salt springs, mines, and army posts.

The frontier army post, serving to protect the settlers from the Indians, has also acted as a wedge to open the Indian country, and has been a nucleus for settlement. In this connection mention should also be made of the government military and exploring expeditions in determining the lines of settlement. But all the more important expeditions were greatly indebted to the earliest pathmakers, the Indian guides, the traders and trappers, and the French voyageurs, who were inevitable parts of governmental expeditions from the days of Lewis and Clark. Each expedition was an epitome of the previous factors in western advance.

From the time the mountains rose between the pioneer and the seaboard, a new order of Americanism arose. The West and the East began to get out of touch of each other. The settlements from the sea to the mountains kept connection with the rear and had a certain solidarity. But the over-mountain men grew more and more independent. The East took a narrow view of American advance, and nearly lost these men. Kentucky and Tennessee history bears abundant witness to the truth of this statement. The East began to try to hedge and limit westward expansion. Though Webster could declare that there were no Alleghanies in his politics, yet in politics in general they were a very solid factor.

The exploitation of the beasts took hunter and trader to the west, the exploitation of the grasses took the rancher west, and the exploitation of the virgin soil of the river valleys and prairies attracted the farmer. Good soils have been the most continuous attraction to the farmer's frontier. The land hunger of the Virginians drew them down the rivers into Carolina, in early colonial days; the search for soils took the Massachusetts men to Pennsylvania and to New York. As the eastern lands were taken up migration flowed across them to the west. Daniel Boone, the great backwoodsman, who combined the occupations of hunter, trader, cattle raiser, farmer, and surveyor, learning, probably from the traders, of the fertility of the lands of the upper Yadkin, where the traders were wont to rest as they took their way to the Indians, left his Pennsylvania home with his father, and passed down the Great Valley road to that stream. Learning from a trader of the game and rich pastures of Kentucky, he pioneered the way for the farmers to that region. Thence he passed to the frontier of Missouri, where his settlement was long a landmark on the frontier. Here again he helped to open the way for civilization, finding salt licks, and trails, and land. His son was among the earliest trappers in the passes of the Rocky Mountains, and his party are said to have been the first to camp on the present site of Denver. His grandson, Colonel A. J. Boone, of Colorado, was a power among the Indians of the Rocky Mountains, and was appointed an agent by the government. Kit Carson's mother was a Boone. Thus this family epitomizes the backwoodsman's advance across the continent.

The farmer's advance came in a distinct series of waves. In Peck's *New Guide to the West,* published in Boston in 1837, occurs this suggestive passage:

Generally, in all the western settlements, three classes, like the waves of the ocean, have rolled one after the other. First comes the pioneer, who depends for the subsistence of his family chiefly upon the natural growth of vegetation, called the "range," and the proceeds of hunting. His implements of agriculture are crude, chiefly of his own make, and his efforts directed mainly to a crop of corn and a "truck patch." The last is a rude garden for growing cabbage, beans, corn for roasting ears, cucumbers, and potatoes. A log cabin, and, occasionally, a stable and corncrib, and a field of a dozen acres, the timber girdled or "deadened," and fenced, are enough for his occupancy. It is quite immaterial whether he ever becomes the owner of the soil. He is the occupant for the time being, pays no rent, and feels as independent as the "lord of the manor." With a horse, cow, and one or two breeders of swine, he strikes into the woods with his family, and becomes the founder of a new county, or perhaps state. He builds his cabin, gathers around him a few other families of similar tastes and habits, and occupies till the range is somewhat subdued, and hunting a little precarious, or, which is more frequently the case, till the neighbors crowd around, roads, bridges, and fields annoy him, and he lacks elbowroom. The preëmption law enables him to dispose of his cabin and cornfield to the next class of emigrants; and, to employ his own figures, he "breaks for the high timber," "clears out for the New Purchase," or migrates to Arkansas or Texas, to work the same process over. . . .

Another wave rolls on. The men of capital and enterprise come. The settler is ready to sell out and take the advantage of the rise in property, push farther into the interior and become, himself, a man of capital and enterprise in turn. The small village rises to a spacious town or city; substantial edifices of brick, extensive fields, orchards, gardens, colleges, and churches are seen.

Omitting those of the pioneer farmers who move from the love of adventure, the advance of the more steady farmer is easy to understand. Obviously the immigrant was attracted by the cheap lands of the frontier, and even the native farmer felt their influence strongly. Year by year the farmers who lived on soil whose returns were diminished by unrotated crops were offered the virgin soil of the frontier at nominal prices. Their growing families demanded more lands, and these were dear. The competition of the unexhausted, cheap, and easily tilled prairie lands compelled the farmer either to go west and continue the exhaustion of the soil on a new frontier, or to adopt intensive culture. Thus the census of 1890 shows, in the Northwest, many counties in which there is an absolute or a relative decrease of population. These states have been sending farmers to advance the frontier on the plains, and have themselves begun to turn to intensive farming and to manufacture. A decade before this, Ohio had shown the same transition stage. Thus the demand for land and the love of wilderness freedom drew the frontier ever onward.

Having now roughly outlined the various kinds of frontiers, and their modes of advance, chiefly from the point of view of the frontier itself, we may next inquire what were the influences on the East and on the Old World. A rapid enumeration of some of the more noteworthy effects is all that I have time for.

First, we note that the frontier promoted the formation of a composite nationality for the American people. The coast was preponderantly English, but the later tides of continental immigration flowed across to the free lands. This was the case from the early colonial days. The Scotch-Irish and the Palatine Germans, or "Pennsylvania Dutch," furnished the dominant element in the stock of the colonial frontier. With these peoples were also the freed indented servants, or redemptioners, who at the expiration of their time of service passed to the frontier. Governor Spotswood of Virginia writes in 1717, "The inhabitants of our frontiers are composed generally of such as have been transported hither as servants, and, being out of their time, settle themselves where land is to be taken up and that will produce the necessarys of life with little labour." Very generally these redemptioners were of non-English stock. In the crucible of the frontier the immigrants were Americanized, liberated, and fused into a mixed race, English in neither nationality nor characteristics. The process has gone on from the early days to our own. Burke and other writers in the middle of the eighteenth century believed that Pennsylvania was "threatened with the danger of being wholly foreign in language, manners, and perhaps even inclinations." The German and Scotch-Irish elements in the frontier of the South were only less great. In the middle of the present century the German element in Wisconsin was already so considerable that leading publicists looked to the creation of a German state out of the commonwealth by concentrating their colonization. Such examples teach us to beware of misinterpreting the fact that there is a common English speech in America into a belief that the stock is also English.

In another way the advance of the frontier decreased our dependence on

England. The coast, particularly of the South, lacked diversified industries, and was dependent on England for the bulk of its supplies. In the South there was even a dependence on the northern colonies for articles of food. Governor Glenn, of South Carolina, writes in the middle of the eighteenth century: " Our trade with New York and Philadelphia was of this sort, draining us of all the little money and bills we could gather from other places for their bread, flour, beer, hams, bacon, and other things of their produce, all which, except beer, our new townships begin to supply us with, which are settled with very industrious and thriving Germans. This no doubt diminishes the number of shipping and the appearance of our trade, but it is far from being a detriment to us." Before long the frontier created a demand for merchants. As it retreated from the coast it became less and less possible for England to bring her supplies directly to the consumer's wharfs, and carry away staple crops, and staple crops began to give way to diversified agriculture for a time. The effect of this phase of the frontier action upon the northern section is perceived when we realize how the advance of the frontier aroused seaboard cities like Boston, New York, and Baltimore to engage in rivalry for what Washington called " the extensive and valuable trade of a rising empire."

The legislation which most developed the powers of the national government, and played the largest part in its activity, was conditioned on the frontier. Writers have discussed the subjects of tariff, land, and internal improvement, as subsidiary to the slavery question. But when American history comes to be rightly viewed it will be seen that the slavery question is an incident. In the period from the end of the first half of the present century to the close of the Civil War slavery rose to primary, but far from exclusive, importance. But this does not justify Dr. von Holst (to take an example) in treating our constitutional history in its formative period down to 1828 in a single volume, giving six volumes chiefly to the history of slavery from 1828 to 1861, under the title *Constitutional History of the United States*. The growth of nationalism and the evolution of American political institutions were dependent on the advance of the frontier. Even so recent a writer as Rhodes, in his *History of the United States since the Compromise of 1850,* has treated the legislation called out by the western advance as incidental to the slavery struggle.

This is a wrong perspective. The pioneer needed the goods of the coast, and so the grand series of internal improvement and railroad legislation began, with potent nationalizing effects. Over internal improvements occurred great debates, in which grave constitutional questions were discussed. Sectional groupings appear in the votes, profoundly significant for the historian. Loose construction increased as the nation marched westward. But the West was not content with bringing the farm to the factory. Under the lead of Clay — " Harry of the West " — protective tariffs were passed, with the cry of bringing the factory to the farm. The disposition of the public lands was a third important subject of national legislation influenced by the frontier.

The public domain has been a force of profound importance in the nationalization and development of the government. The effects of the struggle of the landed and the landless states, and of the Ordinance of 1787, need no discussion. Administratively the frontier called out some of the highest and most vitalizing activities of the general government. The purchase of Louisiana was perhaps the constitutional turning point in the history of the Republic, inasmuch as it afforded both a new area for national legislation and the occasion of the down-fall of the policy of strict construction. But the purchase of Louisiana was called out by frontier needs and demands. As frontier states accrued to the Union the national power grew. In a speech on the dedication of the Calhoun monument Mr. Lamar explained: " In 1789 the states were the creators of the federal government; in 1861 the federal government was the creator of a large majority of the states."

When we consider the public domain from the point of view of the sale and disposal of the public lands we are again brought face to face with the frontier. The policy of the United States in dealing with its lands is in sharp contrast with the European system of scientific administration. Efforts to make this domain a source of revenue, and to withhold it from emigrants in order that settlement might be compact, were in vain. The jealousy and the fears of the East were powerless in the face of the demands of the frontiersmen. John Quincy Adams was obliged to confess: " My own system of administra-tion, which was to make the national domain the inexhaustible fund for pro-gressive and unceasing internal improvement, has failed." The reason is obvious; a system of administration was not what the West demanded; it wanted land. Adams states the situation as follows: " The slaveholders of the South have bought the coöperation of the western country by the bribe of the western lands, abandoning to the new Western States their own proportions of the public property and aiding them in the design of grasping all the lands into their own hands. Thomas H. Benton was the author of this system, which he brought forward as a substitute for the American system of Mr. Clay, and to supplant him as the leading statesman of the West. Mr. Clay, by his tariff com-promise with Mr. Calhoun, abandoned his own American system. At the same time he brought forward a plan for distributing among all the states of the Union the proceeds of the sales of the public lands. His bill for that purpose passed both Houses of Congress, but was vetoed by President Jackson, who, in his annual message of December, 1832, formally recommended that all public lands should be gratuitously given away to individual adventurers and to the states in which the lands are situated."

" No subject," said Henry Clay, " which has presented itself to the present, or perhaps any preceding, Congress, is of greater magnitude than that of the public lands." When we consider the far-reaching effects of the government's land policy upon political, economic, and social aspects of American life, we are disposed to agree with him. But this legislation was framed under frontier influences, and under the lead of Western statesmen like Benton and Jackson. Said Senator Scott of Indiana in 1841: " I consider the preëmption law merely declaratory of the custom or common law of the settlers."

It is safe to say that the legislation with regard to land, tariff, and internal improvements — the American system of the nationalizing Whig Party — was conditioned on frontier ideas and needs. But it was not merely in legislative action that the frontier worked against sectionalism of the coast. The economic and social characteristics of the frontier worked against sectionalism. The men of the frontier had closer resemblances to the Middle region than to either of the other sections. Pennsylvania had been the seed-plot of frontier emigration, and, although she passed on her settlers along the Great Valley into the west of Virginia and Carolinas, yet the industrial society of these Southern frontiersmen was always more like that of the Middle region than like that of the tidewater portion of the South, which later came to spread its industrial type throughout the South.

The Middle region, entered by New York harbor, was an open door to all Europe. The tidewater part of the South represented typical Englishmen, modified by a warm climate and servile labor, and living in baronial fashion on great plantations; New England stood for a special English movement — Puritanism. The Middle region was less English than the other sections. It had a wide mixture of nationalities, a varied society, the mixed town and county system of local government, a varied economic life, many religious sects. In short, it was a region mediating between New England and the South, and the East and the West. It represented that composite nationality which the contemporary United States exhibits, that juxtaposition of non-English groups, occupying a valley or a little settlement, and presenting reflections of the map of Europe in their variety. It was democratic and non-sectional, if not national; " easy, tolerant, and contented "; rooted strongly in material prosperity. It was typical of the modern United States. It was least sectional, not only because it lay between North and South, but also because with no barriers to shut out its frontiers from its settled region, and with a system of connecting waterways, the Middle region mediated between East and West as well as between North and South. Thus it became the typically American region. Even the New Englander, who was shut out from the frontier by the Middle region, tarrying in New York or Pennsylvania on his westward march, lost the acuteness of his sectionalism on the way.

The spread of cotton culture into the interior of the South finally broke down the contrast between the tidewater region and the rest of the state, and based Southern interests on slavery. Before this process revealed its results the western portion of the South, which was akin to Pennsylvania in stock, society, and industry, showed tendencies to fall away from the faith of the fathers into internal improvement legislation and nationalism. In the Virginia convention of 1829–1830, called to revive the constitution, Mr. Leigh, of Chesterfield, one of the tidewater counties, declared:

One of the main causes of discontent which led to this convention, that which had the strongest influence in overcoming our veneration for the work of our fathers, which taught us to contemn the sentiments of Henry and Mason and Pendleton, which weaned us from our reverence for the constituted authorities of the state, was an overweening passion for internal improvement. I say this with perfect knowledge, for it has been avowed to me by gentlemen from the West over and over again. And let me tell the gentleman from Albermarle (Mr. Gordon) that it has been another principal object of those who set this ball of revolution in motion, to overturn the doctrine of state rights, of which Virginia has been the very pillar, and to remove the barrier she has interposed to the interference of the federal government in that same work of internal improvement, by so reorganizing the legislature that Virginia, too, may be hitched to the federal car.

It was this nationalizing tendency of the West that transformed the democracy of Jefferson into the national republicanism of Monroe and the democracy of Andrew Jackson. The West of the War of 1812, the West of Clay, and Benton and Harrison, and Andrew Jackson, shut off by the Middle States and the mountains from the coast sections, had a solidarity of its own with national tendencies. On the tide of the Father of Waters, North and South met and mingled into a nation. Interstate migration went steadily on — a process of cross fertilization of ideas and institutions. The fierce struggle of the sections over slavery on the western frontier does not diminish the truth of this statement; it proves the truth of it. Slavery was a sectional trait that would not down, but in the West it could not remain sectional. It was the greatest of frontiersmen who declared: "I believe this government can not endure permanently half slave and half free. It will become all of one thing or all of the other." Nothing works for nationalism like intercourse within the nation. Mobility of population is death to localism, and the western frontier worked irresistibly in unsettling population. The effect reached back from the frontier and affected profoundly the Atlantic coast and even the Old World.

But the most important effect of the frontier has been in the promotion of democracy here and in Europe. As has been indicated, the frontier is productive of individualism. Complex society is precipitated by the wilderness into a kind of primitive organization based on the family. The tendency is antisocial. It produces antipathy to control, and particularly to any direct control. The tax-gatherer is viewed as a representative of oppression. Professor Osgood, in an able article, has pointed out that the frontier conditions prevalent in the colonies are important factors in the explanation of the American Revolution, where individual liberty was sometimes confused with the absence of all effective government. The same conditions aid in explaining the difficulty of instituting a strong government in the period of the confederacy. The frontier individualism has from the beginning promoted democracy.

The frontier states that came into the Union in the first quarter of a century of its existence came in with democratic suffrage provisions, and had reactive effects of the highest importance upon the older states whose peoples were being attracted there. An extension of the franchise became essential. It was *western* New York that forced an extension of suffrage in the constitutional convention of that state in 1821; and it was *western* Virginia that compelled the tidewater region to put a more liberal suffrage provision in the constitution framed in 1830, and to give to the frontier region a more nearly proportionate representation with the tidewater aristocracy. The rise of democracy as an effective force in the nation came in with Western preponderance under Jackson and William Henry Harrison, and it meant the triumph of the frontier — with all of its good and with all of its evil elements. An interesting illustration of the tone of frontier democracy in 1830 comes from the same debates in the Virginia convention already referred to. A representative from western Virginia declared:

But, sir, it is not the increase of population in the West which this gentleman ought to fear. It is the energy which the mountain breeze and Western habits impart to those emigrants. They are regenerated, politically I mean, sir. They soon become *working politicians;* and the difference, sir, between a *talking* and a *working* politician is immense. The Old Dominion has long been celebrated for producing great orators; the ablest metaphysicians in policy; men that can split hairs in all abstruse questions of political economy. But at home, or when they return from Congress, they have Negroes to fan them asleep. But a Pennsylvania, a New York, an Ohio, or a western Virginia statesman, though far inferior in logic, metaphysics, and rhetoric to an old Virginia statesman, has this advantage, that when he returns home he takes off his coat and takes hold of the plow. This gives him bone and muscle, sir, and preserves his republican principles pure and uncontaminated.

So long as free land exists, the opportunity for a competency exists, and economic power secures political power. But the democracy born of free land, strong in selfishness and individualism, intolerant of administrative experience and education, and pressing individual liberty beyond its proper bounds, has its dangers as well as its benefits. Individualism in America has allowed a laxity in regard to governmental affairs which has rendered possible the spoils system and all the manifest evils that follow from the lack of a highly developed civic spirit. In this connection may be noted also the influence of frontier conditions in permitting lax business honor, inflated paper currency and wildcat banking. The colonial and Revolutionary frontier was the region whence emanated many of the worst forms of an evil currency. The West in the War of 1812 repeated the phenomenon on the frontier of that day, while the speculation and wildcat banking of the period of the crisis of 1837 occurred on the new frontier belt of the next tier of states. Thus each one of the periods of lax financial integrity coincides with periods when a new set of frontier communities had arisen, and coincides in area with these successive frontiers, for the most part. The recent Populist agitation is a case in point. Many a state that now declines any connection with the tenets of the Populists itself adhered to such ideas in an earlier stage of the development of the state. A primitive society can hardly be expected to show the intelligent appreciation of the complexity of business interests in a developed society. The continual recurrence of these areas of paper-money agitation is another evidence that the frontier can be isolated and studied as a factor in American history of the highest importance.

The East has always feared the result of an unregulated advance of the frontier, and has tried to check and guide it. The English authorities would have checked settlement at the headwaters of the Atlantic tributaries and allowed

the " savages to enjoy their deserts in quiet lest the peltry trade should decrease."
This called out Burke's splendid protest:

If you stopped your grants, what would be the consequence? The people would
occupy without grants. They have already so occupied in many places. You cannot
station garrisons in every part of these deserts. If you drive the people from one place,
they will carry on their annual tillage and remove with their flocks and herds to
another. Many of the people in the back settlements are already little attached to
particular situations. Already they have topped the Appalachian Mountains.

But the English government was not alone in its desire to limit the advance
of the frontier and guide its destinies. Tidewater Virginia and South Carolina
gerrymandered those colonies to insure the dominance of the coast in their
legislatures. Washington desired to settle a state at a time in the Northwest;
Jefferson would reserve from settlement the territory of his Louisiana Purchase
north of the thirty-second parallel, in order to offer it to the Indians in exchange
for their settlements east of the Mississippi. " When we shall be full on this
side," he writes, " we may lay off a range of states on the western bank from
the head to the mouth, and so range after range, advancing compactly as we
multiply." Madison went so far as to argue to the French minister that the
United States had no interest in seeing population extend itself on the right
bank of the Mississippi, but should rather fear it. When the Oregon question
was under debate, in 1824, Smyth of Virginia would draw an unchangeable
line for the limits of the United States at the outer limit of two tiers of states
beyond the Mississippi, complaining that the seaboard states were being drained
of the flower of their population by the bringing of too much land into market.
Even Thomas Benton, the man of widest views of the destiny of the West,
at this stage of his career declared that along the ridge of the Rocky Mountains
" the western limits of the Republic should be drawn, and the statue of the
fabled god Terminus should be raised upon its highest peak, never to be thrown
down." But the attempts to limit the boundaries, to restrict land sales and
settlement, and to deprive the West of its share of political power were all
in vain. Steadily the frontier of settlement advanced and carried with it individualism, democracy, and nationalism, and powerfully affected the East and
the Old World.

From the conditions of frontier life came intellectual traits of profound
importance. The works of travelers along each frontier from colonial days onward describe certain common traits, and these traits have, while softening
down, still persisted as survivals in the place of their origin, even when a higher
social organization succeeded. The result is that to the frontier the American
intellect owes its striking characteristics. That coarseness and strength combined
with acuteness and inquisitiveness; that practical, inventive turn of mind, quick
to find expedients; that masterful grasp of material things, lacking in the artistic
but powerful to effect great ends; that restless, nervous energy; that dominant
individualism, working for good and for evil, and withal that buoyancy and
exuberance which comes with freedom — these are traits of the frontier, or traits

called out elsewhere because of the existence of the frontier. Since the days when the fleet of Columbus sailed into the waters of the New World, America has been another name for opportunity, and the people of the United States have taken their tone from the incessant expansion which has not only been open but has even been forced upon them. He would be a rash prophet who should assert that the expansive character of American life has now entirely ceased. Movement has been its dominant fact, and, unless this training has no effect upon a people, the American energy will continually demand a wider field for its exercise. But never again will such gifts of free land offer themselves. For a moment, at the frontier, the bonds of custom are broken and unrestraint is triumphant. There is no *tabula rasa.* The stubborn American environment is there with its imperious summons to accept its conditions; the inherited ways of doing things are also there; and yet in spite of environment, and, in spite of custom, each frontier did indeed furnish a new field of opportunity, a gate of escape from the bondage of the past; and freshness, and confidence, and scorn of older society, impatience of its restraints and its ideas, and indifference to its lessons, have accompanied the frontier. What the Mediterranean Sea was to the Greeks, breaking the bond of custom, offering new experiences, calling out new institutions and activities, that, and more, the ever retreating frontier has been to the United States directly, and to the nations of Europe more remotely. And now, four centuries from the discovery of America, at the end of a hundred years of life under the Constitution, the frontier has gone, and with its going has closed the first period of American history.

Carl Becker

Kansas

SOME years ago, in a New England college town, when I informed one of my New England friends that I was preparing to go to Kansas, he replied rather blankly, " Kansas?! Oh." The amenities of casual intercourse demanded a reply, certainly, but from the point of view of my New England friend I suppose there was really nothing more to say; and, in fact, standing there under the peaceful New England elms, Kansas did seem tolerably remote. Some months later I rode out of Kansas City and entered for the first time what I had always pictured as the land of grasshoppers, of arid drought, and barren social experimentation. In the seat just ahead were two young women, girls rather, whom I afterwards saw at the university. As we left the dreary yards behind, and entered the half-open country along the Kansas River, one of the pair, breaking abruptly away from the ceaseless chatter that

From *Essays in American History dedicated to Frederick Jackson Turner,* 1910.

had hitherto engrossed them both, began looking out of the car window. Her attention seemed fixed, for perhaps a quarter of an hour, upon something in the scene outside — the fields of corn, or it may have been the sunflowers that lined the track; but at last, turning to her companion with the contented sigh of a returning exile, she said, " *Dear old Kansas!* " The expression somehow recalled my New England friend. I wondered vaguely, as I was sure he would have done, why anyone should feel moved to say " Dear old Kansas! " I had supposed that Kansas, even more than Italy, was only a geographical expression. But not so. Not infrequently, since then, I have heard the same expression — not always from emotional young girls. To understand why people say " Dear old Kansas! " is to understand that Kansas is no mere geographical expression, but a " state of mind," a religion, and a philosophy in one.

The difference between the expression of my staid New England friend and that of the enthusiastic young Kansan is perhaps symbolical, in certain respects, of the difference between those who remain at home and those who, in successive generations, venture into the unknown " West " — New England or Kansas — wherever it may be. In the seventeenth century there was doubtless no lack of Englishmen — prelates for example, in lawn sleeves, comfortably buttressed about by tithes and the Thirty-nine Articles — who might have indicated their point of view quite fully by remarking, " New England?! Oh." Whether any New Englander of that day ever went so far as to say " Dear old New England," I do not know. But that the sentiment was there, furnishing fuel for the inner light, is past question.

There are those who will tell us, and have indeed often told us, with a formidable array of statistics, that Kansas is inhabited only in small part by New Englanders, and that it is therefore fanciful in the extreme to think of it as representing Puritanism transplanted. It is true the people of Kansas came mainly from " the Middle West " — from Illinois, Indiana, Ohio, Iowa, Kentucky, and Missouri. But for our purpose the fact is of little importance, for it is the ideals of a people rather than the geography they have outgrown that determine their destiny; and in Kansas, as has been well said, " it is the ideas of the Pilgrims, not their descendants, that have had dominion in the young commonwealth." Ideas, sometimes, as well as the star of empire, move westward, and so it happens that Kansas is more Puritan than New England of today. It is akin to New England of early days. It is what New England, old England itself, once was — the frontier, an ever changing spot where dwell the courageous who defy fate and conquer circumstance.

For the frontier is more than a matter of location, and Puritanism is itself a kind of frontier. There is an intellectual " West " as well as a territorial " West." Both are heresies, the one as much subject to the scorn of the judicious as the other. Broad classifications of people are easily made and are usually inaccurate; but they are convenient for taking a large view, and it may be worth while to think, for the moment, of two kinds of people — those who like the sheltered life, and those who cannot endure it; those who think the world as they know it is well enough, and those who dream of something better, or, at any rate, something different. From age to age society builds its shelters of various sorts — accumulated traditions, religious creeds, political institutions, and intellectual conceptions, cultivated and well-kept farms, well-built and orderly cities — providing a monotonous and comfortable life that tends always to harden into conventional forms resisting change. With all this the homekeeping and timid are well content. They sit in accustomed corners, disturbed by no fortuitous circumstance. But there are those others who are forever tugging at the leashes of ordered life, eager to venture into the unknown. Forsaking beaten paths, they plunge into the wilderness. They must be always on the frontier of human endeavor, submitting what is old and accepted to conditions that are new and untried. The frontier is thus the seed plot where new forms of life, whether of institutions or types of thought, are germinated, the condition of all progress being in a sense a return to the primitive.

Now, generally speaking, the men who make the world's frontiers, whether in religion or politics, science, or geographical exploration and territorial settlement, have certain essential and distinguishing qualities. They are primarily men of faith. Having faith in themselves, they are individualists. They are idealists because they have faith in the universe, being confident that somehow everything is right at the center of things; they give hostages to the future, are ever inventing God anew, and must be always transforming the world into their ideal of it. They have faith in humanity and in the perfectibility of man; are likely, therefore, to be believers in equality, reformers, intolerant, aiming always to level others up to their own high vantage. These qualities are not only Puritan, they are American; and Kansas is not only Puritanism transplanted, but Americanism transplanted. In the individualism, the idealism, the belief in equality that prevail in Kansas, we shall therefore see nothing strangely new, but simply a new graft of familiar American traits. But as Kansas is a community with a peculiar and distinctive experience, there is something peculiar and distinctive about the individualism, the idealism, and the belief in equality of its people. If we can get at this something peculiar and distinctive, it will be possible to understand why the sight of sunflowers growing beside a railroad track may call forth the fervid expression, " Dear old Kansas! "

I

Individualism is everywhere characteristic of the frontier, and in America, where the geographical frontier has hitherto played so predominant a part, a peculiarly marked type of individualism is one of the most obvious traits of the people. " To the frontier," Professor Turner has said, " the American intellect owes its striking characteristics. That coarseness and strength combined with acuteness and inquisitiveness; that practical, inventive turn of mind, quick to find expedients; that masterful grasp of material things, lacking in the artistic but powerful to effect great ends; that restless nervous energy; that dominant individualism, working for good and for evil; and withal that buoyancy and exuberance that comes from freedom." On the frontier, where everything is done by the individual and nothing by organized society, initiative, resourcefulness, quick, confident, and sure judgment are the essential qualities for success. But as the problems of the frontier are rather restricted and definite, those who succeed there have necessarily much the same kind of initiative and resourcefulness, and their judgment will be sure only in respect to the problems that are familiar to all. It thus happens that the type of individualism produced on the frontier and predominant in America has this peculiarity, that while the sense of freedom is strong, there is nevertheless a certain uniformity in respect to ability, habit, and point of view. The frontier develops strong individuals, but it develops individuals of a particular type, all being after much the same pattern. The individualism of the frontier is one of achievement, not of eccentricity; an individualism of fact arising from a sense of power to overcome obstacles, rather than one of theory growing out of weakness in the face of oppression. It is not because he fears governmental activity, but because he has so often had to dispense with it, that the American is an individualist. Altogether averse from hesitancy, doubt, speculative or introspective tendencies, the frontiersman is a man of faith: of faith, not so much in some external power as in himself, in his luck, his destiny; faith in the possibility of achieving whatever is necessary or he desires. It is this marked self-reliance that gives to Americans their tremendous power of initiative; but the absence of deep-seated differences gives to them an equally tremendous power of concerted social action.

The confident individualism of those who achieve through endurance is a striking trait of the people of Kansas. There, indeed, the trait has in it an element of exaggeration, arising from the fact that whatever has been achieved in Kansas has been achieved under great difficulties. Kansans have been subjected, not only to the ordinary hardships of the frontier, but to a succession of reverses and disasters that could be survived only by those for whom defeat is worse than death, who cannot fail because they cannot surrender. To the border wars succeeded hot winds, droughts, grasshoppers; and to the disasters of nature succeeded in turn the scourge of man, in the form of " mortgage fiends " and a contracting currency. Until 1895 the whole history of the state was a series of disasters, and always something new, extreme, bizarre, until the name Kansas became a byword, a synonym for the impossible and the ridiculous, inviting laughter, furnishing occasion for jest and hilarity. " In God we trusted, in Kansas we busted," became a favorite motto of emigrants, worn out with the struggle, returning to more hospitable climes; and for many years it expressed well enough the popular opinion of that fated land.

Yet there were some who never gave up. They stuck it out. They endured all that even Kansas could inflict. They kept the faith, and they are to be pardoned perhaps if they therefore feel that henceforth there is laid up for them a crown of glory. Those who remained in Kansas from 1875 to 1895 must have originally possessed staying qualities of no ordinary sort, qualities which the experience of those years could only accentuate. And as success has at last rewarded their efforts, there has come, too, a certain pride, an exuberance, a feeling of superiority that accompany a victory long delayed and hardly won. The result has been to give a peculiar flavor to the Kansas spirit of individualism.

With Kansas history back of him, the true Kansan feels that nothing is *too much* for him. How shall he be afraid of any danger, or hesitate at any obstacle, having succeeded where failure was not only human but almost honorable? Having conquered Kansas, he knows well that there are no worse worlds to conquer. The Kansas spirit is therefore one that finds something exhilarating in the challenge of an extreme difficulty. " No one," says Saint Augustine, " loves what he endures, though he may love to endure." With Kansans, it is particularly a point of pride to suffer easily the stings of fortune, and if they find no pleasure in the stings themselves, the ready endurance of them gives a consciousness of merit that is its own reward.

Yet it is with no solemn martyr's air that the true Kansan endures the worst that can happen. His instinct is rather to pass it off as a minor annoyance, furnishing occasion for a pleasantry, for it is the mark of a Kansan to take a reverse as a joke rather than too seriously. Indeed, the endurance of extreme adversity has developed a keen appreciation for that type of humor, everywhere prevalent in the West, which consists in ignoring a difficulty, or transforming it into a difficulty of precisely the opposite kind. There is a tradition surviving from the grasshopper time that illustrates the point. It is said that in the midst of that overwhelming disaster, when the pests were six inches deep in the streets, the editor of a certain local paper fined his comment on the situation down to a single line, which appeared among the trivial happenings of the week: " A grasshopper was seen on the courthouse steps this morning." This type of humor, appreciated anywhere west of the Alleghanies, is the type *par excellence* in Kansas. Perhaps it has rained for six weeks in the spring. The wheat is seemingly ruined; no corn has been planted. A farmer, who sees his profits for the year wiped out, looks at the murky sky, sniffs the damp air, and remarks seriously, " Well, it looks like rain. We may save that crop yet." " Yes," his neighbor replies with equal seriousness, " but it will have to come soon, or it won't do any good." When misfortunes beat down upon one in rapid succession, there comes a time when it is useless to strive against them, and in the end they engender a certain detached curiosity in the victim, who finds a mournful pleasure in observing with philosophical resignation the ultimate caprices of fate. Thus Kansans, " coiners of novel phrases to express their defiance of destiny," have employed humor itself as a refuge against misfortune. They have learned not only to endure adversity, but in a very literal sense to laugh at it as well.

I have already said that the type of individualism that is characteristic of America is one of achievement, not of eccentricity. The statement will bear repeating in this connection, for it is truer of Kansas than of most communities, notwithstanding there is a notion abroad that the state is peopled by freaks and eccentrics. It was once popularly supposed in Europe, and perhaps is so yet, that Americans are all eccentric. Now, Kansans are eccentric in the same sense that Americans are: they differ somewhat from other Americans, just as Americans are distinguishable from Europeans. But a fundamental characteristic of Kansas individualism is the tendency to conform; it is an individualism of conformity, not of revolt. Having learned to endure to the end, they have learned to conform, for endurance is itself a kind of conformity. It has not infrequently been the subject of wondering comment by foreigners that in America, where everyone is supposed to do as he pleases, there should nevertheless be so little danger from violence and insurrection. Certainly one reason is that while the conditions of frontier life release the individual from many of the formal restraints of ordered society, they exact a most rigid adherence to lines of conduct inevitably fixed by the stern necessities of life in a primitive community. On the frontier men soon learn to conform to what is regarded as essential, for the penalty of resistance or neglect is extinction: there the law of survival works surely and swiftly. However eccentric frontiersmen may appear to the tenderfoot, among themselves there is little variation from type in any essential matter. In the new community, individualism means the ability of the individual to succeed, not by submitting to some external formal authority, still less by following the bent of an unschooled will, but by recognizing and voluntarily adapting himself to necessary conditions. Kansas, it is true, has produced its eccentrics, but there is a saying here that freaks are raised for export only. In one sense the saying is true enough, for what strikes one particularly is that, on the whole, native Kansans are all so much alike. It is a community of great solidarity, and to the native it is " the Easterner " who appears eccentric.

The conquest of the wilderness in Kansas has thus developed qualities of patience, of calm, stoical, good-humored endurance in the face of natural difficulties, of conformity to what is regarded as necessary. Yet the patience, the calmness, the disposition to conform, is strictly confined to what is regarded as in the natural course. If the Kansan appears stolid, it is only on the surface that he is so. The peculiar conditions of origin and history have infused into the character of the people a certain romantic and sentimental element. Beneath the placid surface there is something fermenting which is best left alone — a latent energy which trivial events or a resounding phrase may unexpectedly release. In a recent commencement address, Mr. Henry King said that conditions in early Kansas were " *hair-triggered*." Well, Kansans are themselves hair-triggered; slight pressure, if it be of the right sort, sets them off. " Everyone is on the *qui vive,* alert, vigilant, like a sentinel at an outpost." This trait finds expression in the romantic devotion of the people to the state, in a certain alert sensitiveness to criticism from outside, above all in the contagious enthusiasm with which they will without warning espouse a cause, especially when symbolized by a striking phrase, and carry it to an issue. Insurgency is native in Kansas, and the political history of the state, like its climate, is replete with surprises that have made it " alternately the reproach and the marvel of mankind." But this apparent instability is only the natural complement of the extreme and confident individualism of the people: having succeeded in overcoming so many obstacles that were unavoidable, they do not doubt their ability to destroy quickly those that seem artificially constructed. It thus happens that while no people endure the reverses of nature with greater fortitude and good humor than the people of Kansas, misfortunes seemingly of man's making arouse in them a veritable passion of resistance; the mere suspicion of injustice, real or fancied exploitation by those who fare sumptuously, the pressure of laws not self-imposed, touch something explosive in their nature that transforms a calm and practical people into excited revolutionists. Grasshoppers elicited only a witticism, but the " mortgage fiends " produced the Populist regime, a kind of religious crusade against the infidel Money Power. The same spirit was recently exhibited in the " Boss Busters " movement, which in one summer spread over the state like a prairie fire and overthrew an established machine supposed to be in control of the railroads. The " Higher Law " is still a force in Kansas. The spirit which refused to obey " bogus laws " is still easily stirred. A people which has endured the worst of nature's tyrannies, and cheerfully submits to tyrannies self-imposed, is in no mood to suffer hardships that seem remediable.

II

Idealism must always prevail on the frontier, for the frontier, whether geographical or intellectual, offers little hope to those who see things as they are. To venture into the wilderness, one must see it, not as it is, but as it will be. The frontier, being the possession of those only who see its future, is the promised land which cannot be entered save by those who have faith. America, having been such a Promised Land, is therefore inhabited by men of faith: idealism is ingrained in the character of its people. But as the frontier in America has hitherto been geographical and material, American idealism has necessarily a material basis, and Americans have often been mistakenly called materialists. True, they seem mainly interested in material things. Too often they represent values in terms of money: a man is " worth " so much; a university is a great university, having the largest endowment of any; a fine building is a building that cost a million dollars — better still, ten millions. Value is extensive rather than intensive or intrinsic. America is the best country because it is the biggest, the wealthiest, the most powerful; its people are the best because they are the freest, the most energetic, the *most* educated. But to see a materialistic temper in all this is to mistake the form for the spirit. The American cares for material things because they represent the substance of things hoped for. He cares less for money than for making money: a fortune is valued, not because it represents ease, but because it represents struggle, achievement, progress. The first skyscraper in any town is nothing in itself, but much as an evidence of growth; it is a white stone on the road to the ultimate goal.

Idealism of this sort is an essential ingredient of the Kansas spirit. In few communities is the word progress more frequently used, or its meaning less frequently detached from a material basis. It symbolizes the *summum bonum,* having become a kind of dogma. Mistakes are forgiven a man if he is progressive, but to be unprogressive is to be suspect; like Aristotle's nonpolitical animal, the unprogressive is extra-human. This may explain why every Kansan wishes first of all to tell you that he comes from the town of X——, and then that it is the finest town in the state. He does not mean that it is strictly the finest town in the state, as will appear if you take the trouble to inquire a little about the country, its soil, its climate, its rainfall, and about the town itself. For it may chance that he is free to admit that it is hot there, that the soil is inclined to bake when there is no rain, that there is rarely any rain — all of which, however, is nothing to the point, because they are soon to have water by irrigation, which is, after all, much better than rainfall. And then he describes the town, which you have no difficulty in picturing vividly: a single street flanked by nondescript wooden shops; at one end a railroad station, at the other a post office; side streets lined with frame houses, painted or not, as the case may be; a schoolhouse somewhere, and a church with a steeple. It is such a town, to all appearances, as you may see by the hundred anywhere in the West — a dreary place which, you think, the world would willingly let die. But your man is enthusiastic; he can talk of nothing but the town of X——. The secret of his enthusiasm you at last discover in the inevitable " but it will be a great country some day," and it dawns upon you that, after all, the man does not live in the dreary town of X——, but in the great country of *some day*. Such are Kansans. Like Saint Augustine, they have their City of God, the idealized Kansas of some day: it is only necessary to have faith in order to possess it.

Kansas idealism is not a force that expends itself in academic contemplation of the unattainable. It is an idealism that is immensely concrete and practical, requiring always some definite object upon which to expend itself, but once having such an object expending itself with a restless, nervous energy that is appalling: whatever the object, it is pursued with the enthusiasm, the profound conviction, given only to those who have communed with the Absolute. It would seem that preoccupation with the concrete and the practical should develop a keen appreciation of relative values; but in new countries problems of material transformation are so insistent that immediate means acquire the value of ultimate ends. Kansas is a new state, and its inhabitants are so preoccupied with the present, so resolutely detached from the experience of the centuries, that they can compare themselves of today only with themselves of yesterday. Past and future appear foreshortened, and the latest new mechanical device brings us an appreciable step nearer the millennium, which seems always to be just over the next hill. By some odd mental alchemy it thus happens that the concrete and the practical have taken on the dignity of the absolute, and the pursuit of a convenience assumes the character of a crusade. Whether it be religion or paving, education or the disposal of garbage, that occupies for the moment the focus of attention, the same stirring activity, the same zeal and emotional glow are enlisted: all alike are legitimate objects of conquest, to be measured in terms of their visual and transferable assets, and won by concerted and organized attack. I recall reading in a local Kansas newspaper some time ago a brief comment on the neighboring village of X—— (in which was located a small college mistakenly called a university), which ran somewhat as follows: " The University of X—— has established a music festival on the same plan as the one at the State University, and with most gratifying results. The first festival was altogether a success. X—— is a fine town, one of the best in the state. It has a fine university and a fine class of people, who have made it a center of culture. X—— lacks only one thing; it has no sewers." Perhaps there are people who would find the juxtaposition of culture and sewers somewhat bizarre. But to us in Kansas it does not seem so. Culture and sewers are admittedly good things to possess. Well, then, let us pursue them actively and with absolute conviction. Thus may an idealized sewer become an object worthy to stir the moral depths of any right-minded community.

An insistent, practical idealism of this sort, always busily occupied with concrete problems, is likely to prefer ideas cast in formal mold, will be a little at a loss in the midst of flexible play of mind, and look with suspicion upon the emancipated, the critical, and the speculative spirit. It is too sure of itself to be at home with ideas of uncertain pressure. Knowing that it is right, it wishes only to go ahead. Satisfied with certain conventional premises, it hastens on to the obvious conclusion. It thus happens that Americans, for the most part, are complaisantly satisfied with a purely formal interpretation of those resounding words that symbolize for them the ideas upon which their institutions are supposed to rest. In this respect Kansas is truly American. Nowhere is there more loyal devotion to such words as liberty, democracy, equality, education. But preoccupation with the concrete fixes the attention upon the word itself, and upon what is traditionally associated with it. Democracy, for example, is traditionally associated with elections, and many of them. Should you maintain that democracy is not necessarily bound up with any particular institution, that it is in the way of being smothered by the complicated blanket ballot, you will not be understood; or, rather, you will be understood only too well as advocating something aristocratic. Democracy is somehow bound up with a concrete thing, and the move for the shorter ballot is therefore undemocractic and un-American. Or, take the word socialism. Your avowed socialist is received politely, and allowed to depart silently and without regret. But if you tell us of the movement for the governmental control of corporate wealth, we grow enthusiastic. The word socialism has a bad odor in Kansas, but the thing itself, by some other name, smells sweet enough.

If one is interested in getting the essential features of socialism adopted in Kansas, or in America itself, the name to conjure with is indeed not socialism, but equality.

III

In a country like America, where there is such confident faith in the individual, one might naturally expect to find the completest toleration, and no disposition to use the government for the purpose of enforcing uniform conditions: logically, it would seem, so much emphasis on liberty should be incompatible with much emphasis on equality. Yet it is precisely in America, and nowhere in America more than in the West, that liberty and equality always go coupled and inseparable in popular speech; where the sense of liberty is especially strong, there also the devotion to equality is a cardinal doctrine. Throughout our history, the West has been a dominant factor in urging the extension of the powers of the national government, and western states have taken the lead in radical legislation of an equalizing character. This apparent inconsistency strikes one as especially pronounced in Kansas. The doctrine of equality is unquestioned there, and that governments exist for the purpose of securing it is the common belief. " A law against it " is the specific for every malady. The welfare of society is thought to be always superior to that of the individual, and yet no one doubts that perfect liberty is the birthright of every man.

Perhaps the truth is that real toleration is a sentiment foreign to the American temper. Toleration is for the skeptical, being the product of much thought or of great indifference; sometimes, to be sure, a mere *modus vivendi* forced upon a heterogeneous society. In America we imagine ourselves liberal-minded because we tolerate what we have ceased to regard as important. We tolerate religions but not irreligion, and diverse political opinion but not unpolitical opinion, customs but not the negation of custom. The Puritans fought for toleration — for themselves. But having won it for themselves, they straightway denied it to others. No small part of American history has been a repetition of the Puritan struggle; it has been a fight, not for toleration as a general principle, but for recognition of a civilization resting upon particular principles: in exterior relations, a struggle for recognition of America by Europe; in interior relations, a struggle for recognition of " the West " by " the East." The principle of toleration is written in our constitutions but not in our minds, for the motive back of the famous guarantees of individual liberty has been recognition of particular opinion rather than toleration of every opinion. And in the nature of the case it must be so. Those who create frontiers and establish new civilizations have too much faith to be tolerant, and are too thoroughgoing idealists to be indifferent. On the frontier conditions are too hazardous for the speculative and the academic to flourish readily: only those who are right and are sure of it can succeed. Certainly it is characteristic of Americans to know that they are right. Certainly they are conscious of having a mission in the world and of having been faithful to it. They have solved great problems hitherto unsolved, have realized utopias dreamed of but never realized by Europe. They are therefore in the van of civilization, quite sure of the direction, triumphantly leading the march towards the ultimate goal. That everyone should do as he likes is part of the American creed only in a very limited sense. That it is possible to know what is right, and that what is right should be recognized and adhered to, is the more vital belief.

That liberty and equality are compatible terms is, at all events, an unquestioned faith in Kansas. The belief in equality, however, is not so much the belief that all men are equal as the conviction that it is the business of society to establish conditions that will make them so. In Kansas at least, no one holds to the right of the individual to do as he likes, irrespective of what it is that he likes. Faith in the individual is faith in the particular individual, the true Kansan, who has learned through adversity voluntarily to conform to what is necessary. Human nature — or, at all events, Kansas nature — is essentially good, and if the environment is right all men can measure up to that high level. That the right environment can be created is not doubted. It is not possible for men so aggressive and self-reliant, who have overcome so many obstacles, to doubt their ability to accomplish this also. Having conquered nature, they cheerfully confront the task of transforming human nature. It is precisely because Kansans are such thoroughgoing individualists, so resourceful, so profoundly confident in their own judgments, so emancipated from the past, so accustomed to devising expedients for every new difficulty, that they are unimpressed by the record of the world's failures. They have always thrived on the impossible, and the field of many failures offers a challenge not to be resisted.

To effect these beneficent ends, the people of Kansas turn naturally to the government because they have a very simple and practical idea of what the government is and what it is for. Kansans think of the government, as they think of everything else, in terms of the concrete. And why, indeed, should they not? Within the memory of man there was no government in Kansas. They, Kansans, made the government themselves for their own purposes. The government is therefore simply certain men employed by themselves to do certain things; it is the sum of the energy, the good judgment, the resourcefulness of the individuals who originally created it and who periodically renew it. The government is the individual writ large; in it every Kansan sees himself drawn to larger scale. Of a government hostile to the individual, they cannot conceive; such a government is a bogus government, and its laws are bogus laws; to resist and overthrow such a government, all the initiative and resourcefulness is enlisted that is devoted to supporting one regarded as legitimate. There is a higher law than the statute book; the law of the state is no law if it does not represent the will of the individual.

To identify the will of the individual with the will of society in this easy fashion presupposes a certain solidarity in the community: an identity of race, custom, habits, needs; a consensus of opinion in respect to morals and politics. Kansas is such a community. Its people are principally American-born, descended from settlers who came mainly from the Middle West. It is an agricultural state, and the conditions of life are, or have been until recently, much the same for all. And the feeling of solidarity resulting from identity of race and uniformity of custom has been accentuated by the peculiar history of the state. Kansans love each other for the dangers they have passed; a unique experience has created a strong *esprit de corps* — a feeling that while Kansans are different from others, one Kansan is not only as good as any other, but very like any other. The philosophy of numbers, the doctrine of the majority, is therefore ingrained, and little sympathy is wasted on minorities. Rousseau's notion that minorities are only mistaken finds ready acceptance, and the will of the individual is easily identified with the will of society.

And in a sense the doctrine is true enough, for there is little difference of opinion on fundamental questions. In religion there are many creeds and many churches, but the difference between them is regarded as unimportant. There is, however, a quite absolute dogmatism of morality. Baptism is for those who enjoy it, but the moral life is for all. And what constitutes the moral life is well understood: to be honest and pay your debts; to be friendly and charitable, good-humored but not cynical, slow to take offense, but regarding life as profoundly serious; to respect sentiments and harmless prejudices; to revere the conventional great ideas and traditions; to live a sober life and a chaste one — to these they lay hold without questioning. Likewise in politics. One may be a Democrat or Republican, stalwart or square-dealer, insurgent or standpatter: it is no vital matter. But no one dreams of denying democracy, the will of the people, the greatest good to the greatest number, equal justice and equal opportunity to all. Whether in respect to politics or economics, education or morals, the consensus of opinion is very nearly perfect: it is an opinion that unites in the deification of the average, that centers in the dogmatism of the general level.

It goes without saying that the general level in Kansas is thought to be exceptionally high. Kansans do not regard themselves as mere Westerners, like Iowans or Nebraskans. Having passed through a superior heat, they are Westerners seven times refined. " It is the quality of piety in Kansas," says Mr. E. H. Abbott, " to thank God that you are not as other men are, beer-drinkers, shiftless, habitual lynchers, or even as these Missourians." The pride is natural enough, perhaps, in men whose judgment has been vindicated at last in the face of general skepticism. Kansans have endured Job's comforters too long not to feel a little complaisant when their solemn predictions come to naught. " While envious rivals were jeering, . . . pointing with scorn's slow unmoving finger at the droughts, grasshoppers, hot winds, crop failures, and other calamities of Kansas, the world was suddenly startled and dazzled by her collective display of . . . products at the Centennial at Philadelphia, which received the highest awards." It is inevitable that those who think they have fashioned a cornerstone out of the stone rejected by the builders should regard themselves as superior workmen.

To test others by this high standard is an instinctive procedure. There is an alert attention to the quality of those who enter the state from outside. The crucial question is: Are they " our kind of men "? Do they speak " the Kansas language "? Yet the Kansas language is less a form of speech, or the expression of particular ideas, than a certain personal quality. Some time since a distinguished visitor from the East came to the state to deliver a public address. He was most hospitably received, as all visitors are, whether distinguished or otherwise, and his address — permeated with the idealistic liberalism of a half century ago — was attentively listened to and highly praised. But to no purpose all these fine ideas. The great man was found wanting, for there was discovered, among his other impedimenta, a valet. It was a fatal mischance. The poor valet was more commented upon than the address, more observed than his master. The circumstance stamped the misguided man as clearly not our kind of man.

Obviously, no man who carries a valet can speak the Kansas language. Needless to say, there are no valets in Kansas.

The feeling of superiority naturally attaching to a chosen people equally inclines Kansans to dispense readily with the advice or experience of others. They feel that those who have worn the hair shirt cannot be instructed in asceticism by those who wear silk. In discussing the university and its problems with a member of the state legislature, I once hazarded some comparative statistics showing that a number of other states made rather more liberal appropriations for their universities than the state of Kansas did for hers. I thought the comparison might be enlightening, that the man's pride of state might be touched. Not at all. "I know all about that," he replied. "That argument is used by every man who is interested in larger appropriations for any of the state institutions. But it doesn't go with a Kansas legislature. In Kansas, we don't care much what other states are doing. Kansas always leads, but never follows." And, in fact, the disregard of precedent is almost an article of faith; that a thing has been done before is an indication that it is time to improve upon it. History may teach that men cannot be legislated into the kingdom of heaven. Kansans are not ignorant of the fact, but it is no concern of theirs. The experience of history is not for men with a mission and faith to perform it. Let the uncertain and the timid profit by history; those who have at all times the courage of their emotions will make history, not repeat it. Kansans set their own standards, and the state becomes, as it were, an experiment station in the field of social science.

The passion for equality in Kansas is thus the complement of the individualism and the idealism of its people. It has at the basis of it an altruistic motive, aiming not so much to level all men down as to level all men up. The Kansan's sense of individual worth enables him to believe that no one can be better than he is, while his confident idealism encourages him to hope that none need be worse.

IV

The Kansas spirit is the American spirit double-distilled. It is a new grafted product of American individualism, American idealism, American intolerance. Kansas is America in microcosm: as America conceives itself in respect to Europe, so Kansas conceives itself in respect to America. Within its borders Americanism, pure and undefiled, has a new lease of life. It is the mission of this self-selected people to see to it that it does not perish from off the earth. The light on the altar, however neglected elsewhere, must ever be replenished in Kansas. If this is provincialism, it is the provincialism of faith rather than of the province. The devotion to the state is devotion to an ideal, not to a territory, and men can say " Dear old Kansas! " because the name symbolizes for them what the motto of the state so well expresses, *ad astra per aspera*.

Benjamin Franklin

Information to Those Who Would Remove to America

MANY persons in Europe, having directly or by letters expressed to the writer of this, who is well acquainted with North America, their desire of transporting and establishing themselves in that country; but who appear to have formed, through ignorance, mistaken ideas and expectations of what is to be obtained there; he thinks it may be useful, and prevent inconvenient, expensive, and fruitless removals and voyages of improper persons, if he gives some clearer and truer notions of that part of the world than appear to have hitherto prevailed.

He finds it is imagined by numbers that the inhabitants of North America are rich — capable of rewarding, and disposed to reward, all sorts of ingenuity; that they are at the same time ignorant of all the sciences, and, consequently, that strangers possessing talents in the belles-lettres, fine arts, etc., must be highly esteemed and so well paid as to become easily rich themselves; that there are also abundance of profitable offices to be disposed of, which the natives are not qualified to fill; and that, having few persons of family among them, strangers of birth must be greatly respected, and of course easily obtain the best of those offices, which will make all their fortunes; that the governments too, to encourage emigrations from Europe, not only pay the expense of personal transportation but give lands gratis to strangers, with Negroes to work for them, utensils of husbandry, and stocks of cattle. These are all wild imaginations; and those who go to America with expectations founded upon them will surely find themselves disappointed.

The truth is that, though there are in that country few people so miserable as the poor of Europe, there are also very few that in Europe would be called rich; it is rather a general happy mediocrity that prevails. There are few great proprietors of the soil, and few tenants; most people cultivate their own lands or follow some handicraft or merchandise; very few are rich enough to live idly upon their rents or incomes, or to pay the highest prices given in Europe for painting, statues, architecture, and the other works of art that are more curious than useful. Hence the natural geniuses that have arisen in America with such talents have uniformly quitted that country for Europe, where they can be more suitably rewarded. It is true that letters and mathematical knowledge are in esteem there, but they are at the same time more common than is apprehended; there being already existing nine colleges or universities, viz. four in New England, and one in each of the provinces of New York, New Jersey, Pennsylvania,

A pamphlet published in England, c. 1782.

Maryland, and Virginia, all furnished with learned professors; besides a number of smaller academies; these educate many of their youth in the languages and those sciences that qualify men for the professions of divinity, law, or physic. Strangers indeed are by no means excluded from exercising those professions; and the quick increase of inhabitants everywhere gives them a chance of employ, which they have in common with the natives. Of civil offices or employments there are few; no superfluous ones, as in Europe; and it is a rule established in some of the states, that no office should be so profitable as to make it desirable. The thirty-sixth article of the Constitution of Pennsylvania runs expressly in these words: " As every freeman, to preserve his independence (if he has not a sufficient estate), ought to have some profession, calling, trade, or farm, whereby he may honestly subsist, there can be no necessity for, nor use in, establishing offices of profit; the usual effects of which are dependence and servility unbecoming freemen, in the possessors and expectants; faction, contention, corruption, and disorder among the people. Wherefore, whenever an office, through increase of fees or otherwise, becomes so profitable as to occasion many to apply for it, the profits ought to be lessened by the legislature."

These ideas prevailing more or less in all the United States, it cannot be worth any man's while, who has a means of living at home, to expatriate himself, in hopes of obtaining a profitable civil office in America; and as to military offices, they are at an end with the war, the armies being disbanded. Much less is it advisable for a person to go thither who has no other quality to recommend him but his birth. In Europe it has indeed its value; but it is a commodity that cannot be carried to a worse market than that of America, where people do not inquire, concerning a stranger, *What is he?* but *What can he do?* If he has any useful art, he is welcome; and if he exercises it and behaves well, he will be respected by all that know him; but a mere man of quality who, on that account, wants to live upon the public, by some office or salary, will be despised and disregarded. The husbandman is in honor there, and even the mechanic, because their employments are useful. The people have a saying that God Almighty is himself a mechanic, the greatest in the universe; and he is respected and admired more for the variety, ingenuity, and utility of his handiworks than for the antiquity of his family. They are pleased with the observation of a Negro, and frequently mention it, that *Boccarora* (meaning the white man) *make de black man workee, make de horse workee, make de ox workee, make ebery ting workee; only de hog. He, de hog, no workee; he eat, he drink, he walk about, he go to sleep when he please, he libb like a gemtleman.* According to these opinions of the Americans, one of them would think himself more obliged to a genealogist who could prove for him that his ancestors and relations for ten generations had been plowmen, smiths, carpenters, turners, weavers, tanners, or even shoemakers — and consequently that they were useful members of society — than if he could only prove that they were gentlemen, doing nothing of value, but living idly on the labor of others, mere *fruges consumere nati,* and otherwise *good for nothing,* till by their death their estates, like the carcass of the Negro's gentleman-hog, come to be *cut up.*

With regard to encouragements for strangers from government, they are really only what are derived from good laws and liberty. Strangers are welcome because there is room enough for them all, and therefore the old inhabitants are not jealous of them; the laws protect them sufficiently, so that they have no need of the patronage of great men; and everyone will enjoy securely the profits of his industry. But if he does not bring a fortune with him, he must work and be industrious to live. One or two years' residence gives him all the rights of a citizen; but the government does not at present, whatever it may have done in former times, hire people to become settlers, by paying their passages, giving land, Negroes, utensils, stock, or any other kind of emolument whatsoever. In short, America is the land of labor, and by no means what the English called *Lubberland,* and the French *Pays de Cocagne,* where the streets are said to be paved with half-peck loaves, the houses tiled with pancakes, and where the fowls fly about ready roasted, crying, *Come eat me!*

Who then are the kind of persons to whom an emigration to America may be advantageous? And what are the advantages they may reasonably expect?

Land being cheap in that country, from the vast forests still void of inhabitants, and not likely to be occupied in an age to come, insomuch that the propriety of an hundred acres of fertile soil full of wood may be obtained near the frontiers, in many places, for eight or ten guineas, hearty young laboring men, who understand the husbandry of corn and cattle, which is nearly the same in that country as in Europe, may easily establish themselves there. A little money saved of the good wages they receive there, while they work for others, enables them to buy the land and begin their plantation, in which they are assisted by the good will of their neighbors, and some credit. Multitudes of poor people from England, Ireland, Scotland, and Germany have by this means in a few years become wealthy farmers, who in their own countries, where all the lands are fully occupied and the wages of labor low, could never have emerged from the poor condition wherein they were born.

From the salubrity of the air, the healthiness of the climate, the plenty of good provisions, and the encouragement to early marriages by the certainty of subsistence in cultivating the earth, the increase of inhabitants by natural generation is very rapid in America and becomes still more so by the accession of strangers; hence there is a continual demand for more artisans of all the necessary and useful kinds, to supply those cultivators of the earth with houses and with furniture and utensils of the grosser sorts which cannot so well be brought from Europe. Tolerably good workmen in any of those mechanic arts are sure to find employ, and to be well paid for their work, there being no restraints preventing strangers from exercising any art they understand, nor any permission necessary. If they are poor, they begin first as servants or journeymen; and if they are sober, industrious, and frugal, they soon become masters, establish themselves in business, marry, raise families, and become respectable citizens.

Also, persons of moderate fortunes and capitals, who, having a number of children to provide for, are desirous of bringing them up to industry, and to secure estates for their posterity, have opportunities of doing it, in America, which Europe does not afford. There they may be taught and practice profitable mechanic arts without incurring disgrace on that account, but on the contrary acquiring respect by such abilities. There small capitals laid out in lands, which daily become more valuable by the increase of people, afford a solid prospect of ample fortunes thereafter for those children. The writer of this has known several instances of large tracts of land, bought, on what was then the frontier of Pennsylvania, for ten pounds per hundred acres, which, when the settlements had been extended far beyond them, sold readily, without any improvement made upon them, for three pounds per acre. The acre in America is the same with the English acre or the acre of Normandy.

Those who desire to understand the state of government in America would do well to read the constitutions of the several states, and the articles of confederation that bind the whole together for general purposes, under the direction of one assembly, called the Congress. These constitutions have been printed, by order of Congress, in America; two editions of them have also been printed in London; and a good translation of them into French has lately been published at Paris.

Several of the princes of Europe of late, from an opinion of advantage to arise by producing all commodities and manufactures within their own dominions, so as to diminish or render useless their importations, have endeavored to entice workmen from other countries by high salaries, privileges, etc. Many persons, pretending to be skilled in various great manufactures, imagining that America must be in want of them and that the Congress would probably be disposed to imitate the princes above mentioned, have proposed to go over, on condition of having their passages paid, lands given, salaries appointed, exclusive privileges for terms of years, etc. Such persons, on reading the articles of confederation, will find that the Congress have no power committed to them, nor money put into their hands, for such purposes; and that if any such encouragement is given, it must be by the government of some separate state. This, however, has rarely been done in America; and when it has been done, it has rarely succeeded so to establish a manufacture which the country was not yet so ripe for as to encourage private persons to set it up: labor being generally too dear there, and hands difficult to be kept together; everyone desiring to be a master, and the cheapness of lands inclining many to leave trades for agriculture. Some indeed have met with success, and are carried on to advantage; but they are generally such as require only a few hands, or wherein great part of the work is performed by machines. Goods that are bulky, and of so small value as not well to bear the expense of freight, may often be made cheaper in the country than they can be imported; and the manufacture of such goods will be profitable wherever there is a sufficient demand. The farmers in America produce indeed a good deal of wool and flax, and none is exported — it is all worked up; but it is in the way of domestic manufacture, for the use of the family. The buying up of quantities of wool and flax, with the design to employ spinners, weavers, etc., and form great establishments producing quantities of linen and woolen goods for sale, has been several times attempted in different provinces; but those projects have generally failed, goods of equal value being imported cheaper. And when the governments have been solicited to support such schemes by encouragements in money, or by imposing duties on importation of such goods, it has been generally refused, on this principle: that if the country is ripe for the manufacture, it may be carried on by private persons to advantage; and if not, it is a folly to think of forcing nature. Great establishments of manufacture require great numbers of poor to do the work for small wages; those poor are to be found in Europe, but will not be found in America till the lands are all taken up and cultivated and the excess of people, who cannot get land, want employment. The manufacture of silk, they say, is natural in France, as that of cloth in England, because each country produces in plenty the first material; but if England will have a manufacture of silk as well as that of cloth, and France of cloth as well as that of silk, these un-natural operations must be supported by mutual prohibitions, or high duties on the importation of each other's goods; by which means the workmen are en-abled to tax the home consumer by greater prices, while the higher wages they receive makes them neither happier nor richer, since they only drink more and work less. Therefore the governments in America do nothing to encourage such projects. The people, by this means, are not imposed on, either by the mer-chant or mechanic. If the merchant demands too much profit on imported shoes, they buy of the shoemaker; and if he asks too high a price, they take them of the merchant; thus the two professions are checks on each other. The shoemaker, however, has on the whole a considerable profit upon his labor in America, be-yond what he had in Europe, as he can add to his price a sum nearly equal to all the expenses of freight and commission, risk or insurance, etc., necessarily charged by the merchant. And the case is the same with the workmen in every other mechanic art. Hence it is that artisans generally live better and more easily in America than in Europe; and such as are good economists make a comfortable provision for age and for their children. Such may, therefore, remove with ad-vantage to America.

In the long-settled countries of Europe, all arts, trades, professions, farms, etc., are so full that it is difficult for a poor man, who has children, to place them where they may gain, or learn to gain, a decent livelihood. The artisans, who fear creating future rivals in business, refuse to take apprentices but upon condi-tions of money, maintenance, or the like, which the parents are unable to comply with. Hence the youth are dragged up in ignorance of every gainful art and obliged to become soldiers, or servants, or thieves, for a subsistence. In America, the rapid increase of inhabitants takes away that fear of rivalship, and artisans willingly receive apprentices from the hope of profit by their labor, during the remainder of the time stipulated, after they shall be instructed. Hence it is easy for poor families to get their children instructed; for the artisans are so desirous of apprentices that many of them will even give money to the parents to have boys from ten to fifteen years of age bound apprentices to them till the age of twenty-one; and many poor parents have, by that means, on their arrival in the country, raised money enough to buy land sufficient to establish themselves and to subsist the rest of their family by agriculture. These contracts for apprentices are made before a magistrate, who regulates the agreement according to reason and justice and, having in view the formation of a future and useful citizen, obliges the master to engage, by a written indenture, not only that, during the time of service stipulated, the apprentice shall be duly provided with meat, drink, apparel, washing, and lodging, and, at its expiration, with a complete new suit of clothes, but also that he shall be taught to read, write, and cast accounts; and that he shall be well instructed in the art or profession of his master, or some other, by which he may afterwards gain a livelihood and be able in his turn to raise a family. A copy of this indenture is given to the apprentice or his friends, and the magistrate keeps a record of it, to which recourse may be had in case of failure by the master in any point of performance. This desire among the masters, to have more hands employed in working for them, induces them to pay the passages of young persons, of both sexes, who, on their arrival, agree to serve them one, two, three, or four years; those who have already learned a trade agreeing for a shorter term, in proportion to their skill and the consequent immediate value of their service; and those who have none agreeing for a longer term, in consideration of being taught an art their poverty would not permit them to acquire in their own country.

The almost general mediocrity of fortune that prevails in America obliging its people to follow some business for subsistence, those vices that arise usually from idleness are in a great measure prevented. Industry and constant employment are great preservatives of the morals and virtue of a nation. Hence bad examples to youth are more rare in America, which must be a comfortable consideration to parents. To this may be truly added that serious religion, under its various denominations, is not only tolerated but respected and practiced. Atheism is unknown there; infidelity rare and secret; so that persons may live to a great age in that country without having their piety shocked by meeting with either an atheist or an infidel. And the Divine Being seems to have manifested his approbation of the mutual forbearance and kindness with which the different sects treat each other, by the remarkable prosperity with which he has been pleased to favor the whole country.

Vernon L. Parrington

Changing America

I

THE pot was boiling briskly in America in the tumultuous postwar years. The country had definitely entered upon its freedom and was settling its disordered household to suit its democratic taste. Everywhere new ways were feverishly at work transforming the countryside. In the South another order was rising uncertainly on the ruins of the plantation system; in the

From *Main Currents in American Thought*, III, 1930.

East an expanding factory economy was weaving a different pattern of industrial life; in the Middle Border a recrudescent agriculture was arising from the application of the machine to the rich prairie soil. All over the land a spider web of iron rails was being spun that was to draw the remotest outposts into the common whole and bind the nation together with steel bands. Nevertheless two diverse worlds lay on the map of continental America. Facing in opposite directions and holding different faiths, they would not travel together easily or take comfort from the yoke that joined them. Agricultural America, behind which lay two and a half centuries of experience, was a decentralized world, democratic, individualistic, suspicious; industrial America, behind which lay only half a dozen decades of bustling experiment, was a centralizing world, capitalistic, feudal, ambitious. The one was a decaying order, the other a rising; and between them would be friction till one or the other had become master.

Continental America was still half frontier and half settled country. A thin line of homesteads had been thrust westward till the outposts reached well into the Middle Border — an uncertain thread running through eastern Minnesota, Nebraska, Kansas; overleaping the Indian Territory, and then running west into Texas — approximately halfway between the Atlantic and the Pacific. Behind these outposts was still much unoccupied land, and beyond stretched the unfenced prairies till they merged in the sagebrush plains, gray and waste, that stretched to the foothills of the Rocky Mountains. Beyond the mountains were other stretches of plains and deserts, vast and forbidding in their alkali blight, to the wooded coast ranges and the Pacific Ocean. In all this immense territory were only scattered settlements — at Denver, Salt Lake City, Sacramento, San Francisco, Portland, Seattle, and elsewhere — tiny outposts in the wilderness, with scattered hamlets, mining camps, and isolated homesteads lost in the great expanse. On the prairies from Mexico to Canada — across which rumbled great herds of buffalo — roved powerful tribes of hostile Indians who fretted against the forward thrust of settlement and disputed the right of possession. The urgent business of the times was the subduing of this wild region, wresting it from Indians and buffalo and wilderness; and the forty years that lay between the California gold rush of '49 and the Oklahoma land rush of '89 saw the greatest wave of pioneer expansion — the swiftest and most reckless — in all our pioneer experience. Expansion on so vast a scale necessitated building, and the seventies became the railway age, bonding the future to break down present barriers of isolation, and opening new territories for later exploitation. The reflux of the great movement swept back upon the Atlantic coast and gave to life there a fresh note of spontaneous vigor, of which the Gilded Age was the inevitable expression.

It was this energetic East, with its accumulations of liquid capital awaiting investment and its factories turning out the materials needed to push the settlements westward, that profited most from the conquest of the Far West. The impulsion from the frontier did much to drive forward the industrial revolution. The war that brought devastation to the South had been more friendly to Northern interests. In gathering the scattered rills of capital into central reservoirs at Philadelphia and New York, and in expanding the factory system to supply the needs of the armies, it had opened to capitalism its first clear view of the Promised Land. The bankers had come into control of the liquid wealth of the nation, and the industrialists had learned to use the machine for production; the time was ripe for exploitation on a scale undreamed-of a generation before. Up till then the potential resources of the continent had not even been surveyed. Earlier pioneers had only scratched the surface — felling trees, making crops, building pygmy watermills, smelting a little iron. Mineral wealth had been scarcely touched. Tools had been lacking to develop it, capital had been lacking, transportation lacking, technical methods lacking, markets lacking.

In the years following the war, exploitation for the first time was provided with adequate resources and a competent technique, and busy prospectors were daily uncovering new sources of wealth. The coal and oil of Pennsylvania and Ohio, the copper and iron ore of upper Michigan, the gold and silver, lumber and fisheries, of the Pacific coast, provided limitless raw materials for the rising industrialism. The Bessemer process quickly turned an age of iron into an age of steel and created the great rolling mills of Pittsburgh from which issued the rails for expanding railways. The reaper and binder, the sulky plow and the threshing machine, created large-scale agriculture on the fertile prairies. Wild grasslands provided grazing for immense herds of cattle and sheep; the development of the corn belt enormously increased the supply of hogs; and with railways at hand the Middle Border poured into Omaha and Kansas City and Chicago an endless stream of produce. As the line of the frontier pushed westward new towns were built, thousands of homesteads were filed on, and the speculator and promoter hovered over the prairies like buzzards seeking their carrion. With rising land values money was to be made out of unearned increment, and the creation of booms was a profitable industry. The times were stirring and it was a shiftless fellow who did not make his pile. If he had been too late to file on desirable acres, he had only to find a careless homesteader who had failed in some legal technicality and "jump his claim." Good bottom land could be had even by latecomers if they were sharp at the game.

This bustling America of 1870 accounted itself a democratic world. A free people had put away all aristocratic privileges and, conscious of its power, went forth to possess the last frontier. Its social philosophy, which it found adequate to its needs, was summed up in three words — preëmption, exploitation, progress. Its immediate and pressing business was to dispossess the government of its rich holdings. Lands in the possession of the government were so much idle waste, untaxed and profitless; in private hands they would be developed. They would provide work, pay taxes, support schools, enrich the community. Preëmption meant exploitation, and exploitation meant progress. It was a simple philosophy and it suited the simple individualism of the times. The Gilded Age knew nothing of the Enlightenment; it recognized only the acquisitive instinct. That much, at least, the frontier had taught the great American democracy; and, in applying to the resource of a continent the lesson it had been so well taught, the Gilded Age wrote a profoundly characteristic chapter of American history.

II

In a moment of special irritation Edwin Lawrence Godkin called the civilization of the seventies a chromo civilization. Mark Twain, with his slack Western standards, was equally severe. As he contemplated the slovenly reality beneath the gaudy exterior he dubbed it the Gilded Age. Other critics with a gift for pungent phrase have flung their gibes at the ways of a picturesque and uncouth generation. There is reason in plenty for such caustic comment. Heedless, irreverent, unlovely, cultivating huge beards, shod in polished top-boots — the last refinement of the farmer's cowhides — wearing linen dickeys over hickory shirts, moving through pools of tobacco juice, erupting in shoddy and grotesque architecture, cluttering its homes with ungainly walnut chairs and marble-topped tables and heavy lambrequins, the decade of the seventies was only too plainly mired and floundering in a gob of bad taste. A world of triumphant and unabashed vulgarity without its like in our history, it was not aware of its plight, but accounted its manners genteel and boasted of ways that were a parody on sober good sense.

Yet just as such comments are, they do not reach quite to the heart of the age. They emphasize rather the excrescences, the casual lapses, of a generation that underneath its crudities and vulgarities was boldly adventurous and creative — a generation in which the democratic freedoms of America, as those freedoms had taken shape during a drab frontier experience, came at last to spontaneous and vivid expression. If its cultural wealth was less than it thought, if in its exuberance it was engaged somewhat too boisterously in stamping its own plebeian image on the work of its hands, it was only natural to a society that for the first time found its opportunities equal to its desires, a youthful society that accounted the world its oyster and wanted no restrictions laid on its will. It was the ripe fruit of Jacksonian leveling, and if it ran to a grotesque individualism — if in its self-confidence it was heedless of the smiles of older societies — it was nevertheless by reason of its uncouthness the most picturesque generation in our history; and for those who love to watch human nature disporting itself with naïve abandon, running amuck through all the conventions, no other age provides so fascinating a spectacle.

When the cannon at last had ceased their destruction it was a strange new America that looked out confidently on the scene. Something had been released by the upheavals of half a century — something strong and assertive that was prepared to take possession of the continent. It did not issue from the loins of war. Its origins must be sought elsewhere, further back in time. It had been cradled in the vast changes that since 1815 had been reshaping America: in the breakup of the old domestic economy that kept life mean and drab, in the noisy enthusiasms of the new coonskin democracy, in the romanticisms of the California gold rush, in the boisterous freedoms discovered by the forties and fifties. It had come to manhood in the battles of a tremendous war, and as it now surveyed the continent, discovering potential wealth before unknown, it demanded only freedom and opportunity — a fair race and no favors. Everywhere was a welling up of primitive pagan desires after long repressions — to grow rich, to grasp power, to be strong and masterful and lay the world at its feet. It was a violent reaction from the narrow poverty of frontier life and the narrow inhibitions of backwoods religion. It had had enough of skimpy, meager ways — of scrubbing along hoping for something to turn up. It would go out and turn it up. It was consumed with a great hunger for abundance, for the good things of life, for wealth. It was frankly materialistic, and if material goods could be wrested from society it would lay its hands heartily to the work. Freedom and opportunity, to acquire, to possess, to enjoy — for that it would sell its soul.

Society of a sudden was become fluid. With the sweeping away of the last aristocratic restraints the potentialities of the common man found release for self-assertion. Strange figures, sprung from obscure origins, thrust themselves everywhere upon the scene. In the reaction from the mean and skimpy, a passionate will to power was issuing from unexpected sources; undisciplined, confused in ethical values, but endowed with immense vitality. Individualism was being simplified to the acquisitive instinct. These new Americans were primitive souls, ruthless, predatory, capable; single-minded men; rogues and rascals often, but never feeble, never hindered by petty scruple, never given to puling or whining — the raw materials of a race of capitalistic buccaneers. Out of the drab mass of common plebeian life had come this vital energy that erupted in amazing abundance and in strange forms. The new freedoms meant diverse things to different men, and each like Jurgen followed after his own wishes and his own desires. Pirate and priest issued from the common source and played their parts with the same picturesqueness. The romantic age of Captain Kidd was come again, and the black flag and the gospel banner were both in lockers to be flown as the needs of the cruise determined. With all coercive restrictions put away the democratic genius of America was setting out on the road of manifest destiny.

Analyze the most talked-of men of the age and one is likely to find a splendid audacity coupled with an immense wastefulness. A note of tough-mindedness marks them. They had stout nippers. They fought their way encased in rhinoceros hides. There was the Wall Street crowd — Daniel Drew, Commodore Vanderbilt, Jim Fisk, Jay Gould, Russell Sage — blackguards for the most part, railway wreckers, cheaters and swindlers, but picturesque in their rascality. There was the numerous tribe of politicians — Boss Tweed, Fernando Wood, G. Oakey Hall, Senator Pomeroy, Senator Cameron, Roscoe Conkling, James G. Blaine — blackguards also for the most part, looting city treasuries, buying and selling legislative votes like railway stock, but picturesque in their audacity. There were the professional keepers of the public morals — Anthony Comstock, John B. Gough, Dwight L. Moody, Henry Ward Beecher, T. De Witt Talmage — ardent proselytizers, unintellectual, men of one idea, but fiery in zeal and eloquent in description of the particular heaven each wanted to people with his fellow Americans. And springing up like mushrooms after a rain was the goodly company of cranks — Victoria Woodhull and Tennessee Claflin, " Citizen " George Francis Train, Henry Bergh, Ben Butler, Ignatius Donnelly, Bob Ingersoll, Henry George — picturesque figures with a flair for publicity who tilled their special fields with splendid gestures. And finally there was Barnum the Showman, growing rich on the profession of humbuggery, a vulgar greasy genius, pure brass without any gilding, yet in picturesque and capable effrontery the very embodiment of the age. A marvelous company, vital with the untamed energy of a new land. In the presence of such men one begins to understand what Walt Whitman meant by his talk of the elemental.

Created by a primitive world that knew not the machine, they were marked by the rough homeliness of their origins. Whether wizened or fat they were never insignificant or commonplace. On the whole one prefers them fat, and for solid bulk what generation has outdone them? There was Revivalist Moody, bearded and neckless, with his two hundred and eighty pounds of Adam's flesh, every ounce of which "belonged to God." There was a lyric Sankey, afflicted with two hundred and twenty-five pounds of human frailty, yet looking as smug as a banker and singing "There were ninety and nine" divinely through mutton-chop whiskers. There was Boss Tweed, phlegmatic and mighty, overawing re-bellious gangsters at the City Hall with his two hundred and forty pounds of pugnacious rascality. There was John Fiske, a philosophic hippopotamus, warm-ing the chill waters of Spencerian science with his prodigious bulk. There was Ben Butler, oily and puffy and wheezy, like Falstaff larding the lean earth as he walked along, who yearly added more flesh to the scant ninety-seven pounds he carried away from Waterville College. And there was Jim Fisk, dressed like a bartender, huge in nerve as in bulk, driving with the dashing Josie Mansfield down Broadway — prince of vulgarians, who jovially proclaimed, " I worship in the Synagogue of the Libertines," and who on the failure of the Erie coup announced cheerfully, " Nothing is lost save honor! "

Impressive as are the fat kine of Egypt, the lean kine scarcely suffer by con-trast. There were giants of puny physique in those days. There was Uncle Dan'l Drew, thin as a dried herring, yet a builder of churches and founder of Drew Theological Seminary, who pilfered and cheated his way to wealth with tobacco juice drooling from his mouth. There was Jay Gould, a lone-hand gambler, a dynamo in a tubercular body, who openly invested in the devil's tenements as likely to pay better dividends, and went home to potter lovingly amongst his exotic flowers. And there was Oakey Hall, clubman and playwright, small, ele-gant, and unscrupulous; and Victoria Woodhull who stirred up the Beecher case, a wisp of a woman who enraged all the frumpy bluestockings by the smartness of her toilet and the perfection of her manners; and little Libby Tilton with her tiny wistful face and great eyes that looked out wonderingly at the world — eyes that were to go blind with weeping before the candle of her life went out. It was such men and women, individual and colorful, that Whitman and Mark Twain mingled with, and that Herman Melville — colossal and dynamic be-yond them all — looked out upon sardonically from his tomb in the Custom House where he was consuming his own heart.

They were thrown up as it were casually out of the huge caldron of energy that was America. All over the land were thousands like them, self-made men quick to lay hands on opportunity if it knocked at the door, ready to seek it out if it were slow in knocking, recognizing no limitations to their powers, discouraged by no shortcomings in their training. When Moody set out to bring the world to his Protestant God he was an illiterate shoe salesman who stumbled over the hard words of his King James Bible. Anthony Comstock, the roundsman of the Lord, was a salesman in a dry-goods shop, and as careless of his spelling as he was careful of his neighbors' morals. Commodore Vanderbilt, who built up the greatest fortune of the time, was a Brooklyn ferryman, hard-fisted and tough as a burr oak, who in a lifetime of over eighty years read only one book, *Pilgrim's Progress,* and that after he was seventy. Daniel Drew was a shyster cattle-drover, whose arid emotions found outlet in periodic conversions and backslidings, and who got on in this vale of tears by salting his cattle and increasing his — and the Lord's — wealth with every pound of water in their bellies — from which cleverness is said to have come the Wall Street phrase, "stock-watering." Jim Fisk was the son of a Yankee peddler, who, disdaining the unambitious ways of his father, set up for himself in a cart gilded like a circus wagon and drove about the countryside with jingling bells. After he had made his pile in Wall Street he set up his own opera house and proposed to rival the Medici as a patron of the arts — and especially of the artists if they were of the right sex. A surprising number of them — Moody, Beecher, Barnum, Fisk, Comstock, Ben Butler — came from New England; Jay Gould was of Connecticut ancestry; but Oakey Hall was a Southern gentleman; Fernando Wood, with the face of an Apollo and the wit of an Irishman, was the son of a Philadelphia cigar-maker and much of his early income was drawn from sailors' groggeries along the waterfront; Tweed was a stolid New Yorker, and Drew was a York State country boy.

What was happening in New York was symptomatic of the nation. If the temple of Plutus was building in Wall Street, his devotees were everywhere. In Chicago, rising higgledy-piggledy from the ashes of the great fire, Phil Armour and Nelson Morris were laying out stockyards and drawing the cattle and sheep and hogs from remote prairie farms to their slaughterhouses. In Cleveland, Mark Hanna was erecting his smelters and turning the iron ore of Michigan into dollars, while John D. Rockefeller was squeezing the small fry out of the petroleum business and creating the Standard Oil monopoly. In Pittsburgh, Andrew Carnegie was applying the Bessemer process to steelmaking and laying the foundations of the later steel trust. In Minneapolis, C. C. Washburn and Charles A. Pillsbury were applying new methods to milling and turning the northern wheat into flour to ship to the ends of the earth. In San Francisco, Leland Stanford and Collis P. Huntington were amassing huge fortunes out of the Southern Pacific Railway and bringing the commonwealth of California to their feet. Everywhere were boom-town and real-estate promoters, the lust of speculation, the hankering after quick and easy wealth.

In the great spaces from Kansas City to Sacramento the frontier spirit was in the gaudiest bloom. The experiences of three centuries of expansion were being crowded into as many decades. In the fifties the highway of the frontier had run up and down the Mississippi River and the golden age of steamboating had brought a motley life to St. Louis; in the seventies the frontier had passed far beyond and was pushing through the Rocky Mountains, repeating as it went the old frontier story of swagger and slovenliness, of boundless hope and heroic endurance — a story deeply marked with violence and crime and heartbreaking failure. Thousands of veterans from the disbanded armies, Northern and Southern alike, flocked to the West to seek their fortunes, and daily life there soon took on a drab note from the alkali of the plains; yet through the drabness ran a boisterous humor that exalted lying to a fine art — a humor that goes back to Davy Crockett and the Ohio flatboat-men. Mark Twain's *Roughing It* is the epic of this frontier of the Pony Express, as *Life on the Mississippi* is the epic of the preceding generation.

The huge wastefulness of the frontier was everywhere, East and West. The Gilded Age heeded somewhat too literally the Biblical injunction to take no thought for the morrow, but was busily intent on squandering the resources of the continent. All things were held cheap, and human life cheapest of all. Wild Bill Hickok with forty notches on his gun and a row of graves to his credit in Boot Hill Cemetery, and Jesse James, most picturesque of desperadoes, levying toll with his six-shooter on the bankers who were desecrating the free spirit of the plains with their two per cent a month, are familiar heroes in Wild West tales; but the real plainsman of the Gilded Age, the picturesque embodiment of the last frontier, was Captain Carver, the faultless horseman and faultless shot, engaged in his celebrated buffalo hunt for the championship of the prairies. Wagering that he could kill more buffalo in a day than any rival hero of the chase, he rode forth with his Indian marker, and dropping the miles behind him he left an endless trail of dead beasts properly tagged, winning handsomely when his rival's horse fell dead from exhaustion. It was magnificent. Davy Crockett's hundred and five bears in a season was but 'prentice work compared with Captain Carver's professional skill. It is small wonder that he became a hero of the day and his rifle, turned now to the circus business of breaking glass balls thrown from his running horse, achieved a fame far greater than Davy's Betsy. With his bold mustaches, his long black hair flying in the wind, his sombrero and chaps and top-boots, he was a figure matched only by Buffalo Bill, the last of the great plainsmen.

Captain Carver was picturesque, but what shall be said of the thousands of lesser Carvers engaged in the same slaughter, market-hunters who discovered a new industry in buffalo-killing? At the close of the Civil War the number on the western plains was estimated at fifteen millions. With the building of the Union Pacific Railroad they were cut asunder into two vast herds, and upon these herds fell the hunters with the new breech-loading rifles, shooting for the hide market that paid sixty-five cents for a bull's hide and a dollar and fifteen cents for a cow's. During the four years from 1871 to 1874 nearly a million head a year were slain from the southern herd alone, their skins ripped off and the carcasses left for the coyotes and buzzards. By the end of the hunting season of 1875 the vast southern herd had been wiped out, and with the building of the Northern Pacific in 1880 the smaller northern herd soon suffered the same fate. The buffalo were gone with the hostile Indians — Sioux and Blackfeet and Cheyennes and a dozen other tribes. It was the last dramatic episode of the American frontier, and it wrote a fitting climax to three centuries of wasteful conquest. But the prairies were tamed, and Wild Bill Hickok and Captain Carver and Buffalo Bill Cody had become romantic figures to enthrall the imagination of later generations.

It was an abundant harvest of those freedoms that America had long been struggling to achieve, and it was making ready the ground for later harvests that would be less to its liking. Freedom had become individualism, and individualism had become the inalienable right to preëmpt, to exploit, to squander. Gone were the old ideals along with the old restraints. The idealism of the forties, the romanticism of the fifties — all the heritage of Jeffersonianism and the French Enlightenment — were put thoughtlessly away, and with no social conscience, no concern for civilization, no heed for the future of the democracy it talked so much about, the Gilded Age threw itself into the business of money-getting. From the sober restraints of aristocracy, the old inhibitions of Puritanism, the niggardliness of an exacting domestic economy, it swung far back in reaction, and with the discovery of limitless opportunities for exploitation it allowed itself to get drunk. Figures of earth, they followed after their own dreams. Some were builders with grandiose plans in their pockets; others were wreckers with no plans at all. It was an anarchistic world of strong, capable men, selfish, unenlightened, amoral — an excellent example of what human nature will do with undisciplined freedom. In the Gilded Age freedom was the freedom of buccaneers preying on the argosies of Spain.

Within the next half century this picturesque America with its heritage of crude energy — greedy, lawless, capable — was to be transformed into a vast uniform middle-class land, dedicated to capitalism and creating the greatest machine order known to history. A scattered agricultural people, steeped in particularistic jealousies and suspicious of centralization, was to be transformed into an urbanized factory people, rootless, migratory, drawn to the job as by a magnet. It was to come about the more easily because the American farmer had never been a land-loving peasant, rooted to the soil and thriving only in daily contact with familiar acres. He had long been half middle-class, accounting unearned increment the most profitable crop, and buying and selling land as if it were calico. And in consequence the vigorous individualism that had sprung from frontier conditions decayed with the passing of the frontier, and those who had lost in the gamble of preëmption and exploitation were added to the growing multitude of the proletariat. It was from such materials, supplemented by a vast influx of immigrants, that was fashioned the America we know today with its standardized life, its machine culture, its mass psychology — an America to which Jefferson and Jackson and Lincoln would be strangers.

Frederick Lewis Allen

Crash!

I

EARLY in September the stock market broke. It quickly recovered, how-ever; indeed, on September 19 the averages as compiled by the New York *Times* reached an even higher level than that of September 3. Once more it slipped, farther and faster, until by October 4 the prices of a good many stocks had coasted to what seemed first-class bargain levels. Steel, for ex-ample, after having touched 261¾ a few weeks earlier, had dropped as low as 204; American Can, at the closing on October 4, was nearly twenty points below its high for the year; General Electric was over fifty points below its high; Radio had gone down from 114¾ to 82½.

A bad break, to be sure, but there had been other bad breaks, and the specu-lators who escaped unscathed proceeded to take advantage of the lesson they had learned in June and December of 1928 and March and May of 1929: when there was a break it was a good time to buy. In the face of all this tremendous liquidation, brokers' loans as compiled by the Federal Reserve Bank of New York mounted to a new high record on October 2, reaching $6,804,000,000 — a sure sign that margin buyers were not deserting the market but coming into it in numbers at least undiminished. (Part of the increase in the loan figure was probably due to the piling up of unsold securities in dealers' hands, as the spawn-ing of investment trusts and the issue of new common stock by every manner of business concern continued unabated.) History, it seemed, was about to repeat itself, and those who picked up Anaconda at 109¾ or American Telephone at 281 would count themselves wise investors. And sure enough, prices once more began to climb. They had already turned upward before that Sunday in early October when Ramsay MacDonald sat on a log with Herbert Hoover at the Rapidan camp and talked over the prospects for naval limitation and peace.

Something was wrong, however. The decline began once more. The wiseacres of Wall Street, looking about for causes, fixed upon the collapse of the Hatry financial group in England (which had led to much forced selling among for-eign investors and speculators), and upon the bold refusal of the Massachusetts Department of Public Utilities to allow the Edison Company of Boston to split up its stock. They pointed, too, to the fact that the steel industry was undoubtedly slipping, and to the accumulation of "undigested" securities. But there was little real alarm until the week of October 21. The consensus of opinion, in the meantime, was merely that the equinoctial storm of September had not quite blown over. The market was readjusting itself into a "more secure technical position."

From *Only Yesterday,* 1931.

II

In view of what was about to happen, it is enlightening to recall how things looked at this juncture to the financial prophets, those gentlemen whose wiz- ardly reputations were based upon their supposed ability to examine a set of graphs brought to them by a statistician and discover, from the relation of curve to curve and index to index, whether things were going to get better or worse. Their opinons differed, of course; there never has been a moment when the best financial opinion was unanimous. In examining these opinions and the outgiv- ings of eminent bankers, it must furthermore be acknowledged that a bullish statement cannot always be taken at its face value: few men like to assume the responsibility of spreading alarm by making dire predictions, nor is a banker with unsold securities on his hands likely to say anything which will make it more difficult to dispose of them, unquiet as his private mind may be. Finally, one must admit that prophecy is at best the most hazardous of occupations. Nevertheless, the general state of financial opinion in October, 1929, makes an instructive contrast with that in February and March, 1928, when, as we have seen, the skies had not appeared any too bright.

Some forecasters, to be sure, were so unconventional as to counsel caution. Roger W. Babson, an investment adviser who had not always been highly re- garded in the inner circles of Wall Street, especially since he had for a long time been warning his clients of future trouble, predicted early in September a decline of sixty or eighty points in the averages. On October 7 the Standard Trade and Securities Service of the Standard Statistics Company advised its clients to pur- sue an " ultra-conservative policy," and ventured this prediction: " We remain of the opinion that, over the next few months, the trend of common-stock prices will be toward lower levels." Poor's *Weekly Business and Investment Letter* spoke its mind on the " great common-stock delusion " and predicted " further liquidation in stocks." Among the big bankers, Paul M. Warburg had shown months before this that he was alive to the dangers of the situation. These com- mentators — along with others such as the editor of the *Commercial and Finan- cial Chronicle* and the financial editor of the New York *Times* — would appear to deserve the 1929 gold medals for foresight.

But if ever such medals were actually awarded, a goodly number of leather ones would have to be distributed at the same time. Not necessarily to the Har- vard Economic Society, although on October 19, after having explained that business was " facing another period of readjustment," it predicted that " if re- cession should threaten serious consequences for business (as is not indicated at present) there is little doubt that the Reserve System would take steps to ease the money market and so check the movement." The Harvard soothsayers proved themselves quite fallible: as late as October 26, after the first wide-open crack in the stock market, they delivered the cheerful judgment that " despite its severity, we believe that the slump in stock prices will prove an intermediate movement and not the precursor of a business depression such as would entail prolonged further liquidation." This judgment turned out, of course, to be ludicrously wrong; but on the other hand the Harvard Economic Society was far from being really bullish. Nor would Colonel Leonard P. Ayres of the Cleveland Trust Company get one of the leather medals. He almost qualified when, on October 15, he delivered himself of the judgment that "there does not seem to be as yet much real evidence that the decline in stock prices is likely to forecast a serious recession in general business. Despite the slowing down in iron and steel production, in automobile output, and in building, the conditions which result in serious business depressions are not present." But the skies, as Colonel Ayres saw them, were at least partly cloudy. "It seems probable," he said, "that stocks have been passing not so much from the strong to the weak as from the smart to the dumb."

Professor Irving Fisher, however, was more optimistic. In the newspapers of October 17 he was reported as telling the Purchasing Agents Association that stock prices had reached "what looks like a permanently high plateau." He expected to see the stock market, within a few months, "a good deal higher than it is today." On the very eve of the panic of October 24 he was further quoted as expecting a recovery in prices. Only two days before the panic, the *Boston News Bureau* quoted R. W. McNeel, director of McNeel's Financial Service, as suspecting "that some pretty intelligent people are now buying stocks." "Unless we are to have a panic — which no one seriously believes — stocks have hit bottom," said Mr. McNeel. And as for Charles E. Mitchell, chairman of the great National City Bank of New York, he continuously and enthusiastically radiated sunshine. Early in October Mr. Mitchell was positive that, despite the stock-market break, "The industrial situation of the United States is absolutely sound and our credit situation is in no way critical. . . . The interest given by the public to brokers' loans is always exaggerated," he added. "Altogether too much attention is paid to it." A few days later Mr. Mitchell spoke again: "Although in some cases speculation has gone too far in the United States, the markets generally are now in a healthy condition. The last six weeks have done an immense amount of good by shaking down prices. . . . The market values have a sound basis in the general prosperity of our country." Finally, on October 22, two days before the panic, he arrived in the United States from a short trip to Europe with these reassuring words: "I know of nothing fundamentally wrong with the stock market or with the underlying business and credit structure. . . . The public is suffering from 'brokers' loanitis.'"

Nor was Mr. Mitchell by any means alone in his opinions. To tell the truth, the chief difference between him and the rest of the financial community was that he made more noise. One of the most distinguished bankers in the United States, in closing a deal in the early autumn of 1929, said privately that he saw not a cloud in the sky. Habitual bulls like Arthur Cutten were, of course, insisting that they were "still bullish." And the general run of traders presumably endorsed the view attributed to "one large house" in mid-October in the *Boston News Bureau's* "Broad Street Gossip," that "the recent break makes a firm foundation for a big bull market in the last quarter of the year." There is no doubt that a great many speculators who had looked upon the midsummer prices as too high were now deciding that deflation had been effected and were buying again. Presumably most financial opinion agreed also with the further statement which appeared in the " Broad Street Gossip " column on October 16, that " business is now too big and diversified, and the country too rich, to be influenced by stock-market fluctuations "; and with the editorial opinion of the *News Bureau,* on October 19, that " whatever recessions (in business) are noted, are those of the runner catching his breath. . . . The general condition is satisfactory and fundamentally sound."

The disaster which was impending was destined to be as bewildering and frightening to the rich and the powerful and the customarily sagacious as to the foolish and unwary holder of fifty shares of margin stock.

III

The expected recovery in the stock market did not come. It seemed to be beginning on Tuesday, October 22, but the gains made during the day were largely lost during the last hour. And on Wednesday, the 23rd, there was a perfect Niagara of liquidation. The volume of trading was over six million shares, the tape was 104 minutes late when the three o'clock gong ended trading for the day, and the New York *Times* averages for fifty leading railroad and industrial stocks lost 18.24 points — a loss which made the most abrupt declines in previous breaks look small. Everybody realized that an unprecedented number of margin calls must be on their way to insecurely margined traders, and that the situation at last was getting serious. But perhaps the turn would come tomorrow. Already the break had carried prices down a good deal farther than the previous breaks of the past two years. Surely it could not go on much longer.

The next day was Thursday, October 24.

On that momentous day stocks opened moderately steady in price, but in enormous volume. Kennecott appeared on the tape in a block of 20,000 shares, General Motors in another of the same amount. Almost at once the ticker tape began to lag behind the trading on the floor. The pressure of selling orders was disconcertingly heavy. Prices were going down. . . . Presently they were going down with some rapidity. . . . Before the first hour of trading was over, it was already apparent that they were going down with an altogether unprecedented and amazing violence. In brokers' offices all over the country, tape-watchers looked at one another in astonishment and perplexity. Where on earth was this torrent of selling orders coming from?

The exact answer to this question will probably never be known. But it seems probable that the principal cause of the break in prices during that first hour on October 24 was not fear. Nor was it short selling. It was forced selling. It was the dumping on the market of hundreds of thousands of shares of stock held in the name of miserable traders whose margins were exhausted or about to be exhausted. The gigantic edifice of prices was honeycombed with speculative credit and was now breaking under its own weight.

Fear, however, did not long delay its coming. As the price structure crumbled there was a sudden stampede to get out from under. By eleven o'clock traders on the floor of the Stock Exchange were in a wild scramble to " sell at the market." Long before the lagging ticker could tell what was happening, word had gone out by telephone and telegraph that the bottom was dropping out of things, and the selling orders redoubled in volume. The leading stocks were going down two, three, and even five points between sales. Down, down, down. . . . Where were the bargain hunters who were supposed to come to the rescue at times like this? Where were the investment trusts, which were expected to provide a cushion for the market by making new purchases at low prices? Where were the big operators who had declared that they were still bullish? Where were the powerful bankers who were supposed to be able at any moment to support prices? There seemed to be no support whatever. Down, down, down. The roar of voices which rose from the floor of the Exchange had become a roar of panic.

United States Steel had opened at 205½. It crashed through 200 and presently was at 193½. General Electric, which only a few weeks before had been selling above 400, had opened this morning at 315 — now it had slid to 283. Things were even worse with Radio: opening at 68¾, it had gone dismally down through the sixties and the fifties and forties to the abysmal price of 44½. And as for Montgomery Ward, vehicle of the hopes of thousands who saw the chain store as the harbinger of the new economic era, it had dropped headlong from 83 to 50. In the space of two short hours, dozens of stocks lost ground which it had required many months of the bull market to gain.

Even this sudden decline in values might not have been utterly terrifying if people could have known precisely what was happening at any moment. It is the unknown which causes real panic.

Suppose a man walked into a broker's branch office between twelve and one o'clock on October 24 to see how things were faring. First he glanced at the big board, covering one wall of the room, on which the day's prices for the leading stocks were supposed to be recorded. The LOW and LAST figures written there took his breath away, but soon he was aware that they were unreliable: even with the wildest scrambling, the boys who slapped into place the cards which recorded the last prices shown on the ticker could not keep up with the changes — they were too numerous and abrupt. He turned to the shining screen across which ran an uninterrupted procession of figures from the ticker. Ordinarily the practiced tape-watcher could tell from a moment's glance at the screen how things were faring, even though the Exchange now omitted all but the final digit of each quotation. A glance at the board, if not his own memory, supplied the missing digits. But today, when he saw a run of symbols and figures like

R   WX
6.5½.5.4.   9.8⅞¾½¼.8.7½.7.

he could not be sure whether the price of " 6 " shown for Radio meant 66 or 56 or 46; whether Westinghouse was sliding from 189 to 187 or from 179 to 177. And presently he heard that the ticker was an hour and a half late; at one o'clock it was recording the prices of half past eleven! All this that he saw was ancient history. What was happening on the floor now?

At ten-minute intervals the bond ticker over in the corner would hammer off a list of selected prices direct from the floor, and a broker's clerk would grab the uncoiling sheet of paper and shear it off with a pair of scissors and read the figures aloud in a mumbling expressionless monotone to the white-faced men who occupied every seat on the floor and stood packed at the rear of the room. The prices which he read out were *ten or a dozen or more points below those recorded on the ticker*. What about the stocks not included in that select list? There was no way of finding out. The telephone lines were clogged as inquiries and orders from all over the country converged upon the Stock Exchange. Once in a while a voice would come barking out of the broker's rear office where a frantic clerk was struggling for a telephone connection: " Steel at ninety-six! " Small comfort, however, to know what Steel was doing; the men outside were desperately involved in many another stock than Steel; they were almost completely in the dark, and their imaginations had free play. If they put in an order to buy or to sell, it was impossible to find out what became of it. The Exchange's whole system for the recording of current prices and for communicating orders was hopelessly unable to cope with the emergency, and the sequel was an epidemic of fright.

In that broker's office, as in hundreds of other offices from one end of the land to the other, one saw men looking defeat in the face. One of them was slowly walking up and down, mechanically tearing a piece of paper into tiny and still tinier fragments. Another was grinning shamefacedly, as a small boy giggles at a funeral. Another was abjectly beseeching a clerk for the latest news of American & Foreign Power. And still another was sitting motionless, as if stunned, his eyes fixed blindly upon the moving figures on the screen, those innocent-looking figures that meant the smashup of the hopes of years. . . .

GL.   AWW.   JMP.
  8.7.5.2.1.90.89.7.6.   3.2½.2   6.5.3.2½

A few minutes after noon, some of the more alert members of a crowd which had collected on the street outside the Stock Exchange, expecting they knew not what, recognized Charles E. Mitchell, erstwhile defender of the bull market, slipping quietly into the offices of J. P. Morgan & Company on the opposite corner. It was scarcely more than nine years since the House of Morgan had been pitted with the shrapnel-fire of the Wall Street explosion; now its occupants faced a different sort of calamity equally near at hand. Mr. Mitchell was followed shortly by Albert H. Wiggin, head of the Chase National Bank; William Potter, head of the Guaranty Trust Company; and Seward Prosser, head of the Bankers Trust Company. They had come to confer with Thomas W. Lamont of the Morgan firm. In the space of a few minutes these five men, with George F. Baker, Jr., of the First National Bank, agreed in behalf of their respective institutions to put up forty millions apiece to shore up the stock market. The object of the two-hundred-and-forty-million-dollar pool thus formed, as explained subsequently by Mr. Lamont, was not to hold prices at any given level, but simply to make such purchases as were necessary to keep trading on an orderly basis. Their first action, they decided, would be to try to steady the prices of the leading securities which served as bellwethers for the list as a whole. It was a dangerous plan, for with hysteria spreading there was no telling what sort of debacle might be impending. But this was no time for any action but the boldest.

The bankers separated. Mr. Lamont faced a gathering of reporters in the Morgan offices. His face was grave, but his words were soothing. His first sentence alone was one of the most remarkable understatements of all time. " There has been a little distress selling on the Stock Exchange," said he, " and we have held a meeting of the heads of several financial institutions to discuss the situation. We have found that there are no houses in difficulty and reports from brokers indicate that margins are being maintained satisfactorily." He went on to explain that what had happened was due to a " technical condition of the market " rather than to any fundamental cause.

As the news that the bankers were meeting circulated on the floor of the Exchange, prices began to steady. Soon a brisk rally set in. Steel jumped back to the level at which it had opened that morning. But the bankers had more to offer the dying bull market than a Morgan partner's best bedside manner.

At about half past one o'clock Richard Whitney, vice-president of the Exchange, who usually acted as floor broker for the Morgan interests, went into the " Steel crowd " and put in a bid of 205 — the price of the last previous sale — for 10,000 shares of Steel. He bought only 200 shares and left the remainder of the order with the specialist. Mr. Whitney then went to various other points on the floor, and offered the price of the last previous sale for 10,000 shares of each of fifteen or twenty other stocks, reporting what was sold to him at that price and leaving the remainder of the order with the specialist. In short, within the space of a few minutes Mr. Whitney offered to purchase something in the neighborhood of twenty or thirty million dollars' worth of stock. Purchases of this magnitude are not undertaken by Tom, Dick, and Harry; it was clear that Mr. Whitney represented the bankers' pool.

The desperate remedy worked. The semblance of confidence returned. Prices held steady for a while; and though many of them slid off once more in the final hour, the net results for the day might well have been worse. Steel actually closed two points higher than on Wednesday, and the net losses of most of the other leading securities amounted to less than ten points apiece for the whole day's trading.

All the same, it had been a frightful day. At seven o'clock that night the tickers in a thousand brokers' offices were still chattering; not till after 7.08 did they finally record the last sale made on the floor at three o'clock. The volume of trading had set a new record — 12,894,650 shares. (" The time may come when we shall see a five-million-share day," the wise men of the Street had been saying twenty months before!) Incredible rumors had spread wildly during the early afternoon — that eleven speculators had committed suicide, that the Buffalo and Chicago exchanges had been closed, that troops were guarding the New York Stock Exchange against an angry mob. The country had known the bitter taste of panic. And although the bankers' pool had prevented for the moment an utter collapse, there was no gainsaying the fact that the economic structure had cracked wide open.

IV

Things looked somewhat better on Friday and Saturday. Trading was still on an enormous scale, but prices for the most part held. At the very moment when the bankers' pool was cautiously disposing of as much as possible of the stock which it had accumulated on Thursday and was thus preparing for future emergencies, traders who had sold out higher up were coming back into the market again with new purchases, in the hope that the bottom had been reached. (Hadn't they often been told that " the time to buy is when things look blackest "?) The newspapers carried a very pretty series of reassuring statements from the occupants of the seats of the mighty; Herbert Hoover himself, in a White House statement, pointed out that " the fundamental business of the country, that is, production and distribution of commodities, is on a sound and prosperous basis." But toward the close of Saturday's session prices began to slip again. And on Monday the rout was under way once more.

The losses registered on Monday were terrific — 17½ points for Steel, 47½ for General Electric, 36 for Allied Chemical, 34½ for Westinghouse, and so on down a long and dismal list. All Saturday afternoon and Saturday night and Sunday the brokers had been struggling to post their records and go over their customers' accounts and send out calls for further margin, and another avalanche of forced selling resulted. The prices at which Mr. Whitney's purchases had steadied the leading stocks on Thursday were so readily broken through that it was immediately clear that the bankers' pool had made a strategic retreat. As a matter of fact, the brokers who represented the pool were having their hands full plugging up the " airholes " in the list — in other words, buying stocks which were offered for sale without any bids at all in sight. Nothing more than this could have been accomplished, even if it could have been wisely attempted. Even six great banks could hardly stem the flow of liquidation from the entire United States. They could only guide it a little, check it momentarily here and there.

Once more the ticker dropped ridiculously far behind, the lights in the brokers' offices and the banks burned till dawn, and the telegraph companies distributed thousands of margin calls and requests for more collateral to back up loans at the banks. Bankers, brokers, clerks, messengers were almost at the end of their strength; for days and nights they had been driving themselves to keep pace with the most terrific volume of business that had ever descended upon them. It did not seem as if they could stand it much longer. But the worst was still ahead. It came the next day, Tuesday, October 29.

The big gong had hardly sounded in the great hall of the Exchange at ten o'clock Tuesday morning before the storm broke in full force. Huge blocks of stock were thrown upon the market for what they would bring. Five thousand shares, ten thousand shares appeared at a time on the laboring ticker at fearful recessions in price. Not only were innumerable small traders being sold out, but big ones, too, protagonists of the new economic era who a few weeks before had counted themselves millionaires. Again and again the specialist in a stock would find himself surrounded by brokers fighting to sell — and nobody at all even thinking of buying. To give one single example: during the bull market the common stock of the White Sewing Machine Company had gone as high as 48; on Monday, October 28, it had closed at 11⅛. On that black Tuesday, somebody — a clever messenger boy for the Exchange, it was rumored — had the bright idea of putting in an order to buy at 1; and in the temporarily complete absence of other bids he actually got his stock for a dollar a share! The scene on the floor was chaotic. Despite the jamming of the communication system, orders to buy and sell — mostly to sell — came in faster than human beings could possibly handle them; it was on that day that an exhausted broker, at the close of the session, found a large wastebasket which he had stuffed with orders to be executed and had carefully set aside for safekeeping — and then had completely forgotten. Within half an hour of the opening the volume of trading had passed three million shares, by twelve o'clock it had passed eight million, by half-past one it had passed twelve million; and when the closing gong brought the day's madness to an end the gigantic record of 16,410,030 shares had been set. Toward the close there was a rally, but by that time the average prices of fifty leading stocks, as compiled by the New York *Times,* had fallen nearly forty points. Meanwhile there was a near-panic in other markets — the foreign stock exchanges, the lesser American exchanges, the grain market.

So complete was the demoralization of the stock market, and so exhausted were the brokers and their staffs and the Stock Exchange employees, that at noon that day, when the panic was at its worst, the Governing Committee met quietly to decide whether or not to close the Exchange. To quote from an address made some months later by Richard Whitney: " In order not to give occasion for alarming rumors, this meeting was not held in the Governing Committee Room, but in the office of the president of the Stock Clearing Corporation directly beneath the Stock Exchange floor. . . . The forty governors came to the meeting in groups of two and three as unobtrusively as possible. The office they met in was never designed for large meetings of this sort, with the result that most of the governors were compelled to stand, or to sit on tables. As the meeting progressed, panic was raging overhead on the floor. . . . The feeling of those present was revealed by their habit of continually lighting cigarettes, taking a puff or two, putting them out and lighting new ones — a practice which soon made the narrow room blue with smoke. . . ." Two of the Morgan partners were invited to the meeting and, attempting to slip into the building unnoticed so as not to start a new flock of rumors, were refused admittance by one of the guards and had to remain outside until rescued by a member of the Governing Committee. After some deliberation, the governors finally decided not to close the Exchange.

It was a critical day for the banks, that Tuesday the 29th. Many of the corporations which had so cheerfully loaned money to brokers through the banks in order to obtain interest at eight or nine per cent were now clamoring to have these loans called — and the banks were faced with a choice between taking over the loans themselves and running the risk of precipitating further ruin. It was no laughing matter to assume the responsibility of millions of dollars' worth of loans secured by collateral which by the end of the day might prove to have dropped to a fraction of its former value. That the call money rate never rose above six per cent that day, that a money panic was not added to the stock panic, and that several Wall Street institutions did not go down into immediate bankruptcy, was due largely to the nerve shown by a few bankers in stepping into the breach. The story is told of one banker who went grimly on authorizing the taking over of loan after loan until one of his subordinate officers came in with a white face and told him that the bank was insolvent. " I dare say," said the banker, and went ahead unmoved. He knew that if he did not, more than one concern would face insolvency.

The next day — Wednesday, October 30 — the outlook suddenly and providentially brightened. The directors of the Steel Corporation had declared an extra dividend; the directors of the American Can Company had not only declared an extra dividend but had raised the regular dividend. There was another flood of reassuring statements — though by this time a cheerful statement from a financier fell upon somewhat skeptical ears. Julius Klein, Mr. Hoover's Assistant Secretary of Commerce, composed a rhapsody on continued prosperity. John J. Raskob declared that stocks were at bargain prices and that he and his friends were buying. John D. Rockefeller poured Standard Oil upon the waters: " Believing that fundamental conditions of the country are sound and that there is nothing in the business situation to warrant the destruction of values that has taken place on the exchanges during the past week, my son and I have for some days been purchasing sound common stocks." Better still, prices rose — steadily and buoyantly. Now at last the time had come when the strain on the Exchange could be relieved without causing undue alarm. At 1.40 o'clock Vice-President Whitney announced from the rostrum that the Exchange would not open until noon the following day and would remain closed all day Friday and Saturday — and to his immense relief the announcement was greeted, not with renewed panic, but with a cheer.

Throughout Thursday's short session the recovery continued. Prices gyrated wildly — for who could arrive at a reasonable idea of what a given stock was worth, now that all settled standards of value had been upset? — but the worst of the storm seemed to have blown over. The financial community breathed more easily; now they could have a chance to set their houses in order.

It was true that the worst of the panic was past. But not the worst prices. There was too much forced liquidation still to come as brokers' accounts were gradually straightened out, as banks called for more collateral, and terror was renewed. The next week, in a series of short sessions, the tide of prices receded once more — until at last, on November 13, the bottom prices for the year 1929

were reached. Beside the figures hung up in the sunny days of September they
made a tragic showing:

	High price Sept. 3, 1929	Low price Nov. 13, 1929
American Can	181⅞	86
American Telephone & Telegraph	304	197¼
Anaconda Copper	131½	70
General Electric	396¼	168⅛
General Motors	72¾	36
Montgomery Ward	137⅞	49¼
New York Central	256⅜	160
Radio	101	28
Union Carbide & Carbon	137⅞	59
United States Steel	261¾	150
Westinghouse E. & M.	289⅞	102⅝
Woolworth	100⅜	52¼
Electric Bond & Share	186¾	50¼

The New York *Times* averages for fifty leading stocks had been almost cut
in half, falling from a high of 311.90 in September to a low of 164.43 on November 13; and the *Times* averages for twenty-five leading industrials had fared
still worse, diving from 469.49 to 220.95.

The Big Bull Market was dead. Billions of dollars' worth of profits — and
paper profits — had disappeared. The grocer, the window cleaner, and the
seamstress had lost their capital. In every town there were families which had
suddenly dropped from showy affluence into debt. Investors who had dreamed
of retiring to live on their fortunes now found themselves back once more at the
very beginning of the long road to riches. Day by day the newspapers printed
the grim reports of suicides.

Coolidge-Hoover Prosperity was not yet dead, but it was dying. Under the
impact of the shock of panic, a multitude of ills which hitherto had passed unnoticed or had been offset by stock-market optimism began to beset the body
economic, as poisons seep through the human system when a vital organ has
ceased to function normally. Although the liquidation of nearly three billion
dollars of brokers' loans contracted credit, and the Reserve Banks lowered the
rediscount rate, and the way in which the larger banks and corporations of the
country had survived the emergency without a single failure of large proportions offered real encouragement, nevertheless the poisons were there: overproduction of capital; overambitious expansion of business concerns; overproduction of commodities under the stimulus of installment buying and buying
with stock-market profits; the maintenance of an artificial price level for many
commodities; the depressed condition of European trade. No matter how many
soothsayers of high finance proclaimed that all was well, no matter how earnestly the President set to work to repair the damage with soft words and White
House conferences, a major depression was inevitably under way.

Nor was that all. Prosperity is more than an economic condition; it is a state of mind. The Big Bull Market had been more than the climax of a business cycle; it had been the climax of a cycle in American mass thinking and mass emotion. There was hardly a man or woman in the country whose attitude toward life had not been affected by it in some degree and was not now affected by the sudden and brutal shattering of hope. With the Big Bull Market gone and prosperity going, Americans were soon to find themselves living in an altered world which called for new adjustments, new ideas, new habits of thought, and a new order of values. The psychological climate was changing; the ever shifting currents of American life were turning into new channels.

The Post-war Decade had come to its close. An era had ended.

Paul B. Sears

From Longhorn to Combine

THE short-grass and sagebrush country represent about the last stand of that legendary hero, the pioneer, unless one sees in the modern racketeer something more than is really there. Upon the cowpuncher fell the spiritual poncho of Adam Poe, Daniel Boone, and Kit Carson after these shadowy figures had passed to a still more shadowy beyond. From the days of the dime thriller to the " Western " his name has been bathed in glory — a source of constant inspiration and dependable profits. This being the case, exactly who were the cowmen?

Economically, they were hired hands, working for others. Personally, they ranged from the usual type of hired hand one finds anywhere to charming and gifted exiles whose existence elsewhere had been fraught with disappointment. Frequently they had been the source rather than the victims of this disappointment. It was essential that they ride horseback, and desirable that they develop sufficient skill and judgment to keep from getting their guts kicked or trampled out. Riding and even roping are more matters of practice than of divine inspiration. Beyond this the demigods of the range were kept in excellent physical condition by the kind of life they led. Their sense of proportion was kept in order by group discipline — a homemade sort of psychoanalysis known as " sandpapering the ego " or " applying the cactus." All told, they were a good lot, patrolling for their overlords a domain that reached west from the grain belt through the mountains, and extended from Canada to Mexico.

Their employers were enterprising capitalists, engaged in quantity production of beef and hides. By purchase or lease they enjoyed the grazing rights on vast areas. The grazing lands of a single owner might be together, but were frequently scattered, giving thus a better possibility of shifting the load with the

From *Deserts on the March*, 1935.

seasonal and yearly changes in pasture and water supply. Necessarily they were in close touch with the breeding and feeding of their animated wealth, and understood the vital importance of conserving the range. The objects of resentment and envy from the land-hungry to the east of them, they labored under the added handicap of being unable to secure permanent control of much of the land which they used.

After 1870, with the development of transcontinental railroads and the systematic destruction of the buffalo, the livestock industry expanded with amazing rapidity through the plains area of the western states. There was no legitimate mechanism by which an individual owner could secure outright possession from the government of enough land to engage in this industry with any assurance of safety and profit. The homesteads, while large as compared with a typical eastern farm, were too small for a semiarid region. The huge grants made to the great railroads were not consolidated, but scattered. It was of course possible, but often difficult, for the wealthy operator to buy out a number of homesteaders and get the land he needed. If the land so purchased made a solid block, it was unusual.

The other recourse was to use the land of others, with or without rental. Gradually, therefore, a system of leased grazing rights developed throughout the entire western cattle country, resulting in serious, probably permanent damage to the range. Here, as in the great lumbering operations of the same period, we see not a fair trial of a system of responsible private ownership, but the concession system operating in its worst form. Had it been possible to allot as permanent holdings sufficient areas to individual cattlemen, there is reason to think that the quality of the range might have been conserved. For the cattleman, unless he were a nonresident capitalist, differed in certain important respects from the lumber baron. The latter, for example, had about the same interest in trees that the butcher might be expected to have in cattle. The trees were ready at hand. But it had not been necessary to supervise their breeding, birth, and growth, or to move them about to prevent their dying of hunger and thirst. So far as the lumberman was concerned, nature could grow new trees while he made off to fresh sources of supply.

On the other hand, the chief responsibility of the cattle industry was to grow the thing that was to be sold. This meant attention to sources of supply for food and water. The cattleman soon learned that a badly overloaded range meant inferior pasture in succeeding years. But since he so seldom had the title to his pasture, the temptation to make immediate profit while he could was too strong to resist. Resulting directly from this pattern of exploitation has been the periodic overexpansion of the cattle industry, more or less following on the intervals of heavier rainfall and more abundant grass. These events not only produced a surplus of cattle, ruining the market, but threw an abnormally heavy load on the range at the beginning of the several dry periods, furthering rapidly the ultimate destruction of the grassland turf. Under the system of land allotments, any planned and provident economy became well-nigh impossible.

In addition, the livestock industry was faced with other and serious problems. Sheep are as essential as cattle to modern civilization, particularly in cool temperate regions where woolen clothing must be worn. Like goats, however, they are thin-lipped, sharp-biting animals capable of cropping very close to the ground. Their small hoofs are edged and will cut and wear the turf unless care is taken. On the English golf courses sheep are used as lawnmowers. In that moist climate the grass grows rapidly and the animals keep it cropped to a close green velvet. If land in regions of high rainfall were not too valuable for sheep pasture, it would afford the best setting for that purpose. Actually, however, it generally becomes necessary to pasture great flocks of sheep in semiarid regions where the grasses have only a brief growing season, remaining the rest of the year dormant and dried — a sort of half-living hay — on the stalk. Under these conditions considerable care and expense is required to keep the flocks of sheep on the move and prevent lasting damage to the range. Moreover, cattle do not like to graze over ground that has been fed upon by sheep.

It can be appreciated, then, that the entrance of sheep into the cattle country meant the declaration of war. A mild and kindly ranchman who, like Cowper's friend, would not needlessly set foot upon a worm describes without batting an eye how great flocks of sheep, coming too near his demesne, are inexplicably clubbed to death, or have their throats cut. Which suggests again the very practical attitude of the cattleman towards conservation of the range.

Towards the would-be small homesteader he could scarcely defend himself by such direct action, although no doubt the intimate history of the West might produce instances in which he did so. Against the settler his only defense could be, in the long run, previous personal ownership of all of the land which he used. The weakness of his position lay in the fact that he was obliged to count on leasing large areas of the public domain to continue in business. And towards this domain hungry eyes were cast.

Probably the great transcontinental railroads, which at first provided a welcome outlet for his cattle, but which also fostered colonization, were inevitable sources of trouble. Mining operations often enriched him. At the same time they helped build centers of population, creating customers, it is true, but also bringing in hordes of the land-hungry. In the end, it was pressure from this last group, encouraged as often as expressed by professional politicians, which caused the cattle industry to suffer most.

Yet in spite of difficulties, the livestock industry made substantial strides towards permanence. The periodic maladjustments wiped out the plungers and exploiters. The large operators who have survived are those who have been sufficiently farsighted and conservative to prevent their being caught by cycles of overproduction, and in particular those who have steadily used their profits to acquire title to their own ranges. At their best, such men have developed a sense of responsibility for the welfare of the humans, the animals, and the land under them comparing favorably with that of the finer type of great plantation owner in the old South. An additional factor which contributed to stabilize the industry was the recognition of priority lease rights to government land, and in particular the enforcement of regulated grazing thereon. It is quite probable that, if general conditions in the country at large could have remained economically balanced, the livestock industry might have shared in this general stability, and the region which supported it have developed an equilibrium. Such has not been the case. But before examining the latter end of the story, it is well to acquaint ourselves with a region whose history is as graphic as a diagram.

The Sand Hills of Nebraska contain about eleven million acres — an area larger than the agricultural portion of Egypt. It consists of billowing, grass-covered hills lying in a vast rock bowl which holds the meager rainfall and slowly passes it up through the loose sand. In summer, when the pastures east of it are parched and dry, the grass here is green and fresh. But here and there, as fateful warnings which spoke plainly to the practiced eye, were great blowouts. These were funnel-shaped craters dug by the wind into the sand wherever the grass had been removed and the weak turf destroyed. Within these craters is a summertime inferno with temperatures often as high as one hundred and forty degrees, while even a moderate wind converts them into a withering, etching sandblast. With all her resources, nature has a painful task to reclaim these blowouts. Given time, she can do it by means of the wiry creeping rootstocks of Redfield's grass, followed slowly by other venturesome plants, and ultimately by the original turf-forming grasses.

So long as this land remained in public domain, it was leased in large blocks and used as cattle range. Between the hills were numerous lakes where the underground water came to the surface, and about their shores were meadows of grass which could be cut and cured for winter feed. By the use of large areas for each individual operator, overloading of the pasture on the hilltops could be prevented, although this was not always the case, and the turf thus allowed to remain and hold the sand in place. But a kingdom like this, the size of Egypt, was too tempting to be allowed such use. It became a political issue. The Sand Hills should be carved up into homesteads, each one mile square, and given to the people. Finally a man was elected to Congress on the issue — Moses Kincaid. He secured the passage of the necessary homestead law, and the settlers who thronged in on these claims were known after him as " Kincaiders."

The Kincaiders often lacked sufficient capital, as well as previous experience with the difficulties which lay ahead of them. Most unfortunately, the area assigned to each homestead, one square mile, was too small to support a family under the conditions which prevailed there. Some confined their activities to cattle but were faced with the fact that enough cattle to support them made too heavy a load on the range. The close-cropped turf broke through, and the sand began to blow, spreading ruin. Others boldly attempted to plow the ground and plant crops. On the lowland there was some return for this trouble, but at the expense of the hay meadows. On the upland the wind swept down and across the planted rows, swirling the sand into the leaves of the planted crop and shredding them to pieces, finally either burying the crop or uncovering its roots.

Easter week of 1920 a family of these homesteaders extended their hospitality to two foot-travelers, with a grace that would have adorned a more stately mansion than the tiny sod house. In the house was a little flour, a little coffee, a few potatoes and, happily, water with which to prepare all three. No milk, no butter, no eggs, no meat. Not one sign was there that the guests might be making inroads on a scant provision — only regret that the repast was not more varied. These brave people were the lords of six hundred and forty acres — a space which in Egypt keeps alive one thousand — yet they were slowly starving. When the travelers took their leave, they were cheerfully urged to return in August to help eat watermelons because " that's sure one thing we kin grow in these valleys, melons."

As the discouraged and defeated Kincaiders retreated from the picture their homesteads were gradually acquired once more by the larger cattle operators, this time as owners instead of lessors. Gradually the pitted and scarred landscape is resuming its proper function as a range region, but in the meantime the loss, both in potential wealth and in human effort and happiness, has been appalling. Here again, as in the monotonous story of exploitation we have rehearsed, it is not possible to fix individual blame. Certainly not on the homesteaders, nor the cattlemen. Not on the well-meaning, humane politician whose name is associated with the experiment. Rather it rests upon a system which tolerates private privilege in utter disregard of public policy, and which as yet does not understand how science may be made to help in the determining of policy. At the time these measures were planned, there were men who knew the Sand Hills from the scientific side, and who could have predicted exactly the outcome, but their views were not consulted in any effective way. Like the expert witnesses in our courts, scientists are only supposed to talk when they have arguments for, not against, a popular or influential project.

The Sand Hills, although not covered with short grass, but rather with bunch grasses, illustrate the situation in the true short-grass country, which extends from about the hundredth meridian west to the Rockies. In this country, of course, there are many fertile river bottoms where alfalfa and other crops can be grown. There are also many places which would prosper under irrigation, if the water could be made available. The Scottsbluff sugar-beet area in western Nebraska is an example of this, as is much of the plain immediately along the front of the Rocky Mountains. But as for the bulk of the upland, its destiny is pasture, with the load of livestock nicely balanced to seasonal and local conditions. The cheapness with which extensive areas of this land could formerly be acquired was a temptation to speculators. " I saw the time," said an old banker, " when you could get a square mile of this for a pair of boots. The only trouble was, no one had the boots." Such were the conditions following a few years of the regularly recurring drought. Given a few years, on the other hand, of good rainfall, which comes as inevitably as the years of drought, things brighten up, and upland crops may be temporarily successful. At such times speculators could unload, and did so, in smaller parcels than were safe for the purchaser to live on. Let the dry years return, as inevitably they will, and the plowed soil moves on with the whirlwind.

These conditions have been frightfully aggravated since the war by the introduction of power machinery and large-scale upland farming, from western Texas north through the Dakotas. Let it be forever recorded that there was ample information, based on the disastrous small-scale experiments which had been tried in western Kansas and Nebraska, to have forestalled the tragedy which occurred. But those were fabulous years, when the still, small voice of a President urging economy and forethought was put down as a bit of New Englandism which should be laughed off and not allowed to interfere seriously with the general popularity of his quaint, canny character.

During these years, the nineteen-twenties, there were for a time good wheat prices and favorable rainfall in conjunction. Everything in the country was going full blast. It was the most natural thing in the world for the Panhandle farmers, whose cattle business had prospered during the war, and who had been encouraged to try dry farming, to attempt the growing of wheat on a huge scale. The soil was loose and friable, the land was theirs to use as they saw fit, gang plows and disks could be dragged across the level with astounding speed and ease by huge tractors. The wheat grew well — not more than knee-high, sometimes ankle-high; and could be cut by a header and threshed all in one operation, leaving the short stubble standing until again disked under. Although the yield per acre was not high as compared with the eastern wheat land, the capital involved was less per acre, and the whole proceeding seemed very profitable. During thousands of years the slow growth of natural vegetation had stored considerable fertility in the soil. Amazing stories began to appear of the new era of power in agriculture — factory production applied to the land. As in the great spinning mills, where only one attendant was required to keep numbers of machines in smooth running order, here were huge farms which could be operated with ease by mechanical means. For a time it looked as though the small farmer of the eastern states would be driven out of business as surely as his brother who owned the small factory had been " merged " or exterminated. During these years there was actually an astonishing decrease in the number of acres of tilled land in the older states, and the murmur of discontent about the farm depression, which had been growing since the close of the war, swelled to a rumble which disturbed or delighted the politicians, according to their particular commitments. But out in the short-grass country, make no mistake about it, the wheat was being delivered.

Then suddenly, everything collapsed. There was no market for the wheat. Even before this disaster the wheat farmers, although making money, were grumbling. They felt that the manufacturing and shipping industries had been virtually handed gifts of money from the government. In the words of one of them: " Sure, we are raising plenty of good wheat without a great deal of expense, and we are getting along. But these other fellows got rich, why can't we? If they can have money handed out to them by the working of a tariff and in other ways, why shouldn't we get all the traffic will bear? " This authentic comment shows that the " farm relief " business is one of many facets. Protest and distress are not always surely proportioned. Among the wheat farmers there was growing resentment against the marketing agencies, whose million-bushel elevators levied a charge of one cent per bushel per month for storage, but which after all were conducted with an eye to business and under conditions of severe competition. Coöperative storing and marketing agencies were organized, and after the destruction of the wheat market much wheat was stored outdoors in great heaps, where weevils, disease, and weather were free to work.

The causes of the disaster are involved with the whole question of the depression. Competition from other continents, and stagnation of the American foreign trade by high tariffs and European impoverishment, were of course important factors. But the one undoubted fact of overproduction in this country is what concerns us here. To an important extent this was accomplished by the wholesale exploitation of the short-grass plains, whose permanent value for extensive grazing was a demonstrated fact, and whose permanent value as a dry farming center remained to be proved.

Artificial restoratives were applied to relieve the situation. These helped steady matters somewhat, but Mother Nature had a remedy of her own, as shortly appeared. Climate, which had been passing through the humid phase of its cycle, swung back towards the dry side. Months passed without a drop of rain in western Kansas in the summer of 1933. The next year was even worse. Not only did the wheat fail to mature, but so little grass was left unplowed that the livestock were starving and had to be moved or killed. Buyers with a little cash could go through this country and name their own prices — sheep two bits apiece; cattle five to ten dollars. From the first of the drought there was considerable wind-sculpture of the naked fields, and local dust storms such as one finds in a dune area. But by the spring of 1935 these dust storms became matters of national extent, fitly symbolizing to distant Washington and New York the painful distress which existed in the country the dust came from. Whether the dust which fell in a given spot in the East actually came from the plowed-up pastures of the West, or from the desert itself, farther west, is immaterial. Within the newest wheat region fences hidden in dust, houses buried to the eaves, blinded jack rabbits, and suffering humanity were eloquent proof of the penalty incurred by disturbing nature's hard-won balance.

The drought, which was the apparent cause of the disaster, was certainly predictable — not in any exact sense, of course, but as unavoidably due to occur at intervals. A system of agriculture had been put into operation in disregard of the certain hazards of the short-grass region, and the dust storms became the costly, spectacular evidence of this fact.

Louis Adamic

Thirty Million New Americans

I

WITHIN its population of slightly less than one hundred and thirty million, the United States has today over thirty million citizens — the overwhelming majority of them young citizens — who are the American-born children of immigrant parents of various nationalities: German, Italian, Polish, Czech, Slovak, Serbian, Croatian, Slovenian, Bulgarian, Jewish, Russian, Carpatho-Russian, Ukrainian, Lithuanian, Finnish, Hungarian, Norwegian, Swedish, Danish, Dutch, French, Flemish, Spanish, Portuguese, Rumanian, Armenian, Syrian, Lett, Albanian, Greek, Turkish, and, of course, English, Scotch, and Irish. The country as a whole is but dimly cognizant of this fact and its implications which, in my opinion, are of fundamental and urgent importance in America's contemporary social and cultural scene. It should perhaps particularly interest those Americans who consider themselves of the old Anglo-Saxon stock; for here is a tremendous new element. What will it do to the old stock? To the country? How will it affect the development of civilization and culture, of racial types on this continent?

These questions had vaguely interested and perturbed me already in the late nineteen-twenties and the earliest nineteen-thirties, but I did not really go into them till 1934. I have told that in the spring of that year I went on a lecture tour. It took me to the great industrial centers of New York State, New Jersey, Pennsylvania, Ohio, Michigan, Illinois, Indiana, Wisconsin, and Minnesota, where the population is preponderantly " foreign." Actually, however, my trip was not so much a series of speaking engagements as an attempt — a device — to get some clear idea, if possible, of this immense mass of so-called " second-generation " citizens, numerically predominant in some of the most important cities and towns, whom I choose to designate the New Americans. I spoke, or rather tried to speak, more or less on the subject of this essay, to about fifty audiences of anywhere from one hundred to twenty-five hundred men and women and young people, in big towns like Pittsburgh, Cleveland, Akron, Detroit, Chicago, South Bend, Milwaukee, St. Paul, and Duluth, and smaller communities like McKeesport, Canonsburg, Ambridge, Farrell, Sharon, and Strabane, Pennsylvania; Lorain, Ohio; Flint, Michigan; and Hibbing and Eveleth, Minnesota. Some of my audiences were almost wholly " foreign "; others mixed " foreign " and old-stock American. At the time I knew very little about the subject; I merely sensed its importance; and, to keep going for an hour or so, I discussed things more or less akin to it and at the end, admitting

From *My America*, 1938.

my ignorance, invited my listeners to get up and say anything they liked in relation to my remarks. Those who were too diffident to talk in a crowd, I asked to speak to me after the lecture or to call me at the hotel or write me a letter. Many of them, both old-stock Americans and New Americans, responded to this invitation. Some of them then asked me to their homes. Others wrote me long letters. And the result was that before my tour was half over I began to think that these New Americans — twenty-six million of them in 1930 and increasing at the rate of perhaps more than a million a year — constituted one of the greatest and most basic problems in this country; in some respects, greater and more basic perhaps than, say, the problem of unemployment, and almost as urgent.

This problem has existed, in nearly the same proportions that it exists today, for a long time, but few people have shown eagerness and ability to deal with it in a broad, fundamental way, or even to discuss it. Much attention — most of it, as already suggested, ill-focused — has been paid to the problem of the foreign-born; but not to that of their children, the American-born second generation. There is no acute or intelligent appreciation of it. Very little is being done about it; and the longer it is neglected the worse it will become, both for the New Americans and in the long run for America as a whole.

In this essay it is not my ambition to present the problem in all its details, ramifications, significances; for it is a vastly complicated one and different in every locality and in every racial group; and, frankly, I still have a great deal to learn about it. My purpose here is merely to give as strong and broad a general suggestion as I can of its character and what I think might be done concerning it.

II

The chief and most important fact (the only one I shall stress here) about the New Americans is that all too many of them are oppressed by feelings of inferiority in relation to their fellow citizens of older stock, to the main stream of American life, and to the problem of life as a whole; which, of course, is bad for them as individuals, but, since there are so many of them and their number is still rapidly increasing, even worse for the country.

These feelings of inferiority are to some degree extensions of their parents' feelings of inferiority as immigrants in a country so drastically different from their native lands. The fathers and mothers of these millions of New Americans were naturally at a disadvantage even in the most friendly surroundings, and the surroundings were seldom wholly and continually friendly. As foreigners, in many cases not speaking the English language, they occupied inferior positions in the country's social, economic, and political life. Most of them were workers performing, by and large, the meanest tasks and receiving meager wages. All too often, in one form or another, they bumped up against racial or general anti-immigrant prejudice. Old-stock American workers looked askance at them. When work slackened, they were laid off before the native employees. Many of them lived in the worst districts of their cities and towns, and were called Hunkies or Bohunks, Squareheads, Dagoes or Wops, Polacks or Litvaks, Sheenies or Kikes. They were frequently — and unavoidably — discriminated against. And in the face of all this, they inevitably felt, as individuals and as members of their immigrant groups, somewhat inferior in their relation to America and to other people here, and their tendency was to segregate themselves and mingle as much as possible only with their own nationals. And just as inevitably, that feeling and that tendency were extended to the children, these New Americans, who shared their parents' lives and experiences, and who too were (and still are) called Hunkies or Dagoes by children of Anglo-Saxon origin, and whose names — names like Zamblaoskas, Krmpotich, and Wojiezkowski — were (and are) subjects for jokes on the part of ignorant teachers, at which the whole school laughed.

But in this respect the majority of New Americans, as individuals, are in an even more unfortunate and uncomfortable position than were (or still are) their immigrant parents. The latter, even if they were uneducated peasants or laborers, living here on the lowest social-economic levels, had in them a consciousness, or at least a powerful instinctive feeling, of some kind of racial or cultural background. They knew who they were. They remembered their native lands. They were Italians or Croatians, Finns or Slovenians; and that meant something to them. Many came from countries which culturally and perhaps in some other respects were superior to the United States, which as a new country had not yet had time to develop along those lines; and when oppressed by feelings of inferiority induced by their circumstances in America, could take partial refuge in their racial and cultural backgrounds. Some of the better educated ones, who did not have merely instinctive feelings about the culture and history of their old countries, but were also intellectually conscious of their heritage, could even look down upon America and consider themselves superior to old-time Americans, thus counterbalancing or compensating themselves as persons from time to time for the unpleasant feelings about their immigrant status in the New World. This was unhealthy socially in the long run, for it was not reaching out toward an understanding with America, real or basic; but it did help individual immigrants to stand up as men and women.

Unlike their parents, who are (or were) aware not only of their European background but of having made the transition from Europe to America and gained a foothold here, most New Americans have no consciousness or instinctive feeling of any racial or cultural background, of their being part of any sort of continuity in human or historic experience. Some of them seem almost as if they had just dropped off Mars and, during the drop, forgotten all about Mars. I know this to be so; I talked to scores and scores of them in more than a dozen different cities and towns, not only during that tour in 1934, but on several occasions and in various connections since then. In the majority of cases, the immigrant parents — uneducated working people or peasants from the various European countries — were too inarticulate to tell their sons and daughters who they (the parents) really were, and thus transmit to them some feeling or knowledge of their background.

The average Slavic peasant, for instance, who came to this country during the last twenty or thirty years, in nine chances out of ten is unable to inform his children adequately who he is, what his old country is like, what his background (which, *ipso facto,* is his children's background) consists of. He tells his numerous sons and daughters that he is a Pole, a Croatian, a Slovak, a Slovenian; but that is about all. The children do not know what that really means. The man acts as if he were proud of being what he is, at least in the privacy of his home; for his instincts and his memories of the old country occasionally make him act that way. To his children, however, who are growing up under anything but the best influences of American life and who do not know that behind their father's pride is a rich and vital past, he very often seems not a little ridiculous, certainly not worthy of their respect. To them he is just a Hunky or Polack, a " working stiff," a poor, pathetic creature constantly at somebody's mercy and repeatedly stepped upon, and as such not much according to American standards — standards which they pick up in the movies and from other powerful agencies in American life. Often they are half ashamed of him. The immigrant mother frequently finds herself in the same situation. There is a mutual lack of understanding; the children as they grow older have begun to grasp at superficial and obvious American realities, and sink themselves in America as far as they can by adopting the easiest, most obvious ways of the country of their birth. And the results are unsatisfactory family life, personal tragedies of all sorts, maladjustments, social perversities.

It is not unusual for boys and girls in their late or even their middle teens to break away from the homes of their immigrant parents, and eventually to repudiate entirely their origin and to Anglicize their Polish, Croatian, Finnish, or Lithuanian names, which old-time Americans find so difficult to pronounce and so amusing. But that, of course, does not solve their problem. In most instances it only makes it worse, though as a rule they do not realize that. I met New Americans of this type; they were invariably hollow, absurd, objectionable persons.

However, the situation of many of those who do not break with their parents, change their " foreign " names, and wholly repudiate their origin is but little better than that of those who do. They were born here and legally, technically, are citizens of the United States; but few — even in the most fortunate homes — have any strong feeling that they really belong here and are part of this country. For, by and large, the education which is inflicted on them in public schools and high schools and in parochial schools, or in colleges, fails to make them Anglo-Saxon Americans or to give them any vital and lasting appreciation of the American heritage, while their Anglo-Saxon schoolmates, purposefully-by-accident stumbling over their feet and calling them Hunkies and Dagoes, and their teachers, making fun of their names, increase their feeling that they are not indigenous Americans, but outsiders who are more or less tolerated. Their instincts, if they have any, are at cross-purposes. They are bewildered persons, constantly oppressed, as I have said, by feelings of inferiority. Their personalities are faint, lopsided, out of focus.

These feelings of inferiority manifest themselves variously. Some of the New Americans turn them inside out and become chauvinistically patriotic; only their chauvinism has no basis in any vital feeling. It is insincere, empty, mere lip service, intended only to impress the dominant Anglo-Saxon element, with which they have to cope; and hence worse — for the development of their own characters — than chauvinism that has some basis in conviction or feeling in racial or national background. And where there is any sincerity in this sort of " patriotism," it is based solely on shallow materialistic concepts, which they have picked up in school and elsewhere. " This is the greatest country . . . we have the biggest buildings . . . the best ice-cream . . . more automobiles, more bathtubs than all the rest of the world," etc. Without realizing it, these New Americans are ready for almost any sort of shallow, ignorant nationalist or fascist movement which will not directly attack the new racial strains in America's population; and thousands of them perhaps would have no great trouble in bringing themselves to deny their parents, pose as old-stock Americans, and serve even a movement which would terrorize the immigrants and their children as the Hitler movement in Germany terrorized the Jews.

Other New Americans turn their inferiority inside out in another way. They become loud and tough, sometimes actively antisocial. But let me hasten to repeat that this last group is not so numerous as is generally imagined by those who occasionally glance at crime and juvenile delinquency statistics, or who read the headlines. The surprising thing to me is that there is not more delinquency and crime among the New Americans. And I should add too that the chauvinists mentioned above are not very numerous either. These categories together include perhaps less than five per cent of the New Americans.

The majority of the grown-up New Americans just hang back from the main stream of life in this country, forming a tremendous mass of neutral, politically lifeless citizenry; while their younger fellow New Americans, boys and girls in their teens (about twelve million of them), now attending public and parochial schools and high schools, show dangerous signs of becoming the same kind of neutral, unstirring citizens, unless something is done about it. There is among them little aggressiveness, little spirit of any sort. Most of them merely hope to get along, to get by, somehow. Without a vital sense of background, perennially oppressed by the feeling that they are outsiders and thus inferior, they will live outside the main stream of America's national life. This is especially true of groups which linguistically and culturally are farthest removed from the Anglo-Saxon, and still more of groups which, besides being unrelated to the Anglo-Saxon, are (or till lately have been) suppressed or subject nationalities in Europe.

And these widespread personal inferiority feelings are producing in large sections of this New American element *actual* inferiority in character, mind, and physique. There is no doubt that, by and large, in bodily and other personal qualities many of the immigrants' children do not favorably compare with their parents. They cannot look one in the eye. They are shy. They stutter and stammer. If an old-stock American, or anyone of some standing, is due to come to their house, they fuss and fret with their parents. They force their peasant mothers to go to the hairdressers, to put on American ladies' dresses and high-heeled shoes which often make the mothers incongruous figures. Then, when the visitor arrives, they tremble at what the old lady or the old man might say, or that he might mispronounce English words even worse than usually. Their limp handshakes gave me creepy feelings all the way from New York to the Iron Range in Minnesota. Those handshakes symbolized for me the distressing tendency on the part of this vast and growing section of America's population toward characterlessness, lack of force and spirit, and other inferior personal qualities.

From whatever angle one looks at it, this is a serious matter for the New Americans as individuals and for America. Thirty million — or even fifteen or twenty million, a probable number to which most or all of my generalizations here are directly applicable — are a lot of people, and this " second generation " will be (many already are) the fathers and mothers of the third generation, and it is not impossible that in two or three decades half of the population of the United States will be of these new cultural and national strains.

III

What then should be done — what can be done about it?

In going about the country in 1934 and subsequently, I met several New Americans of whom most of the things I say above are not true. None of them was totally free of personal inferiority feelings (in fact, I find that even very few old-stock Americans are entirely free of them), but they were, nevertheless, fine-looking young men and women, boys and girls, keen and alert, articulate, ambitious, personally charming. Some were still in high school, one or two in college, and doing well as students; in fact, rather better than old-stock American students. Three or four of the boys were locally prominent football and baseball players.[1] Their handshakes were firm and they looked me in the eye. A few had a lively sense of humor which they could apply to themselves. Their laughter had a healthy ring. They knew something of what was going on in the country, in the world. Some of them, although still very young, seemed to know what they wanted from life. Two or three had literary ambitions. One told me he would try to get into politics " in a big way," by which I understood that the United States Senate was not beyond his gaze; and his name was Wojciezkowski. Another, attending the University of Pittsburgh, thought he would get a job in a steel mill and become a labor leader. In a bleak iron town in Minnesota I met a pretty girl of Slovenian parentage who was the best student in her school, had a vivid personality, and seemed entirely normal in all her attitudes. And so on, and so on. They impressed me as real, solid persons who would be an asset to any country.

Nearly all of them, in their childhood and later, had been unpleasantly af-

---

[1] Athletes with " foreign " names, as is generally known, are not unusual. But most of them, in high schools and colleges as well as in more or less professional sports, are New Americans who are exceptional in the sense stated in this and the ensuing paragraphs.

fected by their parents' humiliating experiences as immigrants and industrial workers, and had had disagreeable experiences of their own which touched them vitally. They had been called Hunkies, Polacks, Litvaks, Dagoes. Many of them had had (and were still having) difficulties with their names. A young man of Lithuanian parentage in Pittsburgh, attending the university there, who was attractive, " clean-cut " in the best American sense, but whose surname was Lamblagoskas, told me that when he was a young boy in McKeesport the teacher had been too lazy or too indifferent to take the trouble to pronounce his name, so she had called him only Johnnie, while all the other children in class had both a first name and a surname. Then the two-name children had begun to call him " Just Johnnie " or " Johnnie the Litvak," which annoyed him very much. As in hundreds of thousands of similar instances, this, in conjunction with other experiences of that nature, produced in him an acute inferiority complex which oppressed him for years — " until," as he put it, " I sort of worked myself out of it."

A young man of Slavic origin, whose surname also was difficult for Anglo-Saxon tongues, told me that in his boyhood he had suffered a great deal because old-stock American boys called him " Sneeze-it," because in school one day the teacher had said that his name could not be pronounced but thought that perhaps she could maybe sneeze it. " But now," he said to me, " things like that don't bother me very much."

Others in this category with whom I came in contact had had and were still having — inevitably, let me repeat — other troubles on account of being immigrants' children; but these troubles were not seriously affecting them, were not preventing them from developing into balanced, strong and healthy, charming human beings.

Why? There are at least two explanations. One is that most of them lived, during at least part of their lives, in comparatively favorable economic circumstances, and their parents managed to give them some schooling in addition to the legal requirement, which helped them more or less to work themselves out of their various second-generation complexes. The other explanation (probably not unrelated to, but I think more important than, the first) is that, in all cases without exception which came to my attention, their fathers and mothers were wise and articulate enough to convey to them something of their backgrounds in the old countries; tell them what it meant to be a Finn, a Slovenian, a Serbian, a Croatian, a Slovak, a Czech, a Pole, or a Lithuanian, and inspire in them some respect for that meaning; make them conscious of their backgrounds and heritage, give them some sense of continuity, some feeling of their being part of America, in which immigrants like themselves played an important role — part of something bigger and better than the bleak, utterly depressing existence led by them and their neighbors in the grimy steel mill and iron and coal mining towns where they lived.

During my 1934 trip and later, I met, as I say, scores of these New Americans. Among them were some of the most attractive people I have encountered anywhere. Some of these I already have mentioned. Another was a girl born and still living in Cleveland, whose father and mother were Slovenians; and there is no doubt in my mind that much of her charm issued from the fact that she was keenly conscious of her parents' native land and culture. Two years before, they had taken her on a visit to Slovenia, and she had discovered a tiny country which is physically as lovely as anything she had seen in America, with an old, mellow culture, a rich folklore, a considerable modern literature, and interesting folkways behind which there are centuries of wisdom and a long, unbroken chain of experience on the part of a quiet, peace-loving little nation that has lived there for a thousand years.

Still another of these exceptional New Americans was a young six-footer of Finnish parentage on the Iron Range in Minnesota. He had never been to Finland, but knew a good deal about the basic cultural qualities of that country from his mother's word-pictures of it. He also had a fluent command of the Finnish language which did not interfere with (indeed, enriched) his English. He knew dozens of Finnish folk ballads and lyrics and sang them well, and had read and re-read in the original the great Finnish epic poem " The Kalevala." He was quietly proud of his people's achievements on the Iron Range both in the mines and on the land, and thought that Minnesota was his country. Despite the bleakness of the region, and the hard life led there by most of the people, especially the Finns, he loved the Iron Range. His people had worked and suffered there for decades and converted great parts of it into farming country, although before they came nobody had thought it could ever be made suitable for anything.

In short, he was conscious of his background; he had a sense of continuity, of being part of a great human experience which was part of the still greater American adventure. Largely, I think, in consequence of this, a strength of character was discernible in his every move and utterance.

I could give several more such cases of exceptional New Americans, but that would be, in the main, repeating what I have said of the girl in Cleveland and the boy in Minnesota. All of them — representing, however, but a small minority — were conscious and, in a greater or lesser degree, proud of their racial groups' background in the old countries, and some also of their racial groups' background and history in this country. They had a sense of continuity, a feeling of being a part of something. And they, I think, are the answer to the question: What should be done about the problem sketched in this essay?

The answer is that the New Americans, whose inarticulate and otherwise inadequate (through no fault of their own) parents have been unable to give them much along these lines, should be helped to acquire a knowledge of, and pride in, their own heritage and makeup; and this help should come, in very large part, from already established and functioning social and cultural institutions and agencies — schools, libraries, settlement and community houses, newspapers, lecture forums, and so on — in coöperation with a central organization which should be formed for the purpose of devising ways to disseminate information about the several racial or national groups represented among the thirty million " second generation " citizens, and for the purpose of studying the problem and working out programs of action for its gradual solution or amelio-ration, from the point of view of honest, intelligent concern for the country's future.

By now it is obvious to many people interested in the problem that it is impossible and, what is more, *undesirable* to make the offspring of Lithuanians or Serbians into Anglo-Saxons; that the aim should be rather to help them become real men and women on the pattern of their own natural cultures. There should be a recognition of the fact that America is not purely an Anglo-Saxon country; if only by virtue of numbers, it is also something else. *A new conception of America is necessary.* There is no doubt that in the few places where no attempts have been made by " patriotic " old-time Americans to force immigrants' children into the old-stock American mold — as, for instance, in the Bohemian communities in Nebraska and Texas, where Bohemians already are in the fourth generation; in the little city of Hamtramck near Detroit, where the public school system consistently encourages the large Polish group there to keep its individuality; in O. E. Rölvaag's Norwegian settlements in the Northwest; in some of the foreign " colonies " in New York City, notably the Ukrainian one on the Lower East Side; or in several small Polish, Italian, and Finnish rural communities in New England, upstate New York, and elsewhere — the development of character, mentality, and physique in the New American element has been vastly more felicitous than where such attempts have been made.

Social and cultural institutions and agencies in various cities and towns where the problem stares them all in the face, wherever they turn, already are beginning to do things to help New Americans develop more or less on the pattern of their backgrounds. To give a few examples: in Cleveland the excellent public library organization, with its scores of branch libraries, has begun to help the New Americans to learn something about themselves, their parents' native lands and their national groups' history in this coun-try, particularly in Cleveland. All three of the big newspapers there have spe-cial reporters covering the " foreign sections " of the city, and print feature articles about the various foreign groups' contribution to the growth and de-velopment of Cleveland. Public-school and high-school teachers in Cleveland, as in one or two other cities, whose classes are anywhere from forty to eighty per cent " foreign," are becoming eagerly interested in " second-generation problems " which face them in the form of numerous neurotic and backward or " problem " children who, for no apparent reason, burst out crying in the middle of a lesson. Of late teachers nearly everywhere, I am told, have ad-vanced so far that they take the trouble to learn the correct pronunciation of difficult Polish, Yugoslav, Lithuanian, Czech, Finnish, and Slovak names, and to caution the old-stock American boys and girls not to call the New American children Hunkies, Wops, and other such names of derision.

In more than half the cities and towns which I visited in 1934 and since, I found the so-called International Institutes, some of them part of the Y.W.C.A., which — with their clubrooms, reading rooms, lectures, social affairs, exhibits of European peasant arts, and printed matter — are beginning to attempt to do something for the second generation, especially the girls. In Flint, Michigan, in Toledo, Ohio, and in one or two other places, I came upon purely local organizations, some of them officered and run by such exceptional New Americans as I have described above, aiming to help the general run of New Americans to fight their feelings of inferiority.

I came upon professional social workers who were doing research in certain phases of the problem and knew a great deal about the local departments thereof. The directors of most of the settlement houses in Pittsburgh, Detroit, Chicago, and Milwaukee were more or less awake to the situation as it existed locally and — in most cases, however, without having any real understanding of it — were also trying to do something about it. The same could be said of various settlement house workers, teachers, a few ministers, and other agencies elsewhere.

All these efforts, or rather beginnings of efforts, are local, however; usually honest enough but very restricted in scope. The International Institutes, for instance, appeal largely to girls. There is no central or national organization interested in the thing as a countrywide problem, which it undoubtedly is, and, as I have tried to show here, a tremendous and important one — important to old-stock Americans and to Americans of the third and fourth generation no less than to these New Americans, and to America as a whole.

The organization I have in mind, which let us designate here as XYZ, would have, during the next twenty or thirty years, a vast and complicated task to perform — namely, to give these millions of New Americans a knowledge of, and pride in, their own heritage, an understanding of their own makeup, which, to some extent, would operate to counteract their feelings of inferiority about themselves in relation to the rest of the country; and, simultaneously, to create a sympathetic understanding toward them on the part of older Americans, so that the latter's anti-" foreign " prejudice, which is partly to blame for inferiority feelings in the new racial groups, would tend to lessen and ultimately be reduced to a minimum.

It would be a great educational-cultural work, the basic aim of which would be (1) to reach, in one way or another, almost everybody in this country with the fact that socially and culturally the United States, as it stands today, is an extension not only of the British Isles and the Netherlands but, more or less, of all Europe; and (2), with constant reiteration and intelligent elaboration of that fact, to try to harmonize and integrate, so far as possible, the various racial and cultural strains in our population without suppressing or destroying any good cultural qualities in any of them, but using and directing these qualities toward a possible enhancement of the color and quality of our national life in America.

IV

I realize, of course, that the problem I sketch here is closely tied up with the socio-economic system under which we live; that, next to their being more or less strangers here, the worst factors behind the inferiority feelings of these millions of New Americans are poverty and its sister evil, ignorance, both of them brought over by the immigrants and then fostered by conditions here; and that the cure for most of the second-generation ills lies, ultimately, in the solution of our socio-economic problem. I doubt, however, whether the latter problem will be quickly and satisfactorily solved in this country if we permit to develop in our population a vast element, running into tens of millions, which is oppressed by acute feelings of inferiority and, largely as a result of those feelings, is becoming actually inferior human material — bewildered, politically neutral, economically unaggressive, culturally nowhere. If this element is left alone in the face of its growing economic difficulties, and in the face of the organized and unorganized prejudice against it on the part of " patriotic " older Americans, there might eventually be no help for it. I imagine that hundreds of thousands of New Americans already are hopeless as potential constructive elements in any sort of vital, progressive civilization and culture; and if their number is permitted to increase, they will — let me repeat — profoundly affect the future of this country in a way that no one would want to see it affected.

On the other hand, if something is done about the problem in the spirit of the above general suggestions, I believe that the majority of the New Americans and the generation that they will produce will have an opportunity to become a great body of self-respecting, constructive citizenry; and that, with the diverse racial and cultural backgrounds they inherited from their immigrant parents, they will enrich the civilization and deepen the culture of this New World.

The Editors of "Fortune"

To Heaven by Subway

AT night ships heading in to New York pick up the lights of Coney Island thirty miles out; and its voice is a muffled bellow that carries a mile and a half offshore. But on a hot, summer Sunday morning fog lies over the lower bay like a damp, too often slept-on sheet; and the only sounds are the flat clangings of the bell buoys along the channel. Toward six o'clock the fog rolls back, and there is a ten-mile basin of soupy water, empty except for a Hog Island freighter moving into quarantine or a party boat outward-bound, crowded with holiday fishermen. To the south of this basin is the Jersey coast — Atlantic Highlands and the long curving sand bar known as Sandy Hook. To the north are Brooklyn and Long Island — an uneven line of smoke-

From Fortune, August, 1938.

stacks, wharves, warehouses, gas tanks, hotels, bungalow colonies, apartment houses, Victorian mansions, crumbling jetties, and beaches. At the western end of this shore line are two and a quarter miles of sand and boardwalk, a cluster of drab shacks, and a backdrop of grotesque shapes — gigantic upthrust wheels, jigsaw towers, and roller-coaster tracks coiled and contorted like snakes trapped in a bonfire. These two and a quarter miles are Coney Island.

At close range, in the hard early morning light, Coney Island is almost incredibly banal. Shoddy shows through the tinsel; the shuttered false fronts are frankly two-dimensional; the gaily painted manes of the flying horses of the carrousels are shrouded in canvas; and even the forthright, weedy smell of the sea seems weak and flavorless. At six in the morning Coney Island is like the stage of a very old theater before the audience arrives — like the empty waiting room of the Philadelphia Broad Street Station. But the voice and color of Coney Island are its people. And at the end of a five-cent subway fare, and less than two hours away, seven million people are waking to a hot and aimless Sunday.

Coney Island itself wakens slowly. On the sand a few early bathers discard their outer clothing and perform self-conscious calisthenics under a rising sun. Along the Boardwalk men in white sailor suits, from New York's Department of Parks, spear the leavings of last night's mob. Milk wagons and beer trucks rumble down Surf Avenue a block away. And in the Bowery and the side streets concessionaires and ride foremen and spielers and counter men and ticket takers and shills collect in groups . . . and peer anxiously at the sky.

The sun, rising higher, picks up the blue and white and red of the towers of Luna park. Smells of cooking — hot dogs and clams and hamburger and fish and onion and garlic and corn — mix with the sweet smell of cotton candy and frozen custard. The light changes from cold silver to warm canary to hot, liquid brass. A dozen disheveled Shetland ponies patter up West Eighth Street toward the pony run on the Bowery, leaving behind them the acrid stench of stables. A test car slams down the ninety-foot drop of the Cyclone. In Steeplechase park a cleanup squad works on the cropped green lawn between the carrousels and the airplane swing. At the counter of a shooting gallery on the Bowery a freak-show dwarf, off duty, gravely inspects a new target and gravely remarks, " That'll wow 'em, Herman. That'll wow 'em sure." And up and down the island, from auto ride to waxworks to freak show to penny arcade, goes the most important phrase in Coney Island economy, " It looks like a good hot day."

At ten the door, octogenarian Paddy Shea, " the original," " the old reliable," takes his seat at the door of his " Gilsey House " saloon. Coney Island is officially awake. And as though at the appearance of a concertmeister the Coney Island orchestra starts tuning up. A spieler tests his microphone with a sudden blast of sound. " Have you tried it? Have you tried it? It's Fascination — that fascinating game." And a block away another answers, " Learn to play Bingo. Free game now going on." And down the street another picks it up — and another — and another — a growing wave of sound flowing up the island

and returning and flowing back again. " Get your hot dogs here. Red hot." —
" Three balls for a dime. Step right up. The ladies play it too." — " Charlie
McCarthy. Take home a Charlie McCarthy." — " Test your skill. Everybody
wins." — " Get your thrill here. Fastest ride on the island." — " Have you tried
it? You'll like it. Oh boy, you'll like it." — And the shills and the boosters
move up to the game tables — and a carrousel organ breaks into *Bei mir bist du
schön* — and the gaily painted horses with their necks arched high move off
in stately procession — and the tinsel changes to gold — and adventure walks
suddenly in the streets — and under the hot summer sun Coney Island slowly
melts and comes slowly to a boil.

Into this fluid mass the subway pours the people of New York and its
visitors — young girls with firm high breasts and pretty legs and shrill, discordant voices — hat-snatching adolescents and youths on the make — children
in arms and children underfoot and children in trouble — harried, scolding
mothers and heavy-suited, heavy-booted fathers — soldiers and sailors and marines — virgins and couples in love and tarts — Gentiles and Jews and the in-
betweens — whites and blacks and orientals — Irish and Italians and Poles and
Swedes and Letts and Greeks — pushing, plodding, laughing, jostling, shriek-
ing, sweating, posing — shedding their identities, with their inhibitions, in
the voice, the smell, the color of Coney Island.

No one knows exactly how Coney Island came by its name. There are those
who claim that it derives from the cone-shaped sand dunes of the original
beach. And there are others who believe that it is a perversion of Colman —
the name of a sailor on Henry Hudson's *Half Moon* who was killed by Indians
in an unexplained brawl. But the most heavily supported and most plausible
tradition is that the early Dutch settlers found hordes of rabbits scampering
across the sand dunes and called it Konijn Eiland or Rabbit Island, of which
Coney was a logical and gradual derivation.

In any case Coney Island is not an island at all. Part of Coney Island Creek,
which once separated it from the body of Brooklyn and in which the fishing
was once very good indeed, was long ago filled in. And much of what was
historically Coney Island is Coney Island no longer. Its western flank has become the eminently respectable, prosaic residential district known as Sea Gate.
To the east it has become the bungalow colony of Brighton and Joe Day's development at Manhattan Beach. But although Coney Island has been decimated
and although geographically and corporately it is a part of Brooklyn, and therefore a part of New York, it retains an intensely jealous civic consciousness and
a chamber of commerce of its own.

The community that the chamber represents, in theory at least, is a city
of 100,000 that swells in summer to 200,000 and is divided into two parts by a
Main Street known as Surf Avenue. To the north is the year-round Coney
Island of the commuters — a section of drab rooming houses and inferior
residences, tapering off in a blighted area along the polluted waters of Gravesend Bay and what is left of Coney Island Creek. On both sides of the avenue
itself, and in the single long strip of land to the south that ends at the Board-

walk and the beach, is concentrated the Coney Island that lives only four months out of the year.

This narrow strip of land, about eight hundred to one thousand feet in width and two and a quarter miles long, is assessed at $22,000,000. It is the home of sixty bathhouses, two big amusement parks (Steeplechase and Luna), seventy " ball " games, thirteen carrousels, eleven roller coasters, five tunnel rides, three fun houses, two waxworks, six penny arcades, twenty shooting galleries, three freak shows, a variety of other games, rides, shows, and souvenir shops, and some two hundred eating establishments — more than five hundred separate enterprises in violent and continual conflict — perhaps the greatest concentration of independent little businesses in the world. But while each of these little businesses is violently, continuously, and vocally in competition with each of its more than five hundred competitors, each to a greater or lesser degree derives profit from the others. For it is the sum total of all the Coney Island attractions that creates the Coney Island market and its urge to spend. A single pitch-till-you-win concessionaire spieling alone on a Coney Island sand dune would draw few nickels into his till.

As it is, some twenty-five million people pile into this area in a season — as many as a million on a hot Sunday — leaving behind them a sum estimated at anything from $7,500,000 to $35,000,000. But whatever the amount — and whether derived from the family on relief or from the twenty-dollar plunger and his girl friend — it is an accumulation of the smallest coins of the country; a flow of millions of dollars from the aorta of the city into its most minute capillaries. Coney Island is today the empire of the nickel.

This, however, was not always so. Coney Island has gone through three incarnations. In its earliest days — in the middle of the eighteen-hundreds — the island was pretty definitely unsavory. Three-card-monte men pitched their stands along the beach and split their take with roving gangs of blacklegs, spiritual ancestors of the modern racketeer. At low tide bodies were washed up on the shore with startling frequency. A minor politician, Michael Norton, extended his rule over wide areas of South Brooklyn operating from his own notorious roadhouse, the " Old West End." And the oldest trade in the world was plied in sight of the sea.

Toward the end of the century Coney Island, considerably regenerated, entered a period of greater prosperity and greater respectability — a period, however, that was not without its conflicts and uncertainties. The gay blades of Brooklyn and Manhattan and their pretty young women drove their spanking trotters out to the race tracks at Gravesend and Sheepshead Bay and to the luxurious new hotels at Brighton and Manhattan Beach. But in Coney Island people spoke of " a family resort "; and bicycle clubs gave picnic parties on the sand; and the old Iron Steamboat line put a boat in regular service between the Battery and Steeplechase pier; and solid citizens moved in — founders of the present Coney Island " families " — the Tilyous of Steeplechase park, the Feltmans who made the frankfurter an American institution, and William F. Mangels, the gentle recreation philosopher, who invented the neck-cracking

Whip, and who, with his son, still manufactures Whips and carrousels and "kiddie rides" within a half mile of the ocean.

Champagne was the occasional though far from universal drink; and along Surf Avenue were restaurants with kitchens as fine and menus as impressive as those of Rector's and Bustanoby's in Manhattan; and it was possible and not unusual to pay a twenty-dollar check for a dinner for two. But for every venison steak and *purée de marrons* served in Feltman's more exclusive dining rooms a hundred frankfurters were served across its counters.

The nickel empire, the third and greatest period of Coney Island prosperity, arrived with the extension of the subway and its five-cent fare to Coney Island in 1920. Or perhaps, more accurately, 1920 is a convenient line of demarcation between two periods that dovetail. As late as 1910 Coney Island might have gone in either of two directions. It might have emphasized its tonier restaurants and exclusive bathhouses and become a convenient summer resort for the well-to-do New Yorker — a sort of glorified Atlantic City. Or it might have followed the frankfurter and the roller coaster and the public beach and become the playground of the masses. After 1910 it could still strike a compromise of sorts between the two. But the subway in 1920 forced a decision. Coney Island became the empire of the nickel.

Coney Island economy is founded primarily on weather. Most of its money is earned in a season only fourteen week-ends long. Three rainy week-ends may mean the difference between profit and loss; five can easily mean bankruptcy. For a summer Sunday cannot be postponed; once lost it is gone forever. The islanders tell you that you can make money by betting against the weather bureau. And because weather is largely unpredictable, and because the cost of rain insurance is prohibitively high, most Coney Island concessionaires roll their shutters up and down with the thermometer as the clouds roll by. And even big Steeplechase park must be prepared to open its gates on a half hour's notice.

Secondary factor in the nickel empire's economy is the nickel itself — and its abundance in the pockets of the Coney Island customer. The nickel was first a symbol of a new order; it became in time a reality. The mass market slowly forced Coney Island's time-honored price scales downward. The fifty-cent rides became a quarter. The quarter rides became fifteen cents. The ten-cent rides became five. And even the ten-cent frankfurter was by the latter nineteen-twenties reduced to a nickel. But until the depression of the early nineteen-thirties the abundance of nickels was unaffected by war or panic or depression. In 1907, and in 1914, and in 1921 — when business indexes were off from twenty to forty per cent — the Coney Island take varied practically not at all. And the more enlightened Islanders referred to their business as a depression-proof industry. But in the last six or seven years, and more particularly in the first month and a half of the current season, Coney Island has felt the pinch. The empire of the nickel is frankly worried.

In terms of nickels Coney Island is today three-quarters amusement park and one-quarter beach. But in terms of numbers the position is reversed. And it is on the beach that any properly conducted tour of the island must begin.

It is a fairly good beach, but it includes only fifty-seven acres of sand at high tide. Armed with lunch boxes, water wings, baseballs, harmonicas, hot dogs, diapers, beer bottles, olive oil, and peanuts, and employing every conceivable stratagem for the nominal draping of their more essentially private parts, six hundred thousand nature lovers, seventy-five million pounds of flesh, black, white, and yellow, converge on this narrow strip on a good Sunday, occupying it to its last square foot of hot dun-colored sand. Perhaps less than a quarter of this army has passed through one or another of Coney Island's bathhouses. More than three-quarters are there through benefit only of the five-cent subway fare. Most of these have worn their bathing suits as underwear — but a few liberated souls have changed briskly on the spot. So, despite the vigilance of the new beach patrol, one of the first and most lasting impressions of Coney beach is not the clothing that is worn — the frankly homemade concessions to modesty, the patched and darned relics of a past prosperity, or the vivid plumage of Davega's, and Macy's basement, and Klein's — but rather the clothing that has been discarded and lies over Coney beach and flutters from Coney jetties and hangs limply on the superstructure of Steeplechase pier.

The one-quarter or less that has yielded to modesty or comfort or convention and has changed its clothes in a bathhouse has had a wide range of accommodations to choose from. There are first the so-called big ten (including Ravenhall, Tilyou, Washington, McLochlin, Ocean Tide, Ward, and Stauch) whose lockers cost some forty to fifty cents a day — a fee that may include the use of a pool, handball and basketball courts, and a solarium for sun-bathing, and that sometimes includes a bathing suit. (Eighty per cent of the customers used to rent suits. Only twenty per cent do today.) Between them these ten bathhouse aristocrats shelter from a million and a quarter to two million and a half people in a season, collect from $300,000 to $500,000, and account for some fifty per cent of Coney Island's total bathhouse bill. Most of them, however, are doing little better than break even and their take is steadily declining.

Then there are the lesser boardwalk bathhouses, where undressing facilities are as low as fifteen cents, two for a quarter, which do another twenty per cent of the total bathhouse business. And there are the white-elephantine Municipal Baths (one-third closed), now under the supervision of the New York City Department of Parks, which entertained 150,000 people last year at fifteen and twenty-five cents a head — only an estimated seven per cent of the island's business. And along the side streets are scores of rickety bathhouses, thrown together in alleyways and back yards. And north of Surf Avenue are the dozens of frankly illegal bedroom bathhouses whose dubious proprietors solicit business in the streets and where as many as ten mixed couples may share a single bedroom, hanging their clothes from the mantelpiece and draping them across the bed.

Compared with the relatively genteel Jones Beach, twenty-five miles down the shore, Coney Island is disorganized, uncouth, and bawdy. The Department of Parks, which has just taken over the island's beach and the Boardwalk, may hope to turn it into another Jones Beach; but the fact remains that Manhattan families can spend the day at Coney Island with no expenditure other than a ten-cent per person round-trip subway fare, while a day at Jones Beach adds up to several times that sum per person for transportation alone.

To police the fifty-seven acres of Coney beach requires an infinite practical tolerance. This is the job of the park department's eighty lifeguards, who watch over the physical well-being of the splashing thousands in the water and less critically over the moral and esthetic welfare of the tens of thousands on the shore. Chief of the Coney Island lifeguards is John McMonigle. For ten years John McMonigle was a jockey — riding the hurdles and on the flat. But for thirty-seven years he has been a lifeguard at Coney Island. His round Irish face belongs to a man nearing sixty; but his trim body is that of a plenty tough guy of forty, and you have the feeling that John McMonigle would be a good man to have on your side if the going got bad.

Who are the people who come to Coney Island beach?

"Just people. The same ones you meet in the subway or at the movies Saturday night or on the street goin' home from work. Only out here they're having a good time. And maybe they don't care quite so much. Maybe they forget a little. And maybe that's a good thing too."

What about drownings?

"Back in the old days they used to run fifty, sixty a year. Now it's down to three or four on the average. In 1935 there wasn't a one. Rescues are different. We have two, three hundred a year honest-to-God rescues . . . not counting the belly rescues where you just go out in the catamaran and tow 'em in. Who are they mostly? Just dumb kids — eighteen, twenty-one years old — putting on a show for the girl friend back on shore. You get so you can spot 'em after a while — the bad swimmers. All that running in, splashing around, don't mean a thing. Half the time the guy can't swim twenty yards. The fat dames is different. Hell, you don't have to worry about them — can't swim a lick — but they go in, dog paddle around two hours, an' never touch bottom. By God, you can't sink 'em."

It must be hard for a lifeguard to keep his mind on his work with all those pretty little girls . . .

". . . An' especially when the girls make a play for the guy because he's kind of a hero. But we watch that all the time. A lifeguard can't let down at all. Hell, you never know when some poor slob might get in trouble. And the lifeguard off minding somebody else's business. We had a case just the other day. Nice kid . . . working his way through school. We found him down in one of the boats. 'And what were you doing?' I says. 'She was just sittin' on the side of the boat,' he says. 'I didn't ask you what *she* was doin',' I says. But I'm tellin' you that was something."

Does the crowd ever pull any rough stuff?

"Well, not so often. The Communists come down and hold meetings and try to put up banners. And sometimes a guy gets a little too much to drink — and you know, once in a while. But it's all in knowing how to get along with 'em. Be polite — and never put a finger on one of 'em or you're in for a lawsuit. The trick is to talk 'em out of it. Hell, they don't mean it anyhow."

Which is in itself a benediction on Coney beach. And whatever the park department's plans may be it is probable that Coney beach will remain Coney beach for a long time to come. Kosher picnics will litter the sand; youths will chase baseballs across the backs of couples lost in earnest embrace; girls will parade by twos and fours along the water's edge; the physical needs of the youngest generation will be relieved in full sight of God and man; and the fat old women will dog paddle around for hours without being able to swim a lick.

Noon is a scarcely noticeable break in the Coney Island routine. There is simply a slight intensification in the eating that has been more or less general and continuous from early morning and will last until the lights go out — cotton candy, apples on sticks, yellow corn. But now whole families fall to on chunks of rye bread and salami and hot dogs, and in the Negro section in front of the municipal baths there is a certain amount of fried chicken wrapped in oilpaper. As the day progresses, the discards and the leavings and the accidentally dropped portions of these tons of food begin to pile up despite the beach patrol and the numerous but half-empty wastebaskets, and the busy flies.

For those who have not brought their own food supply or who have run short there are many possibilities. There are the small " under the Boardwalk " concessions — dark, sunless booths selling hot dogs and ice cream and beer and *knishes,* Jewish potato cakes flavored with onion and *koisha* and fried in deep fat. Further afield, on the side streets toward Surf Avenue, are dozens of small restaurants and stands, kosher and non-kosher — Rumanian tearooms, pop stands, hot-dog grills, and custard counters. For the very superior there is the chaste dining room of the Half Moon Hotel whose big second-floor windows look out across the Boardwalk and ocean. For the thirsty there are many licensed bars; but hard liquor puts a deep dent in a week-end budget, and beer is the accepted drink of Coney Island.

And then there is Feltman's — Coney Island's largest, most elaborate, and most indigenous eating place.

Feltman's was founded on three things — shrewd German common sense, an act of God, and the ten-cent frankfurter. The common sense and the frankfurter were brought to Coney Island by a German baker named Charles Feltman when he opened a restaurant on a 200 by 150 foot plot in 1871. The act of God was the addition of some 1,200 feet of free land piled on to this plot by an obliging sea. This potent combination founded the first great Coney Island family dynasty and a practical long-time monopoly over Coney's restaurant business — a monopoly carried on by Charles's sons, Charles L. and Alfred, and by Charles A. of the third generation, whose likeness to Franchot Tone of the cinema is frequently noted.

Feltman's bridged the three periods of Coney Island history, prospered in each, and reached its peak during the big days of the nickel empire. At the height of Coney's boom of the middle nineteen-twenties Feltman's employed some 1,200 men, could serve 8,000 meals at one time in its Alpine gardens and frankfurter bars and fisherees, boasted of serving 7,000,000 meals in one year, and illuminated this gargantuan scene with some 42,000 electric lights. Its gross volume and its net profits have never been revealed. But at its peak the gross was probably well above $2,000,000; and the Feltman block is today assessed at $1,200,000.

Unfortunately for Feltman's the ten-cent frankfurter could not be patented, and acts of God have a way of averaging off. What happened to Feltman's was a newcomer named Nathan who preceded the depression into Coney Island with a frankfurter at five cents.

Today Feltman's puts on a brave front. Its chef is from the Roney-Plaza in Miami Beach; its frankfurters are still stubbornly priced at ten cents; it still serves by far the best food on the island; and it is wooing its lost customers with a variety of new attractions. A carrousel blares in one corner of the Surf Avenue restaurant. New games and concessions, including a soul-shattering ride called the Boomerang, have blossomed in the long arcade leading to the Boardwalk. And in what was once an Alpine garden moving pictures of the past are now shown nightly at ten cents. But Feltman's 1,200 employees have dwindled to 300 or 350. And there is a persistent rumor that the entire property has been offered for sale. Meanwhile less than a quarter mile away is Nathan's — a corner lunch counter employing perhaps fifty people and occupying only a tiny fraction of Feltman's acres. But the crowd fills the sidewalk fifteen deep, overflows into the street, and blocks the traffic in Surf Avenue — while above its head in endless succession is repeated the magic symbol — 5¢ — in letters of fire-engine red.

The Coney Island Boardwalk cost the people of New York City $4,000,000, and it is as free as the air, the sun, and the beach. Which is to say that on a Sunday afternoon it is alive from sea rail to concession booth. " H-e-e-r-r y-a-a-r-r. H-e-e-r-r y-a-a-r-r. Three balls for a dime. Test your skill." It's the exhortation of a passionate and profane revivalist. It's the voice of the concessionaire . . .

. . . " I been in this park an' carny racket goin' on forty years — the last ten right here on the island. I got a brother's runnin' a geek show in a carnival that's playin' Harlan County an' another that's got the cookhouse an' a pitch-till-you-win out in Nebraska an' my wife's a mentalist. An' I'm tellin' you I never see a year like this. Three week-ends rainy in a row. And when the people come they don't spend. Why hell, there used to be a time you could set up a bottle game, cost you maybe one, two hundred bucks, an' clear that in a week, three balls for ten cents. Now you're lucky if you take that much in a season. Sure some of them big games is makin' money — but, what the hell, costs you maybe twenty, thirty grand — an' next year where are you? Maybe in business, maybe up the creek. Then there's this guy Moss — Paul Moss, the Commissioner of Licenses — where does he think he gets off cuttin' out the bally an' handin' out tickets an' makin' you pay off in merchandise when the Jersey parks is payin' cash. Sure I believe in runnin' games on the level. You gotta keep this racket clean and decent. It's a family racket, that's what I always says. But where does that guy get off tellin' us how to run our business? Of course maybe some of the games was gimmicked a little, but what the hell. You gotta have a percentage with the house don't you? The people just ain't got no money. If there was another soldier's bonus — Jeeze, we got halfa that the first week they paid it off. But that's all over. This new spendin' gag down in Washington oughta mean somethin' — if they hand it out in cash. But it's too late to catch it this year. World's Fair? Listen, there ain't goin' to be no World's Fair. That's the way I figure it. People ain't goin' to pay the rents Whalen's askin'. The small men can't. It ain't in the cards. An' the big ones won't. But I'm tellin' you, mister, I never see a year like this one — an' if it wasn't for the old woman an' my youngest kid — she has the custard stand — I'd be thinkin' about gettin' out on the road again myself where a guy maybe has a chance to pick up a little decent dough — so help me God."

Further along the Boardwalk, just beyond Steeplechase, is a white-fronted entrance with a sign above it reading, "Life Begins at the Baby Incubators." Pay your twenty cents and go in; the Boardwalk is only a few yards away, but you are in a miniature hospital — white-walled, immaculate, remote. Along the rear, behind a brass rail, is a row of eight airtight, glass-walled boxes, each with a bubbling oxygen tank beside it, each holding from one to two incredibly minute babies wrapped in fleece. To the left, behind a glass window, is a fully equipped modern nursery. Lined up at the rail a group of self-conscious young couples and wide-eyed elderly women listen to a youngish man who speaks in a low voice with a clipped Liverpool accent.

" Now this little baby came in nine days ago. It weighed only one pound ten ounces and we were afraid we might be too late. It was even bluer than that little fellow over in the other incubator. . . . Yes, ma'am, it was a premature birth. About six months . . ."

Baby incubators are one of the major paradoxes that have flowered in Coney Island. They appeal to an unhealthy morbidity; and they have been condemned as rank exploitation. Actually the display is completely humanitarian and has the endorsement of the archconservative American Medical Association. Baby incubators have been the lifework of an astonishing individual, by name Dr. Martin A. Couney, a seventy-year-old physician who combines two diametrically opposed qualities — showmanship and scientific integrity. Dr. Couney developed his first baby incubator in the early eighteen-nineties when he was a young interne in a Paris hospital. His funds were limited, and the medical profession was apathetic. Showmanship came to his rescue. He decided to finance his work by direct public subscription in the form of admission fees. His first public appearance, at the Berlin exposition in 1896, was highly successful. There was, however, one minor embarrassment. The name selected for the new contrivance was *Kinderbrütenanstalt,* or baby-breeding place. And many a literal-minded German was disappointed to find on entering that babies were not being bred at all — merely being kept warm.

Doctor Couney landed at Coney Island in 1904 and has been there ever since — although he has maintained separate establishments at Atlantic City and at the Chicago Century of Progress. In his forty-odd years of work he has saved the lives of some seven thousand prematurely born babies — ninety per cent of all those brought to him. These are as a rule children of the poor. Occasionally, however, when all hospital facilities are in use, he takes the children of well-to-do parents; but in no case does he accept a fee. He keeps the babies for from two to three months, then sends them home. To break even, the display must take in $150 a day at twenty cents a ticket. There are the salaries of five registered nurses (one of whom is Doctor Couney's daughter), two wet nurses, and the attendants to be paid — not to mention the cost of equipment, heat, rent, and oxygen. Currently that $150 is not even covered during week-ends, and there is a weekly deficit of some $600. But there have been times in the past when things have gone better, and following the Chicago exposition Dr. Couney was able to present his entire equipment to the Infant Aid Society and endow it with a $16,000 fund.

Coney Island is peppered with the alumni of Dr. Couney's hospital. One is an electrician at Steeplechase; two others work at Luna park; and recently another won a " high sales " prize as a clerk at the five-and-ten. Dr. Couney himself bought five dollars' worth of knickknacks at the last minute to help her win. At a recent birthday party for one two-year-old alumnus, six others were present to help him celebrate.

On hot summer afternoons thunderstorms rise over Coney Island with little warning. To a large part of the island they mean sheer loss; but to Steeplechase park they return a moderate profit. For many of the more solvent of the fleeing thousands seek shelter in its big pavilion, and the admission charge is fifty cents a head.

Steeplechase believes in a few simple truisms. It believes that most people never grow up and that even adolescents like to escape back into childhood. It believes that half the world likes to show off and that the other and less daring half is perpetually interested in the performance. And it believes that pretty legs, however trite, are never dull, and that ugly ones are always funny. And largely because of these truisms the crowds in Steeplechase park are big and noisy and predominantly young and almost frantically amused, and because of this Steeplechase itself is like all the Sunday-school picnics in the world gathered into a single fifteen-acre park.

Steeplechase has a swimming pool and a roller coaster and a Ferris wheel and an airplane swing and an Old Mill scattered over its acres of green lawn. But the heart of Steeplechase is its pavilion, five acres of hardwood floor under a vaulted ceiling of glass and steel. Around the outer edge of this pavilion sweep the famous Steeplechase horses, eight abreast, a couple astride each horse, on tracks that rise and dip and fall away. By leaning forward at the top of the inclines you can increase your speed and beat your seven competitors; but when you dismount, the only exit is into a labyrinth of passages. You emerge from the labyrinth on to a brightly lighted stage occupied by a clown and a dwarf who eye you beadily. Across the footlights you are dimly conscious of a noisy and delighted audience. As you walk self-consciously toward an exit door downstage right, a sudden gust of wind from below whips your partner's skirt above her waist; the clown touches you with a rod and you get a sharp electric shock; and as you clutch your wounded parts the floor buckles under you. The clown shouts a warning; your partner grabs at her hat; a second gust of wind lifts her skirt; the dwarf whacks you mightily with a dingbat; piles of barrels by the door suddenly totter above your head; and you stumble off stage into the grateful anonymity of the crowd with the applause or derision of the audience in your ears.

Across the pavilion from the stage there is a revolving platter of highly polished wood that spills you off against the sides of a crowd-encircled ring; from a platform under the roof the granddaddy of all slides drops you down into a depressed saucer in the floor; from a funnel you drop out onto a table on which a dozen small plates whirl rapidly in opposite directions; swings carry you out above the heads of the crowd; the giant Hoop-La, powered by four agile acrobats, swoops up and down and around; and on a half acre of ballroom floor, couples gyrate in parodies of eccentric dances.

These are the simple ingredients of Steeplechase — good-natured horseplay and crowd hysteria; exhibitionism and frank adolescent sex. And it is the crowd itself that puts on the show.

The monetary unit at Steeplechase is fifty cents. This covers a combination ticket including admission to the park, the pavilion, the ballroom, and all thirty-one of Steeplechase's rides and attractions. And it is this fifty-cent combination ticket that sets Steeplechase apart from the rest of Coney Island. High enough in price to exclude a vast majority of the Coney Island mob, low enough to attract some thirty thousand on a good Sunday, and a fixed charge so that a couple or a family can budget its expenses for an entire day (it takes a good seven or eight hours to try each Steeplechase attraction once), the combination ticket has helped Steeplechase weather Coney Island's first depression and has made it by far the most profitable enterprise on the island.

Steeplechase, which is assessed at more than $2,000,000, is owned by Coney Island's first family — the Tilyous. It was conceived and built by George C. Tilyou, whose father, a French Huguenot, was one of the early Coney Island pioneers. And it is operated today by his sons, Ed and Frank and George C., Jr., who boast that whenever the park is open at least one Tilyou and usually two are there. The park they operate, however, is not the original Steeplechase; that was burned to the ground in 1907 — in one of Coney Island's six major fires. And a story the Tilyous like to tell is that before the embers were cool George Tilyou, Sr., was selling tickets to the hot ruins at ten cents a head.

The problems of an amusement park begin where those of a more prosaic business end. There are such relatively simple problems as charity; Steeplechase entertained some five thousand orphans last year free of charge. And there are the problems raised by the involved Coney Island economy of weather and the nickel. But the biggest and the most insoluble problem of all is human behavior — the drunk who won't go home, the spinster who was pinched by a strange man in a cap, and the boy who wants to stand up in the roller coaster. Perhaps that's why the Tilyous get such a kick out of their jobs — why it's so hard to leave the business once you're in it. As Frank Tilyou says, and he has tried both real estate and banking, " Once sand gets in your shoes, you're sunk."

There are three freak shows of a sort at Coney Island, but the islanders will tell you that there is only one showman. That's Sam Wagner of the World Circus Side Show, Inc., who has been in the business thirty-five years. Sam's two boys handle the spieling and inside lecturing. Sam didn't think much of the idea — tried to persuade them to get into something else; but it didn't work.

Sam is discouraged — on a big day he used to draw twenty thousand people at ten cents each. Now he thinks he's lucky to get eight thousand on a perfect day, and that eight thousand means a take of only $800. Sam's payroll runs about $1,000 a week and his rent and overhead come to about $600 more; so it takes only a few rainy week-ends to put Sam in the red for the year. Sam believes that one reason business is bad is that people just haven't the money to spend any more. Another is that freaks are harder to find. Sam doesn't know why. It may be the competition and it may be just that fewer freaks are born today. Then there are the new regulations of Commissioner Moss, whose power to issue and revoke licenses is the power of life and death over Coney Island shows. Sam is pretty bitter about the new regulations, which prevent honest outside bally (preview of the show on an outside stand). It's hard enough to get them in off the street with the best spieler in the world.

Sam's present show, and he admits it isn't up to some others he's had, includes: The Spider Boy; Singing Lottie, Fat Girl (O Boy, Some Entertainer); Laurello, the Only Man with a Revolving Head (See Frisco, the Wonder Dog); Professor Bernard, Magician Extraordinary (He will fool you); Professor Graf, Tattoo Artist (Alive); and his star act, Belle Bonita and her Fighting Lions (Action, Thrills). Last year he had Jack Johnson at a whopping big salary, but the take wouldn't stand the strain.

But Sam's favorites are his two famous microcephalic idiots, or pinheads, Pipo and Zipo, whom he dug up in the cracker country nine years ago after a rumor had sent him scurrying south armed with a letter of introduction from Mayor Jimmy Walker of New York to the mayor of Hartwell, Georgia.

Since that time Pipo and Zipo have supported their normal cracker relatives with the money Sam pays them for their four months in Coney. (It's $75 a week this year.) In winter they go home for a visit. Pipo is twenty-six, and has the intelligence of an eighteen-months-old baby. His sister, Zipo, is thirty-eight and is much brighter. In fact she is rather horribly smart and winsome.

They are extremely amiable and are probably better off in the four months they spend with Sam than they are at home. Not only are they well fed, clean, and comfortably housed (their rooms above the side show include a shower). With Sam they have something to do — something to look at; and each enjoys an audience.

Sam plays with his pinheads much as other people might play with a pet dog. He has taught them little tricks and mannerisms, and Zipo adores him. There is not the faintest trace of sadism in Sam as he plays with his pinheads. There is only an enormous kindness.

The Bowery runs from the western entrance of Steeplechase into Feltman's arcade. It is a narrow, congested alley, only three and a half blocks long. But at nine o'clock on a crowded Sunday night its impact is like a hard right hook to the jaw. Only slowly do single voices and smells and faces emerge from the cacophony of the whole. Above the sound of a hundred spielers shouting each other down and a dozen mechanical pianos and radios blasting a dozen different tunes you hear the sudden crash of a roller coaster dropping into space, and high above it all, a short shrill scream. Out of that single complex smell, which has a thick, moist substance of its own, you pick the primary smells of corn and cooking sugar and seaweed and strong perfume. And out of the weaving bobbing sea of faces you catch the quick, primitive technique of the pickup. " Want a ride, baby? " " You want a sock in the puss? " In the Bowery the lifeblood of Coney Island runs rich and red out to its smallest, greediest capillaries. It is the concentrated distillate of all the midways of all the carnivals in America.

There are the games — about evenly divided between those that offer something for nothing and those that provide a chance to show off. Packages of cigarettes and tall thin candy boxes stand alternately on a shelf. You shoot a cork from a popgun. You shoot till you win — but what you win is a tall thin candy box with four gray daubs of taffy, a penny a box by the gross. It's what is known as a gimmick. For the shelf is wide, the cigarettes heavy, the candy light and poorly balanced. But if you know how, you can gimmick the game — slip a thumbtack in the cork.

You throw a baseball at six bottles pyramided on a table — three balls for a dime — and you knock the six bottles down with the first ball. But you can't knock them off. A narrow band extends around the table top and keeps them in place. You may get a bamboo cane anyway. It costs the concessionaire nine-tenths of a cent.

There are the waxworks pandering openly to the morbid curiosity that always lifts newspaper circulations after a kidnaping or a good murder. But the tabloids and the confession magazines and the radio have cut heavily into their take. There are the penny arcades that have blossomed out with dozens of new pin games. But the old favorites remain unchanged — the same titles, *After the Bath, Too Hot to Sleep, Too Many Kisses* — the same hot, choked adolescent discovery of sex. Only the gambling machines are missing. The racketeers were run out of Coney Island years ago.

And then there are the rides — each going back to one of the old fundamentals. The roller coasters are frightening (although they are generally among the safest rides of all) but they also bring young bodies into hard, intimate contact. And the ninety-foot vertical drop of the Bowery's Cyclone is said to be the second highest in America. The carrousels or merry-go-rounds, simplest and oldest rides of all, appeal to the spirit of make-believe. The Wonder Wheel climbing up into the night offers the fear of height and the intimacy of a private seat in the sky. The auto rides and the boat rides with their furious, harmless crashes appeal like the carrousels to the spirit of make-believe but they are also a convenient preliminary to a pickup. The Virginia Reel whirling down a zigzag incline, the Whip cracking around its turns, the long dark tunnel rides, the airplane swing, the fun houses, and the newest rides — the Loop-O-Plane and the Octopus and the Boomerang — the aim of each is to frighten; to color the imagination; or to help boy meet girl.

This nickel empire reached its peak during the middle nineteen-twenties. It has been declining ever since. To explain that decline in the depression-proof industry there are a number of theories. There is the theory that people are increasingly interested in active sports — less so in the passive thrills of the midway. There is the theory that the movies and the automobile and the radio are cutting deeply into the whole amusement-park business. And there is the theory that with sixty-mile-an-hour locomotion an everyday matter, the amusement-park business has been signally lacking in imagination. As one Coney Islander puts it, " Nowadays you have to half kill 'em to get a dime."

But whatever the causes of the decline may be and however serious it may seem at the moment, it is probably a mistake to sell the nickel empire short. Amusement parks have lived a long time and have weathered a great many storms. And they still play a vital part in the lives of an enormous number of urban boys and girls. They are what the Caribbean cruise is to the stenographer — what the chance to visit in a strange city is to the small-town girl. They are an escape from the narrow social boundaries of the factory, the block, and the public school. And garish, tawdry, aphrodisiac Coney Island is to a hundred thousand adolescent New Yorkers heaven at the end of the subway.

The late Frederick Thompson founded Luna park with his famous Trip to the Moon, and then named it, not for the moon at all, but for his partner's sister in Des Moines. But always Luna has meant light, and Barron Collier who owns it now has preserved the tradition.

Luna at night is almost impossibly beautiful — an ultimate Christmas tree — a Hans Christian Andersen magic castle — a spendthrift carnival of light. And the lights of Luna sell romance.

At twelve or one Steeplechase is dark and the lights of Luna follow shortly after. But the Bowery pounds on until after two when the lid goes on and Coney Island goes to sleep. On the deserted Boardwalk two sailors argue with a third who is very drunk and believes that the most desirable girl in the world is out somewhere on the dim sand. A single policeman paces by. The bell buoys sound clear and flat across the harbor water. And fog rolls up from the sea like a damp gray sheet.

Justice Oliver Wendell Holmes

Free Speech in a Democracy

THIS indictment is founded wholly upon the publication of two leaflets which I shall describe in a moment. The first count charges a conspiracy, pending the war with Germany, to publish abusive language about the form of government of the United States, laying the preparation and publishing of the first leaflet as overt acts. The second count charges a conspiracy, pending the war, to publish language intended to bring the form of government into contempt, laying the preparation and publishing of the two leaflets as overt acts. The third count alleges a conspiracy to encourage resistance to the United States in the same war and to attempt to effectuate the purpose by publishing the same leaflets. The fourth count lays a conspiracy to incite curtailment of production of things necessary to the prosecution of the war and to attempt to accomplish it by publishing the second leaflet to which I have referred.

The first of these leaflets says that the President's cowardly silence about the intervention in Russia reveals the hypocrisy of the plutocratic gang in Washington. It intimates that " German militarism combined with Allied capitalism to crush the Russian revolution," goes on that the tyrants of the world fight each other until they see a common enemy — working-class enlightenment — when they combine to crush it; and that now militarism and capitalism combined, though not openly, to crush the Russian revolution. It says that there is only one enemy of the workers of the world and that is capitalism; that it is a crime for workers of America, etc., to fight the workers' republic of Russia, and ends " Awake! Awake, you workers of the world! " Signed " Revolutionists." A note adds, " It is absurd to call us pro-German. We hate and despise German militarism more than do you hypocritical tyrants. We have more reasons for denouncing German militarism than has the coward of the White House."

The other leaflet, headed " Workers — Wake Up," with abusive language says that America together with the Allies will march for Russia to help the Czecho-Slovaks in their struggle against the Bolsheviki, and that this time the hypocrites shall not fool the Russian emigrants and friends of Russia in America. It tells the Russian emigrants that they now must spit in the face of false military propaganda by which their sympathy and help to the prosecution of the war have been called forth, and says that with the money they have lent or are going to lend " they will make bullets not only for the Germans but also for the Workers' Soviets of Russia," and further, " Workers in the ammunition factories, you are producing bullets, bayonets, cannon, to murder not only the Germans but also your dearest, best, who are in Russia fighting for freedom." It then appeals to the same Russian emigrants at some length not to consent to

The dissenting opinion in *Abrams* v. *United States* (250 U. S. 616), 1919.

the " inquisitionary expedition to Russia," and says that the destruction of the Russian revolution is " the politics of the march on Russia." The leaflet winds up by saying " Workers, our reply to this barbaric intervention has to be a general strike! " and after a few words on the spirit of revolution, exhortations not to be afraid, and some usual tall talk, ends " Woe unto those who will be in the way of progress. Let solidarity live! The Rebels."

No argument seems to me necessary to show that these pronunciamentos in no way attack the form of government of the United States, or that they do not support either of the first two counts. What little I have to say about the third count may be postponed until I have considered the fourth. With regard to that, it seems too plain to be denied that the suggestion to workers in ammunition factories that they are producing bullets to murder their dearest, and the further advocacy of a general strike, both in the second leaflet, do urge curtailment of production of things necessary to the prosecution of the war within the meaning of the Act of May 16, 1918 amending part 3 of the earlier Act of 1917. But to make the conduct criminal that statute requires that it should be " with intent by such curtailment to cripple or hinder the United States in the prosecution of the war." It seems to me that no such intent is proved.

I am aware, of course, that the word intent as vaguely used in ordinary legal discussion means no more than knowledge at the time of the act that the consequences said to be intended will ensue. Even less than that will satisfy the general principle of civil and criminal liability. A man may have to pay damages, may be sent to prison, at common law might be hanged, if at the time of his act he knew facts from which common experience showed that the consequences would follow, whether he individually could foresee them or not. But, when words are used exactly, a deed is not done with intent to produce a consequence unless that consequence is the aim of the deed. It may be obvious to the actor that the consequence will follow, and he may be liable for it even if he forgets it, but he does not do the act with intent to produce it unless the aim to produce it is the proximate motive of the specific act, although there may be some deeper motive behind.

It seems to me that this statute must be taken to use its words in a strict and accurate sense. They would be absurd in any other. A patriot might think that we were wasting money on aeroplanes, or making more cannon of a certain kind than we needed, and might advocate curtailment with success; yet even if it turned out that the curtailment hindered and was thought by other minds to have been obviously likely to hinder the United States in the prosecution of the war, no one would hold such conduct a crime. I admit that my illustration does not answer all that might be said, but it is enough to show what I think and to let me pass to a more important aspect of the case. I refer to the First Amendment to the Constitution: that Congress shall make no law abridging the freedom of speech.

I never have seen any reason to doubt that the questions of law that alone were before this Court in the cases of *Schenck, Frohwerk,* and *Debs,* were rightly decided. I do not doubt for a moment that by the same reasoning that would justify punishing persuasion to murder, the United States constitutionally may punish speech that produces or is intended to produce a clear and imminent danger that it will bring about forthwith certain substantive evils that the United States constitutionally may seek to prevent. The power undoubtedly is greater in time of war than in time of peace because war opens dangers that do not exist at other times.

But as against dangers peculiar to war, as against others, the principle of the right to free speech is always the same. It is only the present danger of immediate evil or an intent to bring it about that warrants Congress in setting a limit to the expression of opinion where private rights are not concerned. Congress certainly cannot forbid all effort to change the mind of the country. Now nobody can suppose that the surreptitious publishing of a silly leaflet by an unknown man, without more, would present any immediate danger that its opinions would hinder the success of the Government aims or have any appreciable tendency to do so. Publishing these opinions for the very purpose of obstructing, however, might indicate a greater danger and at any rate would have the quality of an attempt. So I assume that the second leaflet, if published for the purpose alleged in the fourth count, might be punishable. But it seems pretty clear to me that nothing less than that would bring these papers within the scope of this law. An actual intent in the sense that I have explained is necessary to constitute an attempt, where a further act of the same individual is required to complete the substantive crime, for reasons given in *Swift & Co.* v. *United States,* 196 U. S. 375, 396. It is necessary where the success of the attempt depends upon others, because if that intent is not present the actor's aim may be accomplished without bringing about the evils sought to be checked. An intent to prevent interference with the revolution in Russia might have been satisfied without any hindrance to carrying on the war in which we were engaged.

I do not see how anyone can find the intent required by the statute in any of the defendants' words. The second leaflet is the only one that affords even a foundation for the charge; and there, without invoking the hatred of German militarism expressed in the former one, it is evident from the beginning to the end that the only object of the paper is to help Russia and stop American intervention there against the popular government — not to impede the United States in the war that it was carrying on. To say that two phrases taken literally might import a suggestion of conduct that would have interference with the war as an indirect and probably undesired effect seems to me by no means enough to show an attempt to produce that effect.

I return for a moment to the third count. That charges an intent to provoke resistance to the United States in its war with Germany. Taking the clause in the statute that deals with that in connection with the other elaborate provisions of the Act, I think that resistance to the United States means some forcible act of opposition to some proceeding of the United States in pursuance of the war. I think the intent must be the specific intent that I have described and for the reasons that I have given. I think that no such intent was proved or existed in fact. I also think that there is no hint at resistance to the United States as I construe the phrase.

In this case sentences of twenty years' imprisonment have been imposed for the publishing of two leaflets that I believe the defendants had as much right to publish as the Government has to publish the Constitution of the United States now vainly invoked by them. Even if I am technically wrong and enough can be squeezed from these poor and puny anonymities to turn the color of legal litmus paper — I will add, even if what I think the necessary intent were shown — the most nominal punishment seems to me all that possibly could be inflicted, unless the defendants are to be made to suffer not for what the indictment alleges but for the creed that they avow — a creed that I believe to be the creed of ignorance and immaturity when honestly held, as I see no reason to doubt that it was held here, but which, although made the subject of examination at the trial, no one has a right even to consider in dealing with the charges before the Court.

Persecution for the expression of opinions seems to me perfectly logical. If you have no doubt of your premises or your power and want a certain result with all your heart, you naturally express your wishes in law and sweep away all opposition. To allow opposition by speech seems to indicate that you think the speech impotent, as when a man says that he has squared the circle, or that you do not care wholeheartedly for the result, or that you doubt either your power or your premises. But when men have realized that time has upset many fighting faiths, they may come to believe, even more than they believe the very foundations of their own conduct, that the ultimate good desired is better reached by free trade in ideas — that the best test of truth is the power of the thought to get itself accepted in the competition of the market, and that truth is the only ground upon which their wishes safely can be carried out. That, at any rate, is the theory of our Constitution. It is an experiment, as all life is an experiment. Every year, if not every day, we have to wager our salvation upon some prophecy based upon imperfect knowledge. While that experiment is part of our system, I think that we should be eternally vigilant against attempts to check the expression of opinions that we loathe and believe to be fraught with death, unless they so imminently threaten immediate interference with the lawful and pressing purposes of the law that an immediate check is required to save the country.

I wholly disagree with the argument of the Government that the First Amendment left the common law as to seditious libel in force. History seems to me against the notion. I had conceived that the United States through many years had shown its repentance for the Sedition Act of 1798 by repaying fines that it imposed. Only the emergency that makes it immediately dangerous to leave the correction of evil counsels to time warrants making any exception to the sweeping command, " Congress shall make no law . . . abridging the freedom of speech." Of course I am speaking only of expressions of opinion and exhortations, which were all that were uttered here, but I regret that I cannot put into more impressive words my belief that in their conviction upon this indictment the defendants were deprived of their rights under the Constitution of the United States.

Mr. Justice Brandeis concurs with the foregoing opinion.

Walt Whitman

The American of the Future

WE have frequently printed the word Democracy. Yet I cannot too often repeat that it is a word the real gist of which still sleeps, quite unawakened, notwithstanding the resonance and the many angry tempests out of which its syllables have come, from pen or tongue. It is a great word, whose history, I suppose, remains unwritten, because that history has yet to be enacted. It is, in some sort, younger brother of another great and often-used word, Nature, whose history also waits unwritten.

As I perceive, the tendencies of our day, in the States, (and I entirely respect them,) are toward those vast and sweeping movements, influences, moral and physical, of humanity, now and always current over the planet, on the scale of the impulses of the elements. Then it is also good to reduce the whole matter to the consideration of a single self, a man, a woman, on permanent grounds. Even for the treatment of the universal, in politics, metaphysics, or anything, sooner or later we come down to one single, solitary soul.

There is, in sanest hours, a consciousness, a thought that rises, independent, lifted out from all else, calm, like the stars, shining eternal. This is the thought of identity — yours for you, whoever you are, as mine for me. Miracle of miracles, beyond statement, most spiritual and vaguest of earth's dreams, yet hardest basic fact, and only entrance to all facts. In such devout hours, in the midst of the significant wonders of heaven and earth, (significant only because of the Me in the centre,) creeds, conventions, fall away and become of no account before this simple idea. Under the luminousness of real vision, it alone takes possession, takes value. Like the shadowy dwarf in the fable, once liberated and looked upon, it expands over the whole earth, and spreads to the roof of heaven.

The quality of BEING, in the object's self, according to its own central idea and purpose, and of growing therefrom and thereto — not criticism by other standards, and adjustments thereto — is the lesson of Nature. True, the full man wisely gathers, culls, absorbs; but if, engaged disproportionately in that, he slights or overlays the precious idiocrasy and special nativity and intention that he is, the man's self, the main thing, is a failure, however wide his general cultivation. Thus, in our times, refinement and delicatesse are not only attended to sufficiently, but threaten to eat us up, like a cancer. Already, the democratic genius watches, ill-pleased, these tendencies. Provision for a little healthy rudeness, savage virtue, justification of what one has in one's self, whatever it is, is demanded. Negative qualities, even deficiencies, would be a relief. Singleness and normal simplicity and separation, amid this more and more complex, more and

From *Democratic Vistas,* 1871.

more artificialized state of society — how pensively we yearn for them! how we would welcome their return!

In some direction, then — at any rate enough to preserve the balance — we feel called upon to throw what weight we can, not for absolute reasons, but current ones. To prune, gather, trim, conform, and ever cram and stuff, and be genteel and proper, is the pressure of our days. While aware that much can be said even in behalf of all this, we perceive that we have not now to consider the question of what is demanded to serve a half-starved and barbarous nation, or set of nations, but what is most applicable, most pertinent, for numerous congeries of conventional, over-corpulent societies, already becoming stifled and rotten with flatulent, infidelistic literature, and polite conformity and art. .

In addition to established sciences, we suggest a science as it were of healthy average personalism, on original-universal grounds, the object of which should be to raise up and supply through the States a copious race of superb American men and women, cheerful, religious, ahead of any yet known.

To help line and put before us the species, or a specimen of the species, of the democratic ethnology of the future, is a work toward which the genius of our land, with peculiar encouragement, invites her well-wishers. Already certain limnings, more or less grotesque, more or less fading and watery, have appeared. We too, (repressing doubts and qualms,) will try our hand.

Attempting, then, however crudely, a basic model or portrait of personality for general use for the manliness of the States, (and doubtless that is most useful which is most simple, comprehensive for all, and toned low enough,) we should prepare the canvas well before-hand. Parentage must consider itself in advance. (Will the time hasten when fatherhood and motherhood shall become a science — and the noblest science?) To our model, a clear-blooded, strong-fibred physique, is indispensable; the questions of food, drink, air, exercise, assimilation, digestion, can never be intermitted. Out of these we descry a well-begotten selfhood — in youth, fresh, ardent, emotional, aspiring, full of adventure; at maturity, brave, perceptive, under control, neither too talkative nor too reticent, neither flippant nor sombre; of the bodily figure, the movements easy, the complexion showing the best blood, somewhat flushed, breast expanded, an erect attitude, a voice whose sound outvies music, eyes of calm and steady gaze, yet capable also of flashing — and a general presence that holds its own in the company of the highest. For it is native personality, and that alone, that endows a man to stand before presidents or generals, or in any distinguished collection, with *aplomb;* and *not* culture, or any knowledge or intellect whatever.

With regard to the mental-educational part of our model, enlargement of intellect, stores of cephalic knowledge, etc., the concentration thitherward of all the customs of our age, especially in America, is so overweening, and provides so fully for that part, that, important and necessary as it is, it really needs nothing from us here — except, indeed, a phrase of warning and restraint.

Manners, costumes, too, though important, we need not dwell upon here. Like beauty, grace of motion, etc., they are results. Causes, original things, being attended to, the right manners unerringly follow. Much is said, among artists, of the grand style, as if it were a thing by itself. When a man, artist or whoever, has health, pride, acuteness, noble aspirations, he has the motive-elements of the grandest style. The rest is but manipulation, (yet that is no small matter.) .

Leaving still unspecified several sterling parts of any model fit for the future personality of America, I must not fail, again and ever, to pronounce myself on one, probably the least attended to in modern times — a hiatus, indeed, threatening its gloomiest consequences after us. I mean the simple, unsophisticated Conscience, the primary moral element. If I were asked to specify in what quarter lie the grounds of darkest dread, respecting the America of our hopes, I should have to point to this particular. I should demand the invariable application to individuality, this day and any day, of that old, ever-true plumb-rule of persons, eras, nations. Our triumphant modern civilizee, with his all-schooling and his wondrous appliances, will still show himself but an amputation while this deficiency remains.

Beyond, (assuming a more hopeful tone,) the vertebration of the manly and womanly personalism of our western world, can only be, and is, indeed, to be, (I hope,) its all penetrating Religiousness. The architecture of individuality will ever prove various, with countless different combinations; but here they rise as into common pinnacles, some higher, some less high, only all pointing upward.

Indeed, the ripeness of Religion is doubtless to be looked for in this field of individuality, and is a result that no organization or church can ever achieve. As history is poorly retained by what the technists call history, and is not given out from their pages, except the learner has in himself the sense of the well-wrapt, never yet written, perhaps impossible to be written, history — so Religion, although casually arrested, and, after a fashion, preserved in the churches and creeds, does not depend at all upon them, but is a part of the identified soul, which, when greatest, knows not bibles in the old way, but in new ways — the identified soul, which can really confront Religion when it extricates itself entirely from the churches, and not before.

Personalism fuses this, and favors it. I should say, indeed, that only in the perfect uncontamination and solitariness of individuality may the spirituality of religion positively come forth at all. Only here, and on such terms, the meditation, the devout ecstasy, the soaring flight. Only here, communion with the mysteries, the eternal problems, whence? whither? Alone, and identity, and the mood — and the soul emerges, and all statements, churches, sermons, melt away like vapors. Alone, and silent thought, and awe, and aspiration — and then the interior consciousness, like a hitherto unseen inscription, in magic ink, beams out its wondrous lines to the sense. Bibles may convey, and priests expound, but it is exclusively for the noiseless operation of one's isolated Self, to enter the pure ether of veneration, reach the divine levels, and commune with the unutterable.

To practically enter into politics is an important part of American personalism. To every young man, North and South, earnestly studying these things, I should here, as an offset to what I have said in former pages, now also say, that may-be to views of very largest scope, after all, perhaps the political, (and perhaps literary and sociological,) America goes best about its development its own way — sometimes, to temporary sight, appalling enough. It is the fashion among dilettants and fops to decry the whole formulation and *personnel* of the active politics of America, as beyond redemption, and to be carefully kept away from. See you that you do not fall into this error. America, it may be, is doing very well upon the whole, notwithstanding these antics of the parties and their leaders, these half-brained nominees, the many ignorant ballots, and many elected failures and blatherers. It is the dilettants, and all who shirk their duty, who are not doing well. As for you, I advise you to enter more strongly yet into politics. I advise every young man to do so. Always inform yourself; always do the best you can; always vote. Disengage yourself from parties. They have been useful, and to some extent remain so; but the floating, uncommitted electors, farmers, clerks, mechanics, the masters of parties — watching aloof, inclining victory this side or that side — such are the ones most needed, present and future. For America, if eligible at all to downfall and ruin, is eligible within herself, not without; for I see clearly that the combined foreign world could not beat her down. But these savage, wolfish parties alarm me. Owning no law but their own will, more and more combative, less and less tolerant of the idea of ensemble and of equal brotherhood, the perfect equality of the States, the ever-over-arching American ideas, it behooves you to convey yourself implicitly to no party, nor submit blindly to their dictators, but steadily hold yourself judge and master over all of them.

So much, (hastily tossed together, and leaving far more unsaid,) for an ideal, or intimations of an ideal, toward American manhood. But the other sex, in our land, requires at least a basis of suggestion.

I have seen a young American woman, one of a large family of daughters, who, some years since, migrated from her meagre country home to one of the northern cities, to gain her own support. She soon became an expert seamstress, but finding the employment too confining for health and comfort, she went boldly to work for others, to housekeep, cook, clean, etc. After trying several places, she fell upon one where she was suited. She told me that she finds nothing degrading in her position; it is not inconsistent with personal dignity, self-respect, and the respect of others. She confers benefits and receives them. She has good health; her presence itself is healthy and bracing; her character is unstained; she has made herself understood, and preserves her independence, and has been able to help her parents and educate and get places for her sisters; and her course of life is not without opportunities for mental improvement, and of much quiet, uncosting happiness and love.

I have seen another woman who, from taste and necessity conjoined, has gone into practical affairs, carries on a mechanical business, partly works at it herself, dashes out more and more into real hardy life, is not abashed by the coarseness of the contact, knows how to be firm and silent at the same time, holds her own with unvarying coolness and decorum, and will compare, any day, with superior carpenters, farmers, and even boatmen and drivers. For all that, she has not lost the charm of the womanly nature, but preserves and bears it fully, though through such rugged presentation.

Then there is the wife of a mechanic, mother of two children, a woman of merely passable English education, but of fine wit, with all her sex's grace and intuitions, who exhibits, indeed, such a noble female personality, that I am fain to record it here. Never abnegating her own proper independence, but always genially preserving it, and what belongs to it — cooking, washing, child-nursing, house-tending — she beams sunshine out of all these duties, and makes them illustrious. Physiologically sweet and sound, loving work, practical, she yet knows that there are intervals, however few, devoted to recreation, music, leisure, hospitality — and affords such intervals. Whatever she does, and where-ever she is, that charm, that indescribable perfume of genuine womanhood, attends her, goes with her, exhales from her, which belongs of right to all the sex, and is, or ought to be, the invariable atmosphere and common aureola of old as well as young.

My mother has described to me a resplendent person, down on Long Island, whom she knew years ago, in early days. She was known by the name of the Peacemaker. She was well toward eighty years old, of happy and sunny temperament, had always lived on a farm, was very neighborly, sensible and discreet, an invariable and welcomed favorite, especially with young married women. She had numerous children and grandchildren. She was uneducated, but possessed a native dignity. She had come to be a tacitly agreed upon domestic regulator, judge, settler of difficulties, shepherdess, and reconciler in the land. She was a sight to draw near and look upon, with her large figure, her profuse, snow-white hair, dark eyes, clear complexion, sweet breath, and peculiar personal magnetism.

The foregoing portraits, I admit, are frightfully out of line from these imported models of womanly personality — the stock feminine characters of the current novelists, or of the foreign court poems, (Ophelias, Enids, princesses, or ladies of one thing or another,) which fill the envying dreams of so many poor girls, and are accepted by our young men, too, as supreme ideals of feminine excellence to be sought after. But I present mine just for a change.

Then there are mutterings, (we will not now stop to heed them here, but they must be heeded,) of something more revolutionary. The day is coming when the deep questions of woman's entrance amid the arenas of practical life, politics, trades, etc., will not only be argued all around us, but may be put to decision, and real experiment.

Of course, in these States, for both man and woman, we must entirely recast the types of highest personality from what the oriental, feudal, ecclesiastical worlds bequeath us, and which yet fully possess the imaginative and esthetic fields of the United States, pictorial and melodramatic, not without use as studies, but making sad work, and forming a strange anachronism upon the scenes and exigencies around us.

Of course, the old undying elements remain. The task is, to successfully adjust them to new combinations, our own days. Nor is this so incredible. I can conceive a community, to-day and here, in which, on a sufficient scale, the perfect personalities, without noise, meet; say in some pleasant Western settlement or town, where a couple of hundred best men and women, of ordinary worldly status, have by luck been drawn together, with nothing extra of genius or wealth, but virtuous, chaste, industrious, cheerful, resolute, friendly and devout. I can conceive such a community organized in running order, powers judiciously delegated — farming, building, trade, courts, mails, schools, elections, all attended to; and then the rest of life, the main thing, freely branching and blossoming in each individual, and bearing golden fruit. I can see there, in every young and old man, after his kind, and in every woman after hers, a true personality, developed, exercised proportionately in body, mind, and spirit. I can imagine this case as one not necessarily rare or difficult, but in buoyant accordance with the municipal and general requirements of our times. And I can realize in it the culmination of something better than any stereotyped *éclat* of history or poems. Perhaps, unsung, undramatized, unput in essays or biographies — perhaps even some such community already exists, in Ohio, Illinois, Missouri, or somewhere, practically fulfilling itself, and thus outvying, in cheapest vulgar life, all that has been hitherto shown in best ideal pictures.

In short, and to sum up, America, betaking herself to formative action, (as it is about time for more solid achievement, and less windy promise,) must, for her purposes, cease to recognize a theory of character grown of feudal aristocracies, or formed by merely esthetic or literary standards, or from any ultramarine, full-dress formulas of culture, polish, caste, etc., and must sternly promulgate her own new standard, yet old enough, and accepting the old, the perennial, elements, and combining them into groups, unities, appropriate to the modern, the democratic, the West, and to the practical occasions and needs of our own cities, and of the agricultural regions. Ever the most precious in the common. Ever the fresh breeze of field, or hill, or lake, is more than any palpitation of fans, though of ivory, and redolent with perfume; and the air is more than the costliest perfumes.

LITERATURE AND THE ARTS

Max Eastman

Humor and America

ONCE I called on a famous psychologist in Europe, and in the course of a not too psychological conversation received some advice.

"I want you to go home," he said, "and write a book on America, and I will tell you what to call it. *Misgeburt* — what is that word in English? No, not *monster*. *Miscarriage* — that's it. The *Miscarriage of American Culture* — that shall be the title of your next book, and you will tell the truth about the whole awful catastrophe."

We laughed, somewhat unsymmetrically, at this jest and I asked: "What makes you hate America so?"

"Hate it?" he said. "I don't hate America, I regret it. I regret that Columbus ever made the mistake of discovering it!"

It happens that I am as a patriot rather slow to boil. I think of myself instinctively as a citizen of the world and have the habit of discussing the defects and merits of my native land — except for its plumbing conveniences, about which I brook no two opinions — in a mood of cool appraisal. Therefore this violence of idea, in a great authority on the manner in which violent ideas are formed, stimulated rather than incensed me. America *has* failed to shine in most branches of human culture which transcend the mood of the matter-of-fact. We are a hard-surfaced folk, or have been. Our serious culture is like one of those modernist plays enacted on a bare stage with no backdrop and no scenery — and withal a sentimental play. We have used our brains well, but not our imaginations, not our emotional perceptions. We lack "depth" — whatever depth is — and we lack fineness.

I recognize all these facts and sense a validity in the viewpoint of the Old World critic. And yet as I left his study I settled back with a very comfortable feeling into being an American, and being a part of the process of creating an American culture. My feeling was not only comfortable, but also a little gleeful,

From *The Enjoyment of Laughter*, 1936.

a little on the laughing side. It was as though I had said to the old man: " It is just as well you don't understand our system — wait till the homestretch and we'll show you."

The basic thing historically is that America was born late, and spent her youth with grown-up brothers and sisters. She is precocious — or she is " old-wise," to translate a better German term. I mean in so far as she is wise at all, and not like all other countries full of dead men and clods. Our earliest heroes — Franklin, Jefferson, Washington, Tom Paine — were disbelievers in the legends in which all other early heroes lived and breathed. They were heroes of the matter-of-fact, and of will and resolution based upon a knowledge of it. A lot of religious and cultural top-hamper that came over with us on the ships, and then the long and pious effort of our second-rate geniuses to imitate it, has obscured this fact. Where other " national minds " were born in an atmosphere of imaginative belief, ours was born in an atmosphere of skeptical common sense. It was born with the industrial revolution and with modern science.

" Poets," said Benjamin Franklin, in a poem almost bad enough to prove it, " are the mere *wastepaper* of mankind."

This does not mean that we are standing still at a goal. It means that we are moving in a different direction. We started in fact and are moving toward imagination; other cultures have moved the other way. I have no assurance where we shall come out. It may be impossible to work this process backward. But if it is not, then those other more imaginative cultures will fade out and die. For facts *are* facts, and once they are known you cannot with inward dignity deny them. I think and hope that American poets will find a way to unleash the imagination, and cultivate subtleties of feeling, without losing that inestimably precious sense of hard fact which is instinctive with us and not a thing that we have slowly had to learn. Nothing could be more interesting than to try to do this. No national mission or adventure could be more exciting.

That is why I felt comfortable in returning to my own nest of Americanness, after agreeing with so much that the great man in Europe said. Why I felt like laughing is not so easy to tell. It may be that I was retreating into the fastnesses of our own cultural territory. I was running up the flag on our sole impregnable fortress. For America *has* unleashed imagination and cultivated feelings in the one realm where, held down by that harsh sense of fact, she instinctively could — the realm of humor. " You may laugh at our crudity and make jokes about Columbus, but we could make a better joke and laugh with more imagination." That is perhaps what I was saying to the old man. That is what I want to say here.

It is no accident that Mark Twain and Abraham Lincoln — both men in whom humor took the place of ideological anchorings — became and have remained in the world's eyes the representative Americans. Their headstrong sensibleness, their steadfast confrontation of fact, and their adjustment through humorous emotion to the predicament in which facts, steadfastly confronted, place the wishful heart of man, is the keynote of our culture if we have one.

There was hardly a bolder and lonelier thing a man could do in Lincoln's place than crash through military discipline with acts of human mercy. There, if anywhere, he needed the support of angels or ideas. " Well, I don't believe shooting will do him any good," he would say to the indignant military. Or: " I put it to you to decide for yourself; if God Almighty gives you a cowardly pair of legs, how can you help their running away with you? " And in this acceptance with a quizzical playful emotion of life's ultimate predicament, his mind would find rest, his will the requisite support. It is not a trivial or incidental thing to be as humorous as Lincoln was.

" I'm quite sure," said Mark Twain, " that . . . I have no race prejudices, and I think I have no color prejudices nor caste prejudices nor creed prejudices. Indeed, I know it. I can stand any society. All that I care to know is that a man is a human being — that is enough for me; he can't be any worse."

In that, it seems to me, you have the whole temper and equilibrium of Mark Twain's mind, the ruthless vision — out of those hawk's eyes — and the laughter. You cannot separate the two as solemn critics do, and arrive at something called " Mark Twain's philosophy." Facts are awful, but you can be honest if you laugh — that was his " philosophy."

I am not saying that these attitudes are final, but just the opposite: that they are the starting point of a distinctively American culture, and that nothing is final. In order to see them so, however, it is necessary to disregard most of what has been done by the historians, for they call American culture everything that developed on this continent. I can find roots running back, but I think American culture as a distinct entity began not so very early in the nineteenth century. And it has its natural beginning, just as all national cultures have, in a mythology — a mythology which has been described, rather unfortunately, as the " tall talk " of the western frontier. If you want to see how much more it is than that, you should read a few pages of Lowell Thomas's sapless collection of " Tall Stories," and compare it with a page of Constance Rourke's chapter on " The Gamecock of the Wilderness " in her book about *American Humor*. I spare you the sample from Lowell Thomas, but here is a page from Constance Rourke's rich book. She is describing the legends which grew up around the historic figure of Davy Crockett.

The story of his life in one of the almanacs began by picturing him as a baby giant planted in a rock bed as soon as he was born and watered with wild buffalo's milk. Another declared that as a boy he tied together the tails of two buffaloes and carried home five tiger cubs in his cap. In another he wrung the tail off a comet, and announced that he could " travel so all lightnin' fast that I've been known to strike fire agin the wind." . . . On one of his adventures he was barred by an " Injun rock so 'tarnal high, so all flinty hard that it will turn off a common streak of lightnin' and make it point downward and look as flat as a cow's tail." Once he escaped up Niagara Falls on an alligator. " The alligator walked up the great hill of water as slick as a wildcat up a white oak."

In the end he became a demigod, and spoke in his own person:

One January morning it was so all screwen cold that the forest trees were stiff and they couldn't shake, and the very daybreak froze fast as it was trying to dawn. The tinderbox in my cabin would no more ketch fire than a sunk raft at the bottom of the sea. Well, seein' daylight war so far behind time I thought creation war in a fair way for freezen fast: so, thinks I, I must strike a little fire from my fingers, light my pipe, an' travel out a few leagues, and see about it. Then I brought my knuckles together like two thunderclouds, but the sparks froze up afore I could begin to collect 'em, so out I walked, whistlin' " Fire in the mountains! " as I went along in three double quick time. Well, arter I had walked about twenty miles up the Peak O'Day and Daybreak Hill I soon discovered what war the matter. The airth had actually friz fast on her axes, and couldn't turn round; the sun had got jammed between two cakes o' ice under the wheels, an' thar he had been shinin' an' workin' to get loose till he friz fast in his cold sweat. C-r-e-a-t-i-o-n! thought I, this ar the toughest sort of suspension, an' it mustn't be endured. Somethin' must be done, or human creation is done for. It war then so anteluvian an' premature cold that my upper and lower teeth an' tongue war all collapsed together as tight as a friz oyster; but I took a fresh twenty-pound bear off my back that I'd picked up on my road, and beat the animal agin the ice till the hot ile began to walk out on him at all sides. I then took an' held him over the airth's axes an' squeezed him till I'd thawed 'em loose, poured about a ton on't over the sun's face, give the airth's cogwheel one kick backward till I got the sun loose — whistled " Push along, keep movin'! " an' in about fifteen seconds the airth gave a grunt an' began movin'. The sun walked up beautiful, salutin' me with sich a wind o' gratitude that it made me sneeze. I lit my pipe by the blaze o' his topknot, shouldered my bear, an' walked home, introducin' people to the fresh daylight with a piece of sunrise in my pocket.

Is it any wonder that this childlike and savage imaginative explosion, crashing in on the refined habits of English literary humor of the genteel tradition, gave rise to the idea that exaggeration is the sole thing at which Americans laugh? Expressing, as Miss Rourke says, " an exhilarated and possessive consciousness of a new earth and even of the wide universe," these legendary heroes found no room to exist in British drawing rooms of the Victorian era. They were indeed too big for that. But among their own companions — and the companions of Davy Crockett are Theseus and Hercules, Thor and Baldur — these American heroes are not distinguished by size, but by humor. All mythical heroes have been exaggerations, but they have been serious ones. America came too late for that. Her demigods were born in laughter; they are consciously preposterous; they are cockalorum demigods. That is the natively American thing — not that her primitive humor is exaggerative, but that her primitive exaggerations were humorous.

I am not very strong in history — it is one of the things I have put off writing until I should have time to read up on it. But it seems to consist of riding some idea through a morass of facts that would bog you down and drown you if you were not mounted. And I should like to propose a brief history of American literature, of American imaginative culture, in which the idea would be that it is only about one hundred years of age, and is not to be regarded as a gradual deposit of calcium in the backbone and vision in the eyes of nice white-handed New England teachers and preachers, mastering a graceful penmanship and learning to write almost as well as the English poets, but as a rough laughing growth springing up out of the struggles of the pioneers, and having its background in a humorous mythology, in legendary heroes taken as a joke.

If imagination is what we failed of in our belated infancy, it is in this humorous mythology rather than our sober poets that we began vigorously to have it. And it is in the humorists, rather than the poets, that, up to recent times at least, this vigor of imagination flourished. This was what made them something of a sensation in the world. They did of course exaggerate. Imaginative humor runs out automatically into exaggeration. How could you play laughing havoc with the qualities of things and not pile them up into quantities that also overwhelm the mind? The two things go together like size and shape — the inordinate quantity and the preposterous image. Ring Lardner said that " if the penalty for selling honest old beer to minors was a $100 fine why, two to fourteen years in a meat grinder would be mild for a guy that sells white pop on the theory that it is a drink." As a modification of the penal code that is indeed extreme, but it is also — is it not — fantastic? And the fantasy, not the extremeness, is what makes Ring Lardner's hand unmistakable in the writing of it.

At high noon the wind was blowing a 2 inch gale backwards and neither scow would move, so the starter postponed it till along came a breath of fresh air, which was a $\frac{1}{4}$ to 2". Then away went the two sloops like a snail with paralysis.

They were in Brock's inner office, the walls of which were adorned with autographed pictures of six or seven of the more celebrated musical comedy stars, and a too-perfect likeness of Brock's wife, whom he had evidently married in a dense fog.

She smiled and Rita noticed her teeth for the first time. Most of the visible ones were of gold, and the work had evidently been done by a dentist for whom three members of a foursome were waiting.

" Does she think," said Stu, " that just because she comes from the golden State she has to run around with a mouthful of nuggets? "

That is the way Ring Lardner exaggerates. And here is Mark Twain:

" Kings " and " kingdoms " were as thick in Britain as they had been in little Palestine in Joshua's time, when people had to sleep with their knees pulled up because they couldn't stretch out without a passport.

I own millions and millions of feet of affluent silver leads in Nevada — in fact the entire undercrust of that country nearly, and if Congress would move that State off my property so that I could get at it, I would be wealthy yet.

Twenty-four years ago, I was strangely handsome. . . . In San Francisco, in the rainy season I was often mistaken for fair weather.

Pa's got a few buckshot in him, but he don't mind it 'cause he don't weigh much anyway.

You can find all the exaggerations you want in Baron Munchausen, but you cannot find a phrase to match those in any writer of English before Mark Twain. Even Lord Byron's wit was not lighted with these exploits of poetic humor. In Charles Dickens you could search all day for a phrase to print on the page with them. " Mark Twain can be quoted in single sentences," says Stephen Leacock, " Dickens mostly in pages." But all vigorously imaginative minds can be quoted in sentences — all of the tribe of Shakespeare. And American humorists, casual and unsustained as their flights are, belong to the tribe of Shakespeare. It is as though that revival of an Elizabethan gleam and range of vision which we call the romantic movement, and which occurred in poetry in England at the beginning of the nineteenth century, occurred a half century later in the United States and in humor instead of poetry.

Comic imagination, then, or what I prefer to call poetic humor, would stand not only at the beginning but close to the center of my briefer history of America's imaginative culture. Another feature of my history would be our humor troubadours. For America has not only a comic mythology; she has had her minstrelsy of laughter too, her jesting tramps or gleemen, who got about by making people smile instead of singing to them. Artemus Ward was the prince of this tribe, a traveling printer who could write " copy," and subsequently a platform entertainer. And he brought something from his eastern home that was not to be found at all in that loud humor of the pioneers. It was not exactly what we call a " dry New England wit," and I am not sure but he got it out of his own bosom rather than out of some abstraction called New England. It was what underlies that dry wit in a laughter-loving rather than a caustic mind — a taste for pure absurdities. Artemus Ward liked to speak out before the public the kind of " foolishness " that is indulged at home. Phrases like " of the same similarness," or " Why is this thus? What is the cause of this thusness? " acquired a delicious drollness on his lips. He made people laugh by saying things that made absolutely no sense, or which there was absolutely no sense in saying.

I was born in the state of Maine of parents.

One of the peculiarities of my lecture is that it contains so many things that haven't anything to do with it.

He used to have with him, when lecturing on the Mormons, a panorama representing what he saw in Utah. In his picture the lion on Brigham Young's gate had a ridiculously elongated tail. He would point to it and say: " Yonder lion, you will observe has a tail. It will be continued a few evenings longer." It appears that his British audience could hardly hold their joy when he pointed to one of the Nevada mountains and said in a modestly informed tone: " The highest part of that mountain is the top."

It is of course impossible to revive the alluring plausibility which his presence could impart to such a statement, how he could make the whole mortal being of a listener move with breathless playful expectation to this simple fall. We merely know that it was true. When it came to making humor humorous

— and it very often does — Artemus Ward seems to have had no equal among men. No man on the platform was ever more successful or more loved.

I think the unique quality of his humor can be conveyed, after a fashion, by saying that his jokes were almost always blunt. If they had a point, he would slur it in the utterance so that you could hardly catch the gleam. And frequently they had no point. And frequently they would seem to lose their point, or forget all about it, and go wandering off in search of some ludicrous situation or image.

"Does this railroad company allow passengers to give it advice, if they do so in a respectful manner?"

The conductor replied in gruff tones that he guessed so.

"Well, it occurred to me that it would be well to detach the cowcatcher from the front of the engine and hitch it to the rear of the train, for you see we are not liable to overtake a cow, but what's to prevent a cow from strolling into this car and biting a passenger?"

Artemus Ward was not perhaps more gifted than other American humorists, but his gift was more unusual. He was, like Poe among our poets, a prodigy. And like Poe he was so recognized in Europe as well as in America. After his first London lecture in 1866, *Punch,* in an editorial ovation, advised "funny men, on or off the stage, to hear Artemus Ward 'speak his piece' at the Egyptian Hall, and then, in so far as in them lies, to go and do likewise.

"To be sure Artemus Ward's delivery of fun is 'un-English.' But there are a good many things English one would like to see un-Englished. Gagging, gross, overdone low comedy is one of them. Snobbishness is another. The two go hand in hand. One of the best of many good points of Artemus Ward's piece is that it is quite free from all trace of either of these English institutions."

Those who think that British humor is a very subtle fluid whose quiet stream has been disturbed by the coarse loud guffaws of the Americans may learn something from these lines. The fact is that Artemus Ward so surprised London with the possibility of a gentle grace and mental quietness in platform humor, that all English society was excited about it. Even the heavy-sitting queen was lifted by the general wave of enthusiasm.

"The most delightful fooling," she said, "that it has ever been our good fortune to hear. During his extraordinary prologue the audience fairly laughed till they could laugh no more, for the strange, quaint, quiet, gentlemanly humor of the lecturer was irresistible."

"Never was an American in London so beloved," said Moncure D. Conway, and Charles Reade nicknamed him "Artemus the delicious." "His jokes," said the London *Times,* "are of the true transatlantic type to which no nation beyond the limits of the States can offer any parallel."

It would be easy, with such a lead, to exaggerate Artemus Ward's Americanness. In his love for pure absurdity, he must take his place with Lewis Carroll as an event in world literature rather than an American event. Chesterton has said that the Victorians "discovered nonsense," and it is true that they were first in the pure love of it. But their nonsense derives some sense from the fact that it was designed for the entertainment of children. Their pointless jokes have always that point. That serious thought sustains many a true lady and gentleman in the indignity of enjoying them. It gives moreover a flavor of condescension, almost a baby-talk flavor, to some of their finest foolishness. Artemus Ward's delicious absurdities were for grown-up minds. He loved nonsense with a manly and mature love.

Unfortunately for the world, he died in the midst of those lectures in London, when he had barely become conscious of his powers. No literary monument exists to perpetuate his rare spirit. Only in the testimony of those who heard him, and in collected fragments — here too like the poetry of Edgar Allan Poe — is the original quality of his mind to be perceived. But almost as Poe stands at the source of a tendency toward " pure poetry," or poetry as an art and not a preachment, so Artemus Ward stands at the source of a tendency toward pure humor — toward the cultivation of absurdity so exquisite that it is treasured without condescension for its own sake.

It is the blending of these two strains — the primitive vigor of imagination and the mature enjoyment of nonsense — that gives its distinct flavor to American humor. Both Mark Twain and Josh Billings were aware of this flavor, and tried to identify it by isolating the word " humor " for the purpose. Mark Twain said that the art of telling a humorous, as opposed to a comic, or a witty story, " was created in America and has remained at home." And Josh Billings apologized for the failings of this art by explaining that " Americans haven't had time yet to bile down their humor and git the wit out ov it."

Josh Billings was a crude character in comparison to Mark Twain — a " crackerbox philosopher," and on some subjects rather more of a crackerbox than a philosopher. But he possessed these two gifts, the comic vision and the liberated taste for foolishness, in a degree that enabled him to create a new artistic form. He would appear in our brief and reckless history as the father of imagism. For he was the first man in English literature to set down on his page, quite like a French painter reared in the tradition of art for art's sake, a series of tiny highly polished verbal pictures, and leave them there for what they might be worth.

The crane is neither flesh, beast, nor fowl, but a sad mixtur ov all theze things.

He mopes along the brinks of kreeks and wet places, looking for sumthing he haz lost.

He haz a long bill, long wings, long legs, and iz long all over.

When he flies thru the air, he is az graceful az a windmill, broke loose from its fastenings.

The gote is a koarse wollen sheep.

They have a good appetite and a sanguine digestion.

A maskuline gote will fite ennything, from an elephant down to his shadder on a ded wall.

They strike from their but-end, instead ov the shoulder, and are as liable to hit as a hammer is a nail-hed.

They kan klime ennything but a greast pole, and know the way up a rock, az natral az a woodbine. . . .

The duk iz a kind ov short-legged hen.
They kan sale on the water as eazy as a grease spot.
Duks hav a broad bill which enables them tew eat their food without enny spoon.
Thare ain't any room on the outside of a duk for enny more feathers.
The duk don't kro like a rooster, but quaks like a duk.

There is little in New England poetry up to that date as graphic as some of this Poughkeepsie auctioneer's metaphors — nothing quite comparable to his statement that goats " know the way up a rock as natural as a woodbine," which is Homeric. Our history would make much of the originality of Josh Billings, and also of his crudity — for our whole history would be of something crude.

We should also devote a considerable and animated section to the great American art of laughing at oneself — that " humor of discomfiture written in the first person," which Leacock again says " absolutely distinguishes " Mark Twain from Dickens. It was not original with us, nor with anyone in history. But with us, I think, it first became a humorous convention. It first seemed the natural and appointed way to engage a reader in the joys of ridicule. One of the most interesting processes in cultural history, and most indisputable, has been the steady playing down of cruelty, and playing up of sympathy, in laughter. And this tendency of American humor stands at the height of that curious, and seemingly almost Christian, development. When you have taken upon your own person a defect or misfortune with which you propose to invite laughter, you are surely not inviting sneers. That is what Constance Rourke means, perhaps, by attributing to American humor as a whole a quality of " tenderness." A more complete and universal understanding of the mood of play would probably describe it better.

We hold ourselves up to laughter because we believe in laughter. We understand it, and know how to distinguish it from snarling and showing of teeth. We believe in being humorous. We believe in it more with our souls than most civilized folk. And this, if my hypothesis about our general culture is correct, is because we have had the energy and the abounding spirits of a young nation, and yet our childhood fell in a day of skepticism instead of animal faith. We have made more of humor because deprived in infancy of serious childish fancies.

Such in outline would be my chapter on humor as the origin and almost the central stem of America's distinctly own imaginative culture. It would go on to tell, of course, how this native tree of laughter, rooted in a humorous mythology, grew to its height in Mark Twain and his contemporaries, and then about the time of his death suddenly burgeoned out all over the sky and with a violent hilarity, and a certain thinning of the life-sap, blossomed. We might call our chapter *The Root, Stem and Petals of American Humor*. It would not agree with the prevailing opinion that this recent phenomenon, this still continuing shower of arrantly hilarious laughter, known variously as the Newer Nonsense, the Larger Lunacy, the Higher Goofyism — or "Humor Gone Nuts," as Donald Ogden Stewart calls it — is an essentially new departure. It is the natural bloom of the tree. It was all foretold and predestined in the riotous mythology of the pioneers and in Artemus Ward's consecration of absurd nonsense — two things which might almost exonerate Columbus for his little mistake, a natural one after all when sailing west for India, in discovering America.

That would not be the whole of our history. It would say much of Edgar Allan Poe, stifled in this cold climate of fact because he lacked the gift of laughter. And it would say more of Walt Whitman, so like Mark Twain in his passion for democracy and fact, and yet unlike him as another world because instead of humor he relied on mystical belief. And with these strands to weave, it would say something about the future — about what might be done by a mind, trained in fact and true to it, equipped as such a mind must be with humor, and yet not ill-at-ease in deeps of feeling and among fervent ventures of imagination, not ill-at-ease among revolutionary ideas, not condemned to make a final resting place of fact and laughter.

John Erskine

Huckleberry Finn

"YOU don't know about me without you have read a book by the name of *The Adventures of Tom Sawyer;* but that ain't no matter," says Huckleberry Finn. He is quite right. We can understand his masterly story even if we have not read the book to which it is the sequel, but most Americans have read both, and a comparison of them helps us to see the greatness of the later one. In the preface to *Tom Sawyer* Mark Twain tells us he is drawing on his own memories of boyhood, and hopes to entertain young readers, but he adds that older folk may be interested in the picture of the Middle West around 1850, and in the incidental record of the odd superstitions which were then prevalent among children and slaves.

In *Huckleberry Finn* the superstitions still appear, and the story certainly fascinates boys and girls, but mature readers value it for the rich picture of human nature — a satirical picture, if you will, but mellow and kind. In the preface to this book Mark Twain calls our attention to the various dialects the characters use, but it is hard not to believe his own interest was chiefly

From *The Delight of Great Books,* 1928.

in providing us with our first and still our best account of Main Street — of the small community, narrow as to their virtues and their vices, and starved in their imaginations, all but the children and the most childlike among them.

Since *The Adventures of Tom Sawyer* and the later book have the same background and much the same characters, it looks as though Mark Twain must have discovered his true subject during the eight years which separated the stories. Huckleberry Finn tells us far more than he knows; through his naïve confessions we see the panorama of his world and become sophisticated. We are really studying ourselves. In the earlier books, however, we have episodes of boyhood, rather loosely strung together, with one terrific stroke of melodrama to help out the plot. No doubt *Tom Sawyer* would be enjoyed by young people even if *Huckleberry Finn* did not lend it fame and keep it alive, but taken by itself it now seems a rather poorly constructed book. The story is built up with anecdotes, each one complete in itself, and none developed beyond the point of the joke.

In this early book Tom Sawyer interests us by his love of mischief and by his exuberant fancy. He contrives more than the usual share of histrionics; other boys make believe, but Tom dramatizes his boyish sentimentality on the grand scale, and we have the suspicion that by emphasizing and isolating the boy, Mark Twain gets the total picture of life out of focus, and makes it difficult for us to interpret the exceptional events in terms of the normal parts of his story.

These comments on the earlier book may help us to see why we instinctively admire *Huckleberry Finn*. The same elements reappear, the same characters, though new persons enter the tale, the same scene is described, though Huckleberry and the Negro Jim have their chief adventures down the river on a raft, and the spirit of adventure in boyhood again is the central theme of the book. But this time the elements are arranged in a proportion which convinces us, and we are sure the picture is true.

When you sit down to write a novel, you find you must have something besides characters and a plot; you must have a philosophy of life. You must decide, for example, what parts of experience are worth writing about, and then you must make up your mind how to dispose of the other parts. Most men and women will take sides on the question whether it is the exceptional experience we should consider important, or whether any experience would seem exceptional if we attached importance to it. Our temperament dictates the answer, but we usually frame it in some kind of philosophy. There are novelists who believe that humdrum experience, the typical daily round of all of us, is the proper material for fiction, and that the novelists, by bearing down hard on it, may bring out the grain of significance under the smooth-worn surface. Another kind of artist portrays the average life remorselessly, to show that it is even less significant than it seems. He is the satirist, and he shows himself frequently in American literature today, a strong critic of narrowness and meanness, especially as observed in village life. A third kind of storyteller, with perhaps the same dislike of what is familiar and trite, turns resolutely to fresh material, to the unusual event; he looks, as we say, for an escape from the world which shuts him in.

In *Huckleberry Finn* Mark Twain is all three kinds of storyteller at once. He gives us a kindly picture of men and women in very small towns along the river, people with no heroic experience, who yet find their lives of considerable importance to themselves.

There is a satiric picture, too, an intermittent glimpse into the smallness of human nature. Huckleberry has learned how to make use of men by appealing to their mean side. When the two oarsmen come near the raft and almost discover the runaway slave, Huckleberry saves Jim by inviting them to come on board and minister to the crew. There's a mild case of smallpox, he explains, and the two men row away, after giving him forty dollars to salve their conscience for thus denying the appeal of the sick.

The way in which the realistic elements and the satiric are combined with extraordinary adventure might well be the envy and the admiration of any novelist. The quiet river towns which Mark Twain remembered from his youth had something of the frontier still; violent death varied the monotony, from time to time, and the outcasts of older parts of the world chanced along, for shelter, or for a last opportunity to play their tricks in a place where they weren't known. The law-abiding portions of the community would condemn such interruptions of the peace, but they would also be fairly hardened to them. If a novelist tried to tell us now that the performance of the two quacks in *Romeo and Juliet,* or in the *Royal Nonesuch,* was ever accepted by any American community we should probably decline to believe him. But when we watch these rascals and their doings through the eyes of Huckleberry Finn, we are free to believe them as exceptional as we please; yet we understand perfectly why the boy took them for granted. Huckleberry has had a bringing-up which has prepared him to be surprised at nothing. We know that his approach to life is peculiar; if his judgments are not those of the average person, we know why they aren't, and we know just how far they depart from the normal, and he has our sympathy. Mark Twain manipulated his material, therefore, so that the most outrageous melodrama could present itself as matter of fact, through the medium of Huckleberry's temperament, and even while we are rearranging the values, and discerning what the boy was blind to, we like him, and concede that he is true to life.

He is not supposed to be an average boy, like Tom Sawyer; he is the son of the village drunkard, a waif who grows up uneducated and uncared for, so far as the community can see. Parents warn their children not to play with him; the schoolmaster whips any boy who is caught in his society. He frankly smokes a corncob pipe; he always wears a tattered hat; trousers and shirt are all his dress; he carries a dead cat by the tail, because he considers a dead cat a treasure, and believes it is good magic.

Huckleberry is explained by his father. The elder Finn is as thorough a study of good-for-nothing propensities as we are likely to find in literature. Whenever he can, he drinks himself into a mad fit and becomes rather dangerous. Huckleberry sits up all night in the hut on the island, with his father's gun in hand, for fear it may be necessary to blow his father's brains out. But in his sober moments the man is even uglier; when he asks Huckleberry next morning what he is doing with the gun, the boy knows he had better invent at once an elaborate lie about a thief who tried to get in during the night.

This extraordinary parent just escapes being lynched for a crime which, oddly enough, he didn't commit, but afterward he is shot in the back during a drunken brawl in a disorderly house. Huckleberry is rather fond of his father — thoroughly afraid of him, of course, and critical of his worst excesses, yet disposed to enjoy the less dangerous periods of his society. From him and from nature has come all the boy's education. His father's temper taught Huckleberry the advantages of falsehood; lying is the better part of discourse, he thinks, one's natural protection against society. He is modest about it, he always believes that Tom Sawyer could make up a far handsomer story, being a superior boy who has had advantages; but we can't see much room for improvement in the gorgeous fables Huckleberry improvises at the slightest challenge of fate. His father's changeable moods taught him also to expect anything of life.

Huckleberry's mother does not exist, so far as the story is concerned. We may imagine her the victim of her husband's brutality, if we are so inclined, and we may endow her with enough virtues to account for her son's kind heart and gentle instincts. But Mark Twain is at his best when he leaves her history a blank. Huckleberry's isolation is complete, and we are under no compulsion to measure him by the accustomed traditions of society.

The handling of the romantic or melodramatic elements in the story can be admired from another angle also. Though the life of the small village may seem unduly quiet, it is the person from the city who chiefly finds it dull; the people involved in it often are aware of excitement. Of course the excitements come at long intervals, and they are cherished most often as scandal. Every small community has its stories about this woman or that man — stories which are often wild enough and improbable, but they really happened. But if a whole and steady view of life seems to us desirable, we can admire the way in which Mark Twain allows us to enjoy the wild adventures of Huckleberry, and at the same time shows us, in the not too remote background, a just picture of the folks who will talk about such experiences, but to whom they will never come. It is extraordinary that this balance is preserved through so long a succession of wild episodes; but even at the end, we still are aware of some surprise when a new accident occurs, we still consider ourselves the inhabitants of a quite normal world.

Several technical devices for securing this sense of the normal, for convincing us that the eccentric character is eccentric, no matter how often he appears, can easily be recognized by anyone who knows the formulas of literary criticism. We can see, for example, that the characters speak for themselves. Though Huckleberry is telling the story, he reports conversations fully, and rarely makes a comment. This is the ancient rule for rendering character vividly, but it is easier to state the principle than to follow it. When the two rascals, driven out of town simultaneously by enraged mobs, happen to meet on the raft, Huck and Jim are wise enough to say nothing until the new arrivals disclose themselves. The younger man, diagnosing their simplicity, as he thinks, breaks the news that he is a duke in disguise, and that his rank entitles him to the only comfortable bed in the raft. Jim and Huck don't care; they know he isn't a duke, but he might as well have the bed. The older man, however, is not so complacent, and in a few moments he has confessed that he is really the lost Dauphin of France, by rights a king. The conversations of the king and the duke are among the great passages of dramatic satire. They know they are not fooling each other, they pretend to be deceiving the Negro and the boy, and yet we half think they would have kept up the nonsense even if they had been alone, so strong in them was the instinct for imposture. The device is the strictly dramatic one of omitting comment and letting the char-acters talk, but the formula is used here by a genius.

It would be in the sound tradition of criticism to say also that Mark Twain established a human scale throughout by descriptions of nature. The broad and changing river, the starry nights, the fogs, the glorious storms, refer us con-stantly to a scheme of things against which man even at his best would seem small. When the first heavy rain makes the river rise, and sweeps away whole villages in the flood, Huck and Jim paddle over to a rather substantial wreck of a house and climb in through the window. Wise as he is in much wicked-ness, Huckleberry seems not to know what sort of house this was before it was swept away, but we see clearly enough. At the time he doesn't know that the murdered man they find in a corner of the room is his own father. We are too much interested ourselves, perhaps, in the description of the room and in the finding of the corpse to grasp the full irony, but later it comes upon us, the contrast between that mighty flood and the wretched occupations it put an end to.

But when we have said this about the descriptions of nature in the story, we ought to add that perhaps Mark Twain put them in for no other reason than his love of them. The joy in grand aspects of weather is so evident that their effect on the story may well have been a happy result, not altogether intended. It is a pagan love of nature — and we might say, a typically American love of the thing for itself, without asking what it means.

The book owes more of its fame than we sometimes recognize to the por-trait of the Negro, Jim, who runs away from a good home and from the neigh-borhood of his wife and children because he has reason to fear he may be sold down the river. He is the one elaborate picture we have of the Negro slave before the war, and in a community in which owner and slave alike take slavery very much for granted. Mrs. Stowe's famous book is full of correct observation; she gives us no doubt a fair account of slavery at its happiest — along with other reports which some Southerners will always think exag-gerated. But *Uncle Tom's Cabin* remains a discussion of slavery as an issue in justice; the problem colors every sentence in the book. There must have been thousands of families in which the issue never suggested itself. That is the version of slavery which Mark Twain has given us — the picture of good Christian homes in which the slaves were as natural an incident as any other human relation. Even as propaganda, if *Huckleberry Finn* had been written early enough to serve that purpose, it would have been more subtly convincing than Mrs. Stowe's book, for the dramatic method, without preaching of any kind, here stirs the emotions deeply.

One of the moving themes of the story is Huck's uneasiness over the fact that by accident he is helping a nigger to run away. He has his own code of morality, where property is concerned; he doesn't wish to be a thief. The refinements of honesty, so to speak, he had learned from his father, who always said it was wrong to take what was another man's, unless you had the intention of paying it back sometime. When he and Jim found themselves obliged to rob orchards and gardens, in order to maintain life, they quieted their conscience by making it a rule never to steal all they could. Crab apples, for instance, they always left untouched. But when it came to stealing niggers! On the other hand, when he thought of Jim's kindness to him, of the Negro's terror of the plantations from which he could never hope to return to his wife and children, Huckleberry was in a tangle. He did go so far as to write Miss Watson and tell her where Jim could be found, but he couldn't bring himself to post the letter. "It was a tight place. I took it up and held it in my hand. I was a-trembling, because I'd got to decide, forever, betwixt two things, and I knowed it. I studied a minute, sort of holding my breath, and then says to myself: 'All right, then, I'll *go* to hell,' and tore it up."

Though our sympathy for the slave is profound, we are allowed to see the Negro on more sides of his character than Mrs. Stowe may have been aware of. She knew that the colored race was deeply religious, but she took religion to mean the reading of the Bible and the attendance on a Christian church. Uncle Tom is religious in this sense. What we have more recently learned to appreciate, the wealth of folklore, superstition, and mysticism which still seems to be the inheritance of Negroes, even when they live among the whites, Mrs. Stowe did not portray. Mark Twain makes the most of it; he shows us the African in Jim, the ignorance which to the casual white seems absurd, but which really is connected with powers the white does not share. Altogether he is a wonderful creation, the more remarkable for the matter-of-fact way in which he is presented, without emphasis or exaggeration. He does not take the important place in the scene — Huckleberry remains the hero of the story, but when we have laid the book down, the patient inscrutable black, with his warm heart and his childlike wisdom, remains not the least vivid of our memories.

Whether the portrait of the Grangerfords and the Shepherdsons, in their famous feud, is true to historical fact, those must decide who know the regions of the South before the war where this feud is supposed to occur. But there is no question that the persons seem real, and that the satire on the follies of human nature bites rather deep in this part of the story. Here again the fact that Huckleberry is telling the story serves to secure a splendid literary effect. Nothing in the book is told with greater restraint, and nothing is quite so tragic. The restraint is art, but it seems the work of nature, because Huck wishes, as he says, to hurry over the details — he tries not to remember them for fear they may spoil his sleep. Yet out of the tragedy the reader seizes a noble emotion. When you reflect on the wickedness of feuds and duels, as on the wickedness of war, you may be troubled that a noble emotion should be roused by such material, but when you let yourself go uncritically you can enjoy the courage, the chivalry, the romance which Mark Twain has put into this episode.

At the end of the story Tom Sawyer reappears. He comes to the place where Jim has been captured as a runaway slave, and Huck is hoping to contrive an escape. Tom happens to know that Jim is no longer a slave, but a freeman. The idea of getting him out of his prison, however, is too fruitful to be resisted; Tom begins to make believe — the log cabin becomes a dungeon; the methods of release must be as elaborate as though there were a moat and high walls to cross, and valiant guards to beat down. From this point on, the story lags. The adventures which Tom imagines are cheap after the real dangers Huck and Jim have gone through. We wonder whether this effect of anticlimax was accidental or intended. Did Mark Twain wish to draw this comparison between the genuine experience and the fanciful? Whether he did or not, the contrast is there.

For that reason I have thought it not unjust to compare the two stories to the advantage of *Huckleberry Finn*. We always think of them together, and here at the close of his masterpiece the author sets the two boys side by side for us to look at. *Tom Sawyer* is a fine story, but the other is one of those books which occur all too rarely in a national literature: a book so close to the life of the people that it can hold any reader, and yet so subtle in its art that the craftsman tries to find out how it was done. I don't see why we shouldn't recognize it as a masterpiece now, without waiting for posterity to cast any more votes. Indeed, we thought a while ago that the ballot was closed. But recently it has been suggested that Mark Twain, poor man, missed his full development as an artist, that American life in his time was not sophisticated enough in matters of art to demand of him perfect workmanship, or to applaud when he gave it. Well, that sort of argument breaks down when we ask to see what men have written who were more fortunately placed than he, and when we set their work beside his. Some things he wrote will suffer by the comparison, but not *The Adventures of Huckleberry Finn*.

Henry James

Hawthorne's Three American Novels

HAWTHORNE'S publisher, Mr. Fields, in a volume entitled *Yesterdays with Authors,* has related the circumstances in which *The Scarlet Letter* came into the world. " In the winter of 1849, after he had been ejected from the Customhouse, I went down to Salem to see him and inquire after his health, for we heard he had been suffering from illness. He was then living in a modest wooden house. . . . I found him alone in a chamber over the sitting room of the dwelling, and as the day was cold he was hovering near a stove. We fell into talk about his future prospects, and he was, as I feared I should find him, in a very desponding mood." His visitor urged him to bethink himself of publishing something, and Hawthorne replied by calling his attention to the small popularity his published productions had yet acquired, and declaring he had done nothing, and had no spirit for doing anything. The narrator of the incident urged upon him the necessity of a more hopeful view of his situation, and proceeded to take leave. He had not reached the street, however, when Hawthorne hurried to overtake him, and, placing a roll of manuscript in his hand, bade him take it to Boston, read it, and pronounce upon it. " It is either very good or very bad," said the author; " I don't know which." " On my way back to Boston," says Mr. Fields, " I read the germ of *The Scarlet Letter;* before I slept that night I wrote him a note all aglow with admiration of the marvelous story he had put into my hands, and told him that I would come again to Salem the next day and arrange for its publication. I went on in such an amazing state of excitement, when we met again in the little house, that he would not believe I was really in earnest. He seemed to think I was beside myself, and laughed sadly at my enthusiasm."

Hawthorne, however, went on with the book and finished it, but it appeared only a year later. His biographer quotes a passage from a letter which he wrote in February, 1850, to his friend Horatio Bridge. " I finished my book only yesterday; one end being in the press at Boston while the other was in my head here at Salem; so that, as you see, my story is at least fourteen miles long. . . . My book, the publisher tells me, will not be out before April. He speaks of it in tremendous terms of approbation; so does Mrs. Hawthorne, to whom I read the conclusion last night. It broke her heart, and sent her to bed with a grievous headache — which I look upon as a triumphant success. Judging from the effect upon her and the publisher, I may calculate on what bowlers call a ten-strike. But I don't make any such calculation." And Mr. Lathrop calls attention, in regard to this passage, to an allusion in the English Note-Books (September 14, 1855). " Speaking of Thackeray, I cannot but wonder

From *Hawthorne,* 1879.

at his coolness in respect to his own pathos, and compare it to my own emotions when I read the last scene of *The Scarlet Letter* to my wife, just after writing it — tried to read it, rather, for my voice swelled and heaved as if I were tossed up and down on an ocean as it subsides after a storm. But I was in a very nervous state then, having gone through a great diversity of emotion while writing it, for many months."

The work has the tone of the circumstances in which it was produced. If Hawthorne was in a somber mood, and if his future was painfully vague, *The Scarlet Letter* contains little enough of gaiety or of hopefulness. It is densely dark, with a single spot of vivid color in it; and it will probably long remain the most consistently gloomy of English novels of the first order. But I just now called it the author's masterpiece, and I imagine it will continue to be, for other generations than ours, his most substantial title to fame. The subject had probably lain a long time in his mind, as his subjects were apt to do; so that he appears completely to possess it, to know it and feel it. It is simpler and more complete than his other novels; it achieves more perfectly what it attempts, and it has about it that charm, very hard to express, which we find in an artist's work the first time he has touched his highest mark — a sort of straightness and naturalness of execution, an unconsciousness of his public, and freshness of interest in his theme.

It was a great success, and he immediately found himself famous. The writer of these lines, who was a child at the time, remembers dimly the sensation the book produced, and the little shudder with which people alluded to it, as if a peculiar horror were mixed with its attractions. He was too young to read it himself; but its title, upon which he fixed his eyes as the book lay upon the table, had a mysterious charm. He had a vague belief, indeed, that the " letter " in question was one of the documents that come by the post, and it was a source of perpetual wonderment to him that it should be of such an unaccustomed hue. Of course it was difficult to explain to a child the significance of poor Hester Prynne's blood-colored *A*. But the mystery was at last partly dispelled by his being taken to see a collection of pictures (the annual exhibition of the National Academy), where he encountered a representation of a pale, hand-some woman, in a quaint black dress and a white coif, holding between her knees an elfish-looking little girl, fantastically dressed, and crowned with flowers. Embroidered on the woman's breast was a great crimson *A,* over which the child's fingers, as she glanced strangely out of the picture, were maliciously playing. I was told that this was Hester Prynne and little Pearl, and that when I grew older I might read their interesting history. But the picture remained vividly imprinted on my mind; I had been vaguely frightened and made uneasy by it; and when, years afterwards, I first read the novel, I seemed to myself to have read it before, and to be familiar with its two strange heroines.

I mention this incident simply as an indication of the degree to which the success of *The Scarlet Letter* had made the book what is called an actuality. Hawthorne himself was very modest about it; he wrote to his publisher, when there was a question of his undertaking another novel, that what had given the history of Hester Prynne its "vogue" was simply the introductory chapter. In fact, the publication of *The Scarlet Letter* was in the United States a literary event of the first importance. The book was the finest piece of imaginative writing yet put forth in the country. There was a consciousness of this in the welcome that was given it — a satisfaction in the idea of America having produced a novel that belonged to literature, and to the forefront of it. Something might at last be sent to Europe as exquisite in quality as anything that had been received, and the best of it was that the thing was absolutely American; it belonged to the soil, to the air; it came out of the very heart of New England.

It is beautiful, admirable, extraordinary; it has in the highest degree that merit which I have spoken of as the mark of Hawthorne's best things — an indefinable purity and lightness of conception, a quality which in a work of art affects one in the same way as the absence of grossness does in a human being. His fancy, as I just now said, had evidently brooded over the subject for a long time; the situation to be represented had disclosed itself to him in all its phases. When I say in all its phases, the sentence demands modification; for it is to be remembered that if Hawthorne laid his hand upon the well-worn theme, upon the familiar combination of the wife, the lover, and the husband, it was, after all, but to one period of the history of these three persons that he attached himself. The situation is the situation after the woman's fault has been committed and the current of expiation and repentance has set in. In spite of the relation between Hester Prynne and Arthur Dimmesdale, no story of love was surely ever less of a "love story." To Hawthorne's imagination the fact that these two persons had loved each other too well was of an interest comparatively vulgar; what appealed to him was the idea of their moral situation in the long years that were to follow. The story, indeed, is in a secondary degree that of Hester Prynne; she becomes really, after the first scene, an accessory figure; it is not upon her the denouement depends. It is upon her guilty lover that the author projects most frequently the cold, thin rays of his fitfully moving lantern, which makes here and there a little luminous circle, on the edge of which hovers the livid and sinister figure of the injured and retributive husband. The story goes on, for the most part, between the lover and the husband — the tormented young Puritan minister, who carries the secret of his own lapse from pastoral purity locked up beneath an exterior that commends itself to the reverence of his flock, while he sees the softer partner of his guilt standing in the full glare of exposure and humbling herself to the misery of atonement — between this more wretched and pitiable culprit, to whom dishonor would come as a comfort and the pillory as a relief, and the older, keener, wiser man, who, to obtain satisfaction for the wrong he has suffered, devises the infernally ingenious plan of conjoining himself with his wronger, living with him, living upon him; and while he pretends to minister to his hidden ailment and to sympathize with his pain, revels in his unsuspected knowledge of these things, and stimulates them by malignant arts.

The attitude of Roger Chillingworth, and the means he takes to compensate himself — these are the highly original elements in the situation that Hawthorne so ingeniously treats. None of his works are so impregnated with that after-sense of the old Puritan consciousness of life to which allusion has so often been made. If, as M. Montégut says, the qualities of his ancestors *filtered* down through generations into his composition, *The Scarlet Letter* was, as it were, the vessel that gathered up the last of the precious drops. And I say this not because the story happens to be of so-called historical cast, to be told of the early days of Massachusetts, and of people in steeple-crowned hats and sad-colored garments. The historical coloring is rather weak than otherwise; there is little elaboration of detail, of the modern realism of research; and the author has made no great point of causing his figures to speak the English of their period. Nevertheless, the book is full of the moral presence of the race that invented Hester's penance — diluted and complicated with other things, but still perfectly recognizable. Puritanism, in a word, is there, not only objectively, as Hawthorne tried to place it there, but subjectively as well. Not, I mean, in his judgment of his characters in any harshness of prejudice, or in the obtrusion of a moral lesson; but in the very quality of his own vision, in the tone of the picture, in a certain coldness and exclusiveness of treatment.

In *The Scarlet Letter* there is a great deal of symbolism; there is, I think, too much. It is overdone at times, and becomes mechanical; it ceases to be impressive, and grazes triviality. The idea of the mystic *A* which the young minister finds imprinted upon his breast and eating into his flesh, in sympathy with the embroidered badge that Hester is condemned to wear, appears to me to be a case in point. This suggestion should, I think, have been just made and dropped; to insist upon it and return to it is to exaggerate the weak side of the subject. Hawthorne returns to it constantly, plays with it, and seems charmed by it; until at last the reader feels tempted to declare that his enjoyment of it is puerile. In the admirable scene, so superbly conceived and beautifully executed, in which Mr. Dimmesdale, in the stillness of the night, in the middle of the sleeping town, feels impelled to go and stand upon the scaffold where his mistress had formerly enacted her dreadful penance, and then, seeing Hester pass along the street, from watching at a sickbed, with little Pearl at her side, calls them both to come and stand there beside him — in this masterly episode the effect is almost spoiled by the introduction of one of these superficial conceits. What leads up to it is very fine — so fine that I cannot do better than quote it as a specimen of one of the striking pages of the book.

But before Mr. Dimmesdale had done speaking, a light gleamed far and wide over all the muffled sky. It was doubtless caused by one of those meteors which the night watcher may so often observe burning out to waste in the vacant regions of the atmosphere. So powerful was its radiance that it thoroughly illuminated the dense medium of cloud betwixt the sky and earth. The great vault brightened, like the dome of an immense lamp. It showed the familiar scene of the street with the distinctness of midday, but also with the awfulness that is always imparted to familiar objects by an unaccustomed light. The wooden houses, with their jutting stories and quaint gable-peaks; the doorsteps and thresholds, with the early grass springing up about them; the garden plots, black with freshly turned earth; the wheel track, little worn and, even in the market place, margined with green on either side — all were visible, but with a singularity of aspect that seemed to give another moral interpretation to the things of this world than they had ever borne before. And there stood the minister, with his hand over his heart; and Hester Prynne, with the embroidered letter glimmering on her bosom; and little Pearl, herself a symbol, and the connecting link between these two. They stood in the noon of that strange and solemn splendor, as if it were the light that is to reveal all secrets, and the daybreak that shall unite all that belong to one another.

That is imaginative, impressive, poetic; but when, almost immediately afterwards, the author goes on to say that "the minister, looking upward to the zenith, beheld there the appearance of an immense letter — the letter A — marked out in lines of dull red light," we feel that he separates the sublime from its intimate neighbor. We are tempted to say that this is not moral tragedy, but physical comedy. In the same way, too much is made of the intimation that Hester's badge had a scorching property, and that if one touched it one would immediately withdraw one's hand.

Hawthorne is perpetually looking for images which shall place themselves in picturesque correspondence with the spiritual facts with which he is concerned, and of course the search is of the very essence of poetry. But in such a process discretion is everything, and when the image becomes importunate it is in danger of seeming to stand for nothing more serious than itself. When Hester meets the minister by appointment in the forest, and sits talking with him while little Pearl wanders away and plays by the edge of the brook, the child is represented as at last making her way over to the other side of the woodland stream, and disporting herself there in a manner which makes her mother feel herself, "in some indistinct and tantalizing manner, estranged from Pearl; as if the child, in her lonely ramble through the forest, had strayed out of the sphere in which she and her mother dwelt together, and was now vainly seeking to return to it." And Hawthorne devotes a chapter to this idea of the child's having, by putting the brook between Hester and herself, established a kind of spiritual gulf, on the verge of which her little fantastic person innocently mocks at her mother's sense of bereavement. This conception belongs, one would say, quite to the lighter order of a storyteller's devices, and the reader hardly goes with Hawthorne in the large development he gives to it. He hardly goes with him either, I think, in his extreme predilection for a small number of vague ideas which are represented by such terms as "sphere" and "sympathies." Hawthorne makes too liberal a use of these two substantives; it is the solitary defect of his style, and it counts as a defect partly because the words in question are a sort of specialty with certain writers immeasurably inferior to himself.

I had not meant, however, to expatiate upon his defects, which are of the slenderest and most venial kind. *The Scarlet Letter* has the beauty and harmony of all original and complete conceptions, and its weaker spots, whatever they are, are not of its essence; they are mere light flaws and inequalities of surface. One can often return to it; it supports familiarity, and has the inexhaustible charm and mystery of great works of art. It is admirably written. Hawthorne afterwards polished his style to a still higher degree; but in his later productions — it is almost always the case in a writer's later productions — there is a touch of mannerism. In *The Scarlet Letter* there is a high degree of polish, and at the same time a charming freshness; his phrase is less conscious of itself. His biographer very justly calls attention to the fact that his style was excellent from the beginning; that he appeared to have passed through no phase of learning how to write, but was in possession of his means, from the first, of his handling a pen.

The House of the Seven Gables was written at Lenox, among the mountains of Massachusetts, a village nestling rather loosely in one of the loveliest corners of New England, to which Hawthorne had betaken himself after the success of *The Scarlet Letter* became conspicuous, in the summer of 1850, and where he occupied for two years an uncomfortable little red house which is now pointed out to the inquiring stranger. The inquiring stranger is now a frequent figure at Lenox, for the place has suffered the process of lionization. It has become a prosperous watering-place, or at least (as there are no waters), as they say in America, a summer resort. It is a brilliant and generous landscape, and thirty years ago a man of fancy, desiring to apply himself, might have found both inspiration and tranquillity there. Hawthorne found so much of both that he wrote more during his two years of residence at Lenox than at any other period of his career.

He began with *The House of the Seven Gables,* which was finished in the early part of 1851. This is the longest of his three American novels; it is the most elaborate, and in the judgment of some persons it is the finest. It is a rich, delightful, imaginative work, larger and more various than its companions, and full of all sorts of deep intentions, of interwoven threads of suggestion. But it is not so rounded and complete as *The Scarlet Letter;* it has always seemed to me more like a prologue to a great novel than a great novel itself. I think this is partly owing to the fact that the subject, the *donnée,* as the French say, of the story, does not quite fill it out, and that we get at the same time an impression of certain complicated purposes on the author's part, which seem to reach beyond it. I call it larger and more various than its companions, and it has, indeed, a greater richness of tone and density of detail. The color, so to speak, of *The House of the Seven Gables* is admirable. But the story has a sort of expansive quality which never wholly fructifies, and as I lately laid it down, after reading it for the third time, I had a sense of having interested myself in a magnificent fragment. Yet the book has a great fascination; and of all of those of its author's productions which I have read over while writing this sketch, it is perhaps the one that has gained most by reperusal. If it be true of the others that the pure, natural quality of the imaginative strain is their great merit, this is at least as true of *The House of the Seven Gables,* the charm of which is in a peculiar degree of the kind that we fail to reduce to its grounds — like that of the sweetness of a piece of music, or the softness of fine September weather. It is vague, indefinable, ineffable; but it is the sort of thing we must always point to in justification of the high claim that we make for Hawthorne. In this case, of course, its vagueness is a drawback, for it is difficult to point to ethereal beauties;

and if the reader whom we have wished to inoculate with our admiration inform us, after looking awhile, that he perceives nothing in particular, we can only reply that, in effect, the object is a delicate one.

The House of the Seven Gables comes nearer being a picture of contemporary American life than either of its companions; but on this ground it would be a mistake to make a large claim for it. It cannot be too often repeated that Hawthorne was not a realist. He had a high sense of reality — his Note-Books superabundantly testify to it; and fond as he was of jotting down the items that make it up, he never attempted to render exactly or closely the actual facts of the society that surround him. I have said — I began by saying — that his pages were full of its spirit, and of a certain reflected light that springs from it; but I was careful to add that the reader must look for his local and national qualities between the lines of his writing and in the *indirect* testimony of his tone, his accent, his temper, of his very omissions and suppressions. *The House of the Seven Gables* has, however, more literal actuality than the others, and if it were not too fanciful an account of it, I should say that it renders, to an initiated reader, the impression of a summer afternoon in an elm-shadowed New England town. It leaves upon the mind a vague correspondence to some such reminiscence, and in stirring up the association it renders it delightful. The comparison is to the honor of the New England town, which gains in it more than it bestows. The shadows of the elms, in *The House of the Seven Gables,* are exceptionally dense and cool; the summer afternoon is peculiarly still and beautiful; the atmosphere has a delicious warmth, and the long daylight seems to pause and rest. But the mild provincial quality is there, the mixture of shabbiness and freshness, the paucity of ingredients. The end of an old race — this is the situation that Hawthorne has depicted, and he has been admirably inspired in the choice of the figures in whom he seeks to interest us. They are all figures rather than characters — they are all pictures rather than persons.

But if their reality is light and vague, it is sufficient, and it is in harmony with the low relief and dimness of outline of the objects that surround them. They are all types, to the author's mind, of something general, of something that is bound up with the history at large of families and individuals, and each of them is the center of a cluster of those ingenious and meditative musings, rather melancholy, as a general thing, than joyous, which melt into the current and texture of the story and give it a kind of moral richness. A grotesque old spinster, simple, childish, penniless, very humble at heart, but rigidly conscious of her pedigree; an amiable bachelor, of an epicurean temperament and an enfeebled intellect, who has passed twenty years of his life in penal confinement for a crime of which he was unjustly pronounced guilty; a sweet-natured and bright-faced young girl from the country, a poor relation of these two ancient decrepitudes, with whose moral mustiness her modern freshness and soundness are contrasted; a young man still more modern, holding the latest opinions, who has sought his fortune up and down the world and, though he has not found it, takes a genial and enthusiastic view of the future: these, with two or three remarkable accessory figures, are the persons concerned in the little drama.

The drama is a small one, but as Hawthorne does not put it before us for its own superficial sake, for the dry facts of the case, but for something in it which he holds to be symbolic and of large application, something that points a moral and that it behoves us to remember, the scenes in the rusty wooden house whose gables give its name to the story have something of the dignity both of history and of tragedy. Miss Hephzibah Pyncheon, dragging out a disappointed life in her paternal dwelling, finds herself obliged in her old age to open a little shop for the sale of penny toys and gingerbread. This is the central incident of the tale; and as Hawthorne relates it, it is an incident of the most impressive magnitude and most touching interest. Her dishonored and vague-minded brother is released from prison at the same moment, and returns to the ancestral roof to deepen her perplexities. But, on the other hand, to alleviate them, and to introduce a breath of the air of the outer world into this long unventilated interior, the little country cousin also arrives, and proves the good angel of the feebly distracted household. All this episode is exquisite — admirably conceived and executed, with a kind of humorous tenderness, an equal sense of everything in it that is picturesque, touching, ridiculous, worthy of the highest praise. Hephzibah Pyncheon, with her nearsighted scowl, her rusty joints, her antique turban, her map of a great territory to the eastward which ought to have belonged to her family, her vain terrors, and scruples, and resentments, the ineptitude and repugnance of an ancient gentlewoman to the vulgar little commerce which a cruel fate has compelled her to engage in — Hephzibah Pyncheon is a masterly picture. I repeat that she is a picture, as her companions are pictures; she is a charming piece of descriptive writing, rather than a dramatic exhibition. But she is described, like her companions, too, so subtly and lovingly that we enter into her virginal old heart and stand with her behind her abominable little counter.

Clifford Pyncheon is a still more remarkable conception, though he is, perhaps, not so vividly depicted. It was a figure needing a much more subtle touch, however, and it was of the essence of his character to be vague and unemphasized. Nothing can be more charming than the manner in which the soft, bright, active presence of Phoebe Pyncheon is indicated, or than the account of her relations with the poor, dimly sentient kinsman for whom her light-handed sisterly offices, in the evening of a melancholy life, are a revelation of lost possibilities of happiness. " In her aspect," Hawthorne says of the young girl, " there was a familiar gladness, and a holiness that you could play with, and yet reverence it as much as ever. She was like a prayer offered up in the homeliest beauty of one's mother tongue. Fresh was Phoebe, moreover, and airy, and sweet in her apparel; as if nothing that she wore — neither her gown, nor her small straw bonnet, nor her little kerchief, any more than her snowy stockings — had ever been put on before; or, if worn, were all the fresher for it, and with a fragrance as if they had lain among the rosebuds." Of the influence of her maidenly salubrity upon poor Clifford, Hawthorne gives the prettiest description, and then, breaking off suddenly, renounces the attempt in language which, while pleading its inadequacy, conveys an exquisite satisfaction to the reader.

I have not mentioned the personage in *The House of the Seven Gables* upon whom Hawthorne evidently bestowed most pains, and whose portrait is the most elaborate in the book; partly because he is, in spite of the space he occupies, an accessory figure, and partly because, even more than the others, he is what I have called a picture rather than a character. Judge Pyncheon is an ironical portrait, very richly and broadly executed, very sagaciously composed and rendered — the portrait of a superb, full-blown hypocrite, a large-based, full-nurtured Pharisee, bland, urbane, impressive, diffusing about him a " sultry " warmth of benevolence, as the author calls it again and again, and basking in the noontide of prosperity and the consideration of society; but in reality hard, gross, and ignoble. Judge Pyncheon is an elaborate piece of description, made up of a hundred admirable touches, in which satire is always winged with fancy, and fancy is linked with a deep sense of reality. It is difficult to say whether Hawthorne followed a model in describing Judge Pyncheon; but it is tolerably obvious that the picture is an impression — a copious impression — of an individual. It has evidently a definite starting point in fact, and the author is able to draw, freely and confidently, after the image established in his mind.

Holgrave, the modern young man, who has been a Jack-of-all-trades, and is at the period of the story a daguerreotypist, is an attempt to render a kind of national type — that of the young citizen of the United States whose fortune is simply in his lively intelligence, and who stands naked, as it were, unbiased and unencumbered alike, in the center of the far-stretching level of American life. Holgrave is intended as a contrast; his lack of traditions, his democratic stamp, his condensed experience, are opposed to the desiccated prejudices and exhausted vitality of the race of which poor feebly scowling, rusty-jointed Hephzibah is the most heroic representative. It is, perhaps, a pity that Hawthorne should not have proposed to himself to give the old Pyncheon qualities some embodiment which would help them to balance more fairly with the elastic properties of the young daguerreotypist — should not have painted a lusty conservative to match his strenuous radical. As it is, the mustiness and moldiness of the tenants of the House of the Seven Gables crumble away rather too easily. Evidently, however, what Hawthorne designed to represent was not the struggle between an old society and a new, for in this case he would have given the old one a better chance; but simply, as I have said, the shrinkage and extinction of a family. This appealed to his imagination; and the idea of long perpetuation and survival always appears to have filled him with a kind of horror and disapproval. Conservative, in a certain degree, as he was himself, and fond of retrospect and quietude and the mellowing influences of time, it is singular how often one encounters in his writings some expression of mistrust of old houses, old institutions, long lines of descent. He was disposed, apparently, to allow a very moderate measure in these respects, and he condemns the dwelling of the Pyncheons to disappear from the face of the earth because it has been standing a couple of hundred years. In this he was an American of Americans; or, rather, he was more American than many of his countrymen, who, though they are accustomed to work for the short run rather than the long, have often a lurking esteem for things that show the marks of having lasted. I will add that Holgrave is one of the few figures, among those which Hawthorne created, with regard to which the absence of the realistic mode of treatment is felt as a loss. Holgrave is not sharply enough characterized; he lacks features; he is not an individual, but a type. But my last word about this admirable novel must not be a restrictive one. It is a large and generous production, pervaded with that vague hum, that indefinable echo, of the whole multitudinous life of man, which is the real sign of a great work of fiction.

After the publication of *The House of the Seven Gables,* which brought him great honor and, I believe, a tolerable share of a more ponderable substance, he composed a couple of little volumes for children — *The Wonder-Book,* and a small collection of stories entitled *Tanglewood Tales.* They are not among his most serious literary titles, but if I may trust my own early impression of them, they are among the most charming literary services that have been rendered to children in an age (and especially in a country) in which the exactions of the infant mind have exerted much too palpable an influence upon literature. Hawthorne's stories are the old Greek myths, made more vivid to the childish imagination by an infusion of details which both deepen and explain their marvels. I have been careful not to read them over, for I should be very sorry to risk disturbing in any degree a recollection of them that has been at rest since the appreciative period of life to which they are addressed. They seem at that period enchanting, and the ideal of happiness of many American children is to lie upon the carpet and lose themselves in *The Wonder-Book*. It is in its pages that they first make the acquaintance of the heroes and heroines of the antique mythology, and something of the nursery fairy-tale quality of interest which Hawthorne imparts to them always remains.

I have said that Lenox was a very pretty place; and that he was able to work there, Hawthorne proved by composing *The House of the Seven Gables* with a good deal of rapidity. But, at the close of the year in which this novel was published, he wrote to a friend (Mr. Fields, his publisher) that, " to tell you a secret, I am sick to death of Berkshire, and hate to think of spending another winter here. . . . The air and climate do not agree with my health at all, and for the first time since I was a boy I have felt languid and dispirited. . . . Oh, that Providence would build me the merest little shanty, and mark me out a rood or two of garden ground, near the seacoast! " He was at this time for a while out of health; and it is proper to remember that though the Massachusetts Berkshire, with its mountains and lakes, was charming during the ardent American summer, there was a reverse to the medal, consisting of December snows prolonged into April and May. Providence failed to provide him with a cottage by the sea; but he betook himself for the winter of 1852 to the little town of West Newton, near Boston, where he brought into the world *The Blithedale Romance.*

This work, as I have said, would not have been written if Hawthorne had not spent a year at Brook Farm; and though it is in no sense of the word an account of the manners or the inmates of that establishment, it will preserve the memory of the ingenious community at West Roxbury for a generation unconscious of other reminders. I hardly know what to say about it, save that it is very charming; this vague, unanalytic epithet is the first that comes to one's pen in treating Hawthorne's novels, for their extreme amenity of form invariably suggests it; but if, on the one hand, it claims to be uttered, on the other it frankly confesses its inconclusiveness. Perhaps, however, in this case it fills out the measure of appreciation more completely than in others, for *The Blithedale Romance* is the lightest, the brightest, the liveliest, of this company of unhumorous fictions.

The story is told from a more joyous point of view — from a point of view comparatively humorous — and a number of objects and incidents touched with the light of the profane world — the vulgar, many-colored world of actuality, as distinguished from the crepuscular realm of the writer's own reveries — are mingled with its course. The book, indeed, is a mixture of elements, and it leaves in the memory an impression analogous to that of an April day — an alternation of brightness and shadow, of broken sun-patches and sprinkling clouds. Its denouement is tragical — there is, indeed, nothing so tragical in all Hawthorne, unless it be the murder of Miriam's persecutor by Donatello, in *The Marble Faun,* as the suicide of Zenobia; and yet, on the whole, the effect of the novel is to make one think more agreeably of life. The standpoint of the narrator has the advantage of being a concrete one; he is no longer, as in the preceding tales, a disembodied spirit, imprisoned in the haunted chamber of his own contemplations, but a particular man, with a certain human grossness.

Of Miles Coverdale I have already spoken, and of its being natural to assume that, in so far as we may measure this lightly indicated identity of his, it has a great deal in common with that of his creator. Coverdale is a picture of the contemplative, observant, analytic nature, nursing its fancies, and yet, thanks to an element of strong good sense, not bringing them up to be spoiled children; having little at stake in life, at any given moment, and yet indulging, in imagination, in a good many adventures; a portrait of a man, in a word, whose passions are slender, whose imagination is active, and whose happiness lies, not in doing, but in perceiving — half a poet, half a critic, and all a spectator. He is contrasted excellently with the figure of Hollingsworth, the heavily treading Reformer, whose attitude with regard to the world is that of the hammer to the anvil, and who has no patience with his friend's indifferences and neutralities. Coverdale is a gentle skeptic, a mild cynic; he would agree that life is a little worth living — or worth living a little; but would remark that, unfortunately, to live little enough, we have to live a great deal. He confesses to a want of earnestness, but in reality he is evidently an excellent fellow, to whom one might look, not for any personal performance on a great scale, but for a good deal of generosity of detail. " As Hollingsworth once told me, I lack a purpose," he writes, at the close of his story. " How strange! He was ruined, morally, by an overplus of the same ingredient the want of which, I occasionally suspect, has rendered my own life all an emptiness. I by no means wish to die. Yet, were there any cause in this whole chaos of human struggle worth a sane

man's dying for, and which my death would benefit, then — provided, however, the effort did not involve an unreasonable amount of trouble — methinks
I might be bold to offer up my life. If Kossuth, for example, would pitch the
battlefield of Hungarian rights within an easy ride of my abode, and choose a
mild, sunny morning, after breakfast, for the conflict, Miles Coverdale would
gladly be his man for one brave rush upon the leveled bayonets. Further than
that I should be loath to pledge myself."

The finest thing in *The Blithedale Romance* is the character of Zenobia,
which I have said elsewhere strikes me as the nearest approach that Hawthorne
has made to the complete creation of a *person*. She is more concrete than Hester
or Miriam, or Hilda or Phoebe; she is a more definite image, produced by a
greater multiplicity of touches. It is idle to inquire too closely whether Hawthorne had Margaret Fuller in his mind in constructing the figure of this
brilliant specimen of the strong-minded class, and endowing her with the genius
of conversation; or, on the assumption that such was the case, to compare the
image at all strictly with the model. There is no strictness in the representation by
novelists of persons who have struck them in life, and there can in the nature
of things be none. From the moment the imagination takes a hand in the game,
the inevitable tendency is to divergence, to following what may be called new
scents. The original gives hints, but the writer does what he likes with them,
and imports new elements into the picture. If there is this amount of reason for
referring the wayward heroine of Blithedale to Hawthorne's impression of the
most distinguished woman of her day in Boston; that Margaret Fuller was the
only literary lady of eminence whom there is any sign of his having known; that
she was proud, passionate, and eloquent; that she was much connected with the
little world of Transcendentalism out of which the experiment of Brook Farm
sprang; and that she had a miserable end and a watery grave — if these are
facts to be noted on one side, I say; on the other, the beautiful and sumptuous
Zenobia, with her rich and picturesque temperament and physical aspects, offers
many points of divergence from the plain and strenuous invalid who represented feminine culture in the suburbs of the New England metropolis. This
picturesqueness of Zenobia is very happily indicated and maintained; she is a
woman in all the force of the term, and there is something very vivid and powerful in her large expression of womanly gifts and weaknesses. Hollingsworth is,
I think, less successful, though there is much reality in the conception of the
type to which he belongs — the strong-willed, narrow-hearted apostle of a
special form of redemption for society.

The most touching element in the novel is the history of the grasp that this
barbarous fanatic has laid upon the fastidious and high-tempered Zenobia,
who, disliking him and shrinking from him at a hundred points, is drawn into
the gulf of his omnivorous egotism. The portion of the story that strikes me as
least felicitous is that which deals with Priscilla and with her mysterious relation to Zenobia — with her mesmeric gifts, her clairvoyance, her identity with
the Veiled Lady, her divided subjection to Hollingsworth and Westervelt, and
her numerous other graceful but fantastic properties — her Sibylline attributes,

as the author calls them. Hawthorne is rather too fond of Sibylline attributes —
a taste of the same order as his disposition, to which I have already alluded,
to talk about spheres and sympathies. As the action advances, in *The Blithedale
Romance,* we get too much out of reality, and cease to feel beneath our feet the
firm ground of an appeal to our own vision of the world — our observation.
I should have liked to see the story concern itself more with the little community
in which its earlier scenes are laid, and avail itself of so excellent an opportunity
for describing unhackneyed specimens of human nature. I have already spoken
of the absence of satire in the novel, of its not aiming in the least at satire, and
of its offering no grounds for complaint as an invidious picture. Indeed, the
brethren of Brook Farm should have held themselves slighted rather than
misrepresented, and have regretted that the admirable genius who for a while
was numbered among them should have treated their institution mainly as a
perch for starting upon an imaginative flight. But when all is said about a
certain want of substance and cohesion in the latter portions of *The Blithedale
Romance,* the book is still a delightful and beautiful one. Zenobia and Hollingsworth live in the memory; and even Priscilla and Coverdale, who linger there
less importunately, have a great deal that touches us and that we believe in. I
said just now that Priscilla was infelicitous; but immediately afterwards I open
the volume at a page in which the author describes some of the out-of-door
amusements at Blithedale, and speaks of a foot race across the grass, in which
some of the slim young girls of the society joined. " Priscilla's peculiar charm
in a foot race was the weakness and irregularity with which she ran. Growing
up without exercise, except to her poor little fingers, she had never yet acquired
the perfect use of her legs. Setting buoyantly forth, therefore, as if no rival less
swift than Atalanta could compete with her, she ran falteringly, and often
tumbled on the grass. Such an incident — though it seems too slight to think
of — was a thing to laugh at, but which brought the water into one's eyes, and
lingered in the memory after far greater joys and sorrows were wept out of it,
as antiquated trash. Priscilla's life, as I beheld it, was full of trifles that affected
me in just this way." That seems to me exquisite, and the book is full of touches
as deep and delicate.

Hawthorne's work will remain; it is too original and exquisite to pass away;
among the men of imagination he will always have his niche. No one has had
just that vision of life, and no one has had a literary form that more successfully
expressed his vision. He was not a moralist, and he was not simply a poet. The
moralists are weightier, denser, richer, in a sense; the poets are more purely
inconclusive and irresponsible. He combined in a singular degree the spon-
taneity of the imagination with a haunting care for moral problems. Man's
conscience was his theme, but he saw it in the light of a creative fancy which
added, out of its own substance, an interest and, I may almost say, an importance.

Ralph Waldo Emerson

The American Scholar

MR. President and Gentlemen, I greet you on the recommencement of our literary year. Our anniversary is one of hope, and, perhaps, not enough of labor. We do not meet for games of strength or skill, for the recitation of histories, tragedies, and odes, like the ancient Greeks; for parliaments of love and poesy, like the troubadours; nor for the advancement of science, like our contemporaries in the British and European capitals. Thus far, our holiday has been simply a friendly sign of the survival of the love of letters amongst a people too busy to give to letters any more. As such it is precious as the sign of an indestructible instinct. Perhaps the time is already come when it ought to be, and will be, something else; when the sluggard intellect of this continent will look from under its iron lids and fill the postponed expectation of the world with something better than the exertions of mechanical skill. Our day of dependence, our long apprenticeship to the learning of other lands, draws to a close. The millions that around us are rushing into life cannot always be fed on the sere remains of foreign harvests. Events, actions, arise that must be sung, that will sing themselves. Who can doubt that poetry will revive and lead in a new age, as the star in the constellation Harp, which now flames in our zenith, astronomers announce, shall one day be the polestar for a thousand years?

In this hope I accept the topic which not only usage but the nature of our association seems to prescribe to this day: The American Scholar. Year by year we come up hither to read one more chapter of his biography. Let us inquire what light new days and events have thrown on his character and his hopes.

It is one of those fables which out of an unknown antiquity convey an unlooked-for wisdom, that the gods, in the beginning, divided Man into men, that he might be more helpful to himself; just as the hand was divided into fingers, the better to answer its end.

The old fable covers a doctrine ever new and sublime: that there is One Man — present to all particular men only partially, or through one faculty; and that you must take the whole society to find the whole man. Man is not a farmer, or a professor, or an engineer, but he is all. Man is priest, and scholar, and statesman, and producer, and soldier. In the *divided* or social state these functions are parceled out to individuals, each of whom aims to do his stint of the joint work, whilst each other performs his. The fable implies that the individual, to possess himself, must sometimes return from his own labor to embrace all the other laborers. But, unfortunately, this original unit, this fountain of power, has been so distributed to multitudes, has been so minutely subdivided and peddled out, that it is spilled into drops and cannot be gathered. The state of society is one in

Delivered before the Harvard Phi Beta Kappa Society on August 31, 1837.

which the members have suffered amputation from the trunk, and strut about so many walking monsters — a good finger, a neck, a stomach, an elbow, but never a man.

Man is thus metamorphosed into a thing, into many things. The planter, who is Man sent out into the field to gather food, is seldom cheered by any idea of the true dignity of his ministry. He sees his bushel and his cart, and nothing beyond, and sinks into the farmer, instead of Man on the farm. The tradesman scarcely ever gives an ideal worth to his work, but is ridden by the routine of his craft, and the soul is subject to dollars. The priest becomes a form; the attorney a statute book; the mechanic a machine; the sailor a rope of the ship.

In this distribution of functions the scholar is the delegated intellect. In the right state he is *Man Thinking*. In the degenerate state, when the victim of society, he tends to become a mere thinker or, still worse, the parrot of other men's thinking.

In this view of him, as Man Thinking, the theory of his office is contained. Him nature solicits with all her placid, all her monitory pictures; him the past instructs; him the future invites. Is not indeed every man a student, and do not all things exist for the student's behoof? And, finally, is not the true scholar the only true master? But the old oracle said, " All things have two handles: beware of the wrong one." In life, too often, the scholar errs with mankind and forfeits his privilege. Let us see him in his school, and consider him in reference to the main influences he receives.

I. The first in time and the first in importance of the influences upon the mind is that of nature. Every day, the sun; and, after sunset, night and her stars. Ever the winds blow; ever the grass grows. Every day, men and women, conversing, beholding and beholden. The scholar is he of all men whom this spectacle most engages. He must settle its value in his mind. What is nature to him? There is never a beginning, there is never an end, to the inexplicable continuity of this web of God, but always circular power returning into itself. Therein it resembles his own spirit, whose beginning, whose ending, he never can find — so entire, so boundless. Far too as her splendors shine, system on system shooting like rays, upward, downward, without center, without circumference — in the mass and in the particle, nature hastens to render account of herself to the mind. Classification begins. To the young mind every thing is individual, stands by itself. By and by, it finds how to join two things and see in them one nature; then three, then three thousand; and so, tyrannized over by its own unifying instinct, it goes on tying things together, diminishing anomalies, discovering roots running under ground whereby contrary and remote things cohere and flower out from one stem. It presently learns that since the dawn of history there has been a constant accumulation and classifying of facts. But what is classification but the perceiving that these objects are not chaotic, and are not foreign, but have a law which is also a law of the human mind? The astronomer discovers that geometry, a pure abstraction of the human mind, is the measure of planetary motion. The chemist finds proportions and intelligible method throughout matter; and science is nothing but the finding of analogy, identity, in the most remote parts. The ambitious soul sits down before each refractory fact; one after another reduces all strange constitutions, all new powers, to their class and their law, and goes on forever to animate the last fiber of organization, the outskirts of nature, by insight.

Thus to him, to this schoolboy under the bending dome of day, is suggested that he and it proceed from one root; one is leaf and one is flower, relation, sympathy, stirring in every vein. And what is that root? Is not that the soul of his soul? A thought too bold; a dream too wild. Yet when this spiritual light shall have revealed the law of more earthly natures — when he has learned to worship the soul, and to see that the natural philosophy that now is, is only the first gropings of its gigantic hand, he shall look forward to an ever expanding knowledge as to a becoming creator. He shall see that nature is the opposite of the soul, answering to it part for part. One is seal and one is print. Its beauty is the beauty of his own mind. Its laws are the laws of his own mind. Nature then becomes to him the measure of his attainments. So much of nature as he is ignorant of, so much of his own mind does he not yet possess. And, in fine, the ancient precept, " Know thyself," and the modern precept, " Study nature," become at last one maxim.

II. The next great influence into the spirit of the scholar is the mind of the past — in whatever form, whether of literature, of art, of institutions, that mind is inscribed. Books are the best type of the influence of the past, and perhaps we shall get at the truth — learn the amount of this influence more conveniently — by considering their value alone.

The theory of books is noble. The scholar of the first age received into him the world around; brooded thereon; gave it the new arrangement of his own mind, and uttered it again. It came into him life; it went out from him truth. It came to him short-lived actions; it went out from him immortal thoughts. It came to him business; it went from him poetry. It was dead fact; now, it is quick thought. It can stand, and it can go. It now endures, it now flies, it now inspires. Precisely in proportion to the depth of mind from which it issued, so high does it soar, so long does it sing.

Or, I might say, it depends on how far the process had gone, of transmuting life into truth. In proportion to the completeness of the distillation, so will the purity and imperishableness of the product be. But none is quite perfect. As no air pump can by any means make a perfect vacuum, so neither can any artist entirely exclude the conventional, the local, the perishable from his book, or write a book of pure thought, that shall be as efficient, in all respects, to a remote posterity as to contemporaries, or rather to the second age. Each age, it is found, must write its own books; or rather, each generation for the next succeeding. The books of an older period will not fit this.

Yet hence arises a grave mischief. The sacredness which attaches to the act of creation, the act of thought, is transferred to the record. The poet chanting was felt to be a divine man: henceforth the chant is divine also. The writer was a just and wise spirit: henceforward it is settled the book is perfect; as love of the hero corrupts into worship of his statue. Instantly the book becomes noxious: the guide is a tyrant. The sluggish and perverted mind of the multitude, slow to open to the incursions of reason, having once so opened, having once received this book, stands upon it, and makes an outcry if it is disparaged. Colleges are built on it. Books are written on it by thinkers, not by Man Thinking; by men of talent, that is, who start wrong, who set out from accepted dogmas, not from their own sight of principles. Meek young men grow up in libraries, believing it their duty to accept the views which Cicero, which Locke, which Bacon, have given; forgetful that Cicero, Locke, and Bacon were only young men in libraries when they wrote these books.

Hence, instead of Man Thinking, we have the bookworm. Hence the book-learned class, who value books as such; not as related to nature and the human constitution, but as making a sort of Third Estate with the world and the soul. Hence the restorers of readings, the emendators, the bibliomaniacs of all degrees.

Books are the best of things, well used; abused, among the worst. What is the right use? What is the one end which all means go to effect? They are for nothing but to inspire. I had better never see a book than to be warped by its attraction clean out of my own orbit, and made a satellite instead of a system. The one thing in the world, of value, is the active soul. This every man is entitled to; this every man contains within him, although in almost all men obstructed, and as yet unborn. The soul active sees absolute truth and utters truth, or creates. In this action it is genius; not the privilege of here and there a favorite, but the sound estate of every man. In its essence it is progressive. The book, the college, the school of art, the institution of any kind, stop with some past utterance of genius. This is good, say they; let us hold by this. They pin me down. They look backward and not forward. But genius looks forward: the eyes of man are set in his forehead, not in his hindhead: man hopes: genius creates. Whatever talents may be, if the man create not, the pure efflux of the Deity is not his; cinders and smoke there may be, but not yet flame. There are creative manners, there are creative actions and creative words; manners, actions, words, that is, indicative of no custom or authority, but springing spontaneous from the mind's own sense of good and fair.

On the other part, instead of being its own seer, let it receive from another mind its truth, though it were in torrents of light, without periods of solitude, inquest, and self-recovery, and a fatal disservice is done. Genius is always sufficiently the enemy of genius by overinfluence. The literature of every nation bears me witness. The English dramatic poets have Shakespearized now for two hundred years.

Undoubtedly there is a right way of reading, so it be sternly subordinated. Man Thinking must not be subdued by his instruments. Books are for the scholar's idle times. When he can read God directly, the hour is too precious to be wasted in other men's transcripts of their readings. But when the intervals of darkness come, as come they must — when the sun is hid and the stars withdraw their shining — we repair to the lamps which were kindled by their ray, to guide our steps to the East again, where the dawn is. We hear, that we may speak. The Arabian proverb says, " A fig tree, looking on a fig tree, becometh fruitful."

It is remarkable, the character of the pleasure we derive from the best books. They impress us with the conviction that one nature wrote and the same reads. We read the verses of one of the great English poets, of Chaucer, of Marvell, of Dryden, with the most modern joy — with a pleasure, I mean, which is in great part caused by the abstraction of all *time* from their verses. There is some awe mixed with the joy of our surprise, when this poet, who lived in some past world, two or three hundred years ago, says that which lies close to my own soul, that which I also had well-nigh thought and said. But for the evidence thence afforded to the philosophical doctrine of the identity of all minds, we should suppose some preëstablished harmony, some foresight of souls that were to be, and some preparation of stores for their future wants, like the fact observed in insects, who lay up food before death for the young grub they shall never see.

I would not be hurried by any love of system, by any exaggeration of instincts, to underrate the book. We all know, that as the human body can be nourished on any food, though it were boiled grass and the broth of shoes, so the human mind can be fed by any knowledge. And great and heroic men have existed who had almost no other information than by the printed page. I only would say that it needs a strong head to bear that diet. One must be an inventor to read well. As the proverb says, " He that would bring home the wealth of the Indies, must carry out the wealth of the Indies." There is then creative reading as well as creative writing. When the mind is braced by labor and invention, the page of whatever book we read becomes luminous with manifold allusion. Every sentence is doubly significant, and the sense of our author is as broad as the world. We then see, what is always true, that as the seer's hour of vision is short and rare among heavy days and months, so is its record, perchance, the least part of his volume. The discerning will read, in his Plato or Shakespeare, only that least part, only the authentic utterances of the oracle; all the rest he rejects, were it never so many times Plato's and Shakespeare's.

Of course there is a portion of reading quite indispensable to a wise man. History and exact science he must learn by laborious reading. Colleges, in like manner, have their indispensable office: to teach elements. But they can only highly serve us when they aim not to drill but to create; when they gather from far every ray of various genius to their hospitable halls, and by the concentrated fires, set the hearts of their youth on flame. Thought and knowledge are natures in which apparatus and pretension avail nothing. Gowns and pecuniary foundations, though of towns of gold, can never countervail the least sentence or syllable of wit. Forget this, and our American colleges will recede in their public importance whilst they grow richer every year.

III. There goes in the world a notion that the scholar should be a recluse, a valetudinarian — as unfit for any handiwork or public labor as a penknife for an axe. The so-called " practical men " sneer at speculative men, as if, because they speculate or *see,* they could do nothing. I have heard it said that the clergy — who are always, more universally than any other class, the scholars of their day — are addressed as women; that the rough, spontaneous conversation of men they do not hear, but only a mincing and diluted speech. They are often virtually disfranchised; and indeed there are advocates for their celibacy. As far as this is true of the studious classes, it is not just and wise. Action is with the scholar subordinate, but it is essential. Without it he is not yet man. Without it thought can never ripen into truth. Whilst the world hangs before the eye as a cloud of beauty, we cannot even see its beauty. Inaction is cowardice, but there can be no scholar without the heroic mind. The preamble of thought, the transition through which it passes from the unconscious to the conscious, is action. Only so much do I know, as I have lived. Instantly we know whose words are loaded with life, and whose not.

The world — this shadow of the soul, or *other me* — lies wide around. Its attractions are the keys which unlock my thoughts and make me acquainted with myself. I run eagerly into this resounding tumult. I grasp the hands of those next me, and take my place in the ring to suffer and to work, taught by an instinct that so shall the dumb abyss be vocal with speech. I pierce its order; I dissipate its fear; I dispose of it within the circuit of my expanding life. So much only of life as I know by experience, so much of the wilderness have I vanquished and planted, or so far have I extended my being, my dominion. I do not see how any man can afford, for the sake of his nerves and his nap, to spare any action in which he can partake. It is pearls and rubies to his discourse. Drudgery, calamity, exasperation, want, are instructors in eloquence and wisdom. The true scholar grudges every opportunity of action past by, as a loss of power. It is the raw material out of which the intellect molds her splendid products. A strange process too, this by which experience is converted into thought, as a mulberry leaf is converted into satin. The manufacture goes forward at all hours.

The actions and events of our childhood and youth are now matters of calmest observation. They lie like fair pictures in the air. Not so with our recent actions — with the business which we now have in hand. On this we are quite unable to speculate. Our affections as yet circulate through it. We no more feel or know it than we feel the feet, or the hand, or the brain of our body. The new deed is yet a part of life — remains for a time immersed in our unconscious life. In some contemplative hour it detaches itself from the life like a ripe fruit, to become a thought of the mind. Instantly it is raised, transfigured; the corruptible has put on incorruption. Henceforth it is an object of beauty, however base its origin and neighborhood. Observe too the impossibility of antedating this act. In its grub state, it cannot fly, it cannot shine, it is a dull grub. But suddenly, without observation, the selfsame thing unfurls beautiful wings and is an angel of wisdom. So is there no fact, no event, in our private history, which shall not, sooner or later, lose its adhesive, inert form and astonish us by soaring from our body into the empyrean. Cradle and infancy, school and playground, the fear of boys, and dogs, and ferules, the love of little maids and berries, and many another fact that once filled the whole sky, are gone already; friend and relative, profession and party, town and country, nation and world, must also soar and sing.

Of course, he who has put forth his total strength in fit actions has the richest return of wisdom. I will not shut myself out of this globe of action, and transplant an oak into a flowerpot, there to hunger and pine; nor trust the revenue of some single faculty, and exhaust one vein of thought, much like those Savoyards who, getting their livelihood by carving shepherds, shepherdesses, and smoking Dutchmen, for all Europe, went out one day to the mountain to find stock, and discovered that they had whittled up the last of their pine trees. Authors we have, in numbers, who have written out their vein, and who, moved by a commendable prudence, sail for Greece or Palestine, follow the trapper into the prairie, or ramble round Algiers, to replenish their merchantable stock.

If it were only for a vocabulary, the scholar would be covetous of action. Life is our dictionary. Years are well spent in country labors; in town; in the insight into trades and manufactures; in frank intercourse with many men and women; in science; in art; to the one end of mastering in all their facts a language by which to illustrate and embody our perceptions. I learn immediately from any speaker how much he has already lived, through the poverty or the splendor of his speech. Life lies behind us as the quarry from whence we get tiles and copestones for the masonry of today. This is the way to learn grammar. Colleges and books only copy the language which the field and the work-yard made.

But the final value of action, like that of books, and better than books, is that it is a resource. That great principle of undulation in nature, that shows itself in the inspiring and expiring of the breath; in desire and satiety; in the ebb and flow of the sea; in day and night; in heat and cold; and, as yet more deeply ingrained in every atom and every fluid, is known to us under the name of polarity — these " fits of easy transmission and reflection," as Newton called them, are the law of nature because they are the law of spirit.

The mind now thinks, now acts, and each fit reproduces the other. When the artist has exhausted his materials, when the fancy no longer paints, when thoughts are no longer apprehended and books are a weariness — he has always the resource *to live*. Character is higher than intellect. Thinking is the function. Living is the functionary. The stream retreats to its source. A great soul will be strong to live, as well as strong to think. Does he lack organ or medium to impart his truth? He can still fall back on this elemental force of living them. This is a total act. Thinking is a partial act. Let the grandeur of justice shine in his affairs. Let the beauty of affection cheer his lowly roof. Those " far from fame," who dwell and act with him, will feel the force of his constitution in the doings and passages of the day better than it can be measured by any public and designed display. Time shall teach him that the scholar loses no hour which the man lives. Herein he unfolds the sacred germ of his instinct, screened from influence. What is lost in seemliness is gained in strength. Not out of those on whom systems of education have exhausted their culture comes the helpful giant to destroy the old or to build the new, but out of unhandseled savage nature; out of terrible Druids and Berserkers come at last Alfred and Shakespeare.

I hear therefore with joy whatever is beginning to be said of the dignity and necessity of labor to every citizen. There is virtue yet in the hoe and the spade, for learned as well as for unlearned hands. And labor is everywhere welcome; always we are invited to work; only be this limitation observed, that a man shall not for the sake of wider activity sacrifice any opinion to the popular judgments and modes of action.

I have now spoken of the education of the scholar by nature, by books, and by action. It remains to say somewhat of his duties.

They are such as become Man Thinking. They may all be comprised in self-trust. The office of the scholar is to cheer, to raise, and to guide men by showing them facts amidst appearances. He plies the slow, unhonored, and unpaid task of observation. Flamsteed and Herschel, in their glazed observatories, may catalogue the stars with the praise of all men; and the results being splendid and useful, honor is sure. But he, in his private observatory, cataloguing obscure and nebulous stars of the human mind, which as yet no man has thought of as such — watching days and months sometimes for a few facts; correcting still his old records — must relinquish display and immediate fame. In the long period of his preparation he must betray often an ignorance and shiftlessness in popular arts, incurring the disdain of the able who shoulder him aside. Long he must stammer in his speech; often forego the living for the dead. Worse yet, he must accept — how often! — poverty and solitude. For the ease and pleasure of treading the old road, accepting the fashions, the education, the religion of society, he takes the cross of making his own, and, of course, the self-accusation, the faint heart, the frequent uncertainty and loss of time, which are the nettles and tangling vines in the way of the self-relying and self-directed; and the state of virtual hostility in which he seems to stand to society, and especially to educated society. For all this loss and scorn, what offset? He is to find consolation in exercising the highest functions of human nature. He is one who raises himself from private considerations and breathes and lives on public and illustrious thoughts. He is the world's eye. He is the world's heart. He is to resist the vulgar prosperity that retrogrades ever to barbarism, by preserving and communicating heroic sentiments, noble biographies, melodious verse, and the conclusions of history. Whatsoever oracles the human heart, in all emergencies, in all solemn hours, has uttered as its commentary on the world of actions — these he shall receive and impart. And whatsoever new verdict reason from her inviolable seat pronounces on the passing men and events of today — this he shall hear and promulgate.

These being his functions, it becomes him to feel all confidence in himself, and to defer never to the popular cry. He and he only knows the world. The world of any moment is the merest appearance. Some great decorum, some fetish of a government, some ephemeral trade, or war, or man, is cried up by half mankind and cried down by the other half, as if all depended on this particular up or down. The odds are that the whole question is not worth the poorest thought which the scholar has lost in listening to the controversy. Let him not quit his belief that a popgun is a popgun, though the ancient and honorable of the earth affirm it to be the crack of doom. In silence, in steadiness, in severe abstraction, let him hold by himself; add observation to observation, patient of neglect, patient of reproach, and bide his own time — happy enough if he can satisfy himself alone that this day he has seen something truly. Success treads on every right step. For the instinct is sure, that prompts him to tell his brother what he thinks. He then learns that in going down into the secrets of his own mind he has descended into the secrets of all minds. He learns that he who has mastered any law in his private thoughts, is master to that extent of all men whose language he speaks, and of all into whose language his own can be translated. The poet, in utter solitude remembering his spontaneous thoughts and recording them, is found to have recorded that which men in crowded cities find true for them also. The orator distrusts at first the fitness of his frank confessions, his want of knowledge of the persons he addresses, until he finds that he is the complement of his hearers — that they drink his words because he fulfils for them their own nature; the deeper he dives into his privatest, secretest presentiment, to his wonder he finds this is the most acceptable, most public, and universally true. The people delight in it; the better part of every man feels: This is my music; this is myself.

In self-trust all the virtues are comprehended. Free should the scholar be — free and brave. Free even to the definition of freedom, " without any hindrance that does not arise out of his own constitution." Brave; for fear is a thing which a scholar by his very function puts behind him. Fear always springs from ignorance. It is a shame to him if his tranquillity, amid dangerous times, arise from the presumption that, like children and women, his is a protected class; or if he seek a temporary peace by the diversion of his thoughts from politics or vexed questions, hiding his head like an ostrich in the flowering bushes, peeping into microscopes, and turning rhymes, as a boy whistles to keep his courage up. So is the danger a danger still; so is the fear worse. Manlike let him turn and face it. Let him look into its eye and search its nature, inspect its origin — see the whelping of this lion — which lies no great way back; he will then find in himself a perfect comprehension of its nature and extent; he will have made his hands meet on the other side, and can henceforth defy it and pass on superior. The world is his who can see through its pretension. What deafness, what stone-blind custom, what overgrown error you behold, is there only by sufferance — by your sufferance. See it to be a lie, and you have already dealt it its mortal blow.

Yes, we are the cowed — we the trustless. It is a mischievous notion that we are come late into nature; that the world was finished a long time ago. As the world was plastic and fluid in the hands of God, so it is ever to so much of His attributes as we bring to it. To ignorance and sin, it is flint. They adapt themselves to it as they may; but in proportion as a man has anything in him divine, the firmament flows before him and takes his signet and form. Not he is great who can alter matter, but he who can alter my state of mind. They are the kings of the world who give the color of their present thought to all nature and all art, and persuade men, by the cheerful serenity of their carrying the matter, that this thing which they do is the apple which the ages have desired to pluck, now at last ripe, and inviting nations to the harvest. The great man makes the great thing. Wherever Macdonald sits, there is the head of the table. Linnæus makes botany the most alluring of studies, and wins it from the farmer and the herb-woman; Davy, chemistry; and Cuvier, fossils. The day is always his who works in it with serenity and great aims. The unstable estimates of men crowd to him whose mind is filled with a truth, as the heaped waves of the Atlantic follow the moon.

For this self-trust, the reason is deeper than can be fathomed, darker than can be enlightened. I might not carry with me the feeling of my audience in stating my own belief. But I have already shown the ground of my hope, in adverting to the doctrine that man is one. I believe man has been wronged; he has wronged himself. He has almost lost the light that can lead him back to his prerogatives. Men are become of no account. Men in history, men in the world of today, are bugs, are spawn, and are called " the mass " and " the herd." In a century, in a millennium, one or two men; that is to say, one or two approximations to the right state of every man. All the rest behold in the hero or the poet their own green and crude being, ripened; yes, and are content to be less, so *that* may attain to its full stature. What a testimony, full of grandeur, full of pity, is borne to the demands of his own nature by the poor clansman, the poor partisan, who re-joices in the glory of his chief. The poor and the low find some amends to their immense moral capacity, for their acquiescence in a political and social inferior-ity. They are content to be brushed like flies from the path of a great person, so that justice shall be done by him to that common nature which it is the dearest desire of all to see enlarged and glorified. They sun themselves in the great man's light, and feel it to be their own element. They cast the dignity of man from their downtrod selves upon the shoulders of a hero, and will perish to add one drop of blood to make that great heart beat, those giant sinews combat and con-quer. He lives for us, and we live in him.

Men, such as they are, very naturally seek money or power; and power be-cause it is as good as money — the " spoils," so called, " of office." And why not? For they aspire to the highest, and this, in their sleepwalking, they dream is highest. Wake them and they shall quit the false good and leap to the true, and leave governments to clerks and desks. This revolution is to be wrought by the gradual domestication of the idea of culture. The main enterprise of the world for splendor, for extent, is the upbuilding of a man. Here are the materials strewn along the ground. The private life of one man shall be a more illustrious mon-archy, more formidable to its enemy, more sweet and serene in its influence to its friend, than any kingdom in history. For a man, rightly viewed, comprehend-eth the particular natures of all men. Each philosopher, each bard, each actor has only done for me, as by a delegate, what one day I can do for myself. The books which once we valued more than the apple of the eye, we have quite ex-hausted. What is that but saying that we have come up with the point of view which the universal mind took through the eyes of one scribe; we have been that man, and have passed on. First one, then another, we drain all cisterns; and waxing greater by all these supplies, we crave a better and more abundant food. The man has never lived that can feed us ever. The human mind cannot be enshrined in a person who shall set a barrier on any one side to this unbounded, unboundable empire. It is one central fire, which, flaming now out of the lips of Etna, lightens the capes of Sicily, and now out of the throat of Vesuvius, illuminates the towers and vineyards of Naples. It is one light which beams out of a thousand stars. It is one soul which animates all men.

But I have dwelt perhaps tediously upon this abstraction of the scholar. I ought not to delay longer to add what I have to say of nearer reference to the time and to this country.

Historically, there is thought to be a difference in the ideas which predominate over successive epochs, and there are data for marking the genius of the Classic, of the Romantic, and now of the Reflective or Philosophical age. With the views I have intimated of the oneness or the identity of the mind through all individuals, I do not much dwell on these differences. In fact, I believe each individual passes through all three. The boy is a Greek; the youth, romantic; the adult, reflective. I deny not, however, that a revolution in the leading idea may be distinctly enough traced.

Our age is bewailed as the age of Introversion. Must that needs be evil? We, it seems, are critical; we are embarrassed with second thoughts; we cannot enjoy anything for hankering to know whereof the pleasure consists; we are lined with eyes; we see with our feet; the time is infected with Hamlet's unhappiness — " sicklied o'er with the pale cast of thought." It is so bad then? Sight is the last thing to be pitied. Would we be blind? Do we fear lest we should outsee nature and God, and drink truth dry? I look upon the discontent of the literary class as a mere announcement of the fact that they find themselves not in the state of mind of their fathers, and regret the coming state as untried; as a boy dreads the water before he has learned that he can swim. If there is any period one would desire to be born in, is it not the age of Revolution; when the old and the new stand side by side and admit of being compared; when the energies of all men are searched by fear and by hope; when the historic glories of the old can be compensated by the rich possibilities of the new era? This time, like all times, is a very good one, if we but knew what to do with it.

I read with some joy of the auspicious signs of the coming days, as they glimmer already through poetry and art, through philosophy and science, through church and state.

One of these signs is the fact that the same movement which effected the elevation of what was called the lowest class in the state, assumed in literature a very marked and as benign an aspect. Instead of the sublime and beautiful, the near, the low, the common, was explored and poetized. That which had been negligently trodden underfoot by those who were harnessing and provisioning themselves for long journeys into far countries is suddenly found to be richer than all foreign parts. The literature of the poor, the feelings of the child, the philosophy of the street, the meaning of household life, are the topics of the time. It is a great stride. It is a sign — is it not? — of new vigor when the extremities are made active, when currents of warm life run into the hands and the feet. I ask not for the great, the remote, the romantic; what is doing in Italy or Arabia; what is Greek art or Provençal minstrelsy; I embrace the common; I explore and sit at the feet of the familiar, the low. Give me insight into today, and you may have the antique and future worlds. What would we really know the meaning of? The meal in the firkin, the milk in the pan, the ballad in the street, the news of the boat, the glance of the eye, the form and the gait of the body — show me the ultimate reason of these matters; show me the sublime presence of the highest spiritual cause lurking, as always it does lurk, in these suburbs and extremities of nature; let me see every trifle bristling with the polarity that ranges it instantly on an eternal law; and the shop, the plow, and the ledger referred to the like cause by which light undulates and poets sing — and the world lies no longer a dull miscellany and lumber-room, but has form and order; there is no trifle, there is no puzzle, but one design unites and animates the farthest pinnacle and the lowest trench.

This idea has inspired the genius of Goldsmith, Burns, Cowper, and, in a newer time, of Goethe, Wordsworth, and Carlyle. This idea they have differently followed and with various success. In contrast with their writing, the style of Pope, of Johnson, of Gibbon, looks cold and pedantic. This writing is blood-warm. Man is surprised to find that things near are not less beautiful and wondrous than things remote. The near explains the far. The drop is a small ocean. A man is related to all nature. This perception of the worth of the vulgar is fruitful in discoveries. Goethe, in this very thing the most modern of the moderns, has shown us, as none ever did, the genius of the ancients.

There is one man of genius who has done much for this philosophy of life, whose literary value has never yet been rightly estimated — I mean Emanuel Swedenborg. The most imaginative of men, yet writing with the precision of a mathematician, he endeavored to engraft a purely philosophical ethics on the popular Christianity of his time. Such an attempt, of course, must have difficulty which no genius could surmount. But he saw and showed the connection between nature and the affections of the soul. He pierced the emblematic or spiritual character of the visible, audible, tangible world. Especially did his shade-loving muse hover over and interpret the lower parts of nature; he showed the mysterious bond that allies moral evil to the foul material forms, and has given in epical parables a theory of insanity, of beasts, of unclean and fearful things.

Another sign of our times, also marked by an analogous political movement, is the new importance given to the single person. Everything that tends to insulate the individual — to surround him with barriers of natural respect, so that each man shall feel the world is his, and man shall treat with man as a sovereign state with a sovereign state—tends to true union as well as greatness. " I learned," said the melancholy Pestalozzi, " that no man in God's wide earth is either willing or able to help any other man." Help must come from the bosom alone. The scholar is that man who must take up into himself all the ability of the time, all the contributions of the past, all the hopes of the future. He must be a university of knowledges. If there be one lesson more than another which should pierce his ear, it is: The world is nothing, the man is all; in yourself is the law of all nature, and you know not yet how a globule of sap ascends; in yourself slumbers the whole of reason; it is for you to know all; it is for you to dare all. Mr. President and Gentlemen, this confidence in the unsearched might of man belongs, by all motives, by all prophecy, by all preparation, to the American Scholar. We have listened too long to the courtly muses of Europe. The spirit of the American freeman is already suspected to be timid, imitative, tame. Public and private avarice make the air we breathe thick and fat. The scholar is decent, indolent, complaisant. See already the tragic consequence. The mind of this country, taught to aim at low objects, eats upon itself. There is no work for any but the decorous and the complaisant. Young men of the fairest promise, who begin life upon our shores, inflated by the mountain winds, shined upon by all the stars of God, find the earth below not in unison with these, but are hindered from action by the disgust which the principles on which business is managed inspire, and turn drudges, or die of disgust, some of them suicides. What is the remedy? They did not yet see, and thousands of young men as hopeful now crowding to the barriers for the career do not yet see, that if the single man plant himself indomitably on his instincts, and there abide, the huge world will come round to him. Patience — patience; with the shades of all the good and great for company; and for solace the perspective of your own infinite life; and for work the study and the communication of principles, the making those instincts prevalent, the conversion of the world. Is it not the chief disgrace in the world not to be a unit; not to be reckoned one character; not to yield that peculiar fruit which each man was created to bear, but to be reckoned in the gross, in the hundred, or the thousand, of the party, the section, to which we belong; and our opinion predicted geographically, as the north, or the south? Not so, brothers and friends; please God, ours shall not be so. We will walk on our own feet; we will work with our own hands; we will speak our own minds. The study of letters shall be no longer a name for pity, for doubt, and for sensual indulgence. The dread of man and the love of man shall be a wall of defense and a wreath of joy around all. A nation of men will for the first time exist, because each believes himself inspired by the Divine Soul which also inspires all men.

Granville Hicks

The Poetic "Renaissance"

THE appearance of volume after volume of original and effective poetry in the years from 1912 to the end of the war was the most dramatic evidence of the emergence of new forces in American literature. Poetry had been peculiarly under the influence of the genteel tradition, and the weakening of that tradition was essential to its emancipation. The poets who wished

From *The Great Tradition*, 1933, 1935.

to take advantage of the new freedom were less fortunate than the novelists, for poetry had been weaker than fiction, and there was little in the American past that they could use. Whitman they made the most of, and they rescued Emily Dickinson from something like oblivion; otherwise they could find few predecessors worthy of anything but contempt. The progress of economic forces, however, had narrowed the gulf between Europe and America, and many of the new poets turned to France for inspiration. In particular the imagists — Ezra Pound, Hilda Doolittle, John Gould Fletcher, and Amy Lowell — studied the experiments that had been undertaken on the French Parnassus. Imagism met the needs of the times, in the United States as in France. For several decades French poets — as well as critics and painters — had insisted that, in the eternal flux, only the immediate impression was certain, and this was consoling doctrine to poets who had nothing else to write about. Moreover, concentration of the concrete image permitted poetry to ignore problems that the poets could not solve.

Not because she was the greatest of the American imagists, but because she remained closest to her native land and propagandized most vigorously for her faith, Amy Lowell, frankly relying on the publicity value of her personality, succeeded in establishing herself, at least in the popular mind, as queen of the new-found realms of poetry. In her manners she violated the conventions of the prosperous and conservative society into which she was born, and in her poems she shattered the traditions of generations of respectable versifiers. She was openly and even noisily a poet in revolt. Emphatically an individualist, she insisted on the supreme value of the immediate impression, and for her a poem was either a single image or a succession of images — and often no more than that.

The complete subjectivism Miss Lowell advocated had, without doubt, a tonic effect on her own poetry and that of her contemporaries. It was one way of breaking down the old traditions of the literary poets, with their stock themes and their threadbare phrases, and of restoring the poet to the rank of creator. But her absolute individualism, her utter rootlessness, destroyed the possibility of growth. She wrote in twenty different manners, and yielded to this influence and that. This woman, who was so belligerently determined to be herself and to express only herself, left no body of work that we can point to as purely her own, the complete and distinct record of a unique vision of life. She seems gradually to have realized her fate, for the enthusiasm of her early work gave place to the melancholy of the posthumous volumes.

Vachel Lindsay was wiser than Amy Lowell. Whether he realized or not that the weakness of the respectable poets was the weakness of their class and its shoddy, superficial culture, he turned for his inspiration to the common people. He wrote of their heroes: Lincoln, Booth, Jackson, Bryan, John L. Sullivan, and P. T. Barnum. He used their language and often the simple verse forms their spokesmen employed. He espoused their causes — prohibition, evangelistic Christianity, populism, and socialism. He borrowed many of his devices from their preachers and their actors. And he went out among them, preaching the gospel of beauty. This contact with people uncontaminated by the small talk of display-counter culture gave Lindsay the vigor and the firm, unsullied language of "The Congo," "The Broncho That Would Not Be Broken," "General William Booth Enters Heaven," and "In Praise of Johnny Appleseed." It set his imagination moving along the paths that the makers of myths have trodden.

But merely to accept the common people was not enough, as Lindsay knew; he had to create for them a vision of the future. And in his vision he could find no place for the machines. He hated industrialism and all its fruits:

> Factory windows are always broken.
> Other windows are let alone.
> No one throws through the chapel window
> The bitter, snarling, derisive stone.

He could think of the future only in terms of the farms and small towns:

> O you who lose the art of hope,
> Whose temples seem to shrine a lie,
> Whose sidewalks are but stones of fear,
> Who weep that Liberty must die,
> Turn to the little prairie towns,
> Your higher hope shall yet begin.
> On every side awaits you there
> Some gate where glory enters in.

His heroes were men like Altgeld and Bryan, who fought "against the towns of Tubal Cain . . . against the ways of Tubal Cain, too cunning for the young." He vituperated the whole race of money getters and dreamt of their extirpation:

> You,
> Short-legged, short-armed, short-minded men,
> Your short-sighted days are over,
> Your habits of strutting through clover,
> Your movie-thugs, killing off souls and dreams,
> Your magazines, drying up healing streams,
> Your newspapers, blasting truth and splendor,
> Your shysters, ruining progress and glory,
> Babbitt, your story is passing away.
> The Virginians are coming again.

But Lindsay was obviously no prophet, leading his people to deliverance. He preached the gospel of beauty, which for him was the beauty of rural life. He sang of the days that were past, and refused to face the problems that the common people were being forced to face. Unable to accept the role of leader, he was compelled to accept the role of entertainer. He became more interested in the art of recitation and the playing of games than in writing poetry. His weaknesses became fixed mannerisms, and in a kind of second childhood he spun his poems out of endless repetitions of commonplaces.

Carl Sandburg did not feel Lindsay's fear of the machines. He sang out the praises of Chicago, wicked, dishonest, brutal, but strong, courageous, laughing —

Laughing the stormy, husky, brawling laughter of Youth, half-naked, sweating, proud to be Hog Butcher, Tool Maker, Stacker of Wheat, Player with Railroads and Freight Handler to the Nation.

In his little sketches of lake boats, docks, streetcars, skyscrapers, and parks, of teamsters, ditchdiggers, miners, shopgirls, and soldiers, of Dagoes, Niggers, and Bohunks, the tenderness of a rich imagination touched a world that hitherto had been unknown to poetry. His seeing eye, finding beauty on the drab prairie and in the smoky factory, not merely extended the province of the poet; it began the difficult but essential task of humanizing the waste places of American life:

> A bar of steel — it is only
> Smoke at the heart of it, smoke and the blood of a man.
> A runner of fire ran in it, ran out, ran somewhere else,
> And left — smoke and the blood of a man
> And the finished steel, chilled and blue.
> So fire runs in, runs out, runs somewhere else again,
> And the bar of steel is a gun, a wheel, a·nail, a shovel,
> A rudder under the sea, a steering-gear in the sky;
> And always dark in the heart and through it,
>   Smoke and the blood of a man.
> Pittsburgh, Youngstown, Gary — they make their steel with men.

Like Lindsay he came from the common people — porter, sceneshifter, dishwasher — and he writes about them. His literary methods are not, as Lindsay's were, akin to those of the newspaper versifiers; like Whitman he has written for the common people, not as they are, but as they may become. But he is close to them as they are, and he is never unaware of their lot. If he has seen the beauty of the machines, he has never ignored their cost in human suffering. The strange loveliness of skyscrapers does not blind him to the tragedies of poverty, nor does the tender grace of cornflowers obscure for him the bitter, unrewarded toil of the farmers.

It is these two qualities — the quick perception of unsuspected beauty and a deep sympathy with the oppressed — that make it so easy to forgive the faults in *Chicago Poems, Cornhuskers,* and *Smoke and Steel.* But it is true that Sandburg seems always to be dealing with unrelated entities. In his world everything is disparate; each object, each person, each event stands by itself. Perhaps that is why, in *Good Morning, America* (1928), he seems to have yielded, like so many of his contemporaries, to despair. The title poem of that volume is not merely an attempt to depict contemporary life; it is a series of questions for which Sandburg has no answers. Like the man from Chillicothe, whose self-examination he describes, he is always seeking for explanations that always elude him. It is no wonder that, unable to see how beauty and goodness can triumph over evil and squalor, he finds his kind of poetry rather futile. That may be why he has spent most of his time, of late, writing stories for children, collecting old songs, and writing a romantic biography of a national hero.

Long before Amy Lowell announced her credo, before Lindsay began preaching the gospel of beauty, before Sandburg discovered Chicago, Edwin Arlington Robinson was quietly studying the people of his Maine town. The enthusiasms of the renaissance and the consequent growth of his own popularity did not make an evangelist of him; he calmly continued on his solitary way. Neither Amy Lowell's theories of prosody nor Sandburg's zeal for the precise accents of modern life moved him. He had his own world, undefined in either space or time, made up of the kind of persons that interested him, and to this he devoted himself. Whether this world was called Tilbury Town, London, or Camelot, whether its inhabitants were named Captain Craig, Shakespeare, or Merlin, it was one world, a unit in the poet's imagination; and nothing outside it existed for him.

One should not underestimate the advantages to a poet of having a world of his own. There have been ages in which a poet could feel the underlying unity of all the forms of life he observed, and could move freely and confidently through all the provinces of experience; but in our day the complication of the social structure, the extension of the bounds of knowledge, and the multiplication of human contacts have broken the world into apparently unrelated atoms. If a poet draws indiscriminately on his experience, as Sandburg has done, his work is very likely to be as fragmentary and imperfect as Sandburg's work. If, on the other hand, he concerns himself only with the elements of his experience whose relations he can understand, as Robinson does, he may achieve order and proportion.

Robinson's world is, obviously, an abstraction. He is primarily interested in problems of personality, especially in the problem of success and failure. To see this problem clearly he deliberately isolates his characters from many of the complexities of modern life. In any of his poems the men and women stand, like the Man Against the Sky, at a certain distance from the routine difficulties of daily existence. He permits himself to concentrate on Avon's passion for revenge or Bartholow's jealousy or Cavender's remorse. His world includes many historical personages — Crabbe, Shakespeare, Rembrandt, Paul — and it extends into the realm of mythology, to embrace Merlin, Lancelot, and Tristram. Robinson's method of treating these men from the past is no different from his method of treating his contemporaries: Merlin and Captain Craig are the same sort of bewildered sages, Lancelot and Penn-Raven the same sort of disloyal lovers, Rembrandt and Fernando Nash the same sort of inspired artists. Only such kinds of experience as are apparently unaffected by changes in politics and economics, developments in science and technology, and fashions in art and morality, exist for his poetry.

Robinson's admirers defend this method of abstraction by saying that he concerns himself with the eternal problems. But the only problems we really know are those that are posed by our own age. There are no eternal problems; each age has its own dilemmas, and, though some of these recur, they take their character from a particular situation. Robinson's fine dignity, the nobility of much of his blank verse, the subtlety of such poems as " A Poor Relation " and " Eros Turannos," the wisdom of some passages in *Captain Craig,* the interpretation of history in " Ben Jonson Entertains a Man from Stratford " and " Rembrandt to Rembrandt," and the lyric beauty of the beginning of *Tristram* have enriched American literature. At times, in other words, he speaks directly to us, and we listen. But we cannot forget the interminable dialogues in *Merlin* and *Lancelot,* the triviality of *Roman Bartholow* and *The Glory of the Nightingales,* the tenuous arguments in *Tristram,* and the utter emptiness of at least half the poems in *Nicodemus.* Is it possible for the poet to touch the enduring strands of humanity's thought and emotion and endeavor unless he finds them, as in daily experience we ourselves do, inextricably part of the warp and woof of man's concrete struggle with a particular environment in a particular age? Whence came Robinson's skepticism if not from the intellectual currents of his day? Could he have been so interested in failure if he had not seen real defeats and been conscious of specific frustrations? By taking attitudes that are the product of a particular situation and projecting them into a world of his own design, he has gained poise of a sort that was impossible for Sandburg and Lindsay: his poems are precisely planned and firmly molded. But much of his poetry is cold and remote, and some of it has no significance at all for Robinson's America.

Robert Frost also has a world of his own, and his great advantage over Robinson lies in the fact that his world is, to some extent, identified with a particular area as it has existed at a particular time. Though his world is as compact and as nearly self-sufficient as the less tangible realm over which Robinson rules, anyone who has traveled north of Boston can recognize the language he speaks, the scenery he describes, and the people he presents. Yet it cannot be denied that Frost has achieved unity by a definite process of exclusion. One not only realizes that life in New Hampshire is not altogether representative of life in the United States as a whole; one has to admit that Frost disregards many elements in New Hampshire life, and especially the elements that link that state with the rest of the country. For example, northern New England has been greatly affected by the growth of industrialism, and yet one would never suspect this from Frost's poetry. Can one believe that it is by accident that he has never written of the factory towns, now so abjectly in decay, or of the exodus to the cities and its failure, now so apparent, to bring deliverance? Has he never heard of the railroads and their influence on the state's politics, touching the smallest hamlet? Do not automobiles and radios exist in New Hampshire? No, Frost is too shrewd not to be well aware that he is excluding from his poems whatever might destroy their unity. He knows the full value of his self-imposed limitations, and he is even willing to boast of his good fortune in the parable of the star in the stone boat:

Such as it is, it promises the prize
Of the one world complete in any size
That I am like to compass, fool or wise.

Much of Frost's experience is close to ours, and we can share his apprecia-
tions and his insights. His strong narratives, his clear and unpretentious lyrics,
and his thoughtful, sensible allegories are more satisfying than most poetry of
our day. But, to the extent that his imagination concerns itself only with what
is personally congenial and poetically available, he too leaves us discontented.
For all his common sense and his originality, he has chosen to identify himself
with a moribund tradition. Many poets, these hundred and fifty years, have
written of mountains, fields, and brooks, and of farmers at their humble tasks;
these things have become part of our imaginative inheritance, and one must
be insensitive indeed not to be conscious of the beauty in them. But there are
other objects now more frequently before our eyes — factories, skyscrapers, machines. We see mechanics, shopgirls, truck drivers, more often than we do
farmers, and we see the farmer not as a romantic figure but as the victim of
cruel economic forces. There is new territory that we beg the poet to conquer
for us. Perhaps today no poet is capable of that conquest, but, if the task is ever
to be accomplished, someone with the talent of a Robert Frost must make a
beginning.

Henry Seidel Canby

Fiction Tells All

AUTOBIOGRAPHY — the desire to tell the world all about it — lifts its
voice in a wail or a shout once every so often, and usually when the
shoe of experience pinches the light foot of the imagination. The Ro-
mans had a spell of near-autobiography when the disintegration of the morale
of the empire began. A great literature of autobiography accompanied and
followed the political and religious tensions of the English seventeenth century. *Pilgrim's Progress* is in its way as autobiographical as the diary of Pepys.
The decline of the Italian Renaissance had its Benvenuto Cellini. The stretched
and throbbing egoes of the romantic movement gave birth to " Childe Harold "
and *Wilhelm Meister*. And the tense transcendentalism of New England led
on to the autobiographical fiction of Melville's *Moby Dick,* the autobiographical poetry of Whitman's " Song of Myself," and four million words in the
Journal of Henry Thoreau.
But our nineteen-twenties and nineteen-thirties were to suffer from a new
and virulent form of this impulse to tell it all, this complaint which is some-

From *Seven Years' Harvest,* 1936.

times a disease. And until one studies the particular kind of egoism that has been plaguing our contemporaries it is quite impossible to understand why we have been showered with books which our grandfathers would have burned for their indecency, which the pastors of the early nineteenth century would have regarded as written by Satan himself, and which many a wise physician even then might have recognized as the truth at last about many aspects of the sick mind for which not even names had been invented.

Very little of this characteristically modern literature is frankly autobiographical. Some of it is biographical. A little is poetry and drama. It is in fiction that its throbbing waves find their best mouthpiece. Its motive is not that sense of *sin* which has produced so many great autobiographies. Nor is it the *joy* which, as spiritual exaltation, has been the inspiration of the famous autobiographical books of the Catholic mystics. It is not *faith,* which has written great poetry, autobiographical in nature, and some of our noblest prose. This modern literature, and especially the fiction, has been more characteristically (let us say, in Joyce, Hemingway, Proust) confession for the sake of confession — a nudism of the ego, exactly parallel to certain kinds of religious confession, except that it is inspired by the natural, not the supernatural, and deals not with God in the mind but with the mind itself.

It is easy to see now that these " frank," revealing books, which try so hard to tell all that " genteel " literature had concealed, were inevitable, although the intensity of the more pathological specimens evidently has been due to special circumstances deriving from the distress and warpings of the war and the depression. The humanism of the Renaissance was sure before it ran its course to encounter some changed conception of the value of the individual which would bring an equivalent change in its emphasis upon the purely human; and this happened, of course, when the rise of the middle class and later of the masses into an importance never before known led to that literary realism which is probably the outstanding characteristic of the literature of the last century. But the great change came with the growth of the science of physiology and the pseudo, or part, science of psychology. When the students of abnormal psychology had done their work, and especially after Freud had made his generalizations, it required no genius of criticism to prophesy that fiction would follow the trail. For if the scientist could learn much about normal man from studying abnormality, it was clear that the literary realist would soon begin to put into his imaginative pictures of everyday humanity dark tones and subtle colors drawn from the phantasies of fear or desire which all but the most stolid among us carry somewhere near the heart.

But artists are not scientists. They are sensitive souls who record and express, who use theories, and indeed facts, only when these help them to make sense of what they see and feel. And here was humanity set before them in a new aspect by psychologists who professed to give new explanations of that human tendency to make a mess of things which is what plots are made of and at the same time invented a new language with such admirable terms in it as " complex " and " introvert " and " phantasy," so that any hack could write his old stories over again using entirely new words. Here also were interesting and often convincing explanations of the mental wounds which the sensitive writer is always the first to feel in himself and to see in others. Naturally these writers told the world, rushing into one form or another of autobiography.

I am not writing here a history of recent literature and, therefore, I need only say that the first stirrings of all this began long before the war. But surely it was the intensities of war experience that brought on the flood. One remembers the painful vividness of Barbusse's *Le Feu,* written early in the great conflict, which seemed to be the cry of man saying " such things as these never happened to me before "; or Wells's *Mr. Britling Sees It Through,* which was the detailed account of one man trying to make up his mind; or the passionate autobiography of the first poets of the war, lovers of English soil, and the equally autobiographical disillusion of those that followed.

The real significance, however, is revealed later, and especially in that lengthy story of *un homme moyen sensuel,* Joyce's *Ulysses,* and his Mr. Bloom whose reflections take place in lavatories and whose most gross or trivial phantasies are the very thread of the plot, or in the painfully minute and subtle analyses of sophisticated sensation that emanated like radio waves from the darkened room of that sensitive ego, Proust.

And thus the stage was set for the redressing of a great injustice in literature — and for an orgy which celebrated one of the greatest defeats in all time of the Greek principle of measure, balance, not anything too much. The age of reticence ended with a bang.

The plain man — not the primitive peasant, not the poor, not the oppressed; but the very ordinary individual who best represents the unheroic, undistinguished, largely incapable millions who make up most of the modern world — never had a show in literature until the new realism sought him out. Perhaps he never had a show then until minds as unpoetic, as unheroic, as unesthetic as his own made him their task and wrote of him, as Theodore Dreiser did in *The American Tragedy,* in a style as undistinguished as the style of the newspapers he read. That job was done, and it seemed that the novelty of being ordinary would soon wear off and that the novelists would seek other material; but now a new vista opened. The class consciousness of Marxism began to give a significance to the masses which they never had before, and if only an undistinguished individual happened to be a " worker," he became valuable for fiction. Unfortunately the so-called proletarian novelists, like Halper, Greenwood, Cantwell, have been photographers, not painters, and their books are with few exceptions deadly dull, so that even the " workers " will not read them. Their authors are all bourgeois on slumming expeditions, and that probably explains why even the best of their stories lack the conviction of the great novels of the middle class. The writers have told the world what they saw, not what they were. We shall have to wait for some time before this attempt to right a literary wrong and put the class struggle into fiction becomes more than a worthy experiment.

A far less theoretical and far more intimate problem was waiting just round the corner of the twentieth century, and this is the injustice to which I referred above. The sick mind, sick from war, sick from the speeds of industrialism, sick from too much knowledge and too fevered thinking, sick from those complicated ills which psychology had been studying, never had been given its day in literature. Oh yes, there were Hamlets, and Iphigenias, and Wilhelm Meisters, and Frankensteins; these, however, were all heroes and their phantasies were heroic phantasies. But psychology had been showing that the abnormal was normal in every man if you only looked deep enough. The sick mind was common enough in our twenties and thirties. Its day had come.

II

An eminent psychiatrist, Dr. Laurence Kubie, in the *Saturday Review of Literature,* made an elaborate psychoanalysis of a book by one of these writers, Faulkner, and of another book by Erskine Caldwell, who belongs in the same gallery. His findings were unusually specific and intelligible for psychology. He discovered definite phantasies such as are familiar to all psychologists with clinical experience, and showed that upon these phantasies the stories were erected, and that from them they drew their intensity and their symbolism. The horror behind Faulkner's *Sanctuary* was the universal fear of impotence. The phantasy behind Caldwell's book was (to oversimplify) the child's craving for the protection of the womb.

I need not go into these technical aspects of this literature of pathology, for my purpose here differs from that of Dr. Kubie, who made no attempt to evaluate either its artistic worth or the temporal causes. I am interested in the reason why this outbreak of a literature of the underworld of the mind should come now, and what it portends for ourselves and for our reading.

Here is Hemingway with his eruptive, monosyllabic style, from which all the fluent rhythms of the old romanticists have been carefully eliminated. He tells a vivid and painful story, dragged from him it seems by reluctant need. His characters are always afraid — afraid often, as has been suggested, of being afraid. They are usually clearly pathological types, and felt to be so, like his killers, or men and women once normal but warped until their egoes can no longer stand the strain of experience — women like Brett in *The Sun Also Rises,* men such as the hero of *A Farewell to Arms* whose mind is a wound. And Hemingway writes like a man seeking release, the release of confession. I do not mean to imply that his books are autobiography in a literal sense, although it is obvious that the autobiographical element is strong. But news of what war does to the soul, or fear of one's father, or of impotence, or of the lust to kill, or of great crowd masses broken, flying, and regardless — such news of the ego they all contain. They will out, these secrets the surface normality of society has so well concealed, and they come with a lurid tensity which is the more vivid because the writing seems to be so restrained.

Little need be added for William Faulkner except to point out again the confessional nature in his stories. This man's tongue has been unleashed to tell of simple, dull people who have the horrors or make them. His Mississippi is a madhouse for the mildly insane, who act so much like poor whites limited merely by education and intelligence that it is only slowly that one realizes why their stories are so poignant. Poverty, drink, frustration have made the phantasies that plague us all dominate them. Faulkner, like many a super-sensitive person, has seen the obsessions of cruelty, fear, and blind hate just under the surface of plain men and women, and has not waited to balance them with their opposites, but rushed into the news with his experience, pre-cisely as the tabloid reporter rushes into the news the exploits of a fiend in a sober community. The pained ego must cleanse its bosom of this perilous stuff, and does not take much care to see where and how the mess splashes.

As for Thomas Wolfe, here is autobiographical realism at its peak. Mil-lions of words recording every act, every thought, every opinion in the youth of a character who wears the thinnest of disguises and is clearly most of the time the author himself. Pen portraits of contemporaries, attacks on fads and cults, close analyses of frustrated types, long descriptions of eccentrics, passionate appeals to an America that keeps rushing on and on without regard for what makes healthy minds and good living — a continuous performance of narrative, description, oratory, satire, poetry, gusto, and complaint, circling endlessly like a drunken genius shouting and reciting as he whirls about on a merry-go-round.

I'll tell the world what it does to a youth, says Wolfe. I'll tell the world what fear can do to man, says Faulkner. I'll tell the world what fear and dis-illusion can do to the mind, says Hemingway. And they tell it, brilliantly or confusedly, profusely or in terse explosions, crassly or with brutal honesty — and especially those cranks and quiddities of the sick mind which psychology plus the responsibilities of realism have made to seem important. Hamlet wanted to tell the world, but Horatio reminded him that it was not so im-portant to describe what way madness lay as to show that one could rise above it. There is less literature but more news in the modern method.

A delusive air of youth blows through all these books. They are usually, not always, about the young, or rather the relatively young, and especially those whose true youth was nipped in the war, and who (as in Hemingway's stories) carry on the abandon, the gaiety, the pursuit of risk, chance, and variety char-acteristic of youth in a mood of strain and disillusion. But it is a delusive air. These are old souls writing, even though they are Americans, and it does not seem too fanciful to say that in these pseudo-autobiographies one feels the sensitive mind of yesterday's culture trying to adjust itself to a mechanical mass civilization. Note the man-mass that so oppresses Wolfe in Boston and New York, and the facial strain of a nervous life that he speaks of again and again. Remember how Hemingway's sad revelers kept drinking so that they should think little and feel less; how they madly pursued fatigue as if it were a new law of life. And these old tired souls in youthful bodies run about hold-ing up their arms and telling their stories, or in fierce restraint they create a warped society of sufferers like themselves, and with cold impartiality tell all that happens in phantasy-ridden minds. Hence the note of defeatism, of cruelty, of pity veiled in scorn, which as much as the subtlety, sincerity, and power of this fiction sharply differentiates it from the success stories of the magazines, which are pathological in another sense, since they represent wish phantasies.

III

Hence of course the emphasis upon sex which has spread far beyond the limits of these realistic autobiographies of the ego. It was D. H. Lawrence who, long before the war, showed that the sexual faculties suffered more than any other from both the mechanization and the intellectualizing of modern society. The baleful effect of the overworked intellect upon instincts native and vital to man was the hidden villain in all his important stories. But it was not thinking that he attacked. He himself loved to argue and to speculate like other would-be philosophers. What excited his wrath were the ghastly results when too much logic or too cold a reason was applied to the business of living. Men had come to believe that they could think themselves out of all their difficulties, but mere thinking was no good in love, and without love what was man or woman either? He demanded a release of the primitive passions whose home was in the instincts of sex.

Lawrence was a prophet. When once *Lady Chatterley's Lover* had broken the seals of reticence, sex flowed out of the yeasty egoes of the age. Two new fictitious characters attained a bad eminence: the frigid woman and the impotent man — the woman frigid by convention and habit more often than by nature, the man relatively impotent for anything except the production of children, because his mind was set upon keeping busy or getting rich. A curious essay could be written comparing these villains of the novel of the first third of the twentieth century with the chaste heroines and self-restraining heroes of the middle third of the nineteenth.

But it would be a sad error to suppose that the extraordinary wave of sex literature which has just washed over us, and is now rapidly subsiding into the scum of the film magazines, was due entirely to such a philosophy of back-to-nature as Lawrence preached. Nine tenths of that sex writing which has been ranging all the way from notable frankness to frank obscenity was release-and-protest literature. You can keep the ordinary talk and interests of ordinary men and women, and literature in separate compartments for just about so long; then back they swing together, both fouling and enriching each other. The talk in Victorian smoking rooms was no more prudish than in clubs and cafés today, and probably more obscene. The facts of life were certainly not omitted from Victorian women's conversations among themselves. The novels of the day omitted both. A reaction was overdue; and if it was the war that set it off in English, and Lawrence who philosophized it, under no circumstances could it have been delayed much longer. Shaw knew this in the early nineteen-hundreds, and Kipling must have guessed it in the nineties.

But it takes more than a decade to get the snicker out of sex, nor is it possible to give authors freedom to write of what they like, and word it honestly, without ungagging many a foul mouth.

Now of all remembered autobiography sex experience is likely to be the most poignant. Hence when the disturbed egoes of the twenties began to pour forth the confessions of their youth, and to write about their own experiences in the guise of fiction, sex memories boiled up in them. Here was something that could not be told in English before in our time. Here were incidents, trivial in themselves, that because the elders had not used their like, were still fresh, unminted, salable. It was often a dishwater soup that resulted, but served as consommé piquant it got a cheap reputation for the writer, and gave the better ones a much needed release. Freud has made us all sex conscious, but it took no Freud, once the inquiring mind was set in that direction, to see how sex suppression or sex release permeated at least two thirds of the events suitable for drama or fiction. Indeed, it would have been far better for literature if Freud had not published his researches, for then we should have seen the writers finding their own way into the just opened frontier of sex and making their own language to use in the new freedom of expression, instead of being led by a formula into what often proved to be both bad science and bad art. Freud was worth thousands of dollars in royalties to the novelists of the twenties, especially the weak ones, but he double-crossed them. The plots they borrowed from him already refuse to stand up alone.

And to those voluble souls whose idea of a novel was a complete confession, this breakdown of sex inhibition was a godsend. Without it most of them would never have been able to make their stories interesting enough to be printed. As for those fiercely bitter writers of the mental underworld, who were bound that the warped minds and the maimed minds should get their place in literature, and who, refusing to stop there, went on to the perverted, the subnormal, the hag-ridden by phantasies, the obsessed by fright — to such writers the ban on sex if it had lasted would have been an insuperable obstacle. They could not have written at all.

IV

What then are we to say of this literature which I have called autobiographical to indicate its intensely egoistic character? It might be called nervous, though the term does not go deep. It might be called morbid, but that word is too narrow. It certainly is not abnormal, for these immense desires for confession, like the egoisms, the perversions, the fears that get expressed, are typical, even though exaggerated, of humanity as psychology knows it and sociology describes it. Jung would call it an introverted literature. I prefer to say that human nature in one of its more rapid moments of adaptation to environment and circumstance (how rapid only the historians who later describe the onset of the age of machines will know) is relieving its hurt ego by voluble and intimate expression. The brakes squeal as the automobile rounds the corner.

Certainly it is an unbalanced literature, unbalanced in both form and content. Its masterpiece in English, Joyce's *Ulysses,* would seem, by every literary test that can be applied to it, to have little chance of survival — except in an excerpt or two and in paragraphs of literary history. It is incredible that the next century will take the pains to read *Ulysses* — quite as incredible as that we should read all of *Euphues* or *The Faerie Queene* or *Clarissa Harlowe* today.

But should it not be said that our balanced literature (especially in fiction), our literature where sanity, proportion, measure, prevail, is too superficial for either great comedy or great tragedy? The *Forsyte Saga* of John Galsworthy represents about the best we could do in English in our time in this way. That is perhaps the only work of this kind in which the creative imagination has portrayed human nature not satirically or symbolically, but straight, in an edifice of real magnitude in this generation. But the *Forsyte Saga* became pitifully weak as it approached these modern years in which not manners but the causes of manners have seemed to be of the greater importance. Why, any tuppenny psychological or proletarian novelist will offer to rewrite you the last volumes of Galsworthy, showing you what all the muddle is about over which the characters skate so sketchily! And he could explain better than Galsworthy, even though his book would prove to be unreadable.

Beneath that sanity which was the subject of the Victorians lies unbalance, and it has been the particular good luck and misfortune of the writers of the last decades to bring this to our attention. It has been their good fortune because, the bars being down for the moment, not only could they write of anything but they were more praised, by the intellectuals at least, than those who wrote of success. And note that by success I do not mean success in terms of the *American Magazine* or the *Saturday Evening Post,* but success as Shakespeare and Sophocles understood it: the persistence of man's potential nobility in the teeth of circumstance and up to tragedy and beyond it. This kind of success has not been popular in our defeatist decade, which if it is to be optimistic at all prefers a cheaper variety. There is a world of difference between the sensualist Antony putting on his antique Roman virtues in disaster and Mr. Salesman marrying his girl with a million in spite of his B.O. and her halitosis. After a little reading of advertisements and the stories written to accompany them, one's sympathies go out to Messrs. Faulkner, Hemingway, *et al.,* who maintain that in spite of cosmetics all is not right with the world.

But it is also a misfortune for these novelists, and with them I include semidetached poets like T. S. Eliot and Robinson Jeffers, that the unhappy struggle between human nature and the demands of a mechanized world for rapid adaptation gives them poorish material to work with. Mr. Eliot was far stronger when he wrote destructively of the Waste-Land than when in his essays he endeavors to turn parched intellectuals into Tory humanists. Mr. Jeffers's imagination riots in an incredible California, whose only antidote seems to be blood. And the phantasies which oppress Mr. Hemingway and cause him to create with magnificent technique killers who, like the centaurs, are only half human, set up repulsions among readers who are blessed with the healthy instinct to make the best even of bad men in bad times. It has been good for us to realize imaginatively what sicknesses beset the human spirit; but sick literature, even when its disease is merely a tendency to tell everything to anybody, is a greater contribution to news than to art — or, if the term " art " seems precious in this context, a better reflection of the unhappier actualities of some human nature than of its potentialities as a whole. I had rather believe with the Quakers that all humanity is potentially good than run with these fellows who are obsessed with its imperfections. One conclusion is quite as scientific as the other.

Therefore, the frequent repulsion which all types of literature that can be called modernistic set up in the populace has some justification. Often it is merely intellectual laziness which makes them refuse to read " unpleasant " books. They do not want to know what lies beneath the surface, and they will not listen to those who write of it unless they are drawn in by inordinate cleverness, crass sensationalism, or a superb technique of narrative. Yet often they have strong right on their side. They are seeking — if the reading instinct of the public can be called by so strong a term — for synthesis, for a building up into revealing character of the life which they vaguely feel and know; and they get autobiography, the analysis of an individual complaining of his defeats. And so, after a brief excursion into *A Farewell to Arms* or *Of Time and the River,* back they flock to Southern columns draped with clematis or the adventures of an icebox salesman in the Middle West.

It is highly improbable that this literature of autobiography will ever take its place beside the outstanding books of the past that have been not only an influence upon posterity but masterpieces in themselves. The warped mind, the complaining body, the defeated, the desperate, the neurotic, are obligatory subjects for literature; but the literature made of them is itself inhibited. It tends to be analytic rather than synthetic; it clogs instead of purging the imagination. No Plato would choose its authors for his ideal state. Indeed, it may have been the tendency of sensitive writers to tell the world about its neurotics which led him to exclude poets from his republic.

> Of the maimed, of the halt and the blind in the rain and the cold —
> Of these shall my songs be fashioned, my tales be told,

said that poet of pity, Masefield. But the mentally maimed and the spiritually halt, in which our modern autobiographers specialize, leave one a little cold at the end — sorry, disturbed, disillusioned, and never with that sense of wings spreading in the imagination which is the effect of great art. And perhaps that is why the moderns are so voluble about themselves and their friends. If they cannot give us what we want, at least they will tell us what we ought to know. To bring Stevenson up to date —

> The world is so full of a number of things,
> I am sure we should all be as nervous as kings.

Great literature is not nervous.

H. L. Mencken

The American Language

THE first Englishman to notice an Americanism sneered at it aloofly, thus setting a fashion that many of his countrymen have been following ever since. He was one Francis Moore, a ruffian who came out to Georgia with Oglethorpe in 1735, and the word that upset him was *bluff,* in the sense of " a cliff or headland with a broad precipitous face." He did not deign to argue against it; he simply dismissed it as " barbarous," apparently assuming that all Englishmen of decent instincts would agree with him. For nearly a century they seem to have done so, and *bluff* lingered sadly below the salt. When it was printed at all in Great Britain it was set off by sanitary quotation marks, or accompanied by other hints of deprecation, as *rubberneck, hot spot,* and *nerts* are accompanied today. But then, in 1830, the eminent Sir Charles Lyell used it shamelessly in the first volume of his monumental *Principles of Geology,* and from that day to this it has been a perfectly respectable if somewhat unfamiliar word in England, with a place in every dictionary.

Its history is the history of almost countless other Americanisms. They have been edging their way into English since early colonial times, and, for more than a century past, in constantly increasing volume; but I can't recall one that didn't have to run a gantlet of opposition in the motherland, at times verging upon the frantic. After the Revolution, that opposition took on the proportions of a holy war. Never an American book came out that the English reviewers did not belabor its vocabulary violently. The brunt of the attack, of course, had to be borne by the poetasters of the era — for example, Joel Barlow, whose *Columbiad* (1807) loosed a really terrifying geyser of abuse. But even the most serious writers got their share — among them, Jefferson, John Marshall, Noah Webster, and John Quincy Adams. Jefferson's crime was that he had invented the verb *to belittle*. It was, one may argue plausibly, a very logical, useful, and perhaps even nifty word, and seventy-five years later the prissy Anthony Trollope was employing it without apology. But when Jefferson ventured to use it in his *Notes on Virginia* (1787) the *London Review* tossed and raged in a manner befitting the discovery of a brace of dueling pistols beneath the cope of the Archbishop of Canterbury; and for several years following, its dudgeon was supported virtuously by most of the other reviews. " What an expression! " roared the *London*. " It may be an elegant one in Virginia, but for our part, all we can do is to *guess* at its meaning. For shame, Mr. Jefferson! Freely, good sir, will we forgive all your attacks, impotent as they are illiberal, upon our national character; but for the future spare — O spare, we beseech you, our mother tongue! "

The underscoring of *guess* was a fling in passing at another foul Americanism. It was the belief of most Englishmen then, as it is today, that the use of the verb in the sense of *to suppose* or *assume* originated in this country. It is actually to be found, in that meaning precisely, in *Measure for Measure* and *Henry VI;* nay, in Chaucer, Wycliffe, and Gower. But such historical considerations have never daunted the more ardent preservers of the King's English. When a word acquires an American flavor it becomes anathema to them, even though it may go back to Boadicea. *To advocate* offers an instructive example. It appeared in English in the dark backward and abysm of time, but during the eighteenth century it seems to have dropped out of general use, though Burke used it. Towards the end of the century it came into vogue in this country, and soon it made its way back to the land of its birth. It was received with all the honors proper to an invasion of Asiatic cholera. The reviews denounced it as loutish, " Gothic," and against God, and lumped it with *to compromit* and *to happify* as proof that civilization was impossible in America, and would be so forevermore. Even Benjamin Franklin, returning from England in 1789, was alarmed into begging Noah Webster to " reprobate " it, along with *to notice, to progress,* and *to oppose.* There is no record of Noah's reply, but it is most unlikely that he did any reprobating, for when he began to make dictionaries he included all four verbs, and they have been listed in every considerable dictionary published since, whether in this country or in England.

The leader of the heroic struggle to keep Americanisms out of Britain, in its early stages, was the celebrated William Gifford, editor of the *Quarterly Review.* Gifford was a killer in general practice, and his savage assaults on Wordsworth, Shelley, and Keats are still unpleasantly remembered. He was the first magazine editor in history to make the trade pay, and when he died in 1828 he left £25,000 and was buried in Westminster Abbey. One of his major specialties was the villainousness of everything American, from politics to table manners and from theology to speechways. Among the allegations that he either made himself or permitted his contributors to make were these: (*a*) that the Americans employed naked colored women to wait upon them at table, (*b*) that they kidnapped Scotsmen, Irishmen, Hollanders, and Welshmen and sold them into slavery, and (*c*) that they were planning to repudiate the English language altogether, and adopt Hebrew in its place. This last charge, as it flew from tongue to tongue, acquired variorum readings. One of them made the new American language an Indian dialect, another made it Greek, and a third was to the effect that the people of Britain would be forced to acquire Greek, thus leaving English to the wicked will of the barbaric Yankees. It all sounds idiotic today, but in 1814 it was taken quite seriously by many Englishmen. Gifford was a tyrannical editor and so vastly enjoyed slashing his contributors' copy that Southey once denounced him as " a butcherly review-gelder." But anything that was against the damyankee passed his eye unscathed, and he piled up accusations in a manner so shameless that the *North American Review* was moved to protest that if the tirade went on it would " turn into bitterness the last drops of good will towards England that exist in the United States."

In the early twenties of that century there was some amelioration, and when

Gifford retired from the *Quarterly* in 1824, voices that were almost conciliatory began to be heard. They heaped praises on Niagara Falls, found something to commend in Cooper's *Spy,* and even had kind words for the speed and luxuriousness of American canalboats. But my most diligent researches have failed to unearth anything complimentary to the American language. It continued to be treated as a grotesque and immoral gibberish, full of uncouth terms and at war with all the canons of English. Every British traveler who came to these shores between the War of 1812 and the Civil War had something to say about the neologisms his ears and eyes encountered on his tour, and nearly all were constrained to deplore them. Captain Basil Hall, who was here in 1827 and 1828, went about in a palpitating daze, confounded and outraged by the signs on American places of business. *Clothing Store* he interpreted after long thought, and *Flour and Feed Store* after prayer and soul-searching, but what on earth was a *Leather and Finding Store?* Captain Thomas Hamilton, who followed five years later, found it impossible to penetrate to "the precise import" of *Dry-Goods Store,* and when he encountered an establishment offering *Hollow Ware, Spiders, and Fire-Dogs* he gave up in despair.

Hall was not one to take it lying down. He decided to call upon Noah Webster, whose American Dictionary of the English Language had just come out, to find out what the Yankees meant by using the mother tongue so cruelly. Webster shocked him by arguing stoutly that "his countrymen had not only a right to adopt new words, but were obliged to modify the language to suit the novelty of the circumstances, geographical and political, in which they were placed." The great lexicographer "who taught millions to spell but not one to sin" went on to observe judicially that it was "quite impossible to stop the progress of language — it is like the course of the Mississippi, the motion of which, at times, is scarcely perceptible; yet even then it possesses a momentum quite irresistible. Words and expressions will be forced into use in spite of all the exertions of all the writers in the world."

"But surely," persisted Hall, "such innovations are to be deprecated?"

"I don't think that," replied old Noah. "If a word becomes universally current in America, where English is spoken, why should it not take its station in the language?"

"Because," declared Hall with magnificent pertinacity, "there are words enough already."

This heroic dogma is still heard in England, where even native novelties are commonly opposed violently, and not infrequently strangled at birth. There seems to be, in the modern Englishman, very little of that ecstasy in wordmaking which so prodigiously engrossed his Elizabethan forebears. Shakespeare alone probably put more new words into circulation than all the English writers since Carlyle, and they were much better ones. The ideal over there today is not picturesque and exhilarating utterance, but correct and reassuring utterance, and one of its inevitable fruits is that bowwow jargon which Sir Arthur Quiller-Couch describes in *On the Art of Writing* as "the medium through which boards of government, county councils, syndicates, committees, commercial firms, express the processes as well as the conclusions of their thought, and so voice the reason of their being." It is, at its worst, at least in accord with what are taken to be the principles of English grammar, and at its best it shows excellent manners and even a kind of mellifluous elegance; indeed, the English, taking one with another, may be said to write much better than we do — at all events by the standards of the schoolmaster. But what they write is seldom animated by anything properly describable as bounce. It lacks novelty, variety, audacity. There is little juice in it. The reader confronted by it is treated politely and lulled pleasantly, but he seldom enjoys the enchantment of surprise. That diligent search for new and racy locutions which occupied so much of the workday of Walt Whitman and William Dean Howells alike, and is practiced so assiduously by scores of saucy Andersons and Hemingways, Sandburgs and Saroyans today, is carried on across the ocean by only a few extravagant eccentrics, virtually all of whom — for example, James Joyce and Ezra Pound — are non- and even anti-Englishmen. The hundred-per-cent English writers, save when they stoop to conscious wickedness, seldom depart very far from the jargon of Quiller-Couch. It is by no means a monopoly of the classes he named, nor is it reserved for solemn occasions. I find it also in my favorite English weekly, the *News of the World,* which is devoted principally to sports, the theaters, and the more scabrous varieties of crime, and is probably a far better mirror of England than the *Times.* When the *News of the World* reports the downfall of a rural dean or a raid on a Mayfair night club, the thing is done in a style so tight and brittle that nothing to match it is discoverable in this country, at least outside the pages of the *Homiletic Review.* " When we want to freshen our speech," Mrs. Virginia Woolf was lately saying, " we borrow from American — *poppycock, rambunctious, flip-flop, booster, good mixer.* All the expressive, ugly, vigorous slang which creeps into use among us, first in talk, later in writing, comes from across the Atlantic."

But whether slang or something better, it always encounters opposition — sometimes merely sullen, but at other times extremely violent. At more or less regular intervals, war upon the invasion is declared formally, and there ensues a long uproar, with the papers full of choleric letters to the editor. One such sharpening of activity was loosed early in 1933, when the chief constable of Wallasey, a suburb of Liverpool, reported in alarm that his policemen were being called *cops* by the tougher youngsters of the place, and otherwise insulted with blasphemies picked up from American movies. " *Oh-yeahs,"* he said, " are frequent in answer to charges, and we are promised *shoots-up in the burg* [*sic*] and threatened to be *bumped-off."* Half the amateur publicists who took a hand in the discussion which followed, advocated using the cat on the offenders, and the other half demanded that American movies be barred from England as intolerable public menaces, like cattle infected with foot-and-mouth disease. As usual, the debate ended in philological futilities. Was *oh yeah* actually English, even bad English, insane English? Or was it only an American borrowing from one of the dialects of the savage Red Indians, or maybe from Polish, Pennsylvania Dutch, Gullah, Yiddish, or some other such godless and anti-British lingo? No matter! *Oh yeah* continues to flourish from the Lizard to Unst, and with it *cop* flourishes too. The latter, in fact, has swept upward from the level of bad boys baiting constables to that of bishops following their transcendental occasions. Even before the chief constable of Wallasey sounded his cry of "Wolf!" a right reverend father in God had been charged before the Farnham (Surrey) magistrates with applying *speed-cop* on a public road to a member of the *mobile police.* Overhauled in his car, so the testimony went, he had demanded, "Are you a *speed-cop?*" His Lordship denied with some heat that he had used the term, or anything else so unseemly, but the magistrates apparently concluded that he must have let it slip, for they took a serious view of his very modest adventure in speeding, fined him £10, and suspended his driving license for three months. I give his name and dignities as a warning to lesser evildoers. He was the Right Reverend Cyril Henry Gelding-Bird, D.D. (Oxon.), Assistant Bishop of Guildford and Archdeacon of Dorking, and a man previously unknown to the police.

Whenever an Americanism comes publicly into question in England, there are efforts to track down its etymology, and sometimes the theories offered are extremely bizarre. In January, 1935, for example, the London *Morning Post* opened its columns to a furious and fantastic discussion of the verb-phrase, *to get his goat.* I content myself with one of the explanations: "Among the Negroes in Harlem it is the custom for each household to keep a goat to act as general scavenger. Occasionally one man will steal another's goat, and the household débris then accumulates to the general annoyance." The truth is that *to get his goat* seems to be of French origin; and in the form of *prendre sa chèvre,* philological genealogists have traced it back to the year 1585. But whatever is strange and upsetting is put down, in England, to the hellish ingenuity of Americans — save, of course, when genuine Americanisms are claimed as really English. This last happens often enough to give what may be called a cockeyed aspect to the perennial pother. In 1934 even the learned Dr. C. T. Onions, one of the editors of the great Oxford Dictionary, succumbed to the madness by offering to find in the dictionary any alleged Americanism that a reporter for the London *Evening News* could name. The reporter began discreetly with *fresh* (in the sense of *saucy*), *to figure* (in the sense of *to believe* or *conclude*), and *to grill* (in the sense of *to question*), and Dr. Onions duly found them all. But when the reporter proceeded to *bunkum,* the learned editor had to forget conveniently that its progenitor was the thoroughly American *buncombe,* when *rake-off* followed he had to admit that the earliest example in the dictionary was from an American work, and when *boloney* and *nerts* were hurled at him he blew up with a bang.

Here, of course, Dr. Onions and his interlocutor ended on the level of slang, but there is no telling where they would be if they could be translated to the year 2036. *Boloney,* like *to belittle,* has the imprimatur of an eminent tribune of the people, and is quite as respectable, philologically speaking, as *buncombe, gerrymander, pork barrel, filibuster, carpetbagger, gag rule,* or *on the fence.* All these came into American from the argot of politics, and got only frowns from the schoolmarm, but they are all quite sound American today, and most of them have gone into English. As for *nerts*, it seems to be but one more member of an endless dynasty of euphemisms, beginning with *zounds* and coming down to *son-of-a-gun, gee,* and *darn. Darn,* like *nerts,* is an Americanism, and Dr. Louise Pound has demonstrated that it descends from *eternal,* which first turned into *tarnal* and then lost its tail and borrowed the head of *damn.* I have heard a bishop use it freely in private discourse, with a waggish sprinkling of actual *damns. Son-of-a-gun* is now so feeble and harmless that the Italians in America use it as a satirical designation for native Americans, who seem to them to fall far behind the Italian talent for profanity and objurgation. It is, I believe, a just criticism. Some time ago I was engaged by a magazine to do an article on American and English swearwords. After two or three attempts I had to give it up, for I found that neither branch of our ancient Frisian tongue could show anything worthy of serious consideration. The antinomians of England stick to two or three banal obscenities, one of which, *bloody,* is obscene only formally, and we Americans seldom get beyond variations of *hell* and *damn.* A single Neapolitan boatman could swear down the whole population of Anglo-Saxondom.

Bloody is perfectly innocuous in the United States, and it may be innocuous in England also on some near tomorrow — or even more disreputable than it is today. There is no predicting the social career of words. Dr. Leonard Bloomfield says that even " our word *whore,* cognate with the Latin *carus* (dear), must have been at one time a polite substitute for some term now lost." Prophecy fails just as dismally when propriety does not come into question. Shakespeare's numerous attempts to introduce new words, some of them his own inventions and others borrowed from the slang of the Bankside, failed almost as often as they succeeded. He found ready takers for *courtship, lonely, sportive, multitudinous, hubbub* and *bump,* but his audiences would have none of *definement,* in the sense of description, or of *citizen* as an adjective, and both seem strange and uncouth to us today, though all the others are as familiar and as decorous as *cat* or *rat.* When John Marston used *strenuous* in 1599 it was attacked by Ben Jonson as barbarous, but a dozen years later it had got into Chapman's Homer, and by 1670 it was being used by Milton. It remained perfectly respectable until 1900, when Theodore Roosevelt announced the Strenuous Life. Both the idea and the term struck the American fancy, and in a little while the latter passed into slang and was worn so threadbare that all persons of careful speech sickened of it. To this day it carries a faintly ridiculous connotation, and is seldom used seriously. But by 1975 it may be restored to the dignity of *psychopath* or *homoousian.* No one can say yes with any confidence, and no one can say no. " Even the greatest purist," observes Robert Lynd, " does not object to the inclusion of *bogus* in a literary English vocabulary, though a hundred years ago it was an American slang word meaning an apparatus for coining false money. *Carpetbagger* and *bunkum* are other American slang words that have naturalized themselves in English speech, and *mob* is an example of English slang that was once as vulgar as *photo.*"

Three Americanisms borrowed by English to one Briticism come into American! The true score, I suspect, is even more favorable to the Yankee as word-maker. Down to 1820, according to Sir William Craigie, the trans-Atlantic trade in neologisms ran mainly westward, but then it began to shift, and today it is very heavily eastward. It would be difficult to recall a dozen British inventions that have entered the common American vocabulary since the World War, but the number of Americanisms taken into English must run to hundreds, and perhaps even to thousands. The American movie and talkie, of course, have been responsible for the introduction of many of them, but there is something beyond that, and something more fundamental. They are adopted in England simply because England has nothing to offer in competition with them — that is, nothing so apt or pungent, nothing so good. His Lordship of Guildford did not apply *speed-cop* to that *mobile policeman* as a voluntary act of subversion, born of a desire to shock and insult the realm; he let it slip for the single reason that it was an irresistibly apposite and satisfying term. And so with all the other Americanisms that challenge and consume their British congeners. They win fairly on palpable points and by every rule of the game. Confronted by the same novelty, whether in object or in situation, the Americans always manage to fetch up a name for it that not only describes it but also illuminates it, whereas the English, since the Elizabethan stimulant oozed out of them, have been content merely to catalogue it. There was a brilliant exemplification of the two approaches in the early days of railways. The English, having to name the wedge-shaped fender that was put in front of the first locomotives, called it a *plow,* which was almost exactly what it was, but the Americans gave it the bold and racy appellation of *cowcatcher.* For the casting which guides the wheels from one rail to another the English coined the depressingly obvious name of *crossing-plate;* the Americans, setting their imaginations free, called it a *frog.* The same sharp contrast appears every time there is a call for a new word today. The American *movie* is obviously much better than the English *cinema;* it is even better English. So is *radio* better than *wireless,* though it may be Latin, and *job-holder* better than *public servant,* though it is surely literal enough, and *shock absorber* vastly better than *anti-bounce clip,* and *highball* than *whisky and soda,* and *bouncer* than *chucker-out,* and *chain store* than *multiple shop,* and *string bean* than *French bean,* and *union suit* than *combination.* Confronting the immensely American *rubberneck,* Dr. J. Y. T. Greig of Newcastle could only exclaim, " One of the best words ever coined! " And in the face of *lounge lizard,* Horace Annesley Vachell fell silent like Sir Isaac Newton on the seashore, overwhelmed by the solemn grandeur of the linguistic universe.

One finds in current American all the characters and tendencies that marked the rich English of Shakespeare's time — an eager borrowing of neologisms from other languages, a bold and often very ingenious use of metaphor, and a fine disdain of the barricades separating the parts of speech. The making of new words is not carried on only, or even principally, to fill gaps in the vocabulary; indeed, one may well agree with Captain Hall that " there are words enough already." It is carried on because there survives in the American something that seems to have faded out of the Englishman: an innocent joy in wordmaking for its own sake, a voluptuous delight in the vigor and elasticity of the language. The search for the *mot juste* is an enterprise that is altogether too pedantic for him; he much prefers to solve his problem by non-Euclidian devices. *Hoosegow* was certainly not necessary when it appeared, for we already had a large repertory of synonyms for *jail*. But when the word precipitated itself from the Spanish *juzgado* somewhere along the Rio Grande it won quick currency, and in a little while it was on the march through the country, and soon or late, I suppose, it will produce its inevitable clipped forms, *hoose* and *gow,* and its attendant adjective and verb. *Corral,* which entered by the same route in the forties of the last century, had hatched a verb before the Civil War, and that verb, according to Webster's New International (1934) now has four separate and distinct meanings. *Bummer,* coming in from the German, is now clipped to *bum,* and is not only noun, verb, and adjective but also adverb. *Buncombe,* borrowed by the English as *bunkum,* has bred *bunco* and *bunk* at home, both of which rove the parts of speech in a loose and easy way, and the last of which has issue in the harsh verb *to debunk,* still under heavy fire in England.

The impact of such lawless novelties upon the more staid English of the motherland is terrific. The more they are denounced as heathen and outlandish, the quicker they get into circulation. Nor do they prosper only on the level of the vulgate, and among careless speakers. There are constant complaints in the English newspapers about their appearance in the parliamentary debates, and even in discourses from the sacred desk, and they begin to show themselves also in belles-lettres, despite the English dislike of new ways of writing. Their progress, in fact, is so widespread and so insidious that they often pop up in the diatribes that revile them; the Englishman, conquered at last, can no longer protest against Americanisms without using them. Moreover, they are now supported actively by a definitely pro-American party of writers and scholars, and though it is still small in numbers, at least compared to the patriot band, it shows some distinguished names. The later Robert Bridges, Poet Laureate, was an active member of it, and among its other adherents are Wyndham Lewis, Edward Shanks, Richard Aldington, and Sir John Foster Fraser. Sir William Craigie, perhaps the first of living lexicographers, is so greatly interested in the American form of English that he has spent the years since 1925 in a scientific examination of it, and will presently begin the publication of an elaborate dictionary. If only because of the greater weight of the population behind it, it seems destined to usurp the natural leadership of British English and to determine the general course of the language hereafter. But its chief advantage in this struggle is really not the numerical one, but the fact that its daring experiments and iconoclasms lie in the grand tradition of English and are signs of its incurable normalcy and abounding vigor.

How far it will move away from the theorizing of grammarians and the policing of schoolmarms remains to be seen. They still make valiant efforts to curb its wayward spirit, but with gradually diminishing success. When, a few years ago, the late Sterling A. Leonard of the University of Wisconsin submitted a long series of their admonitions to a committee of educated Americans, including many philologians, he found that opinion was against them on that high level almost as decidedly as it was on lower ones. His judges favored scores of forms that the school grammars and popular handbooks of usage still condemn. Since then a more direct attack upon the conservative position has been made by Dr. Robert C. Pooley of the same university. He shows that some of the rules laid down with most assurance by pedants have no support in either history or logic, and are constantly violated by writers of unquestionable authority. There have even been rumblings of revolt in the conservative camp. The late George Philip Krapp of Columbia, who was surely anything but a radical, was of the opinion that English would undergo profound changes in the United States, and that many of them would be of such a character that its very grammatical structure would be shaken. Dr. George O. Curme of Northwestern University is another eminent grammarian who warns his colleagues that the rules they cherish have no genuine authority, and must be overhauled from time to time. Once they steel themselves to that sacrifice of their professional dignity, he says, " it will give a thrill to English-speaking students to discover that the English language does not belong to the schoolteacher but belongs to them, and that its future destiny will soon rest entirely in their hands."

Dr. Curme is always careful to think and speak of American as no more than a variation of English. But it must be obvious that, in late years, the tail has begun a vigorous wagging of the dog. " The facts that we ought to realize," says Edward Shanks to his fellow Britons, " and that we ignore when we talk loftily about Americanisms, are that America is making a formidable contribution to the development of our language, and that all our attempts to reject that contribution will in the long run be vain."

James Weldon Johnson

The Negro's Creative Genius

THE status of the Negro in the United States is more a question of national mental attitude toward the race than of actual conditions. And nothing will do more to change that mental attitude and raise his status than a demonstration of intellectual parity by the Negro through the production of literature and art.

Is there likelihood that the American Negro will be able to do this? There is, for the good reason that he possesses the innate powers. He has the emotional endowment, the originality and artistic conception, and, what is more important, the power of creating that which has universal appeal and influence.

I make here what may appear to be a more startling statement by saying that the Negro has already proved the possession of these powers by being the

From *The Book of American Negro Poetry,* 1922.

creator of the only things artistic that have yet sprung from American soil and been universally acknowledged as distinctive American products.

These creations by the American Negro may be summed up under four heads. The first two are the Uncle Remus stories, which were collected by Joel Chandler Harris, and the " spirituals " or slave songs, to which the Fisk Jubilee Singers made the public and the musicians of both the United States and Europe listen. The Uncle Remus stories constitute the greatest body of folklore that America has produced, and the " spirituals " the greatest body of folk song. I shall speak of the " spirituals " later because they are more than folk songs, for in them the Negro sounded the depths, if he did not scale the heights, of music.

The other two creations are the cakewalk and ragtime. We do not need to go very far back to remember when cakewalking was the rage in the United States, Europe, and South America. Society in this country and royalty abroad spent time in practicing the intricate steps. Paris pronounced it the " poetry of motion." The popularity of the cakewalk passed away but its influence remained. The influence can be seen today on any American stage where there is dancing.

The influence which the Negro has exercised on the art of dancing in this country has been almost absolute. For generations the " buck and wing " and the " stop-time " dances, which are strictly Negro, have been familiar to American theater audiences. A few years ago the public discovered the " turkey trot," the " eagle rock," " ballin' the jack," and several other varieties that started the modern dance craze. These dances were quickly followed by the " tango," a dance originated by the Negroes of Cuba and later transplanted to South America. (This fact is attested by no less authority than Vincente Blasco Ibañez in his *Four Horsemen of the Apocalypse*.) Half the floor space in the country was then turned over to dancing, and highly paid exponents sprang up everywhere. The most noted, Mr. Vernon Castle, and, by the way, an Englishman, never danced except to the music of a colored band, and he never failed to state to his audiences that most of his dances had long been done by " your colored people," as he put it.

As for ragtime, I go straight to the statement that it is the one artistic production by which America is known the world over. It has been all-conquering. Everywhere it is hailed as " American music."

For a dozen years or so there has been a steady tendency to divorce ragtime from the Negro; in fact, to take from him the credit of having originated it. Probably the younger people of the present generation do not know that ragtime is of Negro origin. The change wrought in ragtime and the way in which it is accepted by the country have been brought about chiefly through the change which has gradually been made in the words and stories accompanying the music. Once the text of all ragtime songs was written in Negro dialect, and was about Negroes in the cabin or in the cotton field or on the levee or at a jubilee or on Sixth Avenue or at a ball, and about their love affairs. Today, only a small proportion of ragtime songs relate at all to the Negro. The truth is, ragtime is now national rather than racial. But that does not abolish in any way the claim of the American Negro as its originator.

Ragtime music was originated by colored piano players in the questionable resorts of St. Louis, Memphis, and other Mississippi River towns. These men did not know any more about the theory of music than they did about the theory of the universe. They were guided by their natural musical instinct and talent, but above all by the Negro's extraordinary sense of rhythm. Anyone who is familiar with ragtime may note that its chief charm is not in melody, but in rhythms. These players often improvised crude and, at times, vulgar words to fit the music. This was the beginning of the ragtime song.

Ragtime music got its first popular hearing at Chicago during the World's Fair in that city. From Chicago it made its way to New York, and then started on its universal triumph.

The earliest ragtime songs, like Topsy, " jes' grew." Some of these earliest songs were taken down by white men, the words slightly altered or changed, and published under the names of the arrangers. They sprang into immediate popularity and earned small fortunes. The first to become widely known was " The Bully," a levee song which had been long used by roustabouts along the Mississippi. It was introduced in New York by Miss Mary Irwin, and gained instant popularity. Another one of these " jes' grew " songs was one which for a while disputed for place with " Yankee Doodle "; perhaps, disputes it even today. That song was " A Hot Time in the Old Town Tonight," introduced and made popular by the colored regimental bands during the Spanish-American War.

Later there came along a number of colored men who were able to transcribe the old songs and write original ones. I was, about that time, writing words to music for the music show stage in New York. I was collaborating with my brother, J. Rosamond Johnson, and the late Bob Cole. I remember that we appropriated about the last one of the old " jes' grew " songs. It was a song which had been sung for years all through the South. The words were unprintable but the tune was irresistible, and belonged to nobody. We took it, rewrote the verses, telling an entirely different story from the original, left the chorus as it was, and published the song, at first under the name of " Will Handy." It became very popular with college boys, especially at football games, and perhaps still is. The song was " Oh, Didn't He Ramble! "

In the beginning, and for quite a while, almost all of the ragtime songs that were deliberately composed were the work of colored song writers. Now the colored composers, even in this particular field, are greatly outnumbered by the white.

In spite of the bans which musicians and music teachers have placed on it, the people still demand and enjoy ragtime. In fact, there is not a corner of the civilized world in which it is not known and liked. And this proves its originality, for if it were an imitation, the people of Europe, at least, would not have found it a novelty. And it is proof of a more important thing; it is proof that ragtime possesses the vital spark, the power to appeal universally, without which any artistic production, no matter how approved its form may be, is dead.

Of course, there are those who will deny that ragtime is an artistic production. American musicians, especially, instead of investigating ragtime, dismiss it with a contemptuous word. But this has been the course of scholasticism in every branch of art. Whatever new thing the people like is pooh-poohed; whatever is popular is regarded as not worth while. The fact is, nothing great or enduring in music has ever sprung full-fledged from the brain of any master; the best he gives the world he gathers from the hearts of the people, and runs it through the alembic of his genius.

Ragtime deserves serious attention. There is a lot of colorless and vicious imitation, but there is enough that is genuine. In one composition, " The Memphis Blues," the musician will find not only great melodic beauty but a polyphonic structure that is amazing.

It is obvious that ragtime has influenced, and in a large measure become, our popular music; but not many would know that it has influenced even our religious music. Those who are familiar with gospel hymns can at once see this influence if they will compare the songs of thirty years ago, such as " In the Sweet Bye and Bye," " The Ninety and Nine," etc., with the up-to-date, syncopated tunes that are sung in Sunday Schools, Christian Endeavor Societies, Y.M.C.A.'s and the like gatherings today.

Ragtime has not only influenced American music, it has influenced American life. It has become the popular medium for our national expression musically. And who can say that it does not express the blare and jangle and the surge, too, of our national spirit?

Anyone who doubts that there is a peculiar heel-tickling, smile-provoking, joy-awakening, response-compelling charm in ragtime needs only to hear a skillful performer play the genuine article — needs only to listen to its bizarre harmonies, its audacious resolutions often consisting of an abrupt jump from one key to another, its intricate rhythms in which the accents fall in the most unexpected places but in which the fundamental beat is never lost — in order to be convinced. I believe it has its place as well as the music which draws from us sighs and tears.

Now, these dances which I have referred to and ragtime music may be lower forms of art, but they are evidence of a power that will some day· be applied to the higher forms. And even now we need not stop at the Negro's accomplishment through these lower forms. In the " spirituals," or slave songs, the Negro has given America not only its only folk songs but a mass of noble music. I never think of this music but that I am struck by the wonder, the miracle of its production. How did the men who originated these songs manage to do it? The sentiments are easily accounted for; they are, for the most part, taken from the Bible. But the melodies, where did they come from? Some of them so weirdly sweet, and others so wonderfully strong. Take, for instance, " Go Down, Moses "; I doubt that there is a stronger theme in the whole musical literature of the world.

It is to be noted that whereas the chief characteristic of ragtime is rhythm, the chief characteristic of the " spirituals " is melody. The melodies of " Steal away to Jesus," "Swing Low, Sweet Chariot," "Nobody Knows de Trouble I See," "I Couldn't Hear Nobody Pray," "Deep River," "O, Freedom over Me," and many others of these songs possess a beauty that is — what shall I say? — poignant. In the riotous rhythms of ragtime the Negro expressed his irrepressible buoyancy, his keen response to the sheer joy of living; in the " spirituals " he voiced his sense of beauty and his deep religious feeling.

Naturally, not as much can be said for the words of these songs as for the music. Most of the songs are religious. Some of them are songs expressing faith and endurance and a longing for freedom. In the religious songs, the sentiments and often the entire lines are taken bodily from the Bible text. It is evident that the opening lines of " Go Down, Moses " —

> " Go down, Moses,
> 'Way down in Egypt land;
> Tell old Pharaoh,
> Let my people go " —

have a significance beyond the bondage of Israel in Egypt.

The bulk of the lines to these songs, as is the case in all communal music, is made up of choral iteration and incremental repetition of the leader's lines. If the words are read, this constant iteration and repetition are found to be tiresome; and it must be admitted that the lines themselves are often very trite. And yet there is frequently revealed a flash of real, primitive poetry. I give the following examples:

> " Sometimes I feel like an eagle in de air."

> " You may bury me in de East,
> You may bury me in de West,
> But I'll hear de trumpet sound
> In-a dat mornin'."

> " I know de moonlight, I know de starlight;
> I lay dis body down.
> I walk in de moonlight, I walk in de starlight;
> I lay dis body down.
> I know de graveyard, I know de graveyard,
> When I lay dis body down.
> I walk in de graveyard, I walk troo de graveyard
> To lay dis body down.

> " I lay in de grave an' stretch out my arms;
> I lay dis body down.
> I go to de judgment in de evenin' of de day
> When I lay dis body down.
> An' my soul an' yo' soul will meet in de day
> When I lay dis body down."

The Negro in the United States has achieved or been placed in a certain artistic niche. When he is thought of artistically, it is as a happy-go-lucky, singing, shuffling, banjo-picking being or as a more or less pathetic figure. The picture of him is in a log cabin amid fields of cotton or along the levees. Negro dialect is naturally and by long association the exact instrument for voicing this phase of Negro life; and by that very exactness it is an instrument with but two full stops, humor and pathos. So even when he confines himself to purely racial themes, the Aframerican poet realizes that there are phases of Negro life in the United States which cannot be treated in dialect either adequately or artistically. Take, for example, the phases rising out of life in Harlem, that most wonderful Negro city in the world. I do not deny that a Negro in a log cabin is more picturesque than a Negro in a Harlem flat, but the Negro in the Harlem flat is here, and he is but a part of a group growing everywhere in the country — a group whose ideals are becoming increasingly more vital than those of the traditionally artistic group, even if its members are less picturesque.

What the colored poet in the United States needs to do is something like what Synge did for the Irish; he needs to find a form that will express the racial spirit by symbols from within rather than by symbols from without, such as the mere mutilation of English spelling and pronunciation. He needs a form that is freer and larger than dialect, but which will still hold the racial flavor; a form expressing the imagery, the idioms, the peculiar turns of thought, and the distinctive humor and pathos, too, of the Negro, but which will also be capable of voicing the deepest and highest emotions and aspirations, and allow of the widest range of subjects and the widest scope of treatment.

Negro dialect is at present a medium that is not capable of giving expression to the varied conditions of Negro life in America, and much less is it capable of giving the fullest interpretation of Negro character and psychology. This is no indictment against the dialect as dialect, but against the mold of convention in which Negro dialect in the United States has been set. In time these conventions may become lost, and the colored poet in the United States may sit down to write in dialect without feeling that his first line will put the general reader in a frame of mind which demands that the poem be humorous or pathetic. In the meantime, there is no reason why these poets should not continue to do the beautiful things that can be done, and done best, in the dialect.

In stating the need for Aframerican poets in the United States to work out a new and distinctive form of expression I do not wish to be understood to hold any theory that they should limit themselves to Negro poetry, to racial themes; the sooner they are able to write *American* poetry spontaneously, the better. Nevertheless, I believe that the richest contribution the Negro poet can make to American literature of the future will be the fusion into it of his own individual artistic gifts.

Deems Taylor

Music and the Flag

PEOPLE seem to be worrying almost continuously because they can see
no sign of an American " school " of music. They seem to feel that it is
very slow in getting under way, and keep poking at it in an effort to make
it move faster. Opinions differ as to what kind of school it ought to be, and just
what should be its characteristics. Some think it ought to convey the spirit of
American independence and initiative, the spaciousness of the wind-swept
prairies and the solitude of the Grand Canyon; the uncurbed spirit of the Boston
Tea Party, coupled with a slight hint of the Monroe Doctrine.

There are others who think it should convey the roar of the cities, the mechanical perfection of the airplane engine, and the relentless mechanization of a
Ford plant. Still others want it to be expressive of our idealism and international
good will — the Ku Klux Klan and the brotherhood of man.

All, however, are agreed as to two things. First, that there should be a
school. Apparently composers, in their opinion, are something like flying fish,
and can get nowhere unless they are moving in a body. Second, they are positive
that our music should be founded upon our folk songs. Hardly a week goes
by that some newspaper does not print a letter from some onlooker who wants
to know, with considerable heat, why American composers do not utilize the
mine of native musical lore that lies at their feet.

There are three kinds of folk songs in this country upon which various
enthusiasts think our American school of music should be based. The first is
made up of the songs and dances of the American Indian. These have strength
and simplicity, and are undeniably primitive; but wherein are they particularly
American? That is, wherein do they express anything of *us?* Just what response
is going to be stirred in the blood of a New Yorker of mixed Russian, Italian,
and Irish extraction, or a Chicagoan whose forebears were Swedish, Czechoslovak, and German, when he hears a Zuñi medicine song or an Apache war
dance? We have stolen everything else from the Indian that he ever owned; we
might at least let him have his own music for himself.

Not that good music cannot be written on Indian themes. MacDowell's
" Indian " Suite is proof enough of that. But the " Indian " Suite is Indian,
not American.

The same objection holds, I think, against trying to make Negro spirituals
the basis of American music. They were undoubtedly created in this country,
and they are a mine of magnificent musical material. But they are not American
— that is, in the sense of expressing the soul of the average white American.
We may be thrilled by their beauty. But beauty is not enough, at least in a

From *Of Men and Music,* 1937.

folk song. What we are looking for is some common fund of music that awakens ancestral echoes within us; and so far as blood is concerned, the finale of the Ninth Symphony is more likely to do that than " Swing Low, Sweet Chariot."

There remain certain local folk songs, such as the songs of the Kentucky mountains that Loraine Wyman and Howard Brockway collected, and the cowboy songs. The Kentucky songs are beautiful, but they are English where they are not Scotch. Most of them have easily traceable English archetypes; and the lovely " Nightingale " song from the first Wyman-Brockway book is, if you play it a bit faster, not far removed from " The Campbells Are Coming." This is all very well for the Anglo-Saxon American, but it leaves the Scandinavian, Irish, Italian, Russian, French, Jewish, Greek, Czechoslovak, or what-have-you American out in the cold.

Which brings us to the cowboy songs. As folk poems, as verses that convey something characteristically and inescapably American, they are superb. But their music is deplorable. The words of " Jesse James was a man who killed a-many a man " are grand; but the music to which they are set is pretty meager stuff upon which to base symphonies and tone poems. To read the words of " Whoopy ty-yi-yi, get along, little dogies," and then to hear the music, is a complete course in anticlimax. The cowboy songs, for the most part, are ballads, sung narratives in which the words (as they are everywhere) are of primary importance. Judging from the tunes, and what little I know about horses, it is not easy to compose good music while riding horseback.

There is much talk in contemporary circles of making jazz the basis of American music. Thus far only one composer, the lamented George Gershwin, has done anything memorable in that idiom. The *Rhapsody in Blue,* the Concerto in F, and *An American in Paris* may be reckoned as genuine, if not monumental, contributions to contemporary music; but I am inclined to credit their achievement to Gershwin rather than to jazz. The trouble with jazz, to this observer at least, is twofold. First, it is, so far, extremely limited in its emotional range. The best jazz appeals, as Gilbert Seldes once put it, exclusively to the feet. It stimulates, it stirs, it cheers — even inebriates; but it opens no doors to the unseen and the inexpressible. It neither inspires nor consoles. When it does essay the tragic mood, as in the much-admired " blues," it is merely mawkish.

Moreover, jazz is not a wellspring of music; it is a method of writing music, a rhythmic idiom, a formula. And formulas are pretty sterile ground upon which to grow the flower of art. Those of us who look to jazz to save American music might glance at Spain, whose music is also based on a formula, and most of whose composers have gone from the cradle to the grave with the accursed " TUM-de-UM-tum, TUM-de-UM-tum " rhythm of the fandango and habanera ringing in their ears and echoing throughout their pages.

But the quest continues, the search for an American musical speech, some characteristic turn of harmony, melody, or rhythm that will stamp its creator's nationality beyond the possibility of doubt, the search that has bedeviled American music and musicians for a century. It is a vain one, I think. There is no American school of music, and I doubt if there will ever be one. As a matter of fact, I have an idea that " schools " of art are about over, everywhere. In their heyday they were largely a product of times when the artist was esteemed as a craftsman first, and as an original creator second. In the great Italian and Flemish schools of painting, for instance, it was considered no disgrace for one painter to imitate the technique and even the actual composition and ar-rangement of another. Provided he turned out good work, no one criticized him if it bore a more than superficial resemblance to the work of his master. Even as late as the eighteenth century, composers borrowed themes from one another with no self-consciousness whatsoever, and without exciting any par-ticular adverse comment.

But now the emphasis has shifted from the work as a thing in itself to the work as an expression of the individual artist. We do not expect the pupils of a certain painter to paint indefinitely in faithful imitation of his style. Com-posers no longer borrow or lend themes. The luckless musician who borrows somebody else's tune is regarded, not as a borrower, but as an embezzler. In short, the very people who yearn after definite schools of thought and technique are likewise insistent that the artist be uniquely and recognizably himself. Unless he can create pictures and words and music that are his own and nobody else's they refuse to recognize him as an artist at all.

One other factor made for schools of art: nationalism. A school, in its less obvious aspect, is the result of a common fund of thought and feeling — par-ticularly feeling. Talk to a Paris taxicab driver, and you find the same rigorous sense of logic, the same utter innocence of sentimentality, that make Debussy's *Pelléas,* for all its wraith-like fragility and suggestiveness, a solid, firmly built work of art. The reiterated tonic chords at the close of Beethoven's Fifth Sym-phony are but a sublimated and happier manifestation of the Teutonic habit of laboriously pounding home a point long after the listener has wearily con-ceded it. English painting, on the average, is one vast betrayal of the sentimental-ism for which the average Englishman's monosyllabic matter-of-factness is a cloak.

At that, when it comes to music, I suspect us of being a good deal more confident of detecting national characteristics than we have any right to be. I have often thought what an interesting experiment it would be to find some person who was sensitive to music, but knew neither the name nor nationality of a single composer; to take him to hear operas and concert works, and ask him to guess the countries of their origin.

Some he could undoubtedly guess. I would try him on a Chopin polonaise or mazurka. " Polish," he would say. The " Ritual Dance " from De Falla's *El Amor Brujo*. He would probably guess, " Spanish." A gavotte by Lully he would undoubtedly identify as French (Lully was an Italian who founded French opera), and he might find a waltz by Johann Strauss unmistakably German — or, let us say, Teutonic. If I played him a tarantella he would prob-ably identify it as coming from Italy.

But, just as he was beginning to wax a bit boastful, I would play him the exquisite " Fisherman's Tale " from that same *El Amor Brujo,* and ask him — or, rather, dare him — to tell me the nationality of the composer. I would play him the Russian national anthem by Lvoff, and the Austrian national anthem by Haydn, and ask him to tell me which was the Russian and which was the Austrian, and why. If I played him the *" Marche des Rois "* from the *Arlésienne* suite, and the " Habanera " from *Carmen,* I would be extremely curious to see whether he would guess that the same Frenchman had written both.

It is perfectly true that we associate certain rhythms, and certain conventional phrases of musical speech, with definite nationalities. I think it is equally true, however, that nationalism is only for the middling good artist; that when a composer begins to search for some music that will express universal human ideas and emotions, and succeeds, he generally far transcends the bounds of any national idiom. The Wagner of the first scene of the last act of *Parsifal* is no more German to me than the Debussy of the closing scene of *Pelléas et Mélisande* is French.

Just what is the common characteristic that would make you sure of identifying the music of Corelli, Respighi, Verdi, and Pizzetti as unmistakably Italian? What is there French, beyond the composer's name, about Ravel's *Bolero?* The slow movement of the " From the New World " Symphony is accepted as so completely American that, with words by William Arms Fisher and entitled " Goin' Home," it is accepted by thousands of Americans as a genuine Negro spiritual — in other words, American. (Anyone who lives in America, particularly an Indian or a Negro, is, musically speaking, an American.)

Even if it were true that a common fund of racial experience and emotion invariably produces music whose nationality is unmistakable, we would be no better off. For we Americans are not a race. America is a club, not a motherland. Her people have almost no common thoughts and feelings and instincts. We talk a good deal about the Spirit of '76 and the ideals of the Founding Fathers. They once existed, too; but that was long ago, when we were a race of transplanted Englishmen. By now, our blood is such a conglomeration of diverse racial strains that we have hardly any nationalistic feeling at all, in the European sense. Inland, we are parochial; on our eastern coast we are international-minded; in the extreme west we are anti-Oriental — a purely negative kind of nationalism.

All of which does not make for a national school of music or any sort of art. It is not easy to find in our painting or poetry or music any unmistakably American characteristics; to isolate, as it were, an esthetic bacillus that flourishes exclusively in our own culture. Edward MacDowell, George Chadwick — German composers, both of them, the former with a deliberate added touch of Amerindian. Sargent was a superb painter of the French school, a brilliant blood relation of Boldini. Our best novelists seem purely American — frequently for no other reason than that their subject matter is American. But read a poem by Edna Millay or Archibald MacLeish without knowing the poet's name, and (disregarding geographical allusions) tell me the poet's nationality.

I am not prepared to say that there are absolutely no national characteristics in the music of great composers; but I do believe that they are not nearly so clear-cut or important as we have deluded ourselves into thinking they are. In general, a great composer is national only when he is at his second best. At the height of his powers, when he has ceased being decorative or merely exciting, and becomes eloquent and moving, he is likely to sound merely like himself. The great American music of the future will be a music to which America will listen and respond. But it will not be the music of Sitting Bull or Booker T. Washington — or even George. It will belong to us, because one of us made it; but it will, like all great music, belong to the world. And the world will not be curious regarding the name and address of the composer.

Gerald Bywaters

Contemporary American Artists

DURING most of the past forty years American art has existed under the bewitching influence of France. Beginning with the Impressionists, every French art movement has been reflected in American art. The parade of French movements has included Post-Impressionism, Cubism, Futurism, Dadaism, Surrealism, and others more or less intelligible. In the past five years, however, the popularity and effectiveness of French art in America has diminished to the point where it is now forced to struggle with much dealer manipulation along New York's 57th Street for audience and financial support.

The first logical opposition to the continued European domination of American art was generated by certain artists and writers who were natives of the Middle West. Among these artists destined to change the trend of art in America were Thomas Benton of Missouri, Charles Burchfield of Ohio, John Steuart Curry of Kansas, and Grant Wood of Iowa. The writer who foretold the change and has recorded it with so much benefit to the artists involved is Thomas Craven of Kansas, whose books, *Men of Art* and *Modern Art,* and magazine articles have been the principal means for popularizing the change in contemporary American art.

Sons of men who pioneered the Middle West, these artists are themselves pioneers in spirit and have experienced as much trouble in establishing their art in the East as their fathers had in opening up a new country in the face of Eastern legislative opposition and lack of understanding. Even these native sons did not understand their own country at first — they chased false prophets

From the *Southwest Review*, April, 1938.

for a while in Europe and New York. But they eventually realized that they could only be Americans and that America was not the standardized country which Europe and New York would have them believe. Also, although they had tried hard to be French or New York artists, they fortunately concluded that the ideas expressed in crude drawings as Middle Western youngsters possessed more validity for them than all the cosmopolitan subjects and thoughts they had picked up in their wanderings.

After such discoveries these artists were seized with a passion to interpret the America they knew or wanted to know. They devoted themselves to rediscovering their background, to painting towns, streets, fields, houses, shipyards, mines, factories, and those who people such places. Their work was not done with the unfeeling hand of a reporter nor with the assigned eye of an illustrator. They were all artists of talent and training who had decided after wide experience that it was better to interpret life than *nature morte,* and that a combination of form and content was a more substantial creative art than mere technical exercises in form.

Before long the character of American painting began to change. Exhibitions no longer exposed a majority of still lifes, abstractions, studio portraits, French landscapes, decorative pieces, misty seascapes, and fat nudes. Instead there appeared tornadoes, blizzards, drouths, dust storms, prairie fires; farmhands, threshing crews, hard-shell Baptists, Holy Rollers, miners, fiddlers, factory hands, niggers (not Negroes), poor white trash, gangsters, hillbillies, politicians, blacksmiths, cowpunchers; windmills, silos, farmhouses, barns, shanties, river boats, railroad stations, ranch houses; tank baptisms, rodeos, circuses, corn huskings, strikes, burlesque shows, lynchings, honky-tonks, mail robberies, horseshoe pitching; folk songs, ballads, and spirituals. Here, indeed, American art was becoming American and making of itself a blend of Mark Twain, Bret Harte, Bill Nye, Hamlin Garland, Theodore Dreiser, Sherwood Anderson, Willa Cather, William Faulkner, Thomas Wolfe, Paul Green, Jesse Stuart, Carl Sandburg, T. S. Stribling, and Erskine Caldwell. Called the " American Scene," this movement in art has become in actuality more regional in character than national, although it cannot be denied that it has now assumed the national leadership of American art.

Thomas Benton has been one of the leaders of this change in contemporary American art, and no other artist better represents its purpose and attainments. His youthful background was as peculiarly wholesome and American as that of Tom Sawyer; yet when early manhood came, Benton repudiated his natural heritage with all the false shame of a *nouveau riche.* Only after reaching a mature age did Benton adjust his talent to himself and become a powerful force in American art.

Benton was born in Neosho, Missouri, in 1889. His grand-uncle was Thomas Hart Benton, first and most famous Senator from Missouri and close friend of Andrew Jackson; his father was a lawyer, Congressman, and United States district attorney. From these men Benton inherited an energetic individualism, but he did not choose to continue their illustrious legal and political endeavors.

He wanted to be an artist and his first opportunity toward this goal was as cartoonist on a Joplin newspaper. After several boisterous years of cartooning, studying art in Chicago and adopting the pose but not the working habits of an artist, he went to Paris. Here Benton entered a ten-year period of imitating current French isms and forcing his talent into an impotent pattern. Although few of his pictures from this period are of value, his thousands of studies and analyses of classic paintings were later to lend great importance to his works.

Back in New York, Benton continued to paint French abstractions, but he gradually became American again and readjusted himself to his native background. When the war took him into the navy, he did drafting work which indicated how his talent might be put to fortunate use. He drew people, places, and things and found in these drawings the beginnings of personal satisfaction. After the war he made annual excursions into all parts of America, and from his sketches and experiences on these trips he began to build his art around the collective American spirit.

The first opportunity to paint America as he found it was in the murals in the New School for Social Research in New York in 1931. Executed during a nine-months period of stupendous labor and research, these paintings brought Benton no money and much criticism, but they presented the artist's mature genius and established him as a new leader in American art. In 1932 Benton painted a series of murals in the reading room of the Whitney Museum in New York. He received three thousand dollars for these murals and his fame grew in the press. The Whitney Museum paintings were named *The Arts in American Life,* and they depicted the popular arts rather than professional and conditioned ones. In these murals people drink, sing, dance, pitch horseshoes, get religion, and play politics in a vibrant panorama of the life of our time.

For the Century of Progress in 1933 the state of Indiana erected a large building and commissioned Thomas Benton to execute a mural fifteen feet high and two hundred and fifty feet long which was to be the only exhibit in the building. After careful research and travel through the state, Benton painted the mural in tempera, and it became a landmark in contemporary American art. In 1935 Benton was commissioned by his native state to paint a *Social History of Missouri* in the State House at Jefferson City. The artist spent fifteen months on the murals, nine months reading and making sketches and six months executing the actual paintings on the walls. Covering forty-five thousand square feet, these murals were a social history of actuality rather than of professed ideals and they aroused extensive official objections. After some months of active discussion it was generally agreed that these Benton murals were beyond the capacity of any other living American artist and that because of them Missouri had acquired a shrine of American culture.

The publication in 1937 of Benton's autobiography, *An Artist in America,* did much to explain this artist's attitude toward his art and his background. Illustrated with many sketches made on discovery excursions and recording his varied and intimate contacts with fellow Americans, this book has helped to show the real quality of Benton's talent. Recently he has been commissioned by the Limited Editions Club to illustrate a new edition of *Tom Sawyer*. At present Benton is living in Kansas City and teaching at the Art Institute.

If Benton represents the purpose, energy, and objectivity of the American Scene in art, Charles Burchfield is its pioneer, Grant Wood its chief philosopher, John Sloan and Reginald Marsh its New York representatives, and John Steuart Curry and Alexandre Hogue its most effective regional exponents.

Charles Burchfield was born in Ashtabula Harbor, Ohio, in 1893. A tailor's son, he spent his youth playing around the railroad tracks, haunting old tumble-down houses and deserted false-front store buildings. When he grew up he was one of the first American artists to use the physical background of his experience in painting. He became the painter of any Main Street, and his work was one of the earliest influences in pointing out to other artists the possibilities in their own native environments.

Even before Burchfield painted the streets of Middle Western towns John Sloan was making his etchings and paintings of life in New York City. Although some of his best works date to the early years of the century, no other painter has surpassed them in their expression of the many-sided life of a great metropolis. As a direct follower, Reginald Marsh has enlarged considerably on the theme of American city life which Sloan first explored.

Since 1930 when his painting *American Gothic* was awarded a three-hundred-dollar prize at the Chicago Art Institute, the fame of Grant Wood has grown inordinately. Today his name is more familiar to the general public than any other contemporary artist's, and his picture of the Iowa farmer and his wife is almost as well known as Leutze's *Washington Crossing the Delaware*.

Born of Quaker parents in 1892 at Anamosa, Iowa, Grant Wood enjoyed the life of a typical farm boy but he always found time after chores to make drawings on the lids of crackerboxes. He had some art training in high school and became interested in handicrafts, establishing a metalcraft and jewelry shop in Cedar Rapids. When the war forced him to close the craft shop, he worked as a carpenter and house painter until he was able to provide a house for his mother, and then he joined the army. His ability to draw good portraits of officers made his army life easy.

After the war, Wood taught school for seven years and saved money for art study in Europe. In Paris he affected pink whiskers and a basque beret and made paintings of France and Italy in an impressionistic style. After studying the primitive rooms in German museums, Wood discovered how his own precise, natural style could serve him better than any adopted technique and he returned to America to find that his natural feelings could also give him greater satisfaction than borrowed ones. Despite the prejudices aroused in him during 1927 by Mencken, Wood made friends with his own neighbors and launched himself into a long period of happy and important work.

The first painting Wood made after he settled himself back in Cedar Rapids was a portrait of his mother in a printed apron and holding a pot plant. Soon afterward he produced *American Gothic* and there followed a slow but steady production of important works, including *Daughters of Revolution, Stone City, Midnight Ride of Paul Revere, Young Corn, Birthplace of Herbert Hoover,*

Arbor Day, and the design for a mural named *Dinner for Threshers.* During his development as an artist Wood has always found time to continue with teaching. In 1932 he established a summer school and art colony at Stone City, Iowa, and continued this venture for three seasons. At present he is an instructor in art at the University of Iowa in Iowa City.

Benton and Wood are Midwesterners who have made their native lands the subject of their art, but neither has interpreted his background more capably than John Steuart Curry, the Kansas farm boy who grew up to paint the farm and its life with more conviction than any other American artist. Born in Dunevant, Kansas, in 1897, Curry spent his youth plowing, planting, and harvesting crops, and tending cattle, because it was the only life he knew. Yet instinctively the boy put down on paper in graphic form the things of his experience — windstorms, animals, crops, and life on the great plains.

After three years of high school Curry went to art schools in Kansas City and Chicago where fellow students laughed at his rustic pictures. At the age of twenty-two he was in Philadelphia to begin a five-year tenure as a struggling magazine illustrator. Because his pictures were too real his work soon destroyed its own market in the field of fiction. He turned to painting and journeyed to Paris in an attempt to settle his talent. In 1927 he returned to America much improved in technical ability and determined to paint honestly and from his own experience.

The picture *Baptism in Kansas* pronounced Curry as a possible master of American genre and *The Tornado, The Gospel Train,* and other dramatic treatments of life in the Middle West established his name. After an interlude of painting with Ringling Brothers–Barnum and Bailey Circus he returned to the more fortunate subjects of his youth. In 1936 he executed two murals in the Department of Justice Building in Washington. Despite a national reputation the artist was not acclaimed by his native state until recently when he received a commission to decorate the walls of the Capitol Building at Topeka.

At present Curry occupies the unique position of " artist in residence " under a five-year contract at four thousand dollars a year at the University of Wisconsin in Madison. He does not conduct regular classes but his studio door remains open and the attitude of the artist at work has its influence on the campus. As the poet of the realities of rural life Curry is no propagandist for the farmer. As an artist he exerts less influence than any of the other painters of the American Scene because he arrived at his own method through the necessity of his desire for expression.

In the Southwest, Alexandre Hogue is one of the leaders in a flourishing group of artists who have gained national prominence. For years Hogue painted the Southwestern scene before he climbed to fame with a series of paintings of the Dust Bowl. Like other regional artists, he thoroughly understood his subject. Born in 1898, he spent his boyhood on a cattle ranch in the Texas Panhandle. He saw " suitcase " farmers invade the grassy plains, plow unbroken land, and plant wheat for the boom markets. He heard the ranchers warn these farmers that if the land were plowed it would blow away.

After Hogue taught himself to paint and lived in Dallas painting Texas and New Mexico landscapes, dust storms began to roll out of the Panhandle and he executed his series of works on the Dust Bowl. Most important paintings in the series are *Drouth Stricken Area, Dust Bowl, Drouth Survivors,* and *Erosion.* When these paintings were reproduced widely, unending protests w advanced by chambers of commerce. Money was collected to purchase *Dr Stricken Area* so that it might be destroyed as an unfair and isolated of Dust Bowl conditions. For every objection to these depictions of the de ing of the plains, however, there was an approval by agencies seeking to promo. drouth control.

As the leader of regional realism in the Southwest, Hogue prepared the way for other important artists in Texas. Exhibited in the art centers of America and Europe, his pictures have informed the public of the life of a region until recently omitted from the field of art. In addition to Alexandre Hogue, other painters of the new American school whose fame is not definitive but whose ability is thoroughly established are Everett Spruce and Otis Dozier of Dallas and Tom Lea of El Paso, Texas, Howard Cook and Peter Hurd of New Mexico, Don Brown and John McCrady of Louisiana, Joe Jones and Joseph Meert of Missouri, Frank Mechau of Colorado and many painters in California.

These artists insist that art is relevant to life and they are vitally concerned with the problems of human society. They believe they can paint best what they know best. Their paintings reveal the pattern of a significant creative procedure — first, the discovery of a situation of character peculiar to the region, seen through the medium of the artist's individuality; next, an understanding of the subject from experience and association; and finally, evidence that the special character of the subject has controlled the evolution of the work.

Art produced in this manner is certainly regional and provides a true basis for a national art. Only *after* art has been produced as an honest regional expression can it hope to become universal.

Lewis Mumford

Architecture and Civilization

THE capital sign of the early settlements beyond the seashore was the clearing; and since the great majority of newcomers lived by agriculture, the forest itself appeared merely as an obstacle to be removed. The untouched woods of America were all too lush and generous, and if an occasional Leatherstocking loved them, the new settler saw only land to clear and wood to burn. In the New England village, the tradition of culture was

From *Sticks and Stones,* 1924.

perhaps applied to the land itself, and elsewhere there are occasional elements of good practice, in the ordered neatness of boulder fences. For the most part, however, the deliberate obliteration of the natural landscape became a great national sport, comparable to the extermination of bison which the casual western traveler devoted himself to at a later date.

The stripping of the Appalachian forest was the first step in our campaign against nature. By 1860 the effect was already grave enough to warn an acute observer, like George Perkins Marsh, of the danger to our civilization, and to prompt him in *Earth and Man* to remind his countrymen that other civilizations about the Mediterranean and the Adriatic had lost their topsoil and ruined their agriculture through the wanton destruction of their forests.

In the meanwhile, a new factor had entered. If before the nineteenth century we cleared the forest to make way for the farm, with the entrance of the industrial pioneer we began to clear the farm to parcel out the city. We have called this process the settlement of America, but the name is anomalous, for we formed the habit of using the land not as a home, a permanent seat of culture, but as a means to something else — principally as a means to the temporary advantages of profitable speculation and exploitation.

James Mackay, a charitable Scotch observer in the middle of the nineteenth century, explained our negligence of the earth by the fact that we pinned our affections to institutions rather than places, and cared not how the landscape was massacred as long as we lived under the same flag and enjoyed the same forms of government. There is no doubt a little truth in this observation; but it was not merely our attachment to republican government that caused this behavior: it was even more, perhaps, our disattachment from the affiliations of a settled life. The pioneer, to put it vulgarly, was on the make and on the move; it did not matter to him how he treated the land, since by the time he could realize its deficiencies he had already escaped to a new virgin area. " What had posterity done for him? "

The pioneers who turned their backs on a civilized way of life, in order to extend the boundaries of civilization, left us with a heavy burden — not merely blasted and disorderly landscapes, but the habit of tolerating and producing blasted and disorderly landscapes. As Cobbett pointed out in his attempt to account for the unkempt condition of the American farm, the farmer in this country lacked the example of the great landed estates, where the woods had become cultivated parks, and the meadowland had become lawns. Without this cultivated example in the country, it is no wonder that our cities have been littered, frayed at the edges, ugly; no wonder that our pavements so quickly obliterate trees and grass; no wonder that so many towns are little more than gashes of metal and stone.

Those who had been bred on the land brought into the city none of that disciplined care which might have preserved some of its amenities. They left the smoke of the clearings, which was a sign of rural " progress "; they welcomed the smoke of the towns, and all that accompanied it.

It is scarcely a paradox to say that the improvement of our cities must proceed inwards from the countryside; for it is largely a matter of reversing the process which converts the farm into incipient blocks of real estate. Once we assimilate the notion that soil and site have uses quite apart from sale, we shall not continue to barbarize and waste them. Consider how the water's edge of lower Manhattan was developed without the slightest regard for its potential facilities for recreation; how the Acropolis of Pittsburgh, the Hump, was permitted to turn into a noisome slum; how the unique beauty of Casco Bay has been partly secured only by Portland's inferiority as a shipping center. Indeed, all up and down the country one can pick up a thousand examples of towns misplaced, of recreation areas becoming factory sites, of industries located without intelligent reference to raw materials or power or markets or the human beings who serve them, of agricultural land being turned prematurely into suburban lots, and of small rural communities which need the injection of new industries and enterprises, languishing away whilst a metropolis not fifty miles away continues to absorb more people, who daily pay a heavy premium for their congestion.

To see the interdependence of city and country, to realize that the growth and concentration of one is associated with the depletion and impoverishment of the other, to appreciate that there is a just and harmonious balance between the two — this capacity we have lacked. Before we can build well on any scale we shall, it seems to me, have to develop an art of regional planning, an art which will relate city and countryside in a new pattern from that which was the blind creation of the industrial and the territorial pioneer. Instead of regarding the countryside as so much grist doomed to go eventually into the metropolitan mill, we must plan to preserve and develop all our natural resources to the limit.

It goes without saying that any genuine attempt to provide for the social and economic renewal of a region cannot be constrained to preserve vested land-values and property rights and privileges; indeed, if the land is to be fully loved and cared for again we must recover it in something more than name only. The main objection to keeping our natural resources in the hands of the community — namely, that private capital is more zealous at exploitation — is precisely the reason for urging the first course. Our land has suffered from zeal in exploitation; and it would be much better, for example, that our water-power resources should remain temporarily undeveloped than that they should be incontinently used by private corporations to concentrate population in the centers where a high tariff can be charged. The number of things that are waiting to be done — the planting of town forests, the communal restoration of river banks and beaches, the transformation of bare roads into parkways — will of course differ in each region and locality; and my aim here is only to point to a general objective.

In the building of our cities and villages the main mores we have carried over have been those of the pioneer. We have seen how the animus of the pioneer, " mine and move," is antagonistic to the settled life out of which ordered industries and a great architecture grow. We have seen also how this animus was deepened in the nineteenth century by the extraordinary temptation to profit by the increase in land increments which followed the growth of population, the result being — as Mr. Henry George saw when he came back to the cities of the East from a part of California that was still in the throes of settlement — progress *and* poverty.

Now, to increase the population of a town and to raise the nominal values in ground rents is almost a moral imperative in our American communities. That is why our zoning laws, which attempt to regulate the use of land and provide against unfair competition in obtaining the unearned increment, almost universally leave a loophole through which the property owners, by mutual consent, may transform the character of the neighborhood for more intensive uses and higher ground rents. All our city planning, and more and more our architecture itself, is done with reference to prospective changes in the value of real estate. It is nothing to the real-estate speculator that the growth of a city destroys the very purpose for which it may legitimately exist, as the growth of Atlantic City into a suburb of Broadway and Chestnut Street ruined its charm as a seaside fishing village. Sufficient unto the day is the evil he creates.

Most of the important changes that must be effected in relation to industry and the land cannot be accomplished without departing from these dominant mores — from the customs and laws and uneasy standards of ethics which we carry over from the days of our continental conquest. The pioneer inheritance of the miner, coupled with the imperial inheritance of the hunter-warrior, out for loot, lie at the bottom of our present-day social structure; and it is useless to expect any vital changes in the milieu of architecture until the miner and the hunter are subordinated to relatively more civilized types, concerned with the culture of life rather than with its exploitation and destruction.

I am aware that the statement of the problem in these elementary terms will seem a little crude and unfamiliar in America where, in the midst of our buzzing urban environment, we lose sight of the underlying primitive reality, or — which is worse — speak vaguely of the " cave man " unleashed in modern civilization. I do not deny that there are other elements in our make-up and situation that play an important part; but it is enough to bring forward here the notion that our concern with physical utilities and with commercial values is something more than an abstract defect in our philosophy. On the contrary, it seems to me to inhere in the dominant occupations of the country, and it is less to be overcome by moralizing and exhortation than to be grown out of, by taking pains to provide for the ascendancy and renewal of the more humane occupations.

Our communities have grown blindly and, escaping the natural limitations which curbed even the Roman engineers, have not been controlled, on the other hand, by any normative ideal. One step in the direction of departing from our pioneer customs and habits would be to consider what the nature of a city is, and what functions it performs. The dominant, abstract culture of the nineteenth century was blithely unconcerned with these questions; but, as I have already pointed out, the Puritans not merely recognized their importance but regulated the plan and layout of the city accordingly. The notion that there is anything arbitrary in imposing a limitation upon the area and population of a city is absurd: the limits have already been laid down in the physical conditions of human nature, as Mr. Frederic Harrison once wisely observed, in the fact that men do not walk comfortably faster than three miles an hour, nor can they spend on the physical exertion of locomotion and exercise more than a few hours in every twenty-four. With respect to the needs of recreation, home life, and health, the growth of a city to the point where the outlying citizen must travel two hours a day in the subway between his office and his place of work is unintelligent and arbitrary.

A city, properly speaking, does not exist by the accretion of houses, but by the association of human beings. When the accretion of houses reaches such a point of congestion or expansion that human association becomes difficult, the place ceases to be a city. The institutions that make up the city — schools, clubs, libraries, gymnasia, theaters, churches, and so forth — can be traced in one form or another back to the primitive community: they function on the basis of immediate intercourse, and they can serve through their individual units only a limited number of people. Should the population of a local community be doubled, all its civic equipment must be doubled too; otherwise the life that functions through these institutions and opportunities will lapse and disappear.

It is not my purpose to discuss in detail the various devices by which our practice of endless growth and unlimited increment may be limited. Once the necessary conversion in faith and morals has taken place, the other things will come easily — for example, the social appropriation of unearned land increments, and the exercise of the town planner's art to limit the tendency of a community to straggle beyond its boundaries.

While a great many other ideas and measures are of prime importance for the good life of the community, that which concerns its architectural expression is the notion of the community as limited in numbers and in area; and as formed, not merely by the agglomeration of people, but by their relation to definite social and economic institutions. To express these relations clearly, to embody them in buildings and roads and gardens in which each individual structure will be subordinated to the whole — this is the end of community planning.

With the coherence and stability indicated by this method of planning, architectural effect would not lie in the virtuosity of the architect or in the peculiar ornateness and originality of any particular building: it would tend to be diffused, so that the humblest shop would share in the triumph with the most conspicuous public building. There are examples of this order of comprehensive architectural design in hundreds of little villages and towns in pre-industrial Europe — to say nothing of a good handful in pre-industrial America — and community planning would make it once more our daily practice. That it can be done again the examples of Letchworth and Welwyn in England, and numerous smaller gardened cities created by municipal authorities in England and other parts of Europe, bear evidence; and where the precepts of Mr.

Ebenezer Howard have been to any degree followed, architecture has been quick to benefit.

The difference between community planning and the ordinary method of city extension and suburb building has been very well put in a recent report to the American Institute of Architects, by the Committee on Community Planning. " Community planning," says the report, " does not ask by what desperate means a city of 600,000 people can add another 400,000 during the next generation, nor how a city of 7,000,000 may enlarge its effective borders to include 29,000,000. It begins, rather, at the other end, and it asks with Mr. Ebenezer Howard how big must a city be to perform all of its social, educational, and industrial functions. It attempts to establish minima and maxima for different kinds of communities, depending upon their character and function. If the established practices of industry, commerce, and finance tend to produce monstrous agglomerations which do not contribute to human welfare or happiness, community planning must question these established practices, since the values they create have nothing to do with the essential welfare of the community itself, and since the condition thus created is inimical to the stable architectural development of the community."

The normative idea of the garden city and the garden village is the corrective for the flatulent and inorganic conception of city development that we labor with, and under, today. So far from being a strange importation from Europe, the garden city is nothing more or less than a sophisticated recovery of a form that we once enjoyed on our Atlantic seaboard, and lost through our sudden and almost uncontrollable access of natural resources and people. Here and there an enterprising and somewhat benevolent industrial corporation has attempted to carry out some of the principles of garden-city development; and the United States Housing Corporation and the Shipping Board had begun to build many admirable communities when the end of the war brought this vast initiative to a close. These precedents are better than nothing, it goes without saying; but there will have to be a pretty thorough reorientation in our economic and social life before the garden city will be anything more than a slick phrase, without content or power.

Until our communities are ready to undertake the sort of community planning that leads to garden cities, it will be empty eloquence to talk about the future of American architecture. Sheltered as an enjoyment for the prosperous minority, or used as a skysign for the advertisement of business, architecture will still await its full opportunity for creative achievement.

The signs of promise are plenty, and if I have dealt with the darker side of the picture and have occasionally overemphasized the weakness and defects of the American tradition, it is only because, in our present appreciation of what the American architect has already given form to, we are likely to forget the small area these achievements occupy. So far we have achieved patches of good building; more than once we have achieved the *mot juste,* but we have not learned the more difficult art of consecutive discourse. With respect to the architecture of the whole community, medieval Boston and medieval New Amsterdam had more to boast than their magnificently endowed successors. Just as Mr. Babbitt's great ancestor, Scadder, transformed a swamp into a thriving metropolis by the simple method of calling it New Eden, so do we tend to lighten our burdens by calling them the "blessings of progress"; but it does not avail. Our mechanical and metropolitan civilization, with all its genuine advances, has let certain essential human elements drop out of its scheme; and until we recover these elements our civilization will be at loose ends, and our architecture will unerringly express this situation.

Home, meeting place, and factory; polity, culture, and art, have still to be united and wrought together, and this task is one of the fundamental tasks of our civilization. Once that union is effected, the long breach between art and life, which began with the Renaissance, will be brought to an end. The magnitude of our task might seem a little disheartening, were it not for the fact that, "against or with our will," our civilization is perpetually being modified and altered. If in less than a hundred years the feudal civilization of Japan could adopt our modern mechanical gear, there is nothing to prevent our own civilization from recovering once more its human base — nothing, that is, except our own desires, aims, habits, and ends. This is an ironic consolation, perhaps, but the remedy it offers is real.

LETTERS

George *Washington*

To Martha Washington

PHILADELPHIA, *18 June, 1775.*

MY DEAREST,—

I am now set down to write to you on a subject which fills me with inexpressible concern, and this concern is greatly aggravated and increased when I reflect upon the uneasiness I know it will give you. It has been determined in Congress that the whole army raised for the defense of the American cause shall be put under my care, and that it is necessary for me to proceed immediately to Boston to take upon me the command of it.

You may believe me, my dear Patsy, when I assure you, in the most solemn manner, that, so far from seeking this appointment, I have used every endeavor in my power to avoid it, not only from my unwillingness to part with you and the family, but from a consciousness of its being a trust too great for my capacity, and that I should enjoy more real happiness in one month with you at home than I have the most distant prospect of finding abroad, if my stay were to be seven times seven years. But as it has been a kind of destiny that has thrown me upon this service, I shall hope that my undertaking it is designed to answer some good purpose. You might, and I suppose did perceive, from the tenor of my letters, that I was apprehensive I could not avoid this appointment, as I did not pretend to intimate when I should return. That was the case. It was utterly out of my power to refuse this appointment, without exposing my character to such censures as would have reflected dishonor upon myself and given pain to my friends. This, I am sure, could not, and ought not, to be pleasing to you, and must have lessened me considerably in my own esteem. I shall rely, therefore, confidently on that Providence which has heretofore preserved and been bountiful to me, not doubting but that I shall return safe to you in the fall. I shall feel no pain from the toil or the danger of the campaigning; my unhappiness will flow from the uneasiness I know you will feel from being left alone. I therefore beg that you will summon your whole fortitude, and pass your time as agreeably as possible. Nothing will give me so much sincere satisfaction as to hear this, and to hear it from your own pen. My earnest and ardent desire is that you would pursue any plan that is most likely to produce content and a tolerable degree of tranquillity; as it must add greatly to my uneasy feelings to hear that you are dissatisfied or complaining at what I really could not avoid.

As life is always uncertain, and common prudence dictates to every man the necessity of settling his temporal concerns while it is in his power, and while the mind is calm and undisturbed, I have, since I came to this place (for I had not time to do it before I left home), got Colonel Pendleton to draft a will for me, by the directions I gave him, which will I now enclose. The provision made for you in case of my death will, I hope, be agreeable.

I shall add nothing more, as I have several letters to write, but to desire that you will remember me to your friends, and to assure you that I am, with the most unfeigned regard, my dear Patsy, your affectionate, &c.

Thomas Jefferson

To President James Monroe

MONTICELLO, *October 24, 1823.*

DEAR SIR, —

The question presented by the letters you have sent me is the most momentous which has ever been offered to my contemplation since that of Independence. That made us a nation; this sets our compass and points the course which we are to steer through the ocean of time opening on us. And never could we embark on it under circumstances more auspicious. Our first and fundamental maxim should be, never to entangle ourselves in the broils of Europe. Our second, never to suffer Europe to intermeddle with cis-Atlantic affairs. America, North and South, has a set of interests distinct from those of Europe, and peculiarly her own. She should therefore have a system of her own, separate and apart from that of Europe. While the last is laboring to become the domicile of despotism, our endeavor should surely be, to make our hemisphere that of freedom. One nation, most of all, could disturb us in this pursuit; she now offers to lead, aid, and accompany us in it. By acceding to her proposition, we detach her from the band of despots, bring her mighty weight into the scale of free government, and emancipate a continent at one stroke, which might otherwise linger long in doubt and difficulty. Great Britain is the nation which can do us the most harm of any one, or all, on earth; and with her on our side we need not fear the whole world. With her, then, we should most sedulously cherish a cordial friendship; and nothing would tend more to knit our affections than to be fighting once more, side by side, in the same cause. Not that I would purchase even her amity at the price of taking part in her wars. But the war in which the present proposition might engage us, should that be its consequence, is not her war, but ours. Its object is to introduce and establish the American system, of keeping out of our land all foreign powers, of never permitting those of Europe to intermeddle with the affairs of our nations. It is to maintain our own principle, not to depart from it. And if, to facilitate this, we can effect a division in the body of the European powers, and draw over to our side its most powerful member, surely we should do it. But I am clearly of Mr. Canning's opinion, that it will prevent instead of provoking war. With Great Britain withdrawn from their scale and shifted into that of our two continents, all Europe combined would not undertake such a war. For how would they propose to get at either enemy without superior fleets? Nor is the occasion to be slighted which this proposition offers, of declaring our protest against the atrocious violations of the rights of nations, by the interference of any one in the internal affairs of another, so flagitiously begun by Bonaparte, and now continued by the equally lawless Alliance, calling itself Holy.

But we have first to ask ourselves a question. Do we wish to acquire to our own confederacy any one or more of the Spanish provinces? I candidly confess that I have ever looked on Cuba as the most interesting addition which could ever be made to our system of States. The control which, with Florida Point, this island would give us over the Gulf of Mexico, and the countries and isthmus bordering on it, as well as all those whose waters flow into it, would fill up the measure of our political well-being. Yet, as I am sensible that this can never be obtained, even with her own consent, but by war; and its independence, which is our second interest (and especially its independence of England), can be secured without it, I have no hesitation in abandoning my first wish to future chances, and accepting its independence, with peace and the friendship of England, rather than its association, at the expense of war and her enmity.

I could honestly, therefore, join in the declaration proposed, that we aim not at the acquisition of any of those possessions, that we will not stand in the way of any amicable arrangement between them and the mother country; but that we will oppose, with all our means, the forcible interposition of any other power, as auxiliary, stipendiary, or under any other form or pretext, and most especially, their transfer to any power by conquest, cession, or acquisition in any other way. I should think it therefore advisable that the Executive should encourage the British government to a continuance in the dispositions expressed in these letters, by an assurance of his concurrence with them as far as his authority goes; and that as it may lead to war, the declaration of which requires an act of Congress, the case shall be laid before them for consideration at their first meeting, and under the reasonable aspect in which it is seen by himself.

I have been so long weaned from political subjects, and have so long ceased to take any interest in them, that I am sensible I am not qualified to offer opinions on them worthy of any attention. But the question now proposed involves consequences so lasting, and effects so decisive of our future destinies, as to rekindle all the interest I have heretofore felt on such occasions, and to induce me to the hazard of opinions, which will prove only my wish to contribute still my mite towards anything which may be useful to our country. And praying you to accept it at only what it is worth, I add the assurance of my constant and affectionate friendship and respect.

TH. JEFFERSON

Herman Melville

To Nathaniel Hawthorne

[1851]

MY DEAR HAWTHORNE, —

I should have been rumbling down to you in my pineboard chariot a long time ago, were it not that for some weeks past I have been more busy than you can well imagine, — out of doors, — building and patching and tinkering away in all directions. Besides, I had my crops to get in, — corn and potatoes (I hope to show you some famous ones by and by), — and many other things to attend to, all accumulating upon this one particular season. I work myself; and at night my bodily sensations are akin to those I have so often felt before, when a hired man, doing my day's work from sun to sun. But I mean to continue visiting you until you tell me that my visits are both supererogatory and superfluous. With no son of man do I stand upon any etiquette or ceremony, except the Christian ones of charity and honesty. I am told, my fellow-man, that there is an aristocracy of the brain. Some men have bodily advocated and asserted it. Schiller seems to have done so, though I don't know much about him. At any rate, it is true that there have been those who, while earnest in behalf of political equality, still accept the intellectual estates. And I can well perceive, I think, how a man of superior mind can, by its intense cultivation, bring myself, as it were, into a certain spontaneous aristocracy of feeling, — exceedingly nice and fastidious, — similar to that which, in an English Howard, conveys a torpedo-fish thrill at the slightest contact with a social plebeian. So, when you see or hear of my ruthless democracy on all sides, you may possibly feel a touch of a shrink, or something of that sort. It is but nature to be shy of a mortal who bodily declares that a thief in jail is as honorable a personage as Gen. George Washington. This is ludicrous. But Truth is the silliest thing under the sun. Try to get a living by the Truth — and go to the Soup Societies. Heavens! Let any clergyman try to preach the Truth from its very stronghold, the pulpit, and they would ride him out of his church on his own pulpit bannister. It can hardly be doubted that all Reformers are bottomed upon the truth, more or less; and to the world at large are not reformers almost universally laughing-stocks? Why so? Truth is ridiculous to men. Thus easily in my room here do I, conceited and garrulous, revere the test of my Lord Shaftesbury.

It seems an inconsistency to assert unconditional democracy in all things, and yet confess a dislike to all mankind — in the mass. But not so. — But it's an endless sermon, — and no more of it. I began by saying that the reason I have not been to Lenox is this, — in the evening I feel completely done up, as the phrase is, and incapable of the long jolting to get to your house and back. In a week or so, I go to New York, to bury myself in a third-story room, and work and slave on my "Whale" while it is driving through the press. *That* is the only way I can finish it now, — I am so pulled hither and thither by circumstances. The calm, the coolness, the silent grass-growing mood in which a man *ought* always to compose, — that, I fear, can seldom be mine. Dollars damn me; and the malicious Devil is forever grinning in upon me, holding the door ajar. My dear Sir, a presentiment is on me, — I shall at last be worn out and perish, like an old nutmeg-grater, grated to pieces by constant attrition of the wood, that is, the nutmeg. What I feel most moved to write, that is banned, — it will not pay. Yet, altogether, write the *other* way I cannot. So the product is a final hash, and all my books are botches. I'm rather sore, perhaps, in this letter; but see my hand! — four blisters on this palm, made by hoes and hammers within the last few days. It is a rainy morning; so I am indoors, and all work suspended. I feel cheerfully disposed, and therefore I write a little bluely. Would the Gin were here! If ever, my dear Hawthorne, in the eternal times that are to come, you and I shall sit down in Paradise, in some little shady corner by ourselves; and if we shall by any means be able to smuggle a basket of champagne there (I won't believe in a Temperance Heaven), and if we shall then cross our celestial legs in the celestial grass that is forever tropical, and strike our glasses and our heads together, till both musically ring in concert, — then, O my dear fellow-mortal, how shall we pleasantly discourse of all the things manifold which now so distress us, — when all the earth shall be but a reminiscence, yea, its final dissolution an antiquity. Then shall songs be composed as when wars are over; humorous, comic songs, — "Oh, when I lived in that queer little hole called the world," or "Oh, when I toiled and sweated below," or, "Oh, when I knocked and was knocked in the fight" — yes, let us look forward to such things. Let us swear that, though now we sweat, yet it is because of the dry heat which is indispensable to the nourishment of the vine which is to bear the grapes that are to give us the champagne hereafter.

But I was talking of the "Whale." As the fishermen say, "he's in his flurry" when I left him some three weeks ago. I'm going to take him by the jaw, however, before long, and finish him up in some fashion or other. What's the use of elaborating what, in its very essence, is so short-lived as a modern book? Though I wrote the Gospels in this century, I should die in the gutter. — I talk all about myself, and this is selfishness and egotism. Granted. But how help it? I am writing to you; I know little about you, but something about myself. So I write about myself, — at least, to you. Don't trouble yourself, though, about writing; and don't trouble yourself about visiting; and when you *do* visit, don't trouble yourself about talking. I will do all the writing and visiting and talking myself. — By the way, in the last *Dollar Magazine* I read "The Unpardonable

Sin." He was a sad fellow, that Ethan Brand. I have no doubt you are by this time responsible for many a shake and tremor of the tribe of " general readers." It is a frightful poetical creed that the cultivation of the brain eats out the heart. But it's my *prose* opinion that in most cases, in those men who have fine brains and work them well, the heart extends down to hams. And though you smoke them with the fire of tribulation, yet, like veritable hams, the head only gives the richer and better flavor. I stand for the heart. To the dogs with the head! I had rather be a fool with a heart, than Jupiter Olympus with his head. The reason the mass of men fear God, and *at bottom dislike* Him, is because they rather distrust His Heart, and fancy Him all Brain like a watch. (You perceive I employ a capital initial in the pronoun referring to the Deity; don't you think there is a slight dash of flunkeyism in that usage?) Another thing. I was in New York for four-and-twenty hours the other day, and saw a portrait of N. H. And I have seen and heard many flattering (in a publisher's point of view) allusions to the *Seven Gables*. And I have seen *Tales,* and " A New Volume " announced, by N. H. So upon the whole, I say to myself, this N. H. is in the ascendant. My dear Sir, they begin to patronize. All Fame is patronage. Let me be infamous: there is no patronage in *that*. What " reputation " H. M. has is horrible. Think of it! To go down to posterity is bad enough, any way; but to go down as a " man who lived among the cannibals "! When I speak of posterity, in reference to myself, I only mean the babies who will probably be born in the moment immediately ensuing upon my giving up the ghost. I shall go down to some of them, in all likelihood. *Typee* will be given to them, perhaps, with their gingerbread. I have come to regard this matter of Fame as the most transparent of all vanities. I read Solomon more and more, and every time see deeper and deeper and unspeakable meanings in him. I did not think of Fame, a year ago, as I do now. My development has been all within a few years past. I am like one of those seeds taken out of the Egyptian Pyramids, which, after being three thousand years a seed and nothing but a seed, being planted in English soil, it developed itself, grew to greenness, and then fell to mould. So I. Until I was twenty-five, I had no development at all. From my twenty-fifth year I date my life. Three weeks have scarcely passed, at any time between then and now, that I have not unfolded within myself. But I feel that I am now come to the inmost leaf of the bulb, and that shortly the flower must fall to the mould. It seems to me now that Solomon was the truest man who ever spoke, and yet that he a little *managed* the truth with a view to popular conservatism; or else there have been many corruptions and interpolations of the text. — In reading some of Goethe's sayings, so worshipped by his votaries, I came across this, " *Live in the all.*" That is to say, your separate identity is but a wretched one, — good; but get out of yourself, spread and expand yourself, and bring to yourself the tinglings of life that are felt in the flowers and the woods, that are felt in the planets Saturn and Venus, and the Fixed Stars. What nonsense! Here is a fellow with a raging toothache. " My dear boy," Goethe says to him, " you are sorely afflicted with that tooth; but you must *live in the all,* and then you will be happy! " As with all great genius, there is an immense deal of flummery in Goethe, and in proportion to my own contact with him, a monstrous deal of it in me.

H. MELVILLE

P. S. " Amen! " saith Hawthorne.

N. B. This " all " feeling, though, there is some truth in. You must often have felt it, lying on the grass on a warm summer's day. Your legs seem to send out shoots into the earth. Your hair feels like leaves upon your head. This is the *all* feeling. But what plays the mischief with the truth is that men will insist upon the universal application of a temporary feeling or opinion.

P. S. You must not fail to admire my discretion in paying the postage on this letter.

Abraham Lincoln

To Horace Greeley

EXECUTIVE MANSION, WASHINGTON,
August 22, 1862

DEAR SIR, —

I have just read yours of the 19th, addressed to myself through the New York *Tribune.* If there be in it any statements or assumptions of fact which I may know to be erroneous, I do not, now and here, controvert them. If there be in it any inferences which I may believe to be falsely drawn, I do not, now and here, argue against them. If there be perceptible in it an impatient and dictatorial tone, I waive it in deference to an old friend whose heart I have always supposed to be right.

As to the policy I " seem to be pursuing," as you say, I have not meant to leave anyone in doubt.

I would save the Union. I would save it the shortest way under the Constitution. The sooner the national authority can be restored, the nearer the Union will be " the Union as it was." If there be those who would not save the Union unless they could at the same time save slavery, I do not agree with them. If there be those who would not save the Union unless they could at the same time destroy slavery, I do not agree with them. My paramount object in this struggle is to save the Union, and is not either to save or to destroy slavery. If I could have the Union without freeing any slave, I would do it; and if I could save it by freeing all the slaves, I would do it; and if I could save it by freeing some and leaving others alone, I would also do that. What I do about slavery and the colored race, I do because I believe it helps to save the Union; and what I forbear, I forbear because I do not believe it would help to save the Union. I shall do less whenever I shall believe what I am doing hurts the cause, and I shall do more whenever I shall believe doing more will help the cause. I shall try to correct errors when shown to be errors, and I shall adopt new views so fast as they shall appear to be true views.

I have here stated my purpose according to my view of official duty; and I intend no modification of my oft-expressed personal wish that all men everywhere could be free.

Yours,
A. LINCOLN

Artemus Ward

To His Wife

DEAR BETSY, —

I write you this from Boston, " the Modern Atkins," as it is denomyunated, altho' I skurcely know what those air. I'll giv you a kursoory view of this city. I'll klassify the paragrafs under seprit headins, arter the stile of those Emblems of Trooth and Poority, the Washington correspongdents!

COPPS' HILL.

The winder of my room commands a exileratin view of Copps' Hill, where Cotton Mather, the father of the Reformers and sich, lies berrid. There is men even now who worship Cotton, and there is wimin who wear him next their harts. But I do not weep for him. He's bin ded too lengthy. I ain't going to be absurd, like old Mr. Skillins, in our naberhood, who is ninety-six years of age, and gets drunk every 'lection day, and weeps Bitturly because he hain't got no Parents. He's a nice Orphan, *he* is.

BUNKER HILL.

Bunker Hill is over yonder in Charleston. In 1776 a thrillin' dramy was acted out over there, in which the " Warren Combination " played star parts.

MR. FANUEL.

Old Mr. Fanuel is ded, but his Hall is still into full blarst. This is the Cradle in which the Goddess of Liberty was rocked, my Dear. The Goddess hasn't bin very well durin' the past few years, and the num'ris quack doctors she called in

From *Artemus Ward: His Travels,* 1865.

didn't help her any; but the old gal's physicians now are men who understand their bizness, Major-generally speakin', and I think the day is near when she'll be able to take her three meals a day, and sleep nights as comf'bly as in the old time.

THE COMMON.

It is here, as ushil; and the low cuss who called it a Wacant Lot, and wanted to know why they didn't ornament it with sum Bildins', is a onhappy Outcast in Naponsit.

THE LEGISLATUR.

The State House is filled with Statesmen, but sum of 'em wear queer hats. They buy 'em, I take it, of hatters who carry on hat stores down stairs in Dock Square, and whose hats is either ten years ahead of the prevalin' stile, or ten years behind it — jest as a intellectooal person sees fit to think about it. I had the pleasure of talkin' with sevril members of the legislatur. I told 'em the Eye of 1,000 ages was onto we American peple of to-day. They seemed deeply impressed by the remark, and wantid to know if I had seen the Grate Orgin?

HARVARD COLLEGE.

This celebrated institootion of learnin' is pleasantly situated in the Bar-room of Parker's, in School street, and has poopils from all over the country.

I had a letter yes'd'y, by the way, from our mootual son, Artemus, Jr., who is at Bowdoin College in Maine. He writes that he's a Bowdoin Arab. & is it cum to this? Is this Boy, as I nurtered with a Parent's care into his childhood's hour — is he goin' to be a Grate American humorist? Alars! I fear it is too troo. Why didn't I bind him out to the Patent Travellin' Vegetable Pill Man, as was struck with his appearance at our last County Fair, & wanted him to go with him and be a Pillist? Ar, these Boys — they little know how the old folks worrit about 'em. But my father he never had no occasion to worrit about me. You know, Betsy, that when I fust commenced my career as a moral exhibitor with a six-legged cat and a Bass drum, I was only a simple peasant child — skurce 15 Summers had flow'd over my yoothful hed. But I had sum mind of my own. My father understood this. "Go," he said — " go, my son, and hog the public! " (he ment, " knock em," but the old man was allus a little given to slang). He put his withered han' tremblinly onto my hed, and went sadly into the house. I thought I saw tears tricklin' down his venerable chin, but it might hav been tobacker jooce. He chaw'd.

LITERATOOR.

The *Atlantic Monthly,* Betsy, is a reg'lar visitor to our westun home. I like it because it has got sense. It don't print stories with piruts and honist young men into 'em, makin' the piruts splendid fellers and the honist young men dis'gree'ble idiots — so that our darters very nat'rally prefer the piruts to the honist young idiots; but it gives us good square American literatoor. The chaps that write for the *Atlantic,* Betsy, understand their bizness. They can sling ink, they can. I went in and saw 'em. I told 'em that theirs was a high and holy mission. They seemed quite gratified, and asked me if I had seen the Grate Orgin.

WHERE THE FUST BLUD WAS SPILT.

I went over to Lexington yes'd'y. My Boosum hove with sollum emotions. "& this," I said to a man who was drivin' a yoke of oxen, "this is where our revolutionary forefathers asserted their independence and spilt their Blud. Classic ground! "

"Wall," the man said, "it's good for white beans and potatoes, but as regards raisin' wheat, t'ain't worth a damn. But hav' you seen the Grate Orgin? "

THE POOTY GIRL IN SPECTACLES.

I returned in the Hoss Cars, part way. A pooty girl in spectacles sot near me, and was tellin' a young man how much he reminded her of a man she used to know in Waltham. Pooty soon the young man got out, and smilin' in a seductive manner, I said to the girl in spectacles, " Don't *I* remind you of somebody you used to know? "

"Yes," she said, " you do remind me of one man, but he was sent to the penitentiary for stealin' a Bar'l of mackril — he died there, so I conclood you ain't *him.*" I didn't pursoo the conversation. I only heard her silvery voice once more durin' the remainder of the jerney. Turnin' to a respectable lookin' female of advanced summers, she asked her if she had seen the Grate Orgin.

We old chaps, my dear, air apt to forget that it is sum time since we was infants, and et lite food. Nothin' of further int'rist took place on the cars excep' a colored gentleman, a total stranger to me, asked if I'd lend him my diamond Brestpin to wear to a funeral in South Boston. I told him I wouldn't — not a *purpuss.*

COMMON SKOOLS.

A excellent skool sistim is in vogy here. John Slurk, my old pardner, has a little son who has only bin to skool two months, and yet he exhibertid his father's performin' Bear in the show all last summer. I hope they pay partic'lar 'Tention to Spelin' in these Skools, because if a man can't Spel wel he's of no 'kount.

SUMMIN' UP.

I ment to have allooded to the Grate Orgin in this letter, but I haven't seen it. Mr. Reveer, whose tavern I stop at, informed me that it can be distinctly heard through a smoked glass in his nativ town in New Hampshire, any clear day. But settin' the Grate Orgin aside (and indeed, I don't think I heard it mentioned all the time I was there), Boston is one of the grandest, sure-footedest, clear headedest, comfortablest cities on the globe. Onlike ev'ry other large city I was ever in, the most of the hackmen don't seem to hav' bin speshully intended by natur for the Burglery perfession, and it's about the only large city I know of where you don't enjoy a brilliant opportunity of bein' swindled in sum way, from the Risin of the sun to the goin down thereof. There4 I say, loud and continnered applaus' for Boston!

DOMESTIC MATTERS.

Kiss the children for me. What you tell me 'bout the Twins greeves me sorely. When I sent 'em that Toy Enjine I had not contempyulated that they would so fur forgit what wos doo the dignity of our house as to squirt dishwater on the Incum Tax Collector. It is a disloyal act, and shows a prematoor leanin' tords cussedness that alarms me. I send to Amelia Ann, our oldest dawter, sum new music, viz. " I am Lonely sints My Mother-in-law Died "; " Dear Mother, What tho' the Hand that Spanked me in my Childhood's Hour is withered now? " &c. These song writers, by the way, air doin' the Mother Bizness rather too muchly.

Your Own Troo husban',
ARTEMUS WARD

William James

To Henry James

SALISBURY, CONN., May 4, 1907.

DEAREST H., —

I've been so overwhelmed with work, and the mountain of the *Unread* has piled up so, that only in these days here have I really been able to settle down to your *American Scene,* which in its peculiar way seems to me *supremely great.* You know how opposed your whole " third manner " of execution is to the literary ideals which animate my crude and Orson-like breast, mine being to say a thing in one sentence as straight and explicit as it can be made, and then to drop it forever; yours being to avoid naming it straight, but by dint of breathing and sighing all round and round it, to arouse in the reader who may have had a similar perception already (Heaven help him if he hasn't!) the illusion of a solid object, made (like the " Ghost " at the Polytechnic) wholly out of impalpable materials, air, and the prismatic interferences of light, ingeniously focused by mirrors upon empty space. But you *do* it, that's the queerness! And the complication of innuendo and associative reference on the enormous scale

From *The Letters of William James,* edited by Henry James, 1920.

to which you give way to it does so *build out* the matter for the reader that the result is to solidify, by the mere bulk of the process, the like perception from which he has to start. As air, by dint of its volume, will weigh like a corporeal body; so his own poor little initial perception, swathed in this gigantic envelopment of suggestive atmosphere, grows like a germ into something vastly bigger and more substantial. But it's the rummest method for one to employ systematically as you do nowadays; and you employ it at your peril. In this crowded and hurried reading age, pages that require such close attention remain unread and neglected. You can't skip a word if you are to get the effect, and 19 out of 20 worthy readers grow intolerant. The method seems perverse: " Say it *out,* for God's sake," they cry, " and have done with it." And so I say now, give us *one* thing in your older directer manner, just to show that, in spite of your paradoxical success in this unheard-of method, you *can* still write according to accepted canons. Give us that interlude; and then continue like the " curiosity of literature " which you have become. For gleams and innuendoes and felicitous verbal insinuations you are unapproachable, but the *core* of literature is solid. Give it to us *once* again! The bare perfume of things will not support existence, and the effect of solidity you reach is but perfume and simulacrum.

For God's sake don't *answer* these remarks, which (as Uncle Howard used to say of Father's writings) are but the peristaltic belchings of my own crabbed organism. For one thing, your account of America is largely one of its omissions, silences, vacancies. You work them up like solids, for those readers who already germinally perceive them (to others you are *totally* incomprehensible). I said to myself over and over in reading: " How much greater the triumph, if instead of dwelling thus only upon America's vacuities, he could make positive suggestion of what in ' Europe ' or Asia may exist to fill them." That would be nutritious to so many American readers whose souls are only too ready to leap to suggestion, but who are now too inexperienced to know what is meant by the contrast-effect from which alone your book is written. If you could supply the background which is the foil, in terms more full and positive! At present it is supplied only by the abstract geographic term " Europe." But of course anything of that kind is excessively difficult; and you will probably say that you *are* supplying it all along by your novels. Well, the verve and animal spirits with which you can keep your method going, first on one place then on another, through all those tightly printed pages is something marvelous; and there are pages surely doomed to be immortal — those on the " drummers," e.g., at the beginning of " Florida." They are in the best sense Rabelaisian.

But a truce, a truce! I had no idea, when I sat down, of pouring such a bath of my own subjectivity over you. Forgive! forgive! and don't reply; don't at any rate in the sense of defending yourself, but only in that of attacking *me,* if you feel so minded. I have just finished the proofs of a little book called *Pragmatism* which even you *may* enjoy reading. It is a very " sincere " and, from the point of view of ordinary philosophy-professorial manners, a very unconventional utterance, not particularly original at any one point, yet, in the midst of the literature of the way of thinking which it represents, with just that amount of squeak or shrillness in the voice that enables one book to *tell,* when others don't, to supersede its brethren, and be treated later as " representative." I shouldn't be surprised if ten years hence it should be rated as " epoch-making," for of the definitive triumph of that general way of thinking I can entertain no doubt whatever — I believe it to be something quite like the protestant reformation.

You can't tell how happy I am at having thrown off the nightmare of my " professorship." As a " professor " I always felt myself a sham, with its chief duties of being a walking encyclopedia of erudition. I am now at liberty to be a *reality,* and the comfort is unspeakable — literally unspeakable, to be my own man, after 35 years of being owned by others. I can now live for truth pure and simple, instead of for truth accommodated to the most unheard-of requirements set by others. . . . Your affectionate

W. J.

POETRY

Nathan Hale

The breezes went steadily through the
    tall pines,
  A-saying " Oh! hu-ush! " a-saying
    " Oh! hu-ush! "
As stilly stole by a bold legion of horse,
  For Hale in the bush, for Hale in the
    bush.

" Keep still! " said the thrush, as she
    nestled her young
  In a nest by the road, in a nest by the
    road;
" For the tyrants are near, and with them
    appear
  What bodes us no good, what bodes us
    no good."

The brave captain heard it, and thought
    of his home
  In a cot by the brook, in a cot by the
    brook,   10
With mother and sister and memories
    dear,
  He so gaily forsook, he so gaily forsook.

Cooling shades of the night were coming
    apace,
  The tattoo had beat, the tattoo had
    beat;
The noble one sprang from his dark lurk-
    ing-place
  To make his retreat, to make his re-
    treat.

He warily trod on the dry rustling leaves,
  As he passed through the wood, as he
    passed through the wood,
And silently gained his rude launch on
    the shore,
  As she played with the flood, as she
    played with the flood.   20

The guards of the camp on that dark
    dreary night,
  Had a murderous will, had a murder-
    ous will:
They took him and bore him afar from
    the shore,
  To a hut on the hill, to a hut on the hill.

No mother was there, nor a friend who
    could cheer,
  In that little stone cell, in that little
    stone cell;
But he trusted in love from his Father
    above —
  In his heart all was well, in his heart
    all was well.

An ominous owl with his solemn bass
    voice
  Sat moaning hard by, sat moaning
    hard by: 30
" The tyrant's proud minions most gladly
    rejoice,
  For he must soon die, for he must soon
    die."

The brave fellow told them, no thing he
restrained —
The cruel gen'ral, the cruel gen'ral! —
His errand from camp, of the ends to be
gained,
And said that was all, and said that
was all.

They took him and bound him and bore
him away,
Down the hill's grassy side, down the
hill's grassy side.
'Twas there the base hirelings, in royal
array,
His cause did deride, his cause did deride.   40

Five minutes were given, short moments,
no more,
For him to repent, for him to repent.
He prayed for his mother — he asked not
another, —
To heaven he went, to heaven he went.

The faith of a martyr the tragedy showed,
As he trod the last stage, as he trod the
last stage.
And Britons will shudder at gallant
Hale's blood,
As his words do presage, as his words
do presage:

"Thou pale king of terrors, thou life's
gloomy foe,
Go frighten the slave, go frighten the
slave;   50
Tell tyrants, to you their allegiance they
owe —
No fears for the brave, no fears for the
brave!"

I Got Shoes

You got shoes, I got shoes,
All God's chillun got shoes,
When I git to Heb'n goin' to put on my
shoes

Goin' to walk all over God's Heb'n,
Heb'n, Heb'n, goin' to walk all over
God's Heb'n.

I got a derby, you got a derby,
All God's chillun got a derby,
When I git to Heb'n goin' to put on my
derby
Goin' to walk all over God's Heb'n,
Heb'n, Heb'n, goin' to walk all over
God's Heb'n.   10

I got a robe, you got a robe,
All God's chillun got a robe,
When I git to Heb'n goin' to put on my
robe
Goin' to walk all over God's Heb'n,
Heb'n, Heb'n, goin' to walk all over
God's Heb'n.

I got a crown, you got a crown,
All God's chillun got a crown,
When I git to Heb'n goin' to put on my
crown
Goin' to walk all over God's Heb'n,
Heb'n, Heb'n, goin' to walk all over
God's Heb'n.   20

I got a harp, you got a harp,
All God's chillun got a harp,
When I git to Heb'n goin' to put on my
harp
Goin' to play all over God's Heb'n,
Heb'n, Heb'n, goin' to play all over
God's Heb'n.

John Henry

When John Henry was a little babe,
A-holding to his mama's hand,
Says, "If I live till I'm twenty-one,
I'm going to make a steel-driving man,
my babe,
I'm going to make a steel-driving
man."

When John Henry was a little boy,
  A-sitting on his father's knee,
Says, " The Big Bend Tunnel on the
    C. & O. Road
  Is going to be the death of me, my
    babe,
  Is going to be the death of me."   10

John he made a steel-driving man,
  They took him to the tunnel to drive;
He drove so hard he broke his heart,
  He laid down his hammer and he died,
    my babe,
  He laid down his hammer and he died.

O now John Hardy is a steel-driving
    man,
  He belongs to the steel-driving crew,
And every time his hammer comes down,
  You can see that steel walking through,
    my babe,
  You can see that steel walking through.

The steam drill standing on the right-
    hand side,   21
  John Henry standing on the left;
He says, " I'll beat that steam drill down,
  Or I'll die with my hammer in my
    breast, my babe,
  Or I'll die with my hammer in my
    breast."

He placed his drill on the top of the rock,
  The steam drill standing close at hand;
He beat it down one inch and a half
  And laid down his hammer like a man,
    my babe,
  And laid down his hammer like a
    man.   30

Johnny looked up to his boss-man and
    said,
  " O boss-man, how can it be?
For the rock is so hard and the steel is so
    tough,

I can feel my muscles giving way, my
    babe,
I can feel my muscles giving way."

Johnny looked down to his turner and
    said,
  " O turner, how can it be?
The rock is so hard and the steel is so
    tough
  That everybody's turning after me, my
    babe,
  That everybody's turning after me." 40

They took poor Johnny to the steep hill-
    side,
  He looked to his heavens above;
He says, " Take my hammer and wrap it
    in gold
  And give it to the girl I love, my babe,
  And give it to the girl I love."

They took his hammer and wrapped it in
    gold
  And gave it to Julia Ann;
And the last word John Hardy said to her
  Was, " Julia, do the best you can, my
    babe,
  Julia, do the best you can.   50

" If I die a railroad man,
  Go bury me under the tie,
So I can hear old Number Four,
  As she goes rolling by, my babe,
  As she goes rolling by.

" If I die a railroad man,
  Go bury me under the sand,
With a pick and shovel at my head and
    feet,
  And a nine-pound hammer in my
    hand, my babe,
  And a nine-pound hammer in my
    hand."   60

The Roving Gambler

I am a roving gambler, I've gambled all
    around,
Whenever I meet with a deck of cards, I
    lay my money down.
I've gambled down in Washington, I've
    gambled over in Spain,
I'm on my way to Georgia to knock
    down my last game.

I had not been in Washington many
    more weeks than three,
Till I fell in love with a pretty little girl,
    and she fell in love with me;
She took me in her parlor, she cooled me
    with her fan,
She whispered low in her mother's ears,
    " I love this gambling man."

" Oh, daughter, oh, dear daughter, how
    could you treat me so,
To leave your dear old mother and with
    a gambler go? "   10
" Oh, mother, oh, dear mother, you know
    I love you well,
But the love I hold for this gambling
    man no human tongue can tell.

" I wouldn't marry a farmer, for he's al-
    ways in the rain;
The man I want to marry is the gam-
    bling man who wears the big gold
    chain.
I wouldn't marry a doctor, he is always
    gone from home;
All I want is the gambling man, for he
    won't leave me alone.

" I wouldn't marry a railroad man, and
    this is the reason why,
I never seen a railroad man that wouldn't
    tell his wife a lie.
I hear the train a-coming, she's coming
    around the curve,

Whistling and a-blowing and straining
    every nerve.   20

" Oh, mother, oh, dear mother, I'll tell
    you if I can
If you ever see me coming back, I'll be
    with the gambling man."

The Erie Canal

I've got a mule, her name is Sal,
Fifteen miles on the Erie Canal;
She's a good old worker and a good old
    pal,
Fifteen miles on the Erie Canal.
We've hauled some barges in our day,
Filled with lumber, coal, and hay,
And we know ev'ry inch of the way
From Albany to Buffalo.

Refrain:
    Low bridge, ev'rybody down!
    Low bridge, for we're going through a
      town;   10
    And you'll always know your neighbor,
    You'll always know your pal,
    If you ever navigated on the Erie
      Canal.

We better get along on our way, old gal,
Fifteen miles on the Erie Canal,
'Cause you bet your life I'd never part
    with Sal,
Fifteen miles on the Erie Canal.
Git up there, mule, here comes a lock,
We'll make Rome 'bout six o'clock.
One more trip and back we'll go,   20
Right back home to Buffalo.

The Jealous Lover of Lone Green Valley

Way down in lone green valley,
    Where roses bloom and fade,
There was a jealous lover,
    In love with a beautiful maid.

One night the moon was shining,
  The stars were shining, too,
When to the maiden's cottage
  The jealous lover drew.

"Come, love, and we will wander
  Down where the woods are gay,   10
And strolling we will ponder
  Upon our wedding day."

The night grew dark and dreary,
  Says she, "I'm afraid to stay,
I am so tired and weary
  I must retrace my way."

"Retrace your steps, no, never,
  For you have met your doom;
So bid farewell forever
  To parents, friends, and home,"   20

"O Willie, won't you tell me,
  I know there's something wrong;
You must not harm me, Willie,
  Cause we've been friends too long."

Down on her knees before him
  She pleaded for her life;
But deep into her bosom
  He plunged the fatal knife.

"O Willie, my poor darling,
  Why have you tak'n my life?   30
You know I've always loved you,
  And wanted to be your wife.

"I never have deceived you,
  And with my dying breath
I do forgive you, Willie,
  And close my eyes in death."

The Old Chisholm Trail

Come along, boys, and listen to my tale,
I'll tell you of my troubles on the old
  Chisholm trail.

Refrain:
  Coma ti yi youpy, youpy ya, youpy ya,
  Coma ti yi youpy, youpy ya.

I started up the trail October twenty-
  third,
I started up the trail with the 2-U herd.

Oh, a ten dollar hoss and a forty dollar
  saddle, —
And I'm goin' to punchin' Texas cattle.

I woke up one morning on the old Chisholm trail,
Rope in my hand and a cow by the
  tail.   10

I'm up in the mornin' afore daylight
And afore I sleep the moon shines bright.

Old Ben Bolt was a blamed good boss,
But he'd go to see the girls on a sore-
  backed hoss.

Old Ben Bolt was a fine old man
And you'd know there was whiskey
  wherever he'd land.

My hoss throwed me off at the creek
  called Mud,
My hoss throwed me off round the 2-U
  herd.

Last time I saw him he was going cross
  the level
A-kicking up his heels and a-running like
  the devil.   20

It's cloudy in the West, a-looking like
  rain,
And my damned old slicker's in the
  wagon again.

Crippled my hoss, I don't know how,
Ropin' at the horns of a 2-U cow.

We hit Caldwell and we hit her on the fly,
We bedded down the cattle on the hill
close by.

No chaps, no slicker, and it's pouring
down rain,
And I swear, by god, I'll never night-herd
again.

Feet in the stirrups and seat in the saddle,
I hung and rattled with them long-horn
cattle.   30

Last night I was on guard and the leader
broke the ranks,
I hit my horse down the shoulders and I
spurred him in the flanks.

The wind commenced to blow, and the
rain began to fall,
Hit looked, by grab, like we was goin' to
lose 'em all.

I jumped in the saddle and grabbed holt
the horn,
Best blamed cow-puncher ever was born.

I popped my foot in the stirrup and gave
a little yell,
The tail cattle broke and the leaders went
to hell.

I don't give a damn if they never do stop;
I'll ride as long as an eight day clock.   40

Foot in the stirrup and hand on the horn,
Best damned cowboy ever was born.

I herded and I hollered and I done very
well,
Till the boss said, " Boys, just let 'em go
to hell."

Stray in the herd and the boss said, " Kill
it,"
So I shot him in the rump with the
handle of the skillet.

We rounded 'em up and put 'em on the
cars,
And that was the last of the old Two
Bars.

Oh it's bacon and beans most every
day, —
I'd as soon be a-eatin' prairie hay.   50

I'm on my best horse and I'm goin' at a
run,
I'm the quickest shootin' cowboy that
ever pulled a gun.

I went to the wagon to get my roll,
To come back to Texas, dad-burn my
soul.

I went to the boss to draw my roll,
He had it figgered out I was nine dollars
in the hole.

I'll sell my outfit just as soon as I can,
I won't punch cattle for no damned man.

Goin' back to town to draw my money,
Goin' back home to see my honey.   60

With my knees in the saddle and my seat
in the sky,
I'll quit punching cows in the sweet by
and by.

Good-by, Old Paint

My foot in the stirrup, my pony won't
stan',
I'm a-leavin' Cheyenne, I'm off for Montan'.

Refrain:
   Good-by, old Paint, I'm a-leavin' Cheyenne,
   Good-by, old Paint, I'm a-leavin' Cheyenne.

I'm a-ridin' old Paint, I'm a-leadin' old
   Dan,
Good-by, little Annie, I'm off for Chey-
   enne.

Old Paint's a good pony, he paces when
   he can,
Good morning, young lady, my hosses
   won't stan'.

Oh, hitch up your hosses and feed 'em
   some hay,
And seat yourself by me, as long as you
   stay.   10

My hosses ain't hungry, they'll not eat
   your hay,
My wagon is loaded and rolling away.

I'm a-ridin' old Paint, I'm a-leadin' old
   Dan,
I'm goin' to Montan' for to throw the
   hoolihan.

They feed in the coulees, they water in
   the draw,
Their tails are all matted, their backs are
   all raw.

Old Bill Jones had two daughters and a
   song:
One went to Denver, and the other went
   wrong.

His wife she died in a pool room fight,
And still he sings from morning to night.

Oh, when I die, take my saddle from the
   wall,   21
Put it on my pony, lead him from the
   stall.

Tie my bones to his back, turn our faces
   to the West,
And we'll ride the prairie that we love
   the best.

O Bury Me Not on the Lone Prairie

"O bury me not on the lone prairie,"
These words came slowly and mourn-
   fully
From the pallid lips of a youth who lay
On his cold damp bed at the close of day.

  "O bury me not on the lone prairie
  Where the wild coyote will howl o'er
   me,
  Where the cold wind weeps and the
   grasses wave;
  No sunbeams rest on a prairie grave."

He has wasted and pined till o'er his
   brow
Death's shades are slowly gathering
   now;   10
He thought of his home with his loved
   ones nigh,
As the cowboys gathered to see him die.

Again he listened to well known words,
To the wind's soft sigh and the song of
   birds;
He thought of his home and his native
   bowers,
Where he loved to roam in his childhood
   hours.

"I've ever wished that when I died,
My grave might be on the old hillside,
Let there the place of my last rest be —
O bury me not on the lone prairie!   20

"O'er my slumbers a mother's prayer
And a sister's tears will be mingled there;
For 'tis sad to know that the heart-throb's
   o'er,
And that its fountain will gush no more.

"In my dreams I say" — but his voice
   failed there;

And they gave no heed to his dying
prayer;
In a narrow grave six feet by three,
They buried him there on the lone prairie.

May the light-winged butterfly pause to
rest
O'er him who sleeps on the prairie's
crest;   30
May the Texas rose in the breezes wave
O'er him who sleeps in a prairie's grave.

And the cowboys now as they roam the
plain
(For they marked the spot where his
bones have lain)
Fling a handful of roses over his grave,
With a prayer to Him who his soul will
save.

Git Along, Little Dogies

As I walked out one morning for pleasure,
I spied a cow-puncher come all riding
alone;
His hat was throwed back and his spurs
was a-jingling,
As he approached me a-singin' this song.

Refrain:
    Whoopie ti yi yo, git along, little
    dogies,
    It's your misfortune, and none of my
    own.
    Whoopie ti yi yo, git along, little
    dogies,
    For you know Wyoming will be your
    new home.

Early in the spring we round up the
dogies,

Mark 'em and brand 'em and bob off
their tails;   10
Drive up our horses, load up the chuck-
wagon,
Then throw the dogies out on the trail.

It's whoopin' and yellin' and a-drivin'
them dogies;
Oh, how I wish that you would go on;
It's a-whoopin' and punchin' and go on-a,
little dogies,
For you know Wyoming is to be your
new home.

Some boys goes up the trail for pleasure,
But that's where you get in most awfully
wrong;
For you haven't any idea the trouble they
give us
While we go driving them along.   20

When the night comes on and we hold
them on the bed-ground,
These little dogies that roll on so slow;
Round up the herd and cut out the strays,
And roll the little dogies that never rolled
before.

Your mother she was raised way down in
Texas,
Where the jimson weed and sand-burrs
grow;
Now we'll fix you up on prickly pear and
cholla
Till you're ready for the trail to Idaho.

Oh, you'll be beef for Uncle Sam's Injuns;
"It's beef, heap beef," I hear them
cry.   30
Git along, git along, git along-a, little
dogies,
You're gonna be beef steers by and by.

Jesse James

Jesse James was a lad that killed a-many
    a man;
He robbed the Danville train.
But the dirty little coward that shot Mis-
    ter Howard
Has laid poor Jesse in his grave.

Refrain:

  Poor Jesse had a wife to mourn for his
    life,
  Three children, they were brave.
  But that dirty little coward that shot
    Mister Howard
  Has laid poor Jesse in his grave.

It was Robert Ford, that dirty little cow-
    ard,
I wonder how does he feel. 10
For he ate of Jesse's bread, and he slept
    in Jesse's bed,
Then laid poor Jesse in his grave.

Jesse was a man, a friend to the poor,
He never would see a man suffer pain;
And with his brother Frank he robbed
    the Chicago bank,
And stopped the Glendale train.

It was his brother Frank that robbed the
    Glendale bank,
And carried the money from the town;
It was in this very place that they had a
    little race,
For they shot Captain Sheets to the
    ground. 20

They went to the crossing not very far
    from there,
And there they did the same;

With the agent on his knees, he delivered
    up the keys
To the outlaws, Frank and Jesse James.

It was on a Wednesday night, the moon
    was shining bright,
They robbed the Glendale train;
The people, they did say, for many miles
    away,
It was robbed by Frank and Jesse James.

It was on a Saturday night, Jesse was at
    home,
Talking with his family brave; 30
Robert Ford came along like a thief in
    the night
And laid poor Jesse in his grave.

The people held their breath when they
    heard of Jesse's death,
And wondered how he ever came to die;
It was one of the gang called little Robert
    Ford,
He shot poor Jesse on the sly.

Jesse went to his rest with his hand upon
    his breast;
The Devil will be upon his knee.
He was born one day in the county of
    Clay
And came from a solitary race. 40

Jesse went down to the City of Hell,
Thinking for to do as he pleased;
But when Jesse come down to the City
    of Hell,
The Devil quickly had him on his knees.

This song was made by Billy Gashade,
As soon as the news did arrive;
He said there was no man with the law
    in his hand
Who could take Jesse James when alive.

Walt Whitman

One's-Self I Sing

One's-self I sing, a simple separate person,
Yet utter the word Democratic, the word En-Masse.

Of physiology from top to toe I sing,
Not physiognomy alone nor brain alone is worthy for the Muse, I say the Form
    complete is worthier far,
The Female equally with the Male I sing.

Of Life immense in passion, pulse, and power,
Cheerful, for freest action form'd under the laws divine,
The Modern Man I sing.

1867

FROM Song of Myself

I

I celebrate myself, and sing myself,
And what I assume you shall assume,
For every atom belonging to me as good belongs to you.

I loafe and invite my soul,
I lean and loafe at my ease observing a spear of summer grass.

My tongue, every atom of my blood, form'd from this soil, this air,
Born here of parents born here from parents the same, and their parents the same,
I, now thirty-seven years old in perfect health begin,
Hoping to cease not till death.

Creeds and schools in abeyance,   10
Retiring back a while sufficed at what they are, but never forgotten,
I harbor for good or bad, I permit to speak at every hazard,
Nature without check with original energy.

6

A child said *What is the grass?* fetching it to me with full hands;
How could I answer the child? I do not know what it is any more than he.

I guess it must be the flag of my disposition, out of hopeful green stuff woven.

Or I guess it is the handkerchief of the Lord,
A scented gift and remembrancer designedly dropt,
Bearing the owner's name someway in the corners, that we may see and remark,
    and say *Whose?*

Or I guess the grass is itself a child, the produced babe of the vegetation.   20

Or I guess it is a uniform hieroglyphic,
And it means, Sprouting alike in broad zones and narrow zones,
Growing among black folks as among white,
Kanuck, Tuckahoe, Congressman, Cuff, I give them the same, I receive them the
    same.

And now it seems to me the beautiful uncut hair of graves.

Tenderly will I use you curling grass,
It may be you transpire from the breasts of young men,
It may be if I had known them I would have loved them,
It may be you are from old people, or from offspring taken soon out of their
    mothers' laps,
And here you are the mothers' laps.   30

This grass is very dark to be from the white heads of old mothers,
Darker than the colorless beards of old men,
Dark to come from under the faint red roofs of mouths.

O I perceive after all so many uttering tongues,
And I perceive they do not come from the roofs of mouths for nothing.

I wish I could translate the hints about the dead young men and women,
And the hints about old men and mothers, and the offspring taken soon out of
    their laps.

What do you think has become of the young and old men?
And what do you think has become of the women and children?

They are alive and well somewhere,   40
The smallest sprout shows there is really no death,
And if ever there was it led forward life, and does not wait at the end to arrest it,
And ceas'd the moment life appear'd.

All goes onward and outward, nothing collapses,
And to die is different from what any one supposed, and luckier.

16

I am of old and young, of the foolish as much as the wise,
Regardless of others, ever regardful of others,
Maternal as well as paternal, a child as well as a man,
Stuff'd with the stuff that is coarse and stuff'd with the stuff that is fine,
One of the Nation of many nations, the smallest the same and the largest the
     same,   50
A Southerner soon as a Northerner, a planter nonchalant and hospitable down
     by the Oconee I live,
A Yankee bound my own way ready for trade, my joints the limberest joints on
     earth and the sternest joints on earth,
A Kentuckian walking the vale of the Elkhorn in my deer-skin leggings, a
     Louisianian or Georgian,
A boatman over lakes or bays or along coasts, a Hoosier, Badger, Buckeye;
At home on Kanadian snow-shoes or up in the bush, or with fishermen off
     Newfoundland,
At home in the fleet of ice-boats, sailing with the rest and tacking,
At home on the hills of Vermont or in the woods of Maine, or the Texan ranch,
Comrade of Californians, comrade of free North-Westerners, (loving their big
     proportions,)
Comrade of raftsmen and coalmen, comrade of all who shake hands and wel-
     come to drink and meat,
A learner with the simplest, a teacher of the thoughtfullest,   60
A novice beginning yet experient of myriads of seasons,
Of every hue and caste am I, of every rank and religion,
A farmer, mechanic, artist, gentleman, sailor, quaker,
Prisoner, fancy-man, rowdy, lawyer, physician, priest.

I resist any thing better than my own diversity,
Breathe the air but leave plenty after me,
And am not stuck up, and am in my place.

(The moth and the fish-eggs are in their place,
The bright suns I see and the dark suns I cannot see are in their place,
The palpable is in its place and the impalpable is in its place.)   70

17

These are really the thoughts of all men in all ages and lands, they are not origi-
nal with me,
If they are not yours as much as mine they are nothing, or next to nothing,
If they are not the riddle and the untying of the riddle they are nothing,
If they are not just as close as they are distant they are nothing.

This is the grass that grows wherever the land is and the water is,
This the common air that bathes the globe.

21

I am the poet of the Body and I am the poet of the Soul,
The pleasures of heaven are with me and the pains of hell are with me,
The first I graft and increase upon myself, the latter I translate into a new tongue.

I am the poet of the woman the same as the man,   80
And I say it is as great to be a woman as to be a man,
And I say there is nothing greater than the mother of men.

I chant the chant of dilation or pride,
We have had ducking and deprecating about enough,
I show that size is only development.

Have you outstript the rest? are you the President?
It is a trifle, they will more than arrive there every one, and still pass on.

I am he that walks with the tender and growing night,
I call to the earth and sea half-held by the night.

Press close bare-bosom'd night — press close magnetic nourishing night!   90
Night of south winds — night of the large few stars!
Still nodding night — mad naked summer night.

Smile O voluptuous cool-breath'd earth!
Earth of the slumbering and liquid trees!
Earth of departed sunset — earth of the mountains misty-topt!
Earth of the vitreous pour of the full moon just tinged with blue!

Earth of shine and dark mottling the tide of the river!
Earth of the limpid gray of clouds brighter and clearer for my sake!
Far-swooping elbow'd earth — rich apple-blossom'd earth!
Smile, for your lover comes.   100

Prodigal, you have given me love — therefore I to you give love!
O unspeakable passionate love.

52

The spotted hawk swoops by and accuses me, he complains of my gab and my
    loitering.

I too am not a bit tamed, I too am untranslatable,
I sound my barbaric yawp over the roofs of the world.

The last scud of day holds back for me,
It flings my likeness after the rest and true as any on the shadow'd wilds,
It coaxes me to the vapor and the dusk.

I depart as air, I shake my white locks at the runaway sun,
I effuse my flesh in eddies, and drift it in lacy jags.   110

I bequeath myself to the dirt to grow from the grass I love,
If you want me again look for me under your boot-soles.

You will hardly know who I am or what I mean,
But I shall be good health to you nevertheless,
And filter and fibre your blood.

Failing to fetch me at first keep encouraged,
Missing me one place search another,
I stop somewhere waiting for you.

1855

I Hear America Singing

I hear America singing, the varied carols I hear,
Those of mechanics, each one singing his as it should be blithe and strong,
The carpenter singing his as he measures his plank or beam,
The mason singing his as he makes ready for work, or leaves off work,
The boatman singing what belongs to him in his boat, the deck-hand singing on
    the steamboat deck,
The shoemaker singing as he sits on his bench, the hatter singing as he stands,
The wood-cutter's song, the plowboy's on his way in the morning, or at noon
    intermission or at sundown,
The delicious singing of the mother, or of the young wife at work, or of the girl
    sewing or washing,
Each singing what belongs to him or her and to none else,
The day what belongs to the day — at night the party of young fellows, robust,
    friendly,   10
Singing with open mouths their strong melodious songs.

1860

Night on the Prairies

Night on the prairies,
The supper is over, the fire on the ground burns low,
The wearied emigrants sleep, wrapt in their blankets;
I walk by myself — I stand and look at the stars, which I think now I never re-
    alized before.

Now I absorb immortality and peace,
I admire death and test propositions.

How plenteous! how spiritual! how resumé!
The same old man and soul — the same old aspirations, and the same content.

I was thinking the day most splendid till I saw what the not-day exhibited,
I was thinking this globe enough till there sprang out so noiseless around me
    myriads of other globes.   10

Now while the great thoughts of space and eternity fill me I will measure myself
    by them,
And now touch'd with the lives of other globes arrived as far along as those of
    the earth,
Or waiting to arrive, or pass'd on farther than those of the earth,
I henceforth no more ignore them than I ignore my own life,
Or the lives of the earth arrived as far as mine, or waiting to arrive.

O I see now that life cannot exhibit all to me, as the day cannot,
I see that I am to wait for what will be exhibited by death.

                                                                    1860

For You O Democracy

Come, I will make the continent indissoluble,
I will make the most splendid race the sun ever shone upon,
I will make divine magnetic lands,
    With the love of comrades,
        With the life-long love of comrades.

I will plant companionship thick as trees along all the rivers of America, and
      along the shores of the great lakes, and all over the prairies,
I will make inseparable cities with their arms about each other's necks,
  By the love of comrades,
    By the manly love of comrades.

For you these from me, O Democracy, to serve you ma femme!   10
For you, for you I am trilling these songs.

1860

Crossing Brooklyn Ferry

1

Flood-tide below me! I see you face to face!
Clouds of the west — sun there half an hour high — I see you also face to face.

Crowds of men and women attired in the usual costumes, how curious you are to
    me!
On the ferry-boats the hundreds and hundreds that cross, returning home, are
    more curious to me than you suppose,
And you that shall cross from shore to shore years hence are more to me, and
    more in my meditations, than you might suppose.

2

The impalpable sustenance of me from all things at all hours of the day,
The simple, compact, well-join'd scheme, myself disintegrated, every one disinte-
    grated yet part of the scheme,
The similitudes of the past and those of the future,
The glories strung like beads on my smallest sights and hearings, on the walk in
    the street and the passage over the river,
The current rushing so swiftly and swimming with me far away,   10
The others that are to follow me, the ties between me and them,
The certainty of others, the life, love, sight, hearing of others.

Others will enter the gates of the ferry and cross from shore to shore,
Others will watch the run of the flood-tide,
Others will see the shipping of Manhattan north and west, and the heights of
    Brooklyn to the south and east,
Others will see the islands large and small;
Fifty years hence, others will see them as they cross, the sun half an hour high,
A hundred years hence, or ever so many hundred years hence, others will see
    them,
Will enjoy the sunset, the pouring-in of the flood-tide, the falling-back to the sea
    of the ebb-tide.

3

It avails not, time nor place — distance avails not,   20
I am with you, you men and women of a generation, or ever so many generations
    hence,
Just as you feel when you look on the river and sky, so I felt,
Just as any of you is one of a living crowd, I was one of a crowd,
Just as you are refresh'd by the gladness of the river and the bright flow, I was
    refresh'd,
Just as you stand and lean on the rail, yet hurry with the swift current, I stood yet
    was hurried,
Just as you look on the numberless masts of ships and the thick-stemm'd pipes of
    steamboats, I look'd.

I too many and many a time cross'd the river of old,
Watched the Twelfth-month sea-gulls, saw them high in the air floating with
    motionless wings, oscillating their bodies,
Saw how the glistening yellow lit up parts of their bodies and left the rest in
    strong shadow,
Saw the slow-wheeling circles and the gradual edging toward the south,   30
Saw the reflection of the summer sky in the water,
Had my eyes dazzled by the shimmering track of beams,
Look'd at the fine centrifugal spokes of light round the shape of my head in the
    sunlit water,
Look'd on the haze on the hills southward and south-westward,
Look'd on the vapor as it flew in fleeces tinged with violet,
Look'd toward the lower bay to notice the vessels arriving,
Saw their approach, saw aboard those that were near me,
Saw the white sails of schooners and sloops, saw the ships at anchor,
The sailors at work in the rigging or out astride the spars,
The round masts, the swinging motion of the hulls, the slender serpentine pen-
    nants,   40
The large and small steamers in motion, the pilots in their pilot-houses,
The white wake left by the passage, the quick tremulous whirl of the wheels,
The flags of all nations, the falling of them at sunset,
The scallop-edged waves in the twilight, the ladled cups, the frolicsome crests
    and glistening,
The stretch afar growing dimmer and dimmer, the gray walls of the granite
    storehouses by the docks,
On the river the shadowy group, the big steam-tug closely flank'd on each side by
    the barges, the hay-boat, the belated lighter,
On the neighboring shore the fires from the foundry chimneys burning high and
    glaringly into the night,
Casting their flicker of black contrasted with wild red and yellow light over the
    tops of houses, and down into the clefts of streets.

4

These and all else were to me the same as they are to you,
I loved well those cities, loved well the stately and rapid river, 50
The men and women I saw were all near to me,
Others the same — others who look back on me because I look'd forward to them,
(The time will come, though I stop here to-day and to-night.)

5

What is it then between us?
What is the count of the scores or hundreds of years between us?

Whatever it is, it avails not — distance avails not, and place avails not,
I too lived, Brooklyn of ample hills was mine,
I too walk'd the streets of Manhattan island, and bathed in the waters around it,
I too felt the curious abrupt questionings stir within me,
In the day among crowds of people sometimes they came upon me, 60
In my walks home late at night or as I lay in my bed they came upon me,
I too had been struck from the float forever held in solution,
I too had receiv'd identity by my body,
That I was I knew was of my body, and what I should be I knew I should be of my body.

6

It is not upon you alone the dark patches fall,
The dark threw its patches down upon me also,
The best I had done seem'd to me blank and suspicious,
My great thoughts as I supposed them, were they not in reality meagre?
Nor is it you alone who know what it is to be evil,
I am he who knew what it was to be evil, 70
I too knitted the old knot of contrariety,
Blabb'd, blush'd, resented, lied, stole, grudg'd,
Had guile, anger, lust, hot wishes I dared not speak,
Was wayward, vain, greedy, shallow, sly, cowardly, malignant,
The wolf, the snake, the hog, not wanting in me,
The cheating look, the frivolous word, the adulterous wish, not wanting,
Refusals, hates, postponements, meanness, laziness, none of these wanting,
Was one with the rest, the days and haps of the rest,
Was call'd by my nighest name by clear loud voices of young men as they saw me approaching or passing,
Felt their arms on my neck as I stood, or the negligent leaning of their flesh against me as I sat, 80
Saw many I loved in the street or ferry-boat or public assembly, yet never told them a word,
Lived the same life with the rest, the same old laughing, gnawing, sleeping,

Play'd the part that still looks back on the actor or actress,
The same old role, the role that is what we make it, as great as we like,
Or as small as we like, or both great and small.

7

Closer yet I approach you,
What thought you have of me now, I had as much of you — I laid in my stores
in advance,
I consider'd long and seriously of you before you were born.

Who was to know what should come home to me?
Who knows but I am enjoying this?   90
Who knows, for all the distance, but I am as good as looking at you now, for all
you cannot see me?

8

Ah, what can ever be more stately and admirable to me than mast-hemm'd Manhattan?
River and sunset and scallop-edg'd waves of flood-tide?
The sea-gulls oscillating their bodies, the hay-boat in the twilight, and the belated
lighter?

What gods can exceed these that clasp me by the hand, and with voices I love call
me promptly and loudly by my nighest name as I approach?
What is more subtle than this which ties me to the woman or man that looks in
my face?
Which fuses me into you now, and pours my meaning into you?

We understand then do we not?
What I promis'd without mentioning it, have you not accepted?
What the study could not teach — what the preaching could not accomplish is
accomplish'd, is it not?   100

9

Flow on, river! flow with the flood-tide, and ebb with the ebb-tide!
Frolic on, crested and scallop-edg'd waves!
Gorgeous clouds of the sunset! drench with your splendor me, or the men and
women generations after me!
Cross from shore to shore, countless crowds of passengers!
Stand up, tall masts of Mannahatta! stand up, beautiful hills of Brooklyn!
Throb, baffled and curious brain! throw out questions and answers!
Suspend here and everywhere, eternal float of solution!
Gaze, loving and thirsting eyes, in the house or street or public assembly!
Sound out, voices of young men! loudly and musically call me by my nighest
name!
Live, old life! play the part that looks back on the actor or actress!   110

Play the old role, the role that is great or small according as one makes it!

Consider, you who peruse me, whether I may not in unknown ways be looking upon you;

Be firm, rail over the river, to support those who lean idly, yet haste with the hasting current;

Fly on, sea-birds! fly sideways, or wheel in large circles high in the air;

Receive the summer sky, you water, and faithfully hold it till all downcast eyes have time to take it from you!

Diverge, fine spokes of light, from the shape of my head, or any one's head, in the sunlit water!

Come on, ships from the lower bay! pass up or down, white-sail'd schooners, sloops, lighters!

Flaunt away, flags of all nations! be duly lower'd at sunset!

Burn high your fires, foundry chimneys! cast black shadows at nightfall! cast red and yellow light over the tops of the houses!

Appearances, now or henceforth, indicate what you are,   120

You necessary film, continue to envelop the soul,

About my body for me, and your body for you, be hung our divinest aromas,

Thrive, cities — bring your freight, bring your shows, ample and sufficient rivers,

Expand, being than which none else is perhaps more spiritual,

Keep your places, objects than which none else is more lasting.

You have waited, you always wait, you dumb, beautiful ministers,

We receive you with free sense at last, and are insatiate henceforward,

Not you any more shall be able to foil us, or withhold yourselves from us,

We use you, and do not cast you aside — we plant you permanently within us,

We fathom you not — we love you — there is perfection in you also,   130

You furnish your parts toward eternity,

Great or small, you furnish your parts toward the soul.

                                                              1856

O Magnet-South

O Magnet-South! O glistening perfumed South! my South!

O quick mettle, rich blood, impulse and love! good and evil! O all dear to me!

O dear to me my birth-things — all moving things and the trees where I was born — the grains, plants, rivers,

Dear to me my own slow sluggish rivers where they flow, distant, over flats of silvery sands or through swamps,

Dear to me the Roanoke, the Savannah, the Altamahaw, the Pedee, the Tombigbee, the Santee, the Coosa and the Sabine,

O pensive, far away wandering, I return with my soul to haunt their banks again,

Again in Florida I float on transparent lakes, I float on the Okeechobee, I cross
 the hummock-land or through pleasant openings or dense forests,
I see the parrots in the woods, I see the papaw-tree and the blossoming titi;
Again, sailing in my coaster on deck, I coast off Georgia, I coast up the
 Carolinas,
I see where the live-oak is growing, I see where the yellow-pine, the scented bay-
 tree, the lemon and orange, the cypress, the graceful palmetto,   10
I pass rude sea-headlands and enter Pamlico sound through an inlet, and dart
 my vision inland;
O the cotton plant! the growing fields of rice, sugar, hemp!
The cactus guarded with thorns, the laurel-tree with large white flowers,
The range afar, the richness and barrenness, the old woods charged with
 mistletoe and trailing moss,
The piney odor and the gloom, the awful natural stillness, (here in these dense
 swamps the freebooter carries his gun, and the fugitive has his conceal'd
 hut;)
O the strange fascination of these half-known half-impassable swamps, infested
 by reptiles, resounding with the bellow of the alligator, the sad noises of the
 night-owl and the wild-cat, and the whirr of the rattlesnake,
The mocking-bird, the American mimic, singing all the forenoon, singing
 through the moon-lit night,
The humming-bird, the wild turkey, the raccoon, the opossum;
A Kentucky corn-field, the tall, graceful, long-leav'd corn, slender, flapping,
 bright green, with tassels, with beautiful ears each well-sheathed in its
 husk;
O my heart! O tender and fierce pangs, I can stand them not, I will depart;   20
O to be a Virginian where I grew up! O to be a Carolinian!
O longings irrepressible! O I will go back to old Tennessee and never wander
 more.

                 1860

Cavalry Crossing a Ford

A line in long array where they wind betwixt green islands.
They take a serpentine course, their arms flash in the sun — hark to the musical
 clank,
Behold the silvery river, in it the splashing horses loitering stop to drink,
Behold the brown-faced men, each group, each person, a picture, the negligent
 rest on the saddles,
Some emerge on the opposite bank, others are just entering the ford — while,
Scarlet and blue and snowy white,
The guidon flags flutter gayly in the wind.

                 1865

Come Up from the Fields Father

Come up from the fields father, here's a letter from our Pete,
And come to the front door mother, here's a letter from thy dear son.

Lo, 'tis autumn,
Lo, where the trees, deeper green, yellower and redder,
Cool and sweeten Ohio's villages with leaves fluttering in the moderate wind,
Where apples ripe in the orchards hang and grapes on the trellis'd vines,
(Smell you the smell of the grapes on the vines?
Smell you the buckwheat where the bees were lately buzzing?)

Above all, lo, the sky so calm, so transparent after the rain, and with wondrous
     clouds,
Below too, all calm, all vital and beautiful, and the farm prospers well.   10

Down in the fields all prospers well,
But now from the fields come father, come at the daughter's call,
And come to the entry mother, to the front door come right away.

Fast as she can she hurries, something ominous, her steps trembling,
She does not tarry to smooth her hair nor adjust her cap.

Open the envelope quickly,
O this is not our son's writing, yet his name is sign'd,
O a strange hand writes for our dear son, O stricken mother's soul!
All swims before her eyes, flashes with black, she catches the main words only,
Sentences broken, *gunshot wound in the breast, cavalry skirmish, taken to
     hospital,*   20
At present low, but will soon be better.

Ah now the single figure to me,
Amid all teeming and wealthy Ohio with all its cities and farms,
Sickly white in the face and dull in the head, very faint,
By the jamb of a door leans.

Grieve not so, dear mother, (the just-grown daughter speaks through her sobs,
The little sisters huddle around speechless and dismay'd)
See, dearest mother, the letter says Pete will soon be better.
Alas poor boy, he will never be better, (nor may-be needs to be better, that brave
     and simple soul.)
While they stand at home at the door he is dead already,   30
The only son is dead.

But the mother needs to be better,
She with thin form presently drest in black,
By day her meals untouch'd, then at night fitfully sleeping, often waking,
In the midnight waking, weeping, longing with one deep longing,
O that she might withdraw unnoticed, silent from life escape and withdraw,
To follow, to seek, to be with her dear dead son.

1865

As Toilsome I Wander'd Virginia's Woods

As toilsome I wander'd Virginia's woods,
To the music of rustling leaves kick'd by my feet, (for 'twas autumn,)
I mark'd at the foot of a tree the grave of a soldier;
Mortally wounded he and buried on the retreat, (easily all could I understand,)
The halt of a mid-day hour, when up! no time to lose — yet this sign left,
On a tablet scrawl'd and nail'd on the tree by the grave,
Bold, cautious, true, and my loving comrade.

Long, long I muse, then on my way go wandering,
Many a changeful season to follow, and many a scene of life,
Yet at times through changeful season and scene, abrupt, alone, or in the
    crowded street,   10
Comes before me the unknown soldier's grave, comes the inscription rude in
    Virginia's woods,
Bold, cautious, true, and my loving comrade.

1865

Pioneers! O Pioneers!

Come my tan-faced children,
Follow well in order, get your weapons ready,
Have you your pistols? have you your sharp-edged axes?
  Pioneers! O pioneers!

For we cannot tarry here,
We must march my darlings, we must bear the brunt of danger,
We the youthful sinewy races, all the rest on us depend,
  Pioneers! O pioneers!

O you youths, Western youths,
So impatient, full of action, full of manly pride and friendship,   10
Plain I see you Western youths, see you tramping with the foremost,
  Pioneers! O pioneers!

Have the elder races halted?
Do they droop and end their lesson, wearied over there beyond the seas?
We take up the task eternal, and the burden and the lesson,
  Pioneers! O pioneers!

All the past we leave behind,
We debouch upon a newer mightier world, varied world,
Fresh and strong the world we seize, world of labor and the march,
  Pioneers! O pioneers!   20

We detachments steady throwing,
Down the edges, through the passes, up the mountains steep,
Conquering, holding, daring, venturing as we go the unknown ways,
  Pioneers! O pioneers!

We primeval forests felling,
We the rivers stemming, vexing we and piercing deep the mines within,
We the surface broad surveying, we the virgin soil upheaving,
  Pioneers! O pioneers!

Colorado men are we,
From the peaks gigantic, from the great sierras and the high plateaus,   30
From the mine and from the gully, from the hunting trail we come,
  Pioneers! O pioneers!

From Nebraska, from Arkansas,
Central inland race are we, from Missouri, with the continental blood inter-
    vein'd,
All the hands of comrades clasping, all the Southern, all the Northern,
  Pioneers! O pioneers!

O resistless restless race!
O beloved race in all! O my breast aches with tender love for all!
O I mourn and yet exult, I am rapt with love for all,
  Pioneers! O pioneers!   40

Raise the mighty mother mistress,
Waving high the delicate mistress, over all the starry mistress, (bend your
    heads all,)
Raise the fang'd and warlike mistress, stern, impassive, weapon'd mistress,
  Pioneers! O pioneers!

See my children, resolute children,
By those swarms upon our rear we must never yield or falter,
Ages back in ghostly millions frowning there behind us urging,
   Pioneers! O pioneers!

On and on the compact ranks,
With accessions ever waiting, with the places of the dead quickly fill'd,   50
Through the battle, through defeat, moving yet and never stopping,
   Pioneers! O pioneers!

O to die advancing on!
Are there some of us to droop and die? has the hour come?
Then upon the march we fittest die, soon and sure the gap is fill'd,
   Pioneers! O pioneers!

All the pulses of the world,
Falling in they beat for us, with the Western movement beat,
Holding single or together, steady moving to the front, all for us,
   Pioneers! O pioneers!   60

Life's involv'd and varied pageants,
All the forms and shows, all the workmen at their work,
All the seamen and the landsmen, all the masters with their slaves,
   Pioneers! O pioneers!

All the hapless silent lovers,
All the prisoners in the prisons, all the righteous and the wicked,
All the joyous, all the sorrowing, all the living, all the dying,
   Pioneers! O pioneers!

I too with my soul and body,
We, a curious trio, picking, wandering on our way,   70
Through these shores amid the shadows, with the apparitions pressing,
   Pioneers! O pioneers!

Lo, the darting bowling orb!
Lo, the brother orbs around, all the clustering suns and planets,
All the dazzling days, all the mystic nights with dreams,
   Pioneers! O pioneers!

These are of us, they are with us,
All for primal needed work, while the followers there in embryo wait behind,
We to-day's procession heading, we the route for travel clearing,
   Pioneers! O pioneers!   80

O you daughters of the West!
O you young and elder daughters! O you mothers and you wives!
Never must you be divided, in our ranks you move united,
   Pioneers! O pioneers!

   Minstrels latent on the prairies!
(Shrouded bards of other lands, you may rest, you have done your work,)
Soon I hear you coming warbling, soon you rise and tramp amid us,
   Pioneers! O pioneers!

   Not for delectations sweet,
Not the cushion and the slipper, not the peaceful and the studious,   90
Not the riches safe and palling, not for us the tame enjoyment,
   Pioneers! O pioneers!

   Do the feasters gluttonous feast?
Do the corpulent sleepers sleep? have they lock'd and bolted doors?
Still be ours the diet hard, and the blanket on the ground,
   Pioneers! O pioneers!

   Has the night descended?
Was the road of late so toilsome? did we stop discouraged nodding on our way?
Yet a passing hour I yield you in your tracks to pause oblivious,
   Pioneers! O pioneers!   100

   Till with sound of trumpet,
Far, far off the daybreak call — hark! how loud and clear I hear it wind,
Swift! to the head of the army! — swift! spring to your places,
   Pioneers! O pioneers!

                                  1865

To a Certain Civilian

Did you ask dulcet rhymes from me?
Did you seek the civilian's peaceful and languishing rhymes?
Did you find what I sang erewhile so hard to follow?
Why I was not singing erewhile for you to follow, to understand — nor am I
    now;
(I have been born of the same as the war was born,
The drum-corps' rattle is ever to me sweet music, I love well the martial dirge,
With slow wail and convulsive throb leading the officer's funeral;)
What to such as you anyhow such a poet as I? therefore leave my works,
And go lull yourself with what you can understand, and with piano-tunes,   10
For I lull nobody, and you will never understand me.

                                  1865

Oliver Wendell Holmes

The Height of the Ridiculous

I wrote some lines once on a time
  In wondrous merry mood,
And thought, as usual, men would say
  They were exceeding good.

They were so queer, so very queer,
  I laughed as I would die;
Albeit, in the general way,
  A sober man am I.

I called my servant, and he came;
  How kind it was of him   10
To mind a slender man like me,
  He of the mighty limb!

" These to the printer," I exclaimed,
  And, in my humorous way,
I added, (as a trifling jest,)
  " There'll be the devil to pay."

He took the paper, and I watched,
  And saw him peep within;
At the first line he read, his face
  Was all upon the grin.   20

He read the next; the grin grew broad,
  And shot from ear to ear;
He read the third; a chuckling noise
  I now began to hear.

The fourth; he broke into a roar;
  The fifth; his waistband split;
The sixth; he burst five buttons off,
  And tumbled in a fit.

Ten days and nights, with sleepless eye,
  I watched that wretched man,   30
And since, I never dare to write
  As funny as I can.

              1830

My Aunt

My aunt! my dear unmarried aunt!
  Long years have o'er her flown;
Yet still she strains the aching clasp
  That binds her virgin zone;
I know it hurts her, — though she looks
  As cheerful as she can;
Her waist is ampler than her life,
  For life is but a span.

My aunt! my poor deluded aunt!
  Her hair is almost gray;   10
Why will she train that winter curl
  In such a spring-like way?
How can she lay her glasses down,
  And say she reads as well,
When, through a double convex lens,
  She just makes out to spell?

Her father — grandpapa! forgive
  This erring lip its smiles —
Vowed she should make the finest girl
  Within a hundred miles;   20
He sent her to a stylish school;
  'Twas in her thirteenth June;
And with her, as the rules required,
  " Two towels and a spoon."

They braced my aunt against a board,
  To make her straight and tall;
They laced her up, they starved her down,
  To make her light and small;
They pinched her feet, they singed her
    hair,
  They screwed it up with pins; —   30
O never mortal suffered more
  In penance for her sins.

So, when my precious aunt was done,
  My grandsire brought her back;
(By daylight, lest some rabid youth
  Might follow on the track;)

"Ah!" said my grandsire, as he shook
  Some powder in his pan,
"What could this lovely creature do
  Against a desperate man!"   40

Alas! nor chariot, nor barouche,
  Nor bandit cavalcade,
Tore from the trembling father's arms
  His all-accomplished maid.
For her how happy had it been!
  And heaven had spared to me
To see one sad, ungathered rose
  On my ancestral tree.

                                    1831

The Last Leaf

I saw him once before,
As he passed by the door,
  And again
The pavement stones resound,
As he totters o'er the ground
  With his cane.

They say that in his prime,
Ere the pruning-knife of Time
  Cut him down,
Not a better man was found   10
By the Crier on his round
  Through the town.

But now he walks the streets,
And he looks at all he meets
  Sad and wan,
And he shakes his feeble head,
That it seems as if he said,
  "They are gone."

The mossy marbles rest
On the lips that he has prest   20
  In their bloom,
And the names he loved to hear
Have been carved for many a year
  On the tomb.

My grandmama has said —
Poor old lady, she is dead
  Long ago —
That he had a Roman nose,
And his cheek was like a rose
  In the snow.   30

But now his nose is thin,
And it rests upon his chin
  Like a staff,
And a crook is in his back,
And a melancholy crack
  In his laugh.

I know it is a sin
For me to sit and grin
  At him here;
But the old three-cornered hat,   40
And the breeches, and all that,
  Are so queer!

And if I should live to be
The last leaf upon the tree
  In the spring,
Let them smile, as I do now,
At the old forsaken bough
  Where I cling.

                                    1833

Old Ironsides

Ay, tear her tattered ensign down!
  Long has it waved on high,
And many an eye has danced to see
  That banner in the sky;
Beneath it rung the battle shout,
  And burst the cannon's roar; —
The meteor of the ocean air
  Shall sweep the clouds no more!

Her deck, once red with heroes' blood,
  Where knelt the vanquished foe,   10
When winds were hurrying o'er the flood,
  And waves were white below,
No more shall feel the victor's tread,
  Or know the conquered knee; —

The harpies of the shore shall pluck
  The eagle of the sea!

Oh, better that her shattered hulk
  Should sink beneath the wave;
Her thunders shook the mighty deep,
  And there should be her grave;   20
Nail to the mast her holy flag,
  Set every threadbare sail,
And give her to the god of storms,
  The lightning and the gale!

                         1830

Brother Jonathan's Lament for Sister Caroline

She has gone, — she has left us in passion
  and pride, —
Our stormy-browed sister, so long at our
  side!
She has torn her own star from our firmament's glow,
And turned on her brother the face of a
  foe!

O Caroline, Caroline, child of the sun,
We can never forget that our hearts have
  been one, —
Our foreheads both sprinkled in Liberty's
  name,
From the fountain of blood with the finger of flame!

You were always too ready to fire at a
  touch;
But we said, "She is hasty, — she does
  not mean much."   10
We have scowled, when you uttered some
  turbulent threat;
But Friendship still whispered, "Forgive
  and forget!"

Has our love all died out? Have its altars
  grown cold?
Has the curse come at last which the
  fathers foretold?

Then Nature must teach us the strength
  of the chain
That her petulant children would sever
  in vain.

They may fight till the buzzards are
  gorged with their spoil,
Till the harvest grows black as it rots
  in the soil,
Till the wolves and the catamounts troop
  from their caves,
And the shark tracks the pirate, the lord
  of the waves: 20

In vain is the strife! When its fury is past,
Their fortunes must flow in one channel
  at last,
As the torrents that rush from the mountains of snow
Roll mingled in peace through the valleys below.

Our Union is river, lake, ocean, and sky:
Man breaks not the medal, when God
  cuts the die!
Though darkened with sulphur, though
  cloven with steel,
The blue arch will brighten, the waters
  will heal!

O Caroline, Caroline, child of the sun,
There are battles with Fate that can never
  be won!   30
The star-flowering banner must never be
  furled,
For its blossoms of light are the hope of
  the world!

Go, then, our rash sister! afar and aloof,
Run wild in the sunshine away from our
  roof;
But when your heart aches and your feet
  have grown sore,
Remember the pathway that leads to our
  door!

                         1861

John Greenleaf Whittier

The Shoemakers

Ho! workers of the old time styled
 The Gentle Craft of Leather!
Young brothers of the ancient guild,
 Stand forth once more together!
Call out again your long array,
 In the olden merry manner!
Once more, on gay St. Crispin's day,
 Fling out your blazoned banner!

Rap, rap! upon the well-worn stone
 How falls the polished hammer! 10
Rap, rap! the measured sound has grown
 A quick and merry clamor.
Now shape the sole! now deftly curl
 The glossy vamp around it,
And bless the while the bright-eyed girl
 Whose gentle fingers bound it!

For you, along the Spanish main
 A hundred keels are ploughing;
For you, the Indian on the plain
 His lasso-coil is throwing; 20
For you, deep glens with hemlock dark
 The woodman's fire is lighting;
For you, upon the oak's gray bark,
 The woodman's axe is smiting.

For you, from Carolina's pine
 The rosin-gum is stealing;
For you, the dark-eyed Florentine
 Her silken skein is reeling;
For you, the dizzy goatherd roams
 His rugged Alpine ledges; 30
For you, round all her shepherd homes
 Bloom England's thorny hedges.

The foremost still, by day or night,
 On moated mound or heather,
Where'er the need of trampled right
 Brought toiling men together;

Where the free burghers from the wall
 Defied the mail-clad master,
Than yours at Freedom's trumpet-call,
 No craftsmen rallied faster. 40

Let foplings sneer, let fools deride, —
 Ye heed no idle scorner;
Free hands and hearts are still your pride,
 And duty done, your honor.
Ye dare to trust, for honest fame,
 The jury Time empanels,
And leave to truth each noble name
 Which glorifies your annals.

Thy songs, Hans Sachs, are living yet,
 In strong and hearty German; 50
And Bloomfield's lay, and Gifford's wit,
 And patriot fame of Sherman;
Still from his book, a mystic seer,
 The soul of Behmen teaches,
And England's priesthood shakes to hear
 Of Fox's leathern breeches.

The foot is yours; where'er it falls,
 It treads your well-wrought leather,
On earthen floor, in marble halls,
 On carpet, or on heather. 60
Still there the sweetest charm is found
 Of matron grace or vestal's,
As Hebe's foot bore nectar round
 Among the old celestials!

Rap, rap! — your stout and bluff brogan,
 With footsteps slow and weary,
May wander where the sky's blue span
 Shuts down upon the prairie.
On Beauty's foot your slippers glance,
 By Saratoga's fountains, 70
Or twinkle down the summer dance
 Beneath the Crystal Mountains!

The red brick to the mason's hand,
 The brown earth to the tiller's,

The shoe in yours shall wealth command,
　Like fairy Cinderella's!
As they who shunned the household maid
　Beheld the crown upon her,
So all shall see your toil repaid
　With hearth and home and honor. 80

Then let the toast be freely quaffed,
　In water cool and brimming, —
" All honor to the good old Craft,
　Its merry men and women! "
Call out again your long array,
　In the old time's pleasant manner:
Once more, on gay St. Crispin's day,
　Fling out his blazoned banner!

　　　　　1845

Massachusetts to Virginia

The blast from Freedom's Northern hills,
　upon its Southern way,
Bears greeting to Virginia from Massa-
　chusetts Bay:
No word of haughty challenging, nor
　battle bugle's peal,
Nor steady tread of marching files, nor
　clang of horsemen's steel.

No trains of deep-mouthed cannon along
　our highways go, —
Around our silent arsenals untrodden
　lies the snow;
And to the land-breeze of our ports, upon
　their errands far,
A thousand sails of commerce swell, but
　none are spread for war.

We hear thy threats, Virginia! thy stormy
　words and high,
Swell harshly on the Southern winds
　which melt along our sky;　10
Yet, not one brown, hard hand foregoes
　its honest labor here,
No hewer of our mountain oaks suspends
　his axe in fear.

Wild are the waves which lash the reefs
　along St. George's bank, —
Cold on the shore of Labrador the fog
　lies white and dank;
Through storm, and wave, and blinding
　mist, stout are the hearts which man
The fishing-smacks of Marblehead, the
　sea-boats of Cape Ann.

The cold north light and wintry sun
　glare on their icy forms,
Bent grimly o'er their straining lines or
　wrestling with the storms;
Free as the winds they drive before,
　rough as the waves they roam,
They laugh to scorn the slaver's threat
　against their rocky home.　20

What means the Old Dominion? Hath
　she forgot the day
When o'er her conquered valleys swept
　the Briton's steel array?
How side by side, with sons of hers, the
　Massachusetts men
Encountered Tarleton's charge of fire,
　and stout Cornwallis, then?

Forgets she how the Bay State, in answer
　to the call
Of her old House of Burgesses, spoke out
　from Faneuil Hall?
When, echoing back her Henry's cry,
　came pulsing on each breath
Of Northern winds, the thrilling sounds
　of " Liberty or Death! "

What asks the Old Dominion? If now
　her sons have proved
False to their fathers' memory, — false
　to the faith they loved;　30
If she can scoff at Freedom, and its great
　charter spurn,
Must we of Massachusetts from truth and
　duty turn?

We hunt your bondmen, flying from
    Slavery's hateful hell, —
Our voices, at your bidding, take up the
    bloodhound's yell, —
We gather, at your summons, above our
    fathers' graves,
From Freedom's holy altar-horns to tear
    your wretched slaves!

Thank God! not yet so vilely can Massa-
    chusetts bow;
The spirit of her early time is with her
    even now;
Dream not because her Pilgrim blood
    moves slow and calm and cool,
She thus can stoop her chainless neck, a
    sister's slave and tool!   40

All that a *sister* State should do, all that
    a *free* State may,
Heart, hand, and purse we proffer, as in
    our early day;
But that one dark loathsome burden ye
    must stagger with alone,
And reap the bitter harvest which ye
    yourselves have sown!

Hold, while ye may, your struggling
    slaves, and burden God's free air
With woman's shriek beneath the lash,
    and manhood's wild despair;
Cling closer to the " cleaving curse " that
    writes upon your plains
The blasting of Almighty wrath against
    a land of chains.

Still shame your gallant ancestry, the
    cavaliers of old,
By watching round the shambles where
    human flesh is sold, —   50
Gloat o'er the new-born child, and count
    his market value, when
The maddened mother's cry of woe shall
    pierce the slaver's den!

Lower than plummet soundeth, sink the
    Virginia name;
Plant, if ye will, your fathers' graves with
    rankest weeds of shame;
Be, if ye will, the scandal of God's fair
    universe, —
We wash our hands forever of your sin
    and shame and curse.

A voice from lips whereon the coal from
    Freedom's shrine hath been,
Thrilled, as but yesterday, the hearts of
    Berkshire's mountain men:
The echoes of that solemn voice are sadly
    lingering still
In all our sunny valleys, on every wind-
    swept hill.   60

And when the prowling man-thief came
    hunting for his prey
Beneath the very shadow of Bunker's
    shaft of gray,
How, through the free lips of the son, the
    father's warning spoke;
How, from its bonds of trade and sect,
    the Pilgrim city broke!

A hundred thousand right arms were
    lifted up on high,
A hundred thousand voices sent back
    their loud reply;
Through the thronged towns of Essex
    the startling summons rang,
And up from bench and loom and wheel
    her young mechanics sprang!

The voice of free, broad Middlesex, of
    thousands as of one,
The shaft of Bunker calling to that of
    Lexington, —   70
From Norfolk's ancient villages, from
    Plymouth's rocky bound
To where Nantucket feels the arms of
    ocean close her round; —

From rich and rural Worcester, where
  through the calm repose
Of cultured vales and fringing woods the
  gentle Nashua flows,
To where Wachuset's wintry blasts the
  mountain larches stir,
Swelled up to Heaven the thrilling cry
  of " God save Latimer! "

And sandy Barnstable rose up, wet with
  the salt sea spray, —
And Bristol sent her answering shout
  down Narragansett Bay!
Along the broad Connecticut old Hamp-
  den felt the thrill,
And the cheer of Hampshire's woodmen
  swept down from Holyoke Hill.   80

The voice of Massachusetts! Of her free
  sons and daughters, —
Deep calling unto deep aloud, — the
  sound of many waters!
Against the burden of that voice what
  tyrant power shall stand?
*No fetters in the Bay State! No slave
  upon her land!*

Look to it well, Virginians! In calmness
  we have borne,
In answer to our faith and trust, your insult and your scorn;
You've spurned our kindest counsels, —
  you've hunted for our lives, —
And shaken round our hearths and
  homes your manacles and gyves!

We wage no war, — we lift no arm, —
  we fling no torch within
The fire-damps of the quaking mine beneath your soil of sun;   90
We leave ye with your bondmen, to
  wrestle, while ye can,
With the strong upward tendencies and
  godlike soul of man!

But for us and for our children, the vow
  which we have given
For freedom and humanity is registered
  in heaven;
*No slave-hunt in our borders, — no
  pirate on our strand!*
*No fetters in the Bay State, — no slave
  upon our land!*

1843

Telling the Bees

Here is the place; right over the hill
  Runs the path I took;
You can see the gap in the old wall still,
  And the stepping-stones in the shallow
    brook.

There is the house, with the gate red-
    barred,
  And the poplars tall;
And the barn's brown length, and the
    cattle-yard,
  And the white horns tossing above the
    wall.

There are the beehives ranged in the sun;
  And down by the brink   10
Of the brook are her poor flowers, weed-
    o'errun,
  Pansy and daffodil, rose and pink.

A year has gone, as the tortoise goes,
  Heavy and slow;
And the same rose blows, and the same
    sun glows,
  And the same brook sings of a year
    ago.

There's the same sweet clover-smell in
    the breeze;
  And the June sun warm
Tangles his wings of fire in the trees,
  Setting, as then, over Fernside farm.

I mind me how with a lover's care   21
 From my Sunday coat
I brushed off the burrs, and smoothed my
 hair,
  And cooled at the brookside my brow
  and throat.

Since we parted, a month had passed, —
 To love, a year;
Down through the beeches I looked at
 last
  On the little red gate and the well-
  sweep near.

I can see it all now, — the slantwise rain
 Of light through the leaves,   30
The sundown's blaze on her window-
 pane,
  The bloom of her roses under the
  eaves.

Just the same as a month before, —
 The house and the trees,
The barn's brown gable, the vine by the
 door, —
  Nothing changed but the hives of bees.

Before them, under the garden wall,
 Forward and back,
Went drearily singing the chore-girl
 small,
  Draping each hive with a shred of
  black.   40

Trembling, I listened: the summer sun
 Had the chill of snow;
For I knew she was telling the bees of
 one
  Gone on the journey we all must go!

Then I said to myself, " My Mary weeps
 For the dead today:
Haply her blind old grandsire sleeps
  The fret and the pain of his age away."

But her dog whined low; on the doorway
 sill
 With his cane to his chin,   50
The old man sat; and the chore-girl still
 Sung to the bees stealing out and in.

And the song she was singing ever since
 In my ear sounds on: —
" Stay at home, pretty bees, fly not hence!
 Mistress Mary is dead and gone! "
       1858

The Eternal Goodness

O friends! with whom my feet have trod
 The quiet aisles of prayer,
Glad witness to your zeal for God
 And love of man I bear.

I trace your lines of argument;
 Your logic linked and strong
I weigh as one who dreads dissent,
 And fears a doubt as wrong.

But still my human hands are weak
 To hold your iron creeds: 10
Against the words ye bid me speak
 My heart within me pleads.

Who fathoms the Eternal Thought?
 Who talks of scheme and plan?
The Lord is God! He needeth not
 The poor device of man.

I walk with bare, hushed feet the ground
 Ye tread with boldness shod;
I dare not fix with mete and bound
 The love and power of God.   20

Ye praise his justice; even such
 His pitying love I deem:
Ye seek a king; I fain would touch
 The robe that hath no seam.

Ye see the curse which overbroods
  A world of pain and loss;
I hear our Lord's beatitudes
  And prayer upon the cross.

More than your schoolmen teach, within
  Myself, alas! I know;   30
Too dark ye cannot paint the sin,
  Too small the merit show.

I bow my forehead to the dust,
  I veil mine eyes for shame,
And urge, in trembling self-distrust,
  A prayer without a claim.

I see the wrong that round me lies,
  I feel the guilt within;
I hear, with groan and travail-cries,
  The world confess its sin.   40

Yet, in the maddening maze of things,
  And tossed by storm and flood,
To one fixed trust my spirit clings;
  I know that God is good!

Not mine to look where cherubim
  And seraphs may not see,
But nothing can be good in Him
  Which evil is in me.

The wrong that pains my soul below
  I dare not throne above;   50
I know not of His hate, — I know
  His goodness and His love.

I dimly guess from blessings known
  Of greater out of sight,
And, with the chastened Psalmist, own
  His judgments too are right.

I long for household voices gone,
  For vanished smiles I long,
But God hath led my dear ones on,
  And He can do no wrong.   60

I know not what the future hath
  Of marvel or surprise,
Assured alone that life and death
  His mercy underlies.

And if my heart and flesh are weak
  To bear an untried pain,
The bruisèd reed He will not break,
  But strengthen and sustain.

No offering of my own I have,
  Nor works my faith to prove;   70
I can but give the gifts He gave,
  And plead His love for love.

And so beside the Silent Sea
  I wait the muffled oar;
No harm from Him can come to me
  On ocean or on shore.

I know not where His islands lift
  Their fronded palms in air;
I only know I cannot drift
  Beyond His love and care.   80

O brothers! if my faith is vain,
  If hopes like these betray,
Pray for me that my feet may gain
  The sure and safer way.

And Thou, O Lord! by whom are seen
  Thy creatures as they be,
Forgive me if too close I lean
  My human heart on Thee!

                                          1865

Robert Frost

Mending Wall

Something there is that doesn't love a
  wall,
That sends the frozen-ground-swell
  under it,

And spills the upper boulders in the sun;
And makes gaps even two can pass
   abreast.
The work of hunters is another thing:
I have come after them and made repair
Where they have left not one stone on a
   stone,
But they would have the rabbit out of
   hiding,
To please the yelping dogs. The gaps I
   mean,
No one has seen them made or heard
   them made,   10
But at spring mending-time we find
   them there.
I let my neighbor know beyond the hill;
And on a day we meet to walk the line
And set the wall between us once again.
We keep the wall between us as we
   go.
To each the boulders that have fallen to
   each.
And some are loaves and some so nearly
   balls
We have to use a spell to make them bal-
   ance:
" Stay where you are until our backs are
   turned! "
We wear our fingers rough with han-
   dling them.   20
Oh, just another kind of outdoor game,
One on a side. It comes to little more:
There where it is we do not need the
   wall:
He is all pine and I am apple-orchard.
My apple trees will never get across
And eat the cones under his pines, I tell
   him.
He only says, " Good fences make good
   neighbors."
Spring is the mischief in me, and I won-
   der
If I could put a notion in his head:
" *Why* do they make good neighbors?
   Isn't it   30

Where there are cows? But here there are
   no cows.
Before I built a wall I'd ask to know
What I was walling in or walling out,
And to whom I was like to give offense.
Something there is that doesn't love a
   wall,
That wants it down." I could say
   " Elves " to him,
But it's not elves exactly, and I'd rather
He said it for himself. I see him there
Bringing a stone grasped firmly by the
   top
In each hand, like an old-stone savage
   armed.   40
He moves in darkness as it seems to me,
Not of woods only and the shade of trees,
He will not go behind his father's saying,
And he likes having thought of it so well
He says again, " Good fences make good
   neighbors."

              1914

Stopping by Woods on a Snowy Evening

Whose woods these are I think I know.
His house is in the village though;
He will not see me stopping here
To watch his woods fill up with snow.

My little horse must think it queer
To stop without a farmhouse near
Between the woods and frozen lake
The darkest evening of the year.

He gives his harness bells a shake
To ask if there is some mistake.   10
The only other sound's the sweep
Of easy wind and downy flake.

The woods are lovely, dark and deep,
But I have promises to keep,
And miles to go before I sleep,
And miles to go before I sleep.

              1923

Two Tramps in Mud Time

Out of the mud two strangers came
And caught me splitting wood in the
      yard.
And one of them put me off my aim
By hailing cheerily " Hit them hard! "
I knew pretty well why he dropped be-
      hind
And let the other go on a way.
I knew pretty well what he had in mind:
He wanted to take my job for pay.

Good blocks of beech it was I split,
As large around as the chopping block;
And every piece I squarely hit   11
Fell splinterless as a cloven rock.
The blows that a life of self-control
Spares to strike for the common good
That day, giving a loose to my soul,
I spent on the unimportant wood.

The sun was warm but the wind was
      chill.
You know how it is with an April day
When the sun is out and the wind is still,
You're one month on in the middle of
      May.   20
But if you so much as dare to speak,
A cloud comes over the sunlit arch,
A wind comes off a frozen peak,
And you're two months back in the
      middle of March.

A bluebird comes tenderly up to alight
And fronts the wind to unruffle a plume,
His song so pitched as not to excite
A single flower as yet to bloom.
It is snowing a flake: and he half knew
Winter was only playing possum.   30
Except in color he isn't blue,
But he wouldn't advise a thing to blos-
      som.

The water for which we may have to look
In summertime with a witching-wand,
In every wheelrut's now a brook,
In every print of a hoof a pond.
Be glad of water, but don't forget
The lurking frost in the earth beneath
That will steal forth after the sun is set
And show on the water its crystal
      teeth.   40

The time when most I loved my task
These two must make me love it more
By coming with what they came to ask.
You'd think I never had felt before
The weight of an ax-head poised aloft,
The grip on earth of outspread feet,
The life of muscles rocking soft
And smooth and moist in vernal heat.

Out of the woods two hulking tramps
(From sleeping God knows where last
      night,   50
But not long since in the lumber camps).
They thought all chopping was theirs of
      right.
Men of the woods and lumberjacks,
They judged me by their appropriate
      tool.
Except as a fellow handled an ax,
They had no way of knowing a fool.

Nothing on either side was said.
They knew they had but to stay their stay
And all their logic would fill my head:
As that I had no right to play   60
With what was another man's work for
      gain.
My right might be love but theirs was
      need.
And where the two exist in twain
Theirs was the better right — agreed.

But yield who will to their separation,
My object in living is to unite
My avocation and my vocation

As my two eyes make one in sight.
Only where love and need are one,
And the work is play for mortal stakes,
Is the deed ever really done   71
For Heaven and the future's sakes.

                                    1936

Birches

When I see birches bend to left and right
Across the lines of straighter darker trees,
I like to think some boy's been swinging
    them.
But swinging doesn't bend them down to
    stay.
Ice-storms do that. Often you must have
    seen them
Loaded with ice a sunny winter morning
After a rain. They click upon themselves
As the breeze rises, and turn many-
    colored
As the stir cracks and crazes their enamel.
Soon the sun's warmth makes them shed
    crystal shells   10
Shattering and avalanching on the snow-
    crust —
Such heaps of broken glass to sweep away
You'd think the inner dome of heaven
    had fallen.
They are dragged to the withered
    bracken by the load,
And they seem not to break; though once
    they are bowed
So low for long, they never right them-
    selves:
You may see their trunks arching in the
    woods
Years afterwards, trailing their leaves on
    the ground
Like girls on hands and knees that throw
    their hair
Before them over their heads to dry in
    the sun.   20
But I was going to say when Truth broke
    in

With all her matter-of-fact about the ice-
    storm
(Now am I free to be poetical?)
I should prefer to have some boy bend
    them
As he went out and in to fetch the
    cows —
Some boy too far from town to learn base-
    ball,
Whose only play was what he found him-
    self,
Summer or winter, and could play alone.
One by one he subdued his father's trees
By riding them down over and over
    again   30
Until he took the stiffness out of them,
And not one but hung limp, not one was
    left
For him to conquer. He learned all there
    was
To learn about not launching out too
    soon
And so not carrying the tree away
Clear to the ground. He always kept his
    poise
To the top branches, climbing carefully
With the same pains you use to fill a cup
Up to the brim, and even above the brim.
Then he flung outward, feet first, with a
    swish,   40
Kicking his way down through the air to
    the ground.
So was I once myself a swinger of birches.
And so I dream of going back to be.
It's when I'm weary of considerations,
And life is too much like a pathless wood
Where your face burns and tickles with
    the cobwebs
Broken across it, and one eye is weeping
From a twig's having lashed across it
    open.
I'd like to get away from earth awhile
And then come back to it and begin
    over.   50
May no fate willfully misunderstand me

And half grant what I wish and snatch
  me away
Not to return. Earth's the right place for
  love:
I don't know where it's likely to go better.
I'd like to go by climbing a birch tree,
And climb black branches up a snow-
  white trunk
Toward heaven, till the tree could bear
  no more,
But dipped its top and set me down again.
That would be good both going and com-
  ing back.
One could do worse than be a swinger
  of birches.   60
                          1916

The Road Not Taken

Two roads diverged in a yellow wood,
  And sorry I could not travel both
And be one traveler, long I stood
And looked down one as far as I could
  To where it bent in the undergrowth;

Then took the other, as just as fair,
  And having perhaps the better claim,
Because it was grassy and wanted wear;
Though as for that the passing there
  Had worn them really about the
    same,   10

And both that morning equally lay
  In leaves no step had trodden black.
Oh, I kept the first for another day!
Yet knowing how way leads on to way,
  I doubted if I should ever come back.

I shall be telling this with a sigh
  Somewhere ages and ages hence:
Two roads diverged in a wood, and I —
I took the one less traveled by,
  And that has made all the differ-
    ence.   20
                          1916

A Lone Striker

The swinging mill bell changed its rate
To tolling like the count of fate,
And though at that the tardy ran,
One failed to make the closing gate.
There was a law of God or man
That on the one who came too late
The gate for half an hour be locked,
His time be lost, his pittance docked.
He stood rebuked and unemployed.
The straining mill began to shake.   10
The mill, though many, many eyed,
Had eyes inscrutably opaque;
So that he couldn't look inside
To see if some forlorn machine
Was standing idle for his sake.
(He couldn't hope its heart would
  break.)

And yet he thought he saw the scene:
The air was full of dust of wool.
A thousand yarns were under pull,
But pull so slow, with such a twist,   20
All day from spool to lesser spool,
It seldom overtaxed their strength;
They safely grew in slender length.
And if one broke by any chance,
The spinner saw it at a glance.
The spinner still was there to spin.

That's where the human still came in.
Her deft hand showed with finger rings
Among the harp-like spread of strings.
She caught the pieces end to end   30
And, with a touch that never missed,
Not so much tied as made them blend.
Man's ingenuity was good.
He saw it plainly where he stood,
Yet found it easy to resist.

He knew another place, a wood,
And in it, tall as trees, were cliffs;
And if he stood on one of these,
'Twould be among the tops of trees,

Their upper branches round him wreath-
ing,   40
Their breathing mingled with his breath-
ing.
If — if he stood! Enough of ifs!
He knew a path that wanted walking;
He knew a spring that wanted drinking;
A thought that wanted further thinking;
A love that wanted re-renewing.
Nor was this just a way of talking
To save him the expense of doing.
With him it boded action, deed.

The factory was very fine;   50
He wished it all the modern speed.
Yet, after all, 'twas not divine,
That is to say, 'twas not a church.
He never would assume that he'd
Be any institution's need.
But he said then and still would say
If there should ever come a day
When industry seemed like to die
Because he left it in the lurch,
Or even merely seemed to pine   60
For want of his approval, why
Come get him — they knew where to
search.
                                       1936

An Old Man's Winter Night

All out of doors looked darkly in at him
Through the thin frost, almost in sepa-
rate stars,
That gathers on the pane in empty rooms.
What kept his eyes from giving back the
gaze
Was the lamp tilted near them in his
hand.
What kept him from remembering the
need
That brought him to that creaking room
was age.
He stood with barrels round him — at a
loss.

And having scared the cellar under him
In clomping there, he scared it once
again   10
In clomping off; — and scared the outer
night,
Which has its sounds, familiar, like the
roar
Of trees and crack of branches, common
things,
But nothing so like beating on a box.
A light he was to no one but himself
Where now he sat, concerned with he
knew what,
A quiet light, and then not even that.
He consigned to the moon, such as she
was,
So late-arising, to the broken moon
As better than the sun in any case   20
For such a charge, his snow upon the
roof,
His icicles along the wall to keep;
And slept. The log that shifted with a
jolt
Once in the stove, disturbed him and he
shifted,
And eased his heavy breathing, but still
slept.
One aged man — one man — can't keep
a house,
A farm, a countryside, or if he can,
It's thus he does it of a winter night.
                                       1916

Henry Wadsworth Longfellow

Hawthorne

May 23, 1864

How beautiful it was, that one bright day
  In the long week of rain!
Though all its splendor could not chase
  away
    The omnipresent pain.

The lovely town was white with apple-
    blooms,
  And the great elms o'erhead
Dark shadows wove on their aerial looms,
  Shot through with golden thread.

Across the meadows, by the gray old
    manse,
  The historic river flowed: 10
I was as one who wanders in a trance,
  Unconscious of his road.

The faces of familiar friends seemed
    strange;
  Their voices I could hear,
And yet the words they uttered seemed to
    change
  Their meaning to my ear.

For the one face I looked for was not
    there,
  The one low voice was mute;
Only an unseen presence filled the air,
  And baffled my pursuit.   20

Now I look back, and meadow, manse,
    and stream
  Dimly my thought defines;
I only see — a dream within a dream —
  The hill-top hearsed with pines.

I only hear above his place of rest
  Their tender undertone,
The infinite longings of a troubled breast,
  The voice so like his own.

There in seclusion and remote from men
  The wizard hand lies cold,   30
Which at its topmost speed let fall the
    pen,
  And left the tale half told.

Ah! who shall lift that wand of magic
    power,

And the lost clew regain?
The unfinished window in Aladdin's
    tower
  Unfinished must remain!

                    1864

FROM The Song of Hiawatha

10

HIAWATHA'S WOOING

" As unto the bow the cord is,
So unto the man is woman,
Though she bends him, she obeys him,
Though she draws him, yet she follows,
Useless each without the other! "
  Thus the youthful Hiawatha
Said within himself and pondered,
Much perplexed by various feelings,
Listless, longing, hoping, fearing,
Dreaming still of Minnehaha,   10
Of the lovely Laughing Water,
In the land of the Dacotahs.
  " Wed a maiden of your people,"
Warning said the old Nokomis;
" Go not eastward, go not westward,
For a stranger, whom we know not!
Like a fire upon the hearth-stone
Is a neighbor's homely daughter,
Like the starlight or the moonlight
Is the handsomest of strangers! "   20
  Thus dissuading spake Nokomis,
And my Hiawatha answered
Only this: " Dear old Nokomis,
Very pleasant is the firelight,
But I like the starlight better,
Better do I like the moonlight! "
  Gravely then said old Nokomis:
" Bring not here an idle maiden,
Bring not here a useless woman,
Hands unskillful, feet unwilling;   30
Bring a wife with nimble fingers,
Heart and hand that move together,
Feet that run on willing errands! "

Smiling answered Hiawatha:
" In the land of the Dacotahs
Lives the Arrow-maker's daughter,
Minnehaha, Laughing Water,
Handsomest of all the women.
I will bring her to your wigwam,
She shall run upon your errands,   40
Be your starlight, moonlight, firelight,
Be the sunlight of my people! "

Still dissuading said Nokomis:
" Bring not to my lodge a stranger
From the land of the Dacotahs!
Very fierce are the Dacotahs,
Often is there war between us,
There are feuds yet unforgotten,
Wounds that ache and still may open! "

Laughing answered Hiawatha: 50
" For that reason, if no other,
Would I wed the fair Dacotah,
That our tribes might be united,
That old feuds might be forgotten,
And old wounds be healed forever! "

Thus departed Hiawatha
To the land of the Dacotahs,
To the land of handsome women;
Striding over moor and meadow,
Through interminable forests,   60
Through uninterrupted silence.

With his moccasins of magic,
At each stride a mile he measured;
Yet the way seemed long before him,
And his heart outran his footsteps;
And he journeyed without resting,
Till he heard the cataract's laughter,
Heard the Falls of Minnehaha
Calling to him through the silence.
" Pleasant is the sound! " he murmured,
" Pleasant is the voice that calls me! " 71

On the outskirts of the forests,
'Twixt the shadow and the sunshine,
Herds of fallow deer were feeding,
But they saw not Hiawatha;
To his bow he whispered, " Fail not! "
To his arrow whispered, " Swerve not! "
Sent it singing on its errand,

To the red heart of the roebuck;
Threw the deer across his shoulder,   80
And sped forward without pausing.

At the doorway of his wigwam
Sat the ancient Arrow-maker,
In the land of the Dacotahs,
Making arrow-heads of jasper,
Arrow-heads of chalcedony.
At his side, in all her beauty,
Sat the lovely Minnehaha,
Sat his daughter, Laughing Water,
Plaiting mats of flags and rushes;   90
Of the past the old man's thoughts were,
And the maiden's of the future.

He was thinking, as he sat there,
Of the days when with such arrows
He had struck the deer and bison,
On the Muskoday, the meadow;
Shot the wild goose, flying southward,
On the wing, the clamorous Wawa;
Thinking of the great war-parties,
How they came to buy his arrows,   100
Could not fight without his arrows.
Ah, no more such noble warriors
Could be found on earth as they were!
Now the men were all like women,
Only used their tongues for weapons!

She was thinking of a hunter,
From another tribe and country,
Young and tall and very handsome,
Who one morning, in the Spring-time,
Came to buy her father's arrows,   110
Sat and rested in the wigwam,
Lingered long about the doorway,
Looking back as he departed.
She had heard her father praise him,
Praise his courage and his wisdom;
Would he come again for arrows
To the Falls of Minnehaha?
On the mat her hands lay idle,
And her eyes were very dreamy.

Through their thoughts they heard a
   footstep,   120
Heard a rustling in the branches,
And with glowing cheek and forehead,

With the deer upon his shoulders,
Suddenly from out the woodlands
Hiawatha stood before them.

Straight the ancient Arrow-maker
Looked up gravely from his labor,
Laid aside the unfinished arrow,
Bade him enter at the doorway,
Saying, as he rose to meet him,   130
"Hiawatha, you are welcome!"

At the feet of Laughing Water
Hiawatha laid his burden,
Threw the red deer from his shoulders;
And the maiden looked up at him,
Looked up from her mat of rushes,
Said with gentle look and accent,
"You are welcome, Hiawatha!"

Very spacious was the wigwam,
Made of deer-skins dressed and whitened,
With the Gods of the Dacotahs   141
Drawn and painted on its curtains,
And so tall the doorway, hardly
Hiawatha stooped to enter,
Hardly touched his eagle-feathers
As he entered at the doorway.

Then uprose the Laughing Water,
From the ground fair Minnehaha,
Laid aside her mat unfinished,
Brought forth food and set before them,
Water brought them from the brook-
      let,   151
Gave them food in earthen vessels,
Gave them drink in bowls of bass-wood,
Listened while the guest was speaking,
Listened while her father answered,
But not once her lips she opened,
Not a single word she uttered.

Yes, as in a dream she listened
To the words of Hiawatha,
As he talked of old Nokomis,   160
Who had nursed him in his childhood,
As he told of his companions,
Chibiabos, the musician,
And the very strong man, Kwasind,
And of happiness and plenty
In the land of the Ojibways,

In the pleasant land and peaceful.
"After many years of warfare,
Many years of strife and bloodshed,
There is peace between the Ojibways
And the tribe of the Dacotahs."   171
Thus continued Hiawatha,
And then added, speaking slowly,
"That this peace may last forever,
And our hands be clasped more closely,
And our hearts be more united,
Give me as my wife this maiden,
Minnehaha, Laughing Water,
Loveliest of Dacotah women!"

And the ancient Arrow-maker   180
Paused a moment ere he answered,
Smoked a little while in silence,
Looked at Hiawatha proudly,
Fondly looked at Laughing Water,
And made answer very gravely:
"Yes, if Minnehaha wishes;
Let your heart speak, Minnehaha!"

And the lovely Laughing Water
Seemed more lovely as she stood there,
Neither willing nor reluctant,   190
As she went to Hiawatha,
Softly took the seat beside him,
While she said, and blushed to say it,
"I will follow you, my husband!"

This was Hiawatha's wooing!
Thus it was he won the daughter
Of the ancient Arrow-maker,
In the land of the Dacotahs!

From the wigwam he departed,
Leading with him Laughing Water;   200
Hand in hand they went together,
Through the woodland and the meadow,
Left the old man standing lonely
At the doorway of his wigwam,
Heard the Falls of Minnehaha
Calling to them from the distance,
Crying to them from afar off,
"Fare thee well, O Minnehaha!"

And the ancient Arrow-maker
Turned again unto his labor,   210
Sat down by his sunny doorway,

Murmuring to himself, and saying:
" Thus it is our daughters leave us,
Those we love, and those who love us!
Just when they have learned to help us,
When we are old and lean upon them,
Comes a youth with flaunting feathers,
With his flute of reeds, a stranger
Wanders piping through the village,
Beckons to the fairest maiden,   220
And she follows where he leads her,
Leaving all things for the stranger! "

   Pleasant was the journey homeward,
Through interminable forests,
Over meadow, over mountain,
Over river, hill, and hollow.
Short it seemed to Hiawatha,
Though they journeyed very slowly,
Though his pace he checked and
    slackened
To the steps of Laughing Water.   230
   Over wide and rushing rivers
In his arms he bore the maiden;
Light he thought her as a feather,
As the plume upon his head-gear;
Cleared the tangled pathway for her,
Bent aside the swaying branches,
Made at night a lodge of branches,
And a bed with boughs of hemlock,
And a fire before the doorway
With the dry cones of the pine-tree.   240
   All the traveling winds went with
    them,
O'er the meadows, through the forest;
All the stars of night looked at them,
Watched with sleepless eyes their slum-
    ber;
From his ambush in the oak-tree
Peeped the squirrel, Adjidaumo,
Watched with eager eyes the lovers;
And the rabbit, the Wabasso,
Scampered from the path before them,
Peering, peeping from his burrow,   250
Sat erect upon his haunches,
Watched with curious eyes the lovers.
   Pleasant was the journey homeward!

All the birds sang loud and sweetly
Songs of happiness and heart's-ease;
Sang the bluebird, the Owaissa,
" Happy are you, Hiawatha,
Having such a wife to love you! "
Sang the robin, the Opechee,
" Happy are you, Laughing Water,   260
Having such a noble husband! "
   From the sky the sun benignant
Looked upon them through the branches,
Saying to them, " O my children,
Love is sunshine, hate is shadow,
Life is checkered shade and sunshine,
Rule by love, O Hiawatha! "
   From the sky the moon looked at them,
Filled the lodge with mystic splendors,
Whispered to them, " O my children,
Day is restless, night is quiet,   271
Man imperious, woman feeble;
Half is mine, although I follow;
Rule by patience, Laughing Water! "
   Thus it was they journeyed homeward;
Thus it was that Hiawatha
To the lodge of old Nokomis
Brought the moonlight, starlight, fire-
    light,
Brought the sunshine of his people,
Minnehaha, Laughing Water,   280
Handsomest of all the women
In the land of the Dacotahs,
In the land of handsome women.

               1855

The Birds of Killingworth

It was the season, when through all the
    land
   The merle and mavis build, and build-
    ing sing
Those lovely lyrics, written by His hand,
   Whom Saxon Caedmon calls the
    Blithe-heart King;
When on the boughs the purple buds
    expand, .

The banners of the vanguard of the
    Spring,
And rivulets, rejoicing, rush and leap,
And wave their fluttering signals from
    the steep.

The robin and the bluebird, piping loud,
    Filled all the blossoming orchards with
        their glee;   10
The sparrows chirped as if they still were
    proud
    Their race in Holy Writ should men-
        tioned be;
And hungry crows, assembled in a crowd,
    Clamored their piteous prayer inces-
        santly,
Knowing who hears the ravens cry, and
    said:
"Give us, O Lord, this day, our daily
    bread!"

Across the Sound the birds of passage
    sailed,
    Speaking some unknown language
        strange and sweet
Of tropic isle remote, and passing hailed
    The village with the cheers of all their
        fleet;   20
Or quarreling together, laughed and
    railed
    Like foreign sailors, landed in the
        street
Of seaport town, and with outlandish
    noise
Of oaths and gibberish frightening girls
    and boys.

Thus came the jocund Spring in Killing-
    worth,
    In fabulous days, some hundred years
        ago;
And thrifty farmers, as they tilled the
    earth,
    Heard with alarm the cawing of the
        crow,

That mingled with the universal mirth,
    Cassandra-like, prognosticating woe;
They shook their heads, and doomed
    with dreadful words   31
To swift destruction the whole race of
    birds.

And a town-meeting was convened
    straightway
    To set a price upon the guilty heads
Of these marauders, who, in lieu of pay,
    Levied black-mail upon the garden
        beds
And cornfields, and beheld without dis-
    may
    The awful scarecrow, with his flutter-
        ing shreds;
The skeleton that waited at their feast,
Whereby their sinful pleasure was in-
    creased.   40

Then from his house, a temple painted
    white,
    With fluted columns, and a roof of red,
The Squire came forth, august and splen-
    did sight!
    Slowly descending, with majestic tread,
Three flights of steps, nor looking left nor
    right,
    Down the long street he walked, as
        one who said,
"A town that boasts inhabitants like me
Can have no lack of good society!"

The Parson, too, appeared, a man austere,
    The instinct of whose nature was to
        kill;   50
The wrath of God he preached from
    year to year,
    And read, with fervor, Edwards on the
        Will;
His favorite pastime was to slay the deer
    In Summer on some Adirondac hill;
E'en now, while walking down the rural
    lane,

He lopped the wayside lilies with his
    cane.

From the Academy, whose belfry
    crowned
    The hill of Science with its vane of
      brass,
Came the Preceptor, gazing idly round,
    Now at the clouds, and now at the
      green grass,   60
And all absorbed in reveries profound
    Of fair Almira in the upper class,
Who was, as in a sonnet he had said,
As pure as water, and as good as bread.

And next the Deacon issued from his
    door,
    In his voluminous neck-cloth, white as
      snow;
A suit of sable bombazine he wore;
    His form was ponderous, and his step
      was slow;
There never was so wise a man before;
    He seemed the incarnate " Well, I told
      you so! "   70
And to perpetuate his great renown
There was a street named after him in
    town.

These came together in the new town-
    hall,
    With sundry farmers from the region
      round.
The Squire presided, dignified and tall,
    His air impressive and his reasoning
      sound;
Ill fared it with the birds, both great and
    small;
    Hardly a friend in all that crowd they
      found,
But enemies enough, who every one
Charged them with all the crimes be-
    neath the sun.   80

When they had ended, from his place
    apart

Rose the Preceptor, to redress the
    wrong,
And, trembling like a steed before the
    start,
    Looked round bewildered on the ex-
      pectant throng;
Then thought of fair Almira, and took
    heart
    To speak out what was in him, clear
      and strong,
Alike regardless of their smile or frown,
And quite determined not to be laughed
    down.

" Plato, anticipating the Reviewers,
    From his Republic banished without
      pity   90
The Poets; in this little town of yours,
    You put to death, by means of a Com-
      mittee,
The ballad-singers and the Troubadours,
    The street-musicians of the heavenly
      city,
The birds, who make sweet music for us
    all
In our dark hours, as David did for Saul.

" The thrush that carols at the dawn of
    day
    From the green steeples of the piny
      wood;
The oriole in the elm; the noisy jay,
    Jargoning like a foreigner at his
      food;   100
The bluebird balanced on some topmost
    spray,
    Flooding with melody the neighbor-
      hood;
Linnet and meadow-lark, and all the
    throng
That dwell in nests, and have the gift of
    song.

" You slay them all! and wherefore? for
    the gain

Of a scant handful more or less of
    wheat,
Or rye, or barley, or some other grain,
    Scratched up at random by industrious
    feet,
Searching for worm or weevil after rain!
    Or a few cherries, that are not so
    sweet   110
As are the songs these uninvited guests
Sing at their feast with comfortable
    breasts.

" Do you ne'er think what wondrous
    beings these?
    Do you ne'er think who made them,
    and who taught
The dialect they speak, where melodies
    Alone are the interpreters of thought?
Whose household words are songs in
    many keys,
    Sweeter than instrument of men e'er
    caught!
Whose habitations in the tree-tops even
Are half-way houses on the road to
    heaven!   120

" Think, every morning when the sun
    peeps through
    The dim, leaf-latticed windows of the
    grove,
How jubilant the happy birds renew
    Their old, melodious madrigals of
    love!
And when you think of this, remember
    too
    'Tis always morning somewhere, and
    above
The awakening continents, from shore to
    shore,
Somewhere the birds are singing ever-
    more.

" Think of your woods and orchards
    without birds!
    Of empty nests that cling to boughs
    and beams   130

As in an idiot's brain remembered words
    Hang empty 'mid the cobwebs of his
    dreams!
Will bleat of flocks or bellowing of herds
    Make up for the lost music, when your
    teams
Drag home the stingy harvest, and no
    more
The feathered gleaners follow to your
    door?

" What! would you rather see the inces-
    sant stir
    Of insects in the windrows of the hay,
And hear the locust and the grasshopper
    Their melancholy hurdy-gurdies play?
    Is this more pleasant to you than the
    whir   141
    Of meadow-lark, and her sweet roun-
    delay,
Or twitter of little field-fares, as you take
Your nooning in the shade of bush and
    brake?

" You call them thieves and·pillagers;
    but know,
    They are the wingèd wardens of your
    farms,
Who from the cornfields drive the insid-
    ious foe,
    And from your harvests keep a hun-
    dred harms;
Even the blackest of them all, the crow,
    Renders good service as your man-at-
    arms,   150
Crushing the beetle in his coat of mail,
And crying havoc on the slug and snail.

" How can I teach your children gentle-
    ness,
    And mercy to the weak, and reverence
For life, which, in its weakness or excess,
    Is still a gleam of God's omnipotence,
Or Death, which, seeming darkness, is no
    less

The selfsame light, although averted
  hence,
When by your laws, your actions, and
  your speech,
You contradict the very things I teach?"

With this he closed; and through the
  audience went   161
  A murmur, like the rustle of dead
    leaves;
The farmers laughed and nodded, and
  some bent
  Their yellow heads together like their
    sheaves;
Men have no faith in fine-spun sentiment
  Who put their trust in bullocks and in
    beeves.
The birds were doomed; and, as the
  record shows,
A bounty offered for the heads of crows.

There was another audience out of reach,
  Who had no voice nor vote in making
    laws,   170
But in the papers read his little speech,
  And crowned his modest temples with
    applause;
They made him conscious, each one more
  than each,
  He still was victor, vanquished in their
    cause.
Sweetest of all the applause he won from
  thee,
O fair Almira at the Academy!

And so the dreadful massacre began;
  O'er fields and orchards, and o'er wood-
    land crests,
The ceaseless fusillade of terror ran.
  Dead fell the birds, with blood-stains
    on their breasts,   180
Or wounded crept away from sight of
  man,
  While the young died of famine in
    their nests;

A slaughter to be told in groans, not
  words,
The very St. Bartholomew of Birds!

The Summer came, and all the birds
  were dead;
  The days were like hot coals; the very
    ground
Was burned to ashes; in the orchards fed
  Myriads of caterpillars, and around
The cultivated fields and garden beds
  Hosts of devouring insects crawled,
    and found   190
No foe to check their march, till they had
  made
The land a desert without leaf or shade.

Devoured by worms, like Herod, was the
  town,
  Because, like Herod, it had ruthlessly
Slaughtered the Innocents. From the trees
  spun down
  The canker-worms upon the passers-
    by,
Upon each woman's bonnet, shawl, and
  gown,
  Who shook them off with just a little
    cry;
They were the terror of each favorite
  walk,
The endless theme of all the village
  talk.   200

The farmers grew impatient, but a few
  Confessed their error, and would not
    complain,
For after all, the best thing one can do
  When it is raining, is to let it rain.
Then they repealed the law, although
  they knew
  It would not call the dead to life again;
As school-boys, finding their mistake too
  late,
Draw a wet sponge across the accusing
  slate.

That year in Killingworth the Autumn
came
  Without the light of his majestic
  look,   210
The wonder of the falling tongues of
flame,
  The illumined pages of his Doom's-
  Day book.
A few lost leaves blushed crimson with
their shame,
  And drowned themselves despairing in
  the brook,
While the wild wind went moaning
everywhere,
Lamenting the dead children of the air!

But the next Spring a stranger sight was
seen,
  A sight that never yet by bard was
  sung,
As great a wonder as it would have been
  If some dumb animal had found a
  tongue!   220
A wagon, overarched with evergreen,
  Upon whose boughs were wicker cages
  hung,
All full of singing birds, came down the
street,
Filling the air with music wild and sweet.

From all the country round these birds
were brought,
  By order of the town, with anxious
  quest,
And, loosened from their wicker prisons,
sought
  In woods and fields the places they
  loved best,
Singing loud canticles, which many
thought
  Were satires to the authorities addressed,   230
While others, listening in green lanes,
averred
Such lovely music never had been heard!

But blither still and louder caroled they
  Upon the morrow, for they seemed to
  know
It was the fair Almira's wedding-day,
  And everywhere, around, above, be-
  low,
When the Preceptor bore his bride away,
  Their songs burst forth in joyous over-
  flow,
And a new heaven bent over a new earth
Amid the sunny farms of Killing-
worth.   240
           1863

The Harvest Moon

It is the Harvest Moon! On gilded vanes
  And roofs of villages, on woodland
  crests
  And their aerial neighborhoods of
  nests
Deserted, on the curtained window-
panes
Of rooms where children sleep, on coun-
try lanes
  And harvest-fields, its mystic splendor
  rests!
Gone are the birds that were our sum-
mer guests,
  With the last sheaves return the labor-
  ing wains!
All things are symbols: the external
shows
  Of Nature have their image in the
  mind,   10
  As flowers and fruits and falling of the
  leaves;
The song-birds leave us at the summer's
close,
  Only the empty nests are left behind,
  And pipings of the quail among the
  sheaves.
          1878

The Tide Rises, the Tide Falls

The tide rises, the tide falls,
The twilight darkens, the curlew calls;
Along the sea-sands damp and brown
The traveler hastens toward the town,
    And the tide rises, the tide falls.

Darkness settles on roofs and walls,
But the sea, the sea in the darkness calls;
The little waves, with their soft, white
    hands,
Efface the footprints in the sands,
    And the tide rises, the tide falls.   10

The morning breaks; the steeds in their
    stalls
Stamp and neigh, as the hostler calls;
The day returns, but nevermore
Returns the traveler to the shore,
    And the tide rises, the tide falls.
                                    1880

Ralph Waldo Emerson

Concord Hymn

SUNG AT THE COMPLETION OF THE BATTLE
MONUMENT, JULY 4, 1837

By the rude bridge that arched the flood,
    Their flag to April's breeze unfurled,
Here once the embattled farmers stood,
    And fired the shot heard round the
    world.

The foe long since in silence slept;
    Alike the conqueror silent sleeps;
And Time the ruined bridge has swept
    Down the dark stream which seaward
    creeps.

On this green bank, by this soft stream,
    We set today a votive stone;   10
That memory may their deed redeem,
    When, like our sires, our sons are gone.

Spirit, that made those heroes dare
    To die, and leave their children free,
Bid Time and Nature gently spare
    The shaft we raise to them and thee.
                                    1837

Each and All

Little thinks, in the field, yon red-cloaked
    clown,
Of thee from the hill-top looking down;
The heifer that lows in the upland farm,
Far-heard, lows not thine ear to charm;
The sexton, tolling his bell at noon,
Deems not that great Napoleon
Stops his horse, and lists with delight,
Whilst his files sweep round yon Alpine
    height;
Nor knowest thou what argument
Thy life to thy neighbor's creed has lent.
All are needed by each one;   11
Nothing is fair or good alone.
I thought the sparrow's note from heaven,
Singing at dawn on the alder bough;
I brought him home, in his nest, at even;
He sings the song, but it cheers not now,
For I did not bring home the river and
    sky; —
He sang to my ear, — they sang to my
    eye.
The delicate shells lay on the shore;
The bubbles of the latest wave   20
Fresh pearls to their enamel gave,
And the bellowing of the savage sea
Greeted their safe escape to me.
I wiped away the weeds and foam,
I fetched my sea-born treasures home;
But the poor, unsightly, noisome things
Had left their beauty on the shore

With the sun and the sand and the wild
  uproar.
The lover watched his graceful maid,
As 'mid the virgin train she strayed, 30
Nor knew her beauty's best attire
Was woven still by the snow-white choir.
At last she came to his hermitage,
Like the bird from the woodlands to the
  cage; —
The gay enchantment was undone,
A gentle wife, but fairy none.
Then I said, " I covet truth;
Beauty is unripe childhood's cheat;
I leave it behind with the games of
  youth: " —
As I spoke, beneath my feet 40
The ground-pine curled its pretty wreath,
Running over the club-moss burrs;
I inhaled the violet's breath;
Around me stood the oaks and firs;
Pine-cones and acorns lay on the ground;
Over me soared the eternal sky,
Full of light and of deity;
Again I saw, again I heard,
The rolling river, the morning bird; —
Beauty through my senses stole; 50
I yielded myself to the perfect whole.
1839

The Humble-Bee

Burly, dozing humble-bee,
Where thou art is clime for me.
Let them sail for Porto Rique,
Far-off heats through seas to seek;
I will follow thee alone,
Thou animated torrid-zone!
Zigzag steerer, desert cheerer,
Let me chase thy waving lines;
Keep me nearer, me thy hearer,
Singing over shrubs and vines. 10

Insect lover of the sun,
Joy of thy dominion!
Sailor of the atmosphere;
Swimmer through the waves of air;
Voyager of light and noon;
Epicurean of June;
Wait, I prithee, till I come
Within earshot of thy hum, —
All without is martyrdom.

When the south wind, in May days, 20
With a net of shining haze
Silvers the horizon wall,
And with softness touching all,
Tints the human countenance
With the color of romance,
And infusing subtle heats,
Turns the sod to violets,
Thou, in sunny solitudes,
Rover of the underwoods,
The green silence dost displace 30
With thy mellow, breezy bass.

Hot midsummer's petted crone,
Sweet to me thy drowsy tone
Tells of countless sunny hours,
Long days, and solid banks of flowers;
Of gulfs of sweetness without bound
In Indian wildernesses found;
Of Syrian peace, immortal leisure,
Firmest cheer, and bird-like pleasure.

Aught unsavory or unclean 40
Hath my insect never seen;
But violets and bilberry bells,
Maple-sap and daffodels,
Grass with green flag half-mast high,
Succory to match the sky,
Columbine with horn of honey,
Scented fern, and agrimony,
Clover, catchfly, adder's-tongue
And brier-roses, dwelt among;
All beside was unknown waste, 50
All was picture as he passed.

Wiser far than human seer,
Yellow-breeched philosopher!
Seeing only what is fair,
Sipping only what is sweet,

Thou dost mock at fate and care,
Leave the chaff and take the wheat.
When the fierce northwestern blast
Cools sea and lands so far and fast,
Thou already slumberest deep;　　　60
Woe and want thou canst outsleep;
Want and woe, which torture us,
Thy sleep makes ridiculous.

1839

The Snow-Storm

Announced by all the trumpets of the
　　sky,
Arrives the snow, and, driving o'er the
　　fields,
Seems nowhere to alight: the whited air
Hides hills and woods, the river, and the
　　heaven,
And veils the farm-house at the garden's
　　end.
The sled and traveler stopped, the couri-
　　er's feet
Delayed, all friends shut out, the house-
　　mates sit
Around the radiant fireplace, enclosed
In a tumultuous privacy of storm.

Come see the north wind's masonry.　10
Out of an unseen quarry evermore
Furnished with tile, the fierce artificer
Curves his white bastions with projected
　　roof
Round every windward stake, or tree, or
　　door.
Speeding, the myriad-handed, his wild
　　work
So fanciful, so savage, naught cares he
For number or proportion. Mockingly,
On coop or kennel he hangs Parian
　　wreaths;
A swan-like form invests the hidden
　　thorn;
Fills up the farmer's lane from wall to
　　wall,　　　　　　　　　　　　　20

Maugre the farmer's sighs; and at the
　　gate
A tapering turret overtops the work.
And when his hours are numbered, and
　　the world
Is all his own, retiring, as he were not,
Leaves, when the sun appears, astonished
　　Art
To mimic in slow structures, stone by
　　stone,
Built in an age, the mad wind's night-
　　work,
The frolic architecture of the snow.

1841

Terminus

It is time to be old,
To take in sail: —
The god of bounds,
Who sets to seas a shore,
Came to me in his fatal rounds,
And said: " No more!
No farther shoot
Thy broad ambitious branches, and thy
　　root.
Fancy departs: no more invent;
Contract thy firmament　　　　　　10
To compass of a tent.
There's not enough for this and that,
Make thy option which of two;
Economize the failing river,
Not the less revere the Giver,
Leave the many and hold the few.
Timely wise accept the terms,
Soften the fall with wary foot;
A little while
Still plan and smile,　　　　　　20
And, — fault of novel germs, —
Mature the unfallen fruit.
Curse, if thou wilt, thy sires,
Bad husbands of their fires,
Who, when they gave thee breath,
Failed to bequeath
The needful sinew stark as once,

The Baresark marrow to thy bones,
But left a legacy of ebbing veins,
Inconstant heat and nerveless reins, — 30
Amid the Muses, left thee deaf and dumb,
Amid the gladiators, halt and numb."

As the bird trims her to the gale,
I trim myself to the storm of time,
I man the rudder, reef the sail,
Obey the voice at eve obeyed at prime:
" Lowly faithful, banish fear,
Right onward drive unharmed;
The port, well worth the cruise, is near,
And every wave is charmed." 40
1867

Edgar Allan Poe

Romance

Romance, who loves to nod and sing,
With drowsy head and folded wing,
Among the green leaves as they shake
Far down within some shadowy lake,
To me a painted paroquet
Hath been — a most familiar bird —
Taught me my alphabet to say —
To lisp my very earliest word
While in the wild wood I did lie,
A child — with a most knowing eye. 10

Of late, eternal Condor years
So shake the very Heaven on high
With tumult as they thunder by,
I have no time for idle cares
Through gazing on the unquiet sky.
And when an hour with calmer wings
Its down upon my spirit flings —
That little time with lyre and rhyme
To while away — forbidden things!
My heart would feel to be a crime 20
Unless it trembled with the strings!
1829

To Helen

Helen, thy beauty is to me
  Like those Nicaean barks of yore,
That gently, o'er a perfumed sea,
  The weary, wayworn wanderer bore
  To his own native shore.

On desperate seas long wont to roam,
  Thy hyacinth hair, thy classic face,
Thy Naiad airs have brought me home
  To the glory that was Greece
And the grandeur that was Rome.

Lo! in yon brilliant window-niche
  How statue-like I see thee stand,
  The agate lamp within thy hand!
Ah, Psyche, from the regions which
  Are Holy Land!
1831

Lenore

Ah, broken is the golden bowl! the spirit
  flown forever!
Let the bell toll! — a saintly soul floats on
  the Stygian river;
And, Guy De Vere, hast *thou* no tear? —
  weep now or never more!
See! on yon drear and rigid bier low lies
  thy love, Lenore!
Come! let the burial rite be read — the
  funeral song be sung! —
An anthem for the queenliest dead that
  ever died so young —
A dirge for her the doubly dead in that
  she died so young.

" Wretches! ye loved her for her wealth
  and hated her for her pride,
And when she fell in feeble health, ye
  blessed her — that she died!
How *shall* the ritual, then, be read — the
  requiem how be sung 10
By you — by yours, the evil eye, — by
  yours, the slanderous tongue

That did to death the innocence that died,
and died so young? "

Peccavimus; but rave not thus! and let a
Sabbath song
Go up to God so solemnly the dead may
feel no wrong!
The sweet Lenore hath " gone before,"
with Hope, that flew beside,
Leaving thee wild for the dear child
that should have been thy bride —
For her, the fair and *debonair,* that now
so lowly lies,
The life upon her yellow hair but not
within her eyes —
The life still there, upon her hair — the
death upon her eyes.

" Avaunt! tonight my heart is light. No
dirge will I upraise,   20
But waft the angel on her flight with a
Paean of old days!
Let *no* bell toll, then, — lest her soul,
amid its hallowed mirth,
Should catch the note, as it doth float —
up from the damnèd Earth!
To friends above, from fiends below, the
indignant ghost is riven —
From Hell unto a high estate far up
within the Heaven —
From grief and groan, to a golden throne,
beside the King of Heaven."

                                          1831

Ulalume

The skies they were ashen and sober;
   The leaves they were crisped and
   sere —
   The leaves they were withering and
   sere;
It was night in the lonesome October
Of my most immemorial year;
It was hard by the dim lake of Auber,
   In the misty mid region of Weir —

It was down by the dank tarn of Auber,
   In the ghoul-haunted woodland of
   Weir.

Here once, through an alley Titanic,   10
   Of cypress, I roamed with my Soul —
   Of cypress, with Psyche, my Soul.
These were days when my heart was vol-
   canic
   As the scoriac rivers that roll —
   As the lavas that restlessly roll
Their sulphurous currents down Yaanek
   In the ultimate climes of the pole —
That groan as they roll down Mount
   Yaanek
   In the realms of the boreal pole.

Our talk had been serious and sober,   20
   But our thoughts they were palsied and
   sere —
   Our memories were treacherous and
   sere —
For we knew not the month was Octo-
   ber,
   And we marked not the night of the
   year —
   (Ah, night of all nights in the year!)
We noted not the dim lake of Auber —
   (Though once we had journeyed down
   here) —
Remembered not the dank tarn of Auber,
   Nor the ghoul-haunted woodland of
   Weir.

And now, as the night was senescent   30
   And star-dials pointed to morn —
   As the star-dials hinted of morn —
At the end of our path a liquescent
   And nebulous lustre was born,
Out of which a miraculous crescent
   Arose with a duplicate horn —
Astarte's bediamonded crescent
   Distinct with its duplicate horn.

And I said — " She is warmer than Dian:
   She rolls through an ether of sighs —

She revels in a region of sighs: 41
She has seen that the tears are not dry on
  These cheeks, where the worm never
    dies,
And has come past the stars of the Lion
  To point us the path to the skies —
  To the Lethean peace of the skies —
Come up, in despite of the Lion,
  To shine on us with her bright eyes —
Come up through the lair of the Lion,
  With love in her luminous eyes." 50

But Psyche, uplifting her finger,
  Said — " Sadly this star I mistrust —
  Her pallor I strangely mistrust: —
Oh, hasten! — oh, let us not linger!
Oh, fly! — let us fly! — for we must."
In terror she spoke, letting sink her
  Wings till they trailed in the dust —
In agony sobbed, letting sink her
  Plumes till they trailed in the dust —
  Till they sorrowfully trailed in the
    dust. 60

I replied — " This is nothing but dream-
    ing:
Let us on by this tremulous light!
Let us bathe in this crystalline light!
Its Sibyllic splendor is beaming
  With Hope and in Beauty tonight: —
  See! — it flickers up the sky through
    the night!
Ah, we safely may trust to its gleaming,
  And be sure it will lead us aright —
We safely may trust to a gleaming
  That cannot but guide us aright, 70
  Since it flickers up to Heaven through
    the night."

Thus I pacified Psyche and kissed her,
  And tempted her out of her gloom —
  And conquered her scruples and
    gloom;
And we passed to the end of the vista,
  But were stopped by the door of a
    tomb —

By the door of a legended tomb;
And I said — " What is written, sweet
  sister,
  On the door of this legended tomb? "
She replied — " Ulalume — Ulalume —
  'Tis the vault of thy lost Ulalume! " 81

Then my heart it grew ashen and sober
  As the leaves that were crisped and
    sere —
  As the leaves that were withering and
    sere;
And I cried — " It was surely October
  On *this* very night of last year
  That I journeyed — I journeyed down
    here —
  That I brought a dread burden down
    here —
  On this night of all nights in the
    year,
  Ah, what demon has tempted me
    here? 90
Well I know, now, this dim lake of
  Auber —
  This misty mid region of Weir —
Well I know, now, this dank tarn of
  Auber,
  This ghoul-haunted woodland of
    Weir."

Said *we,* then — the two, then — " Ah,
  can it
  Have been that the woodlandish
    ghouls,
  The pitiful, the merciless ghouls —
To bar up our way and to ban it
  From the secret that lies in these
    wolds —
  From the thing that lies hidden in
    these wolds — 100
Had drawn up the spectre of a planet
  From the limbo of lunary souls,
This sinfully scintillant planet
  From the Hell of the planetary souls? "
            1847

Eldorado

Gaily bedight,
  A gallant knight,
In sunshine and in shadow,
  Had journeyed long,
  Singing a song,
In search of Eldorado.

But he grew old —
  This knight so bold —
And o'er his heart a shadow
  Fell as he found   10
  No spot of ground
That looked like Eldorado.

And, as his strength
  Failed him at length,
He met a pilgrim shadow —
  "Shadow," said he,
  "Where can it be —
This land of Eldorado?"

"Over the Mountains
  Of the Moon,   20
Down the Valley of the Shadow,
  Ride, boldly ride,"
  The shade replied, —
"If you seek for Eldorado!"

                1849

Annabel Lee

It was many and many a year ago,
  In a kingdom by the sea,
That a maiden there lived whom you
    may know
  By the name of Annabel Lee:
And this maiden she lived with no other
    thought
  Than to love and be loved by me.

She was a child and *I* was a child,
  In this kingdom by the sea;
But we loved with a love that was more
    than love —

  I and my Annabel Lee —   10
With a love that the wingèd seraphs of
    Heaven
  Coveted her and me.

And this was the reason that, long ago,
  In this kingdom by the sea,
A wind blew out of a cloud, chilling
  My beautiful Annabel Lee —
So that her highborn kinsmen came
  And bore her away from me,
To shut her up in a sepulchre
  In this kingdom by the sea.   20

The angels, not half so happy in Heaven,
  Went envying her and me: —
Yes, that was the reason (as all men
    know,
  In this kingdom by the sea)
That the wind came out of the cloud by
    night
  Chilling and killing my Annabel Lee.

But our love it was stronger by far than
    the love
  Of those who were older than we —
  Of many far wiser than we —
And neither the angels in Heaven
    above,   30
  Nor the demons down under the sea,
Can ever dissever my soul from the soul
  Of the beautiful Annabel Lee: —

For the moon never beams, without
    bringing me dreams
  Of the beautiful Annabel Lee;
And the stars never rise, but I feel the
    bright eyes
  Of the beautiful Annabel Lee;
And so, all the night-tide, I lie down by
    the side
Of my darling, my darling, my life and
    my bride
  In her sepulchre there by the sea —   40
  In her tomb by the sounding sea.

                1849

Sidney Lanier

Song of the Chattahoochee

Out of the hills of Habersham,
  Down the valleys of Hall,
I hurry amain to reach the plain,
Run the rapid and leap the fall,
Split at the rock and together again,
Accept my bed, or narrow or wide,
And flee from folly on every side
With a lover's pain to attain the plain
  Far from the hills of Habersham,
  Far from the valleys of Hall.   10

All down the hills of Habersham,
  All through the valleys of Hall,
The rushes cried *Abide, abide,*
The willful waterweeds held me thrall,
The laving laurel turned my tide,
The ferns and the fondling grass said
    Stay,
The dewberry dipped for to work delay,
And the little reeds sighed *Abide, abide,*
  Here in the hills of Habersham,
  Here in the valleys of Hall.   20

High o'er the hills of Habersham,
  Veiling the valleys of Hall,
The hickory told me manifold
Fair tales of shade, the poplar tall
Wrought me her shadowy self to hold,
The chestnut, the oak, the walnut, the
    pine,
Overleaning, with flickering meaning
    and sign,
Said, *Pass not, so cold, these manifold
  Deep shades of the hills of Habersham,
  These glades in the valleys of Hall.*   30

And oft in the hills of Habersham,
  And oft in the valleys of Hall,
The white quartz shone, and the smooth
    brook-stone

Did bar me of passage with friendly
    brawl,
And many a luminous jewel lone
—Crystals clear or a-cloud with mist,
Ruby, garnet and amethyst —
Made lures with the lights of streaming
    stone
  In the clefts of the hills of Habersham,
  In the beds of the valleys of Hall.   40

But oh, not the hills of Habersham,
  And oh, not the valleys of Hall
Avail: I am fain for to water the plain.
Downward the voices of Duty call —
Downward, to toil and be mixed with the
    main,
The dry fields burn, and the mills are to
    turn,
And a myriad flowers mortally yearn,
And the lordly main from beyond the
    plain
  Calls o'er the hills of Habersham,
  Calls through the valleys of Hall.   50

                                    1883

The Mocking Bird

Superb and sole, upon a plumèd spray
  That o'er the general leafage boldly
    grew,
  He summ'd the woods in song; or typic
    drew
The watch of hungry hawks, the lone
    dismay
Of languid doves when long their lovers
    stray,
  And all birds' passion-plays that sprin-
    kle dew
  At morn in brake or bosky avenue.
Whate'er birds did or dreamed, this bird
    could say.
Then down he shot, bounced airily along

The sward, twitched-in a grasshopper,
   made song   10
  Midflight, perched, prinked, and to
   his art again.
  Sweet Science, this large riddle read
   me plain:
How may the death of that dull insect be
The life of yon trim Shakespeare on the
   tree?

                      1877

The Stirrup-Cup

Death, thou'rt a cordial old and rare:
Look how compounded, with what care!
Time got his wrinkles reaping thee
Sweet herbs from all antiquity.

David to thy distillage went,
Keats, and Gotama excellent,
Omar Khayyám, and Chaucer bright,
And Shakespeare for a king-delight.

Then, Time, let not a drop be spilt:
Hand me the cup whene'er thou wilt;
'Tis thy rich stirrup-cup to me;   11
I'll drink it down right smilingly.

                      1877

Corn

Today the woods are trembling through
   and through
With shimmering forms, that flash be-
   fore my view,
Then melt in green as dawn-stars melt
   in blue.
  The leaves that wave against my cheek
   caress
  Like women's hands; the embracing
   boughs express
  A subtlety of mighty tenderness;
  The copse-depths into little noises start,
  That sound anon like beatings of a
   heart,

Anon like talk 'twixt lips not far apart.
The beech dreams balm, as a dreamer
   hums a song;   10
  Through that vague wafture, expira-
   tions strong
Throb from young hickories breathing
   deep and long
With stress and urgence bold of prisoned
   spring
   And ecstasy of burgeoning.
Now, since the dew-plashed road of
   morn is dry,
Forth venture odors of more quality
And heavenlier giving. Like Jove's
   locks awry,
   Long muscadines
Rich-wreathe the spacious foreheads of
   great pines,
And breathe ambrosial passion from
   their vines.   20
  I pray with mosses, ferns and flowers
   shy
  That hide like gentle nuns from hu-
   man eye
  To lift adoring perfumes to the sky.
I hear faint bridal-sighs of brown and
   green
Dying to silent hints of kisses keen
As far lights fringe into a pleasant sheen.
  I start at fragmentary whispers, blown
  From undertalks of leafy souls un-
   known,
  Vague purports sweet, of inarticulate
   tone.
Dreaming of gods, men, nuns and brides,
   between   30
Old companies of oaks that inward lean
To join their radiant amplitudes of green
  I slowly move, with ranging looks that
   pass
  Up from the matted miracles of grass
Into yon veined complex of space
Where sky and leafage interlace
  So close, the heaven of blue is seen
  Inwoven with a heaven of green.

I wander to the zigzag-cornered fence
Where sassafras, intrenched in brambles
    dense,   40
Contests with stolid vehemence
  The march of culture, setting limb and
    thorn
  As pikes against the army of the corn.

There, while I pause, my fieldward-
    faring eyes
Take harvests, where the stately corn-
    ranks rise,
    Of inward dignities
And large benignities and insights wise,
  Graces and modest majesties.
Thus, without theft, I reap another's
    field;
Thus, without tilth, I house a wondrous
    yield,   50
And heap my heart with quintuple crops
    concealed.

Look, out of line one tall corn-captain
    stands
Advanced beyond the foremost of his
    bands,
  And waves his blades upon the very
    edge
  And hottest thicket of the battling
    hedge.
Thou lustrous stalk, that ne'er mayest
    walk nor talk,
  Still shalt thou type the poet-soul sub-
    lime
  That leads the vanward of his timid
    time
  And sings up cowards with command-
    ing rhyme —
Soul calm, like thee, yet fain, like thee,
    to grow   60
By double increment, above, below;
  Soul homely, as thou art, yet rich in
    grace like thee,
  Teaching the yeomen selfless chivalry

That moves in gentle curves of cour-
    tesy;
Soul filled like thy long veins with sweet-
    ness tense,
    By every godlike sense
Transmuted from the four wild elements.
    Drawn to high plans,
  Thou lift'st more stature than a mortal
    man's,
Yet ever piercest downward in the mould
    And keepest hold   71
Upon the reverend and steadfast earth
    That gave thee birth;
  Yea, standest smiling in thy future
    grave,
    Serene and brave,
  With unremitting breath
  Inhaling life from death,
Thine epitaph writ fair in fruitage elo-
    quent,
    Thyself thy monument.

    As poets should,   80
Thou hast built up thy hardihood
With universal food,
    Drawn in select proportion fair
    From honest mould and vagabond air;
From darkness of the dreadful night,
    And joyful light;
  From antique ashes, whose departed
    flame
  In thee has finer life and longer fame;
From wounds and balms,
From storms and calms,   90
From potsherds and dry bones
    And ruin-stones.
Into thy vigorous substance thou hast
    wrought
Whate'er the hand of Circumstance hath
    brought;
  Yea, into cool solacing green hast spun
  White radiance hot from out the sun.
So thou dost mutually leaven
Strength of earth with grace of heaven;
  So thou dost marry new and old

Into a one of higher mould;   100
So thou dost reconcile the hot and cold,
   The dark and bright,
And many a heart-perplexing opposite,
   And so,
   Akin by blood to high and low,
Fitly thou playest out thy poet's part,
Richly expending thy much-bruisèd
   heart
   In equal care to nourish lord in hall
     Or beast in stall:
   Thou took'st from all that thou mightst
     give to all.   110

O steadfast dweller on the selfsame spot
Where thou wast born, that still repinest
   not —
Type of the home-fond heart, the happy
   lot! —
   Deeply thy mild content rebukes the
     land
   Whose flimsy homes, built on the
     shifting sand
Of trade, for ever rise and fall
With alternation whimsical,
   Enduring scarce a day,
   Then swept away
By swift engulfments of incalculable
   tides   120
Whereon capricious Commerce rides.
Look, thou substantial spirit of content!
Across this little vale, thy continent,
   To where, beyond the mouldering mill,
   Yon old deserted Georgian hill
Bares to the sun his piteous aged crest
   And seamy breast,
   By restless-hearted children left to lie
Untended there beneath the heedless
   sky,
As barbarous folk expose their old to
   die.   130
Upon that generous-rounding side,
   With gullies scarified
   Where keen Neglect his lash hath
     plied,

Dwelt one I knew of old, who played
   at toil
And gave to coquette Cotton soul and
   soil.
   Scorning the slow reward of patient
     grain,
   He sowed his heart with hopes of
     swifter gain,
   Then sat him down and waited for the
     rain.
He sailed in borrowed ships of usury —
A foolish Jason on a treacherous sea,   140
Seeking the Fleece and finding misery.
   Lulled by smooth-rippling loans, in
     idle trance
   He lay, content that unthrift Circum-
     stance
   Should plough for him the stony field
     of Chance.
Yea, gathering crops whose worth no
   man might tell,
He staked his life on games of Buy-and-
   Sell,
And turned each field into a gambler's
   hell.
   Aye, as each year began,
   My farmer to the neighboring city ran;
Passed with a mournful anxious face   150
Into the banker's inner place;
Parleyed, excused, pleaded for longer
   grace;
   Railed at the drought, the worm, the
     rust, the grass;
   Protested ne'er again 'twould come to
     pass;
   With many an *oh* and *if* and *but alas*
Parried or swallowed searching questions
   rude,
And kissed the dust to soften Dives'
   mood.
At last, small loans by pledges great re-
   newed,
   He issues smiling from the fatal door,
   And buys with lavish hand his yearly
     store   160

Till his small borrowings will yield no
    more.
Aye, as each year declined,
With bitter heart and ever-brooding
    mind
He mourned his fate unkind.
    In dust, in rain, with might and main,
    He nursed his cotton, cursed his grain,
    Fretted for news that made him fret
      again,
Snatched at each telegram of Future Sale,
And thrilled with Bulls' or Bears' alter-
    nate wail —
In hope or fear alike for ever pale.   170
    And thus from year to year, through
      hope and fear,
    With many a curse and many a secret
      tear,
Striving in vain his cloud of debt to clear,
    At last
He woke to find his foolish dreaming
    past,
    And all his best-of-life the easy prey
    Of squandering scamps and quacks
      that lined his way
      With vile array,
From rascal statesman down to petty
    knave;
Himself, at best, for all his bragging
    brave,   180
A gamester's catspaw and a banker's
    slave.
    Then, worn and gray, and sick with
      deep unrest,
    He fled away into the oblivious West,
    Unmourned, unblest.

Old hill! old hill! thou gashed and hairy
    Lear
Whom the divine Cordelia of the
    year,
E'en pitying Spring, will vainly strive to
    cheer —
    King, that no subject man nor beast
    may own,

Discrowned,   undaughtered   and
    alone —
Yet shall the great God turn thy fate,   190
And bring thee back into thy monarch
    state
    And majesty immaculate.
Lo, through hot waverings of the
    August morn,
Thou givest from thy vasty sides for-
    lorn
Visions of golden treasuries of corn —
Ripe largesse lingering for some bolder
    heart
That manfully shall take thy part,
    And tend thee,
    And defend thee,
With antique sinew and with modern
    art.   200

                1875

Thar's More in the Man than Thar Is in the Land

I knowed a man, which he lived in Jones,
Which Jones is a county of red hills and
    stones,
And he lived pretty much by gittin' of
    loans,
And his mules was nuthin' but skin and
    bones,
And his hogs was flat as his corn-bread
    pones,
And he had 'bout a thousand acres o'
    land.

This man — which his name it was also
    Jones —
He swore that he'd leave them old red
    hills and stones,
Fur he couldn't make nuthin' but yaller-
    ish cotton,
And little o' *that,* and his fences was
    rotten,   10

And what little corn he had, *hit* was
  boughten
And dinged ef a livin' was in the land.

And the longer he swore the madder he
  got,
And he riz and he walked to the stable
  lot,
And he hollered to Tom to come thar and
  hitch
Fur to emigrate somewhar whar land
  was rich,
And to quit raisin' cock-burrs, thistles
  and sich,
And a wastin' ther time on the cussed
  land.

So him and Tom they hitched up the
  mules,
Pertestin' that folks was mighty big
  fools   20
That 'ud stay in Georgy ther lifetime out,
Jest scratchin' a livin' when all of 'em
  mought
Git places in Texas whar cotton would
  sprout
By the time you could plant it in the land.

And he driv by a house whar a man
  named Brown
Was a livin', not fur from the edge o'
  town,
And he bantered Brown fur to buy his
  place,
And said that bein' as money was skace,
And bein' as sheriffs was hard to face,
Two dollars an acre would git the
  land.   30

They closed at a dollar and fifty cents,
And Jones he bought him a waggin and
  tents,
And loaded his corn, and his wimmin,
  and truck,
And moved to Texas, which it tuck

His entire pile, with the best of luck,
To git thar and git him a little land.

But Brown moved out on the old Jones
  farm,
And he rolled up his breeches and bared
  his arm,
And he picked all the rocks from off'n
  the groun',
And he rooted it up and he plowed it
  down,   40
Then he sowed his corn and his wheat in
  the land.

Five years glid by, and Brown, one day
(Which he'd got so fat that he wouldn't
  weigh),
Was a settin' down, sorter lazily,
To the bulliest dinner you ever see,
When one o' the children jumped on his
  knee
And says, "Yan's Jones, which you
  bought his land."

And thar was Jones, standin' out at the
  fence,
And he hadn't no waggin, nor mules,
  nor tents,
Fur he had left Texas afoot and cum   50
To Georgy to see if he couldn't git sum
Employment, and he was a lookin' as
  hum-
Ble as ef he had never owned any land.

But Brown he axed him in, and he sot
Him down to his vittles smokin' hot,
And when he had filled hisself and the
  floor
Brown looked at him sharp and riz and
  swore
That, "whether men's land was rich or
  poor
Thar was more in the *man* than thar was
  in the *land*."

                                              1884

Evening Song

Look off, dear Love, across the sallow
    sands,
  And mark yon meeting of the sun and
    sea,
How long they kiss in sight of all the
    lands.
    Ah! longer, longer, we.

Now in the sea's red vintage melts the
  sun,

As Egypt's pearl dissolved in rosy wine,
  And Cleopatra night drinks all. 'Tis done,
    Love, lay thine hand in mine.

Come forth, sweet stars, and comfort
    heaven's heart;
  Glimmer, ye waves, round else-un-
    lighted sands.   10
O night! divorce our sun and sky apart
    Never our lips, our hands.

                      1877

Stephen Vincent Benét

FROM John Brown's Body

INVOCATION

American muse, whose strong and diverse heart
So many men have tried to understand
But only made it smaller with their art,
Because you are as various as your land,

As mountainous-deep, as flowered with blue rivers,
Thirsty with deserts, buried under snows,
As native as the shape of Navajo quivers,
And native, too, as the sea-voyaged rose.

Swift runner, never captured or subdued,
Seven-branched elk beside the mountain stream,   10
That half a hundred hunters have pursued
But never matched their bullets with the dream,

Where the great huntsmen failed, I set my sorry
And mortal snare for your immortal quarry.

You are the buffalo-ghost, the broncho-ghost
With dollar-silver in your saddle-horn,
The cowboys riding in from Painted Post,
The Indian arrow in the Indian corn,

And you are the clipped velvet of the lawns
Where Shropshire grows from Massachusetts sods,   20
The grey Maine rocks — and the war-painted dawns
That break above the Garden of the Gods.

The prairie-schooners crawling toward the ore
And the cheap car, parked by the station-door.

Where the skyscrapers lift their foggy plumes
Of stranded smoke out of a stony mouth
You are that high stone and its arrogant fumes,
And you are ruined gardens in the South

And bleak New England farms, so winter-white
Even their roofs look lonely, and the deep   30
The middle grainland where the wind of night
Is like all blind earth sighing in her sleep.

A friend, an enemy, a sacred hag
With two tied oceans in her medicine-bag.

They tried to fit you with an English song
And clip your speech into the English tale.
But, even from the first, the words went wrong,
The catbird pecked away the nightingale.

The homesick men begot high-cheekboned things
Whose wit was whittled with a different sound   40
And Thames and all the rivers of the kings
Ran into Mississippi and were drowned.

They planted England with a stubborn trust.
But the cleft dust was never English dust.

Stepchild of every exile from content
And all the disavouched, hard-bitten pack
Shipped overseas to steal a continent
With neither shirts nor honor to their back.

Pimping grandee and rump-faced regicide,
Apple-cheeked younkers from a windmill-square,   50
Puritans stubborn as the nails of Pride,
Rakes from Versailles and thieves from County Clare,

The black-robed priests who broke their hearts in vain
To make you God and France or God and Spain.

These were your lovers in your buckskin-youth.
And each one married with a dream so proud
He never knew it could not be the truth
And that he coupled with a girl of cloud.

And now to see you is more difficult yet
Except as an immensity of wheel   60
Made up of wheels, oiled with inhuman sweat
And glittering with the heat of ladled steel.

All these you are, and each is partly you,
And none is false, and none is wholly true.

So how to see you as you really are,
So how to suck the pure, distillate, stored
Essence of essence from the hidden star
And make it pierce like a riposting sword.

For, as we hunt you down, you must escape
And we pursue a shadow of our own   70
That can be caught in a magician's cape
That has the flatness of a painted stone.

Never the running stag, the gull at wing,
The pure elixir, the American thing.

And yet, at moments when the mind was hot
With something fierier than joy or grief,
When each known spot was an eternal spot
And every leaf was an immortal leaf,

I think that I have seen you, not as one,
But clad in diverse semblances and powers,   80
Always the same, as light falls from the sun,
And always different, as the differing hours.

Yet, through each altered garment that you wore
The naked body, shaking the heart's core.

All day the snow fell on that Eastern town
With its soft, pelting, little, endless sigh
Of infinite flakes that brought the tall sky down
Till I could put my hands in the white sky

And taste cold scraps of heaven on my tongue
And walk in such a changed and luminous light   90
As gods inhabit when the gods are young.
All day it fell. And when the gathered night

Was a blue shadow cast by a pale glow
I saw you then, snow-image, bird of the snow.

And I have seen and heard you in the dry
Close-huddled furnace of the city street
When the parched moon was planted in the sky
And the limp air hung dead against the heat.

I saw you rise, red as that rusty plant,
Dizzied with lights, half-mad with senseless sound,   100
Enormous metal, shaking to the chant
Of a triphammer striking iron ground.

Enormous power, ugly to the fool,
And beautiful as a well-handled tool.

These, and the memory of that windy day
On the bare hills, beyond the last barbed wire,
When all the orange poppies bloomed one way
As if a breath would blow them into fire,

I keep forever, like the sea-lion's tusk
The broken sailor brings away to land,   110
But when he touches it, he smells the musk,
And the whole sea lies hollow in his hand.

So, from a hundred visions, I make one,
And out of darkness build my mocking sun.

And should that task seem fruitless in the eyes
Of those a different magic sets apart
To see through the ice-crystal of the wise
No nation but the nation that is Art,

Their words are just. But when the birchbark-call
Is shaken with the sound that hunters make   120
The moose comes plunging through the forest-wall
Although the rifle waits beside the lake.

Art has no nations — but the mortal sky
Lingers like gold in immortality.

This flesh was seeded from no foreign grain
But Pennsylvania and Kentucky wheat,
And it has soaked in California rain
And five years tempered in New England sleet

To strive at last, against an alien proof
And by the changes of an alien moon,   130
To build again that blue, American roof
Over a half-forgotten battle-tune

And call unsurely, from a haunted ground,
Armies of shadows and the shadow-sound.

In your Long House there is an attic-place
Full of dead epics and machines that rust,
And there, occasionally, with casual face,
You come awhile to stir the sleepy dust;

Neither in pride nor mercy, but in vast
Indifference at so many gifts unsought,   140
The yellowed satins, smelling of the past,
And all the loot the lucky pirates brought.

I only bring a cup of silver air,
Yet, in your casualness, receive it there.

Receive the dream too haughty for the breast,
Receive the words that should have walked as bold
As the storm walks along the mountain-crest
And are like beggars whining in the cold.

The maimed presumption, the unskilful skill,
The patchwork colors, fading from the first,   150
And all the fire that fretted at the will
With such a barren ecstasy of thirst.

Receive them all — and should you choose to touch them
With one slant ray of quick, American light,
Even the dust will have no power to smutch them,
Even the worst will glitter in the night.

If not — the dry bones littered by the way
May still point giants toward their golden prey.

MOUNTAINEERS

Up in the mountains where the hogs are thin
And razorbacked, wild Indians of hogs,
The laurel's green in April — and if the nights
Are cold as the cold cloud of watersmoke
Above a mountain-spring, the midday sun
Has heat enough in it to make you sweat.

They are a curious and most native stock,
The lanky men, the lost, forgotten seeds
Spilled from the first great wave-march toward the West
And set to sprout by chance in the deep cracks   10
Of that hill-billy world of laurel-hells.
They keep the beechwood-fiddle and the salt
Old-fashioned ballad-English of our first
Rowdy, corn-liquor-drinking, ignorant youth;
Also the rifle and the frying-pan,
The old feud-temper and the old feud-way
Of thinking strangers better shot on sight
But treating strangers that one leaves unshot
With border-hospitality.
                          The girls
Have the brief-blooming, rhododendron-youth   20
Of pioneer women, and the black-toothed age.
And if you yearn to meet your pioneers,
You'll find them there, the same men, inbred sons
Of inbred sires perhaps, but still the same;
A pioneer-island in a world that has
No use for pioneers — the unsplit rock
Of Fundamentalism, calomel,
Clan-virtues, clannish vices, fiddle-tunes
And a hard God.
                    They are our last frontier.
They shot the railway-train when it first came,   30
And when the Fords first came, they shot the Fords.
It could not save them. They are dying now
Of being educated, which is the same.
One need not weep romantic tears for them,
But when the last moonshiner buys his radio,
And the last, lost, wild-rabbit of a girl
Is civilized with a mail-order dress,
Something will pass that was American
And all the movies will not bring it back.

They are misfit and strange in our new day,   40
In Sixty-One they were not quite so strange,
Before the Fords, before the day of the Fords. . . .

Luke Breckinridge, his rifle on his shoulder,
Slipped through green forest alleys toward the town,
A gawky boy with smoldering eyes, whose feet
Whispered the crooked paths like moccasins.
He wasn't looking for trouble, going down,
But he was on guard, as always. When he stopped
To scoop some water in the palm of his hand
From a sweet trickle between moss-grown rocks,   50
You might have thought him careless for a minute,
But when the snapped stick cracked six feet behind him
He was all sudden rifle and hard eyes.
The pause endured a long death-quiet instant,
Then he knew who it was.
                    " Hi, Jim," he said,
Lowering his rifle. The green laurel-screen
Hardly had moved, but Jim was there beside him.
The cousins looked at each other. Their rifles seemed
To look as well, with much the same taut silentness.

" Goin' to town, Luke? "
                    " Uh-huh, goin' to town,   60
You goin'? "
                    " Looks as if I was goin'."
                                        " Looks
As if you was after squirrels."
                    " I might be.
You goin' after squirrels? "
                    " I might be, too."
" Not so many squirrels near town."
                                        " No, reckon there's not."

Jim hesitated. His gaunt hands caressed
The smooth guard of his rifle. His eyes were sharp.
" Might go along a piece together," he said.
Luke didn't move. Their eyes clashed for a moment,
Then Luke spoke, casually.
                    " I hear the Kelceys
Air goin' to fight in this here war," he said.   70
Jim nodded slowly, " Yuh, I heerd that too."
He watched Luke's trigger-hand.

> "I might be goin'
Myself sometime," he said reflectively
Sliding his own hand down. Luke saw the movement.
"We-uns don't like the Kelceys much," he said
With his eyes down to pinpoints.

> Then Jim smiled.
"We-uns neither," he said.

> His hand slid back.

They went along together after that
But neither of them spoke for half-a-mile,
Then finally, Jim said, half-diffidently,   80
"You know who we air goin' to fight outside?
I heard it was the British. Air that so?"
"Hell, no," said Luke, with scorn. He puckered his brows.
"Dunno's I rightly know just who they air."
He admitted finally, "But 'tain't the British.
It's some trash-lot of furriners, that's shore.
They call 'em Yankees near as I kin make it,
But they ain't Injuns neither."

> "Well," said Jim
Soothingly, "Reckon it don't rightly matter
Long as the Kelceys take the other side."   90

APPOMATTOX

So this week, this death-march, these final, desperate strokes,
These last blood-spots on the harvest — until, at length,
The battered grey advance guard, hoping to break
A last, miraculous hole through the closing net,
Sees Ord's whole corps as if risen out of the ground
Before them, blocking all hope.

> The letters are written,
The orders given, while stray fighting goes on
And grey men and blue men die in odd clumps of ground
Before the orders can reach them.

> An aide-de-camp
Seeks a suitable house for the council from a chance farmer.   10
The first one found is too dirty to please his mind,
He picks another.

> The chiefs and the captains meet,
Lee erect in his best dress uniform,

His dress-sword hung at his side and his eyes unaltered.
Chunky Grant in his mudsplashed private's gear
With the battered stars on his shoulders.
                                    They talk a while
Of Mexico and old days.
                        Then the terms are stated.
Lee finds them generous, says so, makes a request.
His men will need their horses for the spring-ploughing.
Grant assents at once.
                        There is no parade of bright swords   20
Given or taken. Grant saw that there should not be.
It is over, then. . . .
                        Lee walks from the little room.
His face is unchanged. It will not change when he dies.
But as he steps on the porch and looks toward his lines
He strikes his hands together once with a sound. . . .

In the room he has left, the blue men stare at each other
For a space of heartbeats, silent. The grey ride off.
They are gone — it is over. . . .

The room explodes like a bomb, they are laughing and shouting,
Yelling strange words, dragging chairs and tables outdoors,   30
Bearded generals waltzing with one another
For a brief, wild moment, punching each other's ribs,
Everyone talking at once and nobody listening,
" It's over — it's done — it's finished! "
                                    Then, order again.
The grey ghost-army falls in for the last time,
Marching to stack its arms.
                        As the ranks move forward
The blue guns go to " Present." Gordon sees the gesture.
He sweeps his sabre down in the full salute.
There are no cheers or words from blue lines or grey.
Only the sound of feet. . . .   40
It is over, now. . . .
                        The arms are stacked from the war.
A few bronzed, tattered grey men, weeping or silent,
Tear some riddled bits of cloth from the color-staffs
And try to hide them under their uniforms.

                                            1928

James Russell Lowell

The Pious Editor's Creed

I du believe in Freedom's cause,
 Ez fur away ez Payris is;
I love to see her stick her claws
 In them infarnal Phayrisees;
It's wal enough agin a king
 To dror resolves an' triggers, —
But libbaty's a kind o' thing
 Thet don't agree with niggers.

I du believe the people want
 A tax on teas an' coffees, 10
Thet nothin' ain't extravygunt, —
 Purvidin' I'm in office;
Fer I hev loved my country sence
 My eye-teeth filled their sockets,
An' Uncle Sam I reverence,
 Partic'larly his pockets.

I du believe in *any* plan
 O' levyin' the taxes,
Ez long ez, like a lumberman,
 I git jest wut I axes; 20
I go free-trade thru thick an' thin,
 Because it kind o' rouses
The folks to vote, — an' keeps us in
 Our quiet custom-houses.

I du believe it's wise an' good
 To sen' out furrin missions,
Thet is, on sartin understood
 An' orthydox conditions; —
I mean nine thousan' dolls. per ann.,
 Nine thousan' more fer outfit, 30
An' me to recommend a man
 The place 'ould jest about fit.

I du believe in special ways
 O' prayin' an' convartin';
The bread comes back in many days,
 An' buttered, tu, fer sartin;

I mean in preyin' till one busts
 On wut the party chooses,
An' in convartin' public trusts
 To very privit uses. 40

I du believe hard coin the stuff
 Fer 'lectioneers to spout on;
The people's ollers soft enough
 To make hard money out on;
Dear Uncle Sam pervides fer his,
 An' gives a good-sized junk to all, —
I don't care *how* hard money is,
 Ez long ez mine's paid punctooal.

I du believe with all my soul
 In the gret Press's freedom, 50
To pint the people to the goal
 An' in the traces lead 'em;
Palsied the arm thet forges yokes
 At my fat contracts squintin',
An' withered be the nose thet pokes
 Inter the gov'ment printin'!

I du believe thet I should give
 Wut's hisn unto Caesar,
Fer it's by him I move an' live,
 Frum him my bread an' cheese air; 60
I du believe thet all o' me
 Doth bear his superscription, —
Will, conscience, honor, honesty,
 An' things o' thet description.

I du believe in prayer an' praise
 To him thet hez the grantin'
O' jobs, — in every thin' thet pays,
 But most of all in CANTIN';
This doth my cup with marcies fill,
 This lays all thought o' sin to rest; —
I *don't* believe in princerple, 71
 But oh, I *du* in interest.

I du believe in bein' this
 Or thet, ez it may happen

One way or t'other hendiest is
  To ketch the people nappin';
It ain't by princerples nor men
  My preudunt course is steadied, —
I scent wich pays the best, an' then
  Go into it baldheaded.   80

I du believe thet holdin' slaves
  Comes nat'ral to a Presidunt,
Let 'lone the rowdedow it saves
  To hev a wal-broke precedunt;
Fer any office, small or gret,
  I couldn't ax with no face,
Without I'd ben, thru dry an' wet,
  Th' unrizzest kind o' doughface.

I du believe wutever trash
  'll keep the people in blindness, —   90
Thet we the Mexicuns can thrash
  Right inter brotherly kindness,
Thet bombshells, grape, an' powder 'n'
    ball
  Air good-will's strongest magnets,
Thet peace, to make it stick at all,
  Must be druv in with bagnets.

In short, I firmly du believe
  In Humbug generally,
Fer it's a thing thet I perceive
  To hev a solid vally;   100
This heth my faithful shepherd ben,
  In pasturs sweet heth led me,
An' this'll keep the people green
  To feed ez they hev fed me.
                              1848

The Courtin'

God makes sech nights, all white an' still
  Fur'z you can look or listen,
Moonshine an' snow on field an' hill,
  All silence an' all glisten.

Zekle crep' up quite unbeknown
  An' peeked in thru the winder,

An' there sot Huldy all alone,
  'ith no one nigh to hender.

A fireplace filled the room's one side
  With half a cord o' wood in —   10
There warn't no stoves (tell comfort
    died)
  To bake ye to a puddin'.

The wa'nut logs shot sparkles out
  Towards the pootiest, bless her,
An' leetle flames danced all about
  The chiny on the dresser.

Agin the chimbley crook-necks hung,
  An' in amongst 'em rusted
The ole queen's-arm thet gran'ther
    Young
  Fetched back f'om Concord busted. 20

The very room, coz she was in,
  Seemed warm from floor to ceilin',
An' she looked full ez rosy agin
  Ez the apples she was peelin'.

'Twas kin' o' kingdom-come to look
  On sech a blessed cretur,
A dogrose blushin' to a brook
  Ain't modester nor sweeter.

He was six foot o' man, A 1,
  Clear grit an' human natur';   30
None couldn't quicker pitch a ton
  Nor dror a furrer straighter.

He'd sparked it with full twenty gals,
  He'd squired 'em, danced 'em, druv
    'em,
Fust this one, an' then thet, by spells —
  All is, he couldn't love 'em.

But long o' her his veins 'ould run
  All crinkly like curled maple,
The side she breshed felt full o' sun
  Ez a south slope in Ap'il.   40

She thought no v'ice hed sech a swing
   Ez hisn in the choir;
My! when he made Old Hunderd ring,
   She *knowed* the Lord was nigher.

An' she'd blush scarlit, right in prayer,
   When her new meetin'-bunnet
Felt somehow thru its crown a pair
   O' blue eyes sot upun it.

Thet night, I tell ye, she looked *some!*
   She seemed to 've gut a new soul,   50
For she felt sartin-sure he'd come,
   Down to her very shoe-sole.

She heered a foot, an' knowed it tu,
   A-raspin' on the scraper, —
All ways to once her feelin's flew
   Like sparks in burnt-up paper.

He kin' o' l'itered on the mat
   Some doubtfle o' the sekle,
His heart kep' goin' pity-pat,
   But hern went pity Zekle.   60

An' yit she gin her cheer a jerk
   Ez though she wished him furder,
An' on her apples kep' to work,
   Parin' away like murder.

" You want to see my Pa, I s'pose? "
   " Wal . . . no . . . I come dasignin' " —
" To see my Ma? She's sprinklin' clo'es
   Agin tomorrer's i'nin'."

To say why gals acts so or so,
   Or don't, 'ould be presumin';   70
Mebby to mean *yes* an' say *no*
   Comes nateral to women.

He stood a spell on one foot fust,
   Then stood a spell on t'other,
An' on which one he felt the wust
   He couldn't ha' told ye nuther.

Says he, " I'd better call agin ";
   Says she, " Think likely, Mister ":
Thet last word pricked him like a pin,
   An' . . . Wal, he up an' kist her.   80

When Ma bimeby upon 'em slips,
   Huldy sot pale ez ashes,
All kin' o' smily roun' the lips
   An' teary roun' the lashes.

For she was jes' the quiet kind
   Whose naturs never vary,
Like streams that keep a summer mind
   Snowhid in Jenooary.

The blood clost roun' her heart felt glued
   Too tight for all expressin',   90
Tell mother see how metters stood,
   And gin 'em both her blessin'.

Then her red come back like the tide
   Down to the Bay o' Fundy,
An' all I know is they was cried
   In meetin' come nex' Sunday.

                    1866

Ode Recited at the Harvard Commemoration

JULY 21, 1865

I

Weak-winged is song,
Nor aims at that clear-ethered height
Whither the brave deed climbs for light:
   We seem to do them wrong,
Bringing our robin's-leaf to deck their
       hearse
Who in warm life-blood wrote their
       nobler verse,
Our trivial song to honor those who come
With ears attuned to strenuous trump
       and drum,
And shaped in squadron-strophes their
       desire, ·

Live battle-odes whose lines were steel
    and fire: 10
Yet sometimes feathered words are
    strong,
A gracious memory to buoy up and save
From Lethe's dreamless ooze, the com-
    mon grave
    Of the unventurous throng.

2

To-day our Reverend Mother welcomes
    back
  Her wisest Scholars, those who under-
    stood
The deeper teaching of her mystic tome,
  And offered their fresh lives to make it
    good:
    No lore of Greece or Rome,
No science peddling with the names of
    things, 20
Or reading stars to find inglorious fates,
    Can lift our life with wings
Far from Death's idle gulf that for the
    many waits,
    And lengthen out our dates
With that clear fame whose memory
    sings
In manly hearts to come, and nerves them
    and dilates:
Nor such thy teaching, Mother of us all!
    Not such the trumpet-call
    Of thy diviner mood,
    That could thy sons entice 30
From happy homes and toils, the fruitful
    nest
Of those half-virtues which the world
    calls best,
    Into War's tumult rude;
    But rather far that stern device
The sponsors chose that round thy cradle
    stood
    In the dim, unventured wood,
    The Veritas that lurks beneath
    The letter's unprolific sheath,

Life of whate'er makes life worth liv-
    ing,
Seed-grain of high emprise, immortal
    food, 40
One heavenly thing whereof earth
    hath the giving.

3

Many loved Truth, and lavished life's
    best oil
Amid the dust of books to find her,
Content at last, for guerdon of their toil,
  With the cast mantle she hath left be-
    hind her.
  Many in sad faith sought for her,
  Many with crossed hands sighed for
    her;
  But these, our brothers, fought for
    her,
  At life's dear peril wrought for her,
  So loved her that they died for her,
  Tasting the raptured fleetness 51
  Of her divine completeness:
    Their higher instinct knew
Those love her best who to themselves are
    true,
And what they dare to dream of, dare to
    do;
  They followed her and found her
  Where all may hope to find,
Not in the ashes of the burnt-out mind,
But beautiful, with danger's sweetness
    round her.
  Where faith made whole with deed
  Breathes its awakening breath 61
  Into the lifeless creed,
  They saw her plumed and mailed,
  With sweet, stern face unveiled,
And all-repaying eyes, look proud on
    them in death.

4

Our slender life runs rippling by, and
    glides
  Into the silent hollow of the past;

What is there that abides
To make the next age better for the
    last?
    Is earth too poor to give us   70
Something to live for here that shall
    outlive us?
    Some more substantial boon
Than such as flows and ebbs with For-
    tune's fickle moon?
    The little that we see
    From doubt is never free;
    The little that we do
    Is but half-nobly true;
    With our laborious hiving
What men call treasure, and the gods call
    dross,
Life seems a jest of Fate's contriv-
    ing   80
    Only secure in every one's conniving,
A long account of nothings paid with
    loss,
Where we poor puppets, jerked by un-
    seen wires,
After our little hour of strut and rave,
With all our pasteboard passions and de-
    sires,
Loves, hates, ambitions, and immortal
    fires,
    Are tossed pell-mell together in the
    grave.
But stay! no age was e'er degenerate,
Unless men held it at too cheap a rate,
For in our likeness still we shape our
    fate.   90
    Ah, there is something here
    Unfathomed by the cynic's sneer,
Something that gives our feeble light
A high immunity from Night,
Something that leaps life's narrow bars
To claim its birthright with the hosts of
    heaven;
A seed of sunshine that can leaven
Our earthy dullness with the beams of
    stars,
    And glorify our clay

With light from fountains elder than the
    Day;   100
A conscience more divine than we,
A gladness fed with secret tears,
A vexing, forward-reaching sense
Of some more noble permanence;
    A light across the sea,
Which haunts the soul and will not let
    it be,
Still beaconing from the heights of
    undegenerate years.

5

    Whither leads the path
    To ampler fates that leads?
    Not down through flowery
    meads,
    To reap an aftermath   III
    Of youth's vainglorious weeds,
    But up the steep, amid the wrath
And shock of deadly-hostile creeds,
Where the world's best hope and
    stay
By battle's flashes gropes a desperate way,
And every turf the fierce foot clings to
    bleeds.
    Peace hath her not ignoble wreath,
    Ere yet the sharp, decisive word
Light the black lips of cannon, and the
    sword   120
    Dreams in its easeful sheath;
But some day the live coal behind the
    thought,
    Whether from Baäl's stone ob-
    scene,
    Or from the shrine serene
    Of God's pure altar brought,
Bursts up in flame; the war of tongue
    and pen
Learns with what deadly purpose it was
    fraught,
And, helpless in the fiery passion caught,
Shakes all the pillared state with shock of
    men:

Some day the soft Ideal that we
    wooed   130
Confronts us fiercely, foe-beset, pursued,
And cries reproachful: " Was it, then, my
    praise,
And not myself was loved? Prove now
    thy truth;
I claim of thee the promise of thy youth;
Give me thy life, or cower in empty
    phrase,
The victim of thy genius, not its mate! "
    Life may be given in many ways,
    And loyalty to Truth be sealed
As bravely in the closet as the field,
    So bountiful is Fate;   140
    But then to stand beside her,
    When craven churls deride her,
To front a lie in arms and not to yield,
    This shows, methinks, God's plan
    And measure of a stalwart man,
    Limbed like the old heroic breeds,
    Who stands self-poised on man-
    hood's solid earth,
    Not forced to frame excuses for his
    birth,
Fed from within with all the strength he
    needs.

6

Such was he, our Martyr-Chief,   150
    Whom late the Nation he had led,
    With ashes on her head,
Wept with the passion of an angry grief:
Forgive me, if from present things I turn
To speak what in my heart will beat and
    burn,
And hang my wreath on his world-
    honored urn.
    Nature, they say, doth dote,
    And cannot make a man
    Save on some worn-out plan,
    Repeating us by rote: 160
For him her Old-World moulds aside
    she threw,

And, choosing sweet clay from the
    breast
    Of the unexhausted West,
With stuff untainted shaped a hero new,
Wise, steadfast in the strength of God,
    and true.
    How beautiful to see
Once more a shepherd of mankind in-
    deed,
Who loved his charge, but never loved to
    lead;
One whose meek flock the people joyed
    to be,
    Not lured by any cheat of birth 170
    But by his clear-grained human
    worth,
And brave old wisdom of sincerity!
    They knew that outward grace is
    dust;
    They could not choose but trust
In that sure-footed mind's unfaltering
    skill,
    And supple-tempered will
That bent like perfect steel to spring
    again and thrust.
    His was no lonely mountain-peak of
    mind,
    Thrusting to thin air o'er our cloudy
    bars,
    A sea-mark now, now lost in vapors
    blind;   180
    Broad prairie rather, genial, level-
    lined,
    Fruitful and friendly for all human
    kind,
Yet also nigh to heaven and loved of
    loftiest stars.
    Nothing of Europe here,
Or, then, of Europe fronting mornward
    still,
    Ere any names of Serf and Peer
    Could Nature's equal scheme deface
    And thwart her genial will;
    Here was a type of the true elder
    race,

And one of Plutarch's men talked with
    us face to face.   190
  I praise him not; it were too late;
And some innative weakness there must
    be
In him who condescends to victory
Such as the Present gives, and cannot
    wait,
    Safe in himself as in a fate.
      So always firmly he:
      He knew to bide his time,
      And can his fame abide,
Still patient in his simple faith sublime,
    Till the wise years decide.   200
  Great captains, with their guns and
    drums,
    Disturb our judgment for the
    hour,
    But at last silence comes;
  These all are gone, and, standing
    like a tower,
  Our children shall behold his fame,
    The kindly-earnest, brave, fore-
    seeing man,
Sagacious, patient, dreading praise,
    not blame,
  New birth of our new soil, the first
    American.

7

Long as man's hope insatiate can dis-
    cern
  Or only guess some more inspiring
    goal   210
  Outside of Self, enduring as the pole,
Along whose course the flying axles
    burn
Of spirits bravely-pitched, earth's man-
    lier brood;
  Long as below we cannot find
The meed that stills the inexorable
    mind;
So long this faith to some ideal Good,
Under whatever mortal names it
    masks,

Freedom, Law, Country, this ethereal
    mood
That thanks the Fates for their severer
    tasks,
  Feeling its challenged pulses leap, 220
  While others skulk in subterfuges
    cheap,
And, set in Danger's van, has all the boon
    it asks,
  Shall win man's praise and woman's
    love,
  Shall be a wisdom that we set above
All other skills and gifts to culture dear,
  A virtue round whose forehead we
    inwreathe
  Laurels that with a living passion
    breathe
When other crowns grow, while we
    twine them, sear.
  What brings us thronging these high
    rites to pay,
And seal these hours the noblest of our
    year,   230
  Save that our brothers found this better
    way?

8

We sit here in the Promised Land
That flows with Freedom's honey and
    milk;
But 't was they won it, sword in hand,
Making the nettle danger soft for us as
    silk.
We welcome back our bravest and our
    best; —
Ah me! not all! some come not with
    the rest,
Who went forth brave and bright as any
    here!
I strive to mix some gladness with my
    strain,
    But the sad strings complain,
    And will not please the ear: 241
I sweep them for a paean, but they wane
    Again and yet again

Into a dirge, and die away, in pain.
In these brave ranks I only see the gaps,
Thinking of dear ones whom the dumb
    turf wraps,
Dark to the triumph which they died to
    gain:
    Fitlier may others greet the living,
    For me the past is unforgiving;
        I with uncovered head   250
        Salute the sacred dead,
Who went, and who return not. — Say
    not so!
'Tis not the grapes of Canaan that repay,
But the high faith that failed not by the
    way;
Virtue treads paths that end not in the
    grave;
No bar of endless night exiles the brave;
    And to the saner mind
We rather seem the dead that stayed be-
    hind.
Blow, trumpets, all your exultations
    blow!
For never shall their aureoled presence
        lack: 260
I see them muster in a gleaming row,
With ever-youthful brows that nobler
    show;
We find in our dull road their shining
    track;
    In every nobler mood
We feel the orient of their spirit glow,
Part of our life's unalterable good,
Of all our saintlier aspiration;
    They come transfigured back,
Secure from change in their high-hearted
    ways,
Beautiful evermore, and with the rays
Of morn on their white Shields of Ex-
        pectation!   271

9
    But is there hope to save
    Even this ethereal essence from the
        grave?

Whatever 'scaped Oblivion's subtle
    wrong
Save a few clarion names, or golden
    threads of song?
    Before my musing eye
    The mighty ones of old sweep by,
Disvoicèd now and insubstantial
    things,
As noisy once as we; poor ghosts of
    kings,
Shadows of empire wholly gone to
    dust,   280
And many races, nameless long ago,
To darkness driven by that imperious
    gust
Of ever-rushing Time that here doth
    blow:
O visionary world, condition strange,
Where naught abiding is but only
    Change,
Where the deep-bolted stars themselves
    still shift and range!
Shall we to more continuance make
    pretense?
Renown builds tombs; a life-estate is
    Wit;
    And, bit by bit,
The cunning years steal all from us but
    woe;   290
    Leaves are we, whose decays no harvest
    sow.
    But, when we vanish hence,
Shall they lie forceless in the dark be-
    low,
Save to make green their little length
    of sods,
Or deepen pansies for a year or two,
Who now to us are shining-sweet as
    gods?
Was dying all they had the skill to
    do?
That were not fruitless: but the Soul
    resents
Such short-lived service, as if blind
    events

Ruled without her, or earth could so
    endure;   300
She claims a more divine investiture
Of longer tenure than Fame's airy
    rents;
Whate'er she touches doth her nature
    share;
Her inspiration haunts the ennobled
    air
    Gives eyes to mountains blind,
Ears to the deaf earth, voices to the
    wind,
And her clear trump sings succor
    everywhere
By lonely bivouacs to the wakeful
    mind;
For soul inherits all that soul could
    dare: 309
    Yea, Manhood hath a wider span
And larger privilege of life than man.
The single deed, the private sacrifice,
So radiant now through proudly-hid-
    den tears,
Is covered up erelong from mortal eyes
With thoughtless drift of the decidu-
    ous years;
But that high privilege that makes all
    men peers,
That leap of heart whereby a people
    rise
    Up to a noble anger's height,
And, flamed on by the Fates, not shrink,
    but grow more bright,
    That swift validity in noble veins,
    Of choosing danger and disdaining
    shame,   321
    Of being set on flame
By the pure fire that flies all contact
    base,
But wraps its chosen with angelic might,
    These are imperishable gains,
Sure as the sun, medicinal as light,
These hold great futures in their lusty
    reins
And certify to earth a new imperial race.

10

    Who now shall sneer?
Who dare again to say we trace   330
Our lines to a plebeian race?
    Roundhead and Cavalier!
Dumb are those names erewhile in battle
    loud;
Dream-footed as the shadow of a cloud,
    They flit across the ear:
That is best blood that hath most iron
    in 't,
To edge resolve with, pouring without
    stint
    For what makes manhood dear.
    Tell us not of Plantagenets,
Hapsburgs, and Guelfs, whose thin
    bloods crawl   340
Down from some victor in a border-
    brawl!
    How poor their outworn coronets,
Matched with one leaf of that plain civic
    wreath
Our brave for honor's blazon shall be-
    queath,
    Through whose desert a rescued Na-
    tion sets
Her heel on treason, and the trumpet
    hears
Shout victory, tingling Europe's sullen
    ears
    With vain resentments and more vain
    regrets!

11

    Not in anger, not in pride,
    Pure from passion's mixture rude
    Ever to base earth allied,   351
    But with far-heard gratitude,
    Still with heart and voice renewed,
To heroes living and dear martyrs dead,
The strain should close that consecrates
    our brave.
    Lift the heart and lift the head!
    Lofty be its mood and grave,

Not without a martial ring,
Not without a prouder tread
And a peal of exultation: 360
Little right has he to sing
Through whose heart in such an
      hour
Beats no march of conscious
      power,
Sweeps no tumult of elation!
'T is no Man we celebrate,
By his country's victories great,
A hero half, and half the whim of
      Fate,
But the pith and marrow of a
      Nation
Drawing force from all her men,
Highest, humblest, weakest,
      all,   370
For her time of need, and then
Pulsing it again through them,
Till the basest can no longer cower,
Feeling his soul spring up divinely tall,
Touched but in passing by her mantle-
      hem.
Come back, then, noble pride, for 't is
      her dower!
How could poet ever tower,
If his passions, hopes, and fears,
If his triumphs and his tears,
Kept not measure with his peo-
      ple?   380
Boom, cannon, boom to all the winds and
      waves!
Clash out, glad bells, from every rocking
      steeple!
Banners, advance with triumph, bend
      your staves!
And from every mountain-peak
Let beacon-fire to answering beacon
      speak,
Katahdin tell Monadnock, White-
      face he,
And so leap on in light from sea to sea,
Till the glad news be sent
Across a kindling continent,

Making earth feel more firm and air
      breathe braver: 390
" Be proud! for she is saved, and all have
      helped to save her!
She that lifts up the manhood of the
      poor,
She of the open soul and open door,
With room about her hearth for all
      mankind!
The fire is dreadful in her eyes no
      more;
From her bold front the helm she
      doth unbind,
Sends all her handmaid armies back
      to spin,
And bids her navies, that so lately
      hurled
Their crashing battle, hold their
      thunders in,
Swimming like birds of calm along
      the unharmful shore.   400
No challenge sends she to the elder
      world,
That looked askance and hated; a
      light scorn
Plays o'er her mouth, as round her
      mighty knees
She calls her children back, and
      waits the morn
Of nobler day, enthroned between her
      subject seas."

12

Bow down, dear Land, for thou hast
      found release!
Thy God, in these distempered days,
Hath taught thee the sure wisdom of
      His ways,
And through thine enemies hath wrought
      thy peace!
Bow down in prayer and praise!
No poorest in thy borders but may
      now   411
Lift to the juster skies a man's enfran-
      chised brow.

O Beautiful! my Country! ours once
        more!
Smoothing thy gold of war-disheveled
        hair
O'er such sweet brows as never other
        wore,
        And letting thy set lips,
        Freed from wrath's pale eclipse,
The rosy edges of their smile lay bare,
What words divine of lover or of poet
Could tell our love and make thee know
        it,   420
Among the Nations bright beyond com-
        pare?
        What were our lives without thee?
        What all our lives to save thee?
        We reck not what we gave thee;
        We will not dare to doubt thee,
But ask whatever else, and we will dare!
                                          1865

Edwin Arlington Robinson

Credo

I cannot find my way: there is no star
In all the shrouded heavens anywhere;
And there is not a whisper in the air
Of any living voice but one so far
That I can hear it only as a bar
Of lost, imperial music, played when fair
And angel fingers wove, and unaware,
Dead leaves to garlands where no roses
    are.

No, there is not a glimmer, nor a call,
For one that welcomes, welcomes when
    he fears,   10
The black and awful chaos of the night;
For through it all — above, beyond it
    all —

I know the far-sent message of the years,
I feel the coming glory of the Light.
                                          1897

Richard Cory

Whenever Richard Cory went down
    town,
    We people on the pavement looked at
    him:
He was a gentleman from sole to crown,
    Clean favored, and imperially slim.

And he was always quietly arrayed,
    And he was always human when he
    talked;
But still he fluttered pulses when he said,
    "Good morning," and he glittered
    when he walked.

And he was rich — yes, richer than a
    king —
    And admirably schooled in every grace:
In fine, we thought that he was every-
    thing   11
    To make us wish that we were in his
    place.

So on we worked, and waited for the
    light,
    And went without the meat, and
    cursed the bread;
And Richard Cory, one calm summer
    night,
    Went home and put a bullet through
    his head.
                                          1897

How Annandale Went Out

"They called it Annandale — and I was
    there
To flourish, to find words, and to attend:
Liar, physician, hypocrite, and friend,

I watched him; and the sight was not so
   fair
As one or two that I have seen elsewhere:
An apparatus not for me to mend —
A wreck, with hell between him and the
   end,
Remained of Annandale; and I was
   there.

"I knew the ruin as I knew the man;
So put the two together, if you can,   10
Remembering the worst you know of me.
Now view yourself as I was, on the
   spot —
With a slight kind of engine. Do you
   see?
Like this. . . . You wouldn't hang me?
   I thought not."

                        1910

Miniver Cheevy

Miniver Cheevy, child of scorn,
   Grew lean while he assailed the sea-
     sons;
He wept that he was ever born,
   And he had reasons.

Miniver loved the days of old
   When swords were bright and steeds
     were prancing;
The vision of a warrior bold
   Would set him dancing.

Miniver sighed for what was not,
   And dreamed, and rested from his
     labors;   10
He dreamed of Thebes and Camelot,
   And Priam's neighbors.

Miniver mourned the ripe renown
   That made so many a name so fra-
     grant;
He mourned Romance, now on the town,
   And Art, a vagrant.

Miniver loved the Medici,
   Albeit he had never seen one;
He would have sinned incessantly
   Could he have been one.   20

Miniver cursed the commonplace
   And eyed a khaki suit with loathing;
He missed the medieval grace
   Of iron clothing.

Miniver scorned the gold he sought,
   But sore annoyed was he without it;
Miniver thought, and thought, and
     thought,
   And thought about it.

Miniver Cheevy, born too late,
   Scratched his head and kept on think-
     ing;   30
Miniver coughed and called it fate,
   And kept on drinking.

                        1910

Amy Lowell

The Dinner-Party

FISH

"So . . ." they said,
With their wine-glasses delicately poised,
Mocking at the thing they cannot under-
   stand.
"So . . ." they said again,
Amused and insolent.
The silver on the table glittered,
And the red wine in the glasses
Seemed the blood I had wasted
In a foolish cause.

GAME

The gentleman with the grey-and-black
   whiskers   10

Sneered languidly over his quail.
Then my heart flew up and labored,
And I burst from my own holding
And hurled myself forward.
With straight blows I beat upon him,
Furiously, with red-hot anger, I thrust
    against him.
But my weapon slithered over his
    polished surface,
And I recoiled upon myself,
Panting.

Drawing-Room

In a dress all softness and half-tones,   20
Indolent and half-reclined,
She lay upon a couch,
With the firelight reflected in her jewels.
But her eyes had no reflection,
They swam in a grey smoke,
The smoke of smoldering ashes,
The smoke of her cindered heart.

Coffee

They sat in a circle with their coffee-cups.
One dropped in a lump of sugar,
One stirred with a spoon.   30
I saw them as a circle of ghosts
Sipping blackness out of beautiful china,
And mildly protesting against my coarse-
    ness
In being alive.

Talk

They took dead men's souls
And pinned them on their breasts for
    ornament;
Their cuff-links and tiaras
Were gems dug from a grave;
They were ghouls battening on exhumed
    thoughts;
And I took a green liqueur from a serv-
    ant   40
So that he might come near me
And give me the comfort of a living
    thing.

Eleven o'Clock

The front door was hard and heavy,
It shut behind me on the house of
    ghosts.
I flattened my feet on the pavement
To feel it solid under me;
I ran my hand along the railings
And shook them,
And pressed their pointed bars
Into my palms.   50
The hurt of it reassured me,
And I did it again and again
Until they were bruised.
When I woke in the night
I laughed to find them aching,
For only living flesh can suffer.

                                    1916

Vachel Lindsay

The Proud Farmer

Into the acres of the newborn state
He poured his strength, and plowed his ancient name,
And, when the traders followed him, he stood
Towering above their furtive souls and tame.

That brow without a stain, that fearless eye
Oft left the passing stranger wondering
To find such knighthood in the sprawling land,
To see a democrat well-nigh a king.

He lived with liberal hand, with guests from far,
With talk and joke and fellowship to spare, —   10
Watching the wide world's life from sun to sun,
Lining his walls with books from everywhere.

He read by night, he built his world by day.
The farm and house of God to him were one.
For forty years he preached and plowed and wrought —
A statesman in the fields, who bent to none.

His plowmen-neighbors were as lords to him.
His was an ironside, democratic pride.
He served a rigid Christ, but served him well —
And, for a lifetime, saved the countryside.   20

Here lie the dead, who gave the church their best
Under his fiery preaching of the word.
They sleep with him beneath the ragged grass . . .
The village withers, by his voice unstirred.

And tho' his tribe be scattered to the wind
From the Atlantic to the China Sea,
Yet do they think of that bright lamp he burned
Of family worth and proud integrity.

And many a sturdy grandchild hears his name
In reverence spoken, till he feels akin   30
To all the lion-eyed who build the world —
And lion-dreams begin to burn within.

1912

General William Booth Enters into Heaven

(To be sung to the tune of " The Blood of the Lamb " with indicated instrument.)

I

Booth led boldly with his big bass drum —　　　　　　　*Bass drum beaten*
(Are you washed in the blood of the Lamb?)　　　　　　*loudly.*
The Saints smiled gravely and they said: " He's come."
(Are you washed in the blood of the Lamb?)
Walking lepers followed, rank on rank,
Lurching bravos from the ditches dank,
Drabs from the alleyways and drug fiends pale —
Minds still passion-ridden, soul-powers frail: —
Vermin-eaten saints with moldy breath,
Unwashed legions with the ways of Death —　　　　　　　　　　10
(Are you washed in the blood of the Lamb?)

Every slum had sent its half-a-score　　　　　　　　*Banjos.*
The round world over. (Booth had groaned for more.)
Every banner that the wide world flies
Bloomed with glory and transcendent dyes.
Big-voiced lasses made their banjos bang;
Tranced, fanatical they shrieked and sang: —
" Are you washed in the blood of the Lamb? "
Hallelujah! It was queer to see
Bull-necked convicts with that land make free.　　　　　　　20
Loons with trumpets blowed a blare, blare, blare
On, on upward thro' the golden air!
(Are you washed in the blood of the Lamb?)

II

Booth died blind and still by faith he trod,　　　　　*Bass drum slower*
Eyes still dazzled by the ways of God.　　　　　　　*and softer.*
Booth led boldly, and he looked the chief,
Eagle countenance in sharp relief,
Beard a-flying, air of high command
Unabated in that holy land.

Jesus came from out the court-house door,　　　　　　*Sweet flute music.*
Stretched his hands above the passing poor.　　　　　　　31
Booth saw not, but led his queer ones there
Round and round the mighty court-house square.

Then, in an instant all that blear review
Marched on spotless, clad in raiment new.
The lame were straightened, withered limbs uncurled
And blind eyes opened on a new, sweet world.

Drabs and vixens in a flash made whole!   *Bass drum louder.*
Gone was the weasel-head, the snout, the jowl!
Sages and sibyls now, and athletes clean,   40
Rulers of empires, and of forests green!

The hosts were sandalled, and their wings were fire!   *Grand chorus of all*
(Are you washed in the blood of the Lamb?)   *instruments. Tam-*
But their noise played havoc with the angel-choir.   *bourines to the*
(Are you washed in the blood of the Lamb?)   *foreground.*
Oh, shout Salvation! It was good to see
Kings and Princes by the Lamb set free.
The banjos rattled and the tambourines
Jing-jing-jingled in the hands of Queens.

And when Booth halted by the curb for prayer   *Reverently   sung,*
He saw his Master thro' the flag-filled air.   *no instruments.*
Christ came gently with a robe and crown
For Booth the soldier, while the throng knelt down.   52
He saw King Jesus. They were face to face,
And he knelt a-weeping in that holy place.
Are you washed in the blood of the Lamb?

                                                                    1913

The Eagle That Is Forgotten

(JOHN P. ALTGELD. BORN DECEMBER 30, 1847; DIED MARCH 12, 1902.)

Sleep softly . . . eagle forgotten . . . under the stone.
Time has its way with you there, and the clay has its own.

" We have buried him now," thought your foes, and in secret rejoiced.
They made a brave show of their mourning, their hatred unvoiced.
They had snarled at you, barked at you, foamed at you day after day.
Now you were ended. They praised you, . . . and laid you away.

The others that mourned you in silence and terror and truth,
The widow bereft of her crust, and the boy without youth,
The mocked and the scorned and the wounded, the lame and the poor
That should have remembered forever, . . . remember no more.   10

Where are those lovers of yours, on what name do they call,
The lost, that in armies wept over your funeral pall?
They call on the names of a hundred high-valiant ones;
A hundred white eagles have risen the sons of your sons;
The zeal in their wings is a zeal that your dreaming began,
The valor that wore out your soul in the service of man.

Sleep softly, . . . eagle forgotten, . . . under the stone,
Time has its way with you there, and the clay has its own.
Sleep on, O brave-hearted, O wise man, that kindled the flame —
To live in mankind is far more than to live in a name,   20
To live in mankind, far, far more . . . than to live in a name.

1913

In Praise of Johnny Appleseed

(BORN 1775; DIED 1847.)

I. OVER THE APPALACHIAN BARRICADE

In the days of President Washington,
The glory of the nations,
Dust and ashes,
Snow and sleet,
And hay and oats and wheat,
Blew west,
Crossed the Appalachians,
Found the glades of rotting leaves, the soft deer-pastures,
The farms of the far-off future
In the forest.   10
Colts jumped the fence,
Snorting, ramping, snapping, sniffing,
With gastronomic calculations,
Crossed the Appalachians,
The east walls of our citadel,
And turned to gold-horned unicorns,
Feasting in the dim, volunteer farms of the forest.
Stripedest, kickingest kittens escaped,
Caterwauling "Yankee Doodle Dandy,"
Renounced their poor relations,   20

*To be read like old
leaves on the elm
tree of Time,
Sifting soft winds
with sentence and
rhyme.*

Crossed the Appalachians,
And turned to tiny tigers
In the humorous forest.
Chickens escaped
From farmyard congregations,
Crossed the Appalachians,
And turned to amber trumpets
On the ramparts of our Hoosiers' nest and citadel,
Millennial heralds
Of the foggy mazy forest.   30
Pigs broke loose, scrambled west,
Scorned their loathsome stations,
Crossed the Appalachians,
Turned to roaming, foaming wild boars
Of the forest.
The smallest, blindest puppies toddled west
While their eyes were coming open,
And, with misty observations,
Crossed the Appalachians,
Barked, barked, barked   40
At the glow-worms and the marsh lights and the lightning-bugs
And turned to ravening wolves
Of the forest.
Crazy parrots and canaries flew west,
Drunk on May-time revelations,
Crossed the Appalachians,
And turned to delirious, flower-dressed fairies
Of the lazy forest.
Haughtiest swans and peacocks swept west,
And, despite soft derivations,   50
Crossed the Appalachians,
And turned to blazing warrior souls
Of the forest,
Singing the ways
Of the Ancient of Days.
And the " Old Continentals
In their ragged regimentals,"
With bard's imaginations,
Crossed the Appalachians.
And   60
A boy
Blew west,
And with prayers and incantations,
And with " Yankee Doodle Dandy,"
Crossed the Appalachians,

And was " young John Chapman,"
Then
" Johnny Appleseed, Johnny Appleseed,"
Chief of the fastnesses, dappled and vast,
In a pack on his back,   70
In a deer-hide sack,
The beautiful orchards of the past,
The ghosts of all the forests and the groves —
In that pack on his back
In that talisman sack,
Tomorrow's peaches, pears, and cherries,
Tomorrow's grapes and red raspberries,
Seeds and tree-souls, precious things,
Feathered with microscopic wings,
All the outdoors and the child heart knows,   80
And the apple, green, red, and white,
Sun of his day and his night —
The apple allied to the thorn,
Child of the rose.
Porches untrod of forest houses
All before him, all day long,
" Yankee Doodle " his marching song;
And the evening breeze
Joined his psalms of praise
As he sang the ways   90
Of the Ancient of Days.
Leaving behind august Virginia,
Proud Massachusetts, and proud Maine,
Planting the trees that would march and train
On, in his name to the great Pacific,
Like Birnam wood to Dunsinane,
Johnny Appleseed swept on,
Every shackle gone,
Loving every sloshy brake,
Loving every skunk and snake,   100
Loving every leathery weed,
Johnny Appleseed, Johnny Appleseed,
Master and ruler of the unicorn-ramping forest,
The tiger-mewing forest,
The rooster-trumpeting, boar-foaming, wolf-ravening forest,
The spirit-haunted forest, fairy-enchanted,
Stupendous and endless,
Searching its perilous ways
In the name of the Ancient of Days.

1921

Carl Sandburg

Chicago

Hog-butcher for the world,
Tool-maker, Stacker of Wheat,
Player with Railroads and the Nation's Freight-handler;
Stormy, husky, brawling,
City of the Big Shoulders:
They tell me you are wicked and I believe them, for I have seen your painted
    women under the gas lamps luring the farm boys.
And they tell me you are crooked and I answer: Yes, it is true I have seen the
    gunmen kill and go free to kill again.
And they tell me you are brutal and my reply is: On the faces of women and
    children I have seen the marks of wanton hunger.
And having answered so I turn once more to those who sneer at this my city,
    and I give them back the sneer and say to them:
Come and show me another city with lifted head singing so proud to be alive
    and coarse and strong and cunning.   10
Flinging magnetic curses amid the toil of piling job on job, here is a tall bold
    slugger set vivid against the little soft cities;
Fierce as a dog with tongue lapping for action, cunning as a savage pitted
    against the wilderness,
      Bareheaded,
      Shoveling,
      Wrecking,
      Planning,
      Building, breaking, rebuilding,
Under the smoke, dust all over his mouth, laughing with white teeth,
Under the terrible burden of destiny laughing as a young man laughs,
Laughing even as an ignorant fighter laughs who has never lost a battle,   20
Bragging and laughing that under his wrist is the pulse, and under his ribs the
    heart of the people.
      Laughing!
Laughing the stormy, husky, brawling laughter of youth, half-naked, sweating,
    proud to be Hog-butcher, Tool-maker, Stacker of Wheat, Player with Rail-
    roads and Freight-handler to the Nation.

                               1914

To a Contemporary Bunkshooter

You come along . . . tearing your shirt . . . yelling about Jesus.
     Where do you get that stuff?
     What do you know about Jesus?

Jesus had a way of talking soft and outside of a few bankers and higher-ups among the con men of Jerusalem everybody liked to have this Jesus around because he never made any fake passes and everything he said went and he helped the sick and gave the people hope.

You come along squirting words at us, shaking your fist and call us all dam fools so fierce the froth slobbers over your lips . . . always blabbing we're all going to hell straight off and you know all about it.

I've read Jesus' words. I know what he said. You don't throw any scare into me. I've got your number. I know how much you know about Jesus.

He never came near clean people or dirty people but they felt cleaner because he came along. It was your crowd of bankers and business men and lawyers hired the sluggers and murderers who put Jesus out of the running.

I say the same bunch backing you nailed the nails into the hands of this Jesus of Nazareth. He had lined up against him the same crooks and strong-arm men now lined up with you paying your way.

This Jesus was good to look at, smelled good, listened good. He threw out something fresh and beautiful from the skin of his body and the touch of his hands wherever he passed along.

You slimy bunkshooter, you put a smut on every human blossom in reach of your rotten breath belching about hell-fire and hiccupping about this Man who lived a clean life in Galilee.   10

When are you going to quit making the carpenters build emergency hospitals for women and girls driven crazy with wrecked nerves from your gibberish about Jesus? — I put it to you again: Where do you get that stuff? What do you know about Jesus?

Go ahead and bust all the chairs you want to. Smash a whole wagon-load of furniture at every performance. Turn sixty somersaults and stand on your nutty head. If it wasn't for the way you scare the women and kids I'd feel sorry for you and pass the hat.

I like to watch a good four-flusher work, but not when he starts people puking and calling for the doctors.

I like a man that's got nerve and can pull off a great original performance, but you — you're only a bug-house peddler of second-hand gospel — you're only shoving out a phoney imitation of the goods this Jesus wanted free as air and sunlight.

You tell people living in shanties Jesus is going to fix it up all right with them
    by giving them mansions in the skies after they're dead and the worms
    have eaten 'em.
You tell $6 a week department store girls all they need is Jesus; you take a steel
    trust wop, dead without having lived, gray and shrunken at forty years of
    age, and you tell him to look at Jesus on the cross and he'll be all right.
You tell poor people they don't need any more money on pay day and even if it's
    fierce to be out of a job, Jesus'll fix that up all right, all right — all they
    gotta do is take Jesus the way you say.
I'm telling you Jesus wouldn't stand for the stuff you're handing out. Jesus
    played it different. The bankers and lawyers of Jerusalem got their sluggers
    and murderers to go after Jesus just because Jesus wouldn't play their game.
    He didn't sit in with the big thieves.

I don't want a lot of gab from a bunkshooter in my religion.
I won't take my religion from any man who never works except with his mouth
    and never cherishes any memory except the face of the woman on the
    American silver dollar.   20

I ask you to come through and show me where you're pouring out the blood of
    your life.
I've been to this suburb of Jerusalem they call Golgotha, where they nailed Him,
    and I know if the story is straight it was real blood ran from His hands and
    the nail-holes, and it was real blood spurted in red drops where the spear
    of the Roman soldier rammed in between the ribs of this Jesus of Nazareth.
                                                                    1916

Caboose Thoughts

It's going to come out all right — do you know?
The sun, the birds, the grass — they know.
They get along — and we'll get along.

Some days will be rainy and you will sit waiting
And the letter you wait for won't come,
And I will sit watching the sky tear off gray and gray
And the letter I wait for won't come.

There will be ac-ci-dents.
I know ac-ci-dents are coming.
Smash-ups, signals wrong, washouts, trestles rotten,   10
Red and yellow ac-ci-dents.
But somehow and somewhere the end of the run
The train gets put together again
And the caboose and the green tail lights
Fade down the right of way like a new white hope.

I never heard a mockingbird in Kentucky
Spilling its heart in the morning.

I never saw the snow on Chimborazo.
It's a high white Mexican hat, I hear.

I never had supper with Abe Lincoln,   20
Nor a dish of soup with Jim Hill.

But I've been around.
I know some of the boys here who can go a little.
I know girls good for a burst of speed any time.

I heard Williams and Walker
Before Walker died in the bughouse.

I knew a mandolin player
Working in a barber shop in an Indiana town,
And he thought he had a million dollars.

I knew a hotel girl in Des Moines.   30
She had eyes; I saw her and said to myself
The sun rises and the sun sets in her eyes.
I was her steady and her heart went pit-a-pat.
We took away the money for a prize waltz at a Brotherhood dance.
She had eyes; she was safe as the bridge over the Mississippi at Burlington; I
    married her.

Last summer we took the cushions going west.
Pike's Peak is a big old stone, believe me.
It's fastened down; something you can count on.

It's going to come out all right — do you know?
The sun, the birds, the grass — they know.   40
They get along — and we'll get along.

1918

Threes

I was a boy when I heard three red words
a thousand Frenchmen died in the streets
for: Liberty, Equality, Fraternity — I asked
why men die for words.

I was older; men with mustaches, sideburns,
lilacs, told me the high golden words are:
Mother, Home, and Heaven — other older men with
face decorations said: God, Duty, Immortality
— they sang these threes slow from deep lungs.

Years ticked off their say-so on the great clocks
of doom and damnation, soup and nuts: meteors flashed
their say-so: and out of great Russia came three
dusky syllables workmen took guns and went out to die
for: Bread, Peace, Land.

And I met a marine of the U.S.A., a leatherneck with
a girl on his knee for a memory in ports circling the
earth and he said: Tell me how to say three things
and I always get by — gimme a plate of ham and eggs —
how much? — and — do you love me, kid?

1920

Archibald MacLeish

Speech to Those Who Say Comrade

The brotherhood is not by the blood certainly:
But neither are men brothers by speech — by saying so:
Men are brothers by life lived and are hurt for it:

Hunger and hurt are the great begetters of brotherhood:
Humiliation has gotten much love:
Danger I say is the nobler father and mother:

Those are as brothers whose bodies have shared fear
Or shared harm or shared hurt or indignity.
Why are the old soldiers brothers and nearest?

For this: with their minds they go over the sea a little   10
And find themselves in their youth again as they were in
Soissons and Meaux and at Ypres and those cities:

A French loaf and the girls with their eyelids painted
Bring back to aging and lonely men
Their twentieth year and the metal odor of danger:

It is this in life which of all things is tenderest —
To remember together with unknown men the days
Common also to them and perils ended:

It is this which makes of many a generation —
A wave of men who having the same years   20
Have in common the same dead and the changes.

The solitary and unshared experience
Dies of itself like the violations of love
Or lives on as the dead live eerily:

The unshared and single man must cover his
Loneliness as a girl her shame for the way of
Life is neither by one man nor by suffering.

Who are the born brothers in truth? The puddlers
Scorched by the same flame in the same foundries:
Those who have spit on the same boards with the blood in it: 30

Ridden the same rivers with green logs:
Fought the police in the parks of the same cities:
Grinned for the same blows: the same flogging:

Veterans out of the same ships — factories —
Expeditions for fame: the founders of continents:
Those that hid in Geneva a time back:

Those that have hidden and hunted and all such —
Fought together: labored together: they carry the
Common look like a card and they pass touching.

Brotherhood! No word said can make you brothers!   40
Brotherhood only the brave earn and by danger or
Harm or by bearing hurt and by no other.

Brotherhood here in the strange world is the rich and
Rarest giving of life and the most valued:
Not to be had for a word or a week's wishing.

1936

DRAMA

CAUTION

Professionals and amateurs are hereby warned that *Green Grow the Lilacs,* being fully protected under the copyright laws of the United States of America, the British Empire, including the Dominion of Canada, and all other countries of the Copyright Union, is subject to a royalty. All rights, including professional, amateur, motion pictures, recitation, public reading, radio broadcasting, and the rights of translation into foreign languages, are strictly reserved. Amateurs may produce this play upon payment of a royalty of Twenty-Five Dollars for each performance, payable one week before the play is to be given, to Samuel French, at 25 West 45th St., New York, N. Y., or 811 West 7th St., Los Angeles, Cal., or, if in Canada, to Samuel French (Canada) Ltd., at 480 University Ave., Toronto, Ont.

Lynn Riggs

Green Grow the Lilacs

PEOPLE

Curly McClain	Ado Annie Carnes
Aunt Eller Murphy	A Pedler
Laurey Williams	Cord Elam
Jeeter Fry	Old Man Peck

and Others of the Countryside

SCENES

SCENE 1. The "front" room of the Williams farmhouse, a June morning.
SCENE 2. Laurey's bedroom.
SCENE 3. The smoke-house.
SCENE 4. The porch of Old Man Peck's house, that night.
SCENE 5. The hayfield, a month later.
SCENE 6. The "front" room, three nights later.
The action of the play takes place in Indian Territory in 1900.

SCENE 1

It is a radiant summer morning several years ago, the kind of morning which, enveloping the shapes of earth — men, cattle in a meadow, blades of the young corn, streams — makes them seem to exist now for the first time, their images giving off a visible golden emanation that is partly true and partly a trick of imagination focusing to keep alive a loveliness that may pass away.

The unearthly sunlight pours through the crocheted curtains of a window in the living room — the "front" room — of a farmhouse in Indian Territory.

It rests upon, and glorifies, scrubbed floors of oak, bright rag rugs, rough hide-bottomed hairy chairs, a rock fireplace, a settee, an old organ magnificently mirrored, ancestral enlargements in their gilt and oval frames. A double sliding door of pine, now closed, is at the back of the room; other heavier doors of oak lead to other parts of the house and to the outside. Somewhere a dog barks twice and stops quickly, reassured; a turkey gobbler makes his startled, swallowing noise.

And, like the voice of the morning, a rich male voice outside somewhere begins to sing:

VOICE:

As I walked out one bright sunny morning,
I saw a cowboy way out on the plain.
His hat was throwed back and his spurs was a-jingling,
And as I passed by him, he was singing this refrain:

Ta whoop ti aye ay, git along, you little dogies!
Way out in Wyoming shall be your bright home —
A-whooping and a-yelling and a-driving those dogies,
And a-riding those bronchos that are none of my own.

The people all say we're goin' to have a picnic,
But I tell you, my boy, they've got 'er down wrong,
For 'f it hadn't a-been for those troublesome dogies,
I never woulda thought of composing this song.

Ta whoop ti aye ay, git along, you little dogies!
Way out in Wyoming shall be your bright home —
A-whooping and a-yelling and a-driving those dogies,
And a-riding those bronchos that are none of my own.

[Before the first verse is finished, part of the singer comes into sight at a window — a tall, waggish, curly-headed young cowboy in a checked shirt and a ten-gallon hat. He looks about the room singing. Just as he finishes he withdraws, hearing footsteps. A moment later, AUNT ELLER MURPHY, *a buxom, hearty woman about fifty, with a tall wooden brass-banded churn in her arms, comes in from the kitchen. She puts the churn down quickly by the fireplace, goes over to the window and looks out, squinting. She grins, good-humoredly.]*

AUNT ELLER: Oh, I see you, Mr. Curly McClain! Don't need to be a-hidin' 'hind that horse of your'n. Couldn't hide them feet of your'n even if yer head wasn't showin'. So you may as well come on in.

[She turns away from the window, takes off her apron, and comes back into the room. CURLY *appears again at the window.]*

CURLY: Hi, Aunt Eller.

AUNT ELLER *[shortly]*: Skeer me to death! Whut're you doin' around here?

CURLY: Come a-singin' to you only you never give me no time to finish.

[*Their speech is lazy, drawling, not Southern, not " hick " — but rich, half-conscious of its rhythms, its picturesque imagery.*]

AUNT ELLER: Go on and finish then. [*She smiles at him.*] You do sing purty, Curly.

CURLY: Nobody never said I didn't.

AUNT ELLER: Yeah, purty. If I wasn't an old womern, and if you wasn't so young and smart-alecky — why, I'd marry you and git you to set around at night and sing to me.

CURLY: No, you wouldn't, neither. If I was to marry — anyone — I wouldn't set around at night a-singin'. They ain't no tellin' *whut* I'd do. But I wouldn't marry you ner none of yer kinfolks, I could he'p it.

AUNT ELLER [*wisely*]: Oh! None of my kinfolks neither, huh?

CURLY: And you c'n tell 'em that, *all* of 'em, includin' that niece of your'n, Miss Laurey Williams, if she's about anywhurs.

AUNT ELLER: Mebbe I will, and mebbe I won't. Whut you doin' over this-a-way, Curly? Thought you was over at Skidmore's ranch, tother side of Justus. Well, air you comin' in or gonna stay there like a Jack-in-the-box?

[CURLY *vaults into the room. He wears dark trousers stuffed into high boots. His heavy roweled spurs clink against the floor.*]

CURLY [*deliberately*]: Aunt Eller, if you was to tell me whur Laurey was at — *whur* would you tell me she was at?

AUNT ELLER: I wouldn't tell you a-tall, less'n you sung me another song.

CURLY: Must think I'm a medicine man a-singin' and passin' the hat around, the way you talk! Got to save my voice, got to take keer of it, so I'll have it. Don't want to do the way ole man Comer done. When he was a kid he squalled so much, and when he was growed he sung so much, now he's a ole man he cain't git a squawk out of him, nary a squawk. 'Cept a whistle. And a whistle don't mean nuthin' — the way a song do.

AUNT ELLER [*unimpressed*]: Sing me a song, Curly McClain.

CURLY: Aw, I *cain't* sing now! I *told* you. Not if I tried and tried, and even et cat-gut. And even 'f I drunk the gall of a turkey gobbler's liver, I couldn't sing a-tall.

AUNT ELLER: Liar and a hypocrite and a shikepoke! Ain't I heared you? Jist now. *You sing!* Er I'll run you off the place.

CURLY: I cain't sing, I told you! 'Ceptin' when I'm lonesome. Out in the saddle when it ain't so sunny, er on a dark night close to a fa'r when you feel so lonesome to God you could die. Looky here, you're old, my, you're old, you'd orter be so smart! Whur you been, anyhow, whose side meat you been eatin' all yer life, not to know nobody cain't sing good 'ceptin' when he's lonesome?

AUNT ELLER: Lonesome? Then if I was you I'd be a-singin' and a-singin' then. A long song, with forty 'leven verses and a chorus 'tween ever' verse. Fer as fur as I c'n make out, Laurey ain't payin' you no heed a-tall. You might jist as well be ridin' the rails as ridin' that range of your'n. So sing yer head off, you lonesome dogie, 'cause you shore have got into a lonesome side-pocket 'thout no grass, you dehorned maverick, you!

CURLY: Whut'd I keer about that?

[*He takes cigaret papers out of his hat-band, Bull Durham from his shirt pocket, and begins to roll a cigaret, with elaborate unconcern.*]

AUNT ELLER: She goes around with her head some'eres else, don't she?

CURLY: How'd I know? Ain't looked at her nary a time since Christmas.

AUNT ELLER: 'Twasn't yore fault though, if you didn't. [*Jeering, good-naturedly.*] She don't see you, does she, Mr. Adam's Off Ox! You've got onto the wrong side of the wagon tongue!

CURLY: Go on, you mean ole womern! Brand a steer till you burn a hole in his hide!

AUNT ELLER: *Mr.* Cowboy! A-ridin' high, wide, and handsome, his spurs a-jin-glin', and the Bull Durham tag a-whippin' outa his pocket! Oh, *Mr.* Cow-puncher! 'Thout no home, ner no wife, ner no one to muss up his curly hair, er keep him warm on a winter's night!

CURLY [*swelling up, defensively*]: So she don't take to me much, huh? Whur'd you get sich a uppity niece 'at wouldn't pay no heed to *me?* Who's the best bronc buster in this yere state?

AUNT ELLER: You, I bet.

CURLY: And the best bull-dogger in seventeen counties? *Me,* that's who! And looky here, I'm handsome, ain't I?

AUNT ELLER: Purty as a pitcher.

CURLY: Curly-headed, ain't I? And bow-legged from the saddle fer God knows how long, ain't I?

AUNT ELLER [*agreeing*]: Couldn't stop a pig in the road.

CURLY: Well, whut else does she want then, the damn she-mule?

AUNT ELLER: I don't know. But I'm shore sartin it ain't *you.*

CURLY: Anh! Quit it, you'll have me a-cryin'!

AUNT ELLER [*triumphantly*]: You better sing me a song then, like I told you to in the first place!

CURLY: Aw, whut'll I sing then?

AUNT ELLER: "A-ridin' ole Paint."

CURLY: And nen whut'll I sing?

AUNT ELLER: Lands, you better git one sung 'fore you start in on another'n!

[*But* CURLY *has already leaned against the wall with his head thrown back, and his feet crossed, and begun to sing in his rich, liquid, mock-heroic voice.*]

CURLY [*singing*]:

> A-ridin' ole Paint and a-leadin' ole Dan,
> I'm goin' to Montana for to throw the hoolian.
> They feed in the hollers and they water in the draw,
> Their tails are all matted and their backs are all raw.

Ride around the little dogies, ride around them slow,
For the fiery and the snuffy are a-rarin' to go.

Ole Bill Jones had two daughters and a son,
One went to Denver and the other went wrong,
One was killed in a pool room fight,
But still he goes singing from morn till night:

Ride around the little dogies, ride around them slow,
For the fiery and the snuffy are a-rarin' to go.

When I die take my saddle from the wall,
Put it on my pony, lead him out of his stall,
Tie my bones to the saddle, turn our faces to the west,
And we'll ride the trail that we love best.

Ride around the little dogies, ride around them slow,
For the fiery and the snuffy are a-rarin' to go.

Now whur's Laurey at?

AUNT ELLER [*pointing*]: Settin' in there in her room a-sewin' er sump'n, when she
orta be in here a-churnin' like I told her. Ain't you gonna sing another song?

CURLY: Ain't you a bother though — keep on a-pesterin'! You go and tell
Laurey to drop a stitch, and see whut Sandy Claus brung her.

AUNT ELLER: Meanin' you, I guess. Whut'd you want with her, Curly, nohow? I'm
her aunt, so you better tell me first, and see if I like the looks of it.

CURLY: You're jist nosy. Well, if you have to know my business, ole man Peck
over acrost Dog Crick's givin' a play-party and I come to ast if Laurey ud
go with me.

AUNT ELLER: And me, too, huh?

CURLY: Yeow, you too. If you'll go and knock on the door there, and bring Laurey
out whur a man c'n git a look at her.

AUNT ELLER [*knocking*]: Laurey! Peck's is givin' a play-party.

LAUREY [*inside*]: Who's givin' a play-party?

AUNT ELLER: Ole man Peck acrost Dog Crick.

LAUREY: Cain't hear a word you say. Who?

AUNT ELLER [*shouting*]: Come on out. Someone's come to see you. He'll tell you.

LAUREY: Who's come to see me? Who's givin' a party?

AUNT ELLER: Well, open up the door, you crazy youngun, I cain't holler my head
off!

[*The door slides back, and* LAUREY *comes out. She is a fair, spoiled, lovely young
girl about eighteen in a long white dress with many ruffles. She sees* CURLY.]

LAUREY: Oh! Thought you was somebody. [*To* AUNT ELLER.] Is this all that's
come a-callin' and it a'ready ten o'clock of a Satiddy mornin'?

CURLY [*sullenly*]: You knowed it was me 'fore you opened the door.

LAUREY: No sich of a thing.

CURLY: You did, too! You heared my voice and knowed it was me.

LAUREY: I did not, I tell you! Heared a voice a-talkin' rumbly along with Aunt Eller. And heared someone a-singin' like a bull-frog in a pond —

CURLY: I don't talk rumbly. And I don't sing like no bull-frog —

LAUREY: Bull-frog in a pond, I told you. But how'd I know it was you, Mr. Curly McClain? You ain't so special. All men sounds alike to me.

CURLY [*doggedly*]: You knowed it was me, so you set in there a-thinkin' up sump'n mean to say. I'm a good mind not to tell you nuthin' about the play-party now. You c'n jist stay at home, for yer tongue. Don't you tell her whur it is, Aunt Eller. Me'n you'll go and leave her at home.

LAUREY: If you *did* ast me, I wouldn't go with you. Besides, how'd you take me? You ain't bought a new buggy with red wheels onto it, have you?

CURLY: No, I ain't.

LAUREY: And a spankin' team with their bridles all jinglin'?

CURLY: No.

LAUREY: 'Spect me to ride on behind ole Dun, I guess. You better ast that ole Cummins girl you've tuck sich a shine to, over acrost the river.

CURLY: If I was to ast you, they'd be a way to take you, Miss Laurey Smarty.

LAUREY: *Oh,* they would?

CURLY: A bran' new surrey with fringe on the top four inches long — and *yeller!* And two white horses a-rarin' and faunchin' to go! You'd shore ride like a queen settin' up in *that* carriage! Feel like you had a gold crown set on yer head, 'th diamonds in it big as goose eggs.

LAUREY: Look out, you'll be astin' me in a minute!

CURLY: I ain't astin' you, I'm *tellin'* you. And this yere rig has got four fine side-curtains, case of a rain. And isinglass winders to look out of! And a red and green lamp set on the dashboard, winkin' like a lightnin' bug!

LAUREY: Whur'd you git sich a rig at? [*With explosive laughter.*] Anh, I bet he's went and h'ard it over to Claremore, thinkin' I'd go with him!

CURLY: 'S all you know about it —

LAUREY [*jeering*]: Went and h'ard it! Spent all his money h'arin' a rig, and now ain't got nobody to ride in it.

CURLY: Have, too! Did *not* h'ar it. Made the whole thing up outa my head —

LAUREY: What! Made it up?

CURLY: Dashboard and all!

LAUREY [*flying at him*]: Oh! Git outa the house, you! Aunt Eller, make him git hisself outa here 'fore I take a stove arn to him! Tellin' me lies —!

CURLY [*dodging her*]: Makin' up a few — Look out, now! Makin' up a few purties ain't agin no law 'at I know of. Don't you wish they *was* sich a rig, though? Nen you could go to the party and do a hoe-down till mornin' 'f you was a mind to. Nen drive home 'th the sun a-peekin' at you over the ridge, purty and fine.

LAUREY: I ain't wantin' to do no hoe-down till mornin'. And whut would I want to see the sun come up fer, a-peekin' purty and fine — alongside of you, anyhow?

AUNT ELLER: Whyn't you jist grab her and kiss her when she acts that-a-way, Curly? She's jist achin' fer you to, I bet.

LAUREY [*with mock fury*]: Oh! I won't even *speak* to him, let alone 'low him to kiss me, the braggin', saddle-awk'ard, wish-'t-he-had-a-sweetheart bum!

[*She flounces into her room, and bangs the sliding door.*]

AUNT ELLER [*turning to* CURLY, *sagely*]: She likes you — quite a little.

CURLY: Whew! 'F she liked me quite a *lot,* she'd sic the dogs onto me, or shoot me full of buckshot!

AUNT ELLER: No, come 'ere, Curly, while I tell you sump'n. A womern that won't let you tetch her 'th a ten foot pole like that is jist dyin' fer you to git closer'n *that* to her.

CURLY: Mebbe. But they's women and women. And some of 'em is accordin' to the rules, and some of 'em ain't never *heared* no rules to be accordin' *to.* Guess I better be movin' my camp some'eres else.

AUNT ELLER: No, look here, Curly. I've knowed Laurey all her born days, ain't I? And since her paw and maw died five year ago, I been paw and maw both to her. And whutever I tell you about her way of feelin' is the truth. Er if it *ain't* I'll give her a everlastin' good spankin', nen it *will* be! Fer I don't know whur her eyes was set in her head 'f she didn't see you, you purty thing, right from the start, the time you come over of a Sunday a year ago and broke them three broncs all in one evenin', 'thout tetchin' leather er yellin' calf-rope. 'Member?

CURLY [*feeling a little better*]: Yeah, I remember. Mean as sin they was, too! That one-eyed un 'th the star in his forehead liked to set me over his head right smack into them lilac bushes the first crack outa the bucket, didn't he? Yeah, onct I break 'em, they're purty apt to stay broke, fer a fact. [*Cryptically.*] You c'n *count* on a horse. [*Suddenly.*] Look here, Aunt Eller, I wanta know sump'n and if you lie to me, I'll ketch thirteen bulgy-eyed toad-frogs and put 'em in yer bed —

AUNT ELLER: Laws a-mercy!

CURLY: Er make you chew Indian turnip till yer tongue feels like a thousand needles run through it, and no way of pullin' 'em out —

AUNT ELLER: Feel 'em a'ready.

CURLY: Listen, whut low, filthy, sneakin' man has Laurey got her cap set fer?

AUNT ELLER: You.

CURLY: Now! —

AUNT ELLER: Fer a fact, I'm tellin' you! From the way she flew at you jist now, I got my mind all made up. 'F she don't git *you,* Curly, she'll waste away to the shadder of a pin point. Yes, sir. Be put in a sateen coffin dead of a broke heart.

CURLY [*ironically*]: I wouldn't want her to do *that.* I'd consider lettin' her *have* me, 'f that ud keep her from dyin'.

AUNT ELLER [*wisely*]: She's a young girl — and don't know her mind. She don't know her feelin's. You c'n he'p her, Curly — and they's few that can.

CURLY: They must be plenty of men a-tryin' to spark her. And she shorely leans to one of 'em, now don't she?

AUNT ELLER: Ain't no one a-sparkin' her. Well, they is that ole widder man at Claremore, makes out he's a doctor er a vet'nary. And that fine farmer, Jace Hutchins, jist this side of Lone Ellum —

CURLY: That's whut I thought!

AUNT ELLER: Not to say nuthin' about someone nearer home that's got her on his mind most of the time, till he don't know a plow from a thrashin' machine —

CURLY: Who'd you mean by that?

AUNT ELLER: Jeeter.

CURLY: Jeeter who?

AUNT ELLER: Don't you know Jeeter Fry, our h'ard hand?

CURLY: What! That bullet-colored growly man 'th the bushy eyebrows that's alwys orderin' the other hands how to work the mowin' machine er sump'n!

AUNT ELLER: Now you don't need to go and say nuthin' agin him! He's a big help around here. Jist about runs the farm by hisself. Well, two women couldn't do it, you orta know that.

CURLY: Laurey'd take up 'th a man like that!

AUNT ELLER: I ain't said she's tuck up with him.

CURLY: Well, he's around all the time, ain't he? Eats his meals with you like one of the fambly, don't he? Sleeps around here some'eres, don't he?

AUNT ELLER: Out in the smoke-house.

CURLY: Laurey sees him all the time, then, don't she? Whyn't you say so in the first place! Whur is this Jeeter, till I git a look at him and mebbe black his eyes fer him?

AUNT ELLER [*slyly*]: Thought you'd moved yer camp some'eres else?

CURLY [*with exaggerated bravado*]: My camp's right here till I git ready to break it. And moreover — whoever puts his foot in it's liable to git shot fer a stinkin' skunk er a sneakin' wildcat!

[*As if waiting for this declaration, the front door bangs open, and the bullet-colored, growly man, with an armful of wood for the fireplace, comes in. He throws the wood in the wood-box, and turns to* AUNT ELLER.]

JEETER: Whur's Laurey at?

AUNT ELLER: In her room there.

[JEETER *gives a surly grunt by way of response, and without another word goes out again, leaving the door wide open behind him.*]

CURLY: Now is that Jeeter?

AUNT ELLER: Yeah.

CURLY: Thought it was. [*He goes over and looks out after him.*] Why ain't he a-workin'?

AUNT ELLER: It's Satiddy.

CURLY: Oh! I'd forgot. He's went in the smoke-house.

AUNT ELLER: It's *his* house. Used to be the *dog*-house.

CURLY [*chuckling*]: That's the place fer him!

[*The sliding door opens a crack, and* LAUREY *sticks her head out.*]

LAUREY: I forgot to tell you, Aunt Eller, you'll have to do the churnin' yerself, less'n you c'n git someone to do it fer you.

AUNT ELLER: Why, you lazy youngun, I'll do no sich of a thing! I got dinner on the stove —

LAUREY: It takes time fer a girl to git herself fixed up, it looks to me like. I'm goin' to a party tonight.

AUNT ELLER: To a party?

LAUREY: Well, stand there 'th yer mouth open! Didn't I tell you? — At ole man Peck's over acrost Dog Crick.

AUNT ELLER: Now whoever went and — Did you, Curly?

LAUREY: I heared about it a week ago. Jeeter told me. I'm goin' with Jeeter.

[*She withdraws.* CURLY *stands very still.*]

CURLY [*after a moment*]: Ever hear that song, Aunt Eller?

AUNT ELLER [*frowning*]: A thousand pins it takes 'em to dress —

CURLY [*grins, ruefully*]: Now wouldn't that jist make you bawl!

[*He goes over, touches a few chords on the organ soberly, and then recovering, seats himself, and after a moment begins to sing, half-satirically. But by the time he has reached the first chorus, the song with its absurd yet plaintive charm has absorbed him. And he sings the rest of its sentimental periods, his head back, his eyes focused beyond the room, beyond himself — upon the young man having his sad say, the young man who'll go into the army, by God, and put an end to his distemper, his unrequited fervor.*]

CURLY [*singing*]:

> I used to have a sweetheart, but now I've got none,
> Since she's gone and left me, I care not for one,
> Since she's gone and left me, contented I'll be,
> For she loves another one better than me.
>
> Green grow the lilacs, all sparkling with dew,
> I'm lonely, my darling, since parting with you,
> And by the next meeting I hope to prove true
> To change the green lilacs to the red, white and blue.
>
> I passed my love's window, both early and late,
> The look that she gave me, it made my heart ache,
> The look that she gave me was harmful to see,
> For she loves another one better than me.
>
> Green grow the lilacs, all sparkling with dew,
> I'm lonely, my darling, since parting with you,
> And by the next meeting I hope to prove true
> To change the green lilacs to the red, white and blue.

I wrote my love a letter in red rosy lines,
She sent me an answer all twisted in twines,
Saying " Keep your love letters and I will keep mine,
Just write to your sweetheart and I'll write to mine."

Green grow the lilacs, all sparkling with dew,
I'm lonely, my darling, since parting with you,
And by the next meeting I hope to prove true
To change the green lilacs to the red, white and blue.

[*He swings off the organ stool, miraculously healed, and makes for the door.*]

AUNT ELLER [*following him over*]: Now don't you be discouraged none, Curly. Laurey's good. She's got sense. She don't let you know too much — keeps you guessin'. And you shore got *her* to wonderin', too! You're shore a pair — full of life — made for each other! Got to have each other. *Got* to. [*She laughs.*] Thought I'd die when you made up all that about the rig and told her —

CURLY [*whistles softly*]: Jesus! [*He turns round with a grin.*] Well, we got a date together, you and me, Aunt Eller.

AUNT ELLER: We have?

CURLY: We shore have. We goin' to that party we've heared so much about.

AUNT ELLER: How we goin', Curly? In that rig you made up? [*She chuckles.*] I'll ride a-straddle of them lights a-winkin' like lightnin' bugs, myself!

CURLY: That there rig ain't no made-up rig, you hear me! I h'ard it over to Clare-more.

AUNT ELLER: Lands, you did!

CURLY: And when I come callin' fer you right after supper, see that you got yer beauty spots fastened onto you proper, so you won't lose 'em off, you hear? Now then. [*He strides away to the door again, enigmatically.*] I think I'll jist go out here to the smoke-house awhile.

AUNT ELLER [*puzzled*]: Whur Jeeter's at?

CURLY: Yeow, whur Jeeter's at. Thought mebbe I'd play a game of pitch with him, 'fore I mosey on home. You reckon he'd like that?

[*He goes out the door.* AUNT ELLER *stares after him, figuring out things.*]

CURTAIN

SCENE 2

LAUREY'S *bedroom, behind its sliding doors, is small, primitive, but feminine. There's a bed, covered with a beautiful crazy-quilt, a dresser, very ornate, with little souvenir shell boxes, combs, hair receivers, hairpins, a vase of buttercups and daisies, etc. There's a small table with pitchers of water under it, and comfortable chairs. A small window looks out into the brilliant day. At the left is a door which goes out to the swept yard in front of the kitchen. The walls are papered, and several small photographs are tacked up — one of a man on*

*horseback, obviously for the first time, one of a young girl with enormous
sleeves in her dress.*

LAUREY *is combing her hair. She seems, in this setting, younger, more glowing, more complete than before, as if the room were necessary to her. It is immediately after Scene 1.* AUNT ELLER *has come in from the door at the left to
see what* LAUREY *is up to.*

AUNT ELLER: Is that all you got to do?

LAUREY [*abstractedly*]: When I was a little girl I had my hair in pigtails. It hung
down and down, till I'd wrap it around my head. Nen I'd look like sump'n
crawled out of a hole.

AUNT ELLER: I ain't got time to listen to sich craziness.

LAUREY: When I got a little older, I cut it off. Maw licked me.

AUNT ELLER: Well, she'd orta licked you.

LAUREY: Why?

AUNT ELLER: Fer cuttin' yer hair off. Don't you know that ain't right?

LAUREY: I ast you fer a answer and all I git is another question.

AUNT ELLER: Oh, I'm goin' back in the kitchen. You ain't started on that churnin'.
I jist come in to see what you was up to so long. Here I find you a-primpin'
and a-talkin' crazy.

LAUREY: Wait a minute. Why don't you set down here a minute?

AUNT ELLER: They's work to do. Ain't time to set.

LAUREY: Then redd up that table if you won't set. And put some fresh water
onto them flowers I picked day before yistiddy. Them buttercups. In the
meader back of the wheat field — walkin' in the tall grass and the sumakes,
you know what I seen? A snake 'th its tail in its mouth —

AUNT ELLER: And a terrapin carryin' a elephant, too, didn't you?

LAUREY: Won't hurt you none to put some water on them flowers.

AUNT ELLER [*acquiescing, judicially*]: Well. You ain't always so lazy, I must say.

LAUREY: Dance at yer weddin'.

AUNT ELLER: I don't know whut's got into you, though.

LAUREY: You don't?

AUNT ELLER [*wisely*]: Yes, I do.

LAUREY [*cryptically*]: I thought you did.

[*Silence.* AUNT ELLER *fills the vase.* LAUREY *combs her hair slowly, and begins
to sing.*]

LAUREY [*singing*]:

>   One morning as I rambled o'er
>   The fields I took my way
>   In hopes of meeting my miner boy
>   And for a while to stray,
>   In hopes of meeting my miner boy,
>   My hope, my joy, my own.
>   My heart was blessed, it could find no rest
>   For the thoughts of my miner boy.

The mother to her daughter,
" I'll comfort you to your room,
You never shall marry a miner boy,
It will certainly be your doom.
They're never, never satisfied,
But always on a drunk.
And all they have in this wide wide world
Is a satchel and a trunk."

The daughter to her mother,
" What makes you be unkind?
I never shall marry another one
But the one that suits my mind.
His trousers are made of corduroy,
His jacket of true blue.
I'd rather marry a miner boy
As to reign with the waters true."

Then fill your glasses to the brim,
Let's all go merry round,
And drink to the health of the miner boy
Who works down in the ground,
When work is o'er comes whistling home
With a heart so full of joy,
And happy, happy is the girl
That marries a miner boy.

Would you marry a miner boy, Aunt Eller?

AUNT ELLER: I don't know no miner boys.

LAUREY: Oh, 'f you did, you would, I bet. [*After a moment.*] Wish 't I lived in the White House, and had diamonds on my shoes, and a little nigger boy to fan me — when it was hot. Does it git hot in the White House, Aunt Eller?

AUNT ELLER: How do I know?

LAUREY: Er I wish 't I lived in Virginia or Californie. In Californie, they's oranges growin', and snow fallin' at the same time. I seen a pitcher of it. In the Verdigree bottom the other day, a man found thirty-three arrowheads — thirty-three — whur they'd been a Indian battle —

AUNT ELLER: Whut's that got to do with the White House and livin' in Californie?

LAUREY: Who said anything about Californie?

AUNT ELLER [*whistles*]: Land's alive! [*After a moment.*] Curly's out in the smoke-house.

LAUREY: Who is?

AUNT ELLER: Curly. Him and Jeeter.

LAUREY [*as if she hadn't heard*]: Bet they'll be a hundred people at Peck's. They'll come in buggies and surreys, a-horseback, in the wagon, and some'll come afoot. Gracie Denham will come all the way from Catoosie to be there, I bet. When she married Dan Denham, everybody thought — " Good-by, good times " — fer Gracie. She fooled 'em, though. How big is Indian Territory, Aunt Eller?

AUNT ELLER: Oh, big.

LAUREY: It's a funny place to live, ain't it?

AUNT ELLER: Whut's funny about it?

LAUREY: Well, take me, if paw and maw hadn't come here, I'd a-been livin' in Missouri now, 'stid of here. I'd a-had education, I'll bet. [*She puts down her comb and stares thoughtfully out the window.*] I lied about the White House, Aunt Eller. I'd ruther be married to a man — if he was a real good man — than to live in the old White House.

AUNT ELLER [*chuckling*]: Hope you do one of the two!

LAUREY: Wouldn't you, Aunt Eller?

AUNT ELLER: I've done about all the marryin' I'm gonna do. Onct is quite a plenty. [*She chortles with delight.*] Less'n I marry Curly and bring him up right. Me and Curly, we're a-goin' to that there party —

LAUREY [*jumps up, runs over and begins shaking the astounded* AUNT ELLER]: You ain't, you air not! He ain't got no way to take you to no party. You got to go with Jeeter and me —

AUNT ELLER: Curly's h'ard a rig. That un he told you about. [LAUREY *drops her hands, backs away, and looks at* AUNT ELLER *with such an amazed and startled expression, that the older woman cries out.*] Why, you look so funny! — Like you'd saw sump'n. [LAUREY *goes over to the window, hangs on to the curtains.*] Besides, you turned him down. [*Teasing her.*] If you jist got to go with Jeeter, they ain't no way out of it, I reckon. Well, me'n Curly, we'll make out —

LAUREY [*quietly, strangely*]: Onct I passed by a farmhouse and it was night. Paw and maw and me was in a covered wagon on our way to here. And this farmhouse was burnin' up. It was burnin' bright, too. Black night, it was like I said. Flames licked and licked at the red-hot chimbley and finally it fell, too, and that was the last of that house. And that was turrible! I cried and cried. [*A sudden slightly-hysterical note in her voice.*] And the farmer's wife jist set there by the side of the road, moanin' and takin' on. Had on a sunbonnet, a *sunbonnet,* and it night! She kept sayin' over and over — " Now my home's burnt up. 'F I'd jist a-give him a piece of cold pork or sump'n. If I'd jist a-fed him! — " [*She shakes her head, as if shutting it out.*] Now ain't that silly! — Don't you listen to a word I said. Ever onct in a while sump'n makes me think about it, the way that womern cried, and said whut she did. Don't you pay no attention to me —

AUNT ELLER: I b'lieve to my soul you got sump'n worryin' on yer mind. Never seen you ack before like a chicken 'th its head cut off, Laurey.

LAUREY [*flippantly*]: Worried to death.

AUNT ELLER: Whut about? Now tell yer ole Aunt. Whut is it, honey?

LAUREY: Ain't got a thing to wear tonight.

AUNT ELLER: You make me so mad — !

LAUREY: Well, I ain't. That ole flowered dewdad of a dress looks like sump'n the cat drug in. And my sash is tore. Sylvie Roberts has got a new kind of a shoe with high heels onto 'em like stilts — and I ain't got none.

AUNT ELLER: You'd shore look purty a-wearin' stilts — like a sandhill crane a-wadin' shaller water! That ain't whut's a-worryin' you, though —

LAUREY: I thought it was. Listen to that mockin' bird a-singin'! Ever' mornin' he sets in that ellum and sings like a tree full of birds all by hisself.

AUNT ELLER: He's lonesome.

LAUREY: He's hungry.

AUNT ELLER: Well, it's the same thing.

LAUREY [with real passion]: If we ever had to leave this here place, Aunt Eller, I'd shore miss it. I like it. I like that thicket down by the branch whur the 'possums live, don't you? And the way we set around in the evenings in thrashin' time, a-eatin' mushmelons and singin', and oh! lots of things! Runnin' to the cellar in a storm, and them yeller trumpet tomaters even, you make jam out of, and the branch and the pond to skate on — They's only one thing I don't to say *like*. And that's Sunday in fall, when it's windy, and the sun shines, and the leaves piles up thick agin the house. I'm 'fraid of my life to go from here to the kitchen — like sump'n was gonna ketch me!

AUNT ELLER: Well, you *air* a silly.

LAUREY: But I'd shore hate to leave here, though, and go some'eres else — like to a town or some place —

AUNT ELLER: Well, the ole Scratch! Whut makes you keep talkin' about leavin' here?

LAUREY: Whut if we had to?

AUNT ELLER: Won't have to. We got money in the bank.

LAUREY: Bank might break.

AUNT ELLER: Well, let it. It's gonna be another good year fer corn and oats, like it's been now fer three year —

LAUREY: Whut if sump'n happened?

AUNT ELLER: Like whut?

LAUREY: Oh, things change. Things don't last the way they air. Besides, whut if they'd be a prairie f'ar — like the one that burnt up a thousand acres by Chambers School House five year ago?

AUNT ELLER: Ain't apt to be no prairie f'ar.

LAUREY: Or a cyclone ud come, like that un did at Sweetwater. Made hash outa three whole sections.

AUNT ELLER: Cain't stop a cyclone by worryin'.

LAUREY: No? Well, whut if Jeeter ud set the house on f'ar?

AUNT ELLER: Jeeter set the — Whut in the name of Jerusalem air you talkin' about! Jeeter set the — My goodness, git yer things ready, gonna start you right off to Vinita to the crazy house!

LAUREY: Well, I told you, anyway —

AUNT ELLER: Git 'em ready!

LAUREY: You don't have to listen.

AUNT ELLER: Whut if I'd put rat poison in the turnip greens? Now whut on earth would Jeeter want to set the house on f'ar fer?

LAUREY: I jist said he might.

AUNT ELLER: Might take a notion to rope a freight train, too. Fiddlesticks! I got my dinner on the stove a-cookin'. [*She makes for the door, slows her pace, and turns around again.*] Now, whut do you mean, anyway — Jeeter set the house on f'ar? —

LAUREY: They's a horse and buggy turnin' off up the road this-a-way.

AUNT ELLER: I won't look till you tell me whut you're a-meanin'.

LAUREY: It's a roan horse 'th a long tail. He's string-haltered. Look at the way he walks —

AUNT ELLER: Not *gonna* look, I tell you!

LAUREY: You know whut a f'ar is, don't you? And you know Jeeter?

AUNT ELLER: That's jist it.

LAUREY [*gravely, queerly*]: Sump'n funny about him. Sump'n black a-pilin' up. Ever since a year ago. Sump'n boilin' up inside of him — *mean.*

AUNT ELLER [*relieved*]: Is that it! Well, I guess you don't mind that so much — goin' to parties with him, and all.

LAUREY [*her face white — in a low voice*]: I'm afraid to tell him I won't, Aunt Eller. 'F I done whut I wanted to, I'd f'ar him off the place so quick! Whut're we gonna do, Aunt Eller! He'd do sump'n turrible, he makes me shiver ever' time he gits close to me — [*With a frightened look around, as if he were in the room.*] Have you ever looked out there in the smoke-house — whur he sleeps?

AUNT ELLER: Course I have, plenty of times.

LAUREY: Whut'd you see?

AUNT ELLER: Nuthin' — but a lot of dirt. Why, whut's out there?

LAUREY [*her voice tight with excitement — creating it*]: I don't know, sump'n awful. I hook my door at night and fasten the winders agin it. Agin *it* — and the sound of feet a-walkin' up and down out there under that tree, and around the corner of the house, and down by the barn — and in the front room there!

AUNT ELLER: Laurey!

LAUREY [*as before*]: I wake up and hear the boards creakin', I tell you! The rafters jist over my head here shakes a little — *easy.* Next mornin', he comes to his breakfast and looks at me out from under his eyebrows like sump'n back in the bresh some'eres. I know what I'm talkin' about —

AUNT ELLER: Why, I didn't have an idy you felt that-a-way about him! Why, we'll run him off the place if you're skeered of him —

LAUREY [*with deep premonition*]: Don't you do it! Don't you say nuthin' to him! *That's* whut skeers me — he'd do sump'n, I tell you! He'd set the house on f'ar, like I told you!

AUNT ELLER: Land's sakes! Jist let me ketch him at it! [*She laughs.*] Now you've went and made all this up, and I don't believe a word of it —

LAUREY: You'll find out some day —

AUNT ELLER: Onct when you was a little girl you know what you done? Looked outa the winder and seen a cow standin' in the tool shed, and you said to yer maw, "I knowed it, I knowed it! I knowed the cow ud eat the grind-stone up!" Didn't you? But the cow didn't, though!

LAUREY [*smiling with great relief*]: No, the cow didn't.

AUNT ELLER: *Well,* then! You didn't know's much's you thought you did. [*She goes and looks out the window.*] Now who'd you reckon that is drove up? [*A dog begins barking angrily.*] Why, it's that ole pedler! The one that sold me that egg-beater. Jist let me git my hands onto him — 'f I don't fix him — !

[*She rushes toward the door.*]

LAUREY: He's got someone with him. Why, it's Ado Annie Carnes! Now ain't she a sight! Ridin' around with that ole pedler.

AUNT ELLER: I'll th'ow him in the branch, that's whut I'll do to him! You know whut he done? Told me that egg-beater ud beat up eggs, and wring out dish rags, and turn the ice cream freezer, and I don't know whut all! —

[*She dashes out the door.*]

LAUREY [*leaning out the window*]: Yoohoo! Ado Annie! C'm here. And bring yer pedler man in too, 'f you ain't afeard I'll take him away from you. [*She snickers with delight.*] I want to buy some things.

[*She flies to the dresser, catches up her hair in the back, straightens her dress, and by the time* ADO ANNIE CARNES *appears in the door is humming softly to herself, apparently having forgotten her uneasiness of the moment before.*]

ADO ANNIE [*coming in*]: Hi.

[*She is an unattractive, stupid-looking farm girl, with taffy-colored hair pulled back from a freckled face. Her dress is of red gingham, and very unbecoming.*]

LAUREY: Hi, yerself. Ridin' a piece?

ADO ANNIE [*non-committally*]: Rode over yere.

LAUREY: Well, set. Whur's yer pedler?

ADO ANNIE [*hiding a grin*]: Aw, he ain't *mine.* He's out there fightin' with Aunt Eller 'bout that ole egg-beater.

LAUREY [*teasing her*]: Now listen here, have you tuck up with a pedler that ud sell a pore old womern a egg-beater that wasn't no good? Ado Annie Carnes, I'm plum ashamed of you! You ort to be strapped.

ADO ANNIE: Ain't tuck up with him. Rode a piece in his ole buggy for I was comin' over here, anyway, to ast about — to ast you sump'n.

LAUREY: Whut was you gonna ast me, then?

ADO ANNIE: 'F you was goin' to that there party over to Peck's.

LAUREY: Course I am.

ADO ANNIE: Well.

LAUREY: Don't I go to all the parties?

ADO ANNIE: I guess. You got fellers, lots of fellers.

LAUREY: Three hundred and fifty.

ADO ANNIE: Oh, you ain't!

LAUREY: Oh, I have.

ADO ANNIE: I kinda wondered 'f you wouldn't take *me*.

LAUREY: *Me*, take *you?*

[*She becomes strange and thoughtful.*]

ADO ANNIE: Well, someone's takin' you, ain't they? You could take me along.

LAUREY: Why, my goodness! [*She beams ecstatically.*] Why, I'd jist love to have you, Ado Annie! You git yerself over here to supper all diked up and fancy, and I'll see that you got a way to go, all right. I'll put myself out! — [*She has another brilliant idea, which amuses her very much.*] Oh, and I'm gonna buy you sump'n so purty the fellers'll all fall over a wagon tongue a-lookin' at you! Whur *is* that man! [*She rushes to the door, in a fever of delight.*] Aunt Eller, Aunt Eller! Quit a-botherin' that man from his business! I want to buy some of his dewdads. [*To* ADO ANNIE, *with mock gravity.*] You don't want to git to like a pedler man *too* good, Ado Annie. You hear me? They got wives in ever' state in the Union.

ADO ANNIE: Oh, foot!

LAUREY: They have! And other places besides. Why, Alaska's jist full of women a-livin' in ice-houses, and freezin' to death 'cause of pedlers runnin' off and leavin' 'em 'thout no kindlin' er nuthin' —

ADO ANNIE: Aw!

LAUREY: A man *told* me! Shore as shootin'! He knowed a Eskimo womern that a pedler up there went off and left, and she had to sell her hair — a hundred hairs at a time — jist cut it right off — to keep from starvin' to death. Finally, she looked like a ole shave head, bald-headed as a turkey buzzard, and she tuck cold and died.

ADO ANNIE: *Who* did?

LAUREY: The *womern!*

ADO ANNIE: My goodness!

[AUNT ELLER *and the* PEDLER *come in. He is a little wiry, swarthy Syrian, neatly dressed, and with a red bandanna around his neck. He is very acquisitive, very cunning. He sets down his bulging suitcases, his little beady eyes sparkling professionally. He rushes over and, to* LAUREY'S *alarm, kisses her hand.*]

PEDLER: My, oh, my! But you are grown lady, Miss Laurey!

[*He gives a grunt of surprised pleasure. His speech is some blurred European tongue with Middle Western variations, from dealing almost entirely with farmers.*]

LAUREY [*backing away*]: Heavens and earth!

PEDLER: Growed up, and sich a be-*youty,* too! My, oh, my! I don't see you in a whole year. Last time you was little, like that, all sunburnt and bony, and now you've turned into a be-*you*tiful young lady. Yum, yum!

[*He kisses her hand again.*]

LAUREY: Quit it, a-bitin' me! 'F you ain't had no breakfast go and eat yerself a green apple. Lands a goodness! You'd think I was angel food cake er sump'n.

[*But she is a little pleased, in spite of herself.*]

PEDLER: Angel cake, that's jist whut you air! Angel cake, and jist hot outa the oven!

LAUREY: My, listen at him! Shet up yer mouth, and show me sump'n. Is that the way he talks to you, Ado Annie?

ADO ANNIE: Aw, he don't talk to me!

LAUREY: Mercy, whut does he *do* to you!

PEDLER: Now Aunt Eller, jist listen at the way she does me —

AUNT ELLER [*snapping at him*]: I ain't yer *Aunt Eller!* Don't you *call* me Aunt Eller, you little wart! I'm mad at you.

PEDLER: Don't you go and be mad with me. Tell you what. I'll give you sump'n — give you another egg-beater.

AUNT ELLER: Don't you go and say *egg-beater* to me *again!*

PEDLER: Well, I'll give you sump'n — sump'n purty.

AUNT ELLER: Whut'll it be, and it'd better be good?

PEDLER: You wait. Sump'n purty for to wear.

AUNT ELLER [*snorting*]: Foot! I got things for to wear. Wouldn't have it. Whur is it?

PEDLER: You wait. I'll show you.

AUNT ELLER: Biggest liar I ever knowed! You'll be tellin' me next you got it hid some'eres, tied onto the horse's belly band —

PEDLER: That's whur it is, exactly! You guessed it!

AUNT ELLER: Lands, you big — I won't listen at you, won't stay in the same room whur you're at. [*She marches out of the room and slams the door. Then she opens it and comes back in.*] Thought I was gone, didn't you? Well, I ain't. I'm gonna stay right here, fer spite. Not gonna leave you and two girls in no bedroom, all by yerselves.

[*She sits down, in the corner.*]

LAUREY [*in a kind of abstracted ecstasy*]: Want some hairpins, a fine-tooth comb, a pink un. Want a buckle made out of shiny silver to fasten onto my shoes! Want a dress with lace! Want pe'fume, face whitenin'! Wanta be purty, wanta smell like a honeysuckle vine!

AUNT ELLER [*from her corner*]: Give her a cake of soap.

LAUREY [*her mood rising*]: Want things I c'n see and put my hands on. Want things I've heared of and never had before — pearls in a plush box, diamonds, a rubber-t'ard buggy, a cut glass sugar bowl. Want things I cain't tell you about. Cain't see 'em clear. Things nobody ever heared of. [*Passionately, in a low voice.*] Not only things to look at and hold in yer hands. Things to *happen* to you! Things so nice if they ever did happen yer heart ud quit beatin', you'd fall down dead. They ain't no end to the things I want. Everything you got wouldn't be a starter fer me, Mister Pedler Man! [*Breaking off.*] So jist give me a bottle of shoe blackin', and make it quick!

PEDLER [*on his knees, at his suitcases, handing them out*]: Some nice garters? Silk in 'em, real silk, too, and bows on 'em! Look at 'em. Made in Persia. Brought to this country —

AUNT ELLER [*satirically*]: Brought to this country at great riskin' of life and limb — like them Monsters from Madagascar. [*She giggles.*] Lemme look at 'em.

LAUREY [*taking them*]: Jist whut I was a-wantin' —

PEDLER: Try 'em on.

LAUREY: Fer Ado Annie.

ADO ANNIE [*overcome*]: Aw!

PEDLER: Four bits apiece.

LAUREY: Four bits a pair.

PEDLER: Apiece.

LAUREY: Keep 'em, then.

PEDLER: Oh, take 'em.

LAUREY [*taking them*]: Here, Ado Annie. Put 'em on when no one ain't a-lookin'. [*To the* PEDLER.] You got any face whitenin'?

PEDLER [*finding it*]: The best they is, Miss Laurey. Liquid powder. Smells like the Queen of Egyp'! Put it on you, they cain't no one stay away from you. Reg'ler love drops! And only six bits a bottle — with a sponge throwed in.

LAUREY: Lemme see it. C'm here, Ado Annie. [*She puts* ADO ANNIE *in a chair.*] Now be still, I'm gonna try it on you. Now don't scrooge around like you had a ringworm or sump'n. Gonna hide them freckles 'f I have to put it on a inch thick.

[*She begins putting the liquid powder on a sponge and dabbing at* ADO ANNIE'S *face.* AUNT ELLER *leans back in her chair and begins to sing, in derision.*]

AUNT ELLER [*singing*]:

> Young men they'll go courting, they'll dress up so fine,
> To cheat the poor girls is all their design,
> They'll hug and they'll kiss and they'll cheat and they'll lie,
> They'll keep the girls up till they're ready to die.
>   Sing down, hidery down!
>
> Those girls will get angry, they'll rise up and say:
> "I am so sleepy, I wish you'd go 'way."
> Those boys will get angry to hear the girls' scorn —
> Before they'll go home, they'll sleep in some barn.
>   Sing down, hidery down!
>
> Oh, early next morning those laddies will rise,
> Brush off the straws and rub up their eyes,
> They'll saddle their horses and away they will ride
> Like all true lovers dressed up in their pride.
>   Sing down, hidery down!

Let us turn from those boys and turn from those lads
And turn to those girls which are twice as bad.
They'll flour up their faces and comb up their hair
Till they look like an owl in the bresh, I'll declare!
    Wo, larry, wo!

It's two long hours they'll stand at the glass,
And a thousand pins it will take them to dress,
They'll dress up so neat, and vanish away,
The devil himself couldn't look half so gay.
    Wo, larry, wo!

You can tell a good girl wherever she goes —
No foolish marks about her clothes,
No ribbons or rings or any such things,
But an old straw bonnet tied under her chin.
    Wo, larry, wo!

Of all the good lives 'tis bachelor's best.
Be drunk or be sober, lie down and take rest,
No wife to scold, no children to squall —
How happy's the man that keeps bachelor's hall.
    Wo, larry, wo!

[*She gets up from her chair to see what* LAUREY *is doing.*] Let's see whut you're a-doin' to her. [*She turns* ADO ANNIE *about in her chair, and bursts into a loud guffaw.* ADO ANNIE's *face is plastered with white.*] Mercy! She's plum whitewashed you! Look like a nigger angel turned all white and shinin'. Whur's yer wings at, Angel?

ADO ANNIE [*scrubbing at her face*]: I'll take ever' bit of it off! Won't have no sich of a mess on me. I'm goin' right home! You've made a plumb sight outa me!

[*She makes for the door, flustered to death.*]

LAUREY [*holding on to her*]: Don't you b'lieve her, Ado Annie! Why, you look purty as one of them rider ladies in the circus — 'cept fer not havin' on no pink tights. Well, jist look in the lookin' glass, you don't b'lieve me.

[*There is a muffled pistol shot somewhere outside. They all start violently.*]

AUNT ELLER: Now, whut in the name of —

PEDLER: Shootin' —

ADO ANNIE: I'm goin' home —

LAUREY [*her face white*]: Wait a minute! Whur was that shot, Aunt Eller? It wasn't out there — out there — ?

AUNT ELLER: Sounded like it come from the smoke-house —

LAUREY: Don't you say it! It couldn't be, couldn't!

AUNT ELLER: It *was,* I tell you.

[*There is another shot.*]

LAUREY [*shaken with fear*]: Curly!

AUNT ELLER [*looking at her in alarm*]: Why, you're 's white as a sheet, Laurey!

LAUREY [*rushing toward the door*]: Why'd you let him go out there whur Jeeter is!

AUNT ELLER: It couldn't be nuthin', honey!

LAUREY: We got to go see!

[*She hurries out the door,* AUNT ELLER *and the* PEDLER *following.* ADO ANNIE *takes out her garters, puts them on hastily, and flies out after them.*]

CURTAIN

SCENE 3

It is immediately after Scene 1 — at the same time as Scene 2.

The smoke-house is a dark, dirty building where the meat was once kept. But now, the floor is full of holes; at night the field mice scurry about the room. The rafters are worn and decayed, smoky, covered with dust and cobwebs. On a low loft, many things are stored — horse-collars, plowshares, bridles, jars of fruit, a saddle, binder twine, a keg of nails. Under it, the four-poster bed is grimy and never made. A pair of muddy shoes and a pair of gum boots are lying on their sides under the bed. On the walls, of unpainted two-by-twelves, soiled clothes are hanging, also tobacco advertisements, an enlisting poster, a pink cover off the Police Gazette, *a large framed picture of Dan Patch, several postcard pictures of teams pulling heavy loads of logs, etc. In one corner, there are hoes, rakes and an ax. In another, a bale of hay covered with a red saddle blanket. In the room also, a tool box, several rough chairs, a table, a spittoon, a wash-stand, several farm lanterns, a rope, a mirror for shaving. A small window lets in a little light, but not much. The door at back is closed.*

JEETER *sits in a low chair looking at some postcards, leaning forward now and then to spit at the spittoon. He is about thirty-five, with a curious earth-colored face and hairy hands. He wears heavy brogans, a greasy pair of trousers, two shirts open at the neck, and both dirty. He is always absorbed, dark, and sullen. Hearing a knock, he shifts about in his chair, spits again, shoves the pictures quickly back into his pocket, and says crossly:*

JEETER: Well, cain't you open it?

[CURLY *opens the door and comes in.*]

CURLY: Howdy —

JEETER [*unpleasantly*]: Is that yore plug tied to that peach tree?

CURLY: 'F you mean that horse, that's my horse. He ain't no plug.

JEETER: Plug or no plug, you mighta tied him some'eres else.

CURLY: They ain't nary a peach on that tree.

JEETER: And they *won't* be, if everbody's gonna tie his saddle horse to it.

CURLY: I'll go and move him.

JEETER: 'S too late, pardner. I done moved him.

CURLY: Whur'd you put him at?

JEETER: Turned him a-loose.

CURLY [*unruffled*]: That's all right.

JEETER: He's prob'ly tuck off up the road by this time, and serve you right.

CURLY: Left the reins a-draggin', didn't you?

JEETER: Yes, I did.

CURLY: Well, that's a cow pony, that is. He'll stand all day if the reins is down.

JEETER [*disappointed*]: You orten't to go around a-tyin' him to peach trees.

CURLY: You know, I don't know a peach tree from a corn stalk.

JEETER: Better learn, then. Whut'd you want around here, anyhow?

CURLY: I done got th'ough my business — up here at the house. I jist thought I'd come in and see you.

JEETER: I ain't got time to see no one. I'm a-takin' a bath.

CURLY [*facetiously*]: Thought you was balin' hay.

JEETER: How's that?

CURLY: I say, that's a good-lookin' rope you got there. [*He points.*] Buy it at Claremore?

JEETER: Cain't see that that's none of *yore* business.

CURLY: I know you didn't steal it.

JEETER [*shortly*]: That rope was *give* to me. It's a used un.

CURLY: Ort to spin, then. [*He goes over, takes it down and begins spinning it.*] You know Will Parker?

JEETER: Never heared of him.

CURLY: Ole man Parker's boy up here by Claremore? He can shore spin a rope. Chews gum when he spins it. Gum ain't healthy, I always say. [*Holding on to one end of the rope, he tosses the other over a rafter, and catches it. He pulls down on both ends, tentatively.*] 'S a good strong rafter you got there. You could hang yerself on that, Jeeter.

JEETER: I could — what?

CURLY [*cheerfully*]: Hang yerself. It ud be easy as fallin' off a log! Fact is, you could stand on a log — er a cheer if you'd ruther — right about here, see, and put this here around yer neck. Tie that good up there first, of course. Then, all you'd have to do would be to fall off the log — er the cheer, whichever you'd ruther fall off of. In five minutes, er less, with good luck, you'd be dead as a door nail.

JEETER [*suspiciously*]: Whut'd you mean by that?

CURLY: The folks ud all gether around and sing. *Sad* songs, of course. And some of 'em ud say whut a good man you was, and others ud say what a pig-stealer and a hound dog you was, and you'd orter been in the penitentiary long ago, fer orneriness.

JEETER: You better be keerful, now!

CURLY: *I* ain't sayin' it. I'm sayin' *they'd* say it. You know the way people talks — like a swarm of mud wasps. [*Looking about the room.*] So this is whur *you* live? Always like to see whur a man's a-livin' at. You got a fine place here, Mr. Jeeter. Matches you.

[*He grins mischievously.* JEETER *gets up, goes over close to him, dangerously.*]

JEETER: I don't know who you air er nuthin' — but I think you'd better tell me whut you come bustin' in here fer, makin' free 'th my things and talkin' the way you talk.

CURLY: Why, my name's Curly. Thought you knowed. Curly McClain. Born on a farm in Kansas. Cowpuncher by trade and by profession. I break broncs, mean uns. I bull-dog steers. I ain't never been licked, and I ain't never been shot. Shot *at,* but not *shot.* I got a good disposition, too, and when anything seems like to me it's funny, why I let loose and laugh till my belt breaks in two and my socks falls down. Whut on earth air *you* doin' 'th a pitcher of Dan Patch?

[*He points to the picture.*]

JEETER [*nonplused*]: Got a right to have a pitcher of Dan Patch, ain't I?

CURLY: Yeah, and you shore have. And that there pink pitcher there, now that's a naked womern, ain't it?

JEETER: Yer eyes don't lie to you.

CURLY: Plumb stark naked as a jaybird! No. No, she ain't, not *quite.* Got a couple of thingumabobs tied on to her.

JEETER: That's a cover off the *Police Gazette.*

CURLY: Wouldn't do fer me to have sich a pitcher around.

JEETER: Whut's wrong with it?

CURLY: I never seen sich a pitcher! That ud give me idys, that would!

JEETER [*at home now and at ease with his guest*]: Shucks, that ain't a thing to whut I got here!

[*He draws out his postcards.*]

CURLY [*covering his eyes*]: I'll go blind! Whew! Lose my eyesight in a minute! I wonder now if we couldn't have a little game of pitch?

JEETER: Look at this here un. That's a dinger, that is!

CURLY [*looking at it gravely*]: Yeah, that shore *is* a dinger.

JEETER: The girls these is tuck of can shore make it interestin' for a man! God, cain't they! Over at Tulsa, I had me another whole pack of these — but I lost 'em —

CURLY: That's too bad. That was sump'n to lose.

JEETER: Yeah, stole off me over to a dance at Bushyhead. Shore, I'll play a game of pitch with you, all right. Here, set down.

[*They sit at the table.* JEETER *fishes in the drawer and pulls out two pistols and a pack of dirty Bicycle playing cards, and lays them on the table.*]

CURLY: You — you got pistols, too?

JEETER: Good uns. Colt 45.

CURLY: Whut do you do 'th pistols?

JEETER: Shoot things.

CURLY: Oh. You deal.

JEETER: No, you deal.

CURLY: Shore, I'll deal. [*He shuffles the cards and begins to deal.*] Is this draw?

JEETER: Suit yerself.

CURLY: Draw, then. With the Jick, and not the left Jack. It's yore first bid.
JEETER: Two.
CURLY: Three.
JEETER: It's your'n.
CURLY: Spades. [*He takes up the deck again.*] How many?
JEETER: One.

[CURLY *deals one to* JEETER, *two to himself, picks up his hand. They begin to play.*]

CURLY [*with lyric warmth — for he is stating something about his own life — and his feeling about life*]: Outside, the sun's jist crazy 'th the heat, beatin' on the prairie and the corn stalks. Passed a field in the bottom this mornin' whur the backwater had been. Ground all cracked and blistered and bakin' in the sun. Likin' it, though! Likin' it good. The crawfish put up their pinchers and hustled about, 'cause their holes is all goin' dry. Seen fields of wheat and oats — fine as a fiddle! The crows went to honkin' at me when I rode th'ough the Dog Crick timber, and I could see hundreds of squirrels friskin' in the blackjacks. I could smell them green walnuts, too, whenever ole Dan ud tromp on 'em. Shore the purtiest mornin' in a long time! Felt like hollerin' and shoutin'. I raired away back in my saddle and ole Dan stepped out a-prancin' and we come th'ough Claremore like a streak of forked lightnin'! An' it's shore a funny end to a fine purty mornin' to find yerself shet up in a dark hole bent over a table a-fingerin' a pack of cards 's greasy 's a ole tin spoon, ain't it? Yeah, that's the way it is, though, in this here life. Got to git used to it. [*He begins to sing.*]

> Oh, my name it is Sam Hall, it is Sam Hall,
> My name it is Sam Hall, it is Sam Hall,
> My name it is Sam Hall, and I hate you one and all,
> I hate you one and all, damn yer eyes!
>
> To the gallows I must go, I must go,
> To the gallows I must go, I must go,
> To the gallows I must go, for I've killed a man you know,
> Because he loved her so, damn his eyes!
>
> I must hang till I am dead, I am dead,
> I must hang till I am dead, I am dead,
> I must hang till I am dead, for I killed a man, they said,
> And I left him there for dead, damn his eyes!
>
> I saw Mollie in the crowd, in the crowd,
> I saw Mollie in the crowd, in the crowd,
> I saw Mollie in the crowd, and I hollered right out loud:
> " Hey, Mollie, ain't you proud, damn yer eyes! "

[*As he sings the game goes slower and slower,* CURLY *interested in the song and in* JEETER, JEETER *frowning and strangely excited. Suddenly a dog begins barking angrily.* JEETER *goes to the door quickly and looks out.*]

JEETER: Who would that be, I wonder? In a buggy. Got a girl with him. Oh! [*He is relieved.*] It's that Syrian pedler. Yeah, that's who. [*He closes the door and comes down again. After a moment.*] Did that — did that Sam Hall kill the feller? [CURLY *nods.*] He'd orta killed the girl, too.

CURLY: They wouldn't a-been much fun in that.

JEETER: Fun! Whut was fun about it, anyway! [*Strangely, darkly, his tongue unloosed.*] I knowed a feller onct killed a girl. He'd been keepin' comp'ny with her and aimed to marry her. One day he found her up in the barn loft with another man. He didn't do nuthin' at first. But this girl lived on a farm with her folks. One night her paw and maw couldn't sleep fer the dog a-barkin' so. Next mornin' the old man went down to feed the stock like he always did, and when he come to the horse troft, he seen sump'n white a-layin' there. It was his daughter, in her nightgown, layin' there in the water all covered with blood, dead. They never did find out who done it. But I met up with a man onct on the road-gang a-makin' that road from here to Collinsville, and he told me he done it. Only — you know what he done? Made out this murder tuck place ten year ago back in Missouri. It didn't, though! It was up here by Sweetwater not two year ago — and I'd saw all about it in the paper! But I didn't let on. Whut a liar he was!

CURLY: And a kind of a — a kind of a murderer, too, wasn't he?

JEETER [*absorbed*]: I couldn't make out why he cut her throat and then throwed her in the horse troft, too. Less'n — he thought — why, that's why! He'd got blood all over him, and he couldn't stand havin' blood on him, so that's why he done it! I knowed another case, too, of a man got a girl in trouble —

CURLY: I was jist goin' to ast you 'f you didn't know some other stories.

JEETER: This man was a married farmer, and he knowed this girl. It had been goin' on a long time till the man it looked like he couldn't live 'thout her. He was kinda crazy and wild if she'd even speak to anyone. One night, it was moonlight, and they'd met out back of an old mowin' machine left in the meader a-rustin' — She told him about the way she was, gonna have a baby. He went jist hog-wild, and found a piece of old rope in the tool box of the mowin' machine, tied her hands and feet with it, nen throwed her up on top of a stack of hay, and set f'ar to it. Burned her to death! Do you know why? He didn't keer about her goin' to have the baby, that wasn't it. He jist didn't know how he was goin' to live 'thout *havin'* her all the time while she was carryin' it! So he killed her. Yeow, it's funny the things people do, like that.

[CURLY *gets up, goes over, throws the door open. A shaft of brilliant sunlight pours in, alive with millions of dust motes.*]

CURLY: Git a little air in here. [*He goes back and sits down.*] Yore mind seems to run on two things, don't it? Before you come here to work fer the Williams, whur did you work?

JEETER [*hostile again*]: I don't know as that concerns no one but me.

CURLY: That's right, pardner. That's yore look-out.

JEETER: I'll tell you, though. Up by Quapaw. And before that over by Tulsa. Bastards to work fer, both of 'em!

CURLY: Whut'd they do?

JEETER: Always makin' out they was *better*. Yeah, *lots* better! Farmers they was, like me, wasn't they? Only not half as good.

CURLY: And whut'd you do — git even?

JEETER [*looks up at him, suspiciously*]: Who said anything about gittin' even?

CURLY: No one, that I recollect. It jist come in my head.

JEETER: Oh, it did? [*He gets up, goes over and shuts the door, turns in the gloom, comes and sits down again, and looks at* CURLY.] Whut was that business you had up here at the house?

CURLY [*after a moment*]: I don't know as that concerns you, does it?

JEETER: It does, though! If it's anything to do with this farm.

CURLY: I forgot you owned it.

JEETER: Never mind that! It couldn't be to buy hay, fer you got plenty of hay.

CURLY: How'd you know that?

JEETER: You work for Skidmore, don't you, tother side of Justus?

CURLY: Thought you didn't know me.

JEETER: I know you, all right. If he's sent you over to buy up the oat crop, why it's done spoke fer.

CURLY: Glad to find that out.

JEETER: We ain't got no cattle to sell, ner no cow ponies, you know that. And the farm ain't fer sale, and won't be.

CURLY: You shore relieved my mind considerable.

JEETER: They's only one thing left you could come snoopin' around here fer. And it ud better not be that!

CURLY [*easily*]: That's exactly whut it is!

JEETER [*white with anger*]: Better not be!

CURLY: It *is*, I tell you.

JEETER: I wouldn't come on the place if I was you! I wouldn't come here —

CURLY: Whut'll happen if I decide that's jist the right thing fer me to do?

JEETER: I'd git on my horse and go quick! Don't you come around that girl, you hear me?

CURLY [*scornfully*]: You shore got it bad. So you're takin' her to that party tonight? Jesus! She's got a taste. I don't know as it's worth fightin' about if she'd ruther go with you. I step out — cheerful as anything. You're welcome. [*Thoughtfully.*] Only — somebody ort to tell her whut you air. And fer that matter somebody ort to tell you onct about yerself.

JEETER: I've had jist about enough!

CURLY: If you'd like to do anything to me, now's the best chanct you'll ever have. [*Softly.*] You got two pistols, good uns, all loaded and ready to bark. They's a ax a-standin' in the corner. A bright bright sickle, right off the grindstone hangs over there on a nail and shines. Yer hoes is sharp, yer razor's got two edges onto it, and nary a one of 'em is rusty. And it ain't very light in here, is it? Not half light enough. A feller wouldn't feel very safe in here 'th you, 'f he didn't know you. [*Acidly.*] But I *know* you, Jeeter. I've knowed you fer a long time.

JEETER [*half rising*]: You don't know a thing about me—

CURLY: The country's full of people like you! I been around. [*His voice rises dramatically.*] In this country, they's two things you c'n do if you're a man. Live out of doors is one. Live in a hole is the other. I've set by my horse in the bresh some'eres and heared a rattlesnake many a time. Rattle, rattle, rattle!—he'd go, skeered to death. Skeered—and *dangerous!* Somebody comin' close to his hole! Somebody gonna step on him! Git his old fangs ready, full of pizen! Curl up and wait! Fer as long's you live in a hole, you're skeered, you got to have pertection. You c'n have muscles, oh, like arn— and still be as weak as a empty bladder—less'n you got things to barb yer hide with. [*Suddenly, harshly, directly to* JEETER.] How'd you git to be the way you air, anyway—settin' here in this filthy hole—and thinkin' the way you're thinkin'? Why don't you do sump'n healthy onct in a while, 'stid of staying shet up here a-crawlin' and festerin'!

JEETER: Shet up, you!

CURLY: You'll die of yer own pizen, I tell you!

JEETER: Anh!

[*He seizes a gun in a kind of reflex, a kind of desperate frenzy, and pulls the trigger. The wall across the room is splintered by the shot.*]

CURLY: Jesus! What was you shootin' at, Jeeter?

JEETER [*his hands on the two pistols, hoarsely*]: Never mind, now!

CURLY [*in a high excitement, but apparently cool and calm*]: You orta feel better now. Hard on the wall, though. I wish 't you'd let me show you sump'n. Jist reach me one of them pistols acrost here a minute— [JEETER *does not move, but sits staring into* CURLY's *eyes.*] They's a knot-hole over there about as big as a dime. See it a-winkin'? I jist want to see if I c'n hit it. [*He leans over unhurriedly, with catlike tension, picks up one of the pistols, turns in his chair, and fires at the wall high up. He turns in triumph.*] Didn't make a splinter! Bullet right through the knot-hole, 'thout tetchin', slick as a whistle, didn't I? I knowed I could do it. You saw it, too, didn't you? Somebody's comin', I 'spect. It's my play, ain't it?

[*He throws down a card.* JEETER *looks at the floor.* LAUREY, AUNT ELLER, *and the* PEDLER, *followed a moment later by* ADO ANNIE, *come running in at the door without knocking.*]

AUNT ELLER [*gasping for breath*]: Whut's this? Who's been a-shootin'? Skeer the liver and lights out of a feller! Was that you, Curly? Don't set there, you lummy, answer when you're spoke to!

CURLY: Well, I shot onct.

AUNT ELLER: What was you shootin' at?

CURLY: See that knot-hole over there?

AUNT ELLER: I see lots of knot-holes.

CURLY: Well, it was one of them.

AUNT ELLER: Don't tell me you was shootin' at a knot-hole!

CURLY: I was, though.

AUNT ELLER [*exasperated*]: Well, ain't you a pair of purty nuthin's, settin' here a-pickin' away at knot-holes 'th a pair of ole pistols and skeerin' everybody to death! You've give that ole turkey gobbler conniption fits. Ort to give you a good Dutch rub and arn some of the craziness out of you! Come 'ere, you all, they ain't nobody hurt. Jist a pair of fools a-swappin' noises.

ADO ANNIE [*dumbly*]: Did someone shoot, Aunt Eller?

AUNT ELLER: Did someone *shoot!*

ADO ANNIE: Whut'd they shoot *at,* Aunt Eller?

AUNT ELLER: Yer grandmaw, silly!

[*She goes out.*]

ADO ANNIE: My lands!

[*She follows her out.* LAUREY *and the* PEDLER *stand in the door.*]

LAUREY [*after a moment*]: Curly.

CURLY: Yeah.

LAUREY: Did you *hit* that knot-hole?

CURLY: How's that?

LAUREY: I say, did you *hit* that knot-hole?

CURLY [*puzzled*]: Yeah, I — I hit it.

LAUREY [*cryptically*]: Well. That was good, wasn't it?

[*She goes out, smiling. The* PEDLER *bounds into life and comes forward with great animation.*]

PEDLER: Well, well. Mr. Jeeter! Don't trouble yerself. Fine day, and a good crop comin'. You too, Mr. Curly. [*Lowering his voice.*] Now then, we're all by ourselves, I got a few little purties, private knick-knacks for to show you. Special for the men folks. [*He winks mysteriously, and draws out of his inside coat pocket a thin flat box and opens it out on the table.*] Yes sir, special. The things you cain't get and 've got to have. All them little things a man needs in his business, eh? [*He points.*] Jist look at them things. Agin the law, ever one of 'em! There's brass knucks, lay a man out jist like he was dead in one good hard hit. Fit any knuckle and break any head. And — in the little package, well, I won't tell you! — Jist open her up, and you'll see — The little dinguses that you got to have. Fancy! Lots of colors and jiggers onto 'em. French! Yes, sir! French — right out of Paris. And jackknives and frog-stickers. Steel and never rusty. Kill a hog or a bastard eh, it's all the same to them little ones! And postcards! Kansas City Best. Made right. Take 'em away, they're hard on the eyes! And here's dice, playing cards. Everything you need, everything a man could want. Look 'em over and if they's any little thing you need, jist point, jist make the signs, and I'm right here — Now then, how's that?

JEETER [*rousing himself*]: How much is that frog-sticker?

PEDLER [*taking out a long wicked-looking knife and opening it*]: That frog-
sticker. That's reasonable, reasonable. I won't charge you much for a knife
like that. 'F you got it in Claremore, you know whut you pay? Twice my
price, jist twice. 'F you could get it. That's a good frog-sticker, that is, and
I'm sellin' it cheap to you, Mr. Jeeter — fer a man hadn't ort to be *without*
a good frog-sticker, it ain't safe, he might need it. He never knows why and
he never knows when. Don't see nuthin' to interest you, Mr. Curly?

CURLY [*slowly*]: I was jist thinkin' myself — that mebbe — jist fer the looks of
the thing — and to kinda have it around — I might consider — buyin' —
if they're good and not too high — and can be depended on — a nice hard
pair of them brass knucks you got there —

[*He reaches over and picks them up.*]

CURTAIN

SCENE 4

Lead her up and down the little brass wagon,
Lead her up and down the little brass wagon,
Lead her up and down the little brass wagon,
For she's the one, my darling!

One wheel off and the axle draggin',
One wheel off and the axle draggin',
One wheel off and the axle draggin',
For she's the one, my darling!

Spokes all broke and the tongue a-waggin',
Spokes all broke and the tongue a-waggin',
Spokes all broke and the tongue a-waggin',
For she's the one, my darling!

Blistered brakes and sides all saggin',
Blistered brakes and sides all saggin',
Blistered brakes and sides all saggin',
For she's the one, my darling!

The party is in full swing in the back yard of OLD MAN PECK's *place across
Dog Creek. There are a few benches on the porch and a large coal stove. A primitive, rough-hewn built-in cabinet runs along one end of the porch and on it are
piled all manner of miscellaneous things — ropes, cans of nails, a vinegar bottle,
sacks of salt and sugar, home-dried apricots and peaches, a guitar, a fiddle, jars
of home-made preserves. On the walls are hanging strings of popcorn on the cob,
red peppers, onions hanging by their tops, the dried pelt of a possum, etc. Kero-
sene lanterns hung to the wall light up the yard. Light streams out from the*

house. Around the corner of the house can be seen the stone well with its wide arch of iron and its pulley, a tremendous walnut tree and the night sky.

The farm boys and the cowboys have forgotten their corn plowing, their day in the hayfield, their day on the range. They have put up the mules, doused themselves at the pump, bolted a supper of fried salt pork, potatoes and gravy and hot biscuits, and now in their store clothes and their chaps and their overalls they grin and sweat and stomp, their voices loud and harsh in the singing. Those who are not playing at the moment lounge in the doorway, chewing tobacco and smoking; some have gone out behind the barn or to their buggies and saddle pockets for a shot of liquor.

Most of the girls are dressed in white and wear bright bows. Some have tiny watches pinned to their dresses, and carry handkerchiefs. OLD MAN PECK *is clapping his hands. He is an old-timer, grizzled and genial, about seventy. He has gone to play-parties and dances now for fifty years, and knows every trick, every extra stomp, every variation in the songs, every sly elaboration of the do si do.*

The voices crack on the high notes, the feet pound, hands clap, the jars on the high cabinet rattle, dust clouds the air. "The Little Brass Wagon" ends in a burst of high, excited, exhausted laughter. Immediately, on a peak of gaiety, hardly stopping to mop their brows, the men begin getting partners for a square dance, calling loudly, grabbing the girls carelessly around the waist and getting slapped for their temerity.

OLD MAN PECK [*leaping out into the middle of the floor and holding up his hands*]: Hey! Boys and gals! Git in the kitchen fer the candy pullin'.

[*The crowd breaks, and dashes in the house noisily.* OLD MAN PECK *is about to follow.*]

AUNT ELLER [*calling from the darkness off left*]: Land's sake, I'm all tangled up in it. Curly, help me cain't you?

CURLY [*off*]: Well, be still, quit a-buckin' up.

AUNT ELLER: Mr. Peck! Mr. Peck, you ole fool, come an' help a lady, cain't you!

OLD MAN PECK: Is that you, Aunt Eller? Whut's the matter?

AUNT ELLER [*entering with* CURLY]: Matter! Say, do you have to have barbed w'ar layin' around all over the yard? Gettin' me all tangled up in it! 'F it hadn't a-been fer *me* I'd a-lost a leg. Whur's Mary?

OLD MAN PECK: Oh, I got the ole womern out in the smoke-house.

AUNT ELLER: Doin' all the work, I bet.

OLD MAN PECK: Yep, that's right. You're kinda late, ain't you?

AUNT ELLER: Got here quick 's I could make it. Say, is this whur the party's at — out here in the yard?

OLD MAN PECK: It's too hot in the house.

AUNT ELLER: Well, it's kinda purty out here, I must say. Here — hang this up.

OLD MAN PECK [*taking the lamp she holds out*]: Whur'd you get that?

AUNT ELLER [*grinning*]: Pulled it off the dashboard. Guess I'll go in and take off my fascinator. [*Taking* CURLY *by the arm.*] How'd you like my feller I went and ketched?

CURLY [*smiling, and taking her by the arm*]: How'd you like my girl I went and ketched?

OLD MAN PECK: Both of you is all right, I reckon. Whur's Laurey at?

CURLY [*pausing as he realizes what this means*]: Laurey, ain't she here yit?

OLD MAN PECK: *Course* not. Thought you was gonna bring her.

CURLY [*concerned*]: They ort to be here, Aunt Eller. Whutta you reckon's happened? They started 'fore we did — half a hour before.

AUNT ELLER [*quieting him*]: Aw, they're jist poky. They're drivin' Old Eighty, and that fool mare is alwys wantin' to graze 'long side the road. Now don't look so worried, Curly, they'll git here. Come on in, and le's see *who's* come with *who*.

[*They go in. A burst of greeting floats out.*]

SHORTY [*a cowboy, staggers in, drunk*]: Say, Mr. Peck, is that yore big old white cow standin' out there by the grainary?

OLD MAN PECK: Hi, Shorty. Yeah, she's mine. Give two gallon and a half a day.

SHORTY: Whew, she like to skeered me to death. Thought she was a ghost — till she said *Moo*.

OLD MAN PECK: You must be drinkin' a little, Shorty.

SHORTY [*speaking as he makes for the door*]: Me? I ain't drinkin'. I'm drunk.

[*He goes into the house.*]

OLD MAN PECK [*spying* JEETER, ADO ANNIE, *and* LAUREY. JEETER *is carrying a lighted lantern which he hangs up*]: Oh, *here* you air. We been wonderin' whur you was.

ADO ANNIE *and* LAUREY: Hi, Mr. Peck.

OLD MAN PECK: Most everbody's here that's comin', I 'spect. I got to go out to the smoke-house, and see about the ice cream freezin'. Go on in, and git yer pardners for the next set.

[*He disappears around the corner of the house.* LAUREY *starts in the house.*]

JEETER [*stopping her*]: I wanta see you.

LAUREY [*a little frightened*]: Well, here I am, so look yer eyes full.

JEETER: Ado Annie, go inside.

LAUREY [*grabbing her*]: Ado Annie, you stay here a minute.

ADO ANNIE [*pulling loose*]: Shoot! I wanta see 'f I cain't git me a pardner, 'fore they're all gone.

[*She dashes in.*]

JEETER: Whut'd you ast that Ado Annie to ride with us fer?

LAUREY: She didn't have no way to go.

JEETER: That ain't yore lookout. Why don't you wanta be with me by yerself?

LAUREY: Why, I don't know whut you're talkin' about! I'm with you by myself now, ain't I?

JEETER: You wouldn't a-been, you coulda got out of it.

LAUREY [*impatiently*]: Well, now 'at I *am*, whut'd you want?

JEETER: Nuthin' — but —

LAUREY: Well, fer land's-livin'! [*She makes for the door.*] Of all the crazies!

JEETER [*getting in front of the door*]: Mornin's you stay hid in yer room all the time. Nights you set in the front room and won't git outa Aunt Eller's sight — [*In a strange hoarse excitement.*] Ain't saw you by yerself in a long time! Why ain't I? First time was last year's thrashin'. You was watchin' the chaff fly and them knives a-cloppin' at the bundles. I come around the corner of the stack and you stood there a-wavin' yer sunbonnet to keep some of the dust offen you, and you said to me to git you a drink of water. I *got* you a drink of water. I brung the jug around. I give it to you. I *did* give it to you, didn't I?

LAUREY [*frightened*]: I don't know whut you mean.

JEETER [*as before*]: Last time it was winter 'th snow six inches deep in drifts when I was sick. You brung me that hot soup out to the smoke-house and give it to me, and me in bed. I hadn't shaved in two weeks. You ast me 'f I had any fever and you put yer hand on my head to see. Why'd you do that? Whut'd you tetch me for! [*He suddenly seizes her in his arms, his voice thick with excitement.*] You won't git away from me — !

LAUREY [*trying to free herself*]: You better le' me alone!

JEETER: You've kep' outa my way, and kep' outa my way —

LAUREY: Quit it, quit it — !

JEETER: Cain't think of nuthin' else! It's killin' me. Lay awake at nights. God damn you, quit a-tryin' to git away — I got you now —

[*He holds her closer.*]

LAUREY [*in revulsion*]: Oh!

[*She turns her head aside, frightened and shaken.*]

JEETER: So goddamned purty!

[*She frees an arm and strikes him in the face, with desperate strength. He releases her, and stands uncomprehending, tranced. She backs away, watching him.*]

LAUREY [*almost hysterically*]: Now le' me go, le' me outa here 'fore I holler and tell on you!

JEETER [*after a moment, slowly*]: You hit me — [*Breaking out, violently.*] Like 'em all! I ain't good enough, am I? I'm a h'ard hand, ain't I? Got dirt on my hands, pig slop — Ain't fitten to tetch you! You're better, so goddamned much better! Yeah, we'll see who's better — we'll see who's better, Miss Laurey! Nen you'll wish 't you wasn't so free 'th yer airs, you're sich a fine lady — !

LAUREY [*suddenly so angry, all her fear vanishes*]: Air you makin' threats — to *me?* Air you standin' there tryin' to tell me 'f I don't 'low you to slobber over me like a hog, why you're gonna do sump'n about it! Why, you're a mangy dog and somebody'd orta shoot you! [*With enormous scorn.*] Yeah, I ort to 'low you yer own way, I reckon. Sich a great, big, fine strappin' man so full of dazzle I ort to git down on my knees to him! Christ all hemlock! [*Sharply, her eyes blazing.*] You think so much about bein' h'ard hand. Well, I'll jist tell you sump'n that'll rest yer brain, Mr. Jeeter! You ain't a h'ard hand fer me, no more! You c'n jist pack up yer duds and scoot! Oh, and I even got better idys 'n that! You ain't to come on the place again, you hear me? I'll send yer stuff any place you say, but don't you 's much 's set foot inside the pasture gate or I'll sic the dogs onto you! Now then, next time you go makin' threats to people, you better think a few thinks first and spit on yer hands fer good luck!

JEETER [*standing quite still, absorbed, dark, his voice low*]: Said yer say. Brought it on yerself. [*In a voice harsh with an inner frenzy.*] Cain't he'p it, I tell you! Sump'n brung it on you. On me, too. Cain't never rest. Cain't be easy. That's the way it is. Ay, I told you the way it was! You wouldn't listen —

[*He goes out, passes the corner of the house and disappears.* LAUREY *stands a moment, held by his strangeness, then she starts toward the house, changes her mind and sinks onto a bench, a frightened little girl again.* ADO ANNIE *bounds out of the house, excited. She sees* LAUREY.]

ADO ANNIE [*worried*]: Laurey, I got sump'n to tell you.

LAUREY [*standing up quickly*]: Ado Annie, is Curly in there?

ADO ANNIE: Yes he's in there, but . . . Laurey, now look, Laurey, it's turrible — I gotta tell you —

LAUREY [*starting swiftly towards the house*]: Don't bother me.

ADO ANNIE [*catching at her*]: Now, Laurey, please, my lands, it's all yore fault, so you gotta tell me whut to do.

LAUREY: Well, whut is it?

ADO ANNIE: Them ole garters is s' tight they 'bout cut my laigs plum in two.

LAUREY: Well, take 'em off.

ADO ANNIE: Take 'em off? Have my stockings rollin' down onto my shoes? Wouldn't I be a purty sight?

LAUREY: You'd have all the boys a-runnin' after you right, you done that.

ADO ANNIE: You shore?

LAUREY: Shore, I'm shore.

ADO ANNIE: Aw, I wouldn't do it fer nuthin'.

LAUREY: Well I told you whut to do, you won't mind me.

[*She makes for the door.*]

ADO ANNIE [*stopping her*]: Laurey! Them ole boys worries me. The minute I got in the house they started grabbin' at me. Whut'd they mean a-tellin' me, " Come out 'hind the barn 'th me? " That ole Payne boy said that.

LAUREY: Whyn't you ast him whut he meant?

ADO ANNIE: I was skeered he'd tell me.

LAUREY: Fiddlesticks! [*She starts again for the door, turns quickly, struck with an idea.*] Ado Annie, will you do sump'n fer me?

ADO ANNIE: 'F it ain't too hard.

LAUREY: Go in there and find Curly, and tell him to come out here. I want to see him, I got to see him!

[*A man runs out of the house calling out,* "Whee! Here's my girl! Come on here, Ado Annie, I'm goin' to swing you till you're dizzy as a loon!" *He whirls her around and around.* LAUREY, *distressed, starts for the house.*]

A MAN [*coming out boisterously*]: Here, Laurey's *my* partner. Come on, Laurey, you promised me away back last August, purt' near.

[*He swings her into position for the next dance.*]

OLD MAN PECK [*coming from the house*]: Git yore pardners like you done be-fore,

Two big rings in the middle of the floor.

[*The others all sweep out, paired off, and take their places for the square dance*]

CROWD [*falling into position*]: I hope there'll be a big fight!

Be lots of work for the shoemaker, tomorrow!

Watch yer honey, watch her close,

When you meet her, double the dose!

Eight hands up, and circle to the west!

[*They start to dance.*]

OLD MAN PECK [*stopping them before they begin*]: Whoa, whoa, back, Maud! My, you're like a gang of mule colts! Quiet down, cain't you, they ain't no a-stoppin' you! Wanta tell you sump'n!

CROWD: Let 'er rip, grampaw!

Say yer say and git it outa you 'fore you choke on it!

Open up yer mouth and holler yer head off, see 'f I keer!

OLD MAN PECK: Now then, listen to me a minute! We gonna have a little singin' to give us a rest. You all 'll be so broke down in a minute you'll be blowin' like a thrashin' machine. Quiet down now, see 'f we cain't git somebody to sing sump'n — Time we sing a little bit, got a s'prise for you. You all know whur the smoke-house is, don't you?

CROWD: 'Hind that ellum out there.

Shore, we know. Settin' on its foundations!

OLD MAN PECK: Well, I got the ole womern out there a-turnin' the ice cream freezer, and a-makin' popcorn balls. And jist as soon as we sing a little bit, everthing ort to be ready. Er 'f it *ain't* ready, take a scantlin' to the ole womern, I will, and blister her good! Now then, who'll give us a song?

CROWD: Sing one yerself, Mr. Peck.

You ain't winded, air you?

Sing one of them ole ballets —

Sing "The Dyin' Cowboy." Oh, bury me not on the lone prairee!

Sing that there un 'bout the blind child, while we cry and take on, the pore little son of a gun, didn't have no mammy!

OLD MAN PECK [*humorously*]: Aw, I'm bashful 's a blushin' bride! Anyways, all I know is sad songs, make you cry. No, cain't I git someone else — how 'bout you, Lizzie?

CROWD: The sadder the better!

Go on, you start things, git everbody limbered up — !

OLD MAN PECK: Tell you whut I'll do, then! Sing you " Custer's Last Charge " an' 'f I ketch airy grin on any of you, gonna do sump'n, I'm tellin' you. And you better keep quiet and respectable-like, 'cause this yere is a serious piece.

CROWD: Go to it, Mr. Peck!

Serious 's a church.

Got my mouth sewed up like a buttonhole.

Sh!

OLD MAN PECK [*singing in a high, thin voice*]:

> 'Twas just before brave Custer's charge,
> Two soldiers drew the rein,
> In parting words and clasping hands,
> They may never meet again.
>
> One had blue eyes and curly hair,
> Just nineteen years ago,
> With rosy cheeks and down on his chin,
> He was only a boy, you know.
>
> The other was a tall and a dark slim form
> With eyes that glittered like gold,
> With coal-black hair and brown mustache,
> Just twenty-five years old.
>
> The tall dark form was the first to speak,
> Saying, " Charley, our hour has come,
> We will ride together up on yonder's hill,
> But you must ride back alone.
>
> " We have rode together on many a raid,
> We have marched for many a mile,
> But, comrade dear, I fear the last
> Has come with a hopeless smile.
>
> " I have a face, it's all this world to me,
> And it shines like a morning's light,
> Like a morning's light it has been to me
> To cheer my lonesome life.

" Like a morning's light it has been to me
To cheer my lonesome life,
And little did I care for the flow of fate
When she promised to be my wife.

" Write to her, Charley, when I am gone,
Send back this fair-formed face,
And gently tell her how I died
And where is my resting place.

" And tell her I'll meet her on the other shore,
In the bordering land between,
Yes, heaven and earth, I'll meet her there,
And it won't be long, I mean."

Then tears filled the eyes of the blue-eyed boy
And his kind heart filled with pain —
" I'll do your bidding, my comrade dear,
Though we never meet again.

" If I get killed and you ride back,
You must do as much for me,
For I have a praying mother at home,
She is all the world to me.

" She has prayed at home like a waiting saint,
She has prayed both night and morn,
For I was the last the country called,
She kissed and sent me on."

Just then, the orders came to charge,
An instant with clasped hands,
Then on they went, then on they rode,
This brave and devoted band.

They rode till they come to the crest of the hill
Where the Indians shot like hail,
They poured death's volley on Custer's men,
And scalped them as they fell.

They turned from the crest of the bloody hills
With an awful gathering gloom,
And those that were left of the faithful band
Rode slowly to their doom.

> There was no one left to tell the blue-eyed girl
> The words that her lover said,
> And the praying mother will never know
> That her blue-eyed boy is dead.

[*The crowd applauds and exclaims.*]

CROWD: Shore a good un!

Sings plumb like a church choir, don't he?

Whur's Curly McClain?

Git him to sing.

Here you, Curly, you c'n sing — one of them cowpuncher ones.

CURLY [*appearing from the crowd*]: Well. Hand me down that guitar, will you?

[*Someone gets the guitar off the cabinet, and hands it to him. He drags forward a stool and sits down.*]

CROWD: " Railroad Man."

" Levee Dan."

" Whistlin' Rufus."

" The Girl I Left Behind Me."

" The Pore Lost Dogie."

" Shoot the Buffalo."

Sump'n lively!

" The Mohawk Trail."

CURLY [*He strums a few notes, and begins to sing, very simply.*]:

> There is a lady, sweet and kind,
> Was never face so pleased my mind,
> I did but see her passing by,
> And yet I love her till I die.

> Her gestures, motion, and her smiles,
> Her wit, her voice, my heart beguiles,
> Beguiles my heart I know not why,
> And yet I love her till I die.

> Cupid is wingèd and doth range
> Her country so my love doth change,
> But change she earth or change she sky,
> Yet will I love her till I die.

CROWD [*applauding*]: Sing another'n, Curly.

You shore fooled us. Funny song fer *you* to be a-singin'!

Now, Aunt Eller —

Aunt Eller, come on, you, it's yore time.

AUNT ELLER: Ketch me a-singin'! Got a frog in my throat — I'm t'ard, too. Got a ketch in my leg and cain't sing. Land's alive! Whyn't you git Ado Annie? — Here, Ado Annie, sing one of them songs of yourn.

[*They drag* ADO ANNIE *forward, squirming.*]

CROWD: Here, quit it a-pullin' back, you don't git out of it —

ADO ANNIE [*awkwardly, standing first on one foot, then on the other*]: Done forgot! Done forgot!

CROWD: Well, hurry up and remember —

ADO ANNIE: Don't know none, nary a one. Done forgot ever' one, I tell you!

CROWD: Well, whistle then, you got to do sump'n.

AUNT ELLER: Forgot yer foot! Sing that un about when you was young and single —

ADO ANNIE: Shoot! My th'oat's plumb sore —

AUNT ELLER: Sump'n else 'll be sore you don't start. Hurry up, now —

ADO ANNIE [*singing in a flat mournful voice*]:

> When I was young and single,
> At home by my own f'ar side,
> With my loving brother and sister,
> My mother she never would chide.
>
> Then there came a young man
> His smiles enticèd me.
> — And I was young and foolish
> And easy led astray.
>
> I don't see why I love him,
> He does not keer for me,
> But my thoughts are alwys of him
> Wherever he may be.
>
> They tell me not to believe him,
> Say " He don't keer fer you."
> How little I think that ever
> Them words would ever come true!
>
> Some say that love is pleasure.
> What pleasure do I see?
> For the one I love so dearly
> Has now gone back on me!
>
> The night is dark and dreary,
> A little incline to rain —
> O God, my heart is weary
> For my lover's gone off on a train!

OLD MAN PECK: All out fer the smoke-house now! Git some ice cream in you, you feel better! Got vanilla and strawberry both, so don't be bashful!

[*The crowd begins to stream noisily out, disappearing past the corner of the house.*]

LAUREY [*catching* CURLY *away from his partner, and dragging him back till the others are all gone*]: Curly!

CURLY [*astonished*]: Now what on earth is ailin' the belle of Claremore? By gum, if you ain't a-cryin'!

[LAUREY *runs over to him, leans against him.*]

LAUREY: Curly — I'm 'fraid, 'fraid of my life — !

CURLY [*in a flurry of surprise and delight*]: Jumpin' toadstools! [*He waves his hat, then throws it away wildly, and puts his arms around* LAUREY, *muttering under his breath.*] Great Lord — !

LAUREY: Don't you leave me —

CURLY: Great Godamighty — !

LAUREY: Don't mind me a-cryin', I cain't he'p it —

CURLY: Jesus! Cry yer eyes out — !

LAUREY: Oh, I don't know whut to do!

CURLY: Here. I'll show you. [*He lifts her face and kisses her. She puts her arms about his neck. He exclaims softly.*] Laurey, Laurey — !

[*He kisses her again and again, then takes a step away from her, disengaging her arms gently.*]

LAUREY [*in alarm*]: Curly —

CURLY: My goodness! [*He shakes his head as if coming out of a daze, gives a low whistle, and backs away.*] Whew! 'Bout all a man c'n stand in public — ! Go 'way from me, *you!*

LAUREY: Oh, you don't like me, Curly —

CURLY: *Like* you? My God! Git away from me, I tell you, plumb away from me!

[*He strides across the room and sits down on the stove.*]

LAUREY [*crying out*]: Curly! You're settin' on the stove!

CURLY [*leaping up*]: Godamighty! [*He turns round, puts his hand down gingerly on the lids.*] Aw! 'S cold 's a hunk of ice!

[*He sits down again.*]

LAUREY [*pouting*]: Wish 't ud burnt a hole in yer pants —

CURLY [*grinning at her, understandingly*]: You do, do you?

LAUREY [*turning away, to hide her smile*]: *You* heared me.

CURLY: Laurey, now looky here, you stand over there right whur you air, and I'll set over here — and you tell me whut you wanted with me.

LAUREY [*grave again*]: Well — Jeeter was here. [*She shudders.*] He skeered me — he's crazy. I never saw nobody like him —

CURLY [*harshly*]: Whut'd he do? Aunt Eller told me all about the way you felt — whyn't you tell *me* — why didn't you? Whut'd he do?

LAUREY: Tried to kiss me — Wouldn't let me out of here. Said he'd tried to see me all by myself fer months. He talked wild — and he threatened me.

CURLY: The bastard!

LAUREY: I f'ard him! Told him not to come on the place again. I got mad to see him standin' there like a black cloud, and I told him whut! I wish 't I hadn't-a! They ain't no tellin' whut he'll do now! 'F I'd jist a-kep' my head! Now whut am I gonna do!

CURLY: You f'ard him?

LAUREY: Yes, but —

CURLY: *Well,* then! That's all they is to it! He won't do nuthin'! Tomorrow, I'll git you a new h'ard hand. I'll stay on the place myself tonight, 'f you're nervous about that hound-dog. [*Putting an end to it.*] That's the end of Jeeter, and about time. Now quit yer worryin' about it, er I'll spank you. Hey, while I think of it — how — how 'bout marryin' me?

LAUREY [*flustered*]: Gracious, whut'd I wanta marry *you* fer?

CURLY [*getting down off the stove and going to her, gravely, like a child*]: Laurey, please, ma'am — marry me. I — I don't know whut I'm gonna do if you — if you don't.

LAUREY [*touched*]: Curly — why, you — why, I'll marry you — 'f you want me to —

CURLY [*He takes her in his arms, kisses her gently.*]: I didn't think you would, I didn't dream you'd ever — !

LAUREY: Sh!

[*He leads her over, and lifts her up on the stove. Then he lets down the oven door and sits on it, at her feet.*]

CURLY [*humbly*]: I ain't got no right to ast you — a good-fer-nuthin' cow-puncher like me —

LAUREY: Don't say things like that.

CURLY: If I'd ever a-thought — ! Oh, I'd orta been a farmer, and worked hard at it, and saved, and kep' buyin' more land, and plowed and planted, like somebody — 'stid of doin' the way I've done! Now the cattle business'll soon be over with. The ranches are breakin' up fast. They're puttin' in barbed w'ar, and plowin' up the sod fer wheat and corn. Purty soon they won't be no more grazin' — thousands of acres — no place fer the cowboy to lay his head.

LAUREY: Don't you worry none, Curly —

CURLY: Yer paw done the right way. He knowed. He could see ahead.

LAUREY: But Pap ain't alive now to enjoy it. But we're alive, Curly. Alive! Enjoy all we can! Case things happen.

CURLY: Nuthin' cain't happen now — nuthin' bad — if you — if you love me — and don't mind a-marryin' me.

LAUREY: Sh! I'll marry you. Somebody's comin', don't you reckon?

CURLY: I don't keer. When *will* you marry me?

LAUREY: Oh, purty soon. I'll have to ast Aunt Eller, first.

CURLY: I'll ast her myself! [*Gaily.*] Oh, I 'member the first time I ever seen you!

You was pickin' blackberries long side the road here years and years ago — you was a little tyke. [*He laughs.*] You'd been a-eatin' berries as fast as you could pick 'em, and yer mouth was black as a coal shovel! — 'F you wasn't a sight!

LAUREY [*embarrassed*]: Curly!

CURLY: Nen I seen you onct at the Fair — a-ridin' that little gray filly of Blue Starr's, and I says to someone — " Who's that little thing with a bang down on her forehead? "

LAUREY: Yeow, I 'member. You was ridin' broncs that day, and one th'owed you.

CURLY: Did *not* th'ow me!

LAUREY: Guess you jumped off, then.

CURLY: Shore I jumped off.

LAUREY: Yeow, you shore did!

CURLY [*lyrically, rapturously*]: Anh, and I seen you once — the Sunday a year ago, I'll never forget. I come over to break them broncs. You'd been out a-pickin' flowers next to that sorghum mill standin' in the cane patch. And you had a whole armful of sweet williams and wild roses and mornin' glories, and I don't know what all. My, I nearly fell off my horse a-lookin' at you! And I thought to myself — " if this yere bronc th'ows me, I won't land anywhurs near no sweet williams and wild roses. No sir! No sich luck! I'll find myself 'th my face plowin' up a patch of cuckle burrs and jimson weeds — er most likely a ole cow pile! " —

LAUREY: Curly! The way you talk!

CURLY [*as before*]: Be the happiest man a-livin', soon 's we're married! [*Frowning.*] Oh, but I'll shore be a unsettled man, though, you're so blame purty, worried somebody'll run off with you! 'F I ever have to leave home to be gone all day, gonna shore tie you up to the hitchin' post, so you'll be there 'gin I git back, you hear? [*He shakes her playfully.*] Ain't gonna take no chances! [*Mischievously.*] And looky here, whut're you gonna give me fer a weddin' present? Well, you gonna marry a good-fer-nuthin' cow hand, 'thout a red cent in his breeches, 's yer own fault, they come high! How 'bout a pair of spurs? Er a nice new saddle blanket, eh, 'th red stripes onto it, and 'nitials stitched inside of a bleedin' heart on the corner? Whut's the use of gettin' married, don't git a saddle blanket er sump'n purty out of it! —

LAUREY: Curly! Now I'll know why you married me — to git a saddle blanket!

CURLY: Yeow, out in the open, that's me! A man's got to watch out fer hisself even 'f he has to marry him a homely critter like you — 'th a face like a windmill, make you dizzy to look at it! Come 'ere and kiss me, why don't you?

LAUREY [*gravely, touching his hair shyly*]: I jist set here and listen at you, and don't keer whut you say about me. Say I'm homely 's a mud fence, you want to — why then, I *am* homely 's a mud fence. 'F you say I'm purty, why I'm purty as anything, and got a voice like Jenny Lind. I never thought of anything like this! But I always wondered and wondered, after the first time I ever seen you — [*Her eyes fill with tears, absurdly.*] And here we set, you and me, on the kitchen stove like a pair of skillets, and I don't know whut's come over us to act so silly — and I'm gonna cry in a minute — and it's all yore fault, you orten't to a-made love to me this-a-way —

[CURLY *jumps up, puts his arms around her.*]

CURLY: Laurey — Cry 'f you want to, then. [*He kisses her tenderly.*] Laurey, sweet — [*After a moment.*] Now, then. [*Crying out, suddenly.*] Why, my lands of goodness! I plumb forgot! You ain't had nuthin' to eat! No popcorn er ice cream er nuthin'! You pore thing! Wait a minute. I'll git you sump'n 'fore it's all gone! [*He runs and looks down the well, and comes back quickly very much amused.*] Hey! Look in the cupboard there and see 'f you cain't find two glasses.

[*He goes back to the well and can be seen hauling up a rope.*]

LAUREY: Whut're you up to, Curly?

[*She flies to the cupboard, finds some glasses.* CURLY *has drawn up a small tin bucket, detached it from the rope, and come back, the bucket dripping. He sets it down on the stool, takes off the cover.*]

CURLY: Cream! Good ole rich cream, right outa the well! Cold as ice! Freeze yer wish-bone, might' nigh, a-slidin' down yer throat!

[*Laurey brings the glasses. He pours them full. They are drinking when the crowd, already paired off, sweeps down into the yard hilariously.*]

CROWD [*calling out in excitement*]: Hey! Whut's this!

Two little love birds!

Jist a-dyin' to git on the nest, too, from the look of 'em!

Gonna be a weddin' —

Gonna be a shivoree —

How'd a girl ever take to a feller like you, Curly?

AUNT ELLER [*appearing*]: Land sakes, I feel turrible! I went and ketched me a feller and here he is makin' up to another girl!

A MAN: Let's start the lovin' couple off right!

[JEETER *has leaned against a post and stands brooding. He has been drinking and has a bottle in his hand.*]

JEETER [*with dark scorn*]: Yay, start 'em off right! To the bride and groom — [*He lifts the bottle, darkly, insultingly, and hurls it across the yard, where it breaks with a loud crash.* CURLY *starts toward him angrily,* LAUREY *clinging to him.* OLD MAN PECK, *seeing the situation, grabs the hands of the people nearest him, and they form a circle which quickly grows, shunting* CURLY *and* LAUREY *off from* JEETER *on one side of the yard. Someone begins to sing; the crowd joins in.* LAUREY *and* CURLY *are hoisted up on chairs, the circle around them.*]

CROWD [*singing*]:

> Gone again, skip to my Lou,
> Gone again, skip to my Lou,
> Gone again, skip to my Lou,
> Skip to my Lou, my darling!

Cain't git a redbird, bluebird'll do,
Cain't git a redbird, bluebird'll do,
Cain't git a redbird, bluebird'll do,
Skip to my Lou, my darling!

My girl wears a number ten shoe,
My girl wears a number ten shoe,
My girl wears a number ten shoe,
Skip to my Lou, my darling!

Flies in the buttermilk, two by two,
Flies in the buttermilk, two by two,
Flies in the buttermilk, two by two,
Skip to my Lou, my darling!

CURTAIN

SCENE 5

A July moon is over the hayfield, making silver tents of the mounds of un-baled hay which recede in irregular formation far into the distance, crossing a low hill. A gaunt wire rake with enormous wheels stands at one side. The sky is powdered with stars, but low clouds drift often in front of them and the moon, blotting out the stubble. A soft summer wind, creeping about the meadow, lifts the spears of grass that have escaped the sickle. A low haystack, very near, has a ladder leaning against it.

After a moment, CURLY *and* LAUREY *steal into sight, looking around cautiously. They stop, move forward a little, breathless, begin to speak in hushed voices.*

CURLY [*softly*]: D'you hear anything?

LAUREY [*softly*]: No.

CURLY: Listen. [*They listen. Then he turns to her with relief.*] Not a sound. We've give 'em the slip.

LAUREY: Sh! Whut was that?

[*There is not a sound.*]

CURLY: Don't hear nuthin'.

LAUREY [*relieved*]: Jist the wind, I guess.

CURLY: Listen. We'll leave Old Eighty standin' whur we tied her. We cain't drive up to the house, 'cause 'f anybody's watchin' out fer us, they'd see us. We'll sneak acrost the hayfield and th'ough the plum thicket — and go in the back door. Come on now. Watch whur you step.

LAUREY [*taking his hand, stopping him, hesitantly*]: Curly, — if they ketch us, whut'll happen? Will it be bad?

CURLY [*soberly*]: You know about shivorees, honey. They git purty rough.

LAUREY: I'm afeard.

CURLY: Don't be afeard, honey. Aunt Eller says fer shore nobody seen us gittin' hitched.

LAUREY: They mighta s'pected sump'n, though. [*Her voice low.*] That's the ketch about gittin' married —

CURLY [*reassuringly*]: But here we air, honey. Married — and purt' nigh home. And not a soul in sight.

LAUREY [*after a moment of registering this, relievedly*]: Yeah. We fooled 'em, didn't we?

CURLY: Shore we did.

LAUREY: Course. [*Her voice full of wonder.*] Curly — we're — we're married now.

CURLY [*softly*]: Yeah. Plumb hitched.

LAUREY: Was you skeered when the preacher said that about " Will you take this here womern — " ?

CURLY: Skeered he wouldn't *say* it.

LAUREY: I was skeered you'd back out on me.

CURLY: I *couldn't* back out on you — 'f I *wanted* to. Could you *me*?

LAUREY [*smiling tenderly*]: Not if I tried and tried.

[*They kiss, and embrace for a moment. Then still holding her hand,* CURLY *turns, looking out over the moonlit field.*]

CURLY [*lyrically, feeling the moment*]: Look at the way the hayfield lays out purty in the moonlight. Next it's the pasture, and over yander's the wheat and the corn, and the cane patch next, nen the truck garden and the timber. Ever'thing laid out fine and jim dandy! The country all around it — all Indian Territory — plumb to the Rio Grande, and north to Kansas, and 'way over east to Arkansaw, the same way, with the moon onto it. Trees ain't hardly a-movin'. Branch bubbles over them limestone rocks, you c'n hear it. Wild flower pe'fume smellin' up the air, sweet as anything! A fine night fer anyone to remember fer a weddin' night! A fine night — fer anyone.

[*Caught up in the spell of the night and their feelings, they move softly away across the stubble, and disappear. There is a moment of silence. Then there is a subdued titter, followed by shishing sounds, then more titters and smothered laughter. There pop into sight on top of and from behind the stacks dozens of men carrying noise-making instruments — tin lids, pots, washboilers, cowbells, gourd rattles, tambourines, pans, iron triangles, whistles, drums. They are an excited, huddled, whispering group, nervous at their long wait for the return of the bride and groom from town, disturbed and hysterical with conjecture on the marital scene they have come to despoil. Veterans of the " shivoree," hardly a bridal couple within twenty miles around, for years and years, has escaped their bawdy ministrations. They look off toward the retreating and oblivious couple, holding their voices down.*]

1ST MAN: Sh! They'll hear you!

3RD MAN [*satirically, mockingly*]: " Fine night to remember fer a weddin' night! "

[*Laughter.*]

5TH MAN: Fine night fer anyone! Whee! [*Hushing them.*] Quiet down now! They'll hear you 'fore they git to the house!

9TH MAN: Tee hee! Bet they'll go to bed in the dark!

[*Laughter.*]

10TH MAN [*severely*]: Be keerful! They'll hear us, you hoodlums!

1ST MAN: Sh!

7TH MAN: Cain't you keep yer mouth still a minute!

3RD MAN: Whee! High ole doin's!

5TH MAN: Ketch 'em in the act!

YOUNG FARMER: Whut're we waitin' fer?

OLD FARMER: Give 'em time to git to the house, cain't you?

CORD ELAM: Don't want to give 'em too much time!

10TH MAN: Wish 't I uz in his shoes. Godamighty!

3RD MAN: He shore got him sump'n there!

1ST MAN: Couple of sections!

2ND MAN: Grazin' and timber and plowed land!

4TH MAN: Money!

6TH MAN: Scads of it in the bank, and more comin'!

5TH MAN: And God! She's a purty un, too!

3RD MAN: Got a face fer kissin'!

7TH MAN: Hands white as snow!

5TH MAN: And that ain't all, brother!

YOUNG FARMER: No, and that ain't all! Jesus! Wish't I uz in Curly's shoes! 'F I uz Curly, ud be in my bare feet by this time!

1ST MAN [*in great excitement*]: Look! They's a light!

[*The crowd in an excited frenzy begins jumping off the stacks.*]

3RD MAN: In the bedroom!

4TH MAN: Look at the way them curtains blow!

2ND MAN: Lace curtains!

3RD MAN: Blowin' out like a shirttail a-poppin' in the breeze!

CORD ELAM: Wonder whut they're a-seein', them curtains?

1ST MAN: Bridal couple! Onct in a lifetime —

3RD MAN: By theirselves!

4TH MAN: Night come on!

YOUNG FARMER: Ay, the good ole black night — 'th nobody to spy on you, nobody to see whut you're up to!

8TH MAN: Look at them shadders a-movin'!

1ST MAN: It's them, they're there! See that *there* un!

2ND MAN: Gittin' ready!

3RD MAN: Got to hurry now. Come on! Give 'em a s'prise!

CORD ELAM: Don't fergit now, right by this here stack whur the ladder is, like we said!

3RD MAN: Don't make so goddamned much noise!

[*They go out. An* OLD MAN *stumbles into the moonlight, shaking his head, dismally.*]

OLD MAN: Listen at that ole owl a-hootin' in the timber, and that there coyote away off yander towards the Verdigree River!

[*He goes out. A* YOUNG FARMER, *flushed and drinking, staggers darkly out of the gloom.*]

YOUNG FARMER: Bridegroom a-waitin' and a-waitin'! Don't you wait now, Mr. Bridegroom! The moon's a-shinin'! Yer time has came! Yes, sirree, bob! No time to wait now. Time to git goin'. See that there bride a-glimmerin' there in her white! Waitin' fer you. Been a-standin' there with her hair down her back and her lips a-movin'! Git next to her, brother! Gonna be high ole times, gonna be Jesus into yer heart!

[*The sound of raucous noise and excitement begins.* CORD ELAM *runs from around a stack shoving the* YOUNG FARMER *out of the way.*]

CORD ELAM: Git outa the way now, Homer! [*To the approaching noisy party.*] Hey! Over this-a-way. Yere's the place!

[*The noise of the shivoree grows louder and louder. Voices rise out of the bedlam, in sharp exclamations and cries. A few men drag* CURLY *in, struggling and angry, his hair in his eyes. His shirt has been ripped off in the struggle.*]

CURLY: God damn you, leave her alone! Don't ary son of a bitch put his hands onto her, I'll kill him — !

A MAN: Aw, nobody's a-hurtin' her, Curly —

CURLY: Better hadn't. I tell you. Make 'em git away from her, plumb away from her!

A MAN [*shouting off*]: Git away from her, you all! Bring her on in!

[CURLY *relaxes, but his captors still hold him tightly. A wide circle of men, shouting, whistling, beating their various noise implements, advances across the stubble. In the middle of the group, walking alone, pale and shaken is* LAUREY, *in a nightgown, her hair down about her shoulders. The crowd goes over to the foot of the ladder and stops.*]

5TH MAN: Quiet down now, a minute! [*To* LAUREY.] Right up the ladder with you, you purty thing!

[*The noise stops.*]

6TH MAN: Go on, boost her up!

7TH MAN: Right up on the stack — !

8TH MAN: Make out it's a bed, why don't you!

[LAUREY *looks around at* CURLY, *then climbs up the short ladder, the crowd shouting at her.*]

9TH MAN: Watch it!

10TH MAN: Put yer foot in the right place.

CORD ELAM: Don't wanta fall and break yer neck — cheat pore Curly outa his rights!

10TH MAN: All right, Curly —

6TH MAN: You're next.

10TH MAN: Bring him on over here.

[*The men holding* CURLY *lead him over to the foot of the ladder, and let go of him. The crowd begins to call out in more jubilant, crazier derision.*]

1ST MAN: Go on, Mr. Bridegroom, there's yer bride! —

3RD MAN: Purty's a new bronc a-standin' and a-lookin', cain't hardly keep off her!

7TH MAN: Mane like silk and eyes a-shinin'!

CORD ELAM: Git on, there, cowpuncher — ! [*After a moment,* CURLY *starts up the ladder, the crowd continuing to shout.*] 'F you ain't a world-beater fer bashful!

3RD MAN: Better be glad we didn't ride you on no fence rail!

1ST MAN: Th'ow the ladder down when he gits up.

10TH MAN: Try to git off, you'll break yer neck, so watch out!

[CURLY *reaches the top. Someone throws the ladder down.*]

CURLY [*deeply troubled*]: Laurey, honey — [*She looks at him, in dumb misery.*] I'd give my eyesight, honey — ! Try to stand it — I done all I could. I cain't he'p it —

[*He takes her in his arms. The men break out into derisive and lascivious guffaws, and begin the deafening noises again, circling the haystack, kicking up their heels, in an orgy of delight.*]

3RD MAN: Give us a little kiss, honey lamb, do a man good, 'tain't a-askin' much!

CORD ELAM: Give us a lick and a promise! — Quick's these bad ole mens goes away, — they ain't no a-tellin', no, siree!

5TH MAN: 'Tain't right to stand there like that — Blush to look at you!

7TH MAN: Ain't no right to be in no nightgown!

10TH MAN: Go on, Mr. Moon Man, hide yer face fer shame!

YOUNG FARMER: How's it feel to be married, Laurey, sugar, all safe and proper, to sich a fine purty man with curly hair and a dimple on his chin! Whee! Got you whur I want you — !

1ST MAN: Scrunch you to death, purt' near!

CORD ELAM: Bite them shoulders —

3RD MAN: Eat 'er alive!

5TH MAN: Yay, Curly, and it's one more river to cross!

[*One of the men cries out, excitedly, snickering.*]

A MAN: Hey, Curly! Hey, Laurey! One baby! [*He tosses a grotesque straw baby high in the air and onto the stack.*] Two! [*He tosses another quickly.*] Three! [*He tosses another.*]

ANOTHER MAN [*holding up admonishing hands, grinning delightedly*]: Hold it! Not so many! That'll give Curly *idys, that* will!

[*There is raucous laughter, and beating of instruments. The glow and smoke of something burning which has already crept quietly over the hayfield now leaps up. A haystack is burning.*]

CURLY [*startled, pointing*]: Look! Fer God's sake, that haystack's on fire! [*The men rush toward it.*] Get us a ladder someone, quick! The whole hayfield 'll be on fire!

[*Suddenly a dark figure comes into sight, carrying a flaming torch. It is* JEETER.]

JEETER [*crying out*]: Yanh, you thought you had it over me so big, didn't you? And you, too, Missy! Wanted sump'n purtier to sleep with. Yanh, you won't be a-havin' it long. Burn you to cracklin's!

[*He springs forward like a maddened animal to apply the torch to the stack.* LAUREY *screams. The men start rushing back, as* CURLY *leaps down, knocking the torch out of* JEETER's *hand.*]

CURLY: Godamighty!

[*They struggle. The crowd exclaims.*]

IST MAN: It's Jeeter Fry! Thought he'd flew the country!

3RD MAN: Drunk as a lord —

4TH MAN: Godamighty, he's crazy drunk!

5TH MAN: He was sweet on her too, they tell me. Stop him, somebody!

7TH MAN: Man seen him last week 'way off in Joplin.

8TH MAN: Jeeter, you goddamned —

[*A man beats at the torch with his bare hands, till another man runs up and smothers it quickly with his coat. Someone picks up the torch, stamping out the flames, and runs out to the branch with it.* JEETER *has backed away in the struggle, and drawn out a knife. He throws himself upon* CURLY. *The crowd mutters in excitement and fear. The men struggle over the knife, their arms gripping each other desperately. Suddenly,* JEETER *trips and they go down on the stubble.* JEETER *groans and whimpers and lies very still.*]

CURLY: Now, now — Christ — [*He shakes his hand, crazily, helplessly, in horror.*] Look at — look at him! Fell on it — Stuck it th'ough his ribs!

[*He backs away, shaken, horrified. Some of the men bend over the prostrate man.*]

YOUNG FARMER: Pull that knife out!

MEN: What's the matter?

Don't you tech it!

Turn him over —

He's breathin', ain't he?

Feel his heart.

How'd it happen?

9TH MAN [*wildly*]: Anh, it's went right th'ough his heart —

4TH MAN: Whut'll we do? Ain't he all right?

10TH MAN: 'S he jist stunned?

CORD ELAM [*pushing into the crowd*]: Git away, some of you! Lemme look at him. [*He bends down, the men crowding around,* CURLY *has slumped back against the stack, like a sick man.* LAUREY *stands dazed, watching. After a moment, standing upright.*] Cain't do a thing now. Try to git him to a doctor, but I don't know —

9TH MAN [*hysterically*]: Pull the knife out, cain't you? Leave a knife stuck in a — !

[*He springs forward.*]

CORD ELAM [*grabbing him*]: You can't pull it out, you fool! Git away from there! [*The man staggers away, weakly.*] Here, you, some of you! Carry him down to the branch. Quick! I'm 'fraid it's too late!

[*The men lift* JEETER *up.*]

10TH MAN: Handle him easy!

6TH MAN: Don't shake him!

3RD MAN: Hold on to him careful, there!

5TH MAN: Godamighty! Whut a thing to happen!

[*They carry him out.*]

CORD ELAM [*to* CURLY]: I don't know, Curly. You better give yerself up, I 'spect. They ain't no a-tellin'. You better go in with me, as I go, and tell 'em how it was. Tonight. It might go hard with you, you don't. [CURLY *stands dazed, as if unhearing.*] 'D you hear me, Curly? You know the way ever'body feels about shivoreein'. You got to take it right.

CURLY [*in desperation*]: But f'ar — *f'ar!* He was tryin' to burn us up!

CORD ELAM: I know. But you got to tell the *law*. It'll be easier that way. I'll come back fer you.

[*He goes out toward the branch.*]

LAUREY [*in a fever of horror*]: Curly, Curly —

CURLY [*hardly able to speak*]: Laurey —

LAUREY: Is he — is he — ?

CURLY: Don't say anything —

LAUREY: It cain't be that-a-way!

CURLY: I didn't *go* to.

LAUREY: *Cain't* be! Like that — to happen to us!

CURLY: Sh! Be quiet!

LAUREY: Whyn't they do sump'n? Why'd they let him — lay there — ? Cain't git over the way he —

CURLY: Laurey, Laurey!

LAUREY [*in mounting hysterical feeling*]: He laid there in the stubble, so quiet, 'th his eyes open, and his eyeballs white and starin'! He laid there in the stubble — 'th his eyes open — !

[*She buries her face in her hands, shuddering.* CURLY *turns away, numb, speechless, his shoulders hunched up, like one shielding himself from the wind. The howl of a coyote drifts in on the summer air — near and desperate and forlorn.*]

CURTAIN

SCENE 6

A few nights later. ADO ANNIE *and* AUNT ELLER *are sitting in the front room, sewing. An oil lamp makes an amber pool of light about them. The sliding doors are closed, but a thin crack of light comes from underneath.* ADO ANNIE, *with a piece of plaid across her knees, is snipping at it with scissors.* AUNT ELLER *is very busy over a flour sack; she pushes her iron spectacles up off her nose and looks over at* ADO ANNIE.

AUNT ELLER [*in astonishment*]: In the name of Doodlebug — whut *air* you a-doin'?

ADO ANNIE [*looking up from her work*]: Makin' a buttonhole, cain't you see?

AUNT ELLER: A round buttonhole?

ADO ANNIE: Course.

AUNT ELLER [*amused*]: Whyn't you make a square one? Er I tell you — make one looks like a four-leaf clover, why don't you?

ADO ANNIE [*shortly*]: Guess I know how to make buttonholes.

AUNT ELLER: Yeah, you shore do. Cuttin' a round hole in that plaid. [*They sew in silence. After a moment* AUNT ELLER *glances up toward the closed door, and says*]: She ain't went to bed yit.

ADO ANNIE: 'S nine o'clock about.

AUNT ELLER [*shaking her head*]: Worried about her. She don't eat ner sleep sence Curly was tuck away.

ADO ANNIE: She'll git pore she don't eat.

AUNT ELLER: Well, *course* she'll git pore.

ADO ANNIE: That's whut I said.

AUNT ELLER [*slightly irritated*]: I *heared* you say it.

ADO ANNIE [*blandly*]: Well.

AUNT ELLER: Looky here, Ado Annie Carnes, don't you ever marry.

ADO ANNIE [*self-consciously*]: Gracious, who'd I marry?

AUNT ELLER: Don't you *ever! I* did. And *look* at me. [*Half-seriously.*] First yer man — *he'll* die — like mine did. Nen the baby — *she'll* die. The rest of yer younguns'll grow up and marry and leave you, the way mine did. Nen you'll be all by yerself. Time you're old as me, you'll be settin' around, jist the way *I* am, 'th a wooden leg and a bald head, and a-rippin' up old flour sacks to make yerself a pair of drawers out of.

[*She holds up her work for* ADO ANNIE *to see.*]

ADO ANNIE [*overcome with mirth*]: Hee! Hee!

AUNT ELLER: Trouble shore starts, you git married. Look at Laurey. Better *not* git married, I tell you.

ADO ANNIE: Well, I won't then, if you say so.

AUNT ELLER: Anh, but trouble starts nohow, so you might jist as well *git* married as to *not*.

ADO ANNIE [*bewildered*]: Well, which'll I do, then?

AUNT ELLER: *Both!* I mean — I don't *keer!* [*Her voice sinking to a grave half-whisper, as she says what is really on her mind.*] They *cain't* stick him —

ADO ANNIE: Stick who?

AUNT ELLER: Curly. They *cain't* stick him. Self-defense. Plain's the nose on yer face. Wish 't they'd git it over with, that's whut I wish —

ADO ANNIE: Did — did Curly *kill* Jeeter — 'th that old knife?

AUNT ELLER: Naw! Course not! Jeeter *fell* on his ole knife — and died. And he *ort* to 'a'.

ADO ANNIE: They ain't no fair a-holdin' Curly fer it, then?

AUNT ELLER: *Course* it ain't fair! It's jist the law. They got to have their old hearin' first. Them *town* fools! First the shivoreein' — that was bad enough. And on top of it — Jeeter. Now Laurey all broke up, and Curly settin' in the cooler at Claremore. Shore a happy weddin', I *must* say. Why, them two ain't *railly married* yit.

ADO ANNIE [*her mouth open*]: Ain't they married, Aunt Eller!

AUNT ELLER: Well, they're married, all right, but they ain't — My, 'f you don't know whut I mean, I shore ain't gonna tell you! [*She gets up, and goes over to the window.*] Looks blackened up over yander. " More rain, more rest, more niggers from the West." Hope it don't come a rain er a big wind-storm 'th all that forty of wheat in the shock. Ort to a-stacked it, I reckon. [*She turns back.*] Does yer maw need you tomorrow, Ado Annie?

ADO ANNIE: Naw, she said I could stay all week, 'f you ud feed me.

AUNT ELLER: I'll feed you, all right. Grease-eye gravy and cracklin' corn-bread! And roas'n'ears. Tomorrow we'll start in to can them peaches — clings and all. 'Spect we better be gittin' to bed. Only, I kinda hate to go to bed 'th Laurey still — [*She taps softly at* LAUREY's *door, and calls gently.*] Laurey —

LAUREY [*after a moment, inside*]: Yes.

AUNT ELLER: Ain't you gone to bed yit, honey?

[*The door slides back and* LAUREY *stands there in the lamplight, looking very pale and changed, years older, a woman now.*]

LAUREY: I cain't sleep — so — they ain't no sense in goin' to bed. [*She comes down into the room.*] Whut're you makin', Ado Annie?

ADO ANNIE: Me a dress. Ain't it purty?

LAUREY: Yes. [*Gravely.*] Aunt Eller, did they — Whut *did* they say?

AUNT ELLER: I *told* you, honey. Jist said the hearin' was comin' up tomorrow. Now, I don't want you to worry about it no more. They'll let him off, all right, they got to.

LAUREY: Curly ort to a-let me went into Claremont with him like I wanted to — to testify for him.

AUNT ELLER: Don't you know they wouldn't a-let you say nuthin', Laurey? You're his wife, ain't you?

LAUREY [*slowly*]: Yes. I'm his wife.

AUNT ELLER: Well.

[LAUREY *sinks back in her chair with a disheartened little moan.*]

LAUREY: Oh, I don't see why — I don't see why — when everthing was so fine, this had to happen!

AUNT ELLER [*comfortingly*]: Oh, Laurey — now nuthin' ain't happened.

LAUREY [*distressed*]: Ain't no tellin' whut they'll do to him! And he couldn't he'p it. He *couldn't.* [*Seeing it again.*] It was over in a minute, and Jeeter lay there — dead. He'd a-killed Curly. He *tried* to kill him.

AUNT ELLER [*soothingly*]: Now, now —

LAUREY: Why'd they have to th'ow Curly in jail? Anyone could see how it happened —

AUNT ELLER: Shore they could, honey. But you know the way everbody feels about shivoreein'. They got a right to it somehow. And a thing like this a-happenin' in the middle of a shivoree — why, it looks *bad,* that's all. But Curly'll go free. Why, it's only been three days. They jist got to git everthing straight.

[*She gestures to indicate freedom and happiness for them both.*]

LAUREY: You shore, Aunt Eller?

AUNT ELLER: *Course* I am!

LAUREY: I cain't stand to think of Curly bein' in jail!

AUNT ELLER: Why, it won't be no time now, till it's all over with — and forgot.

LAUREY [*strangely, a new element coming into her concern*]: No, *not* over with, *not* forgot. You didn't see. Other things. Things you cain't git outa yer mind.

[*She shudders.*]

AUNT ELLER: What is it, honey?

LAUREY: Over and over! The way them men done. The things they said. Oh — why'd it have to be that-a-way!

AUNT ELLER: Don't let yer mind run on it. Men is always like that at shivorees. Sump'n gits into 'em.

LAUREY: The one time in a body's life — !

AUNT ELLER: Sh! I know. It musta been bad.

LAUREY: Cain't ferget it, I tell you! I've tried and tried!

AUNT ELLER [*gravely, wisely*]: Don't try, honey. Don't *try.* They's things you cain't git rid of — lots of things. Not if you live to be a hundred. You got to learn. You got to look at all the good on one side and all the bad on the other, and say: " Well, all right, then! " to both of 'em.

LAUREY [*unheeding*]: — On top of everthing! —

AUNT ELLER [*with great compassion*]: Yeah, you've had yer troubles. I know, Laurey. But they's been good things, too. Think about that. You ain't had to slave away a-workin' fer others, the way some girls has to do, — things like that. You've had you a good home —

LAUREY [*her mind temporarily diverted to another trouble*]: Paw and maw —

AUNT ELLER: Yeah, right when you needed 'em most, both gone. But you lived on, didn't you? You been happy since, ain't you? Course. You been strong about it. Why, when yer paw died — and you thought the world of him — you was all by yerself here — and you stood it. When they sent fer me to Pryor, 'fore I could git here, why he was dead, and in his coffin.

LAUREY [*raising her head, and looking back into the room*]: It set right there — on two cheers. The head towards the door.

AUNT ELLER: Yeah. [*Quietly, without self-pity, stating the fact.*] When yore paw died, and laid there — it was *my brother* in his coffin, too. Oh, and they's lots more, Laurey! I couldn't tell you all. Yer Uncle Jack, the children, both of my sisters, my paw and maw. Troubles thick and fast, you got to put up with. My husband — yer Uncle Jack. When *he* died. 'D you know how? A crazy way to die. No use in it! He'd bought some hogs off Lem Slocum, and they turned out to be full of cholery — and all died. Jack walked over jist acrost the pasture to see Lem about it. Didn't show up and it got night. I tuck a lantern and went out to see. When I come to the worm fence, I found him, in a corner, all huddled down, all bloody from a gunshot. Laid there all doubled up — dead — in a patch of yeller daisies. Lem Slocum musta shot him. I didn't know *who* done it. All I knowed was — *my husband was dead*. Oh, lots of things happens to a womern. Sickness, bein' pore and hungry even, bein' left alone in yer old age, bein' afraid to die — it all adds up. That's the way life is — cradle to grave. And you c'n stand it. They's one way. You got to be hearty. You *got* to be.

LAUREY [*moved*]: Oh, Aunt Eller, I'm sich a baby — !

AUNT ELLER: There, there!

LAUREY: Ashamed of myself! I want to be the way you air.

AUNT ELLER [*breaking off*]: Fiddlesticks! *Fat —* and *old?* You couldn't *h'ar* me to be the way I *am!* Why, in a year's time, you'll git so t'ard even of lookin' at me, you and Curly'll run me off the place, 'th a tin can tied onto my tail —

[LAUREY *half-smiles at the spectacle, and leaning over, gives* AUNT ELLER *an affectionate hug.*]

LAUREY [*through tears*]: Oh, whut ud I do 'thout you, you're sich a crazy! —

AUNT ELLER: Shore's you're borned! —

LAUREY: I never could live. I never could. [*Rising, happier.*] I'll go to bed now.

AUNT ELLER: And sleep, huh?

LAUREY [*smiling*]: Tight.

AUNT ELLER: And eat hearty from now on, huh? Fried chicken and everthing?

LAUREY: Tomorrow.

AUNT ELLER: Tomorrow, yer foot! [*She gets an apple out of a basket on the organ.*] Here, eat that.

LAUREY: I don't want it.

AUNT ELLER: *Eat* it, I said.

[LAUREY *takes it, nibbles at it. A dog begins to bark. They all stop abruptly, listening.*]

AUNT ELLER: Now, who could that — [*She stands up, looks at* LAUREY, *questioningly.*] This hour of night —

[LAUREY *stands up, quite still, straight and pale.*]

LAUREY: Curly —

AUNT ELLER: Couldn't be Curly, 'th ole Shep a-actin' up like a — He's stopped barkin'. [*The dog's barks stop suddenly.* AUNT ELLER *goes over to the window.*

ADO ANNIE *has put down her work. All three women are in a breathless tranced state — suspended, curiously conjecturing.*] It's pitch black —

LAUREY [*with quiet conviction*]: 'S Curly come back.

ADO ANNIE [*with a nervous giggle*]: Ole Shep stopped a-barkin' like he was shot!

AUNT ELLER [*angrily — because of her nervous apprehension*]: Sh! Be still, cain't you!

LAUREY: It's Curly!

AUNT ELLER: 'Tain't *no* one. That dog's jist got the colic, I bet. [*There is a noise as of someone trying the door.*] What's that!

ADO ANNIE [*rising*]: I'm goin' home.

AUNT ELLER: Be still. [*She picks up a shovel standing in the fireplace. She calls out sharply.*] Now then. Whoever's there, answer, and answer quick!

[*The door opens quickly, and* CURLY, *disheveled and worn, appears there.*]

CURLY: Laurey!

AUNT ELLER [*joyfully*]: Why, it's Curly!

LAUREY: Curly!

[*She runs to meet him halfway across the room as he comes forward. They go into each other's arms, and cling to each other.*]

AUNT ELLER [*with extravagant delight*]: My, oh my! Look whut the old cat's drug in! Thought we had him safe in jail and here he turns up like a bad penny! Laws a me! Whutta you mean tryin' to skeer us wall-eyed?

ADO ANNIE [*astonished*]: Why, it's Curly!

AUNT ELLER [*gaily*]: Naw! It's Sandy Claus, cain't you see nuthin'! They've let him off! I knowed they would, I knowed it, I knowed it!

[CURLY *backs out of* LAUREY'S *arms, looks round quickly.*]

LAUREY: Curly! Whut is it!

CURLY: Whut was that noise?

LAUREY [*with premonitory alarm*]: Whut's the matter? Everything's all right, ain't it? They've let you off, ain't they? Curley! Tell me and be quick, I —

CURLY: No. They ain't let me off.

LAUREY: Curly! [*Running to him.*] They couldn't a-sent you up! It wasn't yore fault. They couldn't, I won't let 'em — I won't, I —

CURLY: Sh! [*As they become silent.*] They're after me.

[*He goes swiftly across and pulls down the window shade.*]

AUNT ELLER: Never heared of sich a — Who's after you, the old Booger Man?

LAUREY: Curly!

CURLY: When I clumb th'ough the fence jist by that little bridge, I seen lights 'way over towards Claremore. I knowed they'd got onto which way I was headin', so I run acrost the back of the —

AUNT ELLER: Whut *air* you jabberin' about? [*Light dawning on her.*] Oh! I mighta knowed a curly-headed cowhand like him ud come to a bad end! He's went and broke outa jail.

CURLY [*quickly*]: I *had* to see Laurey. I *had* to! I knowed she'd be a-worryin' about everthing, and I couldn't stand it, her a-worryin' and nobody to help her none —

[*He takes* LAUREY *in his arms again.*]

AUNT ELLER [*severely*]: Worryin'! I ort to take a hick'ry to you and beat you plumb to a frazzle! Here you'd a-got off tomorrow, you crazy youngun — everbody *said* so. Now you'll prob'ly git sent up fer five year fer breakin' loose — and I hope you do!

LAUREY: Aunt Eller, they cain't send him up, they *cain't!*

AUNT ELLER: Oh, cain't they? You wait and see. [*To* CURLY.] Didn't you know they'd know whur you was headin' fer, and find you 'fore a cat could lick his front paw?

CURLY: I didn't think.

AUNT ELLER: I reckon you hain't got nuthin' to think *with.* [*Giving him a swat.*] I'd like to give you a good beatin'! [*Smiling at him tolerantly.*] Aw, I reckon you jist had to see yer girl, didn't you?

CURLY: My wife.

AUNT ELLER: Yeow? Well, *call* her that 'f it does you any good. How fur back was it you seen 'em comin' after you?

CURLY: 'Bout half a mile.

AUNT ELLER: You got jist about two minutes to tell Laurey " Good-by " then.

CURLY: They won't ketch me! Hide me till mornin', Aunt Eller. I cain't let 'em take me now, Aunt Eller!

AUNT ELLER: You'll stay *right* here till they come! You've already caused enough trouble to last us all out to doomsday. Now then. Ado Annie, come on out in the kitchen, and git yerself sump'n to eat. Bet you're hungry.

ADO ANNIE: I hain't hungry, Aunt Eller. I jist had a piece of —

AUNT ELLER: Not hungry! Why, you're all fallin' to staves. Feel ever' rib you got! [*She shoves* ADO ANNIE *out and follows her. As she goes out.*] They'll come any minute now.

CURLY [*after a moment, not knowing how to begin*]: You all right, honey?

LAUREY: Yes. I guess. [*She puts her hand to her forehead as if brushing away her darkness.*] I git to thinkin'.

CURLY [*gently*]: I know. Me, too. Thinkin' and thinkin' about you — and be bringin' sich trouble on you. All my fault.

LAUREY: Nobody could he'p it.

CURLY: Listen, Laurey. [*She goes to him, questioningly, disturbed at something in his manner.*] I had to see you 'fore the hearin' tomorrow. That's why I broke out. Fer whut if they'd send me up, and I not see you fer a long time?

LAUREY: Curly! It *couldn't* be. Don't you say that.

CURLY: *Anything* can be. You got to be ready.

LAUREY [*alarmed*]: Have you heared anything, Curly? Tell me, whut'd you hear?

CURLY: Nuthin', honey. Ain't heared nuthin' — but *good.*

LAUREY [*with glad relief*]: Oh, it's all right, then!

CURLY [*gravely*]: That ain't it. I'm shore myself, honey. Er I *was* shore, till I broke out. I never thought whut *that* might do. But sump'n's always happenin' in this here world. Cain't count on a thing. So you got to promise me sump'n. Whutever happens.— *whutever* it is — you got to bear up, you hear me? [*Smiling.*] Why, I'm a purty one to go a-losin' sleep over, ain't I?

LAUREY [*ruefully*]: Oh, a fine start *we* got, ain't it? [*With an effort, painfully working it out in her mind.*] Oh, I've worried about you, shet up in that filthy jail —

CURLY: Don't mind about that.

LAUREY: — And I've thought about that awful night, too, till I thought I'd go crazy —

CURLY: Pore Laurey.

LAUREY: Looked at it time and again, *heared* it — ringin' in my ears! *Cried* about it, cried about everthing! A plumb baby! And I've tried to figger out how it ud be if sump'n *did* happen to you. Didn't know how I could stand it. That was the worst! And nen, I tried to figger out how I'd go on. Oh, I've went th'ough it all, Curly, from the start. Now I feel shore of sump'n, anyway — I'll be growed up — like everbody else. [*With conviction.*] I'll put up with everthing now. You don't need to worry about me no more. Why, I'll stand it — if they send you to the pen fer life —

CURLY [*with mock alarm*]: Here! Don't know's I like that very well!

[LAUREY *bursts out into a peal of amused, hearty, infectious laughter.*]

LAUREY: The look on yore face! 'S the first time I laughed in three days!

CURLY [*his old self again*]: *I* ain't goin' to no pen fer life — a-poundin' up rocks, and a-wearin' stripes around my legs!

LAUREY: Wouldn't you look purty!

CURLY [*with delight*]: You *air* a devil, ain't you? I don't think you even *like* me.

LAUREY [*playfully*]: Like you? Oh, I like you a little bit. [*They stand looking at each other, shyly, happily.*] Whur on earth'd you git them clothes you got on?

CURLY [*gaily*]: Old Man Peck went and got 'em fer me. Shore a good ole man! Thinks the world of you. Shirt come outa Rucker's Dry Goods Store. Brand new, too! He thought I must be a-needin' clean clothes, I reckon, shet up in that ole jail! My, they's things a-crawlin' there, got legs on both sides! Cell next to mine's got a couple of horse thieves into it, the A. H. T. A. caught up by Sequoyah. They gimme a blanket and one of 'em said, " 'Tain't so purty-fer-nice but it's hell-fer-warm."

LAUREY [*amused*]: Curly!

CURLY: 'Nother cell's got a womern into it that smokes and cusses like a mule driver. Caught her stealin' from the Turf Exchange. Don't know whut's got into Indian Territory nohow! They puttin' everbody in jail — women and all!

LAUREY: I think you like yer ole jail!

CURLY: Jist rairin' to git back. Cain't wait! Lay back on that arn cot and dream about featherbeds!

LAUREY [*softly, happily*]: Ever'time I pass by the barn lot, ole Dun lopes acrost and nickers at me, fer all get-out! Shows his teeth. He's astin' about you, I reckon.

CURLY: Oh, he's apt to fall dead of the heaves when he hears about me — settin' in jail 'stid of on the range! Feels like I ain't set in the saddle in a month of Sundays! Listen, Laurey. I been a-thinkin' — Everthing from now on is gonna be different.

LAUREY: Different?

CURLY: It come to me settin' in that cell of mine. [*Dreamily, out of a visionary absorption — like a song, growing in intensity.*] Oh, I got to learn to be a farmer, I see that! Quit a-thinkin' about dehornin' and brandin' and th'owin' the rope, and start in to git my hands blistered a new way! Oh, things is changin' right and left! Buy up mowin' machines, cut down the prairies! Shoe yer horses, drag them plows under the sod! They gonna make a state outa this, they gonna put it in the Union! Country a-changin', got to change with it! Bring up a pair of boys, new stock, to keep up 'th the way things is goin' in this here crazy country! Life jist startin' in fer me now. Work to do! Now I got you to he'p me — I'll 'mount to sump'n yit! Come here, Laurey. Come here, and tell me " Good-by " 'fore they come fer me and take me away.

LAUREY [*wryly*]: All we do is say " Howdy " and " So long." [*Gravely.*] Good-by, Curly. If you come back tomorrow, I'll be here a-waitin'. If you don't come back, I'll be here a-waitin' anyhow.

CURLY: I'll come back, honey. They couldn't hinder me 'th bird-shot!

LAUREY: Promise me.

CURLY: Oh, I hate to go away and leave you! I cain't. [*He takes her in his arms, hungrily. After a moment, there are voices and sounds of an approaching party. The couple listen breathlessly.*] They're here. Oh, I cain't go, I cain't leave you!

LAUREY [*anguishedly, clinging to him*]: I cain't let you go.

[AUNT ELLER *comes in.*]

AUNT ELLER [*gravely*]: Well, here they air, I guess. They's a whole crowd. I seen the lanterns. You all ready, Curly?

CURLY [*in anguish*]: I guess — I —

AUNT ELLER [*tenderly*]: Good-by, honey. I'm sorry it has to be like this. [*There is a knock at the door.* AUNT ELLER *goes over and calls, her hand on the latch.*] Who is that a-knockin'?

VOICE [*outside*]: It's me, Ed Peck — and I got to see you about —

AUNT ELLER [*opening the door, in astonishment*]: Why, Mr. Peck! Come on in. Whutta *you* want around here?

OLD MAN PECK [*coming in, his eyes going to* CURLY]: Curly knows whut I want. I've *come* fer him.

AUNT ELLER: *You* have? You ain't no marshal.

OLD MAN PECK: I know. But Mr. Burnett, the federal marshal, deputized me and some of the boys to come out and find Curly and bring him back. Come on, Curly.

AUNT ELLER: Well, I *must* say! Sidin' with the federal marshal!

OLD MAN PECK: I ain't sidin' with him, Aunt Eller. Curly's hearin' ain't come up yit, and he hadn't no right to run off this-a-way.

AUNT ELLER: No right! Say, looky here, he wanted to see his wife. That ain't agin the *law* in this country, is it?

OLD MAN PECK: No. But breakin' outa *jail* is agin the law.

AUNT ELLER [*disgusted*]: Well, of all the — When'd you go and git so respectful of the law? Looky here, if a law's a *good* law — it can stand a little breakin'. And them out there — Who's out there? Hey, you all! [*She has gone to the window and thrown up the shade.*] Go on home. Nobody's wantin' *you* around here!

VOICES [*outside*]: We've come fer Curly, Aunt Eller. We got to take him back. [*Snickering.*] He's a plumb criminal, he is, breakin' outa jail this-a-way!

AUNT ELLER: Who's that? That you, Zeb? I mighta knowed! Say, you're a purty nuthin' — a ole pig-stealer like you tryin' to represent the govament!

VOICE [*outside, offended, protesting*]: Who's a pig-stealer?

AUNT ELLER: *You* air, Mr. Zeb Walkley.

VOICE: I ain't, either!

AUNT ELLER: You *air!* Why, you gittin' so that — 'stid of talkin' — you plumb grunt like a ole sow! And say, Dave Tyler — you'll feel funny when I tell yer wife you're carryin' on 'th another womern, won't you?

VOICE [*outside*]: I ain't carryin' on 'th no one.

AUNT ELLER: Mebbe not. But you'll shore feel funny when I tell yer *wife* you air.

VOICES: Now, Aunt Eller, we've come fer Curly.

We cain't stand here and listen to you —

Send him on out!

AUNT ELLER [*indignantly*]: Oh, you'll listen to me! I'm gittin' mad! You cain't *take* Curly, that's all they is to it!

VOICES: We *got* to, Aunt Eller.

He'll git off tomorrow, won't he?

Make him come on out, and le's git started!

AUNT ELLER [*severely*]: All right, 'f you won't listen to me, I plumb warsh my hands of all of you. I thought you was a fine bunch of neighbors. Now I see you're jist a gang of fools. Tryin' to take a bridegroom away from his bride! Why, the way you're sidin' with the federal marshal, you'd think us people out here lived in the United States! Why, we're territory folks — we ort to hang together. I don't mean *hang* — I mean *stick.* Whut's the United States? It's jist a furrin country to me. And *you* supportin' it! Jist dirty ole furriners, ever last one of you! •

VOICES [*outside, grumbling, protesting*]: Now, Aunt Eller, we hain't furriners.

My pappy and mammy was *both* borned in Indian Territory! Why, I'm jist plumb full of Indian blood myself.

Me, too! And I c'n prove it!

AUNT ELLER [*full of guile*]: Well, maybe you *ain't* furriners. I musta made a mistake. [*Slyly, smiling.*] Anyway, I ain't astin' you to let Curly *off*. That's up to them ole United Statesers at the hearin'. *I* mean — you don't have to take Curly back *tonight*. Take him in the mornin' jist as well.

VOICES [*uncertainly*]: Well, I don't know —

I ain't no furriner!

Whut does Mr. Peck say?

He's the boss. Ast *him*.

I wouldn't wanta stand in the way of lettin' Curly —

AUNT ELLER [*triumphantly, to* MR. PECK]: See there! They said it was all right to let him stay tonight.

OLD MAN PECK: No, they didn't.

AUNT ELLER: Did too! Cain't you hear nuthin'? I'll take a black-snake whip to you!

OLD MAN PECK [*sheepishly*]: Well, I — If my men is gonna back out on me this-a-way — I reckon I better let Curly stay.

AUNT ELLER [*overjoyed*]: I knowed you'd see daylight, I knowed it, I knowed it!

OLD MAN PECK [*self-consciously, not looking at* CURLY, *and twirling his hat in his hands, sheepishly*]: I was young onct myself.

[*He hugs* AUNT ELLER.]

AUNT ELLER: Why, you ole devil! Tell yer wife on you!

CURLY: 'D you want me to stay, Laurey?

[*She backs away, flushed and embarrassed and joyous at the same time, flings an arm about his neck and kisses him quickly, whirls over to* OLD MAN PECK, *gives him a quick hug and flies into her room.* CURLY *grins and starts after her.*]

OLD MAN PECK [*as* CURLY *reaches the door*]: Curly. I'll be here right after breakfast to fetch you. I'll be here bright and early.

[CURLY *goes in. The door shuts.*]

AUNT ELLER [*slyly, owlishly*]: Well, not *too* early. [*Then, gravely.*] Younguns has a turrible time, don't they? [*She throws it off.*] Oh, well — they git to be old-timers soon enough. *Too* soon. [*She shows* MR. PECK *out with a lantern. She marches over to the window, calling out.*] Hey you all! Go on home. They ain't nuthin' *you* c'n do around here. Curly's *stayin'*!

[*She jerks the shade down. The voices outside exclaim delightedly and move away. From the bedroom has come the sound of* CURLY *beginning to sing softly, "Green Grow the Lilacs."*]

AUNT ELLER [*going to the window*]: Mr. Peck! [*With delight.*] Listen to that fool cowpuncher! His weddin' night — and there he is singin'!

CURTAIN

CAUTION

Professionals and amateurs are hereby warned that *Our Town,* being fully protected under the copyright laws of the United States of America, the British Empire, including the Dominion of Canada, and all other countries of the Copyright Union, is subject to royalty. All rights, including professional, amateur, motion picture, recitation, lecturing, public reading, radio broadcasting, and the rights of translation into foreign languages, are strictly reserved. Particular emphasis is laid on the question of readings, permission for which must be secured from the author's agent in writing. All inquiries should be addressed to the author's agent, Harold Freedman, 101 Park Avenue, New York City.

Thornton Wilder

Our Town

ACT 1

No curtain. No scenery. The audience, arriving, sees an empty stage in half-light.

Presently the STAGE MANAGER, *hat on and pipe in mouth, enters and begins placing a table and several chairs down stage left, and a table and chairs down stage right. " Left " and " right " are from the point of view of the actor facing the audience. " Up " is towards the back wall. As the house lights go down he has finished setting the stage and leaning against the right proscenium pillar watches the late arrivals in the audience.*

When the auditorium is in complete darkness he speaks:

STAGE MANAGER: This play is called *Our Town*. It was written by Thornton Wilder; produced and directed by A—— [*or:* produced by A——; directed by B——]. In it you will see Miss C——, Miss D——, Miss E——, and Mr. F——, Mr. G——, Mr. H——, and many others.

The name of the town is Grover's Corners, New Hampshire, — just across the Massachusetts line; longitude 42 degrees 40 minutes; latitude 70 degrees 37 minutes.

The First Act shows a day in our town. The day is May 7, 1901. The time is just before dawn. [*A rooster crows.*] The sky is beginning to show some streaks of light over in the East there, behind our mount'in. The morning star always gets wonderful bright the minute before it has to go.

[*He stares at it for a moment, then goes up stage.*]

Well, I'd better show you how our town lies. Up here — [*that is, parallel with the back wall*] is Main Street. Way back there is the railway station; tracks go that way. Polish Town's across the tracks and some Canuck families. [*Toward the left.*] Over there is the Congregational Church; across the street's the Presbyterian.

Methodist and Unitarian are over there.

Baptist is down in the holla' by the river.

Catholic Church is over beyond the tracks.

Here's the Town Hall and Post Office combined; jail's in the basement.

Bryan once made a speech from these steps here.

Along here's a row of stores. Hitching-posts and horse blocks in front of them. First automobile's going to come along in about five years, — belonged to Banker Cartwright, our richest citizen . . . lives in the big white house up on the hill.

Here's the grocery store and here's Mr. Morgan's drugstore. Most everybody in town manages to look into those two stores once a day.

Public School's over yonder. High School's still farther over. Quarter of nine mornings, noontimes, and three o'clock afternoons, the hull town can hear the yelling and screaming from those schoolyards.

[*He approaches the table and chairs down stage right.*]

This is our doctor's house, — Doc Gibbs'. This is the back door.

[*Two arched trellises are pushed out, one by each proscenium pillar.*]

There's some scenery for those who think they have to have scenery.

There's a garden here. Corn . . . peas . . . beans . . . hollyhocks . . . heliotrope . . . and a lot of burdock.

[*Crosses the stage.*]

In those days our newspaper come out twice a week, — the *Grover's Corners Sentinel,* — and this is Editor Webb's house.

And this is Mrs. Webb's garden.

Just like Mrs. Gibbs's, only it's got a lot of sunflowers, too.

Right here, — big butternut tree.

[*He returns to his place by the right proscenium pillar and looks at the audience for a minute.*]

Nice town, y'know what I mean?

Nobody very remarkable ever come out of it, — s'far as we know.

The earliest tombstones in the cemetery up there on the mountain say 1670-1680 — they're Grovers and Cartwrights and Gibbses and Herseys — same names as are around here now.

Well, as I said: it's about dawn.

The only lights on in town are in a cottage over by the tracks where a Polish mother's just had twins. And in the Joe Crowell house, where Joe Junior's getting up so as to deliver the paper. And in the depot, where Shorty Hawkins is gettin' ready to flag the 5:45 for Boston.

[*A train whistle is heard. The* STAGE MANAGER *takes out his watch and nods.*]

Naturally, out in the country — all around — they've been lights on for some time, what with milkin's and so on. But town people sleep late.

So — another day's begun.

There's Doc Gibbs comin' down Main Street now, comin' back from that baby case. And here's his wife comin' downstairs to get breakfast.

Doc Gibbs died in 1930. The new hospital's named after him.

Mrs. Gibbs died first — long time ago in fact. She went out to visit her daughter, Rebecca, who married an insurance man in Canton, Ohio, and died there — pneumonia — but her body was brought back here. She's up in the cemetery there now — in with a whole mess of Gibbses and Herseys — she was Julia Hersey 'fore she married Doc Gibbs in the Congregational Church over there.

In our town we like to know the facts about everybody.

— That's Doc Gibbs.

And there comes Joe Crowell, Jr., delivering Mr. Webb's *Sentinel*.

[DR. GIBBS *has been coming along Main Street from the left. At the point where he would turn to approach his house, he stops, sets down his — imaginary — black bag, takes off his hat, and rubs his face with fatigue, using an enormous handkerchief.* MRS. GIBBS *has entered her kitchen, gone through the motions of putting wood into a stove, lighting it, and preparing breakfast. Suddenly,* JOE CROWELL, JR., *starts down Main Street from the right, hurling imaginary newspapers into doorways.*]

JOE CROWELL, JR.: Morning, Doc Gibbs.

DR. GIBBS: Morning, Joe.

JOE CROWELL, JR.: Somebody been sick, Doc?

DR. GIBBS: No. Just some twins born over in Polish Town.

JOE CROWELL, JR.: Do you want your paper now?

DR. GIBBS: Yes, I'll take it. — Anything serious goin' on in the world since Wednesday?

JOE CROWELL, JR.: Yessir. My schoolteacher, Miss Foster, 's getting married to a fella over in Concord.

DR. GIBBS: I declare. — How do you boys feel about that?

JOE CROWELL, JR.: Well, of course, it's none of my business, — but I think if a person starts out to be a teacher, she ought to stay one.

DR. GIBBS: How's your knee, Joe?

JOE CROWELL, JR.: Fine, Doc, I never think about it at all. Only like you said, it always tells me when it's going to rain.

DR. GIBBS: What's it telling you today? Goin' to rain?

JOE CROWELL, JR.: No, sir.

DR. GIBBS: Sure?

JOE CROWELL, JR.: Yessir.

DR. GIBBS: Knee ever make a mistake?

JOE CROWELL, JR.: No, sir.

[JOE *goes off*. DR. GIBBS *stands reading his paper*.]

STAGE MANAGER: Here comes Howie Newsome delivering the milk.

[HOWIE NEWSOME *comes along Main Street, passes* DR. GIBBS, *comes down the center of the stage, leaves some bottles at* MRS. WEBB'S *back door, and crosses the stage to* MRS. GIBBS'S.]

HOWIE NEWSOME: Git-ap, Bessie. What's the matter with you? — Morning, Doc.

DR. GIBBS: Morning, Howie.

HOWIE NEWSOME: Somebody sick?

DR. GIBBS: Pair of twins over to Mrs. Goruslawski's.

HOWIE NEWSOME: Twins, eh? This town's gettin' bigger every year.

DR. GIBBS: Going to rain, Howie?

HOWIE NEWSOME: No, no. Fine day — that'll burn through. Come on, Bessie.

DR. GIBBS: Hello, Bessie. [*He strokes her*.] How old is she, Howie?

HOWIE NEWSOME: Going on seventeen. Bessie's all mixed up about the route ever since the Lockharts stopped takin' their quart of milk every day. She wants to leave 'em a quart just the same — keeps scolding me the hull trip.

[*He reaches* MRS. GIBBS'S *back door. She is waiting for him*.]

MRS. GIBBS: Good morning, Howie.

HOWIE NEWSOME: Morning, Mrs. Gibbs. Doc's just comin' down the street.

MRS. GIBBS: Is he? Seems like you're late today?

HOWIE NEWSOME: Yes. Somep'n went wrong with the separator. Don't know what 'twas.

[*He goes back to Main Street, clucks for Bessie and goes off right*. DR. GIBBS *reaches his home and goes in*.]

MRS. GIBBS: Everything all right?

DR. GIBBS: Yes. I declare — easy as kittens.

MRS. GIBBS: Bacon'll be ready in a minute. Set down and drink your coffee. Child-*run!* Child-*run!* Time to get up. — George! Rebecca! — You can catch a couple hours' sleep this morning, can't you?

DR. GIBBS: Hm! . . . Mrs. Wentworth's coming at eleven. Guess I know what it's about, too. Her stummick ain't what it ought to be.

MRS. GIBBS: All told, you won't get more'n three hours' sleep. Frank Gibbs, I don't know what's goin' to become of you. I do wish I could get you to go away some place and take a rest. I think it would do you good.

MRS. WEBB: Emileeee! Time to get up! Wally! Seven o'clock!

MRS. GIBBS: I declare, you got to speak to George. Seems like something's come over him lately. He's no help to me at all. I can't even get him to cut me some wood.

DR. GIBBS: Is he sassay to you?

MRS. GIBBS: No. He just whines! All he thinks about is that baseball. — George! Rebecca! You'll be late for school.

DR. GIBBS: M-m-m. . . .

MRS. GIBBS: George!

DR. GIBBS: George, look sharp!

GEORGE'S VOICE: Yes, Pa!

DR. GIBBS [*as he goes off the stage*]: Don't you hear your mother calling you?

MRS. WEBB: Walleee! Emileee! You'll be late for school! Walleee! You wash yourself good or I'll come up and do it myself.

REBECCA GIBBS'S VOICE: Ma! What dress shall I wear?

MRS. GIBBS: Don't make a noise. Your father's been out all night and needs his sleep. I washed and ironed the blue gingham for you special.

REBECCA: Ma, I hate that dress.

MRS. GIBBS: Oh, hush-up-with-you.

REBECCA: Every day I go to school dressed like a sick turkey.

MRS. GIBBS: Now, Rebecca, don't be impossible. You always look *very* nice.

REBECCA: Mama, George's throwing soap at me.

MRS. GIBBS: I'll come up and slap the both of you, — that's what I'll do.

[*A factory whistle sounds. The children enter and take their places at the breakfast tables:* EMILY *and* WALLY WEBB; GEORGE *and* REBECCA GIBBS.]

STAGE MANAGER: We've got a factory in our town too, — hear it? Makes blankets. Cartwrights own it and it brung 'em a fortune.

MRS. WEBB: Children! Now I won't have it. Breakfast is just as good as any other meal and I won't have you gobbling like wolves. It'll stunt your growth, — that's a fact. Put away your book, Wally.

WALLY: Aw, Ma!

MRS. WEBB: You know the rule's well as I do — no books at table. As for me, I'd rather have my children healthy than bright.

EMILY: I'm both, Mama: you know I am. I'm the brightest girl in school for my age. I have a wonderful memory.

MRS. WEBB: Eat your breakfast.

WALLY: I'm bright, too, when I'm looking at my stamp collection.

MRS. GIBBS: I'll speak to your father about it when he's rested. Seems to me twenty-five cents a week's enough for a boy your age. I declare I don't know how you spend it all.

GEORGE: Aw, Ma, — I gotta lotta things to buy.

MRS. GIBBS: Strawberry phosphates — that's what you spend it on.

GEORGE: I don't see how Rebecca comes to have so much money. She has more'n a dollar.

REBECCA [*spoon in mouth, dreamily*]: I've been saving it up gradual.

MRS. GIBBS: Well, dear, I think it's a good thing every now and then to spend some.

REBECCA: Mama, do you know what I love most in the world — do you? — Money.

MRS. GIBBS: Eat your breakfast.

[*The school bell is heard.*]

THE CHILDREN: Mama, there's first bell. — I gotta hurry. — I don't want any more.

MRS. WEBB: Walk fast, but you don't have to run. Wally, pull up your pants at the knee. Stand up straight, Emily.

MRS. GIBBS: Tell Miss Foster I send her my best congratulations — can you remember that?

REBECCA: Yes, Ma.

MRS. GIBBS: You look real nice, Rebecca. Pick up your feet.

ALL: Good-by.

[*The children from the two houses join at the center of the stage and go up to Main Street, then off left.* MRS. GIBBS *fills her apron with food for the chickens and comes down to the footlights.*]

MRS. GIBBS: Here, chick, chick, chick.

No, go away, you. Go away.

Here, chick, chick, chick.

What's the matter with *you?* Fight, fight, fight, — that's all you do.

Hm . . . *you* don't belong to me. Where'd you come from?

[*She shakes her apron.*]

Oh, don't be so scared. Nobody's going to hurt you.

[MRS. WEBB *is sitting by her trellis, stringing beans.*]

MRS. GIBBS: Good morning, Myrtle. How's your cold?

MRS. WEBB: Well, it's better; but I told Charles I didn't know as I'd go to choir practice tonight. Wouldn't be any use.

MRS. GIBBS: Just the same, you come to choir practice, Myrtle, and try it.

MRS. WEBB: Well, if I don't feel any worse than I do now I probably will. While I'm resting myself I thought I'd string some of these beans.

MRS. GIBBS: [*rolling up her sleeves as she crosses the stage for a chat*]: Let me help you. Beans have been good this year.

MRS. WEBB: I've decided to put up forty quarts if it kills me. The children say they hate 'em but I notice they're able to get 'em down all winter.

[*Pause.*]

MRS. GIBBS: Now, Myrtle. I've got to tell you something, because if I don't tell somebody I'll burst.

MRS. WEBB: Why, Julia Gibbs!

MRS. GIBBS: Here, give me some more of those beans. Myrtle, did one of those second-hand furniture men from Boston come to see you last Friday?

MRS. WEBB: No—o.

MRS. GIBBS: Well, he called on me. First I thought he was a patient wantin' to see Dr. Gibbs. 'N he wormed his way into my parlor, and, Myrtle Webb, he offered me three hundred and fifty dollars for Grandmother Wentworth's highboy, as I'm sitting here!

MRS. WEBB: Why, Julia Gibbs!

MRS. GIBBS: He did! That old thing! Why, it was so big I didn't know where to put it and I almost give it to Cousin Hester Wilcox.

MRS. WEBB: Well, you're going to take it, aren't you?

MRS. GIBBS: I don't know.

MRS. WEBB: You don't know — three hundred and fifty dollars. What's come over you?

MRS. GIBBS: Well, if I could get the Doctor to take the money and go away some place on a real trip I'd sell it like that. — Myrtle, ever since I was *that* high I've had the thought that I'd like to see Paris, France. I suppose I'm crazy.

MRS. WEBB: Oh, I know what you mean. — How does the Doctor feel about it?

MRS. GIBBS: Well, I did beat about the bush a little and said that if I got a legacy — that's the way I put it — I'd make him take me somewhere.

MRS. WEBB: M-m-m. . . . What did he say?

MRS. GIBBS: You know how he is. I haven't heard a serious word out of him, ever since I've known him. No, he said, it might make him discontented with Grover's Corners to go traipsin' about Europe; better let well enough alone, he says. Every two years he makes a trip to the battlefields of the Civil War and that's enough treat for anybody, he says.

MRS. WEBB: Well, Mr. Webb just *admires* the way Dr. Gibbs knows everything about the Civil War. Mr. Webb's a good mind to give up Napoleon and move over to the Civil War, only Dr. Gibbs being one of the greatest experts in the country just makes him despair.

MRS. GIBBS: It's a fact! Dr. Gibbs is never so happy as when he's at Antietam or Gettysburg. The times I've walked over those hills, Myrtle, stopping at every bush and pacing it all out, like we was going to buy it.

MRS. WEBB: Well, if that second-hand man's really serious about buyin' it, Julia, you sell it. And then you'll get to see Paris, all right.

MRS. GIBBS: Oh, I'm sorry I mentioned it. Only it seems to me that once in your life before you die you ought to see a country where they don't talk and think in English and don't even want to.

[*The* STAGE MANAGER *returns to the center of the stage.*]

STAGE MANAGER: That'll do. That'll do. Thank you very much, ladies.

[MRS. GIBBS *and* MRS. WEBB *gather up their things, return into their homes and disappear.*]

Now we're going to skip a few hours in the day at Grover's Corners.

But before we go on I want you to know some more things about the town, — all kinds of things.

So I've asked Prof. Willard of our State University to come down here and sketch in a few details of our past history, — kind of scientific account, you might say.

Is Prof. Willard here?

[PROF. WILLARD, *a rural savant, pince-nez on a wide satin ribbon, enters from the right with some notes in his hand.*]

May I introduce Prof. Willard of our University.

A few brief notes, thank you, Professor, — unfortunately our time is limited.

PROF. WILLARD: Grover's Corners . . . let me see . . . Grover's Corners lies on the old Archaeozoic granite of the Appalachian range. I may say it's some of the oldest land in the world. We're very proud of that. A shelf of Devonian basalt crosses it with vestiges of Mesozoic shale, and some sandstone outcroppings; but that's all more recent: two hundred, three hundred million years old.

Some highly interesting fossils have been found. . . . I may say: unique fossils . . . two miles out of town, in Silas Peckham's cow pasture. They can be seen at the museum in our University at any time. Did you wish the meteorological conditions?

STAGE MANAGER: Thank you. We would.

PROF. WILLARD: The mean precipitation is 40 inches. The mean annual temperature is 43 degrees, ranging between 102 degrees in the shade and 38 degrees below zero in winter. The . . . the . . . uh . . .

STAGE MANAGER: Thank you, Professor. And have you Prof. Gruber's notes on the history of human life here?

PROF. WILLARD: Hm . . . yes . . . anthropological data: Early Amerindian stock. Cotahatchee tribes . . . no evidence before the tenth century of this era . . . hm . . . now entirely disappeared . . . possible traces in three families. Migration toward the end of the seventeenth century of English brachycephalic blue-eyed stock . . . for the most part. Since then some influx of Slav and Mediterranean types. . . .

STAGE MANAGER: And the population, Prof. Willard?

PROF. WILLARD: Within the town limits: 2,640. The postal district brings in 507 more.

Mortality and birth-rates are constant; by MacPherson's gauge: 6.032.

STAGE MANAGER: Thank you *very* much, Professor. We're all very much obliged to you, I'm sure.

PROF. WILLARD: Not at all, sir; not at all.

STAGE MANAGER: This way, Professor, and thank you again.

[*Exit* PROF. WILLARD.]

Now the political and social report: Editor Webb. — Oh, Mr. Webb?

[MRS. WEBB *appears at her back door.*]

MRS. WEBB: He'll be here in a minute. . . . He just cut his hand while he was eatin' an apple.

STAGE MANAGER: Thank you, Mrs. Webb.

MRS. WEBB: Charles! Everybody's waitin'.

[*Exit* MRS. WEBB.]

STAGE MANAGER: Mr. Webb is Publisher and Editor of the *Grover's Corners Sentinel*. That's our local paper, y'know.

[MR. WEBB *enters from his house, pulling on his coat. His finger is bound in a handkerchief.*]

MR. WEBB: Hm. . . . I don't have to tell you that we're run here by a Board of Selectmen. — All males vote at the age of 21. Women vote indirect. We're lower middle-class, sprinkling of professional men . . . 10% illiterate laborers. Politically, we're 86% Republicans; 6% Democrats; 4% Socialists; rest, indifferent.

Religiously, we're 85% Protestants; 12% Catholics; rest, indifferent.

Do you want the poverty and insanity statistics?

STAGE MANAGER: Thank you, no. Have you any comments, Mr. Webb?

MR. WEBB: Very ordinary town, if you ask me. Little better behaved than most. Probably a lot duller.

But our young people here seem to like it well enough: 90% of 'em graduating from High School settle down right here to live — even when they've been away to college.

STAGE MANAGER: Thank you, Mr. Webb. Now, is there anyone in the audience who would like to ask Editor Webb anything about the town?

WOMAN IN THE BALCONY: Is there much drinking in Grover's Corners?

MR. WEBB: Well, ma'am, I wouldn't know what you'd call *much*. Satiddy nights the farmhands meet down in Ellery Greenough's stable and holler some. Fourth of July I've been known to taste a drop myself — and Decoration Day, of course. We've got one or two town drunks, but they're always having remorses every time an evangelist comes to town. No, ma'am, I'd say likker ain't a regular thing in the home here, except in the medicine chest. Right good for snake-bite, y'know — always was.

TALL MAN AT BACK OF AUDITORIUM: Is there no one in town aware of —

STAGE MANAGER: Come forward, will you, where we can all hear you. — What were you saying?

TALL MAN: Is there no one in town aware of social injustice and industrial inequality?

MR. WEBB: Oh, yes, everybody is, — somethin' terrible. Seems like they spend most of their time talking about who's rich and who's poor.

TALL MAN: Then why don't they do something about it?

MR. WEBB: Well, we're ready to listen to everybody's suggestion as to how you can see that the diligent and sensible'll rise to the top and the lazy and quarrelsome sink to the bottom. We'll listen to anybody. Meantime until that's settled, we try to take care of those that can't help themselves, and those that can we leave alone. — Are there any more questions?

LADY IN A BOX: Oh, Mr. Webb? Mr. Webb, is there any culture or love of beauty in Grover's Corners?

MR. WEBB: Well, ma'am, there ain't much — not in the sense you mean. Come to think of it, there's some girls that play the piano at High School Commencement; but they ain't happy about it. Yes, and I see where my daughter's been made to read *The Merchant of Venice* over to the school. Seems all pretty remote to 'em, y'know what I mean. No, ma'am, there isn't much culture; but maybe this is the place to tell you that we've got a lot of pleasures of a kind here: we like the sun comin' up over the mountain in the morning, and we all notice a good deal about the birds. We pay a lot of attention to them, and trees and plants. And we watch the change of the seasons: yes, everybody knows about them. But those other things — you're right, ma'am — there ain't much — *Robinson Crusoe* and the Bible; and Handel's *Largo,* we all know that; and Whistler's *Mother* — those are just about as far as we go.

LADY IN A BOX: So I thought. Thank you, Mr. Webb.

STAGE MANAGER: All right! All right! Thank you, everybody.

[MR. WEBB *retires.*]

We'll go back to the town now. It's middle of the afternoon. All 2,642 have had their dinners and all the dishes have been washed.

There's an early afternoon calm in our town: a buzzin' and a hummin' from the school buildings; only a few buggies on Main Street — the horses dozing at the hitching-posts; you all remember what it's like. Doc Gibbs is in his office, tapping people and making them say " ah." Mr. Webb's cuttin' his lawn over there; one man in ten thinks it's a privilege to push his own lawn mower.

No, sir. It's later than I thought. There are the children coming home from school already.

[EMILY WEBB *comes sedately down Main Street carrying some schoolbooks. There are some signs that she is imagining herself to be a lady of striking elegance. Her father's movements to and fro with the lawn mower bring him into her vicinity.*]

EMILY: I *can't,* Lois. I've got to go home and help my mother. I *promised.*

MR. WEBB: Emily, walk simply. Who do you think you are today?

EMILY: Papa, you're terrible. One minute you tell me to stand up straight and the next minute you call me names. I just don't listen to you. [*She gives him an abrupt kiss.*]

MR. WEBB: Golly, I never got a kiss from such a great lady before.

[*He goes out of sight.* EMILY *leans over and picks some flowers by the gate of her house.* GEORGE GIBBS *comes careening down Main Street. He is throwing a ball up to dizzying heights, and waiting to catch it again. This sometimes requires his taking six steps backward.*]

GEORGE: Excuse me, Mrs. Forrest.

STAGE MANAGER [*as* MRS. FORREST]: Go out and play in the fields, young man. You got no business playing baseball on Main Street.

GEORGE: Awfully sorry, Mrs. Forrest. — Hello, Emily.

EMILY: H'lo.

GEORGE: You made a fine speech in class.

EMILY: Well . . . I was really ready to make a speech about the Monroe Doctrine, but at the last minute Miss Corcoran made me talk about the Louisiana Purchase instead. I worked an awful long time on both of them.

GEORGE: Gee, it's funny, Emily. From my window up there I can just see your head nights when you're doing your homework over in your room.

EMILY: Why, can you?

GEORGE: You certainly do stick to it, Emily. I don't see how you can sit still that long. I guess you like school.

EMILY: Well, I always feel it's something you have to go through.

GEORGE: Yeah.

EMILY: I don't mind it really. It passes the time.

GEORGE: Yeah. — Emily, what do you think? We might work out a kinda telegraph from there to there; and once in a while you could give me a kinda hint or two about one of those algebra problems. I don't mean the answers, Emily, of course not . . . just some little hint. . . .

EMILY: Oh, I think *hints* are allowed. — So-ah — if you get stuck, George, you whistle to me; and I'll give you some hints.

GEORGE: Emily, you're just naturally bright, I guess.

EMILY: I figure that it's just the way a person's born.

GEORGE: Yeah. But, you see, I want to be a farmer, and my Uncle Luke says whenever I'm ready I can come over and work on his farm and if I'm any good I can just gradually have it.

EMILY: You mean the house and everything?

[*Enter* MRS. WEBB.]

GEORGE: Yeah. Well, thanks . . . I better be getting out to the baseball field. Thanks for the talk, Emily. — Good afternoon, Mrs. Webb.

MRS. WEBB: Good afternoon, George.

GEORGE: So-long, Emily.

EMILY: So-long, George.

MRS. WEBB: Emily, come and help me string these beans for the winter. George Gibbs let himself have a real conversation, didn't he? Why, he's growing up. How old would George be?

EMILY: I don't know.

MRS. WEBB: Let's see. He must be almost sixteen.

EMILY: Mama, I made a speech in class today and I was very good.

MRS. WEBB: You must recite it to your father at supper. What was it about?

EMILY: The Louisiana Purchase. It was like silk off a spool. I'm going to make speeches all my life. — Mama, are these big enough?

MRS. WEBB: Try and get them a little bigger if you can.

EMILY: Mama, will you answer me a question, serious?

MRS. WEBB: Seriously, dear — not serious.

EMILY: Seriously, — will you?

MRS. WEBB: Of course, I will.

EMILY: Mama, am I good-looking?

MRS. WEBB: Yes, of course you are. All my children have got good features; I'd be ashamed if they hadn't.

EMILY: Oh, Mama, that's not what I mean. What I mean is: am I *pretty?*

MRS. WEBB: I've already told you, yes. Now that's enough of that. You have a nice young pretty face. I never heard of such foolishness.

EMILY: Oh, Mama, you never tell us the truth about anything.

MRS. WEBB: I *am* telling you the truth.

EMILY: Mama, were *you* pretty?

MRS. WEBB: Yes, I was, if I do say it. I was the prettiest girl in town next to Mamie Cartwright.

EMILY: But, Mama, you've got to say *some*thing about me. Am I pretty enough . . . to get anybody . . . to get people interested in me?

MRS. WEBB: Emily, you make me tired. Now stop it. You're pretty enough for all normal purposes. Come along now and bring that bowl with you.

EMILY: Oh, Mama, you're no help at all.

STAGE MANAGER: Thank you. Thank you! That'll do. We'll have to interrupt again here. Thank you, Mrs. Webb; thank you, Emily.

[MRS. WEBB *and* EMILY *withdraw.*]

There are some more things we've got to explore about this town.

This time we're going to go about it in another way: we're going to look back on it from the future. I'm not going to tell you what became of these two families we're seeing most of, because the rest of the play will tell you about them.

But take some of these others:

Take Joe Crowell, Jr.:

Joe was a very bright fellow. He graduated with honors and got a scholarship to Boston Tech., — M.I.T., that is. But the War broke out and Joe died in France. All that education for nothing.

Howie Newsome's still delivering milk at Grover's Corners. He's an old man now, has a lot of help, but he still delivers it himself. Says he gets the feel of the town that way. Carries all the accounts in his head; never has to write down a word.

Mr. Morgan's drugstore ain't the same, — it's all citified. Mr. Morgan retired and went out to live in San Diego, California, where his daughter married a real estate man, name of Kerby. Mr. Morgan died there in 1935 and was buried in a lot of palm trees. Kinda lost his religion at the end and took up New Thought or something. They read some newfangled poetry over him and cre-mated him. The New Hampshire in him sort of broke down in him in that climate, seems like.

The Cartwrights got richer and richer. The house is closed most of the year. They're off eating big dinners in hotels now, — in Virginia Hot Springs and

Miami Beach. They say the winters are cold here. I see where they've become 'Piscopalians.

The Cartwright interests have just begun building a new bank in Grover's Corners — had to go to Vermont for the marble, sorry to say. And they've asked a friend of mine what they should put in the cornerstone for people to dig up a thousand years from now. Of course, they've put in a copy of the *New York Times* and a copy of Mr. Webb's *Sentinel*. We're kind of interested in this because some scientific fellas have found a way of painting all that reading matter with a kind of glue — silicate glue — that'll make it keep a thousand — two thousand years.

We're putting in a Bible . . . and the Constitution of the United States and a copy of William Shakespeare's plays. What do you say, folks? What do you think?

Y'know — Babylon once had two million people in it, and all we know about 'em is the names of the kings and some copies of wheat contracts and . . . the sales of slaves. Yes, every night all those families sat down to supper, and the father came home from his work, and the smoke went up the chimney, — same as here. And even in Greece and Rome, all we know about the real life of the people is what we can piece together out of the joking poems and the comedies they wrote for the theater back then. So I'm going to have a copy of this play put in the cornerstone and the people a thousand years from now'll know a few simple facts about us — more than the Treaty of Versailles and the Lindbergh flight.

See what I mean?

Well, people a thousand years from now, this is the way we were in the provinces north of New York at the beginning of the twentieth century, — this is the way we were in our growing-up, in our marrying, in our living, and in our dying.

Now we'll return to our day in Grover's Corners.

A lot of time has gone by. It's evening. You can hear choir practice going on in the Congregational Church. All the children are at home doing their school work. The day is running down like a tired clock.

[*A choir partially concealed in the orchestra pit has begun singing " Blessed be the tie that binds."* SIMON STIMSON *stands directing them. Two ladders have been pushed on to the stage; they serve as indication of the second story in the Gibbs and Webb houses.* GEORGE *and* EMILY *mount them, and apply themselves to their school work.* DR. GIBBS *has entered and is seated in his kitchen reading.*]

SIMON STIMSON: Now look here, everybody. Music come into the world to give pleasure. — Softer! Softer! Get it out of your heads that music's only good when it's loud. You leave loudness to the Methodists. You couldn't beat 'em, even if you wanted to. Now again. Tenors!

GEORGE: Hssst! Emily!

EMILY: Hello.

GEORGE: Hello!

EMILY: I can't work at all. The moonlight's so *terrible*.

GEORGE: Emily, did you get the third problem?

EMILY: Which?

GEORGE: The *third*?

EMILY: Why, yes, George — that's the easiest of them all.

GEORGE: I don't see it. Emily, can you give me a hint?

EMILY: I'll tell you one thing: the answer's in yards.

GEORGE: ! ! ! In yards? How do you mean?

EMILY: In *square* yards.

GEORGE: Oh . . . in square yards.

EMILY: Yes, George, don't you see?

GEORGE: Yeah.

EMILY: In square yards of *wallpaper*.

GEORGE: Wallpaper, — oh, I see. Thanks a lot, Emily.

EMILY: You're welcome. My, isn't the moonlight *terrible*? And choir practice going on. — I think if you hold your breath you can hear the train all the way to Contookuck. Hear it?

GEORGE: M-m-m. — What do you know!

EMILY: Well, I guess I better go back and try to work.

GEORGE: Good night, Emily. And thanks.

EMILY: Good night, George.

SIMON STIMSON: Before I forget it: how many of you will be able to come in Tuesday afternoon and sing at Fred Hersey's wedding, — show your hands. That'll be fine; that'll be right nice. We'll do the same music we did for Jane Trowbridge's last month.

— Now we'll do: " Art thou weary; art thou languid? " It's a question, ladies and gentlemen, make it talk. Ready.

DR. GIBBS: Oh, George, can you come down a minute?

GEORGE: Yes, Pa.

[He descends the ladder.]

DR. GIBBS: Make yourself comfortable, George; I'll only keep you a minute. George, how old are you?

GEORGE: I? I'm sixteen, almost seventeen.

DR. GIBBS: What do you want to do after school's over?

GEORGE: Why, you know, Pa, I want to be a farmer on Uncle Luke's farm.

DR. GIBBS: You'll be willing, will you, to get up early and milk and feed the stock . . . and you'll be able to hoe and hay all day?

GEORGE: Sure, I will. What are you . . . what do you mean, Pa?

DR. GIBBS: Well, George, while I was in my office today I heard a funny sound . . . and what do you think it was? It was your mother chopping wood. There you see your mother — getting up early; cooking meals all day long; washing and ironing — and still she has to go out in the back yard and chop wood. I suppose she just got tired of asking you. She just gave up and decided it was easier to do it herself. And you eat her meals, and put on the clothes she keeps nice for you, and you run off and play baseball, — like she's some hired girl we keep around the house but that we don't like very much. Well, I knew all I had to do was call your attention to it. Here's a handkerchief, son. George, I've decided to raise your spending money twenty-five cents a week. Not, of course, for chopping wood for your mother, because that's a present you give her, but because you're getting older — and I imagine there are lots of things you must find to do with it.

GEORGE: Thanks, Pa.

DR. GIBBS: Let's see — tomorrow's pay day. You can count on it. — Hmm. Probably Rebecca'll feel she ought to have some more too. Wonder what could have happened to your mother. Choir practice never was as late as this before.

GEORGE: It's only half-past eight, Pa.

DR. GIBBS: I don't know why she's in that old choir. She hasn't any more voice than an old crow. . . . Traipsin' around the streets at this hour of the night. . . . Just about time you retired, don't you think?

GEORGE: Yes, Pa.

[GEORGE *mounts to his place on the ladder. Laughter and good nights can be heard on stage left and presently* MRS. GIBBS, MRS. SOAMES, *and* MRS. WEBB *come down Main Street. When they arrive at the center of the stage they stop.*]

MRS. SOAMES: Good night, Martha. Good night, Mr. Foster.

MRS. WEBB: I'll tell Mr. Webb; I know he'll want to put it in the paper.

MRS. GIBBS: My, it's late!

MRS. SOAMES: Good night, Irma.

MRS. GIBBS: Real nice choir practice, wa'n't it? Myrtle Webb! Look at that moon, will you! Tsk-tsk-tsk. Potato weather, for sure.

MRS. SOAMES: Naturally I didn't want to say a word about it in front of those others, but now we're alone — really, it's the worst scandal that ever was in this town!

MRS. GIBBS: What?

MRS. SOAMES: Simon Stimson!

MRS. GIBBS: Now, Louella!

MRS. SOAMES: But, Julia! To have the organist of a church drink and drunk year after year. You know he was drunk tonight.

MRS. GIBBS: Now, Louella! We all know about Mr. Stimson, and we all know about the troubles he's been through, and Dr. Ferguson knows too, and if Dr. Ferguson keeps him on there in his job the only thing the rest of us can do is just not to notice it.

MRS. SOAMES: Not to notice it! But it's getting worse.

MRS. WEBB: No, it isn't, Louella. It's getting better. I've been in that choir twice as long as you have. It doesn't happen anywhere near so often. . . . My, I hate to go to bed on a night like this. — I better hurry. Those children'll be sitting up till all hours. Good night, Louella.

[*She hurries down stage, enters her house and disappears.*]

MRS. GIBBS: Can you get home safe, Louella?

MRS. SOAMES: It's as bright as day. I can see Mr. Soames scowling at the window now. You'd think we'd been to a dance the way the menfolk carry on.

[*Repeated good nights.* MRS. GIBBS *arrives at her home.*]

MRS. GIBBS: Well, we had a real good time.

DR. GIBBS: You're late enough.

MRS. GIBBS: Why, Frank, it ain't any later'n usual.

DR. GIBBS: And you stopping at the corner to gossip with a lot of hens.

MRS. GIBBS: Now, Frank, don't be grouchy. Come out and smell my heliotrope in the moonlight. [*They stroll out arm in arm along the footlights.*] Isn't that wonderful? What did you do all the time I was away?

DR. GIBBS: Oh, I read — as usual. What were the girls gossiping about tonight?

MRS. GIBBS: Well, believe me, Frank — there is something to gossip about.

DR. GIBBS: Hmm! Simon Stimson far gone, was he?

MRS. GIBBS: Worst I've ever seen him. How'll that end, Frank? Dr. Ferguson can't forgive him forever.

DR. GIBBS: I guess I know more about Simon Stimson's affairs than anybody in this town. Some people ain't made for small town life. I don't know how that'll end; but there's nothing we can do but just leave it alone. Come, get in.

MRS. GIBBS: No, not yet. . . . Oh, Frank, I'm worried about you.

DR. GIBBS: What are you worried about?

MRS. GIBBS: I think it's my duty to make plans for you to get a real rest and change. And if I get that legacy, well, I'm going to insist on it.

DR. GIBBS: Now, Julia, there's no sense in going over that again.

MRS. GIBBS: Frank, you're just *unreasonable!*

DR. GIBBS: Come on, Julia, it's getting late. First thing you know you'll catch cold. I gave George a piece of my mind tonight. I reckon you'll have your wood chopped for a while anyway. No, no, start getting upstairs.

MRS. GIBBS: Oh, dear. There's always so many things to pick up, seems like. You know, Frank, Mrs. Fairchild always locks her front door every night. All those people up that part of town do.

DR. GIBBS: They're all getting citified, that's the trouble with them. They haven't got nothing fit to burgle and everybody knows it.

[*They disappear.* REBECCA *climbs up the ladder beside* GEORGE.]

GEORGE: Get out, Rebecca. There's only room for one at this window. You're always spoiling everything.

REBECCA: Well, let me look just a minute.

GEORGE: Use your own window.

REBECCA: I did; but there's no moon there. . . . George, do you know what I think, do you? I think maybe the moon's getting nearer and nearer and there'll be a big 'splosion.

GEORGE: Rebecca, you don't know anything. If the moon were getting nearer, the guys that sit up all night with telescopes would see it first and they'd tell about it, and it'd be in all the newspapers.

REBECCA: George, is the moon shining on South America, Canada and half the whole world?

GEORGE: Well — prob'ly is.

[*The* STAGE MANAGER *strolls on.*]

STAGE MANAGER: Nine-thirty. Most of the lights are out. No, there's Constable Warren trying a few doors on Main Street. And here comes Editor Webb, after putting his newspaper to bed.

MR. WEBB: Good evening, Bill.

CONSTABLE WARREN: Evenin', Mr. Webb.

MR. WEBB: Quite a moon!

CONSTABLE WARREN: Yepp.

MR. WEBB: All quiet tonight?

CONSTABLE WARREN: Simon Stimson is rollin' around a little. Just saw his wife movin' out to hunt for him so I looked the other way — there he is now.

[SIMON STIMSON *comes down Main Street from the left, only a trace of unsteadiness in his walk.*]

MR. WEBB: Good evening, Simon. . . . Town seems to have settled down for the night pretty well. . . .

[SIMON STIMSON *comes up to him and pauses a moment.*]

Good evening. . . . Yes, most of the town's settled down for the night, Simon. . . . I guess we better do the same. Can I walk along a ways with you?

[SIMON STIMSON *continues on his way without a word and disappears at the right.*]

Good night.

CONSTABLE WARREN: Good night, Mr. Webb.

MR. WEBB: Well, he's seen a peck of trouble, one thing after another. . . . Oh, Bill . . . if you see my boy smoking cigarettes, just give him a word, will you? He thinks a lot of you, Bill.

CONSTABLE WARREN: I don't think he smokes no cigarettes, Mr. Webb. Leastways, not more'n two or three a year. He don't belong to that crowd that hangs out down by the gully.

MR. WEBB: Hm. . . . I hope not. — Well, good night, Bill.

CONSTABLE WARREN: Good night, Mr. Webb.

[*Exit.*]

MR. WEBB: Who's that up there? Is that you, Myrtle?

EMILY: No, it's me, Papa.

MR. WEBB: Why aren't you in bed?

EMILY: I don't know. I just can't sleep yet, Papa. The moonlight's so *wonderful*. And the smell of Mrs. Gibbs's heliotrope. Can you smell it?

MR. WEBB: Hm. . . . Yes. Haven't any troubles on your mind, have you, Emily?

EMILY: *Troubles,* Papa? *No.*

MR. WEBB: Well, enjoy yourself, but don't let your mother catch you. Good night, Emily.

EMILY: Good night, Papa.

[MR. WEBB *crosses into the house, whistling " Blessed be the tie that binds" and disappears.*]

REBECCA: I never told you about that letter Jane Crofut got from her minister when she was sick. The minister of her church in the town she was in before she came here. He wrote Jane a letter and on the envelope the address was like this: it said: Jane Crofut; The Crofut Farm; Grover's Corners; Sutton County; New Hampshire; United States of America.

GEORGE: What's funny about that?

REBECCA: But listen, it's not finished: the United States of America; Continent of North America; Western Hemisphere; the Earth; the Solar System; the Universe; the Mind of God, — that's what it said on the envelope.

GEORGE: What do you know!

REBECCA: And the postman brought it just the same.

GEORGE: What do you know!

STAGE MANAGER: That's the end of the First Act, friends. You can go and smoke now, those that smoke.

ACT 2

The tables and chairs of the two kitchens are still on the stage. The ladders have been withdrawn. The STAGE MANAGER *has been at his accustomed place watching the audience return to its seats.*

STAGE MANAGER: Three years have gone by.

Yes, the sun's come up over a thousand times.

Summers and winters have cracked the mountains a little bit more and the rains have brought down some of the dirt.

Some babies that weren't even born before have begun talking regular sentences already; and a number of people who thought they were right young and spry have noticed that they can't bound up a flight of stairs like they used to, without their heart fluttering a little.

Some older sons are sitting at the head of the table, and some people I know are having their meat cut up for them. —

All that can happen in a thousand days.

Nature's been pushing and contriving in other ways, too: a number of young people fell in love and got married.

Yes, the mountain got bit away a few fractions of an inch; millions of gallons of water went by the mill; and here and there a new home was set up under a roof.

Almost everybody in the world gets married, — you know what I mean? In our town there aren't hardly any exceptions. Most everybody in the world climbs into their graves married.

The First Act was called the Daily Life. This act is called Love and Marriage. There's another act coming after this: I reckon you can guess what that's about.

So:

It's three years later. It's 1904.

It's July 7th, just after High School Commencement. That's the time most of our young people jump up and get married. Soon as they've passed their last examinations in solid geometry and Cicero's Orations, looks like they suddenly feel themselves fit to be married.

It's early morning. Only this time it's been raining. It's been pouring and thundering.

Mrs. Gibbs's garden, and Mrs. Webb's here: drenched.

All those bean poles and pea vines: drenched.

All yesterday over there on Main Street, the rain looked like curtains being blown along.

Hm . . . it may begin again any minute.

There! You can hear the 5:45 for Boston.

And here comes Howie Newsome delivering the milk.

And there's Si Crowell delivering the papers like his brother before him. — You remember about his brother? — all that education he's going to get and that'll be wasted.

And there's Mrs. Gibbs and Mrs. Webb come down to make breakfast, just as though it were an ordinary day.

I don't have to point out to the women in my audience that those ladies they see before them, both those ladies cooked three meals a day, — one of 'em for twenty years, the other for forty, — and no summer vacation. They brought up two children apiece; washed; cleaned the house, — and never a nervous breakdown. Never thought themselves hard-used, either.

It's like what one of those Middle West poets said: You've got to love life to have life, and you've got to have life to love life. . . . It's what they call a vicious circle.

[SI CROWELL *has entered hurling imaginary newspapers into doorways;* HOWIE NEWSOME *has come along Main Street with Bessie.*]

HOWIE NEWSOME: Git-ap, Bessie.

SI CROWELL: Morning, Howie.

HOWIE NEWSOME: Morning, Si. — Anything in the papers I ought to know?

SI CROWELL: Nothing much, except we're losing about the best baseball pitcher Grover's Corners ever had.

HOWIE NEWSOME: Reckon he was. He's been standing off the whole of south New Hampshire single-handed, looks like.

SI CROWELL: He could hit and run bases, too.

HOWIE NEWSOME: Yep. Mighty fine ball player. — Bessie! I guess I can stop and talk if I've a mind to!

SI CROWELL: I don't see how he could give up a thing like that just to get married. Would you, Howie?

HOWIE NEWSOME: Can't tell, Si. Never had no talent that way.

[CONSTABLE WARREN *enters. They exchange mornings.*]

You're up early, Bill.

CONSTABLE WARREN: Seein' if there's anything I can do to prevent a flood. River's been risin' all night.

HOWIE NEWSOME: Si Crowell's all worked up here about George Gibbs' retiring from baseball.

CONSTABLE WARREN: Yes, sir; that's the way it goes. Back in '84 we had a player, Si, — even George Gibbs couldn't touch him. Name of Hank Todd. Went down to Maine and become a parson. Wonderful ball player. — Howie, how did the weather look to you?

HOWIE NEWSOME: No, 'tain't bad. Think maybe it'll clear up for good.

[CONSTABLE WARREN *and* SI CROWELL *continue on their way.* HOWIE NEWSOME *brings the milk first to* MRS. GIBBS's *house. She meets him by the trellis.*]

MRS. GIBBS: Good morning, Howie. Do you think it's going to rain again?

HOWIE NEWSOME: Morning, Mrs. Gibbs. It rained so heavy, I think maybe it'll clear up.

MRS. GIBBS: Certainly hope it will.

HOWIE NEWSOME: How much did you want today?

MRS. GIBBS: I guess I'll need three-a-milk and two-a-cream, Howie. I'm going to have a house full of relations.

HOWIE NEWSOME: My wife says to tell you we both hope they'll be very happy, Mrs. Gibbs. Know they *will*.

MRS. GIBBS: Thanks a lot, Howie. Tell your wife I hope she gits there to the wedding.

HOWIE NEWSOME: Yes, she'll be there; she'll be there if she kin.

[HOWIE NEWSOME *crosses to* MRS. WEBB's *house.*]

Morning, Mrs. Webb.

MRS. WEBB: Oh, good morning, Mr. Newsome. I told you four quarts of milk, but I hope you can spare me another.

HOWIE NEWSOME: Yes'm . . . and the two of cream.

MRS. WEBB: Will it rain all day, Mr. Newsome?

HOWIE NEWSOME: No'm. Just sayin' to Mrs. Gibbs as how it may lighten up. Mrs. Newsome told me to tell you as how we hope they'll both be very happy, Mrs. Webb. Know they *will*.

MRS. WEBB: Thank you, and thank Mrs. Newsome and we hope to see you all at the wedding.

HOWIE NEWSOME: Yes, Mrs. Webb. We hope to git there. Couldn't miss that. Chck! Bessie!

[*Exit* HOWIE NEWSOME. DR. GIBBS *descends in shirt sleeves, and sits down at his breakfast table.*]

DR. GIBBS: Well, Ma, the day has come. You're losin' one of your chicks.

MRS. GIBBS: Frank Gibbs, don't you say another word. I feel like crying every minute. Sit down and drink your coffee.

DR. GIBBS: The groom's up shaving himself. Whistling and singing, like he's glad to leave us. — Every now and then he says "I do" to the mirror, but it don't sound convincing to me.

MRS. GIBBS: I declare I don't know how he'll get along. I've arranged his clothes and seen to it he's put warm things on. — Frank! they're too young. Emily won't think of such things. He'll catch his death of cold within a week. — Here's something I made for you.

DR. GIBBS: Why, Julia Hersey! French toast!

MRS. GIBBS: 'Tain't hard to make, and I had to do something.

DR. GIBBS: I remember my wedding morning, Julia.

MRS. GIBBS: Now don't start that, Frank Gibbs. I tell you I can't stand it.

DR. GIBBS: I was the scardest young fella in the State of New Hampshire. I thought I'd made a mistake for sure. And when I saw you comin' down that aisle I thought you were the prettiest girl I'd ever seen, but the only trouble was that I'd never seen you before. There I was in the Congregational Church marryin' a total stranger.

MRS. GIBBS: And how do you think I felt! — Did you hear Rebecca stirring about upstairs?

DR. GIBBS: Only morning in the year she hasn't been managing everybody's business. She's shut up in her room. I got the impression that maybe she's crying.

MRS. GIBBS: Good Lord! This has got to stop. — Rebecca! Rebecca! Everything's getting cold down here.

[GEORGE *comes rattling down the stairs, very brisk.*]

GEORGE: Good morning, everybody. Only five more hours to live. [*Makes the gesture of cutting his throat.*]

MRS. GIBBS: Where are you going?

GEORGE: Just stepping across the grass to see my girl.

MRS. GIBBS: Now, George! You take an umbrella or I won't let you out of this house.

GEORGE: Aw, Ma. It's just a *step!*

MRS. GIBBS: From tomorrow on you can kill yourself in all weathers, but while you're in my house you live wisely, thank you. There are your overshoes right there in the hall. And here's an umbrella.

GEORGE: Aw, Ma!

DR. GIBBS: George, do as your mother tells you.

MRS. GIBBS: Maybe Mrs. Webb isn't used to callers at seven in the morning. Take a cup-a coffee first.

GEORGE: Be back in a minute.

[*He crosses the stage, leaping over the puddles.*]

Good morning, Mother Webb.

MRS. WEBB: Goodness! You frightened me! — Now, George, you can come in a minute out of the wet, but you know I can't ask you in.

GEORGE: Why not — ?

MRS. WEBB: George, you know's well as I do: the groom can't see his bride on his wedding day, not until he sees her in church.

GEORGE: Aw! — that's just a superstition.

[*Enter* MR. WEBB.]

MR. WEBB: Good morning, George.

GEORGE: Mr. Webb, you don't believe in that superstition, do you?

MR. WEBB: There's a lot of common sense in some superstitions, George.

MRS. WEBB: Millions have folla'd it, George, and you don't want to be the first to fly in the face of custom.

GEORGE: How is Emily?

MRS. WEBB: She hasn't waked up yet. I haven't heard a sound out of her.

GEORGE: Emily's *asleep!!!*

MRS. WEBB: No wonder! We were up 'til all hours, — sewing and packing. I'll tell you what I'll do; you set down here a minute with Mr. Webb and drink this cup of coffee; and I'll go upstairs and see she doesn't come down and surprise you. There's some bacon, too; but don't be long about it.

[*Exit* MRS. WEBB. *Embarrassed silence.*]

MR. WEBB: Well, George, how are you?

GEORGE: Oh, fine. I'm fine. [*Pause.*] Mr. Webb, what sense could there be in a superstition like that?

MR. WEBB: Well, you see, — on her wedding morning a girl's head's apt to be full of . . . clothes and things like that. Don't you think that's probably it?

GEORGE: Ye-e-s. I never thought of that.

MR. WEBB: A girl's apt to be a mite nervous on her wedding day.

[*Pause.*]

GEORGE: I wish a fellow could get married without all that marching up and down.

MR. WEBB: Well, every man that's ever lived has felt that way about it, George; but it hasn't done much good. It's the women that have built up weddings, my boy. From now on they have it pretty much as they like. . . . All those good women standing shoulder to shoulder making sure that the knot's tied in a mighty public way.

GEORGE: But . . . you *believe* in it, don't you, Mr. Webb?

MR. WEBB: Oh, yes; oh, yes. Don't you misunderstand me, my boy. Marriage is a wonderful thing, — wonderful thing. And don't you forget that, George.

GEORGE: No, sir. — Mr. Webb, how old were you when you got married?

MR. WEBB: Well, you see: I'd been to college and I'd taken a little time to get settled. But Mrs. Webb, — she wasn't much older than what Emily is. Oh, age hasn't much to do with it, George, — not compared to other things.

GEORGE: What were you going to say, Mr. Webb?

MR. WEBB: Oh, I don't know, — was I going to say something? [*Pause.*] George, I was thinking the other night of some advice my father gave me when I got married. Charles, he said, Charles, start out early showing who's boss, he said. Best thing to do is to give an order, even if it don't make sense; just so she'll learn to obey. And he said: if anything about your wife irritates you, — her conversation, or anything, — just get up and leave the house. That'll make it clear to her, he said. And, oh, yes! he said: never, *never* let your wife know how much money you have, never.

GEORGE: Well, Mr. Webb . . . I don't think I could. . . .

MR. WEBB: So I took the opposite of my father's advice and I've been happy ever since. And let that be a lesson to you, George, never to ask advice on personal matters. — George, are you going to raise chickens on your farm?

GEORGE: What?

MR. WEBB: Are you going to raise chickens on your farm?

GEORGE: Uncle Luke's never been much interested, but I thought —

MR. WEBB: A book came into my office the other day, George, on the Philo System of raising chickens. I want you to read it. I'm thinking of beginning in a small way in the back yard, and I'm going to put an incubator in the cellar —

[*Enter* MRS. WEBB.]

MRS. WEBB: Charles, are you talking about that old incubator again? I thought you two'd be talking about things worth while.

MR. WEBB: Well, Myrtle, if you want to give the boy some good advice, I'll go upstairs and leave you alone with him.

MRS. WEBB: Now, George, I'm sorry, but I've got to send you away so that Emily can come down and get some breakfast. She told me to tell you that she sends you her love but that she doesn't want to lay eyes on you. So good-by, George.

[GEORGE *crosses the stage to his own home and disappears.*]

MR. WEBB: Myrtle, I guess you don't know about that older superstition.

MRS. WEBB: What do you mean, Charles?

MR. WEBB: Since the cave-men: the groom shouldn't be left alone with his father-in-law on the day of the wedding, or near it. Now don't forget that!

STAGE MANAGER: Thank you. Thank you, everybody.

Now I have to interrupt again here. You see, we want to know how all this began, — this wedding, this plan to spend a lifetime together. I'm awfully interested in how big things like that begin.

You know how it is: you're twenty-one or twenty-two and you make some decisions; then whisss! you're seventy; you've been a lawyer for fifty years, and that white-haired lady at your side has eaten over fifty thousand meals with you.

How do such things begin?

George and Emily are going to show you now the conversation they had when they first knew that . . . that . . . as the saying goes . . . they were meant for one another. But before they do it I want you to try and remember what it was like when you were young, when you were fifteen or sixteen. For some reason it is very hard to do: those days when even the little things in life could be almost too exciting to bear.

And particularly the days when you were first in love; when you were like a person sleep-walking, and you didn't quite see the streets you were in, and didn't quite hear everything that was said to you. You're just a little bit crazy. Will you remember that, please?

Now they'll be coming out of High School at three o'clock. George has just been elected President of the Junior Class, and as it's June, that means he'll be President of the Senior Class all next year. And Emily's just been elected Secretary and Treasurer. I don't have to tell you how important that is.

[*He places a board across the backs of two chairs, parallel to the footlights, and places two high stools behind it. This is the counter of* MR. MORGAN's *drugstore.*]

All ready!

[EMILY, *carrying an armful of —imaginary— schoolbooks, comes along Main Street from the left.*]

EMILY: I can't, Louise. I've got to go home. Good-by.

Oh, Earnestine! Earnestine! Can you come over tonight and do algebra? I did the first and third in Study Hall. No, they're not hard. But, Earnestine, that Caesar's awful hard. I don't see why we have to do a thing like that.

Come over about seven. Tell your mother you *have* to. G'by.

G'by, Helen. G'by, Fred.

[GEORGE, *also carrying books, catches up with her.*]

GEORGE: Can I carry your books home for you, Emily?

EMILY [*coldly*]: Thank you. [*She gives them to him.*]

GEORGE: Excuse me a minute, Emily. — Say, Bob, get everything ready. I'll be there in a quarter of an hour. If I'm a little late start practice anyway. And give Herb some long high ones. His eye needs a lot of practice. Seeya later.

EMILY: Good-by, Lizzy.

GEORGE: Good-by, Lizzy. — I'm awfully glad you were elected, too, Emily.

EMILY: Thank you.

[*They have been standing on Main Street, almost against the back wall.* GEORGE *is about to take the first steps towards the audience when he stops again and says:*]

GEORGE: Emily, why are you mad at me?

EMILY: I'm not mad at you.

GEORGE: You . . . you treat me so funny.

EMILY: Well, I might as well say it right out, George. I don't like the whole change that's come over you in the last year. I'm sorry if that hurts your feelings, but I've just got to tell the truth and shame the devil.

GEORGE: I'm awfully sorry, Emily. Wha-a-what do you mean?

EMILY: Well, up to a year ago I used to like you a lot. And I used to watch you as you did everything . . . because we'd been friends so long . . . and then you began spending all your time at baseball . . . and you never even spoke to anybody any more; not even to your own family you didn't . . . and, George, it's a fact, you've got awful conceited and stuck-up, and all the girls say so. They may not say so to your face, but that's what they say about you behind your back, and it hurts me to hear them say it, but I've got to agree with them a little. I'm sorry if it hurts your feelings . . . but I can't be sorry I said it.

GEORGE: I . . . I'm glad you said it, Emily. I never thought that such a thing was happening to me. I guess it's hard for a fella not to have faults creep into his character.

[*They take a step or two in silence, then stand still in misery.*]

EMILY: I always expect a man to be perfect and I think he should be.

GEORGE: Oh . . . I don't think it's possible to be perfect, Emily.

EMILY: Well, my father is, and as far as I can see your father is. There's no reason on earth why you shouldn't be, too.

GEORGE: Well, Emily . . . I feel it's the other way round. That men aren't naturally good; but girls are. Like you and your mother and my mother.

EMILY: Well, you might as well know right now that I'm not perfect. It's not as easy for a girl to be perfect as a man, because we girls are more nervous. — Now I'm sorry I said all that about you. I don't know what made me say it.

GEORGE: No, no, — I guess if it's the truth you ought to say it. You stick to it, Emily.

EMILY: I don't know if it's the truth or not. And I suddenly feel that it isn't important at all.

GEORGE: Emily, would you like an ice-cream soda, or something, before you go home?

EMILY: Well, thank you. . . . I would.

[*They come into the drugstore and seat themselves on the stools.*]

STAGE MANAGER [*as* MR. MORGAN]: Hello, George. Hello, Emily. What'll you have? Why, Emily Webb, what've you been crying about?

GEORGE [*He gropes for an explanation.*]: She . . . she just got an awful scare, Mr. Morgan. She almost got run over by that hardware store wagon. Everybody always says that Tom Huckins drives like a crazy man.

STAGE MANAGER: Here, take a drink of water, Emily. You look all shook up. There! — Now, what'll you have?

EMILY: I'll have a strawberry phosphate, thank you, Mr. Morgan.

GEORGE: No, no. You go and have an ice-cream soda with me, Emily. — Two strawberry ice-cream sodas, Mr. Morgan.

STAGE MANAGER [*working the faucets*]: Yes, sir. I tell you, you've got to look both ways before you cross Main Street these days. Gets worse every year.

There are a hundred and twenty-five horses in Grover's Corners this minute
I'm talking to you. State Inspector was in here yesterday. And now they're
bringing in these auto-mo-biles, the best thing to do is to just stay home.
Why, I can remember the time when a dog could lie down all day in the
middle of Main Street and nothing would come to disturb him. — Yes, Miss
Ellis; be with you in a minute. Here are your sodas. Enjoy 'em.

[*He goes off.*]

EMILY: They're so expensive.

GEORGE: No, no, — don't you think of that. We're celebrating. First, we're celebrating our election. And then do you know what else I'm celebrating?

EMILY: No.

GEORGE: I'm celebrating because I've got a friend who tells me all the things
that ought to be told me.

EMILY: George, *please* don't think of that. I don't know why I said it. It's not
true. You're —

GEORGE: No, you stick to it, Emily. I'm glad you spoke to me like you did. But
you'll see: I'm going to change so quick — you bet I'm going to change.
And, Emily, I want to ask you a favor.

EMILY: What?

GEORGE: Emily, if I go away to State Agriculture College next year, will you
write me a letter once in a while?

EMILY: I certainly will. I certainly will, George. . . . [*Pause.*] It certainly seems
like being away three years you'd get out of touch with things.

GEORGE: No, no. I mustn't do that. You see I'm not only going to be just a
farmer. After a while maybe I'll run for something to get elected. So your
letters'll be very important to me; you know, telling me what's going on
here and everything. . . .

EMILY: Just the same, three years is a long time. Maybe letters from Grover's
Corners wouldn't be so interesting after a while. Grover's Corners isn't a
very important place when you think of all New Hampshire; but I think it's
a very nice town.

GEORGE: The day wouldn't come when I wouldn't want to know everything
that's happening here. I know *that's* true, Emily.

EMILY: Well, I'll try to make my letters interesting.

[*Pause.*]

GEORGE: Y'know, Emily, whenever I meet a farmer I ask him if he thinks it's
important to go to Agriculture School to be a good farmer.

EMILY: Why, George —

GEORGE: Yeah, and some of them say that it's even a waste of time. You can
get all those things, anyway, out of the pamphlets the government sends out.
And Uncle Luke's getting old, — he's about ready for me to start in taking
over his farm tomorrow, if I could.

EMILY: My!

GEORGE: And, like you say, being gone all that time . . . in other places and meeting other people . . . if anything like that can happen I don't want to go away. I guess new people aren't any better than old ones. I'll bet they almost never are. Emily, . . . I feel that you're as good a friend as I've got. I don't need to go and meet the people in other towns.

EMILY: But, George, maybe it's very important for you to go and learn all that about cattle-judging and soils and those things. And if you're going into politics, maybe you ought to meet people from other parts of the State . . . of course, I don't know.

GEORGE [after a pause]: Emily, I'm going to make up my mind right now. I won't go. I'll tell Pa about it tonight.

EMILY: Why, George, I don't see why you have to decide right now. It's a whole year away.

GEORGE: Emily, I'm glad you spoke to me about that . . . that fault in my character. And what you said was right; but there was *one* thing wrong in it, and that was when you said that for a year I wasn't noticing people, and . . . you, for instance. Listen, Emily . . . you say you were watching me when I did everything. . . . Why, I was doing the same about you all the time. Why, sure, — I always thought about you as one of the chief people I thought about. I always made sure where you were sitting on the bleachers, and who you were with. And we've always had lots of talks . . . and joking, in the halls; and they always meant a lot to me. Of course, they weren't as good as the talk we're having now. Lately I'd been noticing that you'd been acting kind of funny to me, and for three days I've been trying to walk home with you, but something's always got in the way. Yesterday I was standing over against the wall waiting for you, and you walked home with Miss Corcoran.

EMILY: George! . . . Life's awful funny! How could I have known that? Why, I thought —

GEORGE: Listen, Emily, I'm going to tell you why I'm not going to Agriculture School. I think that once you've found a person that you're very fond of . . . I mean a person who's fond of you, too, — at least enough to be interested in your character . . . well, I think that's just as important as college is, and even more so. That's what I think.

EMILY: I think it's awfully important, too.

GEORGE: Emily.

EMILY: Yes, George.

GEORGE: Emily, if I improve and make a big change . . . would you be . . . I mean: *could* you be . . .

EMILY: I . . . I am now; I always have been.

GEORGE [pause]: So I guess this is an important talk we've been having.

EMILY: Yes.

GEORGE [takes a deep breath and straightens his back]: Wait just a minute and I'll take you home.

[He rises and goes to the STAGE MANAGER who appears and comes toward him.]

Mr. Morgan, I'll have to go home and get the money to pay you for this. It'll only take me a minute.

STAGE MANAGER: What's that? George Gibbs, do you mean to tell me — !

GEORGE: Yes, but I had reasons, Mr. Morgan. — Look, here's my gold watch to keep until I come back with the money.

STAGE MANAGER: That's all right. Keep your watch. I'll trust you.

GEORGE: I'll be back in five minutes.

STAGE MANAGER: I'll trust you ten years, George, — not a day more. — Got all over your shock, Emily?

EMILY: Yes, thank you, Mr. Morgan. It was nothing.

GEORGE [*taking up the books from the counter*]: I'm ready.

[*They walk in grave silence down the stage, turn, and pass through the trellis at the Webbs' back door and disappear.*]

STAGE MANAGER: Thank you, Emily. Thank you, George.

Now before we go on to the wedding, there are still some more things we ought to know about this — about this marriage.

I want to know some more about how the parents took it; but what I want to know most of all is: oh, you know what I mean, — what Grover's Corners thought about marriage anyway.

You know's well as I do: people are never able to say right out what they think of money, or death, or fame, or marriage. You've got to catch it between the lines; you've got to *over*-hear it.

Oh, Doctor! Mrs. Gibbs!

[*They appear at their side of the stage and exchange a glance of understanding with him. The* STAGE MANAGER *lays the same plank across two chairs that served as a drugstore counter and it has now become* MRS. GIBBS's *ironing board.* DR. GIBBS *sits down in a rocker and smokes.* MRS. GIBBS *irons a moment in silence; then goes to the foot of the stairs and calls:*]

MRS. GIBBS: Rebecca! It's time you turned out your light and went to sleep. George, you'd better get some sleep, too.

REBECCA's VOICE: Ma, I haven't finished my English.

MRS. GIBBS: What? Well, I bet you haven't been working, Rebecca. You've been reading that Sears, Roebuck catalogue, that's what you've been doing. — All right, I'll give you ten more minutes. If you haven't finished by then you'll just have to fail the course and be a disgrace to your father and me. — George, what are you doing?

GEORGE's VOICE [*hurt*]: I'm doing history.

MRS. GIBBS: Well, you'd better go to bed. You're probably sleeping at the desk as it is.

[*She casts an amused eye at her husband and returns to her ironing.*]

DR. GIBBS: I had a long talk with the boy today.

MRS. GIBBS: Did you?

DR. GIBBS: I tell you, Mrs. G., there's nothing so terrifying in the world as a son.

The relation of a father to a son is the damnedest, awkwardest — . I always come away feeling like a soggy sponge of hypocrisy.

MRS. GIBBS: Well, a mother and a daughter's no picnic, let me tell you.

DR. GIBBS: George is set on it: he wants to marry Emily soon as school's out and take her right on to the farm. [*Pause.*] He says he can sit up nights and learn agriculture from government pamphlets, without going to college for it.

MRS. GIBBS: He always was crazy about farming. Gets that from my people.

DR. GIBBS: At a pinch, I guess he could start in farming; — but I swear I think he's too young to get married. Julia, he's just a green half-grown kid. He isn't ready to be a family man.

MRS. GIBBS: No, he ain't. You're right. — But he's a good boy and I wouldn't like to think of him being alone out there . . . coming into town Satiddy nights, like any old farm hand, tuckered out from work and looking for excitement. He might get into bad ways. It wouldn't be enough fun for him to come and sit by our stove, — and holding hands with Emily for a year mightn't be enough either. He might lose interest in her.

DR. GIBBS: Hm.

MRS. GIBBS: Frank, I been watching her. George is a lucky boy when you think of all the silly girls in the world.

DR. GIBBS: But, Julia, — George *married*. That great gangling selfish nincumpoop.

MRS. GIBBS: Yes, I know. [*She takes up a collar and examines it.*] Frank, what do you do to your collars? Do you gnaw 'em? I never saw such a man for collars.

DR. GIBBS: Julia, when I married you, do you know what one of my terrors was in getting married?

MRS. GIBBS: Pshaw! Go on with you!

DR. GIBBS: I was afraid we weren't going to have material for conversation more'n 'ld last us a few weeks. I was afraid we'd run out and eat our meals in silence, that's a fact. You and I've been conversing for twenty years now without any noticeable barren spells.

MRS. GIBBS: Well, good weather, bad weather, 'tain't very choice, but I always manage to find something to say.

[*Pause.*]

DR. GIBBS: What do you think? What do you think, Julia? Shall we tell the boy he can go ahead and get married?

MRS. GIBBS: Seems like it's up to us to decide. Myrtle and Charles Webb are willing. They think it's a good idea to throw the young people into the sea and let'm sink or swim, as soon as they're ready.

DR. GIBBS: What does that mean? Must we decide right now? This minute?

MRS. GIBBS: There you go putting the responsibility on me!

DR. GIBBS: Here it is, almost April. — I'll go up and say a word to him right now before he goes to bed. [*He rises.*] You're sure, Julia? You've nothing more to add?

MRS. GIBBS [*stops ironing a moment*]: I don't know what to say. Seems like it's too much to ask, for a big outdoor boy like that to go and get shut up in classrooms for three years. And once he's on the farm, he might just as well have a companion, seeing he's found a fine girl like Emily. . . . People are meant to live two-by-two in this world. . . . Yes, Frank, go up and tell him it's all right.

[DR. GIBBS *crosses and is about to call when —*]

MRS. GIBBS [*her hands on her cheeks, staring into the audience, in sharp alarm*]: Wait a minute! Wait a minute! — [*Then resuming her ironing.*] No, — go and tell him.

DR. GIBBS: Why did you stop then, Julia?

MRS. GIBBS: Oh, you know: I thought of all those times we went through in the first years when George and Rebecca were babies, — you walking up and down with them at three in the morning; the whooping-cough; the time George fell off the porch. You and I were twenty-five years old, and more. It's wonderful how one forgets one's troubles, like that. — Yes, Frank, go upstairs and tell him. . . . It's worth it.

DR. GIBBS: Yes, they'll have a lot of troubles, but that's none of our business. Let'm. Everybody has a right to his own troubles. — You ought to be present, Julia, — important occasion like that. I'll call him. — George! Oh, George!

GEORGE'S VOICE: Yes, Pa.

DR. GIBBS: Can you come down a minute? Your mother and I want to speak to you.

GEORGE: Yeah, sure.

MRS. GIBBS [*putting her arm through her husband's*]: Lord, what a fool I am: I'm trembling all over. There's nothing to tremble about.

STAGE MANAGER: Thank you! Thank you!

Now we're ready to go on with the wedding.

[*While he talks, the actors remove the chair and tables and trellises from the Gibbs and Webb homes. They arrange the pews for the church in the back of the stage. The congregation will sit facing the back wall. The aisle of the church is in the middle of the scene. A small platform is placed against the back wall on which the* STAGE MANAGER *as minister can stand.*]

There are a lot of things to be said about a wedding; there are a lot of thoughts that go on during a wedding.

We can't get them all into one wedding, naturally, and especially not into a wedding at Grover's Corners where they're awfully plain and short.

In this wedding I play the minister. That gives me the right to say a few more things about it.

For a while now, the play gets pretty serious.

Y'see, some churches say that marriage is a sacrament. I don't quite know what it means, but I can guess. Like Mrs. Gibbs said a few minutes ago:

People were made to live two-by-two.

This is a good wedding, but people are so put together that even at a good wedding there's a lot of confusion way down deep in people's minds and we thought that that ought to be in our play, too.

The real hero of this scene isn't on the stage at all, and you know who that is. It's like what one of those European fellas said: every child born into the world is nature's attempt to make a perfect human being. Well, we've seen nature pushing and contriving for some time now. We all know that nature's interested in quantity; but I think she's interested in quality, too, — that's why I'm in the ministry. — Maybe she's trying to make another good governor for New Hampshire.

And don't forget the other witnesses at this wedding, — the ancestors. Millions of them. Most of them set out to live two-by-two, also. Millions of them.

Well, that's all my sermon. 'Twan't very long, anyway.

[*The organ starts playing Handel's* Largo. *The congregation streams into the church and sits in silence.* MRS. WEBB, *on the way to her place, turns back and speaks to the audience.*]

MRS. WEBB: I don't know why on earth I should be crying. I suppose there's nothing to cry about. It came over me at breakfast this morning; there was Emily eating her breakfast as she's done for seventeen years and now she's going off to eat it in someone else's house. I suppose that's it.

And Emily! She suddenly said: I can't eat another mouthful, and she put her head down on the table and *she* cried.

[*She starts toward her seat in the church, but turns back and adds:*]

Oh, I've got to say it: you know, there's something downright cruel about sending our girls out into marriage this way.

I hope some of her girl friends have told her a thing or two. It's cruel, I know, but I couldn't bring myself to say anything. I went into it blind as a bat myself.

The whole world's wrong, that's what's the matter.

There they come.

[*She hurries to her place in the pew.* GEORGE *starts to come down the right aisle of the theater, through the audience. Suddenly three members of his baseball team appear by the right proscenium pillar and start whistling and catcalling to him. They are dressed for the ball field.*]

THE BASEBALL PLAYERS: Eh, George, George! Hsst — yaow! If things don't go right, call us in. We know what to do. Eh, fellas! Yaow! George, don't look so innocent, you old geezer. We know what you're thinking. Don't disgrace the team, big boy. Whoo-oo-oo.

STAGE MANAGER: All right! All right! That'll do. That's enough of that.

[*Smiling, he pushes them off the stage. They lean back to shout a few more catcalls.*]

There used to be an awful lot of that kind of thing at weddings in the old days, — Rome, and later. We're more civilized now, — so they say.

[*The choir starts singing "Love divine, all love excelling." George has reached the stage. He stares at the congregation a moment, then takes a few steps of withdrawal, toward the right proscenium pillar.*]

GEORGE [*darkly, to himself*]: I wish I were back at school. . . . I don't want to get married.

[*His mother has left her seat and come toward him. She stops, looking at him anxiously.*]

MRS. GIBBS: George, what's the matter?

GEORGE: Ma, I don't want to grow *old*. Why's everybody pushing me so?

MRS. GIBBS: Why, George . . . you wanted it.

GEORGE: Why do I have to get married at all? Listen, Ma, for the last time I ask you —

MRS. GIBBS: No, no, George . . . you're a man now.

GEORGE: Listen, Ma, you never listen to me. All I want to do is to be a fella . . . why do —

MRS. GIBBS: George! If anyone should hear you! Now stop. Why, I'm ashamed of you!

GEORGE [*passing his hand over his forehead*]: What's the matter? I've been dreaming. Where's Emily?

MRS. GIBBS: Gracious! You gave me such a turn.

GEORGE: Cheer up, Ma. What are you looking so funny for? Cheer up; I'm getting married.

MRS. GIBBS: Let me catch my breath a minute.

GEORGE: Now, Ma, you save Thursday nights. Emily and I are coming over to dinner every Thursday night . . . you'll see. Ma, what are you crying for? Come on; we've got to get ready for this.

[*In the meantime, EMILY, in white and wearing her wedding veil, has come through the audience and mounted on to the stage. She too draws back when she sees the congregation in the church. The choir begins: "Blessed be the tie that binds."*]

EMILY: I never felt so alone in my whole life. And George over there, looking so . . . ! I *hate* him. I wish I were dead. Papa! Papa!

MR. WEBB [*leaves his seat in the pews and comes toward her anxiously*]: Emily! Emily! Now don't get upset. . . .

EMILY: But, Papa, — I don't want to get married. . . .

MR. WEBB: Sh-sh — Emily. Everything's all right.

EMILY: Why can't I stay for a while just as I am? Let's go away.

MR. WEBB: No, no, Emily. Now stop and think.

EMILY: Don't you remember that you used to say, — all the time you used to say that I was *your* girl. There must be lots of places we can go to. Let's go away. I'll work for you. I could keep house.

MR. WEBB: Sh. . . . You mustn't think of such things. You're just nervous, Emily. Now, now, — you're marrying the best young fellow in the world. George is a fine fellow.

EMILY: But, Papa, —

MR. WEBB: George! George!

[MRS. GIBBS *returns to her seat.* GEORGE *hears* MR. WEBB *and looks up.* MR. WEBB *beckons to him. They move to the center of the stage.*]

I'm giving away my daughter, George. Do you think you can take care of her?

GEORGE: Mr. Webb, I want to . . . I want to try. Emily, I'm going to do my best. I love you, Emily. I need you.

EMILY: Well, if you love me, help me. All I want is someone to love me.

GEORGE: I will, Emily.

EMILY: If ever I'm sick or in trouble, that's what I mean.

GEORGE: Emily, I'll try. I'll try.

EMILY: And I mean for *ever.* Do you hear? Forever and ever.

[*They fall into each other's arms. The march from* Lohengrin *is heard.*]

MR. WEBB: Come, they're waiting for us. Now you know it'll be all right. Come, quick.

[GEORGE *slips away and takes his place beside the* STAGE MANAGER-CLERGYMAN. EMILY *proceeds up the aisle on her father's arm.*]

STAGE MANAGER: Do you, George, take this woman, Emily, to be your wedded wife, to have —

[MRS. SOAMES *has been sitting in the last row of the congregation. She now turns to her neighbors and in a shrill voice says:*]

MRS. SOAMES: Perfectly lovely wedding! Loveliest wedding I ever saw. Oh, I do love a good wedding, don't you? Doesn't she make a lovely bride?

GEORGE: I do.

STAGE MANAGER: Do you, Emily, take this man, George, to be your wedded husband, —

MRS. SOAMES: Don't know *when* I've seen such a lovely wedding. But I always cry. Don't know why it is, but I always cry. I just like to see young people happy, don't you? Oh, I think it's lovely.

[*The ring. The kiss. The stage is suddenly arrested into silent tableau. The* STAGE MANAGER, *his eyes on the distance, says to the audience:*]

STAGE MANAGER: I've married two hundred couples in my day.

Do I believe in it?

I don't know.

M—— marries N—— Millions of them.

The cottage, the gocart, the Sunday afternoon drives in the Ford, the children leaving the home, the first rheumatism, the grandchildren, the second rheumatism, the deathbed, the reading of the will. — Once in a thousand times it's interesting.

Well, let's have Mendelssohn's *Wedding March!*

[*The organ picks up the march. The bride and groom come down the aisle, radiant, but trying to be very dignified.*]

MRS. SOAMES: Aren't they a lovely couple? Oh, I've never been to such a nice wedding. I'm sure they'll be happy. I always say: *happiness,* that's the great thing! The important thing is to be happy.

[*The bride and groom reach the steps leading into the audience. A bright light is thrown upon them. They descend into the auditorium and run up the aisle joyously.*]

STAGE MANAGER: That's all the Second Act. Ten minutes' intermission, folks.

ACT 3

During the intermission the audience has seen the actors arranging the stage. On the right-hand side, a little right of the center, ten or twelve ordinary chairs have been placed in three openly spaced rows facing the audience. These are graves in the cemetery.

Towards the end of the intermission the actors enter and take their places. The front row contains: toward the center of the stage, an empty chair; then MRS. GIBBS; SIMON STIMSON. *The second row contains, among others,* MRS. SOAMES. *The third row has* WALLY WEBB. *The dead sit in a quiet without stiffness, and in a patience without listlessness.*

The STAGE MANAGER *takes his accustomed place and waits for the house lights to go down.*

STAGE MANAGER: This time nine years have gone by, friends — summer, 1913. Gradual changes in Grover's Corners. Horses are getting rarer. Farmers coming into town in Fords.

Chief difference is in the young people, far as I can see. They want to go to the moving pictures all the time. They want to wear clothes like they see there . . . want to be citified.

Everybody locks their house doors now at night. Ain't been any burglers in town yet, but everybody's heard about 'em.

But you'd be surprised though — on the whole, things don't change much at Grover's Corners.

Guess you want to know what all these chairs are here fur. Smarter ones have guessed it already. I don't know how you feel about such things; but this certainly is a beautiful place. It's on a hilltop — a windy hilltop — lots of sky, lots of clouds, — often lots of sun and moon and stars. You come up here on a fine afternoon and you can see range on range of hills — awful blue they are — up there by Lake Sunapee and Lake Winnapassaukee . . . and way up, if you've got a glass, you can see the White Mountains and Mt. Washington — where North Conway and Conway is. And, of course, our favorite mountain, Mt. Monadnock, 's right here — and all around it lie these towns — Jaffrey, 'n East Jaffrey, 'n Peterborough, 'n Dublin and [*then pointing down in the audience*] there, quite a ways down is Grover's Corners. Yes, beautiful spot up here. Mountain laurel and li-lacks. I often wonder why people like to be buried in Woodlawn and Brooklyn when they might pass the same time up here in New Hampshire. Over in that corner — [*pointing to stage left*] are the old stones, — 1670, 1680. Strong-minded people that come a long way to be independent. Summer people walk around there laughing at the funny words on the tombstones . . . it don't do any harm. And genealogists come up from Boston — get paid by city people for looking up their ancestors. They want to make sure they're Daughters of the American Revolution and of the *Mayflower.* — Well, I guess that don't do any harm, either. Wherever you come near the human race, there's layers and layers of nonsense. . . .

Over there are some Civil War veterans too. Iron flags on their graves. . . . New Hampshire boys . . . had a notion that the Union ought to be kept together, though they'd never seen more than fifty miles of it themselves. All they knew was the name, friends — the United States of America. The United States of America. And they went and died about it.

This here is the new part of the cemetery. Here's your friend, Mrs. Gibbs. 'N let me see — here's Mr. Stimson, organist at the Congregational Church. And over there's Mrs. Soames who enjoyed the wedding so — you remember? Oh, and a lot of others. And Editor Webb's boy, Wallace, whose appendix burst while he was on a Boy Scout trip to Crawford Notch.

Yes, an awful lot of sorrow has sort of quieted down up here. People just wild with grief have brought their relatives up to this hill. We all know how it is . . . and then time . . . and sunny days . . . and rainy days . . . 'n snow . . . tz-tz-tz. We're all glad they're in a beautiful place and we're coming up here ourselves when our fit's over.

This certainly is an important part of Grover's Corners. A lot of thoughts come up here, night and day, but there's no post office.

Now I'm going to tell you some things you know already. You know'm as well as I do; but you don't take'm out and look at'm very often.

I don't care what they say with their mouths — everybody knows that *something* is eternal. And it ain't houses and it ain't names, and it ain't earth, and it ain't even the stars . . . everybody knows in their bones that *something* is eternal, and that something has to do with human beings. All the greatest people ever lived have been telling us that for five thousand years and yet you'd be surprised how people are always losing hold of it. There's something way down deep that's eternal about every human being.

[*Pause.*]

You know as well as I do that the dead don't stay interested in us living people for very long. Gradually, gradually, they let hold of the earth . . . and the ambitions they had . . . and the pleasures they had . . . and the things they suffered . . . and the people they loved.

They get weaned away from earth — that's the way I put it, — weaned away.

Yes, they stay here while the earth-part of 'em burns away, burns out, and all that time they slowly get indifferent to what's goin' on in Grover's Corners.

They're waitin'. They're waitin' for something that they feel is comin'. Something important and great. Aren't they waitin' for the eternal part in them to come out clear?

Some of the things they're going to say maybe'll hurt your feelings — but that's the way it is: mother 'n daughter . . . husband 'n wife . . . enemy 'n enemy . . . money 'n miser . . . all those terribly important things kind of grow pale around here. And what's left? What's left when memory's gone, and your identity, Mrs. Smith?

[*He looks at the audience a minute, then turns to the stage.*]

Well! There are some *living* people. There's Joe Stoddard, our undertaker, supervising a new-made grave. And here comes a Grover's Corners boy, that left town to go out West.

[JOE STODDARD *has hovered about in the background.* SAM CRAIG *enters left, wiping his forehead from the exertion. He carries an umbrella and strolls front.*]

SAM CRAIG: Good afternoon, Joe Stoddard.

JOE STODDARD: Good afternoon, good afternoon. Let me see now: do I know you?

SAM CRAIG: I'm Sam Craig.

JOE STODDARD: Gracious sakes' alive! Of all people! I should'a knowed you'd be back for the funeral. You've been away a long time, Sam.

SAM CRAIG: Yes, I've been away over twelve years. I'm in business out in Buffalo now, Joe. But I was in the East when I got news of my cousin's death, so I thought I'd combine things a little and come and see the old home. You look well.

JOE STODDARD: Yes, yes, can't complain. Very sad, our journey today, Samuel.

SAM CRAIG: Yes.

JOE STODDARD: Yes, yes. I always say, I hate to supervise when a young person is taken. I see you brought your umbrella. It's going to rain and make it sadder still, seems like. They'll be here in a few minutes now. I had to come here early today — my son's supervisin' at the home.

SAM CRAIG [*reading stones*]: Old Farmer McCarty, I used to do chores for him — after school. He had the lumbago.

JOE STODDARD: Yes, we brought Farmer McCarty here a number of years ago now.

SAM CRAIG [*staring at* MRS. GIBBS's *knees*]: Why, this is my Aunt Julia. . . . I'd forgotten that she'd . . . of course, of course.

JOE STODDARD: Yes, Doc Gibbs lost his wife two-three years ago . . . about this time. And today's another pretty bad blow for him, too.

MRS. GIBBS [*to* SIMON STIMSON, *in an even voice*]: That's my sister Carey's boy, Sam . . . Sam Craig.

SIMON STIMSON: I'm always uncomfortable when *they're* around.

MRS. GIBBS: Simon.

SIMON STIMSON: They and their nonsense and their damned glee at being alive. . . .

MRS. GIBBS: Simon, be patient. . . .

SAM CRAIG: Do they choose their own verses much, Joe?

JOE STODDARD: No . . . not usual. Mostly the bereaved pick a verse.

SAM CRAIG: Doesn't sound like Aunt Julia. There aren't many of those Hersey sisters left now. Let me see: where are . . . I wanted to look at my father's and mother's . . .

JOE STODDARD: Over there with the Craigs. . . . Avenue F.

SAM CRAIG [*reading* SIMON STIMSON's *epitaph*]: He was organist at church, wasn't he? — Hm, drank a lot, we used to say.

JOE STODDARD: Nobody was supposed to know about it. He'd seen a peck of trouble. Those musical fellas ain't like the rest of us, I reckon. [*Behind his hand.*] Took his own life, y' know?

SAM CRAIG: Oh, did he?

JOE STODDARD: Hung himself in the attic. They tried to hush it up, but of course it got around. His wife's just married Senator Barstow. Many a time I've seen her, eleven o'clock at night, goin' around the streets huntin' for her husband. Think o' that! Now she's married to Senator Barstow over at Manchester. He chose his own epy-taph. You can see it there. It ain't a verse exactly.

SAM CRAIG: Why, it's just some notes of music — what is it?

JOE STODDARD: Oh, I wouldn't know. It was wrote up in the Boston papers at the time.

SAM CRAIG: Joe, what did she die of?

JOE STODDARD: Who?

SAM CRAIG: My cousin.

JOE STODDARD: Oh, didn't you know? Had some trouble bringing a baby into the world. Let's see, today's Friday — 'twas almost a week ago now.

SAM CRAIG [*putting up his umbrella*]: Did the baby live?

JOE STODDARD [*raising his coat collar*]: No. 'Twas her second, though. There's a little boy 'bout four years old.

SAM CRAIG: The grave's going to be over there?

JOE STODDARD: Yes, there ain't much more room over here among the Gibbses, so they're opening up a whole new Gibbs section over by Avenue B. You'll excuse me now. I see they're comin'.

THE DEAD [*not lugubrious; and strongly New England in accent*]: Rain'll do a lot of good. — Yes, reckon things were gettin' downright parched. Don't look like it's goin' to last long, tho'. — Lemuel, you remember the floods of '79? Carried away all the bridges but one.

[*From left to right, at the back of the stage, comes a procession. Four men carry a casket, invisible to us. All the rest are under umbrellas. One can vaguely see:* DR. GIBBS, GEORGE, *the* WEBBS, *etc. They gather about a grave in the back center of the stage, a little to the left of center.*]

MRS. SOAMES: Who is it, Julia?

MRS. GIBBS [*without raising her eyes*]: My daughter-in-law, Emily Webb.

MRS. SOAMES [*a little surprised, but no emotion*]: Well, I declare! The road up here must have been awful muddy. What did she die of, Julia?

MRS. GIBBS: In childbirth.

MRS. SOAMES: Childbirth. [*Almost with a laugh.*] I'd forgotten all about that! My, wasn't life awful — [*with a sigh*] and wonderful.

SIMON STIMSON [*with a sideways glance*]: Wonderful, was it?

MRS. GIBBS: Simon! Now, remember!

MRS. SOAMES: I remember Emily's wedding. Wasn't it a lovely wedding! And I remember her reading the class poem at Graduation Exercises. Emily was one of the brightest girls ever graduated from High School. I've heard Principal Wilkins say so time after time. I called on them at their new farm, just before I died. Perfectly beautiful farm.

A WOMAN FROM AMONG THE DEAD: It's on the same road we lived on.

A MAN AMONG THE DEAD: Yes, just near the Elks' picnic grounds. Remember, Joe? By the lake where we always used to go Fourth of July? Right smart farm.

[*They subside. The group by the grave starts singing "Blessed be the tie that binds."*]

A WOMAN AMONG THE DEAD: I always liked that hymn. I was hopin' they'd sing a hymn.

A MAN AMONG THE DEAD: My wife — my second wife — knows all the verses of about every hymn there is. It just beats the Dutch . . . she can go through them all by heart.

[*Pause. Suddenly* EMILY *appears from among the umbrellas. She is wearing a white dress. Her hair is down her back and tied by a white ribbon like a little girl's. She comes slowly, gazing wonderingly at the dead, a little dazed. She stops halfway and smiles faintly.*]

EMILY: Hello.

VOICES AMONG THE DEAD: Hello, Emily. H'lo, M's. Gibbs.

EMILY: Hello, Mother Gibbs.

MRS. GIBBS: Emily.

EMILY: Hello.

[*The hymn continues.* EMILY *looks back at the funeral. She says dreamily:*]
    It's raining.

MRS. GIBBS: Yes. . . . They'll be gone soon, dear. Just rest yourself.

[EMILY *sits down in the empty chair by* MRS. GIBBS.]

EMILY: It seems thousands and thousands of years since I. . . . How stupid they all look. They don't have to look like that!

MRS. GIBBS: Don't look at them now, dear. They'll be gone soon.

EMILY: Oh, I wish I'd been here a long time. I don't like being new here. — How do you do, Mr. Stimson?

SIMON STIMSON: How do you do, Emily.

[EMILY *continues to look about her with a wan and wondering smile; but for a moment her eyes do not return to the funeral group. As though to shut out from her mind the thought of that group she starts speaking to* MRS. GIBBS *with a touch of nervousness.*]

EMILY: Mother Gibbs, George and I have made that farm into just the best place you ever saw. We thought of you all the time. We wanted to show you the new barn and a great long ce-ment drinking fountain for the stock. We bought that out of the money you left us.

MRS. GIBBS: I did?

EMILY: Don't you remember, Mother Gibbs — the legacy you left us? Why, it was over three hundred and fifty dollars.

MRS. GIBBS: Yes, yes, Emily.

EMILY: Well, there's a patent device on this drinking fountain so that it never overflows, Mother Gibbs, and it never sinks below a certain mark they have there. It's fine.

[*Her voice trails off and her eyes return to the funeral group.*]

It won't be the same to George without me, but it's a lovely farm.

[*Suddenly she looks directly at* MRS. GIBBS.]

Live people don't understand, do they?

MRS. GIBBS: No, dear — not very much.

EMILY: They're sort of shut up in little boxes, aren't they? I feel as though I knew them last a thousand years ago. . . . My boy is spending the day at Mrs. Carter's. [*She sees* MR. CARTER *among the dead.*] Oh, Mr. Carter, my little boy is spending the day at your house.

MR. CARTER: Is he?

EMILY: Yes, he loves it there. — Mother Gibbs, we have a Ford, too. Never gives any trouble. I don't drive, though. Mother Gibbs, when does this feeling go away? — Of being . . . one of *them*? How long does it . . . ?

MRS. GIBBS: Sh! dear. Just wait and be patient.

EMILY [*with a sigh*]: I know. — Look, they're finished. They're going.

MRS. GIBBS: Sh — .

[*The umbrellas leave the stage.* DR. GIBBS *comes over to his wife's grave and stands before it a moment.* EMILY *looks up at his face.* MRS. GIBBS *does not raise her eyes.*]

EMILY: Look! Father Gibbs is bringing some of my flowers to you. He looks just like George, doesn't he? Oh, Mother Gibbs, I never realized before how troubled and how . . . how in the dark live persons are. From morning till night, that's all they are — troubled.

[DR. GIBBS *goes off.*]

THE DEAD: Little cooler than it was. — Yes, that rain's cooled it off a little. Those north-east winds always do the same thing, don't they? If it isn't a rain, it's a three-day blow. — Reckon it may clear up before night; often does.

[*A patient calm falls on the stage. The* STAGE MANAGER *appears at his proscenium pillar, smoking.* EMILY *sits up abruptly with an idea.*]

EMILY: But, Mother Gibbs, one can go back; one can go back there again . . . into living. I feel it. I know it. Why just then for a moment I was thinking about . . . about the farm . . . and for a minute I *was* there, and my baby was on my lap as plain as day.

MRS. GIBBS: Yes, of course you can.

EMILY: I can go back there and live all those days over again . . . why not?

MRS. GIBBS: All I can say is, Emily, don't.

EMILY [*takes a few steps toward the* STAGE MANAGER]: But it's true, isn't it? I can go and live . . . back there . . . again.

STAGE MANAGER: Yes, some have tried — but they soon come back here.

MRS. GIBBS: Don't do it, Emily.

MRS. SOAMES: Emily, don't. It's not what you think it'd be.

EMILY: But I won't live over a sad day. I'll choose a happy one — I'll choose the day I first knew that I loved George. Why should that be painful?

[*They are silent. Her question turns to the* STAGE MANAGER.]

STAGE MANAGER: You not only live it; but you watch yourself living it.

EMILY: Yes?

STAGE MANAGER: And as you watch it, you see the thing that they — down there — never know. You see the future. You know what's going to happen afterwards.

EMILY: But is that — painful? Why?

MRS. GIBBS: That's not the only reason why you shouldn't do it, Emily. When you've been here longer you'll see that our life here is our hope that soon we'll forget all that, and think only of what's ahead, and be ready for what's ahead. When you've been here longer you'll understand.

EMILY [*softly*]: But, Mother Gibbs, how can I ever forget that life? It's all I know. It's all I had. [MRS. GIBBS *does not answer.*] Mr. Stimson, did you go back?

SIMON STIMSON [*sharply*]: No.

EMILY: Did you, Mrs. Soames?

MRS. SOAMES: Oh, Emily. It isn't wise. Really, it isn't. All we can do is just warn you. It won't be what you expect.

EMILY [*slowly*]: But it's a thing I must know for myself. I'll choose a happy day, anyway.

MRS. GIBBS: No. At least, choose an unimportant day. Choose the least important day in your life. It will be important enough.

EMILY [*to the* STAGE MANAGER]: Then it can't be since I was married; or since the baby was born. I can choose a birthday at least, can't I? — I choose my twelfth birthday.

STAGE MANAGER: All right. February 11th, 1899. A Tuesday. — Do you want any special time of day?

EMILY: Oh, I want the whole day.

STAGE MANAGER: We'll begin at dawn. You remember it had been snowing for several days; but it had stopped the night before, and they had begun clearing the roads. The sun's coming up.

EMILY [*with a cry*]: There's Main Street . . . why, that's Mr. Morgan's drugstore before he changed it! . . . And there's the livery stable.

[*She walks toward the back of the stage.*]

STAGE MANAGER: Yes, it's 1899. This is fourteen years ago.

EMILY: Oh, that's the town I knew as a little girl. And, look, there's the old white fence that used to be around our house. Oh, I'd forgotten that! Oh, I love it so! Are *they* inside?

STAGE MANAGER: Yes, your mother'll be coming downstairs in a minute to make breakfast.

EMILY [*softly*]: Will she?

STAGE MANAGER: And you remember: your father had been away for several days; he came back on the early morning train.

EMILY: No . . . ?

STAGE MANAGER: He'd been back to his college to make a speech — in western New York, at Clinton.

EMILY: Look! There's Howie Newsome. There's our policeman. But he's *dead;* he *died.*

[*The* STAGE MANAGER *retires to his corner. The voices of* HOWIE NEWSOME, CONSTABLE WARREN, *and* JOE CROWELL, JR., *are heard at the left of the stage.*]

HOWIE NEWSOME: Whoa, Bessie! — Bessie! 'Morning, Bill.

BILL: 'Morning, Howie.

HOWIE NEWSOME: You're up early.

BILL: Been rescuin' a party; darn near froze to death, down by Polish Town thar. Got drunk and lay out in the snowdrifts. Thought he was in bed when I shook'm.

EMILY: Why, there's Joe Crowell. . . .

JOE CROWELL: Good morning, Mr. Warren. 'Morning, Howie.

[MRS. WEBB *has appeared in her kitchen, but* EMILY *does not see her until she calls.*]

MRS. WEBB: Chil-*dren!* Wally! Emily! . . . Time to get up.

EMILY: Mama, here I am! Oh! how young Mama looks! I didn't know Mama was ever that young. Oh!

MRS. WEBB: You can come and dress by the kitchen fire, if you like; but hurry.

[HOWIE NEWSOME *has entered along Main Street and brings the milk to* MRS. WEBB'S *door.*]

Good morning, Mr. Newsome. Whhhh — it's cold.

HOWIE NEWSOME: Ten below by my barn, Mrs. Webb.

MRS. WEBB: Think of it! Keep yourself wrapped up.

[*She takes her bottles in, shuddering.*]

EMILY [*with an effort*]: Mama, I can't find my blue hair ribbon anywhere.

MRS. WEBB: Just open your eyes, dear, that's all. I laid it out for you special — on the dresser, there. If it were a snake it would bite you.

EMILY: Yes, yes. . . .

[*She puts her hand on her heart.* MR. WEBB *comes along Main Street, where he meets* CONSTABLE WARREN.]

MR. WEBB: Good morning, Bill.

BILL: Good morning, Mr. Webb. You're up early.

MR. WEBB: Yes, just been back to my old college in New York State. Been any trouble here?

BILL: Well, I was called up this mornin' to rescue a Polish fella — darn near froze to death he was.

MR. WEBB: We must get it in the paper.

BILL: 'Twan't much.

EMILY [*whispers*]: Papa.

[MR. WEBB *shakes the snow off his feet and enters his house.*]

MR. WEBB: Good morning, Mother.

MRS. WEBB: How did it go, Charles?

MR. WEBB: Oh, fine, I guess. I told'm a few things.

MRS. WEBB: Did you sit up on the train all night?

MR. WEBB: Yes. Never could sleep on a Pullman anyway.

MRS. WEBB: Charles, seems to me — we're rich enough so that you could sleep in a train once in a while.

MR. WEBB: Everything all right here?

MRS. WEBB: Yes — can't think of anything that's happened, special. Been right cold. Howie Newsome says it's ten below over to his barn.

MR. WEBB: Yes, well, it's colder than that at Hamilton College. Students' ears are falling off. It ain't Christian. — Paper have any mistakes in it?

MRS. WEBB: None that I noticed. Coffee's ready when you want it.

[*He starts upstairs.*]

Charles! Don't forget; it's Emily's birthday. Did you remember to get her something?

MR. WEBB [*patting his pocket*]: Yes, I've got something here.

MRS. WEBB: Goodness sakes! I hope she likes what I got for her. I hunted hard enough for it. Child*ren!* Hurry up! Hurry up!

MR. WEBB: Where's my girl? Where's my birthday girl?

[*He goes off left.*]

MRS. WEBB: Don't interrupt her now, Charles. You can see her at breakfast. She's

slow enough as it is. Hurry up, children! It's seven o'clock. Now, I don't want
to call you again.

EMILY [*softly, more in wonder than in grief*]: I can't bear it. They're so young
and beautiful. Why did they ever have to get old? Mama, I'm here. I'm
grown up. I love you all, everything. — I can't look at everything hard
enough. There's the butternut tree.

[*She wanders up Main Street.*]

There's Mr. Morgan's drugstore. And there's the High School, forever and
ever, and ever. And there's the Congregational Church where I got married.
Oh, dear. Oh, dear. Oh, dear!

[*The* STAGE MANAGER *beckons partially to her. He points to the house. She says a
breathless " yes" and goes to the house.*]

Good morning, Mama.

MRS. WEBB [*at the foot of the stairs, kissing her in a matter-of-fact way*]: Well,
now, dear, a very happy birthday to my girl and many happy returns. There
are some surprises waiting for you on the kitchen table.

EMILY: Oh, Mama, you *shouldn't* have.

[*She throws an anguished glance at the* STAGE MANAGER.]

I can't — I can't.

MRS. WEBB [*facing the audience, over her stove*]: But birthday or no birthday, I
want you to eat your breakfast good and slow. I want you to grow up and be
a good strong girl.

[*She goes to the stairs and calls.*]

Wally! Wally, wash yourself good. Everything's getting cold down here.

[*She returns to the stove with her back to* EMILY. EMILY *opens her parcels.*]

That in the blue paper is from your Aunt Carrie and I reckon you can guess
who brought the post card album. I found it on the doorstep when I brought
in the milk — George Gibbs . . . must have come over in the cold pretty
early . . . right nice of him.

EMILY [*to herself*]: Oh, George! I'd forgotten that. . . .

MRS. WEBB: Chew that bacon slow. It'll help keep you warm on a cold day.

EMILY [*beginning softly but urgently*]: Oh, Mama, just look at me one minute
as though you really saw me. Mama, fourteen years have gone by. I'm dead.
You're a grandmother, Mama. I married George Gibbs, Mama. Wally's dead,
too. Mama, his appendix burst on a camping trip to North Conway. We felt
just terrible about it — don't you remember? But, just for a moment now
we're all together. Mama, just for a moment we're happy. Let's look at one
another.

MRS. WEBB: That in the yellow paper is something I found in the attic among
your grandmother's things. You're old enough to wear it now, and I thought
you'd like it.

EMILY: And this is from you. Why, Mama, it's just lovely and it's just what I
wanted. It's beautiful!

[*She flings her arms around her mother's neck. Her mother goes on with her cooking, but is pleased.*]

MRS. WEBB: Well, I hoped you'd like it. Hunted all over. Your Aunt Norah couldn't find one in Concord, so I had to send all the way to Boston. [*Laughing.*] Wally has something for you, too. He made it at manual training class and he's very proud of it. Be sure you make a big fuss about it. — Your father has a surprise for you, too; don't know what it is myself. Sh — here he comes.

MR. WEBB [*off stage*]: Where's my girl? Where's my birthday girl?

EMILY [*in a loud voice to the* STAGE MANAGER]: I can't. I can't go on. Oh! Oh! It goes so fast. We don't have time to look at one another.

[*She breaks down sobbing. At a gesture from the* STAGE MANAGER, MRS. WEBB *disappears.*]

I didn't realize. So all that was going on and we never noticed. Take me back — up the hill — to my grave. But first: Wait! One more look. Goodby, good-by, world. Good-by, Grover's Corners . . . Mama and Papa. Good-by to clocks ticking . . . and Mama's sunflowers. And food and coffee. And new-ironed dresses and hot baths . . . and sleeping and waking up. Oh, earth, you're too wonderful for anybody to realize you.

[*She looks toward the* STAGE MANAGER *and asks abruptly, through her tears*:]

Do any human beings ever realize life while they live it? — every, every minute?

STAGE MANAGER: No. [*Pause.*] The saints and poets, maybe — they do some.

EMILY: I'm ready to go back.

[*She returns to her chair beside* MRS. GIBBS.]

Mother Gibbs, I should have listened to you. Now I want to be quiet for a while. — Oh, Mother Gibbs, I saw it all. I saw your garden.

MRS. GIBBS: Did you, dear?

EMILY: That's all human beings are! — Just blind people.

MRS. GIBBS: Look, it's clearing up. The stars are coming out.

EMILY: Oh, Mr. Stimson, I should have listened to them.

SIMON STIMSON [*with mounting violence; bitingly*]: Yes, now you know. Now you know! That's what it was to be alive. To move about in a cloud of ignorance; to go up and down trampling on the feelings of those . . . of those about you. To spend and waste time as though you had a million years. To be always at the mercy of one self-centered passion, or another. Now you know — that's the happy existence you wanted to go back and see. Did you shout to 'em? Did you call to 'em?

EMILY: Yes, I did.

SIMON STIMSON: Now you know them as they are: in ignorance and blindness.

MRS. GIBBS [*spiritedly*]: Simon Stimson, that ain't the whole truth and you know it.

[*The dead have begun to stir.*]

THE DEAD: Lemuel, wind's coming up, seems like. — Oh, dear, — I keep remembering things tonight. — It's right cold for June, ain't it?

MRS. GIBBS: Look what you've done, you and your rebellious spirit stirring us up here. — Emily, look at that star. I forget its name.

THE DEAD: I'm getting to know them all, but I don't know their names. — My boy Joel was a sailor, — knew 'em all. He'd set on the porch evenings and tell 'em all by name. Yes, sir, it was wonderful. — A star's mighty good company. — Yes, yes. — Yes, 'tis.

SIMON STIMSON: Here's one of *them* coming.

THE DEAD: That's funny. 'Tain't no time for one of them to be here. — Goodness sakes.

EMILY: Mother Gibbs, it's George.

MRS. GIBBS: Sh, dear. You just rest yourself.

EMILY: It's George.

[GEORGE *enters from the left, and slowly comes toward them.*]

A MAN FROM AMONG THE DEAD: And my boy, Joel, who knew the stars — he used to say it took millions of years for that speck o' light to git to the earth. Don't seem like a body could believe it, but that's what he used to say — millions of years.

ANOTHER: That's what they say.

[GEORGE *flings himself on* EMILY's *grave.*]

THE DEAD: Goodness! That ain't no way to behave! — He ought to be home.

EMILY: Mother Gibbs?

MRS. GIBBS: Yes, Emily?

EMILY: They don't understand much, do they?

MRS. GIBBS: No, dear, not very much.

[*The* STAGE MANAGER *appears at the right, one hand on a dark curtain which he slowly draws across the scene. In the distance a clock is heard striking the hour very faintly.*]

STAGE MANAGER: Most everybody's asleep in Grover's Corners. There are a few lights on: Shorty Hawkins, down at the depot, has just watched the Albany train go by. And at the livery stable somebody's setting up late and talking. — Yes, it's clearing up. There are the stars — doing their old, old criss-cross journeys in the sky. Scholars haven't settled the matter yet, but they seem to think there are no living beings up there. They're just chalk . . . or fire. Only this one is straining away, straining away all the time to make something of itself. The strain's so bad that every sixteen hours everybody lies down and gets a rest.

[*He winds his watch.*]

Hm. . . . Eleven o'clock in Grover's Corners. — You get a good rest, too. Good night.

AUTHOR'S NOTE

The Green Pastures is an attempt to present certain aspects of a living religion in the terms of its believers. The religion is that of thousands of Negroes in the deep South. With terrific spiritual hunger and the greatest humility, these untutored black Christians — many of whom cannot even read the book which is the treasure house of their faith — have adapted the contents of the Bible to the consistencies of their everyday lives.

Unburdened by the differences of more educated theologians, they accept the Old Testament as a chronicle of wonders which happened to people like themselves in vague but actual places, and of rules of conduct, true acceptance of which will lead them to a tangible, three-dimensional Heaven. In this Heaven, if one has been born in a district where fish fries are popular, the angels do have magnificent fish fries through an eternity somewhat resembling a series of earthly holidays. The Lord Jehovah will be the promised comforter, a just but compassionate patriarch, the summation of all the virtues His follower has observed in the human beings about him. The Lord may look like the Reverend Mr. Dubois, as our Sunday-School teacher speculates in the play, or he may resemble another believer's own grandfather. In any event, His face will be familiar to the one who has come for his reward.

The author is indebted to Mr. Roark Bradford, whose retelling of several of the Old Testament stories in *Ol' Man Adam an' His Chillun* first stimulated his interest in this point of view.

One need not blame a hazy memory of the Bible for the failure to recall the characters of Hezdrel, Zeba, and others in the play. They are the author's apocrypha, but he believes persons much like them have figured in the meditations of some of the old Negro preachers, whose simple faith he has tried to translate into a play.

Marc Connelly

The Green Pastures

CHARACTERS

Mr. Deshee, the Preacher	Zeba	Jacob
Myrtle	Cain the Sixth	Moses
First Boy	Boy Gambler	Zipporah
Second Boy	First Gambler	Aaron
First Cook	Second Gambler	A Candidate Magician
A Voice	Voice in Shanty	Pharaoh
Second Cook	Noah	General
First Man Angel	Noah's Wife	Head Magician
First Mammy Angel	Shem	First Wizard
A Stout Angel	First Woman	Second Wizard
A Slender Angel	Second Woman	Joshua
Archangel	Third Woman	First Scout
Gabriel	First Man	Master of Ceremonies
God	Flatfoot	King of Babylon
Choir Leader	Ham	Prophet
Custard Maker	Japheth	High Priest
Adam	First Cleaner	Corporal
Eve	Second Cleaner	Hezdrel
Cain	Abraham	Second Officer
Cain's Girl	Isaac	

SCENES

PART I. SCENE 1

A corner in a Negro church.
Ten CHILDREN *and an elderly* PREACHER.
The costumes are those that might be seen in any lower Louisiana town at Sunday-School time. As the curtain rises, MR. DESHEE, *the preacher, is reading from a Bible. The* CHILDREN *are listening with varied degrees of interest. Three or four are wide-eyed in their attention. Two or three are obviously puzzled, but interested, and the smallest ones are engaged in more physical concerns. One is playing with a little doll, and another runs his finger on all the angles of his chair.*

DESHEE: " An' Adam lived a hundred and thirty years, an' begat a son in his own likeness, after his image; an' called his name Seth. An' de days of Adam, after he had begotten Seth, were eight hundred years! an' he begat sons an' daughters; an' all de days dat Adam lived were nine hundred an' thirty years; an' he died. An' Seth lived a hundred an' five years an' begat Enos; an' Seth lived after he begat Enos eight hundred an' seven years an' begat sons and daughters. An' all de days of Seth were nine hundred and twelve years; an' he died." An' it go like dat till we come to Enoch an' de Book say: " An' Enoch lived sixty an' five years and begat Methuselah." Den it say: " An' all de days of Methuselah were nine hund'ed an' sixty an' nine years an' he died." An' dat was de oldest man dat ever was. Dat's why we call ol' Mr. Gurney's mammy ol' Mrs. Methuselah, caize she's so ol'. Den a little later it tell about another member of de fam'ly. His name was Noah. Maybe some of you know about him already. I'm gonter tell you all about him next Sunday. Anyway dat's de meat an' substance of de first five chapters of Genesis. Now, how you think you gonter like de Bible?

MYRTLE: I think it's jest wonderful, Mr. Deshee. I cain't understand any of it.

FIRST BOY: Why did dey live so long, Mr. Deshee?

DESHEE: Why? Caize dat was de way God felt.

SECOND BOY: Dat made Adam a way back.

DESHEE: Yes, he certainly 'way back by de time Noah come along. Want to ask me any mo' questions?

SECOND BOY: What de worl' look like when de Lawd begin, Mr. Deshee?

DESHEE: How yo' mean what it look like?

MYRTLE: Carlisle mean who was in N'Orleans den.

DESHEE: Dey wasn't nobody in N'Orleans on' count dey wasn't any N'Orleans. Dat's de whole idea I tol' you at de end of de first chapter. Yo' got to git yo' minds fixed. Dey wasn't any Rampart Street. Dey wasn't any Canal Street. Dey wasn't any Louisiana. Dey wasn't nothin' on de earth at all caize fo' de reason dey wasn't any earth.

MYRTLE: Yes, but what Carlisle wanter know is —

DESHEE [*interrupting and addressing* LITTLE BOY *who has been playing with his chair and paying no attention*]: Now, Randolph, if you don't listen, how yo' gonter grow up and be a good man? Yo' wanter grow up an' be a transgressor?

LITTLE BOY [*frightened*]: No.

DESHEE: You tell yo' mammy yo' sister got to come wid you next time. She kin git things done in time to bring you to de school. You content yo'self. [*The* LITTLE BOY *straightens up in his chair.*] Now, what do Carlisle want to know?

SECOND BOY: How He decide He want de worl' to be right yere and how He git de idea He wanted it?

MYRTLE: Caize de Book say, don't it, Mr. Deshee?

DESHEE: De Book say, but at de same time dat's a good question. I remember when I was a little boy de same thing recurred to me. An' ol' Mr. Dubois, he was a wonderful preacher at New Hope Chapel over in East Gretna, he said: "De answer is dat de Book ain't got time to go into all de details." And he was right. You know sometimes I think de Lawd expects us to figure out a few things for ourselves. We know that at one time dey wasn't anything except Heaven. We don't know jest where it was but we know it was dere. Maybe it was everywhere. Den one day de Lawd got the idea He'd like to make some places. He made de sun and de moon, de stars. An' He made de earth.

MYRTLE: Who was aroun' den, nothin' but angels?

DESHEE: I suppose so.

FIRST BOY: What was de angels doin' up dere?

DESHEE: I suppose dey jest flew aroun' and had a good time. Dey wasn't no sin, so dey musta had a good time.

FIRST BOY: Did dey have picnics?

DESHEE: Sho, dey had the nicest kind of picnics. Dey probably had fish fries, wid b'iled custard and ten-cent seegars for de adults. God gives us humans lotsa ideas about havin' good times. Maybe det were things he'd seen de angels do. Yes, sir, I bet dey had a fish fry every week.

MYRTLE: Did dey have Sunday School, too?

DESHEE: Yes, dey musta had Sunday School for de cherubs.

MYRTLE: What did God look like, Mr. Deshee?

DESHEE: Well, nobody knows exactly what God looked like. But when I was a little boy I used to imagine dat He looked like de Reverend Dubois. He was de finest-looking ol' man I ever knew. Yes, I used to bet de Lawd looked exactly like Mr. Dubois in de days when He walked de earth in de shape of a natchel man.

MYRTLE: When was dat, Mr. Deshee?

DESHEE: Why, when He was gettin' things started down heah. When He talked to Adam and Eve and Noah and Moses and all dem. He made mighty men in dem days. But aldo they was awful mighty dey always knew dat He was beyond dem all. Pretty near one o'clock, time fo' you chillun to go home to dinner, but before I let you go I wan' you to go over wid me de main facts of de first lesson. What's de name of de book?

CHILDREN: Genesis.

DESHEE: Dat's right. And what's de other name?

CHILDREN: First Book of Moses.

DESHEE: Dat's right. And dis yere's Chapter One. [*The lights begin to dim.*] "In de beginnin' God created de heaven and de earth. An' de earth was widout form an' void. An' de darkness was upon de face of de deep."

PART I. SCENE 2

In the darkness many voices are heard singing " Rise, Shine, Give God the Glory." They sing it gayly and rapidly. The lights go up as the second verse ends. The chorus is being sung diminuendo by a mixed company of angels. That is, they are angels in that they wear brightly colored robes and have wings protruding from their backs. Otherwise they look and act like a company of happy Negroes at a fish fry. The scene itself is a pre-Creation Heaven with compromises.

In the distance is an unbroken stretch of blue sky. Companionable vari-colored clouds billow down to the floor of the stage and roll overhead to the branches of a live oak tree which is up left. The tree is leafy and dripping with Spanish moss, and with the clouds makes a frame for the scene. In the cool shade of the tree are the usual appurtenances of a fish fry; a large kettle of hot fat set on two small parallel logs, with a fire going underneath, and a large rustic table formed by driving four stakes into the ground and placing planks on top of the small connecting boards. On the table are piles of biscuits and corn bread and the cooked fish in dish pans. There are one or two fairly large cedar or crock " churns " containing boiled custard, which looks like milk. There is a gourd dipper beside the churns and several glasses and cups of various sizes and shapes from which the custard is drunk.

The principal singers are marching two by two in a small area at the right of the stage. Two MAMMY ANGELS *are attending to the frying beside the kettle.*

Behind the table a MAN ANGEL *is skinning fish and passing them to the cooks. Another is ladling out the custard. A* MAMMY ANGEL *is putting fish on bread for a brood of cherubs, and during the first scene they seat themselves on a grassy bank upstage. Another* MAMMY ANGEL *is clapping her hands disapprovingly and beckoning a laughing* BOY CHERUB *down from a cloud a little out of her reach.*

Another MAMMY ANGEL *is solicitously slapping the back of a* GIRL CHERUB *who has a large fish sandwich in her hand and a bone in her throat. There is much movement about the table, and during the first few minutes several individuals go up to the table to help themselves to the food and drink. Many of the* WOMEN ANGELS *wear hats and a few of the* MEN *are smoking cigars. A large boxful is on the table. There is much laughter and chatter as the music softens, but continues during the early part of the action. The following short scenes are played almost simultaneously.*

FIRST COOK [*at kettle, calling off*]: Hurry up, Cajey. Dis yere fat's cryin' fo' mo' feesh.

A VOICE [*off stage*]: We comin', fas' we kin. Dey got to be ketched, ain't dey? We cain't say, " C'm'on, little fish. C'm'on an' git fried," kin we?

SECOND COOK [*at table*]: De trouble is de mens is all worm fishin'.

FIRST MAN ANGEL [*at table*]: Whut dif'runce do it make? Yo' all de time got to make out like somebody's doin' somethin' de wrong way.

SECOND COOK [*near table*]: I s'pose you got de per'fec' way fo' makin' bait.

FIRST MAN ANGEL: I ain't sayin' dat. I is sayin' whut's wrong wid worm fishin'.

SECOND COOK: Whut's wrong wid worm fishin'? Ever'thing, dat's all. Dey's only one good way fo' catfishin', and dat's minny fishin'. Anybody know dat.

FIRST MAN ANGEL: Well, it jest so happen dat minny fishin' is de doggondest fool way of fishin' dey is. You kin try minny fishin' to de cows come home an' all you catch'll be de backache. De trouble wid you, sister, is you jest got minny fishin' on de brain.

SECOND COOK: Go right on, loud mouf. You tell me de news. My, my! You jest de wisest person in de worl'. First you, den de Lawd God.

FIRST MAN ANGEL [*to the custard ladler*]: You cain't tell dem nothin'. [*Walks away to the custard churn.*] Does you try to 'splain some simple fac' dey git man-deaf.

FIRST MAMMY ANGEL [*to* CHERUB *on the cloud*]: Now, you heerd me. [*The* CHERUB *assumes several mocking poses, as she speaks.*] You fly down yere. You wanter be put down in de sin book? [*She goes to the table, gets a drink for herself and points out the* CHERUB *to one of the men behind the table.*] Dat baby must got imp blood in him he so vexin'. [*She returns to her position under the cloud.*] You want me to fly up dere an' slap you down? Now, I tol' you. [*The* CHERUB *starts to come down.*]

STOUT ANGEL [*to the* CHERUB *with a bone in her throat*]: I tol' you you was too little fo' catfish. What you wanter git a bone in yo' froat fo'? [*She slaps the* CHERUB'S *back.*]

SLENDER ANGEL [*leisurely eating a sandwich as she watches the back-slapping*]: What de trouble wid Leonetta?

STOUT ANGEL: She got a catfish bone down her froat. [*To the* CHERUB.] Doggone, I tol' you to eat grinnel instead.

SLENDER ANGEL: Ef'n she do git all dat et, she gonter have a belly-ache.

STOUT ANGEL: Ain't I tol' her dat? [*To* CHERUB.] Come on now; let go dat bone. [*She slaps* CHERUB's *back again. The bone is dislodged and the* CHERUB *grins her relief.*] Dat's good.

SLENDER ANGEL [*comfortingly*]: Now she all right.

STOUT ANGEL: Go on an' play wid yo' cousins. [*The* CHERUB *joins the* CHERUBS *sitting on the embankment. The concurrency of scenes ends here.*] I ain't see you lately, Lily. How you been?

SLENDER ANGEL: Me, I'm fine. I been visitin' my mammy. She waitin' on de welcome table over by de throne of grace.

STOUT ANGEL: She always was pretty holy.

SLENDER ANGEL: Yes, ma'am. She like it dere. I guess de Lawd's took quite a fancy to her.

STOUT ANGEL: Well, dat's natural. I declare yo' mammy one of de finest lady angels I know.

SLENDER ANGEL: She claim you best one she know.

STOUT ANGEL: Well, when you come right down to it, I suppose we is all pretty near perfec'.

SLENDER ANGEL: Yes, ma'am. Why is dat, Mis' Jenny?

STOUT ANGEL: I s'pose it's caize de Lawd He don' 'low us 'sociatin' wid de devil any mo' so dat dey cain' be no mo' sinnin'.

SLENDER ANGEL: Po' ol' Satan. Whutevah become of him?

STOUT ANGEL: De Lawd put him some place I s'pose.

SLENDER ANGEL: But dey ain't any place but Heaven, is dey?

STOUT ANGEL: De Lawd could make a place, couldn't He?

SLENDER ANGEL: Dat's de truth. Dey's one thing confuses me though.

STOUT ANGEL: What's dat?

SLENDER ANGEL: I do a great deal of travelin' an' I ain't never come across any place but Heaven anywhere. So if de Lawd kick Satan out of Heaven jest whereat did he go? Dat's my question.

STOUT ANGEL: You bettah let de Lawd keep His own secrets, Lily. De way things is goin' now dey ain't been no sinnin' since dey give dat scamp a kick in de pants. Nowadays Heaven's free of sin an' if a lady wants a little constitutional she kin fly 'til she wing-weary widout gittin' insulted.

SLENDER ANGEL: I was jest a baby when Satan lef'. I don't even 'member what he look like.

STOUT ANGEL: He was jest right fo' a devil. [*An* ARCHANGEL *enters. He is older than the others and wears a white beard. His clothing is much darker than that of the others and his wings a trifle more imposing.*] Good mo'nin', Archangel.

[*Others say good morning.*]

ARCHANGEL: Good mo'nin', folks. I wonder kin I interrup' de fish fry an' give out de Sunday-School cyards? [*Cries of "Suttingly!" "Mah goodness, yes" — etc. The marching* CHOIR *stops.*] You kin keep singin' if you want to. Why don' you sing "When de Saints Come Marchin' In"? Seem to me I ain't heard dat lately. [*The* CHOIR *begins "When de Saints Come Marchin' In," rather softly, but does not resume the marching. The* ARCHANGEL *looks off left.*] All right, bring 'em yere. [*A prim-looking* WOMAN TEACHER-ANGEL *enters, shepherding ten* BOY *and* GIRL CHERUBS. *The* TEACHER *carries ten berib-boned diplomas, which she gives to the* ARCHANGEL. *The* CHERUBS *are dressed in stiffly starched white suits and dresses, the little girls having enormous ribbons at the backs of their dresses and smaller ones in their hair and on the tips of their wings. They line up in front of the* ARCHANGEL *and receive the attention of the rest of the company. The* CHOIR *sings through the ceremony.*] Now den, cherubs, why is you yere?

CHILDREN: Because we so good.

ARCHANGEL: Dat's right. Now who de big boss?

CHILDREN: Our dear Lawd.

ARCHANGEL: Dat's right. When you all grow up what you gonter be?

CHILDREN: Holy angels at de throne of grace.

ARCHANGEL: Dat's right. Now, you passed yo' 'xaminations and it gives me great pleasure to hand out de cyards for de whole class. Gineeva Chaproe. [*The* FIRST GIRL CHERUB *goes to him and gets her diploma. The* CHOIR *sings loudly and resumes marching, as the* ARCHANGEL *calls out another name — and presents diplomas.*] Corey Moulter. [SECOND GIRL CHERUB *gets her diploma.*] Nootzie Winebush. [THIRD GIRL CHERUB.] Harriet Prancy. [FOURTH GIRL CHERUB.] I guess you is Brozain Stew't. [*He gives the* FIFTH GIRL CHERUB *the paper. Each of the presentations has been accompanied by handclapping from the bystanders.*] Now you boys know yo' own names. Suppose you come yere and help me git dese 'sorted right?

[BOY CHERUBS *gather about him and receive their diplomas. The little girls have scattered about the stage, joining groups of the* ADULT ANGELS. *The angel* GABRIEL *enters. He is bigger and more elaborately winged than even the* ARCH-ANGEL, *but he is also much younger and beardless. His costume is less conventional than that of the other men, resembling more the Gabriel of the Doré drawings. His appearance causes a flutter among the others. They stop their chattering with the* CHILDREN. *The* CHOIR *stops as three or four audible whispers of "Gabriel!" are heard. In a moment the heavenly company is all attention.*]

GABRIEL [*lifting his hand*]: Gangway! Gangway for de Lawd God Jehovah!

[*There is a reverent hush and* GOD *enters. He is the tallest and biggest of them all. He wears a white shirt with a white bow tie, a long Prince Albert coat of black alpaca, black trousers and congress gaiters. He looks at the assemblage. There is a pause. He speaks in a rich, bass voice.*]

GOD: Is you been baptized?

OTHERS [*chanting*]: Certainly, Lawd.

GOD: Is you been baptized?

OTHERS: Certainly, Lawd.

GOD [*with the beginning of musical notation*]: Is you been baptized?

OTHERS [*now half-singing*]: Certainly, Lawd. Certainly, certainly, certainly, Lawd.

[*They sing the last two verses with equivalent part division.*]

> Is you been redeemed?
>> Certainly, Lawd.
> Is you been redeemed?
>> Certainly, Lawd.
> Is you been redeemed?
>> Certainly, Lawd. Certainly, certainly, certainly, Lawd.

> Do you bow mighty low?
>> Certainly, Lawd.
> Do you bow mighty low?
>> Certainly, Lawd.
> Do you bow mighty low?
>> Certainly, Lawd. Certainly, certainly, certainly, Lawd.

[*As the last response ends, all heads are bowed.* GOD *looks at them for a moment; then lifts His hand.*]

GOD: Let de fish fry proceed.

[*Everyone rises. The* ANGELS *relax and resume their inaudible conversations. The activity behind the table and about the cauldron is resumed. Some of the* CHOIR *members cross to the table and get sandwiches and cups of the boiled custard. Three or four of the* CHILDREN *in the Sunday-School class and the girl who had the bone in her throat affectionately group themselves about* GOD *as He speaks with the* ARCHANGEL. *He pats their heads, they hang to His coattails, etc.*]

ARCHANGEL: Good mo'nin', Lawd.

GOD: Good mo'nin', Deacon. You lookin' pretty spry.

ARCHANGEL: I cain' complain. We just been givin' our cyards to de chillun.

GOD: Dat's good.

[*A small* CHERUB, *his feet braced against one of* GOD's *shoes, is using* GOD's *coattail as a trapeze. One of the* COOKS *offers a fish sandwich which* GOD *politely declines.*]

FIRST MAMMY ANGEL: Now, you leave go de Lawd's coat, Herman. You heah me?

GOD: Dat's all right, sister. He jest playin'.

FIRST MAMMY ANGEL: He playin' too rough.

[GOD *picks up the* CHERUB *and spanks him good-naturedly. The* CHERUB *squeals with delight and runs to his mother.* GABRIEL *advances to* GOD *with a glass of the custard.*]

GABRIEL: Little b'iled custud, Lawd?

GOD: Thank you very kindly. Dis looks nice.

CUSTARD MAKER [*offering a box*]: Ten-cent seegar, Lawd?

GOD [*taking it*]: Thank you, thank you. How de fish fry goin'? [*Ad lib. cries of " O.K., Lawd," " Fine an' dandy, Lawd," " De best one yit, Lawd," etc. To the* CHOIR.] How you shouters gittin' on?

CHOIR LEADER: We been marchin' and singin' de whole mo'nin'.

GOD: I heerd you. You gittin' better all de time. You gittin' as good as de one at de throne. Why don' you give us one dem ol' time jump-ups?

CHOIR LEADER: Anythin' you say, Lawd. [*To the* OTHERS.] " So High! "

[*The* CHOIR *begins to sing " So High You Can't Get Over It." They sing softly, but do not march. An* ANGEL *offers his cigar to* GOD *from which He can light His own.*]

GOD: No, thanks. I'm gonter save dis a bit.

[*He puts His cigar in His pocket and listens to the singers a moment. Then He sips His custard. After the second sip, a look of displeasure comes on His face.*]

GABRIEL: What's de matter, Lawd?

GOD [*sipping again*]: I ain't jest sure, yit. Dey's something 'bout dis custahd.

[*Takes another sip.*]

CUSTARD MAKER: Ain't it all right, Lawd?

GOD: It don't seem seasoned jest right. You make it?

CUSTARD MAKER: Yes, Lawd. I put everythin' in it like I allus do. It's supposed to be perfec'.

GOD: Yeah. I kin taste de eggs and de cream and de sugar. [*Suddenly.*] I know what it is. It needs jest a little bit mo' firmament.

CUSTARD MAKER: Dey's firmament in it, Lawd.

GOD: Maybe, but it ain't enough.

CUSTARD MAKER: It's all we had, Lawd. Dey ain't a drap in de jug.

GOD: Dat's all right. I'll jest r'ar back an' pass a miracle. [CHOIR *stops singing.*] Let it be some firmament! An' when I say let it be some firmament, I don't want jest a little bitty dab o' firmament, caize I'm sick an' tired of runnin' out of it when we need it. Let it be a whole mess of firmament! [*The stage has become misty until* GOD *and the heavenly company are obscured. As He finishes the speech there is a burst of thunder. As the stage grows darker:*] Dat's de way I like it.

[*Murmurs from the others: " Dat's a lot of firmament!" " Look to me He created rain," etc.*]

FIRST MAMMY ANGEL [*when the stage is dark*]: Now, look, Lawd, dat's too much firmament. De cherubs is gettin' all wet.

SECOND MAMMY ANGEL: Look at my Carlotta, Lawd. She's soaked to de skin. Dat's *plenty* too much firmament.

GOD: Well, 'co'se we don't want de chillun to ketch cold. Can't you dreen it off?

GABRIEL: Dey's no place to dreen it, Lawd.

FIRST MAMMY ANGEL: Why don't we jest take de babies home, Lawd?

GOD: No, I don' wonta bust up de fish fry. You angels keep quiet an I'll pass another miracle. Dat's always de trouble wid miracles. When you pass one you always gotta r'ar back an' pass another. [*There is a hush.*] Let dere be a place to dreen off dis firmament. Let dere be mountains and valleys an' let dere be oceans an' lakes. An' let dere be rivers and bayous to dreen it off in, too. As a matter of fac' let dere be de earth. An' when dat's done let dere be de sun, an' let it come out and dry my cherubs' wings.

[*The lights go up until the stage is bathed in sunlight. On the embankment upstage there is now a waist-high wrought iron railing such as one sees on the galleries of houses in the French quarter of New Orleans. The* CHERUBS *are being examined by their parents and there is an ad lib. murmur of " You all right, honey?" " You feel better now, Albert?" " Now you all dry, Vangy?" until the* ARCHANGEL, *who has been gazing in awe at the railing, drowns them out.*]

ARCHANGEL: Look yere!

[*There is a rush to the embankment accompanied by exclamations, " My goodness!" " What's dis?" " I declah!" etc.* GABRIEL *towers above the group on the middle of the embankment.* GOD *is wrapped in thought, facing the audience. The* CHOIR *resumes singing " So High You Can't Get Over It" softly. The babbling at the balustrade dies away as the people lean over the railing.* GABRIEL *turns and faces* GOD *indicating the earth below the railing with his left hand.*]

GABRIEL: Do you see it, Lawd?

GOD [*quietly, without turning His head upstage*]: Yes, Gabriel.

GABRIEL: Looks mighty nice, Lawd.

GOD: Yes.

[GABRIEL *turns and looks over the railing.*]

GABRIEL [*gazing down*]: Yes, suh. Dat'd make mighty nice farming country. Jest look at dat South forty over dere. You ain't going to let dat go to waste is you, Lawd? Dat would be a pity an' a shame.

GOD [*not turning*]: It's a good earth. [GOD *turns, room is made for Him beside* GABRIEL *on the embankment.*] Yes. I ought to have somebody to enjoy it. [*He turns, facing the audience. The others, save for the* CHOIR *who are lined up in two rows of six on an angle up right, continue to look over the embankment.*] Gabriel!

[GOD *steps down from the embankment two paces.*]

GABRIEL [*joining him*]: Yes, Lawd.

GOD: Gabriel, I'm goin' down dere.

GABRIEL: Yes, Lawd.

GOD: I want you to be my working boss yere while I'm gone.

GABRIEL: Yes, Lawd.

GOD: You know dat matter of dem two stars?

GABRIEL: Yes, Lawd.

GOD: Git dat fixed up! You know dat sparrow dat fell a little while ago? 'Tend to dat, too.

GABRIEL: Yes, Lawd.

GOD: I guess dat's about all. I'll be back Saddy. [*To the* CHOIR.] Quiet, angels. [*The* CHOIR *stops singing. Those on the embankment circle downstage.* GOD *goes to embankment. Turns and faces the company.*] I'm gonter pass one more miracle. You all gonter help me an' not make a soun' caize it's one of the most impo'tant miracles of all. [*Nobody moves.* GOD *turns, facing the sky, and raises His arms above His head.*] Let there be man.

[*There is growing roll of thunder as stage grows dark. The* CHOIR *bursts into " Hallelujah," and continues until the lights go up on the next scene.*]

PART I. SCENE 3

Enclosing the stage is a heterogeneous cluster of cottonwood, camphor, live oak, and sycamore trees, youpon and turkey-berry bushes, with their purple and red berries, sprays of fernlike indigo fiera and splashes of various Louisiana flowers. In the middle of the stage, disclosed when the mistiness at rise grows into warm sunlight, stands ADAM.

He is a puzzled man of thirty, of medium height, dressed in the clothing of the average field hand. He is bare-headed. In the distance can be heard the CHOIR *continuing " Bright Mansions Above." A bird begins to sing.* ADAM *smiles and turns to look at the source of this novel sound. He senses his strength and raises his forearms, his fists clenched. With his left hand he carefully touches the muscles of his upper right arm. He smiles again, realizing his power. He looks at his feet, which are stretched wide apart. He stamps once or twice and now almost laughs in his enjoyment. Other birds begin trilling and* ADAM *glances up joyfully toward the foliage.* GOD *enters.*

GOD: Good mo'nin', Son.

ADAM [*with a little awe*]: Good mo'nin', Lawd.

GOD: What's yo' name, Son?

ADAM: Adam.

GOD: Adam which?

ADAM [*frankly, after a moment's puzzled groping*]: Jest Adam, Lawd.

GOD: Well, Adam, how dey treatin' you? How's things goin'?

ADAM: Well, Lawd, you know it's kind of a new line of wukk.

GOD: You'll soon get the hang of it. You know yo' kind of a new style with me.

ADAM: Oh, I guess I'm gonter make out all right soon as I learn de ropes.

GOD: Yes, I guess you will. Yo' a nice job.

ADAM: Yes, Lawd.

GOD: Dey's jest one little thing de matter with you. Did you notice it?

ADAM: Well, now you mentioned it, Lawd, I kind of thought dey was somethin' wrong.

GOD: Yes suh, you ain't quite right. Adam, you need a family. De reason for dat is in yo' heart you is a family man. [*Flicking the ash off His cigar.*] I'd say dat was de main trouble at de moment.

ADAM [*smiling*]: Yes sir. [*His smile fades and he is puzzled again.*] At de same time — dey's one thing puzzlin' me, Lawd. Could I ask you a question?

GOD: Why, certainly, Adam.

ADAM: Lawd, jest what *is* a family?

GOD: I'm gonter show you. [*Indicates a spot.*] Jest lie down dere, Adam. Make out like you was goin' to slumber.

ADAM [*gently*]: Yes, Lawd.

[*He lies down.* GOD *stands beside him and as He raises His arms above His head the lights go down. In the darkness* GOD *speaks.*]

GOD: Eve. [*Lights go up.* EVE *is standing beside* ADAM. *She is about twenty-six, and quite pretty. She is dressed like a country girl. Her gingham dress is quite new and clean.* GOD *is now at the other side of the stage, looking at them critically.* EVE *looks at* ADAM *in timid wonder and slowly turns her head until she meets the glance of* GOD. ADAM *stands beside* EVE. *They gaze at each other for a moment.* GOD *smiles.*] Now you all right, Eve. [ADAM *and* EVE *face Him.*] Now I'll tell you what I'm gonter do. I'm gonter put you in charge here. I'm gonter give you de run of dis whole garden. Eve, you take care of dis man, an' Adam, you take care of dis woman. You belong to each other. I don' want you to try to do much caize yo' both kind of experiment wid me an' I ain't sho' whether yo' could make it. You two jest enjoy yo'self. Drink de water from de little brooks an' de wine from de grapes an' de berries, an' eat de food dat's hangin' for you in de trees. [*He pauses, startled by a painful thought.*] Dat is, in all but one tree. [*He pauses. Then, not looking at them.*] You know what I mean, my children?

ADAM *and* EVE: Yes, Lawd.

[*They slowly turn their heads left, toward the branches of an off-stage tree. Then they look back at* GOD.]

ADAM: Thank you, Lawd.

EVE: Thank you, Lawd.

GOD: I gotter be gittin' along now. I got a hund'ed thousan' things to do 'fo' you take yo' nex' breath. Enjoy yo'selves —

[GOD *exits.* ADAM *and* EVE *stand looking after Him for a moment, then each looks down and watches their hands meet and clasp. After a moment they lift their heads slowly until they are again gazing at the tree.*]

EVE: Adam.

ADAM [*looking at the tree, almost in terror*]: What?

EVE [*softly as she too continues to look at the tree*]: Adam.

[*The* CHOIR *begins singing "Turn You Round" and as the lights go down the* CHOIR *continues until there is blackness. The* CHOIR *suddenly stops. The following scene is played in the darkness.*]

MR. DESHEE'S VOICE: Now, I s'pose you chillun know what happened after God made Adam 'n' Eve. Do you?

FIRST GIRL'S VOICE: I know, Mr. Deshee.

MR. DESHEE'S VOICE: Jest a minute, Randolph. Didn't I tell you you gotta tell yo' mammy let yo' sister bring you? Carlisle, take way dat truck he's eatin'. You sit by him, see kin you keep him quiet. Now, den, Myrtle, what happened?

FIRST GIRL'S VOICE: Why, den dey ate de fo'bidden fruit and den dey got driv' out de garden.

MR. DESHEE'S VOICE: An' den what happened?

FIRST GIRL'S VOICE: Den dey felt ver' bad.

MR. DESHEE'S VOICE: I don' mean how dey feel, I mean how dey do. Do dey have any children or anything like dat?

FIRST GIRL'S VOICE: Oh, yes, suh, dey have Cain 'n' Abel.

MR. DESHEE'S VOICE: Dat's right, dey have Cain an' Abel.

BOY'S VOICE: Dat was a long time after dey got married, wasn't it, Mr. Deshee? My mammy say it was a hund'ed years.

MR. DESHEE'S VOICE: Well, nobody kin be so sure. As I tol' you befo' dey was jest beginnin' to be able to tell de time an' nobody was any too sure 'bout anythin' even den. So de bes' thing to do is jest realize dat de thing happened an' don't bother 'bout how many years it was. Jest remember what I told you about it gittin' dark when you go to sleep an' it bein' light when you wake up. Dat's de way time went by in dem days. One thing we do know an' dat was dis boy Cain was a mean rascal.

[*The lights go up on the next scene.*]

PART I. SCENE 4

A roadside.

CAIN, *a husky young Negro, stands over the body of the dead* ABEL. *Both are dressed as laborers.* CAIN *is looking at the body in awe, a rock in his right hand.* GOD *enters.*

GOD: Cain, look what you done to Abel.

CAIN: Lawd, I was min'in' my own business and he come monkeyin' aroun' wit' me. I wus wukkin' in de fiel' an' he was sittin' in de shade of de tree. He say " Me, I'd be skeered to git out in dis hot sun. I be 'fraid my brains git cooked. Co'se you ain't got no brains so you ain' in no danger." An' so I up and flang de rock. If it miss 'im all right, an' if it hit 'im all right. Dat's de way I feel.

GOD: All right, but I'm yere to tell you dat's called a crime. When de new Judge is done talkin' to you you'll be draggin' a ball and chain de rest of yo' life.

CAIN: Well, what'd he want to come monkeyin' aroun' me fo' den? I was jest plowin', min'in' my own business, and not payin' him no min', and yere he come makin' me de fool. I'd bust anybody what make me de fool.

GOD: Well, I ain't sayin' you right an' I ain't sayin' you wrong. But I do say was I you I'd jest git myself down de road 'til I was clean out of de county. An' you better take an' git married an' settle down an' raise some chillun. Dey ain't nothin' to make a man fo'git his troubles like raisin' a family. Now, you better git.

CAIN: Yessuh.

[CAIN *walks off.* GOD *watches him from the forestage and as the lights begin to dim looks off. The* CHOIR *begins " Run, Sinner, Run."*]

GOD: Adam an' Eve, you better try again. You better have Seth an' a lot mo' chillun.

[*There is darkness. The* CHOIR *continues until the lights go up on the next scene.*]

PART I. SCENE 5

CAIN *is discovered walking on an unseen treadmill. A middle distance of trees, hillsides, and shrubbery passes him on an upper treadmill. Behind is the blue sky. He stops under the branches of a tree to look at a sign on a fence railing. Only half the tree is visible on the stage. The sign reads, " Nod Parish. County Line."*

CAIN [*sitting down with a sigh of relief under a tree*]: At las'! Phew! [*Wipes his forehead with a handkerchief.*] Feels like I been walkin' fo'ty years. [*He looks back.*] Well, dey cain' git me now. Now I kin raise a fam'ly. [*An idea occurs to him, and suddenly he begins looking right and left.*] Well, I'll be hit by a mule! Knock me down for a trustin' baby! Where I gonter git dat family? Dat preacher fooled me. [*He is quite dejected.*] Doggone!

CAIN'S GIRL [*off stage*]: Hello, Country Boy!

[CAIN *glances up to the off-stage branches of the tree.*]

CAIN: Hey-ho, Good-lookin'! Which way is it to town?

CAIN'S GIRL [*off stage*]: What you tryin' to do? You tryin' to mash me? I be doggone if it ain't gittin' so a gal cain't hardly leave de house 'out some of dese fast men ain' passin' remarks at her.

CAIN: I ain' passin' remarks.

CAIN'S GIRL [*off stage*]: If I thought you was tryin' to mash me, I'd call de police an' git you tooken to de first precinct.

CAIN: Look yere, gal, I ast you a question, an' if you don' answer me I'm gonter bend you 'cross my pants an' burn you up.

CAIN'S GIRL [*off stage*]: I'm comin' down.

[CAIN *takes his eyes from the tree.*]

CAIN: Yes, an' you better hurry.

[CAIN'S GIRL *enters. She is as large as* CAIN, *wickedly pretty, and somewhat flushily dressed. She smiles at* CAIN.]

CAIN'S GIRL: I bet you kin handle a gal mean wid dem big stout arms of your'n. I sho' would hate to git you mad at me, Country Boy.

CAIN [*smiling*]: Come yere. [*She goes a little closer to him.*] Don't be 'fraid, I ain' so mean.

CAIN'S GIRL: You got two bad-lookin' eyes. I bet yo' hot coffee 'mong de women folks.

CAIN: I ain' never find out. What was you doin' in dat tree?

CAIN'S GIRL: Jest coolin' myself in de element.

CAIN: Is you a Nod Parish gal?

CAIN'S GIRL: Bo'n an' bred.

CAIN: You know yo' kinda pretty.

CAIN'S GIRL: Who tol' you dat?

CAIN: Dese yere two bad eyes of mine.

CAIN'S GIRL: I bet you say dat to everybody all de way down de road.

CAIN: Comin' down dat road I didn't talk to nobody.

CAIN'S GIRL: Where you boun' for, Beautiful?

CAIN: I'm jest seein' de country. I thought I might settle down yere fo' a spell. Yo' live wit' yo' people?

CAIN'S GIRL: Co'se I does.

CAIN: 'Spose dey'd like to take in a boarder?

CAIN'S GIRL: Be nice if dey would, wouldn't it?

CAIN: I think so. You got a beau?

CAIN'S GIRL: Huh-uh!

CAIN [smiling]: You has now.

CAIN'S GIRL: I guess — I guess if you wanted to kiss me an' I tried to stop you, you could pretty nearly crush me wit' dem stout arms.

CAIN: You wouldn't try too much, would you?

CAIN'S GIRL: Maybe for a little while.

CAIN: An' den what?

CAIN'S GIRL: Why don' we wait an' see?

CAIN: When would dat be?

CAIN'S GIRL: Tonight. After supper. Think you kin walk a little further now, City Boy?

CAIN: Yeh, I ain't so weary now.

[She takes his hand.]

CAIN'S GIRL: What yo' name?

[Takes his arm.]

CAIN: Cain.

CAIN'S GIRL: Then I'm Cain's Gal. Come on, honey, an' meet de folks.

[They go out. The CHOIR is heard singing " You Better Mind," as GOD enters. GOD watches the vanishing CAIN and his girl.]

GOD [after shaking His head]: Bad business. I don' like de way things is goin' a-tall.

[The stage is darkened. The CHOIR continues singing until the lights go up on the next scene.]

PART I. SCENE 6

GOD's private office in Heaven. It is a small room, framed by tableau curtains. A large window up center looks out on the sky. There is a battered roll-top desk. On the wall next to the window is a framed religious oleograph with a calendar *attached to it underneath. A door is at the left. A hat rack is on the wall above the door. There are two or three cheap pine chairs beside the window, and beyond the door. In front of the desk is an old swivel armchair which creaks every time GOD leans back in it. The desk is open and various papers are stuck in the pigeonholes. Writing implements, etc., are on the desk. On a shelf above the desk is a row of law books. A cuspidor is near the desk, and a waste basket by it. The general atmosphere is that of the office of a Negro lawyer in a Louisiana town. As the lights go up GOD takes a fresh cigar from a box on the desk and begins puffing it without bothering to light it. There is no comment on this minor miracle from GABRIEL who is sitting in one of the chairs with a pencil and several papers in his hand. The singing becomes pianissimo.*

GABRIEL [*looking at the papers*]: Well, I guess dat's about all de impo'tant business this mornin', Lawd.

GOD: How 'bout dat cherub over to Archangel Montgomery's house?

GABRIEL: Where do dey live, Lawd?

[*The singing stops.*]

GOD: Dat little two-story gold house, over by de pearly gates.

GABRIEL: Oh, dat Montgomery. I thought you was referrin' to de ol' gentleman. Oh, yeh. [*He sorts through the papers and finds one he is looking for.*] Yere it 'tis. [*Reads.*] " Cherub Christina Montgomery; wings is moltin' out of season an' nobody knows what to do."

GOD: Well, now, take keer of dat. You gotter be more careful, Gabe.

GABRIEL: Yes, Lawd.

[*Folds the papers and put them in a pocket. GOD turns to His desk, takes another puff or two of the cigar, and with a pencil, begins checking off items on a sheet of paper before Him. His back is turned toward GABRIEL. GABRIEL takes his trumpet from the hat rack and burnishes it with his robe. He then wets his lips and puts the mouthpiece to his mouth.*]

GOD [*without turning around*]: Now, watch yo'self, Gabriel.

GABRIEL: I wasn't goin' to blow, Lawd. I jest do dat every now an' den so I can keep de feel of it.

[*He leans trumpet against the wall. GOD picks up the papers and swings His chair around toward GABRIEL.*]

GOD: What's dis yere about de moon?

GABRIEL [*suddenly remembering*]: Oh! De moon people say it's beginnin' to melt a little, on 'count caize de sun's so hot.

GOD: It's goin' 'roun' 'cordin' to schedule, ain't it?

GABRIEL: Yes, Lawd.

GOD: Well, tell 'em to stop groanin'. Dere's nothin' de matter wid dat moon. Trouble is so many angels is flyin' over dere on Saddy night. Dey git to beatin' dere wings when dey dancin' an' dat makes de heat. Tell dem dat from now on dancin' 'roun' de moon is sinnin'. Dey got to stop it. Dat'll cool off de moon. [*He swings back and puts the paper on the desk. He leans back in the chair comfortably, His hands clasped behind His head.*] Is dere anythin' else you ought to remin' me of?

GABRIEL: De prayers, Lawd.

GOD [*puzzled, slowly swinging chair around again*]: De prayers?

GABRIEL: From mankind. You know, down on de earth.

GOD: Oh, yeh, de poor little earth. Bless my soul, I almos' forgot about dat. Mus' be three or four hund'ed years since I been down dere. I wasn't any too pleased wid dat job.

GABRIEL [*laughing*]: You know you don' make mistakes, Lawd.

GOD [*soberly, with introspective detachment*]: So dey tell me. [*He looks at* GABRIEL, *then through the window again.*] So dey tell me. I fin' I kin be displeased though, an' I was displeased wid de mankind I las' seen. Maybe I ought to go down dere agin — I need a little holiday.

GABRIEL: Might do you good, Lawd.

GOD: I think I will. I'll go down an' walk de earth agin an' see how dem poor humans is makin' out. What time is it, by de sun an' de stars?

GABRIEL [*glancing out of the window*]: Jest exactly half-past, Lawd.

[GOD *is taking His hat and stick from the hat rack.*]

GOD [*opening the door*]: Well, take keer o' yo'self. I'll be back Saddy.

[*He exits. The stage is darkened. The* CHOIR *begins "Dere's No Hidin' Place," and continues until the lights go up on the next scene.*]

PART I. SCENE 7

GOD *is walking along a country road. He stops to listen. Church bells are heard in the distance.*

GOD: Dat's nice. Nice an' quiet. Dat's de way I like Sunday to be. [*The sound is broken by a shrill voice of a girl. It is* ZEBA *singing a "blues."*] Now, dat ain't so good. [GOD *resumes His walk and the upper treadmill brings on a tree stump on which* ZEBA *is sitting. She is accompanying her song with a ukulele.* GOD *and the treadmills stop. When the stump reaches the center of the stage, it is seen that* ZEBA *is a rouged and extremely flashily dressed chippy of about eighteen.*] Stop dat!

ZEBA: What's de matter wid you, Country Boy? Pull up yo' pants.

[*She resumes singing.*]

GOD: Stop dat!

ZEBA [*stops again*]: Say, listen to me, Banjo Eyes. What right you got to stop a lady enjoyin' herself?

GOD: Don't you know dis is de Sabbath? Da's no kin' o' song to sing on de Lawd's day.

ZEBA: Who care 'bout de Lawd's day, anymo'? People jest use Sunday now to git over Saddy.

GOD: You a awful sassy little girl.

ZEBA: I come fum sassy people! We even speak mean of de dead.

GOD: What's yo' name?

ZEBA [*flirtatiously*]: "What's my name?" Ain't you de ol'-time gal hunter! Fust, "What's my name?" den I s'pose, what would it be like if you tried to kiss me? You preachers is de debbils.

GOD: I ain't aimin' to touch you, daughter. [*A sudden sternness frightens* ZEBA. *She looks at him sharply.*] What is yo' name?

ZEBA: Zeba.

GOD: Who's yo' fam'ly?

ZEBA: I'm de great-great-gran'daughter of Seth.

GOD: Of Seth? But Seth was a good man.

ZEBA: Yeh, he too good, he die of holiness.

GOD: An' yere's his little gran'daughter reekin' wid cologne. Ain't nobody ever tol' you yo' on de road to Hell?

ZEBA [*smiling*]: Sho' dat's what de preacher say. Exceptin' of course, I happens to know dat I'm on de road to de picnic groun's, an' at de present time I'm waitin' to keep a engagement wid my sweet papa. He don' like people talkin' to me.

[CAIN THE SIXTH *enters. He is a young buck, wearing a "box" coat and the other flashy garments of a Rampart Street swell.*]

CAIN THE SIXTH: Hello, sugah! [*He crosses in front of* GOD *and faces* ZEBA.] Hello, mamma! Sorry I'm late, baby, but de gals in de barrel-house jest wouldn't let me go. Doggone, one little wirehead swore she'd tear me down.

[ZEBA *smiles and takes his hand.*]

GOD: What's yo' name, son?

CAIN THE SIXTH [*contemptuously, without turning*]: Soap 'n' water, Country Boy.

GOD [*sternly*]: What's yo' name, son?

[CAIN *slowly turns and for a moment his manner is civil.*]

CAIN THE SIXTH: Cain the Sixth.

GOD: I was afraid so.

CAIN THE SIXTH [*his impudence returning*]: You a new preacher?

GOD: Where you live?

CAIN THE SIXTH: Me, I live mos' any place.

GOD: Yes, an' you gonter see dem all. Is de udder young men all like you?

CAIN THE SIXTH [*smiling*]: De gals don' think so.

[*He turns towards* ZEBA *again, picks her up and sits on the stump with the laughing* ZEBA *on his lap.*]

ZEBA: Dey ain't nobody in de worl' like my honey-cake.

[CAIN *kisses her and she resumes her song.* GOD *watches them.* ZEBA *finishes a verse of the song and begins another softly.* CAIN THE SIXTH's *eyes have been closed during the singing.*]

CAIN THE SIXTH [*his eyes closed*]: Is de preacher gone?

[ZEBA *looks quickly at* GOD *without seeing him, and then looks off. She stops the song.*]

ZEBA: Yeh, I guess he walks fast.

[CAIN *pushes her off his lap and rises.*]

CAIN THE SIXTH [*with acid sweetness*]: Dey tell me las' night you was talkin' to a creeper man, baby.

ZEBA: Why, you know dey ain't nobody in de world fo' me but you.

CAIN THE SIXTH [*smiling*]: I know dey ain't. I even got dat guaranteed. [*Takes a revolver from his pocket.*] See dat, baby?

ZEBA: Sho' I see it, honey.

CAIN THE SIXTH: Dat jest makes me positive.

[*Puts the gun back.*]

ZEBA [*pushing him back on the stump*]: You don' wanter believe dem stories, papa.

CAIN THE SIXTH [*with sinister lightness*]: No, I didn't believe dem, baby. Co'se dat big gorilla, Flatfoot, from de other side of de river *is* in town ag'in.

ZEBA: Dat don' mean nothin'. Flatfoot ain't nothin' to me.

CAIN THE SIXTH [*sitting again*]: Co'se he ain't. Go 'head, sing some mo', baby.

[ZEBA *resumes singing.*]

GOD: Bad business. [*The treadmills start turning.* GOD *resumes his walk.* ZEBA, *still singing, and* CAIN THE SIXTH *recede with the landscape.* GOD *is again alone on the country road. There is a twitter of birds.* GOD *looks up and smiles.*] De birds is goin' 'bout dere business, all right. [*A patch of flowers goes by, black-eyed susans, conspicuously.*] How you flowers makin' out? [*Children's voices answer, " We O.K. Lawd."*] Yes, an' you looks very pretty. [*Children's voices: " Thank you, Lawd." The flowers pass out of sight.*] It's only de human bein's makes me downhearted. Yere's as nice a Sunday as dey is turnin' out anywhere, an' nobody makin' de right use of it. [*Something ahead of him attracts his attention. His face brightens.*] Well, now dis is mo' like it. Now dat's nice to see people prayin'. It's a wonder dey don' do it in de church. But I fin' I don' min' it if dey do it outdoors.

GAMBLER: Oh, Lawd, de smoke-house is empty. Oh, Lawd, lemme git dem groceries. Oh, Lawd, lemme see dat little six. [*He casts the dice.*] Wham! Dere she is, frien's.

[*Exclamations from the others: " Well, damn my eyes!" " Doggone, dat's de eighth pass he make," " For God's sake, can't you ever crap?" etc. The* BOY *is picking up the money.*]

GOD: Gamblin'! [*Looks over the group's shoulders.*] An' wid frozen dice!

BOY GAMBLER: Dey's a dolla' 'n' a half talkin' fo' me. How much you want of it, Riney?

FIRST GAMBLER: I take fo' bits. Wait a minute. Mebbe I take a little mo'.

[*He counts some money in his hand.*]

SECOND GAMBLER [*glancing up at* GOD]: Hello, Liver Lips. [*To the others.*] Looka ol' Liver Lips.

[*The others look up and laugh good-naturedly, repeating " Liver Lips."*]

FIRST GAMBLER: Ain't his pockets high from de groun'? Ol' High Pockets.

[*The others keep saying, " Ol' Liver Lips," " Ol' Liver Lips don't like to see people dicin','" " Dat's a good name,' High Pockets.' "*]

BOY GAMBLER [*to others*]: Come on, you gonter fade me or not?

[GOD *seizes the* BOY's *ears and drags him to his feet. The others do not move, but watch, amused.*]

GOD: Come yere, son. Why, yo' jest a little boy. Gamblin' an' sinnin'. [GOD *looks at the* BOY's *face.*] You been chewin' tobacco, too, like you was yo' daddy. [GOD *sniffs.*] An' you been drinkin' sonny-kick-mammy wine. You oughta be shamed.

[*To the others.*] An' you gamblers oughta be shamed, leadin' dis boy to sin.

FIRST GAMBLER: He de bes' crap shooter in town, mister.

GOD: I'm gonter tell his mammy. I bet she don' know 'bout dis.

FIRST GAMBLER: No, she don' know. [*The others laugh.*] She don' know anythin'.

SECOND GAMBLER: Dat's de God's truth.

FIRST GAMBLER: See kin you beat 'im, High Pockets. Dey's a dolla' open yere.

GOD: I ain't gonter beat 'im. I'm gonter teach 'im. I may have to teach you all.

[*He starts walking from them. The* BOY *sticks out his tongue the moment* GOD's *back is turned.*]

BOY GAMBLER: If you fin' my mammy you do mo'n I kin. Come on, gamblers, see kin you gimme a little action. Who wants any part of dat dollar?

[*The treadmill carries them off. The* FIRST GAMBLER *is heard saying, " I'll take anoder two bits," and the others, " Gimme a dime's wo'th," " I ain't only got fifteen cents left," etc., as they disappear.*]

GOD [*walking*]: Where's dat little boy's home? [*The front of a shanty appears and* GOD *stops in front of the door.*] Yere's de place. It ain't any too clean, either.

[*Knocks on the door with his cane.*]

VOICE IN SHANTY: Who dar?

GOD: Never you min' who's yere. Open de door.

VOICE IN SHANTY: You gotta search warrant?

GOD: I don' need one.

VOICE IN SHANTY: Who you wanter see?

GOD: I wanter see de mammy of de little gamblin' boy.

VOICE IN SHANTY: You mean little Johnny Rucker?

GOD: Dat may be his name.

VOICE IN SHANTY: Well, Mrs. Rucker ain't home.

GOD: Where's she at?

VOICE IN SHANTY: Who, Mrs. Rucker?

GOD: You heerd me.

VOICE IN SHANTY: Oh, she run away las' night wid a railroad man. She's eloped.

GOD: Where's Rucker?

VOICE IN SHANTY: He's flat under de table. He so drunk he cain't move.

GOD: Who are you?

VOICE IN SHANTY: I'se jest a fren' an' neighbor. I come in las' night to de party, an' everybody in yere's dead drunk but me. De only reason I kin talk is I drank some new white mule I made myself, an' it burn my throat so I cain't drink no mo'. You got any mo' questions?

GOD: Not for you.

[*The shanty begins to move off as* GOD *starts walking again.*]

VOICE IN SHANTY: Good riddance, I say.

[*Shanty disappears.*]

GOD: Dis ain't gittin' me nowheres. All I gotta say dis yere mankind I been peo-plin' my earth wid sho' ain't much. [*He stops and looks back.*] I got good min' to wipe 'em all off an' people de earth wid angels. No. Angels is all right, singin' an' playin' an' flyin' around, but dey ain't much on workin' de crops and buildin' de levees. No, suh, mankind's jest right for my earth, if he wasn't so doggone sinful. I'd rather have my earth peopled wit' a bunch of channel catfish, dan I would mankin' an' his sin. I jest cain't stan' sin.

[*He is about to resume his walk when* NOAH *enters.* NOAH *is dressed like a country preacher. His coat is of the " hammer-tail" variety. He carries a prayer book under his arm.*]

NOAH: Mo'nin', brother.

GOD: Mo'nin', brother. I declare you look like a good man.

NOAH: I try to be, brother. I'm de preacher yere. I don't think I seen you to de meetin'.

[*They resume walking.*]

GOD: I jest come to town a little while ago an' I been pretty busy.

NOAH: Yeh, mos' everybody say dey's pretty busy dese days. Dey so busy dey cain't come to meetin'. It seem like de mo' I preaches de mo' people ain't got time to come to church. I ain't hardly got enough members to fill up de choir. I gotta do de preachin' an' de bassin' too.

GOD: Is dat a fac'?

NOAH: Yes, suh, brother. Everybody is mighty busy, gamblin', good-timin', and goin' on. You jest wait, though. When Gabriel blow de horn you gonter fin' dey got plenty of time to punch chunks down in Hell. Yes, suh.

GOD: Seems a pity. Dey all perfec'ly healthy?

NOAH: Oh, dey healthy, all right. Dey jest all lazy, and mean, and full of sin. You look like a preacher, too, brother.

GOD: Well, I am, in a way.

NOAH: You jest passin' through de neighborhood?

GOD: Yes. I wanted to see how things was goin' in yo' part of de country, an' I been feelin' jest 'bout de way you do. It's enough to discourage you.

NOAH: Yes, but I gotta keep wres'lin' wid 'em. Where you boun' for right now, brother?

GOD: I was jest walkin' along. I thought I might stroll on to de nex' town.

NOAH: Well, dat's a pretty good distance. I live right yere. [*He stops walking.*] Why don' you stop an' give us de pleasure of yo' comp'ny for dinner? I believe my ol' woman has kilt a chicken.

GOD: Why, dat's mighty nice of you, brother. I don't believe I caught yo' name.

NOAH: Noah, jest brother Noah. Dis is my home, brother. Come right in.

[GOD *and* NOAH *start walking towards* NOAH's *house which is coming into view on the treadmill. The stage darkens, the* CHOIR *sings " Feastin' Table," and when the lights go up again, the next scene is disclosed.*]

PART I. SCENE 8

Interior of NOAH's *house. The ensemble suggests the combination living-dining room in a fairly prosperous Negro's cabin. Clean white curtains hang at the window. A table and chairs are in the center of the room. There is a cheerful checked tablecloth on the table, and on the wall, a framed, highly colored picture reading, " God Bless Our Home." NOAH's WIFE, an elderly Negress, simply and neatly dressed,* GOD, *and* NOAH *are discovered grouped about the table.*

NOAH: Company, darlin'. [NOAH's WIFE *takes* NOAH's *and* GOD's *hats.*] Dis gemman's a preacher, too. He's jest passin' through de country.

GOD: Good mo'nin', sister.

NOAH's WIFE: Good mo'nin'. You jest ketch me when I'm gittin' dinner ready. You gonter stay with us?

GOD: If I ain't intrudin'. Brother Noah suggested —

NOAH's WIFE: You set right down yere. I got a chicken in de pot an' it'll be ready in 'bout five minutes. I'll go out de back an' call Shem, Ham, 'n' Japheth. [*To* GOD.] Dey's our sons. Dey live right acrost de way but always have Sunday dinner wid us. You mens make yo'selves comf'table.

GOD: Thank you, thank you very kindly.

NOAH: You run along, we all right.

[GOD *and* NOAH *seat themselves.* NOAH's WIFE *exits.*]

GOD: You got a fine wife, brother Noah.

NOAH: She pretty good woman.

GOD: Yes, suh, an' you got a nice little home. Have a ten-cent seegar?

[GOD *offers him one.*]

NOAH: Thank you, much obliged.

[*Both men lean back restfully in their chairs.*]

GOD: Jest what seems to be the main trouble 'mong mankind, Noah?

NOAH: Well, it seems to me dat de main trouble is dat de whol' distric' is wide open. Now you know dat makes fo' loose livin'. Men folks spen's all dere time fightin', loafin' and gamblin', an' makin' bad likker.

GOD: What about de women?

NOAH: De women is worse dan de men. If dey ain't makin' love powder dey out beg, borrow an' stealin' money for policy tickets. Doggone, I come in de church Sunday 'fo' las' 'bout an' hour befo' de meetin' was to start, and dere was a woman stealin' de altar cloth. She was goin' to hock it. Dey ain't got no moral sense. Now you take dat case las' month, over in East Putney. Case of dat young Willy Roback.

GOD: What about him?

NOAH: Dere is a boy seventeen years old. Doggone, if he didn't elope with his aunt. Now, you know, dat kin' of goin' on is bad fo' a neighborhood.

GOD: Terrible, terrible.

NOAH: Yes, suh. Dis use' to be a nice, decent community. I been doin' my best to preach de Word, but seems like every time I preach de place jest goes a little mo' to de dogs. De good Lawd only knows what's gonter happen.

GOD: Dat's de truth.

[There is a pause. Each puffs his cigar. Suddenly NOAH grasps his knee, as if it were paining him, and twists his foot.]

NOAH: Huh!

GOD: What's de matter?

NOAH: I jest got a twitch. My buckaguer I guess. Every now and den I gets a twitch in de knee. Might be a sign of rain.

GOD: That's just what it is. Noah, what's de mos' rain you ever had 'round dese parts?

NOAH: Well, de water come down fo' six days steady last April an' de ribber got so swole it bust down de levee up 'bove Freeport. Raise cain all de way down to de delta.

GOD: What would you say was it to rain for forty days and forty nights?

NOAH: I'd say dat was a *complete* rain!

GOD: Noah, you don't know who I is, do you?

NOAH [puzzled]: Yo' face looks easy, but I don' think I recall de name. [GOD rises slowly, and as He reaches His full height there is a crash of lightning, a moment's darkness, and a roll of thunder. It grows light again. NOAH is on his knees in front of GOD.] I should have known you. I should have seen de glory.

GOD: Dat's all right, Noah. You didn' know who I was.

NOAH: I'm jes' ol' preacher Noah, Lawd, an' I'm yo' servant. I ain' very much, but I'se all I got.

GOD: Sit down, Noah. Don' let me hear you shamin' yo'se'f, caize yo' a good man. [Timidly NOAH waits until GOD is seated, and then sits, himself.] I jest wanted to fin' out if you was good, Noah. Dat's why I'm walkin' de earth in de shape of a natchel man. I wish dey was mo' people like you. But, far as I kin see, you and yo' family is de only respectable people in de worl'.

NOAH: Dey jest all poor sinners, Lawd.

GOD: I know. I am your Lawd. I am a god of wrath and vengeance an' dat's why I'm gonter destroy dis worl'.

NOAH [*almost in a whisper, drawing back*]: Jest as you say, Lawd.

GOD: I ain't gonter destroy you, Noah. You and yo' fam'ly, yo' sheep an' cattle, an' all de udder things dat ain't human I'm gonter preserve. But de rest is gotta go. [*Takes a pencil and a sheet of paper from His pocket.*] Look yere, Noah. [*Noah comes over and looks over His shoulder.*] I want you to build me a boat. I want you to call it de "Ark," and I want it to look like dis. [*He is drawing on the paper. Continues to write as He speaks.*] I want you to take two of every kind of animal and bird dat's in de country. I want you to take seeds an' sprouts an' everything like dat an' put dem on dat Ark, because dere is gonter be all dat rain. Dey's gonter be a deluge, Noah, an' dey's goin' to be a flood. De levees is gonter bust an' everything dat's fastened down is comin' loose, but it ain't gonter float long, caize I'm gonter make a storm dat'll sink everythin' from a hencoop to a barn. Dey ain't a ship on de sea dat'll be able to fight dat tempest. Dey all got to go. Everythin'. Everythin' in dis pretty worl' I made, except one thing, Noah. You an' yo' fam'ly an' de things I said are going to ride dat storm in de Ark. Yere's de way it's to be.

[*He hands* NOAH *the paper.* NOAH *takes it and reads.*]

NOAH [*pause, looks at paper again*]: Yes, suh, dis seems to be complete. Now 'bout the animals, Lawd, you say you want everythin'?

GOD: Two of everythin'.

NOAH: Dat would include jayraffes an' hippopotamusses?

GOD: Everythin' dat is.

NOAH: Dey was a circus in town las' week. I guess I kin fin' dem. Co'se I kin git all de rabbits an' possums an' wil' turkeys easy. I'll sen' de boys out. Hum, I'm jest wonderin' —

GOD: 'Bout what?

NOAH: 'Bout snakes? Think you'd like snakes, too?

GOD: Certainly I want snakes.

NOAH: Oh, I kin git snakes, lots of 'em. Co'se, some of 'em's a little dangerous. Maybe I better take a kag of likker, too?

GOD: You can have a kag of likker.

NOAH [*musingly*]: Yes, suh, dey's a awful lot of differ'nt kin's of snakes, come to think about it. Dey's water moccasins, cotton-moufs, rattlers — mus' be a hund'ed kin's of other snakes down in de swamps. Maybe I better take two kags of likker.

GOD [*mildly*]: I think de one kag's enough.

NOAH: No. I better take two kags. Besides I kin put one on each side of de boat, an' balance de ship wid dem as well as havin' dem fo' medicinal use.

GOD: You kin put one kag in de middle of de ship.

NOAH [*buoyantly*]: Jest as easy to take de two kags, Lawd.

GOD: I think one kag's enough.

NOAH: Yes, Lawd, but you see forty days an' forty nights —

[*There is a distant roll of thunder.*]

GOD [*firmly*]: One kag, Noah.

NOAH: Yes, Lawd. One kag.

[*The door in the back opens and* NOAH'S WIFE *enters with a tray of dishes and food.*]

NOAH'S WIFE: Now, den, gen'lemen, if you'll jest draw up cheers.

[*The stage is darkened. The* CHOIR *is heard singing " I Want to Be Ready." They continue in the darkness until the lights go up on the next scene.*]

PART I. SCENE 9

In the middle of the stage is the Ark. On the hillside, below the Ark, a dozen or more men and women, townspeople, are watching NOAH, SHEM, HAM, *and* JAPHETH *on the deck of the Ark. The three sons are busily nailing boards on the cabin.* NOAH *is smoking a pipe. He wears a silk hat, captain's uniform, and a " slicker."*

NOAH [*to* SHEM]: You, Shem, tote up some ol' rough lumber; don' bring up any planed-up lumber, caize dat ain't fo' de main deck.

SHEM: Pretty near supper time, daddy.

NOAH: Maybe 'tis, but I got de feelin' we ought to keep goin'.

FIRST WOMAN: You gonter work all night, Noah, maybe, huh?

NOAH [*without looking at her*]: If de speerit move me.

SECOND WOMAN: Look yere, Noah, whyn't you give up all dis damn foolishness? Don' you know people sayin' yo' crazy? What you think you doin' anyway?

NOAH: I'se buildin' a Ark. [*Other men and women join those in the foreground.*] Ham, you better stop for a while 'n see whether dey bringin' de animals up all right. [*He looks at his watch.*] Dey ought to be pretty near de foot o' de hill by dis time; if dey ain't you wait fo' dem and bring 'em yo'se'f.

[HAM *goes down a ladder at the side of the ship and exits during the following scene. The newcomers in group have been speaking to some of the early arrivals.*]

SECOND WOMAN [*to* THIRD WOMAN, *one of the newcomers*]: No, you don't mean it!

THIRD WOMAN: I do so. Dat's what de talk is in de town.

FIRST MAN: You hear dat, Noah? Dey say yo' ol' lady is tellin' everybody it's gonter rain fo' fo'ty days and fo'ty nights. You know people soon gonter git de idea you *all* crazy.

NOAH: Lot I keer what you think. [*To* JAPHETH.] Straighten up dem boards down dere, Japheth. [*Indicating floor of deck.*]

FIRST MAN [*to* THIRD WOMAN]: Was I you, I wouldn' go 'round with Mrs. Noah any more, lady. First thing you know you'll be gittin' a hard name, too.

THIRD WOMAN: Don' I know?

SECOND WOMAN: A lady cain't be too partic'lar dese days.

[ZEBA *and* FLATFOOT, *a tall, black, wicked-looking buck, enter, their arms around each other's waists.*]

ZEBA: Dere it is, baby. Was I lyin'?

FLATFOOT: Well, I'll be split in two!

FIRST MAN: What you think of it, Flatfoot?

FLATFOOT: I must say! Look like a house wit' a warpin' cellar.

NOAH: Dis yere vessel is a boat.

FLATFOOT: When I was a little boy dey used to build boats down near de ribber, where de water was.

[*The others laugh.*]

NOAH: Dis time it's been arranged to have de water come up to de boat. [JAPHETH *looks belligerently over the rail of the Ark at* FLATFOOT. *To* JAPHETH.] Keep yo' shirt on, son.

SECOND WOMAN [*to* THIRD WOMAN]: Now, you see de whole fam'ly's crazy.

THIRD WOMAN: Listen, dey ain't gonter 'taminate me. It was me dat started resolvin' dem both out o' de buryin' society.

ZEBA: When all dis water due up yere, Noah?

NOAH: You won't know when it gits yere, daughter.

ZEBA: Is she goin' to be a side-wheeler, like de *Bessy-Belle?*

FLATFOOT: No! If she was a side-wheeler she'd get her wheels all clogged wid sharks. She gonter have jus' one great big stern wheel, like de *Commodore.* Den if dey ain't 'nuf water why de big wheel kin stir some up.

[*General laughter. Two or three of the* GAMBLERS *enter and join the group, followed by* CAIN THE SIXTH.]

CAIN THE SIXTH: Dere's de fool an' his monument, jest like I said!

[*The* GAMBLERS *and* CAIN THE SIXTH *roar with laughter, slap their legs, etc. The members of the main group talk sotto voce to each other as* CAIN THE SIXTH *catches* ZEBA's *eye.* FLATFOOT *is on her right and is not aware of* CAIN THE SIXTH's *presence.*]

NOAH: See how dey makin' out inside, son.

[*Stops hammering.* JAPHETH *exits into Ark.* NOAH *turns and gazes towards the east.*]

CAIN THE SIXTH: Hello, honey.

ZEBA [*frightened but smiling*]: Hello, sugah.

CAIN THE SIXTH [*pleasantly*]: Ain' dat my ol' frien' Flatfoot wid you?

ZEBA: Why, so 'tis! [FLATFOOT *is now listening. To* FLATFOOT.] He's got a gun.

CAIN THE SIXTH: No, I ain't.

[*He lifts his hands over his head.* ZEBA *quickly advances and runs her hands lightly over his pockets.*]

ZEBA [*relieved*]: I guess he ain't.

CAIN THE SIXTH: No, I ain't got no gun for my ol' frien', Flatfoot.

[*He walks up to him.*]

FLATFOOT [*smiling*]: Hi, Cain. How's de boy?

[CAIN *quickly presses his chest against* FLATFOOT's, *his downstage arm sweeps around* FLATFOOT's *body and his hand goes up to the small of* FLATFOOT's *back.*]

CAIN THE SIXTH [*quietly, but triumphantly*]: I got a little *knife* fo' him.

[FLATFOOT *falls dead. The laughter of the others stops and they look at the scene.* ZEBA *for a moment is terrified, her clenched hand pressed to her mouth. She looks at* CAIN THE SIXTH, *who is smiling at her. He tosses the knife on the ground and holds his hands out to her. She goes to him, smiling.*]

ZEBA: You sho' take keer of me, honey.

CAIN THE SIXTH: Dat's caize I think yo' wo'th takin' keer of. [*To the others.*] It's all right, folks. I jest had to do a little cleanin' up.

FIRST WOMAN [*smiling*]: You is de quickes' scoundrel.

FIRST GAMBLER: It was a nice quick killin'. Who was he?

SECOND WOMAN [*casually*]: Dey called him Flatfoot. From over de river. He wa'nt any good. He owed me for washin' for over a year.

THIRD WOMAN: Used to peddle muggles. Said it had a kick like reg'lar snow. Wasn't no good.

SECOND GAMBLER: Think we ought to bury him?

FIRST MAN: No, just leave him dere. Nobody comes up yere, 'cept ol' Manatee.

[*Indicates* NOAH. *Cries of* " Ol' Manatee! Ol' Manatee, dat's good! "]

NOAH [*still looking off*]: You bettah pray, you po' chillun.

[*They all laugh.*]

FIRST WOMAN: We bettah pray? You bettah pray, Ol' Manatee.

ZEBA: You bettah pray for rain.

[*Laughter again.*]

NOAH: Dat's what I ain't doin', sinners. Shem! Japheth! [*To others, as he points off. Patter of rain.*] Listen!

CAIN THE SIXTH [*casually*]: Doggone, I believe it *is* gonter shower a little.

FIRST GAMBLER: It do looks like rain.

FIRST WOMAN: I think I'll git on home. I got a new dress on.

ZEBA: Me, too. I wants to keep lookin' nice fo' my sweet papa.

[*She pats* CAIN THE SIXTH's *cheek.* CAIN THE SIXTH *hugs her.*]

NOAH [*almost frantically*]: Ham! Is de animals dere?

HAM [*off stage*]: Yes, sir, dere yere. We're comin'.

NOAH: Den bring 'em on.

[SHEM *and* JAPHETH *come on deck with their hammers. The stage begins to darken.*]

THIRD WOMAN: I guess we all might go home 'til de shower's over. Come on, papa.

SECOND GAMBLER: See you after supper, Noah.

[*Crowd starts moving off.*]

NOAH: God's gittin' ready to start, my sons. Let's git dis plankin' done.

ZEBA: Put a big Texas on it, Noah, an' we'll use it fo' excursions.

[*There is a distant roll of thunder, there are cries of " Good night, Admiral,"
" See you later," " So long, Manatee," as the crowd goes off. The thunder
rumbles again. There is the sound of increasing rain. The hammers of* SHEM
and JAPHETH *sound louder and are joined by the sounds of other hammerers.
There is a flash of lightning. The* CHOIR *begins " Dey Ol' Ark's a-Movering,"
the sounds on the Ark become faster and louder. The rush of rain grows
heavier.*]

NOAH: Hurry! Hurry! Where are you, Ham?

HAM [*just off the stage*]: Yere I am, Father, wid de animals.

NOAH: God's give us His sign. Send 'em up de gangplank.

[*An inclined plane is thrown against the Ark from the side of the stage by*
HAM, *who cracks a whip.*]

HAM: Get on, dere.

[*The heads of two elephants are seen.*]

NOAH: Bring 'em on board! De Lawd is strikin' down de worl'!

[*The singing and the noises reach fortissimo as* HAM *cracks his whip again, and
the rain falls on the stage. The stage is darkened. The* CHOIR *continues singing
in the darkness.*]

PART I. SCENE *10*

   *When the lights go up on the scene, the Ark is at sea. Stationary waves run
in front of it. The hillside has disappeared. The Ark is in the only lighted area.*
   SHEM *is smoking a pipe on the deck, leaning on the rail. A steamboat whistle
blows three short and one long blast.* SHEM *is surprised. In a moment* HAM *appears, also with a pipe, and joins* SHEM *at the rail.*

SHEM: Who'd you think you was signalin'?

HAM: Dat wasn't me, dat was daddy.

SHEM: He think he gonter git a reply?

HAM: I don' know. He's been gittin' a heap of comfort out of dat likker.

SHEM: De kag's nearly empty, ain't it?

HAM: Pretty nearly almos'. [*They look over the rail. A pause.*] Seen anythin'?

SHEM: Dis mornin' I seen somethin' over dere migh'a' been a fish.

HAM: Dat's de big news of de week.

SHEM: How long you think dis trip's gonter las'?

HAM: I don' know! Rain fo'ty days 'n' fo'ty nights an' when dat stop' I thought
   sho' we'd come up ag'inst a san' bar o' somethin'. Looks now like all dat
   rain was jest a little incident of de trip. [*The whistle blows again.*] Doggone! I wish he wouldn't do dat. Fust thing we know he'll wake up dem
   animals ag'in.

[JAPHETH *appears.*]

SHEM: What's de matter wit' de ol' man, Jape?

JAPHETH: Doggone, he say he had a dream dat we're nearly dere. Dat's why he pullin' de whistle cord. See kin he git a' answer. [*He looks over the rail.*] Look to me like de same ol' territory.

[MRS. NOAH *appears on deck.*]

NOAH'S WIFE: You boys go stop yo' paw pullin' dat cord. He so full of likker he think he's in a race.

JAPHETH: He claim he know what he's doin'.

NOAH'S WIFE: I claim he gittin' to be a perfec' nuisance. Me an' yo' wives cain't hardly heah ou'sel'es think. [NOAH *appears, his hat rakishly tilted on his head. He goes to the railing and looks out.*] You 'spectin' company?

NOAH: Leave me be, woman. De watah don't look so rough to-day. De ol' boat's ridin' easier.

NOAH'S WIFE: Ridin' like a ol' mule!

NOAH: Yes, suh, de air don't feel so wet. Shem! 'Spose you sen' out 'nother dove. [SHEM *goes into the Ark.*] Ham, go git de soundin' line. Jape, keep yo' eye on de East.

[JAPHETH *goes to the end of the boat.*]

NOAH'S WIFE: As fo' you, I s'pose you'll help things along by takin' a little drink.

NOAH: Look yere, who's de pilot of dis vessel?

NOAH'S WIFE: Ol' Mister Dumb Luck.

NOAH: Well, see dat's where you don' know anythin'.

NOAH'S WIFE: I s'pose you ain't drunk as a fool?

NOAH [*cordially*]: I feel congenial.

NOAH'S WIFE: An' you look it. You look jest wonderful. I wonder if you'd feel so congenial if de Lawd was to show up?

NOAH: De Lawd knows what I'm doin', don' you worry 'bout dat.

NOAH'S WIFE: I wouldn't say anythin' ag'inst de Lawd. He suttinly let us know dey'd be a change in de weather. But I bet even the Lawd wonders sometimes why He ever put you in charge.

NOAH: Well, you let de Lawd worry 'bout dat.

[SHEM *appears with the dove.*]

SHEM: Will I leave her go, Paw?

NOAH: Leave 'er go. [*There's a chorus of " Good Luck, Dove," from the group as the dove flies off stage.* HAM *appears with the sounding line.*] Throw 'er over, boy. [HAM *proceeds to do so.*]

NOAH'S WIFE: An' another thing —

HAM: Hey.

NOAH [*rushing to his side*]: What is it?

HAM: Only 'bout a inch! Look!

[*They lean over.*]

JAPHETH: It's gettin' light in de East.

[*As* HAM *works the cord up and down,* NOAH *and* NOAH'S WIFE *turn toward* JAPHETH. *The* CHOIR *begins " My Soul Is a Witness for the Lord."*]

NOAH: Praise de Lawd, so it is.

NOAH'S WIFE: Oh, dat's pretty.

NOAH [*to* HAM]: An' de boat's stopped. We've landed. Shem, go down 'n' drag de fires an' dreen de boiler. Yo' go help 'im, Ham.

JAPHETH: Look, Paw.

[*The dove wings back to the Ark with an olive branch in its mouth.*]

NOAH: 'N' yere's de little dove wid greenery in its mouth! Take 'er down, Jape, so she kin tell de animals. [JAPHETH *exits after* SHEM *and* HAM *carrying the dove. To* MRS. NOAH.] Now, maybe you feel little different.

NOAH'S WIFE [*contritely*]: It was jes' gettin' to be so tiresome. I'm sorry, Noah.

NOAH: Dat's all right, ol' woman. [NOAH'S WIFE *exits,* NOAH *looks about him. The lights have changed and the water piece is gone and the Ark is again on the hillside. Two mountains can be seen in the distance and a rainbow slowly appears over the Ark. The singing has grown louder.*] Thank you, Lawd, thank you very much indeed. Amen.

[*The singing stops with the "Amen."* GOD *appears on the deck.*]

GOD: Yo' welcome, Noah.

[NOAH *turns and sees Him.*]

NOAH: O Lawd, it's wonderful.

GOD [*looking about Him*]: I sort of like it. I like de way you handled de ship, too, Noah.

NOAH: Was you watchin', Lawd?

GOD: Every minute. [*He smiles.*] Didn't de ol' lady light into you?

NOAH [*apologetically*]: She was kinda restless.

GOD: That's all right. I ain't blamin' nobody. I don't even min' you cussin' an' drinkin'. I figure a steamboat cap'n on a long trip like you had has a right to a little redeye, jest so he don' go crazy.

NOAH: Thank you, Lawd. What's de orders now?

GOD: All de animals safe?

NOAH: Dey all fin'n' dandy, Lawd.

GOD: Den I want you to open dat starboard door, an' leave 'em all out. Let 'em go down de hill. Den you an' de family take all de seeds 'n' de sprouts an' begin plantin' ag'in. I'm startin' all over, Noah.

[NOAH *exits.* GOD *looks around.*]

GOD: Well, now we'll see what happens. [GOD *listens with a smile, as noises accompanying the debarking of the animals are heard. They are the cracks of whips, the voices of the men on the Ark, shouting: "Git along dere," "Whoa, take it easy," "Duck yo' head," "Keep in line dere," etc. Over the Ark there is a burst of centrifugal shadows, and the sound of a myriad of wings.* GOD *smiles at the shadows.*] Dat's right, birds, fin' yo' new homes. [*Bird twitters are heard again.* GOD *listens a moment and rests an arm on the railing. He speaks softly.*] Gabriel, kin you spare a minute?

[GABRIEL *appears.*]

GABRIEL: Yes, Lawd?

[*The sounds from the other side of the Ark are by now almost hushed. The* LORD *indicates the new world with a wave of the hand.*]

GOD: Well, it's did.

GABRIEL [*respectfully, but with no enthusiasm*]: So I take notice.

GOD: Yes, suh, startin' all over again.

GABRIEL: So I see.

GOD [*looking at him suddenly*]: Don' seem to set you up much.

GABRIEL: Well, Lawd, you see — [*He hesitates.*] 'Tain't none of my business.

GOD: What?

GABRIEL: I say, I don' know very much about it.

GOD: I know you don'. I jest wanted you to see it. [*A thought strikes Him.*] Co'se, it ain' yo' business, Gabe. It's my business. 'Twas my idea. De whole thing was my idea. An' every bit of it's my business 'n' nobody else's. De whole thing rests on my shoulders. I declare, I guess dat's why I feel so solemn an' serious, at dis particklar time. You know dis thing's turned into quite a proposition.

GABRIEL [*tenderly*]: But, it's all right, Lawd, as you say, it's did.

GOD: Yes, suh, it's did. [*Sighs deeply. Looks slowly to the right and the left. Then softly.*] I only hope it's goin' to work out all right.

CURTAIN

PART II. SCENE 1

GOD's *office again.*

Somewhere the CHOIR *is singing "A City Called Heaven." In the office are* TWO WOMEN CLEANERS. *One is scrubbing the floor, the other dusting the furniture. The one dusting stops and looks out the window. There is a whirr and a distant faint boom. The* CHOIR *stops.*

FIRST CLEANER: Dat was a long way off.

SECOND CLEANER [*at window*]: Yes ma'am. An' dat must 'a' been a big one. Doggone, de Lawd mus' be mad fo' sho', dis mon'in'. Dat's de fo'ty-six' thunde'-bolt since breakfast.

FIRST CLEANER: I wonder where at He's pitchin' dem.

SECOND CLEANER: My goodness, don' you know?

FIRST CLEANER [*a little hurt*]: Did I know I wouldn't ask de question.

SECOND CLEANER: Every one of dem's bound fo' de earth.

FIRST CLEANER: De earth? You mean dat little ol' dreenin' place?

SECOND CLEANER: Dat's de planet. [*Another faint whirr and boom.*] Dere goes another.

FIRST CLEANER: Well, bless me. *I* didn't know dey was thunde'bolts.

SECOND CLEANER: Wha'd you think dey was?

FIRST CLEANER [*above desk*]: I wasn't sho', but I thought maybe He might be whittlin' a new star o' two, an' de noise was just de chips fallin'.

SECOND CLEANER: Carrie, where you been? Don' you know de earth is de new scandal? Ever'body's talkin' 'bout it.

FIRST CLEANER: Dey kep' it from me.

SECOND CLEANER: Ain't you noticed de Lawd's been unhappy lately?

FIRST CLEANER [*thoughtfully*]: Yeah, He ain't been His old self.

SECOND CLEANER: What did you think was de matteh? Lumbago?

FIRST CLEANER [*petulantly*]: I didn't know. I didn't think it was fo' me t'inquieh.

SECOND CLEANER: Well, it jest so happens dat de Lawd is riled as kin be by dat measly little earth. Or I should say de scum dat's on it.

FIRST CLEANER: Dat's mankind down dere.

SECOND CLEANER: Dey mus' be scum, too, to git de Lawd so wukked up.

FIRST CLEANER: I s'pose so. [*Another whirr and boom.*] Looks like He's lettin' dem feel de wrath. Ain't dat a shame to plague de Lawd dat way?

SECOND CLEANER: From what I hear dey been beggin' fo' what dey're gittin'. My brother flew down to bring up a saint de other day and he say from what he see mos' of de population down dere has made de debbil king an' dey wukkin' in three shifts fo' him.

FIRST CLEANER: You cain't blame de Lawd.

SECOND CLEANER: Co'se you cain't. Dem human bein's 'd make anybody bile oveh. Ev'rytime de Lawd try to do sompin' fô' dem, doggone if dey don't staht some new ruckus.

FIRST CLEANER: I take notice He's been wukkin' in yere mo' dan usual.

SECOND CLEANER: I wish He'd let us ladies fix it up. Wouldn't take a minute to make dis desk gold-plated.

FIRST CLEANER: I s'pose He likes it dis way. De Lawd's kind o' ol' fashioned in some ways. I s'pose He keeps dis office plain an' simple on purpose.

SECOND CLEANER [*finishing her work*]: I don' see why.

FIRST CLEANER [*looking off*]: Well, it's kind of a nice place to come to when He's studyin' somethin' impo'tant. 'Most evahthin' else in heaven's so fin' 'n' gran', maybe ev'ry now an' den He jest gits sick an' tired of de glory.

[*She is also collecting her utensils.*]

SECOND CLEANER: Maybe so. Jest de same I'd like to have a free hand wid dis place for a while, so's I could gold it up.

[GOD *appears in the doorway.*]

GOD: Good mo'nin', daughters.

FIRST AND SECOND CLEANERS: Good mo'nin', Lawd. We was jest finishin'.

GOD: Go ahead den, daughters.

[*Goes to the window.*]

FIRST AND SECOND CLEANERS: Yes, Lawd. [*Exeunt. Off stage.*] Good mo'nin', Gabriel.

[*Off stage* GABRIEL *says, " Good mo'nin', sisters," and enters immediately. He stands in the doorway for a moment watching* GOD — *a notebook and pencil in his hand.*]

GOD: What's de total?

GABRIEL [*consulting the book*]: Eighteen thousand nine hund'ed an' sixty for de mo'nin'. Dat's includin' de village wid de fo'tune tellers. Dey certainly kin breed fast.

GOD [*solemnly*]: Dey displease me. Dey displease me greatly.

GABRIEL: Want some more bolts, Lawd?

GOD [*looking through window*]: Look at 'em dere. Squirmin' an' fightin' an' bearin' false witness. Listen to dat liar, dere. He don' intend to marry dat little gal. He don' even love her. What did you say?

GABRIEL: Should I git mo' bolts?

GOD: Wait a minute. [*He carefully points His finger down through the window.*] I'm goin' to git dat wicked man myself. [*From a great distance comes an agonized cry: " Oh, Lawd! "* GOD *turns from the window.*] No use gittin' mo' thunde'bolts. Dey don' do de trick. [*He goes to the swivel chair and sits.*] It's got to be somethin' else.

GABRIEL: How would it be if you was to doom 'em all ag'in, like dat time you sent down de flood? I bet dat would make dem mind.

GOD: You see how much good de flood did. Dere dey is, jest as bad as ever.

GABRIEL: How about cleanin' up on de whole mess of 'em and sta'tin' all over ag'in wid some new kind of animal?

GOD: An' admit I'm licked?

GABRIEL [*ashamedly*]: No, of co'se not, Lawd.

GOD: No, suh. No, suh. Man is a kind of pet of mine and it ain't right fo' me to give up tryin' to do somethin' wid him. Doggone, mankin' *mus'* be all right at de core or else why did I ever bother wid him in de first place?

[*Sits at desk.*]

GABRIEL: It's jest dat I hates to see you worryin' about it, Lawd.

GOD: Gabe, dere ain't anythin' worth while anywheres dat didn't cause somebody some worryin'. I ain't never tol' you de trouble I had gittin' things started up yere. Dat's a story in itself. No, suh, de more I keep on bein' de Lawd de more I know I got to keep improvin' things. An' dat takes time and worry. De main trouble wid mankin' is he takes up so much of my time. He ought to be able to help hisself a little. [*He stops suddenly and cogitates.*] Hey, dere! I think I got it!

GABRIEL [*eagerly*]: What's de news?

GOD [*still cogitating*]: Yes, suh, dat seems like an awful good idea.

GABRIEL: Tell me, Lawd.

GOD: Gabriel, have you noticed dat every now an' den, mankin' turns out some pretty good specimens?

GABRIEL: Dat's de truth.

GOD: Yes, suh. Dey's ol' Abraham and Isaac an' Jacob an' all dat family.

GABRIEL: Dat's so, Lawd.

GOD: An' every one of dem boys was a hard wukker an' a good citizen. We got to admit dat.

GABRIEL: Dey wouldn't be up yere flyin' wid us if dey hadn't been.

GOD: No, suh. An' I don' know but what de answer to de whole trouble is right dere.

GABRIEL: How you mean, Lawd?

GOD: Why, doggone it, de good man is de man dat keeps busy. I mean I been goin' along on de principle dat he was something like you angels — dat you ought to be able to give him somethin' an' den jest let him sit back an' enjoy it. Now dat I recollec' I put de first one down dere to take keer o' dat garden an' den I let him go ahead an' do nothin' but git into mischief. [*He rises.*] Sure, *dat's* it. He ain't *built* jest to fool 'roun' an' not do nothin'. Gabe, I'm gonter try a new scheme.

GABRIEL [*eagerly*]: What's de scheme, Lawd?

GOD: I'll tell you later. Send in Abraham, Isaac, an' Jacob. [*A voice outside calls:* "*Right away, Lawd.*"] You go tell dem to put dem bolts back in de boxes. I ain' gonter use dem ag'in awhile.

GABRIEL: O.K., Lawd.

GOD: Was you goin' anywhere near de Big Pit?

GABRIEL: I could go.

GOD: Lean over de brink and tell Satan he's jest a plain fool if he thinks he kin beat anybody as big as me.

GABRIEL: Yes, suh, Lawd. Den I'll spit right in his eye.

[GABRIEL *exits.* GOD *looks down through the window again to the earth below.*]

GOD: Dat new polish on de sun makes it powerful hot. [*He " r'ar back."*] Let it be jest a little bit cooler. [*He feels the air.*] Dat's nice. [*Goes to His desk. A knock on the door.*] Come in.

[ABRAHAM, ISAAC, *and* JACOB *enter. All are very old men, but the beard of* ABRAHAM *is the longest and whitest, and they suggest their three generations. They have wings that are not quite so big as those of the native angels.*]

ISAAC: Sorry we so long comin', Lawd. But Pappy and me had to take de boy [*pointing to* JACOB] over to git him a can of wing ointment.

GOD: What was de matter, son?

JACOB: Dey was chafin' me a little. Dey fine now, thank you, Lawd.

GOD: Dat's good. Sit down an' make yo'selves comf'table. [*The three sit.* MEN: "*Thank you, Lawd.*"] Men, I'm goin' to talk about a little scheme I got. It's one dat's goin' to affec' yo' fam'lies an' dat's why I 'cided I'd talk it over wid you, 'fo' it goes into ee-ffect. I don' know whether you boys know it or not, but you is about de three best men of one fam'ly dat's come up yere since I made little apples. Now I tell you what I'm gonter do. Seein' dat you human bein's cain't 'preciate anythin' lessen you fust wukk to git it and den keep strugglin' to hold it, why I'm gonter turn over a very valuable piece of property to yo' fam'ly, and den see what kin dey do with it. De rest of de worl' kin go jump in de river fo' all I keer. I'm gonter be lookin' out fo' yo' descendants only. Now den, seein' dat you boys know de country pretty tho'ly, where at does you think is de choice piece of property in de whole worl'? Think it over for a minute. I'm gonter let you make de s'lection.

ABRAHAM: If you was to ask me, Lawd, I don't think dey come any better dan de Land of Canaan.

GOD [*to* ISAAC *and* JACOB]: What's yo' feelin' in de matter?

JACOB [*after a nod from* ISAAC]: Pappy an' me think do we get a pick, dat would be it.

GOD [*goes to window again; looks out*]: De Land of Canaan. Yes, I guess dat's a likely neighborhood. It's all run over wid Philistines and things right now, but we kin clean dat up. [*He turns from the window and resumes His seat.*] All right. Now who do you boys think is best of yo' men to put in charge down dere? You see I ain't been payin' much attention to anybody in par-tic'lar lately.

ISAAC: Does you want de brainiest or de holiest, Lawd?

[MEN *look up.*]

GOD: I want de holiest. I'll make him brainy.

[MEN *appreciate the miracle.*]

ISAAC [*as* ABRAHAM *and* JACOB *nod to him*]: Well, if you want A Number One goodness, Lawd, I don't know where you'll git more satisfaction dan in a great-great-great-great-grandson of mine.

GOD: Where's he at?

ISAAC: At de moment I b'lieve he's in de sheep business over in Midian County. He got in a little trouble down in Egypt, but 'twan't his doin'. He killed a man dat was abusin' one of our boys in de brick works. Of co'se you know old King Pharaoh's got all our people in bondage.

GOD: I heard of it. [*With some ire.*] Who did you think put them dere? [*The visitors lower their heads.*] It's all right, boys. [*All rise.*] I'm gonter take dem out of it. An' I'm gonter turn over de whole Land of Canaan to dem. An' do you know who's gonter lead dem dere? Yo' great-great-great-great-grandson. Moses, ain't it?

ISAAC: Yes, Lawd.

GOD [*smiling*]: Yes. I been noticin' *him.*

ABRAHAM: It's quite a favor fo' de fam'ly, Lawd.

GOD: Dat's why I tol' you. You see, it so happens I love yo' fam'ly, an' I delight to honor it. Dat's all, gen'lemen. [*The three others rise and cross to the door, murmuring, "Yes, Lawd," "Thank you, Lawd," "Much obliged, Lawd," etc. The* CHOIR *begins "My Lord's A-Writin' All de Time" pianissimo.* GOD *stands watching the men leave.*] Enjoy yo'selves. [*He goes to the window. The singing grows softer. He speaks through the window to the earth.*] I'm comin' down to see you, Moses, an' dis time my scheme's got to wukk.

[*The stage is darkened. The singing grows louder and continues until the lights go up on the next scene.*]

PART II. SCENE 2

The tableau curtains frame the opening of a cave, which is dimly lighted. A large turkey-berry bush is somewhere near the foreground. MOSES *is seated on the grass eating his lunch from a basket in his lap.* ZIPPORAH, *his wife, stands watching him. He is about forty,* ZIPPORAH *somewhat younger. They are dressed inconspicuously.* MOSES *stutters slightly when he speaks. He looks up to see* ZIPPORAH *smiling.*

MOSES: What you smilin' at, Zipporah?

ZIPPORAH: Caize you enjoyin' yo'self.

MOSES: You is a good wife, Zipporah.

ZIPPORAH: You is a good husband, Moses. [*Moses wipes his mouth with a handkerchief and begins putting into the basket the various implements of the meal which had been on the ground about him.*] Why you suppose it's so dark yere today? Dey's no rain in de air.

MOSES: Seems like it's jest aroun' dis cave. Yo' father's house is got de sun on it. [*He looks in another direction.*] Looks all clear down toward Egypt.

ZIPPORAH: Co'se it *would* be fine weather in Egypt. De sky looks all right. Maybe it's gonter rain jest right yere. Why don't you move de sheep over to de other pasture?

MOSES [*a bit puzzled*]: I don' know. It got dark like dis befo' you come along wid de dinner an' I was gonter stop you on de top of de hill. Den somethin' kep' me yere.

ZIPPORAH: S'pose it could be de Lawd warnin' you dat dey's 'Gyptians hangin' 'roun'?

MOSES: Dey may have fo'gotten all about dat killin' by now. Dey got a new Pharaoh down dere.

ZIPPORAH: An' I hear he's jest as mean to yo' people as his pappy was. I wouldn't put it pas' him to send soljahs all the way up yere fo' you.

MOSES: Dat's all right. De Lawd's looked after me so far. I don't 'spect him to fall down on me now. You better be gittin' home.

ZIPPORAH [*taking the basket*]: I'll be worryin' about you.

MOSES [*kissing her and then smiling*]: 'Parently de Lawd ain't. He knows I'm safe as kin be. Lemme see you feel dat way.

ZIPPORAH: You is a good man, Moses.

MOSES: I'se a lucky man. [ZIPPORAH *exits with the basket.* MOSES *looks up at the sky.*] Dat's funny. De sun seems to be shinin' every place but right yere. It's shinin' on de sheep. Why ain't dey no clouds dere?

GOD [*off stage*]: Caize I want it to be like dat, Moses.

MOSES [*looking about him*]: Who's dat?

GOD [*off stage again*]: I'm de Lawd, Moses.

MOSES [*smiling*]: Dat's what you say. Dis yere shadow may be de Lawd's wukk, but dat voice soun' pretty much to me like my ol' brother Aaron.

GOD [*off stage*]: Den keep yo' eyes open, son. [*The turkey-berry bush begins to glow and then turns completely red.* MOSES *looks at it fascinated.*] Maybe you notice de bush ain't burnin' up.

MOSES: Dat's de truth.

[MOSES *is full of awe but not frightened.*]

GOD [*off stage*]: Now you believe me?

MOSES: Co'se I does. It's wonderful.

[*The light in the bush dies and* GOD *appears from behind it.*]

GOD: No, it ain't, Moses. It was jest a trick.

MOSES: 'Scuse me doubtin' you, Lawd. I always had de feelin' you wuz takin' keer of me, but I never 'spected you'd fin' time to talk wid me pussunly. [*He laughs.*] Dat was a good trick, Lawd. I'se seen some good ones, but dat was de beatenest.

GOD: Yo' gonter see lots bigger tricks dan dat, Moses. In fac', yo' gonter perfo'm dem.

MOSES [*incredulously*]: Me? I'm gonter be a tricker?

GOD: Yes, suh.

MOSES: An' do magic? Lawd, my mouth ain't got de quick talk to go wid it.

GOD: It'll come to you now.

MOSES [*now cured of stuttering*]: Is I goin' wid a circus?

GOD [*slowly and solemnly*]: Yo' is goin' down into Egypt, Moses, and lead my people out of bondage. To do dat I'm gonter make you de bes' tricker in de worl'.

MOSES [*a little frightened*]: Egypt! You know I killed a man dere, Lawd. Won't dey kill me?

GOD: Not when dey see yo' tricks. You ain't skeered, is you?

MOSES [*simply and bravely*]: No, suh, Lawd.

GOD: Den yere's what I'm gonter do. Yo' people is my chillun, Moses. I'm sick and tired o' de way ol' King Pharaoh is treatin' dem, so I'se gonter take dem away, and yo' gonter lead dem. You gonter lead 'em out of Egypt an' across de river Jordan. It's gonter take a long time, and you ain't goin' on no excursion train. Yo' gonter wukk awful hard for somethin' yo' goin' to fin' when de trip's over.

MOSES: What's dat, Lawd?

GOD: It's de Land of Canaan. It's de bes' land I got. I've promised it to yo' people, an' I'm gonter give it to dem.

MOSES: Co'se, ol' King Pharaoh will do everything he kin to stop it.

GOD: Yes, an' dat's where de tricks come in. Dey tell me he's awful fond of tricks.

MOSES: I hear dat's *all* he's fon' of. Dey say if you cain't take a rabbit out of a hat you cain't even git in to see him.

GOD: Wait'll you see de tricks you an' me's goin' to show him.

MOSES [*delightedly*]: Doggone! Huh, Lawd?

GOD: Yes, suh. Now de first trick —

[*God is lifting a stick which He carries.*]

MOSES: Jest a minute, Lawd. [GOD *halts the demonstration.*] I'm gonter learn de tricks and do just like you tell me, but I *know* it's gonter take me a little time to learn all dat quick talkin'. Cain't I have my brother Aaron go wid me? He's a good man.

GOD: I was gonter have him help you wid de Exodus. I guess he can watch, too.

MOSES: I'll call 'im.

[*He turns as if to shout.*]

GOD: Wait. [MOSES *turns and looks at* GOD.] I'll bring him. [*Softly.*] Aaron!

[AARON *appears between* GOD *and* MOSES *in the mouth of the cave. He is a little taller than* MOSES *and slightly older. He, too, is dressed like a field hand.*]

AARON [*blankly*]: Hey!

[MOSES *goes to him, takes his hand and leads him, bewildered, down to where* MOSES *had been standing alone.* AARON *then sees* GOD.]

MOSES [*almost in a whisper*]: It's all right.

GOD: Don't worry, son, I'm jest showin' some tricks. Bringin' you yere was one of dem. [AARON *stares at* GOD *as if hypnotized.*] Now den, you see dis yere rod? Looks like a ordinary walkin' stick, don't it?

MOSES: Yes, Lawd.

GOD: Well, it ain't no ordinary walkin' stick, caize look. [MOSES *leans forward.*] When I lays it down on de groun' —

[*The stage is darkened. The* CHOIR *begins " Go Down, Moses," and continues until the lights go up on the next scene.*]

PART II. SCENE 3

The throne room of PHARAOH. *It suggests a Negro lodge room. The plain board walls are colored by several large parade banners of varying sizes, colors, and materials, bordered with gold fringe and tassels on them. Some of the inscriptions on them read:*

SUBLIME ORDER OF PRINCES OF THE HOUSE OF PHARAOH, HOME CHAPTER

MYSTIC BROTHERS OF THE EGYPTIAN HOME GUARD, LADIES' AUXILIARY, NO. 1

SUPREME MAGICIANS AND WIZARDS OF THE UNIVERSE

PRIVATE FLAG OF HIS HONOR OLD KING PHARAOH

ROYAL YOUNG PEOPLE'S PLEASURE CLUB

ENCHANTED AND INVISIBLE CADETS OF EGYPT, BOYS' BRIGADE

There is one door up right and a window. The throne, an ordinary armchair with a drapery over its back, is on a dais. PHARAOH *is seated on the throne. His crown and garments might be those worn by a high officer in a Negro lodge during a ritual. About the throne itself are high officials, several of them with plumed hats, clothing that suggests military uniforms, and rather elaborate sword belts, swords, and scabbards. A few soldiers carrying spears are also in his neighborhood and one or two bearded ancients in brightly colored robes with the word " Wizard" on their conical hats. In the general group of men and women scattered elsewhere in the room Sunday finery is noticeable everywhere. Most of the civilians have bright " parade" ribbons and wear medals. In a cleared space immediately before the throne a* CANDIDATE MAGICIAN *is performing a sleight-of-hand trick with cards.* PHARAOH *watches him apathetically. He is receiving earnest attention from a few of the others, but the majority of the men and women are talking quietly among themselves. Beside the* CANDIDATE MAGICIAN *are several paraphernalia of previously demonstrated tricks.*

CANDIDATE MAGICIAN [*holding up some cards*]: Now den, ol' King Pharaoh, watch dis. [*He completes a trick. There is a murmur of " Not bad," " Pretty good," etc., from a few of the watchers.* PHARAOH *makes no comment.*] Now I believe de cyard I ast you to keep sittin' on was de trey of diamonds, wasn't it?

PHARAOH: Yeah.

CANDIDATE MAGICIAN: Den kin I trouble you to take a look at it now? [PHARAOH *half rises to pick up a card he has been sitting on, and looks at it.*] I believe you'll now notice dat it's de king of clubs? [PHARAOH *nods and shows the card to those nearest him. The* CANDIDATE MAGICIAN *waits for an audible approval and gets practically none.*] An' dat, ol' King Pharaoh, completes de puffohmance.

[*An elderly man in a uniform steps forward.*]

GENERAL: On behalf of my nephew I beg Yo' Honor to let him jine de ranks of de royal trickers and magicians.

PHARAOH [*to the two* WIZARDS]: What do de committee think? [*The* WIZARDS *shake their heads.*] Dat's what I thought. He ain't good enough. I'd like to help you out, General, but you know a man's got to be a awful good tricker to git in de royal society dese days. You better go back an' steddy some mo', son. [*He lifts his voice and directs two* SOLDIERS *guarding the door.*] Is de head magician reached de royal waitin' room yit? [*One of the* SOLDIERS *opens the door to look out.*] If he is, send him in.

[*The* SOLDIER *beckons to someone off stage, throws the door open, and announces to the court:*]

SOLDIER: De Head Magician of de land of Egypt.

[*A very old and villainous man enters. His costume is covered with cabalistic and zodiacal signs. He advances to the* KING, *the other* MAGICIAN *and his uncle making way for him. He bows curtly to* PHARAOH.]

HEAD MAGICIAN: Good mo'nin', ol' King Pharaoh.

PHARAOH: Mo'nin', Professor. What's de news?

HEAD MAGICIAN: Evahthing's bein' carried out like you said.

PHARAOH: How's de killin' of de babies 'mongst de Hebrews comin' 'long?

HEAD MAGICIAN: Jes' like you ordered.

PHARAOH [*genially*]: Dey killed all of 'em, huh?

HEAD MAGICIAN: Do dey see one, dey kill 'em. You teachin' 'em a great lesson. Dey don' like it a-tall.

PHARAOH [*smiling*]: What do dey say?

HEAD MAGICIAN [*pawing the air inarticulately*]: I hates to tell in front of de ladies.

PHARAOH: Dey feels pretty bad, huh?

HEAD MAGICIAN: Dat's jest de beginnin' of it. Betwixt de poleece and de soljahs we killed about a thousan' of 'em las' night. Dat's purty good.

PHARAOH [*thoughtfully*]: Yeh, it's fair. I guess you boys is doin' all you kin. But I fin' I ain't satisfied, though.

HEAD MAGICIAN: How you mean, Yo' Honor?

PHARAOH: I mean I'd like to make dose Hebrew chillun realize dat I kin be even mo' of a pest. I mean I hates dem chillun. An' I'm gonter think of a way of makin' 'em even mo' mizzable.

HEAD MAGICIAN: But dey *ain't* anythin' meaner dan killin' de babies, King.

PHARAOH: Dey must be sump'n. Doggone, you is my head tricker, you put yo' brains on it. [*To the others.*] Quiet, whilst de Head Magician go into de silence.

HEAD MAGICIAN [*after turning completely around twice, and a moment's cogitation*]: I tell you what I kin do. All de Hebrews dat ain't out to de buryin' grounds or in de hospitals is laborin' in de brick wukks.

PHARAOH: Yeh?

HEAD MAGICIAN [*after a cackling laugh*]: How would it be to take de straw away from 'em and tell 'em dey's got to turn out jest as many bricks as usual? Ain't dat nasty?

PHARAOH: Purty triflin', but I s'pose it'll have to do for de time bein'. Where's de extreme inner guard? [*One of the military* ATTENDANTS *comes forward.*] Go on out an' tell de sup'intendent to put dat into ee-ffect. [*The* ATTENDANT *bows and starts for the door. He stops as* PHARAOH *calls to him.*] Wait a minute! Tell 'im to chop off de hands of anybody dat say he cain't make de bricks dat way. [*The* ATTENDANT *salutes and exits, the door being opened and closed by one of the* SOLDIERS.] Now what's de news in de magic line?

HEAD MAGICIAN: I ain't got very many novelties today, King. I been wukkin' too hard on de killin's. I'm so tired I don' believe I could lift a wand.

[*There are murmurs of protest from the assemblage.*]

PHARAOH: Doggone, you was to 'a' been de chief feature o' de meetin' dis mawnin'. Look at de turn-out you got account of me tellin' 'em you was comin'.

HEAD MAGICIAN: Well dat's de way it is, King. Why don' you git de wizards to do some spell castin'?

PHARAOH: Dey say it's in de cyards dat dey cain't wukk till high noon. [*He glances at the* WIZARDS.] Think mebbe you kin cheat a little?

FIRST WIZARD: Oh, dat cain't be done, King.

PHARAOH: Well, we might as well adjourn, den. Looks to me like de whole program's shot to pieces. [*He starts to rise, when there is a furious banging on the door.*] What's de idea, dere? See who dat is. [*The* SOLDIERS *open the door.* MOSES *and* AARON *enter, pushing the two* SOLDIERS *aside and coming down in front of* PHARAOH. *The* SOLDIERS *are bewildered and* PHARAOH *is angry.*] Say, who tol' you two baboons you could come in yere?

MOSES: Is you ol' King Pharaoh?

PHARAOH: Dat's me. Did you heah what I asked you?

MOSES: My name is Moses, and dis is my brother Aaron.

[*Murmur of " Hebrews" spreads through the room.*]

PHARAOH [*in a rage*]: Is you Hebrews?

MOSES: Yes, suh.

PHARAOH [*almost screaming*]: Put 'em to de sword!

[*As the* COURTIERS *approach,* AARON *suddenly discloses the rod, which he swings once over his head. The* COURTIERS *draw back as if their hands had been stung. Cries of "Hey!" "Look out," etc.*]

MOSES: Keep outside dat circle.

[*The* COURTIERS *nearest* MOSES *and* AARON *look at each other, exclaiming ad lib., "Did you feel dat?" "What was that?" "What's goin' on, heah?" "My hands is stingin'!" etc.*]

PHARAOH [*puzzled but threatening*]: What's de idea yere?

MOSES: We is magicians, ol' King Pharaoh.

PHARAOH [*to the* HEAD MAGICIAN]: Put a spell on 'em. [*The* HEAD MAGICIAN *stands looking at them, bewildered. To Moses.*] I got some magicians, too. We'll see who's got de bes' magic. [MOSES *and* AARON *laugh. Most of the* COURTIERS *are cowering. To the* HEAD MAGICIAN.] Go ahead, give 'em gri-gri.

MOSES: Sure, go ahead.

PHARAOH: Hurry up, dey's laughin' at you. What's de matter?

HEAD MAGICIAN: I cain't think of de right spell.

PHARAOH [*now frightened himself*]: You mean dey got even *you* whupped?

HEAD MAGICIAN: Dey's got a new kind of magic.

PHARAOH [*Gazes at* HEAD MAGICIAN *a moment, bewildered. To the* WIZARDS.] I s'pose if de Professor cain't, you cain't.

FIRST WIZARD: Dat's a new trick, King.

HEAD MAGICIAN [*rubbing his fingers along his palms*]: It's got 'lectricity in it!

PHARAOH: Hm, well dat may make it a little diff'rent. So you boys is magicians, too?

MOSES: Yes, suh.

PHARAOH: Well, we's always glad to see some new trickers in de co't, dat is if dey good. [*He glances about him.*] You look like you is O.K.

MOSES: Dat's what we claims, ol' King Pharaoh. We think we's de best in de worl'.

PHARAOH: You certainly kin talk big. Jest what is it you boys would like?

MOSES: We came to show you some tricks. Den we's goin' to ask you to do somethin' for us.

PHARAOH: Well, I s'pose you know I'm a fool for conjurin'. If a man kin show me some tricks I ain't seen, I go out of my way to do him a favor.

MOSES: Dat's good. Want to see de first trick?

PHARAOH: It ain't goin' to hurt nobody?

MOSES: Dis one won't.

PHARAOH: Go ahead.

MOSES: Dis yere rod my brother has looks jes' like a walkin' stick, don't it?

[*The* COURTIERS *now join the* KING *in interest.*]

PHARAOH: Uh huh. Le's see.

[AARON *hands him the rod, which* PHARAOH *inspects and returns.*]

MOSES: Well, look what happens when he lays it on de groun'.

[AARON *places the rod on the second step of the throne. It turns into a lifelike snake. There are exclamations from the assemblage.*]

PHARAOH: Dat's a good trick! Now turn it back into a walkin' stick again. [AARON *picks it up and it is again a rod. Exclamations of " Purty good! " " Dat's all right! " " What do you think of that! " etc.*] Say, you is good trickers!

MOSES: You ain't never seen de beat of us. Now I'm goin' to ask de favor.

PHARAOH: Sure, what is it?

MOSES [*solemnly*]: Let de Hebrew chillun go!

PHARAOH [*Rises and stares at them. There is a murmur of " Listen to 'im! " " He's got nerve! " " I never in my life! " " My goodness! " etc.*]: What did you say?

MOSES: Let de Hebrew chillun go.

[PHARAOH *seats himself again.*]

PHARAOH [*slowly*]: Don' you know de Hebrews is my slaves?

MOSES: Yes, suh.

PHARAOH: Yes, suh, my slaves. [*There is a distant groaning.*] Listen, and you kin hear 'em bein' treated like slaves. [*He calls toward the window.*] What was dey doin' den?

MAN NEAR THE WINDOW: Dey's jest gettin' de news down in de brickyard.

PHARAOH: I won't let them go. [*He snorts contemptuously.*] Let's see another trick.

MOSES: Yes, suh, yere's a better one. [*He lowers his head.*] Let's have a plague of de flies.

[AARON *raises the rod. The room grows dark and a great buzzing of flies is heard. The* COURTIERS *break out in cries of " Get away from me! " " Take 'em away! " " De place is filled with flies! " " Dis is terrible! " " Do sump'n, Pharaoh! "*]

PHARAOH [*topping the others*]: All right — stop de trick!

MOSES: Will you let de Hebrews go?

PHARAOH: Sho' I will. Go ahead stop it!

MOSES [*also above the others*]: Begone!

[*The buzzing stops and the room is filled with light again, as* AARON *lowers the rod. All except* MOSES *and* AARON *are brushing the flies from their persons.*]

PHARAOH [*laughing*]: Doggone, dat was a good trick! [*The others, seeing they are uninjured, join in the laughter, with exclamations of " Doggone! " " You all right? " " Sho' I'm all right," " Didn't hurt me," etc.*] You is good trickers.

MOSES: Will you let de Hebrew chillun go?

PHARAOH [*sitting down again*]: Well, I'll tell you, boys. I'll tell you sump'n you didn' know. You take me, *I'm* a pretty good tricker, an' I jest outtricked you. So, bein' de bes' tricker, I don' think I will let 'em go. You got any mo' tricks yo'self?

MOSES: Yes, suh. Dis is a little harder one. [AARON *lifts the rod.*] Gnats in de mill pon', gnats in de clover, gnats in de tater patch, stingin' all over.

[*The stage grows dark again. There is the humming of gnats and the slapping of hands against faces and arms, and the same protests as were heard with the flies, but with more feeling: "I'm gittin' stung to death!" "I'm all stung!" "Dey're like hornets!" "Dey's on my face!" etc.*]

PHARAOH: Take 'em away, Moses!

MOSES [*his voice drowning the others*]: If I do, will you let 'em go?

PHARAOH: Sho' I will, dis time.

MOSES: Do you mean it?

PHARAOH: Co'se I mean it! Doggone, one just stang me on de nose.

MOSES: Begone! [*Lights come up as* AARON *lowers the rod. There is a moment of general recovery again.* PHARAOH *rubs his nose, looks at his hands, etc., as do the others.*] Now, how about it?

PHARAOH [*smiling*]: Well, I'll tell you, Moses. Now dat de trick's over —

[MOSES *takes a step toward* PHARAOH.]

MOSES: Listen, Pharaoh. You been lyin' to me, and I'm gittin' tired of it.

PHARAOH: I ain't lyin', I'm trickin', too. You been trickin' me and I been trickin' you.

MOSES: I see. Well, I got one mo' trick up my sleeve which I didn't aim to wukk unless I had to. Caize when I does it, I cain't undo it.

PHARAOH: Wukk it an I'll trick you right back. I don' say you ain't a good tricker, Moses. You is one of de best I ever seen. But I kin outtrick you. Dat's all.

MOSES: It ain't only me dat's goin' to wukk dis trick. It's me an' de Lawd.

PHARAOH: Who?

MOSES: De Lawd God of Israel.

PHARAOH: I kin outtrick you an' de Lawd too!

MOSES [*angrily*]: Now you done it, ol' King Pharaoh. You been mean to de Lawd's people, and de Lawd's been easy on you caize you didn' know better. You been givin' me a lot of say-so and no do-so, and I didn' min' dat. But now you've got to braggin' dat you's better dan de Lawd, and dat's too many.

PHARAOH: You talk like a preacher, an' I never did like to hear preachers talk.

MOSES: You ain't goin' to like it any better, when I strikes down de oldes' boy in every one of yo' people's houses.

PHARAOH: Now, you've given up trickin' and is jest lyin'. [*He rises.*] Listen, I'm Pharaoh. I do de strikin' down yere. I strike down my enemies, and dere's no one in all Egypt kin kill who he wants to, 'ceptin' me.

MOSES: I'm sorry, Pharaoh. Will you let de Hebrews go?

PHARAOH: You heard my word. [AARON *is lifting his rod again at a signal from* MOSES.] Now, no more tricks or I'll —

MOSES: Oh, Lawd, you'll have to do it, I guess. Aaron, lift de rod.

[*There is a thunderclap, darkness and screams. The lights go up. Several of the younger men on the stage have fallen to the ground or are being held in the arms of the horrified elders.*]

PHARAOH: What have you done yere? Where's my boy?

[*Through the door come four men bearing a young man's body.*]

FIRST OF THE FOUR MEN: King Pharaoh.

[PHARAOH *drops into his chair, stunned as the dead boy is brought to the throne.*]

PHARAOH [*grief-stricken*]: Oh, my son, my fine son.

[*The* COURTIERS *look at him with mute appeal.*]

MOSES: I'm sorry, Pharaoh, but you cain't fight de Lawd. Will you let his people go?

PHARAOH: Let them go.

[*The lights go out. The* CHOIR *begins " Mary, Don't You Weep," and continues until it is broken by the strains of " I'm Noways Weary and I'm Noways Tired." The latter is sung by many more voices than the former, and the cacophony ends as the latter grows in volume and the lights go up on the next scene.*]

PART II. SCENE 4

The CHILDREN OF ISRAEL *are marching on the treadmill and now singing fortissimo. They are of all ages and most of them are ragged. The men have packs on their shoulders, one or two have hand carts. The line stretches across the stage. It is nearing twilight, and the faces of the assemblage are illumined by the rays of the late afternoon sun. The upper treadmill carries a gradually rising and falling middle distance past the marchers. The foot of a mountain appears; a trumpet call is heard as the foot of the mountain reaches stage center. The marchers halt. The picture now shows the mountain running up out of sight off right. The singing stops. A babel of " What's de matter? " " Why do we stop? " " 'Tain't sundown yet! " " What's happened? " " What's goin' on? " " What are they blowin' for? " etc. Those looking ahead begin to murmur, " It's Moses," " Moses," " What's happened to him? " The others take up the repetition of " Moses," and* MOSES *enters, on the arm of* AARON. *He is now an old man, as is his brother, and he totters toward the center of the stage. Cries of " What's de matter, Moses? " " You ain't hurt, is you? " " Ain't that too bad? " etc. He slowly seats himself on the rock at the foot of the mountain.*

AARON: How you feelin' now, brother?

MOSES: I'm so weary, Aaron. Seems like I was took all of a sudden.

AARON: Do we camp yere?

MOSES [*pathetically*]: No, you got to keep goin'.

AARON: But you cain't go no further tonight, brother.

MOSES: Dis never happened to me befo'.

A YOUNG WOMAN: But you's a ol' man, now, Father Moses. You cain't expect to go as fas' as we kin.

MOSES: But de Lawd said I'd do it. He said I was to show you de Promised Land. Fo'ty years, I bin leadin' you. I led you out o' Egypt. I led you past Sinai, and through de wilderness. Oh, I cain't fall down on you now.

AARON: Le's res' yere fo' de night. Den we'll see how you feel in de mo'nin'.

MOSES: We tol' de scouts we'd meet 'em three miles furder on. I hate fo' 'em to come back all dis way to report. 'Tis gettin' a little dark, ain't it?

AARON: It ain't dark, brother.

MOSES: No, it's my eyes.

AARON: Maybe it's de dust.

MOSES: No, I jest cain't seem to see. Oh, Lawd, dey cain't have a blind man leadin' 'em! Where is you, Aaron?

AARON: I'se right yere, Moses.

MOSES: Do you think — [*Pause.*] Oh! Do you think it's de time He said?

AARON: How you mean, Moses?

[*Crowd looks from one to another in wonder.*]

MOSES: He said I could lead 'em to de Jordan, dat I'd *see* de Promised Land, and dat's all de further I could go, on account I broke de laws. Little while back I thought I *did* see a river ahead, and a pretty land on de other side. [*Distant shouts: " Hooray!" " Yere dey are!" " Dey traveled quick," etc.*] Where's de young leader of de troops? Where's Joshua?

[*The call " Joshua" is taken up by those on the right of the stage, followed almost immediately by " Yere he is!" " Moses wants you!" etc.* JOSHUA *enters. He is a fine-looking Negro of about thirty.*]

JOSHUA [*going to* MOSES' *side*]: Yes, suh.

MOSES: What's de shoutin' 'bout, Joshua?

JOSHUA: De scouts is back wid de news. De Jordan is right ahead of us, and Jericho is jest on de other side. Moses, we're dere! [*There are cries of " Hallelujah!" " De Lawd be praised!" " Hooray!" " De Kingdom's comin'!" etc. With a considerable stir among the marchers, several new arrivals crowd in from right, shouting " Moses, we're dere!"* JOSHUA *seeing the newcomers:*] Yere's de scouts.

[*Three very ragged and dusty young men advance to* MOSES.]

MOSES [*as the shouting dies*]: So it's de River Jordan?

FIRST SCOUT: Yes, suh.

MOSES: All we got to take is de city of Jericho.

FIRST SCOUT: Yes, suh.

MOSES: Joshua, you got to take charge of de fightin' men, an' Aaron's gotta stay by de priests.

JOSHUA: What about you?

MOSES: You are leavin' me behind. Joshua, you gonter get de fightin' men together and take dat city befo' sundown.

JOSHUA: It's a big city, Moses, wid walls all 'round it. We ain't got enough men.

MOSES: You'll take it, Joshua.

JOSHUA: Yes, suh, but how?

MOSES: Move up to de walls wid our people. Tell de priests to go wid you with de rams' horns. You start marchin' 'roun' dem walls, and den —

JOSHUA: Yes, suh.

MOSES: De Lawd'll take charge, jest as He's took charge ev'y time I've led you against a city. He ain't never failed, has He?

SEVERAL VOICES: No, Moses.

[*All raise their heads.*]

MOSES: And He ain't goin' to fail us now. [*He prays. All bow.*] Oh, Lawd, I'm turnin' over our brave young men to you, caize I know you don' want me to lead 'em any further. [*Rises.*] Jest like you said, I've got to de Jordan but I cain't git over it. An' yere dey goin' now to take de city of Jericho. In a little while dey'll be marchin' 'roun' it. An' would you please be so good as to tell 'em what to do? Amen. [*To* JOSHUA.] Go ahead. Ev'ybody follows Joshua now. Give de signal to move on wid ev'ything. [*A trumpet is heard.*] You camp fo' de night in de city of Jericho.

[MOSES *seats himself on the rock.*]

JOSHUA: Cain't we help you, Moses?

MOSES: You go ahead. De Lawd's got his plans fo' me. Soun' de signal to march. [*Another trumpet call is heard. The company starts marching off.* AARON *lingers a moment.*] Take care of de Ark of de Covenant, Aaron.

AARON: Yes, brother. Good-by.

MOSES: Good-by, Aaron. [*The singing is resumed softly and dies away. The last of the marchers has disappeared.*] Yere I is, Lawd. De chillun is goin' into de Promised Land. [GOD *enters from behind the hill. He walks to* MOSES, *puts His hands on his shoulders.*] You's with me, ain't you, Lawd?

GOD: Co'se I is.

MOSES: Guess I'm through, Lawd. Jest like you said I'd be, when I broke de tablets of de law. De ol' machine's broke down.

GOD: Jest what was it I said to you, Moses? Do you remember?

MOSES: You said I couldn't go into de Promised Land.

GOD: Dat's so. But dat ain't all dey was to it.

MOSES: How you mean, Lawd?

GOD: Moses, you been a good man. You been a good leader of my people. You got me angry once, dat's true. And when you anger me I'm a God of Wrath. But I never meant you wasn't gonter have what was comin' to you. An' I ain't goin' to do you out of it, Moses. It's jest de country acrost de River dat you ain't gonter enter. You gonter have a Promised Land. I been gettin' it ready fo' you, fo' a long time. Kin you stand up?

MOSES [*rising, with* GOD's *help*]: Yes, suh, Lawd.

GOD: Come on, I'm goin' to show it to you. We goin' up dis hill to see it. Moses, it's a million times nicer dan de Land of Canaan.

[*They start up the hill.*]

MOSES: I cain't hardly see.

GOD: Don't worry. Dat's jest caize you so old.

[*They take a step or two up the hill, when* MOSES *stops suddenly.*]

MOSES: Oh!

GOD: What's de matter?

MOSES: We cain't be doin' dis!

GOD: Co'se we kin!

MOSES: But I fo'got! I fo'got about Joshua and de fightin' men!

GOD: How about 'em?

MOSES: Dey're marchin' on Jericho. I tol' 'em to march aroun' de walls and den de Lawd would be dere to tell 'em what to do.

GOD: Dat's all right. He's dere.

MOSES: Den who's dis helpin' me up de hill?

GOD: Yo' faith, yo' God.

MOSES: And is you over dere helpin' them too, Lawd? Is you goin' to tell dem poor chillun what to do?

GOD: Co'se I is. Listen, Moses. I'll show you how I'm helpin' dem.

[*From the distance comes the blast of the rams' horns, the sound of crumbling walls, a roar, and a moment's silence. The* CHOIR *begins " Joshua Fit de Battle of Jericho," and continues through the rest of the scene.*]

MOSES: You did it, Lawd! You've tooken it! Listen to de chillun — dey's in de Land of Canaan at last! You's de only God dey ever was, ain't you, Lawd?

GOD [*quietly*]: Come on, ol' man.

[*They continue up the hill. The stage is darkened.*]

MR. DESHEE [*in the dark*]: But even dat scheme didn' work. Caize after dey got into the Land of Canaan dey went to de dogs again. And dey went into bondage again. Only dis time it was in de city of Babylon.

[*The* CHOIR, *which has been singing " Cain't Stay Away," stops as the next scene begins.*]

PART II. SCENE 5

Under a low ceiling is a room vaguely resembling a Negro night club in New Orleans. Two or three long tables run across the room, and on the left is a table on a dais with a gaudy canopy above it. The table bears a card marked " Reserved for King and guests."

Flashy young men and women are seated at the tables. About a dozen couples are dancing in the foreground to the tune of a jazz orchestra. The costumes are what would be worn at a Negro masquerade to represent the debauchees of Babylon.

FIRST MAN: When did yuh git to Babylon?

SECOND MAN: I jes' got in yesterday.

THIRD MAN [*dancing*]: How do you like dis baby, Joe?

FOURTH MAN: Hot damn! She could be de King's pet!

A WOMAN: Anybody seen my papa?

THIRD MAN: Don' fo'git de dance at de High Priest's home tomorrow.

[*The dance stops as a bugle call is heard. Enter* MASTER OF CEREMONIES.]

MASTER OF CEREMONIES: Stop! Tonight's guest of honor, de King of Babylon, an' party of five.

[*Enter the* KING *and five girls. The* KING *has on an imitation ermine cloak over his conventional evening clothes and wears a diamond tiara. All rise as the* KING *enters, and sing, " Hail, de King of Bab — Bab — Babylon."*]

KING: Wait till you see de swell table I got. [*He crosses the stage to his table. The girls are jabbering.*] Remind me to send you a peck of rubies in de mo'nin'.

MASTER OF CEREMONIES: Ev'nin', King!

KING: Good ev'nin'. How's de party goin'?

MASTER OF CEREMONIES: Bes' one we ever had in Babylon, King.

KING: Any Jew boys yere?

MASTER OF CEREMONIES [*indicating some of the others*]: Lot o' dem yere. I kin go git mo' if you want 'em.

KING: I was really referrin' to de High Priest. He's a 'tic'lar frien' o' mine an' he might drop in. You know what he look like?

MASTER OF CEREMONIES: No, suh, but I'll be on de look-out fo' him.

KING: O.K. Now le's have a li'l good time.

MASTER OF CEREMONIES: Yes, suh. [*To the orchestra.*] Let 'er go, boys.

[*The music begins, waiters appear with food and great urns painted gold and silver, from which they pour out wine for the guests. The* MASTER OF CEREMONIES *exits. The* KING'S *dancing-girls go to the middle of the floor, and start to dance. The* KING *puts his arms about the waists of two girls, and draws them to him.*]

KING: Hot damn! Da's de way! Let de Jew boys see our gals kin dance better'n dere's. [*There is an ad lib. babel of " Da's de truth, King! " " I don't know — we got some good gals, too! " etc.*] Dey ain' nobody in de worl' like Babylon gals.

[*The dancing grows faster, the watchers keep time with handclaps. The door at the left opens suddenly, and the* PROPHET, *a patriarchal, ragged figure, enters. He looks belligerently about the room, and is followed almost immediately by the* MASTER OF CEREMONIES.]

PROPHET: Stop!

[*The music and the dancers halt.*]

KING: What's the idea, bustin' up my party?

MASTER OF CEREMONIES: He said he was expected, King. I thought mebbe he was de —

KING: Did you think he was de High Priest of de Hebrews? Why, he's jest an' ol' bum! T'row dis ole bum out o' yere! De High Priest is a fashion plate. T'row dis ole bum out o' yere!

PROPHET: Stop!

[*Those who have been advancing to seize him stop, somewhat amused.*]

KING: Wait a minute. Don't t'row him out. Let's see what he has to say.

PROPHET: Listen to me, King of Babylon! I've been sent yere by de Lawd God Jehovah. Don't you dare lay a hand on de Prophet!

KING: Oh, you're a prophet, is yuh? Well, you know we don't keer much fo' prophets in dis part of de country.

PROPHET: Listen to me, sons and daughters of Babylon! Listen, you children of Israel dat's given yo'selves over to de evil ways of yo' oppressors! You're all wallowin' like hogs in sin, an' de wrath of Gawd ain' goin' to be held back much longer! I'm tellin' you, repent befo' it's too late. Repent befo' Jehovah casts down de same fire dat burned up Sodom and Gomorrah. Repent befo' de —

[*During this scene yells increase as the* PROPHET *continues. The* HIGH PRIEST *enters left. He is a fat voluptuary, elaborately clothed in brightly colored robes. He walks in hand in hand with a gaudily dressed chippy.*]

HIGH PRIEST [*Noise stops.*]: Whoa, dere! What you botherin' the King fo'?

PROPHET [*wheeling*]: And you, de High Priest of all Israel, walkin' de town wid a dirty li'l tramp.

KING: Seems to be a frien' o' yours, Jake.

HIGH PRIEST [*crossing to the* KING *with his girl*]: Aw, he's one of dem wild men, like Jeremiah and Isaiah. Don' let him bother you none.

[*Pushes* PROPHET *aside and goes to* KING'S *table.*]

PROPHET: You consort with harlots, an' yo' pollution in the sight of the Lawd. De Lawd God's goin' to smite you down, jest as he's goin' to smite down all dis wicked world!

[*Grabs* HIGH PRIEST *and turns him around.*]

KING [*angrily against the last part of the preceding speech*]: Wait a minute. I'm getting tired of this. Don't t'row him out. Jest kill him!

[*There is the sound of a shot. The* PROPHET *falls.*]

PROPHET: Smite 'em down, Lawd, like you said. Dey ain't a decent person left in de whole world.

[*He dies.* MASTER OF CEREMONIES, *revolver in hand, looks down at the* PROPHET.]

MASTER OF CEREMONIES: He's dead, King.

KING: Some of you boys take him out.

[*A couple of young men come from the background and walk off with the body.*]

HIGH PRIEST: Don' know whether you should'a done that, King.

KING: Why not?

HIGH PRIEST: I don' know whether de Lawd would like it.

KING: Now, listen, Jake. You know yo' Lawd ain't payin' much attention to dis man's town. Except fo' you boys, it's tho'ly protected by de Gods o' Babylon.

HIGH PRIEST: I know, but jest de same —

KING: Look yere, s'pose I give you a couple hund'ed pieces of silver. Don' you s'pose you kin arrange to persuade yo' Gawd to keep his hands off?

HIGH PRIEST [*oilily*]: Well of co'se we could try. I dunno how well it would work.

[*As the* HIGH PRIEST *speaks, the* KING *claps his hands.* MASTER OF CEREMONIES *enters with bag of money.*]

KING: Yere it is.

HIGH PRIEST [*smiling*]: I guess we kin square things up. [*He prays — whiningly.*] O Lawd, please forgive my po' frien' de King o' Babylon. He didn't know what he was doin' an' —

[*There is a clap of thunder, darkness for a second. The lights go up and* GOD *is standing in the center of the room.*]

GOD: [*in a voice of doom*]: Dat's about enough. [*The guests are horrified.*] I's stood all I kin from you. I tried to make dis a good earth. I helped Adam, I helped Noah, I helped Moses, an' I helped David. What's de grain dat grew out of de seed? Sin! Nothin' but sin throughout de whole world. I've given you ev'y chance. I sent you warriors and prophets. I've given you laws and commandments, an' you betrayed my trust. Ev'ything I've given you, you've defiled. Ev'y time I've fo'given you, you've mocked me. An' now de High Priest of Israel tries to trifle wid my name. Listen, you chillun of darkness, yo' Lawd is tired. I'm tired of de struggle to make you worthy of de breath I gave you. I put you in bondage ag'in to cure you an' yo' worse dan you was amongst de fleshpots of Egypt. So I renounce you. Listen to the words of yo' Lawd God Jehovah, for dey is de last words yo' ever hear from me. I repent of dese people dat I have made and I will deliver dem no more.

[*There is darkness and cries of "Mercy!" "Have pity, Lawd!" "We didn' mean it, Lawd!" "Forgive us, Lawd!" etc. The* CHOIR *sings "Death's Gwinter Lay His Cold Icy Hands on Me" until the lights go up on the next scene.*]

PART II. SCENE 6

GOD *is writing at His desk. Outside, past the door, goes* HOSEA, *a dignified old man, with wings like* JACOB'S. GOD, *sensing his presence, looks up from the paper He is examining, and follows him out of the corner of His eye. Angrily He resumes His work as soon as* HOSEA *is out of sight. There is a knock on the door.*

GOD: Who is it?

[GABRIEL *enters.*]

GABRIEL: It's de delegation, Lawd.

GOD [*wearily*]: Tell 'em to come in. [ABRAHAM, ISAAC, JACOB, *and* MOSES *enter.*] Good mo'nin', gen'lemen.

THE VISTORS: Good mo'nin', Lawd.

GOD: What kin I do for you?

MOSES: You know, Lawd. Go back to our people.

GOD [*shaking His head*]: Ev'ry day fo' hund'eds of years you boys have come in to ask dat same thing. De answer is still de same. I repented of de people I made. I said I would deliver dem no more. Good mo'nin', gen'lemen. [*The four visitors rise and exeunt.* GABRIEL *remains.*] Gabe, why do dey do it?

GABRIEL: I 'spect dey think you gonter change yo' mind.

GOD [*sadly*]: Dey don' know me. [HOSEA *again passes the door. His shadow shows on wall.* GABRIEL *is perplexed, as he watches.* GOD *again looks surreptitiously over His shoulder at the passing figure.*] I don' like dat, either.

GABRIEL: What, Lawd?

GOD: Dat man.

GABRIEL: He's just a prophet, Lawd. Dat's jest old Hosea. He jest come up the other day.

GOD: I know. He's one of de few dat's come up yere since I was on de earth last time.

GABRIEL: Ain' been annoyin' you, has he?

GOD: I don' like him walkin' past de door.

GABRIEL: All you got to do is tell him to stop, Lawd.

GOD: Yes, I know. I don' want to tell him. He's got a right up yere or he wouldn' be yere.

GABRIEL: You needn' be bothered by him hangin' aroun' de office all de time. I'll tell 'im. Who's he think he —

GOD: No, Gabe. I find it ain't in me to stop him. I sometimes jest wonder why he don' jest come in an' say hello.

GABRIEL: You want him to do that?

[*He moves as if to go to the door.*]

GOD: He never has spoke to me, and if he don't wanta come in, I ain't gonter make him. But dat ain't de worst of it, Gabriel.

GABRIEL: What is, Lawd?

GOD: Ev'y time he goes past de door I hears a voice.

GABRIEL: One of de angels?

GOD [*shaking His head*]: It's from de earth. It's a man.

GABRIEL: You mean he's prayin'?

GOD: No, he ain't exactly prayin'. He's jest talkin' in such a way dat I got to lissen. His name is Hezdrel.

GABRIEL: Is he on de books?

GOD: No, not yet. But ev'y time dat Hosea goes past I hear dat voice.

GABRIEL: Den tell *it* to stop.

GOD: I find I don' want to do that, either. Dey's gettin' ready to take Jerusalem down dere. Dat was my big fine city. Dis Hezdrel, he's jest one of de defenders. [*Suddenly and passionately almost wildly.*] I ain't comin' down. You hear me? I ain't comin' down. [*He looks at* GABRIEL.] Go ahead, Gabriel. 'Tend to yo' chores. I'm gonter keep wukkin' yere.

GABRIEL: I hates to see you feelin' like dis, Lawd.

GOD: Dat's all right. Even bein' Gawd ain't a bed of roses. [GABRIEL *exits.* HOSEA'S *shadow is on the wall. For a second* HOSEA *hesitates.* GOD *looks at the wall. Goes to window.*] I hear you. I know yo' fightin' bravely, but I ain't comin' down. Oh, why don' you leave me alone? You know you ain't talkin' to me. *Is* you talkin' to me? I cain't stand yo' talkin' dat way. I kin only hear part of what yo' sayin', and it puzzles me. Don' you know you cain't puzzle God? [*A pause. Then, tenderly.*] Do you want me to come down dere ve'y much? You know I said I wouldn't come down? [*Fiercely.*] Why don' he answer me a little? [*With clenched fists, looks down through the window*.] Listen! I'll tell you what I'll do. I ain't goin' to promise you anythin', and I ain't goin' to do nothin' to help you. I'm jest feelin' a little low, an' I'm only comin' down to make myself feel a little better, dat's all.

[*The stage is darkened.* CHOIR *begins* " *A Blind Man Stood in de Middle of de Road,*" *and continues until the lights go up on the next scene.*]

PART II. SCENE 7

It is a shadowed corner beside the walls of the temple in Jerusalem. The light of campfires flickers on the figure of HEZDREL, *who was* ADAM *in Part I. He stands in the same position* ADAM *held when first discovered but in his right hand is a sword, and his left is in a sling. Around him are several prostrate bodies. Pistol and cannon shots, then a trumpet call. Six young men enter from left in command of a* CORPORAL. *They are all armed.*

CORPORAL: De fightin's stopped fo' de night, Hezdrel.

HEZDREL: Yes?

CORPORAL: Dey're goin' to begin ag'in at cockcrow. [MAN *enters, crosses the stage and exits.*] Herod say he's goin' to take de temple tomorrow, burn de books and de Ark of de Covenant, and put us all to de sword.

HEZDREL: Yo' ready, ain't you?

EVERYBODY: Yes, Hezdrel.

HEZDREL: Did de food get in through de hole in de city wall?

[*Two* SOLDIERS *enter, cross the stage and exeunt.*]

CORPORAL: Yessuh, we's goin' back to pass it out now.

HEZDREL: Good. Any mo' of our people escape today?

CORPORAL: Ol' Herod's got de ol' hole covered up now, but fifteen of our people got out a new one we made.

[*Other* SOLDIERS *enter, cross the stage and exeunt.*]

HEZDREL: Good. Take dese yere wounded men back and git 'em took care of.

CORPORAL: Yes, suh.

[*They pick up the bodies on the ground and carry them off stage as* HEZDREL *speaks.*]

HEZDREL: So dey gonter take de temple in de mo'nin'? We'll be waitin' for 'em. Jest remember, boys, when dey kill us we leap out of our skins, right into de lap of God.

[*The* MEN *disappear with the wounded; from the deep shadow upstage comes* GOD.]

GOD: Hello, Hezdrel — Adam.

HEZDREL [*rubbing his forehead*]: Who is you?

GOD: Me? I'm jest an ol' preacher, from back in de hills.

HEZDREL: What you doin' yere?

GOD: I heard you boys was fightin'. I jest wanted to see how it was goin'.

HEZDREL: Well, it ain't goin' so well.

GOD: Dey got you skeered, huh?

HEZDREL: Look yere, who is you, a spy in my brain?

GOD: Cain't you see I's one of yo' people?

HEZDREL: Listen, Preacher, we ain't skeered. We's gonter be killed, but we ain't skeered.

GOD: I's glad to hear dat. Kin I ask you a question, Hezdrel?

HEZDREL. What is it?

GOD: How is it you is so brave?

HEZDREL: Caize we got faith, dat's why.

GOD: Faith? In who?

HEZDREL: In our dear Lawd God.

GOD: But God say he abandoned ev'y one down yere.

HEZDREL: Who say dat? Who dare say dat of the Lawd God of Hosea?

GOD: De God of Hosea?

HEZDREL: You heard me. Look yere, you *is* a spy in my brain!

GOD: No, I ain't, Hezdrel. I'm jest puzzled. You ought to know dat.

HEZDREL: How come you so puzzled 'bout de God of Hosea?

GOD: I don' know. Maybe I jest don' hear things. You see, I live 'way back in de hills.

HEZDREL: What you wanter find out?

GOD: Ain't de God of Hosea de same Jehovah dat was de God of Moses?

HEZDREL [*contemptuously*]: No. Dat ol' God of wrath and vengeance? We have de God dat Hosea preached to us. He's de one God.

GOD: Who's he?

HEZDREL [*reverently*]: De God of mercy.

GOD: Hezdrel, don' you think dey must be de same God?

HEZDREL: I don' know. I ain't bothered to think much about it. Maybe dey is. Maybe our God is de same ol' God. I guess jest got tired of his appearance dat ol' way.

GOD: What you mean, Hezdrel?

HEZDREL: Oh, dat ol' God dat walked de earth in de shape of a man. I guess he lived with man so much dat all he seen was de sins in man. Dat's what made him de God of wrath and vengeance. Co'se he made Hosea. An' Hosea never woulda found what mercy was unless dere was a little of it in God, too. Anyway, he ain't a fearsome God no mo'. Hosea showed us dat.

GOD: How you s'pose Hosea found dat mercy?

HEZDREL: De only way he could find it. De only way I found it. De only way anyone could find it.

GOD: How's dat?

HEZDREL: Through sufferin'.

GOD [*after a pause*]: What if dey kill you in de mo'nin', Hezdrel?

HEZDREL: If dey do, dey do. Dat's all.

GOD: Herod say he's goin' to burn de temple —

HEZDREL: So he say.

GOD: And burn de Ark an' de books. Den dat's de end of de books, ain't it?

HEZDREL [*buoyantly*]: What you mean? If he burns dem things in dere? Naw. Dem's jest copies.

GOD: Where is de others?

HEZDREL [*tapping his head*]: Dey's a set in yere. Fifteen got out through de hole in the city wall today. A hundred and fifty got out durin' de week. Each of 'em is a set of de books. Dey's scattered safe all over de countryside now, jest waitin' to git pen and paper fo' to put 'em down ag'in.

GOD [*proudly*]: Dey cain't lick you, kin dey, Hezdrel?

HEZDREL [*smiling*]: I know dey cain't. [*Trumpet.*] You better get out o' yere, Preacher, if you wanter carry de news to yo' people. It'll soon be daylight.

GOD: I'm goin'. [*He takes a step upstage and stops.*] Want me to take any message?

HEZDREL: Tell de people in de hills dey ain't nobody like de Lawd God of Hosea.

GOD: I will, if dey kill you tomorrow I'll bet dat God of Hosea'll be waitin' for you.

HEZDREL: I *know* he will.

GOD [*quietly*]: Thank you, Hezdrel.

HEZDREL: Fo' what?

GOD: Fo' tellin' me so much. You see I been so far away, I guess I was jest way behin' de times.

[*He exits. Pause, then trumpet sounds.* HEZDREL *paces back and forth once or twice. Another young* SOLDIER *appears. Other men enter and stand grouped about* HEZDREL.]

SECOND OFFICER [*excitedly*]: De cock's jest crowed, Hezdrel. Dey started de fightin' ag'in.

HEZDREL: We's ready for 'em. Come on, boys. [*From the darkness upstage comes another group of* SOLDIERS.] Dis is de day dey say dey'll git us. Le's fight till de last man goes. What d'you say?

CORPORAL: Le's go, Hezdrel!

HEZDREL [*calling left*]: Give 'em ev'ything, boys!

[*There is a movement toward the left, a bugle call and the sound of distant battle. The lights go out. The* CHOIR *is heard singing, " March On," triumphantly. They continue to sing after the lights go up on the next scene.*]

PART II. SCENE 8

It is the same setting as the Fish Fry Scene in Part I. The same angels are present but the CHOIR, instead of marching, is standing in a double row on an angle upstage right. GOD is seated in an armchair near center. He faces the audience. As the CHOIR continues to sing, GABRIEL enters, unnoticed by the chattering angels. He looks at GOD, who is staring thoughtfully toward the audience.

GABRIEL: You look a little pensive, Lawd. [GOD *nods his head.*] Have a seegar, Lawd?

GOD: No thanks, Gabriel.

[GABRIEL *goes to the table, accepts a cup of custard; chats with the angel behind the table for a moment as he sips, puts the cup down and returns to the side of* GOD.]

GABRIEL: You look awful pensive, Lawd. You been sittin' yere, lookin' dis way, an awful long time. Is it somethin' serious, Lawd?

GOD: Very serious, Gabriel.

GABRIEL [*awed by His tone*]: Lawd, is de time come for me to blow?

GOD: Not yet, Gabriel. I'm just thinkin'.

GABRIEL: What about, Lawd?

[*Puts up hand. Singing stops.*]

GOD: 'Bout somethin' de boy tol' me. Somethin' 'bout Hosea, and himself. How dey foun' somethin'.

GABRIEL: What, Lawd?

GOD: Mercy. [*A pause.*] Through *sufferin',* he said.

GABRIEL: Yes, Lawd.

GOD: I'm tryin' to find it, too. It's awful impo'tant. It's awful impo'tant to all de people on my earth. Did he mean dat even God must suffer?

[GOD *continues to look out over the audience for a moment and then a look of surprise comes into His face. He sighs. In the distance a voice cries.*]

THE VOICE: Oh, look at him! Oh, look, dey goin' to make him carry it up dat high hill! Dey goin' to nail him to it! Oh, dat's a terrible burden for one man to carry!

[GOD *rises and murmurs "Yes!" as if in recognition. The heavenly beings have been watching Him closely, and now, seeing Him smile gently, draw back, relieved. All the angels burst into "Hallelujah, King Jesus."* GOD *continues to smile as the lights fade away. The singing becomes fortissimo.*]

CURTAIN

NARRATION

Thomas Chandler Haliburton

The Clockmaker

I HAD heard of Yankee clock peddlers, tin peddlers, and Bible peddlers, especially of him who sold polyglot Bibles — all in English — to the amount of sixteen thousand pounds. The house of every substantial farmer has three substantial ornaments: a wooden clock, a tin reflector, and a polyglot Bible.

How is it that an American can sell his wares at whatever price he pleases where a Bluenose would fail to make a sale at all? I will inquire of the Clockmaker the secret of his success.

"What a pity it is, Mr. Slick" — for such was his name — "what a pity it is," said I, "that you, who are so successful in teaching these people the value of clocks, could not also teach them the value of time."

"I guess," said he, "they have got that ring to grow on their horns yet which every four-year-old has in our country. We reckon hours and minutes to be dollars and cents. They do nothin' in these parts but eat, drink, smoke, sleep, ride about, lounge at taverns, make speeches at temperance meetings, and talk about *House of Assembly*. If a man don't hoe his corn, and he don't get a crop, he says it is all owin' to the Bank; and if he runs into debt, and is sued, why he says lawyers are a cuss to the country. They are a most idle set of folks, I tell *you*."

"But how is it," said I, "that you manage to sell such an immense number of clocks, which certainly cannot be called necessary articles, among people with whom there seems to be so great a scarcity of money?"

Mr. Slick paused as if considering the propriety of answering the question and, looking me in the face, said in a confidential tone, "Why, I don't care if I do tell you; for the market is glutted, and I shall quit this circuit. It is done by a knowledge of *soft sawder* and *human natur*. But here is Deacon Flint's," said he. "I have but one clock left, and I guess I will sell it to him."

At the gate of a most comfortable-looking farmhouse stood Deacon Flint, a

From *The Clockmaker,* 1836.

respectable old man who had understood the value of time better than most of his neighbors, if one might judge from the appearance of everything about him. After the usual salutation, an invitation to " alight " was accepted by Mr. Slick, who said he wished to take leave of Mrs. Flint before he left Colchester.

We had hardly entered the house before the Clockmaker, pointing to the view from the window, and addressing himself to me, said, " If I was to tell them in Connecticut that there was such a farm as this away down East here in Nova Scotia, they wouldn't believe me. Why, there ain't such a location in all New England. The Deacon has a hundred acres of dyke — "

" Seventy," said the Deacon, " only seventy."

" Well, seventy; but then there is your fine deep bottom. Why, I could run a ramrod into it — "

" *Interval* we call it," said the Deacon, who, though evidently pleased at this eulogium, seemed to wish the experiment of the ramrod to be tried in the right place.

" Well, interval if you please — though Professor Eleazer Cumstick, in his work on Ohio, calls them bottoms — is jist as good as dyke. Then there is that water privilege, worth three or four thousand dollars, twice as good as what Governor Cass paid fifteen thousand dollars for. I wonder, Deacon, you don't put up a carding mill on it; the same works would carry a turning lathe, a shingle machine, a circular saw, grind bark, and — "

" Too old," said the Deacon, " too old for all these speculations — "

" Old! " repeated the Clockmaker. " Not you. Why, you are worth half a dozen of the young men we see nowadays. You are young enough to have — " Here he said something in a lower tone of voice which I did not distinctly hear; but, whatever it was, the Deacon was pleased: he smiled and said he did not think of such things now.

" But your beasts, dear me, your beasts must be put in and have a feed," saying which he went out to order them to be taken to the stable.

As the old gentleman closed the door after him, Mr. Slick drew near to me and said in an undertone, " Now that is what I call *soft sawder*. An Englishman would pass that man as a sheep passes a hog in a pastur, without looking at him. Or," said he, looking rather archly, " if he was mounted on a pretty smart horse, I guess he'd trot away, *if he could*. Now I find — "

Here his lecture on *soft sawder* was cut short by the entrance of Mrs. Flint.

" Jist come to say good-by, Mrs. Flint."

" What, have you sold all your clocks? "

" Yes, and very low too; for money is scarce, and I wished to close the consarn. I am wrong in saying all, for I have jist one left. Neighbor Steel's wife asked to have the refusal of it, but I guess I won't sell it. I had but two of them, this one and the feller of it that I sold Governor Lincoln. Gineral Green, the Secretary of State for Maine, said he'd give me fifty dollars for this here one — it has composition wheels and patent axles; it is a beautiful article — a real first chop — no mistake, genuine superfine, but I guess I'll take it back. And, besides, Squire Hawk might think kinder hard that I didn't give him the offer."

"Dear me," said Mrs. Flint, "I should like to see it. Where is it?"

"It is in a chist of mine over the way, at Tom Tape's store. I guess he can ship it on to Eastport."

"That's a good man," said Mrs. Flint, "jist let's look at it."

Mr. Slick, willing to oblige, yielded to these entreaties and soon produced the clock — a gaudy, highly varnished, trumpery-looking affair. He placed it on the chimney piece, where its beauties were pointed out and duly appreciated by Mrs. Flint, whose admiration was about ending in a proposal when Mr. Flint returned from giving his directions about the care of the horses.

The Deacon praised the clock. He too thought it a handsome one; but the Deacon was a prudent man, he had a watch — he was sorry, but he had no occasion for a clock.

"I guess you're in the wrong furrow this time, Deacon. It an't for sale," said Mr. Slick. "And if it was, I reckon neighbor Steel's wife would have it, for she gives me no peace about it."

Mrs. Flint said Mr. Steel had enough to do, poor man, to pay his interest without buying clocks for his wife.

"It's no consarn of mine," said Mr. Slick, "so long as he pays me what he has to do, but I guess I don't want to sell it, and besides it comes too high; that clock can't be made at Rhode Island under forty dollars.

"Why, it an't possible," said the Clockmaker, in apparent surprise, looking at his watch, "why, as I'm alive it is four o'clock, and if I haven't been two blessed hours here — how on airth shall I reach River Philip tonight? I'll tell you what, Mrs. Flint. I'll leave the clock in your care till I return on my way to the States — I'll set it a-goin', and put it to the right time."

As soon as this operation was performed, he delivered the key to the Deacon with a sort of serio-comic injunction to wind up the clock every Saturday night, which Mrs. Flint said she would take care should be done, and promised to remind her husband of it, in case he should chance to forget it.

"That," said the Clockmaker, as soon as we were mounted, "that I call *human natur!* Now, that clock is sold for forty dollars — it cost me jist six dollars and fifty cents. Mrs. Flint will never let Mrs. Steel have the refusal — nor will the Deacon larn, until I call for the clock, that having once indulged in the use of a superfluity, how difficult it is to give it up. We can do without any article of luxury we never had, but when once obtained, it isn't in *human natur* to surrender it voluntarily. Of fifteen thousand sold by myself and partners in this Province, twelve thousand were left in this manner, and only ten clocks were ever returned — when we called for them, they invariably bought them. We trust to *soft sawder* to get them into the house, and to *human natur* that they never come out of it."

David Crockett

A Useful Coonskin

WHILE on the subject of election matters, I will relate a little anecdote about myself, which will show the people to the East how we manage these things on the frontiers. It was when I first run for Congress; I was then in favor of the Hero [Andrew Jackson], for he had chalked out his course so sleek in his letter to the Tennessee legislature that, like Sam Patch, says I, "There can be no mistake in him," and so I went ahead. No one dreamt about the monster and the deposits at that time, and so, as I afterward found, many like myself were taken in by these fair promises, which were worth about as much as a flash in the pan when you have a fair shot at a fat bear.

But I am losing sight of my story. Well, I started off to the Cross Roads dressed in my hunting shirt, and my rifle on my shoulder. Many of our constituents had assembled there to get a taste of the quality of the candidates at orating. Job Snelling, a gander-shanked Yankee who had been caught somewhere about Plymouth Bay and been shipped to the West with a cargo of codfish and rum, erected a large shantee and set up shop for the occasion. A large posse of the voters had assembled before I arrived, and my opponent had already made considerable headway with his speechifying and his treating, when they spied me about a rifle shot from camp, sauntering along as if I was not a party in business. "There comes Crockett," cried one. "Let us hear the colonel," cried another; and so I mounted the stump that had been cut down for the occasion, and began to bushwhack in the most approved style.

I had not been up long before there was such an uproar in the crowd that I could not hear my own voice, and some of my constituents let me know that they could not listen to me on such a dry subject as the welfare of the nation until they had something to drink, and that I must treat them. Accordingly I jumped down from the rostrum and led the way to the shantee, followed by my constituents, shouting, "Huzza for Crockett!" and "Crockett forever!"

When we entered the shantee Job was busy dealing out his rum in a style that showed he was making a good day's work of it, and I called for a quart of the best; but the crooked crittur returned no other answer than by pointing to a board over the bar, on which he had chalked in large letters, "*Pay today and trust tomorrow.*" Now that idea brought me up all standing; it was a sort of cornering in which there was no back-out, for ready money in the West, in those times, was the shyest thing in all natur, and it was most particularly shy with me on that occasion.

The voters, seeing my predicament, fell off to the other side, and I was left

From Henry Watterson's *Oddities in Southern Life and Character*, 1882.

deserted and alone, as the Government will be when he no longer has any offices to bestow. I saw as plain as day that the tide of popular opinion was against me, and that unless I got some rum speedily I should lose my election as sure as there are snakes in Virginny; and it must be done soon, or even burnt brandy wouldn't save me. So I walked away from the shantee, but in another manner from the way I entered it, for on this occasion I had no train after me, and not a voice shouted, " Huzza for Crockett! " Popularity sometimes depends on a very small matter indeed; in this particular it was worth a quart of New England rum, and no more.

Well, knowing that a crisis was at hand, I struck into the woods, with my rifle on my shoulder, my best friend in time of need; and, as good fortune would have it, I had not been out more than a quarter of an hour before I treed a fat coon, and in the pulling of a trigger he lay dead at the foot of the tree. I soon whipped his hairy jacket off his back, and again bent my steps towards the shantee, and walked up to the bar, but not alone, for this time I had half a dozen of my constituents at my heels. I threw down the coonskin upon the counter and called for a quart, and Job, though busy dealing out rum, forgot to point at his chalked rules and regulations; for he knew that a coon was as good a legal tender for a quart in the West as a New York shilling any day in the year.

My constituents now flocked about me and cried, " Huzza for Crockett! " " Crockett forever! " and finding the tide had taken a turn, I told them several yarns to get them in a good humor; and having soon dispatched the value of the coon, I went out and mounted the stump without opposition, and a clear majority of the voters followed me to hear what I had to offer for the good of the nation. Before I was half through, one of my constituents moved that they would hear the balance of my speech after they had washed down the first part with some more of Job Snelling's extract of cornstalk and molasses, and the question being put, it was carried unanimously. It wasn't considered necessary to tell the yeas and nays, so we adjourned to the shantee, and on the way I began to reckon that the fate of the nation pretty much depended upon my shooting another coon.

While standing at the bar, feeling sort of bashful while Job's rules and regulations stared me in the face, I cast down my eyes and discovered one end of the coonskin sticking between the logs that supported the bar. Job had slung it there in the hurry of business. I gave it a sort of quick jerk, and it followed my hand as natural as if I had been the rightful owner. I slapped it on the counter, and Job, little dreaming that he was barking up the wrong tree, shoved along another bottle, which my constituents quickly disposed of with great good humor, for some of them saw the trick; and then we withdrew to the rostrum to discuss the affairs of the nation.

I don't know how it was, but the voters soon became dry again, and nothing would do but we must adjourn to the shantee; and as luck would have it, the coonskin was still sticking between the logs, as if Job had flung it there on purpose to tempt me. I was not slow in raising it to the counter; the rum followed, of course; and I wish I may be shot if I didn't, before the day was over, get ten quarts for the same identical skin, and from a fellow, too, who in those parts was considered as sharp as a steel trap and as bright as a pewter button.

This joke secured me my election, for it soon circulated like smoke among my constituents, and they allowed, with one accord, that the man who could get the whip hand of Job Snelling, in fair trade, could outwit Old Nick himself and was the real grit for them in Congress. Job was by no means popular; he boasted of always being wide-awake, and that anyone who could take him in was free to do so, for he came from a stock that, sleeping or waking, had always one eye open, and the other not more than half closed. The whole family were geniuses. His father was the inventor of wooden nutmegs, by which Job said he might have made a fortune if he had only taken out a patent and kept the business in his own hands; his mother, Patience, manufactured the first white oak pumpkin seeds of the mammoth kind, and turned a pretty penny the first season; and his aunt Prudence was the first to discover that cornhusks, steeped into tobacco water, would make as handsome Spanish wrappers as ever came from Havana, and that oak leaves would answer all the purpose of filling, for no one could discover the difference except the man who smoked them, and then it would be too late to make a stir about it. Job himself bragged of having made some useful discoveries, the most profitable of which was the art of converting mahogany sawdust into cayenne pepper, which he said was a profitable and safe business; for the people have been so long accustomed to having dust thrown in their eyes that there wasn't much danger of being found out.

The way I got to the blind side of the Yankee merchant was pretty generally known before election day, and the result was that my opponent might as well have whistled jigs to a milestone as attempt to beat up for votes in that district. I beat him out and out, quite back into the old year, and there was scarce enough left of him, after the canvass was over, to make a small grease spot. He disappeared without even leaving a mark behind; and such will be the fate of Adam Huntsman if there is a fair fight and no gouging.

After the election was over, I sent Snelling the price of the rum but took good care to keep the fact from the knowledge of my constituents. Job refused the money, and sent me word that it did him good to be taken in occasionally, as it served to brighten his ideas; but I afterwards learnt when he found out the trick that had been played upon him, he put all the rum I had ordered in his bill against my opponent, who, being elated with the speeches he had made on the affairs of the nation, could not descend to examine into the particulars of a bill of a vender of rum in the small way.

A. B. Longstreet

The Fight

IN the younger days of the Republic there lived in the county of —— two men who were admitted on all hands to be the very *best men* in the county, which in the Georgia vocabulary means they could flog any other two men in the county. Each, through many a hard-fought battle, had acquired the mastery of his own battalion, but they lived on opposite sides of the court-house and in different battalions; consequently they were but seldom thrown together. When they met, however, they were always friendly; indeed, at their first interview they seemed to conceive a wonderful attachment to each other, which rather increased than diminished as they became better acquainted; so that, but for the circumstance which I am about to mention, the question, which had been a thousand times asked, " Which is the best man, Billy Stallions (Stallings) or Bob Durham? " would probably never have been answered.

Billy ruled the upper battalion and Bob the lower. The former measured six feet and an inch in his stockings, and, without a single pound of cumbrous flesh about him, weighed a hundred and eighty. The latter was an inch shorter than his rival, and ten pounds lighter; but he was much the more active of the two. In running and jumping he had but few equals in the county; and in wrestling, not one. In other respects they were nearly equal. Both were admirable specimens of human nature in its finest form. Billy's victories had generally been achieved by the tremendous power of his blows, one of which had often proved decisive of his battles; Bob's by his adroitness in bringing his adversary to the ground. This advantage he had never failed to gain at the onset, and when gained he never failed to improve it to the defeat of his adversary.

These points of difference have involved the reader in a doubt as to the probable issue of a contest between them. It was not so, however, with the two battalions. Neither had the least difficulty in determining the point by the most natural and irresistible deductions *a priori;* and though, by the same course of reasoning, they arrived at directly opposite conclusions, neither felt its confidence in the least shaken by this circumstance. The upper battalion swore " that Billy only wanted one lick at him to knock his heart, liver, and lights out of him, and if he got two at him he'd knock him into a cocked hat." The lower battalion retorted " that he wouldn't have time to double his fist before Bob would put his head where his feet ought to be; and that, by the time he hit the ground, the meat would fly off his face so quick that people would think it was shook off by the fall." These disputes often led to the *argumentum ad hominem,* but with such equality of success on both sides as to leave the main question just where

From *Georgia Scenes*, 1835.

they found it. They usually ended, however, in the common way — with a bet; and many a quart of old Jamaica (whisky had not then supplanted rum) was staked upon the issue. Still, greatly to the annoyance of the curious, Billy and Bob continued to be good friends.

Now, there happened to reside in the county just alluded to a little fellow by the name of Ransy Sniffle: a sprout of Richmond, who, in his earlier days, had fed copiously upon red clay and blackberries. This diet had given to Ransy a complexion that a corpse would have disdained to own, and an abdominal rotundity that was quite unprepossessing. Long spells of the fever and ague, too, in Ransy's youth, had conspired with clay and blackberries to throw him quite out of the order of nature. His shoulders were fleshless and elevated; his head large and flat; his neck slim and translucent; and his arms, hands, fingers, and feet were lengthened out of all proportion to the rest of his frame. His joints were large and his limbs small; and as for flesh, he could not, with propriety, be said to have any. Those parts which nature usually supplies with the most of this article — the calves of the legs, for example — presented in him the appearance of so many well-drawn blisters. His height was just five feet nothing; and his average weight in blackberry season, ninety-five.

I have been thus particular in describing him, for the purpose of showing what a great matter a little fire sometimes kindleth. There was nothing on this earth which delighted Ransy so much as a fight. He never seemed fairly alive except when he was witnessing, fomenting, or talking about a fight. Then, indeed, his deep-sunken gray eye assumed something of a living fire, and his tongue acquired a volubility that bordered upon eloquence. Ransy had been kept for more than a year in the most torturing suspense as to the comparative manhood of Billy Stallings and Bob Durham. He had resorted to all his usual expedients to bring them in collision, and had entirely failed. He had faithfully reported to Bob all that had been said by the people in the upper battalion " agin him," and " he was sure Billy Stallings started it. He heard Billy say himself to Jim Brown that he could whip him, *or any other man in his battalion* "; and this he told to Bob, adding, " Dod darn his soul, if he was a little bigger, if he'd let any man *put upon* his battalion in such a way! " Bob replied, " If he (Stallings) thought so, he'd better come and try it." This Ransy carried to Billy, and delivered it with a spirit becoming his own dignity and the character of his battalion, and with a coloring well calculated to give it effect. These and many other schemes which Ransy laid for the gratification of his curiosity entirely failed of their object. Billy and Bob continued friends, and Ransy had begun to lapse into the most tantalizing and hopeless despair, when a circumstance occurred which led to a settlement of the long-disputed question.

It is said that a hundred gamecocks will live in perfect harmony together if you do not put a hen with them; and so it would have been with Billy and Bob had there been no women in the world. But there were women in the world, and from them each of our heroes had taken to himself a wife. The good ladies were no strangers to the prowess of their husbands, and, strange as it may seem, they presumed a little upon it.

The two battalions had met at the courthouse upon a regimental parade. The two champions were there, and their wives had accompanied them. Neither knew the other's lady, nor were the ladies known to each other. The exercises of the day were just over when Mrs. Stallings and Mrs. Durham stepped simultaneously into the store of Zephaniah Atwater, from " down East."

" Have you any Turkey red? " said Mrs. S.

" Have you any curtain calico? " said Mrs. D. at the same moment.

" Yes, ladies," said Mr. Atwater, " I have both."

" Then help me first," said Mrs. D., " for I'm in a hurry."

" I'm in as great a hurry as she is," said Mrs. S., " and I'll thank you to help me first."

" And, pray, who are you, madam? " continued the other.

" Your betters, madam," was the reply.

At this moment Billy Stallings stepped in. " Come," said he, " Nancy, let's be going; it's getting late."

" I'd 'a' been gone half an hour ago," she replied, " if it hadn't 'a' been for that impudent hussy."

" Who do you call an impudent hussy, you nasty, good-for-nothing, snaggle-toothed gaub of fat, you? " returned Mrs. D.

" Look here, woman," said Billy. " Have you got a husband here? If you have, I'll *lick* him till he learns to teach you better manners, you *sassy* heifer you! "

At this moment something was seen to rush out of the store as if ten thousand hornets were stinging it, crying, " Take care — let me go — don't hold me — where's Bob Durham? " It was Ransy Sniffle, who had been listening in breathless delight to all that had passed.

" Yonder's Bob, setting on the courthouse steps," cried one. " What's the matter? "

" Don't talk to me! " said Ransy. " Bob Durham, you'd better go long yonder and take care of your wife. They're playing hell with her there in Zeph Atwater's store. Dod etarnally darn my soul, if any man was to talk to my wife as Bill Stallions is talking to yours, if I wouldn't drive blue blazes through him in less than no time! "

Bob sprang to the store in a minute, followed by a hundred friends; for a bully of a county never wants friends.

" Bill Stallions," said Bob as he entered, " what have you been saying to my wife? "

" Is that your wife? " inquired Billy, obviously much surprised and a little disconcerted.

" Yes, she is; and no man shall abuse her, I don't care who he is."

" Well," rejoined Billy, " it ain't worth while to go over it; I've said enough for a fight, and if you'll step out we'll settle it."

" Billy," said Bob, " are you for a fair fight? "

" I am," said Billy. " I've heard much of your manhood, and I believe I'm a better man than you are. If you will go into a ring with me we can soon settle the dispute."

" Choose your friends," said Bob; " make your ring, and I'll be in with mine as soon as you will! "

They both stepped out and began to strip very deliberately, each battalion gathering round its champion, except Ransy, who kept himself busy in a most honest endeavor to hear and see all that transpired in both groups at the same time. He ran from one to the other in quick succession; peeped here and listened there; talked to this one, then to that one, and then to himself; squatted under one's legs and another's arms; and, in the short interval between stripping and stepping into the ring, managed to get himself trod on by half of both battalions.

But Ransy was not the only one interested upon this occasion; the most intense interest prevailed everywhere. Many were the conjectures, doubts, oaths, and imprecations uttered while the parties were preparing for the combat. All the knowing ones were consulted as to the issue, and they all agreed, to a man, in one of two opinions — either that Bob would flog Billy, or Billy would flog Bob. We must be permitted, however, to dwell for a moment upon the opinion of Squire Thomas Loggins, a man who, it was said, had never failed to predict the issue of a fight in all his life. Indeed, so unerring had he always proved in this regard that it would have been counted the most obstinate infidelity to doubt for a moment after he had delivered himself. Squire Loggins was a man who said but little, but that little was always delivered with the most imposing solemnity of look and cadence. He always wore the aspect of profound thought, and you could not look at him without coming to the conclusion that he was elaborating truth from its most intricate combinations.

" Uncle Tommy," said Sam Reynolds, " you can tell us all about it if you will; how will the fight go? "

The question immediately drew an anxious group around the squire. He raised his teeth slowly from the head of his walking cane, on which they had been resting, pressed his lips closely and thoughtfully together, threw down his eyebrows, dropped his chin, raised his eyes to an angle of twenty-three degrees, paused about half a minute, and replied, " Sammy, watch Robert Durham close in the beginning of the fight, take care of William Stallions in the middle of it, and see who has the wind at the end." As he uttered the last sentence he looked slyly at Bob's friends and winked very significantly; whereupon they rushed, with one accord, to tell Bob what Uncle Tommy had said. As they retired, the squire turned to Billy's friends and said, with a smile, " Them boys think I mean that Bob will whip." Here the other party kindled into joy, and hastened to inform Billy how Bob's friends had deceived themselves as to Uncle Tommy's opinion.

In the meantime the principals and seconds were busily employed in preparing themselves for the combat. The plan of attack and defense, the manner of improving the various turns of the conflict, " the best mode of saving wind," etc., etc., were all discussed and settled. At length Billy announced himself ready, and his crowd were seen moving to the center of the Courthouse Square, he and his five seconds in the rear. At the same time Bob's party moved to the same point, and in the same order. The ring was now formed, and for a moment the silence of death reigned through both battalions. It was soon interrupted, however, by the cry of " Clear the way! " from Billy's seconds, when the ring opened in the center of the upper battalion (for the order of march had arranged the center of the two battalions on opposite sides of the circle), and Billy stepped into the ring from the east, followed by his friends. He was stripped to the trousers, and exhibited an arm, breast, and shoulders of the most tremendous portent. His step was firm, daring, and martial; and as he bore his fine form a little in advance of his friends an involuntary burst of triumph broke from his side of the ring, and at the same moment an uncontrollable thrill of awe ran along the whole curve of the lower battalion.

" Look at him! " was heard from his friends. " Just look at him! "

" Ben, how much you ask to stand before that man two seconds? "

" Pshaw, don't talk about it! Just thinkin' about it's broke three o' my ribs a'ready! "

" What's Bob Durham going to do when Billy lets that arm loose upon him? "

" God bless your soul, he'll think thunder and lightning a mint julep to it! "

" Oh, look here, men, go take Bill Stallions out o' that ring, and bring in Phil Johnson's studhorse, so that Durham may have some chance! I don't want to see the man killed right away."

These and many other like expressions, interspersed thickly with oaths of the modern coinage, were coming from all points of the upper battalion while Bob was adjusting the girth of his pantaloons, which walking had discovered not to be exactly right. It was just fixed to his mind, his foes becoming a little noisy and his friends a little uneasy at his delay, when Billy called out with a smile of some meaning, " Where's the bully of the lower battalion? I'm getting tired of waiting."

" Here he is! " said Bob, lighting as it seemed from the clouds into the ring, for he had actually bounded clear of the head of Ransy Sniffle into the circle. His descent was quite as imposing as Billy's entry, and excited the same feelings, but in opposite bosoms.

Voices of exultation now rose on his side.

" Where did he come from? "

" Why," said one of his seconds (all having just entered), " we were girting him up, about a hundred yards out yonder, when he heard Billy ask for the bully, and he fetched a leap over the courthouse and went out of sight; but I told them to come on, they'd find him here."

Here the lower battalion burst into a peal of laughter, mingled with a look of admiration which seemed to denote their entire belief of what they had heard.

" Boys, widen the ring, so as to give him room to jump."

" Oh, my little flying wildcat, hold him if you can! And when you get him fast, hold lightning next."

" Ned, what do you think he's made of? "

" " Steel springs and chicken hawk, God bless you! "

"Gentlemen," said one of Bob's seconds, "I understand it is to be a fair fight — catch-as-catch-can, rough-and-tumble; no man touch till one or the other halloos."

"That's the rule," was the reply from the other side.

"Are you ready?"

"We are ready."

"Then blaze away, my gamecocks!"

At the word, Bob dashed at his antagonist at full speed, and Bill squared himself to receive him with one of his most fatal blows. Making his calculation from Bob's velocity of the time when he would come within striking distance, he let drive with tremendous force. But Bob's onset was obviously planned to avoid this blow; for, contrary to all expectations, he stopped short just out of arm's reach, and before Billy could recover his balance Bob had him " all under-hold." The next second, sure enough, " found Billy's head where his feet ought to be." How it was done no one could tell; but, as if by supernatural power, both Billy's feet were thrown full half his own height in the air, and he came down with a force that seemed to shake the earth. As he struck the ground, com-mingled shouts, screams, and yells burst from the lower battalion, loud enough to be heard for miles. " Hurrah, my little hornet! " " Save him! " " Feed him! " " Give him the Durham physic till his stomach turns! " Billy was no sooner down than Bob was on him, and lending him awful blows about the face and breast. Billy made two efforts to rise by main strength, but failed. " Lord bless you, man, don't try to get up! *Lay* still and take it! You *bleege* to have it! "

Billy now turned his face suddenly to the ground and rose upon his hands and knees. Bob jerked up both his hands and threw him on his face. He again recovered his late position, of which Bob endeavored to deprive him as before; but, missing one arm, he failed, and Billy rose. But he had scarcely resumed his feet before they flew up as before and he came again to the ground. " No fight, gentlemen! " cried Bob's friends; " the man can't stand up! Bouncing feet are bad things to fight in." His fall, however, was this time comparatively light; for, having thrown his right arm round Bob's neck, he carried his head down with him. This grasp, which was obstinately maintained, prevented Bob from getting on him, and they lay head to head, seeming, for a time, to do nothing. Presently they rose, as if by mutual consent; and as they rose a shout burst from both bat-talions. " Oh, my lark! " cried the east, " has he foxed you? Do you begin to feel him! He's only beginning to fight; he ain't got warm yet."

"Look yonder! " cried the west. " Didn't I tell you so? He hit the ground so hard it jarred his nose off. Now ain't he a pretty man as he stands? He shall have my sister Sal, just for his pretty looks. I want to get in the breed of them sort o' men, to drive ugly out of my kinfolks."

I looked, and saw that Bob had entirely lost his left ear and a large piece from his left cheek. His right eye was a little discolored, and the blood flowed pro-fusely from his wounds.

Bill presented a hideous spectacle. About a third of his nose, at the lower extremity, was bit off, and his face so swelled and bruised that it was difficult to discover in it anything of the human visage, much more the fine features which he carried into the ring.

They were up only long enough for me to make the foregoing discoveries, when down they went again, precisely as before. They no sooner touched the ground than Bill relinquished his hold upon Bob's neck. In this he seemed to all to have forfeited the only advantage which put him upon an equality with his adversary. But the movement was soon explained. Bill wanted this arm for other purposes than defense; and he had made arrangements whereby he knew that he could make it answer these purposes; for when they rose again he had the middle finger of Bob's left hand in his mouth. He was now secure from Bob's annoying trips; and he began to lend his adversary tremendous blows, every one of which was hailed by a shout from his friends: " Bullets! " " *Hoss* kicking! " " Thunder! " " That'll do for his face; now feel his short ribs, Billy! "

I now considered the contest settled. I deemed it impossible for any human being to withstand for five seconds the loss of blood which issued from Bob's ear, cheek, nose, and finger, accompanied with such blows as he was receiving. Still he maintained the conflict and gave blow for blow with considerable effect. But the blows of each became slower and weaker after the first three or four; and it became obvious that Bill wanted the room which Bob's finger occupied for breathing. He would therefore, probably, in a short time, have let it go, had not Bob anticipated his politeness by jerking away his hand and making him a present of the finger. He now seized Bill again, and brought him to his knees, but he recovered. He again brought him to his knees, but he again recovered. A third effort, however, brought him down, and Bob on top of him. These efforts seemed to exhaust the little remaining strength of both; and they lay, Bill undermost and Bob across his breast, motionless and panting for breath. After a short pause Bob gathered his hand full of dirt and sand and was in the act of grinding it in his adversary's eyes when Bill cried, " Enough! "

Language cannot describe the scene that followed — the shouts, oaths, frantic gestures, taunts, replies, and little fights — and therefore I shall not attempt it. The champions were borne off by their seconds and washed; when many a bleeding wound and ugly bruise was discovered on each which no eye had seen before.

Many had gathered round Bob, and were in various ways congratulating and applauding him, when a voice from the center of the circle cried out, " Boys, hush, and listen to me! " It proceeded from Squire Loggins, who had made his way to Bob's side and gathered his face up into one of its most flattering and intelligible expressions. All were obedient to the squire's command. " Gentlemen," continued he, with a most knowing smile, " is — Sammy Reynolds — in — this — company — of — gentlemen? "

" Yes," said Sam, " here I am."

" Sammy," said the squire, winking to the company and drawing the head of his cane to his mouth with an arch smile as he closed, " I — wish — you — to tell — Cousin — Bobby — and — these — gentlemen here present — what — your — Uncle — Tommy — said — before — the — fight — began."

" Oh, get away, Uncle Tom," said Sam, smiling (the squire winked), " you don't know nothing about *fighting*." (The squire winked again.) "All you know about it is how it'll begin, how it'll go on, how it'll end; that's all. Cousin Bob, when you going to fight again, just go to the old man and let him tell you all about it. If he can't, don't ask nobody else nothing about it, I tell you."

The squire's foresight was complimented in many ways by the bystanders, and he retired advising " the boys to be at peace, as fighting was a bad business."

Durham and Stallings kept their beds for several weeks and did not meet again for two months. When they met, Billy stepped up to Bob and offered his hand, saying, " Bobby, you've *licked* me a fair fight; but you wouldn't have done it if I hadn't been in the wrong. I oughtn't to have treated your wife as I did; and I felt so through the whole fight; and it sort o' cowed me."

" Well, Billy," said Bob, " let's be friends. Once in the fight, when you had my finger in your mouth, and was pealing me in the face and breast, I was going to halloo; but I thought of Petsy, and knew the house would be too hot for me if I got whipped when fighting for her, after always whipping when I fought for myself."

" Now that's what I always love to see," said a bystander. " It's true I brought about the fight, but I wouldn't have done it if it hadn't 'a' been on account of *Miss* (Mrs.) Durham. But dod etarnally darn my soul if I ever could stand by and see any woman put upon, much less *Miss* Durham! If Bobby hadn't been there I'd 'a' took it up myself, be darned if I wouldn't, even if I'd 'a' got whipped for it! But we're all friends now."

The reader need hardly be told that this was Ransy Sniffle.

T. B. Thorpe

The Big Bear of Arkansas

A STEAMBOAT on the Mississippi frequently, in making her regular trips, carries between places varying from one to two thousand miles apart; and as these boats advertise to land passengers and freight at " all intermediate landings," the heterogeneous character of the passengers of one of these upcountry boats can scarcely be imagined by one who has never seen it with his own eyes. Starting from New Orleans in one of these boats, you will find yourself associated with men from every state in the Union, and from every portion of the globe; and a man of observation need not lack for amusement or instruction in such a crowd if he will take the trouble to read the great book of character so favorably opened before him. Here may be seen jostling together the wealthy Southern planter and the peddler of tinware from New England — the Northern merchant and the Southern jockey — a venerable bishop and

From *The Spirit of the Times*, March 27, 1841.

a desperate gambler — the land speculator and the honest farmer — professional men of all creeds and characters — Wolvereens, Suckers, Hoosiers, Buckeyes, and Corncrackers, beside a " plentiful sprinkling " of the half-horse and half-alligator species of men who are peculiar to " old Mississippi," and who appear to gain a livelihood simply by going up and down the river. In the pursuit of pleasure or business, I have frequently found myself in such a crowd.

On one occasion, when in New Orleans, I had occasion to take a trip of a few miles up the Mississippi, and I hurried on board the well-known " high pressure and beat everything " steamboat *Invincible,* just as the last note of the last bell was sounding; and when the confusion and bustle that is natural to a boat's getting under way had subsided, I discovered that I was associated in as heterogeneous a crowd as was ever got together. As my trip was to be of a few hours' duration only, I made no endeavors to become acquainted with my fellow passengers, most of whom would be together many days. Instead of this, I took out of my pocket the " latest paper," and more critically than usual examined its contents; my fellow passengers at the same time disposed themselves in little groups. While I was thus busily employed in reading, and my companions were more busily employed in discussing such subjects as suited their humors best, we were startled most unexpectedly by a loud Indian whoop uttered in the " social hall," that part of the cabin fitted off for a bar. Then was to be heard a loud crowing, which would not have continued to interest us — such sounds being quite common in that place of spirits — had not the hero of these windy accomplishments stuck his head into the cabin and hallooed out, " Hurrah for the Big Bar of Arkansaw! " And then might be heard a confused hum of voices, unintelligible save in such broken sentences as " horse," " screamer," " lightning is slow," and so forth.

As might have been expected, this continued interruption attracted the attention of everyone in the cabin; all conversation dropped, and in the midst of this surprise the " Big Bar " walked into the cabin, took a chair, put his feet on the stove, and, looking back over his shoulder, passed the general and familiar salute of " Strangers, how are you? " He then expressed himself as much at home as if he had been at " the Forks of Cypress," and " perhaps a little more so." Some of the company at this familiarity looked a little angry, and some astonished; but in a moment every face was wreathed in a smile. There was something about the intruder that won the heart on sight. He appeared to be a man enjoying perfect health and contentment: his eyes were as sparkling as diamonds, and good-natured to simplicity. Then his perfect confidence in himself was irresistibly droll. " Perhaps," said he, " gentlemen," running on without a person speaking, " perhaps you have been to New Orleans often; I never made *the first visit before,* and I don't intend to make another in a crow's life. I am thrown away in that ar place, and useless, that ar a fact. Some of the gentlemen thar called me *green* — well, perhaps I am, said I, *but I arn't so at home;* and if I ain't off my trail much, the heads of them perlite chaps themselves wern't much the hardest; for according to my notion, they were real *know-nothings,* green as a pumpkin vine — couldn't, in farming, I'll bet, raise a crop of turnips; and as for shooting, they'd miss a barn if the door was swinging, and that, too, with the best rifle in the country. And then they talked to me 'bout hunting, and laughed at my calling the principal game in Arkansaw poker and high-low-jack. 'Perhaps,' said I, 'you prefer checkers and roulette.' At this they laughed harder than ever, and asked me if I lived in the woods, and didn't know what *game* was. At this I rather think *I* laughed. 'Yes,' I roared, and says, 'Strangers, if you'd asked me *how we got our meat* in Arkansaw, I'd 'a' told you at once, and given you a list of varmints that would make a caravan, beginning with the bar and ending off with the cat. That's *meat* though, not game.' Game, indeed, that's what city folks call it; and with them it means chippen-birds and shitepokes. Maybe such trash live in my diggins, but I arn't noticed them yet: a bird anyway is too trifling. I never did shoot at but one, and I'd never forgiven myself for that, had it weighed less than forty pounds. I wouldn't draw a rifle on anything less than that; and when I meet with another wild turkey of the same weight I will drap him."

"A wild turkey weighing forty pounds!" exclaimed twenty voices in the cabin at once.

"Yes, strangers, and wasn't it a whopper! You see, the thing was so fat that it couldn't fly far; and when he fell out of the tree, after I shot him, on striking the ground he bust open behind, and the way the pound gobs of tallow rolled out of the opening was perfectly beautiful."

"Where did all that happen?" asked a cynical-looking Hoosier.

"Happen! Happened in Arkansaw. Where else could it have happened but in the creation state, the finishing-up country — a state where the *sile* runs down to the center of the 'arth, and government gives you a title to every inch of it? Then its airs — just breathe them, and they will make you snort like a horse. It's a state without a fault, it is."

"Excepting mosquitoes," cried the Hoosier.

"Well, stranger, except them; for it ar a fact that they are rather *enormous,* and do push themselves in somewhat troublesome. But, stranger, they never stick twice in the same place; and give them a fair chance for a few months, and you will get as much above noticing them as an alligator. They can't hurt my feelings, for they lay under the skin; and I never knew but one case of injury resulting from them, and that was to a Yankee: and they take worse to foreigners, anyhow, than they do to natives. But the way they used that fellow up! First they punched him until he swelled up and busted; then he sup-per-a-ted, as the doctor called it, until he was as raw as beef; then he took the ager, owing to the warm weather; and finally he took a steamboat and left the country. He was the only man that ever took mosquitoes to heart that I know of. But mosquitoes is natur, and I never find fault with her. If they ar large, Arkansaw is large, her varmints ar large, her trees ar large, her rivers ar large, and a small mosquito would be of no more use in Arkansaw than preaching in a canebrake."

This knockdown argument in favor of big mosquitoes used the Hoosier up, and the logician started on a new track, to explain how numerous bear were in his " diggins," where he represented them to be " about as plenty as blackberries, and a little plentifuler."

Upon the utterance of this assertion, a timid little man near me inquired if the bear in Arkansaw ever attacked the settlers in numbers.

" No," said our hero, warming with the subject, " no, stranger, for you see it ain't the natur of bar to go in droves; but the way they squander about in pairs and single ones is edifying. And then the way I hunt them the old black rascals know the crack of my gun as well as they know a pig's squealing. They grow thin in our parts, it frightens them so, and they do take the noise dreadfully, poor things. That gun of mine is perfect *epidemic among bar;* if not watched closely, it will go off as quick on a warm scent as my dog Bowie-knife will. And then that dog — whew! Why, the fellow thinks that the world is full of bar, he finds them so easy. It's lucky he don't talk as well as think; for with his natural modesty, if he should suddenly learn how much he is acknowledged to be ahead of all other dogs in the universe, he would be astonished to death in two minutes. Strangers, the dog knows a bar's way as well as a horse jockey knows a woman's; he always barks at the right time, bites at the exact place, and whips without getting a scratch. I never could tell whether he was made expressly to hunt bar, or whether bar was made expressly for him to hunt; anyway, I believe they were ordained to go together as naturally as Squire Jones says a man and woman is, when he moralizes in marrying a couple. In fact, Jones once said, said he, ' Marriage according to law is a civil contract of divine origin; it's common to all countries as well as Arkansaw, and people take to it as naturally as Jim Doggett's Bowie-knife takes to bar.' "

" What season of the year do your hunts take place? " inquired a gentlemanly foreigner, whom, from some peculiarities of his baggage, I suspected to be an Englishman on some hunting expedition, probably at the foot of the Rocky Mountains.

" The season for bar hunting, stranger," said the man of Arkansaw, " is generally all the year round, and the hunts take place about as regular. I read in history that varmints have their fat season and their lean season. That is not the case in Arkansaw; feeding as they do upon the *spontenacious* productions of the sile, they have one continued fat season the year round — though in winter things in this way is rather more greasy than in summer, I must admit. For that reason bar with us run in warm weather, but in winter they only waddle. Fat, fat! It's an enemy to speed; it tames everything that has plenty of it. I have seen wild turkeys, from its influence, as gentle as chickens. Run a bar in this fat condition, and the way it improves the critter for eating is amazing; it sort of mixes the ile up with the meat, until you can't tell tother from which. I've done this often. I recollect one perty morning in particular, of putting an old fellow on the stretch; and considering the weight he carried, he run well. But the dogs soon tired him down, and when I came up with him, wasn't he in a beautiful sweat — I might say fever; and then to see his tongue sticking out of his mouth a feet, and his sides sinking and opening like a bellows, and his cheeks so fat he couldn't look cross. In this fix I blazed at him, and pitch me naked into a briar patch if the steam didn't come out of the bullet hole ten foot in a straight line. The fellow, I reckon, was made on the high-pressure system, and the lead sort of bust his biler."

"That column of steam was rather curious, or else the bear must have been *warm,*" observed the foreigner with a laugh.

"Stranger, as you observe, that bar was WARM, and the blowing off of the steam showed it, and also how hard the varmint had been run. I have no doubt if he had kept on two miles farther his insides would have been stewed; and I expect to meet with a varmint yet of extra bottom, who will run himself into a skinful of bar's grease — it is possible; much onlikelier things have happened."

"Whereabouts are these bears so abundant?" inquired the foreigner with increasing interest.

"Why, stranger, they inhabit the neighborhood of my settlement, one of the prettiest places on old Mississippi — a perfect location, and no mistake; a place that had some defects until the river made the 'cutoff' at 'Shirttail Bend,' and that remedied the evil, as it brought my cabin on the edge of the river — a great advantage in wet weather, I assure you, as you can now roll a barrel of whisky into my yard in high water from a boat, as easy as falling off a log. It's a great improvement, as toting it by land in a jug, as I used to do, *evaporated* it too fast, and it became expensive. Just stop with me, stranger, a month or two, or a year if you like, and you will appreciate my place. I can give you plenty to eat; for beside hog and hominy, you can have bar ham, and bar sausages, and a mattrass of bar skins to sleep on, and a wildcat skin, pulled off hull, stuffed with corn shucks, for a pillow. That bed would put you to sleep if you had the rheumatics in every joint in your body. I call that ar bed a *quietus.* Then look at my land — the government ain' got another such a piece to dispose of. Such timber, and such bottom land! Why, you can't preserve anything natural you plant in it unless you pick it young, things thar will grow out of shape so quick. I once planted in those diggins a few potatoes and beets. They took a fine start, and after that an ox team couldn't have kept them from growing. About that time I went off to old Kentuck on bisiness, and did not hear from them things in three months, when I accidentally stumbled on a fellow who had stopped at my place, with an idea of buying me out. 'How did you like things?' said I. 'Pretty well,' said he; 'the cabin is convenient, and the timber land is good; but that bottom land ain't worth the first red cent.' 'Why?' said I. ''Cause,' said he. ''Cause what?' said I. ''Cause it's full of cedar stumps and Indian mounds,' said he, *'and it can't be cleared.'* 'Lord,' said I, 'them ar "cedar stumps" is beets, and them ar "Indian mounds" ar tater hills.' As I expected, the crop was overgrown and useless: the sile is too rich, *and planting in Arkansaw is dangerous.* I had a good-sized sow killed in that same bottom land. The old thief stole an ear of corn and took it down where she slept at night to eat. Well, she left a grain or two on the ground and lay down on them; before morning the corn shot up, and the percussion killed her dead. I don't plant any more: natur intended Arkansaw for a hunting ground, and I go according to natur."

The questioner who thus elicited the description of our hero's settlement seemed to be perfectly satisfied and said no more; but the " Big Bar of Arkansaw " rambled on from one thing to another with a volubility perfectly astonishing, occasionally disputing with those around him, particularly with a " live Sucker " from Illinois, who had the daring to say that our Arkansaw friend's stories " smelt rather tall."

In this manner the evening was spent; but conscious that my own association with so singular a personage would probably end before morning, I asked him if he would not give me a description of some particular bear hunt; adding that I took great interest in such things, though I was no sportsman. The desire seemed to please him, and he squared himself round towards me, saying that he could give me an idea of a bar hunt that was never beat in this world, or in any other. His manner was so singular that half of his story consisted in his excellent way of telling it, the great peculiarity of which was the happy manner he had of emphasizing the prominent parts of his conversation. As near as I can recollect, I have italicized them, and given the story in his own words.

" Stranger," said he, " in bar hunts *I am numerous,* and which particular one, as you say, I shall tell, puzzles me. There was the old she-devil I shot at the Hurricane last fall — then there was the old hog thief I popped over at the Bloody Crossing, and then — Yes, I have it! I will give you an idea of a hunt in which the greatest bar was killed that ever lived, *none excepted;* about an old fellow that I hunted, more or less, for two or three years; and if that ain't a particular bar hunt, I ain't got one to tell. But in the first place, stranger, let me say I am pleased with you, because you ain't ashamed to gain information by asking, and listening, and that's what I say to Countess's pups every day when I'm home; and I have got great hopes of them ar pups, because they are continually *nosing about;* and though they stick it sometimes in the wrong place, they gain experience anyhow, and may learn something useful to boot.

" Well, as I was saying about this big bar, you see when I and some more first settled in our region, we were drivin to hunting naturally; we soon liked it, and after that we found it an easy matter to make the thing our business. One old chap, who had pioneered afore us, gave us to understand that we had settled in the right place. He dwelt upon its merits until it was affecting, and showed us, to prove his assertions, more marks on the sassafras trees than I ever saw on a tavern door 'lection time. ' Who keeps that ar reckoning?' said I. ' The bar,' said he. ' What for?' said I. ' Can't tell,' said he; ' but so it is: the bar bite the bark and wood too, at the highest point from the ground they can reach, and you can tell by the marks,' said he, ' the length of the bar to an inch.' ' Enough,' said I; ' I've learned something here a'ready, and I'll put it in practice.'

" Well, stranger, just one month from that time I killed a bar, and told its exact length before I measured it, by those very marks; and when I did that, I swelled up considerable — I've been a prouder man ever since. So I went on, larning something every day, until I was reckoned a buster and allowed to be decidedly the best bar hunter in my district; and that is a reputation as much harder to earn than to be reckoned first man in Congress, as an iron ramrod is harder than a toadstool. Did the varmints grow overcunning by being fooled with by greenhorn hunters, and by this means get troublesome, they send for me as a matter of course; and thus I do my own hunting, and most of my neighbors'. I walk into the varmints though, and it has become about as much the same to me as drinking. It is told in two sentences — a bar is started, and he is killed. The thing is somewhat monotonous now — I know just how much they will run, where they will tire, how much they will growl, and what a thundering time I will have in getting them home. I could give you this history of the chase with all particulars at the commencement, I know the signs so well. *Stranger, I'm certain.* Once I met with a match though, and I will tell you about it; for a common hunt would not be worth relating.

"On a fine fall day, long time ago, I was trailing about for bar, and what should I see but fresh marks on the sassafras trees, about eight inches above any in the forests that I knew of. Says I, ' Them marks is a hoax, or it indicates the damnedest bar that was ever grown.' In fact, stranger, I couldn't believe it was real, and I went on. Again I saw the same marks, at the same height, and *I knew the thing lived.* That conviction came home to my soul like an earthquake. Says I, ' Here is something a-purpose for me; that bar is mine, or I give up the hunting business.' The very next morning what should I see but a number of buzzards hovering over my cornfield. ' The rascal has been there,' said I, ' for that sign is certain '; and, sure enough, on examining, I found the bones of what had been as beautiful a hog the day before as was ever raised by a Buckeye. Then I tracked the critter out of the field to the woods, and all the marks he left behind showed me that he was *the bar.*

"Well, stranger, the first fair chase I ever had with that big critter, I saw him no less than three distinct times at a distance: the dogs run him over eighteen miles and broke down, my horse gave out, and I was as nearly used up as a man can be, made on *my* principle, *which is patent.* Before this adventure, such things were unknown to me as possible; but, strange as it was, that bar got me used to it before I was done with him; for he got so at last that he would leave me on a long chase *quite easy.* How he did it, I never could understand. That a bar runs at all is puzzling; but how this one could tire down and bust up a pack of hounds and a horse, that were used to overhauling everything they started after in no time, was past my understanding. Well, stranger, that bar finally got so sassy that he used to help himself to a hog off my premises whenever he wanted one; the buzzards followed after what he left, and so between *bar and buzzard,* I rather think I was *out of pork.*

"Well, missing that bar so often took hold of my vitals, and I wasted away. The thing had been carried too far, and it reduced me in flesh faster than an ager. I would see that bar in everything I did: *he hunted me,* and that, too, like a devil, which I began to think he was. While in this fix, I made preparations to give him a last brush and be done with it. Having completed everything to my satisfaction, I started at sunrise, and to my great joy I discovered from the way the dogs run that they were near him; finding his trail was nothing, for that had become as plain to the pack as a turnpike road. On we went; and coming to an open country, what should I see but the bar very leisurely ascending a hill, and the dogs close at his heels, either a match for him in speed or else he did not care to get out of their way — I don't know which. But wasn't he a beauty, though? I loved him like a brother.

" On he went until he came to a tree the limbs of which formed a crotch about six feet from the ground. Into this crotch he got and seated himself, the dogs yelling all around it; and there he sat eyeing them as quiet as a pond in low water. A greenhorn friend of mine, in company, reached shooting distance before me and blazed away, hitting the critter in the center of his forehead. The bar shook his head as the ball struck it, and then walked down from that tree as gently as a lady would from a carriage. 'Twas a beautiful sight to see him do that — he was in such a rage that he seemed to be as little afraid of the dogs as if they had been sucking pigs; and the dogs warn't slow in making a ring around him at a respectful distance, I tell you; even Bowie-knife himself stood off. Then the way his eyes flashed — why, the fire of them would have singed a cat's hair; in fact that bar was in a *wrath all over*. Only one pup came near him, and he was brushed out so totally with the bar's left paw that he entirely disappeared; and that made the old dogs more cautious still. In the meantime I came up, and taking deliberate aim, as a man should do, at his side, just back of his foreleg, *if my gun did not snap,* call me a coward, and I won't take it personal. Yes, stranger, *it snapped,* and I could not find a cap about my person. While in this predicament, I turned round to my fool friend. Says I, ' Bill,' says I, ' you're an ass — you're a fool — you might as well have tried to kill that bar by barking the tree under his belly, as to have done it by hitting him in the head. Your shot has made a tiger of him, and blast me, if a dog gets killed or wounded when they come to blows, I will stick my knife into your liver, I will.' My wrath was up. I had lost my caps, my gun had snapped, the fellow with me had fired at the bar's head, and I expected every moment to see him close in with the dogs and kill a dozen of them at least.

" In this thing I was mistaken, for the bar leaped over the ring formed by the dogs, and giving a fierce growl was off — the pack, of course, in full cry after him. The run this time was short, for coming to the edge of a lake the varmint jumped in and swam to a little island in the lake, which it reached just a moment before the dogs. ' I'll have him now,' said I, for I had found my caps in the *lining of my coat.* So, rolling a log into the lake, I paddled myself across to the island, just as the dogs had cornered the bar in a thicket. I rushed up and fired. At the same time the critter leaped over the dogs and came within three feet of me, running like mad. He jumped into the lake and tried to mount the log I had just deserted, but every time he got half his body on it, it would roll over and send him under; the dogs, too, got around him and pulled him about, and finally Bowie-knife clenched with him, and they sunk into the lake together. Stranger, about this time I was excited, and I stripped off my coat, drew my knife, and intended to have taken a part with Bowie-knife myself when the bar rose to the surface. But the varmint staid under. Bowie-knife came up alone, more dead than alive, and with the pack came ashore. ' Thank God,' said I, ' the old villain has got his deserts at last.' Determined to have the body, I cut a grape-vine for a rope, and dove down where I could see the bar in the water, fastened my queer rope to his leg, and fished him, with great difficulty, ashore. Stranger, may I be chawed to death by young alligators if the thing I looked at wasn't a *she-bar, and not the old critter after all.*

" The way matters got mixed on that island was onaccountably curious, and thinking of it made me more than ever convinced that I was hunting the devil himself. I went home that night and took to my bed — the thing was killing me. The entire team of Arkansaw in bar hunting acknowledged himself used up, and the fact sunk into my feelings like a snagged boat will in the Mississippi. I grew as cross as a bar with two cubs and a sore tail. The thing got out 'mong my neighbors, and I was asked how come on that individual that never lost a bar when once started, and if that same individual didn't wear telescopes when he turned a she-bar of ordinary size into an old he-one a little larger than a horse. ' Perhaps,' said I, ' friends ' — getting wrathy — ' perhaps you want to call some-body a liar.' ' Oh, no,' said they, ' we only heard such things as being *rather common* of late, but we don't believe one word of it. Oh, no! ' And then they would ride off and laugh like so many hyenas over a dead nigger. It was too much, and I determined to catch that bar, go to Texas, or die — and I made my preparations accordin'. I had the pack shut up and rested. I took my rifle to pieces and iled it. I put caps in every pocket about my person, *for fear of the lining.* I then told my neighbors that on Monday morning — naming the day — I would start THAT BAR and bring him home with me, or they might divide my settlement among them, the owner having disappeared.

" Well, stranger, on the morning previous to the great day of my hunting ex-pedition, I went into the woods near my house, taking my gun and Bowie-knife along just *from habit;* and there sitting down, also from habit, what should I see getting over my fence but *the bar!* Yes, the old varmint was within a hundred yards of me, and the way he walked *over that fence* — stranger, he loomed up like a *black mist,* he seemed so large; and he walked right towards me. I raised myself, took deliberate aim, and fired. Instantly the varmint wheeled, gave a yell, and *walked through the fence* like a falling tree would through a cobweb. I started after, but was tripped up by my inexpressibles, which either from habit or the excitement of the moment were about my heels, and before I had really gathered myself up I heard the old varmint groaning in a thicket near by, like a thousand sinners, and by the time I reached him he was a corpse.

" Stranger, it took five niggers and myself to put that carcase on a mule's back, and old long-ears waddled under the load as if he was foundered in every leg of his body, and with a common whopper of a bar he would have trotted off and enjoyed himself. 'Twould astonish you to know how big he was: I made a *bedspread of his skin,* and the way it used to cover my bar mattress and leave several feet on each side to tuck up would have delighted you. It was in fact a creation bar, and if it had lived in Samson's time and had met him in a fair fight, it would have licked him in the twinkling of a dicebox. But, strangers, I never like the way I hunted *and missed him.* There is something curious about it, I could never understand — and I never was satisfied at his giving in so easy at last. Perhaps he had heard of my preparations to hunt him the next day, so he jist come in, like Captain Scott's coon, to save his wind to grunt with in dying; but that ain't likely. My private opinion is that that bar was an *unhuntable bar, and died when his time come."*

When the story was ended, our hero sat some minutes with his auditors in a grave silence. I saw there was a mystery to him connected with the bear whose death he had just related, that had evidently made a strong impression on his mind. It was also evident that there was some superstitious awe connected with the affair — a feeling common with all " children of the wood " when they meet with anything out of their everyday experience. He was the first one, however, to break the silence; and jumping up, he asked all present to " liquor " before going to bed — a thing which he did, with a number of companions, evidently to his heart's content.

Long before day, I was put ashore at my place of destination, and I can only follow with the reader, in imagination, our Arkansas friend, in his adventures at the " Forks of Cypress " on the Mississippi.

George W. Harris

Sicily Burns's Wedding

"HEY Ge-orge! " rang among the mountain slopes; and looking up to my left, I saw Sut tearing along down a steep point, heading me off, in a long kangaroo lope, holding his flask high above his head, and hat in hand. He brought up near me, banteringly shaking the half-full " tickler " within an inch of my face.

" Whar am yu gwine? Take a suck, hoss? This yere truck's *ole.* I kotch hit myse'f, hot this mornin frum the still wum. Nara durn'd bit ove strike-nine in hit — I put that ar piece ove burnt dried peach in myse'f tu gin hit color — better nur old Bullen's plan: he puts in tan ooze, in what he sells, an' when that hain't handy, he uses the red warter outen a pon' jis' below his barn — makes a pow'ful natral color, but don't help the taste much. Then he correcks that wif red pepper; hits an orful mixtry, that whisky ole Bullen makes; no wonder he seed ' Hell-sarpints.' He's pisent ni ontu three quarters ove the b'levin parts ove his congregashun wif hit, an' tuther quarter he's sot intu ruff stealin an' cussin. Ef his

From *Sut Lovingood's Yarns,* 1867.

still-'ous don't burn down, ur he peg out hisse'f, the neighborhood am ruinated a-pas salvashun. Hain't he the durndes sampil ove a passun yu ever seed enyhow?

"Say George, du yu see these yere well-poles what I uses fur laigs? Yu sez yu sees em, dus yu?"

"Yes."

"Very well; I passed 'em a-pas' each uther tuther day, right peart. I put one out a-head jis' so, an' then tuther 'bout nine feet a-head ove hit agin jis' so, an' then kep on a-duin hit. I'll jis' gin yu leav tu go tu the devil ha'f hamon, ef I didn't make fewer tracks tu the mile, an' more tu the minit, than wer ever made by eny human man body since Bark Wilson beat the sawlog frum the top ove the Frog Mountin intu the Oconee River, an' dove, an' dodged hit at las'. I hes allers look'd ontu that performince ove Bark's as onekel'd in histery, allers givin way tu dad's ho'net race, however.

"George, every livin thing hes hits pint, a pint ove sum sort. Ole Bullen's pint is a durn'ed fust rate, three bladed, dubbil barril'd, warter-proof, hypock-racy, an' a niver-tirein appertite fur bal'face. Sicily Burns's pint am tu drive men folks plum crazy, an' then bring em too agin. Gin em a rale Orleans fever in five minits, an' then in five minits more, gin them a Floridy ager. Durn her, she's down on her heels flat-footed now. Dad's pint is tu be king ove all durn'd fools, ever since the day ove that feller what cribb'd up so much co'n down in Yegipt, long time ago (he run outen his coat yu minds). The Bibil tell us hu wer the stronges' man — hu wer the bes' man — hu wer the meekis' man, an' hu the wises' man, but leaves yu tu guess hu wer the bigges' fool.

"Well, any man what cudent guess arter readin that ar scrimmage wif an 'oman 'bout the coat, haint sense enuf tu run intu the hous', ef hit wer rainin ded cats, that's all. Mam's pint am in kitchen insex, bakin hoecake, bilin greens, an' runnin bar laiged. My pint am in taking aboard big skeers, an' then beatin enybody's hoss, ur skared dorg, a-running frum onder em agin. I used tu think my pint an' dad's wer jis' the same, sulky, unmix'd king durn'd fool; but when he acted hoss, an' mistook hossflies fur ho'nets, I los' heart. Never mine, when I gits his 'sperence, I may be king fool, but yet great golly, he gets frum bad tu wus, monstrus fas'.

"Now ef a feller happens tu know what his pint am, he kin allers git along, sumhow, purvided he don't swar away his liberty tu a temprins s'ciety, live tu fur frum a still-'ous, an' too ni a chu'ch ur a jail. Them's my sentimints on 'pints'—an' yere's my sentimints ontu folks: Men wer made a-purpus jis' tu eat, drink, an' fur stayin awake in the yearly part ove the nites: an' wimen wer made tu cook the vittils, mix the sperits, an' help the men du the stayin awake. That's all, an' nuthin more, onless hits fur the wimen tu raise the devil atwix meals, an' knit socks atwix drams, an' the men to play short kerds, swap hosses wif fools, an' fite fur exercise, at odd spells.

"George, yu don't onderstan life yet scarcely at all; got a heap tu larn, a heap. But 'bout my swappin my laigs so fas'—these yere very par ove laigs. I hed got about a fox squirril skin full ove biled co'n juice packed onder my shut, an' onder my hide too, I mout es well add, an' wer aimin fur Bill Carr's on foot.

When I got in sight ove ole man Burns's, I seed ni ontu fifty hosses an' muels hitch'd tu the fence. Durnashun! I jis' then tho't ove hit, 'twer Sicily's wedding day. She married old Clapshaw, the suckit rider. The very feller hu's faith gin out when hc mct me sendin sody all over creashun. Suckit-riders am surjestif things tu me. They preaches agin me, an' I hes no chance tu preach back at them. Ef I cud I'd make the institushun behave hitsef better nur hit dus. They hes sum wunderful pints, George. Thar am two things nobody never seed; wun am a dead muel, an' tuther is a suckit-rider's grave. Kaze why, the he muels all turn intu old field school-masters, an' the she ones intu strong minded wimen, an' then when thar time cums, they dies sorter like uther folks. An' the suckit-riders ride ontil they marry; ef they marrys money, they turns intu store-keepers, swaps hosses, an' stays away ove colleckshun Sundays. Them what marrys, an' by sum orful mistake *misses the money,* jis' turns intu polertishuns, sells ' ile well stock,' an' dies sorter in the human way too.

"But 'bout the wedding. Ole Burns hed a big black an' white bull, wif a ring in his snout, an' the rope tied up roun his ho'ns. They rid 'im tu mill, an' sich like wif a saddil made outen two dorgwood forks, an' two clapboards, kivered wif a ole piece ove carpet, rope girth, an' rope stirrups wif a loop in hit fur the foot. Ole ' Sock,' es they call'd the bull, hed jis' got back frum mill, an' wer turn'd intu the yard, saddil an' all, tu solace hissef a-pickin grass. I wer slungin roun the outside ove the hous', fur they hedn't hed the manners tu ax me in, when they sot down tu dinner. I wer pow'fully hurt 'bout hit, an' happen'd tu think — SODY. So I sot in a-watchin fur a chance tu du sumthin. I fus' tho't I'd shave ole Clapshaw's hoss's tail, go tu the stabil an' shave Sicily's mare's tail, an' ketch ole Burns out, an' shave his tail too. While I wer a-studyin 'bout this, ole Sock wer a-nosin 'roun, an' cum up ontu a big baskit what hilt a littil shattered co'n; he dipp'd in his head tu git hit, an' I slipp'd up an' jerked the handil over his ho'ns.

" Now, George, ef yu knows the nater ove a cow brute, they is the durndes fools amung all the beastes ('scept the Lovingoods); when they gits intu tribulashun, they knows nuffin but tu shot thar eyes, beller, an' back, an' keep a-backin. Well, when ole Sock raised his head an' foun hissef in darkness, he jis' twisted up his tail, snorted the shatter'd co'n outen the baskit, an' made a tremenjus lunge agin the hous'. I hearn the picters a-hangin agin the wall on the inside a-fallin. He fotch a deep loud rusty beller, mout been hearn a mile, an' then sot intu a onendin sistem ove backin. A big craw-fish wif a hungry coon a-reachin fur him, wer jis' nowhar. Fust agin one thing, then over anuther, an' at las' agin the bee-bainch, knockin hit an' a dozen stan ove bees heads over heels, an' then stompin back'ards thru the mess. Hit haint much wuf while tu tell what the bees did, ur how soon they sot intu duin hit. They am pow'ful quick-tempered littil critters, enyhow. The air wer dark wif 'em, an' Sock wer kivered all over, frum snout tu tail, so clost yu cudent a-sot down a grain ove wheat fur bees, an' they wer a-fitin one anuther in the air, fur a place on the bull. The hous' stood on sidelin groun, an' the back door wer even wif hit. So Sock happen tu hit hit plum, jis' backed intu the hous' onder 'bout two hundred an' fifty pouns ove steam, bawlin orful, an' every snort he fotch he snorted away a quart ove bees ofen his sweaty snout. He wer the leader ove the bigges' an' the madest army ove bees in the worild. Thar wer at leas' five solid bushels ove 'em. They hed filled the baskit, an' hed lodged ontu his tail, ten deep, ontil hit wer es thick es a waggin tung. He hed hit stuck strait up in the air, an' hit looked adzackly like a dead pine kivered wif ivey. I think he wer the hottes' and wus hurtin bull then livin; his temper, too, seemed tu be pow'fully flustrated. Ove *all* the durn'd times an' kerryins on yu *ever* hearn tell on wer thar an' thar abouts.

" He cum tail fust agin the ole two story Dutch clock, an' fotch hit, bustin hits runnin geer outen hit, the littil wheels a-trundlin over the floor, an' the bees even chasin them. Nex pass, he fotch up agin the foot ove a big dubbil injine bedstead, rarin hit on aind, an' punchin one ove the posts thru a glass winder. The next tail fus' experdishun wer made aginst the caticorner'd cupboard, outen which he made a perfeck momox. Fus' he upsot hit, smashin in the glass doors, an' then jis' sot in an' stomp'd everything on the shelves intu giblits, a-tryin tu back furder in that direckshun, an' tu git the bees ofen his laigs.

" Pickil crocks, perserves jars, vinegar jugs, seed bags, yarb bunches, para-gorick bottils, aig baskits, an' delf war — all mix'd dam permiskusly, an' not worth the sortin, by a duller an' a 'alf. Nex he got a far back acrost the room agin the board pertishun; he went thru hit like hit hed been paper, takin wif him 'bout six foot squar ove hit in splinters, an' broken boards, intu the nex room, whar they wer eatin dinner, an' rite yere the fitin becum gineral, an' the dancin, squawkin, cussin, an' dodgin begun.

" Clapshaw's ole mam wer es deaf es a dogiron, an sot at the aind ove the tabil, nex tu whar old Sock busted thru the wall; tail fus' he cum agin her cheer, a-histin her an' hit ontu the tabil. Now, the smashin ove delf, an' the mixin ove vittils begun. They hed sot severil tabils tugether tu make hit long enuf. So he jis' rolled 'em up a-top ove one anuther, an' thar sot ole Missis Clapshaw, a-straddil ove the top ove the pile, a-fitin bees like a mad wind-mill, wif her caliker cap in one han, fur a wepun, an' a cract frame in tuther, an' a-kickin, an' a-spurrin like she wer ridin a lazy hoss arter the doctor, an' a-screamin rape, fire, an' murder, es fas' es she cud name 'em over.

" Taters, cabbige, meat, soup, beans, sop, dumplins, an' the truck what yu wallers 'em in; milk, plates, pies, puddins, an' every durn fixin yu cud think ove in a week, wer thar, mix'd an' mashed, like hit had been thru a thrashin-meesheen. Ole Sock still kep a-backin, an' backed the hole pile, ole 'oman an' all, also sum cheers, outen the frunt door, an' down seven steps intu the lane, an' then by golly, turn'd a fifteen hundred poun summerset hissef arter em, lit a-top ove the mix'd up mess, flat ove his back, an' then kicked hissef ontu his feet agin. About the time he ris, ole man Burns — yu know how fat, an' stumpy, an' cross-grained he is, enyhow — made a vigrus mad snatch at the baskit, an' got a savin holt ontu hit, but cudent *let go quick enuf;* fur ole Sock jis' snorted, bawled, an' histed the ole cuss heels fust up intu the air, an' he lit on the bull's back, an' hed the baskit in his han.

" Jis' es soon es ole Blackey got the use ove his eyes, he tore off down the lane tu out-run the bees, so durn'd fas' that ole Burns wer feard tu try tu git off. So he jis' socked his feet intu the rope loops, an' then cummenc'd the durndes' bull-ride ever mortal man ondertuck. Sock run atwix the hitched critters an' the rail-fence, ole Burns fust fitin him over the head wif the baskit tu stop him, an' then fitin the bees wif hit. I'll jis' be durn'd ef I didn't think he hed four ur five baskits, hit wer in so meny places at onst. Well, Burns, baskit, an' bull, an' bees, skared every durn'd hoss an' muel loose frum that fence — bees ontu all ove 'em, bees, by golly, everywhar. Mos' on 'em, too, tuck a fence-rail along, fas' tu the bridil reins. Now I'll jis gin ju leave tu kiss my sister Sall till she squalls, ef ever sich a sight wer seed ur sich nises hearn, es filled up that long lane. A heavy cloud ove dus', like a harycane hed been blowin, hid all the hosses, an' away abuv hit yu cud see tails, an' ainds ove fence-rails a-flyin about; now an' then a par ove bright hine shoes wud flash in the sun like two sparks, an' away ahead wer the baskit a-sirklin round an' about at random. Brayin, nickerin, the bel-lerin ove the bull, clatterin ove runnin hoofs, an' a mons'ous rushin soun, made up the noise. Lively times in that lane jis' then, warn't thar?

"I swar ole Burns kin beat eny man on top ove the yeath a-fitin bees wif a baskit. Jis' set 'im a-straddil ove a mad bull, an' let thar be bees enuf tu exhite the ole man, an' the man what beats him kin break me. Hosses an' muels wer tuck up all over the county, an' sum wer forever los'. Yu cudent go eny course, in a cirkil ove a mile, an' not find buckils, stirrups, straps, saddil blankits, ur sumthin belongin tu a saddil hoss. Now don't forgit that about that hous' thar wer a good time bein had ginerally. Fellers an' gals loped outen windows, they rolled outen the doors in bunches, they clomb the chimleys, they darted onder the house jis' tu dart out agin, they tuck tu the thicket, they rolled in the wheat field, lay down in the krick, did everything but stan still. Sum made a straight run *fur* home, an' sum es strait a run *frum* home; livelyest folks I ever did see. Clapshaw crawled onder a straw pile in the barn, an' sot intu prayin — yu cud a-hearn him a mile — sumthin 'bout the plagues ove Yegipt, an' the pains ove the secon death. I tell yu now he lumbered.

"Sicily, she squatted in the cold spring, up tu her years, an' turn'd a milk crock over her head, while she wer a drownin a mess ove bees onder her coats. I went to her, an' sez I, 'Yu hes got anuther new sensashun, haint yu?'

"Sez she, 'Shet yer mouth, yu cussed fool!'

"Sez I, 'Power'ful sarchin feelin bees gins a body, don't they?'

"'Oh, lordy, lordy, Sut, these yere 'bominabil insex is jis' burnin me up!'

"'Gin 'em a mess ove soDY,' sez I, 'that'll cool 'em off, an' skeer the las' durn'd one ofen the place.'

"She lifted the crock, so she cud flash her eyes at me, an' sed, 'Yu go tu hell!' *jis es plain.* I thought, takin all things tugether, that p'raps I mout es well put the mountin atwix me an' that plantashun; an' I did hit.

"Thar warnt an' 'oman ur a gal at that weddin, but what thar frocks an' stockins wer too tite fur a week. Bees am wus on wimen than men, enyhow. They hev a farer chance at 'em. Nex day I passed ole Hawley's, an' his gal Betts wer sittin in the porch, wif a white handkerchef tied roun her jaws; her face wer es red es a beet, an' her eyebrows hung 'way over heavy. Sez I, ' Hed a fine time at the weddin, didn't yu? ' ' Yu mus' be a durn'd fool,' wer every word she sed. I hadent gone a hundred yards, ontil I met Missis Brady, her hans fat, an' her ankils swelled ontil they shined.

" Sez she, ' Whar yu gwine, Sut? '

" ' Bee huntin,' sez I.

" ' Yu jis' say bees agin, yu infunel gallinipper, an' I'll scab yer head wif a rock.'

" Now haint hit strange how tetchus they am, on the subjick ove bees?

" Ove all the durn'd misfortinit weddins ever since ole Adam married that heifer what wer so fon' ove talkin tu snaix an' eatin appils, down ontil now, that one ove Sicily's an' Clapshaw's wer the worst one fur noise, disappintment, skeer, breakin things, hurtin, trubbil, vexashun ove spirrit, an' gineral swellin. Why, George, her an' him cudent sleep tugether fur ni ontu a week, on account ove the doins ove them ar hot-footed, 'vengeful, 'bominabil littil insex. They never will gee tugether, got tu bad a start, mine what I tell yu. Yu haint time now tu hear how ole Burns finished his bull-ride, an' how I cum tu du that lofty, topliftical speciment ove fas' runnin. I'll tell yu all that, sum other time. Ef eny ove 'em axes after me, tell 'em that I'm over in Fannin, on my way tu Dahlonega. They is huntin me tu kill me, I is fear'd.

" Hit am an orful thing, George, tu be a natral born durn'd fool. Yu'se never 'sperienced hit pussonally, hev yu? Hits made pow'fully agin our famerly, an all owin tu dad. I orter bust my head open agin a bluff ove rocks, an' jis' wud du it, ef I warnt a cussed coward. All my yeathly 'pendence is in these yere laigs —d'ye see 'em? Ef they don't fail, I may turn human sum day, that is sorter human, enuf tu be a Squire, ur school cummisiner. Ef I wer jis' es smart es I am mean an' ornary, I'd be President ove a Wild Cat Bank in less nor a week. Is sperrits plenty over wif yu? "

Joel Chandler Harris

Uncle Remus

I. THE WONDERFUL TAR–BABY STORY

"DIDN'T the fox *never* catch the rabbit, Uncle Remus? " asked the little boy the next evening.

" He come mighty nigh it, honey, sho's you born — Brer Fox did. One day atter Brer Rabbit fool 'im wid dat calamus root, Brer Fox went ter wuk en got 'im some tar, en mix it wid some turkentime, en fix up a contrapshun w'at

From *Uncle Remus: His Songs and His Sayings,* 1880.

he call a Tar-Baby, en he tuck dish yer Tar-Baby en he sot 'er in de big road, en den he lay off in de bushes fer to see w'at de news wuz gwineter be. En he didn't hatter wait long, nudder, kaze bimeby here come Brer Rabbit pacin' down de road — lippity-clippity, clippity-lippity — des ez sassy ez a jay-bird. Brer Fox, he lay low. Brer Rabbit come prancin' 'long twel he spy de Tar-Baby, en den he fotch up on his behime legs like he wuz 'stonished. De Tar-Baby, she sot dar, she did, en Brer Fox, he lay low.

" ' Mawnin'! ' sez Brer Rabbit, sezee — ' nice wedder dis mawnin',' sezee.

" Tar-Baby ain't sayin' nothin', en Brer Fox, he lay low.

" ' How duz yo' symtums seem ter segashuate? ' sez Brer Rabbit, sezee.

" Brer Fox, he wink his eye slow, en lay low, en de Tar-Baby, she ain't sayin' nothin'.

" ' How you come on, den? Is you deaf? ' sez Brer Rabbit, sezee. ' Kaze if you is, I kin holler louder,' sezee.

" Tar-Baby stay still, en Brer Fox, he lay low.

" ' Youer stuck up, dat's w'at you is,' says Brer Rabbit, sezee, ' en I'm gwineter kyore you, dat's w'at I'm a gwineter do,' sezee.

" Brer Fox, he sorter chuckle in his stummuck, he did, but Tar-Baby ain't sayin' nothin'.

" ' I'm gwineter larn you how ter talk ter 'specttubble fokes ef hit's de las' ack,' sez Brer Rabbit, sezee. ' Ef you don't take off dat hat en tell me howdy, I'm gwineter bus' you wide open,' sezee.

" Tar-Baby stay still, en Brer Fox, he lay low.

" Brer Rabbit keep on axin' 'im, en de Tar-Baby, she keep on sayin' nothin', twel present'y Brer Rabbit draw back wid his fis', he did, en blip he tuck 'er side de head. His fis' stuck, en he can't pull loose. De tar hilt 'im. But Tar-Baby, she stay still, en Brer Fox, he lay low.

" ' Ef you don't lemme loose, I'll knock you agin,' sez Brer Rabbit, sezee, en wid dat he fotch 'er a wipe wid de udder han', en dat stuck. Tar-Baby, she ain't sayin' nothin', en Brer Fox, he lay low.

" ' Tu'n me loose, fo' I kick de natal stuffin' outen you,' sez Brer Rabbit, sezee, but de Tar-Baby, she ain't sayin' nothin'. She des hilt on, en den Brer Rabbit lose de use er his feet in de same way. Brer Fox, he lay low. Den Brer Rabbit squall out dat ef de Tar-Baby don't tu'n 'im loose he butt 'er cranksided. En den he butted, en his head got stuck. Den Brer Fox, he sa'ntered fort', lookin' des ez innercent ez one er yo' mammy's mockin'-birds.

" ' Howdy, Brer Rabbit,' sez Brer Fox, sezee. ' You look sorter stuck up dis mawnin',' sezee, en den he rolled on de groun', en laft en laft twel he couldn't laff no mo'. ' I speck you'll take dinner wid me dis time, Brer Rabbit. I done laid in some calamus root, en I ain't gwineter take no skuse,' sez Brer Fox, sezee."

Here Uncle Remus paused, and drew a two-pound yam out of the ashes.

" Did the fox eat the rabbit? " asked the little boy to whom the story had been told.

" Dat's all de fur de tale goes," replied the old man. " He mout, en den agin he moutent. Some say Jedge B'ar come 'long en loosed 'im — some say he didn't. I hear Miss Sally callin'. You better run 'long."

II. HOW MR. RABBIT WAS TOO SHARP FOR MR. FOX

"Uncle Remus," said the little boy one evening, when he found the old man with little or nothing to do, "did the fox kill and eat the rabbit when he caught him with the Tar-Baby?"

"Law, honey, ain't I tell you 'bout dat?" replied the old darkey, chuckling slyly. "I 'clar ter grashus I ought er tole you dat, but old man Nod wuz ridin' on my eyeleds twel a leetle mo'n I'd a dis'membered my own name, en den on to dat here come yo' mammy hollerin' atter you.

"W'at I tell you w'en I fus' begin? I tole you Brer Rabbit wuz a monstus soon beas'; leas' ways dat's w'at I laid out fer ter tell you. Well, den, honey, don't you go en make no udder calkalashuns, kaze in dem days Brer Rabbit en his fambly wuz at de head er de gang w'en enny racket wuz on han', en dar dey stayed. 'Fo' you begins ter wipe yo' eyes 'bout Brer Rabbit, you wait en see whar'bouts Brer Rabbit gwineter fetch up at. But dat's needer yer ner dar.

"W'en Brer Fox fine Brer Rabbit mixt up wid de Tar-Baby, he feel mighty good, en he roll on de groun' en laff. Bimeby he up'n say, sezee:

"'Well, I spect I got you dis time, Brer Rabbit,' sezee; 'maybe I ain't, but I speck I is. You been runnin' roun' here sassin' atter me a mighty long time, but I speck you done come ter de een' er de row. You bin cuttin' up yo' capers en bouncin' roun' in dis naberhood ontwel you come ter b'leeve yo'se'f de boss er de whole gang. En den youer allers some'rs whar you got no bizness,' sez Brer Fox, sezee. 'Who ax you fer ter come en strike up a 'quaintance wid dish yer Tar-Baby? En who stuck you up dar whar you iz? Nobody in de roun' worril. You des tuck en jam yo'se'f on dat Tar-Baby widout waitin' fer enny invite,' sez Brer Fox, sezee, 'en dar you is, en dar you'll stay twel I fixes up a bresh-pile and fires her up, kaze I'm gwineter bobbycue you dis day, sho,' sez Brer Fox, sezee.

"Den Brer Rabbit talk mighty 'umble.

"'I don't keer w'at you do wid me, Brer Fox,' sezee, 'so you don't fling me in dat brier-patch. Roas' me, Brer Fox,' sezee, 'but don't fling me in dat brier-patch,' sezee.

"'Het's so much trouble fer ter kindle a fier,' sez Brer Fox, sezee, 'dat I speck I'll hatter hang you,' sezee.

"'Hang me des ez high as you please, Brer Fox,' sez Brer Rabbit, sezee, 'but do fer de Lord's sake don't fling me in dat brier-patch,' sezee.

"'I ain't got no string,' sez Brer Fox, sezee, 'en now I speck I'll hatter drown you,' sezee.

"'Drown me des ez deep ez you please, Brer Fox,' sez Brer Rabbit, sezee, 'but do don't fling me in dat brier-patch,' sezee.

"'Dey ain't no water nigh,' sez Brer Fox, sezee, 'en now I speck I'll hatter skin you,' sezee.

" 'Skin me, Brer Fox,' sez Brer Rabbit, sezee, 'snatch out my eyeballs, t'ar out my years by de roots, en cut off my legs,' sezee, 'but do please, Brer Fox, don't fling me in dat brier-patch,' sezee.

" Co'se Brer Fox wanter hurt Brer Rabbit bad ez he kin, so he cotch 'im by de behime legs en slung 'im right in de middle er de brier-patch. Dar wuz a considerbul flutter whar Brer Rabbit struck de bushes, en Brer Fox sorter hang roun' fer ter see w'at wuz gwineter happen. Bimeby he hear somebody call 'im, en way up de hill he see Brer Rabbit settin' cross-legged on a chinkapin log koamin' de pitch outen his har wid a chip. Den Brer Fox know dat he bin swop off mighty bad. Brer Rabbit wuz bleedzed fer ter fling back some er his sass, en he holler out:

" 'Bred en bawn in a brier-patch, Brer Fox — bred en bawn in a brier-patch!' en wid dat he skip out des ez lively ez a cricket in de embers."

Esther Shephard

The Buckskin Harness

I SUPPOSE everybody's seen pictures of the big log loads we used to haul in the woods in the old times. Loads piled up, ten or twelve rows of logs on top of each other, and the teamster standin' alongside the load, and the top log way up in the air there above his head, and I can tell you them pictures ain't no exaggeration nor nothin' out of the ordinary. Three or four times as high as a man's head I've seen them loads many times. Naturally you had to have a good top-loader to get 'em that high, but that was the top-loader's business to be a good top-loader, and if he knowed what he was about he knowed how to build 'em as high as you'd a mind to have 'em.

In Paul's camp, though, we had 'em higher'n any you could ever of seen in any of the pictures. They used to be so high we had to have a telephone to phone up to the loader, and noontime they always sent his dinner up to him in a balloon. Generally he used to write a letter before he went up in the mornin' to send to his mother in case he shouldn't never come down again.

Course they couldn't of drawed them big loads if it hadn't of been for the buckskin harness that was invented about that time. That come in just before Paul went into Minnesota to log in them big white pine woods there. He used to hitch up Babe by Lake Vermilion and then the logs would be drawed down to Duluth or Two Harbors in one pull.

Everybody knows how buckskin stretches when it gets wet, and then shrinks all up to nothin' almost when it gets dry and warm in the sun. Well, that's the principle the buckskin harness was invented on; and the same as with many

From *Paul Bunyan,* 1924.

inventions, I guess, it was invented practically by pure accident. Look at the way Watt invented the steam engine, just watchin' an old teakettle boil.

But I was goin' to tell about the buckskin harness, and the way that come to be invented was, one of the bull-cooks was goin' to haul the wood in for the cookhouse stove. They'd used up all the wood that was near by already, and so he had to go out a good ways out in the woods to get it. The cook was a pretty cranky feller and he'd told him he'd better bring home something dry that would burn if he knowed what was good for him, and so the bull-cook took his ox and went away over to the south of the camp where the burnt-over land was. Figgured some of them burnt trunks would be dry on the inside anyway. It was rainin' pitchforks that mornin' and nothin' couldn't happen to be dry on the outside by any way or chance.

The ox he had was a big one, though of course not big like Babe, and he had a bran'-new buckskin harness on him.

And so when he got there he cut down a couple of dozen burnt trees and put the logs on the sled and then he starts out for home with 'em, over the trail. First part of it was just kind of a narrow sledtrack through the woods, but about half way that road turned out on one of the big main loggin' roads. He was glad he hit that part of the road and from there on he drove a little faster, walkin' along beside the ox and not botherin' to look back any. And course it was rainin' all the time hard as ever.

Well, when he got to camp it was about noon, and he drove his ox up right close to the door back of the cookhouse, and then when he turned around he seen he didn't have no load at all, but the harness was stretched out all the way down the road to the big tree where the turn was, where the log trail went into the woods, and he knowed his load of stovewood must be somewheres down there behind the tree standin' there. He was just goin' to start back and get it when the dinner horn commenced to toot, and he calculated he might as well go in and eat his dinner and go and tend to his load afterwards.

" That'll be the best thing I can do," he says.

And then while he was eatin' his dinner and while all of the rest of us was eatin' dinner, the sun come out.

And so, in about fifteen minutes, when the bull-cook come back out again, there was his load of wood standin' there right in front of him, and pretty near climbin' up on the old ox's back, so he had to holler for help and hurry and cut him loose before it went right up on top of him.

You know, what happened was, when the sun come out, that buckskin harness had begun to shrink. And that's how it had pulled the load up by itself, without the ox doin' no pullin' at all on his part.

One of the cookees called Paul to see it, and Paul took out a patent on the harness, and the buckskin harness was used for all long hauls in Paul's camp ever since. A fine invention, you see, that come about that way, only the sun hadn't dried out the wood enough, and the cook swore at the bull-cook just the same, like as if he hadn't tried to do his best.

Paul did some great loggin' in Minnesota. Them forests up there was sure fine forests — stretches of pine and spruce and hemlock, with sometimes some white birches in between. Get up on a rise and you could see them all below you like a great ocean, big dark waves where the spruce was, and light patches of jack pine climbin' up on the hills, and the red willows that used to grow along the cricks. Paul used to climb up on Jasper Point sometimes just to enjoy the sight of it, and at the same time to make sure that the three rivers that make their start there was doin' their job of keepin' his three loggin' operations apart — he'd put 'em in on purpose for that, so he wouldn't get 'em mixed up. They're the Nelson-Saskatchewan, you know, and the St. Lawrence and the Mississippi. Jasper Point is the height of land between 'em.

Paul always liked it in Minnesota, though. There was plenty of Swedes around all the time that he could get hold of to work for him whenever he wanted, and then the huntin' was good in them there woods too.

One time, I know, Paul went huntin' spruce patridges. And he hadn't got out in the woods very far yet and hadn't been lookin' around very long till all of a sudden he seen five hundred forty of 'em sittin' in a row on a spruce bough, and he begun figgurin' how was the best way to get 'em.

Course he had his shotgun along and his rifle too, and with his shotgun he could of got 'em all, because there was just enough shot in the load for one shot for each patridge, but he didn't like to get 'em that way if he could help, because he knowed they would be so much trouble to pick up afterwards each one by itself that way.

So what he done was, he took his rifle and went over to the end of the limb and fired and sent the bullet right through the length of the limb and split it open all the way to the tree, and then, just as he figgured, the patridges all got their toes caught in the rebound in the crack he'd made and stuck fast. And then he reloaded his rifle, leavin' the ramrod in, and shot that right through all the patridges. That way he got all but four that he didn't get quite big enough a hold on to make 'em stick on the rod.

He'd finished that shot, and had just turned round, when he seen a fine big buck standin' there not so very far away. He fired his shotgun at him quick and he seen the buck tumble over the ledge just as he fired.

It was such a fine carcass he couldn't hardly wait to get there to get hold of it, so he run as fast as he could to the place where the buck had been. Well, he run too fast. Result was, he run faster than the load, and got ahead of it, and got the whole charge of buckshot in his own back. For the buck'd got scared to death when he seen Paul, and hadn't waited for the shot to reach him.

Ole the Blacksmith come out and helped Paul back to camp and carried the patridges and the buck in for him. The buck when dressed weighed nine hundred seventy-five pounds.

There in Minnesota, the Minneapolis millmen used to want peeled logs, and Paul never liked that much. Oh, there was some sense to it, I spose — would keep the logs from rottin' if they had to lay in the water a long time — but not much. Paul always said it was nothin' but folderol, and I think he was about right. Anyway, it used to make him all-fired plaguy mad. The way he'd peel 'em when he got mad, he'd just hitch the Blue Ox to 'em and jerk 'em out whole. Even, he didn't bother to cut the trees down sometimes but just pulled 'em out from the top, so he got the heart out and left the limbs and bark standin'. That way a good deal was wasted, of course, and it was a lot of trouble, because he couldn't do but one at a time. I don't know how mad he would of got, but they quit askin' for 'em after a while — maybe the sawmill men heard how Paul felt about it, and thought they'd better not ask to get peeled logs no more.

What Paul liked best to do was a whole lot of trees at a time. There in Minnesota he got himself a long fallin' saw that would reach across half a mile or more. Of course if the country was a little hilly or there was a hollow or rise of ground, it didn't work so good, because they'd just get the tops of the trees that growed down in the hollows, and up on the hills the saw would hit in the ground and get dulled on the rocks. Paul had to keep a gang of two hundred filers to keep that saw filed. And that was the saw that Paul always pulled one end of himself. He didn't care who pulled the other end, and he didn't care if they'd ride the saw, he said, if they felt like it, but what he didn't want was for 'em to drag their feet — he drawed the line on that.

Paul always liked to do things on a big scale. One of his ways was just to hitch Babe on to a whole section of timber at a time and haul it into camp and clear it off. If he got one in about sundown, after the day's work was over, he'd generally get it all cleared before supper.

That was efficient so far as the time it took was concerned anyway. But he couldn't of done it without Babe to haul it in for him.

Like one of these here efficiency experts would say, the overhead cost and maintenance for Babe was high, but on account of low operatin' expense and great efficiency, he was pretty economical camp equipment. And Paul couldn't of done much without him, I know that.

Like the time when they drove the wrong logs down the river and over the St. Anthony Falls; Babe just drank the river dry above the falls and sucked 'em all back again.

SHORT STORIES

Nathaniel Hawthorne

Lady Eleanore's Mantle

NOT long after Colonel Shute had assumed the government of Massachusetts Bay, now nearly a hundred and twenty years ago, a young lady of rank and fortune arrived from England to claim his protection as her guardian. He was her distant relative, but the nearest who had survived the gradual extinction of her family; so that no more eligible shelter could be found for the rich and highborn Lady Eleanore Rochcliffe than within the Province House of a transatlantic colony. The consort of Governor Shute, moreover, had been as a mother to her childhood, and was now anxious to receive her, in the hope that a beautiful young woman would be exposed to infinitely less peril from the primitive society of New England than amid the artifices and corruptions of a court. If either the Governor or his lady had especially consulted their own comfort, they would probably have sought to devolve the responsibility on other hands; since with some noble and splendid traits of character, Lady Eleanore was remarkable for a harsh, unyielding pride, a haughty consciousness of her hereditary and personal advantages, which made her almost incapable of control. Judging from many traditional anecdotes, this peculiar temper was hardly less than a monomania; or, if the acts which it inspired were those of a sane person, it seemed due from Providence that pride so sinful should be followed by as severe a retribution. That tinge of the marvelous which is thrown over so many of these half-forgotten legends has probably imparted an additional wildness to the strange story of Lady Eleanore Rochcliffe.

The ship in which she came passenger had arrived at Newport, whence Lady Eleanore was conveyed to Boston in the Governor's coach, attended by a small escort of gentlemen on horseback. The ponderous equipage, with its four black horses, attracted much notice as it rumbled through Cornhill, surrounded by the prancing steeds of half a dozen cavaliers, with swords dangling to their stirrups and pistols at their holsters. Through the large glass windows of the coach as

From *Twice-Told Tales*, 1842.

it rolled along, the people could discern the figure of Lady Eleanore, strangely combining an almost queenly stateliness with the grace and beauty of a maiden in her teens. A singular tale had gone abroad among the ladies of the province, that their fair rival was indebted for much of the irresistible charm of her appearance to a certain article of dress — an embroidered mantle — which had been wrought by the most skillful artist in London, and possessed even magical properties of adornment. On the present occasion, however, she owed nothing to the witchery of dress, being clad in a riding habit of velvet, which would have appeared stiff and ungraceful on any other form.

The coachman reined in his four black steeds, and the whole cavalcade came to a pause in front of the contorted iron balustrade that fenced the Province House from the public street. It was an awkward coincidence that the bell of the Old South was just then tolling for a funeral; so that, instead of a gladsome peal with which it was customary to announce the arrival of distinguished strangers, Lady Eleanore Rochcliffe was ushered by a doleful clang, as if calamity had come embodied in her beautiful person.

"A very great disrespect!" exclaimed Captain Langford, an English officer who had recently brought dispatches to Governor Shute. "The funeral should have been deferred, lest Lady Eleanore's spirits be affected by such a dismal welcome."

"With your pardon, sir," replied Doctor Clarke, a physician and a famous champion of the popular party, "whatever the heralds may pretend, a dead beggar must have precedence of a living queen. King Death confers high privileges."

These remarks were interchanged while the speakers waited a passage through the crowd which had gathered on each side of the gateway, leaving an open avenue to the portal of the Province House. A black slave in livery now leaped from behind the coach and threw open the door; while at the same moment Governor Shute descended the flight of steps from his mansion, to assist Lady Eleanore in alighting. But the Governor's stately approach was anticipated in a manner that excited general astonishment. A pale young man, with his black hair all in disorder, rushed from the throng and prostrated himself beside the coach, thus offering his person as a footstool for Lady Eleanore Rochcliffe to tread upon. She held back an instant; yet with an expression as if doubting whether the young man were worthy to bear the weight of her footstep, rather than dissatisfied to receive such awful reverence from a fellow mortal.

"Up, sir," said the Governor sternly, at the same time lifting his cane over the intruder. "What means the Bedlamite by this freak?"

"Nay," answered Lady Eleanore playfully, but with more scorn than pity in her tone, "your Excellency shall not strike him. When men seek only to be trampled upon, it were a pity to deny them a favor so easily granted — and so well deserved!"

Then, though as lightly as a sunbeam on a cloud, she placed her foot upon the cowering form and extended her hand to meet that of the Governor. There was a brief interval during which Lady Eleanore retained this attitude; and never, surely, was there an apter emblem of aristocracy and hereditary pride trampling on human sympathies and the kindred of nature than these two figures presented at that moment. Yet the spectators were so smitten with her beauty, and so essential did pride seem to the existence of such a creature, that they gave a simultaneous acclamation of applause.

"Who is this insolent young fellow?" inquired Captain Langford, who still remained beside Doctor Clarke. "If he be in his senses, his impertinence demands the bastinado. If mad, Lady Eleanore should be secured from further inconvenience by his confinement."

"His name is Jervase Helwyse," answered the Doctor; "a youth of no birth or fortune or other advantages save the mind and soul that nature gave him; and being secretary to our colonial agent in London, it was his misfortune to meet this Lady Eleanore Rochcliffe. He loved her — and her scorn has driven him mad."

"He was mad so to aspire," observed the English officer.

"It may be so," said Doctor Clarke, frowning as he spoke. "But I tell you, sir, I could well-nigh doubt the justice of the heaven above us if no signal humiliation overtake this lady who now treads so haughtily into yonder mansion. She seeks to place herself above the sympathies of our common nature, which envelops all human souls. See if that nature do not assert its claim over her in some mode that shall bring her level with the lowest."

"Never!" cried Captain Langford indignantly. "Neither in life nor when they lay her with her ancestors."

Not many days afterwards the Governor gave a ball in honor of Lady Eleanore Rochcliffe. The principal gentry of the colony received invitations which were distributed to their residences, far and near, by messengers on horseback, bearing missives sealed with all the formality of official dispatches. In obedience to the summons, there was a general gathering of rank, wealth, and beauty; and the wide door of the Province House had seldom given admittance to more numerous and honorable guests than on the evening of Lady Eleanore's ball. Without much extravagance of eulogy, the spectacle might even be termed splendid; for, according to the fashion of the times, the ladies shone in rich silks and satins outspread over wide-projecting hoops; and the gentlemen glittered in gold embroidery laid unsparingly upon the purple, or scarlet, or sky-blue velvet which was the material of their coats and waistcoats. The latter article of dress was of great importance, since it enveloped the wearer's body nearly to the knees and was perhaps bedizened with the amount of his whole year's income, in golden flowers and foliage. The altered taste of the present day — a taste symbolic of a deep change in the whole system of society — would look upon almost any of those gorgeous figures as ridiculous; although that evening the guests sought their reflections in the pier glasses and rejoiced to catch their own glitter amid the glittering crowd. What a pity that one of the stately mirrors has not preserved a picture of the scene, which, by the very traits that were so transitory, might have taught us much that would be worth knowing and remembering!

Would, at least, that either painter or mirror could convey to us some faint idea of a garment already noticed in this legend, the Lady Eleanore's embroidered mantle, which the gossips whispered was invested with magic properties, so as to lend a new and untried grace to her figure each time that she put it on! Idle fancy as it is, this mysterious mantle has thrown an awe around my image of her, partly from its fabled virtues and partly because it was the handiwork of a dying woman and, perchance, owed the fantastic grace of its conception to the delirium of approaching death.

After the ceremonial greetings had been paid, Lady Eleanore Rochcliffe stood apart from the mob of guests, insulating herself within a small and distinguished circle, to whom she accorded a more cordial favor than to the general throng. The waxen torches threw their radiance vividly over the scene, bringing out its brilliant points in strong relief; but she gazed carelessly, and with now and then an expression of weariness or scorn, tempered with such feminine grace that her auditors scarcely perceived the moral deformity of which it was the utterance. She beheld the spectacle not with vulgar ridicule, as disdaining to be pleased with the provincial mockery of a court festival, but with the deeper scorn of one whose spirit held itself too high to participate in the enjoyment of other human souls. Whether or no the recollections of those who saw her that evening were influenced by the strange events with which she was subsequently connected, so it was that her figure ever after recurred to them as marked by something wild and unnatural; although, at the time, the general whisper was of her exceeding beauty and of the indescribable charm which her mantle threw around her. Some close observers, indeed, detected a feverish flush and alternate paleness of countenance, with a corresponding flow and revulsion of spirits, and once or twice a painful and helpless betrayal of lassitude, as if she were on the point of sinking to the ground. Then, with a nervous shudder, she seemed to arouse her energies, and threw some bright and playful, yet half-wicked sarcasm into the conversation. There was so strange a characteristic in her manners and sentiments that it astonished every right-minded listener; till looking in her face, a lurking and incomprehensible glance and smile perplexed them with doubts both as to her seriousness and sanity.

Gradually Lady Eleanore Rochcliffe's circle grew smaller, till only four gentlemen remained in it. These were Captain Langford, the English officer before mentioned; a Virginian planter, who had come to Massachusetts on some political errand; a young Episcopal clergyman, the grandson of a British Earl; and lastly, the private secretary of Governor Shute, whose obsequiousness had won a sort of tolerance from Lady Eleanore.

At different periods of the evening the liveried servants of the Province House passed among the guests, bearing huge trays of refreshments, and French and Spanish wines. Lady Eleanore Rochcliffe, who refused to wet her beautiful lips even with a bubble of champagne, had sunk back into a large damask chair, apparently overwearied either with the excitement of the scene or its tedium; and while, for an instant, she was unconscious of voices, laughter, and music, a young man stole forward and knelt down at her feet. He bore a salver in his hand, on which was a chased silver goblet filled to the brim with wine, which he offered as reverentially as to a crowned queen, or rather with the awful devotion of a priest doing sacrifice to his idol. Conscious that someone touched her robe, Lady Eleanore started, and unclosed her eyes upon the pale, wild features and dishevelled hair of Jervase Helwyse.

"Why do you haunt me thus?" said she in a languid tone, but with a kindlier feeling than she ordinarily permitted herself to express. "They tell me that I have done you harm."

"Heaven knows if that be so," replied the young man solemnly. "But, Lady Eleanore, in requital of that harm, if such there be, and for your own earthly and heavenly welfare, I pray you to take one sip of this holy wine, and then to pass the goblet round among the guests. And this shall be a symbol that you have not sought to withdraw yourself from the chain of human sympathies — which whoso would shake off must keep company with fallen angels."

"Where has this mad fellow stolen that sacramental vessel?" exclaimed the Episcopal clergyman.

This question drew the notice of the guests to the silver cup, which was recognized as appertaining to the communion plate of the Old South Church; and for aught that could be known, it was brimming over with the consecrated wine.

"Perhaps it is poisoned," half whispered the Governor's secretary.

"Pour it down the villain's throat!" cried the Virginian fiercely.

"Turn him out of the house!" cried Captain Langford, seizing Jervase Helwyse so roughly by the shoulder that the sacramental cup was overturned and its contents sprinkled upon Lady Eleanore's mantle. "Whether knave, fool, or Bedlamite, it is intolerable that the fellow should go at large."

"Pray, gentlemen, do my poor admirer no harm," said Lady Eleanore with a faint and weary smile. "Take him out of my sight, if such be your pleasure; for I can find in my heart to do nothing but laugh at him; whereas, in all decency and conscience, it would become me to weep for the mischief I have wrought!"

But while the bystanders were attempting to lead away the unfortunate young man, he broke from them and with a wild, impassioned earnestness offered a new and equally strange petition to Lady Eleanore. It was no other than that she should throw off the mantle which, while he pressed the silver cup of wine upon her, she had drawn more closely around her form, so as almost to shroud herself within it.

"Cast it from you!" exclaimed Jervase Helwyse, clasping his hands in an agony of entreaty. "It may not yet be too late. Give the accursed garment to the flames."

But Lady Eleanore, with a laugh of scorn, drew the rich folds of the embroidered mantle over her head, in such a fashion as to give a completely new aspect to her beautiful face, which — half hidden, half revealed — seemed to belong to some being of mysterious character and purposes.

"Farewell, Jervase Helwyse!" said she. "Keep my image in your remembrance, as you behold it now."

"Alas, lady!" he replied, in a tone no longer wild, but sad as a funeral bell.

" We must meet shortly, when your face may wear another aspect; and that shall be the image that must abide within me."

He made no more resistance to the violent efforts of the gentlemen and servants, who almost dragged him out of the apartment, and dismissed him roughly from the iron gate of the Province House. Captain Langford, who had been very active in this affair, was returning to the presence of Lady Eleanore Rochcliffe, when he encountered the physician, Doctor Clarke, with whom he had held some casual talk on the day of her arrival. The Doctor stood apart, separated from Lady Eleanore by the width of the room, but eyeing her with such keen sagacity that Captain Langford involuntarily gave him credit for the discovery of some deep secret.

" You appear to be smitten, after all, with the charms of this queenly maiden," said he, hoping thus to draw forth the physician's hidden knowledge.

" God forbid! " answered Doctor Clarke, with a grave smile; " and if you be wise, you will put up the same prayer for yourself. Woe to those who shall be smitten by this beautiful Lady Eleanore! But yonder stands the Governor, and I have a word or two for his private ear. Good night! "

He accordingly advanced to Governor Shute and addressed him in so low a tone that none of the bystanders could catch a word of what he said; although the sudden change of his Excellency's hitherto cheerful visage betokened that the communication could be of no agreeable import. A very few moments afterwards, it was announced to the guests that an unforeseen circumstance rendered it necessary to put a premature close to the festival.

The ball at the Province House supplied a topic of conversation for the colonial metropolis for some days after its occurrence, and might still longer have been the general theme, only that a subject of all-engrossing interest thrust it, for a time, from the public recollection. This was the appearance of a dreadful epidemic which, in that age and long before and afterwards, was wont to slay its hundreds and thousands on both sides of the Atlantic. On the occasion of which we speak, it was distinguished by a peculiar virulence, insomuch that it has left its traces — its pit-marks, to use an appropriate figure — on the history of the country, the affairs of which were thrown into confusion by its ravages. At first, unlike its ordinary course, the disease seemed to confine itself to the higher circles of society, selecting its victims from among the proud, the well-born, and the wealthy, entering unabashed into stately chambers and lying down with the slumberers in silken beds. Some of the most distinguished guests of the Province House — even those whom the haughty Lady Eleanore Rochcliffe had deemed not unworthy of her favor — were stricken by this fatal scourge. It was noticed, with an ungenerous bitterness of feeling, that the four gentlemen — the Virginian, the British officer, the young clergyman, and the Governor's secretary — who had been her most devoted attendants on the evening of the ball were the foremost on whom the plague stroke fell. But the disease, pursuing its onward progress, soon ceased to be exclusively a prerogative of aristocracy. Its red brand was no longer conferred like a noble's star or an order of knighthood. It threaded its way through the narrow and crooked streets, and entered the low, mean, darksome dwellings, and laid its hand of death upon the artisans and laboring classes of the town. It compelled rich and poor to feel themselves brethren then; and stalking to and fro across the Three Hills, with a fierceness which made it almost a new pestilence, there was that mighty conqueror, that scourge and horror of our forefathers, the smallpox!

We cannot estimate the affright which this plague inspired of yore, by contemplating it as the fangless monster of the present day. We must remember, rather, with what awe we watched the gigantic footsteps of the Asiatic cholera striding from shore to shore of the Atlantic and marching like destiny upon cities far remote, which flight had already half depopulated. There is no other fear so horrible and unhumanizing as that which makes man dread to breathe heaven's vital air lest it be poison, or to grasp the hand of a brother or friend lest the gripe of the pestilence should clutch him. Such was the dismay that now followed in the track of the disease or ran before it throughout the town. Graves were hastily dug, and the pestilential relics as hastily covered, because the dead were enemies of the living and strove to draw them headlong, as it were, into their own dismal pit. The public councils were suspended, as if mortal wisdom might relinquish its devices, now that unearthly usurper had found his way into the ruler's mansion. Had an enemy's fleet been hovering on the coast, or his armies trampling on our soil, the people would probably have committed their defense to that same direful conqueror who had wrought their own calamity and would permit no interference with his sway. This conqueror had a symbol of his triumphs. It was a blood-red flag that fluttered in the tainted air, over the door of every dwelling into which the smallpox had entered.

Such a banner was long since waving over the portal of the Province House; for thence, as was proved by tracking its footsteps back, had all this dreadful mischief issued. It had been traced back to a lady's luxurious chamber; to the proudest of the proud; to her that was so delicate, and hardly owned herself of earthly mold; to the haughty one who took her stand above human sympathies; to Lady Eleanore! There remained no room for doubt that the contagion had lurked in that gorgeous mantle which threw so strange a grace around her at the festival. Its fantastic splendor had been conceived in the delirious brain of a woman on her deathbed, and was the last toil of her stiffening fingers, which had interwoven fate and misery with its golden threads. This dark tale, whispered at first, was now bruited far and wide. The people raved against the Lady Eleanore, and cried out that her pride and scorn had evoked a fiend, and that, between them both, this monstrous evil had been born. At times their rage and despair took the semblance of grinning mirth; and whenever the red flag of the pestilence was hoisted over another and yet another door, they clapped their hands and shouted through the streets in bitter mockery, "Behold a new triumph for the Lady Eleanore!"

One day, in the midst of these dismal times, a wild figure approached the portal of the Province House and, folding his arms, stood contemplating the scarlet banner, which a passing breeze shook fitfully, as if to fling abroad the contagion that it typified. At length, climbing one of the pillars by means of the iron balustrade, he took down the flag and entered the mansion, waving it above his head. At the foot of the staircase he met the Governor, booted and spurred, with his cloak drawn around him, evidently on the point of setting forth upon a journey.

"Wretched lunatic, what do you seek here?" exclaimed Shute, extending his cane to guard himself from contact. "There is nothing here but Death. Back — or you will meet him!"

"Death will not touch me, the banner-bearer of the pestilence!" cried Jervase Helwyse, shaking the red flag aloft. "Death and the Pestilence, who wears the aspect of the Lady Eleanore, will walk through the streets tonight, and I must march before them with this banner!"

"Why do I waste words on the fellow?" muttered the Governor, drawing his cloak across his mouth. "What matters his miserable life, when none of us are sure of twelve hours' breath? On, fool, to your own destruction!"

He made way for Jervase Helwyse, who immediately ascended the staircase but, on the first landing place, was arrested by the firm grasp of a hand upon his shoulder. Looking fiercely up, with a madman's impulse to struggle with and rend asunder his opponent, he found himself powerless beneath a calm, stern eye which possessed the mysterious property of quelling frenzy at its height. The person whom he had now encountered was the physician, Doctor Clarke, the duties of whose sad profession had led him to the Province House, where he was an infrequent guest in more prosperous times.

"Young man, what is your purpose?" demanded he.

"I seek the Lady Eleanore," answered Jervase Helwyse submissively.

"All have fled from her," said the physician. "Why do you seek her now? I tell you, youth, her nurse fell death-stricken on the threshold of that fatal chamber. Know ye not, that never came such a curse to our shores as this lovely Lady Eleanore? That her breath has filled the air with poison? That she has shaken pestilence and death upon the land, from the folds of her accursed mantle?"

"Let me look upon her!" rejoined the mad youth more wildly. "Let me behold her in her awful beauty, clad in the regal garments of the pestilence! She and Death sit on a throne together. Let me kneel down before them!"

"Poor youth!" said Doctor Clarke; and, moved by a deep sense of human weakness, a smile of caustic humor curled his lip even then. "Wilt thou still worship the destroyer, and surround her image with fantasies the more magnificent, the more evil she has wrought? Thus man doth ever to his tyrants! Approach, then! Madness, as I have noted, has that good efficacy, that it will guard you from contagion; and perchance its own cure may be found in yonder chamber."

Ascending another flight of stairs, he threw open a door and signed to Jervase Helwyse that he should enter. The poor lunatic, it seems probable, had cherished a delusion that his haughty mistress sat in state, unharmed herself by the pestilential influence, which, as by enchantment, she scattered round about her. He dreamed, no doubt, that her beauty was not dimmed, but brightened into superhuman splendor. With such anticipations, he stole reverentially to the door at which the physician stood, but paused upon the threshold, gazing fearfully into the gloom of the darkened chamber.

" Where is the Lady Eleanore? " whispered he.

" Call her," replied the physician.

" Lady Eleanore! Princess! Queen of Death! " cried Jervase Helwyse, advancing three steps into the chamber. " She is not here! There, on yonder table, I behold the sparkle of a diamond which once she wore upon her bosom. There " — and he shuddered — " there hangs her mantle, on which a dead woman embroidered a spell of dreadful potency. But where is the Lady Eleanore? "

Something stirred within the silken curtains of a canopied bed; and a low moan was uttered, which, listening intently, Jervase Helwyse began to distinguish as a woman's voice, complaining dolefully of thirst. He fancied, even, that he recognized its tones.

" My throat! My throat is scorched," murmured the voice. " A drop of water! "

" What thing art thou? " said the brain-stricken youth, drawing near the bed and tearing asunder its curtains. " Whose voice hast thou stolen for thy murmurs and miserable petitions, as if Lady Eleanore could be conscious of mortal infirmity? Fie! Heap of diseased mortality, why lurkest thou in my lady's chamber? "

" O Jervase Helwyse," said the voice — and as it spoke, the figure contorted itself, struggling to hide its blasted face — " look not now on the woman you once loved! The curse of heaven hath stricken me, because I would not call man my brother, nor woman sister. I wrapped myself in PRIDE as in a MANTLE, and scorned the sympathies of nature; and therefore has nature made this wretched body the medium of a dreadful sympathy. You are avenged — they are all avenged — nature is avenged — for I am Eleanore Rochcliffe! "

The malice of his mental disease, the bitterness lurking at the bottom of his heart, mad as he was, for a blighted and ruined life, and love that had been paid with cruel scorn, awoke within the breast of Jervase Helwyse. He shook his finger at the wretched girl, and the chamber echoed, the curtains of the bed were shaken, with his outburst of insane merriment.

" Another triumph for the Lady Eleanore! " he cried. " All have been her victims! Who so worthy to be the final victim as herself? " Impelled by some new fantasy of his crazed intellect, he snatched the fatal mantle and rushed from the chamber and the house.

That night a procession passed, by torchlight, through the streets, bearing in the midst the figure of a woman, enveloped with a richly embroidered mantle; while in advance stalked Jervase Helwyse, waving the red flag of the pestilence. Arriving opposite the Province House, the mob burned the effigy, and a strong wind came and swept away the ashes. It was said that, from that very hour, the pestilence abated, as if its sway had some mysterious connection, from the first plague stroke to the last, with Lady Eleanore's mantle. A remarkable uncertainty broods over that unhappy lady's fate. There is a belief, however, that in a certain chamber of this mansion a female form may sometimes be duskily discerned, shrinking into the darkest corner and muffling her face within an embroidered mantle. Supposing the legend true, can this be other than the once proud Lady Eleanore?

Edgar Allan Poe

The Tell-Tale Heart

TRUE! Nervous — very, very dreadfully nervous I had been and am; but why *will* you say that I am mad? The disease had sharpened my senses — not destroyed, not dulled them. Above all was the sense of hearing acute. I heard all things in the heaven and in the earth. I heard many things in hell. How, then, am I mad? Hearken, and observe how healthily, how calmly, I can tell you the whole story.

It is impossible to say how first the idea entered my brain; but once conceived, it haunted me day and night. Object there was none. Passion there was none. I loved the old man. He had never wronged me. He had never given me insult. For his gold I had no desire. I think it was his eye! Yes, it was this! He had the eye of a vulture — a pale blue eye, with a film over it. Whenever it fell upon me, my blood ran cold; and so by degrees — very gradually — I made up my mind to take the life of the old man and thus rid myself of the eye forever.

Now this is the point. You fancy me mad. Madmen know nothing. But you should have seen *me*. You should have seen how wisely I proceeded — with what caution, with what foresight, with what dissimulation, I went to work! I was never kinder to the old man than during the whole week before I killed him. And every night, about midnight, I turned the latch of his door and opened it — oh so gently! And then, when I had made an opening sufficient for my head, I put in a dark lantern, all closed, closed, so that no light shone out; and then I thrust in my head. Oh, you would have laughed to see how cunningly I thrust it in! I moved it slowly — very, very slowly, so that I might not disturb the old man's sleep. It took me an hour to place my whole head within the opening so far that I could see him as he lay upon his bed. Ha! Would a madman have been so wise as this? And then, when my head was well in the room, I undid the lantern cautiously — oh, so cautiously; cautiously (for the hinges creaked). I undid it just so much that a single thin ray fell upon the vulture eye. And this I did for seven long nights — every night just at midnight. But I found the eye always closed, and so it was impossible to do the work; for it was not the old man who vexed me, but his Evil Eye. And every morning, when the day broke, I went boldly into the chamber and spoke courageously to him, calling him by name in a hearty tone, and inquiring how he had passed the night. So you see

From *Pioneer,* January, 1843.

he would have been a very profound old man, indeed, to suspect that every night, just at twelve, I looked in upon him while he slept.

Upon the eighth night I was more than usually cautious in opening the door. A watch's minute hand moves more quickly than did mine. Never, before that night, had I *felt* the extent of my own powers — of my sagacity. I could scarcely contain my feeling of triumph. To think that there I was, opening the door, little by little, and he not even to dream of my secret deeds or thoughts. I fairly chuckled at the idea; and perhaps he heard me, for he moved on the bed suddenly, as if startled. Now you may think that I drew back — but no. His room was as black as pitch with the thick darkness (for the shutters were close fastened, through fear of robbers), and so I knew that he could not see the opening of the door, and I kept pushing it on steadily, steadily.

I had my head in, and was about to open the lantern, when my thumb slipped upon the tin fastening, and the old man sprang up in the bed, crying out, " Who's there? "

I kept quite still and said nothing. For a whole hour I did not move a muscle, and in the meantime I did not hear him lie down. He was still sitting up in the bed, listening — just as I have done, night after night, hearkening to the death watches in the wall.

Presently I heard a slight groan, and I knew it was the groan of mortal terror. It was not a groan of pain or of grief — oh, no! — it was the low stifled sound that arises from the bottom of the soul when overcharged with awe. I knew the sound well. Many a night, just at midnight, when all the world slept, it has welled up from my own bosom, deepening, with its dreadful echo, the terrors that distracted me. I say I knew it well. I knew what the old man felt, and pitied him, although I chuckled at heart. I knew that he had been lying awake ever since the first slight noise, when he had turned in the bed. His fears had been ever since growing upon him. He had been trying to fancy them causeless, but could not. He had been saying to himself: " It is nothing but the wind in the chimney "; " It is only a mouse crossing the floor "; or " It is merely a cricket which has made a single chirp." Yes, he had been trying to comfort himself with these suppositions; but he had found all in vain. *All in vain;* because Death, in approaching him, had stalked with his black shadow before him and enveloped the victim. And it was the mournful influence of the unperceived shadow that caused him to feel — although he neither saw nor heard — to *feel* the presence of my head within the room.

When I had waited a long time, very patiently, without hearing him lie down, I resolved to open a little — a very, very little — crevice in the lantern. So I opened it — you cannot imagine how stealthily, stealthily — until at length a single dim ray, like the thread of the spider, shot from out the crevice and fell full upon the vulture eye.

It was open — wide, wide open — and I grew furious as I gazed upon it. I saw it with perfect distinctness — all a dull blue, with a hideous veil over it that chilled the very marrow in my bones. But I could see nothing else of the old man's face or person; for I had directed the ray, as if by instinct, precisely upon the damned spot.

And now have I not told you that what you mistake for madness is but over-acuteness of the senses? Now, I say, there came to my ears a low, dull, quick sound, such as a watch makes when enveloped in cotton. I knew *that* sound well, too. It was the beating of the old man's heart. It increased my fury, as the beating of a drum stimulates the soldier into courage.

But even yet I refrained and kept still. I scarcely breathed. I held the lantern motionless. I tried how steadily I could maintain the ray upon the eye. Meantime the hellish tattoo of the heart increased. It grew quicker and quicker, and louder and louder every instant. The old man's terror *must* have been extreme! It grew louder, I say, louder every moment — do you mark me well? I have told you that I am nervous — so I am. And now at the dead hour of the night, amid the dreadful silence of that old house, so strange a noise as this excited me to uncontrollable terror. Yet for some minutes longer I refrained and stood still. But the beating grew louder, louder! I thought the heart must burst. And now a new anxiety seized me — the sound would be heard by a neighbor! The old man's hour had come! With a loud yell, I threw open the lantern and leaped into the room.

He shrieked once — once only. In an instant I dragged him to the floor and pulled the heavy bed over him. I then smiled gaily, to find the deed so far done. But, for many minutes, the heart beat on with a muffled sound. This, however, did not vex me; it would not be heard through the wall. At length it ceased. The old man was dead. I removed the bed and examined the corpse. Yes, he was stone, stone dead. I placed my hand upon the heart and held it there many minutes. There was no pulsation. He was stone dead. His eye would trouble me no more.

If still you think me mad, you will think so no longer when I describe the wise precautions I took for the concealment of the body. The night waned, and I worked hastily but in silence. First of all I dismembered the corpse. I cut off the head and the arms and the legs. I then took up three planks from the flooring of the chamber and deposited all between the scantlings. I then replaced the boards so cleverly, so cunningly, that no human eye — not even *his* — could have detected anything wrong. There was nothing to wash out — no stain of any kind — no blood spot whatever. I had been too wary for that. A tub had caught all — ha! ha!

When I had made an end of these labors it was four o'clock — still dark as midnight. As the bell sounded the hour, there came a knocking at the street door. I went down to open it with a light heart — for what had I *now* to fear? There entered three men who introduced themselves, with perfect suavity, as officers of the police. A shriek had been heard by a neighbor during the night; suspicion of foul play had been aroused; information had been lodged at the police office, and they (the officers) had been deputed to search the premises.

I smiled — for *what* had I to fear? I bade the gentlemen welcome. The shriek, I said, was my own in a dream. The old man, I mentioned, was absent in the country. I took my visitors all over the house. I bade them search — search *well*. I led them, at length, to *his* chamber. I showed them his treasures, secure, undisturbed. In the enthusiasm of my confidence, I brought chairs into the room, and desired them *here* to rest from their fatigues, while I myself, in the wild audacity of my perfect triumph, placed my own seat upon the very spot beneath which reposed the corpse of the victim.

The officers were satisfied. My *manner* had convinced them. I was singularly at ease. They sat, and while I answered cheerily, they chatted of familiar things. But, ere long, I felt myself getting pale and wished them gone. My head ached, and I fancied a ringing in my ears; but still they sat and still chatted. The ringing became more distinct. It continued and became more distinct. I talked more freely to get rid of the feeling, but it continued and gained definitiveness — until, at length, I found that the noise was *not* within my ears.

No doubt I now grew *very* pale; but I talked more fluently, and with a heightened voice. Yet the sound increased — and what could I do? It was *a low, dull, quick sound — much such a sound as a watch makes when enveloped in cotton*. I gasped for breath — and yet the officers heard it not. I talked more quickly — more vehemently; but the noise steadily increased. I arose and argued about trifles, in a high key and with violent gesticulations; but the noise steadily increased. Why *would* they not be gone? I paced the floor to and fro with heavy strides, as if excited to fury by the observations of the men — but the noise steadily increased. Oh, God! what *could* I do? I foamed — I raved — I swore! I swung the chair upon which I had been sitting, and grated it upon the boards, but the noise arose over all and continually increased. It grew louder — louder — *louder!* And still the men chatted pleasantly, and smiled. Was it possible they heard not? Almighty God! — no, no! They heard — they suspected — they *knew!* They were making a mockery of my horror! This I thought, and this I think. But anything was better than this agony! Anything was more tolerable than this derision! I could bear those hypocritical smiles no longer! I felt that I must scream or die! — and now — again! — hark! louder! louder! louder! *louder!*

"Villains," I shrieked, "dissemble no more! I admit the deed! Tear up the planks! Here, here! It is the beating of his hideous heart!"

Edward Everett Hale

The Man Without a Country

I SUPPOSE that very few casual readers of the New York *Herald* of August 13th observed, in an obscure corner, among the "Deaths," the announcement:

NOLAN. Died, on board U. S. Corvette *Levant,* Lat. 2° 11′ S., Long. 131° W., on the 11th of May, PHILIP NOLAN.

From the *Atlantic Monthly,* December, 1863.

I happened to observe it, because I was stranded at the old Mission House in Mackinaw, waiting for a Lake Superior steamer which did not choose to come, and I was devouring to the very stubble all the current literature I could get hold of, even down to the deaths and marriages in the *Herald*. My memory for names and people is good, and the reader will see, as he goes on, that I had reason enough to remember Philip Nolan. There are hundreds of readers who would have paused at that announcement if the officer of the *Levant* who reported it had chosen to make it thus: " Died, May 11th, THE MAN WITHOUT A COUNTRY." For it was as " The Man Without a Country " that poor Philip Nolan had generally been known by the officers who had him in charge during some fifty years; as, indeed, by all the men who sailed under them. I dare say there is many a man who has taken wine with him once a fortnight, in a three years' cruise, who never knew that his name was Nolan, or whether the poor wretch had any name at all.

There can now be no possible harm in telling this poor creature's story. Reason enough there has been till now, ever since Madison's administration went out in 1817, for very strict secrecy, the secrecy of honor itself, among the gentlemen of the navy who have had Nolan in successive charge. And certainly it speaks well for the *esprit de corps* of the profession and the personal honor of its members, that to the press this man's story has been wholly unknown — and, I think, to the country at large also. I have reason to think, from some investigations I made in the Naval Archives when I was attached to the Bureau of Construction, that every official report relating to him was burned when Ross burned the public buildings at Washington. One of the Tuckers, or possibly one of the Watsons, had Nolan in charge at the end of the war; and when, on returning from his cruise, he reported at Washington to one of the Crownin-shields — who was in the Navy Department when he came home — he found that the Department ignored the whole business. Whether they really knew nothing about it, or whether it was a *non mi ricordo,* determined on as a piece of policy, I do not know. But this I do know, that since 1817, and possibly before, no naval officer has mentioned Nolan in his report of a cruise.

But, as I say, there is no need for secrecy any longer. And now the poor creature is dead, it seems to me worth while to tell a little of his story, by way of showing young Americans of today what it is to be

A MAN WITHOUT A COUNTRY

Philip Nolan was as fine a young officer as there was in the " Legion of the West," as the Western division of our army was then called. When Aaron Burr made his first dashing expedition down to New Orleans in 1805, at Fort Massac, or somewhere above on the river, he met, as the devil would have it, this gay, dashing, bright young fellow, at some dinner party, I think. Burr marked him, talked to him, walked with him, took him a day or two's voyage in his flatboat, and, in short, fascinated him. For the next year, barrack life was very tame to poor Nolan. He occasionally availed of the permission the great man had given him to write to him. Long, high-worded, stilted letters the poor boy wrote and rewrote and copied. But never a line did he have in reply from the gay deceiver. The other boys in the garrison sneered at him, because he sacrificed in this unrequited affection for a politician the time which they devoted to Monongahela, sledge, and high-low-jack. Bourbon, euchre, and poker were still unknown.

But one day Nolan had his revenge. This time Burr came down the river, not as an attorney seeking a place for his office, but as a disguised conqueror. He had defeated I know not how many district attorneys; he had dined at I know not how many public dinners; he had been heralded in I know not how many Weekly Arguses, and it was rumored that he had an army behind him and an empire before him. It was a great day — his arrival — to poor Nolan. Burr had not been at the fort an hour before he sent for him. That evening he asked Nolan to take him out in his skiff, to show him a canebrake or a cotton-wood tree, as he said — really to seduce him; and by the time the sail was over, Nolan was enlisted body and soul. From that time, though he did not yet know it, he lived as " A Man Without a Country."

What Burr meant to do I know no more than you, dear reader. It is none of our business just now. Only, when the grand catastrophe came, and Jefferson and the House of Virginia of that day undertook to break on the wheel all the possible Clarences of the then House of York, by the great treason trial at Richmond, some of the lesser fry in that distant Mississippi Valley, which was farther from us than Puget's Sound is today, introduced the like novelty on their provincial stage and, to while away the monotony of the summer at Fort Adams, got up, for *spectacles,* a string of court-martials on the officers there. One and another of the colonels and majors were tried, and, to fill out the list, little Nolan, against whom, heaven knows, there was evidence enough — that he was sick of the service, had been willing to be false to it, and would have obeyed any order to march anywhither with anyone who would follow him, had the order only been signed, " By command of His Exc. A. Burr." The courts dragged on. The big flies escaped — rightly for all I know. Nolan was proved guilty enough, as I say; yet you and I would never have heard of him, reader, but that, when the president of the court asked him at the close, whether he wished to say anything to show that he had always been faithful to the United States, he cried out, in a fit of frenzy:

" Damn the United States! I wish I may never hear of the United States again! "

I supposed he did not know how the words shocked old Colonel Morgan, who was holding the court. Half the officers who sat in it had served through the Revolution, and their lives, not to say their necks, had been risked for the very idea which he so cavalierly cursed in his madness. He, on his part, had grown up in the West of those days, in the midst of " Spanish plot," " Orleans plot," and all the rest. He had been educated on a plantation where the finest company was a Spanish officer or a French merchant from Orleans. His education, such as it was, had been perfected in commercial expeditions to Vera Cruz, and I think he told me his father once hired an Englishman to be a private tutor for a winter on the plantation. He had spent half his youth with an older brother, hunting horses in Texas; and, in a word, to him " United States " was scarcely a reality. Yet he had been fed by " United States " for all the years since he had been in the army. He had sworn on his faith as a Christian to be true to " United States." It was " United States " which gave him the uniform he wore, and the sword by his side. Nay, my poor Nolan, it was only because " United States " had picked you out first as one of her own confidential men of honor that A. Burr cared for you a straw more than for the flatboat men who sailed his ark for him. I do not excuse Nolan; I only explain to the reader why he damned his country and wished he might never hear her name again.

He never did hear her name but once again. From that moment, September 23, 1807, till the day he died, May 11, 1863, he never heard her name again. For that half-century and more he was a man without a country.

Old Morgan, as I said, was terribly shocked. If Nolan had compared George Washington to Benedict Arnold, or had cried, " God save King George! " Morgan would not have felt worse. He called the court into his private room, and returned in fifteen minutes, with a face like a sheet, to say:

" Prisoner, hear the sentence of the Court! The Court decides, subject to the approval of the President, that you never hear the name of the United States again."

Nolan laughed. But nobody else laughed. Old Morgan was too solemn, and the whole room was hushed dead as night for a minute. Even Nolan lost his swagger in a moment. Then Morgan added: " Mr. Marshal, take the prisoner to Orleans in an armed boat, and deliver him to the naval commander there."

The Marshal gave his orders and the prisoner was taken out of court.

" Mr. Marshal," continued old Morgan, " see that no one mentions the United States to the prisoner. Mr. Marshal, make my respects to Lieutenant Mitchell at Orleans, and request him to order that no one shall mention the United States to the prisoner while he is on board ship. You will receive your written orders from the officer on duty here this evening. The Court is adjourned without day."

I have always supposed that Colonel Morgan himself took the proceedings of the court to Washington City and explained them to Mr. Jefferson. Certain it is that the President approved them — certain, that is, if I may believe the men who say they have seen his signature. Before the *Nautilus* got round from New Orleans to the Northern Atlantic coast with the prisoner on board, the sentence had been approved and he was a man without a country.

The plan then adopted was substantially the same which was necessarily followed ever after. Perhaps it was suggested by the necessity of sending him by water from Fort Adams and Orleans. The Secretary of the Navy — it must have been the first Crowninshield, though he is a man I do not remember — was requested to put Nolan on board a government vessel bound on a long cruise, and to direct that he should be only so far confined there as to make it certain that he never saw or heard of the country. We had few long cruises then, and the navy was very much out of favor; and as almost all of this story is traditional, as I have explained, I do not know certainly what his first cruise was. But the commander to whom he was intrusted — perhaps it was Tingey or Shaw, though I think it was one of the younger men; we are all old enough now — regulated the etiquette and the precautions of the affair, and according to his scheme they were carried out, I suppose, till Nolan died.

When I was second officer of the *Intrepid* some thirty years after, I saw the original paper of instructions. I have been sorry ever since that I did not copy the whole of it. It ran, however, much in this way:

Washington (with the date, which
must have been late in 1807)

Sir, — You will receive from Lieutenant Neale the person of Philip Nolan, late a Lieutenant in the United States Army.

This person on his trial by court-martial expressed with an oath the wish that he might " never hear of the United States again."

The Court sentenced him to have his wish fulfilled.

For the present the execution of the order is intrusted by the President to this department.

You will take the prisoner on board your ship and keep him there with such precautions as shall prevent his escape.

You will provide him with such quarters, rations, and clothing as would be proper for an officer of his late rank, if he were a passenger on your vessel on the business of his Government.

The gentlemen on board will make any arrangements agreeable to themselves regarding his society. He is to be exposed to no indignity of any kind, nor is he ever unnecessarily to be reminded that he is a prisoner.

But under no circumstances is he ever to hear of his country or to see any information regarding it; and you will specially caution all the officers under your command to take care that, in the various indulgences which may be granted, this rule, in which his punishment is involved, shall not be broken.

It is the intention of the Government that he shall never again see the country which he has disowned. Before the end of your cruise you will receive orders which will give effect to this intention.

Respectfully yours,
W. Southard, for the
Secretary of the Navy

If I had only preserved the whole of this paper, there would be no break in the beginning of my sketch of this story. For Captain Shaw, if it was he, handed it to his successor in the charge, and he to his, and I suppose the commander of the *Levant* has it today as his authority for keeping this man in his mild custody.

The rule adopted on board the ships on which I have met " The Man Without a Country " was, I think, transmitted from the beginning. No mess liked to have him permanently, because his presence cut off all talk of home or of the prospect of return, of politics or letters, of peace or of war — cut off more than half the talk men like to have at sea. But it was always thought too hard that he should never meet the rest of us, except to touch hats, and we finally sank into one system. He was not permitted to talk with the men unless an officer was by. With officers he had unrestrained intercourse, as far as they and he chose. But he grew shy, though he had favorites — I was one. Then the captain always asked him to dinner on Monday. Every mess in succession took up the invitation in its turn. According to the size of the ship, you had him at your mess more or less often at dinner. His breakfast he ate in his own state-room — he always had a stateroom — which was where a sentinel, or somebody on the watch, could see the door. And whatever else he ate or drank he ate or drank alone. Sometimes, when the marines or sailors had any special jollifica-tion, they were permitted to invite " Plain Buttons," as they called him. Then Nolan was sent with some officer, and the men were forbidden to speak of home while he was there. I believe the theory was that the sight of his punish-ment did them good. They called him "Plain Buttons " because, while he always chose to wear a regulation army uniform, he was not permitted to wear the army button, for the reason that it bore either the initials or the insignia of the country he had disowned.

I remember, soon after I joined the navy, I was on shore with some of the older officers from our ship and from the *Brandywine,* which we had met at Alexandria. We had leave to make a party and go up to Cairo and the Pyramids. As we jogged along (you went on donkeys then) some of the gentlemen (we boys called them " Dons," but the phrase was long since changed) fell to talking about Nolan, and someone told the system which was adopted from the first about his books and other reading. As he was almost never permitted to go on shore, even though the vessel lay in port for months, his time, at the best, hung heavy; and everybody was permitted to lend him books if they were not pub-lished in America and made no allusion to it. These were common enough in the old days, when people in the other hemisphere talked of the United States as little as we do of Paraguay. He had almost all the foreign papers that came into the ship, sooner or later; only somebody must go over them first and cut out any advertisement or stray paragraph that alluded to America. This was a little cruel sometimes, when the back of what was cut out might be as innocent as Hesiod. Right in the midst of one of Napoleon's battles, or one of Canning's speeches, poor Nolan would find a great hole, because on the back of the page of that paper there had been an advertisement of a packet for New York, or a scrap from the President's message. I say this was the first time I ever heard of this plan, which afterwards I had enough, and more than enough, to do with. I remember it because poor Phillips, who was of the party, as soon as the allusion to reading was made, told a story of something which happened at the Cape of Good Hope on Nolan's first voyage; and it is the only thing I ever knew of that voyage. They had touched at the Cape and had done the civil thing with the English Admiral and the fleet; and then, leaving for a long cruise up the Indian Ocean, Phillips had borrowed a lot of English books from an officer, which, in those days, as indeed in these, was quite a windfall. Among them, as the devil would order, was the " Lay of the Last Minstrel," which they had all of them heard of, but which most of them had never seen. I think it could not have been published long. Well, nobody thought there could be any risk of anything national in that, though Phillips swore old Shaw had cut out " The Tempest " from Shakespeare before he let Nolan have it, because he said " the Bermudas ought to be ours, and, by Jove, should be one day." So Nolan was permitted to join the circle one afternoon when a lot of them sat on deck smoking and reading aloud. People do not do such things so often now; but when I was young we got rid of a great deal of time so. Well, so it happened that in his turn Nolan took the book and read to the others; and he read very well, as I know. Nobody in the circle knew a line of the poem, only it was all magic and Border chivalry, and was ten thousand years ago. Poor Nolan read steadily through the fifth canto, stopped a minute and drank something, and then began, without a thought of what was coming:

> " Breathes there the man, with soul so dead,
> Who never to himself hath said," —

It seems impossible to us that anybody ever heard this for the first time; but all these fellows did then, and poor Nolan himself went on, still unconsciously or mechanically:

> " This is my own, my native land! "

Then they all saw something was to pay; but he expected to get through, I suppose, turned a little pale, but plunged on:

> " Whose heart hath ne'er within him burned,
> As home his footsteps he hath turned
> From wandering on a foreign strand? —
> If such there breathe, go, mark him well."

By this time the men were all beside themselves, wishing there was any way to make him turn over two pages; but he had not quite presence of mind for that; he gagged a little, colored crimson, and staggered on:

> " For him no minstrel raptures swell;
> High though his titles, proud his name,
> Boundless his wealth as wish can claim,
> Despite these titles, power, and pelf,
> The wretch, concentred all in self," —

and here the poor fellow choked, could not go on, but started up, swung the book into the sea, vanished into his stateroom, " and by Jove," said Phillips, " we did not see him for two months again. And I had to make up some beggarly story to that English surgeon why I did not return his Walter Scott to him."

That story shows about the time when Nolan's braggadocio must have broken down. At first, they said, he took a very high tone, considered his imprisonment a mere farce, affected to enjoy the voyage, and all that; but Phillips said that after he came out of his stateroom he never was the same man again. He never read aloud again, unless it was the Bible or Shakespeare, or something else he was sure of. But it was not that merely. He never entered in with the other young men exactly as a companion again. He was always shy afterwards, when I knew him — very seldom spoke, unless he was spoken to, except to a very few friends. He lighted up occasionally — I remember late in his life hearing him fairly eloquent on something which had been suggested to him by one of Fléchier's sermons — but generally he had the nervous, tired look of a heart-wounded man.

When Captain Shaw was coming home — if, as I say, it was Shaw — rather to the surprise of everybody they made one of the Windward Islands, and lay off and on for nearly a week. The boys said the officers were sick of salt junk and meant to have turtle soup before they came home. But after several days the *Warren* came to the same rendezvous. They exchanged signals; she sent to Phillips and these homeward-bound men letters and papers, and told them she was outward-bound, perhaps to the Mediterranean, and took poor Nolan and his traps on the boat back to try his second cruise. He looked very blank when he was told to get ready to join her. He had known enough of the signs of the sky to know that till that moment he was going " home." But this was a distinct evidence of something he had not thought of, perhaps — that there was no going home for him, even to a prison. And this was the first of some twenty such transfers, which brought him sooner or later into half our best vessels, but which kept him all his life at least some hundred miles from the country he had hoped he might never hear of again.

It may have been on that second cruise — it was once when he was up the Mediterranean — that Mrs. Graff, the celebrated Southern beauty of those days, danced with him. They had been lying a long time in the Bay of Naples, and the officers were very intimate in the English fleet, and there had been great festivities, and our men thought they must give a great ball on board the ship. How they ever did it on board the *Warren* I am sure I do not know. Perhaps it was not the *Warren,* or perhaps ladies did not take up so much room as they do now. They wanted to use Nolan's stateroom for something, and they hated to do it without asking him to the ball; so the captain said they might ask him, if they would be responsible that he did not talk with the wrong people, " who would give him intelligence." So the dance went on, the finest party that had ever been known, I dare say; for I never heard of a man-of-war ball that was not. For ladies they had the family of the American consul, one or two travelers who had adventured so far, and a nice bevy of English girls and matrons, perhaps Lady Hamilton herself.

Well, different officers relieved each other in standing and talking with Nolan in a friendly way, so as to be sure that nobody else spoke to him. The dancing went on with spirit, and after a while even the fellows who took this honorary guard of Nolan ceased to fear any *contretemps*. Only when some English lady — Lady Hamilton, as I said, perhaps — called for a set of " American dances," an odd thing happened. Everybody then danced contradances. The black band, nothing loath, conferred as to what " American dances " were, and started off with " Virginia Reel," which they followed with " Money-Musk," which, in its turn in those days, should have been followed by " The Old Thirteen." But just as Dick, the leader, tapped for his fiddlers to begin, and bent forward, about to say, in true Negro state, " ' The Old Thirteen,' gentlemen and ladies! " as he had said " ' Virginny Reel,' if you please! " and " ' Money-Musk,' if you please! " the captain's boy tapped him on the shoulder, whispered to him, and he did not announce the name of the dance; he merely bowed, began on the air, and they all fell to — the officers teaching the English girls the figure, but not telling them why it had no name.

But that is not the story I started to tell. As the dancing went on, Nolan and our fellows all got at ease, as I said — so much so, that it seemed quite natural for him to bow to that splendid Mrs. Graff, and say: " I hope you have not forgotten me, Miss Rutledge. Shall I have the honor of dancing? "

He did it so quickly that Fellows, who was by him, could not hinder him. She laughed, and said: " I am not Miss Rutledge any longer, Mr. Nolan; but I will dance all the same," just nodded to Fellows, as if to say he must leave Mr. Nolan to her, and led him off to the place where the dance was forming.

Nolan thought he had got his chance. He had known her at Philadelphia, and at other places had met her, and this was a godsend. You could not talk in contradances, as you do in cotillions, or even in the pauses of waltzing; but there were chances for tongues and sounds, as well as for eyes and blushes. He began with her travels, and Europe, and Vesuvius, and the French; and then, when they had worked down, and had that long talking-time at the bottom of the set, he said, boldly — a little pale, she said, as she told me the story, years after: " And what do you hear from home, Mrs. Graff? "

And that splendid creature looked through him. Jove! how she must have looked through him!

" Home!! Mr. Nolan!!! I thought you were the man who never wanted to hear of home again! " And she walked directly up the deck to her husband and left poor Nolan alone, as he always was. He did not dance again.

I cannot give any history of him in order — nobody can now; and, indeed, I am not trying to. These are the traditions, which I sort out, as I believe them, from the myths which have been told about this man for forty years. The lies that have been told about him are legion. The fellows used to say he was the " Iron Mask "; and poor George Pons went to his grave in the belief that this was the author of " Junius," who was being punished for his celebrated libel on Thomas Jefferson. Pons was not very strong in the historical line. A happier story than either of these I have told is of the War. That came along soon after. I have heard this affair told in three or four ways — and, indeed, it may have happened more than once. But which ship it was on I cannot tell. However, in one, at least, of the great frigate duels with the English, in which the navy was really baptized, it happened that a round-shot from the enemy entered one of our ports square, and took right down the officer of the gun himself, and almost every man of the gun's crew. Now you may say what you choose about courage, but that is not a nice thing to see. But, as the men who were not killed picked themselves up, and as they and the surgeon's people were carrying off the bodies, there appeared Nolan, in his shirt-sleeves, with the rammer in his hand, and, just as if he had been the officer, told them off with authority — who should go to the cockpit with the wounded men, who should stay with him — perfectly cheery, and with that way which makes men feel sure all is right and is going to be right. And he finished loading the gun with his own hands, aimed it, and bade the men fire. And there he stayed, captain of that gun, keeping those fellows in spirits, till the enemy struck — sitting on the carriage while the gun was cooling, though he was exposed all the time; showing them easier ways to handle heavy shot; making the raw hands laugh at their own blunders; and when the gun cooled again, getting it loaded and fired twice as often as any other gun on the ship. The captain walked forward by way of encouraging the men, and Nolan touched his hat and said:

"I am showing them how we do this in the artillery, sir."

And this is the part of the story where all legends agree; that the Commodore said, "I see you do, and I thank you, sir; and I shall never forget this day, sir, and you never shall, sir."

And after the whole thing was over, and he had the Englishman's sword, in the midst of the state and ceremony of the quarter-deck, he said, "Where is Mr. Nolan? Ask Mr. Nolan to come here."

And when Nolan came, the captain said, "Mr. Nolan, we are all very grateful to you today; you are one of us today; you will be named in the dispatches."

And then the old man took off his own sword of ceremony, and gave it to Nolan, and made him put it on. The man told me this who saw it. Nolan cried like a baby, and well he might. He had not worn a sword since that infernal day at Fort Adams. But always afterwards, on occasions of ceremony, he wore that quaint old French sword of the Commodore's.

The captain did mention him in the dispatches. It was always said he asked that he might be pardoned. He wrote a special letter to the Secretary of War. But nothing ever came of it. As I said, that was about the time when they began to ignore the whole transaction at Washington, and when Nolan's imprisonment began to carry itself on because there was nobody to stop it without any new orders from home.

I have heard it said that he was with Porter when he took possession of the Nukahiwa Islands. Not this Porter, you know, but old Porter, his father, Essex Porter — that is, the old Essex Porter, not this Essex. As an artillery officer, who had seen service in the West, Nolan knew more about fortifications, embrasures, ravelins, stockades, and all that, than any of them did; and he worked with a right good will in fixing that battery all right. I have always thought it was a pity Porter did not leave him in command there with Gamble. That would have settled all the question about his punishment. We should have kept the islands, and at this moment we should have one station in the Pacific Ocean. Our French friends, too, when they wanted this little watering place, would have found it was preoccupied. But Madison and the Virginians, of course, flung all that away.

All that was near fifty years ago. If Nolan was thirty then, he must have been near eighty when he died. He looked sixty when he was forty. But he never seemed to me to change a hair afterwards. As I imagine his life, from what I have seen and heard of it, he must have been in every sea, and yet almost never on land. He must have known, in a formal way, more officers in our service than any man living knows. He told me once, with a grave smile, that no man in the world lived so methodical a life as he. " You know the boys say I am the Iron Mask, and you know how busy he was." He said it did not do for anyone to try to read all the time, more than to do anything else all the time; but that he read just five hours a day. " Then," he said, " I keep up my notebooks, writing in them at such and such hours from what I have been reading; and I include in these my scrapbooks." These were very curious indeed. He had six or eight, of different subjects. There was one of History, one of Natural Science, one which he called " Odds and Ends." But they were not merely books of extracts from newspapers. They had bits of plants and ribbons, shells tied on, and carved scraps of bone and wood, which he had taught the men to cut for him, and they were beautifully illustrated. He drew admirably. He had some of the funniest drawings there, and some of the most pathetic, that I have ever seen in my life. I wonder who will have Nolan's scrapbooks.

Well, he said his reading and his notes were his profession, and that they took five hours and two hours respectively of each day. " Then," said he, " every man should have a diversion as well as a profession. My Natural History is my diversion." That took two hours a day more. The men used to bring him birds and fish, but on a long cruise he had to satisfy himself with centipedes and cockroaches and such small game. He was the only naturalist I ever met who knew anything about the habits of the housefly and the mosquito. All those people can tell you whether they are *Lepidoptera* or *Steptopotera;* but as for telling how you can get rid of them, or how they get away from you when you strike them — why, Linnæus knew as little of that as John Foy the idiot did. These nine hours made Nolan's regular daily " occupation." The rest of the time he talked or walked. Till he grew very old, he went aloft a great deal. He always kept up his exercise; and I never heard that he was ill. If any other man was ill, he was the kindest nurse in the world; and he knew more than half the surgeons do. Then if anybody was sick or died, or if the captain wanted him to on any other occasion, he was always ready to read prayers. I have said that he read beautifully.

My own acquaintance with Philip Nolan began six or eight years after the War, on my first voyage after I was appointed a midshipman. It was in the first days after our slave-trade treaty, while the Reigning House, which was still the House of Virginia, had still a sort of sentimentalism about the suppression of the horrors of the Middle Passage, and something was sometimes done that way.

We were in the South Atlantic on that business. From the time I joined, I believe I thought Nolan was a sort of lay chaplain — a chaplain with a blue coat. I never asked about him. Everything in the ship was strange to me. I knew it was green to ask questions, and I suppose I thought there was a " Plain Buttons " on every ship. We had him to dine in our mess once a week, and the caution was given that on that day nothing was to be said about home. But if they had told us not to say anything about the planet Mars or the Book of Deuteronomy, I should not have asked why; there were a great many things which seemed to me to have as little reason. I first came to understand anything about " The Man Without a Country " one day when he overhauled a dirty little schooner which had slaves on board. An officer was sent to take charge of her, and after a few minutes he sent back his boat to ask that someone might be sent him who could speak Portuguese. We were all looking over the rail when the message came, and we all wished we could interpret, when the captain asked who spoke Portuguese. But none of the officers did; and just as the captain was sending forward to ask if any of the people could, Nolan stepped out and said he should be glad to interpret, if the captain wished, as he understood the language. The captain thanked him, fitted out another boat with him, and in this boat it was my luck to go.

When we got there, it was such a scene as you seldom see, and never want to. Nastiness beyond account, and chaos run loose in the midst of the nastiness. There were not a great many of the Negroes; but by way of making what there were understand that they were free, Vaughan had had their handcuffs knocked off, and for convenience' sake was putting them upon the rascals of the schooner's crew. The Negroes were, most of them, out of the hold and swarming all round the dirty deck, with a central throng surrounding Vaughan and addressing him in every dialect and *patois* of a dialect, from the Zulu click up to the Parisian of Beledeljereed.

As we came on deck, Vaughan looked down from a hogshead, on which he had mounted in desperation, and said: " For God's love, is there anybody who can make these wretches understand something? The men gave them rum, and that did not quiet them. I knocked that big fellow down twice, and that did not soothe him. And then I talked Choctaw to all of them together; and I'll be hanged if they understood that as well as they understood the English."

Nolan said he could speak Portuguese, and one or two fine-looking Kroomen were dragged out, who, as it had been found already, had worked for the Portuguese on the coast at Fernando Po.

" Tell them they are free," said Vaughan; " and tell them that these rascals are to be hanged as soon as we can get rope enough."

Nolan " put that into Spanish " — that is, he explained it in such Portuguese as the Kroomen could understand, and they in turn to such of the Negroes as could understand them. Then there was such a yell of delight, clinching of fists, leaping and dancing, kissing of Nolan's feet, and a general rush made to the hogshead by way of spontaneous worship of Vaughan as the *deus ex machina* of the occasion.

"Tell them," said Vaughan, well pleased, "that I will take them all to Cape Palmas."

This did not answer so well. Cape Palmas was practically as far from the homes of most of them as New Orleans or Rio Janeiro was; that is, they would be eternally separated from home there. And their interpreters, as we could understand, instantly said, "*Ah, non Palmas,*" and began to propose infinite other expedients in most voluble language. Vaughan was rather disappointed at this result of his liberality, and asked Nolan eagerly what they said. The drops stood on poor Nolan's white forehead as he hushed the men down and said:

"He says, 'Not Palmas.' He says, 'Take us home, take us to our own country, take us to our own house, take us to our own pickaninnies and our own women.' He says he has an old father and mother who will die if they do not see him. And this one says he left his people all sick, and paddled down to Fernando to beg the white doctor to come and help them, and that these devils caught him in the bay just in sight of home, and that he has never seen anybody from home since then. And this one says," choked out Nolan, "that he has not heard a word from his home in six months, while he has been locked up in an infernal barracoon."

Vaughan always said he grew gray himself while Nolan struggled through this interpretation. I, who did not understand anything of the passion involved in it, saw that the very elements were melting with fervent heat, and that something was to pay somewhere. Even the Negroes themselves stopped howling as they saw Nolan's agony and Vaughan's almost equal agony of sympathy. As quick as he could get words, he said:

"Tell them yes, yes, yes; tell them they shall go to the Mountains of the Moon if they will. If I sail the schooner through the Great White Desert, they shall go home!"

And after some fashion Nolan said so. And then they all fell to kissing him again, and wanted to rub his nose with theirs.

But he could not stand it long; and getting Vaughan to say he might go back, he beckoned me down into our boat. As we lay back in the stern-sheets and the men gave way, he said to me: "Youngster, let that show you what it is to be without a family, without a home, and without a country. And if you are ever tempted to say a word or to do a thing that shall put a bar between you and your family, your home, and your country, pray God in His mercy to take you that instant home to His own heaven. Stick by your family, boy; forget you have a self, while you do everything for them. Think of your home, boy; write and send, and talk about it. Let it be nearer and nearer to your thought, the farther you have to travel from it; and rush back to it, when you are free, as that poor black slave is doing now. And for your country, boy," and the words rattled in his throat, "and for that flag," and he pointed to the ship, "never dream a dream but of serving her as she bids you, though the service carry you through a thousand hells. No matter what happens to you, no matter who flatters you or who abuses you, never look at another flag, never let a night pass but you pray God to bless that flag. Remember, boy, that behind all these men you have to do with, behind officers, and government, and people even, there is the Country Herself, your country, and that you belong to her as you belong to your own mother. Stand by her, boy, as you would stand by your mother, if those devils there had got hold of her today! "

I was frightened to death by his calm, hard passion; but I blundered out that I would, by all that was holy, and that I had never thought of doing anything else. He hardly seemed to hear me; but he did, almost in a whisper, say: "Oh, if anybody had said so to me when I was of your age! "

I think it was this half-confidence of his, which I never abused, for I never told this story till now, which afterward made us great friends. He was very kind to me. Often he sat up, or even got up, at night to walk the deck with me, when it was my watch. He explained to me a great deal of my mathematics, and I owe to him my taste for mathematics. He lent me books, and helped me about my reading. He never alluded so directly to his story again; but from one and another officer I have learned, in thirty years, what I am telling. When we parted from him in St. Thomas harbor, at the end of our cruise, I was more sorry than I can tell. I was very glad to meet him again in 1830; and later in life, when I thought I had some influence in Washington, I moved heaven and earth to have him discharged. But it was like getting a ghost out of prison. They pretended there was no such man, and never was such a man. They will say so at the Department now! Perhaps they do not know. It will not be the first thing in the service of which the Department appears to know nothing!

There is a story that Nolan met Burr once on one of our vessels, when a party of Americans came on board in the Mediterranean. But this I believe to be a lie; or, rather, it is a myth, *ben trovato,* involving a tremendous blowing-up with which he sunk Burr — asking him how he liked to be " without a country." But it is clear, from Burr's life, that nothing of the sort could have happened; and I mention this only as an illustration of the stories which get a-going where there is the least mystery at bottom.

So poor Philip Nolan had his wish fulfilled. I know but one fate more dreadful: it is the fate reserved for those men who shall have one day to exile themselves from their country because they have attempted her ruin, and shall have at the same time to see the prosperity and honor to which she rises when she has rid herself of them and their iniquities. The wish of poor Nolan, as we all learned to call him, not because his punishment was too great, but because his repentance was so clear, was precisely the wish of every Bragg and Beauregard who broke a soldier's oath two years ago, and of every Maury and Barron who broke a sailor's. I do not know how often they have repented. I do know that they have done all that in them lay that they might have no country — that all the honors, associations, memories, and hopes which belong to " country " might be broken up into little shreds and distributed to the winds. I know, too, that their punishment, as they vegetate through what is left of life to them in wretched Boulognes and Leicester Squares, where they are destined to upbraid each other till they die, will have all the agony of Nolan's, with the added pang that everyone who sees them will see them to despise and to execrate them. They will have their wish, like him.

For him, poor fellow, he repented of his folly, and then, like a man, submitted to the fate he had asked for. He never intentionally added to the difficulty or delicacy of the charge of those who had him in hold. Accidents would happen; but they never happened from his fault. Lieutenant Truxton told me that, when Texas was annexed, there was a careful discussion among the officers whether they should get hold of Nolan's handsome set of maps and cut Texas out of it — from the map of the world and the map of Mexico. The United States had been cut out when the atlas was bought for him. But it was voted, rightly enough, that to do this would be virtually to reveal to him what had happened, or, as Harry Cole said, to make him think Old Burr had succeeded. So it was from no fault of Nolan's that a great botch happened at my own table when, for a short time, I was in command of the *George Washington* corvette, on the South American station. We were lying in the La Plata, and some of the officers, who had been on shore and had just joined again, were entertaining us with accounts of their misadventures in riding the half-wild horses of Buenos Aires. Nolan was at table and was in an unusually bright and talkative mood. Some story of a tumble reminded him of an adventure of his own when he was catching wild horses in Texas with his brother Stephen, at a time when he must have been quite a boy. He told the story with a good deal of spirit — so much so, that the silence which often follows a good story hung over the table for an instant, to be broken by Nolan himself. For he asked, perfectly unconsciously:

" Pray, what has become of Texas? After the Mexicans got their independence, I thought that province of Texas would come forward very fast. It is really one of the finest regions on earth; it is the Italy of this continent. But I have not seen or heard a word of Texas for near twenty years."

There were two Texan officers at the table. The reason he had never heard of Texas was that Texas and her affairs had been painfully cut out of his newspapers since Austin began his settlements; so that, while he read of Honduras and Tamaulipas, and, till quite lately, of California, this virgin province, in which his brother had traveled so far and, I believe, had died, had ceased to be to him. Waters and Williams, the two Texas men, looked grimly at each other and tried not to laugh. Edward Morris had his attention attracted by the third link in the chain of the captain's chandelier. Watrous was seized with a convulsion of sneezing. Nolan himself saw that something was to pay, he did not know what. And I, as master of the feast, had to say: " Texas is out of the map, Mr. Nolan. Have you seen Captain Back's curious account of Sir Thomas Roe's Welcome? "

After that cruise I never saw Nolan again. I wrote to him at least twice a year, for in that voyage we became even confidentially intimate; but he never wrote to me. The other men tell me that in those fifteen years he aged very fast, as well he might indeed, but that he was still the same gentle, uncomplaining, silent sufferer that he ever was, bearing as best he could his self-appointed punishment — rather less social, perhaps, with new men whom he did not know, but more anxious, apparently, than ever to serve and befriend and teach the boys, some of whom fairly seemed to worship him. And now it seems that the dear old fellow is dead. He has found a home at last, and a country.

Since writing this, and while considering whether or no I would print it, as a warning to the young Nolans and Vallandighams and Tatnals of today of what it is to throw away a country, I have received from Danforth, who is on board the *Levant*, a letter which gives an account of Nolan's last hours. It removes all my doubts about telling this story.

To understand the first words of the letter, the non-professional reader should remember that after 1817 the position of every officer who had Nolan in charge was one of the greatest delicacy. The government had failed to renew the order of 1807 regarding him. What was a man to do? Should he let him go? What, then, if he were called to account by the Department for violating the order of 1807? Should he keep him? What, then, if Nolan should be liberated some day, and should bring an action for false imprisonment or kidnapping against every man who had had him in charge? I urged and pressed this upon Southard, and I have reason to think that other officers did the same thing. But the Secretary always said, as they so often do at Washington, that there were no special orders to give, and that we must act on our own judgment. That means, " If you succeed, you will be sustained; if you fail, you will be disavowed." Well, as Danforth says, all that is over now, though I do not know but I expose myself to a criminal prosecution on the evidence of the very revelation I am making.

Here is the letter:

LEVANT, 2° 2′ S. @ 131° W.

DEAR FRED, — I try to find heart and life to tell you that it is all over with dear old Nolan. I have been with him on this voyage more than I ever was, and I can understand wholly now the way in which you used to speak of the dear old fellow. I could see that he was not strong, but I had no idea the end was so near. The doctor has been watching him very carefully, and yesterday morning came to me and told me that Nolan was not so well, and had not left his stateroom — a thing I never remember before. He had let the doctor come and see him as he lay there — the first time the doctor had been in the stateroom — and he said he should like to see me. O dear! do you remember the mysteries we boys used to invent about his room, in the old *Intrepid* days? Well, I went in, and there, to be sure, the poor fellow lay in his berth, smiling pleasantly as he gave me his hand, but looking very frail. I could not help a glance round, which showed me what a little shrine he had made of the box he was lying in. The stars and stripes were triced up above and around a picture of Washington, and he had painted a majestic eagle, with lightnings blazing from his beak and his foot just clasping the whole globe, which his wings overshadowed. The dear old boy saw my glance, and said, with a sad smile, " Here, you see, I have a country! " And then he pointed to the foot of his bed, where I had not seen before a great map of the United States, as he had drawn it from memory, and which he had there to look upon as he lay. Quaint, queer old names were on it, in large letters: "Indiana Territory," "Mississippi Territory," and "Louisiana Territory," as I suppose our fathers learned such things: but the old fellow had patched in Texas, too; he had carried his western boundary all the way to the Pacific, but on that shore he had defined nothing.

"O Danforth," he said, "I know I am dying. I cannot get home. Surely you will tell me something now? Stop! stop! Do not speak till I say what I am sure you know: that there is not in this ship, that there is not in America — God bless her! — a more loyal man than I. There cannot be a man who loves the old flag as I do, or prays for it as I do, or hopes for it as I do. There are thirty-four stars in it now, Danforth. I thank God for that, though I do not know what their names are. There has never been one taken away: I thank God for that. I know by that, that there has never been any successful Burr. O Danforth, Danforth," he sighed out, "how like a wretched night's dream a boy's idea of personal fame or of separate sovereignty seems, when one looks back on it after such a life as mine! But tell me — tell me something — tell me everything, Danforth, before I die!"

Ingham, I swear to you that I felt like a monster that I had not told him everything before. Danger or no danger, delicacy or no delicacy, who was I, that I should have been acting the tyrant all this time over this dear, sainted old man, who had years ago expiated, in his whole manhood's life, the madness of a boy's treason? "Mr. Nolan," said I, "I will tell you everything you ask about. Only, where shall I begin?"

O the blessed smile that crept over his white face! And he pressed my hand and said, "God bless you!" "Tell me their names," he said, and he pointed to the stars on the flag. "The last I know is Ohio. My father lived in Kentucky. But I have guessed Michigan and Indiana and Mississippi — that was where Fort Adams is; they make twenty. But where are your other fourteen? You have not cut up any of the old ones, I hope?"

Well, that was not a bad text, and I told him the names in as good order as I could, and he bade me take down his beautiful map and draw them in as I best could with my pencil. He was wild with delight about Texas, told me how his brother died there: he had marked a gold cross where he supposed his brother's grave was; and he had guessed at Texas. Then he was delighted as he saw California and Oregon; that, he said, he had suspected, partly because he had never been permitted to land on that shore, though the ships were there so much. "And the men," said he, laughing, "brought off a good deal besides furs." Then he went back — heavens, how far! — to ask about the *Chesapeake,* and what was done to Barron for surrendering her to the *Leopard,* and whether Burr ever tried again — and he ground his teeth with the only passion he showed. But in a moment that was over, and he said, "God forgive me, for I am sure I forgive him." Then he asked about the old war — told me the true story of his serving the gun the day we took the *Java;* asked about dear old David Porter, as he called him. Then he settled down more quietly, and very happily, to hear me tell in an hour the history of fifty years.

How I wished it had been somebody who knew something! But I did as well as I could. I told him of the English war. I told him about Fulton and the steamboat beginning. I told him about old Scott, and Jackson; told him all I could think about the Mississippi, and New Orleans, and Texas, and his own old Kentucky. And do you think, he asked who was in command of the "Legion of the West." I told him it was a very gallant officer named Grant, and that, by our last news, he was about to establish his headquarters at Vicksburg. Then, "Where was Vicksburg?" I worked that out on the map; it was about a hundred miles, more or less, above his old Fort Adams; and I thought Fort Adams must be a ruin now. "It must be at old Vick's plantation," said he; "well, that is a change!"

I tell you, Ingham, it was a hard thing to condense the history of half a century into that talk with a sick man. And I do not now know what I told him — of emigration and the means of it; of steamboats, and railroads, and telegraphs; of inventions, and books, and literature; of the colleges, and West Point, and the Naval School — but with the queerest interruptions that ever you heard. You see, it was Robinson Crusoe asking all the accumulated questions of fifty-six years!

I remember he asked, all of a sudden, who was President now; and when I told him, he asked if old Abe was General Benjamin Lincoln's son. He said he met old General Lincoln, when he was quite a boy himself, at some Indian treaty. I said no, that old Abe was a Kentuckian like himself, but I could not tell him of what family; he had worked up from the ranks. "Good for him!" cried Nolan. "I am glad of that. As I have brooded and wondered, I have thought our danger was in keeping up those regular successions in the first families." Then I got talking about my visit to Washington. I told him of meeting the Oregon Congressman, Harding; I told him about the Smithsonian and the Exploring Expedition; I told him about the Capitol, and the statues for the pediment, and Crawford's "Liberty," and Greenough's "Washington." Ingham, I told him everything I could think of that would show the grandeur of his country and its prosperity; but I could not make up my mouth to tell him a word about this infernal Rebellion!

And he drank it in, and enjoyed it as I cannot tell you. He grew more and more silent; yet I never thought he was tired or faint. I gave him a glass of water, but he just wet his lips and told me not to go away. Then he asked me to bring the Presbyterian *Book of Public Prayer*, which lay there, and said, with a smile, that it would open at the right place — and so it did. There was his double red mark down the page; and I knelt down and read, and he repeated with me, "For ourselves and our country, O gracious God, we thank Thee, that, notwithstanding our manifold transgressions of Thy holy laws, Thou hast continued to us Thy marvelous kindness" — and so to the end of that thanksgiving. Then he turned to the end of the same book, and I read the words more familiar to me: "Most heartily we beseech Thee with Thy favor to behold and bless Thy servant, the President of the United States, and all others in authority" — and the rest of the Episcopal collect. "Danforth," said he, "I have repeated those prayers night and morning, it is now fifty-five years." And then he said he would go to sleep. He bent me down over him and kissed me; and he said, "Look in my Bible, Danforth, when I am gone." And I went away.

But I had no thought it was the end. I thought he was tired and would sleep. I knew he was happy and I wanted him to be alone.

But in an hour, when the doctor went in gently, he found Nolan had breathed his life away with a smile. He had something pressed close to his lips. It was his father's badge of the Order of Cincinnati.

We looked in his Bible, and there was a slip of paper, at the place where he had marked the text: "They desire a country, even a heavenly: wherefore God is not ashamed to be called their God: for he hath prepared for them a city."

On this slip of paper he had written: Bury me in the sea; it has been my home, and I love it. But will not someone set up a stone for my memory at Fort Adams or at Orleans, that my disgrace may not be more than I ought to bear? Say on it:

In Memory of

PHILIP NOLAN

Lieutenant in the Army of the United States

He loved his country as no other man has loved her;
but no man deserved less at her hands.

Bret Harte

Tennessee's Partner

I DO not think that we ever knew his real name. Our ignorance of it certainly never gave us any social inconvenience, for at Sandy Bar in 1854 most men were christened anew. Sometimes these appellatives were derived from some distinctiveness of dress, as in the case of " Dungaree Jack "; or from some peculiarity of habit, as shown in " Saleratus Bill," so called from an undue proportion of that chemical in his daily bread; or from some unlucky slip, as exhibited in " The Iron Pirate," a mild, inoffensive man, who earned that baleful title by his unfortunate mispronunciation of the term " iron pyrites." Perhaps this may have been the beginning of a rude heraldry; but I am constrained to think that it was because a man's real name in that day rested solely upon his own unsupported statement. " Call yourself Clifford, do you? " said Boston, addressing a timid newcomer with infinite scorn; " hell is full of such Cliffords! " He then introduced the unfortunate man, whose name happened to be really Clifford, as " Jaybird Charley " — an unhallowed inspiration of the moment that clung to him ever after.

But to return to Tennessee's Partner, whom we never knew by any other than this relative title. That he had ever existed as a separate and distinct individuality we only learned later. It seems that in 1853 he left Poker Flat to go to San Francisco, ostensibly to procure a wife. He never got any farther than Stockton. At that place he was attracted by a young person who waited upon the table at the hotel where he took his meals. One morning he said something to her which caused her to smile not unkindly, to somewhat coquettishly break a plate of toast over his upturned, serious, simple face, and to retreat to the kitchen. He followed her, and emerged a few moments later, covered with more toast and victory. That day week they were married by a justice of the peace, and returned to Poker Flat. I am aware that something more might be made of this episode, but I prefer to tell it as it was current at Sandy Bar —

From *The Luck of Roaring Camp,* 1870.

in the gulches and barrooms — where all sentiment was modified by a strong sense of humor.

Of their married felicity but little is known, perhaps for the reason that Tennessee, then living with his partner, one day took occasion to say something to the bride on his own account, at which, it is said, she smiled not unkindly and chastely retreated — this time as far as Marysville, where Tennessee followed her, and where they went to housekeeping without the aid of a justice of the peace. Tennessee's Partner took the loss of his wife simply and seriously, as was his fashion. But to everybody's surprise, when Tennessee one day returned from Marysville, without his partner's wife — she having smiled and retreated with somebody else — Tennessee's Partner was the first man to shake his hand and greet him with affection. The boys who had gathered in the cañon to see the shooting were naturally indignant. Their indignation might have found vent in sarcasm but for a certain look in Tennessee's Partner's eye that indicated a lack of humorous appreciation. In fact, he was a grave man, with a steady application to practical detail which was unpleasant in a difficulty.

Meanwhile a popular feeling against Tennessee had grown up on the Bar. He was known to be a gambler; he was suspected to be a thief. In these suspicions Tennessee's Partner was equally compromised; his continued intimacy with Tennessee after the affair above quoted could only be accounted for on the hypothesis of a copartnership of crime. At last Tennessee's guilt became flagrant. One day he overtook a stranger on his way to Red Dog. The stranger afterward related that Tennessee beguiled the time with interesting anecdote and reminiscence, but illogically concluded the interview in the following words: " And now, young man, I'll trouble you for your knife, your pistols, and your money. You see your weppings might get you into trouble at Red Dog, and your money's a temptation to the evilly disposed. I think you said your address was San Francisco. I shall endeavor to call." It may be stated here that Tennessee had a fine flow of humor, which no business preoccupation could wholly subdue.

This exploit was his last. Red Dog and Sandy Bar made common cause against the highwayman. Tennessee was hunted in very much the same fashion as his prototype, the grizzly. As the toils closed around him, he made a desperate dash through the Bar, emptying his revolver at the crowd before the Arcade Saloon, and so on up Grizzly Cañon; but at its farther extremity he was stopped by a small man on a gray horse. The men looked at each other a moment in silence. Both were fearless, both self-possessed and independent, and both types of a civilization that in the seventeenth century would have been called heroic, but in the nineteenth simply " reckless."

" What have you got there? — I call," said Tennessee quietly.

" Two bowers and an ace," said the stranger as quietly, showing two revolvers and a bowie-knife.

" That takes me," returned Tennessee; and, with this gambler's epigram, he threw away his useless pistol and rode back with his captor.

It was a warm night. The cool breeze which usually sprang up with the going down of the sun behind the chaparral-crested mountain was that evening withheld from Sandy Bar. The little cañon was stifling with heated resinous odors, and the decaying driftwood on the Bar sent forth faint sickening exhalations. The feverishness of day and its fierce passions still filled the camp. Lights moved restlessly along the bank of the river, striking no answering reflection from its tawny current. Against the blackness of the pines the windows of the old loft above the express office stood out staringly bright; and through their curtainless panes the loungers below could see the forms of those who were even then deciding the fate of Tennessee. And above all this, etched on the dark firmament, rose the Sierra, remote and passionless, crowned with remoter passionless stars.

The trial of Tennessee was conducted as fairly as was consistent with a judge and jury who felt themselves to some extent obliged to justify, in their verdict, the previous irregularities of arrest and indictment. The law of Sandy Bar was implacable, but not vengeful. The excitement and personal feeling of the chase were over; with Tennessee safe in their hands, they were ready to listen patiently to any defense, which they were already satisfied was insufficient. There being no doubt in their own minds, they were willing to give the prisoner the benefit of any that might exist. Secure in the hypothesis that he ought to be hanged on general principles, they indulged him with more latitude of defense than his reckless hardihood seemed to ask. The Judge appeared to be more anxious than the prisoner, who, otherwise unconcerned, evidently took a grim pleasure in the responsibility he had created. " I don't take any hand in this yer game," had been his invariable but good-humored reply to all questions. The Judge — who was also his captor — for a moment vaguely regretted that he had not shot him " on sight " that morning, but presently dismissed this human weakness as unworthy of the judicial mind. Nevertheless, when there was a tap at the door, and it was said that Tennessee's Partner was there on behalf of the prisoner, he was admitted at once without question. Perhaps the younger members of the jury, to whom the proceedings were becoming irksomely thoughtful, hailed him as a relief.

For he was not, certainly, an imposing figure. Short and stout, with a square face, sunburned into a preternatural redness, clad in a loose duck " jumper " and trousers streaked and splashed with red soil, his aspect under any circumstances would have been quaint, and was now even ridiculous. As he stooped to deposit at his feet a heavy carpetbag he was carrying, it became obvious, from partially developed legends and inscriptions, that the material with which his trousers had been patched had been originally intended for a less ambitious covering. Yet he advanced with great gravity, and after shaking the hand of each person in the room with labored cordiality, he wiped his serious perplexed face on a red bandanna handkerchief a shade lighter than his complexion, laid his powerful hand upon the table to steady himself, and thus addressed the Judge:

" I was passin' by," he began, by way of apology, " and I thought I'd just step in and see how things was gittin' on with Tennessee thar — my pardner. It's a hot night. I disremember any sich weather before on the Bar."

He paused a moment, but nobody volunteering any other meteorological recollection, he again had recourse to his pocket handkerchief, and for some moments mopped his face diligently.

"Have you anything to say on behalf of the prisoner?" said the Judge finally.

"Thet's it," said Tennessee's Partner, in a tone of relief. "I come yar as Tennessee's pardner — knowing him nigh on four year, off and on, wet and dry, in luck and out o' luck. His ways ain't aller my ways, but thar ain't any pints in that young man, thar ain't any liveliness as he's been up to, as I don't know. And you sez to me, sez you — confidential-like, and between man and man — sez you, 'Do you know anything in his behalf?' and I sez to you, sez I — confidential-like, as between man and man — 'What should a man know of his pardner?'"

"Is this all you have to say?" asked the Judge impatiently, feeling, perhaps, that a dangerous sympathy of humor was beginning to humanize the court.

"Thet's so," continued Tennessee's Partner. "It ain't for me to say anything agin him. And now, what's the case? Here's Tennessee wants money, wants it bad, and doesn't like to ask it of his old pardner. Well, what does Tennessee do? He lays for a stranger, and he fetches that stranger; and you lays for *him,* and you fetches *him;* and the honors is easy. And I put it to you, bein' a fa'r-minded man, and to you, gentlemen all, as fa'r-minded men, ef this isn't so."

"Prisoner," said the Judge, interrupting, "have you any questions to ask this man?"

"No! No!" continued Tennessee's Partner hastily. "I play this yer hand alone. To come down to the bedrock, it's just this: Tennessee, thar, has played it pretty rough and expensive-like on a stranger, and on this yer camp. And now, what's the fair thing? Some would say more, some would say less. Here's seventeen hundred dollars in coarse gold and a watch — it's about all my pile — and call it square!" And before a hand could be raised to prevent him, he had emptied the contents of the carpetbag upon the table.

For a moment his life was in jeopardy. One or two men sprang to their feet, several hands groped for hidden weapons, and a suggestion to "throw him from the window" was only overridden by a gesture from the Judge. Tennessee laughed. And apparently oblivious of the excitement, Tennessee's Partner improved the opportunity to mop his face again with his handkerchief.

When order was restored and the man was made to understand, by the use of forcible figures and rhetoric, that Tennessee's offense could not be condoned by money, his face took a more serious and sanguinary hue, and those who were nearest to him noticed that his rough hand trembled slightly on the table. He hesitated a moment as he slowly returned the gold to the carpetbag, as if he had not yet entirely caught the elevated sense of justice which swayed the tribunal, and was perplexed with the belief that he had not offered enough. Then he turned to the Judge, and saying, "This yer is a lone hand, played alone, and without my pardner," he bowed to the jury and was about to withdraw, when the Judge called him back:

"If you have anything to say to Tennessee, you had better say it now."

For the first time that evening the eyes of the prisoner and his strange advocate met. Tennessee smiled, showed his white teeth, and saying, " Euchred, old man! " held out his hand. Tennessee's Partner took it in his own, and saying, " I just dropped in as I was passin' to see how things was gettin' on," let the hand passively fall, and adding that " it was a warm night," again mopped his face with his handkerchief, and without another word withdrew.

The two men never again met each other alive. For the unparalleled insult of a bribe offered to Judge Lynch — who, whether bigoted, weak, or narrow, was at least incorruptible — firmly fixed in the mind of that mythical personage any wavering determination of Tennessee's fate; and at the break of day he was marched, closely guarded, to meet it at the top of Marley's Hill.

How he met it, how cool he was, how he refused to say anything, how perfect were the arrangements of the committee, were all duly reported, with the addition of a warning moral and example to all future evildoers in the *Red Dog Clarion*, by its editor, who was present, and to whose vigorous English I cheerfully refer the reader. But the beauty of that midsummer morning, the blessed amity of earth and air and sky, the awakened life of the free woods and hills, the joyous renewal and promise of nature, and above all, the infinite serenity that thrilled through each, was not reported, as not being a part of the social lesson. And yet, when the weak and foolish deed was done, and a life, with its possibilities and responsibilities, had passed out of the misshapen thing that dangled between earth and sky, the birds sang, the flowers bloomed, the sun shone, as cheerily as before; and possibly the *Red Dog Clarion* was right.

Tennessee's Partner was not in the group that surrounded the ominous tree. But as they turned to disperse, attention was drawn to the singular appearance of a motionless donkey-cart halted at the side of the road. As they approached, they at once recognized the venerable " Jenny " and the two-wheeled cart as the property of Tennessee's Partner, used by him in carrying dirt from his claim; and a few paces distant the owner of the equipage himself, sitting under a buckeye tree, wiping the perspiration from his glowing face. In answer to an inquiry, he said he had come for the body of the " diseased," " if it was all the same to the committee." He didn't wish to " hurry anything "; he could " wait." He was not working that day; and when the gentlemen were done with the " diseased," he would take him. " Ef thar is any present," he added, in his simple, serious way, " as would care to jine in the fun'l, they kin come." Perhaps it was from a sense of humor, which I have already intimated was a feature of Sandy Bar — perhaps it was from something even better than that — but two thirds of the loungers accepted the invitation at once.

It was noon when the body of Tennessee was delivered into the hands of his partner. As the cart drew up to the fatal tree, we noticed that it contained a rough oblong box — apparently made from a section of sluicing and half filled with bark and the tassels of pine. The cart was further decorated with slips of willow and made fragrant with buckeye blossoms. When the body was deposited in the box, Tennessee's Partner drew over it a piece of tarred canvas, and gravely mounting the narrow seat in front, with his feet upon the shafts, urged the little donkey forward. The equipage moved slowly on, at that decorous pace which was habitual with Jenny even under less solemn circumstances. The men

— half curiously, half jestingly, but all good-humoredly — strolled along beside the cart, some in advance, some a little in the rear of the homely catafalque. But whether from the narrowing of the road or some present sense of decorum, as the cart passed on, the company fell to the rear in couples, keeping step, and otherwise assumed the external show of a formal procession. Jack Folinsbee, who had at the outset played a funeral march in dumb show upon an imaginary trombone, desisted from a lack of sympathy and appreciation — not having, perhaps, your true humorist's capacity to be content with the enjoyment of his own fun.

The way led through Grizzly Cañon, by this time clothed in funereal drapery and shadows. The redwoods, burying their moccasined feet in the red soil, stood in Indian file along the track, trailing an uncouth benediction from their bending boughs upon the passing bier. A hare, surprised into helpless in-activity, sat upright and pulsating in the ferns by the roadside as the cortège went by. Squirrels hastened to gain a secure outlook from higher boughs; and the bluejays, spreading their wings, fluttered before them like outriders, until the outskirts of Sandy Bar were reached, and the solitary cabin of Tennessee's Partner.

Viewed under more favorable circumstances, it would not have been a cheer-ful place. The unpicturesque site, the rude and unlovely outlines, the unsavory details, which distinguish the nest-building of the California miner, were all here with the dreariness of decay superadded. A few paces from the cabin there was a rough inclosure, which, in the brief days of Tennessee's Partner's matri-monial felicity, had been used as a garden, but was now overgrown with fern. As we approached it, we were surprised to find that what we had taken for a recent attempt at cultivation was the broken soil about an open grave.

The cart was halted before the inclosure, and rejecting the offers of assistance with the same air of simple self-reliance he had displayed throughout, Ten-nessee's Partner lifted the rough coffin on his back and deposited it unaided within the shallow grave. He then nailed down the board which served as a lid, and mounting the little mound of earth beside it, took off his hat and slowly mopped his face with his handkerchief. This the crowd felt was a pre-liminary to speech, and they disposed themselves variously on stumps and boulders, and sat expectant.

" When a man," began Tennessee's Partner slowly, " has been running free all day, what's the natural thing for him to do? Why, to come home. And if he ain't in a condition to go home, what can his best friend do? Why, bring him home. And here's Tennessee has been running free, and we brings him home from his wandering." He paused and picked up a fragment of quartz, rubbed it thoughtfully on his sleeve, and went on: " It ain't the first time that I've packed him on my back, as you seed me now. It ain't the first time that I brought him to this yer cabin when he couldn't help himself; it ain't the first time that I and Jinny have waited for him on yon hill, and picked him up and so fetched him home, when he couldn't speak and didn't know me. And now that it's the last time, why " — he paused and rubbed the quartz gently on his sleeve

— "you see it's sort of rough on his pardner. And now, gentlemen," he added abruptly, picking up his long-handled shovel, "the fun'l's over; and my thanks, and Tennessee's thanks, to you for your trouble."

Resisting any proffers of assistance, he began to fill in the grave, turning his back upon the crowd, that after a few moments' hesitation gradually withdrew. As they crossed the little ridge that hid Sandy Bar from view, some, looking back, thought they could see Tennessee's Partner, his work done, sitting upon the grave, his shovel between his knees, and his face buried in his red bandanna handkerchief. But it was argued by others that you couldn't tell his face from his handkerchief at that distance, and this point remained undecided.

In the reaction that followed the feverish excitement of that day, Tennessee's Partner was not forgotten. A secret investigation had cleared him of any complicity in Tennessee's guilt, and left only a suspicion of his general sanity. Sandy Bar made a point of calling on him and proffering various uncouth but well-meant kindnesses. But from that day his rude health and great strength seemed visibly to decline; and when the rainy season fairly set in, and the tiny grass-blades were beginning to peep from the rocky mound above Tennessee's grave, he took to his bed.

One night, when the pines beside the cabin were swaying in the storm and trailing their slender fingers over the roof, and the roar and rush of the swollen river were heard below, Tennessee's Partner lifted his head from the pillow, saying, "It is time to go for Tennessee; I must put Jinny in the cart"; and would have risen from his bed but for the restraint of his attendant. Struggling, he still pursued his singular fancy: "There, now, steady, Jinny — steady, old girl. How dark it is! Look out for the ruts — and look out for him, too, old gal. Sometimes, you know, when he's blind drunk, he drops down right in the trail. Keep on straight up to the pine on the top of the hill. Thar! I told you so! Thar he is — coming this way, too — all by himself, sober, and his face a-shining. Tennessee! Pardner!"

And so they met.

Mary Noailles Murfree

The "Harnt" that Walks Chilhowee

JUNE had crossed the borders of Tennessee. Even on the summit of Chilhowee Mountain the apples in Peter Giles's orchard were beginning to redden, and his Indian corn, planted on so steep a declivity that the stalks seemed to have much ado to keep their footing, was crested with tassels and plumed with silk. Among the dense forests, seen by no man's eye, the elder was

From *In the Tennessee Mountains*, 1884.

flying its creamy banners in honor of June's coming, and, heard by no man's ear, the pink and white bells of the azalea rang out melodies of welcome.

"An' it air a toler'ble for'ard season. Yer wheat looks likely; an' yer gyarden truck air thrivin' powerful. Even that cold spell we-uns hed about the full o' the moon in May ain't done sot it back none, it 'pears like ter me. But, 'cording ter my way o' thinkin', ye hev got chickens enough hyar ter eat off every pea-bloom ez soon ez it opens." And Simon Burney glanced with a gardener's disapproval at the numerous fowls, lifting their red combs and tufted topknots here and there among the thick clover under the apple trees.

"Them's Clarsie's chickens — my darter, ye know," drawled Peter Giles, a pale, listless, and lank mountaineer. "An' she hev been gin ter onderstand ez they hev got ter be kep' out'n the gyarden; 'thout," he added indulgently — " 'thout I'm a-plowin', when I lets 'em foller in the furrow ter pick up worms. But law! Clarsie is so spry that she don't ax no better 'n ter be let ter run them chickens off'n the peas."

Then the two men tilted their chairs against the posts of the little porch in front of Peter Giles's log cabin, and puffed their pipes in silence. The panorama spread out before them showed misty and dreamy among the delicate spiral wreaths of smoke. But was that gossamer-like illusion, lying upon the far horizon, the magic of nicotian, or the vague presence of distant heights? As ridge after ridge came down from the sky in ever graduating shades of intenser blue, Peter Giles might have told you that this parallel system of enchantment was only " the mountings ": that here was Foxy, and there was Big Injun, and still beyond was another, which he had " hearn tell ran spang up into Virginny." The sky that bent to clasp this kindred blue was of varying moods. Floods of sunshine submerged Chilhowee in liquid gold and revealed that dainty outline limned upon the northern horizon; but over the Great Smoky mountains clouds had gathered, and a gigantic rainbow bridged the valley.

Peter Giles's listless eyes were fixed upon a bit of red clay road which was visible through a gap in the foliage far below. Even a tiny object, that antlike crawled upon it, could be seen from the summit of Chilhowee. " I reckon that's my brother's wagon an' team," he said as he watched the moving atom pass under the gorgeous triumphal arch. "He 'lowed he war goin' ter the Cross-Roads ter-day."

Simon Burney did not speak for a moment. When he did, his words seemed widely irrelevant. "That's a likely gal o' yourn," he drawled, with an odd constraint in his voice; "a likely gal, that Clarsie."

There was a quick flash of surprise in Peter Giles's dull eyes. He covertly surveyed his guest, with an astounded curiosity rampant in his slow brains. Simon Burney had changed color; an expression of embarrassment lurked in every line of his honest, florid, hard-featured face. An alert imagination might have detected a deprecatory self-consciousness in every gray hair that striped the black beard raggedly fringing his chin.

"Yes," Peter Giles at length replied, " Clarsie air a likely enough gal. But she air mightily sot ter hevin' her own way. An' ef tain't give ter her peaceable-like, she jes' takes it, whether or no."

This statement, made by one presumably fully informed on the subject, might have damped the ardor of many a suitor — for the monstrous truth was dawning on Peter Giles's mind that suitor was the position to which this slow, elderly widower aspired. But Simon Burney, with that odd, all-pervading constraint still prominently apparent, mildly observed, " Waal, ez much ez I hev seen of her goin's-on, it 'pears ter me ez her way air a mighty good way. An' it ain't comical that she likes it."

Urgent justice compelled Peter Giles to make some amends to the absent Clarissa. " That's a fac'," he admitted. " An' Clarsie ain't no hand ter jaw. She don't hev no words. But then," he qualified, truth and consistency alike constraining him, " she air a toler'ble hard-headed gal. That air a true word. Ye mought ez well try ter hender the sun from shining ez ter make that thar Clarsie Giles do what she don't want ter do."

To be sure, Peter Giles had a right to his opinion as to the hardness of his own daughter's head. The expression of his views, however, provoked Simon Burney to wrath; there was something astir within him that in a worthier subject might have been called a chivalric thrill, and it forbade him to hold his peace. He retorted: " Of course ye kin say that, ef so minded; but ennybody ez hev got eyes kin see the change ez hev been made in this hyar place sence that thar gal hev been growed. I ain't a-purtendin' ter know that thar Clarsie ez well ez you-uns knows her hyar at home, but I hev seen enough, an' a deal more'n enough, of her goin's-on, ter know that what she does ain't done fur *herself*. An' ef she will hev her way, it air fur the good of the whole tribe of ye. It 'pears ter me ez thar ain't many gals like that thar Clarsie. An' she air a merciful critter. She air mighty savin' of the feelin's of everything, from the cow an' the mare down ter the dogs, an' pigs, an' chickens; always a-feedin' of 'em jes' ter the time, an' never draggin', an' clawin', an' beatin' of 'em. Why, that thar Clarsie can't put her foot out'n the door, that every dumb beastis on this hyar place ain't a-runnin' ter git nigh her. I hev seen them pigs mos' climb the fence when she shows her face at the door. 'Pears ter me ez that thar Clarsie could tame a bar ef she looked at him a time or two, she's so savin' o' the critter's feelin's! An' thar's that old yaller dog o' yourn," pointing to an ancient cur that was blinking in the sun, " he's older 'n Clarsie, an' no 'count in the worl'. I hev hearn ye say forty times that ye would kill him, 'ceptin' that Clarsie purtected him an' hed sot her heart on his a-livin' along. An' all the home folks, an' everybody that kems hyar to sot an' talk awhile, never misses a chance ter kick that thar old dog, or poke him with a stick, or cuss him. But Clarsie! — I hev seen that gal take the bread an' meat off'n her plate an' give it ter that ol dog, ez 'pears ter me ter be the worst dispositionest dog I ever see, an' no thanks lef' in him. He hain't hed the grace ter wag his tail fur twenty year. That thar Clarsie air surely a merciful critter, an' a mighty spry, likely young gal, besides."

Peter Giles sat in stunned astonishment during this speech, which was delivered in a slow, drawling monotone, with frequent meditative pauses, but nevertheless emphatically. He made no reply, and as they were once more silent there rose suddenly the sound of melody upon the air. It came from beyond that tumultuous stream that raced with the wind down the mountain's side. A great log thrown from bank to bank served as bridge. The song grew momentarily more distinct. Among the leaves there were fugitive glimpses of blue and white, and at last Clarsie appeared, walking lightly along the log, clad in her checked homespun dress, and with a pail upon her head.

She was a tall, lithe girl, with that delicately transparent complexion often seen among the women of these mountains. Her lusterless black hair lay along her forehead without a ripple or wave. There was something in the expression of her large eyes that suggested those of a deer — something free, untamable, and yet gentle. " 'Tain't no wonder ter me ez Clarsie is all tuk up with the wild things, an' critters ginerally," her mother was wont to say. " She sorter looks like 'em, I'm a-thinkin'."

As she came in sight there was a renewal of that odd constraint in Simon Burney's face and manner, and he rose abruptly. " Waal," he said hastily, going to his horse, a rawboned sorrel, hitched to the fence, " it's about time I war a-startin' home, I reckons."

He nodded to his host, who silently nodded in return, and the old horse jogged off with him down the road as Clarsie entered the house and placed the pail upon a shelf.

" Who d'ye think hev been hyar a-speakin' of compli*mints* on ye, Clarsie? " exclaimed Mrs. Giles, who had overheard through the open door every word of the loud, drawling voice on the porch.

Clarsie's liquid eyes widened with surprise, and a faint tinge of rose sprang into her pale face as she looked an expectant inquiry at her mother.

Mrs. Giles was a slovenly, indolent woman, anxious, at the age of forty-five, to assume the prerogatives of advanced years. She had placed all her domestic cares upon the shapely shoulders of her willing daughter, and had betaken herself to the chimney corner and a pipe.

" Yes, thar hev been somebody hyar a-speakin' of compli*mints* on ye, Clarsie," she reiterated, with chuckling amusement. " He war a mighty peart, likely boy — that he war! "

Clarsie's color deepened.

" Old Simon Burney! " exclaimed her mother, in great glee at the incongruity of the idea. " *Old Simon Burney!* Jes' a-sittin' out thar, a-wastin' the time, an' a-burnin' of daylight — jes' ez perlite an' smilin' ez a basket of chips — a-speakin' of compli*mints* on ye! "

There was a flash of laughter among the sylvan suggestions of Clarsie's eyes — a flash as of sudden sunlight upon water. But despite her mirth she seemed to be unaccountably disappointed. The change in her manner was not noticed by her mother, who continued banteringly:

" Simon Burney air a mighty pore old man. Ye oughter be sorry fur him,

Clarsie. Ye mustn't think less of folks than ye does of the dumb beastis — that ain't religion. Ye knows ye air sorry fur mos' everything; why not fur this comical old consarn? Ye oughter marry him ter take keer of him. He said ye war a merciful critter; now is yer chance ter show it! Why, air ye a-goin' ter weavin', Clarsie, jes' when I wants ter talk ter ye 'bout'n old Simon Burney? But law! I knows ye kerry him with ye in yer heart."

The girl summarily closed the conversation by seating herself before a great hand-loom. Presently the persistent thump, thump, of the batten and the noisy creak of the treadle filled the room, and through all the long, hot afternoon her deft, practiced hands lightly tossed the shuttle to and fro.

The breeze freshened, after the sun went down, and the hop and gourd vines were all astir as they clung about the little porch where Clarsie was sitting now, idle at last. The rain clouds had disappeared, and there bent over the dark, heavily wooded ridges a pale blue sky, with here and there the crystalline sparkle of a star. A halo was shimmering in the east, where the mists had gathered about the great white moon, hanging high above the mountains. Noiseless wings flitted through the dusk; now and then the bats swept by so close as to wave Clarsie's hair with the wind of their flight. What an airy, glittering, magical thing was that gigantic spider-web suspended between the silver moon and her shining eyes! Ever and anon there came from the woods a strange, weird, long-drawn sigh, unlike the stir of the wind in the trees, unlike the fret of the water on the rocks. Was it the voiceless sorrow of the sad earth? There were stars in the night besides those known to astronomers: the stellular fireflies gemmed the black shadows with a fluctuating brilliancy; they circled in and out of the porch and touched the leaves above Clarsie's head with quivering points of light. A steadier and an intenser gleam was advancing along the road, and the sound of languid footsteps came with it; the aroma of tobacco graced the atmosphere, and a tall figure walked up to the gate.

"Come in, come in," said Peter Giles, rising, and tendering the guest a chair. "Ye air Tom Pratt, ez well ez I kin make out by this light. Waal, Tom, we hain't furgot ye sence ye done been hyar."

As Tom had been there on the previous evening, this might be considered a joke or an equivocal compliment. The young fellow was restless and awkward under it, but Mrs. Giles chuckled with great merriment.

"An' how air ye a-comin' on, Mrs. Giles?" he asked propitiatorily.

"Jes' toler'ble, Tom. Air they all well ter yer house?"

"Yes, they're toler'ble well, too." He glanced at Clarsie, intending to address to her some polite greeting, but the expression of her shy, half-startled eyes, turned upon the faraway moon, warned him. "Thar never war a gal so skittish," he thought. "She'd run a mile, skeered ter death, ef I said a word ter her."

And he was prudently silent.

"Waal," said Peter Giles, "what's the news out yer way, Tom? Ennything a-goin' on?"

"Thar war a shower yander on the Backbone; it rained toler'ble hard fur a while an' sot up the corn wonderful. Did ye git enny hyar?"

" Not a drap."

" 'Pears ter me ez I kin see the clouds a-circlin' round Chilhowee, an' a-rainin' on everybody's cornfield 'ceptin' ourn," said Mrs. Giles. " Some folks is the fa-vored of the Lord, an' tothers hev ter work fur everything an' git nuthin'. Waal, waal; we'uns will see our reward in the nex' worl'. Thar's a better worl' than this, Tom."

" That's a fac'," said Tom, in orthodox assent.

" An' when we leaves hyar once, we leaves all trouble an' care behind us, Tom; fur we don't come back no more." Mrs. Giles was drifting into one of her pious moods.

" I dunno," said Tom. " Thar hev been them ez hev."

" Hev what? " demanded Peter Giles, startled.

" Hev come back ter this hyar yearth. Thar's a harnt that walks Chilhowee every night o' the worl'. I know them ez hev seen him."

Clarsie's great dilated eyes were fastened on the speaker's face. There was a dead silence for a moment, more eloquent with these looks of amazement than any words could have been.

" I reckons ye remember a puny, shriveled little man, named Reuben Crabb, ez used ter live yander, eight mile along the ridge ter that thar big sulphur spring," Tom resumed, appealing to Peter Giles. " He war born with only one arm."

" I 'members him," interpolated Mrs. Giles vivaciously. " He war a mighty porely, sickly little critter, all the days of his life. 'Twar a wonder he war ever raised ter be a man — an' a pity, too. An' 'twar powerful comical, the way of his takin' off; a stunted, one-armed little critter a-ondertakin' ter fight folks an' shoot pistols. He hed the use o' his one arm, sure."

" Waal," said Tom, " his house ain't thar now, 'kase Sam Grim's brothers burned it ter the ground fur his a-killin' of Sam. That warn't all that war done ter Reuben fur killin' of Sam. The sheriff run Reuben Crabb down this hyar road 'bout a mile from hyar — mebbe less — an' shot him dead in the road, jes' whar it forks. Waal, Reuben war in company with another evildoer — he war from the Cross-Roads, an' I furgits what he hed done, but he war a-tryin' ter hide in the mountings, too; an' the sheriff lef' Reuben a-lying thar in the road, while he tries ter ketch up with the tother; but his horse got a stone in his hoof, an' he los' time an' hed ter gin it up. An' when he got back ter the forks o' the road whar he had lef' Reuben a-lyin' dead, thar war nuthin' thar 'ceptin' a pool o' blood. Waal, he went right on ter Reuben's house, an' them Grim boys hed burnt it ter the ground; but he seen Reuben's brother Joel. An' Joel, he tole the sheriff that late that evenin' he hed tuk Reuben's body out'n the road an' buried it, 'kase it hed been lyin' thar in the road ever sence early in the mornin', an' he couldn't leave it thar all night, an' he hadn't no shelter fur it, sence the Grim boys hed burnt down the house. So he war obleeged ter bury it. An' Joel showed the sheriff a new-made grave an' Reuben's coat whar the sheriff's bullet hed gone in at the back an' kem out'n the breast. The sheriff 'lowed ez they'd fine Joel fifty dollars fur a-buryin' of Reuben afore the cor'ner kem; but they never done it, ez I knows on. The sheriff said that when the cor'ner kem the body would be tuk up fur a 'quest. But thar hed been a powerful big frishet, an' the river 'twixt the cor'ner's house an' Chilhowee couldn't be forded fur three weeks. The cor'ner never kem, an' so thar it all stayed. That war four year ago."

"Waal," said Peter Giles dryly, "I ain't seen no harnt yit. I knowed all that afore."

Clarsie's wondering eyes upon the young man's moonlit face had elicited these facts, familiar to the elders, but strange, he knew, to her.

"I war jes' a-goin' on ter tell," said Tom abashed. "Waal, ever sence his brother Joel died this spring, Reuben's harnt walks Chilhowee. He war seen week afore las', 'bout daybreak, by Ephraim Blenkins, who hed been a-fishin' an' war a-goin' home. Eph happened ter stop in the laurel ter wind up his line, when all in a minit he seen the harnt go by, his face white, an' his eyeballs like fire, an' puny an' one-armed, jes' like he lived. Eph, he owed me a haffen day's work; I holped him ter plow las' month, an' so he kem ter-day an' hoed along cornsider'ble ter pay fur it. He say he believes the harnt never seen him, 'kase it went right by. He 'lowed ef the harnt hed so much ez cut one o' them blazin' eyes round at him he couldn't but hev drapped dead. Waal, this mornin', 'bout sunrise, my brother Bob's little gal, three year old, strayed off from home while her mother war out milkin' the cow. An' we went a-huntin' of her, mightily worked up, 'kase thar hev been a bar prowlin' round our cornfield twict this summer. An' I went to the right, an' Bob went to the lef'. An' he say ez he war a-pushin' 'long through the laurel, he seen the bushes ahead of him a-rustlin'. An' he jes' stood still an' watched 'em. An' fur a while the bushes war still too; an' then they moved jes' a little, fust this way an' then that, till of a suddint the leaves opened, like the mouth of hell mought hev done, an' thar he seen Reuben Crabb's face. He say he never seen sech a face! Its mouth war open an' its eyes war a-startin' out'n its head, an' its skin war white till it war blue; an' ef the devil hed hed it a-hangin' over the coals that minit it couldn't hev looked no more skeered. But that war all that Bob seen, 'kase he jes' shet his eyes an' screeched an' screeched like he war destracted. An' when he stopped a second ter ketch his breath he hearn suthin' a-answerin' him back, sorter weak-like, an' thar war little Peggy a-pullin' through the laurel. Ye know she's too little ter talk good, but the folks down ter our house believes she seen the harnt, too."

"My Lord!" exclaimed Peter Giles. "I 'low I couldn't live a minit ef I war ter see that thar harnt that walks Chilhowee!"

"I know I couldn't," said his wife.

"Nor me, nuther," murmured Clarsie.

"Waal," said Tom, resuming the thread of his narrative, "we hev all been a-talkin' down yander ter our house ter make out the reason why Reuben Crabb's harnt hev sot out ter walk *jes' sence his brother Joel died* — 'kase it war never seen afore then. An' ez nigh ez we kin make it out, the reason is 'kase thar's nobody lef' in this hyar worl' what believes he warn't ter blame in that thar killin' o' Sam Grim. Joel always swore ez Reuben never killed him no more'n nuthin'; that Sam's own pistol went off in his own hand an' shot him through the heart jes' ez he war a-drawin' of it ter shoot Reuben Crabb. An' I hev hearn other men ez war a-standin' by say the same thing, though them Grims tells another tale; but ez Reuben never owned no pistol in his life, nor kerried one, it don't 'pear ter me ez what them Grims say air reasonable. Joel always swore ez Sam Grim war a mighty mean man — a great big feller like him a-rockin' of a deformed little critter, an' a-mockin' of him, an' a-hittin' of him. An' the day of the fight Sam jes' knocked him down fur nuthin' at all; an' afore ye could wink Reuben jumped up suddint, an' flew at him like an eagle, an' struck him in the face. An' then Sam drawed his pistol, an' it went off in his own hand, an' shot him through the heart, an' killed him dead. Joel said that ef he could hev kep' that pore little critter Reuben still, an' let the sheriff arrest him peaceable-like, he war sure the jury would hev let him off; 'kase how war Reuben a-goin' ter shoot ennybody when Sam Grim never left a-holt of the only pistol between 'em, in life or in death? They tells me they hed ter bury Sam Grim with that thar pistol in his hand; his grip war too tight fur death to unloose it. But Joel said that Reuben war sartain they'd hang him. He hedn't never seen no jestice from enny one man, an' he couldn't look fur it from twelve men. So he jes' sot out ter run through the woods, like a painter or a wolf, ter be hunted by the sheriff, an' he war run down an' kilt in the road. Joel said *he* kep' up arter the sheriff ez well ez he could on foot — fur the Crabbs never hed no horse — ter try ter beg fur Reuben, ef he war cotched, an' tell how little an' how weakly he war. I never seen a young man's head turn white like Joel's done; he said he reckoned it war his troubles. But ter the las' he stuck ter his rifle faithful. He war a powerful hunter; he war out rain or shine, hot or cold, in sech weather ez other folks would think thar warn't no use in tryin' ter do nuthin' in. I'm mightily afeard o' seein' Reuben, now, that's a fac'," concluded Tom, frankly; " 'kase I hev hearn tell, an' I believes it, that ef a harnt speaks ter ye, it air sartain ye're bound ter die right then."

" 'Pears ter me," said Mrs. Giles, " ez many mountings ez thar air round hyar, he mought hev tuk ter walkin' some o' them, stidder Chilhowee."

There was a sudden noise close at hand: a great inverted splint-basket, from which came a sound of flapping wings, began to move slightly back and forth. Mrs. Giles gasped out an ejaculation of terror, the two men sprang to their feet, and the coy Clarsie laughed aloud in an exuberance of delighted mirth, forgetful of her shyness. " I declar' ter goodness, you-uns air all skeered fur true! Did ye think it war the harnt that walks Chilhowee? "

" What's under that thar basket? " demanded Peter Giles, rather sheepishly, as he sat down again.

" Nuthin' but the duck-legged Dominicky," said Clarsie, " what air bein' broke up from settin'." The moonlight was full upon the dimpling merriment in her face, upon her shining eyes and parted red lips; and her gurgling laughter was pleasant to hear. Tom Pratt edged his chair a trifle nearer as he, too, sat down.

" Ye oughtn't never ter break up a duck-legged hen, nor a Dominicky, nuther," he volunteered, " 'kase they air sech a good kind o' hen ter kerry chickens; but a hen that is duck-legged an' Dominicky too oughter be let ter set, whether or no."

Had he been warned in a dream, he could have found no more secure road to Clarsie's favor and interest than a discussion of the poultry. " I'm a-thinkin'," she said, " that it air too hot fur hens ter set now, an' 'twill be till the las' of August."

" It don't 'pear ter me ez it air hot much in June up hyar on Chilhowee — thar's a differ, I know, down in the valley; but till July, on Chilhowee, it don't 'pear ter me ez it air too hot ter set a hen. An' a duck-legged Dominicky air mighty hard ter break up."

" That's a fac'," Clarsie admitted; " but I'll hev ter do it, somehow, 'kase I ain't got no eggs fur her. All my hens air kerryin' of chickens."

" Waal! " exclaimed Tom, seizing his opportunity, " I'll bring ye some ter-morrer night, when I come agin. We-uns hev got eggs ter our house."

" Thanky," said Clarsie, shyly smiling.

This unique method of courtship would have progressed very prosperously but for the interference of the elders, who are an element always more or less adverse to love-making. " Ye oughter turn out yer hen now, Clarsie," said Mrs. Giles, " ez Tom air a-goin' ter bring ye some eggs ter-morrer. I wonder ye don't think it's mean ter keep her up longer'n ye air obleeged ter. Ye oughter remember ye war called a merciful critter jes' ter-day."

Clarsie rose precipitately, raised the basket, and out flew the " duck-legged Dominicky," with a frantic flutter and hysterical cackling. But Mrs. Giles was not to be diverted from her purpose; her thoughts had recurred to the absurd episode of the afternoon, and with her relish of the incongruity of the joke she opened upon the subject at once.

" Waal, Tom," she said, " we'll be hevin' Clarsie married, afore long, I'm a-thinkin'." The young man sat bewildered. He, too, had entertained views concerning Clarsie's speedy marriage, but with a distinctly personal application; and this frank mention of the matter by Mrs. Giles had a sinister suggestion that perhaps her ideas might be antagonistic. " An' who d'ye think hev been hyar ter-day, a-speakin' of compli*mints* on Clarsie? " He could not answer, but he turned his head with a look of inquiry, and Mrs. Giles continued, " He is a mighty peart, likely boy — *he* is."

There was a growing anger in the dismay on Tom Pratt's face; he leaned forward to hear the name with a fiery eagerness, altogether incongruous with his usual lackluster manner.

" Old Simon Burney! " cried Mrs. Giles with a burst of laughter. " *Old Simon Burney!* Jes' a-speakin' of compli*mints* on Clarsie! "

The young fellow drew back with a look of disgust. " Why, he's a old man; he ain't no fit husband fur Clarsie."

" Don't ye be too sure ter count on that. I war jes' a-layin' off ter tell Clarsie that a gal oughter keep mighty clar o' widowers, 'thout she wants ter marry one. Fur I believes," said Mrs. Giles with a wild flight of imagination, " ez them men hev got some sort'n trade with the Evil One, an' he gives 'em the power ter witch the gals, somehow, so's ter git 'em ter marry; 'kase I don't think that any gal that's got good sense air a-goin' ter be a man's second ch'ice, an' the mother of a whole pack of stepchil'ren, 'thout she air under some sort'n spell. But them men carries the day with the gals ginerally, an' I'm a-thinkin' they're banded with the devil. Ef I war a gal, an' a smart, peart boy like Simon Burney kem around a-speakin' of compli*mints,* an' sayin' I war a merciful critter, I'd jes' give it up an' marry him fur second ch'ice. Thar's one blessin'," she continued, contemplating the possibility in a cold-blooded fashion positively revolting to Tom Pratt: "he ain't got no tribe of chil'ren fur Clarsie ter look arter; nary chick nor child hev old Simon Burney got. He hed two, but they died."

The young man took leave presently, in great depression of spirit — the idea that the widower was banded with the powers of evil was rather overwhelming to a man whose dependence was in merely mortal attractions; and after he had been gone a little while Clarsie ascended the ladder to a nook in the roof, which she called her room.

For the first time in her life her slumber was fitful and restless, long intervals of wakefulness alternating with snatches of fantastic dreams. At last she rose and sat by the rude window, looking out through the chestnut leaves at the great moon, which had begun to dip toward the dark uncertainty of the western ridges, and at the shimmering, translucent, pearly mists that filled the intermediate valleys. All the air was dew and incense; so subtle and penetrating an odor came from that fir tree beyond the fence that it seemed as if some invigorating infusion were thrilling along her veins; there floated upward, too, the warm fragrance of the clover, and every breath of the gentle wind brought from over the stream a thousand blended, undistinguishable perfumes of the deep forests beyond. The moon's idealizing glamour had left no trace of the uncouthness of the place which the daylight revealed; the little log house, the great overhanging chestnut oaks, the jagged precipice before the door, the vague outlines of the distant ranges, all suffused with a magic sheen, might have seemed a stupendous alto-rilievo in silver repoussé. Still, there came here and there the sweep of the bat's dusky wings; even they were a part of the night's witchery. A tiny owl perched for a moment or two amid the dew-tipped chestnut leaves, and gazed with great round eyes at Clarsie as solemnly as she gazed at him.

"I'm thankful enough that ye hed the grace not ter screech while ye war hyar," she said after the bird had taken his flight. "I ain't ready ter die yit, an' a screech ow*el* air the sure sign."

She felt now and then a great impatience with her wakeful mood. Once she took herself to task: "Jes' a-sittin' up hyar all night, the same ez ef I war a fox, or that thar harnt that walks Chilhowee!"

And then her mind reverted to Tom Pratt, to old Simon Burney, and to her mother's emphatic and oracular declaration that widowers are in league with Satan, and that the girls upon whom they cast the eye of supernatural fascination have no choice in the matter. " I wish I knowed ef that thar sayin' war true," she murmured, her face still turned to the western spurs and the moon sinking so slowly toward them.

With a sudden resolution she rose to her feet. She knew a way of telling fortunes which was, according to tradition, infallible, and she determined to try it and ease her mind as to her future. Now was the propitious moment. " I hev always hearn that it won't come true 'thout ye try it jes' before daybreak, an' a-kneelin' down at the forks of the road." She hesitated a moment and listened intently. " They'd never git done a-laffin' at me ef they fund it out," she thought.

There was no sound in the house, and from the dark woods arose only those monotonous voices of the night, so familiar to her ears that she accounted their murmurous iteration as silence too. She leaned far out of the low window, caught the wide-spreading branches of the tree beside it, and swung herself noiselessly to the ground. The road before her was dark with the shadowy foliage and dank with the dew; but now and then, at long intervals, there lay athwart it a bright bar of light where the moonshine fell through a gap in the trees. Once, as she went rapidly along her way, she saw speeding across the white radiance, lying just before her feet, the ill-omened shadow of a rabbit. She paused, with a superstitious sinking of the heart, and she heard the animal's quick, leaping rush through the bushes near at hand; but she mustered her courage and kept steadily on. " Tain't no use a-goin' back ter git shet o' bad luck," she argued. " Ef old Simon Burney air my fortune, he'll come whether or no — ef all they say air true."

The serpentine road curved to the mountain's brink before it forked, and there was again that familiar picture of precipice, and faraway ridges, and shining mist, and sinking moon, which was visibly turning from silver to gold. The changing luster gilded the feathery ferns that grew in the marshy dip. Just at the angle of the divergent paths there rose into the air a great mass of indistinct white blossoms, which she knew were the exquisite mountain azaleas, and all the dark forest was starred with the blooms of the laurel.

She fixed her eyes upon the mystic sphere dropping down the sky, knelt among the azaleas at the forks of the road, and repeated the time-honored invocation:

" Ef I'm a-goin' ter marry a young man, whistle, Bird, whistle. Ef I'm a-goin' ter marry an old man, low, Cow, low. Ef I ain't a-goin' ter marry nobody, knock, Death, knock."

There was a prolonged silence in the matutinal freshness and perfume of the woods. She raised her head and listened attentively. No chirp of half-awakened bird, no tapping of woodpecker, or the mysterious death watch; but from far along the dewy aisles of the forest, the ungrateful Spot, that Clarsie had fed more faithfully than herself, lifted up her voice and set the echoes vibrating. Clarsie, however, had hardly time for a pang of disappointment. While she still knelt among the azaleas her large, deerlike eyes were suddenly dilated with terror. From around the curve of the road came the quick beat of hastening footsteps, the sobbing sound of panting breath, and between her and the sinking moon there passed an attenuated, one-armed figure with a pallid, sharpened face, outlined for a moment on its brilliant disk, and dreadful starting eyes, and quivering open mouth. It disappeared in an instant among the shadows of the laurel, and Clarsie, with a horrible fear clutching at her heart, sprang to her feet.

Her flight was arrested by other sounds. Before her reeling senses could distinguish them, a party of horsemen plunged down the road. They reined in suddenly as their eyes fell upon her, and their leader, an eager, authoritative man, was asking her a question. Why could she not understand him? With her nerveless hands feebly catching at the shrubs for support, she listened vaguely to his impatient, meaningless words, and saw with helpless deprecation the rising anger in his face. But there was no time to be lost. With a curse upon the stupidity of the mountaineer, who couldn't speak when she was spoken to, the party sped on in a sweeping gallop, and the rocks and the steeps were hilarious with the sound.

When the last faint echo was hushed, Clarsie tremblingly made her way out into the road; not reassured, however, for she had a frightful conviction that there was now and then a strange stir in the laurel, and that she was stealthily watched. Her eyes were fixed upon the dense growth with a morbid fascination as she moved away; but she was once more rooted to the spot when the leaves parted and in the golden moonlight the ghost stood before her. She could not nerve herself to run past him, and he was directly in her way homeward. His face was white, and lined, and thin; that pitiful quiver was never still in the parted lips; he looked at her with faltering, beseeching eyes. Clarsie's merciful heart was stirred. " What ails ye, ter come back hyar an' foller me? " she cried out abruptly. And then a great horror fell upon her. Was not one to whom a ghost should speak doomed to death, sudden and immediate?

The ghost replied in a broken, shivering voice, like a wail of pain, " I war a-starvin' — I war a-starvin'," with despairing iteration.

It was all over, Clarsie thought. The ghost had spoken, and she was a doomed creature. She wondered that she did not fall dead in the road. But while those beseeching eyes were fastened in piteous appeal on hers, she could not leave him. " I never hearn that 'bout ye," she said, reflectively. " I knows ye hed awful troubles while ye war alive, but I never knowed ez ye war starved."

Surely that was a gleam of sharp surprise in the ghost's prominent eyes, succeeded by a sly intelligence.

" Day is nigh ter breakin'," Clarsie admonished him as the lower rim of the moon touched the silver mists of the west. " What air ye a-wantin' of me? "

There was a short silence. Mind travels far in such intervals. Clarsie's thoughts had overtaken the scenes when she should have died that sudden terrible death: when there would be no one left to feed the chickens; when no one would care if the pigs cried with the pangs of hunger, unless, indeed, it were time for them to be fattened before killing. The mare — how often would she be taken from the plow and shut up for the night in her shanty without a drop of water after her hard day's work! Who would churn, or spin, or weave?

Clarsie could not understand how the machinery of the universe could go on without her. And Towse, poor Towse! He was a useless cumberer of the ground, and it was hardly to be supposed that after his protector was gone he would be spared a blow or a bullet, to hasten his lagging death. But Clarsie still stood in the road and watched the face of the ghost as he, with his eager, starting eyes, scanned her open, ingenuous countenance.

" Ye do ez ye air bid, or it'll be the worse for ye," said the " harnt," in the same quivering, shrill tone. " Thar's hunger in the nex' worl' ez well ez in this, an' ye bring me some vittles hyar this time ter-morrer, an' don't ye tell nobody ye hev seen me, nuther, or it'll be the worse for ye."

There was a threat in his eyes as he disappeared in the laurel and left the girl standing in the last rays of moonlight.

A curious doubt was stirring in Clarsie's mind when she reached home, in the early dawn, and heard her father talking about the sheriff and his posse, who had stopped at the house in the night, and roused its inmates, to know if they had seen a man pass that way.

" Clarsie never hearn none o' the noise, I'll be bound, 'kase she always sleeps like a log," said Mrs. Giles as her daughter came in with the pail after milking the cow. " Tell her 'bout'n it."

" They kem a-bustin' along hyar a while afore daybreak, a-runnin' arter the man," drawled Mr. Giles, dramatically. " An' they knocked me up, ter know ef ennybody hed passed. An' one o' them men — I never seen none of 'em afore; they's all valley folks, I'm a-thinkin' — an' one of 'em bruk his saddle-girt' a good piece down the road, an' he kem back ter borrer mine; an' ez we war a-fixin' of it, he tole me what they war all arter. He said that word war tuk ter the sheriff down yander in the valley — 'pears ter me them townfolks don't think nobody in the mountings hev got good sense — word war tuk ter the sheriff 'bout this one-armed harnt that walks Chilhowee; an' he sot it down that Reuben Crabb warn't dead at all, an' Joel jes' purtended ter hev buried him, an' it air Reuben hisself that walks Chilhowee. An' thar air two hundred dollars blood money reward fur ennybody ez kin ketch him. These hyar valley folks air powerful cur'ous critters — two hundred dollars blood money reward fur that thar harnt that walks Chilhowee! I jes' sot myself ter laffin' when that thar cuss tole it so solemn. I jes' 'lowed ter him ez he couldn't shoot a harnt nor hang a harnt, an' Reuben Crabb hed about got done with his persecutions in this worl'. An' he said that by the time they hed scoured this mounting, like they hed laid off ter do, they would find that thar puny little harnt war nuthin' but a mortal man an' could be kep' in a jail ez handy ez enny other flesh an' blood. He said the sheriff 'lowed ez the reason Reuben hed jes' taken ter walk Chilhowee sence Joel died is 'kase thar air nobody ter feed him, like Joel done, mebbe, in the nights; an' Reuben always war a pore, one-armed, weakly critter what can't even kerry a gun, an' he air driv by hunger out'n the hole whar he stays, ter prowl round the cornfields an' hen coops ter steal suthin' — an' that's how he kem ter be seen frequent. The sheriff 'lowed that Reuben can't find enough

roots an' yerbs ter keep him up; but law! — a harnt eatin' ! It jes' sot me off
ter laffin'. Reuben Crabb hev been too busy in torment fur the las' four year
ter be a-studyin' 'bout eatin'; an' it air his harnt that walks Chilhowee."

The next morning, before the moon sank, Clarsie, with a tin pail in her
hand, went to meet the ghost at the appointed place. She understood now why
the terrible doom that falls upon those to whom a spirit may chance to speak
had not descended upon her, and that fear was gone; but the secrecy of her
errand weighed heavily. She had been scrupulously careful to put into the pail
only such things as had fallen to her share at the table, and which she had saved
from the meals of yesterday. " A gal that goes a-robbin' fur a hongry harnt," was
her moral reflection, " oughter be throwed bodaciously off'n the bluff."

She found no one at the forks of the road. In the marshy dip were only the
myriads of mountain azaleas, only the masses of feathery ferns, only the con-
stellated glories of the laurel blooms. A sea of shining white mist was in the
valley, with glinting golden rays striking athwart it from the great cresset of the
sinking moon; here and there the long, dark, horizontal line of a distant mountain's summit rose above the vaporous shimmer, like a dreary, somber island in
the midst of enchanted waters. Her large, dreamy eyes, so wild and yet so
gentle, gazed out through the laurel leaves upon the floating gilded flakes of
light, as in the deep coverts of the mountain, where the fulvous-tinted deer were
lying, other eyes, as wild and as gentle, dreamily watched the vanishing moon.
Overhead, the filmy, lacelike clouds, fretting the blue heavens, were tinged
with a faint rose. Through the trees she caught a glimpse of the red sky of dawn,
and the glister of a great lucent, tremulous star. From the ground, misty blue
exhalations were rising, alternating with the long lines of golden light yet drifting through the woods. It was all very still, very peaceful, almost holy. One
could hardly believe that these consecrated solitudes had once reverberated with
the echoes of man's death-dealing ingenuity, and that Reuben Crabb had fallen,
shot through and through, amid that wealth of flowers at the forks of the road.
She heard suddenly the faraway baying of a hound. Her great eyes dilated, and
she lifted her head to listen. Only the solemn silence of the woods, the slow sinking of the noiseless moon, the voiceless splendor of that eloquent daystar.

Morning was close at hand, and she was beginning to wonder that the ghost
did not appear, when the leaves fell into abrupt commotion and he was standing
in the road, beside her. He did not speak, but watched her with an eager, questioning intentness as she placed the contents of the pail upon the moss at the
roadside. " I'm a-comin' agin ter-morrer," she said, gently. He made no reply,
quickly gathered the food from the ground, and disappeared in the deep shades
of the woods.

She had not expected thanks, for she was accustomed only to the gratitude
of dumb beasts; but she was vaguely conscious of something wanting as she
stood motionless for a moment and watched the burnished rim of the moon
slip down behind the western mountains. Then she slowly walked along her
misty way in the dim light of the coming dawn. There was a footstep in the
road behind her; she thought it was the ghost once more. She turned, and met

Simon Burney face to face. His rod was on his shoulder, and a string of fish was in his hand.

"Ye air a-doin' wrongful, Clarsie," he said sternly. "It air agin the law fur folks ter feed an' shelter them ez is a-runnin' from jestice. An' ye'll git yerself into trouble. Other folks will find ye out, besides me, an' then the sheriff'll be up hyar arter ye."

The tears rose to Clarsie's eyes. This prospect was infinitely more terrifying than the awful doom which follows the horror of a ghost's speech.

"I can't help it," she said, however, doggedly swinging the pail back and forth. "I can't gin my consent ter starvin' of folks, even ef they air a-hidin' an' a-runnin' from justice."

"They mought put ye in jail, too — I dunno," suggested Simon Burney.

"I can't help that, nuther," said Clarsie, the sobs rising and the tears falling fast. "Ef they comes an' gits me, and puts me in the pen'tiary away down yander, somewhars in the valley, like they done Jane Simpkins, fur a-cuttin' of her stepmother's throat with a butcher knife, while she war asleep — though some said Jane war crazy — I can't gin my consent ter starvin' of folks."

A recollection came over Simon Burney of the simile of "hendering the sun from shining."

"She hev done sot it down in her mind," he thought, as he walked on beside her and looked at her resolute face. Still he did not relinquish his effort.

"Doin' wrong, Clarsie, ter aid folks what air a-doin' wrong, an' mebbe *hev* done wrong, air powerful hurtful ter everybody, an' henders the law an' jestice."

"I can't help it," said Clarsie.

"It 'pears toler'ble comical ter me," said Simon Burney, with a sudden perception of a curious fact which has proved a marvel to wiser men, "that no matter how good a woman is, she ain't got no respect fur the laws of the country, an' don't sot no store by jestice." After a momentary silence he appealed to her on another basis. "Somebody will ketch him arter a while, ez sure ez ye air born. The sheriff's a-sarchin' now, an' by the time that word gits around, all the mounting boys'll turn out, 'kase thar air two hundred dollars blood money fur him. An' then he'll think, when they ketches him — an' everybody'll say so, too — ez ye war constant in feedin' him jes' ter 'tice him ter comin' ter one place, so ez ye could tell somebody whar ter go ter ketch him, an' make them gin ye haffen the blood money, mebbe. That's what the mounting will say, mos' likely."

"I can't help it," said Clarsie once more.

He left her walking on toward the rising sun, and retraced his way to the forks of the road. The jubilant morning was filled with the song of birds; the sunlight flashed on the dew; all the delicate enameled bells of the pink and white azaleas were swinging tremulously in the wind; the aroma of ferns and mint rose on the delicious fresh air. Presently he checked his pace, creeping stealthily on the moss and grass beside the road rather than in the beaten path. He pulled aside the leaves of the laurel with no more stir than the wind might have made, and stole cautiously through its dense growth, till he came suddenly upon the puny little ghost, lying in the sun at the foot of a tree. The frightened creature sprang to his feet with a wild cry of terror, but before he could move a step he was caught and held fast in the strong grip of the stalwart mountaineer beside him. "I hev kem hyar ter tell ye a word, Reuben Crabb," said Simon Burney. "I hev kem hyar ter tell ye that the whole mounting air a-goin' ter turn out ter sarch fur ye; the sheriff air a-ridin' now, an' ef ye don't come along with me they'll hev ye afore night, 'kase thar air two hundred dollars reward fur ye."

What a piteous wail went up to the smiling blue sky, seen through the dappling leaves above them! What a horror, and despair, and prescient agony were in the hunted creature's face! The ghost struggled no longer; he slipped from his feet down upon the roots of the tree and turned that woful face, with its starting eyes and drawn muscles and quivering parted lips, up toward the unseeing sky.

"God A'mighty, man!" exclaimed Simon Burney, moved to pity. "Whyn't ye quit this hyar way of livin' in the woods like ye war a wolf? Whyn't ye come back an' stand yer trial? From all I've hearn tell, it 'pears ter me ez the jury air obleeged ter let ye off, an' I'll take keer of ye agin them Grims."

"I hain't got no place ter live in," cried out the ghost, with a keen despair.

Simon Burney hesitated. Reuben Crabb was possibly a murderer — at the best could but be a burden. The burden, however, had fallen in his way, and he lifted it.

"I tell ye now, Reuben Crabb," he said, "I ain't a-goin' ter holp no man ter break the law an' hender jestice; but ef ye will go an' stand yer trial, I'll take keer of ye agin them Grims ez long ez I kin fire a rifle. An' arter the jury hev done let ye off, ye air welcome ter live along o' me at my house till ye die. Ye air no-'count ter work, I know, but I ain't a-goin' ter grudge ye fur a livin' at my house."

And so it came to pass that the reward set upon the head of the harnt that walked Chilhowee was never claimed.

With his powerful ally, the forlorn little specter went to stand his trial, and the jury acquitted him without leaving the box. Then he came back to the mountains to live with Simon Burney. The cruel gibes of his burly mockers that had beset his feeble life from his childhood up, the deprivation and loneliness and despair and fear that had filled those days when he walked Chilhowee, had not improved the harnt's temper. He was a helpless creature, not able to carry a gun or hold a plow, and the years that he spent smoking his cob pipe in Simon Burney's door were idle years and unhappy. But Mrs. Giles said she thought he was "a mighty lucky little critter: fust, he hed Joel ter take keer of him an' feed him, when he tuk ter the woods ter pertend he war a harnt; an' they do say now that Clarsie Pratt, afore she war married, used ter kerry him vittles, too; an' then old Simon Burney tuk him up an' fed him ez plenty ez ef he war a good workin' hand, an' gin him clothes an' houseroom, an' put up with his jawin' jes' like he never hearn a word of it. But law! some folks dunno when they air well off."

There was only a sluggish current of peasant blood in Simon Burney's veins, but a prince could not have dispensed hospitality with a more royal hand. Ungrudgingly he gave of his best; valiantly he defended his thankless guest at the risk of his life; with a moral gallantry he struggled with his sloth, and worked early and late, that there might be enough to divide. There was no possibility of a recompense for him, not even in the encomiums of discriminating friends, nor the satisfaction of tutored feelings and a practiced spiritual discernment; for he was an uncouth creature, and densely ignorant.

The grace of culture is, in its way, a fine thing, but the best that art can do — the polish of a gentleman — is hardly equal to the best that nature can do in her higher moods.

Mary E. Wilkins Freeman

On the Walpole Road

WALPOLE was a lively little rural emporium of trade; thither the villagers from the small country hamlets thereabouts went to make the bulk of their modest purchases.

One summer afternoon two women were driving slowly along a road therefrom, in a dusty, old-fashioned chaise whose bottom was heaped up with brown-paper parcels.

One woman might have been seventy, but she looked younger, she was so hale and portly. She had a double, bristling chin, her gray eyes twinkled humorously over her spectacles, and she wore a wide-flaring black straw bonnet with purple bows on the inside of the rim. The afternoon was very warm, and she held in one black-mitted hand a palm-leaf fan, which she waved gently, now and then, over against her capacious bosom.

The other woman was younger — forty, perhaps; her face was plain-featured and energetic. She wore a gray serge dress and drab cotton gloves, and held tightly on to the reins as she drove. Now and then she would slap them briskly upon the horse's back. He was a heavy, hard-worked farm animal, and was disposed to jog along at an easy pace this warm afternoon.

There had not been any rain for a long time, and everything was very dusty. This road was not much traveled, and grass was growing between the wheel ruts; but the soil flew up like smoke from the horse's hoofs and the wheels. The blackberry vines climbing over the stone walls on either side, and the meadowsweet and hardhack bushes were powdered thickly with dust, and had gray leaves instead of green. The big-leaved things, such as burdock, growing close to the ground, had their veins all outlined in dust.

The two women rode in a peaceful sort of way; the old lady fanned herself

From *A Humble Romance,* 1887.

mildly, and the younger one slapped the horse mechanically. Neither spoke, till they emerged into a more open space on a hill crest. There they had an uninterrupted view of the northwest sky; the trees had hidden it before.

"I declare, Almiry," said the old lady, "we air goin' to hev a thundershower."

"It won't get up till we get home," replied the other, "an' ten chances to one it'll go round by the north, anyway, and not touch us at all. That's the way they do half the time here. If I'd 'a' seen a cloud as black as that down where I used to live, I'd 'a' known for sure there was goin' to be a heavy tempest, but here there's no knowin' anything about it. I wouldn't worry, anyway, Mis' Green, if it should come up before we get home: the horse ain't afraid of lightnin'."

The old lady looked comical. "He ain't afraid of anything, is he, Almiry?"

"No," answered her companion, giving the horse a spiteful slap; "he don't know enough to get scared even, that's a fact. I don't believe anything short of Gabriel's trumpet would start him up a bit."

"I don't think you ought to speak that way, Almiry," said the old lady; "it's kinder makin' light o' sacred things, seems to me. But as long as you've spoke of it, I don't believe that would start him up either. Though I'll tell you one thing, Almiry: I don't believe thar's goin' to be anything very frightful 'bout Gabriel's trumpet. I think it's goin' to come kinder like the robins an' the flowers do in the spring, kinder meltin' right into everything else, sweet an' nateral-like."

"That ain't accordin' to Scripture," said Almira stoutly.

"It's accordin' to my Scripture. I tell you what 'tis, Almiry, I've found out one thing a-livin' so long, an' that is, thar ain't so much difference in things on this airth as thar is in the folks that see 'em. It's me a-seein' the Scripturs, an' it's you a-seein' the Scripturs, Almiry, an' you see one thing an' I another, an' I dare say we both see crooked mostly, with maybe a little straight mixed up with it, an' we'll never reely know how much is straight till we see to read it by the light of the New Jerusalem."

"You ought to ha' ben a minister, Mis' Green."

"Wa'al, so I would ha' ben ef I had ben a man; I allers thought I would. But I s'pose the Lord thought there was more need of an extra hand just then to raise up children, an' bake an' brew an' wash dishes. You'd better drive along a leetle faster ef you kin, Almiry."

Almira jerked the reins viciously and clucked, but the horse jogged along undisturbed. "It ain't no use," said she. "You might as well try to start up a stone post."

"Wa'al, mebbe the shower won't come up," said the old lady, and she leaned back and began peacefully fanning herself.

"That cloud makes me think of Aunt Rebecca's funeral," she broke out suddenly. "Did I ever tell you about it, Almiry?"

"No; I don't think you ever did, Mis' Green."

"Wa'al, mebbe you'll like to hear it, as we're joggin' along. It'll keep us from gettin' aggervated at the horse — poor, dumb thing!

"Wa'al, you see, Almiry, Aunt Rebecca was my aunt on my mother's side — my mother's oldest sister she was — an' I'd allers thought a sight of her. This happened twenty year ago or more, before Israel died. She was allers such an own-folks sort of a woman, an' jest the best hand when anyone was sick. I'll never forgit how she nussed me through the typhus fever the year after mother died. Thar I was took sick all of a sudden, an' four leetle children cryin', an' Israel couldn't get anybody but that shiftless Lyons woman, far and near, to come an' help. When Aunt Rebecca heerd of it she jest left everything an' come. She packed off that Lyons woman, bag an' baggage, an' tuk right hold as nobody but her could ha' known how to. I allers knew I should ha' died ef it hadn't been for her.

"She lived ten miles off, on this very road, too, but we allers used to visit back an' forth. I couldn't get along without goin' to see Aunt Rebecca once in so often; I'd get jest as lonesome an' homesick as could be.

"So, feelin' that way, it ain't surprisin' that it gave me an awful shock when I heerd she was dead that mornin'. They sent the word by a man that they hailed, drivin' by. He was comin' down here to see about sellin' a horse, an' he said he'd jest as soon stop an' tell us as not. A real nice sort of a man he was — a storekeeper from Comstock. Wa'al, I see Israel standin' out in the road an' talkin' with the man, an' I wondered what it could be about. But when he came in an' told me that Aunt Rebecca was dead, I jest sat right down, kinder stunned-like. I couldn't ha' felt much worse ef it had been my mother. An' it was so awful sudden! Why, I'd seen her only the week before, an' she looked uncommon smart for her, I thought. Ef it had been Uncle Enos, her husband, I shouldn't ha' wondered. He'd had the heart disease for years, an' we'd thought he might die any minute; but to think of her —

"I jest stared at Israel. I felt too bad to cry. I didn't, till I happened to look down at the apron I had on. It was like a dress she had; she had a piece left, an' she gave it to me for an apron. When I saw that, I bust right out sobbin'.

"'O Lord,' says I, 'this apron she give me! Oh, dear! dear! dear!'

"'Sarah,' says Israel, 'it's the will of the Lord.'

"'I know it,' says I, 'but she's dead, an' she gave me this apron, dear blessed woman'; an' I went right on cryin', though he tried to stop me. Every time I looked at that apron, it seemed as if I should die.

"Thar wa'n't any particulars, Israel said. All the man that told him knew was that a woman hailed him from one of the front windows as he was drivin' by, and asked him to stop an' tell us. I s'posed most likely the woman that hailed him was Mis' Simmons, a widder woman that used to work for Aunt Rebecca busy times.

"Wa'al, Israel kinder hurried me to get ready. The funeral was app'inted at two o'clock, an' we had a horse that wa'n't much swifter on the road than the one you're drivin' now.

"So I got into my best black gown the quickest I could. I had a good black shawl, and a black bunnit too; so I looked quite decent. I felt reel glad I had 'em. They were things I had when mother died. I don't see hardly how I had happened to keep the bunnit, but it was lucky I did. I got ready in such a flutter that I got on my black gown over the caliker one I'd been wearin', an' never knew it till I came to go to bed that night, but I don't think it was much wonder.

"We'd been havin' a terrible dry spell, jest as we've been havin' now, an' everything was like powder. I thought my dress would be spoilt before we got thar. The horse was dreadful lazy, an' it was nothin' but g'langin' an' slappin' an' whippin' all the way, an' it didn't amount to nothin' then.

"When we'd got halfway thar or so, thar come up an awful thundershower from the northwest, jest as it's doin' today. Wa'al, thar wa'n't nowhar to stop, an' we driv right along. The horse wa'n't afraid of lightnin', an' we got in under the shay top as far as we could, an' pulled the blanket up over us; but we got drippin' wet. An' thar was Israel in his meetin' coat, an' me in my best gown. Take it with the dust an' everything, they never looked anyhow again.

"Wa'al, Israel g'langed to the horse, an' put the whip over her, but she jest jogged right along. What with feelin' so about Aunt Rebecca, an' worryin' about Israel's coat an' my best gown, I thought I should never live to git thar.

"When we driv by the meetin' house at Four Corners, where Aunt Rebecca lived, it was five minutes after two, an' two was the time sot for the funeral. I did feel reel worked up to think we was late, an' we chief mourners. When we got to the house thar seemed to be consider'ble goin' on around it, folks goin' in an' out, an' standin' in the yard; an' Israel said he didn't believe we was late, after all. He hollered to a man standin' by the fence, an' asked him if they had had the funeral. The man said no; they was goin' to hev it at the meetin' house at three o'clock. We was glad enough to hear that, an' Israel said he would drive round an' hitch the horse, an' I'd better go in an' get dried off a little, an' see the folks.

"It had slacked up then, an' was only drizzlin' a leetle, an' lightnin' a good ways off now an' then.

"Wa'al, I got out an' went up to the house. Thar was quite a lot of men I knew standin' round the door an' in the entry, but they only bowed kinder stiff an' solemn, an' moved to let me pass. I noticed the entry floor was drippin' wet too. 'Been rainin' in,' thinks I. 'I wonder why they didn't shet the door.' I went right into the room on the left-hand side of the entry — that was the settin' room — an' thar, a-settin' in a cheer by the winder, jest as straight an' smart as could be, in her new black bunnit an' gown, was — Aunt Rebecca.

"Wa'al, ef I was to tell you what I did, Almiry, I s'pose you'd think it was awful. But I s'pose the sudden change from feelin' so bad made me kinder high-stericky. I jest sot right down in the first cheer I come to an' laughed; I laughed till the tears was runnin' down my cheeks, an' it was all I could do to breathe. There was quite a lot of Uncle Enos's folks settin' round the room — his brother's family an' some cousins — an' they looked at me as ef they thought I was crazy. But seein' them look only sot me off again. Some of the folks came in from the entry, an' stood starin' at me, but I jest laughed harder. Finally Aunt Rebecca comes up to me.

" 'For mercy's sake, Sarah,' says she, ' what air you doin' so for? '

" 'Oh, dear! ' says I. ' I thought you was dead, an' thar you was a-settin'. Oh, dear! '

" And then I begun to laugh again. I was awful 'shamed of myself, but I couldn't stop to save my life.

" ' For the land's sake, Aunt Rebecca,' says I, ' is thar a funeral or a weddin'? An' ef thar is a funeral, who's dead? '

" ' Come into the bedroom with me a minute, Sarah,' says she.

" Then we went into her bedroom, that opened out of the settin' room, an' sot down, an' she told me that it was Uncle Enos that was dead. It seems she was the one that hailed the man, an' he was a little hard of hearin', an' thar was a misunderstandin' between 'em some way.

" Uncle Enos had died very sudden, the day before, of heart disease. He went into the settin' room after breakfast an' sot down by the winder, an' Aunt Rebecca found him thar dead in his cheer when she went in a few minutes afterwards.

" It was such awful hot weather they had to hurry about the funeral. But that wa'n't all. Then she went on to tell me the rest. They had had the awfulest time that ever was. The shower had come up about one o'clock, and the barn had been struck by lightnin'. It was a big new one that Uncle Enos had sot great store by. He had laid out consider'ble money on it, an' they'd jest got in twelve ton of hay. I s'pose that was how it happened to be struck. A barn is a good deal more likely to be when they've jest got hay in. Well, everybody sot to an' put the fire in the barn out. They handed buckets of water up to the men on the roof, an' put that out without much trouble by takin' it in time.

" But after they'd got that put out they found the house was on fire. The same thunderbolt that struck the barn had struck that too, an' it was blazin' away at one end of the roof pretty lively.

" Wa'al, they went to work at that then, an' they'd just got that fairly put out a few minutes before we come. Nothin' was hurt much, only thar was a good deal of water round; we had hard work next day cleanin' of it up.

" Aunt Rebecca allers was a calm sort of woman, an' she didn't seem near as much flustered by it all as most folks would have been.

" I couldn't help wonderin' an' lookin' at her pretty sharp to see how she took Uncle Enos's death, too. You see, thar was something kinder curious about their gittin' married. I'd heerd about it all from mother. I don't s'pose she ever wanted him, nor cared about him the best she could do, any more than she would have about any good, respectable man that was her neighbor. Uncle Enos was a pretty good sort of a man, though he was allers dreadful sot in his ways, an' I believe it would have been wuss than death, any time, for him to have given up anything he had determined to hev. But I must say I never thought so much of him after mother told me what she did. You see, the way of it was, my grandmother Wilson, Aunt Rebecca's mother, was awful sot on her hevin' him, an' she was dreadful nervous an' feeble, an' Aunt Rebecca jest give in to her. The wust of it was, thar was someone else she wanted too, an' he wanted her. Abner Lyons his name was; he wa'n't any relation to the Lyons woman I had when I was sick. He was a real likely young feller, an' thar wa'n't a thing agin him that anyone else could see; but grandmother fairly hated him, an' mother said she did believe her mother would rather hev buried Rebecca than seen her married to him. Well, grandmother took on, an' acted so, that Aunt Rebecca give in an' said she'd marry Uncle Enos, an' the weddin' day come.

"Mother said she looked handsome as a pictur', but thar was somethin' kinder awful about her when she stood up before the minister with Uncle Enos to be married.

"She was dressed in green silk an' had some roses in her hair. I kin imagine jest how she must hev looked. She was a good-lookin' woman when I knew her, an' they said when she was young there wa'n't many to compare with her.

"Mother said Uncle Enos looked nice, but he had his mouth kinder hard sot, as ef now he'd got what he wanted, an' meant to hang on to it. He'd known all the time jest how matters was. Aunt Rebecca'd told him the whole story; she declared she wouldn't marry him without she did.

"I s'pose, at the last minute, that Aunt Rebecca got kinder desp'rate, an' a realizin' sense of what she was doin' come over her, an' she thought she'd make one more effort to escape; for when the minister asked that question 'bout thar bein' any obstacles to their gittin' married, an' ef thar were, let 'em speak up, or forever hold their peace, Aunt Rebecca did speak up. Mother said she looked straight at the parson, an' her eyes was shinin' and her cheeks white as lilies.

"'Yes,' says she, ' thar is an obstacle, an' I will speak, an' then I will forever hold my peace. I don't love this man I'm standin' beside of, an' I love another man. Now ef Enos Fairweather wants me after what I've said, I've promised to marry him, an' you kin go on; but I won't tell or act a lie before God an' man.'

"Mother said it was awful. You could hev heerd a pin drop anywheres in the room. The minister jest stopped short an' looked at Uncle Enos, an' Uncle Enos nodded his head for him to go on.

"But then the minister begun to hev doubts as to whether or no he ought to marry 'em after what Aunt Rebecca had said, an' it seemed for a minute as ef thar wouldn't be any weddin' at all.

"But grandmother begun to cry, an' take on, an' Aunt Rebecca jest turned round an' looked at her. ' Go on,' says she to the minister.

"Mother said ef thar was ever anybody looked fit to be a martyr, Aunt Rebecca did then. But it never seemed to me 'twas right. Marryin' to please your relations an' dyin' to please the Lord is two things.

"Wa'al, I never thought much of Uncle Enos after I heerd that story, though, as I said before, I guess he was a pretty good sort of a man. The principal thing that was bad about him, I guess, was, he was bound to hev Aunt Rebecca, an' he didn't let anything, even proper self-respect, stand in his way.

"Aunt Rebecca allers did her duty by him, an' was a good wife an' good housekeeper. They never had any children. But I don't s'pose she was ever really happy or contented, an' I don't see how she could hev respected Uncle Enos, scursly, for my part, but you'd never hev known but what she did.

"So I looked at her pretty sharp, as we sot thar in her little bedroom that opened out of the settin' room; thar was jest room for one cheer beside the bed, an' I sot on the bed. It seemed rather awful, with *him* a-layin' dead in the best room, but I couldn't help wonderin' ef she wouldn't marry Abner Lyons now. He'd never got married, but lived all by himself jest at the rise of the hill from where Aunt Rebecca lived. He'd never had a houseckeeper, but jest shifted for himself; an' folks said his house was as neat as wax, an' he could cook an' wash dishes as handy as a woman. He used to hev his washin' out on the line by seven o'clock of a Monday mornin', anyhow; that I know, for I've seen it myself; an' the clothes looked white as snow. I shouldn't hev been ashamed of 'em myself.

"Aunt Rebecca looked very calm, an' I don't think she'd ben cryin'. But then that wa'n't nothin' to go by; 'twa'n't her way. I don't believe she'd 'a' cried ef it had been Abner Lyons. Though I don't know, maybe, ef she'd married the man she'd wanted, she'd cried easier. For all Aunt Rebecca was so kind an' sympathizin' to other folks, she'd always seemed like a stone 'bout her own troubles. I don't s'pose, ef the barn an' house had both burned down, an' left her without a roof over her head, she'd 'a' seemed any different. I kin see her now, jest as she looked, settin' thar, tellin' me the story that would hev flustrated any other woman 'most to death. But her voice was jest as low an' even, an' never shook. Her hair was gray, but it was kinder crinkly, an' her forehead was as white an' smooth as a young girl's.

"Aunt Rebecca's troubles always stayed in her heart, I s'pose, an' never pricked through. Except for her gray hair, she never looked as ef she'd had one.

"She never took on any more when she went to the funeral, for they buried him at last, poor man. He had 'most as hard a time gittin' buried as he did gittin' married. I couldn't help peekin' 'round to see ef Abner Lyons was thar, an' he was, on the other side of the aisle from me. An' he was lookin' straight at Uncle Enos's coffin, that stood up in front under the pulpit, with the curiousest expression that I ever did see.

"He didn't look glad reely. I couldn't say he did, but all I could think of was a man who'd been runnin' an' runnin' to get to a place, an' at length had got in sight of it.

"Maybe 'twas dreadful for him to go to a man's funeral an' look that way, but natur' is natur', an' I always felt somehow that ef Uncle Enos chose to do as he did 'twa'n't anythin' more than he ought to hev expected when he was dead.

"But I did feel awful ashamed an' wicked, thinkin' of such things with the poor man layin' dead before me. An' when I went up to look at him, layin' thar so helpless, I cried like a baby. Poor Uncle Enos! It ain't for us to be down on folks after everything's all over.

"Well, Aunt Rebecca married Abner Lyons 'bout two years after Uncle Enos died, an' they lived together jest five years an' seven months; then she was took sudden with cholera morbus from eatin' currants, an' died. He lived a year an' a half or so longer, an' then he died in a kind of consumption.

"'Twa'n't long they had to be happy together, an' sometimes I used to think they wa'n't so happy after all; for thar's no mistake about it, Abner Lyons was awful fussy. I s'pose his livin' alone so long made him so; but I don't believe Aunt Rebecca ever made a loaf of bread, after she was married, without his havin' something to say about it; an' ef thar's anything that's aggervatin' to a woman, it's havin' a man fussin' around in her kitchen.

"But ef Aunt Rebecca didn't find anything just as she thought it was goin' to be, she never let on she was disapp'inted.

"I declare, Almiry, thar's the house in sight, an' the shower has gone round to the northeast, an' we ain't had a speck of rain to lay the dust.

"Well, my story's gone round to the northeast too. Ain't you tired out hearin' me talk, Almiry?"

"No, indeed, Mis' Green," replied Almira, slapping the reins; "I like to hear you, only it's kind of come to me, as I've been listening, that I *had* heard it before. The last time I took you to Walpole, I guess, you told it."

"Wa'al, I declare, I shouldn't wonder ef I did."

Then the horse turned cautiously around the corner and stopped willingly before the house.

Ambrose Bierce

One of the Missing

JEROME SEARING, a private soldier of General Sherman's army, then confronting the enemy at and about Kenesaw Mountain, Georgia, turned his back upon a small group of officers with whom he had been talking in low tones, stepped across a light line of earthworks, and disappeared in a forest. None of the men in line behind the works had said a word to him, nor had he so much as nodded to them in passing, but all who saw understood that this brave man had been entrusted with some perilous duty.

Jerome Searing, though a private, did not serve in the ranks; he was detailed for service at division headquarters, being borne upon the rolls as an orderly. "Orderly" is a word covering a multitude of duties. An orderly may be a messenger, a clerk, an officer's servant — anything. He may perform services for which no provision is made in orders and army regulations. Their nature may depend upon his aptitude, upon favor, upon accident. Private Searing, an incomparable marksman, young — it is surprising how young we all were in those days — hardy, intelligent, and insensible to fear, was a scout. The general commanding his division was not content to obey orders blindly without knowing what was in his front, even when his command was not on detached service, but formed a fraction of the line of the army; nor was he satisfied to receive his knowledge of his *vis-à-vis* through the customary channels; he wanted to know

From *In the Midst of Life*, 1891.

more than he was apprised of by the corps commander and the collisions of pickets and skirmishers. Hence Jerome Searing — with his extraordinary daring, his woodcraft, his sharp eyes and truthful tongue. On this occasion his instructions were simple: to get as near to the enemy's lines as possible and learn all that he could.

In a few moments he had arrived at the picket line, the men on duty there lying in groups of from two to four behind little banks of earth scooped out of the slight depressions in which they lay, their rifles protruding from the green boughs with which they had masked their small defenses. The forest extended without a break toward the front, so solemn and silent that only by an effort of the imagination could it be conceived as populous with armed men, alert and vigilant — a forest formidable with possibilities of battle. Pausing a moment in one of the rifle pits to apprise the men of his intention, Searing crept stealthily forward on his hands and knees and was soon lost to view in a dense thicket of underbrush.

" That is the last of him," said one of the men. " I wish I had his rifle; those fellows will hurt some of us with it."

Searing crept on, taking advantage of every accident of ground and growth to give himself better cover. His eyes penetrated everywhere, his ears took note of every sound. He stilled his breathing, and at the cracking of a twig beneath his knee stopped his progress and hugged the earth. It was slow work, but not tedious; the danger made it exciting, but by no physical sign was the excitement manifest. His pulse was as regular, his nerves were as steady, as if he were trying to trap a sparrow.

" It seems a long time," he thought, " but I cannot have come very far; I am still alive."

He smiled at his own method of estimating distance and crept forward. A moment later he suddenly flattened himself upon the earth and lay motionless, minute after minute. Through a narrow opening in the bushes he had caught sight of a small mound of yellow clay — one of the enemy's rifle pits. After some little time, he cautiously raised his head, inch by inch, then his body upon his hands, spread out on each side of him, all the while intently regarding the hillock of clay. In another moment he was upon his feet, rifle in hand, striding rapidly forward with little attempt at concealment. He had rightly interpreted the signs, whatever they were; the enemy was gone.

To assure himself beyond a doubt before going back to report on so important a matter, Searing pushed forward across the line of abandoned pits, running from cover to cover in the more open forest, his eyes vigilant to discover possible stragglers. He came to the edge of a plantation — one of those forlorn, deserted homesteads of the last years of the war, upgrown with brambles, ugly with broken fences, and desolate with vacant buildings having blank apertures in place of doors and windows. After a keen reconnaissance from the safe seclusion of a clump of young pines, Searing ran lightly across a field and through an orchard to a small structure which stood apart from the other farm buildings, on a slight elevation, which he thought would enable him to overlook a large scope of country in the direction that he supposed the enemy to have taken in withdrawing. This building, which had originally consisted of a single room, elevated upon four posts about ten feet high, was now little more than a roof; the floor had fallen away, the joists and planks loosely piled on the ground below or resting on end at various angles, not wholly torn from their fastenings above. The supporting posts were themselves no longer vertical. It looked as if the whole edifice would go down at the touch of a finger. Concealing himself in the débris of joists and flooring, Searing looked across the open ground between his point of view and a spur of Kenesaw Mountain, a half mile away. A road leading up and across this spur was crowded with troops — the rearguard of the retiring enemy, their gun barrels gleaming in the morning sunlight.

Searing had now learned all that he could hope to know. It was his duty to return to his own command with all possible speed and report his discovery. But the gray column of infantry toiling up the mountain road was singularly tempting. His rifle — an ordinary Springfield, but fitted with a globe sight and hair trigger — would easily send its ounce and a quarter of lead hissing into their midst. That would probably not affect the duration and result of the war, but it is the business of a soldier to kill. It is also his pleasure if he is a good soldier. Searing cocked his rifle and set the trigger.

But it was decreed from the beginning of time that Private Searing was not to murder anybody that bright summer morning, nor was the Confederate retreat to be announced by him. For countless ages events had been so matching themselves together, in that wondrous mosaic to some parts of which, dimly discernible, we give the name of history, that the acts which he had in will would have marred the harmony of the pattern.

Some twenty-five years previously the Power charged with the execution of the work according to the design had provided against that mischance by causing the birth of a certain male child in a little village at the foot of the Carpathian Mountains, had carefully reared it, supervised its education, directed its desires into a military channel, and in due time made it an officer of artillery. By the concurrence of an infinite number of favoring influences and their preponderance over an infinite number of opposing ones, this officer of artillery had been made to commit a breach of discipline and fly from his native country to avoid punishment. He had been directed to New Orleans (instead of New York), where a recruiting officer awaited him on the wharf. He was enlisted and promoted, and things were so ordered that he now commanded a Confederate battery some three miles along the line from where Jerome Searing, the Federal scout, stood cocking his rifle. Nothing had been neglected; at every step in the progress of both these men's lives, and in the lives of their ancestors and contemporaries and of the lives of the contemporaries of their ancestors, the right thing had been done to bring about the desired result. Had anything in all this vast concatenation been overlooked, Private Searing might have fired on the retreating Confederates that morning, and would perhaps have missed. As it fell out, a captain of artillery, having nothing better to do while awaiting his turn to pull out and be off, amused himself by sighting a fieldpiece obliquely to his right at what he took to be some Federal officers on the crest of a hill, and discharged it. The shot flew high of its mark.

As Jerome Searing drew back the hammer of his rifle and, with his eyes upon the distant Confederates, considered where he could plant his shot with the best hope of making a widow or an orphan or a childless mother — perhaps all three, for Private Searing, although he had repeatedly refused promotion, was not without a certain kind of ambition — he heard a rushing sound in the air, like that made by the wings of a great bird swooping down upon its prey. More quickly than he could apprehend the gradation, it increased to a hoarse and horrible roar, as the missile that made it sprang at him out of the sky, striking with a deafening impact one of the posts supporting the confusion of timbers above him, smashing it into matchwood, and bringing down the crazy edifice with a loud clatter, in clouds of blinding dust!

Lieutenant Adrian Searing, in command of the picket guard on that part of the line through which his brother Jerome had passed on his mission, sat with attentive ears in his breastwork behind the line. Not the faintest sound escaped him; the cry of a bird, the barking of a squirrel, the noise of the wind among the pines — all were anxiously noted by his overstrained sense. Suddenly, directly in front of his line, he heard a faint, confused rumble, like the clatter of a falling building translated by distance. At the same moment an officer approached him on foot from the rear and saluted.

"Lieutenant," said the aide, "the colonel directs you to move forward your line and feel the enemy if you find him. If not, continue the advance until directed to halt. There is reason to think that the enemy has retreated."

The lieutenant nodded and said nothing; the other officer retired. In a moment the men, apprised of their duty by the non-commissioned officers in low tones, had deployed from their rifle pits and were moving forward in skirmishing order, with set teeth and beating hearts. The lieutenant mechanically looked at his watch. Six o'clock and eighteen minutes.

When Jerome Searing recovered consciousness, he did not at once understand what had occurred. It was, indeed, some time before he opened his eyes. For a while he believed that he had died and been buried, and he tried to recall some portions of the burial service. He thought that his wife was kneeling upon his grave, adding her weight to that of the earth upon his breast. The two of them, widow and earth, had crushed his coffin. Unless the children should persuade her to go home, he would not much longer be able to breathe. He felt a sense of wrong. "I cannot speak to her," he thought; "the dead have no voice; and if I open my eyes I shall get them full of earth."

He opened his eyes — a great expanse of blue sky, rising from a fringe of the tops of trees. In the foreground, shutting out some of the trees, a high, dun mound, angular in outline and crossed by an intricate, patternless system of straight lines; in the center a bright ring of metal — the whole an immeasurable distance away — a distance so inconceivably great that it fatigued him, and he closed his eyes. The moment that he did so he was conscious of an insufferable light. A sound was in his ears like the low, rhythmic thunder of a distant sea breaking in successive waves upon the beach, and out of this noise, seeming a part of it, or possibly coming from beyond it, and intermingled with its ceaseless undertone, came the articulate words: " Jerome Searing, you are caught like a rat in a trap — in a trap, trap, trap."

Suddenly there fell a great silence, a black darkness, an infinite tranquillity, and Jerome Searing, perfectly conscious of his rathood, and well assured of the trap that he was in, remembered all, and, nowise alarmed, again opened his eyes to reconnoiter, to note the strength of his enemy, to plan his defense.

He was caught in a reclining posture, his back firmly supported by a solid beam. Another lay across his breast, but he had been able to shrink a little way from it so that it no longer oppressed him, though it was immovable. A brace joining it at an angle had wedged him against a pile of boards on his left, fastening the arm on that side. His legs, slightly parted and straight along the ground, were covered upward to the knees with a mass of débris which towered above his narrow horizon. His head was as rigidly fixed as in a vice; he could move his eyes, his chin — no more. Only his right arm was partly free. " You must help us out of this," he said to it. But he could not get it from under the heavy timber athwart his chest, nor move it outward more than six inches at the elbow.

Searing was not seriously injured, nor did he suffer pain. A smart rap on the head from a flying fragment of the splintered post, incurred simultaneously with the frightfully sudden shock to the nervous system, had momentarily dazed him. His term of unconsciousness, including the period of recovery, during which he had had the strange fancies, had probably not exceeded a few seconds, for the dust of the wreck had not wholly cleared away as he began an intelligent survey of the situation.

With his partly free right hand he now tried to get hold of the beam which lay across, but not quite against, his breast. In no way could he do so. He was unable to depress the shoulder so as to push the elbow beyond the edge of the timber which was nearest his knees; failing in that, he could not raise the forearm and hand to grasp the beam. The brace that made an angle with it downward and backward prevented him from doing anything in that direction, and between it and his body the space was not half as wide as the length of his forearm. Obviously he could not get his hand under the beam nor over it; he could not, in fact, touch it at all. Having demonstrated his inability, he desisted, and began to think if he could reach any of the débris piled upon his legs.

In surveying the mass with a view to determining that point, his attention was arrested by what seemed to be a ring of shining metal immediately in front of his eyes. It appeared to him at first to surround some perfectly black substance, and it was somewhat more than a half inch in diameter. It suddenly occurred to his mind that the blackness was simply shadow, and that the ring was in fact the muzzle of his rifle protruding from the pile of débris. He was not long in satisfying himself that this was so — if it was a satisfaction. By closing either eye he could look a little way along the barrel — to the point where it was hidden by the rubbish that held it. He could see the one side, with the corresponding eye, at apparently the same angle as the other side with the other eye. Looking with the right eye, the weapon seemed to be directed at a point to the left of his head, and *vice versa*. He was unable to see the upper surface of the barrel, but could see the under surface of the stock at a slight angle. The piece was, in fact, aimed at the exact center of his forehead.

In the perception of this circumstance, in the recollection that just previously to the mischance of which this uncomfortable situation was the result, he had cocked the gun and set the trigger so that a touch would discharge it, Private Searing was affected with a feeling of uneasiness. But that was as far as possible from fear; he was a brave man, somewhat familiar with the aspect of rifles from that point of view, and of cannon, too; and now he recalled, with something like amusement, an incident of his experience at the storming of Missionary Ridge, where, walking up to one of the enemy's embrasures from which he had seen a heavy gun throw charge after charge of grape among the assailants, he thought for a moment that the piece had been withdrawn; he could see nothing in the opening but a brazen circle. What that was he had understood just in time to step aside as it pitched another peck of iron down that swarming slope. To face firearms is one of the commonest incidents in a soldier's life — firearms, too, with malevolent eyes blazing behind them. That is what a soldier is for. Still, Private Searing did not altogether relish the situation, and turned away his eyes.

After groping, aimless, with his right hand for a time, he made an ineffectual attempt to release his left. Then he tried to disengage his head, the fixity of which was the more annoying from his ignorance of what held it. Next he tried to free his feet, but while exerting the powerful muscles of his legs for that purpose it occurred to him that a disturbance of the rubbish which held them might discharge the rifle; how it could have endured what had already befallen it he could not understand, although memory assisted him with various instances in point. One in particular he recalled, in which, in a moment of mental abstraction, he had clubbed his rifle and beaten out another gentleman's brains, observing afterward that the weapon which he had been diligently swinging by the muzzle was loaded, capped, and at full cock — knowledge of which circumstance would doubtless have cheered his antagonist to longer endurance. He had always smiled in recalling that blunder of his " green and salad days " as a soldier, but now he did not smile. He turned his eyes again to the muzzle of the gun, and for a moment fancied that it had moved; it seemed somewhat nearer.

Again he looked away. The tops of the distant trees beyond the bounds of the plantation interested him; he had not before observed how light and feathery they seemed, nor how darkly blue the sky was, even among their branches, where they somewhat paled it with their green; above him it appeared almost black. " It will be uncomfortably hot here," he thought, " as the day advances. I wonder which way I am looking."

Judging by such shadows as he could see, he decided that his face was due north; he would at least not have the sun in his eyes; and north — well, that was toward his wife and children.

"Bah!" he exclaimed aloud, "what have they to do with it?"

He closed his eyes. "As I can't get out, I may as well go to sleep. The rebels are gone, and some of our fellows are sure to stray out here foraging. They'll find me."

But he did not sleep. Gradually he became sensible of a pain in his forehead — a dull ache, hardly perceptible at first, but growing more and more uncomfortable. He opened his eyes and it was gone — closed them and it returned. "The devil!" he said irrelevantly, and stared again at the sky. He heard the singing of birds, the strange metallic note of the meadow lark, suggesting the clash of vibrant blades. He fell into pleasant memories of his childhood, played again with his brother and sister, raced across the fields, shouting to alarm the sedentary larks, entered the somber forest beyond, and with timid steps followed the faint path to Ghost Rock, standing at last with audible heart-throbs before the Dead Man's Cave and seeking to penetrate its awful mystery. For the first time he observed that the opening of the haunted cavern was encircled by a ring of metal. Then all else vanished, and left him gazing into the barrel of his rifle as before. But whereas before it had seemed nearer, it now seemed an inconceivable distance away, and all the more sinister for that. He cried out, and, startled by something in his own voice — the note of fear — lied to himself in denial: "If I don't sing out I may stay here till I die."

He now made no further attempt to evade the menacing stare of the gun barrel. If he turned away his eyes an instant, it was to look for assistance (although he could not see the ground on either side the ruin), and he permitted them to return, obedient to the imperative fascination. If he closed them, it was from weariness; and instantly the poignant pain in his forehead — the prophecy and menace of the bullet — forced him to reopen them.

The tension of nerve and brain was too severe; nature came to his relief with intervals of unconsciousness. Reviving from one of these, he became sensible of a sharp, smarting pain in his right hand, and when he worked his fingers together, or rubbed his palm with them, he could feel that they were wet and slippery. He could not see the hand, but he knew the sensation; it was running blood. In his delirium he had beaten it against the jagged fragments of the wreck, had clutched it full of splinters. He resolved that he would meet his fate more manly. He was a plain, common soldier, had no religion and not much philosophy; he could not die like a hero, with great and wise last words, even if there were someone to hear them, but he could die "game," and he would. But if he could only know when to expect the shot!

Some rats which had probably inhabited the shed came sneaking and scampering about. One of them mounted the pile of débris that held the rifle; another followed, and another. Searing regarded them at first with indifference, then with friendly interest; then, as the thought flashed into his bewildered mind that they might touch the trigger of his rifle, he screamed at them to go away. "It is no business of yours," he cried.

The creatures left; they would return later, attack his face, gnaw away his nose, cut his throat — he knew that, but he hoped by that time to be dead.

Nothing could now unfix his gaze from the little ring of metal with its black interior. The pain in his forehead was fierce and constant. He felt it gradually penetrating the brain more and more deeply, until at last its progress was arrested by the wood at the back of his head. It grew momentarily more insufferable; he began wantonly beating his lacerated hand against the splinters again to counteract that horrible ache. It seemed to throb with a slow, regular recurrence, each pulsation sharper than the preceding, and sometimes he cried out, thinking he felt the fatal bullet. No thoughts of home, of wife and children, of country, of glory. The whole record of memory was effaced. The world had passed away — not a vestige remained. Here, in this confusion of timbers and boards, is the sole universe. Here is immortality in time — each pain an everlasting life. The throbs tick off eternities.

Jerome Searing, the man of courage, the formidable enemy, the strong, resolute warrior, was as pale as a ghost. His jaw was fallen; his eyes protruded; he trembled in every fiber; a cold sweat bathed his entire body; he screamed with fear. He was not insane — he was terrified.

In groping about with his torn and bleeding hand he seized at last a strip of board and, pulling, felt it give way. It lay parallel with his body, and by bending his elbow as much as the contracted space would permit, he could draw it a few inches at a time. Finally it was altogether loosened from the wreckage covering his legs; he could lift it clear of the ground its whole length. A great hope came into his mind: perhaps he could work it upward, that is to say backward, far enough to lift the end and push aside the rifle; or, if that were too tightly wedged, so hold the strip of board as to deflect the bullet. With this object he passed it backward inch by inch, hardly daring to breathe, lest that act somehow defeat his intent, and more than ever unable to remove his eyes from the rifle, which might perhaps now hasten to improve its waning opportunity. Something at least had been gained; in the occupation of his mind in this attempt at self-defense he was less sensible of the pain in his head and had ceased to scream. But he was still dreadfully frightened, and his teeth rattled like castanets.

The strip of board ceased to move to the suasion of his hand. He tugged at it with all his strength, changed the direction of its length all he could, but it had met some extended obstruction behind him, and the end in front was still too far away to clear the pile of débris and reach the muzzle of the gun. It extended, indeed, nearly as far as the trigger guard, which, uncovered by the rubbish, he could imperfectly see with his right eye. He tried to break the strip with his hand, but had no leverage. Perceiving his defeat, all his terror returned, augmented tenfold. The black aperture of the rifle appeared to threaten a sharper and more imminent death in punishment of his rebellion. The track of the bullet through his head ached with an intenser anguish. He began to tremble again.

Suddenly he became composed. His tremor subsided. He clinched his teeth and drew down his eyebrows. He had not exhausted his means of defense; a new design had shaped itself in his mind — another plan of battle. Raising the front end of the strip of board, he carefully pushed it forward through the wreckage at the side of the rifle until it pressed against the trigger guard. Then he moved the end slowly outward until he could feel that it had cleared it; then, closing his eyes, thrust it against the trigger with all his strength!

There was no explosion; the rifle had been discharged as it dropped from his hand when the building fell. But Jerome Searing was dead.

A line of Federal skirmishers swept across the plantation toward the mountain. They passed on both sides of the wrecked building, observing nothing. At a short distance in their rear came their commander, Lieutenant Adrian Searing. He casts his eyes curiously upon the ruin and sees a dead body half buried in boards and timbers. It is so covered with dust that its clothing is Confederate gray. Its face is yellowish white; the cheeks are fallen in, the temples sunken, too, with sharp ridges about them, making the forehead forbiddingly narrow; the upper lip, slightly lifted, shows the white teeth, rigidly clinched. The hair is heavy with moisture, the face as wet as the dewy grass all about. From his point of view the officer does not observe the rifle; the man was apparently killed by the fall of the building.

"Dead a week," said the officer curtly, moving on, mechanically pulling out his watch as if to verify his estimate of time. Six o'clock and forty minutes.

Hamlin Garland

The Return of a Private

THE nearer the train drew toward La Crosse, the soberer the little group of "vets" became. On the long way from New Orleans they had beguiled tedium with jokes and friendly chaff; or with planning with elaborate detail what they were going to do now, after the war. A long journey, slowly, irregularly, yet persistently pushing northward. When they entered on Wisconsin territory they gave a cheer, and another when they reached Madison, but after that they sank into a dumb expectancy. Comrades dropped off at one or two points beyond, until there were only four or five left who were bound for La Crosse County.

Three of them were gaunt and brown; the fourth was gaunt and pale, with signs of fever and ague upon him. One had a great scar down his temple, one limped, and they all had unnaturally large, bright eyes, showing emaciation. There were no bands greeting them at the station, no banks of gaily dressed ladies waving handkerchiefs and shouting "Bravo!" as they came in on the caboose of a freight train into the towns that had cheered and blared at them on their way to war. As they looked out or stepped upon the platform for a moment, while the train stood at the station, the loafers looked at them indiffer-

From *Main-Travelled Roads*, 1891.

ently. Their blue coats, dusty and grimy, were too familiar now to excite notice, much less a friendly word. They were the last of the army to return, and the loafers were surfeited with such sights.

The train jogged forward so slowly that it seemed likely to be midnight before they should reach La Crosse. The little squad grumbled and swore, but it was no use; the train would not hurry, and, as a matter of fact, it was nearly two o'clock when the engine whistled " down brakes."

All of the group were farmers, living in districts several miles out of the town, and all were poor.

" Now, boys," said Private Smith, he of the fever and ague, " we are landed in La Crosse in the night. We've got to stay somewhere till mornin'. Now I ain't got no two dollars to waste on a hotel. I've got a wife and children, so I'm goin' to roost on a bench and take the cost of a bed out of my hide."

" Same here," put in one of the other men. " Hide'll grow on again, dollars'll come hard. It's goin' to be mighty hot skirmishin' to find a dollar these days."

" Don't think they'll be a deputation of citizens waitin' to 'scort us to a hotel, eh? " said another. His sarcasm was too obvious to require an answer.

Smith went on, " Then at daybreak we'll start for home — at least, I will."

" Well, I'll be dummed if I'll take two dollars out o' *my* hide," one of the younger men said. " I'm goin' to a hotel, ef I don't never lay up a cent."

" That'll do f'r you," said Smith; " but if you had a wife an' three young uns dependin' on yeh — "

" Which I ain't, thank the Lord! and don't intend havin' while the court knows itself."

The station was deserted, chill and dark, as they came into it at exactly a quarter to two in the morning. Lit by the oil lamps that flared a dull red light over the dingy benches, the waiting room was not an inviting place. The younger man went off to look up a hotel, while the rest remained and prepared to camp down on the floor and benches. Smith was attended to tenderly by the other men, who spread their blankets on the bench for him and, by robbing themselves, made quite a comfortable bed, though the narrowness of the bench made his sleeping precarious.

It was chill, though August, and the two men, sitting with bowed heads, grew stiff with cold and weariness, and were forced to rise now and again and walk about to warm their stiffened limbs. It did not occur to them, probably, to contrast their coming home with their going forth, or with the coming home of the generals, colonels, or even captains — but to Private Smith, at any rate, there came a sickness at heart almost deadly as he lay there on his hard bed and went over his situation.

In the deep of the night, lying on a board in the town where he had enlisted three years ago, all elation and enthusiasm gone out of him, he faced the fact that with the joy of home-coming was already mingled the bitter juice of care. He saw himself sick, worn out, taking up the work on his half-cleared farm, the inevitable mortgage standing ready with open jaw to swallow half his earnings. He had given three years of his life for a mere pittance of pay, and now — !

Morning dawned at last, slowly, with a pale yellow dome of light rising silently above the bluffs, which stand like some huge storm-devastated castle, just east of the city. Out to the left the great river swept on its massive yet silent way to the south. Bluejays called across the water from hillside to hillside through the clear, beautiful air, and hawks began to skim the tops of the hills. The older men were astir early, but Private Smith had fallen at last into a sleep, and they went out without waking him. He lay on his knapsack, his gaunt face turned toward the ceiling, his hands clasped on his breast, with a curious pathetic effect of weakness and appeal.

An engine switching near woke him at last, and he slowly sat up and stared about. He looked out of the window and saw that the sun was lightening the hills across the river. He rose and brushed his hair as well as he could, folded his blankets up, and went out to find his companions. They stood gazing silently at the river and at the hills.

" Looks natcher'l, don't it? " they said as he came out.

" That's what it does," he replied. " An' it looks good. D'yeh see that peak? " He pointed at a beautiful symmetrical peak, rising like a slightly truncated cone, so high that it seemed the very highest of them all. It was touched by that morning sun and it glowed like a beacon, and a light scarf of gray morning fog was rolling up its shadowed side.

" My farm's just beyond that. Now, if I can only ketch a ride, we'll be home by dinnertime."

" I'm talkin' about breakfast," said one of the others.

" I guess it's one more meal o' hardtack f'r me," said Smith.

They foraged around, and finally found a restaurant with a sleepy old German behind the counter, and procured some coffee, which they drank to wash down their hardtack.

" Time'll come," said Smith, holding up a piece by the corner, " when this'll be a curiosity."

" I hope to God it will! I bet I've chawed hardtack enough to shingle every house in the coolly. I've chawed it when my lampers was down and when they wasn't. I've took it dry, soaked, and mashed. I've had it wormy, musty, sour, and blue-moldy. I've had it in little bits and big bits; 'fore coffee an' after coffee. I'm ready f'r a change. I'd like t' git holt jest about now o' some of the hot biscuits my wife c'n make when she lays herself out f'r company."

" Well, if you set there gabblin', you'll never see yer wife."

" Come on," said Private Smith. " Wait a moment, boys; le's take suthin'. It's on me." He led them to the rusty tin dipper which hung on a nail beside the wooden water-pail, and they grinned and drank. Then shouldering their blankets and muskets, which they were " takin' home to the boys," they struck out on their last march.

" They called that coffee Jayvy," grumbled one of them, " but it never went by the road where government Jayvy resides. I reckon I know coffee from peas."

They kept together on the road along the turnpike, and up the winding road by the river, which they followed for some miles. The river was very lovely, curving down along its sandy beds, pausing now and then under broad basswood trees, or running in dark, swift, silent currents under tangles of wild grape vines, and drooping alders, and haw trees. At one of these lovely spots the three vets sat down on the thick green sward to rest, " on Smith's account." The leaves of the trees were as fresh and green as in June, the jays called cheery greetings to them, and kingfishers darted to and fro with swooping, noiseless flight.

" I tell yeh, boys, this knocks the swamps of Loueesiana into kingdom come."

" You bet. All they c'n raise down there is snakes, niggers, and p'rticler hell."

" An' fightin' men," put in the older man.

" An' fightin' men. If I had a good hook an' line I'd sneak a pick'rel out o' that pond. Say, remember that time I shot that alligator — "

" I guess we'd better be crawlin' along," interrupted Smith, rising and shouldering his knapsack, with considerable effort, which he tried to hide.

" Say, Smith, lemme give you a lift on that."

" I guess I c'n manage," said Smith grimly.

" Course. But, yo' see, I may not have a chance right off to pay yeh back for the times you've carried my gun and hull caboodle. Say, now, gimme that gun, anyway."

" All right, if yeh feel like it, Jim," Smith replied, and they trudged along doggedly in the sun, which was getting higher and hotter each half mile.

" Ain't it queer there ain't no teams comin' along," said Smith after a long silence.

" Well, no, seein's it's Sunday."

" By jinks, that's a fact. It *is* Sunday. I'll git home in time f'r dinner, sure! " he exulted. " She don't hev dinner usially till about *one* on Sundays." And he fell into a muse, in which he smiled.

" Well, I'll git home jest about six o'clock, jest about when the boys are milkin' the cows," said old Jim Cranby. " I'll step into the barn, an' then I'll say, ' He*ah!* why ain't this milkin' done before this time o' day? ' An' then won't they yell! " he added, slapping his thigh in great glee.

Smith went on. " I'll jest go up the path. Old Rover'll come down the road to meet me. He won't bark — he'll know me — an' he'll come down waggin' his tail an' showin' his teeth. That's his way of laughin'. An' so I'll walk up to the kitchen door, an' I'll say, ' *Dinner* f'r a hungry man! ' An' then she'll jump up, an' — "

He couldn't go on. His voice choked at the thought of it. Saunders, the third man, hardly uttered a word, but walked silently behind the others. He had lost his wife the first year he was in the army. She died of pneumonia, caught in the autumn rains while working in the fields in his place.

They plodded along till at last they came to a parting of the ways. To the right the road continued up the main valley; to the left it went over the big ridge.

" Well, boys," began Smith as they grounded their muskets and looked away up the valley, " here's where we shake hands. We've marched together a good many miles, an' now I s'pose we're done."

"Yes, I don't think we'll do any more of it f'r a while. I don't want to, I know."

"I hope I'll see yeh once in a while, boys, to talk over old times."

"Of course," said Saunders, whose voice trembled a little, too. "It ain't *exactly* like dyin'." They all found it hard to look at each other.

"But we'd ought'r go home with you," said Cranby. "You'll never climb that ridge with all them things on yer back."

"Oh, I'm all right! Don't worry about me. Every step takes me nearer home, yeh see. Well, good-by, boys."

They shook hands. "Good-by. Good luck!"

"Same to you. Lemme know how you find things at home."

"Good-by."

"Good-by."

He turned once before they passed out of sight, and waved his cap, and they did the same, and all yelled. Then all marched away with their long, steady, loping, veteran step. The solitary climber in blue walked on for a time, with his mind filled with the kindness of his comrades, and musing upon the many wonderful days they had had together in camp and field.

He thought of his chum, Billy Tripp. Poor Billy! A "minie" ball fell into his breast one day, fell wailing like a cat, and tore a great ragged hole in his heart. He looked forward to a sad scene with Billy's mother and sweetheart. They would want to know all about it. He tried to recall all that Billy had said, and the particulars of it; but there was little to remember — just that wild wailing sound high in the air, a dull slap, a short, quick, expulsive groan, and the boy lay with his face in the dirt in the plowed field they were marching across.

That was all. But all the scenes he had since been through had not dimmed the horror, the terror of that moment, when his boy comrade fell, with only a breath between a laugh and a death groan. Poor handsome Billy! Worth millions of dollars was his young life.

These somber recollections gave way at length to more cheerful feelings as he began to approach his home coolly. The fields and houses grew familiar, and in one or two he was greeted by people seated in the doorways. But he was in no mood to talk, and pushed on steadily, though he stopped and accepted a drink of milk once at the well-side of a neighbor.

The sun was burning hot on that slope, and his step grew slower in spite of his iron resolution. He sat down several times to rest. Slowly he crawled up the rough, reddish-brown road, which wound along the hillside, under great trees, through dense groves of jack oaks, with treetops far below him on his left hand, and the hills far above him on his right. He crawled along like some minute, wingless variety of fly.

He ate some hardtack, sauced with wild berries, when he reached the summit of the ridge, and sat there for some time, looked down into his home coolly.

Somber, pathetic figure! His wide, round, gray eyes gazing down into the beautiful valley, seeing and not seeing, the splendid cloud-shadows sweeping over the western hills and across the green and yellow wheat far below. His head dropped forward on his palm, his shoulders took on a tired stoop, his cheekbones showed painfully. An observer might have said, " He is looking down upon his own grave."

II

Sunday comes in a Western wheat harvest with such sweet and sudden relaxation to man and beast that it would be holy for that reason if for no other, and Sundays are usually fair in harvest time. As one goes out into the field in the hot morning sunshine, with no sound abroad save the crickets and the indescribably pleasant silken rustling of the ripened grain, the reaper and the very sheaves in the stubble seem to be resting, dreaming.

Around the house, in the shade of the trees, the men sit, smoking, dozing, or reading the papers, while the women, never resting, move about at the housework. The men eat on Sundays about the same as on other days, and breakfast is no sooner over and out of the way than dinner begins.

But at the Smith farm there were no men dozing or reading. Mrs. Smith was alone with her three children, Mary, nine, Tommy, six, and little Ted, just past four. Her farm, rented to a neighbor, lay at the head of a coolly or narrow gully, made at some far-off post-glacial period by the vast and angry floods of water which gullied these tremendous furrows in the level prairie — furrows so deep that undisturbed portions of the original level rose like hills on either side, rose to quite considerable mountains.

The chickens wakened her as usual that Sabbath morning from dreams of her absent husband, from whom she had not heard for weeks. The shadows drifted over the hills, down the slopes, across the wheat, and up the opposite wall in leisurely way, as if, being Sunday, they could take it easy also. The fowls clustered about the housewife as she went out into the yard. Fuzzy little chickens swarmed out from the coops, where their clucking and perpetually disgruntled mothers tramped about, petulantly thrusting their heads through the spaces between the slats.

A cow called in a deep, musical bass, and a calf answered from a little pen near by, and a pig scurried guiltily out of the cabbages. Seeing all this, seeing the pig in the cabbages, the tangle of grass in the garden, the broken fence which she had mended again and again — the little woman, hardly more than a girl, sat down and cried. The bright Sabbath morning was only a mockery without him!

A few years ago they had bought this farm, paying part, mortgaging the rest in the usual way. Edward Smith was a man of terrible energy. He worked " nights and Sundays," as the saying goes, to clear the farm of its brush and of its insatiate mortgage. In the midst of his Herculean struggle came the call for volunteers, and with the grim and unselfish devotion to his country which made the Eagle Brigade able to " whip its weight in wildcats," he threw down his scythe and grub-axe, turned his cattle loose, and became a blue-coated cog in a vast machine for killing men and not thistles. While the millionaire sent his money to England for safekeeping, this man, with his girl-wife and three babies, left them on a mortgaged farm and went away to fight for an idea. It was foolish, but it was sublime for all that.

That was three years before, and the young wife, sitting on the well-curb on this bright Sabbath harvest morning, was righteously rebellious. It seemed to her that she had borne her share of the country's sorrow. Two brothers had been killed, the renter in whose hands her husband had left the farm had proved a villain; one year the farm had been without crops, and now the over-ripe grain was waiting the tardy hand of the neighbor who had rented it, and who was cutting his own grain first.

About six weeks before, she had received a letter saying, " We'll be discharged in a little while." But no other word had come from him. She had seen by the papers that his army was being discharged, and from day to day other soldiers slowly percolated in blue streams back into the state and county, but still her hero did not return.

Each week she had told the children that he was coming, and she had watched the road so long that it had become unconscious; and as she stood at the well, or by the kitchen door, her eyes were fixed unthinkingly on the road that wound down the coolly.

Nothing wears on the human soul like waiting. If the stranded mariner, searching the sun-bright seas, could once give up hope of a ship, that horrible grinding on his brain would cease. It was this waiting, hoping, on the edge of despair, that gave Emma Smith no rest.

Neighbors said, with kind intentions: " He's sick, maybe, an' can't start north just yet. He'll come along one o' these days."

" Why don't he write? " was her question, which silenced them all. This Sunday morning it seemed to her as if she could not stand it longer. The house seemed intolerably lonely. So she dressed the little ones in their best calico dresses and homemade jackets, and, closing up the house, set off down the coolly to old Mother Gray's.

" Old Widder Gray " lived at the " mouth of the coolly." She was a widow woman with a large family of stalwart boys and laughing girls. She was the visible incarnation of hospitality and optimistic poverty. With Western openheartedness she fed every mouth that asked food of her, and worked herself to death as cheerfully as her girls danced in the neighborhood harvest dances.

She waddled down the path to meet Mrs. Smith with a broad smile on her face.

" Oh, you little dears! Come right to your granny. Gimme a kiss! Come right in, Mis' Smith. How are yeh, anyway? Nice mornin', ain't it? Come in an' set down. Everything's in a clutter, but that won't scare you any."

She led the way into the best room, a sunny, square room, carpeted with a faded and patched rag carpet, and papered with white and green striped wallpaper, where a few faded effigies of dead members of the family hung in variously sized oval walnut frames. The house resounded with singing, laughter, whistling, tramping of heavy boots, and riotous scufflings. Half-grown boys came to the door and crooked their fingers at the children, who ran out and were soon heard in the midst of the fun.

"Don't s'pose you've heard from Ed?" Mrs. Smith shook her head. "He'll turn up some day, when you ain't lookin' for 'im." The good old soul had said that so many times that poor Mrs. Smith derived no comfort from it any longer.

"Liz heard from Al the other day. He's comin' some day this week. Anyhow, they expect him."

"Did he say anything of — "

"No, he didn't," Mrs. Gray admitted. "But then it was only a short letter, anyhow. Al ain't much for writin', anyhow. But come out and see my new cheese. I tell yeh, I don't believe I ever had better luck in my life. If Ed should come, I want you should take him up a piece of this cheese."

It was beyond human nature to resist the influence of that noisy, hearty, loving household, and in the midst of the singing and laughing the wife forgot her anxiety, for the time at least, and laughed and sang with the rest.

About eleven o'clock a wagonload more drove up to the door, and Bill Gray, the widow's oldest son, and his whole family from Sand Lake Coolly piled out amid a good-natured uproar. Everyone talked at once, except Bill, who sat in the wagon with his wrists on his knees, a straw in his mouth, and an amused twinkle in his blue eyes.

"Ain't heard nothin' o' Ed, I s'pose?" he asked in a kind of bellow. Mrs. Smith shook her head. Bill, with a delicacy very striking in such a great giant, rolled his quid in his mouth, and said:

"Didn't know but you had. I hear two or three of the Sand Lake boys are comin'. Left New Orleens some time this week. Didn't write nothin' about Ed, but no news is good news in such cases, mother always says."

"Well, go put out yer team," said Mrs. Gray, "an' go'n bring me in some taters. An', Sim, you go see if you c'n find some corn. Sadie, you put on the water to bile. Come now, hustle yer boots, all o' yeh. If I feed this yer crowd, we've got to have some raw materials. If y' think I'm goin' to feed yeh on pie — you're jest mightily mistaken."

The children went off into the fields; the girls put dinner on to boil, and then went to change their dresses and fix their hair. "Somebody might come," they said.

"Land sakes, I *hope* not! I don't know where in time I'd set 'em, 'less they'd eat at the second table," Mrs. Gray laughed, in pretended dismay.

The two older boys, who had served their time in the army, lay out on the grass before the house, and whittled and talked desultorily about the war and the crops, and planned buying a threshing machine. The older girls and Mrs. Smith helped enlarge the table and put on the dishes, talking all the time in that cheery, incoherent, and meaningful way a group of such women have — a conversation to be taken for its spirit rather than for its letter, though Mrs. Gray at last got the ear of them all and dissertated at length on girls.

"Girls in love ain't no use in the whole blessed week," she said. "Sundays they're a-lookin' down the road, expectin' he'll come. Sunday afternoons they can't think o' nothin' else, 'cause he's *here*. Monday mornin's they're sleepy and kind o' dreamy and slimpsy, and good f'r nothin' on Tuesday and Wednesday. Thursday they git absent-minded an' begin to look off toward Sunday again, an' mope aroun' an let the dishwater git cold, right under their noses. Friday they break dishes, an' go off in the best room an' snivel, an' look out o' the winder. Saturdays they have queer spurts o' workin' like all p'ssessed, an' spurts o' frizzin' their hair. An' Sunday they begin it all over again."

The girls giggled and blushed all through this tirade from their mother, their broad faces and powerful frames anything but suggestive of lackadaisical sentiment. But Mrs. Smith said:

" Now, Mrs. Gray, I hadn't ought to stay to dinner. You've got — "

" Now you set right down! If any of them girls' beaux comes, they'll have to take what's left, that's all. They ain't s'posed to have much appetite, nohow. No, you're goin' to stay if they starve, an' they ain't no danger o' that."

At one o'clock the long table was piled with boiled potatoes, cords of boiled corn on the cob, squash and pumpkin pies, hot biscuits, sweet pickles, bread and butter, and honey. Then one of the girls took down a conch shell from a nail and, going to the door, blew a long, fine, free blast that showed there was no weakness of lungs in her ample chest.

Then the children came out of the forest of corn, out of the creek, out of the loft of the barn, and out of the garden.

" They come to their feed f'r all the world jest like the pigs when y' holler 'Poo-ee!' See 'em scoot! " laughed Mrs. Gray, every wrinkle on her face shining with delight.

The men shut up their jackknives, and surrounded the horse trough to souse their faces in the cold, hard water, and in a few moments the table was filled with a merry crowd, and a row of wistful-eyed youngsters circled the kitchen wall, where they stood first on one leg and then on the other, in impatient hunger.

" Now pitch in, Mrs. Smith," said Mrs. Gray, presiding over the table. " You know these men critters. They'll eat every grain of it if yeh give 'em a chance. I swan, they're made o' India rubber, their stomachs is, I know it."

" Haf to eat to work," said Bill, gnawing a cob with a swift, circular motion that rivaled a corn sheller in results.

" More like workin' to eat," put in one of the girls, with a giggle. " More eat 'n work with *you*."

" You needn't say anything, Net. Anyone that'll eat seven ears — "

" I didn't no such thing. You piled your cobs on my plate."

" That'll do to tell Ed Varney. It won't go down here where we know yeh."

" Good land! Eat all yeh want! They's plenty more in the fiel's, but I can't afford to give you young uns tea. The tea is for us womenfolks, an' 'specially f'r Mis' Smith an' Bill's wife. We're a-goin' to tell fortunes by it."

One by one the men filled up and shoved back, and one by one the children slipped into their places, and by two o'clock the women alone remained around the débris-covered table, sipping their tea and telling fortunes.

As they got well down to the grounds in the cup, they shook them with a circular motion in the hand, and then turned them bottom side up quickly in the saucer, then twirled them three or four times one way, and three or four times the other, during a breathless pause. Then Mrs. Gray lifted the cup and, gazing into it with profound gravity, pronounced the impending fate.

It must be admitted that, to a critical observer, she had abundant preparation for hitting close to the mark, as when she told the girls that " somebody was comin'." " It's a man," she went on gravely. " He is cross-eyed — "

" Oh, you hush! " cried Nettie.

" He has red hair, and is death on b'iled corn and hot biscuit."

The others shrieked with delight.

" But he's goin' to get the mitten, that red-headed feller is, for I see another feller comin' up behind him."

" Oh, lemme see, lemme see! " cried Nettie.

" Keep off," said the priestess, with a lofty gesture. " His hair is black. He don't eat so much, and he works more."

The girls exploded in a shriek of laughter and pounded their sister on the back.

At last came Mrs. Smith's turn, and she was trembling with excitement as Mrs. Gray again composed her jolly face to what she considered a proper solemnity of expression.

" Somebody is comin' to *you*," she said, after a long pause. " He's got a musket on his back. He's a soldier. He's almost here. See? "

She pointed at two little tea stems, which really formed a faint suggestion of a man with a musket on his back. He had climbed nearly to the edge of the cup. Mrs. Smith grew pale with excitement. She trembled so, she could hardly hold the cup in her hand as she gazed into it.

" It's Ed," cried the old woman. " He's on the way home. Heavens an' earth! There he is now! " She turned and waved her hand out toward the road. They rushed to the door to look where she pointed.

A man in a blue coat, with a musket on his back, was toiling slowly up the hill on the sun-bright, dusty road — toiling slowly, with bent head half hidden by a heavy knapsack. So tired it seemed that walking was indeed a process of falling. So eager to get home he would not stop, would not look aside, but plodded on, amid the cries of the locusts, the welcome of the crickets, and the rustle of the yellow wheat. Getting back to God's country, and his wife and babies!

Laughing, crying, trying to call him and the children at the same time, the little wife, almost hysterical, snatched her hat and ran out into the yard. But the soldier had disappeared over the hill into the hollow beyond, and, by the time she had found the children, he was too far away for her voice to reach him. And, besides, she was not sure it was her husband, for he had not turned his head at their shouts. This seemed so strange. Why didn't he stop to rest at his old neighbor's house? Tortured by hope and doubt, she hurried up the coolly as fast as she could push the baby wagon, the blue-coated figure just ahead pushing steadily, silently forward up the coolly.

When the excited, panting little group came in sight of the gate they saw the blue-coated figure standing, leaning upon the rough rail fence, his chin on his palms, gazing at the empty house. His knapsack, canteen, blankets, and musket lay upon the dusty grass at his feet.

He was like a man lost in a dream. His wide, hungry eyes devoured the scene. The rough lawn, the little unpainted house, the field of clear yellow wheat behind it, down across which streamed the sun, now almost ready to touch the high hill to the west, the crickets crying merrily, a cat on the fence near by, dreaming, unmindful of the stranger in blue —

How peaceful it all was. O God! How far removed from all camps, hospitals, battle lines. A little cabin in a Wisconsin coolly, but it was majestic in its peace. How did he ever leave it for those years of tramping, thirsting, killing?

Trembling, weak with emotion, her eyes on the silent figure, Mrs. Smith hurried up to the fence. Her feet made no noise in the dust and grass, and they were close upon him before he knew of them. The oldest boy ran a little ahead. He will never forget that figure, that face. It will always remain as something epic, that return of the private. He fixed his eyes on the pale face covered with a ragged beard.

" Who *are* you, sir? " asked the wife — or, rather, started to ask; for he turned, stood a moment, and then cried:

" Emma! "

" Edward! "

The children stood in a curious row to see their mother kiss this bearded, strange man, the elder girl sobbing sympathetically with her mother. Illness had left the soldier partly deaf, and this added to the strangeness of his manner.

But the youngest child stood away, even after the girl had recognized her father and kissed him. The man turned then to the baby and said in a curiously unpaternal tone:

" Come here, my little man. Don't you know me? " But the baby backed away under the fence and stood peering at him critically.

" My little man! " What meaning in those words! This baby seemed like some other woman's child, and not the infant he had left in his wife's arms. The war had come between him and his baby — he was only a strange man to him, with big eyes; a soldier, with mother hanging to his arm, and talking in a loud voice.

" And this is Tom," the private said, drawing the oldest boy to him. " *He'll* come and see me. *He* knows his poor old pap when he comes home from the war."

The mother heard the pain and reproach in his voice and hastened to apologize.

" You've changed so, Ed. He can't know yeh. This is papa, Teddy; come and kiss him — Tom and Mary do. Come, won't you? " But Teddy still peered through the fence with solemn eyes, well out of reach. He resembled a half-wild kitten that hesitates, studying the tones of one's voice.

" I'll fix him," said the soldier, and sat down to undo his knapsack, out of which he drew three enormous and very red apples. After giving one to each of the older children, he said:

" *Now* I guess he'll come. Eh, my little man? Now come see your pap."

Teddy crept slowly under the fence, assisted by the overzealous Tommy, and a moment later was kicking and squalling in his father's arms. Then they entered the house, into the sitting room, poor, bare, art-forsaken little room, too, with its rag carpet, its square clock, and its two or three chromos and pictures from *Harper's Weekly* pinned about.

"Emma, I'm all tired out," said Private Smith as he flung himself down on the carpet as he used to do, while his wife brought a pillow to put under his head, and the children stood about munching their apples.

"Tommy, you run and get me a pan of chips, and Mary, you get the teakettle on, and I'll go and make some biscuit."

And the soldier talked. Question after question he poured forth about the crops, the cattle, the renter, the neighbor. He slipped his heavy government brogan shoes off his poor, tired, blistered feet and lay out with utter, sweet relaxation. He was a free man again, no longer a soldier under command. At supper he stopped once, listened and smiled. "That's old Spot. I know her voice. I s'pose that's her calf out there in the pen. I can't milk her tonight, though. I'm too tired. But I tell you, I'd like a drink o' her milk. What's become of old Rove?"

"He died last winter. Poisoned, I guess." There was a moment of sadness for them all. It was some time before the husband spoke again, in a voice that trembled a little.

"Poor old feller! He'd 'a' known me half a mile away. I expected him to come down the hill to meet me. It 'ud 'a' been more like comin' home if I could 'a' seen him comin' down the road an' waggin' his tail, an' laughin' that way he had. I tell yeh, it kind o' took hold o' me to see the blinds down an' the house shut up."

"But, yeh see, we — we expected you'd write again 'fore you started. And then we thought we'd see you if you *did* come," she hastened to explain.

"Well, I ain't worth a cent on writin'. Besides, it's just as well yeh didn't know when I was comin'. I tell you, it sounds good to hear them chickens out there, an' turkeys, an' the crickets. Do you know they don't have just the same kind o' crickets down South? Who's Sam hired t' help cut yer grain?"

"The Ramsey boys."

"Looks like a good crop; but I'm afraid I won't do much gettin' it cut. This cussed fever an' ague has got me down pretty low. I don't know when I'll get rid of it. I'll bet I've took twenty-five pounds of quinine if I've taken a bit. Gimme another biscuit. I tell yeh, they taste good, Emma. I ain't had anything like it — say, if you'd 'a' hear'd me braggin' to th' boys about your butter 'n' biscuits I'll bet your ears 'ud 'a' burnt."

The private's wife colored with pleasure. "Oh, you're always a-braggin' about your things. Everybody makes good butter."

"Yes; old lady Snyder, for instance."

"Oh, well, she ain't to be mentioned. She's Dutch."

"Or old Mis' Snively. One more cup o' tea, Mary. That's my girl! I'm feeling better already. I just b'lieve the matter with me is, I'm *starved*."

This was a delicious hour, one long to be remembered. They were like lovers again. But their tenderness, like that of a typical American family, found utterance in tones rather than in words. He was praising her when praising her biscuit, and she knew it. They grew soberer when he showed where he had been struck, one ball burning the back of his hand, one cutting away a lock of hair from his temple, and one passing through the calf of his leg. The wife shuddered to think how near she had come to being a soldier's widow. Her waiting no longer seemed hard. This sweet, glorious hour effaced it all.

Then they rose, and all went out into the garden and down to the barn. He stood beside her while she milked old Spot. They began to plan fields and crops for next year.

His farm was weedy and encumbered, a rascally renter had run away with his machinery (departing between two days), his children needed clothing, the years were coming upon him, he was sick and emaciated, but his heroic soul did not quail. With the same courage with which he had faced his southern march he entered upon a still more hazardous future.

Oh, that mystic hour! The pale man with big eyes standing there by the well, with his young wife by his side. The vast moon swinging above the eastern peaks, the cattle winding down the pasture slopes with jangling bells, the crickets singing, the stars blooming out sweet and far and serene; the katydids rhythmically calling, the little turkeys crying querulously, as they settled to roost in the poplar tree near the open gate. The voices at the well drop lower, the little ones nestle in their father's arms at last, and Teddy falls asleep there.

The common soldier of the American volunteer army had returned. His war with the South was over, and his fight, his daily running fight with Nature and against the injustice of his fellow men, was begun again.

O. Henry

A Municipal Report

The cities are full of pride,
  Challenging each to each —
This from her mountainside,
  That from her burthened beach.
            — R. Kipling

Fancy a novel about Chicago or Buffalo, let us say, or Nashville, Tennessee! There are just three big cities in the United States that are " story cities " — New York, of course, New Orleans, and, best of the lot, San Francisco. — Frank Norris

EAST is East, and West is San Francisco, according to Californians. Californians are a race of people; they are not merely inhabitants of a state. They are the Southerners of the West. Now, Chicagoans are no less loyal to their city; but when you ask them why, they stammer and speak of lake fish and the new Odd Fellows' Building. But Californians go into detail.

From *Strictly Business*, 1910.

Of course they have, in the climate, an argument that is good for half an hour while you are thinking of your coal bills and heavy underwear. But as soon as they come to mistake your silence for conviction, madness comes upon them, and they picture the city of the Golden Gate as the Bagdad of the New World. So far, as a matter of opinion, no refutation is necessary. But, dear cousins all (from Adam and Eve descended), it is a rash one who will lay his finger on the map and say: " In this town there can be no romance — what could happen here? " Yes, it is a bold and a rash deed to challenge in one sentence history, romance, and Rand and McNally.

NASHVILLE. — A city, port of delivery, and the capital of the State of Tennessee, is on the Cumberland River and on the N. C. & St. L. and the L. & N. railroads. This city is regarded as the most important educational center in the South.

I stepped off the train at 8 P.M. Having searched the thesaurus in vain for adjectives, I must, as a substitution, hie me to comparison in the form of a recipe.

Take of London fog 30 parts; malaria 10 parts; gas leaks 20 parts; dewdrops gathered in a brickyard at sunrise 25 parts; odor of honeysuckle 15 parts. Mix.

The mixture will give you an approximate conception of a Nashville drizzle. It is not so fragrant as a moth ball nor as thick as pea soup; but 'tis enough — 'twill serve.

I went to a hotel in a tumbril. It required strong self-suppression for me to keep from climbing to the top of it and giving an imitation of Sidney Carton. The vehicle was drawn by beasts of a bygone era and driven by something dark and emancipated.

I was sleepy and tired; so when I got to the hotel I hurriedly paid it the fifty cents it demanded (with approximate lagniappe, I assure you). I knew its habits; and I did not want to hear it prate about its old " marster " or anything that happened " befo' de wah."

The hotel was one of the kind described as " renovated." That means twenty thousand dollars' worth of new marble pillars, tiling, electric lights and brass cuspidors in the lobby, and a new L. & N. timetable and a lithograph of Lookout Mountain in each one of the great rooms above. The management was without reproach, the attention full of exquisite Southern courtesy, the service as slow as the progress of a snail and as good-humored as Rip Van Winkle. The food was worth traveling a thousand miles for. There is no other hotel in the world where you can get such chicken livers *en brochette*.

At dinner I asked a Negro waiter if there was anything doing in town. He pondered gravely for a minute and then replied: " Well, boss, I don't really reckon there's anything at all doin' after sundown."

Sundown had been accomplished; it had been drowned in the drizzle long before. So that spectacle was denied me. But I went forth upon the streets in the drizzle to see what might be there.

It is built on undulating grounds; and the streets are lighted by electricity at a cost of $32,470 per annum.

As I left the hotel there was a race riot. Down upon me charged a company of freedmen, or Arabs, or Zulus, armed with — no, I saw with relief that they were not rifles, but whips. And I saw dimly a caravan of black, clumsy vehicles; and at the reassuring shouts, " Kyar you anywhere in the town, boss, fuh fifty cents," I reasoned that I was merely a " fare " instead of a victim.

I walked through long streets, all leading uphill. I wondered how those streets ever came down again. Perhaps they didn't until they were " graded." On a few of the " main streets " I saw lights in stores here and there; saw streetcars go by, conveying worthy burghers hither and yon; saw people pass engaged in the art of conversation; and heard a burst of semi-lively laughter issuing from a soda-water and ice-cream parlor. The streets other than " main " seemed to have enticed upon their borders houses consecrated to peace and domesticity. In many of them lights shone behind discreetly drawn window shades; in a few, pianos tinkled orderly and irreproachable music. There was, indeed, little " doing." I wished I had come before sundown. So I returned to my hotel.

In November, 1864, the Confederate General Hood advanced against Nashville, where he shut up a National force under General Thomas. The latter then sallied forth and defeated the Confederates in a terrible conflict.

All my life I have heard of, admired, and witnessed the fine marksmanship of the South in its peaceful conflicts in the tobacco-chewing regions. But in my hotel a surprise awaited me. There were twelve bright, new, imposing, capacious brass cuspidors in the great lobby, tall enough to be called urns and so wide-mouthed that the crack pitcher of a lady baseball team should have been able to throw a ball into each one of them at five paces distant. But, although a terrible battle had raged and was still raging, the enemy had not suffered. Bright, new, imposing, capacious, untouched, they stood. But, shades of Jefferson Brick! the tile floor — the beautiful tile floor! I could not avoid thinking of the battle of Nashville, and trying to draw, as is my foolish habit, some deductions about hereditary marksmanship.

Here I first saw Major (by misplaced courtesy) Wentworth Caswell. I knew him for a type the moment my eyes suffered from the sight of him. A rat has no geographical habitat. My old friend, A. Tennyson, said, as he so well said almost everything:

> Prophet, curse me the blabbing lip,
> And curse me the British vermin, the rat.

Let us regard the word " British " as interchangeable *ad lib*. A rat is a rat.

This man was hunting about the hotel lobby like a starved dog that had forgotten where he had buried a bone. He had a face of great acreage, red, pulpy, and with a kind of sleepy massiveness like that of Buddha. He possessed one single virtue — he was smoothly shaven. The mark of the beast is not indelible upon a man until he goes about with a stubble. I think that if he had not used his razor that day I would have repulsed his advances, and the criminal calendar of the world would have been spared the addition of one murder.

I happened to be standing within five feet of a cuspidor when Major Caswell opened fire upon it. I had been observant enough to perceive that the attacking force was using Gatlings instead of squirrel rifles; so I side-stepped so promptly that the Major seized the opportunity to apologize to a noncombatant. He had the blabbing lip. In four minutes he had become my friend and had dragged me to the bar.

I desire to interpolate here that I am a Southerner. But I am not one by profession or trade. I eschew the string tie, the slouch hat, the Prince Albert, the number of bales of cotton destroyed by Sherman, and plug chewing. When the orchestra plays " Dixie " I do not cheer. I slide a little lower on the leather-cornered seat and — well — order another Würzburger and wish that Longstreet had — but what's the use?

Major Caswell banged the bar with his fist, and the first gun at Fort Sumter reëchoed. When he fired the last one at Appomattox I began to hope. But then he began on family trees, and demonstrated that Adam was only a third cousin of a collateral branch of the Caswell family. Genealogy disposed of, he took up, to my distaste, his private family matters. He spoke of his wife, traced her descent back to Eve, and profanely denied any possible rumor that she may have had relations in the land of Nod.

By this time I began to suspect that he was trying to obscure by the noise the fact that he had ordered the drinks, on the chance that I would be bewildered into paying for them. But when they were down he crashed a silver dollar loudly upon the bar. Then, of course, another serving was obligatory. And when I had paid for that I took leave of him brusquely; for I wanted no more of him. But before I had obtained my release he had prated loudly of an income that his wife received, and showed a handful of silver money.

When I got my key at the desk the clerk said to me courteously: " If that man Caswell has annoyed you, and if you would like to make a complaint, we will have him ejected. He is a nuisance, a loafer, and without any known means of support, although he seems to have money most of the time. But we don't seem to be able to hit upon any means of throwing him out legally."

" Why, no," said I, after some reflection; " I don't see my way clear to make a complaint. But I would like to place myself on record as asserting that I do not care for his company. Your town," I continued, " seems to be a quiet one. What manner of entertainment, adventure, or excitement have you to offer to the stranger within your gates? "

" Well, sir," said the clerk, " there will be a show here next Thursday. It is — I'll look it up and have the announcement sent up to your room with the ice water. Good night."

After I went up to my room I looked out of the window. It was only about ten o'clock, but I looked upon a silent town. The drizzle continued, spangled with dim lights, as far apart as currants in a cake sold at the Ladies' Exchange.

" A quiet place," I said to myself, as my first shoe struck the ceiling of the occupant of the room beneath mine. " Nothing of the life here that gives color and variety to the cities in the East and West. Just a good, ordinary, humdrum, business town."

Nashville occupies a foremost place among the manufacturing centers of the country. It is the fifth boot and shoe market in the United States, the largest candy and cracker manufacturing city in the South, and does an enormous wholesale dry-goods, grocery, and drug business.

I must tell you how I came to be in Nashville, and I assure you the digression brings as much tedium to me as it does to you. I was traveling elsewhere on my own business, but I had a commission from a Northern literary magazine to stop over there and establish a connection between the publication and one of its personal contributors, Azalea Adair.

Adair (there was no clue to the personality except the handwriting) had sent in some essays (lost art!) and poems that had made the editors swear approvingly over their one o'clock luncheon. So they had commissioned me to round up said Adair and corner by contract his or her output at two cents a word before some other publisher offered her ten or twenty.

At nine o'clock the next morning, after my chicken livers *en brochette* (try them if you find that hotel), I strayed out into the drizzle, which was still on for an unlimited run. At the first corner, I came upon Uncle Caesar. He was a stalwart Negro older than the pyramids, with gray wool and a face that reminded me of Brutus, and a second afterwards of the late King Cetewayo. He wore the most remarkable coat that I ever had seen or expect to see. It reached to his ankles and had once been a Confederate gray in color. But rain and sun and age had so variegated it that Joseph's coat, beside it, would have faded to a pale monochrome. I must linger with that coat, for it has to do with the story — the story that is so long in coming, because you can hardly expect anything to happen in Nashville.

Once it must have been the military coat of an officer. The cape of it had vanished, but all adown its front it had been frogged and tasseled magnificently. But now the frogs and tassels were gone. In their stead had been patiently stitched (I surmise by some surviving " black mammy ") new frogs made of cunningly twisted common hempen twine. This twine was frayed and disheveled. It must have been added to the coat as a substitute for vanished splendors, with tasteless but painstaking devotion, for it followed faithfully the curves of the long-missing frogs. And, to complete the comedy and pathos of the garment, all its buttons were gone save one. The second button from the top alone remained. The coat was fastened by other twine strings tied through the buttonholes and other holes rudely pierced on the opposite side. There was never such a weird garment so fantastically bedecked and of so many mottled hues. The lone button was the size of a half dollar, made of yellow horn and sewed on with coarse twine.

This Negro stood by a carriage so old that Ham himself might have started a hack line after he left the ark with the two animals hitched to it. As I approached he threw open the door, drew out a feather duster, waved it without using it, and said in deep, rumbling tones:

" Step right in, suh; ain't a speck of dust in it — jus' got back from a funeral, suh."

I inferred that on such gala occasions carriages were given an extra cleaning. I looked up and down the street and perceived that there was little choice among the vehicles for hire that lined the curb. I looked in my memorandum book for the address of Azalea Adair.

"I want to go to 861 Jessamine Street," I said, and was about to step into the hack.

But for an instant the thick, gorilla-like arm of the old Negro barred me. On his massive and saturnine face a look of sudden suspicion and enmity flashed for a moment. Then, with quickly returning conviction, he asked blandishingly: "What are you gwine there for, boss?"

"What is that to you?" I asked a little sharply.

"Nothin', suh, jus' nothin'. Only it's a lonesome kind of part of town and few folks ever has business there. Step right in. The seats is clean — jes' got back from a funeral, suh."

A mile and a half it must have been to our journey's end. I could hear nothing but the fearful rattle of the ancient hack over the uneven brick paving; I could smell nothing but the drizzle, now further flavored with coal smoke and something like a mixture of tar and oleander blossoms. All I could see through the streaming windows were two rows of dim houses.

The city has an area of 10 square miles; 181 miles of streets of which 137 miles are paved; a system of waterworks that cost $2,000,000, with 77 miles of mains.

Eight-sixty-one Jessamine Street was a decayed mansion. Thirty yards back from the street it stood, outmerged in a splendid grove of trees and untrimmed shrubbery. A row of box bushes overflowed and almost hid the paling fence from sight; the gate was kept closed by a rope noose that encircled the gatepost and the first paling of the gate. But when you got inside you saw that Eight-sixty-one was a shell, a shadow, a ghost of former grandeur and excellence. But in the story, I have not yet got inside.

When the hack had ceased from rattling and the weary quadrupeds came to a rest, I handed my Jehu his fifty cents with an additional quarter, feeling a glow of conscious generosity as I did so. He refused it.

"It's two dollars, suh," he said.

"How's that?" I asked. "I plainly heard you call out at the hotel: 'Fifty cents to any part of the town.'"

"It's two dollars, suh," he repeated obstinately. "It's a long ways from the hotel."

"It is within the city limits and well within them," I argued. "Don't think that you have picked up a greenhorn Yankee. Do you see those hills over there?" I went on, pointing toward the east (I could not see them, myself, for the drizzle); "well, I was born and raised on their other side. You old fool nigger, can't you tell people from other people when you see 'em?"

The grim face of King Cetewayo softened. "Is you from the South, suh? I reckon it was them shoes of yourn fooled me. They is somethin' sharp in the toes for a Southern gen'l'man to wear."

"Then the charge is fifty cents, I suppose?" said I inexorably.

His former expression, a mingling of cupidity and hostility, returned, remained ten seconds, and vanished.

"Boss," he said, "fifty cents is right; but I *needs* two dollars, suh; I'm *obleeged* to have two dollars. I ain't *demandin'* it now, suh, after I knows whar you's from; I'm jus' sayin' that I *has* to have two dollars tonight, and business is mighty po'."

Peace and confidence settled upon his heavy features. He had been luckier than he had hoped. Instead of having picked up a greenhorn, ignorant of rates, he had come upon an inheritance.

"You confounded old rascal," I said, reaching down to my pocket, "you ought to be turned over to the police."

For the first time I saw him smile. He knew; he *knew*; HE KNEW.

I gave him two one-dollar bills. As I handed them over I noticed that one of them had seen parlous times. Its upper right-hand corner was missing, and it had been torn through the middle, but joined again. A strip of blue tissue paper, pasted over the split, preserved its negotiability.

Enough of the African bandit for the present: I left him happy, lifted the rope, and opened the creaky gate.

The house, as I said, was a shell. A paint brush had not touched it in twenty years. I could not see why a strong wind should not have bowled it over like a house of cards until I looked again at the trees that hugged it close — the trees that saw the battle of Nashville and still drew their protecting branches around it against storm and enemy and cold.

Azalea Adair, fifty years old, white-haired, a descendant of the cavaliers, as thin and frail as the house she lived in, robed in the cheapest and cleanest dress I ever saw, with an air as simple as a queen's, received me.

The reception room seemed a mile square, because there was nothing in it except some rows of books, on unpainted white-pine bookshelves, a cracked marble-top table, a rag rug, a hairless horsehair sofa, and two or three chairs. Yes, there was a picture on the wall, a colored crayon drawing of a cluster of pansies. I looked around for the portrait of Andrew Jackson and the pinecone hanging basket, but they were not there.

Azalea Adair and I had conversation, a little of which will be repeated to you. She was a product of the old South, gently nurtured in the sheltered life. Her learning was not broad, but was deep and of splendid originality in its somewhat narrow scope. She had been educated at home, and her knowledge of the world was derived from inference and by inspiration. Of such is the precious, small group of essayists made. While she talked to me I kept brushing my fingers, trying, unconsciously, to rid them guiltily of the absent dust from the half-calf backs of Lamb, Chaucer, Hazlitt, Marcus Aurelius, Montaigne, and Hood. She was exquisite, she was a valuable discovery; nearly everybody nowadays knows too much — oh, so much too much — of real life.

I could perceive clearly that Azalea Adair was very poor. A house and a dress she had — not much else, I fancied. So, divided between my duty to the magazine and my loyalty to the poets and essayists, who fought Thomas in the valley of the Cumberland, I listened to her voice, which was like a harpsichord's, and found that I could not speak of contracts. In the presence of the nine Muses and the three Graces one hesitated to lower the topic to two cents. There would have to be another colloquy after I had regained my commercialism. But I spoke of my mission, and three o'clock of the next afternoon was set for the discussion of the business proposition.

"Your town," I said, as I began to make ready to depart (which is the time for smooth generalities), "seems to be a quiet, sedate place. A home town, I should say, where few things out of the ordinary ever happen."

It carries an extensive trade in stoves and hollow ware with the West and South, and its flouring mills have a daily capacity of more than two thousand barrels.

Azalea Adair seemed to reflect.

"I have never thought of it that way," she said, with a kind of sincere intensity that seemed to belong to her. "Isn't it in the still, quiet places that things do happen? I fancy that when God began to create the earth on the first Monday morning one could have leaned out one's window and heard the drops of mud splashing from His trowel as He built up the everlasting hills. What did the noisiest project in the world — I mean the building of the tower of Babel — result in finally? A page and a half of Esperanto in the *North American Review.*"

"Of course," I said platitudinously, "human nature is the same everywhere; but there is more color — er — more drama and movement and — er — romance in some cities than in others."

"On the surface," said Azalea Adair. "I have traveled many times round the world in a golden airship wafted on two wings — print and dreams. I have seen (on one of my imaginary tours) the Sultan of Turkey bowstring with his own hands one of his wives who had uncovered her face in public. I have seen a man in Nashville tear up his theater tickets because his wife was going out with her face covered — with rice powder. In San Francisco's Chinatown I saw the slave girl Sing Yee dipped slowly, inch by inch, in boiling almond oil to make her swear she would never see her American lover again. She gave in when the boiling oil had reached three inches above her knee. At a euchre party in East Nashville the other night, I saw Kitty Morgan cut dead by seven of her schoolmates and lifelong friends because she had married a house painter. The boiling oil was sizzling as high as her heart; but I wish you could have seen the fine little smile that she carried from table to table. Oh, yes, it is a humdrum town. Just a few miles of red brick houses and mud stores and lumber yards."

Someone knocked hollowly at the back of the house. Azalea Adair breathed a soft apology and went to investigate the sound. She came back in three minutes with brightened eyes, a faint flush on her cheeks, and ten years lifted from her shoulders.

"You must have a cup of tea before you go," she said, "and a sugar cake."

She reached and shook a little iron bell. In shuffled a small Negro girl about twelve, barefoot, not very tidy, glowering at me with thumb in mouth and bulging eyes.

Azalea Adair opened a tiny, worn purse and drew out a dollar bill, with the upper right-hand corner missing, torn in two pieces and pasted together again with a strip of blue tissue paper. It was one of the bills I had given the piratical Negro — there was no doubt of it.

" Go up to Mr. Baker's store on the corner, Impy," she said, handing the girl the dollar bill, " and get me a quarter of a pound of tea — the kind he always sends me — and ten cents' worth of sugar cakes. Now, hurry. The supply of tea in the house happens to be exhausted," she explained to me.

Impy left by the back way. Before the scrape of her hard, bare feet had died away on the back porch, a wild shriek — I was sure it was hers — filled the hollow house. Then the deep, gruff tones of an angry man's voice mingled with the girl's further squeals and unintelligible words.

Azalea Adair rose without surprise or emotion and disappeared. For two minutes I heard the hoarse rumble of the man's voice; then something like an oath and a slight scuffle, and she returned calmly to her chair.

" This is a roomy house," she said, " and I have a tenant for part of it. I am sorry to have to rescind my invitation to tea. It was impossible to get the kind I always use at the store. Perhaps tomorrow Mr. Baker will be able to supply me."

I was sure that Impy had not had time to leave the house. I inquired concerning streetcar lines and took my leave. After I was well on my way I remembered that I had not learned Azalea Adair's name. But tomorrow would do.

That same day I started in on the course of iniquity that this uneventful city forced upon me. I was in the town only two days, but in that time I managed to lie shamelessly by telegraph, and to be an accomplice — after the fact, if that is the correct legal term — to a murder.

As I rounded the corner nearest my hotel the Afrite coachman of the polychromatic, nonpareil coat seized me, swung open the dungeony door of his peripatetic sarcophagus, flirted his feather duster, and began his ritual: " Step right in, boss. Carriage is clean — jus' got back from a funeral. Fifty cents to any — "

And then he knew me and grinned broadly. " 'Scuse me, boss; you is de gen'l'man what rid out with me dis mawnin'. Thank you kindly, suh."

" I am going out to Eight-sixty-one again tomorrow afternoon at three," said I, " and if you will be here, I'll let you drive me. So you know Miss Adair? " I concluded, thinking of my dollar bill.

" I belonged to her father, Judge Adair, suh," he replied.

" I judge that she is pretty poor," I said. " She hasn't much money to speak of, has she? "

For an instant I looked again at the fierce countenance of King Cetewayo, and then he changed back to an extortionate old Negro hack-driver.

" She ain't gwine to starve, suh," he said slowly. " She has reso'ces, suh; she has reso'ces."

" I shall pay you fifty cents for the trip," said I.

" Dat is puffeckly correct, suh," he answered humbly. " I jus' had to have dat two dollars dis mawnin', boss."

I went to the hotel and lied by electricity. I wired the magazine: " A. Adair holds out for eight cents a word."

The answer that came back was: " Give it to her quick, you duffer."

Just before dinner " Major " Wentworth Caswell bore down upon me with the greetings of a long-lost friend. I have seen few men whom I have so instantaneously hated, and of whom it was so difficult to be rid. I was standing at the bar when he invaded me; therefore I could not wave the white ribbon in his face. I would have paid gladly for the drinks, hoping, thereby, to escape another; but he was one of those despicable, roaring, advertising bibbers who must have brass bands and fireworks attend upon every cent that they waste in their follies.

With an air of producing millions he drew two one-dollar bills from a pocket and dashed one of them upon the bar. I looked once more at the dollar bill with the upper right-hand corner missing, torn through the middle, and patched with a strip of blue tissue paper. It was my dollar bill again. It could have been no other.

I went up to my room. The drizzle and the monotony of a dreary, eventless Southern town had made me tired and listless. I remember that just before I went to bed I mentally disposed of the mysterious dollar bill (which might have formed the clue to a tremendously fine detective story of San Francisco) by saying to myself sleepily: " Seems as if a lot of people here own stock in the Hack-Driver's Trust. Pays dividends promptly, too. Wonder if — " Then I fell asleep.

King Cetewayo was at his post the next day, and rattled my bones over the stones out to Eight-sixty-one. He was to wait and rattle me back again when I was ready.

Azalea Adair looked paler and cleaner and frailer than she had looked on the day before. After she had signed the contract at eight cents per word, she grew still paler and began to slip out of her chair. Without much trouble I managed to get her up on the antediluvian horsehair sofa and then I ran out to the sidewalk and yelled to the coffee-colored pirate to bring a doctor. With a wisdom that I had not suspected in him, he abandoned his team and struck off up the street afoot, realizing the value of speed. In ten minutes he returned with a grave, gray-haired, and capable man of medicine. In a few words (worth much less than eight cents each) I explained to him my presence in the hollow house of mystery. He bowed with stately understanding and turned to the old Negro.

" Uncle Caesar," he said calmly, " run up to my house and ask Miss Lucy to give you a cream pitcher full of fresh milk and half a tumbler of port wine. And hurry back. Don't drive — run. I want you to get back sometime this week."

It occurred to me that Dr. Merriman also felt a distrust as to the speeding powers of the land pirate's steeds. After Uncle Caesar was gone, lumberingly but swiftly, up the street, the doctor looked me over with great politeness and as much careful calculation until he had decided that I might do.

" It is only a case of insufficient nutrition," he said. " In other words, the result of poverty, pride, and starvation. Mrs. Caswell has many devoted friends who would be glad to aid her, but she will accept nothing except from that old Negro, Uncle Caesar, who was once owned by her family."

" Mrs. Caswell! " said I, in surprise. And then I looked at the contract and saw that she had signed it " Azalea Adair Caswell."

" I thought she was Miss Adair," said I.

" Married to a drunken, worthless loafer, sir," said the doctor. " It is said that he robs her even of the small sums that her old servant contributes toward her support."

When the milk and wine had been brought, the doctor soon revived Azalea Adair. She sat up and talked of the beauty of the autumn leaves that were then in season, and their height of color. She referred lightly to her fainting seizure as the outcome of an old palpitation of the heart. Impy fanned her as she lay on the sofa. The doctor was due elsewhere, and I followed him to the door. I told him that it was within my power and intentions to make a reasonable advance of money to Azalea Adair on future contributions to the magazine, and he seemed pleased.

" By the way," he said, " perhaps you would like to know that you have had royalty for a coachman. Old Caesar's grandfather was a king in Congo. Caesar himself has royal ways, as you may have observed."

As the doctor was moving off I heard Uncle Caesar's voice inside: " Did he git bofe of dem two dollars from you, Mis' Zalea? "

" Yes, Caesar," I heard Azalea Adair answer weakly.

And then I went in and concluded business negotiations with our contributor. I assumed the responsibility of advancing fifty dollars, putting it as a necessary formality in binding our bargain. And then Uncle Caesar drove me back to the hotel.

Here ends all of the story as far as I can testify as a witness. The rest must be only bare statements of facts.

At about six o'clock I went out for a stroll. Uncle Caesar was at his corner. He threw open the door of his carriage, flourished his duster, and began his depressing formula: " Step right in, suh. Fifty cents to anywhere in the city — hack's puffickly clean, suh — jus' back from a funeral — "

And then he recognized me. I think his eyesight was getting bad. His coat had taken on a few more faded shades of color, the twine strings were more frayed and ragged, the last remaining button — the button of yellow horn — was gone. A motley descendant of kings was Uncle Caesar!

About two hours later I saw an excited crowd besieging the front door of the drugstore. In a desert where nothing happens this was manna; so I edged my way inside. On an extemporized couch of empty boxes and chairs was stretched the mortal corporeality of Major Wentworth Caswell. A doctor was testing him for the immortal ingredient. His decision was that it was conspicuous by its absence.

The erstwhile Major had been found dead on a dark street and brought by curious and ennuied citizens to the drugstore. The late human being had been engaged in terrific battle — the details showed that. Loafer and reprobate though he had been, he had been also a warrior. But he had lost. His hands were yet clinched so tightly that his fingers would not be opened. The gentle citizens who had known him stood about and searched their vocabularies to find some good words, if it were possible, to speak of him. One kind-looking man said, after much thought: " When ' Cas ' was about fo'teen he was one of the best spellers in school."

While I stood there the fingers of the right hand of " the man that was," which hung down the side of a white-pine box, relaxed and dropped something at my feet. I covered it with one foot quickly, and a little later on I picked it up and pocketed it. I reasoned that in his last struggle his hand must have seized that object unwittingly and held it in a death grip.

At the hotel that night the main topic of conversation, with the possible exceptions of politics and prohibition, was the demise of Major Caswell. I heard one man say to a group of listeners:

" In my opinion, gentlemen, Caswell was murdered by some of those no-account niggers for his money. He had fifty dollars this afternoon which he showed to several gentlemen in the hotel. When he was found the money was not on his person."

I left the city the next morning at nine, and as the train was crossing the bridge over the Cumberland River, I took out of my pocket a yellow horn overcoat button the size of a fifty-cent piece, with frayed ends of coarse twine hanging from it, and cast it out of the window into the slow, muddy waters below.

I wonder what's doing in Buffalo!

Sherwood Anderson

I'm a Fool

IT was a hard jolt for me, one of the most bitterest I ever had to face. And it all came about through my own foolishness, too. Even yet sometimes, when I think of it, I want to cry or swear or kick myself. Perhaps, even now, after all this time, there will be a kind of satisfaction in making myself look cheap by telling of it.

It began at three o'clock one October afternoon as I sat in the grandstand at the fall trotting and pacing meet at Sandusky, Ohio.

To tell the truth, I felt a little foolish that I should be sitting in the grandstand at all. During the summer before, I had left my home town with Harry Whitehead and, with a nigger named Burt, had taken a job as swipe with one of the two horses Harry was campaigning through the fall race meets that year. Mother cried and my sister Mildred, who wanted to get a job as a schoolteacher

From *Horses and Men*, 1923.

in our town that fall, stormed and scolded about the house all during the week before I left. They both thought it something disgraceful that one of our family should take a place as a swipe with race horses. I've an idea Mildred thought my taking the place would stand in the way of her getting the job she'd been working so long for.

But after all I had to work, and there was no other work to be got. A big lumbering fellow of nineteen couldn't just hang around the house, and I had got too big to mow people's lawns and sell newspapers. Little chaps who could get next to people's sympathies by their sizes were always getting jobs away from me. There was one fellow who kept saying to everyone who wanted a lawn mowed or a cistern cleaned, that he was saving money to work his way through college, and I used to lay awake nights thinking up ways to injure him without being found out. I kept thinking of wagons running over him and bricks falling on his head as he walked along the street. But never mind him.

I got the place with Harry and I liked Burt fine. We got along splendid together. He was a big nigger with a lazy sprawling body and soft, kind eyes, and when it came to a fight he could hit like Jack Johnson. He had Bucephalus, a big black pacing stallion that could do 2.09 or 2.10, if he had to, and I had a little gelding named Doctor Fritz that never lost a race all fall when Harry wanted him to win.

We set out from home late in July in a boxcar with the two horses; and after that, until late November, we kept moving along to the race meets and the fairs. It was a peachy time for me, I'll say that. Sometimes now I think that boys who are raised regular in houses, and never have a fine nigger like Burt for best friend, and go to high schools and college, and never steal anything, or get drunk a little, or learn to swear from fellows who know how, or come walking up in front of a grandstand in their shirt sleeves and with dirty horsey pants on when the races are going on and the grandstand is full of people all dressed up — What's the use of talking about it? Such fellows don't know nothing at all. They've never had no opportunity.

But I did. Burt taught me how to rub down a horse and put the bandages on after a race and steam a horse out and a lot of valuable things for any man to know. He could wrap a bandage on a horse's leg so smooth that if it had been the same color you would think it was his skin, and I guess he'd have been a big driver, too, and got to the top like Murphy and Walter Cox and the others if he hadn't been black.

Gee whizz, it was fun. You got to a county seat town, maybe say on a Saturday or Sunday, and the fair began the next Tuesday and lasted until Friday afternoon. Doctor Fritz would be, say, in the 2.25 trot on Tuesday after-noon, and on Thursday afternoon Bucephalus would knock 'em cold in the " free for all " pace. It left you a lot of time to hang around and listen to horse talk, and see Burt knock some yap cold that got too gay, and you'd find out about horses and men and pick up a lot of stuff you could use all the rest of your life, if you had some sense and salted down what you heard and felt and saw.

And then at the end of the week when the race meet was over, and Harry had run home to tend to his livery stable business, you and Burt hitched the two horses to carts and drove slow and steady across the country to the place for the next meeting, so as to not overheat the horses, etc., you know.

Gee whizz, Gosh amighty, the nice hickory nut and beechnut and oaks and other kinds of trees along the roads, all brown and red, and the good smells, and Burt singing a song that was called " Deep River," and the country girls at the windows of houses and everything. You can stick your colleges up your nose for all me. I guess I know where I got my education.

Why, one of those little burgs of towns you come to on the way, say now on a Saturday afternoon, and Burt says, " Let's lay up here." And you did.

And you took the horses to a livery stable and fed them, and you got your good clothes out of a box and put them on.

And the town was full of farmers gaping, because they could see you were race horse people, and the kids maybe never see a nigger before and was afraid and run away when the two of us walked down their main street.

And that was before prohibition and all that foolishness, and so you went into a saloon, the two of you, and all the yaps come and stood around, and there was always someone pretended he was horsey and knew things and spoke up and began asking questions, and all you did was to lie and lie all you could about what horses you had, and I said I owned them, and then some fellow said " Will you have a drink of whisky? " and Burt knocked his eye out the way he could say, offhand like, " Oh, well, all right, I'm agreeable to a little nip. I'll split a quart with you." Gee whizz.

But that isn't what I want to tell my story about. We got home late in November and I promised mother I'd quit the race horses for good. There's a lot of things you've got to promise a mother because she don't know any better.

And so, there not being any work in our town any more than when I left there to go to the races, I went off to Sandusky and got a pretty good place taking care of horses for a man who owned a teaming and delivery and storage and coal and real estate business there. It was a pretty good place with good eats, and a day off each week, and sleeping on a cot in a big barn, and mostly just shoveling in hay and oats to a lot of big good-enough skates of horses that couldn't have trotted a race with a toad. I wasn't dissatisfied and I could send money home.

And then, as I started to tell you, the fall races come to Sandusky and I got the day off and I went. I left the job at noon and had on my good clothes and my new brown derby hat, I'd just bought the Saturday before, and a stand-up collar.

First of all I went downtown and walked about with the dudes. I've always thought to myself, " Put up a good front," and so I did it. I had forty dollars in my pocket and so I went into the West House, a big hotel, and walked up to the cigar stand. " Give me three twenty-five cent cigars," I said. There was a lot of horsemen and strangers and dressed-up people from other towns standing around in the lobby and in the bar, and I mingled amongst them. In the bar there was a fellow with a cane and a Windsor tie on, that it made me sick to look at him. I like a man to be a man and dress up, but not to go put on that kind of airs. So I pushed him aside, kind of rough, and had me a drink of whisky. And then he looked at me, as though he thought maybe he'd get gay, but he changed his mind and didn't say anything. And then I had another drink of whisky, just to show him something, and went out and had a hack out to the races, all to myself, and when I got there I bought myself the best seat I could get, up in the grandstand, but didn't go in for any of those boxes. That's putting on too many airs.

And so there I was, sitting up in the grandstand as gay as you please and looking down on the swipes coming out with their horses, and with their dirty horsey pants on and the horse blankets swung over their shoulders, same as I had been doing all the year before. I liked one thing about the same as the other, sitting up there and feeling grand and being down there and looking up at the yaps and feeling grander and more important, too. One thing's about as good as another, if you take it just right. I've often said that.

Well, right in front of me, in the grandstand that day, there was a fellow with a couple of girls and they was about my age. The young fellow was a nice guy all right. He was the kind maybe that goes to college and then comes to be a lawyer or maybe a newspaper editor or something like that, but he wasn't stuck on himself. There are some of that kind are all right and he was one of the ones.

He had his sister with him and another girl, and the sister looked around over his shoulder, accidental at first, not intending to start anything — she wasn't that kind — and her eyes and mine happened to meet.

You know how it is. Gee, she was a peach! She had on a soft dress, kind of a blue stuff and it looked carelessly made, but was well sewed and made and everything. I knew that much. I blushed when she looked right at me and so did she. She was the nicest girl I've ever seen in my life. She wasn't stuck on herself and she could talk proper grammar without being like a schoolteacher or something like that. What I mean is, she was O. K. I think maybe her father was well-to-do, but not rich to make her chesty because she was his daughter, as some are. Maybe he owned a drugstore or a dry-goods store in their home town, or something like that. She never told me and I never asked.

My own people are all O. K. too, when you come to that. My grandfather was Welsh and over in the old country, in Wales he was — But never mind that.

The first heat of the first race come off and the young fellow setting there with the two girls left them and went down to make a bet. I knew what he was up to, but he didn't talk big and noisy and let everyone around know he was a sport, as some do. He wasn't that kind. Well, he came back and I heard him tell the two girls what horse he'd bet on, and when the heat was trotted they all half got to their feet and acted in the excited, sweaty way people do when they've got money down on a race, and the horse they bet on is up there pretty close at the end, and they think maybe he'll come on with a rush, but he never does because he hasn't got the old juice in him, come right down to it.

And then, pretty soon, the horses came out for the 2.18 pace and there was a horse in it I knew. He was a horse Bob French had in his string but Bob didn't own him. He was a horse owned by a Mr. Mathers down at Marietta, Ohio.

This Mr. Mathers had a lot of money and owned some coal mines or something, and he had a swell place out in the country, and he was stuck on race horses, but was a Presbyterian or something, and I think more than likely his wife was one, too, maybe a stiffer one than himself. So he never raced his horses hisself, and the story round the Ohio race tracks was that when one of his horses got ready to go to the races he turned him over to Bob French and pretended to his wife he was sold.

So Bob had the horses and he did pretty much as he pleased and you can't blame Bob — at least, I never did. Sometimes he was out to win and sometimes he wasn't. I never cared much about that when I was swiping a horse. What I did want to know was that my horse had the speed and could go out in front, if you wanted him to.

And, as I'm telling you, there was Bob in this race with one of Mr. Mathers' horses, was named " About Ben Ahem " or something like that, and was fast as a streak. He was a gelding and had a mark of 2.21, but could step in .08 or .09.

Because when Burt and I were out, as I've told you, the year before, there was a nigger Burt knew, worked for Mr. Mathers and we went out there one day when we didn't have no race on at the Marietta Fair and our boss Harry was gone home.

And so everyone was gone to the fair but just this one nigger and he took us all through Mr. Mathers' swell house and he and Burt tapped a bottle of wine Mr. Mathers had hid in his bedroom, back in a closet, without his wife knowing, and he showed us this Ahem horse. Burt was always stuck on being a driver but didn't have much chance to get to the top, being a nigger, and he and the other nigger gulped that whole bottle of wine and Burt got a little lit up.

So the nigger let Burt take this About Ben Ahem and step him a mile in a track Mr. Mathers had all to himself, right there on the farm. And Mr. Mathers had one child, a daughter, kinda sick and not very good-looking, and she came home and we had to hustle and get About Ben Ahem stuck back in the barn.

I'm only telling you to get everything straight. At Sandusky, that afternoon I was at the fair, this young fellow with the two girls was fussed, being with the girls and losing his bet. You know how a fellow is that way. One of them was his girl and the other his sister. I had figured that out.

" Gee whizz," I says to myself, " I'm going to give him the dope."

He was mighty nice when I touched him on the shoulder. He and the girls were nice to me right from the start and clear to the end. I'm not blaming them.

And so he leaned back and I give him the dope on About Ben Ahem. " Don't bet a cent on this first heat because he'll go like an oxen hitched to a plow, but when the first heat is over go right down and lay on your pile." That's what I told him.

Well, I never saw a fellow treat anyone sweller. There was a fat man sitting beside the little girl, that had looked at me twice by this time, and I at her, and both blushing, and what did he do but have the nerve to turn and ask the fat man to get up and change places with me so I could set with his crowd.

Gee whizz, craps amighty. There I was. What a chump I was to go and get gay up there in the West House bar, and just because that dude was standing there with a cane and that kind of a necktie on, to go and get all balled up and drink that whisky, just to show off.

Of course she would know, me setting right beside her and letting her smell of my breath. I could have kicked myself right down out of that grand-stand and all around that race track and made a faster record than most of the skates of horses they had there that year.

Because that girl wasn't any mutt of a girl. What wouldn't I have give right then for a stick of chewing gum to chew, or a lozenger, or some licorice, or most anything. I was glad I had those twenty-five cent cigars in my pocket and right away I give that fellow one and lit one myself. Then that fat man got up and we changed places and there I was, plunked right down beside her.

They introduced themselves and the fellow's best girl, he had with him, was named Miss Elinor Woodbury, and her father was a manufacturer of barrels from a place called Tiffin, Ohio. And the fellow himself was named Wilbur Wessen and his sister was Miss Lucy Wessen.

I suppose it was their having such swell names got me off my trolley. A fellow, just because he has been a swipe with a race horse, and works taking care of horses for a man in the teaming, delivery, and storage business, isn't any better or worse than anyone else. I've often thought that, and said it too.

But you know how a fellow is. There's something in that kind of nice clothes, and the kind of nice eyes she had, and the way she had looked at me, awhile before, over her brother's shoulder, and me looking back at her, and both of us blushing.

I couldn't show her up for a boob, could I?

I made a fool of myself, that's what I did. I said my name was Walter Mathers from Marietta, Ohio, and then I told all three of them the smashingest lie you ever heard. What I said was that my father owned the horse About Ben Ahem and that he had let him out to this Bob French for racing purposes, because our family was proud and had never gone into racing that way, in our own name, I mean. Then I had got started and they were all leaning over and listening, and Miss Lucy Wessen's eyes were shining, and I went the whole hog.

I told about our place down at Marietta, and about the big stables and the grand brick house we had on a hill, up above the Ohio River, but I knew enough not to do it in no bragging way. What I did was to start things and then let them drag the rest out of me. I acted just as reluctant to tell as I could. Our family hasn't got any barrel factory, and, since I've known us, we've always been pretty poor, but not asking anything of anyone at that, and my grand-father, over in Wales — but never mind that.

We set there talking like we had known each other for years and years, and I went and told them that my father had been expecting maybe this Bob French wasn't on the square, and had sent me up to Sandusky on the sly to find out what I could.

And I bluffed it through I had found out all about the 2.18 pace, in which About Ben Ahem was to start.

I said he would lose the first heat by pacing like a lame cow and then he would come back and skin 'em alive after that. And to back up what I said I took thirty dollars out of my pocket and handed it to Mr. Wilbur Wessen and asked him, would he mind, after the first heat, to go down and place it on About Ben Ahem for whatever odds he could get. What I said was that I didn't want Bob French to see me and none of the swipes.

Sure enough the first heat come off and About Ben Ahem went off his stride, up the back stretch, and looked like a wooden horse or a sick one, and come in to be last. Then this Wilbur Wessen went down to the betting place under the grandstand and there I was with the two girls, and when that Miss Woodbury was looking the other way once, Lucy Wessen kinda, with her shoulder you know, kinda touched me. Not just tucking down, I don't mean. You know how a woman can do. They get close, but not getting gay either. You know what they do. Gee whizz.

And then they give me a jolt. What they had done, when I didn't know, was to get together, and they had decided Wilbur Wessen would bet fifty dollars, and the two girls had gone and put in ten dollars each, of their own money, too. I was sick then, but I was sicker later.

About the gelding, About Ben Ahem, and their winning their money, I wasn't worried a lot about that. It come out O. K. Ahem stepped the next three heats like a bushel of spoiled eggs going to market before they could be found out, and Wilbur Wessen had got nine to two for the money. There was something else eating at me.

Because Wilbur came back, after he had bet the money, and after that he spent most of his time talking to that Miss Woodbury, and Lucy Wessen and I was left alone together like on a desert island. Gee, if I'd only been on the square or if there had been any way of getting myself on the square. There ain't any Walter Mathers, like I said to her and them, and there hasn't ever been one, but if there was, I bet I'd go to Marietta, Ohio, and shoot him tomorrow.

There I was, big boob that I am. Pretty soon the race was over, and Wilbur had gone down and collected our money, and we had a hack downtown, and he stood us a swell supper at the West House, and a bottle of champagne beside.

And I was with that girl and she wasn't saying much, and I wasn't saying much either. One thing I know. She wasn't stuck on me because of the lie about my father being rich and all that. There's a way you know. . . . Craps amighty. There's a kind of girl, you see just once in your life, and if you don't get busy and make hay, then you're gone for good and all, and might as well go jump off a bridge. They give you a look from inside of them somewhere, and it ain't no vamping, and what it means is — you want that girl to be your wife, and you want nice things around her like flowers and swell clothes, and you want her to have the kids you're going to have, and you want good music played and no ragtime. Gee whizz.

There's a place over near Sandusky, across a kind of bay, and it's called Cedar Point. And after we had supper we went over to it in a launch, all by ourselves. Wilbur and Miss Lucy and that Miss Woodbury had to catch a ten o'clock train back to Tiffin, Ohio, because, when you're out with girls like that you can't get careless and miss any trains and stay out all night, like you can with some kinds of Janes.

And Wilbur blowed himself to the launch and it cost him fifteen cold punks, but I wouldn't never have knew if I hadn't listened. He wasn't no tin horn kind of a sport.

Over at the Cedar Point place, we didn't stay around where there was a gang of common kind of cattle at all.

There was big dance halls and dining places for yaps, and there was a beach you could walk along and get where it was dark, and we went there.

She didn't talk hardly at all and neither did I, and I was thinking how glad I was my mother was all right, and always made us kids learn to eat with a fork at table, and not swill soup, and not be noisy and rough like a gang you see around a race track that way.

Then Wilbur and his girl went away up the beach and Lucy and I sat down in a dark place, where there was some roots of old trees, the water had washed up, and after that the time, till we had to go back in the launch and they had to catch their trains, wasn't nothing at all. It went like winking your eye.

Here's how it was. The place we were setting in was dark, like I said, and there was the roots from that old stump sticking up like arms, and there was a watery smell, and the night was like — as if you could put your hand out and feel it — so warm and soft and dark and sweet like an orange.

I most cried and I most swore and I most jumped up and danced, I was so mad and happy and sad.

When Wilbur come back from being alone with his girl, and she saw him coming, Lucy she says, " We got to go to the train now," and she was most crying too, but she never knew nothing I knew, and she couldn't be so all busted up. And then, before Wilbur and Miss Woodbury got up to where we was, she put her face up and kissed me quick and put her head up against me and she was all quivering and — Gee whizz.

Sometimes I hope I have cancer and die. I guess you know what I mean. We went in the launch across the bay to the train like that, and it was dark, too. She whispered and said it was like she and I could get out of the boat and walk on the water, and it sounded foolish, but I knew what she meant.

And then quick we were right at the depot, and there was a big gang of yaps, the kind that goes to the fairs, and crowded and milling around like cattle, and how could I tell her? "It won't be long because you'll write and I'll write to you." That's all she said.

I got a chance like a hay barn afire. A swell chance I got.

And maybe she would write me, down at Marietta that way, and the letter would come back, and stamped on the front of it by the U.S.A. "There ain't any such guy," or something like that, whatever they stamp on a letter that way.

And me trying to pass myself off for a big bug and a swell — to her, as decent a little body as God ever made. Craps amighty — a swell chance I got!

And then the train come in, and she got on it, and Wilbur Wessen he come and shook hands with me, and that Miss Woodbury was nice too and bowed to me, and I at her, and the train went and I busted out and cried like a kid.

Gee, I could have run after that train and made Dan Patch look like a freight train after a wreck but, socks amighty, what was the use? Did you ever see such a fool?

I'll bet you what — if I had an arm broke right now or a train had run over my foot — I wouldn't go to no doctor at all. I'd go set down and let her hurt and hurt — that's what I'd do.

I'll bet you what — if I hadn't a drunk that booze I'd a never been such a boob as to go tell such a lie — that couldn't never be made straight to a lady like her.

I wish I had that fellow right here that had on a Windsor tie and carried a cane. I'd smash him for fair. Gosh darn his eyes. He's a big fool — that's what he is.

And if I'm not another you just go find me one and I'll quit working and be a bum and give him my job. I don't care nothing for working, and earning money, and saving it for no such boob as myself.

Ring Lardner

The Golden Honeymoon

MOTHER says that when I start talking I never know when to stop. But I tell her the only time I get a chance is when she ain't around, so I have to make the most of it. I guess the fact is neither one of us would be welcome in a Quaker meeting, but as I tell Mother, what did God give us tongues for if He didn't want we should use them? Only she says He didn't give them to us to say the same thing over and over again, like I do, and repeat myself. But I say:

"Well, Mother," I say, "when people is like you and I and been married fifty years, do you expect everything I say will be something you ain't heard

From *How to Write Short Stories*, 1924.

me say before? But it may be new to others, as they ain't nobody else lived with me as long as you have."

So she says: "You can bet they ain't, as they couldn't nobody else stand you that long."

"Well," I tell her, "you look pretty healthy."

"Maybe I do," she will say, "but I looked even healthier before I married you."

You can't get ahead of Mother.

Yes, sir, we was married just fifty years ago the seventeenth day of last December and my daughter and son-in-law was over from Trenton to help us celebrate the Golden Wedding. My son-in-law is John H. Kramer, the real estate man. He made $12,000 one year and is pretty well thought of around Trenton; a good, steady, hard worker. The Rotarians was after him a long time to join, but he kept telling them his home was his club. But Edie finally made him join. That's my daughter.

Well, anyway, they come over to help us celebrate the Golden Wedding and it was pretty crimpy weather and the furnace don't seem to heat up no more like it used to and Mother made the remark that she hoped this winter wouldn't be as cold as the last, referring to the winter previous. So Edie said if she was us, and nothing to keep us home, she certainly wouldn't spend no more winters up here and why didn't we just shut off the water and close up the house and go down to Tampa, Florida? You know we was there four winters ago and stayed five weeks, but it cost us over three hundred and fifty dollars for hotel bill alone. So Mother said we wasn't going no place to be robbed. So my son-in-law spoke up and said that Tampa wasn't the only place in the South, and besides we didn't have to stop at no high price hotel but could rent us a couple rooms and board out somewheres, and he had heard that St. Petersburg, Florida, was *the* spot and if we said the word he would write down there and make inquiries.

Well, to make a long story short, we decided to do it and Edie said it would be our Golden Honeymoon and for a present my son-in-law paid the difference between a section and a compartment so as we could have a compartment and have more privatecy. In a compartment you have an upper and lower berth just like the regular sleeper, but it is a shut in room by itself and got a wash bowl. The car we went in was all compartments and no regular berths at all. It was all compartments.

We went to Trenton the night before and stayed at my daughter and son-in-law and we left Trenton the next afternoon at 3.23 P.M.

This was the twelfth day of January. Mother set facing the front of the train, as it makes her giddy to ride backwards. I set facing her, which does not affect me. We reached North Philadelphia at 4.03 P.M. and we reached West Philadelphia at 4.14, but did not go into Broad Street. We reached Baltimore at 6.30 and Washington, D.C., at 7.25. Our train laid over in Washington two hours till another train come along to pick us up and I got out and strolled up the platform and into the Union Station. When I come back, our car had been switched on to another track, but I remembered the name of it, the La Belle, as I had once visited my aunt out in Oconomowoc, Wisconsin, where there was a lake of that name, so I had no difficulty in getting located. But Mother had nearly fretted herself sick for fear I would be left.

" Well," I said, " I would of followed you on the next train."

" You could of," said Mother, and she pointed out that she had the money.

" Well," I said, " we are in Washington and I could of borrowed from the United States Treasury. I would of pretended I was an Englishman."

Mother caught the point and laughed heartily.

Our train pulled out of Washington at 9.40 P.M. and Mother and I turned in early, I taking the upper. During the night we passed through the green fields of old Virginia, though it was too dark to tell if they was green or what color. When we got up in the morning, we was at Fayetteville, North Carolina. We had breakfast in the dining car and after breakfast I got in conversation with the man in the next compartment to ours. He was from Lebanon, New Hampshire, and a man about eighty years of age. His wife was with him, and two unmarried daughters and I made the remark that I should think the four of them would be crowded in one compartment, but he said they had made the trip every winter for fifteen years and knowed how to sleep out of each other's way. He said they was bound for Tarpon Springs.

We reached Charleston, South Carolina, at 12.50 P.M. and arrived at Savannah, Georgia, at 4.20. We reached Jacksonville, Florida, at 8.45 P.M. and had an hour and a quarter to lay over there, but Mother made a fuss about me getting off the train, so we had the darky make up our berths and retired before we left Jacksonville. I didn't sleep good as the train done a lot of hemming and hawing, and Mother never sleeps good on a train as she says she is always worrying that I will fall out. She says she would rather have the upper herself, as then she would not have to worry about me, but I tell her I can't take the risk of having it get out that I allowed my wife to sleep in an upper berth. It would make talk.

We was up in the morning in time to see our friends from New Hampshire get off at Tarpon Springs, which we reached at 6.53 A.M.

Several of our fellow passengers got off at Clearwater and some at Belleair, where the train backs right up to the door of the mammoth hotel. Belleair is the winter headquarters for the golf dudes and everybody that got off there had their bag of sticks, as many as ten and twelve in a bag. Women and all. When I was a young man we called it shinny and only needed one club to play with and about one game of it would of been a-plenty for some of these dudes, the way we played it.

The train pulled into St. Petersburg at 8.20 and when we got off the train you would think they was a riot, what with all the darkies barking for the different hotels.

I said to Mother, I said: " It is a good thing we have got a place picked out to go to and don't have to choose a hotel, as it would be hard to choose amongst them if every one of them is the best."

She laughed.

We found a jitney and I give him the address of the room my son-in-law had got for us and soon we was there and introduced ourselves to the lady that owns the house, a young widow about forty-eight years of age. She showed us our room, which was light and airy with a comfortable bed and bureau and washstand. It was twelve dollars a week, but the location was good, only three blocks from Williams Park.

St. Pete is what folks calls the town, though they also call it the Sunshine City, as they claim they's no other place in the country where they's fewer days when Old Sol don't smile down on Mother Earth, and one of the newspapers gives away all their copies free every day when the sun don't shine. They claim to of only give them away some sixty-odd times in the last eleven years. Another nickname they have got for the town is " the Poor Man's Palm Beach," but I guess they's men that comes there that could borrow as much from the bank as some of the Willie boys over to the other Palm Beach.

During our stay we paid a visit to the Lewis Tent City, which is the head-quarters for the Tin Can Tourists. But maybe you ain't heard about them. Well, they are an organization that takes their vacation trips by auto and carries everything with them. That is, they bring along their tents to sleep in and cook in and they don't patronize no hotels or cafeterias, but they have got to be bona fide auto campers or they can't belong to the organization.

They tell me they's over 200,000 members to it and they call themselves the Tin Canners on account of most of their food being put up in tin cans. One couple we seen in the Tent City was a couple from Brady, Texas, named Mr. and Mrs. Pence, which the old man is over eighty years of age and they had come in their auto all the way from home, a distance of 1,641 miles. They took five weeks for the trip, Mr. Pence driving the entire distance.

The Tin Canners hails from every state in the Union and in the summer time they visit places like New England and the Great Lakes region but in the winter the most of them comes to Florida and scatters all over the state. While we was down there, they was a national convention of them at Gainesville, Florida, and they elected a Fredonia, New York, man as their president. His title is Royal Tin Can Opener of the World. They have got a song wrote up which everybody has got to learn it before they are a member:

> The tin can forever! Hurrah, boys! Hurrah!
>   Up with the tin can! Down with the foe!
> We will rally round the campfire, we'll rally once again,
>   Shouting, " We auto camp forever! "

That is something like it. And the members has also got to have a tin can fastened on to the front of their machine.

I asked Mother how she would like to travel around that way and she said: " Fine, but not with an old rattlebrain like you driving."

" Well," I said, " I am eight years younger than this Mr. Pence who drove here from Texas."

" Yes," she said, " but he is old enough to not be skittish."

You can't get ahead of Mother.

Well, one of the first things we done in St. Petersburg was to go to the Chamber of Commerce and register our names and where we was from as they's great rivalry amongst the different states in regards to the number of their citizens visiting in town and of course our little state don't stand much of a show, but still every little bit helps, as the fella says. All and all, the man told us, they was eleven thousand names registered, Ohio leading with some fifteen hundred-odd and New York State next with twelve hundred. Then come Michigan, Pennsylvania, and so on down, with one man each from Cuba and Nevada.

The first night we was there, they was a meeting of the New York-New Jersey Society at the Congregational Church and a man from Ogdensburg, New York State, made the talk. His subject was " Rainbow Chasing." He is a Rotarian and a very convicting speaker, though I forget his name.

Our first business, of course, was to find a place to eat and after trying several places we run on to a cafeteria on Central Avenue that suited us up and down. We eat pretty near all our meals there and it averaged about two dollars per day for the two of us, but the food was well cooked and everything nice and clean. A man don't mind paying the price if things is clean and well cooked.

On the third day of February, which is Mother's birthday, we spread our-selves and eat supper at the Poinsettia Hotel and they charged us seventy-five cents for a sirloin steak that wasn't hardly big enough for one.

I said to Mother: " Well," I said, " I guess it's a good thing every day ain't your birthday or we would be in the poorhouse."

" No," says Mother, " because if every day was my birthday, I would be old enough by this time to of been in my grave long ago."

You can't get ahead of Mother.

In the hotel they had a card-room where they was several men and ladies playing five hundred and this newfangled whist bridge. We also seen a place where they was dancing, so I asked Mother would she like to trip the light fantastic toe and she said no, she was too old to squirm like you have got to do now days. We watched some of the young folks at it awhile till Mother got disgusted and said we would have to see a good movie to take the taste out of our mouth. Mother is a great movie heroyne and we go twice a week here at home.

But I want to tell you about the Park. The second day we was there we visited the Park, which is a good deal like the one in Tampa, only bigger, and they's more fun goes on here every day than you could shake a stick at. In the middle they's a big bandstand and chairs for the folks to set and listen to the concerts, which they give you music for all tastes, from " Dixie " up to classical pieces like " Hearts and Flowers."

Then all around they's places marked off for different sports and games — chess and checkers and dominoes for folks that enjoys those kind of games, and roque and horseshoes for the nimbler ones. I used to pitch a pretty fair shoe myself, but ain't done much of it in the last twenty years.

Well, anyway, we bought a membership ticket in the club which costs one dollar for the season, and they tell me that up to a couple years ago it was fifty cents, but they had to raise it to keep out the riffraff.

Well, Mother and I put in a great day watching the pitchers and she wanted I should get in the game, but I told her I was all out of practice and would make a fool of myself, though I seen several men pitching who I guess I could take their measure without no practice. However, they was some good pitchers, too, and one boy from Akron, Ohio, who could certainly throw a pretty shoe. They told me it looked like he would win the championship of the United States in the February tournament. We come away a few days before they held that and I never did hear if he win. I forget his name, but he was a clean-cut young fella and he has got a brother in Cleveland that's a Rotarian.

Well, we just stood around and watched the different games for two or three days and finally I set down in a checker game with a man named Weaver from Danville, Illinois. He was a pretty fair checker player, but he wasn't no match for me, and I hope that don't sound like bragging. But I always could hold my own on a checkerboard and the folks around here will tell you the same thing. I played with this Weaver pretty near all morning for two or three mornings and he beat me one game and the only other time it looked like he had a chance, the noon whistle blowed and we had to quit and go to dinner.

While I was playing checkers, Mother would set and listen to the band, as she loves music, classical or no matter what kind, but anyway she was setting there one day and between selections the woman next to her opened up a conversation. She was a woman about Mother's own age, seventy or seventy-one, and finally she asked Mother's name and Mother told her her name and where she was from and Mother asked her the same question, and who do you think the woman was?

Well, sir, it was the wife of Frank M. Hartsell, the man who was engaged to Mother till I stepped in and cut him out, fifty-two years ago!

Yes, sir!

You can imagine Mother's surprise! And Mrs. Hartsell was surprised, too, when Mother told her she had once been friends with her husband, though Mother didn't say how close friends they had been, or that Mother and I was the cause of Hartsell going out West. But that's what we was. Hartsell left his town a month after the engagement was broke off and ain't never been back since. He had went out to Michigan and become a veterinary, and that is where he had settled down, in Hillsdale, Michigan, and finally married his wife.

Well, Mother screwed up her courage to ask if Frank was still living and Mrs. Hartsell took her over to where they was pitching horseshoes and there was old Frank, waiting his turn. And he knowed Mother as soon as he seen her, though it was over fifty years. He said he knowed her by her eyes.

" Why, it's Lucy Frost! " he says, and he throwed down his shoes and quit the game.

Then they come over and hunted me up and I will confess I wouldn't of knowed him. Him and I is the same age to the month, but he seems to show it more, some way. He is balder for one thing. And his beard is all white, where mine has still got a streak of brown in it. The very first thing I said to him, I said:

"Well, Frank, that beard of yours makes me feel like I was back north. It looks like a regular blizzard."

"Well," he said, "I guess yourn would be just as white if you had it dry cleaned."

But Mother wouldn't stand that.

"Is that so!" she said to Frank. "Well, Charley ain't had no tobacco in his mouth for over ten years!"

And I ain't!

Well, I excused myself from the checker game and it was pretty close to noon, so we decided to all have dinner together and they was nothing for it only we must try their cafeteria on Third Avenue. It was a little more expensive than ours and not near as good, I thought. I and Mother had about the same dinner we had been having every day and our bill was $1.10. Frank's check was $1.20 for he and his wife. The same meal wouldn't of cost them more than a dollar at our place.

After dinner we made them come up to our house and we all set in the parlor, which the young woman had give us the use of to entertain company. We begun talking over old times and Mother said she was a-scared Mrs. Hartsell would find it tiresome listening to we three talk over old times, but as it turned out they wasn't much chance for nobody else to talk with Mrs. Hartsell in the company. I have heard lots of women that could go it, but Hartsell's wife takes the cake of all the women I ever seen. She told us the family history of everybody in the state of Michigan and bragged for a half hour about her son, who she said is in the drug business in Grand Rapids, and a Rotarian.

When I and Hartsell could get a word in edgeways we joked one another back and forth and I chafed him about being a horse doctor.

"Well, Frank," I said, "you look pretty prosperous, so I suppose they's been plenty of glanders around Hillsdale."

"Well," he said, "I've managed to make more than a fair living. But I've worked pretty hard."

"Yes," I said, "and I suppose you get called out all hours of the night to attend births and so on."

Mother made me shut up.

Well, I thought they wouldn't never go home and I and Mother was in misery trying to keep awake, as the both of us generally always takes a nap after dinner. Finally they went, after we had made an engagement to meet them in the Park the next morning, and Mrs. Hartsell also invited us to come to their place the next night and play five hundred. But she had forgot that they was a meeting of the Michigan Society that evening, so it was not till two evenings later that we had our first card game.

Hartsell and his wife lived in a house on Third Avenue North and had a private setting room besides their bedroom. Mrs. Hartsell couldn't quit talking about their private setting room like it was something wonderful. We played cards with them, with Mother and Hartsell partners against his wife and I. Mrs. Hartsell is a miserable card player and we certainly got the worst of it.

After the game she brought out a dish of oranges and we had to pretend it was just what we wanted, though oranges down there is like a young man's whiskers; you enjoy them at first, but they get to be a pesky nuisance.

We played cards again the next night at our place with the same partners and I and Mrs. Hartsell was beat again. Mother and Hartsell was full of compliments for each other on what a good team they made, but the both of them knowed well enough where the secret of their success laid. I guess all and all we must of played ten different evenings and they was only one night when Mrs. Hartsell and I come out ahead. And that one night wasn't no fault of hern.

When we had been down there about two weeks, we spent one evening as their guest in the Congregational Church, at a social give by the Michigan Society. A talk was made by a man named Bitting of Detroit, Michigan, on "How I Was Cured of Story Telling." He is a big man in the Rotarians and give a witty talk.

A woman named Mrs. Oxford rendered some selections which Mrs. Hartsell said was grand opera music, but whatever they was my daughter Edie could of give her cards and spades and not made such a hullaballoo about it neither.

Then they was a ventriloquist from Grand Rapids and a young woman about forty-five years of age that mimicked different kinds of birds. I whispered to Mother that they all sounded like a chicken, but she nudged me to shut up.

After the show we stopped in a drugstore and I set up the refreshments and it was pretty close to ten o'clock before we finally turned in. Mother and I would of preferred tending the movies, but Mother said we mustn't offend Mrs. Hartsell, though I asked her had we came to Florida to enjoy ourselves or to just not offend an old chatterbox from Michigan.

I felt sorry for Hartsell one morning. The womenfolks both had an engagement down to the chiropodist's and I run across Hartsell in the Park and he foolishly offered to play me checkers.

It was him that suggested it, not me, and I guess he repented himself before we had played one game. But he was too stubborn to give up and set there while I beat him game after game and the worst part of it was that a crowd of folks had got in the habit of watching me play and there they all was, looking on, and finally they seen what a fool Frank was making of himself, and they began to chafe him and pass remarks. Like one of them said:

"Who ever told you you was a checker player!"

And: "You might maybe be good for tiddle-de-winks, but not checkers!"

I almost felt like letting him beat me a couple games. But the crowd would of knowed it was a put up job.

Well, the womenfolks joined us in the Park and I wasn't going to mention our little game, but Hartsell told about it himself and admitted he wasn't no match for me.

"Well," said Mrs. Hartsell, "checkers ain't much of a game anyway, is it?" She said: "It's more of a children's game, ain't it? At least, I know my boy's children used to play it a good deal."

"Yes, ma'am," I said. "It's a children's game the way your husband plays it, too."

Mother wanted to smooth things over, so she said: "Maybe they's other games where Frank can beat you."

"Yes," said Mrs. Hartsell, "and I bet he could beat you pitching horseshoes."

"Well," I said, "I would give him a chance to try, only I ain't pitched a shoe in over sixteen years."

"Well," said Hartsell, "I ain't played checkers in twenty years."

"You ain't never played it," I said.

"Anyway," says Frank, "Lucy and I is your master at five hundred."

Well, I could of told him why that was, but had decency enough to hold my tongue.

It had got so now that he wanted to play cards every night and when I or Mother wanted to go to a movie, any one of us would have to pretend we had a headache and then trust to goodness that they wouldn't see us sneak into the theater. I don't mind playing cards when my partner keeps their mind on the game, but you take a woman like Hartsell's wife and how can they play cards when they have got to stop every couple seconds and brag about their son in Grand Rapids?

Well, the New York-New Jersey Society announced that they was goin' to give a social evening too and I said to Mother, I said: "Well, that is one evening when we will have an excuse not to play five hundred."

"Yes," she said, "but we will have to ask Frank and his wife to go to the social with us as they asked us to go to the Michigan social."

"Well," I said, "I had rather stay home than drag that chatterbox everywheres we go."

So Mother said: "You are getting too cranky. Maybe she does talk a little too much but she is goodhearted. And Frank is always good company."

So I said: "I suppose if he is such good company you wished you had of married him."

Mother laughed and said I sounded like I was jealous. Jealous of a cow doctor!

Anyway we had to drag them along to the social and I will say that we give them a much better entertainment than they had given us.

Judge Lane of Paterson made a fine talk on business conditions and a Mrs. Newell of Westfield imitated birds, only you could really tell what they was the way she done it. Two young women from Red Bank sung a choral selection and we clapped them back and they gave us "Home to Our Mountains" and Mother and Mrs. Hartsell both had tears in their eyes. And Hartsell, too.

Well, some way or another the chairman got wind that I was there and asked me to make a talk and I wasn't even going to get up, but Mother made me, so I got up and said:

"Ladies and gentlemen," I said. "I didn't expect to be called on for a speech on an occasion like this or no other occasion as I do not set myself up as a speechmaker, so will have to do the best I can, which I often say is the best anybody can do."

Then I told them the story about Pat and the motorcycle, using the brogue, and it seemed to tickle them and I told them one or two other stories, but altogether I wasn't on my feet more than twenty or twenty-five minutes and you ought to of heard the clapping and hollering when I set down. Even Mrs. Hartsell admitted that I am quite a speechifier and said if I ever went to Grand Rapids, Michigan, her son would make me talk to the Rotarians.

When it was over, Hartsell wanted we should go to their house and play cards, but his wife reminded him that it was after 9.30 P.M., rather a late hour to start a card game, but he had went crazy on the subject of cards, probably because he didn't have to play partners with his wife. Anyway, we got rid of them and went home to bed.

It was the next morning, when we met over to the Park, that Mrs. Hartsell made the remark that she wasn't getting no exercise, so I suggested that why didn't she take part in the roque game.

She said she had not played a game of roque in twenty years, but if Mother would play she would play. Well, at first Mother wouldn't hear of it, but finally consented, more to please Mrs. Hartsell than anything else.

Well, they had a game with a Mrs. Ryan from Eagle, Nebraska, and a young Mrs. Morse from Rutland, Vermont, who Mother had met down to the chiropodist's. Well, Mother couldn't hit a flea and they all laughed at her and I couldn't help from laughing at her myself and finally she quit and said her back was too lame to stoop over. So they got another lady and kept on playing and soon Mrs. Hartsell was the one everybody was laughing at, as she had a long shot to hit the black ball, and as she made the effort her teeth fell out on to the court. I never seen a woman so flustered in my life. And I never heard so much laughing, only Mrs. Hartsell didn't join in and she was madder than a hornet and wouldn't play no more, so the game broke up.

Mrs. Hartsell went home without speaking to nobody, but Hartsell stayed around and finally he said to me, he said:

"Well, I played you checkers the other day and you beat me bad and now what do you say if you and me play a game of horseshoes?"

I told him I hadn't pitched a shoe in sixteen years, but Mother said: "Go ahead and play. You used to be good at it and maybe it will come back to you."

Well, to make a long story short, I give in. I oughtn't to of never tried it, as I hadn't pitched a shoe in sixteen years, and I only done it to humor Hartsell.

Before we started, Mother patted me on the back and told me to do my best, so we started in and I seen right off that I was in for it, as I hadn't pitched a shoe in sixteen years and didn't have my distance. And besides, the plating had wore off the shoes so that they was points right where they stuck into my thumb and I hadn't throwed more than two or three times when my thumb was raw and it pretty near killed me to hang on to the shoe, let alone pitch it.

Well, Hartsell throws the awkwardest shoe I ever seen pitched and to see him pitch you wouldn't think he would ever come nowheres near, but he is also the luckiest pitcher I ever seen and he made some pitches where the shoe lit five and six feet short and then schoonered up and was a ringer. They's no use trying to beat that kind of luck.

They was a pretty fair size crowd watching us and four or five other ladies besides Mother, and it seems like, when Hartsell pitches, he has got to chew and it kept the ladies on the anxious seat as he don't seem to care which way he is facing when he leaves go. You would think a man as old as him would of learnt more manners.

Well, to make a long story short, I was just beginning to get my distance when I had to give up on account of my thumb, which I showed it to Hartsell and he seen I couldn't go on, as it was raw and bleeding. Even if I could of stood it to go on myself, Mother wouldn't of allowed it after she seen my thumb. So anyway I quit and Hartsell said the score was nineteen to six, but I don't know what it was. Or don't care, neither.

Well, Mother and I went home and I said I hoped we was through with the Hartsells as I was sick and tired of them, but it seemed like she had promised we would go over to their house that evening for another game of their ever-lasting cards.

Well, my thumb was giving me considerable pain and I felt kind of out of sorts and I guess maybe I forgot myself, but anyway, when we was about through playing Hartsell made the remark that he wouldn't never lose a game of cards if he could always have Mother for a partner.

So I said: "Well, you had a chance fifty years ago to always have her for a partner, but you wasn't man enough to keep her."

I was sorry the minute I had said it and Hartsell didn't know what to say and for once his wife couldn't say nothing. Mother tried to smooth things over by making the remark that I must of had something stronger than tea or I wouldn't talk so silly. But Mrs. Hartsell had froze up like an iceberg and hardly said good night to us and I bet her and Frank put in a pleasant hour after we was gone.

As we was leaving, Mother said to him: "Never mind Charley's nonsense, Frank. He is just mad because you beat him all hollow pitching horseshoes and playing cards."

She said that to make up for my slip, but at the same time she certainly riled me. I tried to keep ahold of myself, but as soon as we was out of the house she had to open up the subject and begun to scold me for the break I had made.

Well, I wasn't in no mood to be scolded. So I said: "I guess he is such a wonderful pitcher and card player that you wished you had married him."

"Well," she said, "at least he ain't a baby to give up pitching because his thumb has got a few scratches."

" And how about you," I said, " making a fool of yourself on the roque court and then pretending your back is lame and you can't play no more! "

" Yes," she said, " but when you hurt your thumb I didn't laugh at you, and why did you laugh at me when I sprained my back? "

" Who could help from laughing! " I said.

" Well," she said, " Frank Hartsell didn't laugh."

" Well," I said, " why didn't you marry him? "

" Well," said Mother, " I almost wished I had! "

" And I wished so, too! " I said.

" I'll remember that! " said Mother, and that's the last word she said to me for two days.

We seen the Hartsells the next day in the Park and I was willing to apologize, but they just nodded to us. And a couple days later we heard they had left for Orlando, where they have got relatives. I wished they had went there in the first place.

Mother and I made it up setting on a bench.

" Listen, Charley," she said. " This is our Golden Honeymoon and we don't want the whole thing spoilt with a silly old quarrel."

" Well," I said, " did you mean that about wishing you had married Hartsell? "

" Of course not," she said, " that is, if you didn't mean that you wished I had, too."

So I said: " I was just tired and all wrought up. I thank God you chose me instead of him as they's no other woman in the world who I could of lived with all these years."

" How about Mrs. Hartsell? " says Mother.

" Good gracious! " I said. " Imagine being married to a woman that plays five hundred like she does and drops her teeth on the roque court! "

" Well," said Mother, " it wouldn't be no worse than being married to a man that expectorates toward ladies and is such a fool in a checker game."

So I put my arm around her shoulder and she stroked my hand and I guess we got kind of spoony.

They was two days left of our stay in St. Petersburg and the next to the last day Mother introduced me to a Mrs. Kendall from Kingston, Rhode Island, who she had met at the chiropodist's.

Mrs. Kendall made us acquainted with her husband, who is in the grocery business. They have got two sons and five grandchildren and one great-grandchild. One of their sons lives in Providence and is way up in the Elks as well as a Rotarian.

We found them very congenial people and we played cards with them the last two nights we was there. They was both experts and I only wished we had met them sooner instead of running into the Hartsells. But the Kendalls will be there again next winter and we will see more of them, that is, if we decide to make the trip again.

We left the Sunshine City on the eleventh day of February, at 11 A.M.

This give us a day trip through Florida and we seen all the country we had passed through at night on the way down.

We reached Jacksonville at 7 P.M. and pulled out of there at 8.10 P.M. We reached Fayetteville, North Carolina, at nine o'clock the following morning, and reached Washington, D. C., at 6.30 P.M., laying over there half an hour.

We reached Trenton at 11.01 P.M. and had wired ahead to my daughter and son-in-law and they met us at the train and we went to their house and they put us up for the night. John would of made us stay up all night, telling about our trip, but Edie said we must be tired and made us go to bed. That's my daughter.

The next day we took our train for home and arrived safe and sound, having been gone just one month and a day.

Here comes Mother, so I guess I better shut up.

Ernest Hemingway

The Three-Day Blow

THE rain stopped as Nick turned into the road that went up through the orchard. The fruit had been picked and the fall wind blew through the bare trees. Nick stopped and picked up a Wagner apple from beside the road, shiny in the brown grass from the rain. He put the apple in the pocket of his Mackinaw coat.

The road came out of the orchard on to the top of the hill. There was the cottage, the porch bare, smoke coming from the chimney. In back was the garage, the chicken coop and the second-growth timber like a hedge against the woods behind. The big trees swayed far over in the wind as he watched. It was the first of the autumn storms.

As Nick crossed the open field above the orchard the door of the cottage opened and Bill came out. He stood on the porch looking out.

" Well, Wemedge," he said.

" Hey, Bill," Nick said, coming up the steps.

They stood together looking out across the country, down over the orchard, beyond the road, across the lower fields and the woods of the point to the lake. The wind was blowing straight down the lake. They could see the surf along Ten Mile Point.

" She's blowing," Nick said.

" She'll blow like that for three days," Bill said.

" Is your dad in? " Nick asked.

" No. He's out with the gun. Come on in."

From *In Our Time*, 1925.

Nick went inside the cottage. There was a big fire in the fireplace. The wind made it roar. Bill shut the door.

" Have a drink? " he said.

He went out to the kitchen and came back with two glasses and a pitcher of water. Nick reached the whisky bottle from the shelf above the fireplace.

" All right? " he said.

" Good," said Bill.

They sat in front of the fire and drank the Irish whisky and water.

" It's got a swell, smoky taste," Nick said, and looked at the fire through the glass.

" That's the peat," Bill said.

" You can't get peat into liquor," Nick said.

" That doesn't make any difference," Bill said.

" You ever seen any peat? " Nick asked.

" No," said Bill.

" Neither have I," Nick said.

His shoes, stretched out on the hearth, began to steam in front of the fire.

" Better take your shoes off," Bill said.

" I haven't got any socks on."

" Take them off and dry them and I'll get you some," Bill said. He went upstairs into the loft and Nick heard him walking about overhead. Upstairs was open under the roof and was where Bill and his father and he, Nick, sometimes slept. In back was a dressing room. They moved the cots back out of the rain and covered them with rubber blankets.

Bill came down with a pair of heavy wool socks.

" It's getting too late to go around without socks," he said.

" I hate to start them again," Nick said. He pulled the socks on and slumped back in the chair, putting his feet up on the screen in front of the fire.

" You'll dent in the screen," Bill said. Nick swung his feet over to the side of the fireplace.

" Got anything to read? " he asked.

" Only the paper."

" What did the Cards do? "

" Dropped a double-header to the Giants."

" That ought to cinch it for them."

" It's a gift," Bill said. " As long as McGraw can buy every good ball player in the league there's nothing to it."

" He can't buy them all," Nick said.

" He buys all the ones he wants," Bill said. " Or he makes them discontented so they have to trade them to him."

" Like Heinie Zim," Nick agreed.

" That bonehead will do him a lot of good."

Bill stood up.

" He can hit," Nick offered. The heat from the fire was baking his legs.

" He's a sweet fielder, too," Bill said. " But he loses ball games."

" Maybe that's what McGraw wants him for," Nick suggested.

" Maybe," Bill agreed.

" There's always more to it than we know about," Nick said.

" Of course. But we've got pretty good dope for being so far away."

" Like how much better you can pick them if you don't see the horses."

" That's it."

Bill reached down the whisky bottle. His big hand went all the way around it. He poured the whisky into the glass Nick held out.

" How much water? "

" Just the same."

He sat down on the floor beside Nick's chair.

" It's good when the fall storms come, isn't it? " Nick said.

" It's swell."

" It's the best time of year," Nick said.

" Wouldn't it be hell to be in town? " Bill said.

" I'd like to see the World Series," Nick said.

" Well, they're always in New York or Philadelphia now," Bill said. " That doesn't do us any good."

" I wonder if the Cards will ever win a pennant? "

" Not in our lifetime," Bill said.

" Gee, they'd go crazy," Nick said.

" Do you remember when they got going that once before they had the train wreck? "

" Boy! " Nick said, remembering.

Bill reached over to the table under the window for the book that lay there, face down, where he had put it when he went to the door. He held his glass in one hand and the book in the other, leaning back against Nick's chair.

" What are you reading? "

" *Richard Feverel.*"

" I couldn't get into it."

" It's all right," Bill said. " It ain't a bad book, Wemedge."

" What else have you got I haven't read? " Nick asked.

" Did you read the *Forest Lovers?* "

" Yup. That's the one where they go to bed every night with the naked sword between them."

" That's a good book, Wemedge."

" It's a swell book. What I couldn't ever understand was what good the sword would do. It would have to stay edge up all the time because if it went over flat you could roll right over it and it wouldn't make any trouble."

" It's a symbol," Bill said.

" Sure," said Nick, " but it isn't practical."

" Did you ever read *Fortitude?* "

" It's fine," Nick said. " That's a real book. That's where his old man is after him all the time. Have you got any more by Walpole? "

" *The Dark Forest,*" Bill said. " It's about Russia."

"What does he know about Russia?" Nick asked.

"I don't know. You can't ever tell about those guys. Maybe he was there when he was a boy. He's got a lot of dope on it."

"I'd like to meet him," Nick said.

"I'd like to meet Chesterton," Bill said.

"I wish he was here now," Nick said. "We'd take him fishing to the 'Voix tomorrow."

"I wonder if he'd like to go fishing," Bill said.

"Sure," said Nick. "He must be about the best guy there is. Do you remember the 'Flying Inn'?"

> "If an angel out of heaven
> Gives you something else to drink,
> Thank him for his kind intentions;
> Go and pour them down the sink."

"That's right," said Nick. "I guess he's a better guy than Walpole."

"Oh, he's a better guy, all right," Bill said.

"But Walpole's a better writer."

"I don't know," Nick said. "Chesterton's a classic."

"Walpole's a classic, too," Bill insisted.

"I wish we had them both here," Nick said. "We'd take them both fishing to the 'Voix tomorrow."

"Let's get drunk," Bill said.

"All right," Nick agreed.

"My old man won't care," Bill said.

"Are you sure?" said Nick.

"I know it," Bill said.

"I'm a little drunk now," Nick said.

"You aren't drunk," Bill said.

He got up from the floor and reached for the whisky bottle. Nick held out his glass. His eyes fixed on it while Bill poured.

Bill poured the glass half full of whisky.

"Put in your own water," he said. "There's just one more shot."

"Got any more?" Nick asked.

"There's plenty more but dad only likes me to drink what's open."

"Sure," said Nick.

"He says opening bottles is what makes drunkards," Bill explained.

"That's right," said Nick. He was impressed. He had never thought of that before. He had always thought it was solitary drinking that made drunkards.

"How is your dad?" he asked respectfully.

"He's all right," Bill said. "He gets a little wild sometimes."

"He's a swell guy," Nick said. He poured water into his glass out of the pitcher. It mixed slowly with the whisky. There was more whisky than water.

"You bet your life he is," Bill said.

"My old man's all right," Nick said.

"You're damn right he is," said Bill.

"He claims he's never taken a drink in his life," Nick said, as though announcing a scientific fact.

"Well, he's a doctor. My old man's a painter. That's different."

"He's missed a lot," Nick said sadly.

"You can't tell," Bill said. "Everything's got its compensations."

"He says he's missed a lot himself," Nick confessed.

"Well, dad's had a tough time," Bill said.

"It all evens up," Nick said.

They sat looking into the fire and thinking of this profound truth.

"I'll get a chunk from the back porch," Nick said. He had noticed while looking into the fire that the fire was dying down. Also he wished to show he could hold his liquor and be practical. Even if his father had never touched a drop Bill was not going to get him drunk before he himself was drunk.

"Bring one of the big beech chunks," Bill said. He was also being consciously practical.

Nick came in with the log through the kitchen and in passing knocked a pan off the kitchen table. He laid the log down and picked up the pan. It had contained dried apricots, soaking in water. He carefully picked up all the apricots off the floor, some of them had gone under the stove, and put them back in the pan. He dipped some more water on to them from the pail by the table. He felt quite proud of himself. He had been thoroughly practical.

He came in carrying the log and Bill got up from the chair and helped him put it on the fire.

"That's a swell log," Nick said.

"I'd been saving it for the bad weather," Bill said. "A log like that will burn all night."

"There'll be coals left to start the fire in the morning," Nick said.

"That's right," Bill agreed. They were conducting the conversation on a high plane.

"Let's have another drink," Nick said.

"I think there's another bottle open in the locker," Bill said.

He kneeled down in the corner in front of the locker and brought out a square-faced bottle.

"It's Scotch," he said.

"I'll get some more water," Nick said. He went out into the kitchen again. He filled the pitcher with the dipper dipping cold spring water from the pail. On his way back to the living room he passed a mirror in the dining room and looked in it. His face looked strange. He smiled at the face in the mirror and it grinned back at him. He winked at it and went on. It was not his face but it didn't make any difference.

Bill had poured out the drinks.

"That's an awfully big shot," Nick said.

"Not for us, Wemedge," Bill said.

"What'll we drink to?" Nick asked, holding up the glass.

" Let's drink to fishing," Bill said.

" All right," Nick said. " Gentlemen, I give you fishing."

" All fishing," Bill said. " Everywhere."

" Fishing," Nick said. " That's what we drink to."

" It's better than baseball," Bill said.

" There isn't any comparison," said Nick. " How did we ever get talking about baseball? "

" It was a mistake," Bill said. " Baseball is a game for louts."

They drank all that was in their glasses.

" Now let's drink to Chesterton."

" And Walpole," Nick interposed.

Nick poured out the liquor. Bill poured in the water. They looked at each other. They felt very fine.

" Gentlemen," Bill said, " I give you Chesterton and Walpole."

" Exactly, gentlemen," Nick said.

They drank. Bill filled up the glasses. They sat down in the big chairs in front of the fire.

" You were very wise, Wemedge," Bill said.

" What do you mean? " asked Nick.

" To bust off that Marge business," Bill said.

" I guess so," said Wemedge.

" It was the only thing to do. If you hadn't, by now you'd be back home working trying to get enough money to get married."

Nick said nothing.

" Once a man's married he's absolutely bitched," Bill went on. " He hasn't got anything more. Nothing. Not a damn thing. He's done for. You've seen the guys that get married."

Nick said nothing.

" You can tell them," Bill said. " They get this sort of fat married look. They're done for."

" Sure," said Nick.

" It was probably bad busting it off," Bill said. " But you always fall for somebody else and then it's all right. Fall for them but don't let them ruin you."

" Yes," said Nick.

" If you'd have married her you would have had to marry the whole family. Remember her mother and that guy she married? "

Nick nodded.

" Imagine having them around the house all the time and going to Sunday dinners at their house, and having them over to dinner and her telling Marge all the time what to do and how to act."

Nick sat quiet.

" You came out of it damned well," Bill said. " Now she can marry somebody of her own sort and settle down and be happy. You can't mix oil and water and you can't mix that sort of thing any more than if I'd marry Ida that works for Strattons. She'd probably like it, too."

Nick said nothing. The liquor had all died out of him and left him alone. Bill wasn't there. He wasn't sitting in front of the fire or going fishing tomorrow with Bill and his dad or anything. He wasn't drunk. It was all gone. All he knew was that he had once had Marjorie and that he had lost her. She was gone and he had sent her away. That was all that mattered. He might never see her again. Probably he never would. It was all gone, finished.

"Let's have another drink," Nick said.

Bill poured it out. Nick splashed in a little water.

"If you'd gone on that way we wouldn't be here now," Bill said.

That was true. His original plan had been to go down home and get a job. Then he had planned to stay in Charlevoix all winter so he could be near Marge. Now he did not know what he was going to do.

"Probably we wouldn't even be going fishing tomorrow," Bill said. "You had the right dope, all right."

"I couldn't help it," Nick said.

"I know. That's the way it works out," Bill said.

"All of a sudden everything was over," Nick said. "I don't know why it was. I couldn't help it. Just like when the three-day blows come now and rip all the leaves off the trees."

"Well, it's over. That's the point," Bill said.

"It was my fault," Nick said.

"It doesn't make any difference whose fault it was," Bill said.

"No, I suppose not," Nick said.

The big thing was that Marjorie was gone and that probably he would never see her again. He had talked to her about how they would go to Italy together and the fun they would have. Places they would be together. It was all gone now. Something gone out of him.

"So long as it's over that's all that matters," Bill said. "I tell you, Wemedge, I was worried while it was going on. You played it right. I understand her mother is sore as hell. She told a lot of people you were engaged."

"We weren't engaged," Nick said.

"It was all around that you were."

"I can't help it," Nick said. "We weren't."

"Weren't you going to get married?" Bill asked.

"Yes. But we weren't engaged," Nick said.

"What's the difference?" Bill asked judicially.

"I don't know. There's a difference."

"I don't see it," said Bill.

"All right," said Nick. "Let's get drunk."

"All right," Bill said. "Let's get really drunk."

"Let's get drunk and then go swimming," Nick said.

He drank off his glass.

"I'm sorry as hell about her but what could I do?" he said. "You know what her mother was like!"

"She was terrible," Bill said.

" All of a sudden it was over," Nick said. " I oughtn't to talk about it."

" You aren't," Bill said. " I talked about it and now I'm through. We won't ever speak about it again. You don't want to think about it. You might get back into it again."

Nick had not thought about that. It had seemed so absolute. That was a thought. That made him feel better.

" Sure," he said. " There's always that danger."

He felt happy now. There was not anything that was irrevocable. He might go into town Saturday night. Today was Thursday.

" There's always a chance," he said.

" You'll have to watch yourself," Bill said.

" I'll watch myself," he said.

He felt happy. Nothing was finished. Nothing was ever lost. He would go into town on Saturday. He felt lighter, as he had felt before Bill started to talk about it. There was always a way out.

" Let's take the guns and go down to the point and look for your dad," Nick said.

" All right."

Bill took down the two shotguns from the rack on the wall. He opened a box of shells. Nick put on his Mackinaw coat and his shoes. His shoes were stiff from the drying. He was still quite drunk but his head was clear.

" How do you feel? " Nick asked.

" Swell. I've just got a good edge on." Bill was buttoning up his sweater.

" There's no use getting drunk."

" No. We ought to get outdoors."

They stepped out the door. The wind was blowing a gale.

" The birds will lie right down in the grass with this," Nick said.

They struck down towards the orchard.

" I saw a woodcock this morning," Bill said.

" Maybe we'll jump him," Nick said.

" You can't shoot in this wind," Bill said.

Outside now the Marge business was no longer so tragic. It was not even very important. The wind blew everything like that away.

" It's coming right off the big lake," Nick said.

Against the wind they heard the thud of a shotgun.

" That's dad," Bill said. " He's down in the swamp."

" Let's cut down that way," Nick said.

" Let's cut across the lower meadow and see if we jump anything," Bill said.

" All right," Nick said.

None of it was important now. The wind blew it out of his head. Still he could always go into town Saturday night. It was a good thing to have in reserve.

Wilbur Daniel Steele

How Beautiful with Shoes

BY the time the milking was finished, the sow, which had farrowed the past week, was making such a row that the girl spilled a pint of the warm milk down the trough-lead to quiet the animal before taking the pail to the well-house. Then in the quiet she heard a sound of hoofs on the bridge, where the road crossed the creek a hundred yards below the house, and she set the pail down on the ground beside her bare, barn-soiled feet. She picked it up again. She set it down. It was as if she calculated its weight.

That was what she was doing, as a matter of fact, setting off against its pull toward the well-house the pull of that wagon team in the road, with little more of personal will or wish in the matter than has a wooden weathervane between two currents in the wind. And as with the vane, so with the wooden girl — the added behest of a whip-lash cracking in the distance was enough; leaving the pail at the barn door, she set off in a deliberate, docile beeline through the cow-yard, over the fence, and down in a diagonal across the farm's one tilled field toward the willow brake that walled the road at the dip. And once under way, though her mother came to the kitchen door and called in her high, flat voice, " Amarantha, where you goin', Amarantha? " the girl went on apparently unmoved, as though she had been as deaf as the woman in the doorway; indeed, if there was emotion in her it was the purely sensuous one of feeling the clods of the furrows breaking softly between her toes. It was springtime in the mountains.

" Amarantha, why don't you answer me, Amarantha? "

For moments after the girl had disappeared beyond the willows the widow continued to call, unaware through long habit of how absurd it sounded, the name which that strange man her husband had put upon their daughter in one of his moods. Mrs. Doggett had been deaf so long she did not realize that nobody else ever thought of it for the broad-fleshed, slow-minded girl, but called her Mary or, even more simply, Mare.

Ruby Herter had stopped his team this side of the bridge, the mules' heads turned into the lane to his father's farm beyond the road. A big-barreled, heavy-limbed fellow with a square, sallow, not unhandsome face, he took out youth in ponderous gestures of masterfulness; it was like him to have cracked his whip above his animals' ears the moment before he pulled them to a halt. When he saw the girl getting over the fence under the willows he tongued the wad of tobacco out of his mouth into his palm, threw it away beyond the road, and drew a sleeve of his jumper across his lips.

" Don't run yourself out o' breath, Mare; I got all night."

From *Harper's Magazine,* August, 1932.

"I was comin'." It sounded sullen only because it was matter of fact.

"Well, keep a-comin' and give us a smack." Hunched on the wagon seat, he remained motionless for some time after she had arrived at the hub, and when he stirred it was but to cut a fresh bit of tobacco, as if already he had forgotten why he threw the old one away. Having satisfied his humor, he unbent, climbed down, kissed her passive mouth, and hugged her up to him, roughly and loosely, his hands careless of contours. It was not out of the way; they were used to handling animals both of them; and it was spring. A slow warmth pervaded the girl, formless, nameless, almost impersonal.

Her betrothed pulled her head back by the braid of her yellow hair. He studied her face, his brows gathered and his chin out.

"Listen, Mare, you wouldn't leave nobody else hug and kiss you, dang you!"

She shook her head, without vehemence or anxiety.

"Who's that?" She hearkened up the road. "Pull your team out," she added as a Ford came in sight around the bend above the house, driven at speed. "Geddap!" she said to the mules herself.

But the car came to a halt near them, and one of the five men crowded in it called, "Come on, Ruby, climb in. They's a loony loose out o' Dayville Asylum, and they got him trailed over somewheres on Split Ridge, and Judge North phoned up to Slosson's store for ever'body come help circle him — come on, hop the runnin' board!"

Ruby hesitated, an eye on his team.

"Scared, Ruby?" The driver raced his engine. "They say this boy's a killer."

"Mare, take the team in and tell pa." The car was already moving when Ruby jumped it. A moment after it had sounded on the bridge it was out of sight.

"Amarantha, Amarantha, why don't you come, Amarantha?"

Returning from her errand, fifteen minutes later, Mare heard the plaint lifted in the twilight. The sun had dipped behind the back ridge, and though the sky was still bright with day, the dusk began to smoke up out of the plowed field like a ground fog. The girl had returned through it, got the milk, and started toward the well-house before the widow saw her.

"Daughter, seems to me you might!" she expostulated without change of key. "Here's some young man friend o' yourn stopped to say howdy, and I been rackin' my lungs out after you. . . . Put that milk in the cool and come!"

Some young man friend? But there was no good to be got from puzzling. Mare poured the milk in the pan in the dark of the low house over the well, and as she came out, stooping, she saw a figure waiting for her, black in silhouette against the yellowing sky.

"Who are you?" she asked, a native timidity making her sound sulky.

"'Amarantha!'" the fellow mused. "That's poetry." And she knew then that she did not know him.

She walked past, her arms straight down and her eyes front. Strangers always affected her with a kind of muscular terror simply by being strangers. So she gained the kitchen steps, aware by his tread that he followed. There, taking courage at sight of her mother in the doorway, she turned on him, her eyes down at the level of his knees.

"Who are you and what d' y' want?"

He still mused. "Amarantha! Amarantha in Carolina! That makes me happy!"

Mare hazarded one upward look. She saw that he had red hair, brown eyes, and hollows under his cheekbones, and though the green sweater he wore on top of a gray overall was plainly not meant for him, sizes too large as far as girth went, yet he was built so long of limb that his wrists came inches out of the sleeves and made his big hands look even bigger.

Mrs. Doggett complained. "Why don't you introduce us, daughter?"

The girl opened her mouth and closed it again. Her mother, unaware that no sound had come out of it, smiled and nodded, evidently taking to the tall, homely fellow and tickled by the way he could not seem to get his eyes off her daughter. But the daughter saw none of it, all her attention centered upon the stranger's hands.

Restless, hard-fleshed, and chap-bitten, they were like a countryman's hands; but the fingers were longer than the ordinary, and slightly spatulate at their ends, and these ends were slowly and continuously at play among themselves.

The girl could not have explained how it came to her to be frightened and at the same time to be calm, for she was inept with words. It was simply that in an animal way she knew animals, knew them in health and ailing, and when they were ailing she knew by instinct, as her father had known, how to move so as not to fret them.

Her mother had gone in to light up; from beside the lamp-shelf she called back, "If he's aimin' to stay to supper you should've told me, Amarantha, though I guess there's plenty of the side-meat to go 'round, if you'll bring me in a few more turnips and potatoes, though it is late."

At the words the man's cheeks moved in and out. "I'm very hungry," he said.

Mare nodded deliberately. Deliberately, as if her mother could hear her, she said over her shoulder, "I'll go get the potatoes and turnips, ma." While she spoke she was moving, slowly, softly, at first, toward the right of the yard, where the fence gave over into the field. Unluckily her mother spied her through the window.

"Amarantha, where *are* you goin'?"

"I'm goin' to get the potatoes and turnips." She neither raised her voice nor glanced back, but lengthened her stride. "He won't hurt her," she said to herself. "He won't hurt her; it's me, not her," she kept repeating, while she got over the fence and down into the shadow that lay more than ever like a fog on the field.

The desire to believe that it actually did hide her, the temptation to break from her rapid but orderly walk grew till she could no longer fight it. She saw the road willows only a dash ahead of her. She ran, her feet floundering among the furrows.

She neither heard nor saw him, but when she realized he was with her she knew he had been with her all the while. She stopped, and he stopped, and so they stood, with the dark open of the field all around. Glancing sidewise presently, she saw he was no longer looking at her with those strangely importunate brown eyes of his, but had raised them to the crest of the wooded ridge behind her.

By and by, "What does it make you think of?" he asked. And when she made no move to see, "Turn around and look!" he said, and though it was low and almost tender in its tone, she knew enough to turn.

A ray of the sunset hidden in the west struck through the tops of the topmost trees, far and small up there, a thin, bright hem.

"What does it make you think of, Amarantha? . . . Answer!"

"Fire," she made herself say.

"Or blood."

"Or blood, yeh. That's right, or blood." She had heard a Ford going up the road beyond the willows, and her attention was not on what she said.

The man soliloquized. "Fire and blood, both; spare one or the other, and where is beauty, the way the world is? It's an awful thing to have to carry, but Christ had it. Christ came with a sword. I love beauty, Amarantha. . . . I say, I love beauty!"

"Yeh, that's right, I hear." What she heard was the car stopping at the house.

"Not prettiness. Prettiness'll have to go with ugliness, because it's only ugliness trigged up. But beauty!" Now again he was looking at her. "Do you know how beautiful you are, Amarantha, *Amarantha sweet and fair?*" Of a sudden, reaching behind her, he began to unravel the meshes of her hair-braid, the long, flat-tipped fingers at once impatient and infinitely gentle. *"Braid no more that shining hair!"*

Flat-faced Mare Doggett tried to see around those glowing eyes so near to hers, but wise in her instinct, did not try too hard. "Yeh," she temporized. "I mean, no, I mean."

"Amarantha, I've come a long, long way for you. Will you come away with me now?"

"Yeh — that is — in a minute I will, mister — yeh . . ."

"Because you want to, Amarantha? Because you love me as I love you? Answer!"

"Yeh — sure — uh . . . *Ruby!*"

The man tried to run, but there were six against him, coming up out of the dark that lay in the plowed ground. Mare stood where she was while they knocked him down and got a rope around him; after that she walked back toward the house with Ruby and Older Haskins, her father's cousin.

Ruby wiped his brow and felt of his muscles. "Gees, you're lucky we come, Mare. We're no more'n past the town, when they come hollerin' he'd broke over this way."

When they came to the fence the girl sat on the rail for a moment and rebraided her hair before she went into the house, where they were making her mother smell ammonia.

Lots of cars were coming. Judge North was coming, somebody said. When Mare heard this she went into her bedroom off the kitchen and got her shoes and put them on. They were brand-new two-dollar shoes with cloth tops, and she had only begun to break them in last Sunday; she wished afterwards she had put her stockings on too, for they would have eased the seams. Or else that she had put on the old button pair, even though the soles were worn through.

Judge North arrived. He thought first of taking the loony straight through to Dayville that night, but then decided to keep him in the lock-up at the court-house till morning and make the drive by day. Older Haskins stayed in, gentling Mrs. Doggett, while Ruby went out to help get the man into the Judge's sedan. Now that she had them on, Mare didn't like to take the shoes off till Older went; it might make him feel small, she thought.

Older Haskins had a lot of facts about the loony.

"His name's Humble Jewett," he told them. "They belong back in Breed County, all them Jewetts, and I don't reckon there's none on 'em that's not a mite unbalanced. He went to college though, worked his way, and he taught somethin' 'rother in some academy-school a spell, till he went off his head all of a sudden and took after folks with an axe. I remember it in the paper at the time. They give out one while how the Principal wasn't goin' to live, and there was others — there was a girl he tried to strangle. That was four-five year back."

Ruby came in guffawing. "Know the only thing they can get 'im to say, Mare? Only God thing he'll say is, 'Amarantha, she's goin' with me.' . . . Mare!"

"Yeh, I know."

The cover of the kettle the girl was handling slid off on the stove with a clatter. A sudden sick wave passed over her. She went out to the back, out into the air. It was not till now she knew how frightened she had been.

Ruby went home, but Older Haskins stayed to supper with them and helped Mare do the dishes afterward; it was nearly nine when he left. The mother was already in bed, and Mare was about to sit down to get those shoes off her wretched feet at last, when she heard the cow carrying on up at the barn, lowing and kicking, and next minute the sow was in it with a horning note. It might be a fox passing by to get at the henhouse, or a weasel. Mare forgot her feet, took a broom-handle they used in boiling clothes, opened the back door, and stepped out. Blinking the lamplight from her eyes, she peered up toward the outbuildings and saw the gable end of the barn standing like a red arrow in the dark, and the top of a butternut tree beyond it drawn in skeleton traceries, and just then a cock crowed.

She went to the right corner of the house and saw where the light came from, ruddy above the woods down the valley. Returning into the house, she bent close to her mother's ear and shouted, "Somethin's a-fire down to the town, looks like," then went out again and up to the barn. "Soh! Soh!" she called in to the animals. She climbed up and stood on the top rail of the cowpen fence, only to find she could not locate the flame even there.

Ten rods behind the buildings a mass of rock mounted higher than their ridgepoles, a chopped-off buttress of the back ridge, covered with oak scrub and wild grapes and blackberries, whose thorny ropes the girl beat away from her skirt with the broom-handle as she scrambled up in the wine-colored dark. Once at the top, and the brush held aside, she could see the tongue-tip of the conflagration half a mile away at the town. And she knew by the bearing of the two church steeples that it was the building where the lock-up was that was burning.

There is a horror in knowing animals trapped in a fire, no matter what the animals.

" Oh, my God! " Mare said.

A car went down the road. Then there was a horse galloping. That would be Older Haskins probably. People were out at Ruby's father's farm; she could hear their voices raised. There must have been another car up from the other way, for lights wheeled and shouts were exchanged in the neighborhood of the bridge. Next thing she knew, Ruby was at the house below, looking for her probably.

He was telling her mother. Mrs. Doggett was not used to him, so he had to shout even louder than Mare had to.

" What y' reckon he done, the hellion! He broke the door and killed Lew Fyke and set the courthouse afire! . . . Where's Mare? "

Her mother would not know. Mare called. " Here, up the rock here."

She had better go down. Ruby would likely break his bones if he tried to climb the rock in the dark, not knowing the way. But the sight of the fire fascinated her simple spirit, the fearful element, more fearful than ever now, with the news. " Yes, I'm comin'," she called sulkily, hearing feet in the brush. " You wait; I'm comin'."

When she turned and saw it was Humble Jewett, right behind her among the branches, she opened her mouth to screech. She was not quick enough. Before a sound came out he got one hand over her face and the other arm around her body.

Mare had always thought she was strong, and the loony looked gangling; yet she was so easy for him that he need not hurt her. He made no haste and little noise as he carried her deeper into the undergrowth. Where the hill began to mount it was harder though. Presently he set her on her feet. He let the hand that had been over her mouth slip down to her throat, where the broad-tipped fingers wound, tender as yearning, weightless as caress.

" I was afraid you'd scream before you knew who 'twas, Amarantha. But I didn't want to hurt your lips, dear heart, your lovely, quiet lips."

It was so dark under the trees she could hardly see him, but she felt his breath on her mouth, near to. But then, instead of kissing her, he said, " No! No! " took from her throat for an instant the hand that had held her mouth, kissed its palm, and put it back softly against her skin.

" Now, my love, let's go before they come."

She stood stock-still. Her mother's voice was to be heard in the distance, strident and meaningless. More cars were on the road. Nearer, around the rock, there were sounds of tramping and thrashing. Ruby fussed and cursed. He shouted, " Mare, dang you, where are you, Mare? " his voice harsh with uneasy anger. Now, if she aimed to do anything, was the time to do it. But there was neither breath nor power in her windpipe. It was as if those yearning fingers had paralyzed the muscles.

"Come!" The arm he put around her shivered against her shoulder blades. It was anger. "I hate killing. It's a dirty, ugly thing. It makes me sick." He gagged, judging by the sound. But then he ground his teeth. "Come away, my love!"

She found herself moving. Once when she broke a branch underfoot with an instinctive awkwardness he chided her. "Quiet, my heart, else they'll hear!" She made herself heavy. He thought she grew tired and bore more of her weight till he was breathing hard.

Men came up the hill. There must have been a dozen spread out, by the angle of their voices as they kept touch. Always Humble Jewett kept caressing Mare's throat with one hand; all she could do was hang back.

"You're tired and you're frightened," he said at last. "Get down here."

There were twigs in the dark, the overhang of a thicket of some sort. He thrust her in under this, and lay beside her on the bed of groundpine. The hand that was not in love with her throat reached across her; she felt the weight of its forearm on her shoulder and its fingers among the strands of her hair, eagerly, but tenderly, busy. Not once did he stop speaking, no louder than breathing, his lips to her ear.

"*Amarantha sweet and fair — Ah, braid no more that shining hair . . .*"

Mare had never heard of Lovelace, the poet; she thought the loony was just going on, hardly listened, got little sense. But the cadence of it added to the lethargy of all her flesh.

"*Like a clew of golden thread — Most excellently ravelléd . . .*"

Voices loudened; feet came tramping; a pair went past not two rods away.

"*. . . Do not then wind up the light — In ribbands, and o'ercloud in night . . .*"

The search went on up the woods, men shouting to one another and beating the brush.

"*. . . But shake your head and scatter day!* I've never loved, Amarantha. They've tried me with prettiness, but prettiness is too cheap, yes, it's too cheap."

Mare was cold, and the coldness made her lazy. All she knew was that he talked on.

"But dogwood blowing in the spring isn't cheap. The earth of a field isn't cheap. Lots of times I've lain down and kissed the earth of a field, Amarantha. That's beauty, and a kiss for beauty." His breath moved up her cheek. He trembled violently. "No, no, not yet!" He got to his knees and pulled her by an arm. "We can go now."

They went back down the slope, but at an angle, so that when they came to the level they passed two hundred yards to the north of the house, and crossed the road there. More and more her walking was like sleepwalking, the feet numb in their shoes. Even where he had to let go of her, crossing the creek on stones, she stepped where he stepped with an obtuse docility. The voices of the searchers on the back ridge were small in distance when they began to climb the face of Coward Hill, on the opposite side of the valley.

There is an old farm on top of Coward Hill, big hayfields as flat as tables. It had been half past nine when Mare stood on the rock above the barn; it was toward midnight when Humble Jewett put aside the last branches of the woods and led her out on the height, and half a moon had risen. And a wind blew there, tossing the withered tops of last year's grasses, and mists ran with the wind, and ragged shadows with the mists, and mares'-tails of clear moonlight among the shadows, so that now the boles of birches on the forest's edge beyond the fences were but opal blurs and now cut alabaster. It struck so cold against the girl's cold flesh, this wind, that another wind of shivers blew through her, and she put her hands over her face and eyes. But the madman stood with his eyes wide open and his mouth open, drinking the moonlight and the wet wind.

His voice, when he spoke at last, was thick in his throat.

" Get down on your knees." He got down on his and pulled her after. " And pray! "

Once in England a poet sang four lines. Four hundred years have forgotten his name, but they have remembered his lines. The daft man knelt upright, his face raised to the wild scud, his long wrists hanging to the dead grass. He began simply:

> " O western wind, when wilt thou blow
> That the small rain down can rain? "

The Adam's-apple was big in his bent throat. As simply he finished.

> " Christ, that my love were in my arms
> And I in my bed again! "

Mare got up and ran. She ran without aim or feeling in the power of the wind. She told herself again that the mists would hide her from him, as she had done at dusk. And again, seeing that he ran at her shoulder, she knew he had been there all the while, making a race of it, flailing the air with his long arms for joy of play in the cloud of spring, throwing his knees high, leaping the moon-blue waves of the brown grass, shaking his bright hair; and her own hair was a weight behind her, lying level on the wind. Once a shape went bounding ahead of them for instants; she did not realize it was a fox till it was gone.

She never thought of stopping; she never thought anything, except once, " Oh, my God, I wish I had my shoes off! " And what would have been the good in stopping or in turning another way, when it was only play? The man's ecstasy magnified his strength. When a snake-fence came at them he took the top rail in flight, like a college hurdler and, seeing the girl hesitate and half turn as if to flee, he would have releaped it without touching a hand. But then she got a loom of buildings, climbed over quickly, before he should jump, and ran along the lane that ran with the fence.

Mare had never been up there, but she knew that the farm and the house belonged to a man named Wyker, a kind of cousin of Ruby Herter's, a violent, bearded old fellow who lived by himself. She could not believe her luck. When she had run half the distance and Jewett had not grabbed her, doubt grabbed her instead. " Oh, my God, go careful! " she told herself. " Go slow! " she implored herself, and stopped running, to walk.

Here was a misgiving the deeper in that it touched her special knowledge. She had never known an animal so far gone that its instincts failed it; a starving rat will scent the trap sooner than a fed one. Yet, after one glance at the house they approached, Jewett paid it no further attention, but walked with his eyes to the right, where the cloud had blown away, and wooded ridges, like black waves rimed with silver, ran down away toward the Valley of Virginia.

" I've never lived! " In his single cry there were two things, beatitude and pain.

Between the bigness of the falling world and his eyes the flag of her hair blew. He reached out and let it whip between his fingers. Mare was afraid it would break the spell then, and he would stop looking away and look at the house again. So she did something almost incredible; she spoke.

" It's a pretty — I mean — a beautiful view down that-a-way."

" God Almighty beautiful, to take your breath away. I knew I'd never loved, Belovéd — " He caught a foot under the long end of one of the boards that covered the well and went down heavily on his hands and knees. It seemed to make no difference. " But I never knew I'd never lived," he finished in the same tone of strong rapture, quadruped in the grass, while Mare ran for the door and grabbed the latch.

When the latch would not give, she lost what little sense she had. She pounded with her fists. She cried with all her might: " Oh — hey — in there — hey — in there! " Then Jewett came and took her gently between his hands and drew her away, and then, though she was free, she stood in something like an awful embarrassment while he tried shouting.

" Hey! Friend! whoever you are, wake up and let my love and me come in! "

" No! " wailed the girl.

He grew peremptory. " Hey, wake up! " He tried the latch. He passed to full fury in a wink's time; he cursed, he kicked, he beat the door till Mare thought he would break his hands. Withdrawing, he ran at it with his shoulder; it burst at the latch, went slamming in, and left a black emptiness. His anger dissolved in a big laugh. Turning in time to catch her by a wrist, he cried joyously, " Come, my Sweet One! "

" No! No! Please — aw — listen. There ain't nobody there. He ain't to home. It wouldn't be right to go in anybody's house if they wasn't to home, you know that."

His laugh was blither than ever. He caught her high in his arms.

" I'd do the same by his love and him if 'twas my house, I would." At the threshold he paused and thought, " That is, if she was the true love of his heart forever."

The room was the parlor. Moonlight slanted in at the door, and another shaft came through a window and fell across a sofa, its covering dilapidated, showing its wadding in places. The air was sour, but both of them were farm-bred.

"Don't, Amarantha!" His words were pleading in her ear. "Don't be so frightened."

He set her down on the sofa. As his hands let go of her they were shaking.

"But look, I'm frightened too." He knelt on the floor before her, reached out his hands, withdrew them. "See, I'm afraid to touch you." He mused, his eyes rounded. "Of all the ugly things there are, fear is the ugliest. And yet, see, it can be the very beautifulest. That's a strange queer thing."

The wind blew in and out of the room, bringing the thin, little bitter sweetness of new April at night. The moonlight that came across Mare's shoulders fell full upon his face, but hers it left dark, ringed by the aureole of her disordered hair.

"Why do you wear a halo, Love?" He thought about it. "Because you're an angel, is that why?" The swift, untempered logic of the mad led him to dismay. His hands came flying to hers, to make sure they were of earth; and he touched her breast, her shoulders, and her hair. Peace returned to his eyes as his fingers twined among the strands.

"*Thy hair is as a flock of goats that appear from Gilead . . .*" He spoke like a man dreaming. "*Thy temples are like a piece of pomegranate within thy locks.*"

Mare never knew that he could not see her for the moonlight.

"Do you remember, Love?"

She dared not shake her head under his hand. "Yeh, I reckon," she temporized.

"You remember how I sat at your feet, long ago, like this, and made up a song? And all the poets in all the world have never made one to touch it, have they, Love?"

"Ugh-ugh — never."

"*How beautiful are thy feet with shoes . . .* Remember?"

"Oh, my God, what's he sayin' now?" she wailed to herself.

"*How beautiful are thy feet with shoes, O prince's daughter! the joints of thy
    thighs are like jewels, the work of the hands of a cunning workman.
Thy navel is like a round goblet, which wanteth not liquor; thy belly is like
    an heap of wheat set about with lilies.
Thy two breasts are like two young roes that are twins.*"

Mare had not been to church since she was a little girl, when her mother's black dress wore out. "No, no!" she wailed under her breath. "You're awful to say such awful things." She might have shouted it; nothing could have shaken the man now, rapt in the immortal, passionate periods of Solomon's song.

"*. . . now also thy breasts shall be as clusters of the vine, and the smell of thy
    nose like apples.*"

Hotness touched Mare's face for the first time. "Aw, no, don't talk so!"

"*And the roof of thy mouth like the best wine for my belovéd . . . causing
    the lips of them that are asleep to speak.*"

He had ended. His expression changed. Ecstasy gave place to anger, love to hate. And Mare felt the change in the weight of the fingers in her hair.

"What do you mean, I mustn't say it like that?" But it was not to her his fury spoke, for he answered himself straightway. "Like poetry, Mr. Jewett; I won't have blasphemy around my school."

"Poetry! My God! if that isn't poetry — if that isn't music —" . . . "It's Bible, Jewett. What you're paid to teach here is *literature.*"

"Doctor Ryeworth, you're the blasphemer and you're an ignorant man." . . . "And your Principal. And I won't have you going around reading sacred allegory like earthly love."

"Ryeworth, you're an old man, a dull man, a dirty man, and you'd be better dead."

Jewett's hands had slid down from Mare's head. "Then I went to put my fingers around his throat, so. But my stomach turned, and I didn't do it. I went to my room. I laughed all the way to my room. I sat in my room at my table and I laughed. I laughed all afternoon and long after dark came. And then, about ten, somebody came and stood beside me in my room."

"'Wherefore dost thou laugh, son?'

"Then I knew who He was. He was Christ.

"'I was laughing about that dirty, ignorant, crazy old fool, Lord.'

"'Wherefore dost thou laugh?'

"I didn't laugh any more. He didn't say any more. I kneeled down, bowed my head.

"'Thy will be done! Where is he, Lord?'

"'Over at the girls' dormitory, waiting for Blossom Sinckley.'

"Brassy Blossom, dirty Blossom . . ."

It had come so suddenly it was nearly too late. Mare tore at his hands with hers, tried with all her strength to pull her neck away.

"Filthy Blossom! and him an old filthy man, Blossom! and you'll find him in hell when you reach there, Blossom . . ."

It was more the nearness of his face than the hurt of his hands that gave her power of fright to choke out three words.

"I — ain't — Blossom!"

Light ran in crooked veins. Through the veins she saw his face bewildered. His hands loosened. One fell down and hung; the other he lifted and put over his eyes, took it away again and looked at her.

"Amarantha!" His remorse was fearful to see. "What have I done!" His hands returned to hover over the hurts, ravening with pity, grief and tenderness. Tears fell down his cheeks. And with that, dammed desire broke its dam.

"Amarantha, my love, my dove, my beautiful love —"

"*And I ain't Amarantha neither, I'm Mary! Mary, that's my name!*"

She had no notion what she had done. He was like a crystal crucible that a chemist watches, changing hue in a wink with one adeptly added drop; but hers was not the chemist's eye. All she knew was that she felt light and free of him; all she could see of his face as he stood away above the moonlight were the whites of his eyes.

" Mary! " he muttered. A slight paroxysm shook his frame. So in the transparent crucible desire changed its hue. He retreated farther, stood in the dark by some tall piece of furniture. And still she could see the whites of his eyes.

" Mary! Mary Adorable! " A wonder was in him. " Mother of God! "

Mare held her breath. She eyed the door, but it was too far. And already he came back to go on his knees before her, his shoulders so bowed and his face so lifted that it must have cracked his neck, she thought; all she could see on the face was pain.

" Mary Mother, I'm sick to my death. I'm so tired."

She had seen a dog like that, one she had loosed from a trap after it had been there three days, its caught leg half gnawed free. Something about the eyes.

" Mary Mother, take me in your arms . . ."

Once again her muscles tightened. But he made no move.

". . . and give me sleep."

No, they were worse than the dog's eyes.

" Sleep, sleep! why won't they let me sleep? Haven't I done it all yet, Mother? Haven't I washed them yet of all their sins? I've drunk the cup that was given me; is there another? They've mocked me and reviled me, broken my brow with thorns and my hands with nails, and I've forgiven them, for they knew not what they did. Can't I go to sleep now, Mother? "

Mare could not have said why, but now she was more frightened than she had ever been. Her hands lay heavy on her knees, side by side, and she could not take them away when he bowed his head and rested his face upon them.

After a moment he said one thing more. " Take me down gently when you take me from the Tree."

Gradually the weight of his body came against her shins, and he slept.

The moon streak that entered by the eastern window crept north across the floor, thinner and thinner; the one that fell through the southern doorway traveled east and grew fat. For a while Mare's feet pained her terribly and her legs too. She dared not move them, though, and by and by they did not hurt so much.

A dozen times, moving her head slowly on her neck, she canvassed the shadows of the room for a weapon. Each time her eyes came back to a heavy earthenware pitcher on a stand some feet to the left of the sofa. It would have had flowers in it when Wyker's wife was alive; probably it had not been moved from its dust-ring since she died. It would be a long grab, perhaps too long; still, it might be done if she had her hands.

To get her hands from under the sleeper's head was the task she set herself. She pulled first one, then the other, infinitesimally. She waited. Again she tugged a very, very little. The order of his breathing was not disturbed. But at the third trial he stirred.

" Gently! gently! " His own muttering waked him more. With some drowsy instinct of possession he threw one hand across her wrists, pinning them to-

gether between thumb and fingers. She kept dead quiet, shut her eyes, lengthened her breathing, as if she too slept.

There came a time when what was pretense grew a peril; strange as it was,
she had to fight to keep her eyes open. She never knew whether or not she
really napped. But something changed in the air, and she was wide awake again.
The moonlight was fading on the doorsill, and the light that runs before dawn
waxed in the window behind her head.

And then she heard a voice in the distance, lifted in maundering song. It
was old man Wyker coming home after a night, and it was plain he had had
some whisky.

Now a new terror laid hold of Mare.

" Shut up, you fool you! " she wanted to shout. " Come quiet, quiet! " She
might have chanced it now to throw the sleeper away from her and scramble
and run, had his powers of strength and quickness not taken her simple imagination utterly in thrall.

Happily the singing stopped. What had occurred was that the farmer had
espied the open door and, even befuddled as he was, wanted to know more
about it quietly. He was so quiet that Mare began to fear he had gone away.
He had the squirrel-hunter's foot, and the first she knew of him was when she
looked and saw his head in the doorway, his hard, soiled, whiskery face half up-
side-down with craning.

He had been to the town. Between drinks he had wandered in and out of
the night's excitement; had even gone a short distance with one search party
himself. Now he took in the situation in the room. He used his forefinger. First
he held it to his lips. Next he pointed it with a jabbing motion at the sleeper.
Then he tapped his own forehead and described wheels. Lastly, with his whole
hand, he made pushing gestures, for Mare to wait. Then he vanished as silently
as he had appeared.

The minutes dragged. The light in the east strengthened and turned rosy.
Once she thought she heard a board creaking in another part of the house, and
looked down sharply to see if the loony stirred. All she could see of his face was
a temple with freckles on it and the sharp ridge of a cheekbone, but even from
so little she knew how deeply and peacefully he slept. The door darkened.
Wyker was there again. In one hand he carried something heavy; with the
other he beckoned.

" Come jumpin'! " he said out loud.

Mare went jumping, but her cramped legs threw her down halfway to the
sill; the rest of the distance she rolled and crawled. Just as she tumbled through
the door it seemed as if the world had come to an end above her; two barrels
of a shotgun discharged into a room make a noise. Afterwards all she could
hear in there was something twisting and bumping on the floor boards. She
got up and ran.

Mare's mother had gone to pieces; neighbor women put her to bed when
Mare came home. They wanted to put Mare to bed, but she would not let them.

She sat on the edge of her bed in her lean-to bedroom off the kitchen, just as she was, her hair down all over her shoulders and her shoes on, and stared away from them, at a place in the wallpaper.

"Yeh, I'll go myself. Lea' me be!"

The women exchanged quick glances, thinned their lips, and left her be. "God knows," was all they would answer to the questionings of those that had not gone in, "but she's gettin' herself to bed."

When the doctor came, though, he found her sitting just as she had been, still dressed, her hair down on her shoulders and her shoes on.

"What d' y' want?" she muttered and stared at the place in the wallpaper.

How could Doc Paradise say, when he did not know himself?

"I didn't know if you might be — might be feeling very smart, Mary."

"I'm all right. Lea' me be."

It was a heavy responsibility. Doc shouldered it. "No, it's all right," he said to the men in the road. Ruby Herter stood a little apart, chewing sullenly and looking another way. Doc raised his voice to make certain it carried. "Nope, nothing."

Ruby's ears got red, and he clamped his jaws. He knew he ought to go in and see Mare, but he was not going to do it while everybody hung around waiting to see if he would. A mule tied near him reached out and mouthed his sleeve in idle innocence; he wheeled and banged a fist against the side of the animal's head.

"Well, what d' y' aim to do 'bout it?" he challenged its owner.

He looked at the sun then. It was ten in the morning. "Hell, I got work!" he flared, and set off down the road for home. Doc looked at Judge North, and the Judge started after Ruby. But Ruby shook his head angrily. "Lea' me be!" He went on, and the Judge came back.

It got to be eleven and then noon. People began to say, "Like enough she'd be as thankful if the whole neighborhood wasn't camped here." But none went away.

As a matter of fact they were no bother to the girl. She never saw them. The only move she made was to bend her ankles over and rest her feet on edge; her shoes hurt terribly and her feet knew it, though she did not. She sat all the while staring at that one figure in the wallpaper, and she never saw the figure.

Strange as the night had been, this day was stranger. Fright and physical pain are perishable things once they are gone. But while pain merely dulls and telescopes in memory and remains diluted pain, terror looked back upon has nothing of terror left. A gambling chance taken, at no matter what odds, and won was a sure thing since the world's beginning; perils come through safely were never perilous. But what fright does do in retrospect is this — it heightens each sensuous recollection, like a hard, clear lacquer laid on wood, bringing out the color and grain of it vividly.

Last night Mare had lain stupid with fear on groundpine beneath a bush, loud footfalls and light whispers confused in her ear. Only now, in her room, did she smell the groundpine. Only now did the conscious part of her brain begin to make words of the whispering.

"*Amarantha*," she remembered, "*Amarantha sweet and fair*." That was as far as she could go for the moment, except that the rhyme with "fair" was "hair." But then a puzzle, held in abeyance, brought other words. She wondered what "ravel Ed" could mean. "*Most excellently ravelléd*." It was left to her mother to bring the end.

They gave up trying to keep her mother out at last. The poor woman's prostration took the form of fussiness.

"Good gracious, daughter, you look a sight. Them new shoes, half ruined; ain't your feet *dead?* And look at your hair, all tangled like a wild one!"

She got a comb.

"Be quiet, daughter; what's ailin' you. Don't shake your head!"

"*But shake your head and scatter day*."

"What you say, Amarantha?" Mrs. Doggett held an ear down.

"Go 'way! Lea' me be!"

Her mother was hurt and left. And Mare ran, as she stared at the wallpaper.

"*Christ, that my love were in my arms . . .*"

Mare ran. She ran through a wind white with moonlight and wet with "the small rain." And the wind she ran through, it ran through her, and made her shiver as she ran. And the man beside her leapéd high over the waves of the dead grasses and gathered the wind in his arms, and her hair was heavy and his was tossing, and a little fox ran before them across the top of the world. And the world spread down around in waves of black and silver, more immense than she had ever known the world could be, and more beautiful.

"*God Almighty beautiful, to take your breath away!*"

Mare wondered, and she was not used to wondering. "Is it only crazy folks ever run like that and talk that way?"

She no longer ran; she walked; for her breath was gone. And there was some other reason, some other reason. Oh, yes, it was because her feet were hurting her. So, at last, and roundabout, her shoes had made contact with her brain.

Bending over the side of the bed, she loosened one of them mechanically. She pulled it half off. But then she looked down at it sharply, and she pulled it on again.

"*How beautiful . . .*"

Color overspread her face in a slow wave.

"*How beautiful are thy feet with shoes . . .*"

"Is it only crazy folks ever say such things?"

"*O prince's daughter!*"

"Or call you that?"

By and by there was a knock at the door. It opened, and Ruby Herter came in.

"Hello, Mare old girl!" His face was red. He scowled and kicked at the floor. "I'd 'a' been over sooner, except we got a mule down sick." He looked at his dumb betrothed. "Come on, cheer up, forget it! He won't scare you no more, not that boy, not what's left o' him. What you lookin' at, sourface? Ain't you glad to see me?"

Mare quit looking at the wallpaper and looked at the floor.

" Yeh," she said.

" That's more like it, babe." He came and sat beside her; reached down behind her and gave her a spank. " Come on, give us a kiss, babe! " He wiped his mouth on his jumper sleeve, a good farmer's sleeve, spotted with milking. He put his hands on her; he was used to handling animals. " Hey, you, warm up a little; reckon I'm goin' to do all the lovin'? "

" Ruby, lea' me be! "

" What! "

She was up, twisting. He was up, purple.

" What's ailin' of you, Mare? What you bawlin' about? "

" Nothin' — only go 'way! "

She pushed him to the door and through it with all her strength, and closed it in his face, and stood with her weight against it, crying, " Go 'way! Go 'way! Lea' me be! "

Katherine Anne Porter

He

LIFE was very hard for the Whipples. It was hard to feed all the hungry mouths; it was hard to keep the children in flannels during the winter, short as it was — " God knows what would become of us if we lived north," they would say; keeping them decently clean was hard. " It looks like our luck won't never let up on us," said Mr. Whipple, but Mrs. Whipple was all for taking what was sent and calling it good, anyhow when the neighbors were in earshot. " Don't ever let a soul hear us complain," she kept saying to her husband. She couldn't stand to be pitied. " No, not if it comes to it that we have to live in a wagon and pick cotton around the country," she said, " nobody's going to get a chance to look down on us."

Mrs. Whipple loved her second son, the simple-minded one, better than she loved the other two children put together. She was forever saying so, and when she talked with certain of her neighbors, she would even throw in her husband and her mother for good measure.

" You needn't keep on saying it around," said Mr. Whipple; " you'll make people think nobody else has any feelings about Him but you."

" It's natural for a mother," Mrs. Whipple would remind him. " You know yourself it's more natural for a mother to be that way. People don't expect so much of fathers, some way."

This didn't keep the neighbors from talking plainly among themselves. " A Lord's pure mercy if He should die," they said. " It's the sins of the fathers,"

From *Flowering Judas*, 1935.

they agreed among themselves. " There's bad blood and bad doings somewhere, you can bet on that." This behind the Whipples' backs. To their faces everybody said, " He's not so bad off. He'll be all right yet. Look how He grows! "

Mrs. Whipple hated to talk about it, she tried to keep her mind off it; but every time anybody set foot in the house, the subject always came up, and she had to talk about Him first, before she could get on to anything else. It seemed to ease her mind. " I wouldn't have anything happen to Him for all the world, but it just looks like I can't keep Him out of mischief. He's so strong and active, He's always into everything; He was like that since He could walk. It's actually funny sometimes, the way He can do anything; it's laughable to see Him up to His tricks. Emly has more accidents — I'm forever tying up her bruises, and Adna can't fall a foot without cracking a bone. But He can do anything and not get a scratch. The preacher said such a nice thing once when he was here. He said, and I'll remember it to my dying day, ' The innocent walk with God — that's why He don't get hurt.' " Whenever Mrs. Whipple repeated these words, she always felt a warm pool spread in her breast, and the tears would fill her eyes, and then she could talk about something else.

He did grow and He never got hurt. A plank blew off the chicken house and struck Him on the head and He never seemed to know it. He had learned a few words, and after this He forgot them. He didn't whine for food as the other children did, but waited until it was given Him; He ate squatting in the corner, smacking and mumbling. Rolls of fat covered Him like an overcoat, and He could carry twice as much wood and water as Adna. Emly had a cold in the head most of the time — " She takes that after me," said Mrs. Whipple — so in bad weather they gave her the extra blanket off His cot. He never seemed to mind the cold.

Just the same, Mrs. Whipple's life was a torment for fear something might happen to Him. He climbed the peach trees much better than Adna and went skittering along the branches like a monkey, just a regular monkey. " Oh, Mrs. Whipple, you hadn't ought to let Him do that. He'll lose His balance sometime. He can't rightly know what He's doing."

Mrs. Whipple almost screamed out at the neighbor. " He *does* know what He's doing! He's as able as any other child! Come down out of there, you! " When He finally reached the ground she could hardly keep her hands off Him for acting like that before people, a grin all over His face and her worried sick about Him all the time.

" It's the neighbors," said Mrs. Whipple to her husband. " Oh, I do mortally wish they would keep out of our business. I can't afford to let Him do anything for fear they'll come nosing around about it. Look at the bees, now. Adna can't handle them, they sting him up so; I haven't got time to do everything, and now I don't dare let Him. But if He gets a sting He don't really mind."

" It's just because He ain't got sense enough to be scared of anything," said Mr. Whipple.

" You ought to be ashamed of yourself," said Mrs. Whipple, " talking that way about your own child. Who's to take up for Him if we don't, I'd like to know? He sees a lot that goes on, He listens to things all the time. And anything I tell Him to do He does it. Don't never let anybody hear you say such things. They'd think you favored the other children over Him."

" Well, now I don't, and you know it, and what's the use of getting all worked up about it? You always think the worst of everything. Just let Him alone, He'll get along somehow. He gets plenty to eat and wear, don't He? " Mr. Whipple suddenly felt tired out. " Anyhow, it can't be helped now."

Mrs. Whipple felt tired too, she complained in a tired voice. " What's done can't never be undone, I know that good as anybody; but He's my child, and I'm not going to have people say anything. I get sick of people coming around saying things all the time."

In the early fall Mrs. Whipple got a letter from her brother saying he and his wife and two children were coming over for a little visit next Sunday week. " Put the big pot in the little one," he wrote at the end. Mrs. Whipple read this part out loud twice, she was so pleased. Her brother was a great one for saying funny things. " We'll just show him that's no joke," she said; " we'll just butcher one of the sucking pigs."

" It's a waste and I don't hold with waste the way we are now," said Mr. Whipple. " That pig'll be worth money by Christmas."

" It's a shame and a pity we can't have a decent meal's vittles once in a while when my own family comes to see us," said Mrs. Whipple. " I'd hate for his wife to go back and say there wasn't a thing in the house to eat. My God, it's better than buying up a great chance of meat in town. There's where you'd spend the money! "

" All right, do it yourself then," said Mr. Whipple. " Christamighty, no wonder we can't get ahead! "

The question was how to get the little pig away from his ma, a great fighter, worse than a Jersey cow. Adna wouldn't try it: " That sow'd rip my insides out all over the pen." " All right, old fraidy," said Mrs. Whipple, " *He's* not scared. Watch *Him* do it." And she laughed as though it was all a good joke and gave Him a little push towards the pen. He sneaked up and snatched the pig right away from the teat and galloped back and was over the fence with the sow raging at His heels. The little black squirming thing was screeching like a baby in a tantrum, stiffening its back and stretching its mouth to the ears. Mrs. Whipple took the pig with her face stiff and sliced its throat with one stroke. When He saw the blood He gave a great jolting breath and ran away. " But He'll forget and eat plenty, just the same," thought Mrs. Whipple. Whenever she was thinking, her lips moved making words. " He'd eat it all if I didn't stop Him. He'd eat up every mouthful from the other two if I'd let Him."

She felt badly about it. He was ten years old now and a third again as large as Adna, who was going on fourteen. " It's a shame, a shame," she kept saying under her breath, " and Adna with so much brains! "

She kept on feeling badly about all sorts of things. In the first place it was the man's work to butcher; the sight of the pig scraped pink and naked made her sick. He was too fat and soft and pitiful-looking. It was simply a shame the way things had to happen. By the time she had finished it up, she almost wished her brother would stay at home.

Early Sunday morning Mrs. Whipple dropped everything to get Him all cleaned up. In an hour He was dirty again, with crawling under fences after a possum and straddling along the rafters of the barn looking for eggs in the hayloft. " My Lord, look at you now after all my trying! And here's Adna and Emly staying so quiet. I get tired trying to keep you decent. Get off that shirt and put on another; people will say I don't half dress you! " And she boxed Him on the ears, hard. He blinked and blinked and rubbed His head, and His face hurt Mrs. Whipple's feelings. Her knees began to tremble; she had to sit down while she buttoned His shirt. " I'm just all gone before the day starts."

The brother came with his plump healthy wife and two great roaring hungry boys. They had a grand dinner, with the pig roasted to a crackling in the middle of the table, full of dressing, a pickled peach in his mouth and plenty of gravy for the sweet potatoes.

" This looks like prosperity all right," said the brother; " you're going to have to roll me home like I was a barrel when I'm done."

Everybody laughed out loud; it was fine to hear them laughing all at once around the table. Mrs. Whipple felt warm and good about it. " Oh, we've got six more of these; I say it's as little as we can do when you come to see us so seldom."

He wouldn't come into the dining room, and Mrs. Whipple passed it off very well. " He's timider than my other two," she said, " He'll just have to get used to you. There isn't everybody He'll make up with — you know how it is with children, even cousins." Nobody said anything out of the way.

" Just like my Alfy here," said the brother's wife. " I sometimes got to lick him to make him shake hands with his own grandmammy."

So that was over, and Mrs. Whipple loaded up a big plate for Him first, before everybody. " I always say He ain't to be slighted, no matter who else goes without," she said, and carried it to Him herself.

" He can chin Himself on the top of the door," said Emly, helping along.

" That's fine, He's getting along fine," said the brother.

They went away after supper. Mrs. Whipple rounded up the dishes, and sent the children to bed and sat down and unlaced her shoes. " You see? " she said to Mr. Whipple. " That's the way my whole family is. Nice and considerate about everything. No out-of-the-way remarks — they *have* got refinement. I get awfully sick of people's remarks. Wasn't that pig good? "

Mr. Whipple said, " Yes, we're out three hundred pounds of pork, that's all. It's easy to be polite when you come to eat. Who knows what they had in their minds all along? "

" Yes, that's like you," said Mrs. Whipple. " I don't expect anything else from you. You'll be telling me next that my own brother will be saying around that we made Him eat in the kitchen! Oh, my God! " She rocked her head in her hands, a hard pain started in the very middle of her forehead. " Now it's all spoiled, and everything was so nice and easy. All right, you don't like them and you never did — all right, they'll not come here again soon, never you mind! But they *can't* say He wasn't dressed every lick as good as Adna — oh, honest, sometimes I wish I was dead! "

" I wish you'd let up," said Mr. Whipple. " It's bad enough as it is."

It was a hard winter. It seemed to Mrs. Whipple that they hadn't ever known anything but hard times, and now to cap it all a winter like this. The crops were about half of what they had a right to expect; after the cotton was in, it didn't do much more than cover the grocery bill. They swapped off one of the plow horses and got cheated, for the new one died of the heaves. Mrs. Whipple kept thinking all the time it was terrible to have a man you couldn't depend on not to get cheated. They cut down on everything, but Mrs. Whipple kept saying there are things you can't cut down on, and they cost money. It took a lot of warm clothes for Adna and Emly, who walked four miles to school during the three-months session. " He sets around the fire a lot, He won't need so much," said Mr. Whipple. " That's so," said Mrs. Whipple, " and when He does the outdoor chores He can wear your tarpaullion coat. I can't do no better, that's all."

In February He was taken sick, and lay curled up under His blanket looking very blue in the face and acting as if He would choke. Mr. and Mrs. Whipple did everything they could for Him for two days, and then they were scared and sent for the doctor. The doctor told them they must keep Him warm and give Him plenty of milk and eggs. " He isn't as stout as He looks, I'm afraid," said the doctor. " You've got to watch them when they're like that. You must put more cover on to Him, too."

" I just took off His big blanket to wash," said Mrs. Whipple, ashamed. " I can't stand dirt."

" Well, you'd better put it back on the minute it's dry," said the doctor, " or He'll have pneumonia."

Mr. and Mrs. Whipple took a blanket off their own bed and put His cot in by the fire. " They can't say we didn't do everything for Him," she said, " even to sleeping cold ourselves on His account."

When the winter broke He seemed to be well again, but He walked as if His feet hurt Him. He was able to run a cotton planter during the season.

" I got it all fixed up with Jim Ferguson about breeding the cow next time," said Mr. Whipple. " I'll pasture the bull this summer and give Jim some fodder in the fall. That's better than paying out money when you haven't got it."

" I hope you didn't say such a thing before Jim Ferguson," said Mrs. Whipple. " You oughtn't to let him know we're so down as all that."

" Godamighty, that ain't saying we're down. A man is got to look ahead sometimes. *He* can lead the bull over today. I need Adna on the place."

At first Mrs. Whipple felt easy in her mind about sending Him for the bull. Adna was too jumpy and couldn't be trusted. You've got to be steady around animals. After He was gone she started thinking, and after a while she could hardly bear it any longer. She stood in the lane and watched for Him. It was nearly three miles to go and a hot day, but He oughtn't to be so long about it. She shaded her eyes and stared until colored bubbles floated in her eyeballs. It was just like everything else in life, she must always worry and never know a moment's peace about anything. After a long time she saw Him turn into the side lane, limping. He came on very slowly, leading the big hulk of an animal by a ring in the nose, twirling a little stick in His hand, never looking back or sideways, but coming on like a sleepwalker with His eyes half shut.

Mrs. Whipple was scared sick of bulls; she had heard awful stories about how they followed on quietly enough, and then suddenly pitched on with a bellow and pawed and gored a body to pieces. Any second now that black monster would come down on Him, my God, He'd never have sense enough to run.

She mustn't make a sound nor a move; she mustn't get the bull started. The bull heaved his head aside and horned the air at a fly. Her voice burst out of her in a shriek, and she screamed at Him to come on, for God's sake. He didn't seem to hear her clamor, but kept on twirling His switch and limping on, and the bull lumbered along behind him as gently as a calf. Mrs. Whipple stopped calling and ran towards the house, praying under her breath: "Lord, don't let anything happen to Him. Lord, you *know* people will say we oughtn't to have sent Him. You *know* they'll say we didn't take care of Him. Oh, get Him home, safe home, safe home, and I'll look out for Him better! Amen."

She watched from the window while He led the beast in, and tied him up in the barn. It was no use trying to keep up, Mrs. Whipple couldn't bear another thing. She sat down and rocked and cried with her apron over her head.

From year to year the Whipples were growing poorer and poorer. The place just seemed to run down of itself, no matter how hard they worked. "We're losing our hold," said Mrs. Whipple. "Why can't we do like other people and watch for our best chances? They'll be calling us poor white trash next."

"When I get to be sixteen I'm going to leave," said Adna. "I'm going to get a job in Powell's grocery store. There's money in that. No more farm for me."

"I'm going to be a schoolteacher," said Emly. "But I've got to finish the eighth grade, anyhow. Then I can live in town. I don't see any chances here."

"Emly takes after my family," said Mrs. Whipple. "Ambitious every last one of them, and they don't take second place for anybody."

When fall came Emly got a chance to wait on table in the railroad eating-house in the town near by, and it seemed such a shame not to take it, when the wages were good and she could get her food too, that Mrs. Whipple decided to let her take it, and not bother with school until the next session. "You've got plenty of time," she said. "You're young and smart as a whip."

With Adna gone too, Mr. Whipple tried to run the farm with just Him to help. He seemed to get along fine, doing His work and part of Adna's without noticing it. They did well enough until Christmas time, when one morning He slipped on the ice coming up from the barn. Instead of getting up He thrashed round and round, and when Mr. Whipple got to Him, He was having some sort of fit.

They brought Him inside and tried to make Him sit up, but He blubbered and rolled, so they put Him to bed and Mr. Whipple rode to town for the doctor. All the way there and back he worried about where the money was to come from: it sure did look like he had about all the troubles he could carry.

From then on He stayed in bed. His legs swelled up double their size, and the fits kept coming back. After four months, the doctor said, " It's no use. I think you'd better put Him in the County Home for treatment right away. I'll see about it for you. He'll have good care there and be off your hands."

" We don't begrudge Him any care, and I won't let Him out of my sight," said Mrs. Whipple. " I won't have it said I sent my sick child off among strangers."

" I know how you feel," said the doctor. " You can't tell me anything about that, Mrs. Whipple. I've got a boy of my own. But you'd better listen to me. I can't do anything more for Him, that's the truth."

Mr. and Mrs. Whipple talked it over a long time that night after they went to bed. " It's just charity," said Mrs. Whipple; " that's what we've come to, charity! I certainly never looked for this."

" We pay taxes to help support the place just like everybody else," said Mr. Whipple, " and I don't call that taking charity. I think it would be fine to have Him where He'd get the best of everything . . . and besides, I can't keep up with these doctor bills any longer."

" Maybe that's why the doctor wants us to send Him — he's scared he won't get his money," said Mrs. Whipple.

" Don't talk like that," said Mr. Whipple, feeling pretty sick, " or we won't be able to send Him."

" Oh, but we won't keep Him there long," said Mrs. Whipple. " Soon's He's better, we'll bring Him right back home."

" The doctor has told you and told you time and again He can't ever get better, and you might as well stop talking," said Mr. Whipple.

" Doctors don't know everything," said Mrs. Whipple, feeling almost happy. " But anyhow, in the summer Emly can come home for a vacation, and Adna can get down for Sundays: we'll all work together and get on our feet again, and the children will feel they've got a place to come to."

All at once she saw it full summer again, with the garden going fine, and new white roller shades up all over the house, and Adna and Emly home, so full of life, all of them happy together. Oh, it could happen, things would ease up on them.

They didn't talk before Him much, but they never knew just how much He understood. Finally the doctor set the day and a neighbor who owned a double-seated carryall offered to drive them over. The hospital would have sent an ambulance, but Mrs. Whipple couldn't stand to see Him going away looking so sick as all that. They wrapped Him in blankets, and the neighbor and Mr. Whipple lifted Him into the back seat of the carryall beside Mrs. Whipple, who had on her black shirtwaist. She couldn't stand to go looking like charity.

" You'll be all right, I guess I'll stay behind," said Mr. Whipple. " It don't look like everybody ought to leave the place at once."

"Besides, it ain't as if He was going to stay forever," said Mrs. Whipple to the neighbor. "This is only for a little while."

They started away, Mrs. Whipple holding to the edges of the blankets to keep Him from sagging sideways. He sat there blinking and blinking. He worked His hands out and began rubbing His nose with His knuckles, and then with the end of the blanket. Mrs. Whipple couldn't believe what she saw; He was scrubbing away big tears that rolled out of the corners of His eyes. He sniveled and made a gulping noise. Mrs. Whipple kept saying, "Oh, honey, you don't feel so bad, do you? You don't feel so bad, do you?" for He seemed to be accusing her of something. Maybe He remembered that time she boxed His ears, maybe He had been scared that day with the bull, maybe He had slept cold and couldn't tell her about it; maybe He knew they were sending Him away for good and all because they were too poor to keep Him. Whatever it was, Mrs. Whipple couldn't bear to think of it. She began to cry, frightfully, and wrapped her arms tight around Him. His head rolled on her shoulder: she had loved Him as much as she possibly could, there were Adna and Emly who had to be thought of too, there was nothing she could do to make up to Him for His life. Oh, what a mortal pity He was ever born!

They came in sight of the hospital, with the neighbor driving very fast, not daring to look behind him.

Stephen Vincent Benét

The Devil and Daniel Webster

IT'S a story they tell in the border country, where Massachusetts joins Vermont and New Hampshire.

Yes, Dan'l Webster's dead — or, at least, they buried him. But every time there's a thunderstorm around Marshfield, they say you can hear his rolling voice in the hollows of the sky. And they say that if you go to his grave and speak loud and clear, "Dan'l Webster — Dan'l Webster!" the ground'll begin to shiver and the trees begin to shake. And after a while you'll hear a deep voice saying, "Neighbor, how stands the Union?" Then you better answer the Union stands as she stood, rock-bottomed and copper-sheathed, one and indivisible, or he's liable to rear right out of the ground. At least, that's what I was told when I was a youngster.

You see, for a while, he was the biggest man in the country. He never got to be President, but he was the biggest man. There were thousands that trusted in him right next to God Almighty, and they told stories about him and all the things that belonged to him that were like the stories of patriarchs and such.

From *Thirteen O'Clock,* 1937.

They said, when he stood up to speak, stars and stripes came right out in the sky, and once he spoke against a river and made it sink into the ground. They said, when he walked the woods with his fishing rod, Killall, the trout would jump out of the streams right into his pockets, for they knew it was no use putting up a fight against him; and when he argued a case, he could turn on the harps of the blessed and the shaking of the earth underground. That was the kind of man he was, and his big farm up at Marshfield was suitable to him. The chickens he raised were all white meat down through the drumsticks, the cows were tended like children, and the big ram he called Goliath had horns with a curl like a morning-glory vine and could butt through an iron door. But Dan'l wasn't one of your gentlemen farmers; he knew all the ways of the land, and he'd be up by candlelight to see that the chores got done. A man with a mouth like a mastiff, a brow like a mountain, and eyes like burning anthracite — that was Dan'l Webster in his prime. And the biggest case he argued never got written down in the books, for he argued it against the devil, nip and tuck and no holds barred. And this is the way I used to hear it told.

There was a man named Jabez Stone, lived at Cross Corners, New Hampshire. He wasn't a bad man to start with, but he was an unlucky man. If he planted corn, he got borers; if he planted potatoes, he got blight. He had good-enough land, but it didn't prosper him; he had a decent wife and children, but the more children he had, the less there was to feed them. If stones cropped up in his neighbor's field, boulders boiled up in his; if he had a horse with the spavins, he'd trade it for one with the staggers and give something extra. There's some folks bound to be like that, apparently. But one day Jabez Stone got sick of the whole business.

He'd been plowing that morning and he'd just broke the plowshare on a rock that he could have sworn hadn't been there yesterday. And as he stood at the plowshare, the off horse began to cough — that ropy kind of cough that means sickness and horse doctors. There were two children down with the measles, his wife was ailing, and he had a whitlow on his thumb. It was about the last straw for Jabez Stone. " I vow," he said, and he looked around him kind of desperate, " I vow it's enough to make a man want to sell his soul to the devil! And I would, too, for two cents! "

Then he felt a kind of queerness come over him at having said what he'd said; though, naturally, being a New Hampshireman, he wouldn't take it back. But all the same, when it got to be evening and, as far as he could see, no notice had been taken, he felt relieved in his mind, for he was a religious man. But notice is always taken, sooner or later, just like the Good Book says. And, sure enough, next day, about suppertime, a soft-spoken, dark-dressed stranger drove up in a handsome buggy and asked for Jabez Stone.

Well, Jabez told his family it was a lawyer, come to see him about a legacy. But he knew who it was. He didn't like the looks of the stranger, nor the way he smiled with his teeth. They were white teeth, and plentiful — some say they were filed to a point, but I wouldn't vouch for that. And he didn't like it when the dog took one look at the stranger and ran away howling, with his tail between his legs. But having passed the word, more or less, he stuck to it, and they went out behind the barn and made their bargain. Jabez Stone had to prick his finger to sign, and the stranger lent him a silver pin. The wound healed clean, but it left a little white scar.

After that, all of a sudden, things began to pick up and prosper for Jabez Stone. His cows got fat and his horses sleek, his crops were the envy of the neighborhood, and lightning might strike all over the valley, but it wouldn't strike his barn. Pretty soon he was one of the prosperous people of the county; they asked him to stand for selectman, and he stood for it; there began to be talk of running him for state senate. All in all, you might say the Stone family was as happy and contented as cats in a dairy. And so they were, except for Jabez Stone.

He'd been contented enough the first few years. It's a great thing when bad luck turns; it drives most other things out of your head. True, every now and then, especially in rainy weather, the little white scar on his finger would give him a twinge. And once a year, punctual as clockwork, the stranger with the handsome buggy would come driving by. But the sixth year the stranger lighted, and, after that, his peace was over for Jabez Stone.

The stranger came up through the lower field, switching his boots with a cane — they were handsome black boots, but Jabez Stone never liked the look of them, particularly the toes. And, after he'd passed the time of day, he said, "Well, Mr. Stone, you're a hummer! It's a very pretty property you've got here, Mr. Stone."

"Well, some might favor it and others might not," said Jabez Stone, for he was a New Hampshireman.

"Oh, no need to decry your industry!" said the stranger, very easy, showing his teeth in a smile. "After all, we know what's been done, and it's been according to contract and specifications. So when — ahem — the mortgage falls due next year, you shouldn't have any regrets."

"Speaking of that mortgage, mister," said Jabez Stone, and he looked around for help to the earth and the sky, "I'm beginning to have one or two doubts about it."

"Doubts?" said the stranger not quite so pleasantly.

"Why, yes," said Jabez Stone. "This being the U.S.A. and me always having been a religious man." He cleared his throat and got bolder. "Yes sir," he said, "I'm beginning to have considerable doubts as to that mortgage holding in court."

"There's courts and courts," said the stranger, clicking his teeth. "Still, we might as well have a look at the original document." And he hauled out a big black pocketbook, full of papers. "Sherwin, Slater, Stevens, Stone," he muttered. "'I, Jabez Stone, for a term of seven years —' Oh, it's quite in order, I think."

But Jabez Stone wasn't listening, for he saw something else flutter out of the black pocketbook. It was something that looked like a moth, but it wasn't a moth. And as Jabez Stone stared at it, it seemed to speak to him in a small sort of piping voice, terrible small and thin, but terrible human. " Neighbor Stone! " it squeaked. " Neighbor Stone! Help me! For God's sake, help me! "

But before Jabez Stone could stir hand or foot, the stranger whipped out a big bandanna handkerchief, caught the creature in it, just like a butterfly, and started tying up the ends of the bandanna.

" Sorry for the interruption," he said. " As I was saying — "

But Jabez Stone was shaking all over like a scared horse.

" That's Miser Stevens' voice! " he said in a croak. " And you've got him in your handkerchief! "

The stranger looked a little embarrassed.

" Yes, I really should have transferred him to the collecting box," he said with a simper, " but there were some rather unusual specimens there and I don't want them crowded. Well, well, these little contretemps will occur."

" I don't know what you mean by contertan," said Jabez Stone, " but that was Miser Stevens' voice! And he ain't dead! You can't tell me he is! He was just as spry and mean as a woodchuck Tuesday! "

" In the midst of life . . ." said the stranger, kind of pious. " Listen! " Then a bell began to toll in the valley and Jabez Stone listened, with the sweat running down his face. For he knew it was tolled for Miser Stevens and that he was dead.

" These long-standing accounts," said the stranger with a sigh; " one really hates to close them. But business is business."

He still had the bandanna in his hand, and Jabez Stone felt sick as he saw the cloth struggle and flutter.

" Are they all as small as that? " he asked hoarsely.

" Small? " said the stranger. " Oh, I see what you mean. Why, they vary." He measured Jabez Stone with his eyes, and his teeth showed. " Don't worry, Mr. Stone," he said. " You'll go with a very good grade. I wouldn't trust you outside the collecting box. Now, a man like Dan'l Webster, of course — well, we'd have to build a special box for him, and even at that, I imagine the wing spread would astonish you. He'd certainly be a prize. I wish we could see our way clear to him. But, in your case, as I was saying — "

" Put that handkerchief away! " said Jabez Stone, and he began to beg and to pray. But the best he could get at the end was a three years' extension, with conditions.

But till you make a bargain like that, you've got no idea of how fast four years can run. By the last months of those years Jabez Stone's known all over the state and there's talk of running him for governor — and it's dust and ashes in his mouth. For every day, when he gets up, he thinks, " There's one more night gone," and every night, when he lies down, he thinks of the black pocketbook and the soul of Miser Stevens, and it makes him sick at heart. Till, finally, he can't bear it any longer, and, in the last days of the last year, he hitches up his horse and drives off to seek Dan'l Webster. For Dan'l was born in New Hampshire, only a few miles from Cross Corners, and it's well known that he has a particular soft spot for old neighbors.

It was early in the morning when he got to Marshfield, but Dan'l was up already, talking Latin to the farm hands and wrestling with the ram, Goliath, and trying out a new trotter and working up speeches to make against John C. Calhoun. But when he heard a New Hampshireman had come to see him, he dropped everything else he was doing, for that was Dan'l's way. He gave Jabez Stone a breakfast that five men couldn't eat, went into the living history of every man and woman in Cross Corners, and finally asked him how he could serve him.

Jabez Stone allowed that it was a kind of mortgage case.

" Well, I haven't pleaded a mortgage case in a long time, and I don't generally plead now, except before the Supreme Court," said Dan'l, " but if I can, I'll help you."

" Then I've got hope for the first time in ten years," said Jabez Stone and told him the details.

Dan'l walked up and down as he listened, hands behind his back, now and then asking a question, now and then plunging his eyes at the floor, as if they'd bore through it like gimlets. When Jabez Stone had finished, Dan'l puffed out his cheeks and blew. Then he turned to Jabez Stone and a smile broke over his face like the sunrise over Monadnock.

" You've certainly given yourself the devil's own row to hoe, Neighbor Stone," he said, " but I'll take your case."

" You'll take it? " said Jabez Stone, hardly daring to believe.

" Yes," said Dan'l Webster. " I've got about seventy-five other things to do and the Missouri Compromise to straighten out, but I'll take your case. For if two New Hampshiremen aren't a match for the devil, we might as well give the country back to the Indians."

Then he shook Jabez Stone by the hand and said, " Did you come down here in a hurry? "

" Well, I admit I made time," said Jabez Stone.

" You'll go back faster," said Dan'l Webster, and he told 'em to hitch up Constitution and Constellation to the carriage. They were matched grays with one white forefoot, and they stepped like greased lightning.

Well, I won't describe how excited and pleased the whole Stone family was to have the great Dan'l Webster for a guest, when they finally got there. Jabez Stone had lost his hat on the way, blown off when they overtook a wind, but he didn't take much account of that. But after supper he sent the family off to bed, for he had most particular business with Mr. Webster. Mrs. Stone wanted him to sit in the front parlor, but Dan'l Webster knew front parlors and said he preferred the kitchen. So it was there they sat, waiting for the stranger, with a jug on the table between them and a bright fire on the hearth — the stranger being scheduled to show up on the stroke of midnight, according to specification.

Well, most men wouldn't have asked for better company than Dan'l Webster and a jug. But with every tick of the clock Jabez Stone got sadder and sadder. His eyes roved round, and though he sampled the jug you could see he couldn't taste it. Finally, on the stroke of 11:30 he reached over and grabbed Dan'l Webster by the arm.

"Mr. Webster, Mr. Webster!" he said, and his voice was shaking with fear and a desperate courage. "For God's sake, Mr. Webster, harness your horses and get away from this place while you can!"

"You've brought me a long way, neighbor, to tell me you don't like my company," said Dan'l Webster, quite peaceable, pulling at the jug.

"Miserable wretch that I am!" groaned Jabez Stone. "I've brought you a devilish way, and now I see my folly. Let him take me if he wills. I don't hanker after it, I must say, but I can stand it. But you're the Union's stay and New Hampshire's pride! He mustn't get you, Mr. Webster! He mustn't get you!"

Dan'l Webster looked at the distracted man, all gray and shaking in the firelight, and laid a hand on his shoulder.

"I'm obliged to you, Neighbor Stone," he said gently. "It's kindly thought of. But there's a jug on the table and a case in hand. And I never left a jug or a case half finished in my life."

And just at that moment there was a sharp rap on the door.

"Ah," said Dan'l Webster very coolly, "I thought your clock was a trifle slow, Neighbor Stone." He stepped to the door and opened it. "Come in!" he said.

The stranger came in — very dark and tall he looked in the firelight. He was carrying a box under his arm — a black japanned box with little air holes in the lid. At the sight of the box Jabez Stone gave a low cry and shrank into a corner of the room.

"Mr. Webster, I presume," said the stranger, very polite, but with his eyes glowing like a fox's deep in the woods.

"Attorney of record for Jabez Stone," said Dan'l Webster, but his eyes were glowing too. "Might I ask your name?"

"I've gone by a good many," said the stranger carelessly. "Perhaps Scratch will do for the evening. I'm often called that in these regions."

Then he sat down at the table and poured himself a drink from the jug. The liquor was cold in the jug, but it came steaming into the glass.

"And now," said the stranger, smiling and showing his teeth, "I shall call upon you, as a law-abiding citizen, to assist me in taking possession of my property."

Well, with that the argument began — and it went hot and heavy. At first Jabez Stone had a flicker of hope, but when he saw Dan'l Webster being forced back at point after point, he just sat scrunched in his corner, with his eyes on that japanned box. For there wasn't any doubt as to the deed or the signature — that was the worst of it. Dan'l Webster twisted and turned and thumped his fist on the table, but he couldn't get away from that. He offered to compromise the case; the stranger wouldn't hear of it. He pointed out the property had increased in value, and state senators ought to be worth more; the stranger stuck to the letter of the law. He was a great lawyer, Dan'l Webster, but we know who's the King of Lawyers, as the Good Book tells us, and it seemed as if, for the first time, Dan'l Webster had met his match.

Finally, the stranger yawned a little. "Your spirited efforts on behalf of your client do you credit, Mr. Webster," he said, " but if you have no more arguments to adduce, I'm rather pressed for time . . ." and Jabez Stone shuddered.

Dan'l Webster's brow looked dark as a thundercloud.

" Pressed or not, you shall not have this man! " he thundered. " Mr. Stone is an American citizen, and no American citizen may be forced into the service of a foreign prince. We fought England for that in '12 and we'll fight all hell for it again! "

" Foreign? " said the stranger. " And who calls me a foreigner? "

" Well, I never yet heard of the dev — of your claiming American citizenship," said Dan'l Webster with surprise.

" And who with better right? " said the stranger with one of his terrible smiles. " When the first wrong was done to the first Indian, I was there. When the first slaver put out for the Congo, I stood on her deck. Am I not in your books and stories and beliefs, from the first settlements on? Am I not spoken of still in every church in New England? 'Tis true the North claims me for a Southerner and the South for a Northerner, but I am neither. I am merely an honest American like yourself — and of the best descent — for, to tell the truth, Mr. Webster, though I don't like to boast of it, my name is older in this country than yours."

" Aha! " said Dan'l Webster with the veins standing out in his forehead. " Then I stand on the Constitution! I demand a trial for my client! "

" The case is hardly one for an ordinary court," said the stranger, his eyes flickering. " And, indeed, the lateness of the hour — "

" Let it be any court you choose, so it is an American judge and an American jury! " said Dan'l Webster in his pride. " Let it be the quick or the dead; I'll abide the issue! "

" You have said it," said the stranger, and pointed his finger at the door. And with that, and all of a sudden, there was a rushing of wind outside and a noise of footsteps. They came, clear and distinct, through the night. And yet they were not like the footsteps of living men.

" In God's name, who comes by so late? " cried Jabez Stone in an ague of fear.

" The jury Mr. Webster demands," said the stranger, sipping at his boiling glass. " You must pardon the rough appearance of one or two; they will have come a long way."

And with that the fire burned blue and the door blew open and twelve men entered, one by one.

If Jabez Stone had been sick with terror before, he was blind with terror now. For there was Walter Butler, the loyalist, who spread fire and horror through the Mohawk Valley in the times of the Revolution; and there was Simon Girty, the renegade, who saw white men burned at the stake and whooped with the Indians to see them burn. His eyes were green, like a catamount's, and the stains on his hunting shirt did not come from the blood of the deer. King Philip was there, wild and proud as he had been in life, with the great gash in his head that gave him his death wound, and cruel Governor Dale, who broke men on the wheel. There was Morton of Merry Mount, who so vexed the Plymouth

Colony, with his flushed, loose, handsome face and his hate of the godly. There was Teach, the bloody pirate, with his black beard curling on his breast. The Reverend John Smeet, with his strangler's hands and his Geneva gown, walked as daintily as he had to the gallows. The red print of the rope was still around his neck, but he carried a perfumed handkerchief in one hand. One and all, they came into the room with the fires of hell still upon them, and the stranger named their names and their deeds as they came, till the tale of twelve was told. Yet the stranger had told the truth — they had all played a part in America.

"Are you satisfied with the jury, Mr. Webster?" said the stranger mockingly, when they had taken their places.

The sweat stood upon Dan'l Webster's brow, but his voice was clear.

"Quite satisfied," he said. "Though I miss General Arnold from the company."

"Benedict Arnold is engaged upon other business," said the stranger with a glower. "Ah, you asked for a justice, I believe."

He pointed his finger once more, and a tall man, soberly clad in Puritan garb, with the burning gaze of the fanatic, stalked into the room and took his judge's place.

"Justice Hathorne is a jurist of experience," said the stranger. "He presided at certain witch trials once held in Salem. There were others who repented of the business later, but not he."

"Repent of such notable wonders and undertakings?" said the stern old justice. "Nay, hang them — hang them all!" And he muttered to himself in a way that struck ice into the soul of Jabez Stone.

Then the trial began, and, as you might expect, it didn't look anyways good for the defense. And Jabez Stone didn't make much of a witness in his own behalf. He took one look at Simon Girty and screeched, and they had to put him back in his corner in a kind of swoon.

It didn't halt the trial though; the trial went on, as trials do. Dan'l Webster had faced some hard juries and hanging judges in his time, but this was the hardest he'd ever faced, and he knew it. They sat there with a kind of glitter in their eyes, and the stranger's smooth voice went on and on. Every time he'd raise an objection, it'd be "Objection sustained," but whenever Dan'l objected, it'd be "Objection denied." Well, you couldn't expect fair play from a fellow like this Mr. Scratch.

It got to Dan'l in the end, and he began to heat, like iron in the forge. When he got up to speak he was going to flay that stranger with every trick known to the law, and the judge and jury too. He didn't care if it was contempt of court or what would happen to him for it. He didn't care any more what happened to Jabez Stone. He just got madder and madder, thinking of what he'd say. And yet, curiously enough, the more he thought about it, the less he was able to arrange his speech in his mind.

Till, finally, it was time for him to get up on his feet, and he did so, all ready to bust out with lightnings and denunciations. But before he started he looked over the judge and jury for a moment, such being his custom. And he noticed the glitter in their eyes was twice as strong as before, and they all leaned forward. Like hounds just before they get the fox, they looked, and the blue mist of evil in the room thickened as he watched them. Then he saw what he'd been about to do, and he wiped his forehead, as a man might who's just escaped falling into a pit in the dark.

For it was him they'd come for, not only Jabez Stone. He read it in the glitter of their eyes and in the way the stranger hid his mouth with one hand. And if he fought them with their own weapons, he'd fall into their power; he knew that, though he couldn't have told you how. It was his own anger and horror that burned in their eyes; and he'd have to wipe that out or the case was lost. He stood there for a moment, his black eyes burning like anthracite. And then he began to speak.

He started off in a low voice, though you could hear every word. They say he could call on the harps of the blessed when he chose. And this was just as simple and easy as a man could talk. But he didn't start out by condemning or reviling. He was talking about the things that make a country a country and a man a man.

And he began with the simple things that everybody's known and felt — the freshness of a fine morning when you're young, and the taste of food when you're hungry, and the new day that's every day when you're a child. He took them up and he turned them in his hands. They were good things for any man. But without freedom they sickened. And when he talked of those enslaved, and the sorrows of slavery, his voice got like a big bell. He talked of the early days of America and the men who had made those days. It wasn't a spread-eagle speech, but he made you see it. He admitted all the wrong that had ever been done. But he showed how, out of the wrong and the right, the suffering and the starvations, something new had come. And everybody had played a part in it, even the traitors.

Then he turned to Jabez Stone and showed him as he was — an ordinary man who'd had hard luck and wanted to change it. And, because he'd wanted to change it, now he was going to be punished for all eternity. And yet there was good in Jabez Stone, and he showed that good. He was hard and mean, in some ways, but he was a man. There was sadness in being a man, but it was a proud thing too. And he showed what the pride of it was till you couldn't help feeling it. Yes, even in hell, if a man was a man, you'd know it. And he wasn't pleading for any one person any more, though his voice rang like an organ. He was telling the story and the failures and the endless journey of mankind. They got tricked and trapped and bamboozled, but it was a great journey. And no demon that was ever foaled could know the inwardness of it — it took a man to do that.

The fire began to die on the hearth and the wind before morning to blow. The light was getting gray in the room when Dan'l Webster finished. And his words came back at the end to New Hampshire ground, and the one spot of land that each man loves and clings to. He painted a picture of that, and to each one of that jury he spoke of things long forgotten. For his voice could search the heart, and that was his gift and his strength. And to one his voice was like the forest and its secrecy, and to another like the sea and the storms of the sea; and one heard the cry of his lost nation in it, and another saw a little harmless scene he hadn't remembered for years. But each saw something. And when Dan'l Webster finished he didn't know whether or not he'd saved Jabez Stone. But he knew he'd done a miracle. For the glitter was gone from the eyes of judge and jury, and, for the moment, they were men again, and knew they were men.

"The defense rests," said Dan'l Webster and stood there like a mountain. His ears were still ringing with his speech, and he didn't hear anything else till he heard Judge Hathorne say, "The jury will retire to consider its verdict."

Walter Butler rose in his place and his face had a dark, gay pride on it.

"The jury has considered its verdict," he said and looked the stranger full in the eye. "We find for the defendant, Jabez Stone."

With that, the smile left the stranger's face, but Walter Butler did not flinch.

"Perhaps 'tis not strictly in accordance with the evidence," he said, "but even the damned may salute the eloquence of Mr. Webster."

With that, the long crow of a rooster split the gray morning sky, and judge and jury were gone from the room like a puff of smoke and as if they had never been there. The stranger returned to Dan'l Webster, smiling wryly.

"Major Butler was always a bold man," he said. "I had not thought him quite so bold. Nevertheless, my congratulations, as between two gentlemen."

"I'll have that paper first, if you please," said Dan'l Webster, and he took it and tore it into four pieces. It was queerly warm to the touch. "And now," he said, "I'll have you!" and his hand came down like a bear trap on the stranger's arm. For he knew that once you bested anybody like Mr. Scratch in fair fight, his power on you was gone. And he could see that Mr. Scratch knew it too.

The stranger twisted and wriggled, but he couldn't get out of that grip. "Come, come, Mr. Webster," he said, smiling palely. "This sort of thing is ridic — ouch! — is ridiculous. If you're worried about the costs of the case, naturally, I'd be glad to pay — "

"And so you shall!" said Dan'l Webster, shaking him till his teeth rattled. "For you'll sit right down at that table and draw up a document, promising never to bother Jabez Stone nor his heirs or assigns nor any other New Hampshireman till doomsday! For any hades we want to raise in this state, we can raise ourselves, without assistance from strangers."

"Ouch!" said the stranger. "Ouch! Well, they never did run very big to the barrel, but — ouch! — I agree!"

So he sat down and drew up the document. But Dan'l Webster kept his hand on his coat collar all the time.

"And now may I go?" said the stranger, quite humble, when Dan'l'd seen the document was in proper and legal form.

"Go?" said Dan'l, giving him another shake. "I'm still trying to figure out what I'll do with you. For you've settled the costs of the case, but you haven't settled with me. I think I'll take you back to Marshfield," he said, kind of reflective. "I've got a ram there named Goliath that can butt through an iron door. I'd kind of like to turn you loose in his field and see what he'd do."

Well, with that the stranger began to beg and to plead. And he begged and he pled so humble that finally Dan'l, who was naturally kindhearted, agreed to let him go. The stranger seemed terrible grateful for that and said, just to show they were friends, he'd tell Dan'l's fortune before leaving. So Dan'l agreed to that, though he didn't take much stock in fortunetellers ordinarily. But, naturally, the stranger was a little different.

Well, he pried and he peered at the lines in Dan'l's hands. And he told him one thing and another that was quite remarkable. But they were all in the past.

"Yes, all that's true, and it happened," said Dan'l Webster. "But what's to come in the future?"

The stranger grinned, kind of happily, and shook his head.

"The future's not as you think it," he said. "It's dark. You have a great ambition, Mr. Webster."

"I have," said Dan'l firmly, for everybody knew he wanted to be President.

"It seems almost within your grasp," said the stranger, "but you will not attain it. Lesser men will be made President and you will be passed over."

"And, if I am, I'll still be Daniel Webster," said Dan'l. "Say on."

"You have two strong sons," said the stranger, shaking his head. "You look to found a line. But each will die in war and neither reach greatness."

"Live or die, they are still my sons," said Dan'l Webster. "Say on."

"You have made great speeches," said the stranger. "You will make more."

"Ah," said Dan'l Webster.

"But the last great speech you make will turn many of your own against you," said the stranger. "They will call you Ichabod; they will call you by other names. Even in New England some will say you have turned your coat and sold your country, and their voices will be loud against you till you die."

"So it is an honest speech, it does not matter what men say," said Dan'l Webster. Then he looked at the stranger and their glances locked.

"One question," he said. "I have fought for the Union all my life. Will I see that fight won against those who would tear it apart?"

"Not while you live," said the stranger grimly, "but it will be won. And after you are dead, there are thousands who will fight for your cause, because of words that you spoke."

"Why, then, you long-barreled, slab-sided, lantern-jawed, fortune-telling note shaver," said Dan'l Webster with a great roar of laughter, "be off with you to your own place before I put my mark on you! For, by the thirteen original colonies, I'd go to the Pit itself to save the Union!"

And with that he drew back his foot for a kick that would have stunned a horse. It was only the tip of his shoe that caught the stranger, but he went flying out of the door with his collecting box under his arm.

"And now," said Dan'l Webster, seeing Jabez Stone beginning to rouse from his swoon, "let's see what's left in the jug, for it's dry work talking all night. I hope there's pie for breakfast, Neighbor Stone."

But they say that whenever the devil comes near Marshfield, even now, he gives it a wide berth. And he hasn't been seen in the state of New Hampshire from that day to this. I'm not talking about Massachusetts or Vermont.

John Steinbeck

The Chrysanthemums

THE high gray-flannel fog of winter closed off the Salinas Valley from the sky and from all the rest of the world. On every side it sat like a lid on the mountains and made of the great valley a closed pot. On the broad, level land floor the gang plows bit deep and left the black earth shining like metal where the shares had cut. On the foothill ranches across the Salinas River, the yellow stubble fields seemed to be bathed in pale cold sunshine, but there was no sunshine in the valley now in December. The thick willow scrub along the river flamed with sharp and positive yellow leaves.

It was a time of quiet and of waiting. The air was cold and tender. A light wind blew up from the southwest so that the farmers were mildly hopeful of a good rain before long; but fog and rain do not go together.

Across the river, on Henry Allen's foothill ranch there was little work to be done, for the hay was cut and stored and the orchards were plowed up to receive the rain deeply when it should come. The cattle on the higher slopes were becoming shaggy and rough-coated.

Elisa Allen, working in her flower garden, looked down across the yard and saw Henry, her husband, talking to two men in business suits. The three of them stood by the tractor shed, each man with one foot on the side of the little Fordson. They smoked cigarettes and studied the machine as they talked.

Elisa watched them for a moment and then went back to her work. She was thirty-five. Her face was lean and strong and her eyes were as clear as water. Her figure looked blocked and heavy in her gardening costume, a man's black hat pulled low down over her eyes, clodhopper shoes, a figured print dress almost completely covered by a big corduroy apron with four big pockets to hold the snips, the trowel and scratcher, the seeds, and the knife she worked with. She wore heavy leather gloves to protect her hands while she worked.

She was cutting down the old year's chrysanthemum stalks with a pair of short and powerful scissors. She looked down toward the men by the tractor shed now and then. Her face was eager and mature and handsome; even her work with the scissors was overeager, overpowerful. The chrysanthemum stems seemed too small and easy for her energy.

She brushed a cloud of hair out of her eyes with the back of her glove, and left a smudge of earth on her cheek in doing it. Behind her stood the neat white farmhouse with red geraniums close-banked around it as high as the windows. It was a hard-swept-looking little house, with hard-polished windows, and a clean mud-mat on the front steps.

Elisa cast another glance toward the tractor shed. The strangers were getting

From *The Long Valley*, 1938.

into their Ford coupe. She took off a glove and put her strong fingers down into the forest of new green chrysanthemum sprouts that were growing around the old roots. She spread the leaves and looked down among the close-growing stems. No aphids were there, no sowbugs or snails or cutworms. Her terrier fingers destroyed such pests before they could get started.

Elisa started at the sound of her husband's voice. He had come near quietly, and he leaned over the wire fence that protected her flower garden from cattle and dogs and chickens.

" At it again," he said. " You've got a strong new crop coming."

Elisa straightened her back and pulled on the gardening glove again. " Yes. They'll be strong this coming year." In her tone and on her face there was a little smugness.

"You've got a gift with things," Henry observed. " Some of those yellow chrysanthemums you had this year were ten inches across. I wish you'd work out in the orchard and raise some apples that big."

Her eyes sharpened. " Maybe I could do it, too. I've a gift with things, all right. My mother had it. She could stick anything in the ground and make it grow. She said it was having planters' hands that knew how to do it."

" Well, it sure works with flowers," he said.

" Henry, who were those men you were talking to? "

" Why, sure, that's what I came to tell you. They were from the Western Meat Company. I sold those thirty head of three-year-old steers. Got nearly my own price, too."

" Good," she said. " Good for you."

" And I thought," he continued, " I thought how it's Saturday afternoon, and we might go into Salinas for dinner at a restaurant, and then to a picture show — to celebrate, you see."

" Good," she repeated. " Oh, yes. That will be good."

Henry put on his joking tone. " There's fights tonight. How'd you like to go to the fights? "

" Oh, no," she said breathlessly. " No, I wouldn't like fights."

" Just fooling, Elisa. We'll go to a movie. Let's see. It's two now. I'm going to take Scotty and bring down those steers from the hill. It'll take us maybe two hours. We'll go in town about five and have dinner at the Cominos Hotel. Like that? "

" Of course I'll like it. It's good to eat away from home."

" All right, then. I'll go get up a couple of horses."

She said, " I'll have plenty of time to transplant some of these sets, I guess."

She heard her husband calling Scotty down by the barn. And a little later she saw the two men ride up the pale yellow hillside in search of the steers.

There was a little square sandy bed kept for rooting the chrysanthemums. With her trowel she turned the soil over and over, and smoothed it and patted it firm. Then she dug ten parallel trenches to receive the sets. Back at the chrysanthemum bed she pulled out the little crisp shoots, trimmed off the leaves of each one with her scissors and laid it on a small orderly pile.

A squeak of wheels and plod of hoofs came from the road. Elisa looked up. The country road ran along the dense bank of willows and cottonwoods that bordered the river, and up this road came a curious vehicle, curiously drawn. It was an old spring-wagon, with a round canvas top on it like the cover of a prairie schooner. It was drawn by an old bay horse and a little gray and white burro. A big stubble-bearded man sat between the cover flaps and drove the crawling team. Underneath the wagon, between the hind wheels, a lean and rangy mongrel dog walked sedately. Words were painted on the canvas, in clumsy, crooked letters. " Pots, pans, knives, sisors, lawn mores, Fixed." Two rows of articles, and the triumphantly definitive " Fixed " below. The black paint had run down in little sharp points beneath each letter.

Elisa, squatting on the ground, watched to see the crazy, loose-jointed wagon pass by. But it didn't pass. It turned into the farm road in front of her house, crooked old wheels skirling and squeaking. The rangy dog darted from between the wheels and ran ahead. Instantly the two ranch shepherds flew out at him. Then all three stopped, and with stiff and quivering tails, with taut straight legs, with ambassadorial dignity, they slowly circled, sniffing daintily. The caravan pulled up to Elisa's wire fence and stopped. Now the newcomer dog, feeling outnumbered, lowered his tail and retired under the wagon with raised hackles and bared teeth.

The man on the wagon seat called out, " That's a bad dog in a fight when he gets started."

Elisa laughed. " I see he is. How soon does he generally get started? "

The man caught up her laughter and echoed it heartily. " Sometimes not for weeks and weeks," he said. He climbed stiffly down, over the wheel. The horse and the donkey drooped like unwatered flowers.

Elisa saw that he was a very big man. Although his hair and beard were graying, he did not look old. His worn black suit was wrinkled and spotted with grease. The laughter had disappeared from his face and eyes the moment his laughing voice ceased. His eyes were dark, and they were full of the brooding that gets in the eyes of teamsters and of sailors. The calloused hands he rested on the wire fence were cracked, and every crack was a black line. He took off his battered hat.

" I'm off my general road, ma'am," he said. " Does this dirt road cut over across the river to the Los Angeles highway? "

Elisa stood up and shoved the thick scissors in her apron pocket. " Well, yes, it does, but it winds around and then fords the river. I don't think your team could pull through the sand."

He replied with some asperity, " It might surprise you what them beasts can pull through."

" When they get started? " she asked.

He smiled for a second. " Yes. When they get started."

" Well," said Elisa, " I think you'll save time if you go back to the Salinas road and pick up the highway there."

He drew a big finger down the chicken wire and made it sing. " I ain't in any hurry, ma'am. I go from Seattle to San Diego and back every year. Takes all my time. About six months each way. I aim to follow nice weather."

Elisa took off her gloves and stuffed them in the apron pocket with the scissors. She touched the under edge of her man's hat, searching for fugitive hairs. " That sounds like a nice kind of a way to live," she said.

He leaned confidentially over the fence. " Maybe you noticed the writing on my wagon. I mend pots and sharpen knives and scissors. You got any of them things to do? "

" Oh, no," she said quickly. " Nothing like that." Her eyes hardened with resistance.

" Scissors is the worst thing," he explained. " Most people just ruin scissors trying to sharpen 'em, but I know how. I got a special tool. It's a little bobbit kind of thing, and patented. But it sure does the trick."

" No. My scissors are all sharp."

" All right, then. Take a pot," he continued earnestly, " a bent pot, or a pot with a hole. I can make it like new so you don't have to buy no new ones. That's a saving for you."

" No," she said shortly. " I tell you I have nothing like that for you to do."

His face fell to an exaggerated sadness. His voice took on a whining undertone. " I ain't had a thing to do today. Maybe I won't have no supper tonight. You see I'm off my regular road. I know folks on the highway clear from Seattle to San Diego. They save their things for me to sharpen up because they know I do it so good and save them money."

" I'm sorry," Elisa said irritably. " I haven't anything for you to do."

His eyes left her face and fell to searching the ground. They roamed about until they came to the chrysanthemum bed where she had been working. " What's them plants, ma'am? "

The irritation and resistance melted from Elisa's face. " Oh, those are chrysanthemums, giant whites and yellows. I raise them every year, bigger than anybody around here."

" Kind of a long-stemmed flower? Looks like a quick puff of colored smoke? " he asked.

" That's it. What a nice way to describe them."

" They smell kind of nasty till you get used to them," he said.

" It's a good bitter smell," she retorted, " not nasty at all."

He changed his tone quickly. " I like the smell myself."

" I had ten-inch blooms this year," she said.

The man leaned farther over the fence. " Look. I know a lady down the road a piece, has got the nicest garden you ever seen. Got nearly every kind of flower but no chrysanthemums. Last time I was mending a copper-bottom washtub for her (that's a hard job but I do it good), she said to me, ' If you ever run acrost some nice chrysanthemums I wish you'd try to get me a few seeds.' That's what she told me."

Elisa's eyes grew alert and eager. " She couldn't have known much about chrysanthemums. You can raise them from seed, but it's much easier to root the little sprouts you see there."

" Oh," he said. " I s'pose I can't take none to her, then."

" Why, yes, you can," Elisa cried. " I can put some in damp sand, and you can carry them right along with you. They'll take root in the pot if you keep them damp. And then she can transplant them."

" She'd sure like to have some, ma'am. You say they're nice ones? "

" Beautiful," she said. " Oh, beautiful." Her eyes shone. She tore off the battered hat and shook out her dark pretty hair. " I'll put them in a flowerpot, and you can take them right with you. Come into the yard."

While the man came through the picket gate Elisa ran excitedly along the geranium-bordered path to the back of the house. And she returned carrying a big red flowerpot. The gloves were forgotten now. She kneeled on the ground by the starting bed and dug up the sandy soil with her fingers and scooped it into the bright new flowerpot. Then she picked up the little pile of shoots she had prepared. With her strong fingers she pressed them into the sand and tamped around them with her knuckles. The man stood over her. " I'll tell you what to do," she said. " You remember so you can tell the lady."

" Yes, I'll try to remember."

" Well, look. These will take root in about a month. Then she must set them out, about a foot apart in good rich earth like this, see? " She lifted a handful of dark soil for him to look at. " They'll grow fast and tall. Now remember this: In July tell her to cut them down, about eight inches from the ground."

" Before they bloom? " he asked.

" Yes, before they bloom." Her face was tight with eagerness. " They'll grow right up again. About the last of September the buds will start."

She stopped and seemed perplexed. " It's the budding that takes the most care," she said hesitantly. " I don't know how to tell you." She looked deep into his eyes, searchingly. Her mouth opened a little, and she seemed to be listening. " I'll try to tell you," she said. " Did you ever hear of planting hands? "

" Can't say I have, ma'am."

" Well, I can only tell you what it feels like. It's when you're picking off the buds you don't want. Everything goes right down into your fingertips. You watch your fingers work. They do it themselves. You can feel how it is. They pick and pick the buds. They never make a mistake. They're with the plant. Do you see? Your fingers and the plant. You can feel that, right up your arm. They know. They never make a mistake. You can feel it. When you're like that you can't do anything wrong. Do you see that? Can you understand that? "

She was kneeling on the ground looking up at him. Her breast swelled passionately.

The man's eyes narrowed. He looked away self-consciously. " Maybe I know," he said. " Sometimes in the night in the wagon there — "

Elisa's voice grew husky. She broke in on him, " I've never lived as you do, but I know what you mean. When the night is dark — why, the stars are sharp-pointed, and there's quiet. Why, you rise up and up! Every pointed star gets driven into your body. It's like that. Hot and sharp and — lovely."

Kneeling there, her hand went out toward his legs in the greasy black trousers. Her hesitant fingers almost touched the cloth. Then her hand dropped to the ground. She crouched low like a fawning dog.

He said, " It's nice, just like you say. Only when you don't have no dinner, it ain't."

She stood up then, very straight, and her face was ashamed. She held the flowerpot out to him and placed it gently in his arms. " Here. Put it in your wagon, on the seat, where you can watch it. Maybe I can find something for you to do."

At the back of the house she dug in the can pile and found two old and battered aluminum saucepans. She carried them back and gave them to him. " Here, maybe you can fix these."

His manner changed. He became professional. " Good as new I can fix them." At the back of his wagon he set a little anvil, and out of an oily tool box dug a small machine hammer. Elisa came through the gate to watch him while he pounded out the dents in the kettles. His mouth grew sure and knowing. At a difficult part of the work he sucked his underlip.

" You sleep right in the wagon? " Elisa asked.

" Right in the wagon, ma'am. Rain or shine, I'm dry as a cow in there."

" It must be nice," she said. " It must be very nice. I wish women could do such things."

" It ain't the right kind of a life for a woman."

Her upper lip raised a little, showing her teeth. " How do you know? How can you tell? " she said.

" I don't know, ma'am," he protested. " Of course I don't know. Now here's your kettles, done. You don't have to buy no new ones."

" How much? "

" Oh, fifty cents'll do. I keep my prices down and my work good. That's why I have all them satisfied customers up and down the highway."

Elisa brought him a fifty-cent piece from the house and dropped it in his hand. " You might be surprised to have a rival some time. I can sharpen scissors, too. And I can beat the dents out of little pots. I could show you what a woman might do."

He put his hammer back in the oily box and shoved the little anvil out of sight. " It would be a lonely life for a woman, ma'am, and a scarey life, too, with animals creeping under the wagon all night." He climbed over the singletree, steadying himself with a hand on the burro's white rump. He settled himself in the seat, picked up the lines. " Thank you kindly, ma'am," he said. " I'll do like you told me; I'll go back and catch the Salinas road."

" Mind," she called, " if you're long in getting there, keep the sand damp."

" Sand, ma'am? . . . Sand? Oh, sure. You mean around the chrysanthemums. Sure I will." He clucked his tongue. The beasts leaned luxuriously into their collars. The mongrel dog took his place between the back wheels. The wagon turned and crawled out the entrance road and back the way it had come, along the river.

Elisa stood in front of her wire fence watching the slow progress of the caravan. Her shoulders were straight, her head thrown back, her eyes half closed, so that the scene came vaguely into them. Her lips moved silently, forming the words " Good-by — good-by." Then she whispered, " That's a bright direction. There's a glowing there." The sound of her whisper startled her. She shook herself free and looked about to see whether anyone had been listening. Only the dogs had heard. They lifted their heads toward her from their sleeping in the dust, and then stretched out their chins and settled asleep again. Elisa turned and ran hurriedly into the house.

In the kitchen she reached behind the stove and felt the water tank. It was full of hot water from the noonday cooking. In the bathroom she tore off her soiled clothes and flung them into the corner. And then she scrubbed herself with a little block of pumice, legs and thighs, loins and chest and arms, until her skin was scratched and red. When she had dried herself she stood in front of a mirror in her bedroom and looked at her body. She tightened her stomach and threw out her chest. She turned and looked over her shoulder at her back.

After a while she began to dress, slowly. She put on her newest underclothing and her nicest stockings and the dress which was the symbol of her prettiness. She worked carefully on her hair, penciled her eyebrows and rouged her lips.

Before she was finished she heard the little thunder of hoofs and the shouts of Henry and his helper as they drove the red steers into the corral. She heard the gate bang shut and set herself for Henry's arrival.

His step sounded on the porch. He entered the house calling, " Elisa, where are you? "

" In my room, dressing. I'm not ready. There's hot water for your bath. Hurry up. It's getting late."

When she heard him splashing in the tub, Elisa laid his dark suit on the bed, and shirt and socks and tie beside it. She stood his polished shoes on the floor beside the bed. Then she went to the porch and sat primly and stiffly down. She looked toward the river road where the willow line was still yellow with frosted leaves so that under the high gray fog they seemed a thin band of sunshine. This was the only color in the gray afternoon. She sat unmoving for a long time. Her eyes blinked rarely.

Henry came banging out of the door, shoving his tie inside his vest as he came. Elisa stiffened and her face grew tight. Henry stopped short and looked at her. " Why — why, Elisa. You look so nice! "

" Nice? You think I look nice? What do you mean by ' nice '? "

Henry blundered on. " I don't know. I mean you look different, strong and happy."

" I am strong? Yes, strong. What do you mean ' strong '? "

He looked bewildered. " You're playing some kind of a game," he said helplessly. " It's a kind of a play. You look strong enough to break a calf over your knee, happy enough to eat it like a watermelon."

For a second she lost her rigidity. " Henry! Don't talk like that. You didn't know what you said." She grew complete again. " I'm strong," she boasted. " I never knew before how strong."

Henry looked down toward the tractor shed, and when he brought his eyes back to her, they were his own again. " I'll get out the car. You can put on your coat while I'm starting."

Elisa went into the house. She heard him drive to the gate and idle down his motor, and then she took a long time to put on her hat. She pulled it here and pressed it there. When Henry turned the motor off she slipped into her coat and went out.

The little roadster bounced along on the dirt road by the river, raising the birds and driving the rabbits into the brush. Two cranes flapped heavily over the willow line and dropped into the river bed.

Far ahead on the road Elisa saw a dark speck. She knew.

She tried not to look as they passed it, but her eyes would not obey. She whispered to herself sadly, " He might have thrown them off the road. That wouldn't have been much trouble, not very much. But he kept the pot," she explained. " He had to keep the pot. That's why he couldn't get them off the road."

The roadster turned a bend and she saw the caravan ahead. She swung full around toward her husband so she could not see the little covered wagon and the mismatched team as the car passed them.

In a moment it was over. The thing was done. She did not look back.

She said loudly, to be heard above the motor, " It will be good, tonight, a good dinner."

" Now you're changed again," Henry complained. He took one hand from the wheel and patted her knee. " I ought to take you in to dinner oftener. It would be good for both of us. We get so heavy out on the ranch."

" Henry," she asked, " could we have wine at dinner? "

" Sure we could. Say! That will be fine."

She was silent for a while; then she said, " Henry, at those prize fights, do the men hurt each other very much? "

" Sometimes a little, not often. Why? "

" Well, I've read how they break noses, and blood runs down their chests. I've read how the fighting gloves get heavy and soggy with blood."

He looked around at her. " What's the matter, Elisa? I didn't know you read things like that." He brought the car to a stop, then turned to the right over the Salinas River bridge.

" Do any women ever go to the fights? " she asked.

" Oh, sure, some. What's the matter, Elisa? Do you want to go? I don't think you'd like it, but I'll take you if you really want to go."

She relaxed limply in the seat. " Oh, no. No. I don't want to go. I'm sure I don't." Her face was turned away from him. " It will be enough if we can have wine. It will be plenty." She turned up her coat collar so he could not see that she was crying weakly — like an old woman.

Wallace Stegner

Remembering Laughter

PROLOGUE

THROUGHOUT the latter part of the morning buggies kept turning in from the highway and wheeling up the quarter mile of elm-arched drive to the farm — surreys and democrat wagons; an occasional brougham, an even more occasional automobile whose brass caught the sunlight between the elms. By eleven o'clock there was a long line parked hub-to-hub against the tight windbreak of interlocked spruce at the north and west of the yard, and the house hummed with the subdued noise of many people.

Sitting at the parlor window, old Mrs. Margaret Stuart had the whole yard, the drive, and the highway beyond under her eye. She could see the white tape of the state road looping over a low hill a mile to the west, the white gabled house and high-shouldered red barn of her neighbors the Paxleys, the cornfields standing dry and stripped in the thin October sun. Along the road, clouds of dust crawled slowly, blown by no wind, almost obliterating the vehicles that raised them. Most of the dust clouds paused at the corner, hung briefly at the end of the elm tunnel, and resolved themselves into the dark moving miniatures of carriages or cars, to draw up at last in the growing line against the windbreak.

Expecting many guests, Margaret Stuart was waiting for no one. There was no curiosity in the eyes that watched the road, no expectancy, no anticipation. A gaunt, angular old woman in black poplin, motionless, hands folded in her lap, she sat before the parlor window and stared quietly out across the Iowa fields and the road and away to the horizon hazy with the attenuated smoke of straw fires.

Seen in profile, she gave the impression of great age. Her face was parchment over bone, with a sharp bony nose, high forehead that rose abruptly into the tightly drawn, lifeless hair, and eyesockets sunk so deeply that they looked at first glance like the eyeless hollows of a skull.

But like many another woman, Margaret Stuart had kept in her eyes the life that had dried gradually out of her body, and anyone at whom she looked directly found himself wondering how he could ever have thought her old. Her eyes were a sudden and violent blue, filmless and clear, and hard as ice. Her body was the body of a woman of sixty, her eyes those of a woman of thirty. Actually she was forty-seven.

The big rooms off the dark parlor were full of people, but Margaret Stuart paid no attention to the sound of many feet, or to the faces that looked curiously in the door. No one spoke to her, she spoke to no one. Elspeth was taking care of them until time for the funeral. There was no reason to go out there now. She sat quietly in the little hard mahogany chair, the rockers never stirring, and stared out across the bare yard and the stripped corn and the road with its rolling cumuli of dust. Outside, the great oak at the corner of the house rubbed gently against the shingles, and occasionally a red-brown leaf wavered past the window.

Margaret turned her head as steps came across the bare maple floor of the hall and Elspeth entered. Though Elspeth was seven years younger than Margaret, she looked like her twin. The same tightly drawn hair, the same high forehead and sharp nose with the nostrils bitten in, the same cavernous eye-sockets and ice-blue eyes, and the same rawboned, gaunt, poplin-clad figure. When they spoke, the words of both had a soft Scottish burr.

" Most of them have come," Elspeth said. " The Reverend Hitchcock thinks we should begin."

Margaret looked at the locket watch that hung on a gold chain against the flat stiff poplin of her breast.

" Better wait till eleven-thirty."

" Will you come in soon? They've been asking about you."

" Soon," said Margaret. " Where's Malcolm? "

" In his room."

" Grieving? "

Elspeth nodded. The two were silent, fixed in an awkward stilted tableau, two gaunt black formal figures like identical scarecrows, one standing, one sitting, in the greenish gloom of the parlor. The rockers creaked slightly as Margaret twisted to look at her sister.

" And you? "

Their eyes met briefly, ice-blue and ice-blue, but it was not a cold or hostile look. There was something in it that struggled toward warmth, as if sympathy and affection were fighting to the surface through crusted years of repression and control.

" I'll never be through grieving, I'm thinking," said Elspeth.

The seated woman moved slightly, almost reached out to pat her sister's arm. Then her hands folded again.

" Better get things ready," she said. " I'll be right in."

Elspeth lingered. " How about you? Are you . . . you . . . ? "

Their eyes met again, looked into each other across the barrier of bitter years, wavered aside as each found it hard to meet the other on any intimate ground.

In the minds of both rose like smoke the memory of another day in October eighteen years before, and the lips of the woman in the chair were twisted with the bitterness of it.

The noise of many people in the other rooms was suddenly loud; yet it was quiet in the dark parlor, as if the still air there were a protective cushion against intrusive sounds. Elspeth's hand made a slight silky rustle in the folds of her dress. The oak sawed quietly against the shingles, and three red leaves drifted down in erratic spirals.

" I guess," said Elspeth thickly, " I guess I'd better go see about things."

She rustled out, and Margaret sat still in the little mahogany rocker, her lips tight together, breathing regularly and audibly through her nose, looking out past the burly trunk of the oak at the bare yard and the brittle stripped corn and the road with its clouds of dust rolling toward her husband's funeral.

I

On the afternoon that Elspeth MacLeod was to arrive from Scotland, Alec Stuart and his wife were waiting in the town of Spring Mill a full hour before the train was due. Still pretty at twenty-nine, Margaret hung on her husband's arm and walked him up and down the platform, happy and excited and talking in quick bursts.

Alec, dressed in his best, looking the landowner he was, kept his arm stiff for his wife to hang on, stiffened it still more until the muscles were ridged and hard when she pinched it in anticipation.

They were a handsome couple, and he knew it; and he grinned down at Margaret in her tight-waisted, puff-shouldered, high-necked dress, tipped the absurd bonnet perched on her brown hair. She was tall, but not so tall as he, and she was slender, and the bloom still on her.

" You haven't been so excited since your wedding day," he said.

" I wish the train would hurry."

" Well, she'll never come the sooner for our walking ourselves to death, my lady. Let's sit down."

" I can't keep still," said Margaret.

" You walk, then. I'll sit down," said Alec good-humoredly.

He sank on a rough bench against the wall of the little station, and Margaret sat dutifully beside him. The town ended abruptly at the tracks, and before them across the few rods of cinders and the double bands of ribboned steel was open country sloping up the long roll of a hill, dark cultivated earth lined with spear-ranks of young corn, white gabled houses half hidden by flourishing oaks and elms, tufted green woodlots tonguing down through swales, the angles of fences and rutted country roads cutting off black fields from intense green squares of meadow and pasture.

" Think she'll like it? " Alec asked.

" I hope so. I described it as well as I could, but maybe I didn't say enough about the winters, and the summer heat, and the flies, and the like."

" It's a good country enough," Alec said. " She'll like it."

Two men crossed over from the water tank, angling across the street toward the block of stores and shops concealed from Alec and Margaret by the station building. They waved at Alec, and he craned around the corner to watch them. They went in the swinging doors of the Corn Belt Saloon.

" Where'd they go? " asked Margaret sharply. " Into that tavern? "

" Na, na," Alec said vaguely. "They're just walking down the street."

Margaret took hold of her husband's arm again in an almost fierce gesture, as if to hold him beside her by force, but he made no move to rise. They sat for ten more minutes quietly absorbing the spring sun, waiting, Margaret's excitement cooled now by her distrust.

Finally Alec rose. " The horses'll need their flynets, I'm thinking."

While she watched suspiciously, he strolled to the other end of the platform where the horses were tied, and threw over them bright yellow nets of string. Big and casual, he stood there a moment with his hands in his pockets, staring across the street, before he sauntered back to his wife.

" I see Henning Ahlquist across the street," he said. " You wait here a minute. I want to talk to him about working this summer."

" Alec! "

Alec's overacted look of surprise broke down before his wife's look. He tried to laugh away the guilty air that he felt he wore, but the laugh too died in an embarrassed cough.

" I *did* see Ahlquist," he said.

" Maybe you did. But if you go over there you know as well as I do that you'll come back drunk as a brewer, and Elspeth coming in a few minutes. 'Twouldn't be the welcome she'd like, Alec."

Alec eased himself back down on the bench and leaned his elbows on his knees.

" Ah, weel," he sighed comically. " I can see Ahlquist any time."

Half humorously he studied his wife's face with its little frown and its lips pursed in almost petulant disapproval.

" Why do you drink, Alec? " Margaret's voice was plaintive, the echo of a thousand repetitions. " Why don't I, you mean," Alec said lugubriously. " Ye'll make me a drunkard yet, just by keeping me from getting full once in a while."

Looking at each other, friendly again, reconciled, half joking, they were both aware of the clash of their wills, neither willing to quarrel but with something between them that showed as a pained puzzlement in Margaret's face and an obscure stubborn tightening in Alec's. Alec's stubbornness, his wife thought, was like a rubber wall. It gave, but the more one pushed against it the harder it became. And Margaret's disgust with drink, Alec was thinking, was too extreme. A little nip with a friend was deadly sin. And so they sat with a nebulous cloud of mutual recrimination between them until the whistle of the train announced Elspeth's arrival.

The train slowed for the station, the engine passed them with a prolonged hiss of escaping steam, its iron underparts smoking and its high wheels dragging, slowing, the drivers moving jerkily like a runner's stiff elbows, and before the cars were completely stopped the two waiting saw Elspeth ready at the door. Then she was down, running toward them across the plank platform into Margaret's arms for a long hug, and out to be whirled high and kissed roundly by big Alec, and back to Margaret's arms. There were exclamations and a few tears, and the smiles of the three were broad and delighted, and then, all a little breathless, they were walking over to the buggy with Elspeth rattling about her trip and the things she'd seen, and the miles and miles and days and nights on the train, and what a tremendous country they had here.

As Alec tossed her bags into the buggy and took her arm to help her into the high seat she stopped short.

"Ooooh! Your own carriage!"

Alec laughed. Then, solemnly, as he lifted her in, "I had to get something to haul away the bodies of Indians Margo and I killed prowling around the house."

Margaret answered Elspeth's startled look with a smile.

"He'll tell you more lies in a minute than you can soak up in a year. Never mind a word he says."

"But aren't there . . . Indians?"

"Not many now," Alec said. "Margo got fourteen with the shotgun off the back porch last year. They used to come around to steal feathers off the chickens for their hair, but Margo's discouraged 'em."

Through the six-mile drive back to the farm Alec was in a constant roar of laughter at Elspeth's questions. They passed several farms with new cylindrical silos, and after the third one Elspeth could no longer restrain her curiosity.

"What are the round things?"

"Wells," Alec said.

"Wells? So high?"

"Artesian wells," Alec said. "They have to be capped or they'll flood the country, and sometimes the water is so strong it lifts the cap way up in the air. Then people have to build up walls to support the cap for fear it'll get tipped a little and fall off the water on somebody. Sometimes they get up two or three hundred feet."

"I don't believe you," said Elspeth. Then to Margo, "Is he lying again?"

"Alec," said his wife, "stop teasing the child."

"She's no child," said Alec. "She's twenty-two. She has a right to know about things."

And throughout the rest of the ride he devoted himself to telling her about things. He told her of the Mississippi Valley angleworms that were so long a hen worked a whole day to eat one. The hen, he said, would get hold of one end of the worm and start backing away, to pull it from its hole. If it was a really grown worm, that hen would back away from eight in the morning till three in the afternoon, with an hour's rest at noon. When the tail end finally came loose from the hole the worm, snapping together after its long stretch, would knock down trees for miles; and if it happened to slip around a house or a barn, would snap that off its foundations slick as a whistle. Then the hen, if she recovered from the elastic backlash, would start eating her way back toward home, arriving there generally after nine in the evening, dusty and footsore and completely spent, and so gorged with angleworm that she couldn't get in the door of the henhouse.

And he told her of the corn he had raised last year, with cobs as big as the trunk of an elm and kernels like penny buns. It took a four-horse team to haul one of those ears out of the field, and it was a half-day job for two men with a saw to cut down the stalk. And in the night, before it was ripe, the noise of its growing was like a tornado through a forest, snapping and popping and whining till you couldn't sleep.

And he told her about the winds of winter that piled snow thirty feet high over the roofs of houses, so that it took forty-eight hours for the smoke from the chimney to melt a hole through to the air, and when it finally got out it was too tired to rise but lay panting on top of the drifts and froze solid. He promised to show her a stick of it he had preserved in the icehouse.

And Margaret, watching him delightedly pour out a lavish stream of nonsense, watching her young sister with bright eyes and pert disbelieving merriment drink it all in, was contented to sit sedately beside them and let her own questions wait. There was much about Scotland, about their father's death, about friends and relatives, that she wanted to know; but meanwhile Alec was telling about how the cannibal eels in the Coon River, which saw their own tails following them, turned and snapped and ate themselves at a gulp in a swirling eddy of water.

They rolled along the country lane, past thickets of wild plum, across two muddy, jungly creeks where the hoofs of the horses and the iron wheels of the buggy beat hollow thunder from the plank bridges, over a low hill where workmen putting up a farmhouse waved at them, along a stretch of white dusty road to where the drive turned in between rows of thrifty young elms that Alec had planted six years ago. At the end of that elm-lined drive the two-story white house shone clean and spotless against a spruce windbreak with the barns looming red off to the right and the henhouse a long red bar across the lower lot.

"Here we are, Elspeth," Margaret said. "Here's your new home."

The buggy stopped on the hard-packed drive before a broad sweep of lawn shaded by two wide-crowned elms as graceful as giant ferns. A cement walk bordered with peonies led to the pillared porch, from either side of which flowers and shrubs spread to girdle the foundations of the house. Elspeth noticed that even the yard beyond the grass plot was clean and well-kept; that it was not, like the yards of most of the farms they had passed, cluttered with machinery and rubbish. The house, too, was bigger, the barns redder, the outbuildings more numerous and in better repair.

Margaret was watching her. "Like it?"

"It's big," Elspeth breathed, "and lovely, and grand. You didn't tell me. I expected a farm. This is a great estate."

They jumped down and followed the luggage-laden Alec into the house. A wide hall opened to the left into living and dining rooms, and on the right a closed door indicated either front bedroom or parlor. Back of the dining room was a huge kitchen where a red-faced Scandinavian woman turned to meet them with flour-coated hands outstretched.

" This is Elspeth, Minnie," Margaret said.

The red-faced woman threw her arms about Elspeth and kissed her boisterously, leaving white tracks on the girl's back. Margaret brushed them off, frowning.

" You should be more careful, Minnie. You'll spoil Elspeth's dress."

" I'm sorry," the hired girl said, still grinning. " I've heard so much about you it was like seeing my own sister."

" It's all right," said Elspeth. " Show me your kitchen. It must be gay cooking in such a place."

" Ya," Minnie said. " Look."

For fifteen minutes she opened cupboards and cabinets, displayed flour and sugar bins, showed stove and oven and pantry, led them outside to the cemented dugout, damp and cool and smelling of smoked meat and storage. Behind the cave was a tiny smokehouse, and beyond that the dark windbreak of spruce and Lombardy poplar. As Elspeth looked, two squirrels chased each other across the back lawn and up the oak at the corner of the house, then out of the oak to the roof, where they sat ten feet apart and racketed at each other with flirting tails.

Inside again, Elspeth was shown the two downstairs bedrooms with their tall beds of carved and burled walnut. She examined with a seamstress's approving eye the bright quilt spreads and the dresser covers crocheted in matched patterns of twined ivy leaves.

Everything about the house delighted her except the parlor that opened off the main hall. There, after the light and the bowls of flowers and the comfortable furniture of the other rooms, she was vaguely depressed. The room looked so painfully clean, so formal and unlivable; the sea shells on the mantel looked so rigorously dusted, like a child with scrubbed ears; the walls were so shadowy in the gloom behind the drawn shades; the horsehair couch on which she sat gingerly was so uncompromisingly hard, that for a moment she felt almost like that child with the scrubbed ears, visiting at a strange house with people she did not know.

Margaret saw the look and apologized. " This is the company parlor. I have to keep it closed most of the time, and the shades down so the sun won't fade the carpet."

She walked over and raised the blinds halfway, so that through the window Elspeth could see two men working by the barn, and Alec driving the team down to be unhitched.

Then the older sister came back to sit beside Elspeth, and they talked with Elspeth's hands tight in Margaret's. But even while she was answering questions about how their father had died, and how she had had to live by teaching for almost a year, and saying, " Yes, yes, I'm not lonesome for home one bit," she was thinking: " She's a dear, she's my only sister and I love her dearly, but there *is* something about this room, something about the way Margaret's clothes look so unwrinkled and the way her hair looks as if it could never get out of place . . . There's something in this cold room that matches something in her — it's almost prim, but prim's hardly the word. Prim, starched, stiff, formal, dignified, haughty — none of those. But there's *something,* and it isn't the real Margaret at all, it's only laid on, as this grim parlor is laid on the rest of the house. The rest of the house is really Margaret; but she brings me in here with the sea shells and the drawn blinds and the chairs that dare you to sit down in them. . . ."

Margaret's cool fingers tightened on hers; her voice was soft with maternal fondness.

" Do you think you can learn to like it here? "

" Learn to like it! " Elspeth jumped up as she heard Alec's step on the porch. " I love it already! Let's go up and see my room."

Margaret rose beside her. They were of even height, with the same rosy complexion, the same straight slim figure, the same brown slightly wavy hair, the same bright birdlike eyes. With their arms around each other they went out into the hall.

Pleased by Elspeth's insatiable curiosity, Alec and Margaret devoted much of the next week to showing her about the farm, through sheds and coops and barns, up into the hayloft, almost empty now and smelling faintly of mold and dust, the packed hay in the corners rustly with field mice. Pigeons roosted there, and Elspeth climbed the ladder Alec held so that she could examine a nest with its four spotted eggs.

From the window of the loft they looked out over the gently rolling land quilted with cornfield and pasture, where Alec's Jersey cattle were tawny quiet spots and a Poland China sow with her trailing brood rooted in distant miniature. Across the corner of Alec's land the sunken line of a creek was a belt of vivid jungle.

" And is all this yours? " Elspeth asked.

" That and more," Alec said, " I've four other farms, over beyond, that I lease." He waved vaguely eastward.

" The stream is yours too? "

" About a mile of it. We'll walk down if you like."

With Alec and Elspeth swinging ahead and Margaret trailing behind, composedly taking her time and stepping carefully over the rough ground, they went down through the gate of the vegetable garden and out across a field geometrically lined with hills of six-inch corn, through a barbed-wire fence which Alec held up for them, across a strip of unplowed land, and down into the shallow flood plain of the creek. On each side of the sluggish stream, elms, oaks, cottonwoods, and birch pillared an interlaced roof of branches and leaves so thick that little sunlight pierced through it. Many of the trunks were almost strangled with creeper and wild grape. Cattle trails shouldered through thickets of willow and dogwood, and the black mud of the bank was pocked with deep tracks.

"Don't go near the bank," Alec said. "There's quicksand here that'd swallow a barn. A man fell in here three years ago and his relatives have been putting tombstone on top of tombstone ever since. There must be a hundred feet of granite on top of him by now."

Margaret, who had settled herself carefully on a fallen trunk, shook her head at him with a slight frown.

"Alec!"

But Alec blithely ignored the look. "Fact," he said to Elspeth. "You remember that spotted cow that fell in, Margo? I got a rope around her horns before she went down, and when we got her hauled out she was a perfect giraffe and permanently dry. The suction milked her completely out. Never gave a drop after that."

Elspeth lips curved and her eyes twinkled at him. "Where is this beast now?"

"Oh, I sold her. A circus gave me two hundred dollars for her."

The girl's laugh pealed gaily among the gray trunks and startled a magpie across the stream into investigative flight. Still laughing, Elspeth watched the bird, turning toward the house to follow it, and saw a man approaching across the sunlit field.

"I wonder if that man's looking for us?" she said.

Alec stared a moment.

"It's Ahlquist."

They walked out to the edge of the timber to meet him.

Henning Ahlquist was blond, slow, powerful, dressed in overalls and blue shirt with the sleeves rolled up, showing huge corded forearms matted with golden hair and glistening in the sun as if oiled. He pulled off his cap with a clublike fist when he saw the women.

"Hello," he said. "I hear you need a hand."

"I do," said Alec. "I thought of you when they told me you'd sold out and sent your family back to Norway."

"Ya, I sold out," Ahlquist said. His voice had the plaintive, chanting singsong of the Nordlander. "I don't want to work long. Just while I get enough money to pay some debts and get back myself."

"Aye," Alec said. "As long as you want, Henning. There's an extra bed in with the Grimmitsch boys."

On the way back to the house Elspeth was silent, watching this huge slow Norwegian with the grave face and the melancholy eyes, wondering what would drive such a Viking away from a land of plenty back to some bleak rocky coast, wondering whether or not he was typical, whether or not she too would want to go back.

"Why do you want to leave here, Mr. Ahlquist?"

The heavy head turned; blue eyes, grave and quiet, searched her face.

" I'm a sailor, miss, a fisherman. I don't like this country."

" Have you been here long? "

" Four years. Four years too long."

In the days to come Elspeth went out of her way to speak to Ahlquist, feeling the loneliness around him, pitying him when she saw him lean on a pitchfork and stare out across the growing corn to horizons shortened by the slow oceanic roll of the earth. He was like a great unhappy dog — slow, sad-eyed, indifferent to the people as to the country around him.

The Grimmitsch brothers — lank, grinning, tobacco-chewing farm hands — did not interest her; but this man eaten by homesickness fascinated her until at times she caught herself wanting to reach out and stroke his blond mane as she would have given an encouraging pat to a Saint Bernard.

Sometimes she would hear Ahlquist singing around the barn in a clear tenor that matched oddly with his ponderous size — singing strange Norwegian songs made stranger by the unfamiliar language. Catching him once, she made him spell out the words, and in her room at night she wrote down all she could remember of them, recalling in the quiet lamplight the melancholy nostalgia of the tune, and the tawny quiet Viking who sang the song to her completely without embarrassment, watching her with grave blue eyes:

> Millom bakkar og berg ut med havet
> Hever Nordmannen fjengit sin heim
> Nar han sjolve hever tufterna gravet
> Og han sat sine hus up a deim.

Ahlquist wouldn't, or couldn't, tell her what the song meant. He only said: " It's just a Norsk song. Fishermen sing it a lot."

And in the dreamful reveries before sleeping Elspeth would imagine the little fishing boats sailing in late afternoon into the mouth of a rocky fjord, with fishermen singing across the black water, and women waiting on shore, and skiffs rocking gently against crude wharfs. At such times she could understand Ahlquist's loneliness; she would lie wide-eyed in the breathless summer night and think, " I'm the only one who does understand him, with his wife gone and his children."

Several times too she took apparently aimless walks that brought her up with Ahlquist where he worked in the field, and he would stop his team and sit quietly listening to her talk, wiping his hot face with a soiled bandanna, and after a few minutes he would cover his glistening hair again with the shapeless hat, shake out the lines, and say, " I have to get back to work now, Miss MacLeod," and leave her standing in the rough black field.

Then one day after she had been talking with the hired man while he sharpened a mower blade behind the barn, she came up to the house and met Margaret, who smiled at her reprovingly, maternally, softening the rebuke with smiling fondness but not completely covering the stiff puritan disapproval behind her words.

"I wouldn't be seen too much with Ahlquist, dear," she said. "He's only a hired man, remember, and you've a certain position to keep. People might talk."

"But he's nice," Elspeth said. "And he's lonesome. I think it cheers him up to have me talk to him."

"Yes," said Margaret, as if to a stubborn child; "but he's a married man, Elspeth, and his wife is away."

"Oh!" Elspeth said hotly. "I think that's . . ."

She turned and went out in the back yard, where she threw herself on the bench against the windbreak, thinking furiously how innocent she was of Margaret's suspicions, how Margaret wronged a pleasant friendship with her stiff conventional avoidance of anything that would cause "talk," how she *was* just interested in Ahlquist because he was lonesome. One would think from the way Margaret took it that she was in love with him!

But in her heart she knew that Margaret didn't think that; she knew that this was only what she mentally called the "parlor" part of Margaret speaking. This was only the rural society woman, the style-setter of a county, the rather proud wife of a wealthy farmer who tightened herself up to what she thought her position and built her life on its conventions. In justice to her sister, Elspeth had to admit that the actual suspicion of anything wrong had never entered Margaret's head, and that Margaret had been merely looking out for her respectability. But even so, Elspeth from that time on saw less of Ahlquist.

To compensate for her thwarted interest in the Viking — an interest that still showed itself in greetings and an occasional conversation — Elspeth gave herself to learning about the farm with the abandon of a child. Everything interested her. She spent hours weeding and trimming and cutting flowers with Margaret in the beds that surrounded the house. She took over the daily chore of gathering eggs from the long chicken shed, and every morning the sight of her white dress brought the hens running and cackling to the wire for the wheat she scattered.

The hens amused her immensely. There was nothing, she told Margaret, quite so ridiculous. She could stand for hours watching the stiff, pecking walk of them, the excited scramble when one found a bug, the wandering, aimless search that led them jerkily around the pen.

The imperial strut of the roosters, too, amused her, and she delighted in taunting them aloud — berating them as stupid, conceited coxcombs, putting a hand through the screen to entice them near, and shooing them off with a flutter of her apron to see their suspicious high-toed strut change instantly to dismayed terror and disorderly retreat.

"Poof!" Elspeth would say. "Absurd beasts!" and walk on down to the barn to caress the silky muzzles of two young calves she had adopted, or to scratch between the horns of the placid mothers.

All the animals on the farm the girl liked, except one ugly old brood sow which had littered after her arrival, and which two days later had turned savagely cannibalistic, eating all but two of her own young. Every time she passed the pen Elspeth shuddered at the hideous gray mud-covered brute with the meaty snout and the little bloodshot eyes and the scalloped sagging teats.

" Why don't you kill the beast? " she asked Alec, and when he explained that slaughtering wasn't done until fall, and that anyway the destruction of the litter had been his own fault because he hadn't watched her closely, Elspeth burst out angrily: " Your fault? Is it your fault if a mother eats her own children? I could kill that old cannibal myself! "

" Sows do it all the time if they're not watched," Alec said. " Boars too, only they don't very often get the chance."

" Then I don't have any use for pigs, and I won't eat their filthy meat again, ever! "

" You're tender because of the little ones," Margaret said. " You can't judge animals like humans, Elspeth."

" Why not? A mother's a mother. Even a silly hen takes care of her chicks. I hate that old sow."

Smiling broadly, Alec winked at Margaret, playfully tweaked the girl's ear.

" She's pretty when she's boilin', eh? "

" Oh, you! "

Elspeth flounced out. Watching her thoughtfully throughout the afternoon, Margaret saw her picking tender tufts of grass along the stable wall and poking the green handfuls into the nibbling lips of the two young calves.

A little later the girl was leaning with her fingers hooked into the screen surrounding the chicken pen. Inside the pen the aimless search for bugs and grain was broken suddenly by the amorous rush of a rooster. Hens scattered and flew. The selected victim ducked and scuttled, but at last submitted meekly to her lover, enduring him with a placidity that was almost insulting. Although the rooster pranced a little higher and more pompously for a few minutes, the hen apparently thought no more of it than she did of pecking up a worm.

Elspeth, fresh, high-colored, stood watching, and when it was over she hissed through the wire at the degraded hen.

" You're a disgrace to your sex, you vixen. You've laid too many eggs. Let that pompous dandy treat you so! S-s-s-s-s-s-s-s! " And to the smug rooster: " S-s-s-s-s-s-s-s! You Mormon, you. You Brigham Young! And *so* proud of yoursel'! So ver-ry *ver-r-ry* proud of yoursel'! "

She bent her arms into wings and strutted back and forth outside the screen, mocking him, while the rooster inside watched suspiciously, stopping with one foot in the air, his combed head perking to see her better, ready to fly at the first flutter of her apron.

" Shoo! "

The apron billowed out, and the rooster took off in a stretch-necked run, wings spread, legs desperately pumping. At a safe distance he stopped, adjusted his wings, and resumed his dainty, slow, high-stepping walk, eyeing her suspiciously still.

And Margaret, who had watched the whole thing through the living room window, turned away with a thoughtful face, thinking of the girl's hatred of the cannibal sow, of her ecstatic devotion to the two awkward little calves, of her bright interest in Ahlquist's melancholy expatriation; thinking of the tense fixity of the girl's figure while she watched the rooster cover the hen.

Later, when Alec came up from the garden eating a raw carrot, she met him in the yard. Elspeth was walking slowly down the lane of elms leading to the state road, and the two stood looking after her for some time before Margaret spoke.

" I'm afraid she's lonesome, Alec."

" Na. She has a grand time. What would she be lonesome for? "

" People her own age — boys."

" Boys? "

The carrot stopped halfway to Alec's mouth as he turned on her in surprise.

" She's ripe to fall in love. I've noticed her with the calves and the chickens."

" What've the calves and chickens got to do with it? "

" Oh, nothing. But I know. I'm going to give a party, Alec. Not just a dinner, but a party. Young people."

" Um," said Alec, munching on the carrot, his eyes on the white dress down the row of elms. " I wouldn't go too fast, Margo."

" You think I'm being a matchmaker? "

" Why, it sounds like it," Alec said. " She's met a few people. Give her time. She'll find someone."

Margaret's lips tightened with determination. " I want to give the party anyway. May I? "

Alec hurled the stub of the carrot high and far into the chicken pen.

" Suit yourself," he said.

II

The day of the party was sweltering. Heat waves like writhing smoke lifted from the broad fields, buildings from a distance looked distorted and out of line, the red barn blazed with intolerable heat. In its shade half a dozen pigs lolled in a puddle. The cows came up from the pasture seeking the shade of the woodlot, and in the wire coop the chickens squatted in the dust, their feathers spread and their bills half open.

Even in the house, shaded by its broad oaks, the least movement was the prelude to sticky discomfort. Margaret, miraculously cool and unruffled, divided her attention between supervising Minnie's cooking for the party and keeping Elspeth out of the kitchen. At eleven, when Alec came in from the field announcing that a four-horse team couldn't drag him out there again in this heat, Elspeth was quietly sewing in the darkened parlor. She looked up when his grinning wet face peered around the corner of the door.

" Would you believe it," Alec said, " the ground's so hot it melted down the disk blades like butter."

" Why didn't the horses' hoofs burn? "

" I shod 'em with asbestos before I went out, but even so they wouldn't stay on the ground. They climbed up and rode the tongue."

"I don't see your shoes scorched any," Elspeth said.

"The heat waves held me up," said Alec. "Just like riding a cloud, but you ought to see the seat of my pants."

They laughed at each other. Elspeth twisting back in her chair to look up into his grinning sunburned face topped by the red hair curly and damp with sweat, noticing hardly consciously the way the muscles of chest and shoulders swelled under the wet blue shirt, thinking him very handsome and strong and amusing.

Margaret's voice came from the kitchen.

"Alec!"

"Coming, my lady," Alec said. He tipped Elspeth's nose with a teasing forefinger and skipped out like a boy when she threatened to throw a book at him.

Margaret took her husband carefully into the kitchen, avoiding touching his sweaty shirt.

"She doesn't know yet," she said with satisfaction.

"How's everything going?"

"Fine. It's going to be a lovely party," Margaret said happily. "Only I'm afraid she'll find out what we're doing and it won't be a surprise."

"It's too hot to work in the field," Alec said. "I'll take her for a walk down by the creek where it's cool. You can keep Henning around to do the heavy work."

"That's it. Then I can get everything ready and put away. Take her out right after we eat."

Alec folded her into a long arm and squeezed her, but she wrinkled her nose at the sweaty smell of him and pushed him away.

"Go take a swim in the windmill trough before we eat," she said.

After dinner she took Alec aside again: "Keep her out till almost six. Then she'll just have time to dress before people begin coming."

He winked and nodded. A minute later Margaret heard his voice in the parlor, and Elspeth's "Oh, yes, it's so hot just sitting here," and then Alec's voice again shouting, "You like to come for a walk down by the creek, Margo?"

"Not now," she called back. "You go on. Maybe this evening when it's cooler we can go out again."

Looking through the dining room window she saw them walking down through the garden and into the waist-high corn. She watched them until his blue and her white figure were a quarter of a mile away, moving like tiny boats on the restless green sea, before she called Ahlquist in to move furniture and help in the kitchen.

Because of the heat Elspeth and Alec walked slowly, the sun a punishing weight on neck and shoulders. As they passed between the rows she let the heavy smooth blades run through her hands, stooped to observe the forming ears plumed with green silk, let her eyes range over the green tops stirring in no wind. The rough softness of the soil under her feet, the feel of firm leaves, the wide green ripples of the field, the sense of Alec striding beside her, even the hot burden of the sun on her back, were acute and incommunicable pleasures. She swung her feet out from the soft drag of the soil gaily, crawled laughing through the barbed wire that Alec held up for her, plucked a sunflower as broad as a saucer from its stalk and fastened it in the breast pocket of Alec's blue shirt. And Alec pulled off his hat to make a sweeping bow of thanks, his hair flashing bright copper in the sun, liking the impulsive gaiety of her, a little dizzy with the freshness of her youth.

The transition from the blazing sunlight to the watery green shade of the woods was sharp and pleasant. The furnace of the sky was shut off by a tight canopy of leaves and vines, the hard brilliance gave way to clear filtered light, the soft dry earth of the field was replaced by a softer damp mat of mold.

They sat on a bank overgrown with dandelions and snake-grass, watching the river sliding smoothly like slick brown glass, Elspeth exclaiming as the triangular wake of a muskrat cut obliquely across the stream. Skaters light as air darted about near the shore, and a tanager was a streak of flame against the bright woods.

" The stream looks inviting," Elspeth said. From the grassy bank she stooped to trail a hand in the brown water. " Wouldn't it be nice if we could come down bathing some time? "

" I swim a good bit when I'm working near the creek," said Alec. " But Margo doesn't approve much. She's afraid someone might see me."

" Don't you . . . ? " Elspeth asked, wide-eyed. " Don't you — wear a suit? "

" Na, you can't swim in a suit. Might as well swim in armor."

The girl bent her head in sudden hot embarrassment, dabbling her fingers in the water, pushing a flat palm against the slow surge of the current. The silence between them let in the far caw of a crow from the woods beyond the stream.

" What's the matter with you women? " Alec said finally. " You freeze up just like Margaret at the mention of nakedness."

" No, I don't," Elspeth said hastily. " I don't, really. I was just thinking it was an odd thing to be talking about with Margaret not here."

" Um," Alec said. He studied her averted face. " She probably wouldn't understand. There's a lot of things she doesn't understand. She doesn't understand why I like to tell thundering lies, or take a drink, or go swimming without five yards of wool around me."

Elspeth said nothing aloud, but to herself she was thinking: " I understand. I understand Ahlquist, too, and if I were Margaret I wouldn't be so prim about things." The thought gave her a warm feeling of satisfaction, of tolerant motherly sympathy such as she had felt when she wanted to reach out and pat Ahlquist's blond mane. Now she felt the same impulse toward Alec. Her fingers itched to run through his stiff red curls, and to still the rising excitement in her blood she jumped up.

" Let's walk."

But her excitement did not lessen as they walked. When Alec did not release her hand after helping her over a log, she let it remain in his with a light high laugh and a quick glance at his beaming face. The next time they came to a fallen trunk he put his arm around her and swung her over.

After a time they sat down again at the foot of a tree. Across the stream a flock of crows flapped heavily, to settle in the dead limbs of a cottonwood.

"Let's call 'em," Alec whispered.

He pulled Elspeth down until they were both hidden behind a bush, threw back his head, and called raucously, the hoarse caws rasping in his throat. Elspeth, watching eagerly, saw two crows rise and sail about as if looking. Then three more left their perch and climbed shiny-black into the bright colorless sky. Alec cawed again. One crow dropped lower, wheeled in their direction, and after a minute the whole flock flew so low that the two on the ground could see their heads bent to search the woods below. Again Alec cawed. The flock wheeled sharply and came back. One was just circling to alight in the tree above them when Elspeth moved slightly to straighten a cramped knee. Immediately the crow was off in straight fast flight, with the whole flock behind him. Their discordant cries grew thin with distance and their forms were black specks in the intolerable brightness of sky before the two stopped staring and looked at each other.

"You did it!" Elspeth cried gleefully. "They were coming right down."

"I could have got a couple with a shotgun, maybe," Alec said. "Maybe not, though. Crows are canny. You can walk up and tweak their bills when you haven't a gun along, but when you have you can't get within cannon shot."

"Can you imitate anything else?"

"Na. Naught except chickens and turkeys and the like."

He leaned back against the tree bole, puffed his lips loosely, and gave a perfect imitation of a hen who has just laid an egg. Pleased with Elspeth's laughter, he did it again. Then he rose to a crouch, arms bent: scratched industriously in the mold, clucked in his throat, went into a flurry of excitement when he found a grub, pecked viciously at the ground with his nose, swallowed painfully, adjusted his feathers, and strutted off with head cocked on one side looking for more. He transformed himself into a turkey and gobbled so fiercely at Elspeth that she rose and retreated weak with laughter.

Warming to his work, Alec next did a convincing reproduction of a pen full of little pigs squealing for their dinner. He bawled like a cow, bellowed and pawed the earth like a rampaging bull, rushed Elspeth into the brush with a thundering charge. There he caught her and they stood hanging on each other's shoulders strangling with merriment.

"You great fool," Elspeth gasped. "You're a bigger fool than Margaret says you are."

Walking again, they chattered like children on a picnic. At the edge of the timber, on the upper edge of the farm, they started a mother quail with what seemed to be a dozen quick, squawking young. Instantly Alec was after them — twisting and turning and dodging, lunging at clumps of weed or grass, thundering heavy-footed after the scurrying balls of feathers. Twice they dodged him completely; then he would circle like a hound on a scent, until one would scuttle from under his very feet and duck into another shelter. Elspeth, standing where they had first flushed the covey, heard him ramping through the willows, yelling like an Apache; then deep and tiptoeing silence; then a whoop of joy, and in a moment Alec came back to her with a tiny quail in his hands.

Elspeth took the bright-eyed trembling bird and felt its thumping heart.

" You frightened it, you lummoxing thing."

" He'll get over it. They tame like chickens."

" Won't he fly away when he gets bigger? "

" Clip his wings."

" *Oo-ooh,* he's a bonny wee thing," Elspeth said. She put the quivering bird against her cheek, and held him there.

When she looked up and saw Alec's eyes upon her, something made her laugh confusedly and turn toward the house.

" Hadn't we better get back? "

Alec glanced at the sun. It was almost five o'clock.

" Let's go back through the trees," he said. " It's longer, but it's out of the heat."

On the way back he followed a little behind Elspeth, thoughtfully quiet, studying her as she walked with the tiny quail held in the hollow of her throat.

Before going up to the house Alec, now matter-of-fact, took the bird from her and put it inside the wire of the chicken coop, where it scuttled for cover.

" Some hen will adopt it in a day or two," he said. " They're very mothering things, hens."

" Hens are nice," Elspeth agreed. " Ridiculous, but nice. You're sure the roosters won't hurt him? "

Thinking of the party to come, of the men who would be there to have a look at Elspeth, Alec answered so harshly that she stared.

" Roosters have no quarrel with anybody but other roosters," he said.

At the front door Margaret, who had been watching through the window, intercepted them before Elspeth had a chance to see into the dining room. She cut off the girl's story of her pet quail and pushed her up the stairway.

" The minister's coming for dinner," she said. " You'll want to look nice. He's a fine young man, and a bachelor."

Having no answer for her sister's arch look, Elspeth went upstairs, and Alec stood looking at his wife's rosy face half guiltily, as if he had betrayed her. She was dressed in the white gown she had worn the day Elspeth arrived, and she looked almost as young and pretty as Elspeth herself. He let his eyes crinkle in a grinning wink.

" She doesn't suspect anything, does she? " Margaret asked.

" Na. What's this about the minister? "

" He's coming. So is Dr. Van Steenbock, and the Paxleys, and the two Bisom boys, and the Armstrongs, and the Andersons; fourteen altogether."

" Doing it up in style, eh? " Alec said. " But what if she takes to one of the Bisoms? Would ye care for that? "

"No," Margaret said. "But she's got to pick her own. I'm not the match-maker you think me, Alec. All I'm doing is letting her see them all. Though it would be a shame if she took a liking to one of those wild ones."

"*You're* picking the minister," Alec said with a grin.

"Why not?" said Margaret stubbornly. "He's a good man, and she wouldn't have to reform him out of wild ways. Just because he's not as high-blooded as yourself is no sign he would make a bad husband."

"Maybe so," Alec said. "I was just wondering if he had any blood at all."

Abruptly he went up to his room, and Margaret entered the dining room to arrange bowls and vases on the long white table. As she worked she was thinking that she would have to watch Alec tonight. He was getting restless and rebellious and fidgety again, and that generally led to a drinking bout. The Bisom boys were notorious high-livers, and she had smelled whisky on Ahlquist once or twice, though he never seemed to get drunk. For the first time she felt a twinge of doubt about the wisdom of her party.

The living room and hall were full of guests when Elspeth came downstairs, blushing rosily and surprised enough to please even Margaret. For a moment she fluttered on the lowest step, feeling the eyes of strange friendly people on her, before Margaret came across the hall with regal dignity and led her off for introductions.

The girl moved dazedly from group to group on her sister's arm, trying to fix her first impressions of people into definite mental pictures, trying to remember names and forgetting them as fast as she learned them. Of the first half hour she remembered only three things: that the Reverend Hitchcock was a pale-eyed blond young man with very red lips who held her hand too long, that Dr. Van Steenbock was so young in spite of his baldness that she felt a pang of pity for him, and that the Bisom twins' bold stare and assured, rakish manner left her slightly discomposed. The rest of the people were vague faces, sets of teeth, freckles, high white collars, shy smiles, embarrassed grins.

It was not until dinner, when she sat between the minister and the doctor, that she began to sort out her pictures, to match teeth with hair and smile with freckles and embarrassed grin with guillotine collar. The prominent teeth belonged to Mr. Paxley, their nearest neighbor. The freckles and shy smile were the joint property of all three of the young Anderson girls. The embarrassed grin and high white celluloid collar sat across from her in the person of Jim Paxley, a youth of twenty whose woolen suit and unaccustomed state of full dress made him acutely and obviously miserable. During the dinner he dropped his knife on the floor with a clatter, stooped to pick it up, and came back up above the table edge with the uncomfortable grin stuck with dreadful permanence on his purple face. Sight of so much distress gave Elspeth enough poise to let her feel comparatively at ease. She was able, having located a few landmarks, to pick out others — Mrs. Paxley, large and many-chinned and beaming, slightly out of place, as her son was, in a social gathering; Johnny Armstrong, snub-nosed and mildly vinegarish, sitting next to his snub-nosed and vinegarish sister;

John Anderson, full of the dignity of years and membership in the State Senate, and his slim birdlike wife caged in écru lace.

As her embarrassment left her, Elspeth found the guests very affable, very friendly, very complimentary with looks and words. John Anderson joshed her heavily about the strong probability that she could pick up a model husband out of such a gathering of the county's eligible bachelors, whereupon the Bisom boys grinned knowingly at each other, the minister wet his red lips, the doctor's skull grew violently pink, and Jim Paxley choked on a mouthful of chicken. The saturnine Johnny Armstrong stared coolly at the Senator, and Alec, at the head of the table, looked down the linen length of it at his wife, who squirmed a little and began talking gowns with Mrs. Paxley, who knew rather less about gowns than a Digger Indian.

Once or twice during the dinner Elspeth glanced up to find Alec's eye on her, and at such times she was painfully aware that the minister in his eagerness to talk bent almost over her plate while torrential words rushed from his wet red lips. It made no apparent difference that most of the time she was turned toward the doctor, who did not embarrass her as the other did, and whose hairlessness ensured her respect. The minister still talked, bending farther to catch her attention, and Elspeth, swinging from doctor to preacher and back to doctor in order to be polite, would look up to see Alec's lips curl contemptuously, and the flush would creep again into her temples.

Somehow, during the hectic dinner, she learned that the doctor was a Dutchman born who had been brought to America at the age of six and had studied at Harvard; that the Reverend Hitchcock was of old New England stock, had studied at three different seminaries (there was a flavor of pride about this, she felt), that he was all alone here in this western state and was lonely — yes, it was lonely here for cultured and educated folk. Didn't she find it so? She learned, though she couldn't have told from whom, that the Bisom twins were the sons of an Englishman who owned even more land than Alec, up north of Sac City; that their father had made of his farm an English estate, had imported foxes and hounds, and rode on the hunt every week with his two swashbuckling sons. She learned that the Andersons were comparatively wealthy people blessed (she mentally put a mean question mark after the "blessed") with three unattractive daughters. She guessed that the Paxleys had been invited because they were newcomers and neighbors. Of the Armstrongs she heard nothing, but they too were obviously well-to-do, part of the county aristocracy. Even while she was still slightly ruffled at being plumped suddenly in the midst of all these strangers, Elspeth could smile a little, inwardly, at the assumption of aristocratic position which they wore. Of the lot, she thought, Margaret was the only aristocrat.

After dinner, while the older people sat comfortably about the walls, there were games. By now Elspeth had shed her confusion, and giggled excitedly with the Anderson girls as they walked warily around the circle of chairs playing "Going to Jerusalem." All the unmarried people played, even the Reverend Hitchcock, but Elspeth noticed that by some means or other one of the Bisoms was always next to him, and always shunted him urgently away from the chair he leaped for at the signal. In four games the minister was always the first one out. Jim Paxley was next, again through the agency of a Bisom. After that the Bisoms and Johnny Armstrong and the doctor struggled for chairs with the five girls, and the laughter of players and spectators rang through the long room. There was much bodily contact, much pushing and argument when two people each got a precarious seat on one chair. On the sidelines with the " outs " the Reverend Hitchcock wet his red lips and pursed them in agitation as Elspeth and the doctor fought for a seat and the doctor's arm went around her in the scuffle, or when one of the Bisoms, who were exasperatingly indistinguishable, grasped the girl's shoulders and whirled her gasping out in a wide circle to land on his lap in a shout of mirth.

Then in the panting interim between games, while the boys mopped their brows with conspicuously white handkerchiefs and the girls fanned hot faces, one of the twins proposed " Post Office." The minister pursed his lips more strongly. The group of young people grew quiet, eyes turned toward Margaret. " Post Office " in the presence of the minister was pretty daring.

" Do you think it would do any harm? " Margaret said weakly. She wanted the party to be gay, she wanted Elspeth to have a good time, but " Post Office " . . .

" I cannot, of course, approve," said the Reverend Hitchcock. " But I am only a guest. I would not think of censoring anything in my hostess's home."

He almost bowed. Out of the cluster of waiting boys and girls came a *sotto voce* " Oh, rats! " that sent a titter through the room.

Alec rose from his chair grinning.

" Come on," he said. " We'll all play except those who disapprove. Come on, my lady."

He held a hand out to his wife, but she remained seated with a slight frown and a shake of the head, and while the game went on the martyred defender of decency drifted over to stand by her watching intently, his tongue flicking out to wet his red lips and his eyes alert behind the glasses. Both he and Margaret noticed that one of the Bisom boys seemed always to be kissing a girl, generally Elspeth, and that they frequently fudged and stole kisses they were not entitled to. The little tight frown stayed on Margaret's face. The doctor, bald and pinkly shining, was worse than useless in such competitions, and Alec, who might have had the grace to help, was delightedly bussing his victims with exaggerated clownishness, elaborately unaware of his wife's attempts to catch his eye.

At the very height of the game, when giggles and guffaws of triumph and squeals of simulated terror echoed through the house and quivered in the long slack curtains, when the game had degenerated into a pursuit-and-capture formula, Margaret rose abruptly and went to the piano. Over the heads of the party floated the strains of " A Bicycle Built for Two," and Larry Bisom swung the girl he was kissing at the moment off in a wild polka. Other couples joined the dance, but Alec and Elspeth, with a covert glance at each other, both sheep-

ish now after their defiance of Margaret and the minister, went to the piano
and stood there singing.

Again the Reverend Hitchcock joined them, and before many minutes was
standing with his arms flung, as if carelessly in the abandon of song, over the
shoulders of both Margaret and Elspeth.

"I wonder you're not out stopping the dancing," Alec said.

"Dancing," said the minister, "is, if properly conducted, a refined and entertaining exercise."

He offered his arm to Elspeth, who, unable to refuse, followed him in a
stiff waltz while Alec glowered and Margaret, looking up over her shoulder,
smiled at her husband with a hint of malice and nodded as if in time to the
music she was playing.

After a time Margaret was relieved at the piano by one of the Anderson
girls anxious to show her talents, but when she looked for Alec he had disappeared. The dancers had blown vigorously at the banked candles on mantel
and sideboard, and the rooms were only dimly lighted. A careful count of those
present left Alec and both Bisoms still unaccounted for. In growing apprehension Margaret sat down in the dark parlor and watched the dancers swing by
in the hall, waiting to see if the three would come back, surer every moment that
they would not. She knew Alec, and she had heard a great deal about the Bisom
twins.

At eleven o'clock Alec had not returned, and Margaret's uneasiness had be-
come fidgety certitude. When Paxley, red-faced and beaming, pranced by with
Elspeth, Margaret motioned to her sister, smiled an apology at Paxley, and drew
Elspeth over to the stairway.

"Have you seen Alec?"

"No," said Elspeth. "Not for almost an hour. He went out somewhere. He
didn't seem to like dancing much."

"Stuff!" Margaret said, flushing. "He loves dancing. He's . . ."

The words stopped themselves on her tongue.

"Would you sit with the minister awhile?" she asked. "I'll go find him."

"Oh, no," Elspeth said quickly. "Don't disturb yourself. I'll find him. I
need a breath of air anyway."

She pushed her sister back into the parlor, waved an "I'll be back" which
she didn't mean at Paxley, and went from the hot hall into the warm night air,
relieved to be out of the stuffy uproar, pleased with the ragged moon just showing over the corner of the barn.

Finding no one on the lawn, she walked toward the black bulk of the barn,
and, with the abruptness of stepping from land into water, passed from the
moonlight into the clean-edged rufous shadow. Above her was the sharp thrust
of eaves against the pale sky, and before her the feel of wall, a more solid shadow
than that on the ground. Somewhere ahead was the low mumble of voices.

Feeling her way around the wall, the girl passed the corner, was immersed
again in moonlight that made the folds of her white muslin shimmer blue as

she moved. The voices were louder now, and a square of dirty yellow low down in the end showed her where they came from. In a moment she stood uncertainly outside the window, shivering a little with the night air now that her blood had cooled.

Through the smeared pane she saw Alec and Ahlquist and the Bisom boys sitting around the low table in the harness room with a bottle before them. Their voices seeped through the wall in a deep masculine rumble.

Elspeth's indecision grew. The prospect of interrupting four men at a drinking bout, even though one of them was Alec, was terrifying, but her impulse to turn back was smothered before she had taken a step by the thought of Margaret fretting and worrying in the house. None of these men would hurt her. They could go on drinking till they fell under the table after she got Alec away.

Firmly she pulled open the half-door and stepped into the black interior heavy with stable smell. The door of the harness room, a few inches ajar, laid a guiding finger of light down the three wooden steps, and up these she climbed, walking heavily to give the men warning. Before she knocked she heard the swift exclamation and sudden movement inside, the abrupt cessation of their voices, then the sound of her own knuckles on the boards, so thin and timid that she was ashamed, and Alec's " Come in," in answer.

The girl pushed open the door and remained in the doorway, seeing in a quick glance the confusion behind the Bisoms' grins, seeing Ahlquist's slow nod, the grave, sober look on his face, noticing as significant the alacrity with which Alec jumped up. The bottle was nowhere in sight.

" We were just talking over crops," Alec said lamely. " The party isn't over, is it? "

" No," Elspeth said. " Margaret thought you should come up to the house."

Immediately she felt guilty, as if she had given Margaret away for a suspicious wife, and that guilt, plus the feeling that she had been eavesdropping, made her turn and stumble down the steps to the moonlit barnyard.

Alec followed and stood beside her, his big body black beside the frail white of her gown, his hair tousled and glinting in the moon, the reek of whisky strong upon him.

" I'm sorry," Elspeth said.

" Never mind. Margo sent you, eh? "

" Yes. She thought you'd been . . . drinking."

Alec ran a hand through his hair with a hard little laugh.

" I have," he said.

Automatically they started walking toward the house.

" Why? " Elspeth asked.

The idea that Alec did not like the party, that there had been some reason for his leaving so abruptly, would not down. And below that idea, in some substratum of consciousness, was a feeling that was hardly so much a feeling as a premonition, a hidden, tingling intuition that she herself was somehow involved.

In the shadow under the eaves Alec's hands grasped her shoulders roughly, swung her around to face him in the dark.

"Why?" he rasped. "I'll tell ye why, Elspeth. I couldn't stand that crew looking ye over. If I'd stayed in there a minute longer I'd have smashed that preacher's prissy face. It's too much like putting ye up on a table and taking bids."

Uncomprehending, Elspeth shrank under his rough hands, stammered. Yet when he pulled her close to him, swept her into a tight embrace, she yielded limply, gave her mouth to his furious kiss.

Alec released her so sharply that she staggered. In the shadow she could not see his face, but when his voice came she knew that he was not apologizing.

"I've been wanting to do that for a month," he said.

Elspeth moved closer to him, driven by the guilty shadows, feeling her whole world fray out in love and shame.

"I . . . Oh, Alec!"

Her need rose in her like hot tears, and the moment of their intimacy lengthened into minutes while the creeping moon narrowed the belt of shadow in which they stood and the sound of the piano rose and died through the open doors and windows of the house.

"Margo wanted to give this party so you could find yourself a man," Alec said.

"Poor Margaret!" Elspeth said. And then, shivering close against him, "Poor Alec! Poor Elspeth!"

III

When Elspeth awoke next morning that moment in the shadow of the barn was like something she had dreamed, an image that lurked on the troubled borders of memory, and the meeting with Margaret at the door appalled her with its implications. Margaret straight, quiet, deeply hurt; she and Alec humbled by their sense of treason; the beauty of the moment gone as light goes, and only their shame left . . . Margaret's quiet "You'd better go to bed," to Alec, and Alec's "Right, my lady," and afterward the task of smiling "good night" to departing guests; and then the intolerable minutes sitting with her sister on the horsehair in the parlor, while Margaret's grief at Alec's actions came out of her in disjointed, restrained, tight-lipped words that tried vainly to break through Elspeth's half-hysterical defense against being a confidante . . .

"I can understand Ahlquist," Margaret had said. "His family is gone, and he's lonely, and he misses his country and people. But Alec hasn't that excuse."

And Elspeth, knowing from that brief revelatory intimacy in the shadow the incommunicable excuses Alec did have, sat stiffly on the stiff couch beside her sister hating Margaret but hating herself and Alec more. A few hours earlier they had all been grand people, she thought unhappily, grand people happy in each other's company, none of them with any ill-will or intention of wrong. Now they had succeeded in so tangling the threads of their lives that only misery could come of it.

For a long time the girl lay quietly in bed, watching a squirrel tightrope the eaves outside her window, thinking of that kiss in the shadow of the barn and what it meant, trying to bring those disquieting five minutes into focus, reduce them to scale with the rest of her life, repeating over to herself that neither Alec's action nor her yielding had any meaning, telling herself that he had been heated with whisky and that she had been excited by the party, by the dancing and music, by the laughter and the kissing game. The kissing game . . .

When she had argued herself into the belief that the whole night had been merely a passing incident without significance, and had finally dressed and gone downstairs, Margaret had her breakfast waiting. Alec was in the field with the men.

While Elspeth ate without appetite her sister came over to lay a hand on her shoulder.

" I'm sorry your party ended so badly, dear."

" Don't be! " Elspeth said in a burst of contrite affection. " Please don't be. It was a lovely party."

And later, helping Margaret and Minnie straighten the house, she resolved that at noon she would talk to Alec, tell him that the evening before was a fiction, that she had been foolish and was sorry, that he must not think it important or lasting.

But when Alec came in he avoided her eyes, ate with his eyes on his food, said a few monosyllabic words, and escaped from the constrained table. It was three days before Elspeth could corner him to tell what had become an increasingly fierce monody in her mind.

They met at the chicken pen, Elspeth with her apron full of wheat for the chickens, Alec with a sack of corn for the hogs. He set the sack on the ground and stood silently beside her as she scattered the grain, and she, without turning her head, felt him as an almost sinister presence, so that her voice cracked a little on the clucking " *Choo-oo — ook, chook, chook, chook!* " and she took a very long time carefully casting handfuls to her pet quail which now ran and pecked with the chickens.

" I told you he'd tame," Alec said.

Elspeth's hands shook out her apron, and then went behind her as she turned to lean against the post and look up at him, fright now upon her as her determination weakened.

" I wanted to tell you . . ." she said, and stopped, furious at the unconvincing weakness of her voice. *He won't believe me,* she thought, *he'll think I'm lying, that I really love him and am afraid.* She blushed hotly, and was furious at that too, but her voice steadied.

" We weren't fair to Margaret the other night. You were drunk and I was foolish. Of course it didn't mean anything, but I wanted to tell you — so you wouldn't . . . think . . ."

Her words trailed away to nothing, and under her lashes she looked up at him, ready to laugh with him and forget it at his word and find herself back on the old friendly ground. But the serious stare of Alec's eyes disconcerted her again. He was not ready to laugh. He was not going to say the word. He wasn't going to let her out.

"Ye're faking," Alec said soberly. "It's no use, Elspeth. When I said I'd been wanting to do it for a month, I meant it. It's no good hiding your head in the sand."

Without answering, terrified at the weakness she felt in herself, the girl turned and ran down to the barn. Alec picked up his sack, emptied it in the hog trough, and followed her slowly, his lips stubborn and a hard vertical wrinkle between his eyes.

He found her with her arms around one of the pet calves, crying into its sleek neck. With a quick look to see that the stable was empty, Alec put his arms around her and pulled her against him, kissed her wet face. As before she clung to him, cried for a few minutes against his shoulder, and then, without a look or a word, pulled away and left him.

And Alec, with a pat on the calf's flank that began as a caress and ended as a blow, went out the other door of the barn.

After that experience of how little strength her resolves had, of how smoothly she could be betrayed by her feelings, and knowing also that Alec's stubborn refusal to hide what he wanted might lead to a disclosure of what she took to calling "the whole silly shameful business," Elspeth kept strictly to a program of chaperonage for weeks. She took long drives with Margaret, or with Margaret and Alec together, but never with Alec alone. When she walked, she walked by herself, refusing herself the company even of Ahlquist because Margaret had shown disapproval of that.

During these days she acquired a hard bright gaiety that was able to talk and joke with Alec in Margaret's presence, but that left her instantly when there was danger of their being alone. Her defenses turned the least word of her brother-in-law into a jest, parried his subtlest advances, reduced him to moody silence. Though she grew thin and unnaturally alert from her constant watchfulness, she kept her sparkle.

When September drew on and the blades of tall corn began to dry yellow, and when the ears grew heavy and hard, there were extra hands to feed, threshers and huskers and teamsters; and she threw herself into preparing food for these men with an industry that more than matched Margaret's cool efficiency and Minnie's oxlike capacity for work. She went to the field and made Ahlquist show her how to husk corn, and many afternoons she worked down the long rows with the men, loving the hazy sunlight and the sense of heavy harvest, hands and feet moving rhythmically to the sound of cobs against bang-board, drawing healthy enjoyment from the creak of harnesses and the tinkle of bits and the dusty sneeze of the horses, laboring mightily to leave a clean row and still keep up with the men. And Alec, watching her go down the rows stripping out ears and tossing them into the trailing wagons, said nothing. When Margaret complained that Elspeth was killing herself needlessly doing a man's work, he only grunted and said that she knew best what she wanted to do.

Twice after the party the minister called on Elspeth. The first time he cornered her in the parlor and held her in talk for two hours, leaning over her eagerly, holding her hand until she pulled it away, telling her of his struggles to set up a house of God in the wilderness, the indifference of many of the people, the lack of educated companions, the loneliness of his life. He regretted a thousand times, licking his red lips with a quick tongue, that they did not live in his parish so that he could have the joy of their support and company, and at the end of his two hours he departed, leaving her weak and slightly nauseated.

The second time he came Elspeth was working in the field and came up in answer to Margaret's call, drawing off her heavy gloves and kicking the dirt from her shoes, her clothes dusted with the yellow powder of husking. She was feeling especially alive and quite happy, but the sight of the minister's buggy in the drive stopped her at the edge of the barn.

A quick glance showed her neither Margaret nor the preacher in sight, and on a sudden mischievous impulse the girl ran across the intervening yard, untied the horse, leaped in the buggy, and was off down the lane to the state road. She was a hundred yards away before the two got to the door, and then she blithely waved at them and continued down the lane of elms, ignoring the Reverend Hitchcock's dismayed shout and Margaret's shrill " Elspeth! "

This time, she thought gaily, he'll not keep me listening to his gabble for two hours! Let him visit Margaret! And so she drove slowly out along the road, stopped at Paxley's for a drink and for the pleasure of telling what she had done to the preacher, took Jim Paxley away from his work and out for a fifteen-minute spin, loitered back past the Stuart lane and on down toward Sac City a mile or two, and finally, when she judged that enough time had elapsed, drove back to the lane and up the drive.

Margaret and the minister met her at the door, and she sat in the buggy seat keeping her face straight, waiting for the reprimands.

" I can't imagine what's got into you, Elspeth," Margaret said. " Reverend Hitchcock drove all the way out here to see you, and you steal his horse and go driving."

" I didn't know he came to see me," said Elspeth. " I thought he came to see you, and I didn't think he'd mind my using his buggy. It would be pretty small charity that would begrudge a girl a few minutes' rest from hard work."

She pulled her heavy work gloves back on and stepped down to face the preacher's trembling insultedness. With a visibly tremendous effort he swallowed his rage and hurt pride and essayed a mild rebuke.

" You shouldn't try to work in the field like a man, Miss MacLeod. Farm girls, yes; but not you. You're not a farm girl. You're a young lady. You should grace a parlor, or lighten a good man's home."

" Oh," said the girl airily, " I like working like a man. It's great fun. You ought to try it sometime."

When the minister had climbed to his buggy and flapped the lines across the back of the horse and had rattled down the drive and out of sight, Elspeth dropped her airy innocence and touched Margaret's arm.

"I'm sorry, Margaret, but if I'd had to talk to him for two hours again I'd have burst. He makes me feel as if I had bugs crawling all over me."

"Well," Margaret sighed, "I doubt if you'll be bothered with him any more. You succeeded in insulting him very thoroughly."

"I meant to," said Elspeth.

By the time Indian summer dropped its warm haze over the stripped fields, and the oak and sumac were crimson in the woods, Elspeth had come to believe that everything was right again. Alec had made no advances. Perhaps, she thought, he has forgotten, perhaps I can relax, perhaps the shell can be sloughed and I can be me again. She found that she could talk to him naturally and with the greatest friendliness at dinner or over the whist table. She could cling to his arm with never a secret fear of her own weakness, never a silent thought that she wanted him to be otherwise than friendly, when they walked down through the autumn woods. She could chatter like a magpie at the incredible crimsons of the leaves or the broad fields of late sunflowers, and she could sail milkweed pods with him while Margaret sat on the bank smiling and composed, even her walking clothes reflecting somehow her flair for the immaculate.

The perfect weather of Indian summer lengthened and lingered, warm sunny days were followed by brisk nights with Hallowe'en a presentiment in the air. In the afternoons the smoke of straw fires was blue on the horizon, and the lawn before the house was thick with crisp leaves.

On such an afternoon Elspeth was moping about the house, wishing that someone would call, even Jim Paxley. With the harvest hands gone there was little to do and no one to see. Alec and Ahlquist were taboo. The minister had not called since the stealing of his buggy. The Bisom boys, who had ridden over occasionally in August, were now in Omaha, she had heard. Dr. Van Steenbock was busy with his practice in town and had not visited them since the party, though every time they drove in they met him and had his blushing promise to come out the first time he got a free moment.

Elspeth tried sewing, but her restlessness made her stitches hurried and impatient. She hunted for something to read, but all the books in the house were stale, and Margaret's new batch of fashion magazines would not arrive for another week. At last, as she had done a dozen times before, she wandered outdoors for a walk, down past the chicken pen where she stood for a while watching her quail. But she felt little interest in the bird any more, now that it was tame and unafraid. It was, she decided, a rather dull fowl, little better than a guinea hen and just as stupidly domesticated.

A little below, the vicious old brood sow lay full length dozing in the trampled mud of the sty. As the girl passed, the sow reared upon her front legs, her heavy hindquarters dragging, and stared out of little red eyes, the rubber snout moving, water glistening on meaty shoulders and straight legs.

"You ugly brute," Elspeth said. "In about a week now you'll be slaughtered for your pains, and I'll be glad. You hear? I'll laugh when they cart you away to market, you cannibal you."

She was now definitely on her way to the creek, though she had had no intention of going that way when she started out. And in the sere field, where pumpkins shone orange among the stalks, she felt better. Her body was lighter and freer, her ears caught the papery rustle of the dry blades of corn, and ahead the thinning red and gold of the timber was still vivid enough to bring anticipations of scuffling feet in knee-deep brittle leaves with the quiet of the woods and the water around her, and squirrels nutting and robins thick on their way south.

By the time she reached the woods the girl had lost all her dullness. She whistled at the squirrels, threw them acorns and hickory nuts, laughed delightedly at the undulant grace of their tails. Many times she stopped breathlessly in the crinkling leaves to watch flocks of robins and flickers, or to observe a redheaded woodpecker drilling for an insect. Later, Margaret had told her, the robins would be gone, and all the other birds except the crows, and then the jays would come by on their migration, to fill the air with their clamor for a few hours and vanish. After the jays had come and gone, there would be winter.

Elspeth sat finally on a heaped pile of leaves by the river, and muskrats swam close with their bright button eyes and whiskers above the water, with the suggestion of strong unseen muscular effort in the way they swam, and the long triangular wake streaming out behind to be bent and strained and finally broken by the slow current. The motion of an arm to toss a curling maple leaf in the water, and the swimmers vanished in a swirl of smooth brown. Sometimes she counted thirty before they came up again rods away from where they had dived.

Elspeth was sitting quietly, full of quiet peacefulness, but stirred too by her old restless desire for activity, loving the autumn woods but hating the prospect of long winter days cooped in the house, rebelling with a slow surge of feeling, still only half felt, against something she couldn't have named, when Alec, coming through the woods with a strayed calf, discovered her.

Without speaking, Alec took the rope from the neck of the calf and shooed the animal into the field toward the house. Then he sat down by her with a crackling of leaves.

"You found a nice spot."

"Lovely," Elspeth said. Her pulse was still racing from the start he had given her. "I couldn't stand it in the house any more, so I came out for a walk," she said.

For a long time they were so still that a swimming rat approached within fifteen feet, but swerved suddenly and dived when Alec's head came up to see if Elspeth was watching it too.

"Remember when we called the crows?" he said.

"I was just thinking of it. The wild ones don't seem very afraid of us, do they?"

The old unnamable reckless impulse was rising in her again, to be snubbed short by the old terror at herself. Alec saw her hand shake as she reached out for a leaf to toss into the stream, and he caught the hand before it could throw.

" Elspeth! "

And with only a momentary struggle, like the hidden underwater effort of the swimming rat that showed only as a kind of strained intensity in its moving head, the girl yielded and the watchfulness of more than two months went out like a child's mud dam. She felt his fingers bite into her arms, felt her body broken backward and his hand fumbling at her dress, felt the hot shock to her blood as his calloused palm touched her breast.

The half-grown calf, freed from the rope around its neck, browsed off into the yellow field, nibbling at fallen ears that the gleaners had missed. From the woods beyond the stream came the far derisive caw of a crow.

A half hour later Alec and Elspeth followed the calf, Elspeth clinging tightly to her lover's arm. Their stiff silent march to the house was somehow a penance, a walking barefoot over hot coals, a march to the gallows. We're both damned, she thought, blackened and damned; and stumbling over the rough clods beside Alec she studied him furtively until he turned and smiled down at her, a wavering smile that made his mouth seem suddenly weak. She bent her eyes to the ground again, ashamed of him and of herself, choking back the frantic thought of Margaret and pushing away with numb defensive caution any visions of the future.

With Alec snatching at dried sunflower heads and rasping out with his thumb the sharp brittle seeds, they walked across the field and through the fence toward the lower lot. Past the barn they could see Margaret raking and burning leaves in the yard, and the fragrant smoke of the fires lay upon the still air like incense.

Elspeth tightened her grasp on Alec's arm.

" Alec, I'm afraid! "

They stopped briefly, and Alec's thumb rubbed at the bare seed-head while he looked at her.

" Go in alone," he said. " She's seen us, so don't try to slip in the back. Everything will be all right."

" I can't face her," Elspeth whispered.

" You can," said Alec, " and you will. Go on, now. I'll stop at the barn."

She was led along, desperately afraid of that walk she must make alone past Margaret and into the house, smothering as unworthy and wild the half-formed wish that Alec would lead her boldly up to the house, speak his love for her, and carry her away. She clung to him tightly in the shelter of the barn, and then he was pulling her arms away and talking to her to give her courage.

At last, armored with a tight shell of composure, she stepped out around the barn, across the lawn past Margaret.

" Back again," Margaret said. " Lovely day for a walk, isn't it? "

" Yes," Elspeth said. " A lovely day."

She smiled at her sister with stiff lips, and went on into the house.

Alec, watching Elspeth closely during the following days, soberly following her with his eyes, aware of the mischief he might have done, was surprised
to find that after the first terror the girl seemed happy and even gay. She sang
about the house, and at night when they played whist or sat reading, her words
had a wit and a natural bantering edge that even he could find no hysteria in.
Her eyes were full of laughter when she looked at him generally, but on three
or four occasions they widened luminously and her mouth smiled, and when at
these times she let down the shield of make-believe he knew that she had accepted him as lover, had tossed her watchfulness and her qualms and her affection for Margaret to the reckless winds.

Before a week had passed, after Ahlquist and the Grimmitsch boys had
finished milking, the two met in the barn and clung and kissed in the dim, beast-
smelling twilight, and climbed together into the loft. Frequently in the evening
Elspeth went down with Alec to watch the milking, and there, hidden from
the other men by the high sides of the stall, she could lean against the manger
and watch his hands and hear the soft hiss of milk into foam, and he could
turn his face away from the cow's flank and purse his lips for a kiss, and get it,
and they could talk trivial nonsense for the others, but only they two could
read the real meaning of their words.

Those evenings were often exciting and gay and thoughtless, but over them
was the shadow of discovery, and in Elspeth, despite the excitement of passion,
a sneaking sense of shame and guilt and regret. Wholehearted as her love was,
and fanned by secrecy and broken taboos, there were many times when she
could think of herself and Alec as nothing but criminal and vicious, and many
of their trysts in the loft were begun or ended in shameful tears.

One evening Alec had sent the Grimmitsch brothers to his east farm for
chicken feed. He and Ahlquist were milking, and Elspeth leaned against the
manger in the closed stall. The shame was upon her, and with the ring of the
pail in her ears she stood fixed in a sad catalepsy, wide-eyed, staring, the gloom
of the darkening barn a gelid medium supporting the shadowy thrust of stalls
in a long row like the piers of ruined bridges jutting into a river of liquefied
dark.

She heard Ahlquist's grunt as he finished his last cow, the clatter of metal as
he emptied his bucket into the tall milk can, and his heavy footsteps retreating
as he went up to the men's house to wash for supper.

Then the girl's voice came out of the trance that held her, and she heard it
like no voice, like something frail and brittle that rode the quiet dark as milkweed pods ride a stream.

" We're so horribly lost, Alec! "

The quality of her voice, the strange far-off wail of anguish under its quietness, brought a startled " Eh? " from Alec, and the whish of milk ceased.

" We're lost. We love each other without right and we stab Margaret without reason. I rob her of you, you rob her of me, we leave her nothing, and we
have nothing ourselves but our love, and that's unclean."

The words hung and passed, as if someone upstream had stopped dropping pods on the water. Through the dark barn rose the murmur of obscure life, a stamp or a swish of a tail, the low munch of ruminating cows.

" What do ye want to do? " Alec asked quietly.

" I'm selfish," Elspeth said bitterly. The trance had passed, and her words stung.

" I'm selfish! I want you, and I don't want to hurt Margaret. Oh, Alec! "

Neither of them had heard the steps approaching from the house, neither of them had seen Margaret's figure darken the opaque square of the door. Tight now in each other's arms, Elspeth stammering and passionately clinging, her words a jargon of passion and desire, they neither saw nor heard the woman who stood stricken and unbreathing in the shadow.

When the flame in their blood was hot, Alec drew her to the ladder leading up into the loft, and she climbed willingly. Then they heard the gasp the shadow gave, the stumble of her feet on the sill, and against the almost-dark of the door they saw her running.

Elspeth's hands clawed at the rungs of the ladder, her legs went numb and she half fell into Alec's arms.

" Almighty God! " Alec said.

He held Elspeth tightly, but she slid free and sank on the floor, and her grief came out of her in a long shuddering moan. In the dark a cow moved against the forgotten pail, and the clatter of tumbling tin was like an explosion in the hollow barn.

Alec made no move to recover it, but stood silently above the vague huddle of Elspeth's dress, while the shadowy interior heaved around them with its murmurous swell of beast-sounds.

At last he stooped and lifted the girl to her feet, and his voice was like the voice of one dying in bed after a long illness.

" We'd best go in and face it now," he said.

IV

When Margaret turned and ran stumbling from the barn there was no room for thoughts in her mind. She never knew how she got into the house and up to her room. Numb with black bewildered grief, she sat on the edge of the bed and, gasping for air, ripped loose her high collar with icy shaking hands, convulsed alternately by tears and blasts of hot fury that shook her till she chattered.

The front door opened below, and her body froze erect as she listened. She heard no voices, but she knew they were whispering, wondering where she was, and she could see them in imagination standing like conspirators at the foot of the stairs. Her teeth clicked at the thought that they might be plotting to go away together.

Then there was the bell for the men, and Minnie's strident voice calling supper, and in a moment Alec's answer.

" Oh, aye," she heard him say. " Put ours away for a while, Minnie. We won't be eating just yet."

Margaret's teeth clicked again in furious indignation that he could still speak, still answer a call to dinner, still control the commonplace trivialities of that other life that had been theirs.

She heard no more words, though her breath was held with listening, only a low mutter of Alec's voice to which Elspeth apparently did not answer, and Elspeth's dragging footsteps on the stairs. The steps hesitated at the top, and the listener heard the short jerky breath of sobs before the sounds went down the hall and were lost behind the shutting of Elspeth's door. Almost at the same instant the front door slammed shut below.

Even then it was clear to Margaret that there was no triumph in the two, but that revelation brought her no comfort. Their misery was the reward for deadly sin; hers was undeserved, unearned, unbearable!

" My *sister!* "

She spat the words hissing into the dark, sitting straight on the bed, adding the favors and the kindnesses she had done Elspeth, thinking of Alec and his periodic drinking, transforming subtly her mad jealousy into puritan censure, shifting the burden of furious personal affront to the religion she had been bred in, sublimating her own wrong into deadly sin against the Calvinist God, until she could approach a sad resignation to her lot and to the sinfulness of her relatives. Margaret had lost her husband and her sister; that was undeserved and bitter, but she could bear it. But Alec and Elspeth had lost their immortal souls, and a lifetime of expiation could never make their peace with a stern God.

By slow degrees Margaret's jealousy was transformed and masked, but the progress toward resignation was broken by paroxysms of rebellious fury, and the image that filled her mind was not of the lost souls before the tribunal of a just God, but of two shadows fumbling for the ladder to the loft.

For hours that image kept leaping out of the dark to scald her with hot resentment and burn away in an instant the laborious rationalizations of an hour. In the midst of one of these fits she leaped from the bed, lighted the lamp, and with fingers that trembled clumsily in their haste, stripped off her clothes to the last shred. Then she stood before the mirror studying her naked body — she who had never allowed Alec to watch her undress, who had almost turned her eyes from her own nakedness, now stood peering, lifting the lamp and turning half sidewise to study herself in profile, running an experimental hand down the smooth flank to the swelling of a hip, stiffening her shoulders to correct the almost imperceptible sag of her breasts.

The mirror was high, and so she climbed upon the bed to see herself full length, strenuously ignoring the high flush on the face in the mirror, staring at the slim legs, the white womanly body, thinking " Unwanted wife, unwanted wife, unwanted wife." Her eyes lifted to meet the eyes of the woman in the mirror, she stepped off the bed to stare closely into them, and then with a strong shudder she blew out the lamp and threw herself on the bed where she lay stiff with shame at herself, and the tears came on again.

Through the long sleepless night she lay revolving the bitter cycle from passionate protest to puritan judgment, fumbling for a way out, for a pattern of action, trying to imagine what the others would do, furiously crying that it didn't matter what they did, she could never forgive them. Alec could never again be her husband, Elspeth was irrevocably her sister no longer. Even if she could live on in the same house with them, and even if they wanted that, even if she could continue the patterns of decent and regular life, nothing would ever again be the same, and she could never forgive them. Neither her jealousy nor her religion would allow that.

At the end of the hall Elspeth too lay sleepless in grief as strong as Margaret's own. A half dozen times she half rose from the bed, intending to go to Margaret on her knees, but always the image of herself knocking timidly on a stern unopened door prevented her. There would be no forgiveness behind that door — there shouldn't be. She had no right. There was nothing she could beg for except her sister's pity, and pity would not help what was done. Nothing could help any of them, nothing, nothing. She tried to pray, and shrank from the unclean thing she was.

At two ends of the hall lay two women — the one bitter, hurt, justifying her jealousy in Calvinistic sternness and then tearing off the veil to expose herself as a scorned and insulted woman, the other lacerated by a guilt that admitted no extenuation, a guilt whose enormity was now increased tenfold by the shame of discovery. Both were listening unconsciously for Alec's step below, both caught up by the emotional ionization of the charged air in that dark corridor, whereby all shame and guilt clustered at the door of the miserable girl, all accusation and jealous wrath at the door of the wronged wife. Both were listening for Alec's step on the stair, not because either wanted him to come to her, not because either during that night had any room for love of him, but for a reason that neither could have expressed and that neither would have recognized — that without him their conflict did not exist.

Margaret, naked in the big walnut bed, lay wondering if he would try to come to her, if he would dare; lay wondering what she would do if he did, not wanting him but listening for the sound of his heavy shoes. There was nothing to discuss, she told herself. Everything that needed saying they had said in the barn. Yet when Alec did not come, and the secret boards in walls and floor creaked with the passing of interminable hours, and the light grayed the windows to translucent squares, she was conscious of a dull disappointment, as if his coming might have made some magic that would change this dismal nightmare back into reality, as if she had lain waiting all night to be released from this fear and had found that it was no bad dream to be brushed aside with a word of incantation. And as she rose to dress, the puritan stiffness in her hardened and tightened, and the face that she wore when she went downstairs was gray, expressionless, calm as stone.

Alec spent the night in the barn, pacing up and down the soft beast-smelling corridor between the rows of stalls, puttering at mending a broken tug, climbing to the loft to throw down more hay into the mangers, going on impulse into the box stall where Elspeth's two calves lay and scratching their hard polls. His thoughts drove him to activity, and he lighted the lantern to spend an hour cleaning stalls and pitching manure out the square hole at the end of the barn. He went out into the chilly dark and sacked corn to be carried to the hogs in the morning. In a frenzy of industry he did all the odd jobs he could find, and when those ran out he sat down on the bench in the harness room with the lantern swinging slightly in the draft from a broken pane, and filed all the saws he owned, fiercely pleased with the screech of steel on steel, soothing raw nerves with a noise that he would have ordinarily found unbearable after five minutes.

If he wondered at all about how he and Elspeth would face Margaret in the morning he shouldered his way through the thought and left it behind. In his mind, as in Elspeth's, their guilt was plain and unpardonable. In that brief moment when they were halted at the foot of the ladder by Margaret's gasp and the stumbling of her feet, he had been tied away from Elspeth as if by chains, and linked indissolubly to Margaret by his own realization of her wrong. What happened to them now was in Margaret's hands.

Morning found him huddled in a horseblanket, shivering in the draft from the broken window. He had apparently been asleep, although he remembered nothing about finishing the saws. With the precision of long habit he went to the men's quarters, took the milk pails from their hooks, roused Ahlquist and the Grimmitsch brothers, and went out to the milking. Following that he soused his head in the icy water of the windmill trough, washed his hands carefully, and walked back to the house, calling to Ahlquist to feed the hogs.

As he opened the front door Elspeth was coming downstairs. They stood facing each other for a moment, Elspeth pale and nervous, Alec standing stupidly anguished with his mouth half open and his red wet hair on end, before the girl came down and passed him going into the dining room. In that moment were said all their farewells, as in that other moment last night in the barn their passion had been cut suddenly, as a nerve is cut.

Alec followed her into the dining room, intent on bearing his part in the self-immolation she had apparently decided upon.

But there was no immolation. Margaret, setting the breakfast table, met them with a cold " Good morning " and went on with her work. She was composed, but her greeting had an edge that cut. It drove Elspeth to a pathetic helpfulness that fussed with dishes and cream and sugar and was miserably clumsy. Alec silently sat down to his oatmeal and bacon and eggs. After his eighteen-hour fast and the all-night furious working he was ravenous, and Margaret, bending stolidly to her food, let a twinge of jealous pique show through her stone mask at the sight of his wolfish appetite. She herself ate very little, and Elspeth even less.

Alec rose before his last mouthful was swallowed, and started out.

" Got to get to work," he mumbled.

Elspeth too sprang up to carry their plates into the kitchen, still driven by the need to show her contrition in helpfulness.

To Margaret, as to the others, that first meeting had been stiff, wintry, inhumanly cold. She was thankful that at least it had been free from accusations or appeals for forgiveness, but as she sat quietly finishing her breakfast she looked across the table into the comfortless future, and the sternness of her unforgiving was bleak in her eyes.

They passed the last week of October, and November wore through dismal repetitive days, and December came on. Two or three times Alec took Ahlquist and drove into Sac City or Spring Mill or Wall Lake, and the two women did not see him for forty-eight hours. On those days Margaret would be grimmer than usual, and Elspeth, creeping timidly about the house with dustpan and broom, would see her sitting motionless in the hard mahogany rocker in the darkened parlor, stiff, unmoving, her face showing bonily and her eyes cavernous in the wintry gloom, no ray or gleam of light about her or about the room, not even enough to show on the decorative gold band of the picture molding or on the brooch at her throat. Elspeth knew she was not waiting for Alec, for the blind was tight down on the window that commanded the road from town. Yet she was: she was waiting with every nerve strained, with a seethe of contradictory emotions under the masklike face. She was waiting for Alec with some need to know that he had been drinking again, some positive necessity to find him guilty of more and more and yet more crimes against her and God. In his further damnation was the justification of her vindictiveness; and she sat for hours together in the chilly parlor with the blinds drawn against the sunless light of outdoors, waiting and waiting and waiting for the crunch of wheels in the gravel and the sounds of Ahlquist half carrying him off to the stable to sober up.

Yet she was kind, with a malignant kindness that martyred itself with every gesture of sisterly or wifely solicitude. To Elspeth, mournfully watching the transfiguration of all three of them, her sister's natural impulses to love seemed all to have soured into cold courtesy and unfailing calculated tact. When company called, as it frequently did after snow fouled the roads and stopped any but inside work, she always sent Minnie to bring Alec in from crib or barn; sat composed and charming, drawing her husband and Elspeth into the conversation, listened smiling to their talk; maintained her perfect composure and her old aristocratic dignity. And Alec still, in company, called her " my lady " in a ritual of respect, and Elspeth fought back the strangling desire to cry, learned to smile and nod and inquire about commonplaces. And always behind the united family front was the intangible shadow of estrangement, an atmosphere of loveless frigidity nurtured by wrong and fattened by the silence that seemed to the three to have soaked into the very walls of the house, to have become a haunting presence that shouted soundlessly through the footsteps on the stairs or echoed in the slamming of a door.

They never spoke of the false front they offered to friends and neighbors, never planned it, never agreed upon it. It was simply there, a part of Margaret's implicit insistence on decency and decorum, a part on their side of a hopeless and endless expiation.

One morning Margaret told Ahlquist to hitch up the team, packed a bag, and came down in traveling dress to fling a dare in the face of the two.

"I'm going to Chicago to do my Christmas shopping," she said. "I'll be gone about four days."

Coolly overlooking the fact that in going she left together the two who had betrayed her before, ignoring their situation with an audacity that made Elspeth gasp, she climbed into the buggy.

"I'll have Henning meet you at the station," Alec said.

During the time they were alone Elspeth saw Alec for hardly fifteen minutes altogether. He ate with the men and seldom came into the house during the day, and she was grateful. There was no reason why she should seize the opportunity to tell him. It would come out soon enough. The certainty of that sent her feverishly to her room every day to work over clothes that would conceal her longer, hide this nightmare within nightmare close in the secret darkness of her womb, this feeding parasite that wasted her body and desolated her mind, this child of sin that at almost every meal her body tried to repudiate in nausea. Her strained efforts to eat naturally, her eyes that she knew were sunken and terrified, her face drained of blood in the struggle to keep down her sickness, could not escape Margaret for long, and even if it did there would soon be the shape of her to betray her.

It would come out soon enough; there was no need to tell Alec. There was not even any desire to talk to Alec, any feeling for him as the father of the nightmare. That passion had smothered in the airless prison of guilt.

When Margaret came back and Alec stood by the wheel to help her down, Elspeth was on the steps, her hands clasped in front of her partly from timidity but more from the fear that her shape had already begun to betray her. After four days she half hoped for a smile, for a greeting with a hint of warmth in it, but she saw Margaret take Alec's helping hand as if it were the hand of a groom, and she shrank back to make way as her sister swept up the walk and into the house with a curt nod. Because her eyes were lowered Elspeth did not see the sharp look that Margaret gave them both, the prying glance that searched for guilt even beyond their first immeasurable guilt, and thought it found what it searched for. But Elspeth did not see that look; she only smelled the clean new smell of Margaret's clothes, sensed the air of comfortable opulence in the fur neckpiece and the smart traveling suit, felt only the sickening inferiority of her own plain dress, her own appearance, her own qualities of mind and body and soul, to the high excellence that inhered in everything Margaret's.

She went meekly into the house and helped Minnie prepare dinner while Margaret sat upstairs surrounded by the unopened bags and parcels that Alec had brought in, biting her lips with vexation at her foolishness in leaving the two alone. Their very humility gave them away. She had been a fool, a fool, fool, fool! During the ride out from town she had been almost passionately anxious to see them, to find them innocent and smiling again, but the lugubrious timidity of Elspeth in the doorway twisting her hands in her apron and Alec's frozen stiffness as he helped her down had been too full of the consciousness of guilt. She knew in her heart that they had sinned again, and once more the unforgiving core in her hardened.

Yet she was kind; in spite of herself, in defiance of herself, in defiance of her religion and her jealousy, there would creep out in her words and actions a feeling for their comfort. When, on Christmas Eve, she held the party that had been traditional with them for years, and invited the tenant farmers and their families to the house for games and refreshments and gifts, she made with her own hands, almost lovingly, the haggis that Alec loved, and she swallowed her repugnance for drink to send Ahlquist into Spring Mill for Christmas ale and wine. But when the tenants were gone and she could not find Alec she knew that Ahlquist had brought more than ale and wine, and that if she wanted to look she would find the two in the harness room with a bottle of whisky.

In a scorching fury she waited in the parlor until Elspeth had gone forlornly to bed, waited until the house was quiet and the four candles in the dining room threw wavering shadows in the deserted hall. Then she went to her room, carried downstairs the gifts she had bought in Chicago, and arranged them carefully under the Christmas tree; with furious care she placed them so that the name cards were up. " Christmas Greetings to Elspeth from Margaret." " The Season's Best Wishes to Her Husband from His Loving Wife: Alec from Margaret." Tinseled and gilded paper with snow scenes upon it, and her own careful printing underneath. Above them, when she had finished, she stood with clenched hands — too bitter to smile at the irony of her giving — and then she blew out the candles and went up to the bedroom whose door had never been open to Alec since that night in October, whose door he had never since tried to enter.

When the house was quiet again and the only sound was the rasp of bare oak limbs against the shingles, Elspeth quietly opened her door, tiptoed breathlessly past her sister's room down the stairs to the Christmas tree, and there laid beside the packages of Margaret her own offering, presents for both Alec and Margaret, things she had ordered by letter from Sac City the last time Ahlquist had been in.

And Elspeth had barely crept as soundlessly as a mouse back to her room before Alec opened the front door, creaked drunkenly to the tree, and laid his gifts beside the others in the dark.

None of them ever forgot the mockery of that Christmas, that gift-giving; that intolerable dinner whose turkey and dressing and cranberry sauce and delicate sweet ham and heaped vegetables and pumpkin and mince pie and papery-thin oatcake fairly shrieked for someone to enjoy it; that groaning table about which the three of them sat crushed by the heavy silence of the house, grateful for Minnie's clatter in the kitchen, grim with the cold thanks and the joyless unwrapping of presents, mocked by the Christmas tree glinting with decorations in the hall. None of them ever forgot how the kingly food was ashes in the mouth, how the gifts were bitter hostages to the hollow life they had tacitly consented to lead, derisive burlesques of affection and friendliness. And none of them, sitting without appetite at table, dressed for the holiday, stiff in broadcloth and brocade, could see any hope or promise in a future that stretched through interminable years frozen by the same guilt and shame.

Now December was done and over, and the snow of January piled in heavy curling drifts over fences and coops and against the windward faces of house and barn, and toward the end of January Margaret knew what she had suspected for some time. Elspeth had felt her eyes before; on a day when the snow was falling outside in coin-broad flakes, when the stair door was closed to keep the heat from going upstairs and the heatless parlor was shut tight, the girl sat in the dining room by the window when Margaret entered and stood in the doorway watching her. There were no words. Even Elspeth's impulse to shrink and cry out was never translated into action. Her head did not turn after the first sidelong look; her eyes remained fixed on the quiet flakes outside the window. And Margaret, intently staring, satisfied herself that what she believed was true, and left the room.

Then there were two of them sitting by the windows watching the feathery fall of snow: Elspeth by the boxed geraniums in the dining room, Margaret on the hard mahogany rocker in the icy parlor, both outwardly calm, both lacerated inwardly by emotions made all the stronger by their repression.

Margaret sat in the cold for over an hour, not heeding the periodic tense shivers that ran through her limbs, or the slow retreat of blood from hands and feet, or the tightening of throat and jaw in the chilly air. At last she rose quietly, threw a walking cape over her shoulders, and went outside. Elspeth saw her hurrying through the thick flakes to the men's house, saw her knock and stand waiting, her bare head powdered with white, saw Ahlquist come to the door and motion her in, saw the shake of her head, and then after a moment Ahlquist came out in a mackinaw and the two went across the lot and disappeared in the stable.

The girl felt no curiosity about what she saw. Margaret knew now — what she would do about it was locked behind the inscrutable stone mask she wore. Whatever she did it could not be worse than this endless and hopeless contrition, this purgatory of despairing expiation.

If Margaret could see it, others would soon be able to, but that thought was only a dull unhappiness, a moping wonder that she, Elspeth MacLeod, should be with child, and at the mercy of the sort of people who galloped about the countryside with such news. The tears that came were not tears of anguish, but of defenseless despairing shame; she sat with her knees touching the window box full of winter blooms, and watched the still, hurrying snow build hooded covers for every branch and twig in the oak outside, watched the brown clotted earth left by a recent thaw disappear slowly under the white.

On my grave, she thought, quiet snow on a quiet grave; yes, I do wish it, and the ache gone and the fever and only the cool and the snow. Maybe I'll die with the child, and end it for all of us, and there'll be no more forgetting, no more trying not to remember.

She thought of her quiet life in Glasgow, of her childhood and her mother, and the songs her mother had sung about the house. One particularly, an old ballad, and with the impact of a thrown missile the pertinence of that ballad to her own life struck her.

> Word's gane to the kitchen,
> And word's gane to the ha',
> That Marie Hamilton gangs wi' bairn
> To the hichest Stewart of a'.

Even the name, she thought; even the Stuart, and Margaret the auld Queen. The memory of her mother's figure dusting about the house was sharp reality, and the falling strains of the last stanza with its laconic implications of tragedy brought the tears so thick that she couldn't see the geraniums or the wavering snow.

Over and over, whispering, she sang the last stanza:

> Last nicht there was four Maries,
> The nicht there'll be but three;
> There was Marie Seton, and Marie Beton,
> And Marie Carmichael, and me.

" And me," she said, and caught her tears in her hands.

Out in the barn Margaret faced Ahlquist's unhurried questioning, her face drawn with cold and her eyes fixed on his impassive face. Ahlquist did not speak; he merely stood and waited as he seemed to wait for everything: fatalistic and immobile, like a great sad-eyed dog.

" You still want to go back to Norway? " Margaret asked. The strain she was under gave her words a harsh, snarling quality.

The Viking nodded and waited, patient, apparently not even curious.

" No matter what they say of you, or why they think you went? "

" What will that matter? " said Ahlquist simply. " I won't be here."

He knows! Margaret thought. He knows why I brought him out here and what I'm going to ask.

" I'll give you two hundred dollars to go back to your country," she said swiftly. " On one condition. Two, rather. Do you agree? "

In the Viking's eyes she caught something very like sympathy, and behind that a veiled irony, a quick intuitive intelligence that waited for her to come to the point he had already guessed.

" I never talk," Ahlquist said. " And I want to go right away. Is that it? "

" Tonight," Margaret said. " And you leave secretly. You tell no one you're going."

She pulled her purse from under the cape and opened it. As she began to count out bills the Norwegian interrupted her.

" One hundred is enough," he said. " I'd do it for you and Miss MacLeod for nothing if I had enough of my own to get me there."

Margaret's imperious control of herself gave way like an uncoiling spring. Her hand shook as she wadded an uncounted bundle of money into his hand and turned hastily to the door. Her " Thank you, Ahlquist," was choked and almost inaudible. After the door swung shut behind her Ahlquist stood quietly, his lips puckered and his face like that of a melancholy friendly big dog, and then he shoved the bills in his pocket and went back to his quarters to pack. Sometime before night, in the thick shrouding snowfall, he disappeared.

After dinner, when Elspeth had gone to her room and Alec sat reading the county newspaper, Margaret entered the dining room and spoke to him, her words tight, clipped, coldly restrained, but with something in her tone that hinted hysteria, as if that calm voice could at any moment break into cracked screaming.

" Ahlquist's gone," she said.

Alec lowered his newspaper. " Yes. How did you know? "

" I sent him."

" You what? "

" I gave him the money and asked him to go."

The hard tight vertical line appeared between Alec's brows and he dropped the paper on the floor. His voice, when it came, was flat.

" Why? "

Margaret — facing him squarely, seeing the anger in his eyes, feeling her own control going, fighting for it, hearing the hysteric edge in her words, wanting to blast him with her fury and hurt, and fighting that because she wanted to tell him calmly and cruelly — ended the deadlock of eyes and wills by spitting the words in his face.

" Because Elspeth's going to have a baby. You hear? My sister's going to have a baby! "

Her voice escaped her entirely, rose to a furious scream. " You hear? You hear? Now do you know why I gave him the money and sent him away? He knows. He knew already, and he knows the story we'll allow people to spread around. He knows he'll father a child not his. *But other people won't know!* You see now? You see why I sent him away? "

She caught at breath and control, and the frenzied scream died to a tense monotone.

" You left me no other choice. There's no one would marry her this far along, and there were only two men people could pin it on."

The anger in Alec's eyes had been replaced by something stubborn and defensive.

" I'll no' try to deny the child, Margaret."

" But you will! " said Margaret. " You've left me little enough, but that little I'll keep. If I have to I'll tell it myself, on my own sister, that Ahlquist is the man. You've taken what really counted, but I'll keep the husk of it, the name of it. You hear? "

And Alec, seeing her with the mask off, feeling the depth of her hurt, nodded slowly, knowing that whatever she demanded of him in future he would agree to.

" So be it then," he said.

V

Elspeth's child was born in June, a year almost to the day after she had arrived from Scotland. For three weeks the girl lay in her bed with her sunken bright eyes fixed on Margaret as she came and went with food, with changes and wrappers for the infant, with books and fruit and embroidery — books Elspeth never read, fruit she never ate, embroidery that never occupied her fingers. They piled up on the stand by her elbow while she watched Margaret with stricken eyes, and after a day or two Margaret would take them away and bring others. Always the older sister compelled speech into the narrow channel of the necessary, brief greetings and " good nights," inquiries as to the patient's comfort, suggestions of foods.

For she was kind. Even the armor of her efficiency could not hide that. Elspeth and the child were waited on by no one else. She would hardly even let Minnie prepare the broths and custards that went in to the sick woman. But when Elspeth nursed the baby Margaret would stand watching for a moment — for just a moment — with something lost and hungry on her lips and in her eyes, and then she would turn and go out.

And Elspeth would think of Margaret's letters in the past, telling how she wanted to bear Alec a child, a son, and the disappointment showing in the quiet written words when she told her sister that she apparently never could now. And now one in the house, Elspeth thought; and it not hers, so terribly not hers, and not mine either, not really mine. And she would hug the forlorn sickly little waif to her in an agony of love that could never be love, that could only be fear and reproach and sorrow, that would never quite forgive the agony of its birth and its fatherlessness.

When Margaret spoke to her after she was well again about christening the child, Elspeth shrank, feeling her son a child of darkness, never to be taken brutally out into the light for a public ceremony, unworthy of the ministrations of even such a minister as the Reverend Hitchcock. She could see the reactions of people she knew, hear their tongues wag.

" Must he be . . .? "

" Of course he must," said Margaret. " He has to have a name. Have you thought of one? "

Elspeth shook her head. Then, abruptly, as if offering her baby as an expiatory sacrifice, she said, " Would you give him a name? "

Margaret thought a moment, and when she spoke it was with unconscious cruelty.

" There's never been a Malcolm in our family. Would that do? Malcolm MacLeod? "

And Elspeth, thinking, " That's the way she puts it: *There's never been a Malcolm in our family* — as if he weren't worthy a name any of us have had," assented with a mute nod.

The next Sunday, through the silence and the veiled whispers of the few stragglers who had remained after church to watch, Margaret walked almost proudly up the aisle with the child squalling in her arms, and he was christened Malcolm MacLeod and dedicated to the service of Christ on earth. Elspeth was not there, nor was Alec.

And the years — the stifling nights of summer, windless and humid, the hot oppressive blackness when the three lay awake in different rooms listening to the petulant discomfort of the child and the curtains hung slack in wide-open windows; the interminable days when clothes clung to perspiring bodies and the oaks drooped under the fierce sun and the darkened parlor was the only passably cool room in the house; the slow ripening of September, the golden fields, the farm alive with strange men, huskers and threshers powdered with the bright dust of harvest, and in full view from the window of the haymow the incredible streak of flame that was the creek bed; and in October also the still wavering fall of leaves — and in the intervals between labor and labor the wild regret that was never to die, but was to be fed with silence and unforgiving and the avoidance of outward feeling until it grew into a shell of habit, so that for days at a time the three forgot the reasons for their watchful silence and the bleakness of their house. . . .

Winter swept its drifts against the broad barn; and the chickens (Elspeth's quail among them, now completely forgotten) pecked their wheat gingerly out of the granular snow. Every morning while light still seemed only a ghostly reflection from the drifts there would be the sound of saws as the Grimmitsch brothers worked at the woodpile, and there would be shouts as they drove the cattle out into the pen after milking, and there they would stand quietly with their breath blooming like flowers about their heads.

And the long rains of spring — when fields and roads were impassable quagmires and the overflowing creek spread out into the flats where in summer sunflowers grew; and after a time the green thrust of tulip and crocus blades against the warm south wall of the house, the fat popping of lilac buds, the yellow burgeoning of leafless forsythia, and from the loft window a countryside misted with green as delicate as thin smoke . . .

And the slow timeless revolution of the seasons — while the boy Malcolm grew frailly, and walked, and then talked, and his age became successively two and three and four and five, and he could be taken out in the buggy by Uncle Alec, and the two sharp-featured women in the big house would watch with emotions that they had almost ceased to recognize, but with an inflexible tight-lipped taciturnity as ingrained as the habits of sleeping or eating . . .

More and more they began to look alike. Elspeth, who never went out, even to church, dressed in sober black as if in a kind of mourning, and after the child was born Margaret too lost gradually the delight in dress that had made her the style-setter of a county, that had led her into Chicago or Omaha two or three times a year, that had filled her attic with fashion magazines and patterns and trunks of discarded clothes. In public Alec no longer called her " my lady." Her hair was no longer carefully pompadoured, but combed straight back from her high bony forehead. Her dresses, like Elspeth's, were fusty black relieved only by a bit of lace at the collar and the gold locket watch at her breast. By slow transition her dignity hardened into a stiff-backed formality.

Yet still, rigidly clinging to the patterns of her old life, she entertained neighbors and townspeople, defying their gossip until the passing years made it no longer a matter of any moment. Her table still groaned with food on Christmas and Thanksgiving and Easter, and though her parties lacked the gaiety that in old times had echoed through the rooms, she kept her friends. Even the children, who might have been afraid of her rigid black-frocked figure, were only curious. Something in her led them to come up and stare into her face. Something — perhaps her startling eyes, perhaps some subtly communicated kindliness beneath the forbidding old-maidishness of her person, made them come to her as they never came to Elspeth.

Alec, having given up the night Ahlquist left, poured his energies into his farms. When Malcolm was five years old he bought two full sections of rich bottom land adjoining his east acreage and recorded it in the boy's name. Every autumn when the rents came in he made a special trip to town to deposit them in Malcolm's account. At every opportunity he took the boy with him to the fields, on drives, into Chicago. When he was elected to the State Senate in Malcolm's sixth year they went together to Des Moines and stayed together through the entire session, Alec stuffing his nephew with candy, loading him with skates and sleds and toys, taking him to shows and plays. It was as if, single-handed, he was attempting to counteract the boy's home environment; as if by dragging him into the air, into the city, around the farms, he was trying to eradicate the pallor, blow away the timidity and silence that the child absorbed from the very walls of the house he lived in, relieve him from the psychic repression of the two women who were bringing him up.

The years that had smoothed Margaret's pompadour to a flat mousy wig — that had sunk her eyes and sharpened the straight ridge of her nose, that had transformed her queenly figure to a gaunt shape in sober black — the years that had driven Elspeth out of youth and into middle age before she passed twenty-five, that had made her a soft-stepping, quietly rustling, timid, pallid-faced housekeeper — had touched Alec more lightly. The face was more florid, with almost infinitesimal veins showing on nose and cheekbones. He was heavier, and his very size gave him a senatorial air of solidity and prosperous householdership. In the company of men he was still a great laugher, fond of horseplay and convivial company, and he was admired almost to adulation by the county he dominated. But around the house, with Elspeth or Margaret or even Malcolm, he moved and spoke guardedly, observing the wordless taboos of their relationship. Often he sat with a newspaper or a book for hours, ostensibly reading but actually watching the two women. And they, looking up to find his eyes on them, shifted under the brooding intensity of his look, squirmed like sullen rebuked children.

Malcolm and Alec were so much together that one winter Margaret was visited and revisited by a curious dream in which Alec and the boy walked hand in hand down a long gloomy corridor, and she could see their hands clasped together and their bare feet as they searched the shadowy pavement of the hall. Their hands and their bare feet and the glimmering white wedge of the boy's face she could always see as if a light shone out of the flesh, but Alec's face was no face in any of the recurrences of the dream, only a whitish blur that moved in the stealthy dark beside the white hands and white face and white moving feet of the boy. Miles and miles the two walked, the corridor opening always new gulfs of shadow before them. Sometimes Margaret's sleeping eyes saw them at a distance, the phosphorescent flesh wavering like incandescent moths in the dark. Then they were close, the boy's dark eyes upturned to the blur of Alec's face, and the sinews and cords of their linked hands clear to her watching eyes.

Four times Margaret had this dream, and each time she awoke clammy and trembling. For some reason that she could not define, that vaguely glowing blur above Alec's ghostly shoulders terrified her. And she never dreamed that dream without seeing at least once the close-up of those clinging and tightly clasped hands.

In the house Alec was always grave with Malcolm, but they went out frequently. What they did when they were gone Margaret never knew, but there was always warm color in the boy's cheeks when they returned, and in his eyes a lurking sly laughter as if over a secret joke, a sidelong twinkling glance that hardly ripped the decorum of his indoor face, but that caught its echo several times an evening in Alec's eyes.

Margaret never knew, but Elspeth did. One afternoon when Malcolm was eight she was picking peas and beans in the garden plot when she heard them coming up from the cornfield that now reached all the way to the flood plain of the creek. She heard Malcolm laugh, not the hesitant embarrassed chuckle that was his only evidence of lightheartedness around his two aunts — not that, but a gay, exuberant, whooping peal of merriment with all his lungs behind it, so startling that she bent farther below the protecting strip of sweet corn that screened her.

" You just ought to see one sometime," she heard Alec say. " There never were such caterpillars before or since. I skinned that one and we used his hide for a rug for years. It covered the whole hall floor where those rag ones are now. Finally the moths got to him and we had to throw him away."

" How long was his fur? " The boy's voice, curious, half jeering in good-humored disbelief, still gurgling with laughter.

" Oh, up to your knees, I expect. And thick! Just like a jungle. The cat used to hunt rabbits in it. He had a pelt, I tell you. If you happened to walk across it barefooted before you went to bed you couldn't sleep all night, you were so tickled. Just lie in bed and laugh till you ached."

" How could a moth eat his fur if it was so thick? "

The voices were growing fainter. Elspeth's straining ears just caught part of Alec's reply.

" These were Sac County moths. Big as a buzzard. Their jaws are gimlets that'll bore a two-inch hole . . ."

Standing in the garden behind the protecting fringe of sweet corn, Elspeth could see them walking hand in hand toward the house, and with an intuition that shrank at its own sharpness she predicted the exact moment when, passing the chicken yard, Malcolm's hand dropped from Alec's and the two figures moved apart to become not companions any more but just two people walking with each other.

That evening Malcolm looked up from his book and saw his Aunt Elspeth watching him with something dewy and eager in her bright sunken eyes, saw her prim lips trembling into softness, and he smiled his slow hesitant smile in return, rather surprised to find such an expression on the face of either of his aunts. Then the warmth went out of his aunt's eyes and her lips tightened again, and Malcolm had no way of knowing that she had been trying to come out of the shell that bound her, that she had been urging him to laughter, trying to tell him that she too had known laughter and a light heart. She too remembered angleworms so long that a hen worked ten hours to pull one from its hole. She remembered the spotted cow that fell in the quicksand and came out a giraffe. She remembered nonsense and joyous preposterous horseplay, and all the hunger of nine years had been in her face as she looked at Malcolm.

But Malcolm had no way of knowing, and he did not even suspect that when his Aunt Elspeth left the room a moment later she went up to her room to cry with a bitterness that racked her bony chest and left her exhausted, to cry as she had not cried in nine years, and to lie miserably in the dark looking back through the loveless unforgiving repression that had become her life, remembering as she had never dared remember the few gay months after her arrival from Scotland when she was still a girl and laughter had not yet gone from her life.

And Alec had not forgotten. Away from the house he was teaching Malcolm to laugh, blowing out of him the rheumatic chilly damp of the bleak house, drawing him away from the depressing and frozen-faced kindness of his aunts. His aunts! Elspeth sneered in the face of that lie and what had come of it. Witches, the two of them, hags; one afraid to play with the boy because that would be presuming to show herself his mother, the other refusing because by doing so she condoned the crime of his birth, condoned her own betrayal by stooping to show affection for her sister's and her husband's son.

Hags, Elspeth thought; witches that haunt the child and he growing up crushed and timid and pale, yet all of us loving him as we can love nothing else. Margaret too, I know she does, it shows in her, but she won't let herself admit it. All of us, and only Alec able to help him at all, only Alec remembering laughter and a light heart.

The years passed like sand under the feet of the four, the seasons swung in the same long rhythm from the first robin and the swelling lilac buds to breathless summer heat and the metallic trill of locusts and in the evenings fireflies starring the tangible velvet of the air; from the dying flame of sumac and soft maple into the long pointless waiting of winter, and back to the thrust of crocus blades under the last snow.

The house grew old with its occupants, the horsehair sofa was replaced by a broad oak settee with leather cushions, wallpaper changed at three-year intervals. Wilton rugs covered the floors instead of the worn Brussels carpets, but actually there was little change from the somber coloring of the years, no alleviation of the bleakness that was like a chill in the bones of the building. Its rooms kept their imperviousness to redecoration and warmth; laughter was as unthinkable as a bright dress on one of the sisters.

Nothing, not even the sisters, changed. They might have been twins, and they might have been any age from thirty to fifty. In the two years after Malcolm's birth they had attained a kind of dry agelessness as durable as stone. Only their eyes remained youthful and alive, deeply sunken and ice-blue, bright, alert as the eyes of animals.

Nothing changed. Even Minnie, who had left them to be married to a farmer ten miles away, had seen her husband and her one child die in a flaming barn, and was back in her old place after a four-year absence.

Malcolm was with them only during the summers now. At fourteen he was sent to school in Sac City, where he boarded with friends. When he left, his two aunts silently packed his trunk and stood by the door watching, not waving, not even smiling, yet somehow communicating love, good wishes, solicitude. Having learned observation from his elders the boy had a feeling, as the last bundle was stowed away and as he sat waiting in the front seat of the Case automobile his uncle had bought that spring, that both women were very close to tears. A word or a gesture, he thought, might bring them to him to shower him with kisses and hugs. But he shrank from that possibility as he would have shrunk from cursing them. The thought of either of them displaying any feeling was intolerable.

Alec swung the crank, the motor thundered, and they were off down the lane of perfect elms. When he looked back to wave, Malcolm saw the two black figures still motionless against the white wall of the house, and his wave received no answer.

For three years Malcolm left in this way, wondering at the strangeness of his aunts, but forgetting them in the warmth of his uncle's company before they had passed Paxleys'. For three years he returned in June to find the two women standing just where he had left them the autumn before, as if time had fixed them forever in that attitude of silent hail and farewell. They greeted him with a word and a shake of the hand and something in the eyes like a smile, and there was nothing in their demeanor to tell him that since early morning neither had left her chair by a strategic window, and that what he took for a softening like a smile in the ice-blue eyes might have been caused by the strain of watching the road for hours as intently as one watches at a deathbed.

A few days after returning from his third year of high school Malcolm gave evidence that the long lie about his parentage was beginning to wear thin. Alec was tinkering with the car in the machine shed when the boy entered.

" Want a job? " Alec asked.

" Sure."

" Hold this."

Malcolm held the wrench while Alec fumbled underneath to tighten a nut, and as they leaned together over the motor the boy asked the question that had been burning in him for months.

" Look," he said. " Who am I? "

" Eh? "

Alec dropped the nut and groped for it an unnecessarily long time. When he raised his head whatever had been in his face was carefully veiled.

" Who am I? "

" My nephew. Who did you think you were, the Crown Prince? "

But Alec's jocularity left Malcolm untouched.

" No, I want to know who I really am. You say my mother was Aunt Margaret's sister who died, and that my father's dead too."

" That's right," Alec said quietly.

" Well," said Malcolm, " I met Jim Paxley in Sac City and he said ' Hello, Ahlquist.' Where'd he get that? Is my name really Ahlquist? "

" No," said Alec. " Take my word for it, your name's not Ahlquist."

" Seems to me I've heard that name before," Malcolm said. " Haven't I heard you mention somebody named Ahlquist that used to work for you? "

" Maybe. He went back to Norway before you were born."

" Well, why is my name MacLeod, when that's Aunt Elspeth's name, and Aunt Margaret's maiden name? "

" Accident," Alec said shortly. " Your mother happened to marry a man with the same name. There's plenty of MacLeods in Scotland. Whole clans of 'em."

" Maybe I'm just stupid," Malcolm said. " Paxley seemed to think it was a great joke to call me Ahlquist."

" It wouldn't take much to amuse that Paxley," Alec said. " Here, take the crank and turn it over slow, will you, while I have a look? "

During that summer Malcolm asked no more questions, but Alec was increasingly aware that the two women of the house were not the only ones who could hide their thoughts behind an impenetrable mask, and one night when they were alone he spoke to Margaret.

" We'll send Malcolm to Chicago to school the coming year."

" Why? "

" They're starting to call him Ahlquist in Sac."

The mask of Margaret's face did not change expression.

" In that case he'd better go to Chicago," she said.

Malcolm's departure for Chicago was delayed almost a month by an epidemic that closed the schools, so that it was early October before he packed and got through the preliminaries of leaving. Two nights before he was to go, the boy and his aunts were sitting down to dinner when Alec entered the front door. Margaret, at the kitchen end of the table, looked up to see him standing slumped and nerveless in the hall, with his hand on the knob behind him, and her fingers tightened on the dish she was passing.

Now he's taken to coming drunk to dinner, she thought. Her blood was racing with the old furious protest, but the mask of her face was expressionless, and her " Will you have some asparagus, Malcolm? " was quiet and even.

As Alec came in and sat down only Malcolm spoke, and his ineffectual greeting trailed off into the electric silence. In the lamplight Alec's face looked ghastly: the eyes ringed darkly and the lips touched faintly with blue. *Getting to look like a drunkard,* said Margaret's hissing mind, *and bringing it in here for the boy to see.*

Without a word, in the uncomfortable silence that hung over the table, Alec reached out for the dish Elspeth passed, helped himself, and started to put it down. Then, while the eyes of Malcolm were bent in embarrassment on the food he was eating, while Margaret was burning behind her mask with the old violence that would never down, while Elspeth was rigid with the terror that came upon her when the tension of unspoken and hoarded wrong was in the air — while all three thought him drunk and reacted to that belief — Alec died instantly, with a little gurgle in his throat.

The dish dropped to the table, his body fell forward across the corner of the board, tipping it, and as the two women sprang up, Alec slid sideways, pulling the tablecloth and dishes down upon himself, and Malcolm leaped with a strangling cry to his uncle's side.

Minnie, running in from the kitchen at the crash, saw Margaret and Elspeth standing stiffly, their masks off now, Margaret's hand against her mouth to stifle a scream, Elspeth whimpering through contorted lips, and before them the wrecked table and Malcolm bending over his uncle's body.

Malcolm's head turned.

" Help me," he said.

With Minnie helping he carried Alec to the broad leather settee in the parlor, the two aunts trailing like sleepwalkers behind. There, after a frenzied five minutes of feeling for pulse in the stiffening wrist, Malcolm turned abruptly and ran outside. The three women stood silently in the gloomy parlor, and the bleakness of the house seeped upon them as heavy as black fog.

In the stillness they heard the automobile burst into full roar, heard the clash of its gears and the reckless explosion of gravel as it whirled heavily into the lane. Like one walking in sleep Margaret moved to pull the blinds upon the already dark room, brought the lamp from the dining room and set it, turned low, upon the mantel — moved it because it shed too much light on Alec's dead face.

Across the noise of Minnie's crying the two sisters looked at each other, their eyes meeting frankly for the first time in eighteen years.

" Maybe I'd better fix his bed," Elspeth said weakly. " Malcolm must have gone for the doctor."

" I'll fix it! "

Margaret went up the stairs with firm steps, and Elspeth, alone with the body of Alec, stood watching him, wanting to smooth the twisted lips and straighten the rumpled hair, but not daring. When she realized how fully she did not dare she went into the dining room and wept.

EPILOGUE

There were no more buggies or cars turning into the lane now. With a last look at the quiet spread of level countryside Margaret Stuart rose awkwardly from the little mahogany rocker, and the noise from the other rooms rose with her. The scent of flowers was overpowering, a sticky, decaying sweetness of roses and lilies strong with the smell of death.

Composedly, quietly, Margaret walked into the hall and through the people who greeted her and made way into the dining room where before the windows Alec's coffin lay on a scaffolding completely smothered in flowers.

The noise of conversation and the sympathetic sniffling of women fell off gradually and died to a waiting silence as Margaret stood by the coffin and took a last look at her husband's face. Elspeth, sitting behind and to one side, saw no change in the parchment of her sister's face, no quivering of the lips, no relaxation of the inflexible rigidity of her body. Then Margaret stepped back, nodded to the minister, and sat down between Elspeth and Malcolm while the Reverend Hitchcock wet his red lips and bent his head over the casket.

"Let us pray," he said.

For three quarters of an hour he bleated through a panegyric on Alec Stuart, whom he had never liked, and women standing in the hall wiped their eyes furtively and men coughed. Margaret sat dry-eyed, conscious of Elspeth and Malcolm beside her on the high dining room chairs, sensing with emotionless clearness the violence of the boy's grief and Elspeth's tense self-control, realizing with an almost smiling wonder that the Reverend Hitchcock was even more stupid than Alec and Elspeth had thought him, rebelling at the voice bleating "In my Father's house are m-aaaa-ny m-aaaa-nsions" while she recalled Alec's contemptuous doubt if the preacher had any blood in him at all. Fool to plan a big funeral, she thought. Fool to have Hitchcock preach — the only person in the room who didn't like Alec, who isn't genuinely sorry, and he giving the sermon, lying with every word, doing God's office for the fee in it.

And when the long ride to the cemetery and back was over, and the minister had taken his fee and gone and the buggies and cars had one by one passed through the tunnel of elms to the road, it was with a feeling of tired relief that Margaret took off her plain black bonnet and helped Minnie clear the house of the remaining flowers.

Since Alec's death Malcolm had been gloomily silent, wrapped in profound morbid isolation. After the funeral he spent the afternoon pacing back and forth through the crisp leaves of the back lawn, and both his aunts noticed the haggard weariness in the youth's face, the tight vertical wrinkle between his eyes that was so much like Alec's expression when angry or intent.

The wrinkle was still there at breakfast the next morning, and when the three were finished Malcolm rose.

"Will you come into the living room?" he said. "I have to talk to you."

There was something so troubled and unhappy and miserably stubborn in the boy's eyes that Elspeth sat down with the old freezing anticipation of an emotional crisis, shooting an oblique glance at Margaret to see if she felt it too, but finding no change in the bony masklike face.

For some time the boy sat uncomfortably studying his hands, and when he spoke it was with an effort that strained his voice to the cracking point. What he said, turning full toward Elspeth where she sat with her hands twisted in her apron, was "You're my mother, aren't you?"

Elspeth's breath hissed in her throat. The gaunt figure of Margaret never moved.

"And Uncle Alec was my father, wasn't he?"

Neither of the sisters answered.

"I'm sorry," Malcolm said wretchedly. "I'm awfully sorry; but I've thought so for a long while, and now I've got to know."

He looked at Elspeth stubbornly, and she broke under his look to bury her face in the back of the settee.

"I'm sorry," Malcolm mumbled again. Then he broke out to Margaret: "Did Uncle . . . Did my father leave a will?"

"You're taken care of," Margaret said. Her voice was flat, dead, carefully void of expression. "Two farms are in your name, and there's something like a thousand dollars in your account in Sac City. There's also a thousand dollars in cash left you in his will, and five thousand in bonds for your schooling."

"So much?"

In the boy's words there was no exultation, only a sad moping wonder that death should have left him with what would have been under ordinary circumstances boundless wealth.

"I'm going away," he said. "I'll need some of that money — not all."

"I'll get your bank book."

Margaret went quietly out and returned in a moment with the book.

Malcolm took it, his eyes on the cowering figure of his mother still twisted sideways to cry into the curve of her arm. When he looked back at Margaret her lip was bitten up between her teeth and her eyes filmed with hot tears. With a swift step he was beside her, had stooped and kissed her thin hard mouth, and then he had lifted Elspeth gently, kissed her too, tasting the salt of her tears. The sight of both these hard old women crying unnerved him, and he choked.

"Good-by, Mother," he said. "Good-by, Aunt Margaret."

He started out, but Elspeth leaped to her feet to run after him.

"You'll write, Malcolm? You'll write often?"

"Every week," Malcolm said. "I don't know where I'm going yet — not to school for a while, anyway — but I'll write."

Standing in the doorway before these two old women who had brought him up, the old-woman aunt of forty-seven and the equally old-woman mother of forty — realizing with sentimental, youthful incompleteness the gray imprisonment that their lives must have been — he wanted to bow his head and weep for the bitterness of their living; but the tears choked him and he turned with a wave of the hand and went out. A few minutes later the two sisters, peering sharp-featured out the window, saw him drive out of the machine shed with Tom Grimmitsch and head out toward the road.

They watched until the car turned right up the hill past Paxley's, and then with something like a sigh they turned to face each other in the empty and depressing house.

In that moment, looking at each other for the third time since Alec's death across the barrier of eighteen gray years, they were sisters again. The cause of their trouble was gone, secure and peaceful in October earth. Malcolm was gone, freed from the grimness of the house he had been born in. The guilt and the shame and the unforgiving and the expiation were gone, and both women knew it as surely as if Margaret had put her arms around Elspeth and said, " Oh, Elspeth, the sword has been drawn between us for so many years, the bitterness and the unforgivingness and the regret have already taken so much from us, the acid of our wrongs has eaten the love and kindness and lightheartedness out of our lives through so many seasons . . ."

She might have said it — the impulse was there, the barriers weakened by Alec's death and Malcolm's leaving and Elspeth's tears. The jealous hurt and the wrong were shadows of far away and long ago, and the cause of them buried under mounded earth already drifted with October leaves.

But as surely as they knew that they were sisters again, they knew that they were old women. Eighteen years of sunless living lay upon them like a blight, and with Malcolm had gone their last hold upon that life which still knew laughter and a light heart. They were two old women sentenced to the prison they had made for themselves, doomed to wear away slowly, toughly; to fade and wither and dry up inch by inch in the silence of their house.

Their look broke, and Margaret glanced at the locket watch against the flat stiff poplin of her breast.

" We'd best go and straighten up Malcolm's room," she said.

NOTES

NOTES

Portraits

LINCOLN STEFFENS: I Become a Student

Lincoln Steffens (1866–1936) was one of America's great reporters during the "muckraking" years at the beginning of the century. In a series of scathing essays in *McClure's Magazine,* later published as *The Shame of the Cities* (1904), he laid bare the corruption accompanying boss rule in many of America's large cities. He knew and understood political bosses and reformers, and with a certain cynicism, grew to prefer the bosses — because they were good politicians, and, despite graft and lawlessness, usually gave value received. During the war years Steffens was in Mexico and Russia, and later was a spectator at Versailles. To the end of his life the old spark of "hunting the story" was ever in his eyes. Within the present generation his most influential work has been his provocative *Autobiography,* from which "I Become a Student" is drawn.

"I worked for [Nixon]; I worked more, much more, for myself." This sentence lies at the heart of Steffens' attitude toward knowledge, and in a sense epitomizes the difference between the mature student and the average loafer of whom Steffens is contemptuous. In criticizing his contemporaries in college, is Steffens a cynic, or does his attitude seem thoroughly justified? Are college students today as irresponsible as Steffens considered most of his own classmates? Steffens' methods of preparing for entrance examinations to the University of California may suggest the self-direction often found in present-day progressive schools. Would Steffens' preparation be practical or impractical for work in an average college or university today? Should he have had more orderly discipline before he entered college? Should students be encouraged to follow out their personal interests, as Steffens did, to the neglect of some of their other courses? Discuss any discoveries you have made comparable to Steffens' concerning the relativity of knowledge. Have you encountered any "liberating" mind such as that of Steffens' Mr. Nixon? In what respects were you influenced? Are adults in danger of becoming less well educated as they grow older? Explain the apparent paradox on page 4: "With all their knowledge they knew no essential truth." Do students today still want to be told what to learn? Upon entering college, how did your own state of mind compare to Steffens'? Explain intellectual curiosity, using a concrete example or two. One of the tests of your own intellectual curiosity may be the challenge of Steffens on the subject of the undemocratic Founding Fathers (p. 7). Were you curious to know what Charles A. Beard's *An Economic Interpretation of the Constitution* might say on the subject — and, if he is to be believed, just when America began to be democratic? Consult the library card catalog for titles of books by Beard which might indicate his political and social sympathies.

Suggestions for writing: The inspiring teacher. My private method of preparing for college. The relativity of truth (examine various interpretations of a historical problem — *e.g.* the sinking of the *Lusitania,* the causes of the Mexican War, the Scopes evolution trial). Education outside the classroom. Should college be vocational or cultural? Education for leisure. The pleasures of intellectual curiosity. Compare Steffens at California with Vincent Sheean (*Personal History*) at Chicago.

CLARENCE DARROW: My Home

Clarence Darrow (1857–1938) was for many years America's most prominent criminal lawyer. In spectacular lawsuits he defended, among others, Eugene V. Debs, the socialist leader; the McNamara brothers, on trial for dynamiting the Los Angeles *Times;* Loeb and Leopold, the Chicago kidnapers; and Charles T. Scopes, charged with teaching evolution in Tennessee. Throughout his life he was a liberal and crusaded for the extension of human rights and the spread of tolerance. He was a consummately shrewd lawyer whose every move in a trial attracted front-page publicity. In the Scopes trial, for instance, when he was pitted against William Jennings Bryan, he quoted Scripture to the complete confusion of his fundamentalist opponent who wanted to call him an atheist. A life in the headlines made him seem a garish figure, but in *Farmington* (1904) and *The Story of My Life* (1932), he revealed himself as a person of depth and sensitivity.

In this chapter from his autobiography *Farmington,* Darrow is primarily interested in contrasting the romantic and sentimental stories of family affection with the conditions he knew in his own family circle. If the picture seems somewhat bleak, has Darrow merely removed the warm coloring of fiction, or is his family environment exceptional? What emphasis does he put on the term " Puritanic "? Must all parents seem rather remote in the eyes of their children, or is close companionship frequent enough today to be characteristic? What gains or losses can you see in Darrow's family atmosphere as compared with that in which you grew up? Would urban surroundings alter the relationship of parents and children? What kind of home produces the greatest feeling of family solidarity? Consult the 1925–28 volume of the *Readers' Guide to Periodical Literature* for a list of magazine articles by and about Darrow during a period when he was nationally conspicuous.

Suggestions for writing: On bringing up parents. Clarence Day and his father (as seen in his book, *Life with Father*). On being an only child. Etiquette for parents. The family of tomorrow. Justice to the hard-boiled parent. George Washington as a parent (if the cherry-tree story were true). Steffens on Darrow (see Steffens' *Autobiography,* pp. 658 ff.).

SAMUEL L. CLEMENS: Learning the River

Samuel L. Clemens (Mark Twain) grew up in the Mississippi River country, and became a river pilot in the golden days of the side-wheelers before the Civil War. His autobiographical volume published years later is a genuine period piece, full of characteristic good-humored gusto; and *Life on the Mississippi* not only pictures Clemens' youth, but in a series of nostaligic chapters records the decline of the steamboat and the passing of the unique race of pilots.

In "Learning the River" you will note a different autobiographical method from that followed by Steffens and Darrow. To what extent does each author become philosophical? Compare the amount of narrative content in each of the three essays. Might Steffens have employed Clemens' anecdotal method with good effect? Note Clemens' skillful handling of a basic expository problem in arrangement and chronology — an outline of the essay will reveal the unobtrusive orderliness. The tone of each of the first three essays is distinctive — characterize each in a word or phrase. The derivation of Clemens' pseudonym is explained in "Learning the River" — but "mark twain" itself may need explanation. The unit of nautical depth is the fathom (Old English for "outstretched arms"), 6 feet. Half twain is 2½ fathoms or 15 feet, mark twain exactly 2 fathoms or 12 feet, and so forth. Look up "texas," "leadsman," and "snag" in *Webster's New International Dictionary* (1934) and the *Oxford English Dictionary* (1888–1933). Comment on the different purposes served by each dictionary.

Suggestions for writing: Mr. Nixon and Mr. Bixby as teachers. On being overwhelmed by a new job. The art of kibitzing. The cub pilot's chances of success. "A woman could handle Mr. Bixby." The river steamboat still lives. Showboat, twentieth-century version. If Lincoln Steffens were learning the river.

HENRY DAVID THOREAU: Where I Lived, and What I Lived For

America has given birth to a host of individualists, men who pursued their own way oblivious to the crowd. Henry David Thoreau (1817–1862) was certainly one of these, but he was more than an eccentric. As he went through life he seemed constantly to demand that the traditional, the commonly accepted attitude toward any situation should justify itself anew in his eyes. In a later age he might have been a cynic, but in New England's golden day his skepticism was easily outweighed by an idealism that gave him confidence in his own judgment.

In his zeal for experimenting before arriving at a standard of values, Thoreau built a cabin on Walden Pond and lived in it for two years. But he enjoyed his mother's cooking too much to be a complete hermit, and according to his biographers he was seen frequently about Concord. Nevertheless his experiment was unusual in that, as he says, he wanted to reduce life to its lowest terms, to learn whether it was mean or sublime, to see if renunciation were worth practicing. He recounts with a puckish air building his house for $28.12½ and spending about a dollar a month for food; but it is clear that of first importance was the new perspective on the world which a life of independence and contemplation brought him.

Here is autobiography almost entirely on an intellectual level. But Thoreau, although he is philosophical, is stubbornly seeking the answer to a most important practical problem: what is really important in life? Many of his paradoxes are worth close examination. Consider, for instance, his attitude toward letters and the news (p. 28), and his statement that a poet often enjoys the most valuable part of a farm (p. 22). What does Thoreau mean by the "auroral character" of his first day at Walden? Explain how this idea is symbolically developed later in the essay. Contrast the tone and content of the two parts of the essay. In the light of Thoreau's paragraph on news, how might he interpret the important events of this century? Paraphrase the concluding two sentences of the essay in concrete language. Look at the sketch of Thoreau in the *Dictionary of American Biography* to see how the period at Walden is related to the philosopher's whole career.

Suggestions for writing: " As long as possible live free and uncommitted." The questions Thoreau would have asked on a Mississippi steamer. Thoreau's curiosity. " Things are in the saddle and ride mankind." Was Thoreau antisocial? Parallels between Thoreau and Henry Adams (see *The Education of Henry Adams,* chapters 20, 21).

THOMAS HART BENTON: Rodeo

Thomas Hart Benton (1899–   ) belongs to a generation of American artists who have declared their intellectual independence of Europe, and have turned to native subject-matter and technique with highly significant results. Gerald Bywaters' " Contemporary American Artists " contains an excellent brief biographical and critical sketch of Benton (pp. 270–272). The same wry sense of humor that is evident in his lithographs and murals is present in his prose, and it made *An Artist in America* a best-seller. This volume is not only a *confessio* and a *credo,* but, because Benton discovered the real America by hitchhiking, it is also rich in vignettes of common folk the country over.

Despite his activities near the corrals as " official artist," Benton is primarily interested in people. Notice that for him the rodeo is full of human interest, and very little space is devoted to the actual business of the afternoon. And Benton paints with a few bold strokes; in a very few sentences Montana and Jim quickly come alive. Part of his effect derives from the authentic colloquial dialogue, but it is significant that Montana is depicted without conversation. Why is the informal tone of " Rodeo " preserved throughout? Compare Benton's style with that of Clarence King in " Wayside Pikes," where there is a much greater gulf between King's literary diction and the spoken language. What characteristics of subject-matter and point of view distinguish Benton's vignette from the more formal essay of Thoreau? To what degree are the differences explained by the widely separated dates of composition? Notice the use of the Denver *Post* motif to give " Rodeo " a crisp, effective ending. Benton makes much of the sheepherders; but whether he knew it or not, to a cowboy the word " sheepherder " is not so much a descriptive term as a piece of insulting profanity. Despite Benton's affability he has had his share of controversies. Consult the *New York Times Index* for 1937 for references to the dispute over his murals in the Missouri capitol.

Suggestion for writing: Recount some personal experience, being careful to avoid flatness or banality by giving it genuine human interest and by introducing some recurrent detail which will give a particular fillip to the close.

CLARENCE KING: Wayside Pikes

Clarence King (1842–1901) was perhaps the outstanding public geologist of the nineteenth century. He was trained in the Sheffield Scientific School at Yale, and was responsible for the systematic geological survey of California. He helped to organize the United States Geological Survey and was its first director; he was chief of a group that made the first thorough survey of the 40th parallel; and he occupied his later years as a mining engineer and adviser in mining suits. One of his most widely publicized exploits was the exposure of a great diamond fraud in 1872 (see A. J. Liebling, " The American Golconda," *The New Yorker,* November 16, 1940). His vivid volume, *Mountaineering in the Sierra Nevada,* brought him to the attention of a large public. One of his singular friendships was with Henry Adams, who wrote warmly of him in *The Education.*

In " Wayside Pikes " King is writing of the Sequoia district in the southern Sierras which he first discovered. The Newtys, as he himself says, are a symbol of the tragedies of westward migration, and they are doubly characteristic since they are from the legendary Pike County, Missouri. King impresses one with his ability to see the Newtys completely in perspective, but he never loses his own identity, nor does he drop the pose of objectivity long enough to be intimately sympathetic. Compare his tone and his literary style with that of Benton; how can the significant differences be explained? As for the Newtys themselves, are they to be pitied? What seem to be King's explanations for their " social disintegration "? Has he really understood the cause of Mr. Newty's restlessness — is Newty's " permanent discontent " of his own making? What is to be said in defense of King's occasional condescension? Notice that had he concluded the sketch with Mr. Newty's remark that the man who married Susan would get half the hogs, the anecdote would have assumed major importance. How is the emphasis altered by the paragraphs that follow this remark? Compare the sketches of King's career in the *Encyclopædia Britannica* and the *Encyclopedia Americana.*

Suggestions for writing: Mr. Newty and the Okies. Beyond the frontier with Mark Twain (based upon *Roughing It*). The lure of the far-away. An economic interpretation of the Newtys. The Matanuska migration. Population shifts in the United States. King's California exploits. Unmasking the great diamond fraud.

Heywood Broun: Shooting the Young Idea

The word " militant " has always characterized Heywood Broun (1888–1939). During the first World War he reported inefficiency in the War Department and lost his job as correspondent for the A.E.F. Later he attacked the post-war redbaiting of A. Mitchell Palmer and during the twenties loosed his irony and invective against the Ku Klux Klan and bogus liberals wherever they flourished. He resigned his post on the New York *World* when it refused to print his columns on Sacco and Vanzetti, " the first violent newspaper pieces I had ever done." He was later rehired and discharged, this time for an article in the *Nation* (reprinted in *It Seems to Me*) insisting that the *World* was not a genuinely liberal newspaper. During the thirties his militancy took on a political cast. He ran an unsuccessful race for Congress and was a founder and first president of the Newspaper Guild. He was a constant contributor to the liberal weeklies and his daily column was widely syndicated. A vigorous man, he was usually good-natured, though his ideas were occasionally fumbled under the strain of the daily deadline. " He wedded his wit to his indignation, his pity to his humor," wrote one critic. And the writing reveals the man.

In " Shooting the Young Idea " (the title, by the way, is a playful paraphrase of James Thomson's line, " to teach the young idea to shoot "), Broun casts a half-nostalgic eye upon his schooldays. Like Steffens he does not approve of all that passed for education in his boyhood, and in this respect the two share a hard-boiled anti-sentimental attitude characteristic of much American writing in the twenties and thirties. Underneath, however, both men have room for honest sentiment, both are inclined to assume a misleading air of objectivity. This is especially true of Broun's humility, which is exaggerated for dramatic effect. This essay is provocative because Broun's reactions are lively and extrovert, and also because his criticisms of education have validity. Do similar conflicts between your own technique and the method of the school (p. 47) exist today? Are picayune prohibitions such as the crooked forefinger noticeable in modern school systems? Grammar is threatened with becoming a lost art. Compare Broun's experience (p. 48) with your own. Explain Broun's percentages in the paragraph on " shall " and " will." Broun remembers vividly the occasion when " for the first time in my life I conceived of any great public question as having two sides." Has modern education followed Broun's Canadian teacher very far toward objectivity? Do you agree with Broun's stand on " the expression of dissent " (p. 50)? In this connection Justice Holmes' opinion (a dissenting one, at that) in a free speech case is very enlightening. See pages 185–188. What should be Broun's chief objections to the way he was taught English? What was the single tax? See a brief article on the subject in the *Dictionary of American History*. Expand Broun's references to John Brown and C. T. Copeland.

Suggestions for writing: Shortcomings or conflicts in your own early schooling. Kenneth Roberts' *Oliver Wiswell* as an example of the " other side " of the Revolutionary War. Combating popular prejudices. Free speech — for whom? The difficulties of writing well. Contrast Broun's memories of Kittredge with Stuart P. Sherman's (pp. 53–56).

Stuart P. Sherman: George Lyman Kittredge

Stuart P. Sherman (1881–1926) had a brief but brilliant career as teacher, editor, and author. After graduating at Williams College in 1903 he came to Harvard for his doctorate under Kittredge. Then followed almost two decades of teaching, at Northwestern and at Illinois, where he quickly became prominent through reviews and essays in the *Nation*. In 1924 he became editor of *Books,* the New York *Herald-Tribune* literary supplement, and raised it to a position of national distinction in the two years before his death in 1926. Critically he espoused Matthew Arnold's respect for tradition in *On Contemporary Literature* (1917), a volume which began a somewhat acrimonious duel with H. L. Mencken. Gradually, however, after a period of extreme chauvinism during the first World War, he began to change his position; and where he had stoutly defended the Puritan spirit he came, before his death, to desert humanism and speak favorably of such moderns as Sherwood Anderson, Theodore Dreiser, and D. H. Lawrence. This critical about-face may be traced in *Americans* (1922), *The Genius of America* (1923), *Points of View* (1924) and *Critical Woodcuts* (1926).

The close-up portrait of Professor Kittredge (1860–   ) concentrates almost entirely on his activities as a teacher, perhaps because for Kittredge teaching and the scholarship that inseparably went with it have been his whole life. Sherman's wit and irony are at once unmistakable; and in addition to these rhetorical devices he uses anecdote to make his portrait vivid and intimate. There is a constant " edge " in his style. In his opening paragraph, why does he enclose " productive scholarship " in quotation marks? There are barbed shafts in his description of several " new styles of teaching." From your experience would you extend Sherman's catalog? We are told that Mr. Kittredge " assumes nothing but the general ignorance, indolence, and inattentiveness of undisciplined youth," and that he is therefore " an educational realist." Do you agree? Does Kittredge's method with undergraduates seem negative to you, or would you enjoy a real challenge such as he offers? Why should Kittredge distinguish between his graduate and his undergraduate manner? Do you think he is being two-faced and hypocritical, or do you believe that Sherman makes a good case for the two approaches? Explain " Jupiter Tonans," and justify Sherman's application of the phrase to Kittredge. What are *obiter dicta* that they should be handed down from year to year by graduate students? Sherman speaks (p. 55) of the " unrelenting ardor " with which one fixed attention on minutiae of scholarship in a Kittredge seminar. What is the value of such procedure? Does Sherman offer any explanation for the students' " spellbound gravity "? What, finally, are the characteristics that made Kittredge a great teacher in Sherman's eyes? For a clearer insight to Sherman's personality, see Kunitz and others, *Authors Today and Yesterday.*

Suggestions for writing: If Lincoln Steffens had studied under Kittredge. " Negative psychology is often good psychology in teaching." The most impressive teacher I have known. Is " scholarship " worth its while? " Youth needs a firm hand to discipline it." Explain Heywood Broun's reaction to Kittredge (p. 51). " Giving the students a good show will not perforce educate them."

JAMES PARTON: Charles Goodyear

James Parton (1822–1891) was an outstanding American biographer of the nineteenth century. His success began with *The Life of Horace Greeley* (1855) and continued through a long list whose subjects included Aaron Burr, Jackson, Franklin, John Jacob Astor, Jefferson, and Voltaire. He was the third husband of Sara Payson Willis, the " Fanny Fern " of sentimental fame, and after her death he married his stepdaughter, Ellen Willis Eldredge. In him the crusading spirit frequently came to the fore: he wrote a tract against smoking and drinking, and before he married " Fanny Fern " he championed her cause against her editor brother, N. P. Willis, who had refused to publish her writings. As a biographer he was not always an incisive analyst, but he was painstaking and orderly, and writing in a popular style he created an animated picture of his subject. His lives of Franklin and Jefferson remain to this day the best for the general reader.

Parton's short biography of Charles Goodyear reveals the inventor as a man of less than heroic proportions. Goodyear's career provides Parton with a *chronological* outline which he follows except for a few digressions that are related *logically* to the whole. Notice how he sustains interest through the ever darkening " hard luck " story. Why does Parton seem to be more general from page 73 onward when success finally comes to Goodyear? Aside from the fact that this is more detailed, how does the account of Goodyear differ from that of Kittredge? Of Theodore Roosevelt (" The Happy Warrior," p. 80)? Make a list of words and phrases that date Parton as a nineteenth-century author. In what other respects does his biographical method differ from characteristic twentieth-century approaches? What scientists and inventors share the spotlight with Goodyear in the middle of the nineteenth century? See the *Encyclopedia of World History,* pp. 561–563.

Suggestions for writing: The inventive spirit — Goodyear, Ford, Edison. The rubber industry of today. Pioneers in plastics. Rubber and world economy. How vulcanization works. Bringing Parton up to date in some phase of rubber usage. Latex in home and industry. Nylon or some other branch of industrial chemistry. Living in a synthetic world of tomorrow. The inventor of yesterday versus the researcher of today.

JOHN DOS PASSOS: The Happy Warrior

Among the present-day writers whose views of life have been largely conditioned by the first World War, John Dos Passos (1896–   ) and Ernest Hemingway (p. 703) are at once conspicuous. Dos Passos went to Spain to study architecture but remained to do ambulance work with the Red Cross and with the French and American armies. The experiences of 1916–18 left their mark in his first two books, *One Man's Initiation* and *Three Soldiers.* But his reputation was made with *Manhattan Transfer* (1925), in which he employed the daring technical experiments found also in the trilogy *U.S.A.* (1930–36). In these books Dos Passos sought to create psychological realism not by the stream-of-consciousness method of James Joyce and Virginia Woolf, in which the mind becomes the center of a universe; on the contrary he attempted to contract the breadth of a whole society into the limits of a novel. To do this he employed a large body of shifting characters, and broadened his canvas further by interspersing brief biographies of persons important as period pieces (such is his use of Theodore Roosevelt in *Nineteen-Nineteen*), " newsreels " made up of popular songs and characteristic headlines, and the recurrent " camera eye," a poetic, autobiographical, impressionistic device. Such a redefinition of the method and content of a novel could not but be provocative; and to it Dos Passos added a proletarian sympathy that distressed many gentlefolk. Dos Passos' people are a cross-section, and their behavior is conveyed unsparingly to the reader; but it was shortsighted of humanist critics to dismiss *Manhattan Transfer* as " an explosion in a cesspool." Whatever his limitations — and he has handled his complex literary experiment imperfectly — his *U.S.A.* cannot be ignored as a chronicle of the bitter, gay, and hysterical years from 1900 to 1929.

One is immediately struck by the unconventional appearance of the Dos Passos printed page. What seems to be the basis of paragraphing in the first two pages of " The Happy Warrior "? The semi-poetic quality of the prose becomes increasingly apparent as the tempo increases. Note too that the punctuation (particularly the unorthodox use of commas) is impressionistic. Explain the force of the parenthetical and the italicized passages on pages 80–81. To what extent is Dos Passos' tone patronizing? Point out a few conspicuous examples. Comment on the irony implicit in use of the word " righteous." Find examples of explicit irony. Explain the sentence " Czolgocz made him president." What is a round-robin; a peccary; lyddite? Contrast the biographical technique of Dos Passos and Parton. Which author has the more well-defined approach? Which is more emotional? Compare Dos Passos' sketch of Roosevelt with that found in the *Dictionary of American Biography.*

Suggestions for writing: Dos Passos as a biographer (read the sketches of Burbank, Edison, La Follette, Ford, Hearst, and Wilson in *U.S.A.*). Roosevelt and the Platt machine. T.R. and the Panama Canal. " The Strenuous Life " as Roosevelt understood it. F.D.R. as Dos Passos might have caught him. Roosevelt and Lincoln Steffens. Can a novelist be a good biographer?

Essays on America

DONALD DAVIDSON: Still Rebels, Still Yankees

In 1930 twelve Southerners published a volume entitled *I'll Take My Stand,* in which they deplored the growing uniformity of America and urged the South to preserve its own way of life — a life based upon an agrarian economy. Donald Davidson (1893–   ) was one of the twelve, and he has continued to champion the integrity of the Southern way of life. He has been chiefly interested in genuine regional cultures wherever they exist, and in *The Attack on Leviathan* (1938) he has shown a more realistic attitude than was displayed by some of the " unreconstructed " agrarians. As a professor of English at Vanderbilt University, Davidson has been an important intellectual force in the South ever since the emergence of the *Fugitive* group in the twenties.

In " Still Rebels, Still Yankees," Davidson shows his partiality for a homestead type of existence that harks back to the earlier agrarian days, and he may underestimate the effect of industrial civilization on even the most primitive establishment. But these reservations are slight in comparison to the amount of good, hard sense contained in this trenchant essay. He feels that the diversity of life in Vermont and Georgia is a result of natural evolution, and he is optimistic in believing that they are very likely to survive the gravest shocks. Point out some respects in which American life *is* clearly uniform the country over. In the light of your findings, why do you suppose Davidson chose Vermont and Georgia for his discussion, and not some other pair of states? Explain the allusions to Harlan County, Scottsboro, Dayton, and Gastonia on page 87. Comment on the fairness of his implied criticism of " an overgrown urban America " in the same paragraph. Does the picture of the Vermont or the Georgia scene clash with your own idea about representative life in those states? See if you can account for your own ideas — through travel, residence, reading, personal friendships, and the like — which may differ from his. Why does Davidson single out Aladdin and Wordsworth on page 89? Consult the *Encyclopedia of the Social Sciences* for a discussion of economic determinism, a philosophy to which Davidson (p. 89) is not very devoted. " It is a temptation," he observes, " to say that the people were a great deal like the land," and he points to the influence of New England climate on the Yankee temperament. How does the poetry of Robert Frost (see pp. 331–336) bear out Davidson's observation? Cousin Roderick's father said, " You've got to make this land take care of itself." Davidson is strongly in sympathy with the idea, although he is careful to point out the variations inevitably found between Yankeetown and Rebelville. If one disagrees with Davidson, what are the alternatives? Does *Tobacco Road* illustrate or refute Davidson's thesis? For a more intimate glimpse of the half-understood South, *The Attack on Leviathan* might well be supplemented by *Culture in the South* (1935), edited by W. T. Couch, and *Southern Regions of the United States* (1936), by Howard W. Odum.

Suggestions for writing: Sectionalism in an industrial civilization. Is the country being ruined by the city? The domestic economy of a town in the Middle West, the Southwest, the Far West. Regional prejudices. " The good life " for the urban laborer — a possibility within Davidson's philosophy? A regional vocabulary (words and idiomatic uses not found in the dictionary, but natural in your locality). Can an agrarian philosophy succeed? (see Henry N. Smith, " The Dilemma of Agrarianism," *Southwest Review,* XIX, 215 [April, 1934]).

FREDERICK JACKSON TURNER: The Significance of the Frontier in American History

A new outlook in American history was born when in 1893 Frederick Jackson Turner (1861–1932), then professor in the University of Wisconsin, read his paper on " The Significance of the Frontier " to the American Historical Association. In a statement now classic he declared that " the wilderness masters the colonist." He explained that it finds him a European in dress, manners, industries, modes of thought; that little by little, as he transforms the wilderness, it also transforms him; that the outcome is not the old Europe, but a new product that is American. The idea of the frontier as a determinant of American civilization has proved as fruitful in this country as the idea of the geographic or the economic determination of history — perhaps more so. While Turner himself wrote little — his chief books are *The Rise of the New West* (1906), *The Frontier in American History* (1921), and *The Significance of Sections in American History* (1932) — his essays have been full of ideas at once caught up by others. His doctrine has in fact molded much American thinking ever since 1893. The frontier may of course be made to explain too much in American history; but that it does explain a great deal, and that its passing marked the end of a distinct epoch, cannot be controverted.

Look up the meaning of " terminal moraine," " the fall line," " palimpsest," " loose construction," " gerrymander," all technical terms which Turner uses in his essay. It might be helpful to prepare a map, tracing in colored pencil the successive areas of settlement, to supplement Turner's discussion of American frontiers as of 1790, 1820, 1850, 1880 (pp. 101–102). On page 103, Turner outlines the steps in social evolution of a normal district. Trace the development in your own state or region. Why should the Cumberland Gap and the South Pass in the Rockies have been so important in westward migration? Turner suggests that the location of most cities is no accident. What geographical facts explain the importance of San Francisco, St. Louis, Atlanta, Pittsburgh, Albany, Spokane, Salt Lake City, Detroit, Chicago? (See any good atlas.) Does Turner contradict Davidson when he speaks (p. 105) of the " economic and social consolidation of the country " having welded America into one nation instead of a " collection of isolated states "? Explain the importance of such widely diverse formative factors as salt springs and army posts. It has been said that the settlement of America would have been entirely altered if the Mississippi River ran in an east-west line and emptied into the Atlantic. Discuss. Compare Turner's remarks on frontier individualism on page 112 with Becker's more extended discussion, pages 117 ff. If the frontier dominated the first century of

America's independent life, what has since determined the fundamental character of the land and its people?

Suggestions for writing: Evidences of the frontier still visible in your own region. Lewis and Clark, Daniel Boone, Stephen F. Austin, or Joseph Smith as frontiersmen. The influence of rainfall on the development of the West (see Paul B. Sears, " From Longhorn to Combine," pp. 153–159). Imperialist dreams in America since the disappearance of the frontier. The influence of the barbed-wire fence or the Colt revolver on the growth of America (see Walter Webb, *The Great Plains*). If the Pilgrims had come by air — the significance of Turner's theory if the settlement of America had begun in the twentieth century. The frontier in O. E. Rölvaag's *Giants in the Earth,* Willa Cather's *O Pioneers!* and *Death Comes for the Archbishop.*

CARL BECKER: Kansas

Carl Becker (1873–   ) is Professor of History in Cornell University, but before he went to Ithaca in 1916 he had taught in the University of Kansas for fourteen years. He knew the Middle West well from his early residence in Iowa and Wisconsin, so that when he went to Kansas he was prepared to see far more closely into Kansas individuality than had he been a stranger to the whole region. His account partakes, then, of both the objective and the intimate view; and fortunately Mr. Becker is philosophical.

If Donald Davidson in " Still Rebels, Still Yankees " stresses the diversity of the America he knows, Carl Becker goes one step further to show how Kansas is at once typical of America at large, yet tenacious in her individuality. A similar essay could doubtless be written on other states which have a history quite different from that of either Georgia, Vermont, or Kansas. For the truth is that the two characteristics of uniformity and diversity coexist throughout most of the United States. The formal structure of Becker's essay is easily apparent: notice the threefold division announced at the end of the introduction (p. 117) and re-echoed in the brief conclusion. Moreover, in each of the three principal sections, the opening paragraph introduces the concept to be developed, and a close interrelation is drawn between American and Kansan characteristics. Becker's essay was written in 1910; do his ideas still hold true for the United States as a whole? What was the Populist régime of which he speaks? Explain the reference to Aristotle's " nonpolitical animal." Discuss the paradox of frontier individuality and conformity existing side by side. How has Becker been influenced by Turner's essay on " The Significance of the Frontier "? Comment on the attitude toward democracy discussed at the end of Section II. Amplify the statement that " In America we imagine ourselves liberal-minded because we tolerate what we have ceased to regard as important." How can intolerance be a characteristic of democracy? Is the " leveling-up " process still active today? Where? What seems to be the secret of good government in Davidson's Vermont? His Georgia? Becker's Kansas of 1910?

Suggestions for writing: The " shelters " and the " frontiers " (pp. 116–117) in the region from which you come. " Tolerance is often a negative virtue." Describe some pioneer man or woman you have known, emphasizing particularly the qualities of character he possessed. Compare the frontier periods of Kansas and of your own state. Qualities of individualism, idealism, and equality in Caroline Kirkland's *A*

New Home: Who'll Follow?, Fenimore Cooper's *The Prairie*, George R. Stewart's *Ordeal by Hunger*, Hamlin Garland's *A Son of the Middle Border*.

BENJAMIN FRANKLIN: Information to Those Who Would Remove to America

Benjamin Franklin (1706–1790) was one of America's first internationalists. A man of sagacity and ingenuity, a graduate of the school of experience and the creator of Poor Richard, he represented the American colonies in Europe throughout a long diplomatic career. He strove diligently to avert the Revolution, but afterward negotiated the alliance between America and France, and was one of the signers of the eventual peace treaty. His career is too well known to require detailed comment, but his *Autobiography* has caused many important aspects of his life to receive scant attention in the public eye. Above all, he was a man of supreme intellectual curiosity, motivated by a firm utilitarian sense. His shortcomings are summarized by one critic who speaks of him as "a man of cool calculating reason and broad humanity in politics, rather than of high moral principle." But his limitations were the limitations of his age.

His pamphlet of "Information to Those Who Would Remove to America" was written in England and is an unspectacular yet optimistic brochure of encouragement. It lacks the high pressure of the notorious land companies of the nineteenth and twentieth centuries, and, in typical Franklin vein, is full of facts and figures. To a modern reader its historical interest is obvious. Here is a picture of an America antedating the signing of the Constitution — an America compact yet underdeveloped, homogeneous yet scarcely a unified nation. Here is pictured the equality of opportunity that pushed the frontier ever westward for an exciting century, and left America a world power, but, as Parrington demonstrates, a changed land. Notice evidences of Franklin's utilitarian bent in the third paragraph of the essay. There is a distinct break near the middle of the essay (p. 130); what chief point is developed in each half? "Those poor are to be found in Europe, but will not be found in America till the lands are all taken up and cultivated and the excess of people, who cannot get land, want employment." Comment on this prophecy in the light of Turner's announcement concerning the frontier in 1893. What effect have immigration and the quickened industrial tempo had in hastening the "day of reckoning"? Has the problem in the twentieth century been growing more or less serious? See immigration statistics in the *World Almanac*.

Suggestions for writing: In the manner of Franklin, write a brief paper of "Information" to interest people in "removing" to your state, assuming the year to be about 1882. Franklin's optimism. The Oklahoma land rush. The railroad as colonizer. R. H. Dana's picture of pre-gold California (see his *Two Years Before the Mast*). Twentieth-century population movements.

VERNON L. PARRINGTON: Changing America

One of the most stimulating and provocative works of twentieth-century American scholarship is the three-volume *Main Currents in American Thought* by Vernon L. Parrington (1871–1929). Parrington was Professor of English in the University of Washington, and in his studies of American literature he found himself dissatisfied with traditional evaluations based upon purely aesthetic grounds. His own interpretation grew from a recognition of Taine's race-place-time theories, reinforced by a belief in economic determinism (*i.e.* the belief that " economic forces imprint their mark upon political, social, and religious institutions ") and in the principle that American literature reflects American thought. Under his thesis, Poe and Longfellow receive scant treatment, while persons like Calhoun, Henry George, and Henry Adams become freshly significant. Parrington's judgments have by no means gone unchallenged; but he has explored many fruitful avenues, and his revaluations are those of a liberal of Jeffersonian leanings, dissatisfied with the oversimplifications of the genteel school of criticism.

In his essay " Changing America " he is setting the stage for a detailed discussion of the Gilded Age, as Mark Twain called the post-Civil War period. Parrington preferred to term it " The Great Barbecue," in the belief that economically America was a great outdoor feast to which the whole world — and particularly the exploiting world — thronged. With crackling directness and a sardonic wit Parrington lays down his indictment. It is not wholly a pretty sight, and the nineteenth-century school of patriotic historians had preferred to center their attentions elsewhere. Yet, as he himself says, it is one of the most colorful periods in all our history. And certainly no one can understand present-day America without understanding what the nineteenth century left the nation to recover from. Why did this era of exploitation not dawn until after the Civil War? From the evidence supplied by Parrington, define the contemporary meaning of the terms " preëmption," " exploitation," and " progress." Parrington says that the " acquisitive instinct " had been sharpened by the frontier. Explain. Why does he devote sizable paragraphs to the figures of " solid bulk " and those of " puny physique "? Parrington echoes Franklin's prophecy (p. 132) by pointing to the swelling ranks of the proletariat created with the passing of the frontier, but his concluding sentence seems to contradict Donald Davidson's thesis. Does it, in fact? For a closer view of the Gilded Age, see Matthew Josephson's *The Robber Barons* and *The Politicos,* and Allan Nevins' *The Emergence of Modern America.*

Suggestions for writing: Investigate one of the " figures of earth " named on pages 137–139, and write a paper on the tough-mindedness, the audacity, or the charlatanry conspicuous in his character. Bad taste in the Gilded Age (see Nevins' *Emergence*). " There was a creative side to the buccaneers of the 1870's." Has the Gilded Age disappeared completely?

Frederick Lewis Allen: Crash!

In the last half century the old conception of history as a running account of " battles and kings " has given way before a number of fresh approaches. The economic historian, for instance, has shed much light on the ultimate causes of war and peace; the social historian has re-created people's lives and habits of bygone eras. Mark Sullivan's volumes of *Our Times* gather a great body of raw material for the future historian of the early twentieth century. In a somewhat different vein, Frederick Lewis Allen (1890–   ) has written some important footnotes to the nineteen-twenties in *Only Yesterday,* and the nineteen-thirties in *Since Yesterday.* He calls his volumes informal histories, and they are just that. Here are some chapter head-ings in *Only Yesterday:* " The Big Red Scare," " The Revolution in Manners and Morals," " The Ballyhoo Years," " Alcohol and Al Capone," " Home, Sweet Florida," " The Revolt of the Highbrows." Above all, they catch the atmosphere of the times. Allen was educated at Harvard and has been since 1931 associate editor of *Harper's Magazine.*

In " Crash! " Allen concentrates on the financial débâcle of October, 1929, and by using the chronological method so pointedly, he creates a sense of intimacy and suspense, as if the story were just unfolding before one's eyes. Point out literary devices by which Allen secures vividness. He emphasizes the fact that trading on *margin* was one of the primary causes of the crash. Look up the meaning of the term in the *Encyclopedia of the Social Sciences,* in the article on the stock exchange. What is his purpose in quoting " expert " opinions on pages 143–145? Explain " forced selling." Why did conservative investors as well as speculators feel the terrific slump in prices? Mr. Allen hints that the worst of the panic had passed by November, 1929, but not the worst prices. Compare the quotations on page 152 with those recorded in the New York *Times* on January 1 of subsequent years. In January, 1933, for instance, American Can was down to 54, American Telephone 104, Anaconda Copper 7.

Suggestions for writing: In imitation of Allen, write a paper upon some conspicuous episode about which you can find day-to-day information in newspapers and news magazines (*e.g.* the 1933 Bank Holiday, the 1938 hurricane in New England, the death of Floyd Collins or Rudolf Valentino). The hazards of prophecy. The Securities Exchange Commission and the stock market. Recent market trends. Common misconceptions concerning the market. " The stock market is no place for a lady."

PAUL B. SEARS: From Longhorn to Combine

The problem of conservation is one that America should have faced seriously fifty years ago, when the grazing lands of the arid West were turned into farms and when the merciless lumber drives were denuding our forests and paving the way for wholesale erosion. The nation is, belatedly, conscious of its problem, but not until the thirties were the dramatic effects of our wastefulness shocking enough to impress the general public. With the creation of the vast " dust bowl " in the Southwest, nature gave Americans a stern warning. Among scientists who tried to convey this warning to a complacent public was Paul B. Sears (1891–   ), then Professor of Botany in the University of Oklahoma. His *Deserts on the March* showed how vital is nature's balance, and how dangerous had been the hit-and-miss exploitation of our forests and plains. His volume was reviewed enthusiastically, but it was not until a year or so later, when it was voted the most meritorious " neglected " book of 1935, that it began to reach a wide audience. Since then it has become a standard work for the general reader.

Explain the title of this essay. Why does it symbolize the tragedy of the dust bowl? Why should land in high-rainfall regions be too valuable for grazing? Consult rainfall maps in the *Atlas of American Agriculture* (1936). How were the railroads involved in the exploitation of land during the late nineteenth century? Judging from a physical map of the United States, what areas beside the Nebraska Sand Hills were unfit for grain cultivation? On page 159 Sears speaks of the " undoubted fact of overproduction." Just how should the term be understood in its context? What steps have been taken to improve the conditions of the dust bowl areas? Of deforested areas? Of water-eroded slopes in the East?

Suggestions for writing: The Kincaiders. Willa Cather's *My Ántonia* and the Nebraska plains country. Shelter belts. Contour plowing. Irrigation: salvation or romance? The dust bowl ballads of Woody Guthrie (Victor albums P–27 and P–28). The Scars thesis and the migrations of the Okies (see opening chapters of *The Grapes of Wrath*). Present-day theories of conservation.

Louis Adamic: Thirty Million New Americans

Louis Adamic (1899–   ) came to America from Yugoslavia and, after serving in the United States Army during the first World War, became a free-lance journalist. His first book, *Dynamite,* was published in 1931, and that was followed three years later by *The Native's Return,* which brought him national recognition. Among his other books, *My America* (1938) and *From Many Lands* (1940) are important because in them Adamic focuses upon the problem of foreign minorities in America. He believes, as he says in " Thirty Million New Americans," that a concerted effort should be made to give the second-generation American a feeling of a past, which will in turn, he holds, make him a better citizen. He echoes Donald Davidson's thesis that uniformity is not *per se* to be preferred to honest diversity; and he thinks that it is a mistake for " foreign " groups to feel inferior in the presence of an Anglo-Saxon civilization. The problem Adamic poses is a difficult one; but he understands its difficulties, and for some years has been preaching his message in the manner he outlines on pages 160–161.

Look at the current *World Almanac* for the figures on foreign-born population in your state (the second-generation Americans will number two to three times that figure). What special problems with heterogeneous populations do you observe in the locality from which you come? Why should the problem of the " New Americans " be neglected while so much attention has been paid to immigrant groups? Are you acquainted with any specific instances of prejudice against " foreigners " (the term is sometimes very offensively applied to anyone who has a foreign-sounding name)? How may prejudice best be combated? What is chauvinism? Why does Adamic deprecate it? What, in your judgment, should be done about unpronounceable names? Adamic stresses the importance of making the second-generation American proud of the country of his parents, of giving him a " sense of continuity " (p. 167). Do all Americans possess it? If your parents and you were born in different parts of the world, do you know much about the region they originally lived in? Recall what you were told about your own grandparents' lives and times, about the America in which they lived. Do you agree with Adamic that it is " impossible and . . . undesirable to make offspring of Lithuanians and Serbians into Anglo-Saxons; that the aim should be rather to help them become real men and women on the pattern of their own natural cultures "? What should future generations do about the foreign districts in our large cities?

Suggestions for writing: Your own links with the past. A character sketch of a second-generation American you have known, stressing the side of his make-up in which Adamic would be interested. A letter you might have written to Adamic if you had heard him on his speaking tour of 1934. The Niseis (second-generation

Japanese) of California. "The feeling of 'not belonging' exists in the hearts of many old-stock Americans in some parts of the country." In 1900 it was "America, the melting-pot"; what shall it be by the year 2000?

The Editors of *Fortune:* To Heaven by Subway

In 1929, just as the crash was about to plunge America into half a decade of misery, the editors of the successful *Time* decided to launch a magazine for the businessman and executive. It was to be big and was to "tell the story" of business from tobacco to cans, pianos to aluminum — but in terms of individual companies, not generalized pictures of a whole industry. The journalism that made *Fortune* a success in the face of disastrous conditions is difficult to analyze. But excellent writing, plus a clear idea of how to handle difficult expository problems, and a lavish use of all manner of illustration — these are a part of the secret.

"To Heaven by Subway" is somewhat afield from the major concerns of *Fortune,* but it illustrates an interesting development: the magazine, destined for the successful executive, had a fashionable appeal that attracted a much wider audience, and this in turn led to a broadening of the magazine's scope. Here the editors are surveying an unconventional "industry" that has a perennial attraction for young and old. Notice the problem of organization here, and comment on the Editors' success in handling it. The basic outline is chronological, with the impressionistic beginning and conclusion framing an account of a single Sunday in midsummer. But the outline is actually more complex than this, as one will see by observing the apparent digressions during which time stands still. Characterize some of the various styles of prose found in this essay. Is such a variety appropriate? Point out particular passages in which facts and figures are predominant. Is the "carny" talk necessary for greatest vividness? The article implies that Coney Island's palmiest days have passed, but does not give exhaustive reasons for the partial decline in popularity. Can you add other reasons? What is *Fortune's* circulation? See the current volume of Ayer's *Directory of Newspapers and Periodicals.*

Suggestions for writing: Is the present generation as easy to "shake down" in a carnival atmosphere as were its predecessors? The excitement of carnival rides. The bathing beach as a democratic institution. On being a lifeguard. Some tricks that Barnum would envy today. The streamlined circus of the present. Barnum and Tom Thumb. Are the radio and movies taking the excitement out of the Coney Island type of amusement?

Justice Oliver Wendell Holmes: Free Speech in a Democracy

A perennially young mind in our highest courts is a rarity, but Justice Oliver Wendell Holmes (1841–1935) was an exceptional man in many respects. He was the son of Dr. Oliver Wendell Holmes (see pp. 323–325), and after an eventful army career during the Civil War he taught in the Harvard Law School, wrote legal papers, and for a few years engaged in private practice. His book *The Common Law* (1881), developing the modern conception of law as servant, not master of man, brought him an international reputation, and within a year he was appointed to the Massachusetts Supreme Court. In 1902 Theodore Roosevelt made him a justice of the United States Supreme Court. Here he served for a generation, impressing young and old alike with his trenchant wit, his lucidity and penetration, his liberal interpretation of Constitution and statutes.

He has become best known to the present generation for his dissenting opinions, although he dissented from the majority in no more than ten per cent of the cases before the Court. He deserves more properly to be known for his clear, epigrammatic, and brilliant literary style. Nowhere has the fundamental conception of free speech in a democracy been so simply yet so forcefully stated as in his opinion in the case of *Abrams* v. *United States:* "The best test of truth is the power of the thought to get itself accepted in the competition of the market." And the resilience of his mind is vividly reflected in his statement that "All life is an experiment. Every year, if not every day, we have to wager our salvation upon some prophecy based upon imperfect knowledge."

Why does Justice Holmes distinguish sharply between the two leaflets which he describes? Why does he find one punishable, the other not? How does he interpret the word "intent"? Why does this case have a particular bearing on the problem of free speech in wartime? Explain the sentence, "Persecution for the expression of opinions seems to me perfectly logical," and define the force of "logical." Explain the reference to squaring the circle. Does Holmes believe that "free trade in ideas" should ever be curtailed?

Suggestions for writing: Holmes as a jurist (read some of *The Dissenting Opinions of Mr. Justice Holmes* [1929]). Consult the *Readers' Guide* for the years 1930–1935 for articles upon which you can write a profile of Justice Holmes, emphasizing his personal qualities. Holmes and Darrow. Free speech in wartime. A study of some liberal Justice now on the Supreme Court.

WALT WHITMAN: The American of the Future

A new kind of American poetry made its appearance in 1855 with the publication of Walt Whitman's *Leaves of Grass* (see pp. 306 ff., 835), which its author described as filled "with that vehemence of pride and audacity of freedom necessary to loosen the mind of still-to-be-formed America from the accumulated folds, the superstitions, and all the long, tenacious, and stifling anti-democratic authorities of the Asiatic and European past." In succeeding editions of *Leaves of Grass,* much revised and enlarged, this tone continues, and it is typical of much of his prose as well.

"The American of the Future" is a section of Whitman's *Democratic Vistas,* a fervent and optimistic consideration of the future developments of democracy. The original 1871 edition contains characteristic Whitmanisms — word coinages, occasional long sentences that tie themselves in knots, whimsical punctuation and a rash of parentheses, and a generally rhapsodic style not always free from repetition. The text of this selection follows the original in order that Whitman may be glimpsed in an unmodernized context. After discussing Democracy in general and complaining of a growing effeteness, Whitman urges "a little healthy rudeness," a little less "polite conformity." Then he proceeds to a discussion of the American of the future — both male and female — and concludes by demanding that America free herself from slavish imitation of European "feudal" standards — echoing Emerson's plea of a generation earlier (see "The American Scholar," pp. 224–236 above). Notice that he considers every side of personal development, but is inclined to disparage education and other refining influences in favor of more rugged virtues.

And the West is the symbol of the vitality he envisions for America's future. Is Whitman's attitude toward women consistent with the nineteenth-century Tennysonian conception, or does it seem more modern? Why should Whitman describe an ideal community (p. 194) in just the terms he employs? With what does it contrast? How does his attitude toward the future compare in detail with Emerson's? What has inspired Whitman's close? Compare the interpretations of Whitman's *Democratic Vistas* in the *Cambridge History of American Literature* (II, 270) and in Parrington's *Main Currents in American Thought* (III, 81–86).

Suggestions for writing: A descriptive sketch of two or three Americans of today who possess the characteristics you would like to see perpetuated in future generations. The power of the independent in politics. The dangers of over-education. " America has never prided herself on being civilized." A comparison of Whitman's views on democracy in prose and verse (see also pp. 306–322).

Literature and the Arts

MAX EASTMAN: Humor and America

Max Eastman (1883–   ) was an editor of the *Masses* and the *Liberator* during the first World War, but afterward he broke with the Communist party because of his sympathy toward Trotzky. As a literary critic he has often been a controversialist, but scarcely a radical. His chief volumes of essays are *The Enjoyment of Poetry* (1913), *The Literary Mind* (1931), *Artists in Uniform* (1934), and *The Enjoyment of Laughter* (1936). In *The Literary Mind* he discussed the influence of science on literature, and in *Artists in Uniform* he attacked the regimentation of aesthetic activity in Stalinist Russia. The other two books are less controversial, and if they are not everywhere profound, their point of view is nevertheless stimulating and fresh.

Informality has always been a predominant characteristic of American life, and nowhere is it more generously illustrated than in American humor. In the essay here reprinted, Eastman concentrates particularly on David Crockett, Artemus Ward, and Josh Billings. But had space permitted, he might have mentioned many others. Mark Twain, of course, would lend himself to exhaustive treatment, and there are more recent figures like Mr. Dooley and Will Rogers who with their homespun wit have masked serious comment beneath a humorous exterior. In connection with this essay, notice Artemus Ward's letter to his wife (p. 288) and the section of folk tales beginning on page 559. Why should Eastman object to the term " tall talk " as descriptive of frontier humor? Why does he feel that vigor of imagination has been more characteristic of our humorists than of our poets? Might the poets' dependence on European models of the nineteenth century explain this in part? Distinguish between the humor of Artemus Ward and Josh Billings. Why does Eastman call Billings the first imagist poet? (For a note on Imagism see below, p. 846.) On page 204 Eastman refers to recent tendencies in humor. Why is the fantastic frequently a source of humor? Which seems to you the higher form of art, saying things " that make absolutely no sense," or saying things "which there is absolutely no sense in saying"?

Suggestions for writing: The humor of the *New Yorker.* "The pun is the staple of the radio comedian." Artemus Ward's lecture on the Mormons. The humor of illiterate spelling. Humor in Haliburton and Longstreet (pp. 559 ff., pp. 565 ff.). Select one modern humorist from the list in F. B. Millett's *Contemporary American Authors* (1940), p. 685, and write a paper on some of his work, making use of the bibliographies in the body of the *CAA.*

John Erskine: Huckleberry Finn

John Erskine (1879–   ) is the well-known novelist and Columbia University professor. His most popular work was *The Private Life of Helen of Troy* (1925), a rather racy version of the familiar mythological matter. He has also written textbooks, literary essays, short stories, and a dozen other novels. He has edited much of the writing of Lafcadio Hearn, and he was one of the editors of the *Cambridge History of American Literature* (1917–1921). His interest in music and his official connection with the Juilliard School of Music in New York are of long standing.

In his essay on *Huckleberry Finn,* John Erskine presents not merely an appreciation of the book, but a serious attempt to analyze its merits. The comparison with *Tom Sawyer* is inevitable, yet in his judgment *Huckleberry Finn* seems by far the greater work. By what implied standard of value does he consider *Tom Sawyer* less successful? On page 205 he points to three philosophies common in the modern novel and discusses the presence of all three in *Huckleberry Finn.* Do you think that Erskine implies that they are present in ideal proportions? Why should melodrama be an objectionable feature of any novel? What seems to be the chief melodramatic episode in *Huckleberry Finn?* Why should "the dramatic method, without preaching of any kind," be more effective than the open propaganda of a novel like *Uncle Tom's Cabin?* In his concluding paragraph Erskine alludes to a point of view expressed in Van Wyck Brooks' *The Ordeal of Mark Twain.* A comparison of this book with Bernard De Voto's *Mark Twain's America* will reveal the chief controversy over the humorist since his death.

Suggestions for writing: Huck's idea of right and wrong. Mark Twain and Sinclair Lewis as critics of village life. Mark Twain's low estimation of human nature. "*Huckleberry Finn* is a boy's book, but it has always had a peculiar attraction for the adult reader."

Henry James: Hawthorne's Three American Novels

Henry James (1843–1916) has been the subject of much dispute since fame began to attend him shortly after the close of the Civil War. He was born an American, but spent so much of his time abroad and assumed such a Continental manner that to many people he seemed scarcely an American. Moreover, he was critical of all that was crude and rootless in the United States, and so alienated many would-be admirers, who later resented his becoming a British subject shortly before his death. But these are trivial objections in the face of his merits as a novelist. A superb craftsman, he achieved a remarkable degree of psychological penetration in his studies of conduct. As he developed, he became less and less interested in superficial events and more steadily concerned with the eddies of thought and feeling beneath the surface. His method is seen at its best in novels like *The Ambassadors, The American,* and *The Portrait of a Lady.* Some of the later novels dispense almost entirely with action, and this more introspective manner, to which was added an increased complexity of style, provoked the sharp rebuke from James' brother William, " Say it out, for God's sake " (see the entire letter, p. 291, above). If he is criticized for his " ivory tower " attitude toward life and his affinity for the genteel, he has at least left some superb examples of the " well-made " novel.

James was not primarily a biographer, and in this chapter from the English Men of Letters biography of Hawthorne, we see him laying aside the chronicle of Hawthorne's life for a consideration of his most important fiction. As one might expect of a novelist, James pays most attention to those characteristics which he and Hawthorne have in common. He sympathizes with Hawthorne's interest in moral problems and feels gratified that Hawthorne seldom tells a story " vulgarly " for its own sake. Look closely at his discussion of the three books to see why he calls *The Scarlet Letter* Hawthorne's best work. Does James recount enough plot for those who may not have read the novels? Does he recount too much? What is symbolism in fiction? Do you agree with James' criticism of the symbolism in *The Scarlet Letter* (p. 214)? In *The House of the Seven Gables* (p. 218)? Do you notice any condescension toward America in James' writing? Why should James insist that Hawthorne was not a realist? Point out some evidences of style that make James' work clearly that of a nineteenth-century critic. Why should Hawthorne have been briefly interested in Transcendentalism? See a discussion of the term and the movement in Thrall and Hibbard, *A Handbook to Literature.*

Suggestions for writing: The Blithedale Romance and Brook Farm. Henry James' American prejudices. A detailed criticism of Hawthorne's *Lady Eleanore's Mantle* (pp. 593 ff.). Hawthorne as seen in his Note-Books. The problem of evil in *The Scarlet Letter.*

RALPH WALDO EMERSON: The American Scholar

" A Greek head on right Yankee shoulders " was Lowell's playful yet accurate characterization of the paradox that is Emerson (1803–1882). For if Emerson's philosophical ideas identified him with the Hellenists, his homespun phrase and pungent epigram betokened the independent, hard-headed American. He had the courage of his convictions: at the age of twenty-nine he resigned from the Unitarian ministry because of his changing beliefs; and a few years later he risked the loss of the lecture platform — his only real " profession " aside from that of man of letters — when he expressed his sincere but radical views on independence in religious thought. Today his life seems uneventful — largely, one supposes, because he lived almost entirely in the world of ideas. As a Transcendentalist he seemed to his age a religious freethinker, with his mystical pronouncements concerning the " Over-Soul." But he can be considered simply an idealist who insisted, as one critic has put it, that " the good life is the life of the independent spirit, and not that of material possessions." He questioned the standards of value in his time; but even when he complained that " Things are in the saddle and ride mankind," his belief in human dignity led him to prophesy America's eventual greatness.

The relation of this country to Europe was one of the major critical preoccupations of the nineteenth century. Political independence was one thing, but Sydney Smith, despite his scorn, summed up this nation's intellectual position when in 1820 he asked, " Who reads an American book? " Aside from Philip Freneau and Charles Brockden Brown, the young United States had at that time produced no writers of importance. American literary fashions were hand-me-downs from England, and the lack of copyright laws made piracy of successful English books so easy that it was difficult to see any future for American authorship. As time passed, however, there was an increasing demand for a literature that would mirror America's distinctive qualities (although some critics deplored the " unpoetic " American landscape). In his address to the Harvard Phi Beta Kappa Society in 1837 Emerson delivered a strong plea — by no means the first — for American intellectual independence. Lowell echoed the classic statement a decade later, in *A Fable for Critics,* and it had been taken up by many another writer. A great school of American authors — a flowering of New England, chiefly — reached the height of their powers near the middle of the century; but, as Howard Mumford Jones has observed, it was not until the present century that the European influences were in fact thrown aside.

Does Emerson use the word " scholar " in exactly the meaning current today? He discusses the education of the scholar by nature, by books, and by action. Does the education of the scholar (or, better, the thinking man) derive from these same sources today? Has there been any great change in the importance of any one of the three? Are there other sources of a scholar's strength today? Emerson urges the scholar to " feel all confidence in himself, and . . . defer never to the popular cry." What pitfalls lie in the way of this ideal? Has Emerson underestimated the pull of popular opinion, no matter how illogically formed, upon the professor, the professional man, the writer, the public servant? Point out some examples of effective epigrammatic statement in the essay. What is the relation between epigram and poetry? Discuss Emerson's interest in the commonplace. Is self-conscious nationalism in art necessarily a good thing? When Emerson says that " We have listened too long to the courtly muses of Europe," is he counseling a narrow provincial literature of our own? Does Emerson's faith in the future seem shallow optimism, or is it firmly founded upon reason and an attainable idealism?

Suggestions for writing: Culture for the masses. The importance of the commonplace in twentieth-century American literature. The pitfalls of popularizing. " Pessimism in public utterance is always dangerous." The optimism of Emerson's poetry (see pp. 346 ff., and read additional poems). Is idealism a luncheon-club expedient in present-day America? Parrington's estimate of Emerson.

Granville Hicks: The Poetic " Renaissance "

Granville Hicks (1901–   ) is known today chiefly for his book, *The Great Tradition* (1933), and for his interest in the proletariat and proletarian literature. *The Great Tradition* concerns America since the Civil War; in it Hicks discusses the relation between literature and the economic and political realities of an industrial civilization. In the post-war period described by Parrington (pp. 133–141), for instance, Hicks feels that most of the novelists were occupied with problems of a past generation, or with problems that were distressingly trivial. William Dean Howells, a leading realist of the seventies and eighties, wrote one of the few books that dealt with a rich man; but *The Rise of Silas Lapham* depicts a man who is worth one million dollars, in a period when Carnegie, Rockefeller, and Fisk were pyramiding their fortunes dizzily. Hicks praises Howells' interest in realism, but insists that no novelist really came to grips with the actual problems of the time; no one undertook to explain how fortunes were made, how the masses were shamefully exploited, how government was almost uniformly the tool of business. This is, in general, the tone of Hicks' indictment — an indictment of the " genteel tradition," repeated, for example, in the opening paragraph of " The Poetic ' Renaissance.' "

Hicks deplores aestheticism and the ivory tower attitude, holding that it is the artist's duty to reflect the actual problems current in a world dominated by economic and political forces. Like Parrington (with whose ideas he is in only partial accord), Hicks has been a stimulating critic, although he has his blind spots. But the astringent criticism of liberals and radicals, no matter how unacceptable it may seem to a future generation, has been helpful if only in revising many of the inflated judgments of previous impressionist critics. Why should Hicks, despite his regard for the merits of Lindsay, Sandburg, Robinson, and Frost, feel that they did not create a genuine poetic renaissance? Point out some of Hicks' comments that show his interest in economic forces of the early twentieth century. Why should poetry mirror the industrial civilization of urban America? Read the poems of Vachel Lindsay and Carl Sandburg (pp. 381 ff., 387 ff.) and test Hicks' judgments carefully before you agree or disagree with him. " Robinson's world is, obviously, an abstraction," says Hicks, and he goes on to point out the advantages and disadvantages of a poet's own world. Apply his criticism to the poems of Robinson and Frost reprinted in this volume (pp. 378 f., 331 ff.). Why does Hicks feel that " the talent of a Robert Frost " will be necessary to a poet who measures up to his ideal? Consult the 1933 *Book Review Digest* for some indication of the reception accorded Hicks' *The Great Tradition*.

Suggestions for writing: An analysis of " A Lone Striker " (agreeing or disagreeing with Hicks' interpretation of Frost's world). " There is new territory that we beg the poet to conquer for us." Should one judge a poem by purely aesthetic standards? " The modern poet's search has been for truth oftener than for beauty." Hicks' interpretation of Whitman (see the Poetry section above, and *The Great Tradition*, pp. 20–31).

HENRY SEIDEL CANBY: Fiction Tells All

Henry Seidel Canby (1878–   ) was educated at Yale, and has for many years been on the English faculty of that university. He was the founder of the *Saturday Review of Literature,* and its editor from 1924 to 1936; and from the beginning he has been chairman of the board of judges of the Book-of-the-Month Club. Beside his numerous essays on literary subjects, he has written a biography of Thoreau, several studies of the short story, and two volumes of social history, *The Age of Confidence* and *Alma Mater*.

Mr. Canby is a literary conservative who prefers the Greek principles of measure and restraint to what he finds in the literature he discusses in " Fiction Tells All." At least he explains why the violence of autobiographical revelation has taken place, even if he does not condone it. And a future generation may find Mr. Canby's estimate of his contemporaries juster than that of the more sympathetic criticism they have received. What is " virulent " in the modern impulse to tell all? Do you agree with Canby's characterization of modern autobiographical fiction? Why should little joy and less faith be revealed in the novels of the twenties and thirties? Does the recent preoccupation with psychoanalysis seem entirely unfortunate? Canby speaks of Hemingway's " eruptive, monosyllabic style, from which all the fluent rhythms of the old romanticists have been carefully eliminated." Comment on the justice of this statement with specific reference to *The Three-Day Blow* (pp. 703 ff.). Is Canby's criticism of the literature of the twenties and thirties at heart a criticism of society itself during those periods? If the public temper is disillusioned and cynical, and a realistic writer has his eye on posterity, should he seek some basis for expression other than the life of his own time? Do the Pulitzer awards in fiction bear out Mr. Canby's criticism of the twenties and thirties? Consult the list in the current *World Almanac*.

Suggestions for writing: Is personal tragedy a subject for autobiography? Self-revelation in *Look Homeward, Angel*. William Faulkner's complaint against civilization. Drugstore fiction as an index to popular taste. Hollywood's treatment of serious novels. Should we return to an age of reticence? " Great literature is not nervous."

H. L. MENCKEN: The American Language

In his earlier years H. L. Mencken (1880–   ) was editor of *Smart Set* and the *American Mercury,* and during the twenties was known as one of the " bad boys " of criticism. He crusaded dogmatically against smugness and hypocrisy, ignorance, and what an English critic calls " the ' cruder ' manifestations of American civilization." His style is broadly satiric; his use of an over-formal vocabulary is always tongue-in-cheek, and the self-conscious witticisms elaborately hidden in his every sentence keep his polysyllabic diction from being merely pretentious. But beneath the mock solemnity is genuine seriousness of purpose, for Mencken except in his treatment of the American language is almost always the reformer. His six series of *Prejudices* subjected the weaknesses and inanities of the twenties to merciless attack, and the real mellowness of his character has only recently become apparent, in the series of reminiscences beginning with *Happy Days* (1940).

The American intellectual independence of England urged by Emerson in his " American Scholar " address has been a long time in coming, but linguistically it seems to have been achieved. In 1919 Mencken published the first edition of *The American Language,* developing the thesis that American English was growing away from British English, and that the differences would probably multiply. During the twenties and thirties the influence of American English became so strong even in England that Mencken was forced to modify his original thesis. In his essay here reprinted, and in the fourth edition of *The American Language* (1936), he declares that " the pull of American has become so powerful that it has begun to drag English with it." The strongest argument he urges is that the coinage of racy words and idioms proceeds in America with Elizabethan vigor, and that the freshness of American English is spreading from this country to all other parts of the English-speaking world.

Analyze Mencken's style in some detail, pointing out devices he uses to keep the reader alert and interested. Why does the opening sentence serve as an admirable springboard into the subject under discussion? Point out other topic sentences which serve as division points in the essay. Does Noah Webster's reply to Captain Basil Hall (p. 253) seem a modern way of looking at language? Discuss the function of a dictionary. Is the " bowwow jargon " of which Mencken speaks on page 253 very noticeable in this country? See if you can find some examples (" The answer to the query of the gentleman is in the negative," etc.) in newspaper columns. In the new *Dictionary of American English* (alluded to on p. 258), look up the origin and history of *buncombe, gerrymander, pork barrel, filibuster, carpetbagger, gag rule.* Compile a brief list of picturesque colloquialisms which seem to express ideas more vividly than the corresponding conventional expressions we already have.

Suggestions for writing: A glossary of fresh college slang. Is formal grammar breaking down? The dictionary — arbiter or historian? The language of newspaper advertising. The language of women. Euphemisms of polite society (see *The American Language* [1936], pp. 284 ff. for a starter). The language of Walter Winchell.

James Weldon Johnson: The Negro's Creative Genius

Among the foremost representatives of the Negro race in the United States since the Civil War, James Weldon Johnson (1871–1938) ranks beside Booker T. Washington, educator, and George W. Carver, scientist. Johnson was born in Florida and educated largely in the South, but his ambition soon sought wider scope. After having joined the Florida bar he moved to New York City where he studied at Columbia and for a time supported himself by writing popular songs and free-lancing. Later he was United States Consul in Venezuela and Nicaragua, but in 1912 he returned to this country to spend the remainder of his life working for the advancement of the colored race. Besides editing *The Book of American Negro Poetry* (1922), he wrote several books, notably a novel, *The Autobiography of an Ex-Colored Man* (1912), and a volume of verse, *God's Trombones* (1927). With his brother, J. Rosamond Johnson, he compiled two books of American Negro spirituals.

In his essay " The Negro's Creative Genius " Johnson states his principal beliefs: that within certain spheres where the Negro has been able to compete as an equal, he has made a genuine contribution to American civilization. Indeed, he goes further to say that the Negro has created " the only things artistic that have yet sprung from American soil and been universally acknowledged as distinctive American products." Certainly there is no denying that the Negro influence on music in this country has been profound, especially when one considers the " imported " European quality of most of America's musical life during the nineteenth century. Look closely at the poetic examples Johnson includes in his essay — " crude, but they contain something of real poetry," he says of them. See if you can discover these qualities in each. Do you agree with Johnson's views on Negro dialect expressed near the close of the essay (p. 264)? Does Johnson agree or disagree with Deems Taylor concerning themes for art of the future? Compare the article " Ragtime and Jazz " in the *Oxford Companion to Music* with Johnson's point of view.

Suggestions for writing: The career of W. C. Handy. The Blues: Art or Sham? The emotional quality of Negro spirituals. Negro psychology as reflected in the Uncle Remus stories. The sentimentalizing of the Negro in fiction (read some of the stories in Thomas Nelson Page's *In Ole Virginia*). A modern Negro artist (Marian Anderson, Roland Hayes, Paul Robeson, Bill Robinson). An estimate of the work of Langston Hughes (*The Weary Blues, Not Without Laughter, The Ways of White Folks*), or of Richard Wright (*Uncle Tom's Children, Native Son*).

DEEMS TAYLOR: Music and the Flag

Deems Taylor (1885–   ) is a critic who has been successful also as a creator. He has written two operas, *The King's Henchman* (1927) and *Peter Ibbetson* (1931), and has composed a considerable body of orchestral music, most notable among which is the suite, "Through the Looking Glass." For years Mr. Taylor was critic on various New York newspapers, and more recently as consultant on music to the Columbia Broadcasting System has won a wide audience with his intermission talks at the Philharmonic Symphony Society broadcasts. His books include *Of Men and Music* (1937) and *The Well-Tempered Listener* (1940).

As a critic Deems Taylor is witty and direct, in contrast to the humorless and pompous style of many of his colleagues and most of his predecessors. Occasionally he is led astray in his zeal for phrase-making; in "Music and the Flag," for example, he may underestimate the quality of folk music, in order to say what he does about saddle rhythm. It must be said in his favor, however, that he has done much to popularize the cause of good music by his simple, often homely approach.

"Music and the Flag" has a single unmistakable point. Is it made forcefully? Is it justified in the light of Mr. Taylor's argument within the essay? Is folk music as poor stuff as Mr. Taylor thinks? Has Tin Pan Alley improved or degraded the "blues," the cowboy song, the Negro spiritual? Look up the history of Brahms' "Academic Festival Overture" in Oscar Thompson's *International Encyclopedia of Music and Musicians* to see how several popular German songs have been used in a formal composition. If it is possible, listen to a performance of Roy Harris' *When Johnny Comes Marching Home* (Victor 8629), which may be an interesting commentary on Mr. Taylor's ideas.

Suggestions for writing: The case for nationalism in music. The songs of your own childhood. What makes military music military? The ballads of John Jacob Niles (listen to Victor albums M–604, M–718). The effect of radio on musical standards. Enjoyment versus understanding for the layman. The hidden beauties of folk music.

GERALD BYWATERS: Contemporary American Artists

Gerald Bywaters (1906–   ) has modestly excluded himself from the list of painters among whom he deserves to rank. He is Assistant Professor of Art in Southern Methodist University, and is among the most forceful and original artists of the Southwest. Like Thomas Hart Benton and Grant Wood, he was educated abroad, but found his true metier in the life he knew best. His work shows greater sympathy and less satire than Benton's, but otherwise their treatment of the American scene is alike frank and informal. He has written extensively on art in the Dallas *News* and the *Southwest Review,* and his work in many media has been widely exhibited.

As Bywaters points out in his essay, there have been two recent developments of importance in American art. It has not only been freeing itself from European domination — and here art was a generation or two behind literature — but the artistic capital has shown signs of moving westward from New York City. It is clear that the most significant contributions to American art in recent years have been made by the regionalists. The artists whose work he discusses are vitally concerned with painting what they know best, but, as Bywaters points out, " only after art has been produced as an honest regional expression can it hope to become universal." Does Mr. Canby's criticism of literature apply to the undignified subject-matter which has frequently been the basis for Benton's paintings and lithographs? How does the development in contemporary American art seem to be paralleling that of American humor (Max Eastman's " Humor and America," pp. 195 ff.)? How do you account for the dissatisfaction which came to Grant Wood and Thomas Hart Benton after they had gone to Paris to study? Why should it have required the twentieth-century atmosphere to reveal the wealth of subject-matter in the heart of America hitherto overlooked by the artist? Do you agree with the two concluding paragraphs in Bywaters' essay?

Suggestions for writing: Benton's discovery of America (see *An Artist in America,* 1938). Governmental encouragement of art. The America of Grant Wood (see *Art Digest* for references to reproductions of his paintings mentioned on p. 272). The National Gallery. Regionalism versus universality.

LEWIS MUMFORD: Architecture and Civilization

American interest in community planning has developed tardily, and is almost entirely a product of the twentieth century. Lewis Mumford (1895–   ), along with Frank Lloyd Wright and many younger men trained in Europe, has done much to stimulate a sense of the builder's responsibility toward society. He contributes frequent articles on new building to the *New Yorker,* and in books like *Sticks and Stones* (1924), *Technics and Civilization* (1934), and *The Culture of Cities* (1938) he has emphasized his thesis that planning for the future is everybody's job, and cannot be done whimsically or haphazardly. His interest in American culture has resulted in several provocative studies, including *The Golden Day* (1926), *American Taste* (1929), and *The Brown Decades* (1931).

In so far as Lewis Mumford's essay is critical of American wastefulness, he begins where Parrington left off. He points particularly to the conception of exploitation which laid waste farm and forest lands without any regard for the future; and he is critical of the artificial necessity which drove large portions of our population to dark and airless city tenements. Community planning, as he outlines it, is a remedy for the future, yet admittedly it will be a difficult job not only to make over urban areas, but to change an ingrained national conception of the city. Is it still a common belief in America that every town will one day become a large city? What isolated examples of community planning suggest the possibility of following out Mumford's ideas? Are government public housing projects designed to utilize the maximum of air and sunlight? Mumford mentions housing difficulties during the first World War. What problems have been recurrent in wartime economy?

Suggestions for writing: Work out an ideal development for the area near your college. Progress *and* poverty as the architect sees it. The housing problem as seen in "One-third of a Nation" (*Federal Theater Plays*, Vol. I). The architectural philosophy of Mr. Ebenezer Howard. Frank Lloyd Wright's city of the future. The future of the skyscraper.

Letters

It has been said that speech has been given man to enable him to conceal his thoughts. Except in our conversation, we probably conceal our real thoughts most effectively in letters. Consider how few of our letters reveal more than the dull skeleton of movement from one place to another — disclosing what we did, where we went, now and then what we said, but only seldom what seriously occupied our minds. The good letter wherever it occurs is the letter that reveals the personality of its author and shows the way his mind works. Such letters run the gamut of revelation. There are terse but chilling sentences like those of Cornelius Vanderbilt:

GENTLEMEN:
You have undertaken to cheat me. I will not sue you, for law takes too long. I will ruin you.

Sincerely yours,

This is a far cry from another type, the garrulous and minutely analytical style of Samuel Richardson's epistolary novels. The handful of letters in this volume illustrate a variety of approaches, each characteristic of its author — Lincoln, simple, lean, unpretentious; Artemus Ward, the humorist making the most of misspellings and illiterate formations, yet underneath the vulgarities displaying a subtle vein of criticism; George Washington, grave yet tender, the husband rather than the Gilbert Stuart portrait; Melville and William James, each ebullient in his own way — the former with powerful strokes of wilfulness slashing his way through verbal thickets, the latter bubbling with kind enthusiasm edged with steel; and Thomas Jefferson, an old man of eighty, modestly stating his views on the momentous question of the Monroe Doctrine, ever resourceful in language, only twice altering a phrase as he wrote. Each letter is characteristic of its author, and each has something important to say.

The George Washington letter is self-explanatory. It is unfortunate that the original has disappeared, and we shall therefore never know how he signed himself to his wife.

Thomas Jefferson's letter to President Monroe was written during the summer that the Monroe Doctrine was taking shape. The present-day invocation of Jefferson's ideas on every hand has led to extensive quotation of this and many other pronouncements of the democratic president. The letter is of great importance as a prophecy of America's role in world affairs, although many persons will find his imperialist sentiments distasteful, even if only partially inaccurate.

In the summer of 1851 Melville was reading proof of *Moby Dick*, and he and Hawthorne were both living in western Massachusetts. The letter reveals the apocalyptic character of some of Melville's best writing — and it also reveals him as a somewhat unhappy and disillusioned man, on the eve of what only a future generation would regard as a distinguished contribution to American literature.

Abraham Lincoln, as the opening sentence points out, was answering an open letter Greeley had published in his *Tribune,* accusing Lincoln of improperly conducting the war. Greeley's letter was entitled " A Prayer of Twenty Millions," and urged that the slaves be freed. A month after this public exchange of views, Lincoln issued the Emancipation Proclamation.

Charles Farrar Browne (1834–1867) was known to millions as " Artemus Ward," and during his brief life he was a popular lecturer in both America and England. Although the illiteracies in his written style are humorous at a low level, the man was essentially witty, as one can instantly see by reading his lecture on the Mormons. In the letter to his wife the " Grate Orgin " he constantly mentions was the magnificent instrument installed in Boston's Music Hall in 1863 and a necessary stop in every sight-seer's pilgrimage.

William James (1842–1910) was one of the few persons who could profitably have addressed to his brother Henry the direct criticism his letter contains. He is speaking not of the James manner in the early biography of Hawthorne (a chapter of which is reprinted above, pp. 211 ff.), but of the highly complex style characteristic of such later novels as *The Wings of the Dove* and *The Golden Bowl.* William James' reference to his " little book called *Pragmatism* " may sound immodest, but he was trying to estimate it fairly for his brother in England, and he was correct in feeling that the volume would be a classic statement of pragmatic philosophy.

Ballads and Folk Songs

The interest in collecting and preserving folk song is relatively new in the United States, but it has a long and continuous history in England and other European countries. The famous diarist Pepys assembled a large collection of " broadsides " — printed ballads sold for a penny and usually recounting some historical event or some prodigious occurrence. In the eighteenth century Bishop Thomas Percy made history when he rescued a bundle of manuscript from a Shropshire house in which the pages were being used to light fires. The manuscript included copies of many popular ballads, and Percy published them in 1765 as *Reliques of Ancient English Poetry.* During the nineteenth century collectors became more assiduous, and more careful (the good Bishop had edited and " improved " his texts freely). The most notable monument of ballad scholarship was the painstaking *English and Scottish Popular Ballads* by Professor F. J. Child of Harvard.

Child's work is significant for several reasons. For one thing, he devoted much of his time to discovering analogues in foreign ballads, and his exhaustive notes have proved invaluable to every serious ballad student. For another, it is significant that he should have overlooked the possibilities of balladry in America. But his contribution was so signal that he may be pardoned for not taking the whole world as his province, especially since a host of his successors have turned to this new fertile field.

In the fastness of the Southern mountains, and in many back-country districts all over the eastern United States, remnants of English and Scottish ballads have been found. More than sixty of the three hundred and five independent ballads listed by Child have been discovered in Maine, for example, and the number is almost as large in half a dozen other states. But more immediately important for present considerations, a vast heritage of native American popular song has been discovered — or, more properly, recognized by the scholar, for it had always been familiar to large sections of our population. There were Negro and white spirituals, work songs, "hollers," "sinful songs," play party singing games, and the widely popular cow boy songs. This was not all: in lumber camps, on the Erie canal, in the arroyos of the California mining country — everywhere, in fact, where men could gather in common exploits and make up songs about their deeds — ballads and folk songs abounded. Even today, the old broadside tradition that flourished in Shakespeare's time is still alive. The deaths of the beloved Will Rogers and the notorious John Dillinger were celebrated by " made-up songs "; and there exists today many a singer like Woody Guthrie, whose " Dust Bowl Ballads " (Victor Albums P–27 and P–28) offer us fresh insight into the wellsprings of folk composition.

It has been said that as soon as folklore is collected, it begins to die out in actual life. There is no denying that the phonograph and the radio have been corrupting the historically developed taste of the generation who would normally hand on the songs they have learned from their parents and grandparents. But at least our important folk inheritance has not yet died out; and it may well be that twentieth-century collectors, far from hastening a requiem, are providentially preserving our ballad literature from complete extinction. And not collectors alone: a wider public is today appreciative of songs such as those reprinted in this volume. If these songs are aesthetically far from great, they are yet not such sorry stuff as Deems Taylor's hasty generalization would suggest. And they are alive, especially when the words are wedded to the music. An evening with Carl Sandburg's *The American Songbag*, or the Lomaxes' *American Ballads and Folk Songs* will convince the skeptic who may be doubtful that there can be art where there is not gentility.

In addition to the ballads in this section of *The American Reader,* a large number are included in Lynn Riggs' play *Green Grow the Lilacs* (pp. 395 ff.). A comparison of the two versions of " Git Along, Little Dogies " and " Good-by, Old Paint " will be especially interesting.

Nathan Hale

This is an early example of the broadside ballad, and was circulated in 1776, almost immediately after the American Revolutionary hero was hanged as a spy by British soldiers. In the ballad, Hale's traditional statement that he was sorry he had but one life to give for his country is not repeated, but he is allowed a parting stanza. It was said that his requests for a Bible and religious comfort were denied by the British. The ballad is more charitable in granting him " five . . . short moments . . . to repent."

John Henry

The ballad of John Henry is widely current in America, and the steel-driving man has become a legendary symbol of strength and endurance. According to recent researches, John Henry seems to have been a Negro steel-driver who helped drill the Big Bend tunnel on the Chesapeake and Ohio Railroad around 1870, at about the time the steam drill was being introduced. The confusions in many versions of the ballad — and indeed in two stanzas of the version reprinted here — are explained by the existence of a Negro murderer, John Hardy, who enjoyed a brief period of notoriety in 1894. The John Hardy ballads tell of a crap game and a murder, and are frequently interwoven with elements of railroad building from the John Henry saga. Except for the confusion of names, the version reprinted here is pure John Henry.

The Jealous Lover of Lone Green Valley

This tearful ditty, more often known as " Fair Florella," is perhaps the most widespread single ballad in America. The late Phillips Barry, who studied it in detail, has traced it to an English street ballad, " The Murder of Betsey Smith," and finds it circulating from Nova Scotia to Wyoming, and throughout the South. The present version is from Texas, and was collected by one of the editors of the present volume. Mr. Barry, commenting on the morbid quality of the ballad, called it a " love song about murder in which even the motive is lacking," and observed that in only a few texts was there a stanza of " warning " — " so consistently is the folk satisfied to let the murderer go scot free." There is a slight resemblance between this ballad and " When I Was Young and Single " in *Green Grow the Lilacs,* p. 432, above.

The Old Chisholm Trail

" The name is pronounced *Chizzum.* This song in its entirety would give all the possible experiences of a group of cowboys driving a herd of cattle from Texas to Dodge City, Kansas. Many stanzas are not mailable. Thus far no one has shown that it is not a product of the plains — a genuine cowboy song, both words and music. Of all songs, the most universally sung by cowboys." — John A. Lomax's note in *Cowboy Songs.*

Git Along, Little Dogies

Dogies (pronounced to rhyme with " fogies ") are stunted calves which have lost their mothers and have been forced to begin a grass diet at such an early age that they become pot-bellied and irritable. " You haven't any idea the trouble they give us While we go driving them along," says the cowboy singer with some justice. Compare this version with that in *Green Grow the Lilacs,* p. 396.

Jesse James

Jesse James was an American Robin Hood, and it was inevitable that ballads should retell sensational aspects of his career. This very popular version recounts the central episode — Jesse's death at the hands of the " dirty little coward," Robert Ford. Jesse had been a member of Quantrell's guerilla gang during the Civil War, and afterward had organized his own band of train and bank robbers. A price was on his head; and, under the name of Mr. Howard, he had settled down in St. Joseph, Missouri, when one of his own gang shot him " on the sly " in his home — while hanging a picture, according to legend. The ballad recounts some of Jesse's exploits, but the fact that " Jesse was a man, a friend to the poor " outweighs all the crime of his banditry.

Fifteen Poets

The date given at the conclusion of each poem is that of first publication.

WALT WHITMAN

In an essay on " The Poet " written in 1844, Emerson observed that " We have yet had no genius in America, with tyrannous eye, which knew the value of our incomparable materials, and saw, in the barbarism and materialism of the times, another carnival of the same gods whose picture it so much admires in Homer; then in the middle age; then in Calvinism. . . . Our log-rolling, our stumps and their politics, our fisheries, our Negroes and Indians, our boats, and our repudiations, the wrath of rogues, and the pusillanimity of honest men, the northern trade, the southern planting, the western clearing, Oregon and Texas, are yet unsung. Yet America is a poem in our eyes . . . and it will not wait long for metres."

America did not have long to wait, for in 1855 with the publication of Walt Whitman's *Leaves of Grass* America had a poet who fitted Emerson's specifications to an astonishing degree. Emerson may not have anticipated Whitman's egotism, nor may he have expected the metrical freedom of the new poet. But in other respects Whitman's poetry celebrates, however romantically, the exuberance of man in a democratic world. Whitman was conscious of American regions as no other poet had been; he gave attention to persons of all walks of life; and he deliberately extended the language of poetry beyond the rather stereotyped diction common to the school of " beloved " poets. Whitman was not an instant success, for he broke too many rules and opened too many unusual vistas to his readers. But as further editions of *Leaves of Grass* appeared, revised and enlarged, the poet's work gained recognition — in Europe, where he seemed the first genuine American poet, and, eventually, in his own country. Whitman's faults are obvious; but in his " barbaric yawp " there is energy, vitality, and an expansiveness that makes him America's first modern poet.

The text of Whitman's poems follows that in the 1884 Philadelphia edition of *Leaves of Grass*.

Song of Myself

In this poem Whitman emphasizes his democratic ideas by identifying himself with all manner of men — hence the long catalog, such as that in stanza 16. Beyond that preoccupation with " my own diversity " is the idea that all experience, all persons and things, are equal. He glorifies the commonplace, exalts the sensual, and dignifies the paradoxical.

Crossing Brooklyn Ferry

In Specimen Days (1882) Whitman records that during the fifties and sixties, he rode the Fulton ferry between New York and Brooklyn almost daily, " often up in the pilot-houses where I could get a full sweep, absorbing shows, accompaniments, surroundings. What oceanic currents, eddies, underneath — the great tides of humanity also, with ever-shifting movements! Indeed I have always had a passion for ferries; to me they afford inimitable, streaming, never-failing, living poems."

Whitman again identifies himself with all persons, present, past, and future, and his experience with theirs. In a mystical way, he feels that the common experience of riding on the ferry constitutes an affinity between people of different generations.

Cavalry Crossing a Ford

This and the two poems following grew out of Whitman's own experience in the Civil War. In 1862 he nursed a younger brother in Fredericksburg, Virginia, and for the next three years cared for the wounded in hospitals in and near Washington. " Cavalry Crossing a Ford " and " As Toilsome I Wander'd Virginia's Woods " are brief, sharp etchings. " Come Up from the Fields Father " is a poignant, sincere expression of grief; but despite his sensitiveness to tragedy, he felt that the war must go on, in order that the Union might be preserved.

Pioneers! O Pioneers!

Whitman had great faith in the West. In " The American of the Future " he envisioned an ideal community of the future, " some pleasant Western settlement or town " (see p. 194). The pioneer to him is here a symbol of his democratic ideal. He celebrates the pioneer's strength, his optimism and courage, his willingness to put the past behind him. And he mystically identifies himself with the whole pioneer spirit.

OLIVER WENDELL HOLMES

Although Oliver Wendell Holmes (1809–1894) is known today chiefly as a poet, he was much more than that to nineteenth-century Boston. He was Professor of Anatomy and Physiology in the Harvard Medical School, a brilliant conversationalist at the Saturday Club, and a witty essayist of *Breakfast Table* fame. James Russell Lowell accepted the first editorship of the *Atlantic Monthly* only on condition that Holmes would agree to be a contributor. And the Harvard Class of '29 was immortalized by his affectionate verses. His paper on " The Contagiousness of Puerperal Fever " is still recognized as a genuine contribution to medical science, despite the controversy it aroused in 1843. Holmes wrote what he called " medicated fiction," of which *Elsie Venner* (1861) is best known. But he remains the gifted " occasional " poet, slyly humorous, ever warm, urbane, and graceful.

The Last Leaf

Holmes said that this poem was suggested by the presence of " a venerable relic of the Revolution " on Boston's streets, wearing a cocked hat and knee breeches. The figure reminded him, he said, of a leaf that has clung to its branch through the storms of winter and remains while the new spring growth bursts around it. The " relic " was Major Thomas Melville, grandfather of Herman Melville.

Old Ironsides

When the Secretary of the Navy decided in 1830 that the frigate *Constitution*, familiarly known as *Old Ironsides,* was unfit for further service and should be dismantled, the nation's sentimental affection for this symbol of American naval victories asserted itself. Holmes voiced the general indignation in this poem, which was first printed in the *Boston Daily Advertiser,* September 15, 1830. Popular feeling swayed the officials, and the ship was preserved. In 1927, the ship was reconstructed for the fourth time, the money coming largely from school children. In 1940, President Roosevelt ordered her recommissioned. She was one of the first three ships built for the United States Navy.

Brother Jonathan's Lament for Sister Caroline

South Carolina was the first state to secede from the Union before the Civil War, voting almost unanimously to take the step, December 20, 1860. On March 25, 1861, before the Fort Sumter incident ignited the nation, Holmes wrote this poem. He looked upon the difficulties as slight, and felt that South Carolina was " petulant," that " there are battles with Fate that can never be won." Once the war had begun, however, his tone became almost bitter, as he urged the North to " Smite the bold traitors."

JOHN GREENLEAF WHITTIER

John Greenleaf Whittier (1807–1892) was an up-country New England Quaker who turned to writing at an early age. William Lloyd Garrison, the abolitionist, published Whittier's first poem in 1826. After a brief schooling the young poet became a newspaper editor. For thirty years before the Civil War, Whittier wrote and spoke in favor of the abolition of slavery, and his social conscience turned him from an imitation of the romantic poets to antislavery poems such as " Massachusetts to Virginia," " The Reformer," and " Ichabod," which reveal not only a genuine humanitarian, but also a militant Quaker spirit. The winter idyl " Snow-Bound " brought him widespread fame, and ballads like " Skipper Ireson's Ride " and " Barbara Frietchie " were very popular. He is at his best in picturing the simple New England countryside and in the sincere devotion of such hymns as " Dear Lord and Father of Mankind " and " The Eternal Goodness." He has been unduly neglected by modern readers, partly because of the journalistic quality of much of his verse, and partly because of the general reaction against the whole school of sentimental poets. Undoubtedly he was too effusively praised by his own generation, but he deserves more from his modern readers than a condescending nod for " Snow-Bound."

The Shoemakers

Whittier's *Songs of Labor* (1850) celebrated half a dozen varieties of craftsmen — shipbuilders, shoemakers, drovers, fishermen, cornhuskers, and lumbermen. In the dedication he defends his interest in " life's common things," and hopes that his poems may inspire " a manlier spirit of content " among laboring men. Lines 49 ff. allude to famous men who were shoemakers in their youth. Hans Sachs was the famous sixteenth-century meistersinger (the hero of Wagner's opera); Robert Bloom-field was a minor English poet remembered for his popular poem "The Farmer Boy"; William Gifford was the caustic editor of the *Quarterly Review;* Roger Sherman was a revolutionary political leader whose "patriot fame" was due to his persuasive attitude of moderation; "Behmen" was Jakob Boehme, the seventeenth-century German mystic; and George Fox was the famous English Quaker. St. Crispin (lines 7, 87) was the patron saint of shoemakers.

Massachusetts to Virginia

"Written on reading an account of the proceedings of the citizens of Norfolk, Va., in reference to George Latimer [cf. line 76], the alleged fugitive slave, the result of whose case in Massachusetts will probably be similar to that of the Negro Somerset in England in 1772." — Whittier's note. In a later note, Whittier recalled that when Latimer was arrested in Boston, accused of having escaped from his Norfolk master, fifty thousand Massachusetts citizens signed a petition to Congress calling for laws that would free the state from obligation under the fugitive slave laws. Latimer, contrary to Whittier's prediction, was able to purchase his freedom.

The poem bears similarities to Holmes' "Brother Jonathan's Lament for Sister Caroline" (p. 325, above).

Telling the Bees

"A remarkable custom, brought from the Old Country, formerly prevailed in the rural districts of New England. On the death of a member of the family, the bees were at once informed of the event, and their hives dressed in mourning. This ceremonial was supposed to be necessary to prevent the swarms from leaving their hives and seeking a new home." — Whittier's note.

The drama of the poem, concealed until the very close, arises from the lover's belief that Mary's grandfather has passed away; but when he hears the chore-girl singing, he realizes that his beloved Mary herself is the one who is dead.

ROBERT FROST

Robert Frost (1875–   ) was born in San Francisco, but since the age of ten he has been a New Englander, and his verse has been largely inspired by the country north of Boston. After an irregular schooling and a futile attempt to win recognition in this country, he went to England and published *A Boy's Will* (1913) and *North of Boston* (1914). When the war drove him back to America, his fame preceded him, and with sure technique he produced volume after volume of unhurried poetry. He was soon made a professor of English at Amherst. Three times he was awarded the Pulitzer prize; he has been poet-in-residence at Michigan; and in 1939 was appointed to the Ralph Waldo Emerson Fellowship in poetry at Harvard. Although he is a literary descendant of Wordsworth and Whittier, he is unlike both poets in his use of language. Frost's diction is spare and lean, or, to change the figure, cut from the block of up-country New England dignified colloquialism. For further comment, see Granville Hicks, "The Poetic 'Renaissance,'" pp. 241–242, above.

Henry Wadsworth Longfellow

If the tastes and the literary style of Washington Irving were formed largely in England, Longfellow (1807–1882) was indebted to the whole European continent. For in his years of study in France, Spain, Italy, and Germany he felt the full warmth of Continental romanticism, and later as Smith Professor of Modern Languages at Harvard he ranged widely through the literature of Europe. It is not surprising, therefore, that so many of his narrative poems should be foreign not only in spirit, but also in setting — Old English, Scandinavian, French, Spanish, Italian. But Longfellow was an American and a New Englander, and much of his most popular poetry centers about his home and community. In the light of his later popularity, it is significant that, although he began to write while he was still an undergraduate at Bowdoin College, it was not until 1854 that he felt secure enough as a poet to resign his professorship. *Evangeline* had already appeared in 1847, and his production of poems long and short continued, with *The Song of Hiawatha* in 1855, *The Courtship of Miles Standish* in 1858, *The Tales of a Wayside Inn* in 1863, and the translation of *The Divine Comedy* in 1867, to name but a few volumes. Few persons know Longfellow well: his reputation has rested on a relatively few titles which have tended to become threadbare. But he is far more than a sentimental fireside poet of grade-school textbooks. As a sonneteer, he is probably unsurpassed in America; he handled the long narrative poem skillfully; he stood for clear-cut aesthetic values, and technically his poems have polish. While he wrote much that had its own immediate reward, much remains of worth and profit, and the selections here are a partial indication of his excellences.

Hawthorne

Hawthorne died on May 19, 1864, and was buried four days later in the Sleepy Hollow cemetery in Concord. " The hill-top hearsed with pines " is also the resting place of Emerson and Thoreau, and the spot is not far from the " meadow, manse, and stream " which Longfellow recalls.

The Song of Hiawatha

" This Indian Edda — if I may so call it — is founded on a tradition prevalent among the North American Indians, of a personage of miraculous birth, who was sent among them to clear their rivers, forests, and fishing-grounds, and to teach them the arts of peace. He was known among different tribes by the several names of Michabou, Chiabo, Manabozo, Tarenyawagon, and Hiawatha. . . . Into this old tradition I have woven other curious Indian legends, drawn chiefly from the various writings of Mr. Schoolcraft, to whom the literary world is greatly indebted for his indefatigable zeal in rescuing from oblivion so much of the legendary lore of the Indians.

" The scene of the poem is among the Ojibways on the southern shore of Lake Superior, in the region between the Pictured Rocks and the Grand Sable." — Longfellow's note.

The Birds of Killingworth

The Tales of a Wayside Inn, a series of narrative poems set in a " frame " not unlike that of Chaucer's *Canterbury Tales,* is known to all readers through the Landlord's tale of " Paul Revere's Ride." The final tale in the first series is " The Birds of Killingworth," and is told by the Poet. Longfellow perhaps unconsciously casts a slur on the piece when, in order to keep his storytellers in character, he allows the Landlord to close his eyes during the Poet's story and make a " sonorous sound " like " distant bagpipes," whereupon all laugh and the Landlord bestirs himself and swears he has been listening with eyes closed.

The Wayside Inn is in Sudbury, not far from Boston; Killingworth is in southern Connecticut, only a few miles from Long Island Sound (cf. line 17).

RALPH WALDO EMERSON

For a biographical note on Emerson, see above, p. 824.

Concord Hymn

This poem, to which Emerson gave the less appropriate final title of " Concord Fight," was written to be sung at the unveiling of the monument marking the Concord battleground. The event was to have taken place on April 19, 1836, the anniversary of the battle, but seems to have been deferred until July 4 of the next year.

Terminus

As a poem expressing a philosophical view of old age, " Terminus " invites comparison with Tennyson's " Crossing the Bar " and Browning's " Prospice."

EDGAR ALLAN POE

The brief and unfortunate life of Edgar Allan Poe (1809–1849) is too well known to require detailed comment. It is a story of continued poverty, thankless hack writing, discontent with family, and conflict with sentimental literary conventions of the time. Against this background Poe appears as a paradoxical person, embracing alternately the phantasmagoric and the cold logic of mathematics. Undoubtedly he was handicapped by living at a time when literary artistry was only scantily appreciated. During his stormy life his excellent criticism in the *Southern Literary Messenger* and *Graham's Magazine* was generally underestimated, and only " The Raven " brought him fame. In many respects Poe's work seems foreign, but it is in reality an American outcropping of a widespread romanticism, in a young country where foreign influences were yet dominant. His development of the technique of the short story was notable, and in his poetry, as one critic has pointed out, he has sought, " by blurred image and verbal melody to hypnotize the reader into a willing suspension of disbelief."

To Helen

The poem records the poet's grief at the death of " the first purely ideal love of my soul," Mrs. Jane Stith Stanard of Richmond. Lowell said that the poem was written when Poe was only fourteen years of age, but Professor Killis Campbell pointed out that if it had been written in 1824 it would have appeared in Poe's editions of 1827 and 1829, whereas it first appears in the 1831 volume. Whatever the facts of composition, it remains an almost perfect lyric.

Lenore

Poe is frequently preoccupied with the death of a beautiful woman as being " unquestionably the most poetical topic in the world." This poem is given added dramatic quality by the speeches of Lenore's lover, Guy De Vere, in the second and fourth stanzas; her own relatives speak in the first and third stanzas. The poem underwent considerable revision after its original publication in 1831. Note the interesting rearrangement of the final stanza in 1849:

> " Avaunt! — avaunt! to friends from fiends the
> indignant ghost is riven —
> From Hell unto a high estate within the utmost
> Heaven —
> From moan and groan to a golden throne beside the
> King of Heaven: —
> Let no bell toll, then, lest her soul, amid its
> hallowed mirth,
> Should catch the note as it doth float up from
> the damnèd Earth!
> And I — to-night my heart is light: — no dirge
> will I upraise,
> But waft the angel on her flight with a Paean
> of old days! "

Ulalume

Many interpretations of " Ulalume," some of them autobiographical, have been suggested. But it is difficult to believe, for instance, that the poem is " a cry of utter despair from a man's inmost soul " simply because Poe's child bride Virginia Clemm had died a few months before " Ulalume " was published. Poe tried many experiments in the creation of unusual emotional effects; the use of fantastic geography and such phrases as " alley Titantic," " ghoul-haunted woodland," and " boreal pole " would suggest that whatever the significance of the feminine references in the poem, Poe's chief interest here was creating an impression of a wild other-worldliness.

Eldorado

El Dorado is the name given to the legendary South American city where gold and precious stones abound to a fabulous degree. The poem was probably suggested to Poe by the gold rush of 1849, but the larger implications of a quest for the ideal are also evident.

Annabel Lee

One of Poe's most splendid lyrics, "Annabel Lee" was among Poe's three or four final compositions. Attempts to identify the feminine source of inspiration of this poem have been unsuccessful, and seem peculiarly irrelevant.

SIDNEY LANIER

Sidney Lanier (1842–1881) is one of the South's most distinctive poets. He graduated from Oglethorpe College only a short time before the outbreak of the Civil War, served as a scout and later as officer on blockade runners, and spent the last months of the war in a Federal prison, where his health was seriously imperiled. After almost a decade of discouraging attempts to find a career and to guard his weak constitution, he went to Baltimore in 1873 to join the Peabody Orchestra as flautist. From that time until his death eight years later, his career flourished modestly. In 1875 he published two long poems, "Corn" and "The Symphony"; two years later he issued a volume of verse; in 1879 he was appointed lecturer in English literature at the Johns Hopkins University; and throughout the last ten years of his life he was adding little by little to the store of poetry that was collected by his widow and published in 1884. Most of his life was devoted to the taxing struggle for existence, and his terrier-like courage in the face of tuberculosis reminds one of Keats. Many of his poems are romantic and sentimental, but there is a vein of steel and careful logic in his best work; and his sensitive musical ear assisted him in attaining a high degree of metrical polish. The sectional loyalty of his Southern admirers has often led to personal, rather than aesthetic judgments; some Northern critics have been equally unjust in dismissing him as another local poet. Within a narrow range Lanier just missed greatness, and his poetry, rooted in familiar soil, is addressed to all men.

Song of the Chattahoochee

The Chattahoochee River rises in Habersham County in northern Georgia, flows southward through Hall County and eventually becomes the western boundary of the state before emptying into the Gulf of Mexico.

This has always been Lanier's most popular poem, despite the objection of some critics that Lanier has rather unpoetically linked Duty with the forces of gravity (lines 44 ff.).

Corn

This poem and the dialect piece that follows illustrate Lanier's interest in the economic plight of the South after the Civil War. Here he feels that rotation of crops is necessary and that the popular notion of cotton as a staple cash crop is a delusion. He was right, of course; but it is doubtful that the substitution of corn would alone dispel the evils of the one-crop system. His narrative of the poor farmer at the mercy of a banker's loan (lines 131–184) recalls an oppression which has dogged farmers of every time and place. In an interesting passage earlier (lines 52–110), he sets forth the role of the poet in society.

Stephen Vincent Benét

It is not surprising that Stephen Vincent Benét (1898–   ) should have written a narrative poem about the Civil War, since his ancestors for three generations were army officers. He was educated at Yale, and after several years of successful magazine writing he spent 1926 and 1927 in France on a Guggenheim fellowship. In these years he wrote the uniquely successful *John Brown's Body*. It won the Pulitzer prize in 1928, and was more widely read than almost any poetic narrative since the time of Longfellow and Tennyson. Mr. Benét has written several other volumes of poetry and a number of novels. His *Thirteen O'Clock* (1937) includes some of his best short stories, of which " The Devil and Daniel Webster " is representative, with its folk treatment of the supernatural.

John Brown's Body

John Brown's Body is a kaleidoscopic poem. It is not a history of the Civil War, as Benét is careful to point out, but it is based upon careful research, and it gives a truer picture of some of the psychological realities than can be found in most histories. The method is impressionistic, focusing on many groups of historical and fictitious characters; but in the foreground are a few individuals in whom the tragedy and triumph of the war are symbolized. As Henry Seidel Canby has pointed out, this poem could not have been written before the modern novelists had expanded the subject-matter and sensitized the method of fiction. Here the war becomes a complex of personalities and inanimate forces, and technically the poem is indebted to modern influences as diverse as James Joyce and the movies. Much of its effectiveness lies in Benét's versatility with poetic form and diction — a versatility only suggested in the three excerpts from the poem reprinted in this volume. The " Invocation," suggesting the opening of classical epics, is addressed to the " American muse whose strong and diverse heart So many men have tried to understand "; in it Benét seeks to characterize that amorphous but living thing that is the American spirit. " Mountaineers " not only illustrates characteristic folk attitudes, which Benét has so successfully caught in some of his short stories, but also reveals a dramatic power swift and sure, and an impeccable control of diction. In " Appomattox " his avoidance of the usual romantic heroics makes Lee's surrender a moment of genuine emotion; and the homely details at the conclusion of the scene are worth a hundred maudlin gestures.

James Russell Lowell

Like most poets who try to become lawyers, Lowell (1819–1891) spent several germinal years in an empty office, trying few cases, many literary experiments. After he decided to abandon the law for literature, success came to him quickly. While he was yet in his twenties the " annus mirabilis " of 1848 saw the publication of *A Fable for Critics, The Vision of Sir Launfal,* the first series of *The Biglow Papers,* and the two-volume *Poems.* Thus was this Bostonian launched in a literary world of which Boston was a self-confessed center. In 1855 he succeeded Longfellow as Smith Professor of Modern Languages at Harvard, and in 1857 he became the first editor of the *Atlantic Monthly.* He continued to teach until 1872, when he gave up not only his Harvard post, but also the co-editorship of the *North American Review,* which he had assumed in 1864 after having left the *Atlantic* in 1861. In 1877 he was named minister to Spain, and from 1880 to 1885 he was America's ambassador to Great Britain. In a long and varied career the poet, essayist, professor, editor, and diplomat thus touched public life of his generation at many points. Although some modern critics have seen shallowness in his simplicity, appreciation rather than judgment in his criticism, bookish amateurishness in his scholarship, they can scarcely overlook the masterful pungency of his satiric verse and the nobility of the heroic " Commemoration Ode." As a critic he resembles Lamb in possessing what William Watson called " judgment aërated by wit," and he is genial and urbane even when he is not intellectually rigorous.

The Pious Editor's Creed

This poem appeared in the first series of *The Biglow Papers*. Lowell created Hosea Biglow, a country New Englander, as the author of dialect poems supposedly sent to the editor of the Boston *Courier* by a Rev. Homer Wilbur (who added his own pedantic commentary). The poems were usually political satires, and won a ready audience. They were quoted far and wide, their authorship debated. Wrote Lowell, " I once even, when rumor had at length caught up my name in one of its eddies, had the satisfaction of hearing it demonstrated . . . that *I* was utterly incompetent to have written anything of the kind."

" The Pious Editor's Creed " condemns mercenary editors with an irony that is obvious. But Lowell has Parson Wilbur underline the point with two quotation-sprinkled pages of preface: " Our editor . . . takes up the crook, not that the sheep may be fed, but that he may never want a warm woolen suit and a joint of mutton. . . . For which reason I would derive the name *editor* not so much from *edo,* to publish, as from *edo,* to eat, that being the peculiar profession to which he esteems himself called. He blows up the flames of political discord for no other occasion than that he may thereby handily boil his own pot."

The Courtin'

From *The Biglow Papers,* second series.

Concerning the language of *The Biglow Papers,* Lowell wrote: " In choosing the Yankee dialect, I did not act without forethought. It had long seemed to me that the great vice of American writing and speaking was a studied want of simplicity . . . and that the only chance of escape was by seeking it at its living sources among those who were . . . ' divinely illiterate.' " See the essay of Max Eastman, " Humor and America," pp. 195 ff., above.

Ode Recited at the Harvard Commemoration

This poem, one of the finest pieces of elevated verse that America has produced, was written for a service commemorating the Harvard men who fought in the Civil War. The ninth section was added after the poem was first published in the *Atlantic Monthly,* September, 1865. Briefly summarized by sections, the thought of the poem is as follows: 1. Poetry is "weak-winged" compared with "live battle-odes," but it may preserve the memory of heroic deeds. 2. Harvard's motto "Veritas" symbolizes the principles for which her sons "offered their fresh lives." 3. "Many loved Truth . . . but these, our brothers, fought for her." 4. "Is Earth too poor to give us Something to live for?" 5. "Peace hath her not ignoble wreath," but "To front a lie in arms and not to yield" is "God's plan And measure of a stalwart man." 6. Lincoln, "the first American," was such a man. 7. "Our brothers" were animated by this "faith in some ideal Good." 8. We welcome the returning soldiers, and "salute the sacred dead." 9. "The Soul resents Such short-lived service" as ends in oblivion, and "She claims a more divine investiture" in "a new imperial race." 10. The "rescued Nation," which has set "Her heel on treason" (disunity), is the envy of outworn Europe. 11. "'Tis no Man we celebrate," but the nation saved from civil strife. 12. "O Beautiful! my Country! ours once more!"

EDWIN ARLINGTON ROBINSON

Like Robert Frost, E. A. Robinson (1869–1935) has lived in a modern age yet in some respects has remained strangely aloof from it. Born in Maine and attracted to poetry early in life, he was middle-aged before recognition came to him. After two years at Harvard he held various non-literary jobs — working on the construction gang of a New York subway, writing advertising for a Boston department store. A volume of poems printed at his own expense brought him encouragement but no public. And the reception of his *Children of the Night* (1897), his second book, was satisfactory but not spectacular, until President Theodore Roosevelt reviewed the second edition for the *Outlook* in 1905. Roosevelt not only spread his fame, but found the poet a post in the New York customhouse. In 1910 Robinson published *The Town Down the River,* and from that year devoted himself entirely to poetry. A series of distinguished volumes — among them *The Man Against the Sky* (1916), *Tristram* (1927), *Cavender's House* (1929) — established him as the foremost poet of his time. During the last twenty-five years of his life, many honors came to him, including three Pulitzer awards and several honorary degrees.

Despite the high quality of his work, Robinson has not been a popular poet. *Tristram* reached the largest audience and stimulated the sale of later volumes, but his poems have never produced a liberal financial return. It is not difficult to understand why: Robinson was not a writer of tinkling verses, not a shallow optimist complacent in a world that seemed to him imperfect at so many vital points. In the searching brief narratives reprinted here one sees a severe conscience seriously, though seldom bitterly, examining the vagaries of life. Robinson's ideas are not expressed conventionally or obviously, and the occasional obscurity of his verse has been another barrier to widespread popularity. But there is much to be said for the cool-eyed unpopular poet whose standard is not determined by the tastes of the masses. If he is too much the brooding onlooker, we should remember that he represents an important school of American thought. His attitude is the attitude, *mutatis mutandis,* of Henry Adams, of Lincoln Steffens, of Edgar Lee Masters, of the early Dreiser. Tone aside, his handling of metrics, his skill in epigrammatic expression, is nowhere more brilliantly displayed in short poems than in the four reprinted in this volume. In longer poems like *Merlin, Lancelot,* and *Tristram,* his skill in investing romantic subject-matter with sensuous beauty and occasional humor marks him as a versatile poet who, using traditional forms in an age of almost frantic experimentation, has added distinction and depth to the range of American poetry.

For further comment, see Granville Hicks, " The Poetic ' Renaissance,' " pp. 240–241, above.

AMY LOWELL

" I made myself a poet," Amy Lowell (1874–1925) is said to have quipped, " but God made me a business man." The remark is as characteristic of her as it is revealing. She did not become seriously interested in poetry until 1902, when she was in her late twenties; but when she once determined to become a poet, she bent all her efforts in that direction. For eight years she ranged widely, studying all manner of poetic composition, before she sent any of her own work forth into the world. *A Dome of Many-Coloured Glass* (1912), her first collection of poems, was conventional, and was scarcely a prelude to what was soon to follow. In the next year when she met Ezra Pound, John Gould Fletcher, Hilda Doolittle, and other experimentalists in England, she became a swift convert to " imagism." Indeed, with characteristic aggressiveness, she soon succeeded Pound as the chief spokesman for the new movement. In *Sword Blades and Poppy Seed* (1914) and later volumes she illustrated, in free verse and polyphonic prose, the principles laid down in the Imagist Manifesto:

To use the language of common speech, but to employ always the *exact* word . . . To create new rhythms . . . To allow absolute freedom in the choice of subject . . . To present an Image. We are not a school of painters, but we believe that poetry should render particulars exactly and not deal in vague generalities, however magnificent and sonorous . . . To produce poetry that is hard and clear . . . Finally, most of us believe that concentration is of the very essence of poetry.

Her interest in Keats led her to write a two-volume study of his life and works; and her exhaustion from the labors of the book brought on her death in 1925. She attracted wide, if irrelevant, publicity for eccentricities such as her fondness for reversing the usual working and sleeping hours, her phobia for mirrors, her mannishness (symbolized for most people by her cigar smoking), and her imperious treatment of publishers and critics. In her writing she was a sincere and serious craftsman, searching for the precise image, achieving a mastery of sensuous, rhythmic free verse with the " hard and clear " effect desired by a wider circle than the faddish Imagists. Despite the limitations of the group with which her name is commonly linked — an exuberance of revolt often led them to extravagance — Amy Lowell appears to advantage whenever she can combine vivid clarity of diction with subject-matter that allows a play of intellectual humor. The swift etchings of " The Dinner-Party " are thus characteristic of her style at its best.

VACHEL LINDSAY

Vachel Lindsay (1879–1931) has been called a jazz poet and a jingle man. His early tours of the country with his " Rhymes to be traded for bread " have led critics to speak loosely and very inaccurately of his " deeply degraded beggary." Actually he is more than a jazz poet, just as he was more than a degraded beggar when he went on the road. His parents intended him for medicine, and he himself wanted to be an artist. After very good training in Chicago and New York, and a European sojourn, he failed to find an outlet for his work, and turned to lecturing on art at the New York Y.M.C.A. After he had begun to write poetry, he made several walking tours " as an act of protest against the United States commercial standard," before his work won recognition. But with the publication of " General Booth Enters into Heaven " in 1913, and " Congo " the following year, he became popular. The troubadour role of lecturing now included colleges and universities, and in addition to reading his poems, he crusaded for an increased emphasis upon sound and rhythm in poetry (note his use of directions for reading, pp. 382, 384). Because of his interest in achieving colloquial effects, he has frequently descended to a kind of doggerel which is appropriate to his atmosphere and subject-matter, but which is scarcely great. Lindsay was fond of Poe and Swinburne, and the same emphasis upon rhythm and sensuous effect is present in his verse. The reformer in Lindsay led him to sponsor Anti-Saloon League activities and a shirt-sleeve conception of democracy with almost equal fervor; but his enthusiasm, if it has not made for distinguished poetry, has developed the modern American idiom into a virile and expressive vehicle.

The Proud Farmer

This is the first of three poems which Lindsay often read as a group under the title " A Gospel of Beauty." " Taken as a triad," Lindsay said, " they hold in solution my theory of American civilization."

General Booth Enters into Heaven

During his travels, Lindsay spent several nights in Salvation Army quarters when he was out of funds, and he came to know the organization from the inside. In a note on this poem he added, " In the spring of 1912 the news went around the world that the great founder of the Army [William Booth] had gone blind. . . . Later came the announcement of his death, with elaborate biographies. . . . In my poem I merely turned into rhyme as well as I could, word for word, General Booth's own account of his life, and the telegraph dispatches of his death after going blind. I set it to the tune that is not a tune, but a speech, a refrain used most frequently in the meetings of the Army on any public square to this day."

The Eagle That Is Forgotten

John P. Altgeld was a German immigrant who became a Chicago judge and later a governor of Illinois. While in office he pardoned the anarchists who were serving heavy prison sentences for participating in the Haymarket riot, and by so doing brought down upon himself a storm of protest from conservatives. To Lindsay he stands as a fearless champion of human rights. To workingmen throughout America Altgeld is still a symbol of the enlightened liberal official.

In Praise of Johnny Appleseed

John Chapman was a pioneer herbalist and philosopher who went west, " singing the ways of the Ancient of Days," and planting apple orchards " that would march and train on, in his name to the great Pacific." With the interest of a folk poet,

Lindsay makes the story of the man who became known as Johnny Appleseed symbolic of the whole nineteenth-century pioneer movement. The poet refers the reader to an article on Chapman in *Harper's Monthly Magazine,* November, 1871. See also the account of Chapman in the *Dictionary of American Biography.*

CARL SANDBURG

Amy Lowell, writing of Carl Sandburg (1878–   ) in *A Critical Fable* (1922), said of him: " He has sight of a loveliness no man has seen, and . . . a great flowing power of words to express its hugeness and littleness." She went on to deplore his sense of equalitarian democracy, his " demagogy," his unwillingness to rise from an artisan to an artist. To some extent her criticism is justifiable. Sandburg's poetry was not the poetry of beauty, but a poetry of the life he had known when he knocked about the country doing all sorts of odd jobs, meeting all sorts of people. His idiom is by no means a Middle Western equivalent of Frost's New England folk speech. Where Frost's language is spare but sharp and dignified, Sandburg's, in *Chicago Poems* (1916) and *Smoke and Steel* (1920), at any rate, is the bruising, brawling language of truck drivers and steel workers, of rough men and ready women. The new idiom in American poetry may not have seemed unpoetic to Amy Lowell, but she did dislike Sandburg's Whitmanesque affiliation with the people en masse.

As to the poetry itself, Sandburg has since shown that he was a sensitive craftsman who deliberately sought the effects of unloveliness produced in " Chicago " and " To a Contemporary Bunkshooter." A later volume, *The People, Yes* (1936), renews his faith in the democratic ideal, but the tone is slightly less strenuous. Meantime, if Sandburg's capacities as an artist needed further proof, it was being eloquently supplied in his six-volume biography of Lincoln — *The Prairie Years* (1926) and *The War Years* (1939). This valuable study is penetrating, warm, poetic; and though it does not present any startling new approach to the man, the spiritual affinity between biographer and subject produced a rare understanding of the president's quizzical personality. As a poet of the common people and biographer of one of its heroes, Sandburg has naturally been interested in folk literature, and his *American Songbag* (1927) is a splendid collection of native ballads and folk songs (some of which he has recorded in Musicraft Album 11).

For further comment, see Granville Hicks, " The Poetic ' Renaissance,' " p. 239, above.

ARCHIBALD MACLEISH

Archibald MacLeish (1892–   ) has had a rather complex and constant development as a poet. The influence of T. S. Eliot, Ezra Pound, and the French symbolists in his early work is pronounced, and may be seen characteristically in *The Hamlet of A. MacLeish* (1928). With *Conquistador* (1932), a poem of epic proportions on the conquest of Mexico, he turned to the romantic story of Cortez, where his poetry assumed greater breadth and less of the *Waste Land* variety of preoccupation than had characterized his earlier work. Since *Conquistador,* MacLeish has accepted the social functions of the poet, pointing out that poetry fails to achieve its potentialities as long as it is a " teacup art," divorced from political and social problems. And he urges the poet to drop the private language so characteristic of a generation of post-war poets, and realize the power as well as the obligation of public speech. Whatever the artistic limitations of this point of view, MacLeish illustrated his changing attitude in *Public Speech* (1936), from which " Speech to Those Who Say Comrade " is taken. His diction is simplified, his message more direct, and certainly the impetus to poetry more social. This artistic development of MacLeish somewhat paralleled his personal career: whereas he left a successful legal practice to devote himself to poetry, and spent several years in Europe and Asia during the twenties, in the thirties he became successively an editor of *Fortune,* Curator of the Nieman Collection of Journalism at Harvard, and, in 1939, Librarian of Congress. His verse plays *Panic* (1935), *The Fall of the City* (1937), and *Air Raid* (1938) — the two latter written for radio — have emphasized his intensified effort to reach the widest possible audience with all the poetic intensity that can be brought to bear on poignant problems of humanity. If, as Arthur Mizener has said, MacLeish arrives at a complete rationalization of a point of view just as he is about to abandon it (for most artists theory usually follows practice), at least he has continued to develop, and though his verse is often imitative, no one man has remained his master.

Drama

LYNN RIGGS: Green Grow the Lilacs

Lynn Riggs was born in 1899 in Claremore, Oklahoma, then in Indian Territory. After early schooling he turned to various jobs before he became interested in writing — he was a cowpuncher, a singer, a proofreader, a movie extra, and ranged widely over the country. In the early twenties he entered the University of Oklahoma to further a budding poetic career, but he soon began to write plays, and a comedy *Cuckoo* was produced at the University in 1922. The Santa Fé Players presented his *Knives from Syria,* and in quick succession Riggs wrote *The Primitives, Sump'n Like Wings,* and *Big Lake,* all of them developing Southwestern folk material. None of these plays reached Broadway, but Barrett H. Clark, the theatrical critic, was impressed with Riggs' unusual material and dramatic promise and recommended him for a Guggenheim fellowship, which he was granted in 1928. During a year abroad Riggs wrote two plays. *Borned in Texas,* rechristened *Roadside* and " aimlessly " produced on Broadway, was a failure. The other, *Green Grow the Lilacs,* opened early in 1931 and was a successful play in a season that included *Private Lives, The Barretts of Wimpole Street,* and *Grand Hotel.* Since *Green Grow the Lilacs,* Riggs has worked more slowly. *Russet Mantle* had a four-month Broadway run in 1936, but did not add to Riggs' earlier reputation.

As a regional play, *Green Grow the Lilacs* invites comparison with *The Green Pastures* and *Tobacco Road.* In theme it is of course far removed from either, since Riggs' major emphasis is upon a vanishing way of life rather than a social problem or a semi-fantastic re-creation of a racial myth. Through the distinctive idiom of folk speech and highly atmospheric music Riggs weaves a poetic texture into the realities of the stage. Some of the Broadway critics felt that Riggs' poetic sense was superior to his drama, and though granting the play's high entertainment value, were inclined to credit it to the music and the skillful production rather than to the genius of the playwright. They praised the scene in the smoke-house as being the best-written in the entire play (in order to visualize the strong dramatic effect the reader should remember that Scenes 2 and 3 are played simultaneously), but to some critics Laurey seemed a rather conventional heroine and Jeeter a stock melodramatic villain. Richard Lockridge, in a " morning-after " review which might not have represented his considered judgment, said in the New York *Sun* that the dialogue did not ring true. " It is not that the idiom is strange," he said. " That is a detail. It is that Mr. Riggs has made it all up out of his head, arbitrarily." This criticism raises an interesting problem, but one may not necessarily agree with Mr. Lockridge. John Mason Brown of the *Post,* for example, said of the language: " Mr. Riggs has heard his cowboys, and recorded their speech admirably as folk speech. He has flavored his play with the pungent, welcome flavor of the land in which it is set." Even though *Green Grow the Lilacs* may lack some of the universal elements present in the best plays of the Irish Renaissance, it is full of gusto and authentic insight into folkways, and illustrates an important side of American life ordinarily neglected in the commercial theater.

In a preface to the published version of the play, Mr. Riggs explained his dramatic aims as follows: " It must be fairly obvious from reading or seeing the play that it might have been subtitled *An Old Song.* The intent has been solely to recapture in a kind of nostalgic glow (but in dramatic dialogue more than in song) the great range of mood which has characterized the old folk songs and ballads I used to hear in my Oklahoma childhood — their quaintness, their sadness, their robustness, their simplicity, their hearty or bawdy humors, their sentimentalities, their melodrama, their touching sweetness. For this reason it seemed wise to throw away the conventions of ordinary theatricality — a complex plot, swift action, etc. — and try to exhibit luminously, in the simplest of stories, a wide area of mood and feeling."

The following glossary, prepared by Mr. Riggs, may be of help to readers whose childhood was less spacious than Curly McClain's:

dogies — specifically, an orphaned calf, but used often, affectionately, as a synonym for cattle.

shikepoke — a mythical Middle West bird, whose activities (unprintable) are embarrassing to everyone. A term of opprobrium.

side meat — bacon.

maverick — an unbranded, and hence ownerless, calf or steer.

off-ox — the ox on the off-side (the right side) of the wagon tongue.

bronc buster — a rider of bucking bronchos.

bull-dogger — one who leaps off a running horse, swings on the horns of a bull or steer, and throws and ties him.

stove arn — that is, stove iron, or handle for lifting the lids.

tetchin' leather — to ride a bronc without touching leather is to ride without hanging on to the saddle horn or any other part of the saddle.

yellin' calf-rope — to yell calf-rope signifies defeat.

to change the green lilacs to the red, white and blue — means, " I'm going to join the army."

string-haltered — a corruption of spring-halted, a convulsive movement of the hind legs of a horse.

Dan Patch — a celebrated racing horse, a pacer.

Jick — the joker in a pack of cards.

bottom — that is, river bottom, the low land along a river.

backwater — the water backed up, from being unable to empty into a swollen stream now higher than its tributaries.

shivoree — a corruption of the French *charivari,* a wedding celebration.

the A. H. T. A. — the Anti-Horse Thief Association.

THORNTON WILDER: Our Town

Thornton Wilder (1897–   ) was born in Madison, Wisconsin, was educated in America and the Orient, and graduated from Yale in 1920. For a number of years thereafter he taught French at the Lawrenceville School. He achieved literary prominence in 1927 with his second novel, *The Bridge of San Luis Rey,* and left teaching to devote himself entirely to fiction. *The Woman of Andros* appeared in 1930 and *Heaven's My Destination* four years later, but neither was an advance upon the technical brilliance, if remote content, of his earlier work. After the somewhat unsympathetic critical reception accorded *Heaven's My Destination,* Wilder announced that he was forsaking the novel for the drama. Actually he had published several volumes of plays already, but *Our Town* (1938) was the first to reach Broadway. It was an immediate success and won the Pulitzer prize (as had *The Bridge of San Luis Rey* a decade earlier). The play has been given hundreds of performances on Broadway and in summer theaters, and Wilder himself has upon occasion appeared as the Stage Manager.

The most conspicuous feature of *Our Town* is the absence of scenery and the unconventional way in which the real and the imaginary are mingled. The playgoer is actively a participant in the play, since Wilder is deliberately requiring him to lend his imagination to the action and " restage it inside his own head." The sceneryless play is not new: the Middle English miracle plays depended very little upon the realism of the pageant-wagon; the Shakespearean plays designated " night " or " Bohemia " with a placard and except for scenes on the inner stage were almost completely independent of properties. The Wilder device, then, is not original. Indeed, it was not new even to Wilder himself, for in 1931 he published a volume of one-act plays which included the sceneryless " Happy Journey to Trenton and Camden." He used the device again, he said, because he wished " to record a village's life on the stage, with realism and with generality."

And that is an important consideration here. For Grover's Corners is not only a New Hampshire town. The title points up Wilder's interest in life, love, and death anywhere and everywhere. He seeks to achieve this universality by emphasizing the details we all cherish yet take so much for granted that we are scarcely conscious of them. As he wrote, he was seeking the answer to questions that haunted him: " What is the relation between the countless ' unimportant ' details of our daily life, on the one hand, and the great perspectives of time, social history and current religious ideas on the other? What is trivial and what is significant about any one person's making a breakfast, engaging in a domestic quarrel, in a ' love scene,' in dying? " The answers are implicit throughout the play, but Wilder had originally written a section in which they were stated openly. In an intermediate draft of the play the Stage Manager spoke of mementoes which were being placed in the cornerstone of the new bank; the articles were to be chemically treated so that they would last a thousand or two thousand years. *Our Town* itself was to be included, said the Stage Manager, " so that future ages will know more about the life of the average person: More than just the Treaty of Versailles and the Lindbergh Flight — see what I mean? "

The occasional attack on the play by a school of uncomfortable critics can be anticipated. A few objected that Wilder had presented too idyllic a picture, that he ignored the influence of an industrial civilization and sidestepped the problem of human depravity. Actually, of course, the Stage Manager admits that Grover's Corners may be a little better behaved than some other towns, but he won't claim that the town is perfect. John Mason Brown in *Two on the Aisle* dismisses this criticism by insisting that Wilder's purpose was to be representative, to emphasize " the unexceptional, the average, the personal," a view which Wilder's statements substantiate. " Personally," Brown concluded, " I should as soon think of condemning the Twenty-third Psalm because it lacks the factual observation of Sinclair Lewis and the social point of view of Granville Hicks as I would of accusing *Our Town* of being too unrealistically observed."

MARC CONNELLY: The Green Pastures

Marc Connelly (1890–   ), a Pennsylvanian by birth, worked on several Pittsburgh newspapers before coming to New York in 1915. From writing lyrics for musical comedies he drifted to play-doctoring and contributing to the old *Life,* but his theatrical career really began when he collaborated with George S. Kaufman in *Dulcy* (1921). This successful comedy established both authors and brought recognition also to Lynn Fontanne, who played the title role. The Kaufman-Connelly partnership resulted in three other successful plays during their five years together — *To the Ladies,* a comedy, *Merton of the Movies,* a satire on the Hollywood industry, and the important expressionistic *Beggar on Horseback*. After 1925 Kaufman joined forces successively with Edna Ferber, Morrie Ryskind, and Moss Hart in a long succession of skillful wisecracking plays more important for their topicality and bright satire than for their enduring qualities. Meantime Connelly continued alone. His *Wisdom Tooth* was an engaging fantasy, but of his later plays only *The Green Pastures* (1930) reveals his full stature as a playwright.

In a note immediately preceding the play (p. 500), Connelly explains that he is trying to present " certain aspects of a living religion in terms of its believers." If God created Man in His own image, it is equally true that much of the human race has reversed the process by imagining an anthropomorphic God with human habits and emotions. Connelly therefore assumes that to many uneducated Southern Negroes, God is a kind of " boss-man," with an office, ten-cent cigars, and a benevolent attitude toward saint and sinner alike. If such a conception seems to belittle the deity, it should not be forgotten that the Negro of whom Connelly is thinking is creating a God he can visualize, just as he creates visions of a " tangible, three-dimensional Heaven." Far from being sacrilege, it represents perhaps the sincerest form of belief of which he is capable. And in that spirit Connelly presents parts of the Bible story as the sort of folk myth the old Negro preachers rationalized in order to make the remote pre-Christian world seem real and vivid. The importance of Roark Bradford's *Ol' Man Adam an' His Chillun* to Connelly's success can scarcely be overemphasized. Admittedly Connelly developed Bradford's stories imaginatively, creating a number of non-Biblical characters, and providing a unity which is not in the original. But much of the spirit of Bradford's stories is present in the play, and not a little of the dialogue has been preserved.

"De Lawd" is, significantly, not the God of vengeance, but a compassionate Being, "the summation of all the virtues His follower has observed in the human beings about him." And he is not always omniscient. Because of these two attributes of its chief character, the play can have its moments of comedy without offense; moreover, the serious undertone throughout the play is powerful just because it is human and simple. Finally, to capture the effectiveness of *The Green Pastures* completely, one should not forget the Negro spirituals which form brief interludes between scenes. Sung by an invisible choir, they not only create much of the play's atmosphere, but also prepare the audience for changes in mood from one scene to another. (Most of the spirituals named in the stage directions may be found in *The Books of American Negro Spirituals,* edited by James Weldon Johnson and J. Rosamond Johnson [one-volume edition, 1940].)

Folk Tales

Nothing in our literature is quite so characteristic of the American temper as is our humor. The spirit of braggadocio has given us a rich treasure of tall tales; the sharp-dealing of the Yankee peddler has immortalized the anecdote of shrewdness; the very immensity of the country has contributed to the creation of superhuman folk-heroes; and the frontier society's contempt for pallid gentility has given us the funny-man's playfulness with illiteracy. Holmes and Lowell, Mark Twain and Bret Harte were professional writers and their humorous work enjoyed popularity and acclaim. But until recently the humor of the frontier and the backwoods, like the ballad and the folk song, was considered sub-literary. Now that our social historians have given us a clearer perspective of the past, we can see how the conditions described by Frederick Jackson Turner and Carl Becker produced an oral literature rich in vigor, now scrupulous in its realism, now spinning out fancies without restraint. *The Spirit of the Times,* an antebellum ancestor of the *Police Gazette,* popularized tall tales of the South and West, many of which had been circulating orally before being recorded by the remarkable group of amateur writers who gave them quasi-literary form. And volumes like Longstreet's *Georgia Scenes,* T. B. Thorpe's *The Hive of the Bee Hunter,* Thompson's *Major Jones's Courtship,* Hooper's *Adventures of Simon Suggs,* Baldwin's *Flush Times of Alabama and Mississippi,* and Harris' *Sut Lovingood* — these books and many others — reflect the importance of a virile exuberance lacking in the work of most of America's polite authors of the mid-century.

The writers of the old Southwest were most influential and most numerous, but popular humor was not confined to one region. Seba Smith's Jack Downing letters and Haliburton's series of Sam Slick volumes did for the Northeast what George H. Derby's *Phoenixiana* did for the Far West. And professional humorists, trading on wry spellings and the same frozen-faced method of storytelling, lost their own identity amidst the popularity of their fantastic pseudonyms — "Josh Billings," "Artemus Ward," "Petroleum V. Nasby." Mark Twain was a natural product of all the schools of popular humor, as Bernard DeVoto has made clear in *Mark Twain's America.* And it is but a step from Artemus Ward and Mark Twain to Mr. Dooley and Will Rogers.

For further comment see Max Eastman, "Humor and America," pp. 195 ff., above.

THOMAS CHANDLER HALIBURTON: The Clockmaker

"Down East" extends from eastern New England for an indeterminate distance, and by courtesy we may consider the writing of Judge Haliburton (1796–1865) as American, despite the fact that he was a Nova Scotia judge for many years. He is chiefly remembered for his creation of Sam Slick of Slickville, the shrewd Yankee peddler, whose sayings and doings provided material for four popular volumes. Ironically, Haliburton said he wrote the Slick stories as indirect propaganda for a Nova Scotia railroad; the passage on page 560 is an example of the flattering remarks on the Nova Scotia countryside which Slick utters in the author's behalf. *The Clockmaker* series were popular here and in England for quite another reason, however. As Walter Blair observes in *Native American Humor,* Sam Slick's individuality, his "aphoristic wisdom," and his cleverness all endear him to the reader. Haliburton was not original — the shrewd peddler had long been a source of humorous stories, and though many of his anecdotes were undoubtedly invented, many more came from newspaper clippings and — as with most humorists — from yarns already in oral circulation.

In "The Clockmaker," the narrator of the episode is traveling with Slick and, upon inquiring the secret of the clockmaker's success, discovers a basic rule of psychology — "We can do without any article of luxury we never had, but when once obtained, it isn't in *human natur* to surrender it voluntarily." Sam Slick is an American, but his success is due to a universal quality of the good salesman — a skill in using "soft sawder."

DAVID CROCKETT: A Useful Coonskin

David Crockett (1786–1836), besides being a heroic martyr of Texas independence, was a Tennessee Congressman, a prodigious hunter and fighter, and somewhat of a writer. The Davy Crockett legend is, however, a free improvisation on the facts of his life. In a series of "Crockett" almanacs and apochryphal volumes of adventures purporting to be authentic (Constance Rourke's *Davy Crockett* deals most skillfully with the vexed problems of authorship), some of the best examples of the storyteller's art are to be found. The "Sunrise in His Pocket" quoted by Max Eastman (p. 198) is a characteristic piece of almanac tall talk. "A Useful Coonskin," although far less fantastic, is an anecdote rich in backwoods flavor. It may have been recorded by Crockett himself.

A. B. LONGSTREET: The Fight

The publication in 1835 of *Georgia Scenes* from a small Augusta press was the real beginning of the appearance of humorous frontier material on a national scale. Here was a realistic book "by a native Georgian" which pictured life during the first half-century of the republic, and did it without self-consciousness or condescension. Among the nineteen sketches in the volume were accounts of gander-pullings, militia drills, shooting matches, horse-swappings, and bloody fights. Augustus Baldwin Longstreet (1790–1879) was the author of the volume, but this versatile man, later prominent throughout the South as editor, politician, judge, minister, and president of four colleges, was inclined to shrink from this production of his earlier days. The rest of the country, however, embraced it. As Franklin J. Meine recalls in his introduction to *Tall Tales of the Southwest,* the popularity of *Georgia Scenes* led to the publication of a flood of anecdotes and lively humorous episodes in newspapers all over the country. He considers Longstreet's influence of primary importance, and calls his book the " cornerstone " of antebellum humorous literature.

" The Fight " illustrates the reasons for Longstreet's popularity. The authentic atmosphere of the backwoods brawl is not damped by reticence of the author. Longstreet's honesty and his avoidance of the mere burlesque set the style for vivid narrative which has definitely enriched our literature. In the hands of some, the cult of cruelty and the delight at physical discomfiture went much further; Longstreet does not offend good taste, but his humor possesses an honest gusto, for he was not over-civilized.

T. B. THORPE: The Big Bear of Arkansas

Thomas Bangs Thorpe (1815–1878) was a Massachusetts man who went to Louisiana when he was twenty-one, and thereafter was an artist, an editor of several newspapers, an officer in the Mexican War, and the author of *The Mysteries of the Backwoods* (1846) and *The Hive of the Bee Hunter* (1854). His style is often pretentious, and only a few of his stories escape dullness by modern standards. But " The Big Bear of Arkansas " is in a class by itself: it is by far Thorpe's best work, and is a masterpiece of the tall tale. Here are the vaunting whoops of the frontiersman who is " half horse, half alligator," the fantastic tales of mosquitoes, game birds, and extraordinary Arkansas fertility. This is all but an artful prelude to the disquisition on bears and the story of the " creation bear " who was unhuntable and who " died when his time come." Set in a " frame " of cultured literary English, the monologue of the man from Arkansas is all the more effective because of its racy idiom, its apt metaphors, its constant undertone of poker-faced humor.

GEORGE W. HARRIS: Sicily Burns's Wedding

Although the earliest known edition of *Sut Lovingood's Yarns* is dated 1867, it is possible that this was not the first edition of the distinctive work, since several Sut Lovingood stories appeared in newspapers during the early fifties. In any case, the work of George W. Harris (1814–1869) belongs to the school of Longstreet and Thorpe, although its flavor is much gamier. Harris was a Tennesseean and, like most of his colleagues, was a man of many talents: he was a silversmith and a riverboat captain, a hunter and a writer of political articles. As a storyteller he is superlative. With him the tall tale becomes half fantasy and half the most particular realism, but the tone is set largely by the character of Sut, that prime example of a " natral born durn'd fool." Sut's idea of humor is clearly revealed in " Sicily Burns's Wedding." With lavish innocence he breaks up the wedding dinner to get even with Sicily for an indignity she and her soda (p. 583) had previously dealt him, and he delights in the physical discomfort which Sock and the bees cause. Franklin J. Meine called Sut " the genuinely naïve roughneck mountaineer riotously bent on raising hell." If his antics occasionally verge on the coarse, they are redeemed by their unabashed naturalness. The dialect will be a more serious stumbling-block for the average modern reader, but a little patience should suffice to remove most of the difficulties.

JOEL CHANDLER HARRIS: Uncle Remus

The Uncle Remus stories are so well known that comment is almost superfluous. Uncle Remus and the little boy are real, but no more so than Brer Rabbit and Mr. Fox, who are a source of humor because of the human traits they half-grotesquely exemplify. Harris (1848–1908) was on the staff of the Atlanta *Constitution* when he wrote the stories that comprise *Uncle Remus: His Songs and His Sayings* (1880) and *Nights with Uncle Remus* (1883). Many of the anecdotes were undoubtedly a part of his childhood memories, and he was surprised to be considered an anthropological expert by scholars who found analogues to South American and Indian folk material in his tales. The truth is, of course, that the universality of human nature is mirrored in its folklore, and Harris in telling stories appropriate to the Negro life he had observed and the Negro yarn spinners he had known, was inevitably transcending localism. Even though the rabbit, weak but clever, may subconsciously represent the Negro race itself, more important is the fact that when we listen to Uncle Remus we suspend our disbelief and willingly enter that world where animals talk and act with all the wisdom and guile of human beings.

ESTHER SHEPHARD: The Buckskin Harness

America has created many folk heroes of superhuman mold. We have our Mike Fink, Pecos Bill, Big-Foot Wallace, and the Negro John Henry. But none has been so popular or has gathered around his personage so many stories as has Paul Bunyan, the master logger. The saga of Paul and his blue ox Babe developed in the East, and moving through northern United States and southern Canada, followed the lumbering industry to the west coast. Mrs. Shephard assembled a volume of Paul Bunyan tales from loggers in Washington, Oregon, and British Columbia. She dates the earliest before the Civil War, and says that they reached the height of their popularity in the eighties and nineties. Despite the effect of civilization on folk literature, Paul Bunyan stories still circulate, and story-telling, like ballad-singing, is likely to take the form of contests. On this account, perhaps, many tall tales from other parts of the country — tales originally having nothing to do with logging — have attached themselves to the Paul Bunyan cycle as loggers vie with each other to cap marvel with marvel. " The Buckskin Harness " has all the plausible quality of a Munchausen tale. No single story can give a fair picture of the prodigious logger and his ox, but Mrs. Shephard's *Paul Bunyan* as a whole shows the many-sided figures in characteristic poses.

Short Stories

NATHANIEL HAWTHORNE: Lady Eleanore's Mantle

Henry James' essay, " Hawthorne's Three American Novels," pp. 211 ff., above, characterizes the principal works of the Salem author. He is equally important in the history of the American short story. In two series of *Twice-Told Tales* (1837, 1842), and later in *Mosses from an Old Manse* (1846) and *The Snow Image* (1852), he advanced the power of short fiction over what it had been in Irving's hands. Hawthorne, although inevitably a romantic, dealt not with the exotic subject-matter of gift-books and annuals, but with problems of conduct and conscience. This occasionally led to an allegorical treatment of theme and to a certain remoteness from life itself; but to offset this limitation, Hawthorne brought to the short story general technical excellence and dramatic intensity.

Frequently he elaborated his stories from abstract ethical ideas. In "Lady Eleanore's Mantle," for example, the plot seems to have developed outwardly from the basic theme that pride which separates a person from human sympathies is sure to be followed by severe retribution. The germ of the story is suggested indirectly by two jottings in the *American Note-Books:* " To poison a person or a party of persons with the sacramental wine "; " An ornament to be worn about the person of a lady, — as a jewelled heart. After many years, it happens to be broken or unscrewed, and a poisonous odor comes out." Within the story itself the theme is stated with almost improper emphasis half a dozen times, and there is all manner of foreshadowing. Hawthorne is fond of using concrete symbols to intensify the effect — veils, butterflies, birthmarks, poison plants — and here he employs the mantle, with its aura of magical properties. The net effect of Hawthorne's method of storytelling is frequently to make moral tales of most of his short fiction, but they are redeemed by their singleness of purpose and their polish of form.

Edgar Allan Poe: The Tell-Tale Heart

For a note on Poe, see above, p. 840.

" The Tell-Tale Heart," like many of Poe's other stories, is concerned with a kind of horror that is scarcely human. But such is his skill that he almost convinces us that it *is* phantasmagorically human — until the final sentence, when the truth which we have known all the time bursts forth. This is of course the character of all good surprise endings — that they prove, upon examination, to have been not inconceivable, but inevitable. The use of the first person enables Poe to combine the rational and irrational qualities of the madman in constantly varying proportion; and the orderly factual description of his actions creates an illusion of reality vivid enough to hold the reader. Notice the mechanical means whereby he quickens the tempo of the closing half-page.

Edward Everett Hale: The Man Without a Country

Edward Everett Hale (1822–1909), a descendant of Nathan Hale (see p. 297), was Boston's first prominent short story writer. Writing was a family occupation — his father was editor of the *Daily Advertiser* and his mother was a translator — and he grew up in an atmosphere of books. He graduated from Harvard at the age of seventeen and soon thereafter entered the ministry, but along with his pastoral duties he led a full life as a writer, producing many volumes of fiction, history, travel, and sermons. He is best known for two short stories, " My Double and How He Undid Me " and " The Man Without a Country," both manifestly improbable tales that he has clothed with such circumstantial detail that, like Poe, he captures our complete confidence in spite of ourselves. Hale was overrated by his contemporaries, and his potboilers lie completely forgotten today. But his simplicity and clarity of diction were influential on editors and writers alike, and American prose style has been the better for Hale's influence.

" The Man Without a Country " created a sensation when it appeared in the December, 1863, *Atlantic,* and in the patriotic atmosphere of wartime it became a strong document for promoting unity in the North (note the topical references on p. 618). The story seems to have been suggested to Hale by accounts of a case involving ex-Congressman Clement L. Vallandigham of Dayton, Ohio. Vallandigham had vigorously opposed war with the South, even after Fort Sumter was attacked. When he was defeated for re-election, he continued to lead the peace democrats, or " copperheads," as they were called. He became so outspoken that the War Department issued a General Order making it a crime to embarrass the government. In May, 1863, Vallandigham defied the order in a speech during which he tore up a copy of the order, spat on it, and trampled it. He was arrested and sentenced, but Lincoln decided instead to turn him over to the Southerners. They, however, refused to harbor him, and he became quite literally a man without a country. He fled to Bermuda and thence to Canada, where he directed an unsuccessful campaign for the Ohio governership. After the war he returned to Dayton and resumed his law practice.

Bret Harte: Tennessee's Partner

Bret Harte (1839–1902) is known to most people as a Californian. Actually he lived in New York state until he was nineteen, was twelve years on the west coast, and spent most of the rest of his life abroad. Herein lies one of Harte's chief weaknesses: he sees California after a theatrical fashion, typing its inhabitants with an overweening fondness for melodramatic contrasts; and in his later work he seems to exploit the country rather than to deal seriously with what he must have known. His best stories are contained in his first volume, *The Luck of Roaring Camp* (1870), and he never surpassed the " Luck," " The Outcasts of Poker Flat," and " Tennessee's Partner." These early stories in the *Overland Monthly* aroused such enthusiasm in the East that the *Atlantic Monthly* offered him a fabulous $10,000 contract for a year's output, and his progress across the continent was a continuous triumph. For a few years he lectured on his California experiences, but the financial pressure of his extravagant tastes led him to leave America to recoup. He held consulates in Germany and Scotland and spent his final years in London. His influence in giving the impetus to the local color movement was of vast importance, but as with so many local colorists, his first work was his best.

" Tennessee's Partner " illustrates two common features of frontier society — the informal " lynch law " justice, and the strong sentimental ties of masculine friendship. There is less grotesque contrast in this story than in, say, " The Outcasts of Poker Flat," but it is not absent. The sharp disparity between the idyllic midsummer morning (p. 627) and the scene at the top of Marley's Hill illustrates a favorite Harte mannerism, not always ineffective. The literary English, too, is deliberately contrasted with the colloquialism of a spoken language full of mining and gambling jargon. The author's predominant interest in Tennessee's partner leads not only to the honest sentiment reticently exhibited over the grave, but also to the less restrained close. Here, it may be felt by some readers, he exchanges tragedy for pathos by bringing

Tennessee's partner to his death. But the very fidelity of Harte's scenes keeps them from becoming either perfunctory or maudlin.

MARY NOAILLES MURFREE: The "Harnt" that Walks Chilhowee

In the decade or so following Bret Harte's first appearance before the public, every section of the United States had its local colorist who sought to put into magazine short stories the peculiarities of speech, manners, and landscape of the region. Mary Murfree (1850–1922) did for the Tennessee Mountains what George W. Cable was doing for New Orleans, Thomas Nelson Page for Virginia, Sarah Orne Jewett for rural New England. Under the name of Charles Egbert Craddock Miss Murfree sold a number of short stories to the *Atlantic* in the late seventies and early eighties. She wrote a firm masculine hand, and her stories seemed to be the work of a man. So it was with great surprise that the publishers invited "Craddock" to Boston and planned a banquet in celebration of the visit, only to have a tiny woman appear and announce that she had written the stories which were being gathered as *In the Tennessee Mountains*. This first volume, like Harte's *The Luck of Roaring Camp*, contained the author's best work. In it the mountaineer folk were portrayed in all their vigor of speech, their limited knowledge of the world, their intense love of individualism, their indifference to the natural beauty around them, their honest homeliness. "The 'Harnt' that Walks Chilhowee" captures all these qualities within its limited scope. Perhaps Clarsie is too exotic with her deer-eyes and the odd Cinderella-Tarzan combination of manner; perhaps the landscape weighs down the story with its heavy subtropical lushness. But the folkways are real. Miss Murfree has seen deeply into the character of the primitives, and she is not condescending toward them.

MARY E. WILKINS FREEMAN: On the Walpole Road

Like Miss Murfree, Mary Wilkins Freeman (1852–1930) was strongly influenced by the local color vogue which reached its peak of popularity in the eighties. But in the two women's work there are only slight points of similarity: they both wrote excellent dialect stories, and as novelists they were relatively unsuccessful. Mrs. Freeman wrote of country life in eastern Massachusetts, and most of her stories look at life from a woman's point of view. In *A Humble Romance* (1887), *A New England Nun* (1891), and other volumes of short stories, she achieves dignity by being objective. Her reportorial method, skillfully cultivated to present the reader with all the data needed for the subtlest shades of meaning, makes interpretation on the author's part unnecessary. Whereas Miss Murfree is purely a local colorist, picturing her mountain folk against a highly individualized setting and stressing the unusual aspects of life, Mrs. Freeman concentrates on people in a different fashion. Her folk are products of a New England environment, to be sure, and they speak a recognizable dialect; but she has very wisely treated those aspects of character which are universal, rather than merely picturesque or exotic or unique. This approach distinguishes her somewhat from Sarah Orne Jewett, who was also writing of the New England scene. Mrs. Freeman is dispassionate, while Miss Jewett, eschewing bleakness, is softly sentimental. They both treat a declining New England whose chief glories lie in the past, but the decline is presented by the one author, lamented by the other.

"On the Walpole Road" is a frame story. That is to say, the beginning and ending furnish the provocation for the story proper, which is in turn related by one of the characters (cf. "The Birds of Killingworth," p. 340, above, told by the Poet in *Tales of a Wayside Inn*). The frame can be perfunctorily handled, but here it has a dramatic quality, particularly because of Almira's humorous remark at the close. Notice the sources of humor here, and the way even slight digressions are made to increase verisimilitude.

AMBROSE BIERCE: One of the Missing

In an age when sentimentalism was the keynote in popular fiction, Ambrose Bierce (1842 1914?) stood out from his contemporaries because of his cynicism, his love of irony, his acid wit, his taste for the macabre. His life was long and busy, but his energies were burnt out in journalism. He was connected with several unimportant magazines, and in his later years worked on various Hearst enterprises, despite his dislike for the whole commercial world in which he moved. His *Tales of Soldiers and Civilians* (1891), later called *In the Midst of Life*, contains some excellent short stories of their sort, but they were neglected by his generation. His collected works include such characteristic titles as *The Devil's Dictionary*, *The Fiend's Delight* (a "cold collation of diabolisms"), *Cobwebs from an Empty Skull*. An ironist to the last, in 1913 he begged his friends to "forgive him in not 'perishing' where he was," and disappeared into Mexico. Rumors have multiplied the mystery of his death, but whether he was killed by the Revolutionists or wandered off to die has never been ascertained.

"Bitter Bierce" he was, writing gruesome and terrifying stories almost always built around some irony. His favorite device is to make a sequence of events elaborately convincing in the most intense manner possible, and then to knock all the props from under our credulity as he runs away. "An Occurrence at Owl Creek Bridge," for example, concerns a Civil War hanging, which the victim seems to have escaped through a breaking of the noose; but after pages of circumstantial detail, during which he falls through the bridge into a river, escapes the shots of guards, and makes his way home, we learn finally that this train of events is what went on in Peyton Farquhar's mind during the instant between the springing of the trapdoor and the breaking of his neck. In "The Man and the Snake," Harker Brayton pays a visit to a herpetologist, discovers a snake in his room, is hypnotized by the snake's eyes, and is literally frightened to death. But after building us up to this climax, Bierce puts the mordant ironic touch on the close by calmly telling us that "It was a stuffed snake; its eyes were two shoe buttons." Bierce's interest in the grotesque and uncanny suggests comparison with Poe, by whom he was undoubtedly influenced. The circumstantial detail with which he builds up a picture of Searing's plight is not unlike the manner of "The Pit and the Pendulum"; but "One of the Missing" gains its characteristic Bierce flavor by a final sentence which alters the perspective of the entire story.

HAMLIN GARLAND: The Return of a Private

Hamlin Garland (1860–1940) wrote some of his best stories in protest against the Middle West of his childhood. He had left his family's Iowa farm to educate himself, and after a period in Boston, during which he lived meagerly and read at the

Public Library, he returned to his home to see the whole region with a clear eye. He had read Henry George's *Progress and Poverty* and had become an ardent single-taxer, angry at land speculation and the farmer's unhappy lot. In such a mood he wrote the stories that were gathered in 1891 as *Main-Travelled Roads*. He was consciously avoiding the sentimental and idyllic picture of the farm; rather he emphasized the capriciousness of nature, the unrewarded hard work, the clashing interests of city and country. " The main-travelled road, " said Garland, " is long and wearyful, and has a dull little town at one end and a home of toil at the other. Like the main-travelled road of life it is traversed by many classes of people, but the poor and the weary predominate." This group of stories, several times enlarged and reissued, was the beginning of a promising literary career. But in a few years he succumbed to the lure of the large-circulation magazine and the romantic tale. As he prospered the level of his art sank, and of a shelf of later volumes, almost the only work of real power is *A Son of the Middle Border,* the first of a long series of autobiographical books.

" The Return of a Private " is notable as it foreshadows the modern anti-heroic attitude toward war. It antedated Stephen Crane's *Red Badge of Courage,* and by its realism forms the strongest contrast to the romantic pathos of such a story as Thomas Nelson Page's " Marse Chan." If Garland's Midwest seems here unusually drab and cheerless, it is yet a far more realistic picture than the sentimental Eggleston *Hoosier Schoolmaster* or the sugary poems of James Whitcomb Riley.

O. HENRY: A Municipal Report

The short story in America has been a vehicle for moral allegory, for the creation of terror, for exploiting local oddities, for protesting against social evils. But when William Sydney Porter (1862–1910) began to write, he made it sheer entertainment, with the accent on humor. In the more than four hundred stories which he wrote between 1899 and 1910, he perfected the device of the surprise ending which had been skillfully used by many of his predecessors. The vaudeville mannerisms of O. Henry made for an artful artlessness — he appears to digress, he seems to be wandering into seriousness, but he has calculated his effect beforehand and knows exactly how far he can deceive the reader. During his years in the Columbus penitentiary he wrote stories of Latin America and the Southwest. After his release, his growing popularity led the New York *World* to commission a weekly story for its Sunday supplement, and from 1904 onward, he wrote usually of life in " Bagdad-on-the-Subway."

His stories are frequently expanded anecdotes, and their plot alone would not give them life. Rather it is O. Henry's manner that makes any subject promising under his hand. Like Mark Twain, he was primarily a humorist, but his humor is not necessarily the humor of reality. His style is artificial — a fantastic combination of ephemeral slang and overstuffed literary English — but it admirably serves its purpose of surprising the reader constantly. The rapid pace, journalistic in its liveliness, the concentration on amusement with no ulterior motives lurking beneath the surface, and the careful attention given to form and total effect — all these are ingredients in O. Henry's genius. He was not a great writer; almost no one of his stories is of first rank in every respect. But he made the short story a medium of great popularity, and he brought freshness to the art of characteristic American storytelling.

" A Municipal Report " is one of O. Henry's best stories. Although it seems garrulous in the opening pages, it has been deftly planned; even the interpolated guidebook sentences, carelessly thrown in, are important as a foil for the melodrama with which the story concludes. Since this is a " well-made " story, all the motifs re-enter at the close — even the horn button. Yet once the necessary information is before us, the author quickly withdraws, leaving us to savor the implications which make this a serious story.

SHERWOOD ANDERSON: I'm a Fool

Once O. Henry had loosed the short story from what might be called writer's diction, it was inevitable that the slang, the vulgarities, even the moronic slovenliness of actual speech should be exploited. In a sense, this development, conspicuous in the twenties, was a return to the dialect story — but with a difference. Whereas the local colorists had recorded distinctive regional language, Anderson, Hemingway, Lardner, and many of their contemporaries made us conscious of class dialects. The speech of baseball players, shopgirls, high-school boys, businessmen, housewives, and truck drivers is distinctive, but the difference is not merely a matter of geography. It is no accident that " I'm a Fool " and " The Golden Honeymoon " are first-person stories; for only by giving us the full flavor of a spoken language can either story produce such a strong effect of reality and directness.

Sherwood Anderson (1876–1941) was born in Ohio and spent most of his adolescent years drifting about the country from one small job to another. The Spanish-American War came as an escape from the humdrum. Afterward he settled in Chicago and worked for an advertising firm, all the while trying his hand at writing. After running a paint factory in Elyria, Ohio, for a time, he suddenly wearied of it as he realized that executive and writer were not compatible. He walked out of his office, returned to advertising, and took up his writing more seriously. *Windy McPherson's Son* (1916) was an autobiographic first novel, and it was followed in 1919 by *Winesburg, Ohio,* which brought him general recognition. Anderson's work was fresh, his style individual; but some critics found serious fault with this series of tales because they explored the " hidden life " of many ordinary Midwestern folk, exposing especially the grotesque fancies and aberrations that lay beneath commonplace exteriors. *Poor White* (1920) was a sensitive but strange novel. *Horses and Men* (1923), from which " I'm a Fool " is taken, contains several racetrack stories which reflect his childhood experiences. Abnormality is suppressed in " I'm a Fool," a story which we value simply as an authentic picture of an adolescent dilemma. It is not particularly characteristic of the Anderson about whom controversies have raged, but it is an example of his excellent work in handling colloquial language on a level above mere reporting. His most distinctive contribution to style is the poetic overtone, achieved by artistic selection of detail, without sacrifice of fidelity.

ERNEST HEMINGWAY: The Three-Day Blow

In " Fiction Tells All " (pp. 242 ff.), Mr. Canby voices a common complaint which applies to Hemingway's novels and to many of his short stories. One may well ask whether the age itself was not responsible for the point of view as well as the subject-matter of Hemingway, Wolfe, and Faulkner. For their work represents the effect, rather than the cause of disillusionment. Whatever be the individual judgment on this point, it seems clear that since Mr. Canby wrote, we have begun to see the twenties and thirties as a phase which has now been superseded by a somewhat more positive view — again, mirroring the public temper. Hemingway has expressed a rising faith in humanity in *For Whom the Bell Tolls* (1940), and in that respect has recovered from the feeling which motivated his work of the decade previous.

Hemingway's long fiction has been conditioned largely by war and its effect on the individual. A good many of his early short stories, however, derive from visits to northern Michigan during his youth. Such is " The Three-Day Blow," an interesting study of a rather common problem of youth. Loosely related to it is the brief " End of Something," which immediately precedes it in *In Our Time* (1925). In the earlier story, Nick undertakes to tell Marge that they are " through." Neither of them is very articulate, but it is apparent that they have deep regard for each other. As Marge leaves, Bill appears and we learn that it was his idea to save Nick from assuming any serious responsibilities. " The Three-Day Blow " follows this scene immediately, and presents us with the first stages of the rebound.

Ring Lardner: The Golden Honeymoon

Ring Lardner (1885–1933) was a sports writer during most of his career, and, though talented, was looked upon by the literary fraternity as just a competent journalist. A few years before his death, however, it began to be clear that his was no ephemeral talent riding the waves of daily opportunity. True, most of his fiction had a sports background, and dealt with baseball players, prize-fighters, and similar folk. Many of his characters were almost simple-minded, and spoke a disintegrated, grammarless English. With a masterful gift for humor and satire, he has been a refreshing figure in the recent development of the short story. His ability to caricature the garrulous barber (" Haircut ") or the over-excited young girl of many loves (" I Can't Breathe "), reminds one of Fielding, but his idiom is pointedly modern, his vehicle an uncannily accurate colloquialism.

" The Golden Honeymoon " is not a plotted story, although the presence of the Hartsells does lead to a mild contretemps. The chief interest lies in Lardner's satire of the individual who is unhappily gifted with total recall. Such a man would be undeniably boring in real life, but Lardner has created the illusion without actually boring the reader; and it becomes a brilliant portrait before he has finished. We see old Charley with all his stock responses, his terrific addiction to clichés, his time-table memory, his atrocious taste. He is real, and Lardner has applied the touch of the artist to the ocean of words so that they reveal the character of the other persons in the story with perfect clarity.

Wilbur Daniel Steele: How Beautiful with Shoes

Since O. Henry, most important American writers of the short story have been known primarily as novelists. There are, however, a few exceptions. Ring Lardner, Katherine Anne Porter, and Wilbur Daniel Steele, for example, have all built their present reputation upon short stories. Steele (1886–   ) had extensive training in art, and won several prizes for painting and etching before he decided to forego art for literature. From 1915 until the early thirties he wrote many excellent stories, notable for their clean craftsmanship and sensitive style. Recently he has turned to the drama, and has written a number of plays, among which his *Post Road* (1935) has enjoyed greatest success.

Steele was born in North Carolina and has lived much of his life in the South. " How Beautiful with Shoes " is one of his outstanding stories with Southern setting. Despite its violence, the story is predominantly poetic; yet Steele is not a Southerner of the old school. His milieu is not romantically idyllic, nor are his characters sentimentally beautiful. The story of Amarantha and the madman is deeply moving because it is neither melodramatic nor inherently morbid. The experience has left the simple girl changed, but the hypnosis is beauty, not fright. The story should be compared with " He " and " The ' Harnt ' that Walks Chilhowee."

Katherine Anne Porter: He

The work of Katherine Anne Porter (1894–   ) has slowly but surely won recognition. She has written very little — a volume of stories, *Flowering Judas* (1935), and three short novels gathered as *Pale Horse, Pale Rider* (1939). But her method is painstaking, and her work is characterized by sureness of technique and stylistic finish. As critics have pointed out, she is occasionally too subtle, and " implicit " values tend to become obscure when pushed too far. This is not true, however, of her best stories. Her work is not easily typed, inasmuch as she has approached each story primarily as a problem of technique and has rigorously shaped her style and point of view to produce the effect she desires. Whether the setting be New Orleans, Mexico, or rural America, her insight into character is always penetrating.

" He " is not dependent on sharply localized setting since it is a study of character. Although the people are almost poor-white, and the tone of the story is bleak, a certain tenderness results from the constant reference to the unfortunate Whipple child as " He," and the unhappy conclusion becomes an incident of genuine tragedy.

Stephen Vincent Benét: The Devil and Daniel Webster

For a note on Benét, see above, p. 843.

John Steinbeck: The Chrysanthemums

John Steinbeck (1902–   ) first achieved success in *Tortilla Flat* (1935), a series of delightful and mellow sketches of simple Spanish folk near Monterey, California. *Of Mice and Men* (1937), as a novelette and then as a play, continued this feeling for the little people of earth. *In Dubious Battle* (1936) had, however, revealed Steinbeck's proletarian sympathies in an angry fashion, and served as a prelude to *The Grapes of Wrath* (1939), the best-seller in which he praised the indomitable character of dispossessed dust-bowl farmers and attacked the failure of California and the nation to solve what was an economic as well as a human problem. The two sides of Steinbeck, the tender and the indignant, are by no means irreconcilable; indeed, they complement each other naturally. And the various manners of his books represent, not fumbling experimentation, but a technical virtuosity which marks him in his later work as a skilled craftsman.

" The Chrysanthemums " is set in the district around Salinas, California, which has become known as "the Steinbeck country." It is a finely wrought story in which we come to understand Elisa Allen's character through the scene with the potmender. On the surface very little happens, but the depths of her character are revealed not only by her tenseness before the man, but by her thought as he goes down the road: "That's a bright direction. There's a glowing there." The implications of the closing scene with her husband are likewise significant. Without being over-subtle Steinbeck has gained eloquence and tragic beauty here by the emotional intensity of the closing pages, and the whole story is a model of restraint.

Novelette

WALLACE STEGNER: Remembering Laughter

Wallace Stegner (1909–   ) was born in Iowa and spent his early years in the Far West of the United States and Canada. After graduating from the University of Utah, he studied at California and took his Ph.D. degree at the University of Iowa in 1935. He had already begun to write for the regional magazines, but he first achieved national recognition in 1936 when *Remembering Laughter* won the Little, Brown novelette award. Since then he has had outstanding stories in the *Virginia Quarterly Review, Harper's,* and the *Atlantic,* and has published three books, *The Potter's House* (1938), *On a Darkling Plain* (1940), and *Fire and Ice* (1941). He has taught at the Universities of Utah and Wisconsin and is now Briggs-Copeland Instructor of English at Harvard.

The novelette is a difficult form in which few authors have been able to write successfully. In the hands of the inexpert, it becomes either an attenuated short story or an underdeveloped novel. Stegner's *Remembering Laughter* gives the illusion of the full-length form, and achieves its brevity largely by the marked economy with which character and scene are realized. Throughout the story, it is clash of individual will that dominates; the effect of Elspeth's experience on her own personality and Margaret's is the author's chief concern. It is clear that he is not interested in pointing a moral (if the reader wishes a moral, it would be that unfortunately the wages of sin are not always death); rather he wishes to show, through an objective study of character, how a single episode can turn happiness inside out, can make virtual twins of persons as different as are the two women at the beginning of the story.

One source of power in *Remembering Laughter* is the distinguished prose style. With the sureness of a master Stegner sketches swiftly but never in fragments; his descriptive effects are clear and sharp, highly charged with sensory images, yet always freshly conceived and poetically expressed. Indeed, the dominant impulse here is poetic. It does not limit the complete realism of speech or action, but it frequently determines what shall be developed dramatically in full scenes, what by simple narration. Despite the somberness of the close, there is laughter to be remembered — the tall talk of Alec, so characteristically American, so completely indigenous to the Midwestern locale. The combination of localism and universality is highly important in giving the work its earthiness and its social tensions, side by side with the broader implications of loneliness and immolation. And it is through Alec that the story is unified: in some respects he is the least important of the trio, yet all the threads of the novel — the feeling for the land, the insufficiency of Puritanism, the impulse to reckless independence — all the mainsprings to action and reaction, are centered in him.

The technique of *Remembering Laughter* will repay detailed study. The management of time, for example, is ordinarily difficult when so many years are encompassed in relatively brief space. Direct and indirect methods of character development appear here in skillful variety, with each individual requiring different treatment. The sources of humor, the use of poetic diction, the literal and figurative functions of setting, the occasional pinpricks of satire, the implication of such deliberate repetitions as the sentence "But Margaret was kind," the dramatic value of the two songs — these and kindred inquiries will make clear the technical finish and the total meaning of the novelette.